Ways of Reading

AN ANTHOLOGY FOR WRITERS

NINTH EDITION

David Bartholomae
UNIVERSITY OF PITTSBURGH

Anthony Petrosky
UNIVERSITY OF PITTSBURGH

BEDFORD/ST. MARTIN'S
BOSTON ◆ NEW YORK

For Bedford/St. Martin's

Executive Editor: John E. Sullivan III
Production Editor: Katherine Caruana
Production Supervisor: Samuel Jones
Senior Marketing Manager: Molly Parke
Editorial Assistant: Shannon Walsh
Copyeditor: Linda McLatchie
Senior Art Director: Anna Palchik
Text Design: Tom Carling, carlingdesign.com
Cover Design: Marine Miller
Cover Art: Jaume Plensa, *Glückauf?* 2004, Iron, Dimensions variable. Installation view: *Is art something in between?* Kunsthalle Mannheim, Germany, 2005. © Jaume Plensa. Courtesy Galerie Lelong, New York. Photograph: Jürgen Diemer.
Composition: MPS Limited, a Macmillan Company
Printing and Binding: RR Donnelley & Sons

President: Joan E. Feinberg
Editorial Director: Denise B. Wydra
Editor in Chief: Karen S. Henry
Director of Marketing: Karen R. Soeltz
Director of Editing, Design, and Production: Susan W. Brown
Assistant Director of Editing, Design, and Production: Elise S. Kaiser
Managing Editor: Elizabeth M. Schaaf

Library of Congress Control Number: 2010928381

Manufactured in the United States of America.

5 4 3 2 1
f e d c b

For information, write: Bedford/St. Martin's, 75 Arlington Street, Boston, MA 02116 (617-399-4000)

ISBN-10: 0–312–57091–0
ISBN-13: 978–0–312–57091–0

Acknowledgments

Acknowledgments and copyrights appear at the back of the book on pages 772–74, which constitute an extension of the copyright page. It is a violation of the law to reproduce these selections by any means whatsoever without the written permission of the copyright holder.

Preface

Ways of Reading is designed for a course where students are given the opportunity to work on what they read, and to work on it by writing. When we began developing such courses, we realized the problems our students had when asked to write or talk about what they read were not "reading problems," at least not as these are strictly defined. Our students knew how to move from one page to the next. They could read sentences. They had, obviously, been able to carry out many of the versions of reading required for their education — skimming textbooks, cramming for tests, strip-mining books for term papers.

Our students, however, felt powerless in the face of serious writing, in the face of long and complicated texts — the kinds of texts we thought they should find interesting and challenging. We thought (as many teachers have thought) that if we just, finally, gave them something good to read — something rich and meaty — they would change forever their ways of thinking about English. It didn't work, of course. The issue is not only *what* students read, but what they can learn to *do* with what they read. We learned that the problems our students had lay not in the reading material (it was too hard) or in the students (they were poorly prepared) but in the classroom — in the ways we and they imagined what it meant to work on an essay.

There is no better place to work on reading than in a writing course, and this book is intended to provide occasions for readers to write. You will find a number of distinctive features in *Ways of Reading*. For one thing, it contains selections you don't usually see in a college reader: long, powerful, mysterious, and difficult pieces like Kwame Anthony Appiah's "Race, Culture, Identity: Misunderstood Connections," John Berger's "Ways of Seeing," Judith Butler's "Beside Oneself: On the Limits of Sexual Autonomy," Susan Griffin's "Our Secret,"

Edward Said's "States," John Edgar Wideman's "Our Time," David Foster Wallace's "Authority and American Usage," or Michel Foucault's "Panopticism." These are the sorts of readings we talk about when we talk with our colleagues. We have learned that we can talk about them with our students as well.

When we chose the essays, we were looking for "readable" texts — that is, texts that leave some work for a reader to do. We wanted selections that invite students to be active, critical readers, that present powerful readings of common experience, that open up the familiar world and make it puzzling, rich, and problematic. We wanted to choose selections that invite students to take responsibility for their acts of interpretation. So we avoided the short set-pieces you find in so many anthologies. In a sense, those short selections misrepresent the act of reading. They can be read in a single sitting; they make arguments that can be easily paraphrased; they solve all the problems they raise; they wrap up life and put it into a box; and so they turn reading into an act of appreciation, where the most that seems to be required is a nod of the head. And they suggest that a writer's job is to do just that, to write a piece that is similarly tight and neat and self-contained. We wanted to avoid pieces that were so plainly written or tightly bound that there was little for students to do but "get the point."

We learned that if our students had reading problems when faced with long and complex texts, the problems lay in the way they imagined a reader — the role a reader plays, what a reader does, why a reader reads (if not simply to satisfy the requirements of a course). When, for example, our students were puzzled by what they read, they took this as a sign of failure. ("It doesn't make any sense," they would say, as though the sense was supposed to be waiting on the page, ready for them the first time they read through.) And our students were haunted by the thought that they couldn't remember everything they had read (as though one could store all of Judith Butler's "Beside Oneself: On the Limits of Sexual Autonomy" in memory); or if they did remember bits and pieces, they felt that the fragmented text they possessed was evidence that they could not do what they were supposed to do. Our students were confronting the experience of reading, in other words, but they were taking the problems of reading — problems all readers face — and concluding that there was nothing for them to do but give up.

As expert readers, we have all learned what to do with a complex text. We know that we can go back to a text; we don't have to remember it — in fact, we've learned to mark up a text to ease that reentry. We know that a reader is a person who puts together fragments. Those coherent readings we construct begin with confusion and puzzlement, and we construct those readings by writing and rewriting — by working on a text.

These are the lessons our students need to learn, and this is why a course in reading is also a course in writing. Our students need to learn that there is something they can do once they have first read through a complicated text; successful reading is not just a matter of "getting" an essay the first time. In a very real sense, you can't begin to feel the power a reader has until you realize the problems, until you realize that no one "gets" Appiah or Butler or Wideman all at once. You work on what you read, and then what you have at the end is something that is yours, something you made. And this is what the teaching apparatus in *Ways of Reading* is designed to do. In a sense, it says to students, "OK, let's get to work on these essays; let's see what you can make of them."

This, then, is the second distinctive feature you will find in *Ways of Reading*: reading and writing assignments designed to give students access to the essays. After each selection, for example, you will find "Questions for a Second Reading." We wanted to acknowledge that rereading is a natural way of carrying out the work of a reader, just as rewriting is a natural way of completing the work of a writer. It is not something done out of despair or as a punishment for not getting things right the first time. The questions we have written highlight what we see as central textual or interpretive problems. These questions might serve as preparations for class discussion or ways of directing students' work in journals. Whatever the case, they both honor and direct the work of rereading.

Each selection is also followed by two sets of writing assignments, "Assignments for Writing" and "Making Connections." The first set directs students back into the work they have just read. While the assignments vary, there are some basic principles behind them. They ask students to work on the essay by focusing on difficult or problematic moments in the text; they ask students to work on the author's examples, extending and testing his or her methods of analysis; or they ask students to apply the method of the essay (its way of seeing and understanding the world) to settings or experiences of their own. The last assignments, "Making Connections," invite students to read one essay in the context of another, to see, for example, if Mary Louise Pratt's account of the "literate arts of the contact zone" can be used to frame a reading of Gloria Anzaldúa's prose or Paulo Freire's or Richard E. Miller's account of education. In a sense, then, the essays are offered as models, but not as "prose models" in the strictest sense. What they model is a way of seeing or reading the world, of both imagining problems and imagining methods to make those problems available to a writer.

At the end of the book, we have included several assignment sequences. A single sequence provides structure for an entire course. (There are a number of additional sequences included in the Instructor's Manual.) Most of the sequences include more than one essay in the anthology and require a series of separate drafts and revisions. Alternative essays and assignments are included with the sequences. In academic life, readers seldom read single essays in isolation, as though one were "finished" with Judith Butler after a week or two. Rather, they read with a purpose—with a project in mind or a problem to solve. The assignment sequences are designed to give students a feel for the rhythm and texture of an extended academic project. They offer, that is, one more way of reading and writing. Because these sequences lead students through intellectual projects proceeding from one week to the next, they enable them to develop authority as specialists, to feel the difference between being an expert and being a "common" reader on a single subject. And, with the luxury of time available for self-reflection, students can look back on what they have done, not only to revise what they know, but also to take stock and comment on the value and direction of their work.

Because of their diversity, it is difficult to summarize the assignment sequences. Perhaps the best way to see what we have done is to turn to the back of the book and look at them. They are meant to frame a project for students but to leave open possibilities for new directions. You should feel free to add or drop readings, to mix sequences, and to revise the assignments to fit your course and your schedule.

You will also notice that there are few "glosses" appended to the essays. We have not added many editors' notes to define difficult words or to identify names or allusions to other authors or artists. We've omitted them because their presence suggests something we feel is false about reading. They suggest that good readers know all the words or pick up all the allusions or recognize every name that is mentioned. This is not true. Good readers do what they can and try their best to fill in the blanks; they ignore seemingly unimportant references and look up the important ones. There is no reason for students to feel they lack the knowledge necessary to complete a reading of these texts. We have translated some foreign phrases, but we have kept the selections as clean and open as possible.

We have been asked on several occasions whether the readings aren't finally just too hard for students. The answer is no. Students will have to work on the selections, but that is the point of the course and the reason, as we said before, why a reading course is also a course in writing. College students want to believe that they can strike out on their own, make their mark, do something they have never done before. They want to *be* experts, not just hear from them. This is the great pleasure, as well as the great challenge, of undergraduate instruction. It is not hard to convince students they ought to be able to speak alongside of (or even speak back to) Judith Butler or Edward Said. And, if a teacher is patient and forgiving—willing, that is, to let a student work out a reading of Butler or Said, willing to keep from saying, "No, that's not it," and filling the silence with the "right" reading—then students can, with care and assistance, learn to speak for themselves. It takes a certain kind of classroom, to be sure. A teacher who teaches this book will have to be comfortable turning the essays over to the students, even with the knowledge that they will not do immediately on their own what a professional could do—at least not completely, or with the same grace and authority.

In our own teaching, we have learned that we do not have to be experts on every figure or every area of inquiry represented in this book. And, frankly, that has come as a great relief. We can have intelligent, responsible conversations about Appiah's "Race, Culture, Identity: Misunderstood Connections" without being experts on Appiah's work or current work on race and identity. We needed to prepare ourselves to engage and direct students as readers, but we did not have to prepare ourselves to lecture on Foucault or Butler, on poststructuralism and gender theory. The classes we have been teaching, and they have been some of the most exciting we have ever taught, have been classes where students—together and with their instructors—work on what these essays might mean.

So here we are, imagining students working shoulder to shoulder with Said, Butler, and Foucault, even talking back to them as the occasion arises. There is a wonderful Emersonian bravado in all this. But such is the case with strong and active readers. If we allow students to work on powerful texts, they will want to share the power. This is the heady fun of academic life, the real pleasure of thinking, reading, and writing. There is no reason to keep it secret from our students.

NEW TO THE NINTH EDITION

Half of the selections in the ninth edition of *Ways of Reading* are new. Our principle of selection remained the same—we were looking for "readable" texts, pieces that instructors and students would find challenging and compelling, pieces that offer powerful readings of ordinary experiences, pieces worth extended work.

There are chapter-length selections by David Abram, Kwame Anthony Appiah, Judith Butler, Laura Kipnis, Richard E. Miller, Tommie Shelby, and David Foster Wallace. We have until now included essays, such as these, of substantial length. Yet we have been asked on occasion to include briefer selections, and in this edition we have done so. Also new are five additional selections—by Eula Biss, Anne Carson, Brian Doyle, Antonio Porchia, and Alberto Álvaro Ríos. These "shorts" are much briefer than the pieces we have previously included in *Ways of Reading*; most are just two or three pages long. The shorts offer students opportunities to see how substantial intellectual and analytic work can be taken on with just a few pages or lines. The shorts, like the longer selections, offer students the possibility of articulating the complex and exploring the connections between the experimental and the critical. Except for Porchia, all of the new selections are the work of contemporary writers.

We have also been asked on occasion to provide examples of student work. In response we have added two student essays that reply to the Richard E. Miller selection, under the heading "Engaging with Student Writing." Rather than offering these essays as student samples, as an exhortative *You can do it, too!* we ask that students work with these essays *as* essays, as thoughtful responses to the Miller reading, as essays worth engaging in conversation, as essays to think about and to write with and against.

We have developed three new assignment sequences, "The Uses of Reading (II)," "The Art of Argument," and "Working with Metaphor," and we have revised the existing sequences, some to incorporate the new selections, others because, after teaching them again, we thought about them differently. In addition to sequences focusing on academic writing, we have continued to offer sequences focusing on autobiographical writing and the personal essay. While there have always been assignments in *Ways of Reading* that ask students to use their experience as subject matter, these assignments invite students to look critically and historically at the genre and insist that reading and thinking can *also* be represented as part of one's "personal" experience. Teaching these as examples of reading and writing projects has taught us that they have much to offer that students can study and imitate. We remain convinced that this kind of work helps students to think about sentences in useful ways. And we have continued to focus attention on prose models that challenge conventional forms and idioms, that complicate the usual ways of thinking about and representing knowledge and experience. There are several assignment sequences that ask students to write as though they too could participate in such revisionary work.

RESOURCES FOR INSTRUCTORS AND STUDENTS

Instructor Resources

Ways of Reading doesn't stop with a book. Online, you'll find both free and affordable premium resources to help students get even more out of the book and your course. You'll also find convenient instructor resources and even a nationwide community of teachers. To learn more about or order any of the products below, contact your Bedford/St. Martin's sales representative, e-mail sales support (sales_support@bfwpub.com), or visit the Web site at **bedfordstmartins.com/waysofreading.**

We've updated ***Resources for Teaching Ways of Reading*** by including three new pedagogical essays by Cathy Birkenstein, Tara Lockhart, and Stacey Waite. We continue to offer essays by graduate students; these essays give advice on how to work with the book. They stand as examples of the kinds of papers graduate students might write when they use *Ways of Reading* in conjunction with a teaching seminar. They stand best, however, as examples of graduate students speaking frankly to other graduate students about teaching and about *Ways of Reading*. In addition to the pedagogical essays, the Instructor's Manual includes entries on each selection and sequence, sample syllabi, additional sequences, and extensive resources for using *Ways of Reading* in the classroom, including a section of frequently asked questions. This manual is available in PDF that can be downloaded from the Bedford/St. Martin's Web site. Note: Due to copyright restrictions, pedagogical essays are included in the print version of the manual only. To obtain a print copy of the manual at no charge, contact your Bedford/St. Martin's sales representative.

Teaching Central offers the entire list of Bedford/St. Martin's print and online professional resources in one place. You'll find landmark reference works, sourcebooks on pedagogical issues, award-winning collections, and practical advice for the classroom — all free for instructors.

Bits collects creative ideas for teaching a range of composition topics in an easily searchable blog. A community of teachers — leading scholars, authors, and editors — discuss revision, research, grammar and style, technology, peer review, and much more. Take, use, adapt, and pass the ideas around. Then, come back to the site to comment or share your own suggestion. A group of instructors from the University of Pittsburgh provide insight into teaching with *Ways of Reading* at the place where it all started.

Content cartridges for the most common course management systems — Blackboard, WebCT, Angel, and Desire2Learn — allow you to easily download digital materials from Bedford/St. Martin's for your course.

Student Resources

Send students to free and open resources or upgrade to an expanding collection of innovative digital content.

Re:Writing, the best free collection of online resources for the writing class, offers clear advice on citing sources in *Research and Documentation Online* by

Diana Hacker, 30 sample papers and designed documents, and over 9,000 writing and grammar exercises with immediate feedback and reporting in *Exercise Central*. Updated and redesigned, *Re:Writing* also features five free videos from *VideoCentral* and three new visual tutorials from our popular *ix visual exercises* by Cheryl Ball and Kristin Arola. *Re:Writing* is completely free and open (no codes required) to ensure access to all students. Visit **bedfordstmartins.com/rewriting**.

VideoCentral is a growing collection of videos for the writing class that captures real-world, academic, and student writers talking about how and why they write. Writer and teacher Peter Berkow interviewed hundreds of people—from Michael Moore to Cynthia Selfe—to produce 50 brief videos about topics such as revising and getting feedback. *VideoCentral* can be packaged with *Ways of Reading* at a significant discount. An activation code is required. To learn more, visit **bedfordstmartins.com/videocentral**. To order *VideoCentral* packaged with the print book, use ISBN 10: 0-312-53986-X or ISBN 13: 978-0-312-53986-3.

Re:Writing Plus gathers all of Bedford/St. Martin's premium digital content for composition into one online collection. It includes hundreds of model documents, the first ever peer review game, and *VideoCentral*. *Re:Writing Plus* can be purchased separately or packaged with the print book at a significant discount. An activation code is required. To learn more, visit **bedfordstmartins.com/rewriting**. To order *Re:Writing Plus* packaged with the print book, use ISBN 10: 0-312-53993-2 or ISBN 13: 978-0-312-53993-1.

ACKNOWLEDGMENTS

With our colleagues, we have taught most of the selections in this book, including the new ones. Several of us worked together to prepare the assignment sequences; most of these, too, have been tested in class. As we have traveled around giving talks, we've met many people who have used *Ways of Reading*. We have been delighted to hear them speak about how it has served their teaching, and we have learned much from their advice and example. It is an unusual and exciting experience to see our course turned into a text, to see our work read, critiqued, revised, and expanded. We have many people to thank. The list that follows can't begin to name all those to whom we owe a debt. And it can't begin to express our gratitude.

We owe much to the friendship and wisdom of our colleagues at the University of Pittsburgh. There are old friends and colleagues with whom we have worked for a very long time: Don Bialostosky, Ellen Bishop, Jean Ferguson Carr, Steve Carr, Nick Coles, Kathryn Flannery, Jean Grace, Paul Kameen, Geeta Kothari, Beth Matway, Mariolina Salvatori, Jim Seitz, Phil Smith, and Lois Williams. Jim Seitz worked closely with us in preparing this edition; he and a range of our teaching assistants and teaching fellows taught the eighth edition and some of the new selections for the ninth. A smaller group of graduate students and non-tenure track faculty colleagues played a major role, with Jim, in helping to develop the new edition: Jennifer Lee, Brie Owen, Dahliani Reynolds, Stacey Waite, Emily Wender, and Brenda Whitney. Stacey was there at the beginning, but she also played a major role as we rewrote assignments, worked up the new sequences, and did the final revisions. It is an honor and a pleasure to teach together with such colleagues; we have learned much from their example, their critique, and their suggestions.

And we owe much to colleagues at other schools who have followed our work with interest and offered their support and criticism. We are grateful for the notes, letters, and student papers.

We are fortunate to have a number of outstanding reviewers on the project: Patrick Baliani, University of Arizona; Heather Bastian, University of Kansas; David Carillo, University of Connecticut–Waterbury; Patricia Comitini, Quinnipiac University; Jennifer Coolidge, Truman State University; Pamelyn Dane, Lane Community College; Darren DeFrain, Wichita State University; Patrick A. Dolan Jr., University of Iowa; Kim Donehower, University of North Dakota; Stephen F. Evans, University of Kansas; Nicole Plyler Fisk, University of South Carolina; Gordon Fraser, University of Connecticut; Charlotte Hogg, Texas Christian University; Rebecca Huffman, University of Kentucky; Constance Baucum Little, Colorado State University–Pueblo; Tara Lockhart, San Francisco State University; Cynthia Miecznikowski, University of North Carolina at Pembroke; Laurie Polhemus, University of Central Oklahoma; Glenda Pritchett, Quinnipiac University; Melissa Purdue, Minnesota State University, Mankato; Lori Robison, University of North Dakota; James Schneider, South Puget Sound Community College; Robert A. Smart, Quinnipiac University; Patricia S. Sullivan, Northeastern University; Stacey Waite, University of Pittsburgh; Emily Wender, University of Pittsburgh. We also thank our anonymous reviewers.

We would also like to thank those who responded to our questionnaire: Margaret Bayless, Lane Community College; J. James Bono, University of Pittsburgh; Amy E. Borden, California State University, San Bernardino; Jose Chaves, Lane Community College; John P. Craig, University of Tennessee; Emily Donnelli, Park University; Lynn Dornink, Northeastern University; Stephen F. Evans, University of Kansas; LaToya Faulk, Michigan State University; Nicole Plyler Fisk, University of South Carolina; Paul Fitzjarrald, California State University, Fullerton; Theresa Flynn, Pepperdine University; Gordon Fraser, University of Connecticut; Lisa Giles, University of Southern Maine; Angela L. Glover, Simpson College; Carol V. Hamilton, University of Pittsburgh; Anna Harris, Wichita State University; Robin Hoffman, University of Pittsburgh; Linda Jordan, Platt La Roche College; Ryan Keefe, Virginia Tech; Ralph Leary, Clarion University; Jodie Liedke, Wichita State University; Constance Baucum Little, Colorado State University–Pueblo; Neil Meyer, Queens College; Mary Bauer Morley, University of North Dakota; Laura Neef, Wichita State University; Ellen Noonan, Northeastern University; Gabrielle Owen, University of Pittsburgh; Glenda Pritchett, Quinnipiac University; Dahliani Reynolds, University of Pittsburgh; Leah Schwebel, University of Connecticut; Jennifer Swartz, Lake Erie College; and Kathryn Toof, Whatcom Community College. We are also grateful to those who chose to remain anonymous.

Chuck Christensen and Joan Feinberg at Bedford/St. Martin's helped to shape this project from its very beginning. They remain fine and thoughtful friends as well as fine and thoughtful editors. John Sullivan joined the group for the fifth edition. He had taught from an earlier edition of *Ways of Reading* and had, for us, a wonderful sense of the book's approach to reading, writing, and teaching. John is organized, resourceful, generous, quick to offer suggestions and to take on extra work. He soon became as much a collaborator as an editor. It was a real pleasure to work with him. Sandy Schechter and Linda Finigan handled permissions. Shannon Walsh assisted with many details. Katherine Caruana expertly guided the manuscript through production. Linda McLatchie was an excellent copyeditor, sensitive to the quirks of our prose and attentive to detail.

And, finally, we are grateful to Joyce and Ellen, and to Jesse, Dan, Kate, Matthew, and Ben, for their love and support.

Contents

beings, and consciousness as consciousness intent upon the world. They must abandon the educational goal of deposit-making and replace it with the posing of the problems of human beings in their relations with the world."

[FROM *Pedagogy of the Oppressed*]

SUSAN GRIFFIN, OUR SECRET **335**

"The nightmare images of the German child-rearing practices that one discovers . . . call to mind the catastrophic events of recent German history. I first encountered this pedagogy in the writing of Alice Miller. At one time a psychoanalyst, she was haunted by a question, *What could make a person conceive the plan of gassing millions of human beings to death?* In her work, she traces the origins of this violence to childhood. Of course there cannot be one answer to such a monumental riddle, nor does any event in history have a single cause. Rather a field exists. . . ."

[FROM *A Chorus of Stones*]

LAURA KIPNIS, READER ADVISORY **390**
LOVE'S LABORS **391**

"Might we entertain the possibility that posing philosophical questions isn't restricted to university campuses and learned tomes, that maybe it's something everyone does in the course of everyday life — if not always in an entirely knowing fashion? If adultery is more of a critical practice than a critical theory, well, acting out *is* what happens when knowledge or consciousness about something is foreclosed."

[FROM *Against Love: A Polemic*]

RICHARD E. MILLER, THE DARK NIGHT OF THE SOUL **420**

"Can secular institutions of higher education be taught to use writing to foster a kind of critical optimism that is able to transform idle feelings of hope into viable plans for sustainable action? Can the first year writing course become a place where we engage productively with the dark realities of our time: violence, suicide, war, and terrorism, as well as fraudulence, complicity, and trauma? Can teachers of first year writing be moved beyond praising students for generating arguments without consequence, thought with no interest in action?"

[FROM *Writing at the End of the World*]

WALKER PERCY, THE LOSS OF THE CREATURE **459**

"When a caste system becomes absolute, envy disappears. Yet the caste of layman-expert is not the fault of the expert. It is due altogether to the eager surrender of sovereignty by the layman so that he may take up the role not of the person but of the consumer."

[FROM *The Message in the Bottle*]

Additional Sequences included in *Resources for Teaching Ways of Reading*

Introduction: Ways of Reading

MAKING A MARK

Reading involves a fair measure of push and shove. You make your mark on a book, and it makes its mark on you. Reading is not simply a matter of hanging back and waiting for a piece, or its author, to tell you what the writing has to say. In fact, one of the difficult things about reading is that the pages before you will begin to speak only when the authors are silent and you begin to speak in their place, sometimes for them — doing their work, continuing their projects — and sometimes for yourself, following your own agenda.

This is an unusual way to talk about reading, we know. We have not mentioned finding information or locating an author's purpose or identifying main ideas, useful though these skills are, because the purpose of our book is to offer you occasions to imagine other ways of reading. We think of reading as a social interaction — sometimes peaceful and polite, sometimes not so peaceful and polite.

We'd like you to imagine that when you read the works we've collected here, somebody is saying something to you, and we'd like you to imagine that you are in a position to speak back, to say something of your own in turn. In other words, we are not presenting our book as a miniature library (a place to find information), and we do not think of you, the reader, as a term-paper writer (a person looking for information to summarize or report).

When you read, you hear an author's voice as you move along; you believe a person with something to say is talking to you. You pay attention, even when you don't completely understand what is being said, trusting that it will all make sense in the end, relating what the author says to what you already know or expect to hear or learn. Even if you don't quite grasp everything you are reading at every moment (and you won't), and even if you don't remember everything you've read (no reader does—at least not in long, complex pieces), you begin to see the outlines of the author's project, the patterns and rhythms of that particular way of seeing and interpreting the world.

When you stop to talk or write about what you've read, the author is silent; you take over—it is your turn to write, to begin to respond to what the author said. At that point, this author and his or her text become something you construct out of what you remember or what you notice as you go back through the text a second time, working from passages or examples but filtering them through your own predisposition to see or read in particular ways.

In "The Achievement of Desire," one of the essays in this book, Richard Rodriguez tells the story of his education, of how he was drawn to imitate his teachers because of his desire to think and speak like them. His is not a simple story of hard work and success, however. In a sense, Rodriguez's education gave him what he wanted—status, knowledge, a way of understanding himself and his position in the world. At the same time, his education made it difficult to talk to his parents, to share their point of view; and to a degree, he felt himself becoming consumed by the powerful ways of seeing and understanding represented by his reading and his education. The essay can be seen as Rodriguez's attempt to weigh what he had gained against what he had lost.

If ten of us read his essay, each would begin with the same words on the page, but when we discuss the essay (or write about it), each will retell and interpret Rodriguez's story differently; we will emphasize different sections—some, for instance, might want to discuss the strange way Rodriguez learned to read, others might be taken by his difficult and changing relations to his teachers, and still others might want to think about Rodriguez's remarks about his mother and father.

Each of us will come to his or her own sense of what is significant, of what the point is, and the odds are good that what each of us makes of the essay will vary from one to another. Each of us will understand Rodriguez's story in his or her own way, even though we read the same piece. At the same time, if we are working with Rodriguez's essay (and not putting it aside or ignoring its peculiar way of thinking about education), we will be working within a framework he has established, one that makes education stand, metaphorically, for a complicated interplay between permanence and change, imitation and freedom, loss and achievement.

In "The Achievement of Desire," Rodriguez tells of reading a book by Richard Hoggart, *The Uses of Literacy*. He was captivated by a section of this book in which Hoggart defines a particular kind of student, the "scholarship boy." Here is what Rodriguez says:

> Then one day, leafing through Richard Hoggart's *The Uses of Literacy*, I found, in his description of the scholarship boy, myself. For the first time I realized that there were other students like me, and so I was able to frame the meaning of my academic success, its consequent price—the loss.

For Rodriguez, this phrase, "scholarship boy," became the focus of Hoggart's book. Other people, to be sure, would read that book and take different phrases or sections as the key to what Hoggart has to say. Some might argue that Rodriguez misread the book, that it is really about something else, about British culture, for example, or about the class system in England. The power and value of Rodriguez's reading, however, are represented by what he was able to *do* with what he read, and what he was able to do was not record information or summarize main ideas but, as he says, "frame the meaning of my academic success." Hoggart provided a frame, a way for Rodriguez to think and talk about his own history as a student. As he goes on in his essay, Rodriguez not only uses this frame to talk about his experience, but he resists it, argues with it. He casts his experience in Hoggart's terms but then makes those terms work for him by seeing both what they can and what they cannot do. This combination of reading, thinking, and writing is what we mean by *strong reading*, a way of reading we like to encourage in our students.

When we have taught "The Achievement of Desire" to our students, it has been almost impossible for them not to see themselves in Rodriguez's description of the scholarship boy (and this was true of students who were not minority students and not literally on scholarships). They, too, have found a way of framing (even inventing) their own lives as students — students whose histories involve both success and loss. When we have asked our students to write about this essay, however, some students have argued, and quite convincingly, that Rodriguez had either to abandon his family and culture or to remain ignorant. Other students have argued equally convincingly that Rodriguez's anguish was destructive and self-serving, that he was trapped into seeing his situation in terms that he might have replaced with others. He did not necessarily have to turn his back on his family. Some have contended that Rodriguez's problems with his family had nothing to do with what he says about education, that he himself shows how imitation need not blindly lead a person away from his culture, and these student essays, too, have been convincing.

READERS LEARN TO PUT THINGS TOGETHER BY WRITING.

Reading, in other words, can be the occasion for you to put things together, to notice this idea or theme rather than that one, to follow a writer's announced or secret ends while simultaneously following your own. When this happens, when you forge a reading of a story or an essay, you make your mark on it, casting it in your terms. But the story makes its mark on you as well, teaching you not only about a subject (Rodriguez's struggles with his teachers and his parents, for example) but also about a way of seeing and understanding a subject. The text provides the opportunity for you to see through someone else's powerful language, to imagine your own familiar settings through the images, metaphors, and ideas of others. Rodriguez's essay, in other words, can make its mark on readers, but they, too, if they are strong, active readers, can make theirs on it.

Readers learn to put things together by writing. This is not something you can do, at least not to any degree, while you are reading. It requires that you work on what you have read, and that work best takes shape when you sit down to write. We will have more to say about this kind of thinking in a later section of the introduction, but for now let us say that writing gives you a way of going to work on the text you have read. To write about a story or an essay, you go back to what you have read to find phrases or passages that define what for you are the key moments, that help you interpret sections that seem difficult or troublesome or mysterious. If you are writing an essay of your own, the work that you are doing gives a purpose and a structure to that rereading.

Writing also, however, gives you a way of going back to work on the text of your own reading. It allows you to be self-critical. You can revise not just to make your essay neat or tight or tidy but to see what kind of reader you have been, to examine the pattern and consequences in the choices you have made. Revision, in other words, gives you the chance to work on your essay, but it also gives you an opportunity to work on your reading—to qualify or extend or question your interpretation of, say, "The Achievement of Desire."

We can describe this process of "re-vision," or re-seeing, fairly simply. You should not expect to read "The Achievement of Desire" once and completely understand the essay or know what you want to say. You will work out what you have to say while you write. And once you have constructed a reading—once you have completed a draft of your essay, in other words—you can step back, see what you have done, and go back to work on it. Through this activity—writing and rewriting—we have seen our students become strong, active, and critical readers.

Not everything a reader reads is worth that kind of effort. The pieces we have chosen for this book all provide, we feel, powerful ways of seeing (or framing) our common experience. The selections cannot be quickly summarized. They are striking, surprising, sometimes troubling in how they challenge common ways of seeing the world. Some of them have captured and altered the way our culture sees and understands daily experience. The essays have changed the ways people think and write. In fact, every selection in the book is one that has given us, our students, and our colleagues that dramatic experience, almost like a discovery, when we suddenly saw things as we had never seen them before and, as a consequence, we had to work hard to understand what had happened and how our thinking had changed.

If we recall, for example, the first time we read Susan Griffin's "Our Secret" or John Edgar Wideman's "Our Time," we know that they have radically shaped our thinking. We carry these essays with us in our minds, mulling over them, working through them, hearing Griffin and Wideman in sentences we write or sentences we read. We introduce the essays in classes we teach whenever we can; we are surprised, reading them for the third or fourth time, to find things we didn't see before. It's not that we failed to "get" these essays the first time around. In fact, we're not sure we have captured them yet, at least not in any final sense, and we disagree in basic ways about what Griffin and Wideman are saying or about how these essays might best be used. Essays like these are not the sort that you can "get" like a loaf of bread at the store. We're each convinced that the essays are ours in that we know best what's going on in them, and yet we have also become theirs, creatures of these essays, because of the ways they have come to dominate our seeing, talking, reading, and writing. This captivity is something we welcome, yet it is also something we resist.

Our experience with these texts is a remarkable one and certainly hard to provide for others, but the challenges and surprises are reasons we read—we hope to be taken and changed in just these ways. Or, to be more accurate, it is why we read outside the daily requirements to keep up with the news or conduct our business. And it is why we bring reading into our writing courses.

WAYS OF READING

Before explaining how we organized this book, we would like to say more about the purpose and place of the kind of strong, aggressive, labor-intensive reading we've been referring to.

Readers face many kinds of experiences, and certain texts are written with specific situations in mind and invite specific ways of reading. Some texts, for instance, serve very practical purposes—they give directions or information. Others, like the short descriptive essays often used in English textbooks and anthologies, celebrate common ways of seeing and thinking and ask primarily to be admired. These texts seem self-contained; they announce their own meanings with little effort and ask little from the reader, making it clear how they want to be read and what they have to say. They ask only for a nod of the head or for the reader to take notes and give a sigh of admiration ("yes, that was very well said"). They are clear and direct. It is as though the authors could anticipate all the questions their essays might raise and solve all the problems a reader might imagine. There is not much work for a reader to do, in other words, except, perhaps, to take notes and, in the case of textbooks, to work step-by-step, trying to remember as much as possible.

This is how assigned readings are often presented in university classrooms. Introductory textbooks (in biology or business, for instance) are good examples of books that ask little of readers outside of note-taking and memorization. In these texts the writers are experts, and your job, as novice, is to digest what they have to say. And, appropriately, the task set before you is to summarize—so you can speak again what the author said, so you can better remember what you read. Essay tests are an example of the writing tasks that often follow this kind of reading. You might, for instance, study the human nervous system through textbook readings and lectures and then be asked to write a summary of what you know from both sources. Or a teacher might ask you during a class discussion to paraphrase a paragraph from a textbook describing chemical cell communication to see if you understand what you've read.

Another typical classroom form of reading is reading for main ideas. With this kind of reading you are expected to figure out what most people (or most people within a certain specialized group of readers) would take as the main idea of a selection. There are good reasons to read for main ideas. For one, it is a way to learn how to imagine and anticipate the values and habits of a particular group—test-makers or, if you're studying business, Keynesian economists, perhaps. If you are studying business, to continue this example, you must learn to notice what Keynesian economists notice—for instance, when they analyze the problems of growing government debt—to share key terms, to know the theoretical positions they take, and to adopt for yourself their common examples and interpretations, their jargon, and their established findings.

There is certainly nothing wrong with reading for information or reading to learn what experts have to say about their fields of inquiry. These are not, however, the only ways to read, although they are the ones most often taught. Perhaps because we think of ourselves as writing teachers, we are concerned with presenting other ways of reading in the college and university curriculum.

A danger arises in assuming that reading is only a search for information or main ideas. There are ways of thinking through problems and working with written texts which are essential to academic life, but that are not represented by summary and paraphrase or by note-taking and essay exams.

Student readers, for example, can take responsibility for determining the meaning of the text. They can work as though they were doing something other than finding ideas already there on the page, and they can be guided by their own impressions or questions as they read. We are not, now, talking about finding hidden meanings. If such things as hidden meanings can be said to exist, they are hidden by readers' habits and prejudices (by readers' assumptions that what they read should tell them what they already know) or by readers' timidity and passivity (by their unwillingness to take the responsibility to speak their minds and say what they notice).

Reading to locate meaning in the text places a premium on memory, yet a strong reader is not necessarily a person with a good memory. This point may seem minor, but we have seen too many students haunted because they could not remember everything they read or retain a complete essay in their minds. A reader could set herself the task of remembering as much as she could from Walker Percy's "The Loss of the Creature," an essay filled with stories about tourists at the Grand Canyon and students in a biology class, but a reader could also do other things with that essay; a reader might figure out, for example, how students and tourists might be said to have a common problem seeing what they want to see. Students who read Percy's essay as a memory test end up worrying about bits and pieces (bits and pieces they could go back and find if they had to) and turn their attention away from the more pressing problem of how to make sense of a difficult and often ambiguous essay.

A reader who needs to have access to something in the essay can use simple memory aids. A reader can go back and scan, for one thing, to find passages or examples that might be worth reconsidering. Or a reader can construct a personal index, making marks in the margin or underlining passages that seem interesting or mysterious or difficult. A mark is a way of saying, "This is something I might want to work on later." If you mark the selections in this book as you read them, you will give yourself a working record of what, at the first moment of reading, you felt might be worth a second reading.

If Percy's essay presents problems for a reader, they are problems of a different order from summary and recall. The essay is not the sort that tells you what it says. You would have difficulty finding one sentence that sums up or announces, in a loud and clear voice, what Percy is talking about. At the point you think Percy is about to summarize, he turns to one more example that complicates the picture, as though what he is discussing defies his attempts to sum things up. Percy is talking about tourists and students, about such things as individual "sovereignty" and our media culture's "symbolic packages," but if he has a point to make, it cannot be stated in a sentence or two.

In fact, Percy's essay is challenging reading in part because it does not have a single, easily identifiable main idea. A reader could infer that it has several points to make, none of which can be said easily and some of which, perhaps, are contradictory. To search for information, or to ignore the rough edges in search of a single, paraphrasable idea, is to divert attention from the task at hand, which is not to remember what Percy says but to speak about the essay and what it means to you, the reader. In this sense, the Percy essay is not the sum of its individual parts; it is, more accurately, what its readers make of it.

A reader could go to an expert on Percy to solve the problem of what to make of the essay—perhaps to a teacher, perhaps to the Internet or to a book in the library. And if the reader pays attention, he could remember what the expert said, or she could put down notes on paper (or in an e-file). But in doing either, the reader only rehearses what he or she has been told, abandoning the responsibility to make the essay meaningful. There are ways of reading, in other words, in which Percy's essay "The Loss of the Creature" is not what it means to the experts but what it means to you as a reader willing to take the chance to construct a reading. You can be the authority on Percy; you don't have to turn to others. The meaning of the essay, then, is something you develop as you go along, something for which you must take final responsibility. The meaning is forged from reading the essay, to be sure, but it is determined by what you do with the essay, by the connections you can make and your explanation of why those connections are important, and by your account of what Percy might mean when he talks about "symbolic packages" or a "loss of sovereignty" (phrases Percy uses as key terms in the essay). This version of Percy's essay will finally be yours; it will not be exactly what Percy said. (Only his words in the order he wrote them would say exactly what he said.) You will choose the path to take through his essay and support it as you can with arguments, explanations, examples, and commentary.

AN ESSAY OR A STORY IS NOT THE SUM OF ITS PARTS BUT SOMETHING YOU AS A READER CREATE BY PUTTING TOGETHER THOSE PARTS THAT SEEM TO MATTER.

If an essay or a story is not the sum of its parts but something you as a reader create by putting together those parts that seem to matter personally, then the way to begin, once you have read a selection in this collection, is by reviewing what you recall, by going back to those places that stick in your memory—or, perhaps, to those sections you marked with checks or notes in the margins. You begin by seeing what you can make of these memories and notes. You should realize that with essays as long and complex as those we've included in this book, you will never feel, after a single reading, as though you have command of everything you read. This is not a problem. After four or five readings (should you give any single essay that much attention), you may still feel that there are parts you missed or don't understand. This sense of incompleteness is part of the experience of reading, at least the experience of reading serious work. And it is part of the experience of a strong reader. No reader could retain one of these essays in her mind, no matter how proficient her memory or how experienced she might be. No reader, at least no reader we would trust, would admit that he understood everything that Michel Foucault or Judith Butler or Edward Said had to say. What strong readers know is that they have to begin, and they have to begin regardless of their doubts or hesitations. What you have after your first reading of an essay is a starting place, and you begin with your marked passages or examples or notes, with questions to answer, or with problems to solve. Strong readings, in other words, put a premium on individual acts of attention and composition.

STRONG READERS, STRONG TEXTS

We chose pieces for this book that invite strong readings. Our selections require more attention (or a different form of attention) than a written summary, a reduction to gist, or a recitation of main ideas. They are not "easy" reading. The challenges they present, however, do not make them inaccessible to college students. The essays are not specialized studies; they have interested, pleased, or piqued general and specialist audiences alike. To say that they are challenging is to say, then, that they leave some work for a reader to do. They are designed to teach a reader new ways to read (or to step outside habitual ways of reading), and they anticipate readers willing to take the time to learn. These readers need not be experts on the subject matter. Perhaps the most difficult problem for students is to believe that this is true.

You do not need experts to explain these stories and essays, although you could probably go to the library and find an expert guide to most of the selections we've included. Let's take, for example, John Berger's essay "Ways of Seeing." You could go to the library to find out how Berger is understood and regarded by experts, by literary critics or art historians, for example; you could learn how his work fits into an established body of work on art and representation. You could see what others have said about the writers he cites — Walter Benjamin, for example. You could see how others have read and made use of Berger. You could track one of his key terms, like "mystification."

Though it is often important to seek out other texts and to know what other people are saying or have said, it is often necessary and even desirable to begin on your own. Berger can also be read outside any official system of interpretation. He is talking, after all, about our daily experience. And when he addresses the reader, he addresses a person — not a term-paper writer. When he says, "The way we see things is affected by what we know and what we believe," *you* are part of that construction, part of the "we" he is invoking.

The primary question, then, is not what Berger's words might mean to an art historian or to those with credentials as professors or as cultural critics. The question is what you, the reader, can make of those words given your own experience, your goals, and the work you do with what he has written. In this sense, "Ways of Seeing" is not what it means to others (those who have already decided what it means) but what it means to you, and this meaning is something you compose when you write about the essay; it is your account of what Berger says and how what he says might be said to make sense.

A teacher, poet, and critic we admire, I. A. Richards, once said, "Read as though it made sense and perhaps it will." To take command of complex material like the selections in this book, you need not subordinate yourself to experts; you can assume the authority to provide such a reading on your own. This means you must allow yourself a certain tentativeness and recognize your limits. You should not assume that it is your job to solve all the problems these essays present. You can speak with authority while still acknowledging that complex issues *are* complex.

There is a paradox here. On the one hand, the essays are rich, magnificent, too big for anyone to completely grasp all at once, and before them, as before inspiring spectacles, it seems appropriate to stand humbly, admiringly. And yet, on the other hand, a reader must speak with authority.

In "The American Scholar," Ralph Waldo Emerson says, "Meek young men grow up in libraries, believing it their duty to accept the views, which Cicero, which Locke, which Bacon, have given, forgetful that Cicero, Locke, and Bacon were only young men in libraries when they wrote these books." What Emerson offers here is not a fact but an attitude. There is creative reading, he says, as well as creative writing. It is up to you to treat authors as your equals, as people who will allow you to speak, too. At the same time, you must respect the difficulty and complexity of their texts and of the issues and questions they examine. Little is to be gained, in other words, by turning a complex essay into a message that would fit on a poster in a dorm room: "Be Yourself" or "Stand on Your Own Two Feet."

READING WITH AND AGAINST THE GRAIN

Reading, then, requires a difficult mix of authority and humility. On the one hand, a reader takes charge of a text; on the other, a reader gives generous attention to someone else's (a writer's) key terms and methods, commits his time to her examples, tries to think in her language, imagines that this strange work is important, compelling, at least for the moment.

Most of the questions in *Ways of Reading* will have you moving back and forth in these two modes, reading with and against the grain of a text, reproducing an author's methods, questioning his or her direction and authority. With Susan Bordo's essay "Beauty (Re)discovers the Male Body," for example, we have asked students to look at images from the contemporary media, to think about them in terms of her argument, and to write about them as she might—to see them and to understand them in her terms, through the lens of her essay. We have asked students to give themselves over to this essay, in other words—recognizing that this is not necessarily an easy thing to do. Notice what she would notice. Ask the questions she would ask. Try out her conclusions.

To read generously, to work inside someone else's system, to see your world in someone else's terms—we call this "reading with the grain." It is a way of working *with* a writer's ideas, in conjunction with someone else's text. As a way of reading, it can take different forms. In the reading and writing assignments that follow the selections in this book, you will sometimes be asked to summarize and paraphrase, to put others' ideas into your terms, to provide your account of what they are saying. This is a way of getting a tentative or provisional hold on a text, its examples and ideas; it allows you a place to begin to work.

And sometimes you will be asked to extend a writer's project—to add your examples to someone else's argument, to read your experience through the frame of another's text, to try out the key terms and interpretive schemes in another writer's work. In the assignments that follow Bordo's essay, for example, students are asked both to reproduce her argument and to extend her terms to examples from their own experience.

We have also asked students to read against the grain, to read critically, to turn back, for example, *against* Bordo's project, to ask questions they believe might come as a surprise, to look for the limits of her vision, to provide alternate readings of her examples, to find examples that challenge her argument—to engage her, in other words, in dialogue. Susan Bordo, we say, is quite specific about her age and her experience, her point of view. You are placed at a different moment in time, your experience is different, your schooling and your exposure to images have prepared you differently. Your job, then, is not simply to reproduce Bordo's project in your writing and thinking, but to refine it, to extend it, to put it to the test.

Many of the essays in this book provide examples of writers working against the grain of common sense or everyday language. This is true of John Berger, for example, who redefines the "art museum" against the way it is usually understood. It is true of John Edgar Wideman, who reads against his own text while he writes it—asking questions that disturb the story as it emerges on the page. It is true of Judith Butler, Susan Griffin, and Kwame Anthony Appiah, whose writings show the signs of their efforts to work against the grain of the standard essay, of habitual ways of representing what it means to know something, to be somebody, to speak before others.

MANY OF THE ESSAYS IN THIS BOOK PROVIDE EXAMPLES OF WRITERS WORKING AGAINST THE GRAIN OF COMMON SENSE OR EVERYDAY LANGUAGE.

This, we've found, is the most difficult work for students to do, this working against the grain. For good reasons and bad, students typically define their skill by reproducing rather than questioning or revising the work of their teachers (or the work of those their teachers ask them to read). It is important to read generously and carefully and to learn to submit to projects that others have begun. But it is also important to know what you are doing—to understand where this work comes from, whose interests it serves, how and where it is kept together by will rather than desire, and what it might have to do with you. To fail to ask the fundamental questions—Where am I in this? How can I make my mark? Whose interests are represented? What can I learn by reading with or against the grain?—to fail to ask these questions is to mistake skill for understanding, and it is to misunderstand the goals of a liberal education. All of the essays in this book, we would argue, ask to be read, not simply reproduced; they ask to be read and to be read with a difference. Our goal is to make that difference possible.

WORKING WITH DIFFICULTY

When we chose the selections for this textbook, we chose them with the understanding that they were difficult to read. And we chose them knowing that students were not their primary audience (that the selections were not speaking directly to you). We chose them, in other words, knowing that we would be asking you to read something you were most likely not prepared to read. But this is what it means to be a student, and it was our goal to take our students seriously. Students have to do things they are not yet ready to do; this is how they learn. Students need to read materials that they are not yet ready to read. This is how they get started; this is where they begin. It is also the case that, in an academic setting, difficulty is not necessarily a problem. If something is hard to read, it is not necessarily the case that the writer is at fault. The work can be hard to read because the writer is thinking beyond the usual ways of thinking. It is hard because it is hard, in other words. The text is not saying the same old things in the same old ways.

We believe the best way to work on a difficult text is by *re*reading, and we provide exercises to direct this process ("Questions for a Second Reading"), but you can also work on the difficult text by writing—by taking possession of the work through sentences and paragraphs of your own, through summary, paraphrase, and quotation, by making another writer's work part of your work. The textbook is organized to provide ways for you to work on these difficult selections by writing and rereading. Each of the selections is followed by questions designed to help you get started.

To get a better sense of what we mean by "working with difficulty," it might be useful to look at an example. One of the selections in *Ways of Reading* is a chapter from a book titled *Pedagogy of the Oppressed*, by the Brazilian educator Paulo Freire. The chapter is titled "The 'Banking' Concept of Education," and the title summarizes the argument at its most simple level. The standard forms of education, Freire argues, define the teacher as the active agent and the student as the passive agent. The teacher has knowledge and makes deposits from this storehouse into the minds of students, who are expected to receive these deposits completely and without alteration—like moving money from a wallet to the bank vault. And this, he argues, is not a good thing.

One of the writing assignments attached to this selection asks students to think along with Freire and to use his argument to examine a situation from their own experience with schooling. Here is an essay (a very skillful essay) that we received from a freshman in the opening weeks of class. It is relatively short and to the point. It will be familiar. You should have no trouble following it, even if you haven't read the selection by Freire.

The "Banking" Concept of Education

As a high school senior, I took a sociology class that was a perfect example of the "banking" concept of education, as described by Freire. There were approximately thirty students enrolled in the class. Unless each of our brains was computerized for long-term memorization, I don't understand how we were expected to get anything out of the class.

Each class began with the copying of four to five pages of notes, which were already written on the blackboards when we entered the classroom. Fifteen to twenty minutes later, the teacher proceeded to pass out a worksheet, which was to be filled out using only the notes we previously copied as our reference. If a question was raised, her reply was, "It's in the notes."

With approximately ten minutes left in the period, we were instructed to pass our worksheets back one desk. Then, she read the answers to the worksheets and gave a grade according to how many questions we answered correctly.

During the semester, we didn't have any quizzes, and only one test, which consisted of matching and listing-type questions. All test information was taken directly from the daily worksheets, and on no occasion did she give an essay question. This is an example of a test question:

Name three forms of abuse that occur in the family.

1.

2.

3.

In order to pass the class, each piece of information printed on her handouts needed to be memorized. On one occasion, a fellow classmate summed up her technique of teaching perfectly by stating, "This is nothing but education by memorization!"

Anyone who cared at all about his grade in the class did quite well, according to his report card. Not much intelligence is required to memorize vocabulary terms. Needless to say, not too many of us learned much from the class, except that "education by memorization" and the "banking" concept of education, as Freire puts it, are definitely not an interesting or effective system of education.

The essay is confident and tidy and not wrong in its account of the "banking" concept of education. In five short paragraphs, the writer not only "got" Freire but also worked his high school sociology teacher and her teaching methods into the "banking" narrative. We asked the student (as we have asked many students since then): How did you do this? What was the secret? And he was quick to answer, "I read through the Freire essay, and I worked with what I understood and I ignored the rest." And it's true. He did. And it is true that this is one way to get started. It's OK. You work with what you can.

The difficult sections of Freire's argument (the hard parts, the sections, and the passages our writer ignored) are related to a Marxist analysis of a *system* of education and its interests. Freire does not write just about individuals—a bad teacher and a smart student—although it is certainly easier (and in some ways more comforting) to think that schooling is just a matter of individual moments and individual actors, good and bad. What is happening in our classrooms, Freire argues, is bigger than the intentions or actions of individuals. He says, for example, "Education as the exercise of domination stimulates the credulity of students, with the ideological intent (often not perceived by educators) of indoctrinating them to adapt to the world of oppression." He writes about how schools "regulate the way the world 'enters into' students." He calls for "problem-posing education": "Problem-posing education is revolutionary futurity." What is at stake, he says, is "humanity." What is required is "*conscientização.*" He is concerned to promote education in service of "revolution": "A deepened consciousness of their situation leads people to apprehend that situation as an historical reality susceptible of transformation." There is more going on here, in other words, than can be represented simply by a teacher who is lazy or unimaginative.

The student's essay marks a skillful performance. He takes Freire's chapter and makes it consistent with what he knows how to say. You hear that in this statement: "'education by memorization' and the 'banking' concept of education, as Freire puts it, are definitely not an interesting or effective system of education." Freire's language becomes consistent with his own (the "banking" concept can be filed away under "education by memorization"), and once this is achieved, the writer's need to do any real work with Freire's text becomes unnecessary—"needless to say." Working with difficult readings often requires a willingness to step outside of what you can conveniently control, and this process often begins with revision. As important as it was for this student to use his essay to get hold of Freire, to open a door or to get handhold, a place of purchase, a way to begin, it is equally important for a writer to take the next step—and the next step is to revise, particularly where revision is a way of reworking rather than just "fixing" what you have begun.

This was a student of ours, and after talking with him about the first draft, we suggested that he reread "The 'Banking' Concept of Education," this time paying particular attention to the difficult passages, the passages that were hard to understand, those that he had ignored the first time around. And we suggested that his revised essay should bring some of those passages into the text. He did just this, and by changing the notion of what he was doing (by working with rather than in spite of difficulty), he wrote a very different essay. This was real revision, in other words, not just a matter of smoothing out the rough edges. The revision changed the way the writer read, and it changed the way the reader wrote. The revised essay was quite different (and not nearly so confident and skillful—and this was a good thing, a sign of learning). Here is a representative passage:

> We never really had to "think" in the class. In fact, we were never permitted to "think," we were merely expected to take in the information and store it like a computer. Freire calls this act a "violation of [men's] humanity" (p. 327). He states, "Any situation in which some individuals prevent others from engaging in the process of inquiry is one of violence" (p. 327). I believe what Freire is speaking of here is . . .

We'll keep his conclusion to ourselves, since the conclusion is not nearly so important as what has happened to the writer's understanding of what it means to *work* on a reading. In this revised paragraph, he brings in phrases from the text, and the phrases he brings in are not easy to handle; he has to struggle to put them to use or to make them make sense. The writer is trying to figure out the urgency in Freire's text. The story of the sociology class was one thing, but how do you get from there to a statement about a "violation of men's humanity"?

So the passage that is quoted is not just dumped in for color; it is there for the writer to work with, to try to deploy. And that is what comes next:

> He states, "Any situation in which some individuals prevent others from engaging in the process of inquiry is one of violence" (p. 327). I believe what Freire is speaking of here is . . .

The key moment in writing like this is the moment of translation: "I believe what Freire is speaking of here is . . ." This is where the writer must step forward to take responsibility for working inside the terms of Freire's project.

There is much to admire in this revision. It was early in the semester when writing is always risky, and it took courage and determination for a student to work with what she (or he) couldn't quite understand, couldn't sum up easily, couldn't command. We are a long way from the first draft and "needless to say." You can see, even in this brief passage, that the writing has lost some of the confidence (or arrogance) of the first draft, and as the writer works to think with Freire about education as a system, the characters of the "student" and the "teacher" become different in this narrative. And this is good writing. It may not be as finished as it might need to be later in the semester, but it is writing where something is happening, where thought is taken seriously.

ONCE YOU HAVE AN ENTRY POINT, WHERE YOU HAVE ENTERED AND HOW YOU HAVE ENTERED WILL HELP TO SHAPE YOUR SENSE OF WHAT IS INTERESTING OR IMPORTANT IN THE TEXT.

So, how do you work with a difficult text? You have to get started somewhere and sometime, and you will almost always find yourself writing before you have a sense that you have "mastered" the text, fully comprehended what you have read. (We would argue that these are dangerous goals, "mastery" and "comprehension." We value what students can bring themselves to *do* with what they read, and we measure their success in relation to the success of the project.) You have to get started somewhere, and then you can go back to work again on what you have begun by rereading and rewriting. The textbook provides guidelines for rereading.

When you are looking for help with a particular selection, you can, for example, turn to the "Questions for a Second Reading." Read through *all* of them, whether they are assigned or not, since they provide several entry points, different ways in, many of them suggested to us by our students in class and in their essays. You might imagine that these questions and the writing assignments that follow (and you might read through these writing assignments, too) provide starting points. Each suggests a different path through the essay. No one can hold a long and complicated essay in mind all at once. Every reader needs a starting point, a way in. Having more than one possible starting point allows you to make choices.

Once you have an entry point, where you have entered and how you have entered will help to shape your sense of what is interesting or important in the text. In this sense, you (and not just the author) are organizing the essay or chapter. The text will present its shape in terms of sections or stages. You should look for these road signs — breaks in the text or phrases that indicate intellectual movement, like "on the other hand" or "in conclusion." You can be guided by these, to be sure, but *you* also give shape to what you read—and you do this most deliberately when you reread. This is where you find (and impose) patterns and connections that are not obvious and not already articulated but that make sense to you and give you a way to describe what you see in what you are reading. In our own teaching, we talk to our students about "scaffolds." The scaffold, we say, represents the way you are organizing the text, the way you are putting it together. A scaffold is made up of lines and passages from the text, the terms you've found that you want to work with, ideas that matter to you, your sense of the progress of the piece.

The scaffold can also include the work of others. In groups or in class discussion, take notes on what other students say. This is good advice generally (you can always learn from your colleagues), but it is particularly useful in a class that features reading and writing. Your notes can document the ideas of others, to be sure, but most important they can give you a sense of where other people are beginning, of where they have entered the text and what they are doing once they have started. You can infer the scaffold they have constructed to make sense of what they read, and this can give highlight and relief, even counterpoint, to your own. And use your teacher's comments and questions, including those on your first drafts, to get a sense of the shape of your work as a reader and a writer. This is not a hunt for ideas, for the right or proper or necessary thing to say about a text. It is a hunt for a method, for a way of making sense of a text without resorting only to simple summary.

READING AND WRITING: THE QUESTIONS AND ASSIGNMENTS

Strong readers, we've said, remake what they have read to serve their own ends, putting things together, figuring out how ideas and examples relate, explaining as best they can material that is difficult or problematic, translating phrases like Richard Rodriguez's "scholarship boy" into their own terms. At these moments, it is hard to distinguish the act of reading from the act of writing. In fact, the connection between reading and writing can be seen as almost a literal one, since the best way you can show your reading of a rich and dense essay like "The Achievement of Desire" is by writing down your thoughts, placing one idea against another, commenting on what you've done, taking examples into account, looking back at where you began, perhaps changing your mind, and moving on.

Readers, however, seldom read a single essay in isolation, as though their only job were to arrive at some sense of what an essay has to say. Although we couldn't begin to provide examples of all the various uses of reading in academic life, it is often the case that readings provide information and direction for investigative projects, whether they are philosophical or scientific in nature. The reading and writing assignments that follow each selection in this book are designed to point you in certain directions, to give you ideas and projects to work with, and to challenge you to see one writer's ideas through another's.

Strong readers often read critically, weighing, for example, an author's claims and interpretations against evidence—evidence provided by the author in the text, evidence drawn from other sources, or the evidence that is assumed to be part of a reader's own knowledge and experience. Critical reading can produce results as far-reaching as a biochemist publicly challenging the findings and interpretations in an article on cancer research in the *New England Journal of Medicine* or as quiet as a student offering a personal interpretation of a story in class discussion.

You will find that the questions we have included in our reading and writing assignments often direct you to test what you think an author is saying by measuring it against your own experience. Paulo Freire, for example, in "The 'Banking' Concept of Education" talks about the experience of the student, and one way for you to develop or test your reading of his essay is to place what he says in the context of your own experience, searching for examples that are similar to his and examples that differ from his. If the writers in this book are urging you to give strong readings of your common experience, you have access to what they say because they are talking not only to you but about you. Freire has a method that he employs when he talks about the classroom—one that compares "banking" education with "problem-posing" education. You can try out his method and his terms on examples of your own, continuing his argument as though you were working with him on a common project. Or you can test his argument as though you want to see not only where and how it will work but also where and how it will not.

You will also find questions that ask you to extend the argument of the essay by looking in detail at some of the essay's own examples. John Berger, for example, gives a detailed analysis of two paintings by Frans Hals in "Ways of Seeing." Other paintings in the essay he refers to only briefly. One way of working on his essay is to look at the other examples, trying to do with them what he has done for you earlier.

Readers, as we have said, seldom read an essay in isolation, as though, having once worked out a reading of Kwame Anthony Appiah's "Race, Culture, Identity: Misunderstood Connections," they could go on to something else, something unrelated. It is unusual for anyone, at least in an academic setting, to read in so random a fashion. Readers read most often because they have a project in hand—a question they are working on or a problem they are trying to solve. For example, if as a result of reading Appiah's essay you become interested in questions of race and identity, and you begin to notice things you would not have noticed before, then you can read other essays in the book through this frame. If you have a project in mind, that project will help determine how you read these other essays. Sections of an essay that might otherwise seem unimportant suddenly become important—Gloria Anzaldúa's unusual prose style, or John Wideman's account of his racial politics in Pittsburgh. Appiah may enable you to read Wideman's narrative differently. Wideman may spur you to rethink Appiah. In a sense, then, you do have the chance to become an expert reader, a reader with a project in hand, one who has already done some reading, who has watched others at work, and who has begun to develop a method of analysis and a set of key terms. Imagining yourself operating alongside some of the major figures in contemporary thought can be great fun and heady work—particularly when you have the occasion to speak back to them.

In every case, then, the material we provide to direct your work on the essay, story, or poem will have you constructing a reading, but then doing something with what you have read—using the selection as a frame through which you can understand (through which you can "read") your own experience, the examples of others, or the ideas and methods of other writers.

You may find that you have to alter your sense of who a writer is and what a writer does as you work on your own writing. Writers are often told that they need to begin with a clear sense of what they want to do and what they want to say. The writing assignments we've written, we believe, give you a sense of what you want (or need) to do. We define a problem for you to work on, and the problem will frame the task for you. You will have to decide where you will go in the texts you have read to find materials to work with, the primary materials that will give you a place to begin as you work on your essay. It would be best, however, if you did not feel that you need to have a clear sense of what you want to say before you begin. You may begin to develop a sense of what you want to say while you are writing—as you begin, for example, to examine how and why Anzaldúa's prose could be said to be difficult to read, and what that difficulty might enable you to say about what Anzaldúa expects of a reader. It may also be the case, however, that the subjects you will be writing about are too big for you to assume that you need to have all the answers or that it is up to you to have the final word or to solve the problems once and for all. When you work on your essays, you should cast yourself in the role of one who is exploring a question, examining what might be said, and speculating on possible rather than certain conclusions. If you consider your responses to be provisional, examples of what might be said by a bright and serious student at this point in time, you will be in a position to learn more, as will those who read what you write. Think of yourself, then, as a writer intent on opening a subject up rather than closing one down.

THINK OF YOURSELF, THEN, AS A WRITER INTENT ON OPENING A SUBJECT UP RATHER THAN CLOSING ONE DOWN.

Let us turn briefly now to the three categories of reading and writing assignments you will find in the book.

Questions for a Second Reading

Immediately following each selection are questions designed to guide your second reading. You may, as we've said, prefer to follow your own instincts as you search for the materials to build your understanding of the essay or story or poem. These questions are meant to assist that process or develop those instincts. Most of the selections in the book are longer and more difficult than those you may be accustomed to reading. They are difficult enough that any reader would have to reread them and work to understand them; these questions are meant to suggest ways of beginning that work.

The second-reading questions characteristically ask you to consider the relations between ideas and examples in what you have read or to test specific statements in the essays against your own experience (so that you can get a sense of the author's habit of mind, his or her way of thinking about subjects that are available to you, too). Some turn your attention to what we take to be key terms or concepts, asking you to define these terms by observing how the writer uses them throughout the essay.

These are the questions that seemed "natural" to us; they reflect our habitual way of reading and, we believe, the general habits of mind of the academic community. These questions have no simple answers; you will not find a correct answer hidden somewhere in the selection. In short, they are not the sorts of questions asked on SAT or ACT exams. They are real questions, questions that ask about the basic methods of an essay or about the issues the essay raises. They pose problems for interpretation or indicate sections where, to our minds, there is some interesting work for a reader to do. They are meant to reveal possible ways of reading the text, not to indicate that there is only one correct way, and that we have it.

You may find it useful to take notes as you read through each selection a second time, perhaps in a journal you can keep as a sourcebook for more formal written work. We will often also divide our students into groups, with each group working together with one of the second-reading questions in preparation for a report to the class. There are important advantages for you as a *writer* when you do this kind of close work with the text. Working through a second time, you get a better sense of the argument and of the *shape* of the argument; you get a sense of not only what the author is *saying* but what she is *doing,* and this prepares you to provide not only summary and paraphrase but also a sense of the author and her project. And the work of rereading sends you back to the text; the second time through you can locate passages you might very well want to use in your own writing—passages that are particularly interesting to you, or illustrative, or even puzzling and obscure. These become the block quotations you can use to bring the author's words into your essay, to bring them in as the object of scrutiny and discussion.

Assignments for Writing

This book actually offers three kinds of writing assignments: assignments that ask you to write about a single essay or story, assignments that ask you to read one selection through the frame of another, and longer sequences of assignments that define a project within which three or four of the selections serve as primary sources. All of these assignments serve a dual purpose. Like the second-reading questions, they suggest a way for you to reconsider the essays; they give you access from a different perspective. The assignments also encourage you to be a strong reader and actively interpret what you have read. In one way or another, they all invite you to use a story or an essay as a way of framing experience, as a source of terms and methods to enable you to interpret something else—some other text, events and objects around you, or your own memories and experience. The assignment sequences can be found at the end of the book and in *Resources for Teaching Ways of Reading*. The others (titled "Assignments for Writing" and "Making Connections") come immediately after each selection.

"Assignments for Writing" ask you to write about a single selection. Although some of these assignments call for you to paraphrase or reconstruct difficult passages, most ask you to interpret what you have read with a specific purpose in mind. The work you are to do is generally of two sorts. For most of the essays, one question asks you to interpret a moment from your own experience through the frame of the essay—adapting its method, using its key terms, extending the range of its examples. Other assignments, however, ask you to turn an essay back on itself or to extend the conclusions of the essay by reconsidering the examples the writer has used to make his or her case.

A note on the writing assignments: When we talk with teachers and students using *Ways of Reading*, we are often asked about the wording of these assignments. The assignments are long. The wording is often unusual, unexpected. The assignments contain many questions, not simply one. The directions seem indirect, confusing. "Why?" we're asked. "How should we work with these?" When we write assignments, our goal is to point students toward a project, to provide a frame for their reading, a motive for writing, a way of asking certain kinds of questions. In that sense, the assignments should not be read as a set of directions to be followed literally. In fact, they are written to resist that reading, to forestall a writer's desire to simplify, to be efficient, to settle for the first clear line toward the finish. We want to provide a context to suggest how readers and writers might take time, be thoughtful. And we want the projects students work on to become their own. We hope to provoke varied responses, to leave the final decisions to the students. So the assignments try to be open and suggestive rather than narrow and direct. We ask lots of questions, but students don't need to answer them all (or any of them) once they begin to write. Our questions are meant to suggest ways of questioning, starting points. "What do you want?" Our own students ask this question. We want writers to make the most they can of what they read, including our questions and assignments.

So, what's the best way to work with an assignment? The writing assignments we have written will provide a context for writing, even a set of expectations, but the assignments do not provide a set of instructions. The first thing to do, then, is to ask yourself what, within this context, do you want to write about? What is on your mind? What is interesting or pressing for you? What direction can you take that will best allow you to stretch or to challenge yourself or to do something that will be new and interesting? We will often set aside class time to talk through an assignment and what possibilities it might suggest for each student's work. (We don't insist that everyone take the same track.) And we invite students to be in touch with us and with one another outside of class or via the Internet. At this stage (at least to our minds), sharing your thoughts with others is one way to do the work of the academy. Writers and scholars rely on their friends and colleagues to help them get an angle, think about where to begin, understand what is new and interesting and what is old and dull. And, then, finally, the moment comes and you just sit down to the keyboard and start writing. There is no magic here, unfortunately. You write out what you can, and then you go back to what you have written to see what you are saying and to see what comes next and to think about how to shape it all into an essay to give to readers in the hope that they might say "eloquent," "persuasive," "beautiful."

Making Connections

The connections questions will have you work with two or more readings at a time. These are not so much questions that ask you to compare or contrast the essays or stories as they are directions on how you might use one text as the context for interpreting another. Mary Louise Pratt, for example, in "Arts of the Contact Zone" looks at the work of a South American native, an Inca named Guaman Poma, writing in the seventeenth century to King Philip III of Spain. His work, she argues, can be read as a moment of contact, one in which different cultures and positions of power come together in a single text—in which a conquered person responds to the ways he is represented in the mind and the language of the conqueror. Pratt's reading of Guaman Poma's letter to King Philip, and the terms she uses to describe the way she reads it, provide a powerful context for a reader looking at essays by other writers, like Gloria Anzaldúa, for whom the "normal" or "standard" language of American culture is difficult, troubling, unsatisfactory, or incomplete. There are, then, assignments that ask you both to extend and to test Pratt's reading through your reading of alternative texts.

THE SEQUENCES ALLOW YOU TO PARTICIPATE IN AN EXTENDED ACADEMIC PROJECT.

The purpose of all these assignments is to demonstrate how the work of one author can be used as a frame for reading and interpreting the work of another. This can be exciting work, and it demonstrates a basic principle of liberal arts education: students should be given the opportunity to adopt different points of view, including those of scholars and writers who have helped to shape modern thought. These kinds of assignments give you the chance, even as a novice, to try your hand at the work of professionals.

Reading one essay through the lens of another becomes a focused form of rereading. To write responses to these assignments, you will need to reread both of the assigned selections. The best way to begin is by taking a quick inventory of what you recall as points of connection. You could do this on your own, with a colleague, or in groups, but it is best to do it with pen and paper (or laptop) in hand. And before you reread, you should come to at least a provisional sense of what you want to do with the assignment. Then you can reread with a project in mind. Be sure to mark passages that you can work with later, when you are writing. And look for passages that are interestingly different as well as those that complement each other.

The Assignment Sequences

The assignment sequences are more broad-ranging versions of the "Making Connections" assignments; in the sequences, several reading and writing assignments are linked and directed toward a single goal. They allow you to work on projects that require more time and incorporate more readings than would be possible in a single assignment. And they encourage you to develop your own point of view in concert with those of the professionals who wrote the essays and stories you are reading.

The assignments in a sequence build on one another, each relying on the ones before. A sequence will usually make use of four or five reading selections. The first is used to introduce an area of study or inquiry as well as to establish a frame of reference, a way of thinking about the subject. In the sequence titled "The Aims of Education," you begin with readings by Paulo Freire. The goal of the sequence is to provide a point for you to work from, one that you can open up to question. Subsequent assignments ask you to develop examples from your own schooling as you work through other accounts of education in, for example, Mary Louise Pratt's "Arts of the Contact Zone," Susan Griffin's "Our Secret," or Richard E. Miller's "The Dark Night of the Soul."

The sequences allow you to participate in an extended academic project, one in which you take a position, revise it, look at a new example, hear what someone else has to say, revise it again, and see what conclusions you can draw about your subject. These projects always take time—they go through stages and revisions as a writer develops a command over his material, pushing against habitual ways of thinking, learning to examine an issue from different angles, rejecting quick conclusions, seeing the power of understanding that comes from repeated effort, and feeling the pleasure writers take when they find their own place in the context of others whose work they admire. This is the closest approximation we can give you of the rhythm and texture of academic life, and we offer our book as an introduction to its characteristic ways of reading, thinking, and writing.

THE Readings

DAVID Abram

David Abram has an odd, hybrid, or conflicted relationship with the academy and its ways and its work. His thinking is clearly indebted to traditions of Western scholarship. His writing makes repeated reference to Maurice Merleau-Ponty and a school of philosophy, phenomenology, concerned with human experience and human perception and, in particular, with a fundamental sensory engagement with the outside world that comes before thought and interpretation. He writes with footnotes, in other words, and acknowledges his indebtedness to previous scholarship and thought. Abram graduated summa cum laude from Wesleyan University in 1980; he did graduate work in the Yale School of Forestry and received a PhD in philosophy from SUNY Stony Brook in 1993. He has received fellowships from the Watson and Rockefeller foundations.

Abram, however, gives equal, if not greater, weight to what he learned as a sleight-of-hand magician and through his travels among the indigenous peoples of Southeast Asia and the Americas. While in college, he performed as a magician in bars and restaurants in New England, including a stint in Alice's Restaurant in the Berkshires; he took a year off from college to perform as a street magician in Europe. When he returned to school, he realized that he could use his skills as a magician to study non-Western medical practices. In a National Public Radio interview with Scott London, he said:

> When I decided to return to college to finish my degree, I became very interested in the uses of magic in medicine. It struck me that this was a very old connection — that in traditional societies the healers were often magicians. So I traveled as an itinerant magician into various indigenous, traditional cultures in Southeast Asia — Sri Lanka, various parts of Indonesia, and Nepal — in the hopes of using my own skills as a sleight-of-hand magician to meet and come to know some of the traditional magicians, or medicine people, who apply their craft in those cultures.

One result of this learning was a book, *The Spell of the Sensuous: Perception and Language in a More-Than-Human World* (1996), the book from which the following selection was taken. *The Spell of the Sensuous* has had considerable success and is widely read, both inside and outside the academy. It won the prestigious Lannan Literary Award for Nonfiction. Since its publication, Abram has lectured widely and written on "cultural ecology," on the cultural causes and consequences of the degradation of our environment. He publishes in the journal *Environmental Ethics*. He is the founder and creative director of the Alliance for Wild Ethics (AWE), "a consortium of individuals and organizations working to ease the spreading devastation of the animate earth through a rapid transformation of culture." AWE employs "the arts, often in tandem with the natural sciences, to provoke deeply felt shifts in the human experience of nature." He has taught at Schumacher College in Devon, England, an experimental college that offers short, highly interactive courses in which students can develop "ideas and solutions which serve the short and long term wellbeing of the planet, its people and its ecology." Abram also performs as a "storyteller," and he has done much to promote the traditions and legacies of an oral culture in a world of print.

Storyteller and philosopher. This doubleness is reproduced in the opening of *The Spell of the Sensuous*, where there are two "introductions." The first, "The Ecology of Magic: A Personal Introduction to the Inquiry," opens as follows:

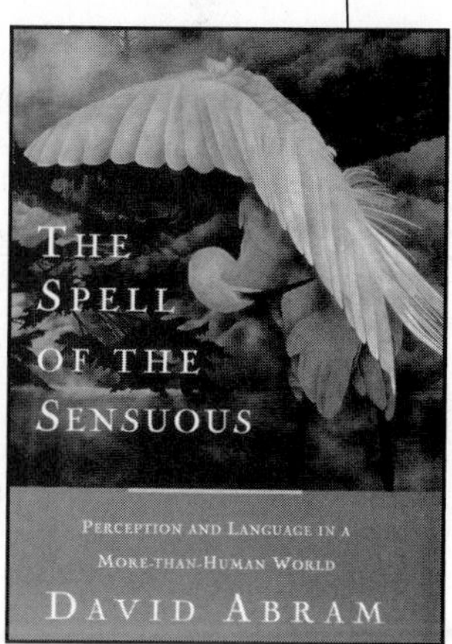

> Late one evening I stepped out of my little hut in the rice paddies of eastern Bali and found myself falling through space. Over my head the black sky was rippling with stars, densely clustered in some regions, almost blocking out the darkness between them, and more loosely scattered in other areas, pulsing and beckoning to each other. Behind them all streamed the great river of light with its several tributaries. Yet the Milky Way churned beneath me as well, for my hut was set in the middle of a large patchwork of rice paddies, separated from each other by narrow two-foot-high dikes, and these paddies were all filled with water. The surface of these pools, by day, reflected perfectly the blue sky, a reflection broken only by the thin, bright green tips of new rice. But by night the stars themselves glimmered from the surface of the paddies, and the river of light whirled through the darkness underfoot as well as above; there seemed no ground in front of my feet, only the abyss of star-studded space falling away forever.
>
> I was no longer simply beneath the night sky, but also *above* it—the immediate impression was of weightlessness. (p. 4)

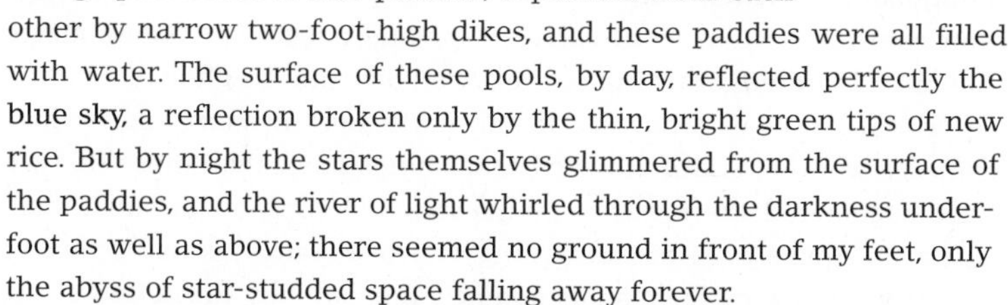

The second introduction, "Philosophy on the Way to Ecology: A Technical Introduction to the Inquiry," provides a summary account of the work of two philosophers, Edmund Husserl and Maurice Merleau-Ponty. It reads like a "review of the literature," a standard opening chapter in academic writing, or at least in the writing of dissertations. It begins:

> It is natural that we turn to the tradition of phenomenology in order to understand the strange difference between the experienced world, or worlds, of indigenous, vernacular cultures and the world of modern European and North American civilization. For phenomenology is the Western philosophical tradition that has most forcefully called into question the modern assumption of a single, wholly determinable, objective reality. (p. 31)

Abram said that he had two goals for his book: "to provide a set of powerful conceptual tools for my colleagues in the broad world of environmental activism" and "to provide some new thinking within the institutional realm of scholars, scientists and educators—many of whom have been strangely silent in response to the rapid deterioration of wild nature, the steady vanishing of other species, and the consequent flattening of our human relationships" (x). In the interview with Scott London, he said that it was important to him to write a book that would speak to "experts," but that would speak to them in a different way.

> That was very much the intent of the book, to bridge the gap between the world of the imagination—the kind of magical world of these indigenous, traditional societies—and the world of academia, the intelligentsia, and the scientific elite. But I didn't want to do that just by writing a scholarly or scientific analysis of indigenous, animistic ways of thinking. I wanted to do the opposite. I wanted to do an animistic analysis of rationality and the Western intellect, and to show that our Western, civilized ways of thinking are themselves a form of magic.

And, in the book's final section, the "Coda," he asks, "What then of writing?"

> The preceding pages have called attention to some unnoticed and unfortunate side-effect of the alphabet—effects that have structured much of the way we now perceive. Yet it would be a perilous mistake for any reader to conclude from these pages that he or she should simply relinquish the written word. Indeed, the story sketched out herein suggests that the written word carries a pivotal magic—the same magic that once sparkled for us in the eyes of an owl and the glide of an otter.
>
> For those of us who care for an earth not encompassed by machines, a world of textures, tastes, and sounds other than those that we have engineered, there can be no question of simply abandoning literacy, or turning away from all writing. Our task, rather, is that of *taking up* the written word, with all its potency, and patiently, carefully, writing language back into the land. Our craft is that of releasing the budded, earthly intelligence of our words, freeing them to respond to the speech of the things themselves—to the green uttering-forth of leaves from the spring branches. It is the practice of spinning stories that have the rhythm and lilt of the local sound-scape, tales for the tongue, tales that want to be told, again and again, sliding off the digital screen and slipping off the lettered page to inhabit these coastal forests, those desert canyons, those whispering grasslands and valleys and swamps.

> Finding phrases that place us in contact with the trembling neck-muscles of a deer holding its antlers high as it swims toward the mainland, or with the ant dragging a scavenged rice-grain through the grasses. Planting words like seeds, under rocks and fallen logs — letting language take root, once again, in the earthen silence of shadow and bone and leaf. (pp. 273–74)

Is there magic here, magic on the page? Is such magic possible? These are the questions Abram invites us to ask. The selection that follows lays out the argument for the problems inherent in writing and in alphabetic literacy. It is a call for us to write (and think and act) differently, all on behalf of the natural world.

Animism and the Alphabet

> Lifting a brush, a burin, a pen, or a stylus is like releasing a bite or lifting a claw.
>
> — GARY SNYDER

The question regarding the origins of the ecological crisis, or of modern civilization's evident disregard for the needs of the natural world, has already provoked various responses from philosophers. There are those who suggest that a generally exploitative relation to the rest of nature is part and parcel of being human, and hence that the human species has from the start been at war with other organisms and the earth. Others, however, have come to recognize that long-established indigenous cultures often display a remarkable solidarity with the lands that they inhabit, as well as a basic respect, or even reverence, for the other species that inhabit those lands. Such cultures, much smaller in scale (and far less centralized) than modern Western civilization, seem to have maintained a relatively homeostatic or equilibrial relation with their local ecologies for vast periods of time, deriving their necessary sustenance from the land without seriously disrupting the ability of the earth to replenish itself. The fecundity and flourishing diversity of the North American continent led the earliest European explorers to speak of this terrain as a primeval and unsettled wilderness — yet this continent had been continuously inhabited by human cultures for at least ten thousand years. That indigenous peoples can have gathered, hunted, fished, and settled these lands for such a tremendous span of time without severely degrading the continent's wild integrity readily confounds the notion that humans are innately bound to ravage their earthly surroundings. In a few centuries of European settlement, however, much of the native abundance of this continent has been lost—its broad animal populations decimated, its many-voiced forests overcut and its prairies overgrazed, its rich soils depleted, its tumbling clear waters now undrinkable.

European civilization's neglect of the natural world and its needs has clearly been encouraged by a style of awareness that disparages sensorial reality, denigrating the visible and tangible order of things on behalf of some absolute source assumed to exist entirely beyond, or outside of, the bodily world. Some historians and philosophers have concluded that the Jewish and Christian traditions, with their otherworldly God, are primarily responsible for civilization's negligent attitude toward the environing earth. They cite, as evidence, the Hebraic God's injunction to humankind in Genesis: "Be fertile and increase, fill the earth and master it; and rule the fish of the sea, the birds of the sky, and all the living things that creep on earth."[1]

Other thinkers, however, have turned toward the Greek origins of our philosophical tradition, in the Athens of Socrates and Plato, in their quest for the roots of our nature-disdain. A long line of recent philosophers, stretching from Friedrich Nietzsche down to the present, have attempted to demonstrate that Plato's philosophical derogation of the sensible and changing forms of the world — his claim that these are mere simulacra of eternal and pure ideas existing in a nonsensorial realm beyond the apparent world — contributed profoundly to civilization's distrust of bodily and sensorial experience, and to our consequent estrangement from the earthly world around us.

So the ancient Hebrews, on the one hand, and the ancient Greeks on the other, are variously taken to task for providing the mental context that would foster civilization's mistreatment of nonhuman nature. Each of these two ancient cultures seems to have sown the seeds of our contemporary estrangement — one seeming to establish the spiritual or religious ascendancy of humankind over nature, the other effecting a more philosophical or rational dissociation of the human intellect from the organic world. Long before the historical amalgamation of Hebraic religion and Hellenistic philosophy in the Christian New Testament, these two bodies of belief already shared — or seem to have shared — a similar intellectual distance from the nonhuman environment.

In every other respect these two traditions, each one originating out of its own specific antecedents, and in its own terrain and time, were vastly different. In every other respect, that is, but one: they were both, from the start, profoundly informed by writing. Indeed, they both made use of the strange and potent technology which we have come to call "the alphabet."

• • • • • • •

Writing, like human language, is engendered not only within the human community but between the human community and the animate landscape, born of the interplay and contact between the human and the more-than-human world. The earthly terrain in which we find ourselves, and upon which we depend for all our nourishment, is shot through with suggestive scrawls and traces, from the sinuous calligraphy of rivers winding across the land, inscribing arroyos and canyons into the parched earth of the desert, to the black slash burned by lightning into the trunk of an old elm. The swooping flight of birds is a kind of cursive script written on the wind; it is this script that was studied by the ancient "augurs," who could read therein the course of the future. Leaf-miner insects make strange hieroglyphic tabloids of the leaves they consume. Wolves urinate on specific stumps and stones to mark off their territory. And today you read these printed words as tribal hunters once read the tracks of deer, moose, and bear printed in the soil of the forest floor. Archaeological evidence suggests that for more than a million years the subsistence of humankind has depended upon the acuity of such hunters, upon their ability to read the traces — a bit of scat here, a broken twig there — of these animal Others. These letters I print across the page, the scratches and scrawls you now focus upon, trailing off across the white surface, are hardly different from the footprints of prey left in the snow. We read these traces with organs honed over millennia by our tribal ancestors, moving instinctively from one track to the next, picking up the trail afresh whenever it leaves off, hunting the *meaning*, which would be the *meeting* with the Other.[2]

The multiform meanings of the Chinese word for writing, *wen*, illustrate well this interpenetration of human and nonhuman scripts:

> The word *wen* signifies a conglomeration of marks, the simple symbol in writing. It applies to the veins in stones and wood, to constellations, represented by the strokes connecting the stars, to the tracks of birds and quadrupeds on the ground (Chinese tradition would have it that the observation of these tracks suggested the invention of writing), to tattoos and even, for example, to the designs that decorate the turtle's shell ("The turtle is wise," an ancient text says — gifted with magico-religious powers — "for it carries designs on its back"). The term *wen* has designated, by extension, literature. . . .[3]

Our first writing, clearly, was our own tracks, our footprints, our handprints in mud or ash pressed upon the rock. Later, perhaps, we found that by copying the distinctive prints and scratches made by other animals we could gain a new power; here was a method of identifying with the other animal, taking on its expressive magic in order to learn of its whereabouts, to draw it near, to make it appear. Tracing the impression left by a deer's body in the snow, or transferring that outline onto the wall of the cave: these are ways of placing oneself in distant contact with the Other, whether to invoke its influence or to exert one's own. Perhaps by multiplying its images on the cavern wall we sought to ensure that the deer itself would multiply, be bountiful in the coming season. . . .

OUR FIRST WRITING, CLEARLY, WAS OUR OWN TRACKS, OUR FOOTPRINTS, OUR HANDPRINTS IN MUD OR ASH PRESSED UPON THE ROCK.

All of the early writing systems of our species remain tied to the mysteries of a more-than-human world. The petroglyphs of pre-Columbian North America abound with images of prey animals, of rain clouds and lightning, of eagle and snake, of the paw prints of bear. On rocks, canyon walls, and caves these figures mingle with human shapes, or shapes part human and part Other (part insect, or owl, or elk).

Some researchers assert that the picture writing of native North America is not yet "true" writing, even where the pictures are strung together sequentially — as they are, obviously, in many of the rock inscriptions (as well as in the calendrical "winter counts" of the Plains tribes). For there seems, as yet, no strict relation between image and utterance.

In a much more conventionalized pictographic system, like the Egyptian hieroglyphics (which first appeared during the First Dynasty, around 3000 B.C.E. and remained in use until the second century C.E.),[4] stylized images of humans and human implements are still interspersed with those of plants, of various kinds of birds, as well as of serpents, felines, and other animals. Such pictographic systems, which were to be found as well in China as early as the fifteenth century B.C.E., and in Mesoamerica by the middle of the sixth century B.C.E., typically include characters that scholars have come to call "ideograms." An ideogram is often a pictorial character that refers not to the visible entity that it explicitly pictures but to some quality or other phenomenon readily associated with that entity. Thus — to invent a simple example — a stylized image of a jaguar with its feet off the ground might come to signify "speed." For the Chinese, even today, a stylized image of the sun and moon together signifies "brightness"; similarly, the word for "east" is invoked by a stylized image of the sun rising behind a tree.[5]

The efficacy of these pictorially derived systems necessarily entails a shift of sensory participation away from the voices and gestures of the surrounding landscape toward our own human-made images. However, the glyphs which constitute the bulk of these ancient scripts continually remind the reading body of its inherence in a more-than-human field of meanings. As signatures not only of the human form but of other animals, trees, sun, moon, and landforms, they continually refer our senses beyond the strictly human sphere.[6]

Yet even a host of pictograms and related ideograms will not suffice for certain terms that exist in the local discourse. Such terms may refer to phenomena that lack any precise visual association. Consider, for example, the English word "belief." How might we signify this term in a pictographic, or ideographic, manner? An image of a phantasmagorical monster, perhaps, or one of a person in prayer. Yet no such ideogram would communicate the term as readily and precisely as the simple image of a bumblebee, followed by the figure of a leaf. We could, that is, resort to a visual pun, to images of things that have nothing overtly to do with belief but which, when named in sequence, carry the same *sound* as the spoken term "belief" ("bee-leaf"). And indeed, such pictographic puns, or *rebuses,* came to be employed early on by scribes in ancient China and in Mesoamerica as well as in the Middle East, to record certain terms that were especially amorphous or resistant to visual representation. Thus, for instance, the Sumerian word *ti*, which means "life," was written in cuneiform with the pictorial sign for "arrow," which in Sumerian is also called *ti.*[7]

An important step has been taken here. With the rebus, a pictorial sign is used to directly invoke a particular sound of the human voice, rather than the outward reference of that sound. The rebus, with its focus upon the sound of a name rather than the thing named, inaugurated the distant possibility of a *phonetic* script (from the Greek *phonein:* "to sound"), one that would directly transcribe the sound of the speaking voice rather than its outward intent or meaning.[8]

However, many factors impeded the generalization of the rebus principle, and thus prevented the development of a fully phonetic writing system. For example, a largely pictographic script can easily be utilized, for communicative purposes, by persons who speak very different dialects (and hence cannot understand one another's speech). The same image or ideogram, readily understood, would simply invoke a different sound in each dialect. Thus a pictographic script allows for commerce between neighboring and even distant linguistic communities – an advance that would be lost if rebuslike signs alone were employed to transcribe the spoken sounds of one community. (This factor helps explain why China, a vast society comprised of a multitude of distinct dialects, has never developed a fully phonetic script.)[9]

Another factor inhibiting the development of a fully phonetic script was the often elite status of the scribes. Ideographic scripts must make use of a vast number of stylized glyphs or characters, since every term in the language must, at least in principle, have its own written character. (In 1716 a dictionary of Chinese – admittedly an extreme example – listed 40,545 written characters! Today a mere 8,000 characters are in use.)[10] Complete knowledge of the pictographic system, therefore, could only be the province of a few highly trained individuals. Literacy, within such cultures, was in fact the literacy of a caste, or cult, whose sacred knowledge was often held in great esteem by the rest of society. It is unlikely that the scribes would willingly develop innovations that could simplify the new technology and so render literacy more accessible to the rest of the society, for this would surely lessen their own importance and status.

> . . . it is clear that ancient writing was in the hands of a small literate elite, the scribes, who manifested great conservatism in the practice of their craft, and, so far from being interested in its simplification, often chose to demonstrate their virtuosity by a proliferation of signs and values. . . .[11]

Nevertheless, in the ancient Middle East the rebus principle was eventually generalized – probably by scribes working at a distance from the affluent and established centers of civilization – to cover all the common sounds of a given language. Thus, "syllabaries" appeared, wherein every basic sound-syllable of the language had its own conventional notation or written character (often rebuslike in origin). Such writing systems employed far fewer signs than the pictographic scripts from which they were derived, although the number of signs was still very much larger than the alphabetic script we now take for granted.

The innovation which gave rise to the alphabet was itself developed by Semitic scribes around 1500 B.C.E.[12] It consisted in recognizing that almost every syllable of their language was composed of one or more silent consonantal elements plus an element of sounded breath – that which we would today call a vowel. The silent consonants provided, as it were, the bodily framework or shape through which the sounded breath must flow. The original Semitic *aleph-beth,* then, established a character, or letter, for each of the consonants of the language. The vowels, the sounded breath that must be added to the written consonants in order to make them come alive and to speak, had to be chosen by the reader, who would vary the sounded breath according to the written context.

By this innovation, the *aleph-beth* was able to greatly reduce the necessary number of characters for a written script to just twenty-two—a simple set of signs that could be readily practiced and learned in a brief period by anyone who had the chance, even by a young child. The utter simplicity of this technical innovation was such that the early Semitic *aleph-beth,* in which were written down the various stories and histories that were later gathered into the Hebrew Bible, was adopted not only by the Hebrews but by the Phonecians (who presumably carried the new technology across the Mediterranean to Greece), the Aramaeans, the Greeks, the Romans, and indeed eventually gave rise (directly or indirectly) to virtually every alphabet known, including that which I am currently using to scribe these words.

With the advent of the *aleph-beth,* a new distance opens between human culture and the rest of nature. To be sure, pictographic and ideographic writing already involved a displacement of our sensory participation from the depths of the animate environment to the flat surface of our walls, of clay tablets, of the sheet of papyrus. However, as we noted above, the written images themselves often related us back to the other animals and the environing earth. The pictographic glyph or character still referred, implicitly, to the animate phenomenon of which it was the static image; it was that worldly phenomenon, in turn, that provoked from us the sound of its name. *The sensible phenomenon and its spoken name were, in a sense, still participant with one another*—the name a sort of emanation of the sensible entity. With the phonetic *aleph-beth,* however, the written character no longer refers us to any sensible phenomenon out in the world, or even to the name of such a phenomenon (as with the rebus), but solely to a gesture to be made by the human mouth. There is a concerted shift of attention away from any outward or worldly reference of the pictorial image, away from the sensible phenomenon that had previously called forth the spoken utterance, to the shape of the utterance itself, now invoked directly by the written character. *A direct association is established between the pictorial sign and the vocal gesture, for the first time completely bypassing the thing pictured.* The evocative phenomena—the entities imaged—are no longer a necessary part of the equation. Human utterances are now elicited, directly, by human-made signs; *the larger, more-than-human life-world is no longer a part of the semiotic, no longer a necessary part of the system.*

Or is it? When we ponder the early Semitic *aleph-beth,* we readily recognize its pictographic inheritance. *Aleph,* the first letter, is written thus: ⋗. *Aleph* is also the ancient Hebrew word for "ox." The shape of the letter, we can see, was that of an ox's head with horns; turned over, it became our own letter *A.*[13] The name of the Semitic letter *mem* is also the Hebrew word for "water"; the letter, which later became our own letter *M,* was drawn as a series of waves: 〰. The letter *ayin,* which also means "eye" in Hebrew, was drawn as a simple circle, the picture of an eye; it is this letter, made over into a vowel by the Greek scribes, that eventually became our letter *O.* The Hebrew letter *qoph,* which is also the Hebrew term for "monkey," was drawn as a circle intersected by a long, dangling, tail ⏀. Our letter *Q* retains a sense of this simple picture.[14]

These are a few examples. By thus comparing the names of the letters with their various shapes, we discern that the letters of the early *aleph-beth* are still implicitly tied to the more-than-human field of phenomena. But these ties to other animals, to natural elements like water and waves, and even to the body itself, are far more tenuous than in the earlier, predominantly nonphonetic scripts. These traces of sensible nature linger in the new script only as vestigial holdovers from the old — they are no longer necessary participants in the transfer of linguistic knowledge. The other animals, the plants, and the natural elements — sun, moon, stars, waves — are beginning to lose their own voices. In the Hebrew Genesis, the animals do not speak their own names to Adam; rather, they are *given* their names by this first man. Language, for the Hebrews, was becoming a purely *human* gift, a human power.

It was only, however, with the transfer of phonetic writing to Greece, and the consequent transformation of the Semitic *aleph-beth* into the Greek "alphabet," that the progressive abstraction of linguistic meaning from the enveloping life-world reached a type of completion. The Greek scribes took on, with slight modifications, both the shapes of the Semitic letters and their Semitic names. Thus *aleph* — the name of the first letter, and the Hebrew word for "ox" — became *alpha*; *beth* — the name of the second letter, as well as the word for "house" — became *beta*; *gimel* — the third letter, and the word for "camel," became *gamma,* etc. But while the Semitic names had older, nongrammatological meanings for those who spoke a Semitic tongue, the Greek versions of those names had no nongrammatological meaning whatsoever for the Greeks. That is, while the Semitic name for the letter was also the name of the sensorial entity commonly imaged by or associated with the letter, the Greek name had no sensorial reference at all.[15] While the Semitic name had served as a reminder of the worldy origin of the letter, the Greek name served only to designate the human-made letter itself. The pictorial (or iconic) significance of many of the Semitic letters, which was memorialized in their spoken names, was now readily lost. The indebtedness of human language to the more-than-human perceptual field, an indebtedness preserved in the names and shapes of the Semitic letters, could now be entirely forgotten.

THE RAPPER'S RHYTHM

". . . I'm a lover of learning, and trees and open country won't teach me anything, whereas men in the town do." These words are pronounced by Socrates, the wise and legendary father of Western philosophy, early in the course of the *Phaedrus* — surely one of the most eloquent and lyrical of the Platonic dialogues.[16] Written by Socrates' most illustrious student,

Plato, these words inscribe a new and curious assumption at the very beginning of the European philosophical tradition.

It is difficult to reconcile Socrates' assertion — that trees and the untamed country have nothing to teach — with the Greece that we have come to know through Homer's epic ballads. In the Homeric songs the natural landscape itself bears the omens and signs that instruct human beings in their endeavors; the gods speak directly through the patterns of clouds, waves, and the flight of birds. Zeus rouses storms, sends thunderclaps, dispatches eagles to swoop low over the heads of men, disrupting their gatherings. Athena herself may take the shape of a seahawk, or may stir a wind to fill a ship's sails. Proteus, "the ancient of the salt sea, who serves under Poseidon," can readily transform into any beast, or into a flaming fire, or into water itself. Indeed, the gods seem indistinguishable at times from the natural elements that display their power: Poseidon, "the blue-maned god who makes the islands tremble," is the very life and fury of the sea itself; Helios, "lord of high noon," is not distinct from the sun (the fiery sun here a willful intelligence able even to father children: Circe, the sorceress, is his daughter). Even "fair Dawn, with her spreading fingertips of rose," is a living power. Human events and emotions are not yet distinct from the shifting moods of the animate earth — an army's sense of relief is made palpable in a description of thick clouds dispersing from the land; Nestor's anguish is likened to the darkening of the sea before a gale; the inward release of Penelope's feelings on listening to news of her husband is described as the thawing of the high mountain snows by the warm spring winds, melting the frozen water into streams that cascade down the slopes — as though the natural landscape was the proper home of those emotions, or as though a common psyche moved between humans and clouds and trees. When Odysseus, half-drowned by Poseidon's wrath and nearly dashed to pieces on the rocky coast of Phaiákia, spies the mouth of a calm river between the cliffs, he prays directly to the spirit of that river to have mercy and offer him shelter — and straightaway the tide shifts, and the river draws him into safety. Here, then, is a land that is everywhere alive and awake, animated by a multitude of capricious but willful forces, at times vengeful and at other times tender, yet always in some sense responsive to human situations. The diverse forms of the earth still speak and offer guidance to humankind, albeit in gestures that we cannot always directly understand.[17]

This participatory and animate earth contrasts vividly with the dismissive view of nature espoused by Socrates in the *Phaedrus*. To make sense of this contrast, it is necessary to realize that the Homeric epics, probably written down in the seventh century B.C.E., are essentially orally evolved creations, oral poems that had been sung and resung, shifting and complexifying, long before they were written down and thus frozen in the precise form in which we now know them.[18] The Platonic dialogues, on the other hand, written in the first half of the fourth century B.C.E., are thoroughly lettered constructions, composed in a literate context by a manifestly literate author. And indeed they inscribe for the first time many of the mental patterns or thought styles that today we of literate culture take for granted.

The Greek alphabet was first invented — or, rather, adapted from the Semitic *aleph-beth* — several centuries before Plato, probably during the eighth century B.C.E.[19] The new technology did not spread rapidly through Greece; rather, it encountered remarkable resistance in the form of a highly developed and ritualized oral culture.[20] That is, the traditions of prealphabetic Greece were actively preserved in numerous oral stories regularly recited and passed along from generation to generation by the Greek bards, or "rhapsodes." The chanted tales carried within their nested narratives much of the accumulated knowledge of the culture. Since they were not written down, they were never wholly fixed, but would shift incrementally with each telling to fit the circumstances or needs of a particular audience, gradually incorporating new practical knowledge while letting that which was obsolete fall away. The sung stories, along with the numerous ceremonies to which they were linked, were in a sense the living encyclopedias of the culture — carrying and preserving the collected knowledge and established customs of the community — and they themselves were preserved through constant repetition and ritual reenactment. There was thus little overt need for the new technology of reading and writing. According to literary historian Eric Havelock, for the first two or three centuries after its appearance in Greece, "[t]he alphabet was an interloper, lacking social standing and achieved use. The elite of society were all reciters and performers."[21]

THE GREEK ALPHABET WAS FIRST INVENTED — OR, RATHER, ADAPTED FROM THE SEMITIC *ALEPH-BETH* — SEVERAL CENTURIES BEFORE PLATO, PROBABLY DURING THE EIGHTH CENTURY B.C.E.

The alphabet, after all, had not here developed gradually, as it had across the Mediterranean, out of a series of earlier scripts, and there was thus no already existing context of related inscriptions and scribal practices for it to latch onto. Moreover, the oral techniques for preserving and transmitting knowledge, and the sensorial habits associated with those techniques, were, as we shall see, largely incompatible with the sensorial patterns demanded by alphabetic literacy.

In a culture as thoroughly and complexly oral as Greek culture in this period, the alphabet could take root only by allying itself, at first, with the oral tradition. Thus, the first large written texts to appear in Greece — namely, the *Iliad* and the *Odyssey* — are, paradoxially, "oral texts." That is, they are not written compositions, as had long been supposed, but rather alphabetic transcriptions of orally chanted poems. Homer, as an oral bard, or rhapsode (from the Greek *rhapsoidein,* which meant "to stitch song together"), improvised the precise form of the poems by "stitching together" an oral tapestry from a vast fund of memorized epithets and formulaic phrases, embellishing and elaborating a cycle of stories that had already been variously improvised or "stitched together" by earlier bards since the Trojan War itself.[22]

We owe our recognition of the oral nature of the Homeric epics to the pioneering research undertaken by the Harvard classicist Milman Parry and his assistant Albert Lord, in the 1930s.[23] Parry had noticed the existence of certain stock phrases — such as "the wine-dark sea," "there spoke clever Odysseus," or "when Dawn spread out her fingertips of rose" — that are continually repeated throughout the poems. Careful study revealed that the poems were composed almost entirely of such expressions (in the twenty-seven thousand hexameters there are twenty-nine thousand repetitions of phrases with two or more words).[24] Moreover, Homer's choice of one particular epithet or formula rather than another seemed at times to be governed less by the exact meaning of the phrase than by the metrical exigencies of the line; the bard apparently called upon one specific formula after another in order to fit the driving meter of the chant, in a trance of rhythmic improvisation. This is not at all to minimize Homer's genius, but simply to indicate that his poetic brilliance was performative as much as creative — less the genius of an author writing a great novel than that of an inspired and eloquent rap artist.

The reliance of the Homeric texts upon repeated verbal formulas and stock epithets — this massive dependence upon that which we today refer to, disparagingly, as "clichés" — offered Parry and subsequent researchers a first insight into the very different world of a European culture without writing. In a literate society, like our own, any verbal discovery or realization can be preserved simply by being written down. Whenever we wish to know how to accomplish a certain task, we need only find the book wherein that knowledge is inscribed. When we wish to ponder a particular historical encounter, we simply locate the text wherein that encounter is recorded. Oral cultures, however, lacking the fixed and permanent record that we have come to count on, can preserve verbal knowledge only by constantly repeating it. Practical knowledge must be embedded in spoken formulas that can be easily recalled — in prayers and proverbs, in continually recited legends and mythic stories. The rhythmic nature of many such spoken formulas is a function of their mnemonic value; such pulsed phrases are much easier for the pulsing, breathing body to assimilate and later recall than the strictly prosaic statements that appear only after the advent of literacy. (For example, the phrase "an apple a day keeps the doctor away" is vastly easier to remember than the phrase "one should always eat fruit in order to stay healthy.") The discourse of nonwriting cultures is, of necessity, largely comprised of such formulaic and rhythmic phrases, which readily spring to the tongue in appropriate situations.[25]

Parry's insights regarding the orally composed nature of the Homeric epics remained somewhat speculative until he was able to meet and observe representatives of an actual bardic tradition still in existence in Eastern Europe. In the 1930s, Parry and his student Albert Lord traveled to Serbia, where they befriended a number of nonliterate Slavic singers whose craft was still rooted in the ancient oral traditions of the Balkans. These singers (or *guslars*) chanted their long stories — for which there existed no written texts — in coffeehouses and at weddings, accompanying themselves on a simple stringed instrument called a *gusla*. Parry and Lord recorded many of these epic songs on early phonographic disks,[26] and so were later able to compare the metrical structure of these chanted stories with the structure and phrasing of the Homeric poems. The parallels were clear and remarkable.[27]

> When one hears the Southern Slavs sing their tales he has the overwhelming feeling that, in some way, he is hearing Homer. This is no mere sentimental feeling that comes from his seeing a way of life and a cast of thought that are strange to him. . . . When the hearer looks closely to see why he should seem to be hearing Homer he finds precise reasons: he is ever hearing the same ideas that Homer expresses, and is hearing them expressed in phrases which are rhythmically the same, and which are grouped in the same order.[28]

Parry carefully documented these strong parallels, and after his early death his research into oral modes of composition was carried on by Albert Lord. Among other things, Lord's research indicated that learning to read and write thoroughly disabled the oral poet, ruining his capacity for oral improvisation.[29]

• • • • • • •

When the Homeric epics were recorded in writing, then the art of the rhapsodes began to lose its preservative and instructive function. The knowledge embedded in the epic stories and myths was now captured for the first time in a visible and fixed form, which could be returned to, examined, and even questioned. Indeed, it was only then, under the slowly spreading influence of alphabetic technology, that "language" was beginning to separate itself from the animate flux of the world, and so becoming a ponderable presence in its own right.

> It is only as language is written down that it becomes possible to think about it. The acoustic medium, being incapable of visualization, did not achieve recognition as a phenomenon wholly separable from the person who used it. But in the alphabetized document the medium became objectified. There it was, reproduced perfectly in the alphabet . . . no longer just a function of "me" the speaker but a document with an independent existence.[30]

The scribe, or author, could now begin to dialogue with his own visible inscriptions, viewing and responding to his own words even as he wrote them down. *A new power of reflexivity was thus coming into existence, borne by the relation between the scribe and his scripted text.*

We can witness the gradual spread of this new power in the written fragments of the pre-Socratic philosophers of the sixth and fifth centuries B.C.E. These thinkers are still under the sway of the oral-poetic mode of discourse – their teachings are commonly couched in an aphoristic or poetic form, and their attention is still turned toward the sensuous terrain that surrounds them. Nevertheless, they seem to stand at a new distance from the natural order, their thoughts inhabiting a different mode of temporality from the flux of nature, which they now question and strive to understand. The written fragments of Heraclitus or of Empedocles give evidence of a radically new, literate reflection combined with a more traditional, oral preoccupation with a sensuous nature still felt to be mysteriously animate and alive, filled with immanent powers. In the words of the pre-Socratic philosopher Thales, "all things are full of gods."[31]

It was not until the early fourth century B.C.E. that such numinous powers, or gods, were largely expelled from the natural surroundings. For it was only at this time that alphabetic literacy became a collective reality in Greece. Indeed, it was only during Plato's lifetime (428–348 B.C.E.) that the alphabet was incorporated within Athenian life to the extent that we might truthfully speak of Athenian Greece as a "literate" culture:

> Plato, in the early fourth century B.C., stands on the threshold between the oral and written cultures of Greece. The earliest epigraphic and iconographic indications of young boys being taught to write date from Plato's childhood. In his day, people had already been reciting Homer from the text for centuries. But the art of writing was still primarily a handicraft. . . . In the fifth century B.C., craftsmen began to acquire the art of carving or engraving letters of the alphabet. But writing was still not a part of recognized instruction: the most a person was expected to be able to write and spell was his own name. . . .[32]

Plato was teaching, then, precisely at the moment when the new technology of reading and writing was shedding its specialized "craft" status and finally spreading, by means of the Greek curriculum, into the culture at large. The significance of this conjunction has not been well recognized by Western philosophers, all of whom stand—to a greater or lesser extent—within Plato's lineage. Plato, or rather the association between the literate Plato and his mostly nonliterate teacher Socrates (469?–399 B.C.E.), may be recognized as the hinge on which the sensuous, mimetic, profoundly embodied style of consciousness proper to orality gave way to the more detached, abstract mode of thinking engendered by alphabetic literacy. Indeed, it was Plato who carefully developed and brought to term the collective thought-structures appropriate to the new technology.

AN ETERNITY OF UNCHANGING IDEAS

Although Socrates himself may have been able to write little more than his own name, he made brilliant use of the new reflexive capacity introduced by the alphabet. Eric Havelock has suggested that the famed "Socratic dialectic"—which, in its simplest form, consisted in asking a speaker to explain what he has said—was primarily a method for disrupting the mimetic thought patterns of oral culture. The speaker's original statement, if it concerned important matters of morality and social custom, would necessarily have been a memorized formula, a poetic or proverbial phrase, which presented a vivid example of the matter being discussed. By asking the speaker to explain himself or to repeat his statement in different terms, Socrates forced his interlocutors to separate themselves, for the first time, from their own words — to separate themselves, that is, from the phrases and formulas that had become habitual through the constant repetition of traditional teaching stories. Prior to this moment, spoken discourse was inseparable from the endlessly repeated stories, legends, and myths that provided many of the spoken phrases one needed in one's daily actions and interactions. To speak was to live within a storied universe, and thus to feel one's closeness to those protagonists and ancestral heroes whose words often seemed to speak through one's own mouth. Such, as we have said, is the way culture preserves itself in the absence of written records. But Socrates interrupted all this. By continually asking his interlocutors to repeat and explain what they had said in other words, by getting them thus to listen to and ponder their own speaking, Socrates stunned his listeners out of the mnemonic trance demanded by orality, and hence out of the sensuous, storied realm to which they were accustomed. Small wonder that some Athenians complained that Socrates' conversation had the numbing effect of a stingray's electric shock.

Prior to the spread of writing, ethical qualities like "virtue," "justice," and "temperance" were thoroughly entwined with the specific situations in which those qualities were exhibited. The terms for such qualities were oral utterances called forth by particular social situations; they had no apparent existence independent of those situations. As utterances, they slipped back into the silence immediately after they were spoken; they had no permanent presence to the senses. "Justice" and "temperance" were thus experienced as living occurrences, as *events*. Arising in specific situations, they were inseparable from the particular persons or actions that momentarily embodied them.

Yet as soon as such utterances were recorded in writing, they acquired an autonomy and a permanence hitherto unknown. Once written down, "virtue" was seen to have an unchanging, visible form independent of the speaker — and independent as well of the corporeal situations and individuals that exhibited it.

Socrates clearly aligned his method with this shift in the perceptual field. Whenever, in Plato's dialogues, Socrates asks his interlocutor to give an account of what "virtue," or "justice," or "courage" actually is, questioning them regarding the real meaning of the qualitative terms they unthinkingly employ in their speaking, they confidently reply by recounting particular instances of the quality under consideration, enumerating specific examples of "justice," yet never defining "justice" itself. When Socrates invites Meno to say what "virtue" is, Meno readily enumerates so many different instances or embodiments of virtue that Socrates retorts sardonically: "I seem to be in luck. I only asked you for one thing, virtue, but you have given me a whole swarm of virtues."[33] In keeping with older, oral modes of discourse, Socrates' fellow Athenians cannot abstract these spoken qualities from the lived situations that seem to exemplify these terms and call them forth. Socrates, however, has little interest in these multiple embodiments of "virtue," except in so far as they all partake of some common, unchanging element, which he would like to abstract and ponder on its own. In every case Socrates attempts to induce a reflection upon the quality as it exists in itself, independent of particular circumstances. The specific embodiments of "justice" that we may encounter in the material world are necessarily variable and fleeting; genuine knowledge, claims Socrates, must be of what is eternal and unchanging.

Socrates, then, is clearly convinced that there is a fixed, unchanging essence of "justice" that unites all the just instances, as there is an eternal essence of "virtue," of "beauty," of "goodness," "courage," and all the rest. Yet Socrates' conviction would not be possible without the alphabet. For only when a qualitative term is written down does it become ponderable as a fixed form independent of both the speakers and of situations.[34]

Not all writing systems foster this thorough abstraction of a spoken quality from its embeddedness in corporeal situations. The ideographic script of China, as we have seen, still retains pictorial ties to the phenomenal world of sensory experience. Thus, the Chinese ideograph for "red" is itself a juxtaposition of lived examples; it is composed of abbreviated pictorial images of a rose, a cherry, iron rust, and a flamingo. And indeed, according to some observers, if one asks a cultured person in China to explain a general quality like "red," or "loyalty," or "happiness," she will likely reply by describing various instances or examples of that quality, much like Socrates' interlocutors.[35] It was not writing per se, but phonetic writing, and the Greek alphabet in particular, that enabled the abstraction of previously ephemeral qualities like "goodness" and "justice" from their inherence in situations, promoting them to a new realm independent of the flux of ordinary experience. For the Greek alphabet had effectively severed all ties between the written letters and the sensible world from which they were derived; it was the first writing system able to render almost any human utterance in a fixed and lasting form.

While Socrates focused his teaching on the moral qualities, his disciple Plato recognized that not just ephemeral qualities but *all* general terms, from "table" to "cloud," could now be pondered as eternal, unchanging forms. In retrospect, we can see that the alphabet had indeed granted a new autonomy and permanence to all such terms. Besides the various meandering rivers, for instance, that one could view, or wade through, in the sensible world, there was also the singular notion "river," which now had its own visibility; "river" itself could now be pondered apart from all those material rivers that were liable to change their course or to dry up from one season to the next. For Plato, as for his teacher, genuine knowledge must be of what is unchanging and eternal — there can be no "true" knowledge of a particular river, but only of the pure Idea (or *eidos*) "river." That Plato often used the Greek term *eidos* (which meant "visible shape or form") to refer to such unchanging essences is itself, I believe, an indication of the affinity between these eternal essences and the unchanging, visible shapes of the alphabet.

For the letters of the alphabet, like the Platonic Ideas, do not exist in the world of ordinary vision. The letters, and the written words that they present, are not subject to the flux of growth and decay, to the perturbations and cyclical changes common to other visible things; they seem to hover, as it were, in another, strangely timeless dimension. Further, the letters defer and dissimulate their common visibility, each one dissolving into sound even as we look at it, trading our eyes for our ears, so that we seem not to be *seeing* so much as *hearing* something. Alphabetic writing deflects our attention from its visible aspect, effectively vanishing behind the current of human speech that it provokes.[36]

As we have already seen, the process of learning to read and to write with the alphabet engenders a new, profoundly reflexive, sense of self. The capacity to view and even to dialogue with one's own words after writing them down, or even in the process of writing them down, enables a new sense of autonomy and independence from others, and even from the sensuous surroundings that had earlier been one's constant interlocutor. The fact that one's scripted words can be returned to and pondered at any time that one chooses, regardless of when, or in what situation, they were first recorded, grants a timeless quality to this new reflective self, a sense of the relative independence of one's verbal, speaking self from the breathing body with its shifting needs. The literate self cannot help but feel its own transcendence and timelessness relative to the fleeting world of corporeal experience.

This new, seemingly autonomous, reflective awareness is called, by Socrates, the *psychê,* a term he thus twists from its earlier, Homeric significance as the invisible breath that animates the living body and that remains, as kind of wraith or ghost, after the body's death. (The term *psychê* was derived from an older Greek term, *psychein,* which meant "to breathe" or "to blow.") For Plato, as for Socrates, the *psychê* is now that aspect of oneself that is refined and strengthened by turning away from the ordinary sensory world in order to contemplate the intelligible Ideas, the pure and eternal forms that, alone, truly exist. The Socratic-Platonic *psychê,* in other words, is none other than the literate intellect, that part of the self that is born and strengthened in relation to the written letters.[37]

THE PROCESS OF LEARNING TO READ AND TO WRITE WITH THE ALPHABET ENGENDERS A NEW, PROFOUNDLY REFLEXIVE, SENSE OF SELF.

Plato himself effects a powerful critique of the influence of writing in the *Phaedrus,* that dialogue from which I quoted earlier in this chapter. In the course of that dialogue, Socrates relates to the young Phaedrus a curious legend regarding the Egyptian king Thamus. According to this story, Thamus was approached directly by the god Thoth — the divine inventor of geometry, mathematics, astronomy, and writing — who offers writing as a gift to the king so that Thamus may offer it, in turn, to the Egyptian people. But Thamus, after considering both the beneficent and the baneful aspects of the god's inventions, concludes that his people will be much better off *without* writing, and so he refuses the gift. Against Thoth's claim that writing will make people wiser and improve their memory, the king asserts that the very opposite is the case:

> If men learn this, it will implant forgetfulness in their souls; they will cease to exercise memory because they rely on that which is written, calling things to remembrance no longer from within themselves, but by means of external marks.[38]

Moreover — according to the king — spoken teachings, once written down, easily find their way into the hands of those who will misunderstand those teachings while nevertheless thinking that they understand them. Thus, the written letters bring not wisdom but only "the conceit of wisdom," making men seem to know much when in fact they know little.[39]

Plato's Socrates clearly agrees with the king's judgment, and it is evident that Plato wishes the reader to take these criticisms of writing quite seriously. Later in the same dialogue we read that "a written discourse on any subject is bound to contain much that is fanciful," and that in any case "nothing that has ever been written whether in verse or prose merits much serious attention."[40] Certainly, it is strange to read such strong remarks against writing from a thinker whose numerous written texts are among the most widely distributed and worshipfully read in the Western world. Here is Plato, from whom virtually all Western philosophers draw their literary ancestry, disparaging writing as nothing more than a pastime! What are we to make of these statements?

Such doubts about the alphabet, and such assertions regarding its potentially debilitating effects, must have been legion in Athens just before or during the time that Plato was writing. It is remarkable that Plato held to such criticisms despite the fact that he was an inveterate participant in the alphabetic universe. Given his multiple and diverse writings, which constitute what is probably the first large corpus of prose by a single author in the history of the alphabet, it seems clear that Plato did not intend his own criticisms to dissuade his students and readers from writing, or from reading him further. Rather, it is as though he meant to build into the very body of his writings a caution that they not be given too much weight. Not because he was uncertain about the genuine and serious worth of his philosophy, but simply because he had strong reservations about the written word and its ability to convey the full meaning of a philosophy that was as much a practice — involving direct, personal interaction and instruction — as it was a set of static formulations and reflections. Writing, according to Socrates, can at best serve as a *reminder* to a reader who already knows those things that have been written.[41] It is possible that Plato wrote his various dialogues to serve just such a restricted function; to act as reminders, for the students of his academy, of the methods and insights that they first learned in direct, face-to-face dialogue with their teacher.

Nevertheless Plato, despite his cautions, did not recognize the extent to which the very content of his teaching — with its dependence upon the twin notions of a purely rational *psychê* and a realm of eternal, unchanging Ideas — was already deeply under the influence of alphabetic writing. In the early fourth century B.C.E., when literacy was gradually spreading throughout Athenian society, it was certainly possible to witness the impact that writing was having upon the dissemination of particular teachings. An astute observer might discern as well the debilitating effects of writing upon the collective practice of memory, as what had previously been accomplished through the memorized repetition of ritual poems, songs, and stories was transferred to an external and fixed artifact. But it was hardly possible to discern the pervasive influence of letters upon patterns of perception and contemplation in general. Similarly, today we are simply unable to discern with any clarity the manner in which our own perceptions and thoughts are being shifted by our sensory involvement with electronic technologies, since any thinking that seeks to discern such a shift is itself subject to the very effect that it strives to thematize. Nevertheless, we may be sure that the shapes of our consciousness *are* shifting in tandem with the technologies that engage our senses — much as we can now begin to discern, in retrospect, how the distinctive shape of Western philosophy was born of the meeting between the human senses and the alphabet in ancient Greece.

OF TONGUES IN TREES

Socrates' critique of writing, in the *Phaedrus,* is occasioned by a written text carried by the young Phaedrus at the very beginning of the dialogue, when Socrates encounters him on his way out of the city. Phaedrus has just heard a friend of his, Lysias, declaiming a newly written speech on the topic of love; impressed by Lysias's speech, Phaedrus has obtained a copy of the speech and is going for a walk outside the city walls to ponder the text at his leisure. Socrates, always eager for philosophical discourse, agrees to accompany Phaedrus into the open country where they may together consider Lysias's text and discuss its merits. It is summer; the two men walk along the Ilissus River, wade across it, then settle on the grass in the shade of a tall, spreading plane tree. Socrates compliments Phaedrus for leading them to this pleasant glen, and Phaedrus replies, with some incredulity, that Socrates seems wholly a stranger to the country, like one who had hardly ever set foot outside the city walls. It is then that Socrates explains himself: "You must forgive me, dear friend. I'm a lover of learning, and trees and open country won't teach me anything, whereas men in the town do."[42]

We have already seen how peculiar this statement seems in relation to the world of the Homeric poems. How much more bizarre Socrates' words would seem to the members of an oral society still less exposed to the influence of literate traders than was Homeric Greece — to a culture, in other words, whose gods were not yet as anthropomorphic as even frothy-haired Poseidon and eruptive Hephaestus. The claim that "trees and open country won't teach anything" would have scant coherence within an indigenous hunting community, for the simple reason that such communities necessarily take their most profound teachings or instructions directly from the more-than-human earth. Whether among the Plains Indians of North America, the bushmen of the Kalahari Desert, or the Pintupi of the Australian outback, the elders and "persons of high degree" within such hunting communities continually defer to the animate powers of the surrounding landscape — to those nonhuman powers from which they themselves draw their deepest inspiration.

When a young person within such a culture is chosen, by whatever circumstance, to become a seer or shaman for the community, he or she may be trained by an elder seer within the tribe. Yet the most learned and powerful shaman will be one who has first learned his or her skills directly from the land itself — from a specific animal or plant, from a river or a storm — during a prolonged sojourn out beyond the boundaries of the human society. Indeed, among many of the tribes once indigenous to North America, a boy could gain the insight necessary to enter the society of grown men only by undertaking a solitary quest for vision — only by rendering himself vulnerable to the wild forces of the land and, if need be, crying to those forces for a vision.[43] The initiatory "Walkabout" undertaken by Aboriginal Australians is again just such an act whereby oral peoples turn toward the more-than-human earth for the teachings that must vitalize and sustain the human community.

In indigenous, oral cultures, nature itself is articulate; it *speaks*. The human voice in an oral culture is always to some extent participant with the voices of wolves, wind, and waves — participant, that is, with the encompassing discourse of an animate earth. There is no element of the landscape that is definitively void of expressive resonance and power: any movement may be a gesture, any sound may be a voice, a meaningful utterance.

Socrates' claim that trees have nothing to teach is a vivid indicator of the extent to which the human senses in Athens had already withdrawn from direct participation with the natural landscape. To directly perceive any phenomenon is to enter into relation with it, to feel oneself in a living interaction with another being. To define the phenomenon as an inert object, to deny the ability of a tree to inform and even instruct one's awareness, is to have turned one's senses away from that phenomenon. It is to ponder the tree from outside of its world, or, rather, from outside of the world in which both oneself and the tree are active participants.

Yet even here Plato seems to waver and vacillate. Indeed, just as the *Phaedrus* is the prime locus of Plato's apparent ambivalence with regard to his own practice of writing, so it is also the locus of a profound ambivalence with regard to nature, or to the expressive power of the natural world. Although the dialogue opens with Socrates' disparagement of trees and the open countryside, it is significant that the dialogue itself takes place in the midst of that very countryside. Unlike the other Platonic dialogues, the *Phaedrus* alone occurs outside the walls of the city, out beyond the laws and formalities that enclose and isolate the human community from the more-than-human earth. Socrates and Phaedrus have themselves embarked, as it were, on a kind of vision quest, stepping outside the city norms in order to test their citified knowledge against the older knowings embedded in the land. Plato is here, in a sense, putting philosophy itself to the test, by opening and exposing it to the nonhuman powers that for so long had compelled the awe and attention of humankind. In direct contrast to *The Republic,* in which Plato vilifies the ancient gods and effectively banishes the oral poets and storytellers from the utopian city that he envisions, in the *Phaedrus,* Plato brings philosophy itself outside the city, there to confront and come to terms with the older, oral ways of knowing which, although they may be banished from the city, nevertheless still dwell in the surrounding countryside. It is only outside the city walls that Plato will allow himself to question and critique the practice of writing to which he (and all later philosophy) is indissolubly tied. And it is only outside those walls that he will allow himself to fully acknowledge and offer respect to the oral, animistic universe that is on the wane.

Thus, shortly after his assertion that trees can teach him nothing, Socrates allows himself to be goaded into making an impromptu speech by an oath that Phaedrus swears upon the spirit of the very tree beneath which they sit![44] Trees, it would seem, still retain a modicum of efficacious power. Later in the dialogue Socrates himself will remind Phaedrus that, according to tradition, "the first prophetic utterances came from an oak tree."[45]

Not just trees but animals, too, have — in the *Phaedrus*—magical powers. Socrates initiates the discussion of writing by speculating that the cicadas chirping and "conversing with one another" in the tree overhead are probably observing the two of them as well; he maintains that the cicadas will intercede with the Muses on their behalf if he and Phaedrus continue to converse on philosophical matters.[46] And he proceeds to recount a story that describes how the cicadas, who were originally persons, were transformed into their present form:

> The story is that once upon a time these creatures were men — men of an age before there were any Muses — and that when the latter came into the world, and music made its appearance, some of the people of those days were so thrilled with pleasure that they went on singing and quite forgot to eat and drink until they actually died without noticing it. From them in due course sprang the race of cicadas, to which the Muses have granted the boon of needing no sustenance right from their birth, but of singing from the very first, without food or drink, until the day of their death, after which they go and report to the Muses how they severally are paid honor among mankind and by whom. . . .[47]

Any student of indigenous, oral cultures will hear a ring of familiarity in this tale. The story of the cicadas is identical in its character to the stories of the "Distant Time" told today by the Koyukon Indians of Alaska, identical to stories from that mysterious realm "long ago, in the future" which are told by the Inuit (or eastern Eskimo), or to the "Dreamtime" stories told by Aboriginal Australians. We may recall, in this context, these Inuit words . . . :"In the very earliest time, when both people and animals lived on earth, a person could become an animal if he wanted to, and an animal could become a human being. . . ." Here is a typical Distant Time story told by the Koyukon:

> When the burbot [ling cod] was human, he decided to leave the land and become a water animal. So he started down the bank, taking a piece of bear fat with him. But the other animal people wanted him to stay and tried to hold him back, stretching him all out of shape in the process. This is why the burbot has such a long, stretched-out body, and why its liver is rich and oily like the bear fat its ancestor carried to the water long ago.[48]

Like all oral stories of the Distant Time or Dreamtime, Socrates' myth of the cicadas is a functional myth; it serves to explain certain observed characteristics of the cicadas, like their endless humming and buzzing, and their apparent lack of any need for nourishment ("when music appeared, some of the people of those days were so thrilled with pleasure that they went on singing, and quite forgot to eat and drink"). Anthropologists have tended to view such stories from the Dreamtime or Distant Time as confused attempts at causal explanation by the primitive mind. Here, however, in the light of our discussion regarding orality and literacy, such stories can be seen to serve a far more practical function.

Without a versatile writing system, there is simply no way to preserve, in any fixed, external medium, the accumulated knowledge regarding particular plants (including where to find them, which parts of them are edible, which poisonous, how they are best prepared, what ailments they may cure or exacerbate), and regarding specific animals (how to recognize them, what they eat, how best to track or hunt them), or even regarding the land itself (how best to orient oneself in the surrounding terrain, what landforms to avoid, where to find water or fuel). Such practical knowledge must be preserved, then, in spoken formulations that can be easily remembered, modified when new facts are learned, and retold from generation to generation. Yet not all verbal formulations are amenable to simple recall — most verbal forms that we are conversant with today are dependent upon a context of writing. To us, for instance, a simple mental list of the known characteristics of a particular plant or animal would seem the easiest and most obvious formulation. Yet such lists have no value in an oral culture; without a visible counterpart that can be brought to mind and scanned by the mind's eye, spoken lists cannot be readily recalled and repeated.[49] Without writing, knowledge of the diverse properties of particular animals, plants, and places can be preserved only by being woven into *stories*, into vital tales wherein the specific characteristics of the plant are made evident through a narrated series of events and interactions. Stories, like rhymed poems or songs, readily incorporate themselves into our felt experience; the shifts of action echo and resonate

WITHOUT WRITING, KNOWLEDGE OF THE DIVERSE PROPERTIES OF PARTICULAR ANIMALS, PLANTS, AND PLACES CAN BE PRESERVED ONLY BY BEING WOVEN INTO *STORIES.*

our own encounters — in hearing or telling the story we vicariously *live* it, and the travails of its characters embed themselves into our own flesh. The sensuous, breathing body is, as we have seen, a dynamic, ever-unfolding form, more a process than a fixed or unchanging object. As such, it cannot readily appropriate inert "facts" or "data" (static nuggets of "information" abstracted from the lived situations in which they arise). Yet the living body can easily assimilate other dynamic or eventful processes, like the unfolding of a story, appropriating each episode or event as a variation of its own unfolding.

And the more lively the story — the more vital or stirring the encounters within it — the more readily it will be in-corporated.[50] Oral memorization calls for lively, dynamic, often violent, characters and encounters. If the story carries knowledge about a particular plant or natural element, then that entity will often be cast, like all of the other characters, in a fully animate form, capable of personlike adventures and experiences, susceptible to the kinds of setbacks or difficulties that we know from our own lives. In this manner the character or personality of a medicinal plant will be easily remembered, its poisonous attributes will be readily avoided, and the precise steps in its preparation will be evident from the sequence of events in the very legend that one chants while preparing it. One has only to recite the appropriate story, from the Distant Time, about a particular plant, animal, or element in order to recall the accumulated cultural knowledge regarding that entity and its relation to the human community.

In this light, that which we literates misconstrue as a naïve attempt at causal explanation may be recognized as a sophisticated mnemonic method whereby precise knowledge is preserved and passed along from generation to generation. The only causality proper to such stories is a kind of cyclical causality alien to modern thought, according to which persons may influence events in the enveloping natural order and yet are themselves continually under the influence of those very events. By invoking a dimension or a time when all entities were in human form, or when humans were in the shape of other animals and plants, these stories affirm human kinship with the multiple forms of the surrounding terrain. They thus indicate the respectful, mutual relations that must be maintained with natural phenomena, the reciprocity that must be practiced in relation to other animals, plants, and the land itself, in order to ensure one's own health and to preserve the well-being of the human community.

This facet of respectful consideration, and its attendant circular causality, is also present in Socrates' tale of the cicadas. By relating the tale to Phaedrus, Socrates indicates, although not without a sense of irony, the respect that is properly due to such insects, who might confer a boon upon the two of them in return. Later, indeed, Socrates will attribute his own loquacious eloquence in this dialogue to the inspiration of the cicadas, "those mouthpieces of the Muses."[51]

It seems clear that in the *Phaedrus,* Plato accords much more consideration to the oral-poetic universe, with its surplus of irrational, sensuous, and animistic powers, than he does in other dialogues. The *Phaedrus* seems to attempt a reconciliation of the transcendent, bodiless world of eternal Ideas proposed in this and other dialogues with the passionate, feeling-toned world of natural magic that still lingered in the common language of his day. But this conciliatory affirmation of the animistic, sensuous universe is effected only within the context of a more subtle devaluation. This is most obviously evident in the allegory at the heart of the dialogue, wherein Socrates gives his own account of love, or "eros." According to Socrates, the divine madness of love is to be honored and praised, for it is love that can most powerfully awaken the soul from its slumber in the bodily world. The lover's soul is stirred by the sensuous beauty of the beloved into remembering, however faintly, the more pure, genuine beauty of the eternal, bodiless Ideas which it once knew. Thus reminded of its own transcendent nature, the previously dormant soul begins to sprout wings, and soon aspires to rise beyond this world of ceaseless "becoming" toward that changeless eternal realm beyond the stars:

> It is there that true being dwells, without color or shape, that cannot be touched; reason alone, the soul's pilot, can behold it, and all true knowledge is knowledge thereof.[52]

In this dialogue, then, the bodily desire for sensuous contact and communion with other bodies and with the bodily earth is honored, but only as an incitement or spur toward the more genuine union of the reasoning soul with the eternal forms of "justice," "temperance," "virtue," and the like, which — according to Plato — lie beyond the sensory world entirely.

We have seen that this affinity between the reasoning soul or *psychê* and the changeless Ideas is inseparable from the relation between the new, literate intellect and the visible letters of the alphabet (which, although not outside of the sensory world, do present an entirely new and stable order of phenomena, relative to which all other phenomenal forms may come to seem remarkedly fleeting, ambiguous, and derivative). Just as Plato's apparent criticisms of alphabetic writing in the *Phaedrus* take place within the context of a much broader espousal of the detached (or disembodied) reflection that writing engenders, so in the same dialogue his apparent affirmation of oral-animistic modes of experience is accomplished only in the context of a broader disparagement. The erotic, participatory world of the sensing body is conjured forth only to be subordinated to the incorporeal world toward which, according to Plato, it points. The literate intellect here certifies its dominion by claiming the sensuous life of the body-in-nature as its subordinate ally. What was previously a threat to the literate mind's clean ascendance is now disarmed by being given a place within the grand project of transcendence. Hence, even and especially in this most pastoral of dialogues, in which the rational intellect seems almost balanced by the desiring body, and in which trees that "can teach nothing" seem balanced by watchful cicadas, we may still discern the seeds of nature's eventual eclipse behind a world of letters, numbers, and texts.

SYNAESTHESIA AND THE ENCOUNTER WITH THE OTHER

It is remarkable that none of the major twentieth-century scholars who have directed their attention to the changes wrought by literacy have seriously considered the impact of writing — and, in particular, phonetic writing — upon the human experience of the wider natural world. Their focus has generally centered upon the influence of phonetic writing on the structure and deployment of human language,[53] on patterns of cognition and thought,[54] or upon the internal organization of human societies.[55] Most of the major research, in other words, has focused upon the alphabet's impact on processes either internal to human society or presumably "internal" to the human mind. Yet the limitation of such research — its restriction within the bounds of human social interaction and personal interiority — itself reflects an anthropocentric bias wholly endemic to alphabetic culture. In the absence of phonetic literacy, neither society, nor language, nor even the experience of "thought" or consciousness, can be pondered in isolation from the multiple nonhuman shapes and powers that lend their influence to all our activities (we need think only of our ceaseless involvement with the ground underfoot, with the air that swirls around us, with the plants and animals that we consume, with the daily warmth of the sun and the cyclic pull of the moon). Indeed, in the absence of formal writing systems, human communities come to know themselves primarily as they are reflected back by the animals and the animate landscapes with which they are directly engaged. This epistemological dependence is readily evidenced, on every continent, by the diverse modes of identification commonly categorized under the single term "totemism."

It is exceedingly difficult for us literates to experience anything approaching the vividness and intensity with which surrounding nature spontaneously presents itself to the members of an indigenous, oral community. Yet as we saw in the previous chapters, Merleau-Ponty's careful phenomenology of perceptual experience had begun to disclose, underneath all of our literate abstractions, a deeply participatory relation to things and to the earth, a felt reciprocity curiously analogous to the animistic awareness of indigenous, oral persons. If we wish to better comprehend the remarkable shift in the human experience of nature that was occasioned by the advent and spread of phonetic literacy, we would do well to return to the intimate analysis of sensory perception inaugurated by Merleau-Ponty. For without a clear awareness of what reading and writing amounts to when considered at the level of our most immediate, bodily experience, any "theory" regarding the impact of literacy can only be provisional and speculative.

Although Merleau-Ponty himself never attempted a phenomenology of reading or writing, his recognition of the importance of synaesthesia — the overlap and intertwining of the senses — resulted in a number of experiential analyses directly pertinent to the phenomenon of reading. For reading, as soon as we attend to its sensorial texture, discloses itself as a profoundly synaesthetic encounter. Our eyes converge upon a visible mark, or a series of marks, yet what they find there is a sequence not of images but of sounds, something heard; the visible letters, as we have said, trade our eyes for our ears. Or, rather, the eye and the ear are brought together at the surface of the text — a new linkage has been forged between seeing and hearing which ensures that a phenomenon apprehended by one sense is instantly transposed into the other. Further, we should note that this sensory transposition is mediated by the human mouth and tongue; it is not just any kind of sound that is experienced in the act of reading, but specifically human, vocal sounds — those which issue from the human mouth. It is important to realize that the now common experience of "silent" reading is a late development in the story of the alphabet, emerging only during the Middle Ages, when spaces were first inserted between the words in a written manuscript (along with various forms of punctuation), enabling readers to distinguish the words of a written sentence without necessarily sounding them out audibly. Before this innovation, to read was necessarily to read aloud, or at the very least to mumble quietly; after the twelfth century it became increasingly possible to internalize the sounds, to listen inwardly to phantom words (or the inward echo of words once uttered).[56]

Alphabetic reading, then, proceeds by way of a new synaesthetic collaboration between the eye and the ear, between seeing and hearing. To discern the consequences of this new synaesthesia, we need to examine the centrality of synaesthesia in our perception of others and of the earth.

The experiencing body . . . is not a self-enclosed object, but an open, incomplete entity. This openness is evident in the arrangement of the senses: I have these multiple ways of encountering and exploring the world — listening with my ears, touching with my skin, seeing with my eyes, tasting with my tongue, smelling with my nose — and all of these various powers or pathways continually open outward from the perceiving body, like different paths diverging from a forest. Yet my experience of the world is not fragmented; I do not commonly experience the visible appearance of the world as in any way separable from its audible aspect, or from the myriad textures that offer themselves to my touch. When the local tomcat comes to visit, I do not have distinctive experiences of a visible cat, an audible cat, and an olfactory cat; rather, the tomcat is precisely the place where these separate sensory modalities join and dissolve into one another, blending as well with a certain furry tactility. Thus, my divergent senses meet up with each other in the surrounding world, converging and commingling in the things I perceive. We may think of the sensing body as a kind of open circuit that completes itself only in things, and in the world. The differentiation of my senses, as well as their spontaneous convergence in the world at large, ensures that I am a being destined for relationship: it is primarily through my engagement with what is *not* me that I effect the integration of my senses, and thereby experience my own unity and coherence.[57]

Indeed, the synaesthetic flowing together of different senses into a dynamic and unified experience is already operative within the single system of vision itself. For ordinary vision is a blending of two unique vistas, two perspectives, *two eyes*. Even here, within a single sensory system, we discern an originary openness or divergence — between, in this case, the two sides of my body, each with its own access to the visible — and it is only via the convergence and meeting of these two perspectives at some point out in front of my body that the visible world becomes present to me in all its depth. The double images common to unfocused vision have only a flimsy reality: if I let my eyes focus upon a shelf across the room, and meanwhile hold my index finger up in front of my face, I find that two images of my finger float before me like insubstantial phantoms and that the shelf, despite its greater distance, is much more substantial and present to my awareness than is my finger. Only when I break my focus upon the shelf and let my eyes reunite at the finger does this appendage with its delicate hairs and gnarly knuckles become fully present.

Ordinary seeing, then, involves the convergence of two views into a single dynamic vision; divergent parts of myself are drawn together by the object, and I thus meet up with myself *over there,* at that tree or that spider upon which I focus. Vision itself, in other words, is already a kind of synaesthesia, a collaboration of different sensory channels or organs.[58]

When we attend carefully to our perceptual experience, we discover that the convergence of the eyes often prompts the added collaboration of the other senses. When, for instance, I gaze through the window toward a blackbird in a nearby bush — my two eyes drawn together by the bird's jerking body as it plucks red berries from the branches — other senses are quite naturally drawn into that same focus. Certain tactile sensations, for instance, may accompany the blackbird's movements, and if I have been watching carefully I may notice, as it squoonches each new berry in its beak, a slightly acidic taste burst within my mouth. Or rather, strangely, I seem to feel this burst of taste over there, in *its* mouth, yet I feel its mouth only with my own.

Similarly, when I watch a stranger learning to ride a bicycle for the first time, my own body, although it is standing solidly on the ground, inadvertently experiences the uncertain equilibrum of the rider, and when that bicycle teeters and falls I feel the harsh impact of the asphalt against my own leg and shoulder. My tactile and proprioceptive senses are, it would seem, caught up over there where my eyes have been focused; the momentary shock and subsequent throbbing in my limbs make me wince. My hearing, as well, had been focused by the crash; the other ambient sounds to which I'd been listening just before (birds, children playing) have no existence for me now, only this stranger's pained breathing as he slowly shoves the bicycle aside and accepts the hand I am offering, pulling himself to his feet. He shakes his head, laughs a bit, then grins — all in a manner that readily communicates to my body that he's okay — and then turns to inspect the bicycle.

The diversity of my sensory systems, and their spontaneous convergence in the things that I encounter, ensures this interpenetration or interweaving between my body and other bodies — this magical participation that permits me, at times, to feel what others feel. The gestures of another being, the rhythm of its voice, and the stiffness or bounce in its spine all gradually draw my senses into a unique relation with one another, into a coherent, if shifting, organization. And the more I linger with this other entity, the more coherent the relation becomes, and hence the more completely I find myself face-to-face with another intelligence, another center of experience.

In the encounter with the cyclist, as in my experience of the blackbird, the visual focus induced and made possible the participation of the other senses. In different situations, other senses may initiate the synaesthesia: our ears, when we are at an orchestral concert; or our nostrils, when a faint whiff of burning leaves suddenly brings images of childhood autumns; our skin, when we are touching or being touched by a lover. Nonetheless, the dynamic conjunction of the eyes has a particularly ubiquitous magic, opening a quivering depth in whatever we focus upon, ceaselessly inviting the other senses into a concentrated exchange with stones, squirrels, parked cars, persons, snow-capped peaks, clouds, and termite-ridden logs. This power — the synaesthetic magnetism of the visual focus — will prove crucial for our understanding of literacy and its perceptual effects.

PHONETIC READING, OF COURSE, MAKES USE OF A *PARTICULAR* SENSORY CONJUNCTION — THAT BETWEEN SEEING AND HEARING.

The most important chapter of Merleau-Ponty's last, unfinished work is entitled "The Intertwining — The Chiasm." The word "chiasm," derived from an ancient Greek term meaning "crisscross," is in common use today only in the field of neurobiology: the "optic chiasm" is that anatomical region, between the right and left hemispheres of the brain, where neuronal fibers from the right eye and the left eye cross and interweave. As there is a chiasm between the two eyes, whose different perspectives continually conjoin into a single vision, so — according to Merleau-Ponty — there is a chiasm between the various sense modalities, such that they continually couple and collaborate with one another. Finally, this interplay of the different senses is what enables the chiasm between the body and the earth, the reciprocal participation — between one's own flesh and the encompassing flesh of the world — that we commonly call perception.[59]

Phonetic reading, of course, makes use of a *particular* sensory conjunction — that between seeing and hearing. And indeed, among the various synaesthesias that are common to the human body, the confluence (or chiasm) between seeing and hearing is particularly acute. For vision and hearing are the two "distance" senses of the human organism. In contrast to touch and proprioception (inner-body sensations), and unlike the chemical senses of taste and smell, seeing and hearing regularly place us in contact with things and events unfolding at a substantial distance from our own visible, audible body.

My visual gaze explores the reflective surfaces of things, their outward color and contour. By following the play of light and shadow, the dance of colors, and the gradients of repetitive patterns, the eyes — themselves gleaming surfaces — keep me in contact with the multiple outward facets, or faces, of the things arrayed about me. The ears, meanwhile, are more inward organs; they emerge from the depths of my skull like blossoms or funnels, and their participation tells me less about the outer surface than the interior substance of things. For the audible resonance of beings varies with their material makeup, as the vocal calls of different animals vary with the size and shape of their interior cavities and hollows. I feel their expressive cries resound in my skull or my chest, echoing their sonorous qualities with my own materiality, and thus learn of their inward difference from myself. Looking and listening bring me into contact, respectively, with the outward surfaces and with the interior voluminosity of things, and hence where these senses come together, I experience, over there, the complex interplay of inside and outside that is characteristic of my own self-experience. It is thus at those junctures in the surrounding landscape where my eyes and my ears are drawn together that I most readily feel myself confronted by another power like myself, another life.

If a native hunter is tracking, alone, in the forest, and a whooping cry reaches his ears from the leafy canopy, he will likely halt in his steps, silencing his breathing in order to hear that sound, when it comes again, more precisely. His eyes scan the cacophony of branches overhead with an unfocused gaze, attentive to minute movements on the periphery of the perceptual field. A slight rustle of branches draws his eyes into a more precise focus, his attention now restricted to a small patch of the canopy, yet still open, questioning, listening. When the cry comes again, the eyes, led by the ears, swiftly converge upon the source of that sound, and suddenly a monkey's form becomes evident, half-hidden from the leaves, its tail twirled around a limb, its body poised, watching. As the tribesman's searching eyes are drawn into a common focus with his listening ears, this conjunction, this chiasm, rebounds upon his own tactile and proprioceptive sensations — he feels himself suddenly confronted, caught up in a dynamic exchange with another entity, another carnal intelligence.

Indeed, the synaesthesia between the human eyes and ears is especially concentrated in our relation to other animals, since for a million years these "distance" senses were most tightly coupled at such moments of extreme excitement, when closing in on prey, or when escaping from predators. When backing slowly away from a mother grizzly protecting her cubs, or when watching intently the movements of an aroused rattlenake in order to avoid its numbing strike — these are moments when visual and auditory foci are virtually indistinguishable. For these senses are functioning here as a single, hyperattentive organ; we feel ourselves listening with our eyes and watching with our ears, ready to respond with our whole body to any change in the Other's behavior.

Yet our ears and our eyes are drawn together not only by animals, but by numerous other phenomena within the landscape. And, strangely, *wherever* these two senses converge, we may suddenly feel ourselves in relation with another expressive power, another center of experience. Trees, for instance, can seem to speak to us when they are jostled by the wind. Different forms of foliage lend each tree a distinctive voice, and a person who has lived among them will easily distinguish the various dialects of pine trees from the speech of spruce needles or Douglas fir. Anyone who has walked through cornfields knows the uncanny experience of being scrutinized and spoken to by whispering stalks. Certain rock faces and boulders request from us a kind of auditory attentiveness, and so draw our ears into relation with our eyes as we gaze at them, or with our hands as we touch them — for it is only through a mode of listening that we can begin to sense the interior voluminosity of the boulder, its particular density and depth. There is an expectancy to the ears, a kind of patient receptivity that they lend to the other senses whenever we place ourselves in a mode of listening — whether to a stone, or a river, or an abandoned house. That so many indigenous people allude to the articulate speech of trees or of mountains suggests the ease with which, in an oral culture, one's auditory attention may be joined with the visual focus in order to enter into a living relation with the expressive character of things.

Far from presenting a distortion of their factual relation to the world, the animistic discourse of indigenous, oral peoples is an inevitable counterpart of their immediate, synaesthetic engagement with the land that they inhabit. The animistic proclivity to perceive the angular shape of a boulder (while shadows shift across its surface) as a kind of meaningful gesture, or to enter into felt conversations with clouds and owls — all of this could be brushed aside as imaginary distortion or hallucinatory fantasy if such active participation were not the very structure of perception, if the creative interplay of the senses in the things they encounter was not our sole way of linking ourselves to those things and letting the things weave themselves into our experience. Direct, prereflective perception is inherently synaesthetic, participatory, and animistic, disclosing the things and elements that surround us not as inert objects but as expressive subjects, entities, powers, potencies.

And yet most of us seem, today, very far from such experience. Trees rarely, if ever, speak to us; animals no longer approach us as emissaries from alien zones of intelligence; the sun and the moon no longer draw prayers from us but seem to arc blindly across the sky. How is it that these phenomena *no longer address us,* no longer compel our involvement or reciprocate our attention? If participation is the very structure of perception, how could it ever have been brought to a halt? To freeze the ongoing animation, to block the wild exchange between the senses and the things that engage them, would be tantamount to freezing the body itself, stopping it short in its tracks. And yet our bodies still move, still live, still breathe. If we no longer experience the enveloping earth as expressive and alive, this can only mean that the animating interplay of the senses has been transferred to another medium, another locus of participation.

• • • • • • •

It is the written text that provides this new locus. For to read is to enter into a profound participation, or chiasm, with the inked marks upon the page. In learning to read we must break the spontaneous participation of our eyes and our ears in the surrounding terrain (where they had ceaselessly converged in the synaesthetic encounter with animals, plants, and streams) in order to recouple those senses upon the flat surface of the page. As a Zuñi elder focuses her eyes upon a cactus and hears the cactus begin to speak, so we focus our eyes upon these printed marks and immediately hear voices. We hear spoken words, witness strange scenes or visions, even experience other lives. As nonhuman animals, plants, and even "inanimate" rivers once spoke to our tribal ancestors, so the "inert" letters on the page now speak to us! *This is a form of animism that we take for granted, but it is animism nonetheless — as mysterious as a talking stone.*

And indeed, it is only when a culture shifts its participation to these printed letters that the stones fall silent. Only as our senses transfer their animating magic to the written word do the trees become mute, the other animals dumb.

But let us be more precise, recalling the distinction between different forms of writing discussed at the start of this chapter. As we saw there, pictographic, ideographic, and even rebuslike writing still makes use of, or depends upon, our sensorial participation with the natural world. As the tracks of moose and bear refer beyond themselves to those entities of whom they are the trace, so the images in early writing systems draw their significance not just from ourselves but from sun, moon, vulture, jaguar, serpent, lightning — from all those sensorial, never strictly human powers, of which the written images were a kind of track or tracing. To be sure, these signs were now inscribed by human hands, not by the hooves of deer or the clawed paws of bear; yet as long as they presented images of paw prints and of clouds, of sun, and of serpent, these characters still held us in relation to a more-than-human field of discourse. Only when the written characters lost all explicit reference to visible, natural phenomena did we move into a new order of participation. Only when those images came to be associated, alphabetically, with purely human-made sounds, and even the names of the letters lost all worldly, extrahuman significance, could speech or language come to be experienced as an exclusively human power. For only then did civilization enter into the wholly self-reflexive mode of animism, or magic, that still holds us in its spell:

> We know what the animals do, what are the needs of the beaver, the bear, the salmon, and other creatures, because long ago men married them and

> acquired this knowledge from their animal wives. Today the priests say we lie, but we know better. The white man has been only a short time in this country and knows very little about the animals; we have lived here thousands of years and were taught long ago by the animals themselves. The white man *writes everything down in a book* so that it will not be forgotten; but our ancestors *married* animals, learned all their ways, and passed on this knowledge from one generation to another.[60]

• • • ● • • •

That alphabetic reading and writing was itself experienced as a form of magic is evident from the reactions of cultures suddenly coming into contact with phonetic writing. Anthropological accounts from entirely different continents report that members of indigenous, oral tribes, after seeing the European reading from a book or from his own notes, came to speak of the written pages as "talking leaves," for the black marks on the flat, leaflike pages seemed to talk directly to the one who knew their secret.

The Hebrew scribes never lost this sense of the letters as living, animate powers. Much of the Kabbalah, the esoteric body of Jewish mysticism, is centered around the conviction that each of the twenty-two letters of the Hebrew *aleph-beth* is a magic gateway or guide into an entire sphere of existence. Indeed, according to some kabbalistic accounts, it was by combining the letters that the Holy One, Blessed Be He, created the ongoing universe. The Jewish kabbalists found that the letters, when meditated upon, would continually reveal new secrets; through the process of *tzeruf,* the magical permutation of the letters, the Jewish scribe could bring himself into successively greater states of ecstatic union with the divine. Here, in other words, was an intensely concentrated form of animism—a participation conducted no longer with the sculpted idols and images worshiped by other tribes but solely with the visible letters of the *aleph-beth.*

Perhaps the most succinct evidence for the potent magic of written letters is to be found in the ambiguous meaning of our common English word "spell." As the roman alphabet spread through oral Europe, the Old English word "spell," which had meant simply to recite a story or tale, took on the new double meaning: on the one hand, it now meant to arrange, in the proper order, the written letters that constitute the name of a thing or a person; on the other, it signified a magic formula or charm. Yet these two meanings were not nearly as distinct as they have come to seem to us today. For to assemble the letters that make up the name of a thing, in the correct order, was precisely to effect a magic, to establish a new kind of influence over that entity, to summon it forth! To spell, to correctly arrange the letters to form a name or a phrase, seemed thus at the same time to *cast a spell,* to exert a new and lasting power over the things spelled. Yet we can now realize that to learn to spell was also, and more profoundly, to step under the influence of the written letters ourselves, to cast a spell upon our own senses. It was to exchange the wild and multiplicitous magic of an intelligent natural world for the more concentrated and refined magic of the written word.

• • • • • • •

The Bulgarian scholar Tzvetan Todorov has written an illuminating study of the Spanish conquest of the Americas, based on extensive study of documents from the first months and years of contact between European culture and the native cultures of the American continent.[61] The lightning-swift conquest of Mexico by Cortéz has remained a puzzle for historians, since Cortéz, leading only a few hundred men, managed to seize the entire kingdom of Montezuma, who commanded *several hundred thousand.* Todorov concludes that Cortéz's astonishing and rapid success was largely a result of the discrepancy between the different forms of participation engaged in by the two societies. The Aztecs, whose writing was highly pictorial, necessarily felt themselves in direct communication with an animate, more-than-human environment. "Everything happens as if, for the Aztecs, [written] signs automatically and necessarily proceed from the world they designate . . ."; the Aztecs are unable to use their spoken words, or their written characters, to hide their true intentions, since these signs belong to the world around them as much as to themselves.[62] To be duplicitous with signs would be, for the Aztecs, to go against the order of nature, against the encompassing speech or logos of an animate world, in which their own tribal discourse was embedded.

The Spaniards, however, suffer no such limitation. Possessed of an *alphabetic* writing system, they experience themselves not in communication with the sensuous forms of the world, but solely with one another. The Aztecs must answer, in their actions as in their speech, to the whole sensuous, natural world that surrounds them; the Spanish need answer only to themselves.

In contact with this potent new magic, with these men who participate solely with their own self-generated signs, whose speech thus seems to float free of the surrounding landscape, and who could therefore be duplicitous and *lie* even in the presence of the sun, the moon, and the forest, the Indians felt their own rapport with those sensuous powers, or gods, beginning to falter:

> The testimony of the Indian accounts, which is a description rather than an explanation, asserts that everything happened because the Mayas and the Aztecs lost control of communication. The language of the gods has become unintelligible, or else these gods fell silent. "Understanding is lost, wisdom is lost" [from the Mayan account of the Spanish invasion]. . . . As for the Aztecs, they describe the beginning of their own end as a silence that falls: the gods no longer speak to them.[63]

In the face of aggression from this new, entirely self-reflexive form of magic, the native peoples of the Americas — like those of Africa and, later, of Australia — felt their own magics wither and become useless, unable to protect them.

NOTES

[1] Perhaps the most influential of such analyses has been historian Lynn White Jr.'s much-reprinted essay "The Historical Roots of Our Ecologic Crisis," originally published in *Science* 155 (1967), pp. 1203–1207.

The Genesis quote is from *Tanakh: The Holy Scriptures,* translated by the Jewish Publication Society according to the traditional Hebrew text (Philadelphia: Jewish Publication Society, 1985). [All notes are Abram's.]

[2] Jacques Derrida and other theorists have claimed that there is no self-identical author or subject standing behind any text that one reads, legislating its "actual" meanings; the precise meaning of a text, like its real origin, can only be indicated by referring to other texts to which this one responds, and since those, in turn, mark divergences from still other texts, the clear source, or the true meaning, is always deferred, always elsewhere. Since neither the origin nor the precise meaning of a text can ever be made wholly explicit, there can be no real meeting between the reader and the writer, at least not in the traditional sense of a pure coinciding of one's "self" with the exact intention of a supposed "author."

My equation of "meaning" with "meeting" would seem, at first blush, to fall easy prey to this critique. Yet Derrida's critique has bite only if one maintains that the other who writes is an exclusively *human* Other, only if one assumes that the written text is borne by an exclusively human subjectivity. Here, however, I am asserting a homology between the act of reading and the ancestral, indigenous act of *tracking.* I am suggesting that that which lurks behind all the texts that we read is not a human subject but another animal, another shape of awareness (ultimately the otherness of animate nature itself). The meeting that I speak of, then, is precisely the encounter with a presence that can never wholly coincide with our own, the confrontation with an enigma that cannot be dispelled by thought, an otherness that can never be fully overcome.

[3] J. Gernet, quoted in Jacques Derrida, *Of Grammatology,* trans. Gayatri Spivak (Baltimore: Johns Hopkins University Press, 1976), p. 123.

[4] The approximate dates referred to in this paragraph are drawn from several texts, including Albertine Gaur, *A History of Writing* (New York: British Library/Cross River Press, 1992); J. T. Hooker et al., *Reading the Past: Ancient Writing from Cuneiform to the Alphabet* (Berkeley: British Museum/University of California Press, 1990); and Jack Goody, *The Interface Between the Written and the Oral* (Cambridge: Cambridge University Press, 1987).

[5] The written characters or glyphs that I have referred to as ideograms are sometimes called logograms (word signs) by contemporary linguists, in order to emphasize that these characters are regularly used to transcribe or invoke particular words. The term "logogram," however, hides or masks the pictorial element that remains subtly operative in many of these written characters, and it is for this reason that I, like many others, have retained the popular terminology. The pictorial, "iconic" nature of many characters within a script inevitably influences the experience of language and linguistic meaning common to those who use that script. In the Mayan languages, for instance, the words for "writing" and "painting" were and are the same — the same artisans practiced both crafts, and the patron deities of both crafts were twin monkey gods. As Dennis Tedlock informs us in his introduction to the Mayan *Popol Vuh,* "In the books made under the patronage of these twin gods . . . the writing not only records words but sometimes has elements that picture or point to their meaning without the necessity of a detour through words." Dennis Tedlock, trans., *Popul Vuh: The Mayan Book of the Dawn of Life* (New York: Simon & Schuster, 1985), p. 30.

[6] That the contemporary Chinese word for "writing," as we saw earlier, also applies to the tracks of animals and the marks on a turtle shell may well be attributed to the fact that China has retained a somewhat iconic or pictorially derived mode of writing down to the present day.

[7] Jack Goody, *The Interface Between the Written and the Oral,* pp. 34, 38.

[8] It is important to realize that many pictorially derived writing systems commonly assumed by Western thinkers to be largely ideographic — like Egyptian hieroglyphs, the Chinese script, and even the recently deciphered Mayan system — utilize a host of conventional rebuses as phonetic indicators in combination with ideographic signs. These phonetic characters, however, commonly retain pictorial ties to the sensuous world. Although a hasty reader might choose to read these phonetic symbols without giving thought to their pictorial significance, according to Dennis Tedlock "the other meanings were still there for a reader who could see and hear them — even the same reader perhaps, in a different mood." A striking demonstration of the imagistic logic that animates such nonalphabetic writing systems may be found in the chapter entitled "Eyes and Ears to the Book" in Tedlock's remarkable study of Mayan culture, *Breath on the Mirror* (San Francisco: HarperCollins, 1993, pp. 109–14).

[9] Walter J. Ong, *Orality and Literacy: The Technologizing of the Word* (New York: Methuen, 1982), pp. 87–88.

[10] Ibid.

[11] J. A. Hawkins, "The Origin and Dissemination of Writing in Western Asia," in P. R. S. Moorey, ed., *Origins of Civilization* (London: Oxford University Press, 1979), p. 132.

[12] Ong, p. 89. See also Hooker et al., pp. 210–11; Gaur, p. 87.

[13] However, the *aleph* in the Hebrew *aleph-beth* does not represent a vowel sound—rather, it signifies the opening of the throat prior to any sound.

[14] Another common version of the early Semitic "qoph" consisted of a *semicircle* intersected by a vertical line: Ϙ. Linguist Geoffrey Sampson writes that "no-one familiar with the look of heavy simian eyebrows ought . . . to find it difficult to see ['qoph'] as a full-face view of an ape." Likewise, the Semitic letter "gimel" (which means camel in Hebrew) consisted of a rising and descending line: ⋀—Sampson believes that this may be a stylized image of a camel's most prominent feature: its hump. Other letters took their forms from a hand, mouth, a snake. See Geoffrey Sampson, *Writing Systems: A Linguistic Introduction* (Stanford: Stanford University Press, 1985), pp. 78–81.

These letter shapes are from the original Hebrew *aleph-beth,* known in the later Jewish tradition as *Ksav Ivri* (literally: "script of the Hebrews"). These letters were eventually replaced, between the fifth and the third century B.C.E., by the square Hebrew letters used today, themselves borrowed from a late Aramaic version of the *aleph-beth.* See Hooker, et al., pp. 226–27; also Gaur, p. 92.

[15] David Diringer, *The Alphabet* (New York: Philosophical Library, 1948), p. 159.

[16] Plato, *Phaedrus,* trans. R. Hackforth, in *Plato: The Collected Dialogues,* ed. Edith Hamilton and Huntington Cairns (Princeton: Princeton University Press, 1982), sec. 230d.

[17] Homer, *The Odyssey,* trans. Robert Fitzgerald (Garden City, N.Y.: Doubleday & Co., 1961); and Homer, *The Iliad,* trans. Robert Fitzgerald (Garden City, N.Y.: Doubleday & Co., 1974).

[18] Eric Havelock, *The Muse Learns to Write: Reflections on Orality and Literacy from Antiquity to the Present* (New Haven: Yale University Press, 1986), pp. 19, 83, 90. See also Havelock's seminal text *Preface to Plato* (Cambridge: Harvard University Press, 1963).

[19] The earliest Greek inscriptions of an alphabetic nature yet to be discovered are from around 740 or 730 B.C.E. (Hooker et al., pp. 230–32). See also Rhys Carpenter, "The Antiquity of the Greek Alphabet," *American Journal of Archaeology* 37 (1933); Havelock, *Preface to Plato,* pp. 49–52; Havelock, *The Muse Learns to Write,* pp. 79–97; Goody, *The Interface Between the Written and the Oral,* pp. 40–47.

[20] The evidence for this resistance is carefully documented by Eric A. Havelock, the most accomplished scholar of the transition from orality to literacy in ancient Greece, particularly in his essay "The Special Theory of Greek Orality," in *The Muse Learns to Write.*

[21] Havelock, *The Muse Learns to Write,* p. 87.

[22] There is a linguistic parallel here with the Vedic *sutras,* so named because they, too, are sewn, or *sutured,* together.

[23] See Adam Parry, ed., *The Making of Homeric Verse: The Collected Papers of Milman Parry* (Oxford: Clarendon Press, 1971). See also Albert Lord, *The Singer of Tales* (Cambridge: Harvard University Press, 1960).

[24] Ivan Illich and Barry Sanders, The *Alphabetization of the Popular Mind* (San Francisco: North Point Press, 1988), p. 18.

[25] See Ong, p. 35: "Fixed, often rhythmically balanced, expressions of this sort and of other sorts can be found occasionally in print, indeed can be 'looked up' in books of sayings, but in oral cultures they are not occasional. They are incessant. They form the substance of thought itself. Thought in any extended form is impossible without them, for it consists in them."

[26] Today these disks are housed in the Parry Collection at Harvard University.

[27] See especially "Whole Formulaic Verses in Greek and Southslavic Heroic Song," as well as other essays in Adam Parry, *The Making of Homeric Verse.*

[28] Ibid., p. 378.

[29] Ong, p. 59. In recent years Milman Parry's conclusion that the Homeric epics originated in a completely oral context has been disputed by Jack Goody, another careful student of oral-literate contrasts. Goody points out that while the Yugoslavian bards recorded by Parry and Lord were themselves nonliterate, the culture in which they sang and improvised their epic poems was not entirely untouched by literacy. Goody himself has worked among the LoDagaa people of northern Ghana—a tribe unacquainted with literacy until quite recently—and he undertook to record their oral myth, "the Bagre," which is ritually recited during the course of a long series of initiatory ceremonies (Jack Goody, *The Myth of the Bagre* [Oxford: Clarendon Press, 1972]). Along with many obvious similarities, he has found marked differences between the LoDagaa recitation and both the Slavic and the Homeric epics. The epic poems of Yugoslavia and of ancient Greece seem much more formal and tightly composed than their African counterparts (see "Africa, Greece and Oral Poetry," in Goody, *The Interface Between the Written and the Oral*). Further, according to Goody, the epic mode of the bardic tales, centered on the legendary acts of a human hero or a group of heroes, is foreign both to the Bagre and to other oral compositions of indigenous Africa (on this, see also Ruth Finnegan, *Oral Literature in Africa* [London: Oxford University Press, 1970]). Goody's evidence suggests that the epic mode is more proper to the poetry of cultures in the earliest stages of literacy, rather than to that of purely oral peoples. He argues from this that the culture in which the *Iliad* and the *Odyssey* took shape should not be considered a pristinely oral culture, since even if the culture

was without writing it had nevertheless been influenced (1) by the much earlier existence of nonalphabetic writing systems (Linear A and Linear B, which had been used, for economic and military accounting, by the Minoan and Mycenaean cultures on the island of Crete, until such writing vanished around 1100 B.C.E.), and (2) by the literacy of the neighboring societies of the Near East, societies with which the Greek merchants must have been in frequent contact ("Africa, Greece and Oral Poetry," pp. 98, 107–9). Goody's premise, that pre-Homeric Greece may have been influenced by the limited literacy of its Minoan and Mycenaean forebears, or by the protophonetic literacy of some cultures across the Mediterranean, may help us to understand why the Homeric gods and goddesses are as anthropomorphic as they are, much more human in form than are the deities of most cultures entirely untouched by literacy. We may, however, accept Goody's argument for the *indirect* influence of literacy without concluding that mainland Greece from 1100 to 750 B.C.E. made any *direct* use of writing, or had any wish to do so. For a lively debate on the orality of the Homeric epics, see "Becoming Homer: An Exchange," in the *New York Review of Books,* May 14, 1992.

[30] Havelock, *The Muse Learns to Write,* p. 112.

[31] Philip Wheelwright, ed., *The Presocratics* (New York: Macmillan Publishing Co., 1985), p. 45.

[32] Illich and Sanders, pp. 22–23.

[33] Plato, *Meno,* trans. W. K. C. Guthrie, in *Plato: The Collected Dialogues,* ed. Hamilton and Cairns, sec. 72a (Princeton: Princeton University Press, 1982).

[34] The reader may object that the alphabet gave a fixed and visible form *not* to the actual quality we call "justice," but only to the word, to the verbal label that "stands for" that quality. Surely Socrates was asking his discussants to ponder the quality itself, not the mere word. However, the clear distinction assumed by this objection, between words and what they "stand for," is a fairly recent distinction, itself made possible by the spread of phonetic writing. Only after spoken words were fixed in writing could they begin to be thought of as arbitrary "labels." In the Athens of Socrates and Plato, however — a society only emerging into literacy — the word was still directly participant with the phenomenon that it invoked, the phenomenon still participant with the spoken word. If the new technology of writing imparted to the spoken word "virtue" a new sense of autonomy and permanence, it brought a new sense of changelessness to the quality itself.

[35] Ernest Fenollosa, cited in Ezra Pound, *ABC of Reading* (New York: New Directions Press, 1960), pp. 19–22.

[36] Jacques Derrida has explored at great length the consequences of this curious vanishing throughout the trajectory of Western (alphabetic) philosophy, a tradition that ceaselessly forgets, or represses, its dependence upon writing. See, for instance, *Of Grammatology,* trans. Gayatri Spivak (Baltimore: Johns Hopkins University Press, 1976). Derrida, however, does not notice some of the most glaring differences between alphabetic and nonalphabetic modes of thought, differences that make themselves evident in our experienced relation to the animate earth. While Derrida assimilates all language to writing (l'écriture), my approach has been largely the reverse, to show that all discourse, even written discourse such as this, is implicitly sensorial and bodily, and hence remains bound, like the sensing body, to a world that is never exclusively human.

[37] By suggesting that the relation, in Plato's writing, between the immortal psyche and the intelligible Ideas is dependent upon the experienced relation between the new, literate intellect and the visible letters of the alphabet, my intention is not to effect a reduction of transcendent, philosophic notions to banal, mundane experience, but rather to reawaken a sense of the profoundly magical, transcendent activity that reading *is*. In this I am simply practicing the method of wakefulness urged by Merleau-Ponty, whose phrase "the primacy of perception" expressed an intuition that even the most transcendental philosophies remain rooted in, and dependent upon, the very corporeal, sensuous world that they seek to forget.

[38] *Phaedrus,* 275a.

[39] Ibid., 275b.

[40] Ibid., 277e.

[41] Ibid., 278a.

[42] Ibid., 230d.

[43] Two reputable and accessible firsthand accounts of how visions and "medicine power" were and sometimes still are invoked among the Plains tribes are *Lame Deer, Seeker of Visions* by John Fire Lame Deer and Richard Erdoes, and *Black Elk Speaks,* by John Neihardt. Both books exist in numerous editions.

[44] *Phaedrus,* 236e.

[45] Ibid., 275b.

[46] Ibid., 259a–d.

[47] Ibid., 259b–c.

[48] Richard Nelson, *Make Prayers to the Raven* (Chicago: University of Chicago, 1983), p. 17.

[49] Jack Goody, in *The Domestication of the Savage Mind* (Cambridge: Cambridge University Press, 1977), has shown the dependence of such "mental" lists upon visible, written lists. See also Walter Ong: "Primary oral cultures commonly situate their equivalent of lists in narrative, as in the catalogue of the ships and captains in the *Iliad* (Book 11, lines 461–879). . . . In the text of the Torah, which set down in writing thought forms still basically oral, the equivalent of geography

(establishing the relationship of one place to another) is put into a formulary action narrative (Numbers 33:16ff.): 'Setting out from the desert of Sinai, they camped at Kibroth-hattaavah. Setting out from Kibroth-hattaavah, they camped at Hazeroth. Setting out from Hazeroth, they camped at Rithmah . . .' and so on for many more verses. Even genealogies out of such orally framed tradition are in effect commonly narrative. Instead of a recitation of names, we find a sequence of 'begats,' of statements of what someone did: 'Irad begat Mahajael, Mahajael begat Methusael, Methusael begat Lamech' (Genesis 4:18)." Ong, p. 99.

[50] Walter Ong writes of this as the "agonistic" requirement in oral storytelling. See Ong, pp. 43–45.

[51] *Phaedrus,* 262d.

[52] Ibid., 247c.

[53] For instance, the research of Milman Parry and Albert Lord (see n. 23 above).

[54] Such is the focus of the research undertaken by such diverse scholars as Eric Havelock, Marshall McLuhan, Walter Ong, Jack Goody, and, most recently, Ivan Illich. See Havelock, *Preface to Plato* and *The Muse Learns to Write: Reflections on Orality and Literacy from Antiquity to the Present;* Marshall McLuhan, *The Gutenberg Galaxy: The Making of Typographic Man* (Toronto: University of Toronto Press, 1962); Ong, *Interfaces of the Word* (London: Cornell University Press, 1977) and *Orality and Literacy: The Technologizing of the Word;* Goody, *The Interface Between the Written and the Oral* and *The Domestication of the Savage Mind* (Cambridge: Cambridge University Press, 1977); Illich and Sanders, *The Alphabetization of the Popular Mind.*

[55] This is a special concern in Illich and Sanders, and in Goody, *The Interface Between the Written and the Oral.*

[56] Ivan Illich, *In the Vineyard of the Text* (Chicago: University of Chicago Press, 1993). Also Illich and Sanders, pp. 45–51.

[57] This reciprocity, the circular manner in which a nuanced sense of self emerges only through a deepening relation with other beings, is regularly acknowledged in Buddhism as the "dependent co-arising of self and other."

[58] Indeed, Merleau-Ponty takes the visual focus to be paradigmatic for synaesthesia in general: ". . . the senses interact in perception as the two eyes collaborate in vision." *Phenomenology of Perception,* translated by Colin Smith (London: Routledge & Kegan Paul, 1962), pp. 233–34.

[59] It is important to realize that the focused structure of perception ensures that I am able to participate with any phenomenon only by *not* participating with other phenomena. I cannot directly perceive a particular entity, in all its synaesthetic depth and otherness, without forfeiting, for the moment, a direct encounter with other entities, which must therefore remain part of the indeterminate background—at least until they themselves succeed in winning the focus of my senses. Thus, among many indigenous, oral peoples, for whom all things are potentially animate, it is nonetheless clear that *not all phenomena are experienced as animate all the time.* Indeed, certain phenomena, certain plants or insects that we ask about, may have little or no overt significance to the tribal community; they may not even have names within the storied language of the culture. Since these phenomena do not solicit the focused attention of the human community, they are rarely, if ever, experienced by them as unique entities with their own intensity and depth. Only those phenomena that regularly engage our synaesthetic attention stand out from the body of the land as autonomous powers in their own right. If there is no focus, no juxtaposition of diverse sensory modalities, then the phenomenon has no chance to move us, no chance to play one part of our experience off another, no chance to teach us. It thus remains flat, without much depth or dynamism, a purely background phenomenon.

[60] A Carrier Indian, quoted in Diamond Jenness, *The Carrier Indians of the Bulkley River,* Bureau of American Ethnology: Bulletin 133 (Washington, D.C.: Smithsonian Institution, 1943), p. 540 (emphasis added).

[61] Tzvetan Todorov, *The Conquest of America,* trans. Richard Howard (New York: Harper & Row, 1984).

[62] Ibid., p. 89.

[63] Ibid., pp. 61–62.

QUESTIONS FOR A SECOND READING

1. It is common to talk about punctuation in relation to the sentence. Writers use marks of punctuation (commas, dashes, colons, semicolons, parentheses, type ornaments) to organize a sentence and to help readers locate themselves in relation to what they are reading. Writers also, however,

punctuate essays or chapters—longer units of text. Abram provides a case in point. For example, notice how he uses white space and subheadings and type ornaments to organize the essay into sections.

As you reread, pay attention to the units or stages in Abram's argument. How are they related? How are you expected to put them together? What is the most difficult or surprising or challenging section? How might these sections be an aid to writing? What help do they provide to a reader? Chart the development of Abram's ideas—the steps by which he tries to persuade us of his unconventional position on the effects of the alphabet. And when you have finished, and as an exercise in understanding, write a paraphrase of the argument in this essay that accounts for its progress from beginning to end.

2. Toward the end of his essay, Abram writes: "Far from presenting a distortion of their factual relation to the world, the animistic discourse of indigenous, oral peoples is an inevitable counterpart of their immediate, synaesthetic engagement with the land that they inhabit" (p. 55). In our experience teaching this essay, students ignore the section on "Synaesthesia and the Encounter with the Other." As you reread, and as an exercise, assume that this is the *most* important section of the essay. What is Abram saying here? What is he *doing* in this section? Why is this argument important to him? Do you buy it?

3. In his discussion of the *Phaedrus*, Abram notes that Socrates, Plato's central character, presents a pointed critique of writing—which raises the question of why Plato would write as much and as seriously as he did if he found writing so problematic:

   > Certainly, it is strange to read such strong remarks against writing from a thinker whose numerous written texts are among the most widely distributed and worshipfully read in the Western world. Here is Plato, from whom virtually all Western philosophers draw their literary ancestry, disparaging writing as nothing more than a pastime! What are we to make of these statements? (p. 43)

   Much of Abram's essay is devoted to describing what we've lost rather than gained as a result of literacy—yet the medium for his critique of alphabetic writing is alphabetic writing.

   As you reread, pay particular attention to the ways Abram's practice as a writer could be said to reproduce what he takes to be the problems of writing. What are these problems, according to Abram? What sentences might you point to for evidence that Abram is prey to them? And pay attention to any attempts Abram might make to overcome those problems, to write differently. Are there any lessons here?

4. In this chapter, David Abram refers to the work of the philosopher Maurice Merleau-Ponty. Elsewhere in the book he refers to Edmund Husserl. Both are important figures in a field of philosophical inquiry called phenomenology.

Using the library as well as the Internet (so that you can put your hands on books and scholarly journals) and, perhaps, working with a group, create brief glosses on these writers and their work. Who are they, and why would they be interesting or important or useful or memorable for Abram? How might they serve those concerned with the crisis of the environment?

ASSIGNMENTS FOR WRITING

1. At several points in the essay, Abram speaks to the experience of reading and writing, and when he does, his prose often becomes rhapsodic. He says, for example, that

> to read is to enter into a profound participation, or chiasm, with the inked marks upon the page. In learning to read we must break the spontaneous participation of our eyes and our ears in the surrounding terrain (where they had ceaselessly converged in the synaesthetic encounter with animals, plants, and streams) in order to recouple those senses upon the flat surface of the page. As a Zuñi elder focuses her eyes upon a cactus and hears the cactus begin to speak, so we focus our eyes upon these printed marks and immediately hear voices. We hear spoken words, witness strange scenes or visions, even experience other lives. As nonhuman animals, plants, and even "inanimate" rivers once spoke to our tribal ancestors, so the "inert" letters on the page now speak to us! *This is a form of animism that we take for granted, but it is animism nonetheless — as mysterious as a talking stone.* (p. 56)

He also says,

> the process of learning to read and to write with the alphabet engenders a new, profoundly reflexive, sense of self. The capacity to view and even to dialogue with one's own words after writing them down, or even in the process of writing them down, enables a new sense of autonomy and independence from others, and even from the sensuous surroundings that had earlier been one's constant interlocutor. The fact that one's scripted words can be returned to and pondered at any time that one chooses, regardless of when, or in what situation, they were first recorded, grants a timeless quality to this new reflective self, a sense of the relative independence of one's verbal, speaking self from the breathing body with its shifting needs. The literate self cannot help but feel its own transcendence and timelessness relative to the fleeting world of corporeal experience. (p. 42)

Write an essay in which you tell your own story of reading and/or writing, one focusing on a particular moment, either representative or formative, in which you felt yourself to be a reader and/or writer. You needn't adopt this rhapsodic tone—in fact, we would encourage you to focus your attention on event, detail, and context. What were you doing? Where were you doing it? Why? In the end, however, your essay should be in conversation with Abram and what he has to say about the effects and consequences of reading and writing, about animism, for example, or a reflexive sense of self. You are putting your story up against his in order to see how the two might be in conversation with each other, in order to see what you might make of the conjunction.

How would Abram read your story of reading or writing? What might he see in your experience that you'd overlooked until reading his essay, and what might he fail to see that you've noticed? What are the consequences of interpreting your stories in your way instead of his?

2. Though he spends most of his essay looking at a significant cultural shift that took place many centuries ago, Abram briefly observes that we are currently undergoing a change of similar magnitude as we move from print-based literacy to electronic literacy. But Abram claims that our immersion in this change makes it impossible for us to analyze it properly:

> Today we are simply unable to discern with any clarity the manner in which our own perceptions and thoughts are being shifted by our sensory involvement with electronic technologies, since any thinking that seeks to discern such a shift is itself subject to the very effect that it strives to thematize. Nevertheless, we may be sure that the shapes of our consciousness *are* shifting in tandem with the technologies that engage our senses. . . . (p. 44)

In other words, we can't yet understand the impact of electronic (and digital) environments for reading and writing because we can't see outside of what is currently shaping our vision. We can only know that we are in the midst of a powerful transformation.

There is a challenge here—and an invitation. How might new media, which combine image, sound, and text, complicate Abram's argument about the effects of writing and our divorce from the natural world? A generation of students is emerging for whom digital environments have been everyday experiences. You can speak for them. Write an essay that extends or challenges Abram's arguments by looking at developments in new media. Your essay should be similar to Abram's in language, spirit, and tone. While generalizing, he also speaks from his own experience. You should too. Your essay should be a response to his, which means that you will need to provide summary and paraphrase; you should also, however, make a point of picking up his key terms or phrases to see how they work in the context of your experience and your argument. And it is probably best, at least at the outset, to take a measured and skeptical stance toward new media.

3. Abram makes much of the difference between what he refers to as "oral" and "literate" cultures. Oral cultures rely on memory, verbal formulas, stories, and stock epithets; literate cultures have text as a tool and so can

value abstraction, questioning, reflexivity, and an attention to words rather than people, places, or things:

> Plato, or rather the association between the literate Plato and his mostly nonliterate teacher Socrates . . . may be recognized as the hinge on which the sensuous, mimetic, profoundly embodied style of consciousness proper to orality gave way to the more detached, abstract mode of thinking engendered by alphabetic literacy. (p. 39)

While Abram is talking about the long sweep of history and the development of Western culture, it is still common for people to distinguish between oral and literate cultures in contemporary life, even within the experience of individuals. We live one way in speech and song, and another way in print or print environments.

Reread "Animism and the Alphabet" paying particular attention to the qualities of life and thought Abram attributes to oral and literate cultures, and to the people shaped by them. Then write an essay in which you use these distinctions to think about familiar scenes and characters. Are your parents or grandparents, for example, more oral or literate than you? Are you yourself, or people like you, more oral or literate in your habits of mind and your uses of language? Do you see contemporary culture split along these lines? Can you put these distinctions to work in ways that seem useful?

4.

> Trees, for instance, can seem to speak to us when they are jostled by the wind. (p. 55)

At various moments in his essay, Abram refers to talking trees, whispering stalks of grass, and animals communicating through footprints. The sun, the moon, the mountains, the streams—all come alive in Abram's writing, as if he himself were an animist.

Trees (or rivers) speak to us, and, for Abram, we are enjoined to speak back. Here is what he wrote in an essay in *Environmental Ethics* (27 [2005]: 171–90) in response to a critic:

> Yet if the river is an expressive power—if the river itself *speaks* — how then can I continue to speak only *about* the river, as though the river itself has no voice? How can I still speak in a manner that denies the river its own part in the conversation? The phenomenologist, originally dedicated to the careful *description* of the way things present themselves to her awareness, gradually discovers through such attentive description that the things are already engaging her as active, expressive powers; she begins to realize that by solely describing things—by using language only to paint a picture of things, *and never to consult or to speak with the things themselves*—she is insulting those things, holding herself aloof from a full encounter with those beings, and hence closing herself off from the wider conversation. If every entity is indeed fathomless, if each has its own dynamism, its own uncertainty and openness, then how

> can she persist in talking about them only *behind their back*, as it were, treating them as closed objects, rather than as open and indeterminate subjects?

And then, as if sensing that this sounds a little goofy, he adds:

> But is it not ludicrous to address the world directly, to speak to other organisms and elements as though they could understand? Certainly not, if such is the simplest way to open our ears toward those others, compelling us to listen, with *all* our senses, for the reply of the things. To be sure, the valleys and the oaks do not speak in words. But neither do humans speak only in words. We speak with our whole bodies, deploying a language of gesture, tone, and rhythm that animates all our discourse. This is most obvious, of course, when we are speaking *aloud*, yet even our written words can be much more than verbal — if, that is, we're awake to the magic of the written medium.

Write an essay in which you carry out an Abram-like project, exploring your own "conversation" with the natural world or the ways you read and understand its signs. (You might prepare for this essay by spending some time outdoors — walking, listening, observing.) In what ways have you sometimes found yourself in significant communication with animals or things, with the natural world, either animate or inanimate? When and where does this happen? What occurs? What comes of your exchange, and what functions does it serve? Write with as much attention to detail as possible.

Or, if there is another way of representing your relationship with the natural world, an experience not well represented by the metaphors of reading, writing, or conversing, use your essay to find a way of articulating this experience.

And, finally, Abram offers both the example of his own such experiences and a way of theorizing about them. At some point in your essay, bring in Abram as a point of reference. How does he write about such experiences? How does he explain them? Where and how is he helpful (or not helpful) to you?

MAKING CONNECTIONS

1. In "Joyas Voladoras" (p. 273), Brian Doyle considers the hearts of hummingbirds and blue whales, one of which is remarkably tiny and the other remarkably large. It is through writing that Doyle attempts to understand these creatures and their bodies; it is through the metaphors and connections wrought by written language that he imagines what it is like to experience their lives. In other words, we might see Doyle's text as an implicit challenge to David Abram's contention that writing detaches us from the natural world. As you reread their essays, consider the kind of conversation

Doyle and Abram might have about the relationship between writing and our recognition of the living beings that populate the environment.

Write an essay that moves between two kinds of writing—one in which you explore, Doyle-like, the inner lives of particular animals, and another in which, Abram-like, you discuss the problem of trying to understand other creatures through writing about them. What does writing enable us to comprehend about nonhuman entities? What are its delusions or limits? Your essay should represent an attempt to imagine that which you cannot experience, and to reflect on the value and difficulty of doing so.

2. In "Arts of the Contact Zone" (p. 485), Mary Louise Pratt defines contact zones as "social spaces where cultures meet, clash, and grapple with each other, often in contexts of highly asymmetrical relations of power." While we don't ordinarily think of the natural world as a culture, David Abram writes about the environment as if it were a culture of sorts—speaking to us, writing to us, attempting to communicate if only we are willing and able to listen. Abram might argue as well that the environment speaks in a context of "highly asymmetrical relations of power," where people—like the Spaniards in Pratt's central example—hold the dominant position, often exhibiting little interest in the "languages" spoken by mountains, rivers, animals, and clouds.

   Write an essay in which you consider how Pratt's concept of the contact zone might be useful in helping us consider our relationship with the natural world. Is the environment trying to speak to us as Guaman Poma tried to speak to his Spanish conquerors? In what ways is this analogy useful or productive, and in what ways does it fall short? Where would we find the "autoethnographic texts" produced by the natural world, and how can we learn to read them? Can you locate environmental versions of what Pratt calls "critique, collaboration, bilingualism, mediation, parody, denunciation, imaginary dialogue, [and] vernacular expression"? What are the possibilities for—and the problems with—"translating" messages from the natural world into languages we understand?

3. There is much that is similar to Abram's concerns in Walker Percy's "The Loss of the Creature" (p. 459). In fact, it is easy to imagine Abram using the same title. They ask similar questions; they write with a similar urgency; they are even similar in method. Why, Percy asks, has it become so difficult to experience the Grand Canyon? "Why is it almost impossible to gaze directly at the Grand Canyon . . . and see it for what it is—as one picks up a strange object from one's back yard and gazes directly at it?"

   Let's take the similarities as a starting point. As you reread the essays, think primarily about the differences. Both are concerned with loss. What, for each, has been lost? What are the reasons? What are the consequences? What options are available for restoration? Write an essay that begins with Abram's point of view, a concern over "modern civilization's evident disregard for the needs of the natural world," and that thinks, then, about Percy's understanding of loss, its origins and consequences.

4. In the final chapter of *Writing at the End of the World,* Richard E. Miller says the following about his own writing:

> While the assessments, evaluations, proposals, reports, commentaries, and critiques I produce help to keep the bureaucracy of higher education going, there is another kind of writing I turn to in order to sustain the ongoing search for meaning in a world no one controls. This writing asks the reader to make imaginative connections between disparate elements; it tracks one path among many possible ones across the glistening water. (p. 196)

We can assume that this is the kind of writing present in "The Dark Night of the Soul" (p. 420). And he says this about English and the humanities:

> The practice of the humanities . . . is not about admiration or greatness or appreciation or depth of knowledge or scholarly achievement; it's about the movement between worlds, arms out, balancing; it's about making the connections that count. (p. 198)

This latter is a pretty bold statement, since English departments have traditionally defined their job as teaching students to read deeply, to conduct scholarly research, and to appreciate great works of literature. What Miller has to offer, rather, is "movement between worlds, arms out, balancing" or "making the connections that count."

Miller and Abram write with a sense of urgency over what we have lost, and what we have lost can be traced to problems of reading and writing, problems that belong not just to this student or to that writer, but to the culture at large. As you reread these two selections, "The Dark Night of the Soul" and "Animism and the Alphabet," think about Miller and Abram in relation to schooling; in fact, think of them as designing writing courses, like the course you are taking right now. How would each approach such a course? What would the course look like? What would its students do? How would they be evaluated? Would you want to take such a course? You need to justify your assumptions with reference to what they say (and do) in their essays.

GLORIA Anzaldúa

Gloria Anzaldúa (1942–2004) grew up in southwest Texas, the physical and cultural borderland between the United States and Mexico, an area she called "*una herida abierta*," an open wound, "where the Third World grates against the first and bleeds." Defining herself as lesbian, feminist, Chicana—a representative of the new *mestiza*—she dramatically revised the usual narrative of American autobiography. "I am a border woman," she said. "I grew up between two cultures, the Mexican (with a heavy Indian influence) and the Anglo (as a member of a colonized people in our own territory). I have been straddling that *tejas*-Mexican border, and others, all my life." Cultural, physical, spiritual, sexual, linguistic—the borderlands defined by Anzaldúa extend beyond geography. "In fact," she said, "the Borderlands are present where two or more cultures edge each other, where people of different races occupy the same territory, where under, lower, middle, and upper classes touch, where the space between two individuals shrinks with intimacy." In a sense, her writing argues against the concept of an "authentic," unified, homogeneous culture, the pure "Mexican experience," a nostalgia that underlies much of the current interest in "ethnic" literature.

In the following selections, which represent two chapters from her book *Borderlands/La frontera: The New Mestiza* (1987), Anzaldúa mixes genres, moving between poetry and prose, weaving stories with sections that resemble the work of a cultural or political theorist. She tells us a story about her childhood, her culture, and her people that is at once both myth and history. Her prose, too, is mixed, shifting among Anglo-American English, Castilian Spanish, Tex-Mex, Northern Mexican dialect, and Nahuatl (Aztec), speaking to us in the particular mix that represents her linguistic heritage: "Presently this infant language, this bastard language, Chicano Spanish, is not approved by any society. But we Chicanos no longer feel that we need to beg entrance, that we need always to make the first overture—to translate to Anglos, Mexicans, and Latinos, apology blurting out of our mouths with every step. Today we ask to be met halfway. This book is our invitation to you." The book is an invitation, but not always an easy one. The chapters that follow make a variety of demands on the reader. The shifting styles, genres, and languages can be confusing or disturbing, but this is part of the effect of Anzaldúa's prose, part of the experience you are invited to share.

In a chapter from the book that is not included here, Anzaldúa gives this account of her writing:

> In looking at this book that I'm almost finished writing, I see a mosaic pattern (Aztec-like) emerging, a weaving pattern, thin here, thick there. I see a preoccupation with the deep structure, the underlying structure, with the gesso underpainting that is red earth, black earth.... This almost finished product seems an assemblage, a montage, a beaded work with several leitmotifs and with a central core, now appearing, now disappearing in a crazy dance. The whole thing has had a mind of its own, escaping me and insisting on putting together the pieces of its own puzzle with minimal direction from my will.

Beyond her prose, she sees the competing values of more traditionally organized narratives, "art typical of Western European cultures, [which] attempts to manage the energies of its own internal system.... It is dedicated to the validation of itself. Its task is to move humans by means of achieving mastery in content, technique, feeling. Western art is always whole and always 'in power.'"

Anzaldúa's prose puts you, as a reader, on the borderland; in a way, it re-creates the position of the *mestiza*. As you read, you will need to meet this prose halfway, generously, learning to read a text that announces its difference.

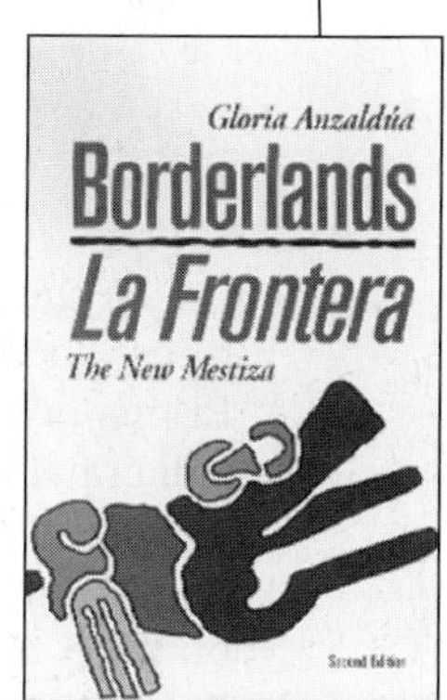

In addition to *Borderlands/La frontera*, Anzaldúa edited *Haciendo Caras: Making Face/Making Soul* (1990) and coedited an anthology, *This Bridge Called My Back: Writings by Radical Women of Color* (1983). She published a book for children, *Prietita and the Ghost Woman* (1996), which retells traditional Mexican folktales from a feminist perspective. A collection of interviews, *Interviews/Entrevistas*, was published in 2000, and a coedited anthology of multicultural feminist theory titled *This Bridge We Call Home: Radical Visions for Transformation* was published in 2002.

Entering into the Serpent

Sueño con serpientes, con serpientes del mar,
Con cierto mar, ay de serpientes sueño yo.
Largas, transparentes, en sus barrigas llevan
Lo que puedan arebatarle al amor.
Oh, oh, oh, la mató y aparese una mayor.
Oh, con mucho más infierno en digestión.

I dream of serpents, serpents of the sea,
A certain sea, oh, of serpents I dream.
Long, transparent, in their bellies they carry
All that they can snatch away from love.
Oh, oh, oh, I kill one and a larger one appears.
Oh, with more hellfire burning inside!

— SILVIO RODRÍGUES,
"Sueño con serpientes"[1]

In the predawn orange haze, the sleepy crowing of roosters atop the trees. *No vayas al escusado en lo oscuro*. Don't go to the outhouse at night, Prieta, my mother would say. *No se te vaya a meter algo pour allá*. A snake will crawl into your *nalgas*,[2] make you pregnant. They seek warmth in the cold. *Dicen que las culebras* like to suck *chiches*,[3] can draw milk out of you.

En el escusado in the half-light spiders hang like gliders. Under my bare buttocks and the rough planks the deep yawning tugs at me. I can see my legs fly up to my face as my body falls through the round hole into the sheen of swarming maggots below. Avoiding the snakes under the porch I walk back into the kitchen, step on a big black one slithering across the floor.

ELLA TIENE SU TONO[4]

Once we were chopping cotton in the fields of Jesus Maria Ranch. All around us the woods. *Quelite*[5] towered above me, choking the stubby cotton that had outlived the deer's teeth.

I swung *el ázadón*[6] hard. *El quelite* barely shook, showered nettles on my arms and face. When I heard the rattle the world froze.

I barely felt its fangs. Boot got all the *veneno*.[7] My mother came shrieking, swinging her hoe high, cutting the earth, the writhing body.

I stood still, the sun beat down. Afterwards I smelled where fear had been: back of neck, under arms, between my legs, I felt its heat slide down my body. I swallowed the rock it had hardened into.

When Mama had gone down the row and was out of sight, I took out my pocketknife. I made an X over each prick. My body followed the blood, fell onto the soft ground. I put my mouth over the red and sucked and spit between the rows of cotton.

I picked up the pieces, placed them end on end. *Culebra de cascabel.*[8] I counted the rattlers: twelve. It would shed no more. I buried the pieces between the rows of cotton.

That night I watched the window sill, watched the moon dry the blood on the tail, dreamed rattler fangs filled my mouth, scales covered my body. In the morning I saw through snake eyes, felt snake blood course through my body. The serpent, *mi tono*, my animal counterpart. I was immune to its venom. Forever immune.

Snakes, *víboras*: since that day I've sought and shunned them. Always when they cross my path, fear and elation flood my body. I know things older than Freud, older than gender. She — that's how I think of *la Víbora*, Snake Woman. Like the ancient Olmecs, I know Earth is a coiled Serpent. Forty years it's taken me to enter into the Serpent, to acknowledge that I have a body, that I am a body and to assimilate the animal body, the animal soul.

COATLALOPEUH, SHE WHO HAS DOMINION OVER SERPENTS

Mi mamagrande Ramona toda su vida mantuvo un altar pequeño en la esquina del comedor. Siempre tenía las velas prendidas. Allí hacía promesas a la Virgen de Guadalupe. My family, like most Chicanos, did not practice Roman Catholicism but a folk Catholicism with many pagan elements. *La Virgen de Guadalupe*'s Indian name is *Coatlalopeuh*. She is the central deity connecting us to our Indian ancestry.

Coatlalopeuh is descended from, or is an aspect of, earlier Mesoamerican fertility and Earth goddesses. The earliest is *Coatlicue*, or "Serpent Skirt." She had a human skull or serpent for a head, a necklace of human hearts, a skirt of twisted serpents, and taloned feet. As creator goddess, she was mother of the celestial deities, and of *Huitzilopochtli* and his sister, *Coyolxauhqui*, She with Golden Bells, Goddess of the Moon, who was decapitated by her brother. Another aspect of *Coatlicue* is *Tonantsi*.[9] The Totonacs, tired of the Aztec human sacrifices to the male god, *Huitzilopochtli*, renewed their reverence for *Tonantsi* who preferred the sacrifice of birds and small animals.[10]

COATLALOPEUH IS DESCENDED FROM, OR IS AN ASPECT OF, EARLIER MESOAMERICAN FERTILITY AND EARTH GODDESSES.

The male-dominated Azteca-Mexica culture drove the powerful female deities underground by giving them monstrous attributes and by substituting male deities in their place, thus splitting the female Self and the female deities. They divided her who had been complete, who possessed both upper (light) and underworld (dark) aspects. *Coatlicue*, the Serpent goddess, and her more sinister aspects, *Tlazolteotl* and *Cihuacoatl*, were "darkened" and disempowered much in the same manner as the Indian *Kali*.

Tonantsi—split from her dark guises, *Coatlicue*, *Tlazolteotl*, and *Cihuacoatl*—became the good mother. The Nahuas, through ritual and prayer, sought to oblige *Tonantsi* to ensure their health and the growth of their crops. It was she who gave *México* the cactus plant to provide her people with milk and pulque. It was she who defended her children against the wrath of the Christian God by challenging God, her son, to produce mother's milk (as she had done) to prove that his benevolence equalled his disciplinary harshness.[11]

After the Conquest, the Spaniards and their Church continued to split *Tonantsi/Guadalupe*. They desexed *Guadalupe*, taking *Coatlalopeuh*, the serpent/sexuality, out of her. They completed the split begun by the Nahuas by making *la Virgen de Guadalupe/Virgen María* into chaste virgins and *Tlazolteotl/Coatlicue/la Chingada* into *putas*; into the Beauties and the Beasts. They went even further; they made all Indian deities and religious practices the work of the devil.

Thus *Tonantsi* became *Guadalupe*, the chaste protective mother, the defender of the Mexican people.

El nueve de diciembre del año 1531
a las cuatro de la madrugada
un pobre indio que se llamaba Juan Diego
iba cruzando el cerro de Tepeyác
cuando oyó un cantó de pájaro.
Alzó al cabeza vío que en la cima del cerro
estaba cubierta con una brillante nube blanca.
Parada en frente del sol
sobre una luna creciente
sostenida por un ángel
estaba una azteca
vestida en ropa de india.
Nuestra Señora María de Coatlalopeuh
se le apareció.
"Juan Diegito, El-que-habla-como-un-águila,"
la Virgen le dijo en el lenguaje azteca.
"Para hacer mi altar este cerro eligo.
Dile a tu gente que yo soy la madre de Dios,
a los indios yo les ayudaré.
Estó se lo contó a Juan Zumarraga
pero el obispo no le creyo.
Juan Diego volvió, lleño su tilma[12]
con rosas de castilla
creciendo milagrosamiente en la nieve.
Se las llevó al obispo,
y cuando abrío su tilma
el retrato de la Virgen
ahí estaba pintado.

Guadalupe appeared on December 9, 1531, on the spot where the Aztec goddess, *Tonantsi* ("Our Lady Mother"), had been worshiped by the Nahuas and where a temple to her had stood. Speaking Nahua, she told Juan Diego, a poor Indian crossing Tepeyac Hill, whose Indian name was *Cuautlaohuac* and who belonged to the *mazehual* class, the humblest within the Chichimeca tribe, that her name was *María Coatlalopeuh*. *Coatl* is the Nahuatl word for serpent. *Lopeuh* means "the one who has dominion over serpents." I interpret this as "the one who is at one with the beasts." Some spell her name *Coatlaxopeuh* (pronounced "*Cuatlash-upe*" in Nahuatl) and say that "*xopeuh*" means "crushed or stepped on with disdain." Some say it means "she who crushed the serpent," with the serpent as the symbol of the indigenous religion, meaning that her religion was to take the place of the Aztec religion.[13] Because *Coatlalopeuh* was homophonous to the Spanish *Guadalupe*, the Spanish identified her with the dark Virgin, *Guadalupe*, patroness of West Central Spain.[14]

From that meeting, Juan Diego walked away with the image of *la Virgen* painted on his cloak. Soon after, Mexico ceased to belong to Spain, and *la Virgen de Guadalupe* began to eclipse all the other male and female religious figures in Mexico, Central America, and parts of the U.S. Southwest. "*Desde entonces para el mexicano ser Guadalupano es algo esencial*/Since then for the Mexican, to be a *Guadalupano* is something essential."[15]

Mi Virgen Morena	My brown virgin
Mi Virgen Ranchera	my country virgin
Eres nuestra Reina	you are our queen
México es tu tierra	Mexico is your land
Y tú su bandera.	and you its flag.

—"LA VIRGEN RANCHERA"[16]

In 1660 the Roman Catholic Church named her Mother of God, considering her synonymous with *la Virgen María*; she became *la Santa Patrona de los mexicanos*. The role of defender (or patron) has traditionally been assigned to male gods. During the Mexican Revolution, Emiliano Zapata and Miguel Hidalgo used her image to move *el pueblo mexicano* toward freedom. During the 1965 grape strike in Delano, California, and in subsequent Chicano farmworkers' marches in Texas and other parts of the Southwest, her image on banners heralded and united the farmworkers. *Pachucos* (zoot suiters) tattoo her image on their bodies. Today, in Texas and Mexico she is more venerated than Jesus or God the Father. In the Lower Rio Grande Valley of south Texas it is *la Virgen de San Juan de los Lagos* (an aspect of *Guadalupe*) that is worshiped by thousands every day at her shrine in San Juan. In Texas she is considered the patron saint of Chicanos. *Cuando Carito, mi hermanito,* was missing in action and, later, wounded in Viet Nam, *mi mamá* got on her knees *y le prometío a Ella que si su hijito volvía vivo* she would crawl on her knees and light novenas in her honor.

Today, *la Virgen de Guadalupe* is the single most potent religious, political, and cultural image of the Chicano/*mexicano*. She, like my race, is a synthesis of the old world and the new, of the religion and culture of the two races in our psyche, the conquerors and the conquered. She is the symbol of the *mestizo* true to his or her Indian values. *La cultura chicana* identifies with the mother (Indian) rather than with the father (Spanish). Our faith is rooted in indigenous attributes, images, symbols, magic, and myth. Because *Guadalupe* took upon herself the psychological and physical devastation of the conquered and oppressed *indio*, she is our spiritual, political, and psychological symbol. As a symbol of hope and faith, she sustains and insures our survival. The Indian, despite extreme despair, suffering, and near genocide, has survived. To Mexicans on both sides of the border, *Guadalupe* is the symbol of our rebellion against the rich, upper and middle class; against their subjugation of the poor and the *indio*.

Guadalupe unites people of different races, religions, languages: Chicano protestants, American Indians, and whites. *"Nuestra abogada siempre serás* / Our *mediatrix* you will always be." She mediates between the Spanish and the Indian cultures (or three cultures as in the case of *mexicanos* of African or other ancestry) and between Chicanos and the white world. She mediates between humans and the divine, between this reality and the reality of spirit entities. *La Virgen de Guadalupe* is the symbol of ethnic identity and of the tolerance for ambiguity that Chicanos-*mexicanos*, people of mixed race, people who have Indian blood, people who cross cultures, by necessity possess.

La gente Chicana tiene tres madres. All three are mediators: *Guadalupe*, the virgin mother who has not abandoned us, *la Chingada (Malinche)*, the raped mother whom we have abandoned, and *la Llorona*, the mother who seeks her lost children and is a combination of the other two.

Ambiguity surrounds the symbols of these three "Our Mothers." *Guadalupe* has been used by the Church to mete out institutionalized oppression: to placate the Indians and *mexicanos* and Chicanos. In part, the true identity of all three has been subverted — *Guadalupe* to make us docile and enduring, *la Chingada* to make us ashamed of our Indian side, and *la Llorona* to make us long-suffering people. This obscuring has encouraged the *virgen/puta* (whore) dichotomy.

Yet we have not all embraced this dichotomy. In the U.S. Southwest, Mexico, Central and South America the *indio* and the *mestizo* continue to worship the old spirit entities (including *Guadalupe*) and their supernatural power, under the guise of Christian saints.[17]

Las invoco diosas mías, ustedes las indias
sumergidas en mi carne que son mis sombras.
Ustedes que persisten mudas en sus cuevas.
Ustedes Señoras que ahora, como yo,
están en desgracia.

FOR WAGING WAR IS MY COSMIC DUTY: THE LOSS OF THE BALANCED OPPOSITIONS AND THE CHANGE TO MALE DOMINANCE

Therefore I decided to leave
The country [Aztlán],
Therefore I have come as one charged with a special duty,

Because I have been given arrows and shields,
For waging war is my duty,
And on my expeditions I
Shall see all the lands,
I shall wait for the people and meet them
In all four quarters and I shall give them
Food to eat and drinks to quench their thirst,
For here I shall unite all the different peoples!

— HUITZILOPOCHTLI
speaking to the Azteca-Mexica[18]

Before the Aztecs became a militaristic, bureaucratic state where male predatory warfare and conquest were based on patrilineal nobility, the principle of balanced opposition between the sexes existed.[19] The people worshiped the Lord and Lady of Duality, *Ometecuhtli* and *Omecihuatl*. Before the change to male dominance, *Coatlicue*, Lady of the Serpent Skirt, contained and balanced the dualities of male and female, light and dark, life and death.

The changes that led to the loss of the balanced oppositions began when the Azteca, one of the twenty Toltec tribes, made the last pilgrimage from a place called Aztlán. The migration south began about the year A.D. 820. Three hundred years later the advance guard arrived near Tula, the capital of the declining Toltec empire. By the eleventh century, they had joined with the Chichimec tribe of Mexitin (afterwards called Mexica) into one religious and administrative organization within Aztlán, the Aztec territory. The Mexitin, with their tribal god *Tetzauhteotl Huitzilopochtli* (Magnificent Humming Bird on the Left), gained control of the religious system.[20] (In some stories *Huitzilopochtli* killed his sister, the moon goddess *Malinalxoch*, who used her supernatural power over animals to control the tribe rather than wage war.)

Huitzilopochtli assigned the Azteca-Mexica the task of keeping the human race (the present cosmic age called the Fifth Sun, *El Quinto Sol*) alive. They were to guarantee the harmonious preservation of the human race by unifying all the people on earth into one social, religious, and administrative organ. The Aztec people considered themselves in charge of regulating all earthly matters.[21] Their instrument: controlled or regulated war to gain and exercise power.

After one hundred years in the central plateau, the Azteca-Mexica went to Chapultepec, where they settled in 1248 (the present site of the park on the outskirts of Mexico City). There, in 1345, the Azteca-Mexica chose the site of their capital, Tenochtitlan.[22] By 1428, they dominated the Central Mexican lake area.

The Aztec ruler, *Itzcoatl*, destroyed all the painted documents (books called codices) and rewrote a mythology that validated the wars of conquest and thus continued the shift from a tribe based on clans to one based on classes. From 1429 to 1440, the Aztecs emerged as a militaristic state tha preyed on neighboring tribes for tribute and captives.[23] The “w flowers” were encounters between local armies with a fixed numb warriors, operating within the Aztec World, and, according to set r fighting ritual battles at fixed times and on predetermined battlefields. The religious purpose of these wars was to procure prisoners of war who could be sacrificed to the deities of the capturing party. For if one "fed" the gods, the human race would be saved from total extinction. The social purpose was to enable males of noble families and warriors of low descent to win honor, fame, and administrative offices, and to prevent social and cultural decadence of the elite. The Aztec people were free to have their own religious faith, provided it did not conflict too much with the three fundamental principles of state ideology: to fulfill the special duty set forth by *Huitzilopochtli* of unifying all peoples, to participate in the wars of flowers, and to bring ritual offerings and do penance for the purpose of preventing decadence.[24]

Matrilineal descent characterized the Toltecs and perhaps early Aztec society. Women possessed property, and were curers as well as priestesses. According to the codices, women in former times had the supreme power in Tula, and in the beginning of the Aztec dynasty, the royal blood ran through the female line. A council of elders of the Calpul headed by a supreme leader, or *tlactlo*, called the father and mother of the people, governed the tribe. The supreme leader's vice-emperor occupied the position of "Snake Woman" or *Cihuacoatl*, a goddess.[25] Although the high posts were occupied by men, the terms referred to females, evidence of the exalted role of women before the Aztec nation became centralized. The final break with the democratic Calpul came when the four Aztec lords of royal lineage picked the king's successor from his siblings or male descendants.[26]

La Llorona's wailing in the night for her lost children has an echoing note in the wailing or mourning rites performed by women as they bid their sons, brothers, and husbands good-bye before they left to go to the "flowery wars." Wailing is the Indian, Mexican, and Chicana woman's feeble protest when she has no other recourse. These collective wailing rites may have been a sign of resistance in a society which glorified the warrior and war and for whom the women of the conquered tribes were booty.[27]

In defiance of the Aztec rulers, the *macehuales* (the common people) continued to worship fertility, nourishment, and agricultural female deities, those of crops and rain. They venerated *Chalchiuhtlicue* (goddess of sweet or inland water), *Chicomecoatl* (goddess of food), and *Huixtocihuatl* (goddess of salt).

Nevertheless, it took less than three centuries for Aztec society to change from the balanced duality of their earlier times and from the egalitarian traditions of a wandering tribe to those of a predatory state. The nobility kept the tribute, the commoner got nothing, resulting in a class split. The conquered tribes hated the Aztecs because of the rape of their women and the heavy taxes levied on them. The *Tlaxcalans* were the Aztec's bitter enemies and it was they who helped the Spanish defeat the Aztec rulers, who were by this time so unpopular with their own common people that they could not even mobilize the populace to defend the city. Thus the Aztec nation fell not because *Malinali (la Chingada)* interpreted for and slept with Cortés, but because the ruling elite had subverted the solidarity between men and women and between noble and commoner.[28]

SUEÑO CON SERPIENTES

Coatl. In pre-Columbian America the most notable symbol was the serpent. The Olmecs associated womanhood with the Serpent's mouth which was guarded by rows of dangerous teeth, a sort of *vagina dentate*. They considered it the most sacred place on earth, a place of refuge, the creative womb from which all things were born and to which all things returned. Snake people had holes, entrances to the body of the Earth Serpent; they followed the Serpent's way, identified with the Serpent deity, with the mouth, both the eater and the eaten. The destiny of humankind is to be devoured by the Serpent.[29]

Dead,
the doctor by the operating table said.
I passed between the two fangs,
the flickering tongue.
Having come through the mouth of the serpent,
swallowed,
I found myself suddenly in the dark,
sliding down a smooth wet surface
down down into an even darker darkness.
Having crossed the portal, the raised hinged mouth,
having entered the serpent's belly,
now there was no looking back, no going back.

Why do I cast no shadow?
Are there lights from all sides shining on me?
Ahead, ahead,
curled up inside the serpent's coils,
the damp breath of death on my face.
I knew at that instant; something must change
or I'd die.
Algo tenía que cambiar.

After each of my four bouts with death I'd catch glimpses of an otherworld Serpent. Once, in my bedroom, I saw a cobra the size of the room, her hood expanding over me. When I blinked she was gone. I realized she was, in my psyche, the mental picture and symbol of the instinctual in its collective impersonal, prehuman. She, the symbol of the dark sexual drive, the chthonic (underworld), the feminine, the serpentine movement of sexuality, of creativity, the basis of all energy and life.

THE PRESENCES

She appeared in white, garbed in white,
standing white, pure white.

— BERNARDINO DE SAHAGÚN[30]

On the gulf where I was raised, *en el Valle del Río Grande* in South Texas — that triangular piece of land wedged between the river *y el golfo* which serves as the Texas-U.S./Mexican border—is a Mexican *pueblito* called Hargill (at one time in the history of this one-grocery-store, two-service-stations town there were thirteen churches and thirteen *cantinas*). Down the road, a little ways from our house, was a deserted church. It was known among the *mexicanos* that if you walked down the road late at night you would see a woman dressed in white floating about, peering out the church window. She would follow those who had done something bad or who were afraid. *Los mexicanos* called her *la Jila*. Some thought she was *la Llorona*. She was, I think, *Cihuacoatl*, Serpent Woman, ancient Aztec goddess of the earth, of war and birth, patron of midwives, and antecedent of *la Llorona*. Covered with chalk, *Cihuacoatl* wears a white dress with a decoration half red and half black. Her hair forms two little horns (which the Aztecs depicted as knives) crossed on her forehead. The lower part of her face is a bare jawbone, signifying death. On her back she carries a cradle, the knife of sacrifice swaddled as if it were her papoose, her child.[31] Like *la Llorona, Cihuacoatl* howls and weeps in the night, screams as if demented. She brings mental depression and sorrow. Long before it takes place, she is the first to predict something is to happen.

Back then, I, an unbeliever, scoffed at these Mexican superstitions as I was taught in Anglo school. Now, I wonder if this story and similar ones were the culture's attempts to "protect" members of the family, especially girls, from "wandering." Stories of the devil luring young girls away and having his way with them discouraged us from going out. There's an ancient Indian tradition of burying the umbilical cord of an infant girl under the house so she will never stray from it and her domestic role.

BACK THEN, I, AN UNBELIEVER, SCOFFED AT THESE MEXICAN SUPERSTITIONS AS I WAS TAUGHT IN ANGLO SCHOOL.

A mis ancas caen los cueros de culebra,
cuatro veces por año los arrastro,
me tropiezo y me caigo
y cada vez que miro una culebra le pregunto
¿Qué traes conmigo?

Four years ago a red snake crossed my path as I walked through the woods. The direction of its movement, its pace, its colors, the "mood" of the trees and the wind and the snake—they all "spoke" to me, told me things. I look for omens everywhere, everywhere catch glimpses of the patterns and cycles of my life. Stones "speak" to Luisah Teish, a Santera; trees whisper their secrets to Chrystos, a Native American. I remember listening to the voices of the wind as a child and understanding its messages. *Los espíritus* that ride the back of the south wind. I remember their exhalation blowing in through the slits in the door during those hot Texas afternoons. A gust of wind raising the linoleum under my feet, buffeting the house. Everything trembling.

We're not supposed to remember such otherworldly events. We're supposed to ignore, forget, kill those fleeting images of the soul's presence and of the spirit's presence. We've been taught that the spirit is outside our bodies or above our heads somewhere up in the sky with God. We're supposed to forget that every cell in our bodies, every bone and bird and worm has spirit in it.

Like many Indians and Mexicans, I did not deem my psychic experiences real. I denied their occurrences and let my inner senses atrophy. I allowed white rationality to tell me that the existence of the "other world" was mere pagan superstition. I accepted their reality, the "official" reality of the rational, reasoning mode which is connected with external reality, the upper world, and is considered the most developed consciousness — the consciousness of duality.

The other mode of consciousness facilitates images from the soul and the unconscious through dreams and the imagination. Its work is labeled "fiction," make-believe, wish-fulfillment. White anthropologists claim that Indians have "primitive" and therefore deficient minds, that we cannot think in the higher mode of consciousness — rationality. They are fascinated by what they call the "magical" mind, the "savage" mind, the *participation mystique* of the mind that says the world of the imagination — the world of the soul — and of the spirit is just as real as physical reality.[32] In trying to become "objective," Western culture made "objects" of things and people when it distanced itself from them, thereby losing "touch" with them. This dichotomy is the root of all violence.

Not only was the brain split into two functions but so was reality. Thus people who inhabit both realities are forced to live in the interface between the two, forced to become adept at switching modes. Such is the case with the *india* and the *mestiza*.

Institutionalized religion fears trafficking with the spirit world and stigmatizes it as witchcraft. It has strict taboos against this kind of inner knowledge. It fears what Jung calls the Shadow, the unsavory aspects of ourselves. But even more it fears the suprahuman, the god in ourselves.

"The purpose of any established religion . . . is to glorify, sanction, and bless with a superpersonal meaning all personal and interpersonal activities. This occurs through the 'sacraments,' and indeed through most religious rites." But it sanctions only its own sacraments and rites. Voodoo, Santeria, Shamanism, and other native religions are called cults and their beliefs are called mythologies. In my own life, the Catholic Church fails to give meaning to my daily acts, to my continuing encounters with the "other world." It and other institutionalized religions impoverish all life, beauty, pleasure.

The Catholic and Protestant religions encourage fear and distrust of life and of the body; they encourage a split between the body and the spirit and totally ignore the soul; they encourage us to kill off parts of ourselves. We are taught that the body is an ignorant animal; intelligence dwells only in the head. But the body is smart. It does not discern between external stimuli and stimuli from the imagination. It reacts equally viscerally to events from the imagination as it does to "real" events.

So I grew up in the interface trying not to give countenance to *el mal aigre*,[33] evil nonhuman, noncorporeal entities riding the wind, that could come in through the window, through my nose with my breath. I was not supposed to believe in *susto*, a sudden shock or fall that frightens the soul out of the body. And growing up between such opposing spiritualities how could I reconcile the two, the pagan and the Christian?

No matter to what use my people put the supranatural world, it is evident to me now that the spirit world, whose existence the whites are so adamant in denying, does in fact exist. This very minute I sense the presence of the spirits of my ancestors in my room. And I think *la Jila* is *Cihuacoatl*, Snake Woman; she is *la Llorona*, Daughter of Night, traveling the dark terrains of the unknown searching for the lost parts of herself. I remember *la Jila* following me once, remember her eerie lament. I'd like to think that she was crying for her lost children, *los* Chicanos/*mexicanos*.

LA FACULTAD

La facultad is the capacity to see in surface phenomena the meaning of deeper realities, to see the deep structure below the surface. It is an instant "sensing," a quick perception arrived at without conscious reasoning. It is an acute awareness mediated by the part of the psyche that does not speak, that communicates in images and symbols which are the faces of feelings, that is, behind which feelings reside/hide. The one possessing this sensitivity is excruciatingly alive to the world.

Those who are pushed out of the tribe for being different are likely to become more sensitized (when not brutalized into insensitivity). Those who do not feel psychologically or physically safe in the world are more apt to develop this sense. Those who are pounced on the most have it the strongest — the females, the homosexuals of all races, the darkskinned, the outcast, the persecuted, the marginalized, the foreign.

When we're up against the wall, when we have all sorts of oppressions coming at us, we are forced to develop this faculty so that we'll know when the next person is going to slap us or lock us away. We'll sense the rapist when he's five blocks down the street. Pain makes us acutely anxious to avoid more of it, so we hone that radar. It's a kind of survival tactic that people, caught between the worlds, unknowingly cultivate. It is latent in all of us.

I walk into a house and I know whether it is empty or occupied. I feel the lingering charge in the air of a recent fight or lovemaking or depression. I sense the emotions someone near is emitting — whether friendly or threatening. Hate and fear — the more intense the emotion, the greater my reception of it. I feel a tingling on my skin when someone is staring at me or thinking about me. I can tell how others feel by the way they smell, where others are by the air pressure on my skin. I can spot the love or greed or generosity lodged in the tissues of another. Often I sense the direction of and my distance from people or objects — in the dark, or with my eyes closed, without looking. It must be a vestige of a proximity sense, a sixth sense that's lain dormant from long-ago times.

Fear develops the proximity sense aspect of *la facultad*. But there is a deeper sensing that is another aspect of this faculty. It is anything that breaks into one's everyday mode of perception, that causes a break in one's defenses and resistance, anything that takes one from one's habitual grounding, causes the depths to open up, causes a shift in perception. This shift in perception deepens the way we see concrete objects and people; the senses become so acute and piercing that we can see through things, view events in depth, a piercing that reaches the underworld (the realm of the soul). As we plunge vertically, the break, with its accompanying new seeing, makes us pay attention to the soul, and we are thus carried into awareness — an experiencing of soul (Self).

We lose something in this mode of initiation, something is taken from us: our innocence, our unknowing ways, our safe and easy ignorance. There is a prejudice and a fear of the dark, chthonic (underworld), material such as depression, illness, death, and the violations that can bring on this break. Confronting anything that tears the fabric of our everyday mode of consciousness and that thrusts us into a less literal and more psychic sense of reality increases awareness and *la facultad*.

NOTES

[1] From the song *"Sueño con serpientes"* by Silvio Rodrígues, from the album *Días y flores*. Translated by Barbara Dane with the collaboration of Rina Benmauor and Juan Flores. [All notes are Anzaldúa's.]

[2] *Nalgas*: vagina, buttocks.

[3] *Dicen que las culebras* like to suck *chiches*: they say snakes like to suck women's teats.

[4] *Ella tiene su tono*: she has supernatural power from her animal soul, the *tono*.

[5] *Quelite*: weed.

[6] *Azadón*: hoe.

[7] *Veneno*: venom, poison.

[8] *Culebra de cascabel*: rattlesnake.

[9] In some Nahuatl dialects *Tonantsi* is called *Tonatzin*, literally "Our Holy Mother." "*Tonan* was a name given in Nahuatl to several mountains, these being the congelations of the Earth Mother at spots convenient for her worship." The Mexica considered the mountain mass southwest of Chapultepec to be their mother. Burr Cartwright Brundage, *The Fifth Sun: Aztec Gods, Aztec World* (Austin, TX: University of Texas Press, 1979), 154, 242.

[10] Ena Campbell, "The Virgin of Guadalupe and the Female Self-image: A Mexican Case History," *Mother Worship: Themes and Variations*, James J. Preston, ed. (Chapel Hill, NC: University of North Carolina Press, 1982), 22.

[11] Alan R. Sandstrom, "The Tonantsi Cult of the Eastern Nahuas," *Mother Worship: Themes and Variations*, James J. Preston, ed.

[12] *Una tela tejida con asperas fibras de agave* [*sic*]: it is an oblong cloth that hangs over the back and ties together across the shoulders.

[13] Andres Gonzales Guerrero, Jr., *The Significance of Nuestra Señora de Guadalupe and La Raza Cósmica in the Development of a Chicano Theology of Liberation* (Ann Arbor, MI: University Microfilms International, 1984), 122.

[14] *Algunos dicen que Guadalupe es una palabra derivida del lenguaje arabe que significa "Río Oculto."* Tomie de Paola, *The Lady of Guadalupe* (New York, NY: Holiday House, 1980), 44.

[15] *"Desde el cielo una hermosa mañana,"* from *Propios de la misa de Nuestra Señora de Guadalupe*, Guerrero, 124.

[16] From *"La Virgen Ranchera,"* Guerrero, 127.

[17] *La Virgin María* is often equated with the Aztec *Teleoinam*, the Maya *Ixchel*, the Inca *Mamacocha*, and the Yoruba *Yemayá*.

[18] Geoffrey Parrinder, ed., *World Religions: From Ancient History to the Present* (New York, NY: Facts on File Publications, 1971), 72.

[19] Lévi-Strauss's paradigm which opposes nature to culture and female to male has no such validity in the early history of our Indian forebears. June Nash, "The Aztecs and the Ideology of Male Dominance," *Signs* (Winter, 1978), 349.

[20] Parrinder, 72.

[21] Parrinder, 77.

[22] Nash, 352.

[23] Nash, 350, 355.

[24] Parrinder, 355.

[25] Jacques Soustelle, *The Daily Life of the Aztecs on the Eve of the Spanish Conquest* (New York, NY: Macmillan Publishing Company, 1962). Soustelle and most other historians got their information from the Franciscan father, Bernardino de Sahagún, chief chronicler of Indian religious life.

[26] Nash, 252–253.

[27] Nash, 358.

[28] Nash, 361–362.

[29] Karl W. Luckert, *Olmec Religion: A Key to Middle America and Beyond* (Norman, OK: University of Oklahoma Press, 1976), 68, 69, 87, 109.

[30] Bernardino de Sahagún, *General History of the Things of New Spain* (Florentine Codex), Vol. I Revised, trans. Arthur Anderson and Charles Dibble (Sante Fe, NM: School of American Research, 1950), 11.

[31] The Aztecs muted Snake Woman's patronage of childbirth and vegetation by placing a sacrificial knife in the empty cradle she carried on her back (signifying a child who died in childbirth), thereby making her a devourer of sacrificial victims. Snake Woman had the ability to change herself into a serpent or into a lovely young woman to entice young men, who withered away and died after intercourse with her. She was known as a witch and a shape-shifter. Brundage, 168–171.

[32] Anthropologist Lucien Levy-Bruhl coined the word *participation mystique*. According to Jung, "It denotes a peculiar kind of psychological connection . . . [in which] the subject cannot clearly distinguish himself from the object but is bound to it by a direct relationship which amounts to partial identity." Carl Jung, "Definitions," in *Psychological Types, The Collected Works of C. G. Jung*, Vol. 6 (Princeton, NJ: Princeton University Press, 1953), par. 781.

[33] Some *mexicanos* and Chicanos distinguish between *aire*, air, and *mal aigre*, the evil spirits which reside in the air.

How to Tame a Wild Tongue

"We're going to have to control your tongue," the dentist says, pulling out all the metal from my mouth. Silver bits plop and tinkle into the basin. My mouth is a motherlode.

The dentist is cleaning out my roots. I get a whiff of the stench when I gasp. "I can't cap that tooth yet, you're still draining," he says.

"We're going to have to do something about your tongue," I hear the anger rising in his voice. My tongue keeps pushing out the wads of cotton, pushing back the drills, the long thin needles. "I've never seen anything as strong or as stubborn," he says. And I think, how do you tame a wild tongue, train it to be quiet, how do you bridle and saddle it? How do you make it lie down?

> Who is to say that robbing a people of
> its language is less violent than war?
>
> —RAY GWYN SMITH[1]

I remember being caught speaking Spanish at recess — that was good for three licks on the knuckles with a sharp ruler. I remember being sent to the corner of the classroom for "talking back" to the Anglo teacher when all I was trying to do was tell her how to pronounce my name. "If you want to be American, speak 'American.' If you don't like it, go back to Mexico where you belong."

"I want you to speak English. *Pa' hallar buen trabajo tienes que saber hablar el inglés bien. Qué vale toda tu educación si todavía hablas inglés con un* 'accent,'" my mother would say, mortified that I spoke English like a Mexican. At Pan American University, I and all Chicano students were required to take two speech classes. Their purpose: to get rid of our accents.

Attacks on one's form of expression with the intent to censor are a violation of the First Amendment. *El Anglo con cara de inocente nos arrancó la lengua*. Wild tongues can't be tamed, they can only be cut out.

OVERCOMING THE TRADITION OF SILENCE

> *Ahogadas, escupimos el oscuro.*
> *Peleando con nuestra propia sombra*
> *el silencio nos sepulta.*

En boca cerrada no entran moscas. "Flies don't enter a closed mouth" is a saying I kept hearing when I was a child. *Ser habladora* was to be a gossip and a liar, to talk too much. *Muchachitas bien criadas*, well-bred girls don't answer back. *Es una falta de respeto* to talk back to one's mother or father. I remember one of the sins I'd recite to the priest in the confession box the few times I went to confession: talking back to my mother, *hablar pa''tras, repelar. Hociocona, repelona, chismosa,* having a big mouth, questioning, carrying tales are all signs of being *mal criada*. In my culture they are all words that are derogatory if applied to women—I've never heard them applied to men.

The first time I heard two women, a Puerto Rican and a Cuban, say the word "*nosotras*," I was shocked. I had not known the word existed. Chicanas use *nosotros* whether we're male or female. We are robbed of our female being by the masculine plural. Language is a male discourse.

> And our tongues have become
> dry the wilderness has
> dried out our tongues and
> we have forgotten speech.
>
> —IRENA KLEPFISZ[2]

Even our own people, other Spanish speakers *nos quieren poner candados en la boca*. They would hold us back with their bag of *reglas de academia*.

OYÉ COMO LADRA: EL LENGUAJE DE LA FRONTERA

> *Quien tiene boca se equivoca.*
>
> —Mexican saying

WE SPEAK A PATOIS, A FORKED TONGUE, A VARIATION OF TWO LANGUAGES.

"*Pocho*, cultural traitor, you're speaking the oppressor's language by speaking English, you're ruining the Spanish language," I have been accused by various Latinos and Latinas. Chicano Spanish is considered by the purist and by most Latinos deficient, a mutilation of Spanish.

But Chicano Spanish is a border tongue which developed naturally. Change, *evolución, enriquecimiento de palabras nuevas por invención o adopción* have created variants of Chicano Spanish, *un nuevo lenguaje. Un lenguaje que corresponde a un modo de vivir*. Chicano Spanish is not incorrect, it is a living language.

For a people who are neither Spanish nor live in a country in which Spanish is the first language; for a people who live in a country in which English is the reigning tongue but who are not Anglo; for a people who cannot entirely identify with either standard (formal, Castilian) Spanish nor standard English, what recourse is left to them but to create their own language? A language which they can connect their identity to, one capable of communicating the realities and values true to themselves—a language with terms that are neither *español ni inglés*, but both. We speak a patois, a forked tongue, a variation of two languages.

Chicano Spanish sprang out of the Chicanos' need to identify ourselves as a distinct people. We needed a language with which we could communicate with ourselves, a secret language. For some of us, language is a homeland closer than the Southwest — for many Chicanos today live in the Midwest and the East. And because we are a complex, heterogeneous people, we speak many languages. Some of the languages we speak are

1. Standard English
2. Working-class and slang English
3. Standard Spanish
4. Standard Mexican Spanish
5. North Mexican Spanish dialect
6. Chicano Spanish (Texas, New Mexico, Arizona, and California have regional variations)
7. Tex-Mex
8. *Pachuco* (called *caló*)

My "home" tongues are the languages I speak with my sister and brothers, with my friends. They are the last five listed, with 6 and 7 being closest to my heart. From school, the media, and job situations, I've picked up standard and working-class English. From Mamagrande Locha and from reading Spanish and Mexican literature, I've picked up Standard Spanish and Standard Mexican Spanish. From *los recién llegados*, Mexican immigrants, and *braceros*, I learned the North Mexican dialect. With Mexicans I'll try to speak either Standard Mexican Spanish or the North Mexican dialect. From my parents and Chicanos living in the Valley, I picked up Chicano Texas Spanish, and I speak it with my mom, younger brother (who married a Mexican and who rarely mixes Spanish with English), aunts, and older relatives.

With Chicanas from *Nuevo México* or *Arizona* I will speak Chicano Spanish a little, but often they don't understand what I'm saying. With most California Chicanas I speak entirely in English (unless I forget). When I first moved to San Francisco, I'd rattle off something in Spanish, unintentionally embarrassing them. Often it is only with another Chicana *tejano* that I can talk freely.

Words distorted by English are known as anglicisms or *pochismos*. The *pocho* is an anglicized Mexican or American of Mexican origin who speaks Spanish with an accent characteristic of North Americans and who distorts and reconstructs the language according to the influence of English.[3] Tex-Mex, or Spanglish, comes most naturally to me. I may switch back and forth from English to Spanish in the same sentence or in the same word. With my sister and my brother Nune and with Chicano *tejano* contemporaries I speak in Tex-Mex.

From kids and people my own age I picked up *Pachuco*. *Pachuco* (the language of the zoot suiters) is a language of rebellion, both against Standard Spanish and Standard English. It is a secret language. Adults of the culture and outsiders cannot understand it. It is made up of slang words from both English and Spanish. *Ruca* means girl or woman, *vato* means guy or dude, *chale* means no, *simón* means yes, *churro* is sure, talk is *periquiar*, *pigionear* means petting, *que gacho* means how nerdy, *ponte águila* means watch out, death is called *la pelona*. Through lack of practice and not having others who can speak it, I've lost most of the *Pachuco* tongue.

CHICANO SPANISH

Chicanos, after 250 years of Spanish/Anglo colonization, have developed significant differences in the Spanish we speak. We collapse two adjacent vowels into a single syllable and sometimes shift the stress in certain words such as *maíz/maiz, cohete/cuete*. We leave out certain consonants when they appear between vowels: *lado/lao, mojado/mojao*. Chicanos from South Texas pronounce *f* as *j* as in *jue (fue)*. Chicanos use "archaisms," words that are no longer in the Spanish language, words that have been evolved out. We say *semos, truje, haiga, ansina*, and *naiden*. We retain the "archaic" *j*, as in *jalar*, that derives from an earlier *h* (the French *halar* or the Germanic *halon* which was lost to standard Spanish in the sixteenth century), but which is still found in several regional dialects such as the one spoken in South Texas. (Due to geography, Chicanos from the Valley of South Texas were cut off linguistically from other Spanish speakers. We tend to use words that the Spaniards brought over from Medieval Spain. The majority of the Spanish colonizers in Mexico and the Southwest came from Extremadura — Hernán Cortés was one of them — and Andalucía. Andalucians pronounce *ll* like a *y*, and their *d*'s tend to be absorbed by adjacent vowels: *tirado* becomes *tirao*. They brought *el lenguaje popular, dialectos, y regionalismos*.)[4]

Chicanos and other Spanish speakers also shift *ll* to *y* and *z* to *s*.[5] We leave out initial syllables, saying *tar* for *estar*, *toy* for *estoy*, *hora* for *ahora* (*cubanos* and *puertorriqueños* also leave out initial letters of some words). We also leave out the final syllable such as *pa* for *para*. The intervocalic *y*, the *ll* as in *tortilla, ella, botella*, gets replaced by *tortia* or *toriya, ea, botea*. We add an additional syllable at the beginning of certain words: *atocar* for *tocar*, *agastar* for *gastar*. Sometimes we'll say *lavaste las vacijas*, other times *lavates* (substituting the *ates* verb endings for the *aste*).

We use anglicisms, words borrowed from English: *bola* from ball, *carpeta* from carpet, *máchina de lavar* (instead of *lavadora*) from washing machine. Tex-Mex argot, created by adding a Spanish sound at the beginning or end of an English word such as *cookiar* for cook, *watchar* for watch, *parkiar* for park, and *rapiar* for rape, is the result of the pressures on Spanish speakers to adapt to English.

We don't use the word *vosotros/as* or its accompanying verb form. We don't say *claro* (to mean yes), *imagínate*, or *me emociona*, unless we picked up Spanish from Latinas, out of a book, or in a classroom. Other Spanish-speaking groups are going through the same, or similar, development in their Spanish.

LINGUISTIC TERRORISM

Deslenguadas. Somos los del español deficiente. We are your linguistic nightmare, your linguistic aberration, your linguistic *mestisaje*, the subject of your *burla*. Because we speak with tongues of fire we are culturally crucified. Racially, culturally, and linguistically *somos huérfanos* — we speak an orphan tongue.

Chicanas who grew up speaking Chicano Spanish have internalized the belief that we speak poor Spanish. It is illegitimate, a bastard language. And because we internalize how our language has been used against us by the dominant culture, we use our language differences against each other.

Chicana feminists often skirt around each other with suspicion and hesitation. For the longest time I couldn't figure it out. Then it dawned on me. To be close to another Chicana is like looking into the mirror. We are afraid of what we'll see there. *Pena*. Shame. Low estimation of self. In childhood we are told that our language is wrong. Repeated attacks on our native tongue diminish our sense of self. The attacks continue throughout our lives.

Chicanas feel uncomfortable talking in Spanish to Latinas, afraid of their censure. Their language was not outlawed in their countries. They had a whole lifetime of being immersed in their native tongue; generations, centuries in which Spanish was a first language, taught in school, heard on radio and TV, and read in the newspaper.

If a person, Chicana or Latina, has a low estimation of my native tongue, she also has a low estimation of me. Often with *mexicanas y latinas* we'll speak English as a neutral language. Even among Chicanas we tend to speak English at parties or conferences. Yet, at the same time, we're afraid the other will think we're *agringadas* because we don't speak Chicano Spanish. We oppress each other trying to out-Chicano each other, vying to be the "real" Chicanas, to speak like Chicanos. There is no one Chicano language just as there is no one Chicano experience. A monolingual Chicana whose first language is English or Spanish is just as much a Chicana as one who speaks several variants of Spanish. A Chicana from Michigan or Chicago or Detroit is just as much a Chicana as one from the Southwest. Chicano Spanish is as diverse linguistically as it is regionally.

By the end of this [the twentieth] century, Spanish speakers will comprise the biggest minority group in the United States, a country where students in high schools and colleges are encouraged to take French classes because French is considered more "cultured." But for a language to remain alive it must be used.[6] By the end of this century English, and not Spanish, will be the mother tongue of most Chicanos and Latinos.

So, if you want to really hurt me, talk badly about my language. Ethnic identity is twin skin to linguistic identity — I am my language. Until I can take pride in my language, I cannot take pride in myself. Until I can accept as legitimate Chicano Texas Spanish, Tex-Mex, and all the other languages I speak, I cannot accept the legitimacy of myself. Until I am free to write bilingually and to switch codes without having always to translate, while I still have to speak English or Spanish when I would rather speak Spanglish, and as long as I have to accommodate the English speaker rather than having them accommodate me, my tongue will be illegitimate.

I will no longer be made to feel ashamed of existing. I will have my voice: Indian, Spanish, white. I will have my serpent's tongue — my woman's voice, my sexual voice, my poet's voice. I will overcome the tradition of silence.

> My fingers
> move sly against your palm
> Like women everywhere, we speak in code. . . .
>
> — MELANIE KAYE / KANTROWITZ[7]

"VISTAS," CORRIDOS, Y COMIDA: MY NATIVE TONGUE

In the 1960s, I read my first Chicano novel. It was *City of Night* by John Rechy, a gay Texan, son of a Scottish father and a Mexican mother. For days I walked around in stunned amazement that a Chicano could write and could get published. When I read *I Am Joaquín*[8] I was surprised to see a bilingual book by a Chicano in print. When I saw poetry written in Tex-Mex for the first time, a feeling of pure joy flashed through me. I felt like we really existed as a people. In 1971, when I started teaching High School English to Chicano students, I tried to supplement the required texts with works by Chicanos, only to be reprimanded and forbidden to do so by the principal. He claimed that I was supposed to teach "American" and English literature. At the risk of being fired, I swore my students to secrecy and slipped in Chicano short stories, poems, a play. In graduate school, while working toward a Ph.D., I had to "argue" with one adviser after the other, semester after semester, before I was allowed to make Chicano literature an area of focus.

Even before I read books by Chicanos or Mexicans, it was the Mexican movies I saw at the drive-in — the Thursday night special of $1.00 a carload — that gave me a sense of belonging. "*Vámonos a las vistas*," my mother would call out and we'd all — grandmother, brothers, sister, and cousins — squeeze into the car. We'd wolf down cheese and bologna white bread sandwiches while watching Pedro Infante in melodramatic tear-jerkers like *Nosotros los pobres*, the first "real" Mexican movie (that was not an imitation of European movies). I remember seeing *Cuando los hijos se van* and surmising that all Mexican movies played up the love a mother has for her children and what ungrateful sons and daughters suffer when they are not devoted to their mothers. I remember the singing-type "westerns" of Jorge Negrete and Miguel Aceves Mejía. When watching Mexican movies, I felt a sense of homecoming as well as alienation. People who were to amount to something didn't go to Mexican movies, or *bailes*, or tune their radios to *bolero*, *rancherita*, and *corrido* music.

The whole time I was growing up, there was *norteño* music sometimes called North Mexican border music, or Tex-Mex music, or Chicano music, or *cantina* (bar) music. I grew up listening to *conjuntos*, three- or four-piece bands made up of folk musicians playing guitar, *bajo sexto*, drums, and button accordion, which Chicanos had borrowed from the German immigrants who had come to Central Texas and Mexico to farm and build breweries. In the Rio Grande Valley, Steven Jordan and Little Joe Hernández were popular, and Flaco Jiménez was the accordion king. The rhythms of

Tex-Mex music are those of the polka, also adapted from the Germans, who in turn had borrowed the polka from the Czechs and Bohemians.

I remember the hot, sultry evenings when *corridos* — songs of love and death on the Texas-Mexican borderlands — reverberated out of cheap amplifiers from the local *cantinas* and wafted in through my bedroom window.

Corridos first became widely used along the South Texas/Mexican border during the early conflict between Chicanos and Anglos. The *corridos* are usually about Mexican heroes who do valiant deeds against the Anglo oppressors. Pancho Villa's song, *"La cucaracha,"* is the most famous one. *Corridos* of John F. Kennedy and his death are still very popular in the Valley. Older Chicanos remember Lydia Mendoza, one of the great border *corrido* singers who was called *la Gloria de Tejas*. Her *"El tango negro,"* sung during the Great Depression, made her a singer of the people. The ever-present *corridos* narrated one hundred years of border history, bringing news of events as well as entertaining. These folk musicians and folk songs are our chief cultural mythmakers, and they made our hard lives seem bearable.

I grew up feeling ambivalent about our music. Country-western and rock-and-roll had more status. In the fifties and sixties, for the slightly educated and *agringado* Chicanos, there existed a sense of shame at being caught listening to our music. Yet I couldn't stop my feet from thumping to the music, could not stop humming the words, nor hide from myself the exhilaration I felt when I heard it.

There are more subtle ways that we internalize identification, especially in the forms of images and emotions. For me food and certain smells are tied to my identity, to my homeland. Woodsmoke curling up to an immense blue sky; woodsmoke perfuming my grandmother's clothes, her skin. The stench of cow manure and the yellow patches on the ground; the crack of a .22 rifle and the reek of cordite. Homemade white cheese sizzling in a pan, melting inside a folded *tortilla*. My sister Hilda's hot, spicy *menudo*, *chile colorado* making it deep red, pieces of *panza* and hominy floating on top. My brother Carito barbequing *fajitas* in the backyard. Even now and 3,000 miles away, I can see my mother spicing the ground beef, pork, and venison with *chile*. My mouth salivates at the thought of the hot steaming *tamales* I would be eating if I were home.

SI LE PREGUNTAS A MI MAMÁ, "¿QUÉ ERES?"

> Identity is the essential core of who
> we are as individuals, the conscious
> experience of the self inside.
>
> — GERSHEN KAUFMAN[9]

Nosotros los Chicanos straddle the borderlands. On one side of us, we are constantly exposed to the Spanish of the Mexicans, on the other side we hear the Anglos' incessant clamoring so that we forget our language.

Among ourselves we don't say *nosotros los americanos, o nosotros los españoles, o nosotros los hispanos*. We say *nosotros los mexicanos* (by *mexicanos* we do not mean citizens of Mexico; we do not mean a national identity, but a racial one). We distinguish between *mexicanos del otro lado* and *mexicanos de este lado*. Deep in our hearts we believe that being Mexican has nothing to do with which country one lives in. Being Mexican is a state of soul — not one of mind, not one of citizenship. Neither eagle nor serpent, but both. And like the ocean, neither animal respects borders.

> *Dime con quien andas y te diré quien eres.*
> (Tell me who your friends are and I'll tell you who you are.)
> — Mexican saying

Si le preguntas a mi mamá, "¿Qué eres?" te dirá, "Soy mexicana." My brothers and sister say the same. I sometimes will answer "*soy mexicana*" and at others will say "*soy Chicana*" *o* "*soy tejana*." But I identified as "*Raza*" before I ever identified as "*mexicana*" or "Chicana."

As a culture, we call ourselves Spanish when referring to ourselves as a linguistic group and when copping out. It is then that we forget our predominant Indian genes. We are 70–80 percent Indian.[10] We call ourselves Hispanic[11] or Spanish-American or Latin American or Latin when linking ourselves to other Spanish-speaking peoples of the Western hemisphere and when copping out. We call ourselves Mexican-American[12] to signify we are neither Mexican nor American, but more the noun "American" than the adjective "Mexican" (and when copping out).

SI LE PREGUNTAS A MI MAMÁ, "¿QUÉ ERES?" TE DIRÁ, "SOY MEXICANA."

Chicanos and other people of color suffer economically for not acculturating. This voluntary (yet forced) alienation makes for psychological conflict, a kind of dual identity — we don't identify with the Anglo-American cultural values and we don't totally identify with the Mexican cultural values. We are a synergy of two cultures with various degrees of Mexicanness or Angloness. I have so internalized the borderland conflict that sometimes I feel like one cancels out the other and we are zero, nothing, no one. *A veces no soy nada ni nadie. Pero hasta cuando no lo soy, lo soy.*

When not copping out, when we know we are more than nothing, we call ourselves Mexican, referring to race and ancestry; *mestizo* when affirming both our Indian and Spanish (but we hardly ever own our Black) ancestry; Chicano when referring to a politically aware people born and/or raised in the United States; *Raza* when referring to Chicanos; *tejanos* when we are Chicanos from Texas.

Chicanos did not know we were a people until 1965 when Cesar Chavez and the farmworkers united and *I Am Joaquín* was published and *la Raza Unida* party was formed in Texas. With that recognition, we became a distinct people. Something momentous happened to the Chicano soul — we became aware of our reality and acquired a name and a language

(Chicano Spanish) that reflected that reality. Now that we had a name, some of the fragmented pieces began to fall together — who we were, what we were, how we had evolved. We began to get glimpses of what we might eventually become.

Yet the struggle of identities continues, the struggle of borders is our reality still. One day the inner struggle will cease and a true integration take place. In the meantime, *tenémos que hacer la lucha. ¿Quién está protegiendo los ranchos de mi gente? ¿Quién está tratando de cerrar la fisura entre la india y el blanco en nuestra sangre? El Chicano, si, el Chicano que anda como un ladrón en su propia casa.*

Los Chicanos, how patient we seem, how very patient. There is the quiet of the Indian about us.[13] We know how to survive. When other races have given up their tongue we've kept ours. We know what it is to live under the hammer blow of the dominant *norteamericano* culture. But more than we count the blows, we count the days the weeks the years the centuries the aeons until the white laws and commerce and customs will rot in the deserts they've created, lie bleached. *Humildes* yet proud, *quietos* yet wild, *nosotros los mexicanos-Chicanos* will walk by the crumbling ashes as we go about our business. Stubborn, persevering, impenetrable as stone, yet possessing a malleability that renders us unbreakable, we, the *mestizas* and *mestizos*, will remain.

NOTES

1 Ray Gwyn Smith, *Moorland Is Cold Country*, unpublished book.

2 Irena Klepfisz, "*Di rayze aheym*/The Journey Home," in *The Tribe of Dina: A Jewish Women's Anthology*, Melanie Kaye/Kantrowitz and Irena Klepfisz, eds. (Montpelier, VT: Sinister Wisdom Books, 1986), 49.

3 R. C. Ortega, *Dialectología Del Barrio*, trans. Hortencia S. Alwan (Los Angeles, CA: R. C. Ortega Publisher & Bookseller, 1977), 132.

4 Eduardo Hernandéz-Chávez, Andrew D. Cohen, and Anthony F. Beltramo, *El Lenguaje de los Chicanos: Regional and Social Characteristics of Language Used by Mexican Americans* (Arlington, VA: Center for Applied Linguistics, 1975), 39.

5 Hernandéz-Chávez, xvii.

6 Irena Klepfisz, "Secular Jewish Identity: Yidishkayt in America," in *The Tribe of Dina*, Kaye/Kantrowitz and Klepfisz, eds., 43.

7 Melanie Kaye/Kantrowitz, "Sign," in *We Speak in Code: Poems and Other Writings* (Pittsburgh, PA: Motheroot Publications, Inc., 1980), 85.

8 Rodolfo Gonzales, *I Am Joaquín/Yo Soy Joaquín* (New York, NY: Bantam Books, 1972). It was first published in 1967.

9 Gershen Kaufman, *Shame: The Power of Caring* (Cambridge, MA: Schenkman Books, Inc., 1980), 68.

10 John R. Chávez, *The Lost Land: The Chicano Images of the Southwest* (Albuquerque, NM: University of New Mexico Press, 1984), 88–90.

11 "Hispanic" is derived from *Hispanis* (*España*, a name given to the Iberian Peninsula in ancient times when it was a part of the Roman Empire) and is a term designated by the U.S. government to make it easier to handle us on paper.

12 The Treaty of Guadalupe Hidalgo created the Mexican-American in 1848.

13 Anglos, in order to alleviate their guilt for dispossessing the Chicano, stressed the Spanish part of us and perpetrated the myth of the Spanish Southwest. We have accepted the fiction that we are Hispanic, that is Spanish, in order to accommodate ourselves to the dominant culture and its abhorrence of Indians. Chávez, 88–91.

QUESTIONS FOR A SECOND READING

1. The most immediate challenge to many readers of these chapters will be the sections that are written in Spanish. Part of the point of a text that mixes languages is to give non-Spanish-speaking readers the feeling of being lost, excluded, left out. What is a reader to do with this prose? One could learn Spanish and come back to reread, but this is not a quick solution and, according to Anzaldúa, not even a completely satisfactory one, since some of her Spanish is drawn from communities of speakers not represented in textbooks and classes.

   So how do you read this text if you don't read Spanish? Do you ignore the words? sound them out? improvise? Anzaldúa gives translations of some words or phrases, but not all. Which ones does she translate? Why? Reread these chapters with the goal of explaining how you handled Anzaldúa's polyglot style.

2. These chapters are made up of shorter sections written in a variety of styles (some as prose poems, some with endnotes, some as stories). And while the sections are obviously ordered, the order is not a conventional argumentative one. The text is, as Anzaldúa says elsewhere in her book, "an assemblage, a montage, a beaded work, . . . a crazy dance":

   > In looking at this book that I'm almost finished writing, I see a mosaic pattern (Aztec-like) emerging, a weaving pattern, thin here, thick there. . . . This almost finished product seems an assemblage, a montage, a beaded work with several leitmotifs and with a central core, now appearing, now disappearing in a crazy dance. The whole thing has had a mind of its own, escaping me and insisting on putting together the pieces of its own puzzle with minimal direction from my will. It is a rebellious, willful entity, a precocious girl-child forced to grow up too quickly, rough, unyielding, with pieces of feather sticking out here and there, fur, twigs, clay. My child, but not for much longer. This female being is angry, sad, joyful, is Coatlicue, dove, horse, serpent, cactus. Though it is a flawed thing—clumsy, complex, groping, blind thing, for me it is alive, infused with spirit. I talk to it; it talks to me.

   This is not, in other words, a conventional text; it makes unexpected demands on a reader. As you reread, mark sections you could use to talk about how, through the text, Anzaldúa invents a reader and/or a way of reading. Who is Anzaldúa's ideal reader? What does he or she need to be able to do?

3. Although Anzaldúa's text is not a conventional one, it makes an argument and proposes terms and examples for its readers to negotiate. How might you summarize Anzaldúa's argument in these two chapters? How do the individual chapters mark stages or parts of her argument? How might you

explain the connections between the chapters? As you reread this selection, mark those passages where Anzaldúa seems to you to be creating a case or an argument. What are its key terms? its key examples? its conclusions?

ASSIGNMENTS FOR WRITING

1. Anzaldúa has described her text as a kind of crazy dance (see the second "Question for a Second Reading"); it is, she says, a text with a mind of its own, "putting together the pieces of its own puzzle with minimal direction from my will." Hers is a prose full of variety and seeming contradictions; it is a writing that could be said to represent the cultural "crossroads" which is her experience / sensibility.

   As an experiment whose goal is the development of an alternate (in Anzaldúa's terms, a mixed or *mestiza*) understanding, write an autobiographical text whose shape and motives could be described in her terms: a mosaic, woven, with numerous overlays; a montage, a beaded work, a crazy dance, drawing on the various ways of thinking, speaking, understanding that might be said to be part of your own mixed cultural position, your own mixed sensibility.

   To prepare for this essay, think about the different positions you could be said to occupy, the different voices that are part of your background or present, the competing ways of thinking that make up your points of view. Imagine that your goal is to present your world and your experience to those who are not necessarily prepared to be sympathetic or to understand. And, following Anzaldúa, you should work to construct a mixed text, not a single unified one. This will be hard, since you will be writing what might be called a "forbidden" text, one you have not been prepared to write.

2. In "*La Conciencia de la Mestiza* / Towards a New Consciousness," the last essaylike chapter in her book (the remaining chapters are made up of poems), Anzaldúa steps forward to define her role as writer and yours as reader. She says, among other things,

   > Many women and men of color do not want to have any dealings with white people. . . . Many feel that whites should help their own people rid themselves of race hatred and fear first. I, for one, choose to use some of my energy to serve as mediator. I think we need to allow whites to be our allies. Through our literature, art, *corridos*, and folktales we must share our history with them so when they set up committees to help Big Mountain Navajos or the Chicano farmworkers or los *Nicaragüenses* they won't turn people away because of their racial fears and ignorances. They will come to see that they are not helping us but following our lead.

> Individually, but also as a racial entity, we need to voice our needs. We need to say to white society: We need you to accept the fact that Chicanos are different, to acknowledge your rejection and negation of us. We need you to own the fact that you looked upon us as less than human, that you stole our lands, our personhood, our self-respect. We need you to make public restitution: to say that, to compensate for your own sense of defectiveness, you strive for power over us, you erase our history and our experience because it makes you feel guilty — you'd rather forget your brutish acts. To say you've split yourself from minority groups, that you disown us, that your dual consciousness splits off parts of yourself, transferring the "negative" parts onto us. . . . To say that you are afraid of us, that to put distance between us, you wear the mask of contempt. Admit that Mexico is your double, that she exists in the shadow of this country, that we are irrevocably tied to her. Gringo, accept the doppelganger in your psyche. By taking back your collective shadow the intracultural split will heal. And finally, tell us what you need from us.

This is only a part of the text — one of the ways it defines the roles of reader and writer — but it is one that asks to be taken account of, with its insistent list of what a white reader must do and say. (Of course not every reader is white, and not all white readers are the same. What Anzaldúa is defining here is a "white" way of reading.)

Write an essay in which you tell a story of reading, the story of your work with the two chapters of *Borderlands / La frontera* reprinted here. Think about where you felt at home with the text and where you felt lost, where you knew what you were doing and where you needed help; think about the position (or positions) you have taken as a reader and how it measures up against the ways Anzaldúa has figured you in the text, the ways she has anticipated a response, imagined who you are and how you habitually think and read.

3. In "How to Tame a Wild Tongue" (p. 85), Anzaldúa says, "I will no longer be made to feel ashamed of existing. I will have my voice: Indian, Spanish, white. I will have my serpent's tongue — my woman's voice, my sexual voice, my poet's voice." Anzaldúa speaks almost casually about "having her voice," not a single, "authentic" voice, but one she names in these terms: Indian, Spanish, white; woman, lesbian, poet. What is "voice" as defined by these chapters? Where does it come from? What does it have to do with the act of writing or the writer?

   As you reread these chapters, mark those passages that you think best represent Anzaldúa's voices. Using these passages as examples, write an essay in which you discuss how these voices are different — both different from one another and different from a "standard" voice (as a "standard" voice is imagined by Anzaldúa). What do these voices represent? How do they figure in your reading? in her writing?

4. Anzaldúa's writing is difficult to categorize as an essay or a story or a poem; it has all of these within it. The writing may appear to have been just put together, but it is more likely that it was carefully crafted to represent the various voices Anzaldúa understands to be a part of her. She speaks directly about her voices — her woman's voice, her sexual voice, her poet's voice; her Indian, Spanish, and white voices on pages 89–90 of "How to Tame a Wild Tongue."

   Following Anzaldúa, write an argument of your own, one that requires you to use a variety of voices, in which you carefully present the various voices that you feel are a part of you or a part of the argument.

   When you have completed this assignment, write a two-page essay in which you explain why the argument you made might be worth a reader's attention.

MAKING CONNECTIONS

1. In "Arts of the Contact Zone" (p. 485), Mary Louise Pratt talks about the "autoethnographic" text, "a text in which people undertake to describe themselves in ways that engage with representations others have made of them," and about "transculturation," the "processes whereby members of subordinated or marginal groups select and invent from materials transmitted by a dominant or metropolitan culture."

   Write an essay in which you present a reading of these two chapters as an example of an autoethnographic and / or transcultural text. You should imagine that you are writing to someone who is not familiar with either Pratt's argument or Anzaldúa's book. Part of your work, then, is to present Anzaldúa's text to readers who don't have it in front of them. You have the example of Pratt's reading of Guaman Poma's *New Chronicle and Good Government*. And you have her discussion of the "literate arts of the contact zone." Think about how Anzaldúa's text might be similarly read, and about how her text does and doesn't fit Pratt's description. Your goal should be to add an example to Pratt's discussion and to qualify it, to give her discussion a new twist or spin now that you have had a chance to look at an additional example.

2. While they do not explicitly use the term or define the genre as Laura Kipnis does in "Love's Labors" (p. 391), Paulo Freire's "The 'Banking' Concept of Education" (p. 318) and the two selections from Gloria Anzaldúa's *Borderlands/La frontera* can be classified as polemics, works that attempt to "shake things up," to provoke readers and poke holes in "cultural pieties." Polemics, Kipnis explains, often bend or break conventional rules or expectations for argumentation. "Be advised," she warns us: "polemics aren't measured; they don't tell 'both sides of the story.' They overstate the case. They toss out provocations and occasionally mockery, usually because they're arguing against something so unquestionable and deeply entrenched it's the only way to make even a dent in the usual story" (p. 390).

Write an essay in which you present the sections from *Borderlands/La frontera* as an example of polemical writing. You may want to begin by thinking about what has drawn the writer to the polemical form. What is "the usual story" that the polemicist wants to dislodge? What kinds of opposition from readers might the writer anticipate, and how does he or she address or attempt to counter resistance? As a reader, how did you respond to this attack on "received wisdom"?

Kipnis also tells us that "polemics aren't necessarily unconflicted (nor are the polemicists); rhetoric and sentiment aren't always identical twins." If you find evidence that the polemicist might be "conflicted," how does he or she deal with such conflicts and/or contradictions? Does your analysis of Anzaldúa's text offer some new insights into polemical writing—its social function, its merits, its risks—that Kipnis has not elucidated?

3. Gloria Anzaldúa, in "Entering into the Serpent," describes *la facultad*, which she explains in the following passage:

> *La facultad* is the capacity to see in surface phenomena the meaning of deeper realities, to see the deep structure below the surface. It is an instant "sensing," a quick perception arrived at without conscious reasoning. It is an acute awareness mediated by the part of the psyche that does not speak, that communicates in images and symbols. . . . (p. 82)

Both Gloria Anzaldúa and Alberto Álvaro Ríos, in "Translating Translation: Finding the Beginning" (p. 506), could be said to be trying to convey this capacity of *la facultad* in their writing—through what both they and their subjects see and say. Write an essay in which you articulate your understanding of *la facultad*.

You may begin with a discussion of the passage above—of particular key words or phrases—to focus your attention on what the term *la facultad* means and how you have arrived at making that particular meaning. It may help to return to Anzaldúa's essay and to reread Ríos in the context of her essay. Once you have offered a meaningful discussion of *la facultad*, use this concept as a lens through which to think about the writing in Ríos's "Translating Translation" and Anzaldúa's "Entering into the Serpent." What sense can you make of the notion that there might be a "part of the psyche that does not speak"? How about the "deep structure below the surface"?

KWAME ANTHONY Appiah

Kwame Anthony Appiah (pronounced AP-eea, with the accent on the first syllable) was born in London; he grew up in Ghana, in the town of Asante; he took his MA and PhD degrees from Cambridge University in England; he is now a citizen of the United States. He has taught at Yale, Cornell, Duke, Harvard, and, most recently, Princeton, where he is the Laurence S. Rockefeller University Professor of Philosophy and a member of the University Center for Human Values. Appiah's father was Ghanaian and a leader in the struggle for Pan-Africanism and Ghanaian independence from Britain; his mother, originally Peggy Cripps, was British and the daughter of a leading figure in the Labour government. Appiah's work circulates widely and has won numerous awards. He was elected to the American Academy of Arts and Sciences and the American Philosophical Society and was inducted in 2008 into the American Academy of Arts and Letters.

Appiah's life illustrates the virtues of a "rooted cosmopolitanism," a term he offers to describe a desired way of living in the world, and it illustrates the difficulties we face in naming someone as black or white or African or American. In the preface to a recent book, *The Ethics of Identity* (2004), he says,

> What has proved especially vexatious, though, is the effort to take account of those social forms we now call identities: genders and sexual orientations, ethnicities and nationalities, professions and vocations. Identities make ethical claims because—and this is just a fact about the world we human beings have created—we make our lives as men and as women, as gay and as straight people, as Ghanaians and as Americans, as blacks and as whites. Immediately, conundrums start to assemble. Do identities represent a curb on autonomy, or do they provide its contours: What claims, if any, can identity groups as such justly make upon the state? These are concerns that have gained a certain measure of salience in recent political philosophy, but, as I hope to show, they are anything but newfangled. What's modern is that we conceptualize identity in particular ways. What's age-old is that when we are asked—and ask ourselves—who we are, we are being asked what we are as well. (p. xiv)

Appiah is a prolific writer; he is both a political philosopher and a cultural theorist. His books include *Assertion and Conditionals* (1985); *For Truth in Semantics* (1986); *In My Father's House: Africa in the Philosophy of Culture* (1992); *Cosmopolitanism: Ethics in a World of Strangers* (2007); and *Experiments in Ethics* (2008). He is also the author of three mystery novels, *Avenging Angel* (1991), *Nobody Likes Letitia* (1994), and *Another Death in Venice* (1995); a textbook, *Thinking It Through: An Introduction to Contemporary Philosophy* (2003); and, with Henry Louis Gates Jr., the *Encarta Africana CD-ROM encyclopedia.* The selection that follows was taken from a book coauthored with Amy Gutmann, *Color Consciousness: The Political Morality of Race* (1996), winner of the 1997 Ralph J. Bunche award from the American Political Science Association. *Color Consciousness* is drawn from the lectures Appiah and Gutmann gave as the Tanner Lectures on Human Values at the University of California, San Diego. We've included Appiah, half of the exchange. In an era when discussions of race are often angry, rigid, and strident, this book provides the best possible example of careful, thoughtful, and constructive debate.

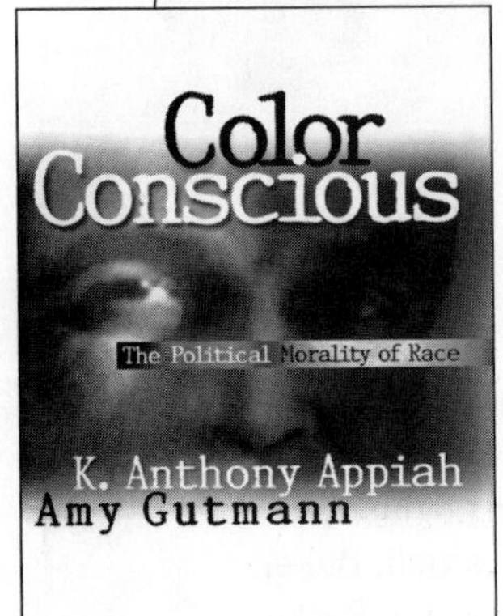

Race, Culture, Identity: Misunderstood Connections

EXPLAINING RACE THINKING

Imagine yourself on Angel Island in the 1920s. You are helping an inquisitive immigrant from Canton to fill in an immigration form. *Name*, it says. You ask her name. She tells you. You write it down. *Date of birth*. She gives it to you (according to the Chinese calendar, of course, so you have to look up your table for translating from one system to another). Then there is an entry that says *Race*. This you do not have to ask. You write "Oriental." And your interlocutor, because she is inquisitive, asks politely: "What are you writing now?" (After all, until now, everything you have written has been in response to her answers.)

Disingenuously, you say: "I am writing down where you are from."

"Ah yes," she replies helpfully, "Canton, I was born in Canton. How did you know?"

"No. Actually, that's the next question I was going to ask. Place of birth."

"So what have you written already?"

How do you answer this question? Seventy years ago, how would you have explained to someone from outside the modern West what our English word "race" meant? Or how would you have explained to a Sicilian across the continent on Ellis Island, thirty years earlier, why the right answer for him was "Caucasian"? (Where he came from, the people of the North of Italy, the ancestors of the modern Lombard league, think of him, as he very well knows, as of a different, darker, *razza* than theirs: how do you explain that here he is going to become white?) And would you give the same explanation today?

Or, again, imagine yourself in North Carolina, in the later nineteenth century, as Reconstruction is coming to an end. You are in a small town,

---

I should like to express my sense of enormous indebtedness to Lawrence Blum, Jorge Garcia, Martha Minow, Richard T. Ford, Maneesha Sinha, David Wilkins, and David Wong, for discussions both together and separately; to Houston Baker and Lucius Outlaw for prompting me (in Lucius's case, regularly!) to rethink these issues; to many people, whose names I have not recorded, to whom I have talked about identity and culture at many universities over the last few years; to several generations of students in my Introduction to Afro-American Studies class at Harvard; and, above all, to Henry Finder, on whom I try out most of my ideas first. I delivered a Tanner lecture on these issues at the University of California at San Diego in 1994, and the occasion provided the first stimulus for me to bring these thoughts together; the very helpful responses of many who responded there helped in the preparation of this more extended version of my thoughts. Naturally, responsibility for the opinions expressed here remains mine alone. [All notes are Appiah's, unless indicated by Eds.]

out of the way, where there are families that come in all shades of skin color, milk through chocolate. A message comes through from the state capitol in Raleigh. Everyone now has to be white or colored. If you're white, step this way; colored, go the other. You are talking to Joe, a teenager, whose skin is milky white, whose eyes are blue, but whose grandmother, Mary, is a brown-skinned woman who remembers *her* mother's stories of Africa. "I was gonna go with my grandma," he tells you. "But then I saw my Uncle Jim was gonna be with her, so I'm gonna cross to the other side of the room. 'Cause one thing I know for sure; I don't want to be anywhere my Uncle Jim's gonna be."[1]

Is Joe making a conceptual mistake? Or is he unintentionally making what will turn out to be a lucky choice for him and his descendants; a choice that will leave him and them with a vote, better schools, better jobs? Can you imagine someone like Joe, in the nineteenth-century South, born after emancipation but raised before the high-water mark of the strange career of Jim Crow, who doesn't know that in America, or at least in the Carolinas, even white-skinned people with black grandmothers are Negroes?

My preliminary aim in this essay is to explore the concept of race that is at work in these cases — an American concept, though also, of course, one that draws on and interacts with ideas from elsewhere. I will go on to argue for three[2] analytical conclusions. First, I want to explain why American social distinctions cannot be understood in terms of the concept of race: the only human race[3] in the United States, I shall argue, is *the* human race. Second, I want to show that replacing the notion of race with the notion of culture is not helpful: the American social distinctions that are marked using racial vocabulary do not correspond to cultural groups, either. And third, I want to propose that, for analytical purposes, we should use instead the notion of a racial identity, which I will try to explore and explain.

THE ONLY HUMAN RACE IN THE UNITED STATES, I SHALL ARGUE, IS *THE* HUMAN RACE.

Finally, I will argue for an ethical conclusion: that there is a danger in making racial identities too central to our conceptions of ourselves; while there is a place for racial identities in a world shaped by racism, I shall argue, if we are to move beyond racism we shall have, in the end, to move beyond current racial identities.

MEANING

If in the 1920s you'd left Angel Island and traveled much farther east than Ellis Island, sailing across to England, landing at Southampton and taking the train up to London and on to Cambridge, you could have consulted the leading experts in the English-speaking world on questions of meaning. In 1923 Charles K. Ogden and I. A. Richards had published *The Meaning of Meaning: A Study of the Influence of Language upon Thought and of the Science of Symbolism*, with supplementary essays by various people including the anthropologist Bronislaw Malinowski. A year earlier Ludwig Wittgenstein had published the *Tractatus Logico-Philosophicus*, which was to become a classic in a field that was not yet called the philosophy of language.

We do not need to delve deeply into that field. But it will help us later, when we turn to some of the difficult philosophical questions about understanding the idea of race, if we make a distinction that was already available when Wittgenstein was writing the *Tractatus*.

Before I introduce that distinction, however, I want to draw attention to the fact that the issues I am going to be discussing next grow out of a tradition of philosophical reflection that is not directly concerned with ethical matters. It is particularly important, I think, to illustrate how technical philosophy can be of the greatest help in clarifying our moral predicament; and to show that what can be helpful lies as much in the spheres of metaphysics and epistemology and philosophy of language as it does in the field of ethics. Now to the theoretical distinction.

In the 1920s there were — and there are still today — two very different and competing philosophical notions of what it is to give an adequate account of the meaning of a word or expression.

One — we can call this the "ideational" view of meaning — which goes back to at least the seventeenth century and the Logic of Port Royal, associates the meaning of a term, like "race," with what the Port Royal Logicians called an "idea." Understanding the idea of race involves grasping how people think about races: what they take to be the central truths about races; under what sorts of circumstances they will apply the idea of race; what consequences for action will flow from that application.

The other picture of meaning — the "referential" view — suggests that to explain what the word "race" means is, in effect, to identify the things to which it applies, the things we refer to when we speak of "races."

These views are not as far apart as they might at first appear. To find out what people are referring to in using the word "race," after all, you might need to know what idea their word "race" expresses: if they had no ideas, no thoughts, about race, and if there were no circumstances when they used the word, no consequences to their applying it, then we could hardly suppose that their making the sound "race" meant anything at all. In practice, at least, access to an idea of race is probably needed to find the referent.

And, conversely, once we have identified the referent — found, that is, the races — we can assume that people who understand the word "race" have some beliefs that are at least roughly true of races. For if people are talking about races, it is because they have, or think they have, experience of races: and, generally speaking, some of that experience will be reliable. A little bit of knowledge of what races are like combined with a little information about what people are like — how sensory experience works, for example — will allow us to predict at least some of people's ideas about races.

My aim is not to decide between these two broad traditions of conceiving of meaning. Anyone concerned to understand our concept of race ought, I think, to be interested both in the reality of race and in the way people think about it, in both the referential and the ideational aspects: we can leave it to the philosophers of language to wrangle about which of these ought to have the central place in semantics (or whether, as I suspect, we need both of them).

THE IDEATIONAL ACCOUNT OF RACE

Perhaps the simplest ideational theory of meaning runs like this: what we learn when we learn a word like "race" is a set of rules for applying the term. Everybody who knows what the word "race" means — which means most competent speakers of English — learns the same rules: so that while people have different beliefs about races, they share some special beliefs — I'll call them the criterial beliefs — that define the concept. These beliefs may not be very high-powered. They might include, for example, the thought that people with very different skin colors are of different races or that your race is determined by the race of your parents. But on this simplest ideational theory, all these criterial beliefs have this property: someone who doesn't believe these things doesn't understand what the English word "race" means.

The simplest theory would also require that if we collected together all these criterial beliefs about race and took them all together, they could be thought of as defining the meaning of the word "race." (This is equivalent to saying that there are things that have to be true of something if it is to be a race — conditions necessary for being a race; and that these necessary conditions are, when taken together, sufficient for being a race.) We can use a device invented by the English philosopher Frank Ramsey in the 1920s to make this an explicit definition: something is a race just in case all the criterial beliefs are true of it.[4] Let's call this the "strict criterial theory."

The Ramsey definition makes clear the connection between defining a term and questions of existence: there are races if, but only if, there are things that satisfy all the criteria.

For a number of reasons, which again I want to skirt, you won't get many philosophers of language to buy into this strict criterial theory today; there is a general skepticism about it, which goes back, I suppose, to W. V. O. Quine's attack on the idea of the analytic truth, which he called one of the "dogmas of empiricism." For if the strict criterial theory were right, those criterial sentences would be analytically true: they would be sentences that were true simply by virtue of their meanings, and Quine urged us to doubt that there *were* any of those.[5]

But you don't need highfalutin semantic arguments to be led to wonder whether we could in fact write a Ramsey-style definition of the word "race." Consider each of the two claims I gave a little while ago. *People with very different skin colors are of different races. Your race is determined by the race of your parents.*

Take the first one. Suppose Jorge were to speak of the Latino "race" and to maintain that the whole range of colors found among people that the U.S. census would classify as Hispanic simply demonstrated that a race didn't have to be fairly monochrome. Is this a mistake about the meaning of the word "race"? Now take the second claim. Two people marry. The wife has one Ghanaian and one British parent. The father's parents are Norwegian. They have children of various shades, one of whom looks, to all intents and purposes, like an average Norwegian. My friend Georg agrees that the mother's parents are of different races and contends that the Norwegian-looking son is Caucasian, but his darker brothers are not. Does Georg not know what "race" means? Apparently, if people with two parents of the same race are of the same race as their parents. For if your race is determined by the race of your parents, you must have the same race as your full siblings.

It seems to me simply unconvincing to insist that Jorge and Georg don't know what the word "race" means; at least if knowing what it means is knowing whatever you need to know to count as a competent user of the English word "race." This fails, of course, to establish that we couldn't find a set of beliefs necessary and sufficient for understanding the word "race"; beliefs, that is, that everybody who understands the word "race" must have and such that everybody who has them understands the concept of race. But if even *these* rather uncontroversial-looking claims turn out to be ones that can be denied by someone who understands the word "race," then one might begin to wonder whether *any* claims will turn out to be necessary: and if none are necessary, then certainly the conjunction of the necessary conditions won't be sufficient.

Such doubts about the strict criterial theory — in terms of criteria individually necessary and jointly sufficient — lead us on to the next obvious proposal, one that might seem to be suggested by Wittgenstein's use of the notion of a criterion.[6] Perhaps what is required to know what "race" means is that you should believe most of the criterial beliefs (or a good number of them) but not that you should believe any particular ones. The explicit definition that captures the common notion of those who understand the word "race" will then be given by a modified Ramsey-style definition: a race is something that satisfies a good number of the criterial beliefs. I'll call this the "vague criterial theory."

Accepting this theory has certain important consequences. First of all, it isn't going to allow us to draw a sharp line between not knowing what the word "race" means and having unusual views about races. That boundary is vague, because the expression "a good number" is vague.

Second, the theory admits that among the criterial beliefs are some that are plainly not held by everybody who uses the word "race." For example, *Most sub-Saharan Africans are of the Negro race. Most Western Europeans are of the white race. Most Chinese are of the yellow race. Everybody has* a *race. There are only a few races.*

There are clearly people who count as understanding the term "race" who don't believe each of these things. Somebody who uses the word "race" may have no thoughts at all about Africa or Western Europe or China, need not know even that they exist. I, as you will see, deny that everybody has *a* race, because I think nobody has a race: but there are more moderate folks who think that people of so-called mixed race are neither of the race of their parents nor of some separate race and deny that everybody has *a* race for that reason.[7] And there have been physical anthropologists who felt that the only useful notion of race classified people into scores of kinds.

If the strict criterial theory had been true, it would have been easy to argue against the existence of races. One would only have had to find the correct definition and then show that nothing in the world actually satisfied it. This looser theory correspondingly makes it harder to argue against the existence of races. But the vague criterial theory does suggest a route to understanding the race concept: to explore the sorts of things people believe about what they call "races" and to see what races would have to be like for these things to be true of them. We can then inquire as to whether current science suggests that there is anything in the world at all like *that*.

Now, suppose there isn't one such thing in the world; then, on this view, there are no races. It will still be important to understand the vague criteria, because these will help us to understand what people who believe in races are thinking. That will be important, even if there are no races: first, because we often want to understand how other people are thinking, for its own sake; and second, because people act on their beliefs, whether or not they are true. Even if there are no races, we could use a grasp of the vague criteria for the concept of race in predicting what their thoughts and their talk about race will lead them to do;[8] we could use it, too, to predict what thoughts about races various experiences would lead them to have.

I have already declared myself very often on the question whether I think there are any races. I think there aren't. So it is important that I am clear that I also believe that understanding how people think about race remains important for these reasons, even though there aren't any races. To use an analogy I have often used before, we may need to understand talk of "witchcraft" to understand how people respond cognitively and how they act in a culture that has a concept of witchcraft, whether or not we think there are, in fact, any witches.

The ideational view might, therefore, lead you to explore contemporary thought and talk about races. But I think—remembering Jorge and Georg—that this is likely to produce a confusing picture. This is because current ways of talking about race are the residue, the detritus, so to speak, of earlier ways of thinking about race; so that it turns out to be easiest to understand contemporary talk about "race" as the pale reflection of a more full-blooded race discourse that flourished in the last [the nineteenth] century. The ideational theory can thus be combined with a historical approach: we can explore the ideational structures of which our present talk is, so to speak, the shadow, and then see contemporary uses of the term as drawing from various different structures, sometimes in ways that are not exactly coherent.

Before we turn to historical questions, however, let me ask what route to understanding the race concept is suggested by the referential account of meaning.

THE REFERENTIAL ACCOUNT OF RACE: PHILOSOPHY OF SCIENCE

The answer is most easily understood by thinking about an issue in the history and philosophy of science. From the point of view of current theory some previous theories — early nineteenth-century chemistry, say — look as though they classified some things — acids and bases, say — by and large correctly, even if a lot of what they said about those things was pretty badly wrong. From the point of view of current theory, you might argue, an acid is, roughly, a proton donor.[9] And our recognition of the fact that the classification of acids and bases was in itself an intellectual achievement is recorded in the fact that we are inclined to say that when Sir Humphrey Davy — who, not having any idea of the proton, could hardly be expected to have understood the notion of a proton donor — used the word "acid," he was nevertheless talking about what we call acids.

The issues here are at the intersection of the philosophy of language and the philosophy of science. And in explaining why it seems proper to think that Sir Humphrey Davy was referring to the things we call "proton donors," even though much of what he believed about acids is not true of proton donors, philosophers of science have borrowed ideas about reference from recent philosophy of language.

One proposal some have borrowed is what is called the "causal theory of reference." The idea is simple enough: if you want to know what object a word refers to, find the thing in the world that gives the best causal explanation of the central features of uses of that word. If you want to know what the name "New York" refers to, find the object in the world that is at the root of most of the causal chains that lead to remarks containing the expression "New York."

THE ISSUES HERE ARE AT THE INTERSECTION OF THE PHILOSOPHY OF LANGUAGE AND THE PHILOSOPHY OF SCIENCE.

So in the case of acids, we are urged to believe that the stuffs "out there" in the world that really accounted for the central features of Davy's "acid"-talk really were acids and that that is what accounts for our sense that Davy was not simply talking about something else (or, of course, about nothing at all). Early physiologists (like Descartes) who talked about "animal spirits" in the nerve fibers, on the other hand, we now say were referring to nothing at all: there is no currently recognized stuff that can account for what they said about animal spirits; instead there are truths about sodium pumps and lipid bilayers and synapses. There simply is no substance that was usually present when and only when the expression "animal spirits" was uttered and that behaves at all as they thought animal spirits behaved.

THE REFERENTIAL ACCOUNT OF RACE: A PROPOSAL

How can we use these ideas to develop a referential account of the concept of race? Well, we need to explore the sorts of things people have said about what they call "races" and see whether there is something in the world that gives a good causal explanation of their talk. If there *is* one thing in the world that best explains that talk, then that will be what the word "race" refers to; and that can be true, even if it would surprise most people to know that that was what they were really talking about—just as Sir Humphrey Davy would have been surprised to discover that when he said "acids," he was talking about—referring to—proton donors.

As a practical matter, at least three things are required for us to allow that a past theorist who spoke of *Y*s and was badly mistaken was nevertheless talking about *some*thing, call it *X*.

First, the existence condition—*we* must acknowledge the existence of *X*.

Second, the adequacy condition—*some* of what was thought to be true of what *Y* denoted must be at least approximately true of *X*.

Third, the uniqueness condition—*X* must be the best candidate for the job of *Y*'s referent, so that no other thing that satisfies the existence condition satisfies the adequacy condition equally well.

On the causal theory, what it is for *X* to be the best candidate for the job of *Y*'s referent in the speech of a community is for *X* to be the thing that best causally explains their talk about *Y*s. So what we need to do, on this view, is explore the history of the way the word "race" has been used and see if we can identify through that history some objective phenomenon that people were responding to when they said what they said about "races."

The difference between ideational and referential theories of meaning, then, is roughly that the referential theory requires that we do a historical version of what the ideational theory permits us to do. On the referential theory, exploring the history of the term is central to understanding what it means. Semantical considerations thus steer us toward historical inquiry.

A NOTE ON METHOD

The history I am going to explore is the history of the ideas of the intellectual and political elites of the United States and the United Kingdom. You might ask why I don't look at the words of more ordinary people: race is statistically most important in ordinary lives. A good question, I say. (This is what you say when you think you have a good answer.) The reason is itself embedded in the history: as we shall see, throughout the nineteenth century the term "race" came increasingly to be regarded, even in ordinary usage, as a scientific term. Like many scientific terms, its being in use among specialists did not stop its being used in everyday life. Treating it as a scientific term meant not that it was only for use by scientists but that scientists and scholars were thought to be the experts on how the term worked. That is, with the increasing prestige of science, people became used to using words whose exact meanings they did not need to know, because their exact meanings were left to the relevant scientific experts.

In short, there developed a practice of *semantic deference*: people used words like "electricity" outside the context of natural philosophy or physical science, assuming that the physicists could say more precisely than they could what it meant. This semantic deference thus instituted a new form of what Hilary Putnam has called "linguistic division of labor," just as older specialties, like theology or law, had for a long time underwritten concepts — the Trinity, landlord — whose precise definition ordinary people didn't know.

The result is that even ordinary users of the term "race," who operated with what I have called vague criteria in applying it, thought of themselves as using a term whose value as a tool for speaking the truth was underwritten by the experts. Ordinary users, when queried about whether their term "race" really referred to anything, would have urged you to go to the experts: the medical doctors and anatomists, and later, the anthropologists and philologists and physiologists, all of whom together developed the scientific idea of race.

This makes the term "race" unlike many other terms in our language: "solid," for example. "Solid" is a term that we apply using everyday criteria: if I tell you that materials scientists say that a hunk of glass is not a solid but a liquid, you may well feel that they are using the term in a special technical sense, resisting semantic deference. Some people might want to defend the word "race" against scientific attacks on its legitimacy by denying, in effect, that semantic deference is appropriate here. Of this strategy, I will make just this observation: if you're going to go that route, you should probably offer some criteria — vague or strict — for applying the term. This is because, as we shall see, the arguments against the use of "race" as a scientific term suggest that most ordinary ways of thinking about races are incoherent.

THOMAS JEFFERSON: ABOLITIONIST

The understandings of "race" I am exploring are American; it seems appropriate enough, then, to begin with a thinker who helped shape the American republic: namely, Thomas Jefferson. And I want to begin with some representative reflections of his from the first quarter of the nineteenth century; for it is in the nineteenth century, I think, that the configuration of ideas about race we have inherited began to take its modern shape.

In Thomas Jefferson's *Autobiography* — begun, as he says, on January 6, 1822, at the age of seventy-seven — the third President of the United States reproduces his original draft of the Declaration of Independence, with the passages deleted by the Congress "distinguished by a black line drawn under them."[10] There are only two paragraphs entirely underlined in black; and the second, and by far the longer of them, gives, as grounds for complaint against "the present king of Great Britain,"[11] the fact that "he has waged cruel war against human nature itself, violating its most sacred rights of life and liberty in the persons of a distant people who never offended him, captivating & carrying them into slavery in another hemisphere, or to incur miserable death in their transportation thither. This piratical warfare, the opprobrium of INFIDEL powers, is the warfare of the CHRISTIAN king of Great Britain."[12] This first failure at gathering the new republic around the banner of antislavery did not discourage him. Not many pages later, Jefferson reports his equally unsuccessful attempts to persuade the legislature of Virginia to proceed, albeit gradually, toward total emancipation: "But it was found that the public mind would not yet bear the proposition, nor will it bear it even at this day. Yet the day is not distant when it must bear and adopt it, or worse will follow. Nothing is more certainly written in the book of fate than that these people are to be free."[13] So far, I think, we can feel that Thomas Jefferson was not simply ahead of his times, at least in the state of Virginia, but that, allowing for changes in rhetorical taste, he is our moral contemporary.

The sentence that follows disrupts this happy illusion: "Nor is it less certain," the former President writes, "that the two races, equally free, cannot live in the same government."[14] For Jefferson, who offers here no defense of his view, this is a piece of common sense. Here is a point at which we see one of the central characteristics of Jefferson's way of thinking about race: *it is a concept that is invoked to explain cultural and social phenomena,* in this case, the alleged political impossibility of a citizenship shared between white and black races.

THOMAS JEFFERSON: RACE THEORIST

If we want to know the sources of Jefferson's stern conviction — "Nor is it less certain . . ." — we can turn to Query XIV of the *Notes on the State of Virginia,* published four decades earlier, in the 1780s. Emancipation is inevitable, Jefferson has argued; and it is right. But blacks, once emancipated, will have to be sent elsewhere. Jefferson anticipates that we may wonder why, especially given "the expense of supplying, by importation of white settlers, the vacancies they will leave."

> Deep rooted prejudices entertained by the whites; ten thousand recollections, by the blacks, of the injuries they have sustained; new provocations; the real distinctions which nature has made; and many other circumstances, will divide us into parties, and produce convulsions which will probably never end but in the extermination of the one or the other race. — To these objections, which are political, may be added others, which are physical and moral. The first difference which strikes us is that of color. Whether the black of the negro resides in the reticular membrane between the skin and scarf-skin, or in the scarf-skin itself; whether it proceeds from the color of the blood, the color of the bile, or from that of some other secretion, the difference is fixed in nature, and is as real as if its seat and cause were better known to us. And is this difference of no importance? Is it not the foundation of a greater or less share of beauty in the two races? Are not the fine

> mixtures of red and white, the expressions of every passion by greater or less suffusions of color in the one, preferable to that eternal monotony, which reigns in the countenances, that immoveable veil of black which covers all the emotions of the other race? Add to these, flowing hair, a more elegant symmetry of form, their own judgment in favor of the whites, declared by their preference for them, as uniformly as is the preference of the Oranootan for the black woman over those of his own species. The circumstance of superior beauty, is thought worthy attention in the propagation of our horses, dogs, and other domestic animals; why not in that of man?[15]

Apart from this difference of color, with its attendant aesthetic consequences, Jefferson observes that there are other relevant differences: blacks have less hair on their face and bodies; "they secrete less by the kidneys, and more by the glands of the skin, which gives them a very strong and disagreeable odor"; "they seem to require less sleep. . . . They are at least as brave and more adventuresome. But this may perhaps proceed from a want of forethought." (Jefferson has forgotten the Aristotelian proposal that bravery is *intelligent* action in the face of danger.) "They are more ardent after their female; but love seems with them to be more an eager desire, than a tender delicate mixture of sentiment and sensation. Their griefs are transient."[16]

> Comparing them by their faculties of memory, reason, and imagination, it appears to me, that in memory they are equal to the whites; in reason much inferior, as I think one could scarcely be found capable of tracing and comprehending the investigations of Euclid; and that in imagination they are dull, tasteless, and anomalous.... [Among African-Americans] some have been liberally educated, and all have lived in countries where the arts and sciences are cultivated to a considerable degree, and have had before their eyes samples of the best works from abroad. The Indians, with no advantages of this kind, will often carve figures on their pipes not destitute of design and merit.... They astonish you with strokes of the most sublime oratory; such as prove their reason and sentiment strong, their imagination glowing and elevated. But never yet could I find that a black had uttered a thought above the level of plain narration; never see even an elementary trait of painting or sculpture. In music they are more generally gifted than the whites with accurate ears for tune and time, and they have been found capable of imagining a small catch.... Misery is often the parent of the most affecting touches in poetry.—Among the blacks is misery enough, God knows, but no poetry.... Religion indeed produced a Phyllis Whately [*sic*]; but it could not produce a poet. The compositions published under her name are below the dignity of criticism.[17]

Jefferson has nicer things to say about Ignatius Sancho, an African whose letters had been published in London in 1782.[18] And the judiciousness of his tone here adds, of course, greatly to the weight of his negative judgments. A little later in the same long paragraph—it is nearly six pages in the Library of America edition — he writes: "Whether further observation will or will not verify the conjecture, that nature has been less bountiful to them in the endowments of the head, I believe that in those of the heart she will be found to have done them justice. That disposition to theft with which they have been branded, must be ascribed to their situation, and not to any depravity of the moral sense."[19] Though he tells us that "the opinion, that they are inferior in the faculties of reason and imagination, must be hazarded with great diffidence,"[20] he nevertheless concludes:

> I advance it as a suspicion only, that the blacks whether originally a distinct race, or made distinct by time and circumstances, are inferior to the whites in the endowments both of body and mind. It is not against experience to suppose, that different species of the same genus, or varieties of the same species, may possess different qualifications. Will not a lover of natural history then, one who views gradations in all the races of animals with the eye of philosophy, excuse an effort to keep those in the department of man as distinct as nature has formed them. This unfortunate difference of color, and perhaps of faculty, is a powerful obstacle to the emancipation of these people.[21]

IT IS EASY TO MISS THE FACT THAT JEFFERSON BELIEVES THAT NEGROES AND WHITES MUST BE KEPT APART, EVEN IF HIS "SUSPICION" IS MISTAKEN.

After so conspicuously fair and balanced a discussion, it would have been hard not to share Jefferson's "suspicion." His very caution here adds to rather than detracting from the force of his conclusions; and after so much attention to the "difference . . . of faculty," it is easy to miss the fact that Jefferson believes that Negroes and whites must be kept apart, even if his "suspicion" is mistaken. For Jefferson the political significance of race begins and ends with color.

Jefferson's claims here about the Negro's faculties went neither unnoticed nor unanswered. And we can find, in his letters as in the *Notes*, evidence that he remained willing to entertain the possibility that his skepticism about the capacities of the Negro was unwarranted. In a letter of August 30, 1791, to Benjamin Banneker, who had worked on the design of the Capitol in Washington — he was one Negro gentleman who was certainly capable of "comprehending the investigations of Euclid" — Jefferson wrote: "No body wishes more than I do to see such proofs as you exhibit, that nature has given to our black brethren, talents equal to those of the other colors of men, and that the appearance of want in them is owing merely to the degraded condition of their existence, both in Africa & America."[22] And he repeats the sentiment in a letter to Henri Grégoire. Thanking the Abbé for sending him a copy of his *La littérature des nègres* (1808) Jefferson writes:

> Be assured that no person living wishes more sincerely than I do, to see a complete refutation of the doubts I have myself entertained and expressed on the grade of understanding allotted to them by nature, and

to find that in that respect they are on a par with ourselves. My doubts were the results of personal observation [one wonders, a little, about the Orangutan here] on the limited sphere of my own State, where the opportunities for the development of their genius were not favorable, and those of exercising it still less so. I expressed them therefore with great hesitation; but whatever be their degree of talent it is no measure of their rights. Because Sir Isaac Newton was superior to others in understanding, he was not therefore lord of the person or property of others.[23]

THE ENLIGHTENMENT IDEA

I have quoted so much of Jefferson in part, of course, because Jefferson is an important figure in the history of American debates about racial politics; but mostly because in these passages I have cited we see something entirely representative of the best thinking of his day: the running together of biology and politics, science and morals, fact and value, ethics and aesthetics. Jefferson is an intelligent, sensitive, educated American shaped by the Western intellectual currents we call the Enlightenment: if we query these conflations, we are querying not so much an individual as the thinking of a whole culture.

Let us explore the structure of Jefferson's explanation of why black and white races cannot live together in equality and harmony. He begins with suggestions that do not especially rely on the character of the race concept: prejudice, on the part of whites, and justified resentment, on the part of blacks. But almost immediately he moves on to speak of "the real distinctions which nature has made." And the first of these "physical and moral" differences is the primary criterion for dividing the black from the white race: skin color. Notice that in a passage devoted to a socio-political question — let me repeat that the issue here is why the races can't live together in harmony — he spends a great deal of time on theories about skin color and its consequences for the physiology of the expression of the emotions. Notice, too, however, that Jefferson holds the dark skin color and the nature of Negro hair to be relevant in part because they mean that whites are of "superior beauty" to blacks; an argument that appears to presuppose that beauty is a condition for fraternity; or, even — something that the passage hints at rather than asserting — that men can share citizenship with other men only if they find each other's women sexually attractive. I think we can assume that if Jefferson had seen that either of these premises was implicit in his argument, he might well have rejected (especially the second of) them: my point is only that it requires some such assumption to make his observations genuinely relevant to the question at hand.

Jefferson continues to talk about physical matters and their aesthetic consequences — hairlessness, kidneys, sweat — before moving on to discuss questions of the moral character of the Negro — bravery, lustfulness, crudeness of feeling (no "tender, delicate mixture of sentiment and sensation"), shallowness (those transient griefs) — and ends, at last, with the intellectual capacities — or rather, incapacities — of black people.

This passage is representative of late eighteenth-century discussions of race because, as I say, it brings together considerations that we are likely to think should be kept distinct. Remember always why the intellectual incapacity of blacks — their inferior reason — is invoked: not to justify unequal treatment — Jefferson, the democrat, clearly believes that intellectual superiority does not warrant greater political power, superior rights — but as part of a catalog of differences, which, taken together, make it certain that blacks and whites cannot live together as fellow citizens.

And it is clear that Jefferson believes that the answer to this question lies in what we would call differences in physiology, and moral and cognitive psychology, distinctions that, if they are real, we too are likely to regard as "distinctions which nature has made."

Not only, then, is race, for Jefferson, *a concept that is invoked to explain cultural and social phenomena,* it is also grounded in the physical and the psychological natures of the different races; it is, in other words, what we would call a *biological concept.*

FROM NATURAL HISTORY TO RACE SCIENCE

I say that it was what *we* would call a biological concept, because the science of biology did not exist when Jefferson was writing the *Notes.*[24] What did exist was natural history; and Jefferson would have agreed that race was a natural historical notion, as much as was the idea of species that Linnaeus had developed and which Buffon had popularized.[25] To think of race as a biological concept is to pull out of the natural history of humans a focus on the body — its structure and function — and to separate it both from mental life — the province of psychology — and from the broader world of behavior and of social and moral life. If Jefferson's discussion, with its movement from questions of the morphology of the skin, to discussions of sexual desire, to music and poetry, strikes us as a hodgepodge, it is because we live on the other side of a great intellectual chasm, which opens up with increasing speed through the nineteenth century. For we live now with a new configuration of the sciences; and, more especially, with the differentiation from the broad field of natural history, of anatomy, physiology, psychology, philology (i.e., historical linguistics), sociology, anthropology, and a whole host of even more specialized fields that gradually divided between them the task of describing and understanding human nature.

Jefferson's discussion is representative of a transition in the way the word "race" is used in reflecting on the characters of different kinds of peoples: the outer manifestations of race — the black skin of the Negro, the white skin and round eyes of the European, the oval eyes of the Oriental — have taken their place for him besides other, less physical, criteria, in defining race. The race of a person is expressed in all these ways, physical, moral, intellectual: they are referred back, so to speak, to a common cause or ground.

BEFORE NATURAL HISTORY

If we look back, for a moment, to the seventeenth-century traditions of English thought that are Jefferson's background, we see a different configuration of ideas, in which the physical body was important not as a cause but as a *sign* of difference.[26] Remember Othello. As G. K. Hunter has well expressed the matter:

> Shakespeare has presented to us a traditional view of what Moors are like, i.e. gross, disgusting, inferior, carrying the symbol of their damnation on their skin; and has caught our over-easy assent to such assumptions in the grip of a guilt which associates us and our assent with the white man representative of such views in the play—Iago. Othello acquires the glamour of an innocent man that *we* have wronged, and an admiration stronger than he could have achieved by virtue plainly represented.[27]

This device works only if the audience accepts that the Moor is *not,* simply by virtue of his Moorish physical inheritance, incorrigibly evil. Othello's blackness is a sign of his Moorishness; and it can associate him, through that sign, with the Infidel (since, unlike the Moor of Venice, most Moors are not Christian) and thus with moral or religious evil.

A similar point applies to the treatment of "the Jew" in both Shakespeare's *Merchant of Venice* and Marlowe's *Jew of Malta.* When Shylock, in what is surely his best-known speech, asks "Hath not a Jew eyes?" he is insisting that his body is a human body: and thus *essentially* the same as the body of a Gentile. He claims a status that depends on accepting that whatever is distinctive about him it is not his physical descent; what we would call his biological inheritance. So too, when Barabas in Marlowe's play is faced, by the Governor of Malta, with the accusation that Christ's blood "is upon the Jews," he replies:

> But say the Tribe that I descended of
> Were all in general cast away for sin,
> Shall I be tried by their transgression?[28]

Barabas here makes the essentially Christian point that sin and righteousness are individual matters; that they are precisely not inherited from "the Tribe that I descended of." If Barabas deserves punishment, it must be for something *he* has done: and, in fact, the Governor's reply demonstrates a grasp of this point. For he asserts that the issue is not Barabas's *descent* but his Jewish *faith:* the issue, therefore, cannot be conceptualized as simply racial. This is (a religious) anti-Judaism, not (a racial) anti-Semitism (which is, of course, not much consolation for Barabas).

There is good reason, then, to interpret these Elizabethan stereotypes, which *we* might naturally think of as rooted in notions of inherited dispositions (that is, of biology), as having much more to do with the idea of the Moor and the Jew as infidels; unbelievers whose physical differences are signs (but not causes or effects) of their unbelief.

But while Jefferson has thus moved toward conceiving of racial difference as both physical and moral, he is not yet *committed* to the view that race explains all the rest of the moral and social and political matter that is drawn into the portrait of the Negro in the *Notes*. The letters to Banneker and Grégoire reveal a man who leaves open — at least in theory — the possibility "that nature has given to our black brethren, talents equal to those of the other colors of men"; and throughout the *Notes* Jefferson writes with real affection and respect about Indians, who "astonish you with strokes of the most sublime oratory; such as prove their reason and sentiment strong, their imagination glowing and elevated." The differences between whites and Indians, for Jefferson, hardly constitute a difference of essential natures.

If we move on another fifty or so years from Jefferson's *Autobiography*, we enter once more a new intellectual landscape: one in which there is no longer any doubt as to the connection between race and what Jefferson calls "talent": and here, of course, the word "talent" — deriving from the New Testament parable of the talents — refers to inherited — to "native" — capacities.

MATTHEW ARNOLD: ON THE STUDY OF CELTIC LITERATURE

Let me turn, then, from Jefferson and move on into the second half of the nineteenth century, to the work of a poet and critic who, like Jefferson, uses the concept of race to explain the moral and the literary but, unlike him, is convinced that biological inheritance helps determine every aspect of racial capacity: Matthew Arnold.

Arnold was the greatest English critic of the nineteenth century. He was also a central Victorian poet, an influential essayist, and a lecturer: in short, a very public intellectual, whose influence was extended into the United States, not least by his lecture tour here in 1883 to 1884 (in his early sixties) which lead to the publication, in 1885, of *Discourses in America*.

In 1857 Matthew Arnold was elected to the Professorship of Poetry at Oxford, a position he held for about a decade. Ten years later, he published a series of lectures he had given as Professor of Poetry, *On the Study of Celtic Literature*. Arnold begins with a somewhat melancholy description of a visit to an Eisteddfod — a festival of Welsh bards — in Llandudno in North Wales. On an "unfortunate" day — "storms of wind, clouds of dust, an angry, dirty sea"[29] — Arnold sits with a meager crowd listening to the last representatives of a great poetic tradition performing for a small audience in a language he admits he does not understand. ("I believe it is admitted," Arnold observes drily, "even by admirers of Eisteddfods in general, that this particular Eisteddfod was not a success."[30])

This sad episode is only the preliminary, however, to an argument for the view that the ancient literature of the Celts — of Ireland and Wales, in particular — is part of the literary heritage of Britain; even of those Britons in England who by then conceived of themselves as heirs to a Saxon heritage and were inclined, by and large, to hold the Irish Celts, in particular, in less than high regard.

Here is how Arnold makes his case:

> Here in our country, in historic times, long after the Celtic embryo had crystallized into the Celt proper, long after the Germanic embryo had crystallized into the German proper, there was an important contact between the two peoples; the Saxons invaded the Britons and settled themselves in the Britons' country. Well, then, here was a contact which one might expect would leave its traces; if the Saxons got the upper hand, as we all know they did, and made our country be England and us be English, there must yet, one would think, be some trace of the Saxon having met the Briton; there must be some Celtic vein or other running through us....
>
> Though, as I have said, even as a matter of science, the Celt has a claim to be known, and we have an interest in knowing him, yet this interest is wonderfully enhanced if we find him to have actually a part in us. The question is to be tried by external and internal evidence; the language and physical type of our race afford certain data for trying it, and other data are afforded by our literature, genius, and spiritual production generally. Data of this second kind belong to the province of the literary critic; data of this first kind to the province of the philologist and the physiologist.
>
> The province of the philologist and the physiologist is not mine; but this whole question as to the mixture of Celt with Saxon in us has been so little explored, people have been so prone to settle it off-hand according to their prepossessions, that even on the philological and physiological side of it I must say a few words in passing.[31]

The ensuing discussion of what Arnold calls "physiology" is not what we should expect: it turns out that he is simply going to discuss the likelihood of mixture — that is, breeding — between the races. He cites, for example, the opinion of a certain Monsieur Edwards that "an Englishman who now thinks himself sprung from the Saxons or the Normans, is often in reality the descendant of the Britons."[32] The appeal to philology, on the other hand, might seem to suggest an alternative mechanism for the transmission of racial traits — namely, through language — but, in fact, philology is, for Arnold and his contemporaries, largely a guide to racial filiation, with those whose languages are most closely related being also most closely related by blood. Arnold is clear that language can, in fact, be misleading: "How little the triumph of the conqueror's laws, manners, and language, proves the extinction of the old race, we may see by looking at France; Gaul was Latinized in language, manners, and laws, and yet her people remained essentially Celtic."[33] But he is also convinced, as I say, that it can be a guide to racial character.

RACIALISM

What Arnold lays out in these passages is the essence of what I call *racialism.* He believed — and in this he was typical of educated people in the English-speaking world of his day — that we could divide human beings into a small number of groups, called "races," in such a way that the members of these groups shared certain fundamental, heritable, physical, moral, intellectual, and cultural characteristics with one another that they did not share with members of any other race.

There are a few complications to this basic picture, which we should bear in mind. First, there are two major ways in which counterexamples to claims about the members of the race could simply be ruled out. It was acknowledged that there were, to begin with, in all races, as there are in animal species, occasional defective members: in animals, the two-headed pigs and three-legged cats so beloved of tabloid journalism in my homeland of Ghana: in human beings, the mute, the mentally disabled, the blind. These individuals were not to count against the general laws governing the racial type. Similarly, the norm for each race might be different for males and females, so that a racial type might be defined by two norms, rather than one.

WHAT ARNOLD LAYS OUT IN THESE PASSAGES IS THE ESSENCE OF WHAT I CALL *RACIALISM.*

A second complication derives from the fact that many of the characteristics of the various races were described as dispositions or tendencies: a single person who was not defective might still differ from the average member of his race because his individual character dominated the natural tendencies he had inherited in his racial essence. Celts might all tend toward the sentimental; but a particular Welshman might, through an exercise of will, conquer his natural racial temper. As a result, the failure of an individual to fit the norm for her race would not by itself refute the theory: for it might be that that person had simply conquered her inherited disposition. Many of what I shall call the characteristics of a race were thus not, to use a modern term, phenotypic: they did not necessarily display themselves in the observable behavior of every individual.[34]

These characteristics, then, that each normal woman (and man) of a race was supposed to share with every other woman (and man) together determined what we can call the *essence* of that race; they were characteristics that were necessary and sufficient, taken together, for someone to be a normal member of the race. Arnold's concept of race should, then, provide the materials for what I have called a strict criterial theory of the meaning of the term "race."

Arnold was uncharacteristic of his age in many ways: and one of them is the cosmopolitanism — or, at least, the Europeanism — of his temperament: he quotes frequently from French and German scholars. And on the question of race his views conformed with what was coming to be the common sense of Western European intellectuals.

Arnold's discussion in *On the Study of Celtic Literature* makes it plain that he believes that the racial essence accounts for more than the obvious visible characteristics of individuals and of groups — skin color, hair, shape of face — on the basis of which we decide whether people are, say, Asian- or Afro-Americans. For a racialist, then, to say someone is "Negro" is not just to say that she has inherited a black skin or curly hair: it is to say that her skin color goes along with other important inherited characteristics — including moral and literary endowments. By the end of the nineteenth century most Western scientists (indeed, most educated Westerners) believed that racialism was correct, and theorists sought to explain many characteristics — including, as we see here, the character of literatures — by supposing that they were inherited along with (or were in fact part of) a person's racial essence.

MIXING ESSENCES

In the British people, Arnold is arguing, not only are there some whose ancestors are Celt — the first Britons — and some whose ancestors are Saxon, but these two lines have become literally joined through intermarriage, and the character of British literature is thus not only the product of a cultural syncretism but a joining of the essences of two races. Thus while the Celtic essence survives, it survives mixed with a Saxon essence: the character of the English thus contains both essences, both are available as driving energies of English poetry.

> All tendencies of human nature are in themselves vital and profitable; when they are blamed, they are to be blamed relatively, not absolutely. This holds true of the Saxon's phlegm as well as the Celt's sentiment. Out of the steady humdrum habit of the creeping Saxon, as the Celt calls him, — out of his way of going near the ground — has come, no doubt, Philistinism, that plane of essentially Germanic growth, flourishing with its genuine marks only in the German fatherland, Great Britain and her colonies, and the United States of America; but what a soul of goodness there is in Philistinism itself! and this soul of goodness I, who am often supposed to be Philistinism's mortal enemy merely because I do not wish it to have things all its own way, cherish as much as anybody. This steady-going habit leads at last . . . up to science, up to the comprehension and interpretation of the world.[35]

Arnold has to account as well for the presence of Norman blood in this brew of racial essences, and once this is done he has all the elements he needs for constructing a picture of the British racial hybrid.

> I have got a rough, but, I hope, clear notion of these three forces, the Germanic genius, the Celtic genius, the Norman genius. The Germanic genius has steadiness as its main basis, with commonness and humdrum for its defect, fidelity to nature for its excellence. The Celtic genius, sentiment as its main basis, with love of beauty, charm, and spirituality for

> its excellence, ineffectualness and self-will for its defect. The Norman genius, talent for affairs as its main basis, with strenuousness and clear rapidity for its excellence, hardness and insolence for its defect. And now to try and trace these in the composite English genius.[36]

Part of the evidence that Arnold offers that the character of England is the product of the intermixing of these racial types is in the contrast between English prose – exemplified in the news pages of the *London Times* – and German – exemplified in the *Cologne Gazett.* "At noon a long line of carriages extended from Pall Mall to the Peer's entrance of the Palace of Westminster," writes the correspondent of the *Times* (we must turn to the editorial pages to discover why it was known as "the Thunderer"). While the *Gazett* has: "Nachdem die Vorbereitungen zu dem auf dem Gürzenich-Saale zu Ehren der Abgeordneten Statt finden sollenden Bankette bereits vollständig getroffen worden waren, fand heute vormittag auf polizeiliche Anordnung die Schliessung sämmtlicher Zugänge zum Gürzenich Statt."[37] Arnold concludes: "Surely the mental habit of people who express their thoughts in so very different a manner, the one rapid, the other slow, the one plain, the other embarrassed, the one trailing, the other striding, cannot be essentially the same."[38] It follows that there must be something other than the common Teutonic racial stock, which Germans and Saxons share, that accounts for the difference: this is evidence, then, on the racialist view, for the proposition that the British stock has been hybridized with some other race.

Arnold makes the same sort of appeal to race – this time at a greater level of generality, discussing the contrast between Indo-European and Semitic races – in *Culture and Anarchy,* a work that is much more widely known. In these essays, based on articles that first appeared in *Cornhill Magazine* in 1867 and 1868, and then in book form in 1869, Arnold wrote:

> Science has now made visible to everybody the great and pregnant elements of difference which lie in race, and in how signal a manner they make the genius and history of an Indo-European people vary from those of a Semitic people. Hellenism is of Indo-European growth, Hebraism of Semitic growth; and we English, a nation of Indo-European stock, seem to belong naturally to the movement of Hellenism. But nothing more strongly marks the essential unity of man than the affinities we can perceive, in this point or that, between members of one family of peoples and members of another; and no affinity of this kind is more strongly marked than that likeness in the strength and prominence of the moral fiber, which, notwithstanding immense elements of difference, knits in some special sort the genius and history of us English, and of our American descendants across the Atlantic, to the genius and history of the Hebrew people. Puritanism, which has been so great a power in the English nation, and in the strongest part of the English nation, was originally the reaction, in the seventeenth century, of the conscience and moral sense of our race,

> against the moral indifference and lax rule of conduct which in the sixteenth century came in with the Renaissance. It was a reaction of Hebraism against Hellenism.[39]

Arnold makes a move here that is similar to the one he makes in the discussion of Celts and Saxons: he invokes race — which in Jefferson is invoked to account for division — in a context where he is arguing toward universality. Hebraism is Arnold's name for the tendencies in Western culture that are owed to what *we* would call its Judeo-Christian religious heritage: Arnold is convinced of the importance of Christianity and insists, in *Culture and Anarchy,* on the necessity of maintaining an established — that is, a state-supported — church in England. He is not, then, an enemy of Hebraism as such: every race, he insists here as much as in *On The Study of Celtic Literature,* has emblematic excellences as well as distinctive defects. The ideal for Britain, Arnold argues, is to construct a judicious mixture of Hebraism and Hellenism: the British, lacking Semitic blood, are not, by nature, Hebraists. The point, then, is that by Arnold's day even someone wanting to point to what was shared between two human groups was likely to do so in terms of the notion of race, a notion that was largely defined in terms of what separates people.[40]

These passages from the two sources, taken together, reveal a great deal of the structure of racialist thinking. Arnold displays both the flexibility of the view and some of its characteristic obscurities. Part of the flexibility flows from the fact that racial classification proceeds, as we see, at different levels: the Saxons and the Celts are both Indo-European. Differences between them are differences within the broader Indo-European race. When we need similarities, we can appeal to the higher level — the subsuming category of the Indo-European; when we need differences we can move lower down the taxonomic tree. In the United States, the differences between the Irish and the Anglo-Saxons could be used to account for the cultural and moral deficiencies—real or imaginary — of Irish immigrants; but their whiteness could be used to distinguish them from the Negro.

But there is also something of a muddle here: if the Celtic and the Saxon essences are so opposite, what is an individual like who inherits both of them? What would a man be like who was steady *and* sentimental; suffered from commonness and humdrummery *and* ineffectualness and self-will; was faithful to nature and loved "beauty, charm, and spirituality"? What is lacking in Arnold's work is any theory of inheritance, any mechanism for explaining how the character of a race survives through the generations, transmitted in the bodies of its members: and any account of the laws that govern the interactions of racial essences. Without these, racialism makes no particular predictions about racial hybrids: a fact that is of the greatest importance since, if we are considering races at the taxonomic level of Celt and Saxon, there were very few peoples known to Arnold and his contemporaries who could plausibly have been thought to be unmixed.

What is also lacking is an answer to the question how we balance the effects of race and the effects of environment. *Culture and Anarchy* is in large measure about why the British are not Hellenic enough. If the British inherit naturally the tendencies of Hellenism with their Indo-European blood and language, why is British culture not too suffused with Hellenism (as the theory should predict) but too dominated by Hebraism? The answer Arnold gives has to do with the role of Christianity in spreading Hebraism, not by racial admixture but by cultural influence. And if the spread of Hebraism is a cultural phenomenon, then the Hellenism carried in the British blood, the racial essence, cannot be determinative of how a people will act. In *Celtic Literature* he says:

> And if, — whereas the Semitic genius placed its highest spiritual life in the religious sentiment, and made that the basis of its poetry, — the Indo-European genius places its highest spiritual life in the imaginative reason, and makes that the basis of its poetry, we are none the better for trying to make ourselves Semitic, when nature has made us Indo-European, and to shift the basis of our poetry. We may mean well; all manner of good may happen to us on the road we go; but we are not on our real right road, the road we must in the end follow.[41]

If this determinism of race is correct, isn't the Hebraism of England, described in *Culture and Anarchy,* evidence that the English are in fact not Indo-European but Semitic? And what significance for the issue of environment versus racial essence should we give to the claim, in a letter of June 21, 1865, that "a nation is really civilized by acquiring the qualities it by nature is wanting in"?[42]

There is no doubt that these questions could have been answered: the idea, to which I referred earlier, that members of races inherited tendencies rather than more strictly phenotypic or behavioral properties could be invoked, for example, in an account of the interaction of racial character, individual traits, and environment. Indeed, in a period before Mendelism, it was possible to believe, with Lamarck, that the environment acted on individuals to produce in them changes that they transmitted to their children not through teaching but through bodily inheritance. After Mendel and Darwin, one can maintain that the environment acts on bodily heredity only slowly and over many generations;[43] but until then the distinction between cultural innovation, on the one hand, which allows a group to develop and transmit a new behavioral response extremely quickly, and biological change, which moves with a stately and glacial torpor, was unavailable. In Arnold's day, one could have argued that the Hebraism of England was both racially inherited and recently acquired: acquired, for example, in the first age of Puritanism.

Without answers to questions such as these, however, what is masquerading as an empirical, even a scientific, theory is remarkably insensitive to evidence. These deficiencies in Arnold are found in other race thinkers of the period — and, as we shall see, they are by no means limited to those who addressed the less physical — that is, the moral or cultural — traits of races.

THE ORIGINS OF LITERARY RACIALISM

Arnold's identification of literature as a key to the national spirit is in a tradition we can trace back a century earlier to Johann Gottfried Herder.

In his *On the New German Literature: Fragments* of 1767, Herder — who is, in some ways, the first important philosopher of modern nationalism — put forward the notion that language, far from being (as the received Aristotelian tradition had it) the merely material cause of a work of literature — that is, just what it happened to be written in — is not just "a tool of the arts and sciences" but "a part of them." "Whoever writes about the literature of a country," Herder continued, "must not neglect its language." Herder's notion of the *Sprachgeist* — literally the "spirit" of the language — embodies the thought that language is more than the medium through which speakers communicate.

Herder's ideas became part of mid-nineteenth-century common sense. The consensus was well expressed by Thomas Carlyle, the British essayist and man of letters, in 1831, less than a decade after Jefferson's *Autobiography* — in a discussion, in the *Edinburgh Review,* of a history of German poetry: "The History of a nation's poetry is the essence of its History, political, scientific, religious. With all these the complete Historian of a national poetry will be familiar: the national physiognomy, in its finest traits, and through its successive stages of growth, will be clear to him; he will discern the grand spiritual Tendency of each period."[44] That the "nation" here is not a political unit but a group defined by descent is evident from the fact that there was, in 1831, no single German state: Bismarck's time had not yet come. Between Carlyle's essay and Arnold's lectures, talk of "nations" was displaced by talk of "race."

ARNOLD'S IDENTIFICATION OF LITERATURE AS A KEY TO THE NATIONAL SPIRIT IS IN A TRADITION WE CAN TRACE.

Herder himself had had to make a sharp distinction between nations and states because in eighteenth-century Europe there was not even an approximate correlation between linguistic and political boundaries.[45] The modern European nationalism, which produced, for example, the German and Italian states, involved trying to create states to correspond to nationalities: nationalities conceived of as sharing a civilization and, more particularly, a language and literature. Exactly because political geography did not correspond to Herder's nationalities, he was obliged to draw a distinction between the nation as a natural entity and the state as the product of culture, as a human artifice.

But with the increasing influence of the natural sciences — the separation out of specialties for natural history, and the increasing professionalization of scientific research — what is natural in human beings — the human nature whose story natural history told—came increasingly to be thought of as the province of such sciences as biology and anthropology. Inevitably, then, the nation comes more and more to be identified not just by common descent but also as a biological unit, defined by the shared essence that flows from that common descent.

Imposing the Herderian identification of the core of the nation with its national literature on top of the racial conception of the nation, we arrive at the racial understanding of literature that Arnold expresses: a way of thinking that flourishes from the mid-nineteenth century in the work of the first modern literary historians. Hippolyte Taine's monumental *History of English Literature,* published in France in the 1860s and perhaps the first modern literary history of English—begins with the words "History has been transformed, within a hundred years in Germany, within sixty in France, and that by the study of their literatures."[46] But he is soon telling us that "a race, like the Old Aryans, scattered from the Ganges as far as the Hebrides, settled in every clime, and every stage of civilization, transformed by thirty centuries of revolutions, nevertheless manifests in its languages, religions, literatures, philosophies, the community of blood and of intellect which to this day binds its offshoots together."[47] What is revealed, in short, by the study of literature that has transformed the discipline of history is the "moral state" of the race whose literature it is. It is because of this conception that Taine finds it proper to start his study of English literature with a chapter on the Saxons; so that chapter 1, book 1, of Taine's *History* begins not in England at all but in Holland: "As you coast the North Sea from Scheldt to Jutland, you will mark in the first place that the characteristic feature is the want of slope: marsh, waster, shoal; the rivers hardly drag themselves along, swollen and sluggish, with long, black-looking waves."[48] The "Saxons, Angles, Jutes, Frisians . . . [and] Danes"[49] who occupied this region of Holland at the beginning of the first millennium are, according to Taine, the ancestors of the English; but since they, themselves, are of German descent, Taine also refers, in describing this "race" a few pages later, to some of the traits ascribed to Germans in Tacitus.

It is the conception of the binding core of the English nation as the Anglo-Saxon race that accounts for Taine's decision to identify the origins of English literature not in its antecedents in the Greek and Roman classics that provided the models and themes of so much of the best-known works of English "poesy"; not in the Italian models that influenced the drama of Marlowe and Shakespeare; but in *Beowulf,* a poem in the Anglo-Saxon tongue, a poem that was unknown to Chaucer and Spenser and Shakespeare, the first poets to write in a version of the English language that we can still almost understand.

DARWIN AND THE RISE OF RACE SCIENCE

Arnold represents, then, a version of an older theory couched in terms of the new vocabulary of "race," whose authority derives, in part, from its association with the increasing prestige of the natural sciences. (You will have noticed that in the excerpts from the *Celtic Literature* lectures Arnold uses the word "data" several times.) And the most important theoretical development in the growth of a biological conception of race had already occurred by the time Arnold published *Culture and Anarchy* in 1869. For on November 24, 1859, Charles Darwin had published a work whose full title reads: *The Origin of Species by Means of Natural Selection or the Preservation of Favored Races in the Struggle for Life.*

The word "race" had been used in this way to refer to kinds of animals and plants, as well as to kinds of people, for some time; but there is no doubt that even for a mid-nineteenth-century ear this title promises something of relevance to the study of human difference. Indeed, the very fact that a single scientific theory promised to account for the variety of kinds of animals, in general, made its application to humans a natural step in the continuing process of placing the study of human anatomy in the context of a comparative zoology.

Darwin suggested, with characteristic caution, in *The Origin of Species,* that his theory might throw light on "the origin of man and his history"; the implication being that human beings developed, like other modern organisms, out of earlier forms. Taken to its "logical conclusion" this view suggested the oneness not only of all human beings — related by common descent — but, at least potentially, the common ancestry and thus unity of all life.

Darwin's theory can be thought of as consisting of two components: one is the claim that kinds of organisms develop by "descent with modification."[50] This claim was immediately widely accepted and applied to understanding the classification of organisms, representing, as it did, a continuation of arguments made five decades earlier by Lamarck.

But Darwin's more distinctive claim was that the mechanism of modification was natural selection: the selective survival of characteristics that gave individuals advantages in the "struggle for life." Darwin here drew on the parallelism with artificial selection of animals that was carried on by horse and cattle breeders and by pigeon fanciers. Just as they worked only with the natural variation among animals, selecting those with characteristics they favored and breeding from them, so, in Darwin's theory, nature "selected" organisms for breeding, not (as the rather colorful talk of the "struggle for life" suggested) by destroying some and allowing others to survive but by affecting differentially rates of reproductive success.

This claim was not so easily accepted. To begin with, it was not clear that there was sufficient variation within most kinds of organisms on which selection could work; and, indeed, though Darwin and Darwinians did stress the variability of natural populations, they had no account of the origin of the variations on which selection could act. More than this, most selective forces did not look as though they applied sufficient selection pressure to lead to any very substantial effects: it was only much later, with the development of population genetics, that it was possible to show that relatively small differences in survival rates could produce cumulatively large effects.

And, finally, Darwin had an inadequate and undeveloped theory of inheritance: the modern account, in terms of the gene, had no real impact until after Mendel's work was rediscovered in 1900. The theory of evolution by natural selection required that organisms should inherit the characteristics of their ancestors: otherwise the surviving offspring of an organism with a trait that gave it an advantage in the struggle for life offered no guarantee that its children would carry the same trait. Indeed, since Darwin believed in a sort of blending theory of inheritance, in which what accounted for a particular observable characteristic was the blended mixture of the factors that determined that characteristic in one's parents, he could not really explain why a factor that was rare in a population could survive at all, since it would be constantly "diluted" by more common forms.

There were other problems: if you want to treat all creatures as derived from a single ancient population, there must be some source of new variations: otherwise every characteristic in any modern organism must have existed in the earliest population. (Darwin was aware of "sports," creatures like the two-headed pigs to which I have already referred; but he thought — rightly, as it turns out — that these were of little importance in evolution.)

It is thus only with the development of Mendelism, with its account of inheritance in terms of genes and its recognition of the possibility of new variety arising by mutation, that the theory of natural selection was placed on a sound footing.

This second part of Darwin's theory — the view of natural selection — was thus rightly greeted with less immediate enthusiasm than the general idea of descent with modification.

Descent with modification was all that was required, however, to allow biology to give a much more straightforward account of how organisms should be classified. Darwin thought of species as essentially classificatory conveniences;[51] he was interested in how populations changed their character and separated from each other, not in drawing boundaries between them. But his theory allowed that the accumulation of differences by selection could gradually produce kinds — varieties or species — that were measurably different; and thus suggested a mode of classification in which kinds that were more closely related by evolution should be classified together.

Thus the general acceptance of descent with modification and the increasing acceptance of Darwin's theory of natural selection gave scientific support to the idea that human kinds — races — could, like animal and plant species, be both evolutionarily related and biologically distinct. Furthermore, even though human races were not mutually infertile, the theory of evolution suggested a way of thinking of varieties as being in the process of speciation: races might not be species, but they were, so to speak, moving in that direction.

THE PROBLEM FOR A BIOLOGY OF RACE

Darwin, as I have said, thought of the species as essentially a classificatory convenience: he was, in philosophical jargon, a nominalist about species, holding that the boundaries between species were not clearly marked "in nature"; and if species were not marked in nature then varieties or subspecies (which is what, on his view, human races were), being even less distinct from one another than species, were presumably classificatory conveniences also.

To believe this was already to move away from the sort of racial essences that we find in Arnold. For Arnold, the interest of the characteristics of a race was exactly that you could suppose that its members all shared certain properties; so that having identified a person's race membership from her appearance one could then make inferences about her moral or literary dispositions. It makes sense that Darwin, whose whole analysis depends on the recognition of variation within populations, was more interested in the ways individuals differed from each other within their varieties than in the ways they were similar.

Once we have the modern genetic picture we can see that each person is the product of enormous numbers of genetic characteristics, interacting with one another and with an environment, and that there is nothing in the theory of evolution to guarantee that a group that shares one characteristic will share all or even most others. Characteristics on different chromosomes are, as the Mendelians said, independently assorted. The theory of evolution will also predict that as you move through a geographical range along a gradient of selection pressure, the frequency of certain characteristics — those that affect skin color, for example — may change fairly continuously, so that populations may blend into one another; and characteristics may drift from one neighboring population into another over time by intermarriage (or, to speak less euphemistically, interbreeding). Indeed, it turns out that, in humans, however you define the major races, the biological variability within them is almost as great as the biological variation within the species as a whole: put another way, while there are some characteristics that we are very good at recognizing — skin color, hair, skull shape — that are very unevenly geographically distributed, the groups produced by these assignments do not cluster much for other characteristics.

This fact was noticed by Ralph Waldo Emerson, only a few years after Arnold's essays. In 1876, in *his* essays on English traits, he wrote:

> An ingenious anatomist has written a book[52] to prove that races are imperishable, but nations are pliant constructions, easily changed or destroyed. But this writer did not found his assumed races on any necessary law, disclosing their ideal or metaphysical necessity; nor did he on the other hand count with precision the existing races and settle the true bounds; a point of nicety, and the popular test of his theory. The individuals at the extremes of divergence in one race of men are as unlike as the wolf to the lapdog. Yet each variety shades down imperceptibly into the next, and you cannot draw the line where a race begins or ends. Hence every writer makes a different count. Blumenbach reckons five races; Humboldt three; and Mr. Pickering, who lately in our Exploring Expedition thinks he saw all kinds of men that can be on the planet, makes eleven.[53]

Even limiting oneself to the range of morphological criteria available to these comparative anatomists it is hard to classify people objectively into a small set of populations; and whichever way you do it, it will turn out that, for biological purposes, your classification will contain almost as much human genetic variation as there is in the whole species.[54]

"Race," then, as a biological concept, picks out, at best, among humans, classes of people who share certain easily observable physical characteristics, most notably skin color and a few visible features of the face and head.

The materials for an evolutionary explanation for skin color variation are easily laid out. The original human population had dark skins, which give you a selective advantage in the tropics, because they protect you somewhat from skin cancer. Lighter skins developed in colder climes, no doubt in part because skin cancer is less of a problem where you are permanently clothed, because of the cold, and the sun's rays pass more obliquely through the atmosphere. There may have been actual selection for white skins — maybe a landscape of mist and snow makes it easier to hide from your enemies — or it may just be that the mutations that make for white skin developed and survived because there was no longer selection pressure against them.[55] This second possibility illustrates a form of evolutionary change that is of some importance, namely the development of populations whose character is the result not of adaptation but of the presence, by chance, in an isolated environment of a particular nonrepresentative sample of the total gene pool. And we may as well mention a third possibility here, one that Darwin noticed as well, which is that skin color was maintained by sexual selection: because, for some reason or other, human beings of one sex or other (or both) developed a preference for mates with lighter skins.

"RACE," THEN, AS A BIOLOGICAL CONCEPT, PICKS OUT, AT BEST, AMONG HUMANS, CLASSES OF PEOPLE WHO SHARE CERTAIN EASILY OBSERVABLE PHYSICAL CHARACTERISTICS, MOST NOTABLY SKIN COLOR.

Why does biological variation in skin color not correlate more with other characteristics? Partly because the other characteristics have been selected (as has, say, sickle-cell disease in parts of West Africa and the Eastern Mediterranean) under pressures not highly correlated with the presence of harmful amounts of sunlight. Perhaps, too, because there are mechanisms that have evolved to maintain the stability of the genotype, reflecting, among other things, the fact that certain combinations of genes are adaptive only when they are present together.[56] As a result, even after long periods — of the order of hundreds of thousands of years — of geographical separation, human populations do not drift apart significantly with respect to most of their biological properties. And finally, because there has been continuous exchange of genes between the major geographical areas of human settlement over the hundreds of thousands of years since the first humans set off out of Africa.

The United States bears witness to the continuing significance of this phenomenon. It is true that Americans still tend, overwhelmingly, to marry people of their own, as we say, "racial identity." But very large numbers (perhaps as many as two-thirds) of African-Americans have some European forebears; up to two-fifths may have American Indian "blood"; and at least 5 percent of white Americans are thought to have African roots. It is estimated that 20 to 30 percent of the genes of the average African-American come from European and American Indian ancestors.[57]

The result is that even if the four roughly separated populations of the four continents from which the ancestors of most Americans came had each been much less genetically variable than was in fact the case, there would still be large numbers of people whose skin color predicted very few other biological properties.

WHY THERE ARE NO RACES

We have followed enough of the history of the race concept and said enough about current biological conceptions to answer, on both ideational and referential views, the question whether there are any races.

On the ideational view, the answer is easy. From Jefferson to Arnold, the idea of race has been used, in its application to humans, in such a way as to require that there be significant correlations between the biological and the moral, literary, or psychological characters of human beings; and that these be explained by the intrinsic nature (the "talents" and "faculties" in Jefferson; the "genius," in Arnold) of the members of the race.[58]

That has turned out not to be true; the recent fuss generated by *The Bell Curve* about the correlation of race and IQ in the United States notwithstanding. Even if you believed Murray and Herrnstein's estimates of the heritability of IQ within groups in the United States — and you shouldn't — they offer almost no evidence relevant to refuting the claim that the differences between American groups are entirely caused by the environment; say, in particular, by the ways that blacks are treated in a racist society.[59]

Once you have the modern theory of inheritance, you can see why there is less correlation than everyone expected between skin color and things we care about: people are the product not of essences but of genes interacting with one another and with environments, and there is little systematic correlation between the genes that fix color and the like and the genes that shape courage or literary genius. So, to repeat, on the ideational view we can say that nothing in the world meets the criteria for being a Jeffersonian or an Arnoldian race.

The biological notion of race was meant to account only for a narrower range of characteristics, namely, the biological ones, by which I mean the ones important for biological theory. There are certainly many ways of classifying people for biological purposes: but there is no single way of doing so that is important for most biological purposes that corresponds, for example, to the majority populations of each continent or subcontinent. It follows that on an ideational view, there are no biological races, either: not, in this case, because nothing fits the loose criteria but because too many things do.[60]

On the referential view we are required to find something in the world that best explains the history of usage of the term. Two candidates suggest themselves for the biological uses of "race": one is the concept of a population that I have been using for a while now. It can be defined as "the community of potentially interbreeding individuals at a given locality."[61] There are interesting discussions in the literature in population genetics as to how one should think about where to draw the boundaries of such communities: sometimes there is geographic isolation, which makes interbreeding in the normal course of things much less likely. But the population concept is generally used in such a way that we speak sometimes of a population defined by one geographical region and also, at other times, of a wider population, defined by a wider range, of which the first population is a part; and at yet other times of populations that are overlapping.

I have no problem with people who want to use the word "race" in population genetics.[62] What Darwin was talking about — evolution, speciation, adaptation — can best be understood in terms of talk of populations. And the fact is that in many plants and animals there are, in fact, local populations that are reproductively isolated from one another, different in clustered and biologically interesting ways, and still capable of interbreeding if brought artificially together; and biologists both before and after Darwin could have called these "races." It's just that this doesn't happen in human beings. In this sense, there are biological races in some creatures, but not in us.

A more ecumenical proposal in this spirit would be to say that the word "race" refers to populations, more generally. The trouble is that, in this sense, while there are human populations that are and have been for some time relatively reproductively isolated, it is not at all plausible to claim that any social subgroup in the United States is such a population. In *this* sense, then, there are human races, because there are human populations, in the geneticists' sense, but no large social group in America is a race. (The Amish, on the other hand, might come out as a race on this view, because they are a relatively reproductively isolated local population.)

A second candidate for the biological referent would simply be groups defined by skin color, hair, and gross morphology, corresponding to the dominant pattern for these characteristics in the major subcontinental regions: Europe, Africa, East and South Asia, Australasia, the Americas, and perhaps the Pacific Islands. This grouping would encompass many human beings quite adequately and some not at all: but it is hard to see of what biological *interest* it would be, since we can study the skin and gross morphology separately, and there is, at any rate, a good deal of variation within all these areas, in skin, hair color, and the morphology of the skull. Certainly this referent would not provide us with a concept that was central to biological thinking about human beings. And once more, in the

United States, large numbers of people would not fit into any of these categories, because they are the products of mixtures (sometimes long ago) between people who do roughly fit this pattern, even though the social distinctions we call "racial" in the United States do, by contrast, cover almost everybody. And so, if we used this biological notion, it would have very little established correlation with any characteristics currently thought to be important for moral or social life.

The bottom line is this: you can't get much of a race concept, ideationally speaking, from any of these traditions; you can get various possible candidates from the referential notion of meaning, but none of them will be much good for explaining social or psychological life, and none of them corresponds to the social groups we call "races" in America.

NOTES

[1] I owe this thought experiment to a conversation with Samuel R. Delany.

[2] The discussion of the second and third conclusions are not included in this selection. They appear in the subsequent section of *Color Consciousness* [Eds.].

[3] I'm going to avoid my normal custom of using scare-quotes around the word "race" throughout, because in this context it would be question begging. It would also be confusing, since a lot of what I have to say is about the alleged relation between the word "race" and allegedly actual races. So quotes around the word "race" in this piece are for the purposes of distinguishing between use and mention.

[4] See "Theories," in Frank Ramsey, *Foundations: Essays in Philosophy, Logic, Mathematics and Economics*, ed. D. H. Mellor (London: Routledge and Kegan Paul, 1978), pp. 101–25.

[5] W. V. O. Quine, "Two Dogmas of Empiricism," in *From a Logical Point of View* (Cambridge: Harvard University Press, 1953), pp. 20–46.

[6] See P. F. Strawson, "Wittgenstein's Conception of a Criterion," in *Wittgenstein and the Problem of Other Minds*, ed. Harold Morick (Brighton, Sussex: Harvester Press, 1981).

[7] See Naomi Zack, *Race and Mixed Race* (Philadelphia: Temple University Press, 1993).

[8] Strictly speaking, if there aren't any races, there's no talk or thought about races. So this is a shorthand for "talk they would assent to (or thoughts they would express) using the word 'race' and its cognates."

[9] This is the so-called Bronsted theory of the Danish physical chemist Johannes Nicolaus Bronsted.

[10] *Autobiography*, in Thomas Jefferson, *Writings* (New York: Library of America, 1984), p. 18.

[11] Ibid., p. 21.

[12] Ibid., p. 22.

[13] Ibid., p. 44.

[14] Jefferson, *Autobiography.*

[15] *Notes of the State of Virginia* (1781–82), in Jefferson, *Writings*, p. 264.

[16] Ibid., p. 265.

[17] Ibid., p. 206.

[18] Ignatius Sancho (1729–80), *Letters of the Late Ignatius Sancho, an African* (London: printed by J. Nichols, 1782).

[19] Jefferson, *Notes of the State of Virginia*, pp. 268–69.

[20] Ibid., p. 269.

[21] Ibid., p. 270.

[22] August 30, 1791, to Benjamin Banneker. "Letters," in Jefferson, *Writings*, p. 982.

[23] February 25, 1806, to Henri Grégoire. Ibid., p. 1202.

[24] "The term 'biology' first appeared in a footnote in an obscure German medical publication of 1800. Two years later it again appeared, apparently independently, and was given ample publicity in treatises by a German naturalist (Gottfried Treviranus) and a French botanist turned zoologist (Jean-Baptiste de Lamarck)." William Coleman, *Biology in the Nineteenth Century: Problems of Form, Function and Transformation*, Cambridge History of Science Series (Cambridge: Cambridge University Press, 1971), p. 1.

[25] Carolus Linnaeus, *Systema Naturae*, in which people are classified as Homo sapiens, appears in 1735.

[26] For more on the background here see Hugh B. MacDougall, *Racial Myth in English History: Trojans, Teutons, and Anglo-Saxons* (Hanover, N.H.: University Press of New England, 1982); and Reginald Horsman, *Race and Manifest Destiny: The Origins of American Racial Anglo-Saxonism* (Cambridge: Harvard University Press, 1981).

[27] George K. Hunter, "Othello and Race-Prejudice," in *Dramatic Identities and Cultural Tradition: Studies in Shakespeare and His Contemporaries* (Liverpool: Liverpool University Press, 1978), pp. 45–46.

[28] Christopher Marlowe, *The Jew of Malta* (London: Methuen, 1987), lines 340–42.

[29] Matthew Arnold, *On the Study of Celtic Literature and on Translating Homer* (New York: MacMillan, 1883), p. 6.

[30] Ibid., p. 8.

[31] Ibid., pp. 66–67.

[32] Ibid., p. 72. Arnold never explicitly discusses sex, of course; and so we are left with the possibility of interpreting this as meaning either that there are Englishmen who are of wholly British (i.e., Celtic) descent or that there are some of partially British descent. Given, however, that some of the former have "passed" many centuries ago, the existence of the latter can be assumed.

[33] Ibid., p. 69.

[34] Nevertheless, it is a point about the logic of dispositional terms that it is hard (though not impossible) to make sense of applying them to the members of a group if no one in the group ever displays the disposition: see Anthony Appiah, *Assertion and Conditionals* (Cambridge: Cambridge University Press, 1985), chap. 2, sec. 4.

[35] Arnold, *On the Study of Celtic Literature,* pp. 83–84.

[36] Ibid., p. 87.

[37] Ibid., p. 88.

[38] Ibid., pp. 88–89.

[39] Matthew Arnold, *Culture and Anarchy,* ed. Samuel Lipman (New Haven: Yale University Press, 1994), p. 95.

[40] Arnold's fairly benign mobilization of the idea of a Celtic race here contrasts favorably with contemporary and later uses of it in discussions of the Irish character both in England and in the United States. In late nineteenth-century America, the place of the Irish "race" within the broader European races was distinctly below that of the Anglo-Saxon and Nordic "races" and, in some contexts, closer to that of the Negro.

[41] Arnold, *On the Study of Celtic Literature,* p. 113.

[42] Joseph Carroll, *The Cultural Theory of Matthew Arnold* (Berkeley and Los Angeles: University of California Press, 1982).

[43] Perhaps one should also add August Weismann's doctrine of the separation of the somatoplasm and the germplasm as a crucial further bolster, from cytology, to this argument. See Garland Allen, *Life Science in the Twentieth Century,* Cambridge History of Science Series (Cambridge: Cambridge University Press, 1978).

[44] Thomas Carlyle, *Critical and Miscellaneous Essays: Collected and Republished,* vol. 3 (London: Chapman and Hall, 1869), p. 225.

[45] It is important to remember that the correlation remains in most parts of the world quite rough and ready.

[46] Hippolyte A. Taine, *History of English Literature,* trans. H. Van Laun (London: Chatto and Windus, 1897), p. 1.

[47] Ibid., p. 17.

[48] Ibid., p. 37.

[49] Ibid., p. 39.

[50] My account here is based on Coleman, *Biology in the Nineteenth Century.*

[51] See George W. Stocking, *Race, Culture, and Evolution* (New York: Free Press, 1968), p. 46: "Darwin's own position on the question of human races was equally congenial to polygenist thinking. Although he thought it a matter of indifference whether human races were called species or subspecies, he granted that a naturalist confronted for the first time with specimens of Negro and European man would doubtless call them 'good and true species.'"

[52] The reference is to Robert Knox's *The Races of Men* (1850).

[53] Ralph Waldo Emerson, *English Traits* (1876), vol. 5, Concord ed. (Boston: Houghton Mifflin, 1904), pp. 44–45.

[54] "On average there's .2 percent difference in genetic material between any two randomly chosen people on Earth. Of that diversity, 85 percent will be found within any local group of people — say, between you and your neighbor. More than half (9 percent) of the remaining 15 percent will be represented by differences between ethnic and linguistic groups within a given race (for example, between Italians and French). Only 6 percent represents differences between races (for example, between Europeans and Asians). And remember that's 6 percent of .2 percent. In other words, race accounts for only a minuscule .012 percent difference in our genetic material." Paul Hoffman, "The Science of Race," *Discover,* November 1994, p. 4.

[55] See Bernard R. Ortiz de Montellano, "Melanin, Afrocentricity and Pseudoscience," *Yearbook of Physical Anthropology* 36 (1993): 33–57.

[56] Ernst Mayr, *Populations, Species, and Evolution* (Cambridge: Harvard University Press, 1970), p. 300.

[57] James Shreve, "Terms of Estrangement," *Discover,* November 1994, p. 58. All these claims should be interpreted bearing in mind the fact that a "recent study found that in the early 1970s, 34 percent of the people participating in a census survey in two consecutive years changed racial groups from one year to the next."

[58] That is, *not* produced by the fact that people who have certain physical appearances are treated in ways that produce differences.

[59] Since this point is elementary it is perhaps worth explaining. Heritability measures the ratio of variance in a characteristic in an environment that is due to genes to the total variance. The heritability of height in the United States, in India, and in the human population in general is large. There is, too, a significant difference in average height between Indians (in India) and Americans (in America). But this interpopulational difference is almost entirely due to differences in nutrition. High heritability is quite consistent with most of the difference between populations being environmental.

Herrnstein and Murray, authors of *The Bell Curve* (New York: Free Press, 1994), are aware of this fact and so seek to offer some rather unconvincing arguments for the suspicion that interracial average differences are in fact significantly genetic in origin. For arguments that they are *not,* see chap. 6 of Thomas Sowell's *Race and Culture: A World View* (New York: Basic Books, 1994).

[60] This is essentially the point of Jared Diamond's essay "Race without Color," in *Discover,* November 1994, pp. 82–89.

[61] Mayr, *Populations, Species, and Evolution,* p. 82.

[62] I think, however, that this usage carries two risks: first, it gives an ill-deserved legitimacy to ideas that are mistaken, because those who listen in on these conversations may not be aware of the fact that the usage here does not correspond at all to the groups that have mostly been called races in Europe and America; second, because speaking this way, you can actually find yourself relying, illicitly, on those other modes of classification. Still, if you can avoid these two dangers, there's no problem.

QUESTIONS FOR A SECOND READING

1. This is a very reader-friendly text—that is, it goes out of its way to address, engage, anticipate, and entertain its readers. It begins, for example: "Imagine yourself on Angel Island in the 1920s. You are helping an inquisitive immigrant from Canton to fill in an immigration form." This engagement is a *technical* feat; it is a strategy; it is the result of something Appiah does as a writer. It is not just a quality of his character. As evidence of technique, his work suggests strategies that you, too, could adopt and use.

   As you reread, take note of the places in the text where the writer addresses you or, if not through direct address, where the writer seems to have you in mind. When you are done, go back over your notes to see if there are distinct strategies, to see if your examples cluster into types. Give them a name and prepare a list of Appiah's Strategies for Engaging the Reader. This is something you can add to your toolkit.

2. Although this is a reader-friendly text, it is also a learned text. It contains quick references to writers and scholars whom you may not recognize, such as Jorge Garcia, David Wong, Houston Baker, Samuel Delaney, I. A. Richards, Frank Ramsey, and W. V. O. Quine—to list just a few. Using the library as well as the Internet (so that you can put your hands on books and scholarly journals) and, perhaps, working with a group, create brief

glosses on some of these writers and their work. Who are they, and why would they be interesting or important or useful or memorable for Appiah?

The text also contains references to complicated ideas, and it includes technical terms, some of them coined by Appiah himself: "racialism," "semantic deference," "biological concept," to name just a few. Make a list of words or phrases that you feel to be key terms, referencing key ideas for Appiah and for his understanding of race. Working with the text, "Race, Culture, Identity: Misunderstood Connections," and looking to see how the word or phrase is used in context, prepare a list of glosses or translations: "What I think this means for Appiah is . . ." This list may also be prepared with a group.

3. It is common to talk about punctuation in relation to the sentence. Writers use marks of punctuation (commas, dashes, colons, semicolons, parentheses) to organize a sentence and to help readers locate themselves in relation to what they are reading.

   Writers also, however, punctuate essays or chapters — longer units of text. Appiah provides an excellent example. You can notice immediately, for example, how he uses white space and subheadings to organize the essay into sections. Often, however, he also speaks as a writer about the text he is writing (and that you are reading). He does this to remind you (and perhaps himself) where you have been and where you are going in relation to this long piece of writing. Here are some examples:

   > Before I introduce that distinction, however, I want to draw attention to the fact that the issues I am going to be discussing next grow out of a tradition of philosophical reflection that is not directly concerned with ethical matters. (p. 103)
   >
   > Before we turn to historical questions, however, let me ask what route to understanding the race concept is suggested by the referential account of meaning. (p. 106)
   >
   > Let us explore the structure of Jefferson's explanation of why black and white races cannot live together in equality and harmony. (p. 113)

   As you reread, take note of the places in the text where the writer speaks as a writer in order to locate what he is doing in relation to the larger project. When you are done, go back over your notes to see if there are distinct strategies, to see if your examples cluster into types. Give them a name and prepare a list of Appiah's Strategies for Punctuating the Essay. This is something you can add to your toolkit.

   Note: If you worked with the first second-reading question, there will surely be overlap between the items on your first list and the items on this one. One way to engage a reader is to engage her as a reader trying to sort out where she is in a long and complicated text.

4. Central to Appiah's method in this essay is his use of two concepts taken from his reading in the philosophy of language: the "ideational" view of

meaning and the "referential" view of meaning. As an exercise in understanding, prepare a paraphrase, one long paragraph, to explain what Appiah means by one of the two and how it serves his argument. As you do this (and again as an exercise in understanding), include a passage in block quotation — perhaps not as long as Appiah's use of Jefferson's words on pages 110 or 111, but in that format. Choose a passage that you find useful or interesting or perplexing or challenging. Introduce the passage and then follow it with sentences of your own in which you explain (or translate) what Appiah is saying.

5. Footnotes, it is sometimes said, are where the real action is in scholarly writing. Footnotes or endnotes — these are where you find the jokes, the fights, the confessions, the second thoughts, the interesting subtexts to the drama unfolding on stage or in the arena. As you reread, pay particular attention to what is going on in the endnotes. What do they say about Appiah as a scholar and a writer? What is he doing in these additions to the text? What conclusions might you draw — or, better yet, what lesson might you learn — about scholarly writing and scholarly work?

ASSIGNMENTS FOR WRITING

1. What might be the consequences of Appiah's argument? If, as a mental exercise (or because you are convinced), you accept Appiah's conclusion that "American social distinctions cannot be understood in terms of the concept of race," what effects might this have on the way we think, act, speak, and write? These questions most certainly provide the starting point for an essay. If you choose to write this essay, you'll need to bring Appiah's argument in this essay to your readers — smart people but people who have not read "Race, Culture, Identity." (Appiah provides examples of this work when he presented Jefferson and Arnold to you.) And then you will need to turn to the question of consequences.

   You should most certainly speak for yourself. What would the consequences be to your own ways of thinking and acting? In Appiah's spirit, however, you should think of this also as a national and ethical issue. What might be the consequences for public life and public policy if, as a nation, we learned the limits of our understanding of the concept of race?

   To do this work well, to make this an intellectual project and not just a rehearsal of opinion, you will need to think carefully about the example or examples you can bring to the discussion. You will need to think about what you can place on the table next to his Jefferson and his Arnold. Your ideas or arguments are certainly an important part of this essay — what you have to say in response to Appiah. But equally important will be the examples you provide, the ways you can focus attention to racial thinking as it is most crucially and most interestingly present to you and to your generation or your cohort, to the people for whom you feel authorized to speak.

2. Central to Appiah's method in this essay is his use of two concepts taken from his reading in the philosophy of language: the "ideational" view of meaning and the "referential" view of meaning. (The fourth second-reading question can provide a preliminary exercise for this writing assignment.) Write an essay in which you use this method to examine a key word (or phrase) in your discursive world—a word or phrase with consequence (like "race"). You'll need to take some time to present your key term and the complications or controversies it entails. And then you can, following Appiah, work from "ideational" to "referential" as you examine the ways it is (and has been) used and understood.

   Appiah says (and shows) that the referential theory requires an examination of the history of the term and its use. Although you may not have the range of reference evident in Appiah's essay, it is important that you do this work, that you look for examples across time. The range may not be as great (from the eighteenth century on), but it is important that you locate your key term in instances of its use in print as well as in common speech. You can turn to historical dictionaries, like the *Oxford English Dictionary*. You can turn to newspapers, magazines, books, films, and popular culture. This is a research project, in other words.

MAKING CONNECTIONS

1. Appiah's essay could be titled "Against Race." Laura Kipnis's essay could be titled "Love, Culture, Identity." But they are not. Kipnis, as she declares, is writing polemically—against something. Appiah, as he declares, is writing to "explore the concept of race," to think of race in relation to culture and identity. These are different *kinds* of writing.

   Both writers have a strong argument to make, and they state it from the beginning. Both write as though something important were at stake—something they feel personally. So what *are* the key differences—the differences that matter to you as a writer, thinker, and citizen?

   As you reread the two essays, take notes on the differences in style and method and mark passages you might use in an essay. If each of these essays is teaching a lesson to writers, what is it? What is required in a polemic? What do you need to learn to write this way? What is required in an essay like Appiah's? (And what name would you give it?) What do you need to learn to write like Appiah? What are the possibilities for each genre? And finally, why do you suppose that scholarly writing might prefer Appiah's style and method over Kipnis's? And what is your position on this?

2. > First, I want to explain why American social distinctions cannot be understood in terms of the concept of race: the only human race in the United States, I shall argue, is *the* human race. (p. 102)
   >
   > —KWAME ANTHONY APPIAH
   >
   > *Race, Culture, Identity: Misunderstood Connections*

> I would urge blacks living in the United States, and by extension those in other parts of the world, to identify with each other on the basis of their experience of racial oppression and commitment to collectively resist it. From the standpoint of black political solidarity, each should be allowed to interpret "blackness" however he or she sees fit, provided the interpretation does not advocate anything immoral and is consistent with the collective struggle for racial justice. In saying this, I am not suggesting, as some have, that individual blacks should give up their various black identities in favor of an American, a cosmopolitan, or simply a "human" identity. (pp. 606–07)
>
> —TOMMIE SHELBY
> *Social Identity and Group Solidarity*

Kwame Anthony Appiah is a generation ahead of Tommie Shelby, who is a young scholar (*We Who Are Dark* is his first book); Shelby credits Appiah's influence on his thinking and his work—even his decision to turn to philosophy and to pursue an academic career. Appiah is present in Shelby's endnotes. It is useful and appropriate, then, to consider "Social Identity and Group Solidarity" as a response to Appiah, who is represented in *Ways of Reading* through his essay "Race, Culture, Identity: Misunderstood Connections," a chapter from the book *Color Conscious: The Political Morality of Race.*

As you reread them (first Appiah, then Shelby), think about questions of priority and influence and take notes where, for example, Appiah could be said to be addressing the next generation, and where Shelby, whether he acknowledges it or not, is addressing Appiah (and his generation). How would you characterize the exchange: a dialogue? a debate? a clash of wills? a failure to communicate? a classic example of . . . what? And where do you stand in relation to the two—how do their essays address you and your concerns?

3. Both Tommie Shelby's "Social Identity and Group Solidarity" (p. 584) and Kwame Anthony Appiah's "Race, Culture, Identity: Misunderstood Connections" call attention to the difficulties of representing and understanding the experience of those whom we call "African Americans"—the difficulty of telling the story, of getting it right, of recovering experience from the representations of others.

   Read one, or both, of these essays alongside John Edgar Wideman's "Our Time" (p. 657) and write an essay in which you represent these texts as examples of writers working on a problem that has a particular urgency for black Americans. How might you name this problem? How might you illustrate it? What examples are available? What do you find compelling in each of these approaches to the problem? And what might this problem have to do with you—as a writer, a thinker, a citizen?

4. Both Kwame Anthony Appiah's "Race, Culture, Identity: Misunderstood Connections" and David Foster Wallace's "Authority and American Usage" (p. 622) have a distinctive style, voice, and method. A character emerges in each essay, a figure representing one version of a well-schooled, learned, and articulate adult, an intellectual; someone who reads widely, who thinks closely and freshly and methodically about big questions, someone with ideas and with style, someone who is defined in relation to sources, to books and other writers; and someone who takes pains to address his readers. This is an intellectual, then, with a desire to reach others, to engage them, and to bring them into his point of view.

   Write an essay in which you discuss the figure of the intellectual represented in these two essays. You'll need to work closely with a few key and representative moments in the texts. And write an essay in which you assess this figure in relation to your own education — better yet, in relation to the figure you intend to cut as a well-schooled adult, as an intellectual, as a person with ideas and knowledge and something to say.

JOHN
Berger

John Berger (b. 1926), like few other art critics, elicits strong and contradictory reactions to his writing. He has been called (sometimes in the same review) "preposterous" as well as "stimulating," "pompous" yet "exciting." He has been accused of falling prey to "ideological excesses" and of being a victim of his own "lack of objectivity," but he has been praised for his "scrupulous" and "cogent" observations on art and culture. He is one of Europe's most influential Marxist critics, yet his work has been heralded and damned by leftists and conservatives alike. Although Berger's work speaks powerfully, its tone is quiet, thoughtful, measured. According to the poet and critic Peter Schjeldahl, "The most mysterious element in Mr. Berger's criticism has always been the personality of the critic himself, a man of strenuous conviction so loath to bully that even his most provocative arguments sit feather-light on the mind."

The first selection is Chapter 1 from *Ways of Seeing*, a book which began as a series on BBC television. In fact, the show was a forerunner of those encyclopedic television series later popular on public television stations in the United States: *Civilization, The Ascent of Man, Cosmos, The Civil War*. Berger's show was less glittery and ambitious, but in its way it was more serious in its claims to be educational. As you watched the screen, you saw a series of images (like those in the following text). These were sometimes presented with commentary, but sometimes in silence, so that you constantly saw one image in the context of another—for example, classic presentations of women in oil paintings interspersed with images of women from contemporary art, advertising, movies, and "men's magazines." The goal of the exercise, according to Berger, was to "start a process of questioning," to focus his viewer's attention not on a single painting in isolation but on "ways of seeing" in general, on the ways we have learned to look at and understand the images that surround us, and on the culture that teaches us to see things as we do. The method of *Ways of Seeing*, a book of art history, was used by Berger in another book, *A Seventh Man*, to document the situation of the migrant worker in Europe.

After the chapter from *Ways of Seeing*, we have added two brief passages from a beautiful, slight, and quite compelling book by Berger, *And Our Faces, My Heart, Brief as Photos*. This book is both a meditation on time and space and a long love letter (if you can imagine such a combination!). At several points in the book, Berger turns his (and his reader's) attention to paintings. We have included two instances, his descriptions of Rembrandt's *Woman in Bed* and Caravaggio's *The Calling of St. Matthew* (and we have included reproductions of the paintings). We offer these as supplements to *Ways of Seeing*, as additional examples of how a writer turns images into words and brings the present to the past.

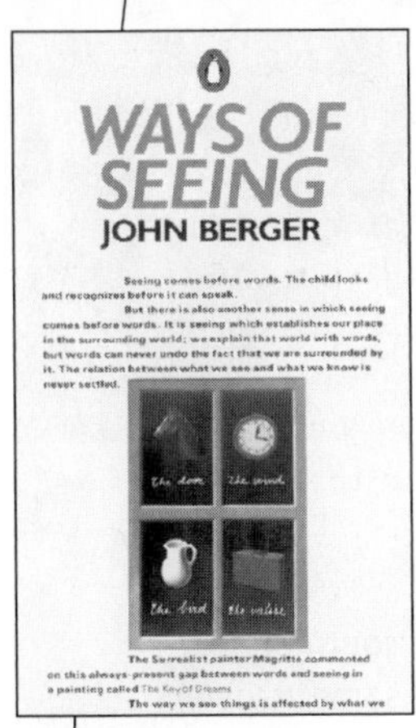

Berger has written poems, novels, essays, and film scripts, including *The Success and Failure of Picasso* (1965), *A Fortunate Man* (1967), *G.* (1971), and *About Looking* (1980). He lived and worked in England for years, but he currently lives in Quincy, a small peasant village in Haute-Savoie, France, where he wrote, over the course of several years, a trilogy of books on peasant life, titled *Into Their Labours*. The first book in the series, *Pig Earth* (1979), is a collection of essays, poems, and stories set in Haute-Savoie. The second, *Once in Europa* (1987), consists of five peasant tales that take love as their subject. The third and final book in the trilogy, *Lilac and Flag: An Old Wives' Tale of the City* (1990), is a novel about the migration of peasants to the city. His most recent books are *Photocopies* (1996), a collection of short stories; *King: A Street Story* (1999), a novel; *I Send You This Cadmium Red: A Correspondence between John Berger and John Christie* (2000); two essay collections, *The Shape of the Pocket* (2001) and *Selected Essays* (2001); *Here Is Where We Meet: A Fiction* (2005), a series of autobiographical vignettes; *Hold Everything Dear: Dispatches on Survival and Resistance* (2007), a meditation on political resistance; and *About Looking* (2009), the follow-up to *Ways of Seeing*.

Ways of Seeing

Seeing comes before words. The child looks and recognizes before it can speak.

But there is also another sense in which seeing comes before words. It is seeing which establishes our place in the surrounding world; we explain that world with words, but words can never undo the fact that we are surrounded by it. The relation between what we see and what we know is never settled. Each evening we *see* the sun set. We *know* that the earth is turning away from it. Yet the knowledge, the explanation, never quite fits the sight. The Surrealist painter Magritte commented on this always-present gap between words and seeing in a painting called *The Key of Dreams*.

The way we see things is affected by what we know or what we believe. In the Middle Ages when men believed in the physical existence of Hell the sight of fire must have meant something different from what it means today. Nevertheless their idea of Hell owed a lot to the sight of fire consuming and the ashes remaining — as well as to their experience of the pain of burns.

When in love, the sight of the beloved has a completeness which no words and no embrace can match: a completeness which only the act of making love can temporarily accommodate.

Yet this seeing which comes before words, and can never be quite covered by them, is not a question of mechanically reacting to stimuli. (It can only be thought of in this way if one isolates the small part of the process which concerns the eye's retina.) We only see what we look at. To look is an act of choice. As a result of this act, what we see is brought within our reach — though not necessarily within arm's reach. To touch something is to situate oneself in relation to it. (Close your eyes, move round the room and notice how the faculty of touch is like a static, limited form of sight.) We never look at just one thing; we are always looking at the relation between things and ourselves. Our vision is continually active, continually

The Key of Dreams by Magritte [1898–1967].

moving, continually holding things in a circle around itself, constituting what is present to us as we are.

Soon after we can see, we are aware that we can also be seen. The eye of the other combines with our own eye to make it fully credible that we are part of the visible world.

If we accept that we can see that hill over there, we propose that from that hill we can be seen. The reciprocal nature of vision is more fundamental than that of spoken dialogue. And often dialogue is an attempt to verbalize this — an attempt to explain how, either metaphorically or literally, "you see things," and an attempt to discover how "he sees things."

In the sense in which we use the word in this book, all images are man-made [see below]. An image is a sight which has been recreated or reproduced. It is an appearance, or a set of appearances, which has been detached from the place and time in which it first made its appearance and preserved — for a few moments or a few centuries. Every image embodies a way of seeing. Even a photograph. For photographs are not, as is often assumed, a mechanical record. Every time we look at a photograph, we are aware, however slightly, of the photographer selecting that sight from an infinity of other possible sights. This is true even in the most casual family snapshot. The photographer's way of seeing is reflected in his choice of subject. The painter's way of seeing is reconstituted by the marks he makes on the canvas or paper. Yet, although every image embodies a way of seeing, our perception or appreciation of an image depends also upon our own way of seeing. (It may be, for example, that Sheila is one figure among twenty; but for our own reasons she is the one we have eyes for.)

EVERY IMAGE EMBODIES A WAY OF SEEING. EVEN A PHOTOGRAPH.

Images were first made to conjure up the appearance of something that was absent. Gradually it became evident that an image could outlast what it represented; it then showed how something or somebody had once looked — and thus by implication how the subject had once been seen by other people. Later still the specific vision of the image-maker was also recognized as part of the record. An image became a record of how X had seen Y. This was the result of an increasing consciousness of individuality, accompanying an increasing awareness of history. It would be rash to try to date this last development precisely. But certainly in Europe such consciousness has existed since the beginning of the Renaissance.

No other kind of relic or text from the past can offer such a direct testimony about the world which surrounded other people at other times. In this respect images are more precise and richer than literature. To say this is not to deny the expressive or imaginative quality of art, treating it as mere documentary evidence; the more imaginative the work, the more profoundly it allows us to share the artist's experience of the visible.

Yet when an image is presented as a work of art, the way people look at it is affected by a whole series of learned assumptions about art. Assumptions concerning:

Beauty
Truth
Genius
Civilization
Form
Status
Taste, etc.

Many of these assumptions no longer accord with the world as it is. (The world-as-it-is is more than pure objective fact, it includes consciousness.) Out of true with the present, these assumptions obscure the past. They

Regents of the Old Men's Alms House by Hals [1580–1666].

Regentesses of the Old Men's Alms House by Hals [1580–1666].

mystify rather than clarify. The past is never there waiting to be discovered, to be recognized for exactly what it is. History always constitutes the relation between a present and its past. Consequently fear of the present leads to mystification of the past. The past is not for living in; it is a well of conclusions from which we draw in order to act. Cultural mystification of the past entails a double loss. Works of art are made unnecessarily remote. And the past offers us fewer conclusions to complete in action.

When we "see" a landscape, we situate ourselves in it. If we "saw" the art of the past, we would situate ourselves in history. When we are prevented from seeing it, we are being deprived of the history which belongs to us. Who benefits from this deprivation? In the end, the art of the past is being mystified because a privileged minority is striving to invent a history which can retrospectively justify the role of the ruling classes, and such a justification can no longer make sense in modern terms. And so, inevitably, it mystifies.

Let us consider a typical example of such mystification. A two-volume study was recently published on Frans Hals.[1] It is the authoritative work to date on this painter. As a book of specialized art history it is no better and no worse than the average.

The last two great paintings by Frans Hals [pp. 143, 144] portray the Governors and the Governesses of an Alms House for old paupers in the Dutch seventeenth-century city of Haarlem. They were officially commissioned portraits. Hals, an old man of over eighty, was destitute. Most of his life he had been in debt. During the winter of 1664, the year he began painting these pictures, he obtained three loads of peat on public charity, otherwise he would have frozen to death. Those who now sat for him were administrators of such public charity.

The author records these facts and then explicitly says that it would be incorrect to read into the paintings any criticism of the sitters. There is no evidence, he says, that Hals painted them in a spirit of bitterness. The author considers them, however, remarkable works of art and explains why. Here he writes of the Regentesses:

> Each woman speaks to us of the human condition with equal importance. Each woman stands out with equal clarity against the *enormous* dark surface, yet they are linked by a firm rhythmical arrangement and the subdued diagonal pattern formed by their heads and hands. Subtle modulations of the *deep*, glowing blacks contribute to the *harmonious fusion* of the whole and form an *unforgettable contrast* with the *powerful* whites and vivid flesh tones where the detached strokes reach *a peak of breadth and strength*. [Berger's italics]

The compositional unity of a painting contributes fundamentally to the power of its image. It is reasonable to consider a painting's composition. But here the composition is written about as though it were in itself the emotional charge of the painting. Terms like *harmonious fusion, unforgettable contrast*, reaching *a peak of breadth and strength* transfer the emotion provoked by the image from the plane of lived experience, to that of disinterested "art appreciation." All conflict disappears. One is left with the unchanging "human condition," and the painting considered as a marvellously made object.

Very little is known about Hals or the Regents who commissioned him. It is not possible to produce circumstantial evidence to establish what their relations were. But there is the evidence of the paintings themselves: the evidence of a group of men and a group of women as seen by another man, the painter. Study this evidence and judge for yourself.

The art historian fears such direct judgment:

> As in so many other pictures by Hals, the penetrating characterizations almost seduce us into believing that we know the personality traits and even the habits of the men and women portrayed.

What is this "seduction" he writes of? It is nothing less than the paintings working upon us. They work upon us because we accept the way Hals saw his sitters. We do not accept this innocently. We accept it in so far as it corresponds to our own observation of people, gestures, faces, institutions. This is possible because we still live in a society of comparable social relations and moral values. And it is precisely this which gives the paintings their psychological and social urgency. It is this — not the painter's skill as a "seducer" — which convinces us that we *can* know the people portrayed.

The author continues:

> In the case of some critics the seduction has been a total success. It has, for example, been asserted that the Regent in the tipped slouch hat, which hardly covers any of his long, lank hair, and whose curiously set eyes do not focus, was shown in a drunken state. [below]

This, he suggests, is a libel. He argues that it was a fashion at that time to wear hats on the side of the head. He cites medical opinion to prove that the Regent's expression could well be the result of a facial paralysis. He insists that the painting would have been unacceptable to the Regents if one of them had been portrayed drunk. One might go on discussing each of these points for pages. (Men in seventeenth-century Holland wore their hats on the side of their heads in order to be thought of as adventurous and pleasure-loving. Heavy drinking was an approved practice. Etcetera.) But such a discussion would take us even farther away from the only confrontation which matters and which the author is determined to evade.

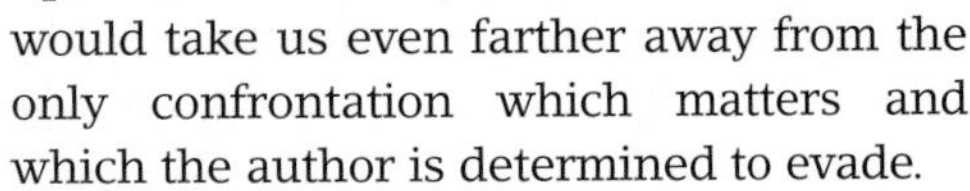

In this confrontation the Regents and Regentesses stare at Hals, a destitute old painter who has lost his reputation and lives off public charity; he examines them through the eyes of a pauper who must nevertheless try to be objective; i.e., must try to surmount the way he sees as a pauper. This is the drama of these paintings. A drama of an "unforgettable contrast."

Mystification has little to do with the vocabulary used. Mystification is the process of explaining away what might otherwise be evident. Hals was the first portraitist to paint the new characters and expressions created by capitalism. He did in pictorial terms what Balzac did two centuries later in literature. Yet the author of the authoritative work on these paintings sums up the artist's achievement by referring to

> Hals's unwavering commitment to his personal vision, which enriches our consciousness of our fellow men and heightens our awe for the ever-increasing power of the mighty impulses that enabled him to give us a close view of life's vital forces.

That is mystification.

In order to avoid mystifying the past (which can equally well suffer pseudo-Marxist mystification) let us now examine the particular relation which now exists, so far as pictorial images are concerned, between the present and the past. If we can see the present clearly enough, we shall ask the right questions of the past.

Today we see the art of the past as nobody saw it before. We actually perceive it in a different way.

This difference can be illustrated in terms of what was thought of as perspective. The convention of perspective, which is unique to European art and which was first established in the early Renaissance, centers everything on the eye of the beholder. It is like a beam from a lighthouse — only instead of light traveling outwards, appearances travel in. The conventions called those appearances *reality*. Perspective makes the single eye the center of the visible world. Everything converges on to the eye as to the vanishing point of infinity. The visible world is arranged for the spectator as the universe was once thought to be arranged for God.

According to the convention of perspective there is no visual reciprocity. There is no need for God to situate himself in relation to others: he is himself the situation. The inherent contradiction in perspective was that it structured all images of reality to address a single spectator who, unlike God, could only be in one place at a time.

After the invention of the camera this contradiction gradually became apparent.

> I'm an eye. A mechanical eye. I, the machine, show you a world the way only I can see it. I free myself for today and forever from human immobility. I'm in constant movement. I approach and pull away from objects. I creep under them. I move alongside a running horse's mouth. I fall and

Still from *Man with a Movie Camera* by Vertov [1895–1954].

rise with the falling and rising bodies. This is I, the machine, maneuvring in the chaotic movements, recording one movement after another in the most complex combinations.

Freed from the boundaries of time and space, I coordinate any and all points of the universe, wherever I want them to be. My way leads towards the creation of a fresh perception of the world. Thus I explain in a new way the world unknown to you.[2]

The camera isolated momentary appearances and in so doing destroyed the idea that images were timeless. Or, to put it another way, the camera showed that the notion of time passing was inseparable from the experience of the visual (except in paintings). What you saw depended upon where you were when. What you saw was relative to your position in time and space. It was no longer possible to imagine everything converging on the human eye as on the vanishing point of infinity.

This is not to say that before the invention of the camera men believed that everyone could see everything. But perspective organized the visual field as though that were indeed the ideal. Every drawing or painting that used perspective proposed to the spectator that he was the unique center of the world. The camera — and more particularly the movie camera — demonstrated that there was no center.

THE INVENTION OF THE CAMERA CHANGED THE WAY MEN SAW.

The invention of the camera changed the way men saw. The visible came to mean something different to them. This was immediately reflected in painting.

For the Impressionists the visible no longer presented itself to man in order to be seen. On the contrary, the visible, in continual flux, became fugitive. For the Cubists the visible was no longer what confronted the single eye, but the totality of possible views taken from points all round the object (or person) being depicted [below].

The invention of the camera also changed the way in which men saw paintings painted long before the camera was invented. Originally paintings were an integral part of the building for which they were

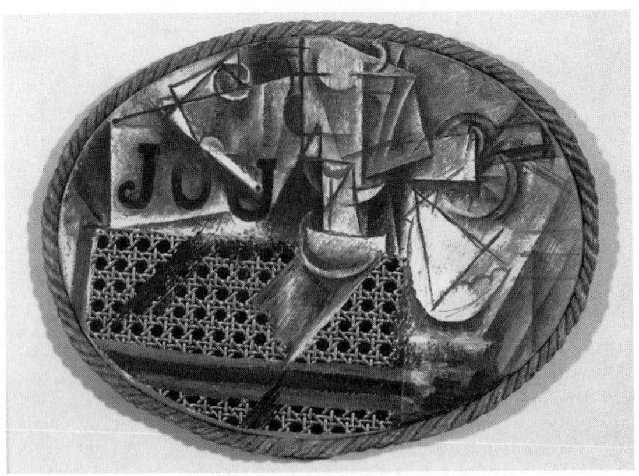

Still Life with Wicker Chair by Picasso [1881–1973].

designed. Sometimes in an early Renaissance church or chapel one has the feeling that the images on the wall are records of the building's interior life, that together they make up the building's memory — so much are they part of the particularity of the building [at right].

Church of St. Francis at Assisi.

The uniqueness of every painting was once part of the uniqueness of the place where it resided. Sometimes the painting was transportable. But it could never be seen in two places at the same time. When the camera reproduces a painting, it destroys the uniqueness of its image. As a result its meaning changes. Or, more exactly, its meaning multiplies and fragments into many meanings.

This is vividly illustrated by what happens when a painting is shown on a television screen. The painting enters each viewer's house. There it is surrounded by his wallpaper, his furniture, his mementos. It enters the atmosphere of his family. It becomes their talking point. It lends its meaning to their meaning. At the same time it enters a million other houses and, in each of them, is seen in a different context. Because of the camera, the painting now travels to the spectator rather than the spectator to the painting. In its travels, its meaning is diversified.

One might argue that all reproductions more or less distort, and that therefore the original painting is still in a sense unique. Here [on the next page] is a reproduction of the *Virgin of the Rocks* by Leonardo da Vinci.

Having seen this reproduction, one can go to the National Gallery to look at the original and there discover what the reproduction lacks. Alternatively one can forget about the quality of the reproduction and simply be reminded, when one sees the original, that it is a famous painting of which somewhere one has already seen a reproduction. But in either case the uniqueness of the original now lies in it being *the original of a reproduction*. It is no longer what its image shows that strikes one as unique; its first meaning is no longer to be found in what it says, but in what it is.

This new status of the original work is the perfectly rational consequence of the new means of reproduction. But it is at this point that a process of mystification again enters. The meaning of the original work no longer lies in what it uniquely says but in what it uniquely is. How is its unique existence evaluated and defined in our present culture? It is defined as an object whose value depends upon its rarity. This market is affirmed and gauged by the

Virgin of the Rocks by Leonardo da Vinci [1452–1519]. Reproduced by courtesy of the Trustees, The National Gallery, London.

price it fetches on the market. But because it is nevertheless "a work of art" — and art is thought to be greater than commerce — its market price is said to be a reflection of its spiritual value. Yet the spiritual value of an object, as distinct from a message or an example, can only be explained in terms of magic or religion. And since in modern society neither of these is a living force, the art object, the "work of art," is enveloped in an atmosphere of entirely bogus religiosity. Works of art are discussed and presented as though they were holy relics: relics which are first and foremost evidence of their own survival. The past in which they originated is studied in order to prove their survival genuine. They are declared art when their line of descent can be certified.

Before the *Virgin of the Rocks* the visitor to the National Gallery would be encouraged by nearly everything he might have heard and read about the painting to feel something like this: "I am in front of it. I can see it. This painting by Leonardo is unlike any other in the world. The National Gallery has the real one. If I look at this painting hard enough, I should somehow be able to feel its authenticity. The *Virgin of the Rocks* by Leonardo da Vinci: it is authentic and therefore it is beautiful."

To dismiss such feelings as naive would be quite wrong. They accord perfectly with the sophisticated culture of art experts for whom the National Gallery catalogue is written. The entry on the *Virgin of the Rocks* is one of the longest entries. It consists of fourteen closely printed pages. They do not deal with the meaning of the image. They deal with who commissioned the painting, legal squabbles, who owned it, its likely date, the families of its owners. Behind this information lie years of research. The aim of the research is to prove beyond any shadow of doubt that the painting is a genuine Leonardo. The secondary aim is to prove that an almost identical painting in the Louvre is a replica of the National Gallery version.

French art historians try to prove the opposite [see p. 151].

The National Gallery sells more reproductions of Leonardo's cartoon of *The Virgin and Child with St. Anne and St. John the Baptist* [on the next page] than any other picture in their collection. A few years ago it was known only to scholars. It became famous because an American wanted to buy it for two and a half million pounds.

Now it hangs in a room by itself. The room is like a chapel. The drawing is behind bullet-proof perspex. It has acquired a new kind of impressiveness.

National Gallery

Virgin of the Rocks by Leonardo da Vinci [1452–1519]. Louvre Museum.

The Virgin and Child with St. Anne and St. John the Baptist by Leonardo da Vinci [1452–1519]. Reproduced by courtesy of the Trustees, The National Gallery, London.

Not because of what it shows — not because of the meaning of its image. It has become impressive, mysterious, because of its market value.

The bogus religiosity which now surrounds original works of art, and which is ultimately dependent upon their market value, has become the substitute for what paintings lost when the camera made them reproducible. Its function is nostalgic. It is the final empty claim for the continuing values of an oligarchic, undemocratic culture. If the image is no longer unique and exclusive, the art object, the thing, must be made mysteriously so.

The majority of the population do not visit art museums. The following table shows how closely an interest in art is related to privileged education.

National proportion of art museum visitors according to level of education: Percentage of each educational category who visit art museums

	Greece	*Poland*	*France*	*Holland*		*Greece*	*Poland*	*France*	*Holland*
With no educational qualification	0.02	0.12	0.15	—	Only secondary education	10.5	10.4	10	20
Only primary education	0.30	1.50	0.45	0.50	Further and higher education	11.5	11.7	12.5	17.3

Source: Pierre Bourdieu and Alain Darbel, *L'Amour de l'art*, Editions de Minuit, Paris 1969, Appendix 5, table 4

The majority take it as axiomatic that the museums are full of holy relics which refer to a mystery which excludes them: the mystery of unaccountable wealth. Or, to put this another way, they believe that original masterpieces belong to the preserve (both materially and spiritually) of the rich. Another table indicates what the idea of an art gallery suggests to each social class.

Of the places listed below which does a museum remind you of most?

	Manual workers	*Skilled and white collar workers*	*Professional and upper managerial*
	%	%	%
Church	66	45	30.5
Library	9	34	28
Lecture hall	—	4	4.5
Department store or entrance hall in public building	—	7	2
Church and library	9	2	4.5
Church and lecture hall	4	2	—
Library and lecture hall	—	—	2
None of these	4	2	19.5
No reply	8	4	9
	100 (n = 53)	100 (n = 98)	100 (n = 99)

Source: as above, Appendix 4, table 8

In the age of pictorial reproduction the meaning of paintings is no longer attached to them; their meaning becomes transmittable: that is to say it becomes information of a sort, and, like all information, it is either put to use or ignored; information carries no special authority within itself. When a painting is put to use, its meaning is either modified or totally changed. One should be quite clear about what this involves. It is not a question of reproduction failing to reproduce certain aspects of an image faithfully; it is a question of reproduction making it possible, even inevitable, that an image will be used for many different purposes and that the reproduced image, unlike an original work, can lend itself to them all. Let us examine some of the ways in which the reproduced image lends itself to such usage.

Venus and Mars by Botticelli [1445–1510]. Reproduced by courtesy of the Trustees, The National Gallery, London.

Reproduction isolates a detail of a painting from the whole. The detail is transformed. An allegorical figure becomes a portrait of a girl [see bottom, p. 153].

When a painting is reproduced by a film camera it inevitably becomes material for the film-maker's argument.

A film which reproduces images of a painting leads the spectator, through the painting, to the film-maker's own conclusions. The painting lends authority to the film-maker. This is because a film unfolds in time and a painting does not. In a film the way one image follows another, their succession, constructs an argument which becomes irreversible. In a painting all its elements are there to be seen simultaneously. The spectator may need time to examine each element of the painting but whenever he reaches a conclusion, the simultaneity of the whole painting is there to reverse or qualify his conclusion. The painting maintains its own authority [below]. Paintings are often reproduced with words around them [see top, p. 156].

Procession to Calvary by Breughel [1525–1569].

This is a landscape of a cornfield with birds flying out of it. Look at it for a moment [below]. Then turn the page [p. 156].

It is hard to define exactly how the words have changed the image but undoubtedly they have. The image now illustrates the sentence.

In this essay each image reproduced has become part of an argument which has little or nothing to do with the painting's original independent meaning. The words have quoted the paintings to confirm their own verbal authority. . . .

Reproduced paintings, like all information, have to hold their own against all the other information being continually transmitted [see bottom, p. 156].

Wheatfield with Crows by Van Gogh [1853–1890].

This is the last picture that Van Gogh painted before he killed himself.

Consequently a reproduction, as well as making its own references to the image of its original, becomes itself the reference point for other images. The meaning of an image is changed according to what one sees immediately beside it or what comes immediately after it. Such authority as it retains, is distributed over the whole context in which it appears [see p. 157].

Because works of art are reproducible, they can, theoretically, be used by anybody. Yet mostly – in art books, magazines, films, or within gilt frames in living-rooms – reproductions are still used to bolster the illusion that nothing has changed, that art, with its unique undiminished authority, justifies most other forms of authority, that art makes inequality seem noble and hierarchies seem thrilling. For example, the whole concept of the National Cultural Heritage exploits the authority of art to glorify the present social system and its priorities.

and the Labour Party

STEPHEN JOHNS

MASS UNEMPLOYMENT is the reality facing the Clyde. This will mean poverty and degradation for thousands of workers and their families.

Going at £1,680,000
'It will fit perfectly over my fireplace...'

British tea planters shot by Khan's troops

Bridge contract

Subject and significance in Titian's Death of Actaeon

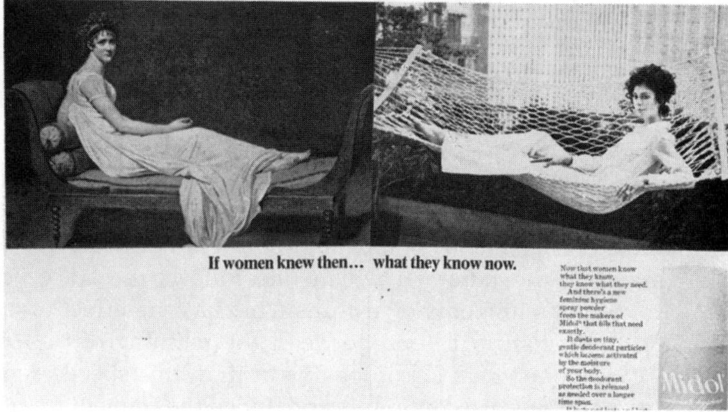

EVERY PACKET CARRIES A GOVERNMENT HEALTH WARNING

If women knew then... what they know now.
Midol

The means of reproduction are used politically and commercially to disguise or deny what their existence makes possible. But sometimes individuals use them differently [p. 158].

Adults and children sometimes have boards in their bedrooms or living-rooms on which they pin pieces of paper: letters, snapshots, reproductions of paintings, newspaper cuttings, original drawings, postcards. On each board all the images belong to the same language and all are more or less equal within it, because they have been chosen in a highly personal way to match and express the experience of the room's inhabitant. Logically, these boards should replace museums.

What are we saying by that? Let us first be sure about what we are not saying.

We are not saying that there is nothing left to experience before original works of art except a sense of awe because they have survived. The way original works of art are usually approached — through museum catalogues, guides, hired cassettes, etc. — is not the only way they might be approached. When the art of the past ceases to be viewed nostalgically, the works will cease to be holy relics — although they will never re-become what they were before the age of reproduction. We are not saying original works of art are now useless.

Original paintings are silent and still in a sense that information never is. Even a reproduction hung on a wall is not comparable in this respect for in the original the silence and stillness permeate the actual material, the paint, in which one follows the traces of the painter's immediate gestures. This has the effect of closing the distance in time between the painting of the picture and one's own act of looking at it. In this special sense all paintings are contemporary. Hence the immediacy of their testimony. Their historical moment is literally there before our eyes. Cézanne made a similar observation from the painter's point of view. "A minute in the world's life passes! To paint it in its reality, and forget everything for that! To become that minute, to be the sensitive plate . . . give the image of what we see, forgetting everything that has appeared before our time. . . ." What we make of that painted moment when it is before our eyes depends upon what we expect of art, and that in turn depends today upon how we have already experienced the meaning of paintings through reproductions.

ORIGINAL PAINTINGS ARE SILENT AND STILL IN A SENSE THAT INFORMATION NEVER IS.

Nor are we saying that all art can be understood spontaneously. We are not claiming that to cut out a magazine reproduction of an archaic Greek head, because it is reminiscent of some personal experience, and to pin it to a board beside other disparate images, is to come to terms with the full meaning of that head.

The idea of innocence faces two ways. By refusing to enter a conspiracy, one remains innocent of that conspiracy. But to remain innocent may also be to remain ignorant. The issue is not between innocence and knowledge (or between the natural and the cultural) but between a total approach to art which attempts to relate it to every aspect of experience and the esoteric approach of a few specialized experts who are the clerks of the nostalgia of a ruling class in decline. (In decline, not before the proletariat, but before the new power of the corporation and the state.) The real question is: to whom does the meaning of the art of the past properly belong? to those who can apply it to their own lives, or to a cultural hierarchy of relic specialists?

The visual arts have always existed within a certain preserve; originally this preserve was magical or sacred. But it was also physical: it was the place, the cave, the building, in which, or for which, the work was made. The experience of art, which at first was the experience of ritual, was set apart from the rest of life — precisely in order to be able to exercise power over it. Later the preserve of art became a social one. It entered the culture of the ruling class, while physically it was set apart and isolated in their palaces and houses. During all this history the authority of art was inseparable from the particular authority of the preserve.

What the modern means of reproduction have done is to destroy the authority of art and to remove it — or, rather, to remove its images which they reproduce — from any preserve. For the first time ever, images of art have become ephemeral, ubiquitous, insubstantial, available, valueless, free. They surround us in the same way as a language surrounds us. They have entered the mainstream of life over which they no longer, in themselves, have power.

Woman Pouring Milk by Vermeer [1632–1675].

Yet very few people are aware of what has happened because the means of reproduction are used nearly all the time to promote the illusion that nothing has changed except that the masses, thanks to reproductions, can now begin to appreciate art as the cultured minority once did. Understandably, the masses remain uninterested and skeptical.

If the new language of images were used differently, it would, through its use, confer a new kind of power. Within it we could begin to define our experiences more precisely in areas where words are inadequate. (Seeing comes before words.) Not only personal experience, but also the essential historical experience of our relation to the past: that is to say the experience of seeking to give meaning to our lives, of trying to understand the history of which we can become the active agents.

The art of the past no longer exists as it once did. Its authority is lost. In its place there is a language of images. What matters now is who uses that language for what purpose. This touches upon questions of copyright for reproduction, the ownership of art presses and publishers, the total policy of public art galleries and museums. As usually presented, these are narrow professional matters. One of the aims of this essay has been to show that what is really at stake is much larger. A people or a class which is cut off from its own past is far less free to choose and to act as a people or class than one that has been able to situate itself in history. This is why — and this is the only reason why — the entire art of the past has now become a political issue.

Many of the ideas in the preceding essay have been taken from another, written over forty years ago by the German critic and philosopher Walter Benjamin.

His essay was entitled The Work of Art in the Age of Mechanical Reproduction. *This essay is available in English in a collection called* Illuminations *(Cape, London, 1970).*

NOTES

[1] Seymour Slive, *Frans Hals* (Phaidon, London). [All notes are Berger's.]

[2] This quotation is from an article written in 1923 by Dziga Vertov, the revolutionary Soviet film director.

On Rembrandt's *Woman in Bed*

It is strange how art historians sometimes pay so much attention, when trying to date certain paintings, to "style," inventories, bills, auction lists, and so little to the painted evidence concerning the model's age. It is as if they do not trust the painter on this point. For example, when they try to date and arrange in chronological order Rembrandt's paintings of Hendrickje Stoffels. No painter was a greater expert about the process of aging, and no painter has left us a more intimate record of the great love of his life. Whatever the documentary conjectures may allow, the paintings make it clear that the love between Hendrickje and the painter lasted for about twenty years, until her death, six years before his.

Woman in Bed by Rembrandt.

She was ten or twelve years younger than he. When she died she was, on the evidence of the paintings, at the very least forty-five, and when he first painted her she could certainly not have been older than twenty-seven. Their daughter, Cornelia, was baptized in 1654. This means that Hendrickje gave birth to their child when she was in her mid-thirties.

The *Woman in Bed* (from Edinburgh) was painted, by my reckoning, a little before or a little after the birth of Cornelia. The historians suggest that it may be a fragment taken from a larger work representing the wedding night of Sarah and Tobias. A biblical subject for Rembrandt was always contemporary. If it is a fragment, it is certain that Rembrandt finished it, and bequeathed it finally to the spectator, as his most intimate painting of the woman he loved.

There are other paintings of Hendrickje. Before the *Bathsheba* in the Louvre, or the *Woman Bathing* in the National Gallery (London), I am wordless. Not because their genius inhibits me, but because the experience from which they derive and which they express — desire experiencing itself as something as old as the known world, tenderness experiencing itself as the end of the world, the eyes' endless rediscovery, as if for the first time, of their love of a familiar body — all this comes before and goes beyond words. No other paintings lead so deftly and powerfully to silence. Yet, in both, Hendrickje is absorbed in her own actions. In the painter's vision of her there is the greatest intimacy, but there is no mutual intimacy between them. They are paintings which speak of his love, not of hers.

In the painting of the *Woman in Bed* there is a complicity between the woman and the painter. This complicity includes both reticence and abandon, day and night. The curtain of the bed, which Hendrickje lifts up with her hand, marks the threshold between daytime and nighttime.

In two years, by daylight, Van Rijn will be declared bankrupt. Ten years before, by daylight, Hendrickje came to work in Van Rijn's house as a nurse for his baby son. In the light of Dutch seventeenth-century accountability and Calvinism, the housekeeper and the painter have distinct and separate responsibilities. Hence their reticence.

At night, they leave their century.

> A necklace hangs loose across her breasts,
> And between them lingers —
>   yet is it a lingering
>   and not an incessant arrival? —
>   the perfume of forever.
>   A perfume as old as sleep,
>   as familiar to the living as to the dead.

Leaning forward from her pillows, she lifts up the curtain with the back of her hand, for its palm, its face, is already welcoming, already making a gesture which is preparatory to the act of touching his head.

She has not yet slept. Her gaze follows him as he approaches. In her face the two of them are reunited. Impossible now to separate the two images: his image of her in bed, as he remembers her: her image of him as she sees him approaching their bed. It is nighttime.

On Caravaggio's *The Calling of St. Matthew*

One night in bed you asked me who was my favorite painter. I hesitated, searching for the least knowing, most truthful answer. Caravaggio. My own reply surprised me. There are nobler painters and painters of greater breadth of vision. There are painters I admire more and who are more admirable. But there is none, so it seems – for the answer came unpremeditated – to whom I feel closer.

The few canvases from my own incomparably modest life as a painter, which I would like to see again, are those I painted in the late 1940s of the streets of Livorno. This city was then war-scarred and poor, and it was there that I first began to learn something about the ingenuity of the dispossessed. It was there too that I discovered that I wanted as little as

The Calling of St. Matthew by Caravaggio.

possible to do in this world with those who wield power. This has turned out to be a lifelong aversion.

The complicity I feel with Caravaggio began, I think, during that time in Livorno. He was the first painter of life as experienced by the popolaccio, the people of the backstreets, les sans-culottes, the lumpenproletariat, the lower orders, those of the lower depths, the underworld. There is no word in any traditional European language which does not either denigrate or patronize the urban poor it is naming. That is power.

Following Caravaggio up to the present day, other painters — Brower, Ostade, Hogarth, Goya, Géricault, Guttuso — have painted pictures of the same social milieu. But all of them — however great — were genre pictures, painted in order to show others how the less fortunate or the more dangerous lived. With Caravaggio, however, it was not a question of presenting scenes but of seeing itself. He does not depict the underworld for others: his vision is one that he shares with it.

In art-historical books Caravaggio is listed as one of the great innovating masters of chiaroscuro and a forerunner of the light and shade later used by Rembrandt and others. His vision can of course be considered art-historically as a step in the evolution of European art. Within such a perspective *a* Caravaggio was almost inevitable, as a link between the high art of the Counter Reformation and the domestic art of the emerging Dutch bourgeoisie, the form of this link being that of a new kind of space, defined by darkness as well as by light. (For Rome and for Amsterdam damnation had become an everyday affair.)

IN ART-HISTORICAL BOOKS CARAVAGGIO IS LISTED AS ONE OF THE GREAT INNOVATING MASTERS OF CHIAROSCURO.

For the Caravaggio who actually existed — for the boy called Michelangelo born in a village near Bergamo, not far from where my friends, the Italian woodcutters, come — light and shade, as he imagined and saw them, had a deeply personal meaning, inextricably entwined with his desires and his instinct for survival. And it is by this, not by any art-historical logic, that his art is linked with the underworld.

His chiaroscuro allowed him to banish daylight. Shadows, he felt, offered shelter as can four walls and a roof. Whatever and wherever he painted he really painted interiors. Sometimes — for *The Flight into Egypt* or one of his beloved John the Baptists — he was obliged to include a landscape in the background. But these landscapes are like rugs or drapes hung up on a line across an inner courtyard. He only felt at home — no, that he felt nowhere — he only felt relatively at ease *inside*.

His darkness smells of candles, overripe melons, damp washing waiting to be hung out the next day: it is the darkness of stairwells, gambling corners, cheap lodgings, sudden encounters. And the promise is not in what will flare against it, but in the darkness itself. The shelter it offers is only relative, for the chiaroscuro reveals violence, suffering, longing, mortality, but at least it reveals them intimately. What has been banished, along with the daylight, are distance and solitude — and both these are feared by the underworld.

Those who live precariously and are habitually crowded together develop a phobia about open spaces which transforms their frustrating lack of space and privacy into something reassuring. He shared those fears.

The Calling of St. Matthew depicts five men sitting round their usual table, telling stories, gossiping, boasting of what one day they will do, counting money. The room is dimly lit. Suddenly the door is flung open. The two figures who enter are still part of the violent noise and light of the invasion. (Berenson wrote that Christ, who is one of the figures, comes in like a police inspector to make an arrest.)

Two of Matthew's colleagues refuse to look up, the other two younger ones stare at the strangers with a mixture of curiosity and condescension. Why is he proposing something so mad? Who's protecting him, the thin one who does all the talking? And Matthew, the tax-collector with a shifty conscience which has made him more unreasonable than most of his colleagues, points at himself and asks: Is it really I who must go? Is it really I who must follow you?

How many thousands of decisions to leave have resembled Christ's hand here! The hand is held out towards the one who has to decide, yet it is ungraspable because so fluid. It orders the way, yet offers no direct support. Matthew will get up and follow the thin stranger from the room, down the narrow streets, out of the district. He will write his gospel, he will travel to Ethiopia and the South Caspian and Persia. Probably he will be murdered.

And behind the drama of this moment of decision in the room at the top of the stairs, there is a window, giving onto the outside world. Traditionally in painting, windows were treated either as sources of light or as frames framing nature or framing an exemplary event outside. Not so this window. No light enters by it. The window is opaque. We see nothing. Mercifully we see nothing because what is outside is bound to be threatening. It is a window through which only the worst news can come.

QUESTIONS FOR A SECOND READING

1. Berger says, "The past is never there waiting to be discovered, to be recognized for exactly what it is. History always constitutes the relation between a present and its past" (p. 144). And he says, "If we 'saw' the art of the past, we would situate ourselves in history. When we are prevented from seeing it, we are being deprived of the history which belongs to us" (p. 144). As you reread this essay, pay particular attention to Berger's uses of the word "history." What does it stand for? What does it have to do with looking at pictures? How might you define the term if your definition were based on its use in this essay?

   You might take Berger's discussion of the Hals paintings as a case in point. What is the relation Berger establishes between the past and the present? If he has not "discovered" the past or recognized it for exactly what it is, what has Berger done in writing about these paintings? What might it mean to say that he has "situated" us in history or has returned a history that belongs to us? And in what way might this be said to be a political act?

2. Berger argues forcefully that the account of the Hals painting offered by the unnamed art historian is a case of "mystification." How would you characterize Berger's account of that same painting? Would you say that he sees what is "really" there? If so, why wasn't it self-evident? Why does it take an expert to see "clearly"? As you read back over the essay, look for passages you could use to characterize the way Berger looks at images or paintings. If, as he says, "The way we see things is affected by what we know or what we believe," what does he know and what does he believe?

ASSIGNMENTS FOR WRITING

1.

> We are not saying that there is nothing left to experience before original works of art except a sense of awe because they have survived. The way original works of art are usually approached — through museum catalogues, guides, hired cassettes, etc. — is not the only way they might be approached. When the art of the past ceases to be viewed nostalgically, the works will cease to be holy relics — although they will never re-become what they were before the age of reproduction. We are not saying original works of art are now useless. (p. 157)

Berger argues that there are barriers to vision, problems in the ways we see or don't see original works of art, problems that can be located in and overcome by strategies of approach.

For Berger, what we lose if we fail to see properly is history: "If we 'saw' the art of the past, we would situate ourselves in history. When we are prevented from seeing it, we are being deprived of the history which belongs to us" (p. 144). It is not hard to figure out who, according to Berger, prevents us from seeing the art of the past. He says it is the ruling class. It is difficult, however, to figure out what he believes gets in the way and what all this has to do with history.

For this assignment, write an essay explaining what, as you read Berger, it is that gets in the way when we look at paintings, and what it is that we might do to overcome the barriers to vision (and to history). You should imagine that you are writing for someone interested in art, perhaps preparing to go to a museum, but someone who has not read Berger's essay. You will, that is, need to be careful in summary and paraphrase.

2. Berger says that the real question is this: "To whom does the meaning of the art of the past properly belong?" Let's say, in Berger's spirit, that it belongs to you. Look again at the painting by Vermeer, *Woman Pouring Milk*, that is included in "Ways of Seeing" (p. 159). Berger includes the painting but without much discussion, as though he were, in fact, leaving it for you.

Write an essay that shows others how they might best understand that painting. You should offer this lesson in the spirit of John Berger. Imagine that you are doing this work for him, perhaps as his apprentice.

3. Original paintings are silent and still in a sense that information never is. Even a reproduction hung on a wall is not comparable in this respect for in the original the silence and stillness permeate the actual material, the paint, in which one follows the traces of the painter's immediate gestures. This has the effect of closing the distance in time between the painting of the picture and one's own act of looking at it. . . . What we make of that painted moment when it is before our eyes depends upon what we expect of art, and that in turn depends today upon how we have already experienced the meaning of paintings through reproductions. (p. 158)

While Berger describes original paintings as silent in this passage, it is clear that these paintings begin to speak if one approaches them properly, if one learns to ask "the right questions of the past." Berger demonstrates one route of approach, for example, in his reading of the Hals paintings, where he asks questions about the people and objects and their relationships to the painter and the viewer. What the paintings might be made to say, however, depends on the viewer's expectations, his sense of the questions that seem appropriate or possible. Berger argues that, because of the way art is currently displayed, discussed, and reproduced, the viewer expects only to be mystified.

For this paper, imagine that you are working against the silence and mystification Berger describes. Go to a museum—or, if that is not possible, to a large-format book of reproductions in the library (or, if that is not possible, to the reproductions on the Web)—and select a painting that seems silent and still, yet invites conversation. Your job is to figure out what sorts of questions to ask, to interrogate the painting, to get it to speak, to engage with the past in some form of dialogue. Write an essay in which you record this process and what you have learned from it. Somewhere in your paper, perhaps at the end, turn back to Berger's essay and speak to it about how this process has or hasn't confirmed what you take to be Berger's expectations.

Note: If possible, include with your essay a reproduction of the painting you select. (Check the postcards at the museum gift shop.) In any event, you want to make sure that you describe the painting in sufficient detail for your readers to follow what you say.

4. In "Ways of Seeing" Berger says,

> If the new language of images were used differently, it would, through its use, confer a new kind of power. Within it we could begin to define our experiences more precisely in areas where words are inadequate. . . . Not only personal experience, but also the essential historical experience of our relation to the past: that is to say the experience of seeking to give meaning to our lives, of trying to understand the history of which we can become the active agents. (p. 160)

As a writer, Berger is someone who uses images (including some of the great paintings of the Western tradition) "to define [experience] more precisely in areas where words are inadequate." In a wonderful book, *And Our Faces, My Heart, Brief as Photos*, a book that is both a meditation on time and space and a long love letter, Berger writes about paintings in order to say what he wants to say to his lover. We have included two examples, descriptions of Rembrandt's *Woman in Bed* and Caravaggio's *The Calling of St. Matthew*.

Read these as examples, as lessons in how and why to look at, to value, to think with, to write about paintings. Then use one or both as a way of thinking about the concluding section of "Ways of Seeing" (pp. 158–60). You can assume that your readers have read Berger's essay but have difficulty grasping what he is saying in that final section, particularly since it is a section that seems to call for action, asking the reader to do something. Of what use might Berger's example be in trying to understand what we might do with and because of paintings?

MAKING CONNECTIONS

1. Walker Percy, in "The Loss of the Creature" (p. 459), like Berger in "Ways of Seeing," talks about the problems people have seeing things. "How can the sightseer recover the Grand Canyon?" Percy asks. "He can recover it in any number of ways, all sharing in common the stratagem of avoiding the approved confrontation of the tour and the Park Service." There is a way in which Berger also tells a story about tourists—tourists going to a museum to see paintings, to buy postcards, gallery guides, reprints, and T-shirts featuring the image of the Mona Lisa. "The way original works of art are usually approached—through museum catalogues, guides, hired cassettes, etc.—is not the only way they might be approached. When the art of the past ceases to be viewed nostalgically, the works will cease to be holy relics—although they will never re-become what they were before the age of reproduction" (p. 157).

   Write an essay in which you describe possible "approaches" to a painting in a museum, approaches that could provide for a better understanding or a more complete "recovery" of that painting than would be possible to a casual viewer, to someone who just wandered in, for example, with no strategy in mind. You should think of your essay as providing real advice to a real person. (You might, if you can, work with a particular painting in a particular museum.) What should that person do? How should that person prepare? What would the consequences be?

   At least one of your approaches should reflect Percy's best advice to a viewer who wanted to develop a successful strategy, and at least one should represent the best you feel Berger would have to offer. When you've finished explaining these approaches, go on in your essay to examine the differences between those you associate with Percy and those you associate with Berger. What are the key differences? And what do they say about the different ways these two thinkers approach the problem of why we do or do not see that which lies before us?

2. Both John Berger in "Ways of Seeing" and Michel Foucault in "Panopticism" (p. 282) discuss what Foucault calls "power relations." Berger claims that "the entire art of the past has now become a political issue," and he makes a case for the evolution of a "new language of images" that could "confer a new kind of power" if people were to understand history in art. Foucault argues that the Panopticon signals an "inspired" change in power relations. "It is," he says, "an important mechanism, for it automatizes and disindividualizes power. Power has its principle not so much in a person as in a certain concerted distribution of bodies, surfaces, lights, gazes; in an arrangement whose internal mechanisms produce the relation in which individuals are caught up" (p. 288).

   Both Berger and Foucault create arguments about power and its methods and goals. As you read through their essays, mark passages you might use to explain how each author thinks about power—where it comes from, who has it, how it works, where you look for it, how you know it when you see it, what it does, where it goes. You should reread the essays as a pair, as part of a single project in which you are seeking to explain theories of power.

   Write an essay in which you present and explain "Ways of Seeing" and "Panopticism" as examples of Berger's and Foucault's theories of power and vision. Both Berger and Foucault are arguing against usual understandings of power and knowledge and history. In this sense, their projects are similar. You should be sure, however, to look for differences as well as similarities.

3. In "Beauty (Re)discovers the Male Body" (p. 189) Susan Bordo refers to John Berger and his work in *Ways of Seeing*, although she refers to a different chapter than the one included here. In general, however, both Berger and Bordo are concerned with how we see and read images; both are concerned to correct the ways images are used and read; both trace the ways images serve the interests of money and power; both are written to teach readers how and why they should pay a different kind of attention to the images around them.

   For this assignment, use Bordo's work to reconsider Berger's. Write an essay in which you consider the two chapters as examples of an ongoing project. Berger's essay precedes Bordo's by about a quarter of a century. If you look closely at one or two of their examples, and if you look at the larger concerns of their arguments, are they saying the same things? doing the same work? If so, how? And why is such work still necessary? If not, how do their projects differ? And how might you explain those differences?

EULA
Biss

Eula Biss (b. 1978) holds a BA from Hampshire College and an MFA from the University of Iowa, both in nonfiction writing, and she is the Artist in Residence at Northwestern University. Biss is one of the important new voices in contemporary nonfiction. Her prose is often formally experimental (as in the essay that follows); as a writer, she takes on difficult subjects: identity, social politics, suffering, and violence. While many writers engage with similar topics, Biss is particularly noted and celebrated for the complex, attentive, and nuanced ways she observes and carefully examines the world around her. A starred review in *Booklist* notes that "Biss calls our attention to things so intrinsic to our lives they have become invisible."

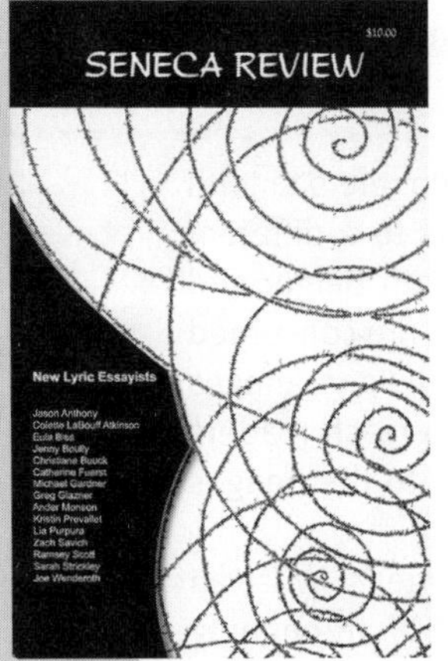

The essay that follows presents pain as one of the invisible things Biss wants her readers to reconsider or redefine. She begins with zero — a concept that, before reading Biss's opening lines, we may not have thought of as a problem. Biss writes, "Zero is a number in the way that Christ was a man." This statement, as with many of Biss's statements, raises more questions than it answers. In fact, as a writer, Biss is most concerned with questions. "Unfortunately, my strength is more in asking questions," Biss tells *Time Out Chicago*. "I would find that great, too, if I were able to come up with a solution, but I tend to generate problems, not fix them."

In addition to "The Pain Scale," Biss has published essays, prose poems, and experimental nonfiction, including two book-length collections: *The Balloonists* (2002) and *Notes from No Man's Land* (2009), a collection of essays that won the Graywolf Nonfiction Prize. She is the founding editor of *Essay Press*, a publisher of innovative creative nonfiction. Her essays have recently appeared in *The Best American Nonrequired Reading* (2009), *The Best Creative Nonfiction* (2007), and the *Touchstone Anthology of Contemporary Nonfiction* (2007), as well as in *The Believer*, *Gulf Coast*, *Columbia*, *Ninth Letter*, the *North American Review*, the *Iowa Review*, the *Seneca Review*, and *Harper's*. "The Pain Scale" appeared in *Harper's Magazine* and *Seneca Review* in 2005.

The Pain Scale

The concept of Christ is considerably older than the concept of zero. Both are problematic — both have their fallacies and their immaculate conceptions. But the problem of zero troubles me significantly more than the problem of Christ.

I am sitting in the exam room of a hospital entertaining the idea that absolutely no pain is not possible. Despite the commercials, I suspect that pain cannot be eliminated. And this may be the fallacy on which we have based all our calculations and all our excesses. All our sins are for zero.

Zero is not a number. Or at least, it does not behave like a number. It does not add, subtract, or multiply like other numbers. Zero is a number in the way that Christ was a man.

Aristotle, for one, did not believe in Zero.

If no pain is possible, then, another question — is no pain desirable? Does the absence of pain equal the absence of everything?

Some very complicated mathematical problems cannot be solved without the concept of zero. But zero makes some very simple problems impossible to solve. For example, the value of zero divided by zero is unknown.

I'm not a mathematician. I'm sitting in a hospital trying to measure my pain on a scale from zero to ten. For this purpose, I need a zero. A scale of any sort needs fixed points.

The upper fixed point on the Fahrenheit scale, ninety-six, is based on a slightly inaccurate measure of normal body temperature. The lower fixed point, zero, is the coldest temperature at which a mixture of salt and water can still remain liquid. I myself am a mixture of salt and water. I strive to remain liquid.

Zero, on the Celsius scale, is the point at which water freezes. And one hundred is the point at which water boils.

But Anders Celsius, who introduced the scale in 1741, originally fixed zero as the point at which water boiled, and one hundred as the point at which water froze. These fixed points were reversed only after his death.

The deepest circle of Dante's *Inferno* does not burn. It is frozen. In his last glimpse of Hell, Dante looks back and sees Satan upside down through the ice.

There is only one fixed point on the Kelvin scale — absolute zero. Absolute zero is 273 degrees Celsius colder than the temperature at which water freezes. There are zeroes beneath zeroes. Absolute zero is the temperature at which molecules and atoms are moving as slowly as possible. But even at absolute zero, their motion does not stop completely. Even the absolute is not absolute. This is comforting, but it does not give me faith in zero.

At night, I ice my pain. My mind descends into a strange sinking calm. Any number multiplied by zero is zero. And so with ice and me. I am nullified. I wake up to melted ice and the warm throb of my pain returning.

EVERY TIME I GO TO THE DOCTOR AND EVERY TIME I VISIT THE PHYSICAL THERAPIST, I AM ASKED TO RATE MY PAIN ON A SCALE FROM ZERO TO TEN.

Grab a chicken by its neck or body — it squawks and flaps and pecks and thrashes like mad. But grab a chicken by its feet and turn it upside down, and it just hangs there blinking in a waking trance. Zeroed. My mother and I hung the chickens like this on the barn door for their necks to be slit. I like to imagine that a chicken at zero feels no pain.

← 1 →

> Major things are wind, evil, a good fighting horse, prepositions, inexhaustible love, the way people choose their king. Minor things include dirt, the names of schools of philosophy, mood and not having a mood, the correct time. There are more major things than minor things overall, yet there are more minor things than I have written here, but it is disheartening to list them. . . .
>
> — ANNE CARSON

My father is a physician. He treats patients with cancer, who often suffer extreme pain. My father raised me to believe that most pain is minor. He was never impressed by my bleeding cuts or even my weeping sores. In retrospect, neither am I.

Every time I go to the doctor and every time I visit the physical therapist, I am asked to rate my pain on a scale from zero to ten. This practice of quantifying pain was introduced by the hospice movement in the 1970s, with the goal of providing better care for patients who did not respond to curative treatment.

My father once told me that an itch is just very mild pain. Both sensations simply signal, he told me, irritated or damaged tissue.

But a nasty itch, I observed, can be much more excruciating than a paper cut, which is also mild pain. Digging at an itch until it bleeds and is transformed into pure pain can bring a kind of relief.

Where does pain worth measuring begin? With poison ivy? With a hang nail? With a stubbed toe? A sore throat? A needle prick? A razor cut?

When I complained of pain as a child, my father would ask, "What kind of pain?" Wearily, he would list for me some of the different kinds of pain, "Burning, stabbing, throbbing, prickling, dull, sharp, deep, shallow . . ."

Hospice nurses are trained to identify five types of pain: physical, emotional, spiritual, social, and financial.

The pain of feeling, the pain of caring, the pain of doubting, the pain of parting, the pain of paying.

Overlooking the pain of longing, the pain of desire, the pain of sore muscles, which I find pleasurable . . .

The pain of learning, and the pain of reading.

The pain of trying.

The pain of living.

A minor pain or a major pain?

There is a mathematical proof that zero equals one. Which, of course, it doesn't.

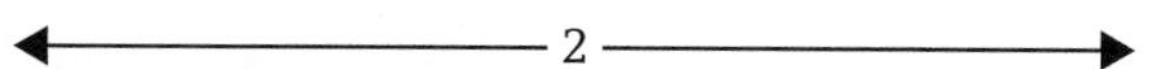

The set of whole numbers is also known as "God's numbers."

The devil is in the fractions.

Although the distance between one and two is finite, it contains infinite fractions. This could also be said of the distance between my mind and my body. My one and my two. My whole and its parts.

The sensations of my own body may be the only subject on which I am qualified to claim expertise. Sad and terrible, then, how little I know. "How do you feel?" the doctor asks, and I cannot answer. Not accurately. "Does this hurt?" he asks. Again, I'm not sure. "Do you have more or less pain than the last time I saw you?" Hard to say. I begin to lie to protect my reputation. I try to act certain.

The physical therapist raises my arm above my head. "Any pain with this?" she asks. Does she mean any pain in addition to the pain I already feel, or does she mean any pain at all? She is annoyed by my question. "Does this cause you pain?" she asks curtly. No. She bends my neck forward, "Any pain with this?" No. "Any pain with this?" No. It feels like a lie every time.

On occasion, an extraordinary pain swells like a wave under the hands of the doctor, or the chiropractor, or the massage therapist, and floods my body. Sometimes I hear my throat make a sound. Sometimes I see spots. I consider this the pain of treatment, and I have come to find it deeply pleasurable. I long for it.

The International Association for the Study of Pain is very clear on this point — pain must be unpleasant. "Experiences which resemble pain but are not unpleasant," reads their definition of pain, "should not be called pain."

In the second circle of Dante's *Inferno*, the adulterous lovers cling to each other, whirling eternally, caught in an endless wind. My next-door neighbor, who loves Chagall, does not think this sounds like Hell. I think it depends on the wind.

Wind, like pain, is difficult to capture. The poor windsock is always striving, and always falling short.

It took sailors more than two hundred years to develop a standardized numerical scale for the measure of wind. The result, the Beaufort scale, provides twelve categories for everything from "Calm" to "Hurricane." The scale offers not just a number, but a term for the wind, a range of speed, and a brief description.

A force 2 wind on the Beaufort scale, for example, is a "Light Breeze" moving between four and seven miles per hour. On land, it is specified as "wind felt on face; leaves rustle; ordinary vanes moved by wind."

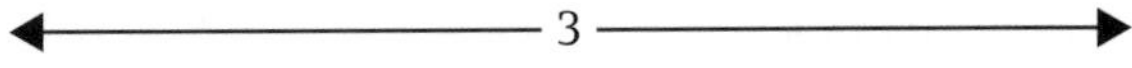

Left alone in the exam room I stare at the pain scale, a simple number line complicated by only two phrases. Under zero: "no pain." Under ten: "the worst pain imaginable."

The worst pain imaginable . . . Stabbed in the eye with a spoon? Whipped with nettles? Buried under an avalanche of sharp rocks? Impaled with hundreds of nails? Dragged over gravel behind a fast truck? Skinned alive?

My father tells me that some things one might expect to be painful are not. I have read that starving to death, at a certain point, is not exactly painful. At times, it may even cause elation. Regardless, it is my sister's worst fear. She would rather die any other way, she tells me.

I do not prefer one death over another. Perhaps this is because I am incapable of imagining the worst pain imaginable. Just as I am incapable of actually understanding calculus, although I could once perform the equations correctly.

Like the advanced math of my distant past, determining the intensity of my own pain is a blind calculation. On my first attempt, I assigned the value of ten to a theoretical experience — burning alive. Then I tried to determine what percentage of the pain of burning alive I was feeling.

I chose 30 percent — three. Which seemed, at the time, quite substantial.

Three. Mail remains unopened. Thoughts are rarely followed to their conclusions. Sitting still becomes unbearable after one hour. Nausea sets in. Grasping at the pain does not bring relief. Quiet desperation descends.

"Three is nothing," my father tells me now. "Three is go home and take two aspirin." It would be helpful, I tell him, if that could be noted on the scale.

The four vital signs used to determine the health of a patient are blood pressure, temperature, breath, and pulse. Recently, it has been suggested that pain be considered a fifth vital sign. But pain presents a unique problem in terms of measurement, and a unique cruelty in terms of suffering — it is entirely subjective.

Assigning a value to my own pain has never ceased to feel like a political act. I am citizen of a country that ranks our comfort above any other concern. People suffer, I know, so that I may eat bananas in February. And then there is history. . . . I struggle to consider my pain in proportion to the pain of a napalmed Vietnamese girl whose skin is slowly melting off as she walks naked in the sun. This exercise itself is painful.

"You are not meant to be rating world suffering," my friend in Honduras advises. "This scale applies only to you and your experience."

At first, this thought is tremendously relieving. It unburdens me of factoring the continent of Africa into my calculations. But the reality that my nerves alone feel my pain is terrifying. I hate the knowledge that I am isolated in this skin — alone with my pain and my own fallibility.

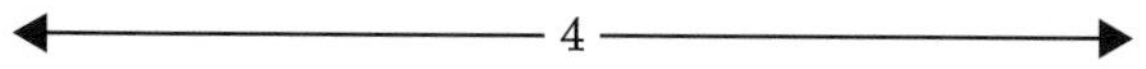

The Wong-Baker Faces scale was developed to help young children rate their pain. It features a smiley face at zero "No Hurt" and a crying face at five "Hurts Worst." In between are a nervous smile, a straight-mouthed stare, a slight grimace, and a deep frown.

The face I remember, always, was on the front page of a local newspaper in an Arizona gas station. The man's face was horrifyingly distorted in an open-mouthed cry of raw pain. His house, the caption explained, had just been destroyed in a wildfire. But the man himself, the article revealed, had not been hurt.

Several studies have suggested that children using the Wong-Baker scale tend to conflate emotional pain and physical pain. A child who is not in physical pain but is very frightened of surgery, for example, might choose the crying face. One researcher observed that "hurting" and "feeling" seemed to be synonymous to some children. I myself am puzzled by the distinction. Both words are used to describe emotions as well as physical sensations, and pain is defined as a "sensory and emotional experience." In an attempt to rate only the physical pain of children, a more emotionally "neutral" scale was developed. The faces on this scale appear alien, and the first four have nearly indistinguishable expressions of blankness followed by a wince and then an open-mouthed shout.

A group of adult patients favored the Wong-Baker scale in a study comparing several different types of pain scales. The patients were asked to identify the easiest scale to use by rating all the scales on a scale from zero, "not easy," to six, "easiest ever seen." The patients were then asked to rate how well the scales represented pain on a scale from zero, "not good," to six, "best ever seen." The patients were not invited to rate the experience of rating.

I stare at a newspaper photo of an Israeli boy with a bloodstained cloth wrapped around his forehead. His face is impassive.

I stare at a newspaper photo of a prisoner standing delicately balanced with electrodes attached to his body, his head covered with a hood.

No face, no pain?

A crying baby, to me, always seems to be in the worst pain imaginable. But when my aunt became a nurse twenty years ago, it was not unusual for surgery to be done on infants without any pain medication. Babies, it was believed, did not have the fully developed nervous systems necessary to feel pain. Medical evidence that infants experience pain in response to anything that would cause an adult pain has only recently emerged.

There is no evidence of pain on my body. No marks. No swelling. No terrible tumor. The X-rays revealed nothing. Two MRIs of my brain and spine revealed nothing. Nothing was infected and festering, as I had suspected and feared. There was no ghastly huge white cloud on the film. There was nothing to illustrate my pain except a number, which I was told to choose from between zero and ten. My proof.

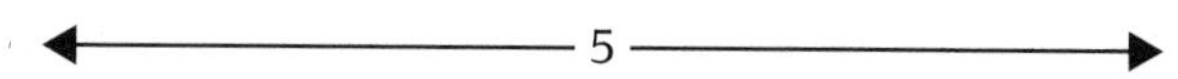

"The problem with scales from zero to ten," my father tells me, "is the tyranny of the mean."

Overwhelmingly, patients tend to rate their pain as a five, unless they are in excruciating pain. At best, this renders the scale far less sensitive to gradations in pain. At worst, it renders the scale useless.

I understand the desire to be average only when I am in pain. To be normal is to be okay in a fundamental way — to be chosen numerically by God.

When I could no longer sleep at night because of my pain, my father reminded me that a great many people suffer from both insomnia and pain. "In fact," he told me, "neck and back pain is so common that it is a cliché — a pain in the neck!"

The fact that 50 million Americans suffer from chronic pain does not comfort me. Rather, it confounds me. "This is not normal," I keep thinking. A thought invariably followed by a doubt, "Is this normal?"

THERE WAS NOTHING TO ILLUSTRATE MY PAIN EXCEPT A NUMBER, WHICH I WAS TOLD TO CHOOSE FROM BETWEEN ZERO AND TEN. MY PROOF.

The distinction between test results that are normal or abnormal is often determined by how far the results deviate from the mean. My X-rays did not reveal a cause for my pain, but they did reveal an abnormality. "See this," the doctor pointed to the string of vertebrae hanging down from the base of my skull like a loose line finding plumb. "Your spine," he told me, "is abnormally straight."

I live in Middle America. I am of average height, although I have always thought of myself as short. I am of average weight, although I tend to believe I am oddly shaped. Although I try to hide it, I have long straight blond hair, like most of the women in this town.

Despite my efforts to ignore it and to despise it, I am still susceptible to the mean — a magnet that pulls even flesh and bone. For some time I entertained the idea that my spine might have been straightened by my long-held misconception that normal spines were perfectly straight. Unknowingly, I may have been striving for a straight spine, and perhaps I had managed to disfigure my body by sitting too straight for too many years. "Unlikely," the doctor told me.

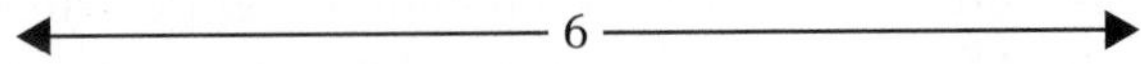
6

A force 6 wind on the Beaufort scale, a "Strong Breeze," is characterized by "large branches in motion; telegraph wires whistle; umbrellas used with difficulty."

Over a century before preliminary scales were developed to quantify the wind, serious efforts were made to produce an accurate map of Hell. Infernal cartography was considered an important undertaking for the architects and mathematicians of the Renaissance, who based their calculations on the distances and proportions described by Dante. The exact depth and circumference of Hell inspired intense debates, despite the fact that all calculations, no matter how sophisticated, were based on a work of fiction.

Galileo Galilei delivered extensive lectures on the mapping of Hell. He applied recent advances in geometry to determine the exact location of the entrance to the underworld and then figured the dimensions that would be necessary to maintain the structural integrity of Hell's interior.

It was the age of the golden rectangle — the divine proportion. Mathematics revealed God's plan. But the very use of numbers required a religious faith, because one could drop off the edge of the earth at any point. The boundaries of the maps at that time faded into oceans full of monsters.

Imagination is treacherous. It erases distant continents, it builds a Hell so real that the ceiling is vulnerable to collapse. To be safe, I think I should only map my pain in proportion to pain I have already felt.

But my nerves have short memories. My mind remembers crashing my bicycle as a teenager, but my body does not. I cannot seem to conjure the sensation of lost skin without actually losing skin. My nerves cannot, or will not, imagine past pain — this, I think, is for the best. Nerves simply register, they do not invent.

After a year of pain, I realized that I could no longer remember what it felt like not to be in pain. I was left anchorless. I tended to think of the time before the pain as easier and brighter, but I began to suspect myself of fantasy and nostalgia.

Although I cannot ask my body to remember feeling pain it does not feel, and I cannot ask it to remember not feeling pain it does feel, I have found that I can ask my body to imagine the pain it feels as something else. For example, with some effort I can imagine the sensation of pain as heat.

Perhaps, with a stronger mind, I could imagine the heat as warmth, and then the warmth as nothing at all.

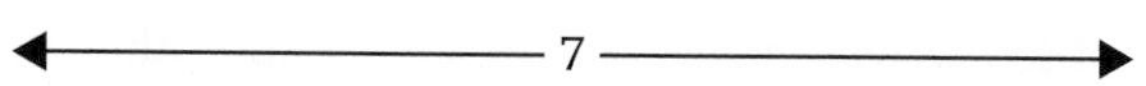
7

I accidentally left a burner on the stove going for two and a half days — a small blue flame, burning, burning, burning . . .

The duration terrified me. How incredibly dangerous, so many hours of fire.

I would happily cut off a finger at this point if I could trade the pain of that cut for the endless pain I have now.

When I cry from it, I cry over the idea of it lasting forever, not over the pain itself. The psychologist, in her rational way, suggests that I do not let myself imagine it lasting forever. "Choose an amount of time that you know you can endure," she suggests, "and then challenge yourself only to make it through that time." I make it through the night, and then sob through half the morning.

The pain scale measures only the intensity of pain, not the duration. This may be its greatest flaw. A measure of pain, I believe, requires at least two dimensions. The suffering of Hell is terrifying not because of any specific torture, but because it is eternal.

The square root of seven results in a decimal that repeats randomly into infinity. The exact figure cannot be known, only a close approximation. Rounding a number to the nearest significant figure is a tool designed for the purpose of making measurements. The practicality of rounding is something my mind can fully embrace. No measurement is ever exact, of course.

Seven is the largest prime number between zero and ten. Out of all the numbers, the very largest primes are unknown. Still, every year, the largest known prime is larger. Euclid proved the number of primes to be infinite, but the infinity of primes is slightly smaller than the infinity of the rest of the numbers. It is here, exactly at this point, that my ability to comprehend begins to fail.

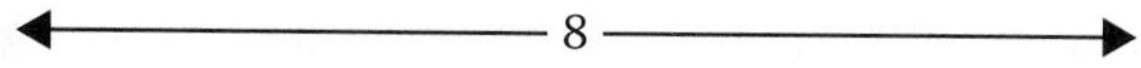
8

Although all the numbers follow each other in a predictable line, many unknown quantities exist.

I do not know how long I have been clenching my teeth when I notice that I am clenching my teeth. My mind, apparently, has not been with my body. I wonder why, when I most want to, I cannot seem to keep my mind from my body.

I no longer know who I am, or if I am in charge of myself.

Experts do not know why some pain resolves and other pain becomes chronic. One theory is that the body begins to react to its own reaction, trapping itself in a cycle of its own pain response. This can go on indefinitely, twisting like the figure eight of infinity.

My father tells me that when he broke his collarbone it didn't hurt. I would like to believe this, but I am suspicious of my father's assessment of his own pain.

The problem of pain is that I cannot feel my father's, and he cannot feel mine. This, I suppose, is also the essential mercy of pain.

Several recent studies have suggested that women feel pain differently than men. Further studies have suggested that pain medications act differently on women than they do on men. I am suspicious of these studies, so favored by *Newsweek*, and so heaped upon waiting-room tables. I dislike the idea that our flesh is so essentially unique that it does not even register pain as a man's flesh does — a fact that renders our bodies, again, objects of supreme mystery.

But I am comforted, oddly, by the possibility that you cannot compare my pain to yours. And, for that reason, cannot prove it insignificant.

The medical definition of pain specifies the "presence or potential of tissue damage." Pain that does not signal tissue damage is not, technically, pain.

"This is a pathology," the doctor assured me when he informed me that there was no definitive cause of my pain, no effective treatment for it, and very probably no end to it. "This is not in your head."

It would not have occurred to me to think that I was imagining the pain. But the longer the pain persisted, and the harder it became for me to imagine what it was like not to be in pain, the more seriously I considered the disturbing possibility that I was not, in fact, in pain.

Another theory of chronic pain is that it is a faulty message sent by malfunctioning nerves. "For example," the Mayo Clinic suggests, "your pain could be similar to the phantom pain some amputees feel in their amputated limbs."

I walked out of a lecture on chronic pain after too many repetitions of the phrase, "We have reason to believe that you are in pain, even if there is no physical evidence of your pain." I had not realized that the fact that I believed myself to be in pain was not reason enough.

We have reason to believe in infinity, but everything we know ends.

9

"I have a very high pain threshold," my mother mentions casually. This is undoubtedly true.

I stand by uselessly and cover my ears as my mother, a very small woman, lifts the blunt end of a pick axe over her head and slams it down on a metal pipe she is driving into the frozen ground. Any portrait of my mother should include a blue-black fingernail.

"I breathe, I have a heartbeat, I have pain . . ." I repeat to myself as I lie in bed at night. I am striving to adopt the pain as a vital sensation. My mother, I know, has already mastered this exercise.

Her existence, like my father's, pains me. This is the upper fixed point of love.

Once, for a study of chronic pain, I was asked to rate not just my pain but also my suffering. I rated my pain as a three. Having been sleepless for nearly a week, I rated my suffering as a seven.

"Pain is the hurt, either physical or emotional, that we experience," writes the Reverend James Chase. "Suffering is the story we tell ourselves of our pain."

Yes, suffering is the story we tell ourselves.

"At the moment we are devoid of any standard criteria as to what constitutes suffering," Reverend Chase writes in his paper on genetic therapy, which is more a meditation on suffering. "Since we do not have agreed-upon criteria, it would be negligent to make decisions for others regarding suffering. We might be able to answer this for ourselves, but not for others. . . .

"If we come to the point where we have no place for suffering, to what lengths will we go to eradicate it? Will we go so far as to inflict suffering to end it?"

Christianity is not mine. I do not know it and I cannot claim it. But I've seen the sacred heart ringed with thorns, the gaping wound in Christ's side, the weeping virgin, the blood, the nails, the cross to bear. . . . Pain is holy, I understand. Suffering is divine.

In my worst pain, I can remember thinking, "This is not beautiful." I can remember being disgusted by the very idea.

But in my worst pain, I also found myself secretly cherishing the phrase, "This too shall pass." The longer the pain lasted, the more beautiful and impossible and absolutely holy this phrase became.

← 10
The Worst Pain Imaginable

Through a failure of my imagination, or of myself, I have discovered that the pain I am in is always the worst pain imaginable.

But I would like to believe that there is an upper limit to pain. That there is a maximum intensity nerves can register.

There is no tenth circle in Dante's Hell.

The digit ten depends on the digit zero, in our current number system. In 1994 Robert Forslund developed an Alternative Number System. "This system," he wrote with triumph, "eliminates the need for the digit zero, and hence all digits behave the same."

In the Alternate Number System, the tenth digit is represented by the character A. Counting begins at one: 1, 2, 3, 4, 5, 6, 7, 8, 9, A, 11, 12 . . . 18, 19, 1A, 21, 22 . . . 28, 29, 2A . . . 98, 99, 9A, A1, A2, A3, A4, A5, A6, A7, A8, A9, AA, 111, 112 . . .

"One of the functions of the pain scale," my father explains, "is to protect doctors — to spare them some emotional pain. Hearing someone describe their pain as a ten is much easier than hearing them describe it as a hot poker driven through their eyeball into their brain."

A better scale, my father thinks, might rate what patients would be willing to do to relieve their pain. "Would you," he suggests, "visit five specialists and take three prescription narcotics?" I laugh because I have done just that. "Would you," I offer, "give up a limb?" I would not. "Would you surrender your sense of sight for the next ten years?" my father asks. I would not. "Would you accept a shorter life span?" I might. We are laughing, having fun with this game. But later, reading statements collected by the American Pain Foundation, I am alarmed by the number of references to suicide.

". . . constant muscle aches, spasms, sleeplessness, pain, can't focus . . . must be depression . . . two suicide attempts later, electroshock therapy and locked-down wards. . . ."

The description of hurricane-force winds on the Beaufort scale is simply "devastation occurs."

Bringing us, of course, back to zero.

QUESTIONS FOR A SECOND READING

1. This essay, "The Pain Scale," has very distinctive style. As you reread, think about the style of this essay as evidence of technique, as an example of something Biss set out to do with the conventions of prose when she sat down to write. (We are asking you, then, to think about style as achievement and *not* as something that just comes naturally. Not all of Biss's essays, for example, have the look, sound, or feel of this one.)

   What do you take to be the distinctive features of this style? What is she doing when she does what she does? What is she *not* doing? What does prose like this do for a reader? What does it do for a writer?

2. This question follows on Question 1, above. Write a paragraph (or cluster of paragraphs) in the style of "The Pain Scale." Same shape. Same number of words. You supply the content. When you are done, write a brief paragraph on what this prose *does*. How does it define the writer? The reader? The exchange of thought or feeling between them? If you had to make the case that everyone should learn to write like this, what might you say?

3. Let's say that pain is the "nominal" subject of this essay, and the nominal subject allows Biss a way of writing about other things as well. As you reread the essay, think about the "aboutness" of the piece. If this essay is an exercise in thought and/or argument, what are its subjects? Make a list of them, and make it as long as you can while still being attentive to the prose on the page. You should be prepared to defend any of the items on the list by turning to a passage for illustration.

4. Biss's essay, "The Pain Scale," raises the question of what it means to measure things. What is a scale? What does it mean to measure something? To define? To organize? To rank or rate? On a common-sense level, these terms are easy to use and easy to understand, yet Biss wants to argue that such simplicity is deceiving.

   The *Oxford English Dictionary* provides not only definitions of words, but a history of their use. Look up at least two of these terms (or terms that seem crucial in your reading of "The Pain Scale"). Read the various definitions, but also read through the etymology, date chart, and the selected quotations to gain a sense of how these words have been used across time.

ASSIGNMENTS FOR WRITING

1. In the third Second Reading question above, we invite you to think about pain as the "nominal" subject of this essay, "The Pain Scale." And we invite you to think of the essay as having multiple subjects; it is a way of thinking about several things at once and not just one thing, or one thing at a time.

With the work you've done as a reader, you've become something of an expert on this essay. Write an essay of your own that teaches someone to read "The Pain Scale" as you do, someone who will be coming to the essay, and to Eula Biss, for the first time. You'll need to be generous in your use of examples. (And you'll need to be skillful in the use of block quotation.) You'll need to think not only about your interest in the essay but in how and why someone else might share that interest.

2. Biss writes, "the sensations of my own body may be the only subject on which I am qualified to claim expertise. Sad and terrible, then, how little I know" (p. 173). Her essay points to the slippage between feeling and knowing (or speaking or writing), between public knowledge and private experience, between one's self and the world. Consider, for example, her struggles to rate her pain proportionally to others':

> "You are not meant to be rating world suffering," my friend in Honduras advises. "This scale applies only to you and your experience."
>
> At first, this thought is tremendously relieving. It unburdens me of factoring the continent of Africa into my calculations. But the reality that my nerves alone feel my pain is terrifying. I hate the knowledge that I am isolated in this skin — alone with my pain and my own fallibility. (p. 175)

Write an essay in which you take up this discussion and these concerns. With Biss as your starting point (and you will need to establish this starting point for your readers, readers who may not have read "The Pain Scale"), work toward examples, observations, and conclusions of your own. What do you have to add? And, from your vantage point, after having written about this topic, what thoughts do you have now about Biss and "The Pain Scale"?

3. Biss uses the pain scale, a medical device, as both a topic (something to write about) and an instrument (something to write with). Choose a similar device — an index, a scale, a system of measurement, a form used for rating, ranking, or ordering — and write a similar essay — one that imitates the style and structure of "The Pain Scale" and one that thinks similarly about the ways we know and understand ourselves and others.

When you are done, prepare a brief "Preface" or "Coda" in which you speak to your readers about this writing project as a *project*. What were you hoping to do? What did you achieve? What couldn't you achieve? What is at stake for you, and for Eula Biss, in writing this way?

MAKING CONNECTIONS

1. A first reading of Eula Biss's "The Pain Scale" might suggest that it is very different in both form and content from David Foster Wallace's "Authority and American Usage" (p. 622). A second reading might reveal similarities

as well as differences. Like Wallace, Biss is interested in a different kind of reading and writing than what we might characterize as "typical," especially in an academic context.

If the two essays each demonstrate a "different" kind of writing, it's worth thinking about what we can learn from those differences. Write an essay in which you present your reading of the "different" kinds of writing exhibited by Biss and Wallace, and what we might learn—as readers and writers—from their respective writing choices.

2. One way to approach Susan Griffin's "Our Secret" (p. 335) and Biss's "The Pain Scale" is to think of them as experiments in writing—attempts to do what can't be done in more conventional forms of the essay. One of the commonalities the two essays share is that they both get at their project by metaphor and analogy. In "Our Secret," Griffin writes about Heinrich Himmler in order to think about larger issues of parenting, education, culture, and human development. In "The Pain Scale," Biss uses the scale to think about epistemologies, about our desire to measure and quantify and pin down the unknowable. Both authors, then, structure their essays around an area of inquiry—not a thesis statement.

   For this assignment, create your own experiment in writing, one in which you work on your own set of questions in ways that subvert more common approaches to essay writing. You might choose to write in fragments, like Griffin, arranging your commentary on various matters in a kind of collage; you might choose to structure your essay in a form more commonly used in other settings, as Biss does, organizing your discussion through a predetermined structure; or you may choose some other approach, one best suited for thinking about the question or problem or concern you want to interrogate.

   Keep in mind that you are not being asked to write a report. However you choose to structure your text, this essay is meant to be an inquiry into a set of questions you find important. For Griffin, Himmler's life raises questions about parenting and education and culture. How, she asks, does a child become this kind of man? As you reflect on the issue/problem/concern you want to think about, consider the questions you might investigate as you pursue this line of inquiry.

3. In writing courses, we often think of writing as a form of inquiry, as a way of developing and sustaining an intellectual investigation into a complex problem. Both Eula Biss, in "The Pain Scale" and Judith Butler, in "Beside Oneself: On the Limits of Sexual Autonomy" (p. 238), demonstrate this kind of work. Both write in a distinctive style. Both refer to pain and loss; both essays consider the difficulties of defining who we are in relation to others.

   Write an essay in which you present the arguments and methods in these two essays. What are they about? How do they understand and represent the difficulties of writing and understanding? Assume that you are writing to an audience not familiar with these particular pieces of writing. You will need to be generous in your use of examples. What might these essays have to say to each other? And, finally, where are you in relation to these two writers and these two essays? What might they allow you to understand that you didn't understand before? What role might they play in your education—including your education as a writer? Do you find one of the essays more useful or compelling than the other?

4. In the opening paragraphs of his essay "Ways of Seeing" (p. 141), John Berger declares that "seeing comes before words" and that "the relation between what we see and what we know is never settled." Moreover, he argues, "the way we see things is affected by what we know or what we believe." With these few sentences, Berger calls into question not only the relationship between seeing and knowing, and between knowledge and language, but also the concept of knowledge itself. How does sight help us know things, and does what we know affect what we can see?

   Like Berger, Biss is exploring the concept of knowledge, this time using measurement as a way of seeing, of conceptualizing and understanding experience. As you reread the two essays, think about the essay form itself, the form of the essay as deployed by each writer, and think about the form of the essay as a "way of seeing" or as a method for measurement and location.

   What do these essays say about the problems of knowledge? How are these essays formally different? How do they approach the problems of knowledge—of thinking, researching, exploring and communicating the results of such efforts? What positions do these writers take on writing as a way of seeing, knowing, and comprehending the world? What lessons might writers of your generation take from their examples?

SUSAN
Bordo

Susan Bordo (b. 1947) is the Otis A. Singletary Chair of Humanities at the University of Kentucky. Bordo is a philosopher, and while her work has touched on figures and subjects traditional to the study of philosophy (René Descartes, for example), she brings her training to the study of culture, including popular culture and its representations of the body. She is a philosopher, that is, who writes not only about Plato but also about Madonna and John Travolta.

In *Unbearable Weight: Feminism, Western Culture, and the Body* (1993), Bordo looks at the complicated cultural forces that have produced our ways of understanding and valuing a woman's body. These powerful forces have shaped not only attitudes and lives but, through dieting, training, and cosmetic surgery, the physical body itself. *Unbearable Weight* was nominated for the 1993 Pulitzer Prize; it won the Association for Women in Psychology's Distinguished Publication Award and was named by the *New York Times* as one of the "Notable Books of 1993." The book had a broad audience and made a significant contribution to the academic study of gender and the body. In fact, Bordo's work (in this book and those that followed) has been central to the newly evolving field of "body studies." Bordo is also the author of *The Flight to Objectivity: Essays on Cartesianism and Culture* (1987) and *Twilight Zones: The Hidden Life of Cultural Images from Plato to O.J.* (1997); she is coeditor (with Alison Jaggar) of *Gender/Body/Knowledge: Feminist Reconstruction of Being and Knowing* (1989) and editor of *Feminist Interpretations of Descartes* (1999).

In 1992, Bordo says, as she was finishing work on *Unbearable Weight*, she received a letter from Laurence Goldstein, editor of *Michigan Quarterly Review*, asking her to write a review article on a surprising series of recently published books concerning men and masculinity. It was as though the feminist work on women as figures of thought and commerce had made the category of the "male" equally available for study and debate. She said,

> It was as if Larry had read my mind. . . . I had known for a long time that I wanted to write about men and their bodies; it seemed the logical, natural, almost inevitable next step. I just wasn't expecting to begin quite so soon. But I couldn't resist the opportunity. . . .

The review essay was the beginning of what became her next major publication, *The Male Body: A New Look at Men in Public and Private* (1999), from which the following selection is drawn. As was the case with *Unbearable Weight, The Male Body* has been read with great interest and care by a wide audience, with favorable reviews in the *New York Times, Elle,* and *Vanity Fair.* In *The Male Body*, Bordo writes about her father, about the 1950s, about gay men and straight men, about movies, and about sex manuals. The chapter we have chosen, "Beauty (Re)discovers the Male Body," comes from a section titled "Public Images" and looks specifically at the use of men in advertising, where men's bodies (rather than the usual case—women's) are presented as objects of pleasure and instances of commerce. There is a powerful argument here about gender, identity, and the media (about how we come to see and value our physical selves). The writing is witty, committed, and engaging—moving from personal history to cultural history, deftly bringing in key concepts from contemporary literary and media theory, like the concept of the "gaze." In this chapter, Bordo provides a compelling example of what it means to read closely, to read images as well as words, and to write those close readings into an extended argument. She brings the concerns of a philosopher to the materials of everyday life.

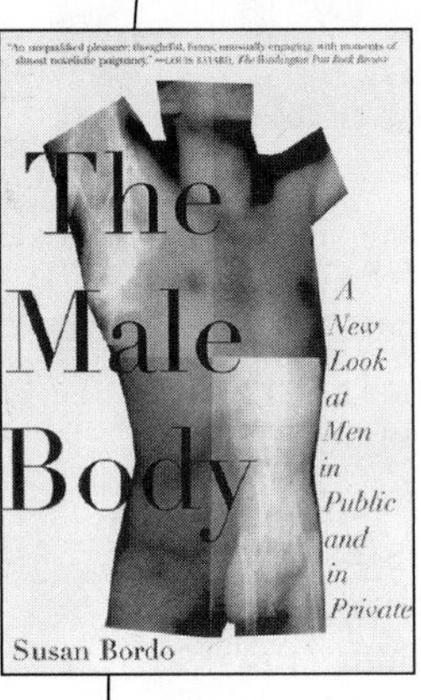

Beauty (Re)discovers the Male Body

MEN ON DISPLAY

Putting classical art to the side for the moment, the naked and near-naked female body became an object of mainstream consumption first in *Playboy* and its imitators, then in movies, and only then in fashion photographs. With the male body, the trajectory has been different. Fashion has taken the lead, the movies have followed. Hollywood may have been a chest-fest in the fifties, but it was male clothing designers who went south and violated the really powerful taboos — not just against the explicit depiction of penises and male bottoms but against the admission of all sorts of forbidden "feminine" qualities into mainstream conceptions of manliness.

It was the spring of 1995, and I was sipping my first cup of morning coffee, not yet fully awake, flipping through *The New York Times Magazine*, when I had my first real taste of what it's like to inhabit this visual culture as a man. It was both thrilling and disconcerting. It was the first time in my experience that I had encountered a commercial representation of a male body that seemed to deliberately invite me to linger over it. Let me make that stronger — that seemed to reach out to me, interrupting my mundane but peaceful Sunday morning, and provoke me into erotic consciousness, whether or not I wanted it. Women — both straight and gay — have always gazed covertly, of course, squeezing our illicit little titillations out of representations designed for — or pretending to — other purposes than to turn us on. *This* ad made no such pretense. It caused me to knock over my coffee cup, ruining the more cerebral pleasures of the *Book Review*. Later, when I had regained my equilibrium, I made a screen-saver out of him, so I could gaze at my leisure.

I'm sure that many gay men were as taken as I was, and perhaps some gay women too. The erotic charge of various sexual styles is not neatly mapped onto sexual orientation (let alone biological sex). Brad Pitt's baby-butch looks are a turn-on to many lesbians, while I — regarded by most of my gay friends as a pretty hard-core heterosexual — have always found Anne Heche irresistible (even before Ellen did). A lesbian friend of mine, reading a draft of my section on biblical S&M, said the same movies influenced her later attraction to butch *women*. Despite such complications, until recently only heterosexual men have continually been inundated by popular cultural images *designed* with their sexual responses (or, at least, what those sexual responses are imagined to be) in mind. It's not entirely a gift. On the minus side is having one's composure continually

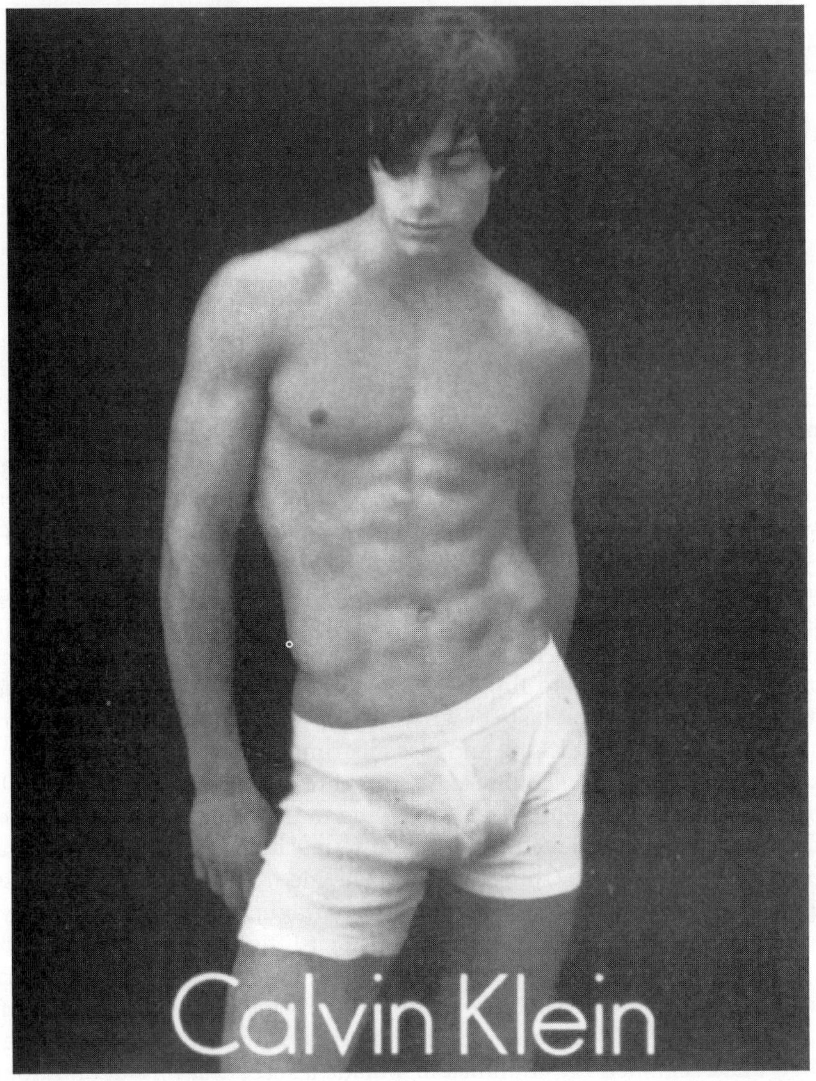

challenged by what Timothy Beneke has aptly described as a culture of "intrusive images," eliciting fantasies, emotions, and erections at times and in places where they might not be appropriate. On the plus side is the cultural permission to be a voyeur.

Some psychologists say that the circuit from eyes to brain to genitals is a quicker trip for men than for women. "There's some strong evidence," popular science writer Deborah Blum reports, citing studies of men's responses to pictures of naked women, "that testosterone is wired for visual response." Maybe. But who is the electrician here? God? Mother Nature? Or Hugh Hefner? Practice makes perfect. And women have had little practice. The Calvin Klein ad made me feel like an adolescent again, brought me back to that day when I saw Barry Resnick on the basketball court of Weequahic High and realized that men's legs could make me weak in the knees. Men's legs? I knew that *women's* legs were supposed to be sexy. I had learned that from all those hose-straightening scenes in the movies. But men's legs? Who had ever seen a woman gaga over some guy's legs in the movies? Or even read about it in a book? Yet the muscular grace of Barry's legs took my breath away. Maybe something was wrong with me. Maybe my sex drive was too strong, too much like a man's. By the time I came across that Calvin Klein ad, several decades of feminism and life experience had left me a little less worried about my sex drive. Still, the sight of that model's body made me feel that my sexual education was still far from complete.

I brought the ad to classes and lectures, asking women what they thought of him. Most began to sweat the moment I unfolded the picture, then got their bearings and tried to explore the bewitching stew of sexual elements the picture has to offer. The model — a young Jackson Browne look-alike — stands there in his form-fitting and rip-speckled Calvin Klein briefs, head lowered, dark hair loosely falling over his eyes. His body projects strength, solidity; he's no male waif. But his finely muscled chest is not so overdeveloped as to suggest a sexuality immobilized by the thick matter of the body. Gay theorist Ron Long, describing contemporary gay sexual aesthetics — lean, taut, sinuous muscles rather than Schwarzenegger bulk — points to a "dynamic tension" that the incredible hulks lack. Stiff, engorged Schwarzenegger bodies, he says, seem to *be* surrogate penises — with nowhere to go and nothing to do but stand there looking massive — whereas muscles like this young man's seem designed for movement, for sex. His body isn't a stand-in phallus; rather, he *has* a penis — the real thing, not a symbol, and a fairly breathtaking one, clearly outlined through the soft jersey fabric of the briefs. It seems slightly erect, or perhaps that's his nonerect size; either way, there's a substantial presence there that's palpable (it looks so touchable, you want to cup your hand over it) and very, very male.

AT THE SAME TIME, HOWEVER, MY GAZE IS INVITED BY SOMETHING "FEMININE" ABOUT THE YOUNG MAN.

At the same time, however, my gaze is invited by something "feminine" about the young man. His underwear may be ripped, but ever so slightly, subtly; unlike the original ripped-underwear poster boy Kowalski, he's hardly a thug. He doesn't stare at the viewer challengingly, belligerently, as do so many models in other ads for male underwear, facing off like a street tough passing a member of the rival gang on the street. ("Yeah, this is an underwear ad and I'm half naked. But I'm still the one in charge here. Who's gonna look away first?") No, this model's languid body posture, his averted look are classic signals, both in the "natural" and the "cultural" world, of willing subordination. He offers himself nonaggressively to the gaze of another. Hip cocked in the snaky S-curve usually reserved for depictions of women's bodies, eyes downcast but not closed, he gives off a sultry, moody, subtle but undeniably seductive consciousness of his erotic allure. Feast on me, I'm here to be looked at, my body is for your eyes. Oh my.

Such an attitude of male sexual supplication, although it has (as we'll see) classical antecedents, is very new to contemporary mainstream representations. Homophobia is at work in this taboo, but so are attitudes about gender that cut across sexual orientation. For many men, both gay and straight, to be so passively dependent on the gaze of another person for one's sense of self-worth is incompatible with being a real man. As we'll see, such notions about manliness are embedded in Greek culture, in contemporary visual representation, and even (in disguised form) in existentialist philosophy. "For the woman," as philosopher Simone de Beauvoir writes, ". . . the absence of her lover is always torture; he is an eye, a judge . . . away from him, she is dispossessed, at once of herself and of the world." For Beauvoir's sometime lover and lifelong soul mate Jean-Paul Sartre, on the other hand, the gaze (or the Look, as he called it) of another person — including the gaze of one's lover — is the "hell" that other people represent. If we were alone in the world, he argues, we would be utterly free — within physical constraints — to be whomever we wanted to be, to be the creatures of our own self-fantasies, to define our behavior however we like. Other people intrude on this solipsism, and have the audacity to see us from their own perspective rather than ours. The result is what Sartre calls primordial Shame under the eyes of the Other, and a fierce desire to reassert one's freedom. The other person has stolen "the secret" of who I am. I must fight back, resist their attempts to define me.

I understand, of course, what Sartre is talking about here. We've all, male and female alike, felt the shame that another pair of eyes can bring. Sartre's own classic example is of being caught peeking through a keyhole by another person. It isn't until those other eyes are upon you that you truly feel not just the "wrongness" of what you are doing, but — Sartre would argue — the very fact that you are doing it. Until the eyes of another are upon us, "catching us" in the act, we can deceive ourselves, pretend. Getting caught in moments of fantasy or vanity may be especially shameful. When I was an adolescent, I loved to pretend I was a radio personality, and talking into an empty coffee can created just the right sound. One day, my mother caught me speaking in the smooth and slightly sultry tones that radio personalities had even in those days. The way I felt is what Sartre means when he describes the Look of another person as the fulcrum of shame-making. My face got hot, and suddenly I saw how ridiculous I must have seemed, my head in the Chock Full O' Nuts, my narcissistic fantasies on full display. I was caught, I wanted to run.

The disjunction between self-conception and external judgment can be especially harsh when the external definitions carry racial and gender stereotypes with them. Sartre doesn't present such examples — he's interested in capturing the contours of an existential situation shared by all rather than in analyzing the cultural differences that affect that situation — but they are surely relevant to understanding the meaning of the Look of the Other. A black man jogs down the street in sweat clothes, thinking of the class he is going to teach later that day; a white woman passes him, clutches her handbag more tightly, quickens her step; in her eyes, the teacher is a potentially dangerous animal. A Latin American student arrives early the first day of college; an administrator, seeing him in the still-deserted hall, asks him if he is the new janitor. The aspiring student has had his emerging identity erased, a stereotype put in its place by another pair of eyes. When women are transformed from professionals to "pussies" by the comments of men on the street, it's humiliating, not so much because we're puritans as because we sense the hostility in the hoots, the desire to bring an uppity woman down to size by reminding her that she's just "the sex" (as Beauvoir put it).

We may all have felt shame, but — as the different attitudes of Beauvoir and Sartre suggest — men and women are socially sanctioned to deal with the gaze of the Other in different ways. Women learn to anticipate, even play to the sexualizing gaze, trying to become what will please, captivate, turn shame into pride. (In the process, we also learn how sexy being gazed at can feel — perhaps precisely because it walks the fine edge of shame.) Many of us, truth be told, get somewhat addicted to the experience. I'm renting a video, feeling a bit low, a bit tired. The young man at the counter, unsolicited, tells me I'm "looking good." It alters everything, I feel fine, alive; it seems to go right down to my cells. I leave the store feeling younger, stronger, more awake. When women sense that they are not being assessed sexually — for example, as we age, or if we are disabled — it may feel like we no longer exist.

Women may dread being surveyed harshly — being seen as too old, too fat, too flat-chested — but men are not supposed to enjoy being surveyed *period*. It's feminine to be on display. Men are thus taught — as my uncle Leon used to say — to be a moving target. Get out of range of those eyes, don't let them catch you — even as the object of their fantasies (or, as Sartre would put it, don't let them "possess," "steal" your freedom). This phobia has even distorted scientific research. . . . Evolutionary theorists have long acknowledged display as an important feature of courting behavior among primates — except when it comes to *our* closest ancestors. With descriptions of hominid behavior, male display behavior "suddenly drops out of the primate evolutionary picture" (Sheets-Johnstone) and is replaced by the concept of year-round female sexual receptivity. It seems that it has been intolerable, unthinkable for male evolutionary theorists to imagine the bodies of their male ancestors being on display, sized up, dependent on selection (or rejection) by female hominids.

Scientists and "ordinary guys" are totally in synch here, as is humorously illustrated in Peter Cattaneo's popular 1997 British film *The Full Monty*. In the film, a group of unemployed metalworkers in Sheffield, England, watch a Chippendale's show and hatch the money-making scheme of presenting their own male strip show in which they will go right down to the "full Monty." At the start of the film, the heroes are hardly pillars of successful manliness (Gaz, their leader, refers to them as "scrap"). Yet even they have been sheltered by their guyhood, as they learn while putting the show together. One gets a penis pump. Another borrows his wife's face cream. They run, they wrap their bellies in plastic, they do jumping jacks, they get artificial tans. The most overweight one among them (temporarily) pulls out of the show. Before, these guys hadn't lived their lives under physical scrutiny, but in male action mode, in which men are judged by their accomplishments. Now, anticipating being on display to a roomful of spectators, they suddenly realize how it feels to be judged as women routinely are, sized up by another pair of eyes. "I pray that they'll be a bit more understanding about us" than they've been with women, David (the fat one) murmurs.

They get past their discomfort, in the end, and their show is greeted with wild enthusiasm by the audience. The movie leaves us with this feel-good ending, not raising the question obvious to every woman watching the film: would a troupe of out-of-shape women be received as warmly, as affectionately? The climactic moment when the men throw off their little pouches is demurely shot from the rear, moreover, so we — the audience — don't get "the full Monty." Nonetheless, the film gently and humorously makes an important point: for a heterosexual man to offer himself up to a sexually evaluating gaze is for him to make a large, scary leap — and not just because of the anxieties about size . . . (the guy who drops out of the show, remember, is embarrassed by his fat, not his penis). The "full Monty" — the naked penis — is not merely a body part in the movie (hence it doesn't really matter that the film doesn't show it). It's a symbol for male exposure, vulnerability to an evaluation and judgment that women — clothed or naked — experience all the time.

I had to laugh out loud at a 1997 *New York Times Magazine* "Style" column, entitled "Overexposure," which complained of the "contagion" of nudity spreading through celebrity culture. "Stars no longer have private parts," the author observed, and fretted that civilians would soon also be measured by the beauty of their buns. I share this author's concern about our body-obsessed culture. But, pardon me, he's just noticing this now??? Actresses have been baring their breasts, their butts, even their bushes, for some time, and ordinary women have been tromping off to the gym in pursuit of comparably perfect bodies. What's got the author suddenly crying "overkill," it turns out, is Sly Stallone's "surreally fat-free" appearance on the cover of *Vanity Fair*, and Rupert Everett's "dimpled behind" in a Karl Lagerfeld fashion spread. Now that *men* are taking off their clothes, the culture is suddenly going too far. Could it be that the author doesn't even "read" all those naked female bodies as "overexposed"? Does he protest a bit too much when he declares in the first sentence of the piece that he found it "a yawn" when Dirk Diggler unsheathed his "prosthetic shillelagh" ("penis" is still a word to be avoided whenever possible) at the end of *Boogie Nights*? A yawn? My friend's palms were sweating profusely, and I was not about to drop off to sleep either.

As for dimpled behinds, my second choice for male pinup of the decade is the Gucci series of two ads in which a beautiful young man, shot from the rear, puts on a pair of briefs. In the first ad, he's holding them in his hands, contemplating them. Is he checking out the correct washing-machine temp? It's odd, surely, to stand there looking at your underwear,

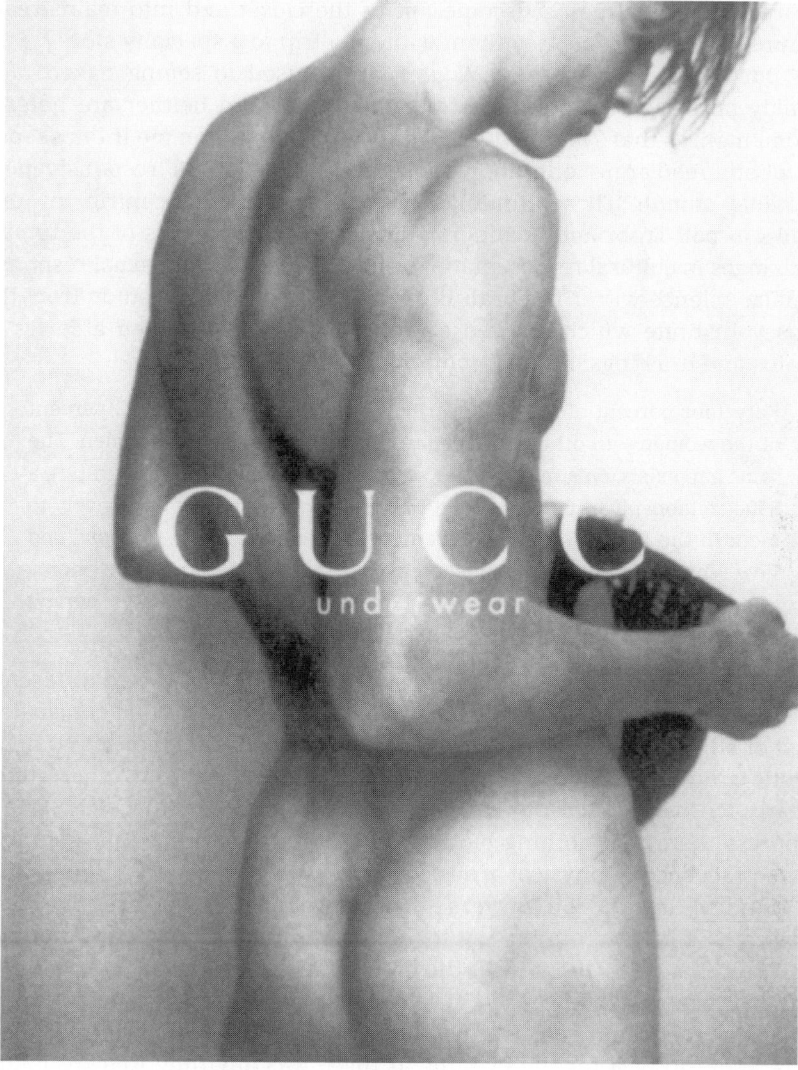

but never mind. The point is: his underwear is in his hands, not on his butt. *It* — his bottom, that is — is gorgeously, completely naked — a motif so new to mainstream advertising (but since then catching on rapidly) that several of my friends, knowing I was writing about the male body, e-mailed me immediately when they saw the ad. In the second ad, he's put the underwear on, and is adjusting it to fit. Luckily for us, he hasn't succeeded yet, so his buns are peeking out the bottom of the underwear, looking biteable. For the *Times* writer, those buns may be an indecent exposure of parts that should be kept private (or they're a boring yawn, I'm afraid he can't have it both ways), but for me — and for thousands of gay men across the country — this was a moment of political magnitude, and a delicious one. The body parts that *we* love to squeeze (those plastic breasts, they're the real yawn for me) had come out of the closet and into mainstream culture, where *we* can enjoy them without a trip to a specialty store.

But all this is very new. Women aren't used to seeing naked men frankly portrayed as "objects" of a sexual gaze (and neither are heterosexual men, as that *Times* writer makes clear). So pardon me if I'm skeptical when I read arguments about men's greater "biological" responsiveness to visual stimuli. These "findings," besides being ethnocentric (no one thinks to poll Trobriand Islanders), display little awareness of the impact of changes in cultural representations on our capacities for sexual response. Popular science writer Deborah Blum, for example, cites a study from the Kinsey Institute which showed a group of men and women a series of photos and drawings of nudes, both male and female:

> Fifty-four percent of the men were erotically aroused versus 12 percent of the women — in other words, more than four times as many men. The same gap exists, on a much larger scale, in the business of pornography, a $500-million-plus industry in the U.S. which caters almost exclusively to men. In the first flush of 1970s feminism, two magazines — *Playgirl* and *Viva* — began publishing male centerfolds. *Viva* dropped the nude photos after surveys showed their readers didn't care for them; the editor herself admitted to finding them slightly disgusting.

Blum presents these findings as suggestive of a hard-wired difference between men and women. I'd be cautious about accepting that conclusion. First of all, there's the question of which physiological responses count as "erotic arousal" and whether they couldn't be evidence of other states. Clearly, too, we can *learn* to have certain physiological responses — and to suppress them — so nothing biologically definitive is proved by the presence or absence of physical arousal.

Studies that rely on viewers' *own* reports need to be carefully interpreted too. I know, from talking to women students, that they sometimes aren't all that clear about *what* they feel in the presence of erotic stimuli, and even when they are, they may not be all that comfortable admitting what they feel. Hell, not just my students! Once, a lover asked me, as we were about to part for the evening, if there was anything that we hadn't done that I'd really like to do. I knew immediately what that was: I wanted him to undress, very slowly, while I sat on the floor and just watched. But I couldn't tell him. I was too embarrassed. Later, alone in my compartment on the train, I sorely regretted my cowardice. The fact is that I love to watch a man getting undressed, and I especially like it if he is conscious of being looked at. But there is a long legacy of shame to be overcome here, for both sexes, and the cultural models are only now just emerging which might help us move beyond it.

Perhaps, then, we should wait a bit longer, do a few more studies, before we come to any biological conclusions about women's failure to get aroused by naked pictures. A newer (1994) University of Chicago study found that 30 percent of women ages eighteen to forty-four and 19 percent of women ages forty-five to fifty-nine said they found "watching a partner undress" to be "very appealing." ("Not a bad percentage," Nancy Friday comments, "given that Nice Girls didn't look.") There's still a gender gap—the respective figures for men of the same age groups were 50 percent and 40 percent. We're just learning, after all, to be voyeuses. Perhaps, too, heterosexual men could learn to be less uncomfortable offering themselves as "sexual objects" if they realized the pleasure women get from it. Getting what you have been most deprived of is the best gift, the most healing gift, the most potentially transforming gift—because it has the capacity to make one more whole. Women have been deprived not so much of the *sight* of beautiful male bodies as the experience of having the male body *offered* to us, handed to us on a silver platter, the way female bodies—in the ads, in the movies—are handed to men. Getting this from her partner is the erotic equivalent of a woman's coming home from work to find a meal prepared and ready for her. Delicious—even if it's just franks and beans.

THANKS, CALVIN!

Despite their bisexual appeal, the cultural genealogy of the ads I've been discussing and others like them is to be traced largely through gay male aesthetics, rather than a sudden blossoming of appreciation for the fact that women might enjoy looking at sexy, well-hung young men who don't appear to be about to rape them. Feminists might like to imagine that Madison Avenue heard our pleas for sexual equality and finally gave us "men as sex objects." But what's really happened is that women have been the beneficiaries of what might be described as a triumph of pure consumerism—and with it, a burgeoning male fitness and beauty culture—over homophobia and the taboos against male vanity, male "femininity," and erotic display of the male body that have gone along with it.

Throughout [the twentieth] century, gay photographers have created a rich, sensuous, and dramatic tradition which is unabashed in eroticizing the male body, male sensuousness, and male potency, including penises. But until recently, such representations have been kept largely in the closet. Mainstream responses to several important exhibits which opened in the seventies—featuring the groundbreaking early work of Wilhelm von Gloeden, George Dureau, and George Platt Lynes as well as then-contemporary artists such as Robert Mapplethorpe, Peter Hujar, and Arthur Tress—would today probably embarrass the critics who wrote about them when they opened. John Ashbery, in *New York* magazine, dismissed the entire genre of male nude photography with the same sexist tautology that covertly underlies that *Times* piece on cultural "overexposure": "Nude women seem to be in their natural state; men, for some reason, merely look undressed. . . . When is a nude not a nude? When it is male." (Substitute "blacks" and "whites" for "women" and "men" and you'll see how offensive the statement is.)

For other reviewers, the naked male, far from seeming "merely undressed," was unnervingly sexual. *New York Times* critic Gene Thompson wrote that "there is something disconcerting about the sight of a man's naked body being presented as a sexual object"; he went on to describe the world of homoerotic photography as one "closed to most of us, fortunately." Vicki Goldberg, writing for the *Saturday Review*, was more appreciative of the "beauty and dignity" of the nude male body, but concluded that so long as its depiction was erotic in emphasis, it will "remain half-private, slightly awkward, an art form cast from its traditions and in search of some niche to call its home."

Goldberg needed a course in art history. It's true that in classical art, the naked human body was often presented as a messenger of spiritual themes, and received as such. But the male bodies sculpted by the Greeks and Michelangelo were not exactly nonerotic. It might be more accurate to say that in modernity, with the spiritual interpretation of the nude body no longer a convention, the contemporary homophobic psyche is not screened from the sexual charge of the nude male body. Goldberg was dead wrong about something else too. Whatever its historical lineage, the frankly sexual representation of the male body was to find, in the next twenty years, a far from private "niche to call its home": consumer culture discovered its commercial potency.

THE MALE BODIES SCULPTED BY THE GREEKS AND MICHELANGELO WERE NOT EXACTLY NONEROTIC.

Calvin Klein had his epiphany, according to one biography, one night in 1974 in New York's gay Flamingo bar:

> As Calvin wandered through the crowd at the Flamingo, the body heat rushed through him like a revelation; this was the cutting edge. . . . [The] men! The men at the Flamingo had less to do about sex for him than the notion of portraying men as gods. He realized that what he was watching was the freedom of a new generation, unashamed, in-the-flesh embodiments of Calvin's ideals: straight-looking, masculine men, with chiseled bodies, young Greek gods come to life. The vision of shirtless young men with hardened torsos, all in blue jeans, top button opened, a whisper of hair from the belly button disappearing into the denim pants, would inspire and inform the next ten years of Calvin Klein's print and television advertisements.

Klein's genius was that of a cultural Geiger counter; his own bisexuality enabled him to see that the phallic body, as much as any female figure, is an enduring sex object within Western culture. In America in 1974, however, that ideal was still largely closeted. Only gay culture unashamedly sexualized the lean, fit body that virtually everyone, gay and straight, now aspires to. Sex, as Calvin Klein knew, sells. He also knew that gay sex wouldn't sell to straight men. But the rock-hard, athletic gay male bodies that Klein admired at the Flamingo did not advertise their sexual preference through the feminine codes — limp wrists, raised pinkie finger, swishy walk — which the straight world then identified with homosexuality. Rather, they embodied a highly masculine aesthetic that — although definitely exciting for gay men — would scream "heterosexual" to (clueless) straights. Klein knew just the kind of clothing to show that body off in too. As Steven Gaines and Sharon Churcher tell it:

> He had watched enough attractive young people with good bodies in tight jeans dancing at the Flamingo and Studio 54 to know that the "basket" and the behind was what gave jeans sex appeal. Calvin sent his assistants out for several pairs of jeans, including the classic five-button Levi's, and cut them apart to see how they were made. Then he cut the "rise," or area from the waistband to under the groin, much shorter to accentuate the crotch and pull the seam up between the buttocks, giving the behind more shape and prominence. The result was instant sex appeal — and a look that somehow Calvin just *knew* was going to sell.

So we come to the mainstream commercialization of the aesthetic legacy of Stanley Kowalski and those inspired innovations of Brando's costumer in *A Streetcar Named Desire*. When I was growing up, jeans were "dungarees" — suitable for little kids, hayseeds, and juvenile delinquents, but not for anyone to wear on a date. Klein transformed jeans from utilitarian garments to erotic second skins. Next, Klein went for underwear. He wasn't the first, but he was the most daring. In 1981, Jockey International had broken ground by photographing Baltimore Oriole pitcher Jim Palmer in a pair of briefs (airbrushed) in one of its ads — selling $100 million worth of underwear by year's end. Inspired by Jockey's success, in 1983 Calvin Klein put a forty-by-fifty-foot Bruce Weber photograph of Olympic pole vaulter Tom Hintinauss in Times Square, Hintinauss's large penis clearly discernible through his briefs. The Hintinauss ad, unlike the Palmer ad, did not employ any of the usual fictional rationales for a man's being in his underwear — for example, the pretense that the man is in the process of getting dressed — but blatantly put Hintinauss's body on display, sunbathing on a rooftop, his skin glistening. The line of shorts "flew off the shelves" at Bloomingdale's and when Klein papered bus shelters in Manhattan with poster versions of the ad they were all stolen overnight.

Images of masculinity that will do double (or triple or quadruple) duty with a variety of consumers, straight and gay, male and female, are not difficult to create in a culture like ours, in which the muscular male body has a long and glorious aesthetic history. That's precisely what Calvin Klein was the first to recognize and exploit — the possibility and profitability of what is known in the trade as a "dual marketing" approach. Since then, many advertisers have taken advantage of Klein's insight. A recent Abercrombie & Fitch ad, for example, depicts a locker room full of young, half-clothed football players getting a postmortem from their coach after a game. Beautiful, undressed male bodies doing what real men are "supposed to do." Dirty uniforms and smudged faces, wounded players, helmets. What could be more straight? But as iconography depicting a culture of exclusively male bodies, young, gorgeous, and well-hung, what could be more "gay"?

Bronzed and beautiful Tom Hintinauss: a breakthrough ad for Calvin Klein — and the beginning of a new era for the unabashed erotic display of the male body.

It required a Calvin Klein to give the new vision cultural form. But the fact is that if we've entered a brave, new world of male bodies it is largely because of a more "material" kind of epiphany — a dawning recognition among advertisers of the buying power of gay men. For a long time prejudice had triumphed over the profit motive, blinding marketers to just how sizable — and well-heeled — a consumer group gay men represent. (This has been the case with other "minorities" too. Hollywood producers, never bothering to do any demographics on middle-class and professional African American women — or the issues that they share with women of other races and classes in this culture — were shocked at the tremendous box office success of *Waiting to Exhale*. They won't make that particular mistake again.) It took a survey conducted by *The Advocate* to jolt corporate America awake about gay consumers. The survey, done between 1977 and 1980, showed that 70 percent of its readers aged twenty to forty earned incomes well above the national median. Soon, articles were appearing on the business pages of newspapers, like one in 1982 in *The New York Times Magazine*, which described advertisers as newly interested in "wooing . . . the white, single, well-educated, well-paid man who happens to be homosexual."

"Happens to be homosexual": the phrasing — suggesting that sexual identity is peripheral, even accidental — is telling. Because of homophobia, dual marketing used to require a delicate balancing act, as advertisers tried to speak to gays "in a way that the straight consumer will not notice." Often, that's been accomplished through the use of play and parody, as in Versace's droll portraits of men being groomed and tended by male servants, and Diesel's overtly narcissistic gay posers. "Thanks, Diesel, for making us so very beautiful," they gush. Or take the ad below, with its gorgeous, mechanically inept model admitting that he's "known more for my superb bone construction and soft, supple hair than my keen intellect." The playful tone reassures heterosexual consumers that the vanity (and

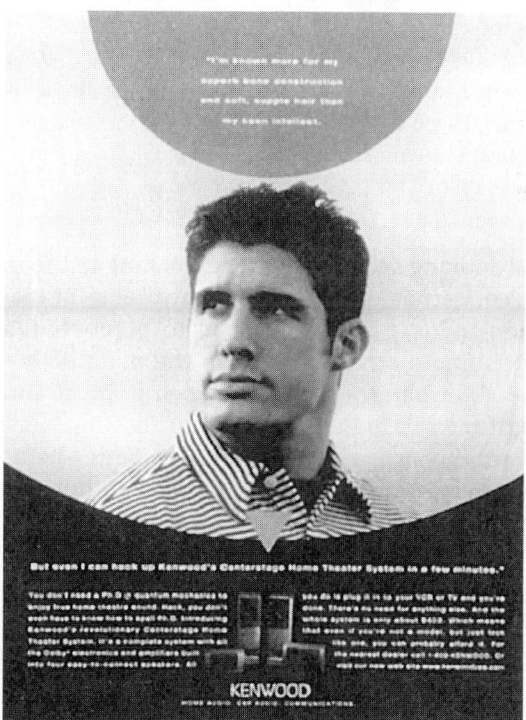

"I'm known more for my superb bone construction and soft, supple hair than my keen intellect. But even I can hook up Kenwood's Centerstage Home Theater System in a few minutes."

mechanical incompetence) of the man selling the product is "just a joke." For gay consumers, on the other hand, this reassurance is *itself* the "joke"; they read the humor in the ad as an insider wink, which says, "This is for *you*, guys." The joke is further layered by the fact that they know the model in the ad is very likely to be gay.

Contrast this ad to the ostentatious heterosexual protest of a Perry Ellis ad which appeared in the early 1990s (and no, it's not a parody):

> I hate this job. I'm not just an empty suit who stands in front of a camera, collects the money and flies off to St. Maarten for the weekend.
>
> I may model for a living, but I hate being treated like a piece of meat. I once had a loud-mouthed art director say "Stand there and pretend you're a human." I wanted to punch him, but I needed the job.
>
> What am I all about? Well, I know I'm very good-looking, and there are days when that is enough. Some nights, when I'm alone, it's not.
>
> I like women — all kinds.
>
> I like music — all kinds.
>
> I like myself so I don't do drugs.
>
> Oh yeah, about this fragrance. It's good. Very good.
>
> When I posed for this picture, the art director insisted that I wear it while the pictures were being taken. I thought it was silly, but I said "What the hell? It's their money."
>
> After a while, I realized I like this fragrance a lot. When the photo shoot was over, I walked right over, picked up the bottle, put it in my pocket and said "If you don't mind, I'd like to take this as a souvenir." Then I smiled my best f—— you smile and walked out.
>
> Next time, I'll pay for it.
>
> It's that good.

Today, good-looking straight guys are flocking to the modeling agencies, much less concerned about any homosexual taint that will cleave to them. It's no longer necessary for an ad to plant its tongue firmly in cheek when lavishing erotic attention on the male body — or to pepper the ad with proofs of heterosexuality. It used to be, if an advertisement aimed at straight men dared to show a man fussing over his looks with seemingly romantic plans in mind, there had better be a woman in the picture, making it clear just *whom* the boy was getting pretty for. To sell a muscle-building product to heterosexuals, of course, you had to link it to virility and the ability to attract women on the beach. Today, muscles are openly sold for their looks; Chroma Lean nutritional supplement unabashedly compares the well-sculpted male body to a work of art (and a gay male icon, to boot) — Michelangelo's "David." Many ads display the naked male body without shame or plot excuse, and often exploit rather than resolve the sexual ambiguity that is generated.

Today, too, the athletic, muscular male body that Calvin plastered all over buildings, magazines, and subway stops has become an aesthetic norm, for straights as well as gays. "No pecs, no sex," is how the trendy David Barton gym sells itself: "My motto is not 'Be healthy'; it's 'Look better naked,'" Barton says. The notion has even made its way into that most determinedly heterosexual of contexts, a Rob Reiner film. In *Sleepless in Seattle*, Tom Hanks's character, who hasn't been on a date in fifteen years, asks his friend (played by Rob) what women are looking for nowadays. "Pecs and a cute butt," his friend replied without hesitation. "You can't even turn on the news nowadays without hearing about how some babe thought some guy's butt was cute. Who the first woman to say this was I don't know, but somehow it caught on." Should we tell Rob that it wasn't a woman who started the craze for men's butts?

ROCKS AND LEANERS

We "nouvelles voyeuses" thus owe a big measure of thanks to gay male designers and consumers, and to the aesthetic and erotic overlap — not uniform or total, but significant — in what makes our hearts go thump. But although I've been using the term for convenience, I don't think it's correct to say that these ads depict men as "sex objects." Actually, I find that whole notion misleading, whether applied to men or women, because it seems to suggest that what these representations offer is a body that is inert, depersonalized, flat, a mere thing. In fact, advertisers put a huge amount of time, money, and creativity into figuring out how to create images of beautiful bodies that are heavy on attitude, style, associations with pleasure, success, happiness. The most compelling images are suffused with "subjectivity" — they *speak* to us, they seduce us. Unlike other kinds of "objects" (chairs and tables, for example), they don't let us use them in any way we like. In fact, they exert considerable power over us — over our psyches, our desires, our self-image.

How do male bodies in the ads speak to us nowadays? In a variety of ways. Sometimes the message is challenging, aggressive. Many models stare coldly at the viewer, defying the observer to view them in any way other than how they have chosen to present themselves: as powerful, armored, emotionally impenetrable. "I am a rock," their bodies (and sometimes their genitals) seem to proclaim. Often, as in the Jackson Browne look-alike ad, the penis is prominent, but *unlike* the penis in that ad, its presence is martial rather than sensual. Overall, these ads depict what I would describe as "face-off masculinity," in which victory goes to the dominant contestant in a game of will against will. Who can stare the other man down? Who will avert his eyes first? Whose gaze will be triumphant? Such moments — "facing up," "facing off," "staring down" — as anthropologist David Gilmore has documented, are a test of macho in many cultures, including our own. "Don't eyeball me!" barks the sergeant to his cadets in training in *An Officer and a Gentleman*; the authority of the stare is a prize to be won only with full manhood. Before then, it is a mark of insolence — or stupidity, failure to understand the codes of masculine rank. In *Get Shorty*, an unsuspecting film director challenges a mob boss to look him in the eye; in return, he is hurled across the room and has his fingers broken.

Face-off masculinity.

"Face-off" ads, except for their innovations in the amount of skin exposed, are pretty traditional — one might even say primal — in their conception of masculinity. Many other species use staring to establish dominance, and not only our close primate relatives. It's how my Jack Russell terrier intimidates my male collie, who weighs over four times as much as the little guy but cowers under the authority of the terrier's macho stare. In the doggie world, size doesn't matter; it's the power of the gaze — which indicates the power to stand one's ground — that counts. My little terrier's dominance, in other words, is based on a convincing acting job — and it's one that is very similar, according to William Pollack, to the kind of performance that young boys in our culture must learn to master. Pollack's studies of boys suggest that a set of rules — which he calls "The Boy Code" — govern their behavior with each other. The first imperative of the code — "Be a sturdy oak" — represents the emotional equivalent of "face-off masculinity": Never reveal weakness. Pretend to be confident even though you may be scared. Act like a rock even when you feel shaky. Dare others to challenge your position.

The face-off is not the only available posture for male bodies in ads today. Another possibility is what I call "the lean" — because these bodies are almost always reclining, leaning against, or propped up against something in the fashion typical of women's bodies. James Dean was probably our first pop-culture "leaner"; he made it stylish for teenagers to slouch. Dean, however, never posed as languidly or was as openly seductive as some of the high-fashion leaners are today. A recent Calvin Klein "Escape" ad depicts a young, sensuous-looking man leaning against a wall, arm raised, dark underarm hair exposed. His eyes seek out the imagined viewer, soberly but flirtatiously. "*Take Me*," the copy reads.

Languid leaners have actually been around for a long time. Statues of sleeping fauns, their bodies draped languorously, exist in classical art alongside more heroic models of male beauty. I find it interesting, though, that Klein has chosen Mr. Take Me to advertise a perfume called "Escape." Klein's "Eternity" ads usually depict happy, heterosexual couples, often with a child. "Obsession" has always been cutting-edge, sexually ambiguous erotica. This ad, featuring a man offering himself up seductively, invitingly to the observer, promises "escape." From what? *To* what? Men have complained, justly, about the burden of always having to be the sexual initiator, the pursuer, the one of whom sexual "performance" is expected. Perhaps the escape is from these burdens, and toward the freedom to indulge in some of the more receptive pleasures traditionally reserved for women. The pleasures, not of staring someone down but of feeling one's body caressed by another's eyes, of being the one who receives the awaited call rather than the one who must build up the nerve to make the call, the one who doesn't have to hump and pump, but is permitted to lie quietly, engrossed in reverie and sensation.

NEVER REVEAL WEAKNESS. PRETEND TO BE CONFIDENT EVEN THOUGH YOU MAY BE SCARED.

Some people describe these receptive pleasures as "passive" — which gives them a bad press with men, and is just plain inaccurate too. "Passive" hardly describes what's going on when one person offers himself or herself to another. Inviting, receiving, responding — these are active behaviors too, and rather thrilling ones. It's a macho bias to view the only *real* activity as that which takes, invades, aggresses. It's a bias, however, that's been with us for a long time, in both straight and gay cultures. In many

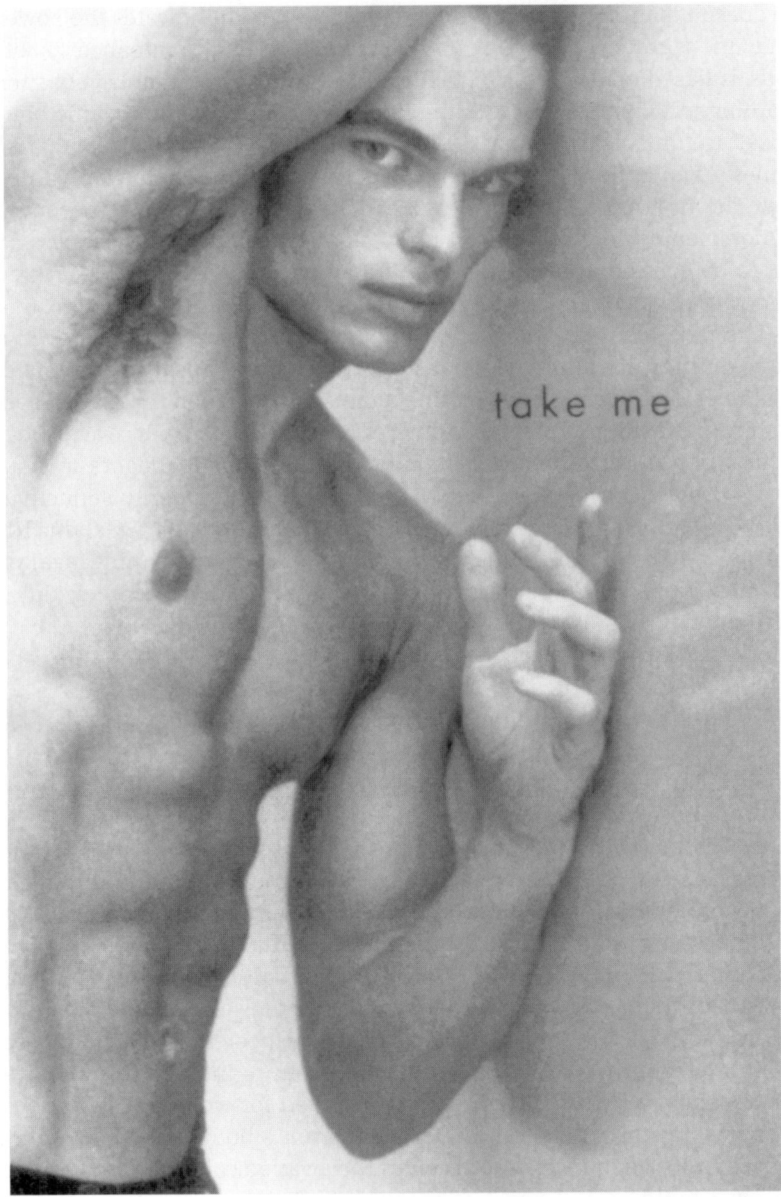

Latin cultures, it's not a disgrace to sleep with other men, so long as one is *activo* (or *machista*) — the penetrator rather than the penetratee. To be a *pasivo*, on the other hand, is to be socially stigmatized. It's that way in prison cultures too — a good indication of the power hierarchies involved. These hierarchies date back to the ancient Greeks, who believed that passivity, receptivity, penetrability were marks of inferior feminine being. The qualities were inherent in women; it was our nature to be passively controlled by our sexual needs. (Unlike us, the Greeks viewed women — not men — as the animalistic ones.) Real Men, who unlike women had the necessary rationality and will, were expected to be judicious in the exercise of their desires. But being judicious and being "active" — deciding when to pursue, whom to pursue, making advances, pleading one's case — went hand in hand.

Allowing oneself to be pursued, flirting, accepting the advances of another, offering one's body — these behaviors were permitted also (but only on a temporary basis) to still-developing, younger men. These young men — not little boys, as is sometimes incorrectly believed — were the true "sex objects" of elite Greek culture. Full-fledged male citizens, on the other hand, were expected to be "active," initiators, the penetrators not the penetratees, masters of their own desires rather than the objects of another's. Plato's *Symposium* is full of speeches on the different sexual behaviors appropriate to adult men with full beards and established professions and glamorous young men still revered more for their beauty than their minds. But even youth could not make it okay for a man to behave *too much* like a woman. The admirable youth was the one who — unlike a woman — was able to remain sexually "cool" and remote, to keep his wits about him. "Letting go" was not seemly.

Where does our culture stand today with respect to these ideas about men's sexuality? Well, to begin with, consider how rarely male actors are shown — on their faces, in their utterances, and not merely in the movements of their bodies — having orgasms. In sex scenes, the moanings and writhings of the female partner have become the conventional cinematic code for heterosexual ecstasy and climax. The male's participation is largely represented by caressing hands, humping buttocks, and — on rare occasions — a facial expression of intense concentration. She's transported to another world; he's the pilot of the ship that takes her there. When men are shown being transported themselves, it's usually been played for comedy (as in Al Pacino's shrieks in *Frankie and Johnny*, Eddie Murphy's moanings in *Boomerang*, Kevin Kline's contortions in *A Fish Called Wanda*), or it's coded to suggest that something is not quite normal about the man — he's sexually enslaved, for example (as with Jeremy Irons in *Damage*). Mostly, men's bodies are presented like action-hero toys — wind them up and watch them perform.

Hollywood — still an overwhelmingly straight-male-dominated industry — is clearly not yet ready to show us a man "passively" giving himself over to another, at least not when the actors in question are our cultural icons. Too feminine. Too suggestive, metaphorically speaking, of penetration by another. But perhaps fashion ads are less uptight? I decided to perform an experiment. I grouped ads that I had collected over recent years into a pile of "rocks" and a pile of "leaners" and found, not surprisingly, that both race and age played a role. African American models, whether in *Esquire* or *Vibe*, are almost always posed facing-off. And leaners tend to be younger than rocks. Both in gay publications and straight ones, the more languid, come-hither poses in advertisements are of boys and very young men. Once a certain maturity line is crossed, the

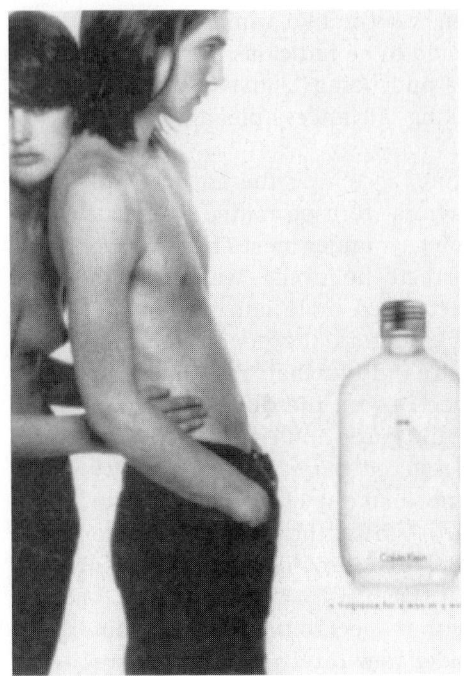

A youthful, androgynous "leaner" — appropriately enough, advertising [CK One] fragrance "for a man or a woman."

challenging stares, the "face-off" postures are the norm. What does one learn from these ads? Well, I wouldn't want to claim too much. It used to be that one could tell a lot about gender and race from looking at ads. Racial stereotypes were transparent, the established formulas for representing men and women were pretty clear (sociologist Erving Goffman even called ads "gender advertisements"), and when the conventions were defied it was usually because advertisers sensed (or discovered in their polls) that social shifts had made consumers ready to receive new images. In this "post-modern" age, it's more of a free-for-all, and images are often more reactive to each other than to social change. It's the viewers' jaded eye, not their social prejudices, that is the prime consideration of every ad campaign, and advertisers are quick to tap into taboos, to defy expectations, simply in order to produce new and arresting images. So it wouldn't surprise me if we soon find languid black men and hairy-chested leaners in the pages of *Gentlemen's Quarterly*.

But I haven't seen any yet. At the very least, the current scene suggests that even in this era of postmodern pastiche racial clichés and gender taboos persist; among them, we don't want grown men to appear too much the "passive" objects of another's sexual gaze, another's desires. We appear, still, to have somewhat different rules for boys and men. As in ancient Greece, boys are permitted to be seductive, playful, to flirt with being "taken." *Men* must still be in command. Leonardo DiCaprio, watch out. Your days may be numbered.

"HONEY, WHAT DO I WANT TO WEAR?"

Just as fifties masculinity was fought over (metaphorically speaking) by Stanley Kowalski and Stanley Banks, the male fashion scene of the nineties involves a kind of contest for the souls of men too. Calvin Klein, Versace, Gucci, Abercrombie & Fitch have not only brought naked bottoms and bulging briefs onto the commercial scene, they present underwear, jeans, shirts, and suits as items for enhancing a man's appearance and sexual appeal. They suggest it's fine for a man to care about how he looks and to cultivate an openly erotic style. In response, aggressively heterosexual Dockers and Haggar ads compete — for the buying dollar of men, but in the process for their gender consciousness too — by stressing the no-nonsense utility of khakis. Consider the Haggar casuals advertisement on this page, and what it says about how "real men" should feel about their clothes:

"I'm damn well gonna wear what I want. ... Honey, what do I want?"

Looked at in one light, the man in the advertisement is being made fun of, as a self-deceived blusterer who asserts his independence "like a man" and in the next breath reveals that he is actually a helpless little boy who needs his mommy to pick out his clothes for him. But fashion incompetence is a species of helplessness that many men feel quite comfortable with, even proud of. Recognizing this, Haggar and Dockers are among those manufacturers who have put a great deal of effort into marketing "nonfashion-guy fashion" to a niche of straight men — working-class and yuppie — who, they presume, would be scared off by even a whiff of "feminine" clothes-consciousness. Here's another one from Haggar's:

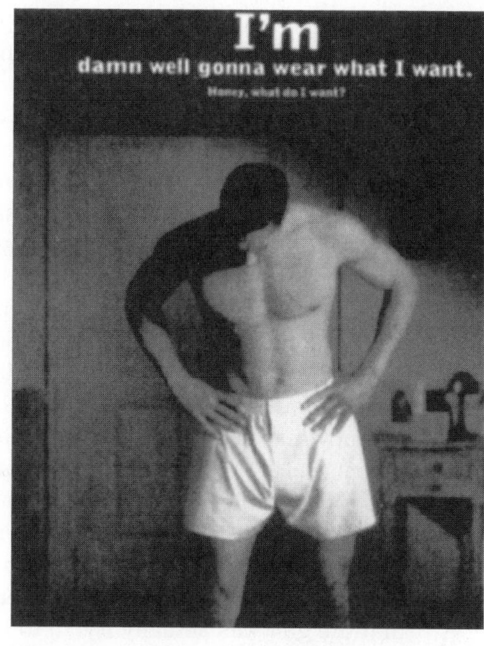

"I'm damn well gonna wear what I want. Honey, what do I want?"

"In the female *the ability to match colors comes at an early age. In the* male *it comes when he marries a female."*

The juxtaposition of inept male/fashion-conscious female, which with one stroke establishes the masculinity *and* the heterosexuality of the depicted man, is a staple of virtually every Haggar ad. In a Haggar television spot with voice-over by John Goodman (Roseanne's beefy former television husband), a man wakes up, sleepily pulls on a pair of khakis, and goes outside to get the paper:

"I am not what I wear. I'm not a pair of pants, or a shirt." (He then walks by his wife, handing her the front section of the paper.) *"I'm not in touch with my inner child. I don't read poetry, and I'm not politically correct."* (He goes down a hall, and his kid snatches the comics from him.) *"I'm just a guy, and I don't have time to think about what I wear, because I've got a lot of important guy things to do."* (Left with only the sports section of the paper, he heads for the bathroom.) *"One-hundred-per-cent-cotton-wrinkle-free khaki pants that don't require a lot of thought. Haggar. Stuff you can wear."*

Yes, it's a bit of a parody, but that only allows Haggar to double its point that real guys have better things to do than think about what they are going to wear or how they appear to others. The guy who would be so worried about his image that he couldn't poke fun at himself wouldn't be a real guy at all. Real guys don't take themselves so seriously! That's for wimps who favor poetry, self-help psychology, and bleeding-heart politics. That's for girls, and for the men who are pussy-whipped by them.

In Haggar's world, real guys don't choose clothing that will enhance the appearance of their bodies or display a sense of style; real guys just put on some "stuff" to wear because they have to, it's socially required. The less decorative, the better. "We would never do anything with our pants that would frighten anyone away," says Dockers designer Gareth Morris as reported in a 1997 piece in *The New Yorker*. "We'd never do too many belt loops, or an unusual base cloth . . . [or] zips or a lot of pocket flaps and details on the back." Pocket flaps, the ultimate signifier of suspect sexuality! In such ads, male naiveté about the sexual potency of clothes, as agency maven David Altschiller claims, is critical. "In women's advertising," he points out, "self-confidence is sexy. But if a man is self-confident — if he knows he is attractive and is beautifully dressed — then he's not a man anymore. He's a fop. He's effeminate." In Dockers' "Nice Pants" television ads, for example, it's crucial that the guy not *know* his pants are "nice" until a gorgeous woman points it out to him.

It's no accident that the pants are described via the low-key understatement "nice" (rather than "great," for example, which would suggest that the guy was actually *trying* to look good). For the real man (according to Dockers), the mirror is a tool, not a captivating pool; if he could, he'd look the other way while he shaves. Many other advertisers capitalize on such notions, encouraging men to take care of their looks, but reassuring them that it's for utilitarian or instrumental purposes. Cosmetic surgeons emphasize the corporate advantage that a face-lift or tummy tuck will give the aging executive: "A youthful look," as one says, "gives the appearance of a more dynamic, charging individual who will go out and get the business." Male grooming products too are often marketed by way of "action hero" euphemisms which obscure their relation to feminine versions of the same product (a male girdle marketed by BodySlimmers is called the Double Agent Boxer) and the fact that their function is to enhance a man's appearance: hair spray as "hair control," exfoliating liquid as "scruffing lotion," astringents as "scrubs," moisturizers and fragrances as "after" or "pre" accompaniments to that most manly of rituals, the shave. They often have names like Safari and Chaps and Lab Series, and come in containers shaped like spaceships and other forms a girl could have some fun with.

The notions about gender that are maintained in this marketing run deeper than a refusal to use the word "perfume" for products designed to make men smell good. In the late seventies, coincident with the development of feminist consciousness about these matters, art historian John Berger discovered what he argued were a set of implicit cultural paradigms of masculinity and femininity, crystallized in a visual "rule" of both classical painting and commercial advertisements: *"men act and women appear."* Here's a contemporary illustration:

The man in the *Nautica* ad on the next page, rigging his sail, seems oblivious to his appearance; he's too busy checking the prevailing winds. The woman, in contrast, seems well aware and well pleased that her legs

Men act and women appear.

have caught the attention of the men gaping at her. A woman's *appearance*, Berger argued, has been socially determined to be "of crucial importance for what is normally thought of as the success of her life." Even walking on a city street, headed for their highpowered executive jobs, women exist to be seen, and they *know* it — a notion communicated by the constant tropes of female narcissism: women shown preening, looking in mirrors, stroking their own bodies, exhibiting themselves for an assumed spectator, asking to be admired for their beauty.

With depictions of men, it's just the opposite. "A man's presence," Berger wrote, "is dependent upon the promise of power which he embodies . . . what he is capable of doing to you or for you." Thus, the classic formula for representing men is always to show them in action, immersed in whatever they are doing, seemingly unaware of anyone who might be looking at them. They never fondle their own bodies narcissistically, display themselves purely as "sights," or gaze at themselves in the mirror. In everything from war paintings to jeans and cologne ads, men have been portrayed as utterly oblivious to their beauty (or lack of it), intent only on getting the job done — raising the flag, baling hay, lassoing a steer, busting up concrete. The ability to move heavy things around, tame wild creatures — that's manly business. Fretting about your love handles, your dry skin, your sagging eyelids? That's for girls.

Women in ads and movies thus require no plot excuse to show off their various body parts in ads, proudly, shyly, or seductively; it's the "business" of *all* of us to be beautiful — whether we are actresses, politicians, homemakers, teachers, or rock stars. This has changed very little since Berger came up with his formula. When *Time* magazine did a story on the new dominance of female stars in the rock world, its cover featured singing star Jewel, not performing, but in a dewy close-up, lips moist and soft eyes smiling from behind curled lashes. This formidable new "force" in the rock world might as well have been modeling Maybelline. True, a beautiful woman today may be depicted puffing away on a cigar, getting "in touch with her masculine side." But in expression she's still a seductress, gazing through long-lashed lids into the eyes of an imagined viewer. "Do you like what you see?" the expressions of the models seem to ask.

Men, according to Berger's formula, must never seem as though they are asking this question, and may display their beauty only if it is an unavoidable side effect of other "business." Thus, a lot of the glistening, naked male chests in the movies of the fifties and sixties were on the bodies of warriors, prisoners, slaves, and prizefighters. No one could claim there was vanity in such nakedness. (No time for preening while nailing spikes on a chain gang or rowing in a slave galley.) So a strong dose of male skin could be sneaked into a movie without disturbing the gender rules. The physical presence of an actor like Richard Gere, who emanates consciousness of his body as the erotic focus of the gaze and invites it, has always annoyed and disconcerted critics. The pomposity of Charlton Heston, on the other hand, his naked (and actually rather gorgeous) chest puffed up in numerous biblical epics, goes unnoticed, because he's doing it all in a builder-of-the-universe rather than narcissus-in-the-mirror mode.

A STRONG DOSE OF MALE SKIN COULD BE SNEAKED INTO A MOVIE WITHOUT DISTURBING THE GENDER RULES.

Saturday Night Fever (1977) deserves mention here, for openly breaking with this convention. Tony Manero (John Travolta), a disco-dancing dandy who knows how to use his walk, was a man who *really* needed a course in masculinity-according-to-Haggar. He blows all his wages on fancy shirts and shoes. On Saturday night, he prepares his body meticulously, shaving, deodorizing, blow-drying, choosing just the right combination of gold chains and amulets, torso-clinging pants, shiny platforms. Eating dinner with his family, he swathes himself in a sheet like a baby to protect his new floral shirt; when his father boxes his ear roughly, his only thought is for his pompadour: "Just watch the hair! I work on my hair a long time and you hit it. He hits the hair!" Manero spends much of his time in front of the mirror, getting himself pretty, posing, anticipating the impression he's going to make when he enters the disco or struts down the street.

Never before *Saturday Night Fever* had a heterosexual male movie hero spent so much time on his toilette. (Even Cary Grant's glamorous looks were never shown as requiring any conscious effort or attention; in *The Awful Truth* he sits under a tanning lamp — but that's to fake a trip to Florida.) Although this was the polyester seventies, and men like Sonny Bono dressed like Tony on television, Bono was very careful (as the Beatles were too) to treat his flamboyant ruffles as showbiz costumes, while Cher proudly strutted her feathers and finery as a second skin for her body and sexuality. Tony, like Cher, chooses his clothes to highlight his sinuous form.

Manero was, in many ways, the cinema equivalent (reassuringly straight and working-class) of the revolution that Calvin Klein was making in more sexually ambiguous form in the fashion world. As a dancer, Tony is unembarrassed — and the camera isn't embarrassed either — to make his hips, groin, and buttocks the mesmerizing center of attention. Travolta was also the first actor to appear on-screen in form-fitting (if discreetly black) briefs. One scene finds him asleep in his underwear, blanket between his legs, hip jutting upward; the camera moves slowly down the length of his body, watches as Tony rouses, sits up, pulls the blanket from between his legs, and puts his hand in his briefs to adjust his penis. (The script originally had called for Travolta to appear naked in a later scene; he balked, suggesting the early morning scene as a compromise.) We then follow him to the mirror (where he compares himself admiringly with a poster of Al Pacino) and into the hall, where he flexes teasingly for his shocked grandmother. This was new stuff, and some people were a bit taken aback by such open male vanity and exhibitionism. (Pauline Kael, for one, seemed to need to convince herself of Tony's sexual orientation. "It's a straight heterosexual film," she wrote, "but with a feeling for the sexiness of young boys who are bursting their britches with energy and desire.")

True, there is the suggestion, in the film, that Tony may grow out of his narcissism once he leaves Brooklyn and the gold chain crowd. Hollywood, of course, had shown men preening, decorating, and oiling themselves before — pimps and homosexuals, usually, but also various unassimilated natives (blacks, Puerto Ricans, Italians) depicted as living more fully in their bodies, with a taste for flashy clothes that marks them as déclassé. Manero fits those stereotypes — but only up to a point. He may have awful taste in jewelry, but he also has boyish charm and "native" intelligence. Unlike his friends — a pathetic trio of racist, homophobic, sexist homeboys — Tony has integrity. He is enraged when, at the "2001" dance contest, racism and favoritism land him first prize over a Puerto Rican couple. He's also the only one of his friends who doesn't taunt a gay couple as they pass on the street. The movie may poke affectionate fun at him, but it also admires him. A hero-narcissus — a very new image for postwar Hollywood.

Of course, most men, gold chains or not, straight or gay, *do* care how they "appear." The gender differences described in Berger's formula and embedded in the Dockers and Haggar advertisements are "fictional," a distillation of certain *ideas* about men and women, not an empirical generalization about their actual behavior. This doesn't mean, however, that they have no impact on "real life." Far from it. As embodied in attractive and sometimes highly manipulative images, "men act and women appear" functions as a visual instruction. Women are supposed to care very much about fashion, "vanity," looking good, and may be seen as unfeminine, man-hating, or lesbian if they don't. The reverse goes for men. The man who cares about his looks the way a woman does, self-esteem on the line, ready to be shattered at the slightest insult or weight gain, is unmanly, sexually suspect.

So the next time you see a Dockers or Haggar ad, think of it not only as an advertisement for khakis but also as an advertisement for a certain notion of what it means to be a man. The ad execs know that's what's going on, they're open about not wanting to frighten men off with touches of feminine decorativeness. What they are less open about is the fact that such ads don't just cater to male phobias about fashion but also perpetuate them. They have to. Nowadays, the Dockers man is competing against other models of masculinity, laughing at him from both the pages of history and from what was previously the "margin" of contemporary culture. Can you imagine Cary Grant, Rupert Everett, or Michael Jordan as the fashion-incompetent man in a Dockers ad? The stylish man, who began to make a new claim on popular cultural representations with the greater visibility of black and gay men — the men consumer culture once ignored — was chiseling cracks in the rule that "men act and women appear" even as Berger was formulating it.

MALE DECORATIVENESS IN CULTURAL PERSPECTIVE

Not all heterosexual men are as uptight about the pocket flaps on their pants as the Haggar executive would have us believe. Several weeks after the piece on khakis appeared in *The New Yorker*, a reader wrote in protesting that the idea "that men don't want to look like they're trying to be fashionable or sexy" was rather culture-bound. Maybe, this reader acknowledged, it applies to American, English, and Japanese men. "But are we really to believe that French, Italian, and Spanish men share this concern? And, when we expand the category 'male' beyond human beings, biologists have shown that the demonstration of male splendor is a key element in the vertebrate mating game. Are American males just an anomalous species?"

The letter reminds us that there are dangers in drawing broad conclusions on the basis of only those worlds with which one is familiar. And it's not just different international attitudes toward men and fashion that cast doubt on the universal applicability of the Dockers/Haggar view of masculinity. To look at the variables of race, class, and history is to produce a picture of male attitudes toward fashionable display that is far from consistently phobic.

First of all, for most of human history, there haven't been radically different "masculine" and "feminine" attitudes toward beauty and decorativeness. On farms, frontiers, and feudal estates, women were needed to work alongside men and beauty was hardly a priority for either. Among aristocrats, it was most important to maintain class privilege (rather than gender difference), and standards of elegance for both sexes (as Anne Hollander's fascinating *Sex and Suits* documents) were largely the same: elaborate headwear, cosmetics, nonutilitarian adornments, and accessories. Attention to beauty was associated not with femininity but with a life that was both privileged and governed by exacting standards. The constrictions, precarious adornments, elaborate fastenings reminded the elite that they were highly civilized beings, not simple peasant "animals." At the same time, decorativeness was a mode of royal and aristocratic competition, as households and courts would try to out-glam each other with jewels and furs. Hollander describes a sixteenth-century summit meeting between Francis I and Henry VIII, in which everyone wore "silver covered with diamonds, except when they were in cloth of gold and covered with rubies. Everything was lined with ermine and everything was 20 yards long, and there were plumes on everybody." Everybody — male or female — had to be as gorgeous as possible. It was a mode of power competition.

Until roughly the fourteenth century, men and women didn't even dress very differently. (Think of the Greeks and Romans and their unisex robes and togas.) Clear differences started to emerge only in the late Middle Ages and early Renaissance: women's breasts began to be exposed and emphasized in tight bodices, while their legs were covered with long skirts. Men's legs — and sometimes their genitals as well — were "fully articulated" and visible through pantaloons (what we call "tights"), with body armor covering the chest. While to our sensibilities, the shapely legs and genitals of men in tights (unless required by a ballet or historical drama) are either to be laughed at or drooled over, Hollander argues that in the Renaissance, to outline the male body was to make it more "real" and "natural," less a template for sexual fantasy (as women's bodies were becoming). This trend continued, with men's clothing getting progressively more unrestrictive, tailored, simple and women's more stiff, tightly fitted, decorative. Still, into the seventeenth century, fashionable gentlemen continued to wear lace and silk, and to don powder and wigs before appearing in public. Hollander regards the nineteenth century as a "great divide," after which not only the styles of men's and women's clothing (trousers for men, increasingly romantic froufrou for women) would become radically different, but ideas about them as well. Men's clothing must now be "honest, comfortable, and utilitarian," while women's begins to develop a reputation for being "frivolous" and "deceptive." The script for "men act and women appear" was being written — right onto male and female clothing.

Looking beyond fashion to the social world (something Hollander refuses to do, but I'll venture), it's hard not to speculate that these changes anticipate the emergence of the middle class and the nineteenth-century development of distinctively separate spheres for men and women within it. In the industrial era, men's sphere — increasingly the world of manufacturing, buying, selling, power brokering — was performance-oriented, and demanded "no nonsense." Women, for their part, were expected not only to provide a comfortable, well-ordered home for men to return to but to offer beauty, fantasy, and charm for a man to "escape" to and restore himself with after the grim grind of the working day. As this division of labor developed, strong dualistic notions about "masculinity" and "femininity" began to emerge, with sanctions against the man or woman who dared to cross over to the side of the divide where they did not belong "by nature."

By the end of the nineteenth century, older notions of manliness premised on altruism, self-restraint, and moral integrity — qualities that women could have too — began to be understood as vaguely "feminine." Writers and politicians (like Teddy Roosevelt) began to complain loudly about the emasculating effects of civilization and the excessive role played by women teachers in stifling the development of male nature. New words like "pussyfoot" and "stuffed shirt" — and, most deadly, "sissy" — came into parlance, and the "homosexual" came to be classified as a perverse personality type which the normal, heterosexual male had to prove himself distinct from. (Before, men's relations with each other had been considerably more fluid, and even the heterosexual male was allowed a certain degree of physical intimacy and emotional connection — indeed, "heterosexuality" as such was a notion that hardly made sense at the time.) A new vogue for bodybuilding emerged. "Women pity weakly men," O. S. Fowler warned, but they love and admire "right hearty feeders, not dainty; sprightly, not tottering; more muscular than exquisite, and more powerful than effeminate, in mind and body." To be "exquisite," to be decorative, to be on display, was now fully woman's business, and the man who crossed that line was a "fop."

From that time on, male "vanity" went into hiding, and when cosmetic products for men began to be marketed (for men *did* use them, albeit in secret), they had to justify themselves, as Kathy Piess documents, through the manly rhetoric of efficiency, rugged individualism, competitive advantage, autonomy. While Pompeian cream promises to "beautify and youthify" women, the same product for men will help them "win success" and "make promotion easier" on the job. Even that most manly of rituals (from our perspective), shaving, required special rhetoric when home shaving was first introduced early in the twentieth century. "The Gillette is typical of the American spirit," claimed a 1910 ad. "Its use starts habits of energy — of initiative. And men who *do* for themselves are men who *think* for themselves." Curley's Easy-Shaving Safety Razor claimed that "the first Roman to shave every day was no fop, but Scipio, conqueror of Africa." When it came to products used also by women — like scents and creams — manufacturers went out of their way to reassure prospective customers of their no-nonsense "difference," through action names (Brisk, Dash, Vim, Keen, Zest) and other means. When Florian, a line of men's toiletries, was introduced in 1929, its creator, Carl Weeks, advised druggists to locate the products near cigar (again!) counters, using displays featuring manly accouterments like boxing gloves, pipes, footballs. This, he argued, "will put over the idea that the mascu-*line* is all *stag*. It's for he-men with no women welcome nohow."

This isn't to say that from the turn of the nineteenth century on, the drive to separate "masculine" and "feminine" attitudes toward self-beautification pushed forward relentlessly. For one thing, culture is never of one piece; it has its dominant images, but also its marginal, recessive, and countercultural images. For another, the history of gender ideology didn't end with the nineteenth century, as dramatic as its changes were. A century of mutations and permutations followed, as demanded by social, economic, and political conditions. Older ideals lingered too and were revived when needed. The Depression, for example, brought a love affair with (a fantasy of) aristocratic "class" to popular culture, and a world of Hollywood representations . . . in which sexual difference was largely irrelevant, the heroes and heroines of screwball comedy a matched set of glamorously attired cutups. In these films, the appeal of actors like Cary Grant, Fred Astaire, and William Powell was largely premised not on assertions of masculine performance but on their elegance, wit, and charm. Their maleness wasn't thrown into question by the cut of their suits. Rather, being fashionable signified that they led an enviable life of pleasure and play. Such associations still persist today. Fashion advertisements for Ralph Lauren, Valentino, Hugo Boss, and many others are crafted to appeal to the class consciousness of consumers; in that universe, one can never be too beautiful or too vain, whatever one's sex.

In the screwball comedies, it didn't matter whether you were a man or a woman, everyone's clothes sparkled and shone. Following the lead of the movies, many advertisements of the thirties promoted a kind of androgynous elegance. But others tried to have their cake and eat it too, as in a 1934 ad for Fougère Royale aftershave, which depicts a group of tony men in tuxedos, hair slicked back, one even wearing a pince-nez, but with the caption "Let's *not* join the ladies!" We may be glamorous, even foppish — but *puh-lease! Ladies* we're not! I should note, too, that while the symbols of "class" can function to highlight equality between men and women, they can also be used to emphasize man's superiority over women — as in a contemporary Cutty Sark ad in which a glamorously attired woman relaxes, dreamily stroking a dog, while the tuxedo-clad men standing around her engage in serious conversation (about stocks, I imagine); these guys don't need to go off into the drawing room in order to escape the ladies; they can keep one around for a bit of decorativeness and sensual pleasure while she remains in her own, more languorous world within their own.

During World War II, movies and magazines continued to celebrate independent, adventurous women, to whom men were drawn "as much for their spirit and character as for their looks."[1] But when the fighting men returned, the old Victorian division of labor was revived with a new commercial avidity, and the world became one in which "men act" (read: *work*) and "women appear" (read: *decorate* — both themselves and their houses) — with a vengeance. Would Barbie get on a horse without the proper accessories? Would the Marlboro Man carry a mirror with him on the trail? By the late fifties and early sixties, the sexy, wisecracking, independent-minded heroine had morphed into a perky little ingenue. Popular actresses Annette Funicello, Connie Stevens, and Sandra Dee were living Barbie dolls, their femininity blatantly advertised on their shirt-waisted bodies. They had perfectly tended bouffant hairdos (which

I achieved for myself by sleeping on the cardboard cylinders from toilet tissue rolls) and wore high heels even when washing dishes (I drew the line at that). And what about the dashing, cosmopolitan male figure in fashionable clothes? He now was usually played as a sissy or a heel — as for example Lester (Bob Evans), the slick playboy of *The Best of Everything*, who seduces gullible April (Diane Baker) with his big-city charm, then behaves like a cad when she gets pregnant.

There have always been ways to market male clothes consciousness, however. Emphasizing neatness is one. Our very own Ronnie Reagan (when he was still a B-movie star) advertised Van Heusen shirts as "the neatest Christmas gift of all" because they "won't wrinkle . . . ever!!" Joining elegance with violence is another. James Bond could get away with wearing beautiful suits because he was ruthless when it came to killing and bedding. (A men's cologne, called 007, was advertised in the sixties with clips from *Thunderball*, the voice-over recommending: "When you use 007, be kind" because "it's loaded" and "licensed to kill . . . women.") The elegant male who is capable of killing is like the highly efficient secretary who takes off her glasses to reveal a passionate, gorgeous babe underneath: a species of tantalizing, sexy disguise.

When elegance marks one man's superior class status over another it gives him a competitive edge (as was the dominant function of elegance before the eighteenth century) rather than turning him into a fop. "We have our caste marks, too" ran a 1928 ad for Aqua Velva, which featured a clean-shaven, top-hatted young man, alongside a turbaned, bejeweled, elite Indian man. This ad, however, proved to be problematic, as Kathy Piess points out. American men didn't like being compared with dark-skinned foreigners, even aristocratic ones. The more dominant tradition — among Europeans as well as Americans — has been to portray an order in which the clean, well-shaven white man is being served or serviced by the dark ones, as in a 1935 American ad for Arrow Shirts in which the black maid is so fashion-clueless that she doesn't even know what a manufacturer's label is, or in a German ad for shaving soap depicting the "appropriate" relation between the master race and the Others.

Such codes were clearly being poked fun at — how successfully I'm not sure — when a 1995 Arid Extra-Dry commercial depicted African American pro basketball player Charles Barkley dressed up as a nineteenth-century British colonial, declaring that anything less than Arid "would be uncivilized." The commercial, however, is not just (arguably) a poke at the racist equation of civilization and whiteness. It's also, more subtly, a playful assertion of some distinctive African American attitudes toward male display. "Primordial perspiration," Barkley says in the commercial, "shouldn't mess with your style." And "style" is a concept whose history and cultural meanings are very different for blacks and whites in this country. Among many young African American men, appearing in high style, "cleaned up" and festooned with sparkling jewelry, is not a sign of effeminacy, but potency and social standing. Consider the following description, from journalist Playthell Benjamin's 1994 memoir, *Lush Life* (while you're

reading it, you might also recall Anne Hollander's description of Henry VIII's summit meeting):

> [Fast Black] was dressed in a pair of white pants, white buck shoes, and a long-sleeve white silk shirt—which was open to his navel and revealed a 24-karat gold chain from which hung a gold medallion set with precious stones: diamonds, rubies, and emeralds. His massively muscled body was strikingly displayed in a white see-through silk shirt, and the trousers strained to contain his linebacker thighs. His eyes were bloodshot and his skin was tight against his face, giving it the look of an ebony mask. He struck me right off as a real dangerous muthafucka; mean enough to kill a rock.

A "real dangerous muthafucka" in a white see-through silk shirt? For the white boys to whom the Dockers and Haggar ads are largely addressed, see-through silk is for girls, and showing off one's body — particularly with sensuous fabrics — is a "fag" thing. Thus, while a Haggar ad may play up the sensual appeal of soft fabrics — *"These clothes are very soft and they'll never wrinkle"* — it makes sure to include a parenthetical (and sexist) reference to a dreamed-of wife: *"Too bad you can't marry them."* But sartorial sensuality and decorativeness, as I've learned, do not necessarily mean "femininity" for African American men.

When I first saw the Charles Barkley commercial, the word "style" slipped by me unnoticed, because I knew very little about the history of African American aesthetics. An early paper of mine dealing with Berger's equation was utterly oblivious to racial differences that might confound the formula "men act and women appear." Luckily, an African American male colleague of mine gently straightened me out, urging me to think about Mike Tyson's gold front tooth as something other than willful masculine defiance of the tyranny of appearance. Unfortunately, at that time not much of a systematic nature had been written about African American aesthetics; I had to find illuminating nuggets here and there. Then, just this year, Shane White and Graham White's *Stylin'* appeared. It's a fascinating account of how the distinctive legacy of African aesthetics was maintained and creatively, sometimes challengingly, incorporated into the fashion practices of American blacks, providing a vibrant (and frequently subversive) way for blacks to "write themselves into the American story."

Under slavery, white ownership of blacks was asserted in the most concrete, humiliating way around the display of the body on the auction block. Slaves were often stripped naked and instructed to show their teeth like horses being examined for purchase. Women might have their hair cut off. Everyone's skin would be polished to shine, as apples are polished in grocery stores today. As a former slave described it:

"The first thing they had to do was wash up and clean up real good and take a fat greasy meat skin and run over their hands, face and also their feet, or in other words, every place that showed about their body so that they would look real fat and shiny. Then they would trot them out before their would-be buyers and let them look over us real good, just like you would a bunch of fat cows that you were going to sell on the market and try to get all you could for them."

It makes perfect sense that with the body so intimately and degradingly under the control of the slave owner, opportunities to "take back" one's own body and assert one's own cultural meanings with it would have a special significance. On Sundays, slaves would dress up for church in the most colorful, vibrant clothes they could put together — a temporary escape from and an active repudiation of the subservience their bodies were forced into during the week. Their outfits, to white eyes, seemed "clashing" and mismatched. But putting together unusual combinations of color, texture, and pattern was an essential ingredient of West African textile traditions, handed down and adapted by African American women.

Color and shape "coordination"—the tyranny of European American fashion until pretty recently—were not the ruling principles of style. "Visual aliveness," *Stylin'* reports, was. The visual aliveness of the slaves' Sunday best, so jangling to white sensibilities, was thus the child both of necessity—they were forced to construct their outfits through a process of bricolage, putting them together from whatever items of clothing were available—and aesthetic tradition.

From the start, whites perceived there was something insubordinate going on when blacks dressed up—and they were not entirely wrong. "Slaves were only too keen to display, even to flaunt, their finery both to slaves and to whites"; the Sunday procession was, as I've noted, a time to reclaim the body as one's own. But at the same time, blacks were not just "flaunting," but preserving and improvising on vibrant African elements of style whose "flashiness" and "insolence" were largely in the eye of the white beholder, used to a very different aesthetic. The cultural resistance going on here was therefore much deeper than offended whites (and probably most blacks too) realized at the time. It wasn't simply a matter of refusal to behave like Stepin Fetchit, with head lowered and eyes down. A new culture of unpredictable, playfully decorative, visually bold fashion was being created—and it would ultimately (although not for some time) transform the world of mainstream fashion as much as Klein's deliberately erotic underwear and jeans.

THE MOST DAZZLINGLY DRESSED MEN, OFTEN JAZZ MUSICIANS, WERE KNOWN AS "SPORTS."

After "emancipation," funeral marches and celebratory promenades were a regular feature of black city life, in which marchers, male and female alike, were "emblazoned in colorful, expensive clothes," the men in "flashy sports outfits: fancy expensive silk shirts, new pants, hats, ties, socks," "yellow trousers and yellow silk shirts," and "bedecked with silk-and-satin-ribboned streamers, badges." Apart from formal processions, streets like Memphis's Beale Street and New Orleans's Decatur Street were ongoing informal sites for "strolling" and display. The most dazzlingly dressed men, often jazz musicians, were known as "sports." As "Jelly Roll" Morton describes it, each "sport" had to have a Sunday suit, with coat and pants that did not match, and crisply pressed trousers as tight as sausage skins. Suspenders were essential and had to be "very loud," with one strap left provocatively "hanging down." These guys knew how to "use their walk" too. The sport would walk down the street in a "very mosey" style: "Your hands is at your sides with your index fingers stuck out and you kind of struts with it." Morton—by all accounts a particularly flashy sport—had gold on his teeth and a diamond in one of them. "Those days," he recalled, "I thought I would die unless I had a hat with the emblem Stetson in it and some Edwin Clapp shoes." Shades of Tony Manero. Or King Henry VIII.

In fact, the flashiest African American male styles have partaken both of the African legacy and European notions of "class." Although the origin of the zoot suit—broad shoulders, long coats, ballooning, peg-legged trousers, usually worn with a wide-brimmed hat—is debated, one widely believed account says it was based on a style of suit worn by the Duke of Windsor. Another claims Rhett Butler in *Gone With the Wind* was the inspiration for the zoot suit (if so, it is a "deep irony," as the authors of *Stylin'* comment). But whatever its origins, the zoot suit, worn during the forties when cloth conservation orders ruled the use of that much fabric illegal, was a highly visible and dramatic statement in *disunity* and defiance of "American Democracy," a refusal to accede to the requirements of patriotism. Even more so than the slave's Sunday promenade, the zoot-suiter used "style" aggressively to assert opposition to the culture that had made him marginal to begin with — without his assent.

The use of high style for conspicuous display or defiance is still a big part of male street culture, as sociologist Richard Majors notes: "Whether it's your car, your clothes, your young body, your new hairdo, your jewelry, you style it. The word 'style' in [African American] vernacular usage means to show off what you've got. And for teenagers with little money and few actual possessions, showing off what you do have takes on increased importance. As one youth puts it, 'It's identity. It's a big ego trip.' "

What's changed since Majors wrote these words in the early nineties is the increasing commercial popularity of hip-hop music and culture, which has turned the rebellious stylings of street youth into an empire of images and products, often promoted (and sometimes designed) by big-name stars. With postmodern sensibilities (grab what you like) ruling the fashion world, moreover, what once were signature elements of black street style have been incorporated — as gay styles have also been incorporated — in the fashions of other worlds, both "high" (designer clothing) and "low" (white high school boys with their pants slung low, trying to look so cool).

Two versions of "style": "Style point" and "life, unity, peace."

Despite the aggressive visibility of hip-hop culture, "showing off what you've got" has not been the only influential definition of style among African Americans. In the late nineteenth and early twentieth century, several etiquette books were published, written by middle-class blacks, promoting a very different fashion ideal. The *National Capital Code of Etiquette*, published in 1889, warned young men to "avoid colors that do not blend with the remainder of your wearing apparel, and above all things shun the so-called 'loud' ties with colors that fairly shriek unto Heaven . . . ." The young black men should also avoid "bright reds, yellows and light greens as you would the plague" and never, ever strut or swagger. Hortense Powdermaker, who studied black life in Indianola, Mississippi, in the late 1930s, noted that better-off African Americans "deliberately avoided bright colors" and were offended when clerks, on the basis of "the Negroe's reputation for wearing gaudy clothes," assumed they wanted something "loud." Those who advocated a less ostentatious style were dismayed by the lower-class practice of adorning healthy front teeth with gold, while leaving bad back teeth unattended.

A recent *Essence* list of fashion "do's and don'ts" emphasizes this deliberately understated — and in today's world, "professional" — conception of black male style. "Yes" to well-groomed hands, well-fitting suit and a "definite sense of self." "No" to "glossy polished nails," "cologne that arrives before he does," "Mr. T jewelry (the T stands for tacky)," and "saggy jeans on anyone old enough to remember when 'Killing Me Softly' was *first* released." Even in their most muted variations, African American styles have done a great deal to add color, playfulness, and unexpected, sexy little fillips to "tasteful," professional male clothing: whimsical ties, internationally inspired shirts and sweaters, and, in general, permission to be slightly dramatic, flirtatious, and ironic with one's clothes. The rule of always matching patterns, too, no longer holds in the world of high fashion, the result of a collaboration (not necessarily conscious, of course) between postmodern sensibilities and the slave legacy of bricolage.

Superstar Michael Jordan (his masculine credentials impeccable, his reputation as a family man solidly established over the years), a very effective spokesperson for style, has done a great deal to make fashionableness, even "feminine" decorativeness, congruous with masculinity. This year, he was named *GQ*'s "Most Stylish Man." "How stylish is Michael Jordan?" *GQ* asks. "Answer: So stylish he can get away with wearing five rings!" Of course, the fact that Jordan can "get away" with wearing five rings reveals *GQ*'s cultural biases. For the magazine, Jordan's stylishness resides in the "drape of his suits, in the plain gold hoop in his left ear, in the tempered, toned-down body language of his late career." For *GQ*, subtlety equals style. For Jordan too. But of course that plain gold hoop would not have been viewed as so tastefully subtle had Jordan not made it an acceptable item of male decorativeness.

Jordan, God bless him, is also unabashed in admitting that he shops more than his wife, and that he gets his inspiration from women's magazines. The night before he goes on the road, he tries on every outfit he's going to wear.

He describes himself as a "petite-type person" who tries to hide this with oversize clothes and fabrics that drape. When questioned about the contradiction between the "manliness" of sports and his "feminine" love of fashion, Jordan replies that "that's the fun part — I can get away from the stigma of being an athlete." Saved by fashion from the "stigma" of being a sweaty brute — that's something, probably, that only an African American man can fully appreciate. The fact that it's being an athlete and not "femininity" that's the "stigma" to be avoided by Jordan — that's something a woman's got to love.

The ultimate affront to Dockers masculinity, however, is undoubtedly the Rockport ad above, with drag superstar RuPaul in a beautifully tailored suit. His feet and his stare are planted — virtually identically to

Michael Jordan's posture in the feature I've just discussed — in that unmistakable (and here, ironic) grammar of face-off ad masculinity. "I'm comfortable being a MAN," declares RuPaul. "I'm comfortable being a woman too," of course, is the unwritten subtext. Man, woman, what's the difference so long as one is "uncompromising" about style?

MY WORLD . . . AND WELCOME TO IT?

Despite everything I've said thus far, I feel decidedly ambivalent about consumer culture's inroads into the male body. I *do* find it wonderful — as I've made abundantly clear — that the male form, both clothed and unclothed, is being made so widely available for sexual fantasy and aesthetic admiration. I like the fact that more and more heterosexual white guys are feeling permission to play with fashion, self-decoration, sensual presentation of the self. Even Dockers has become a little less "me a guy . . . duh!" in its ads and spreads for khakis, which now include spaced-out women as well as men.

But I also know what it's like to be on the other side of the gaze. I know its pleasures, and I know its agonies — intimately. Even in the second half of the twentieth century, beauty remains a prerequisite for female success. In fact, in an era characterized by some as "postfeminist," beauty seems to count more than it ever did before, and the standards for achieving it have become more stringent, more rigorous, than ever. We live in an empire ruled not by kings or even presidents, but by images. The tight buns, the perfect skin, the firm breasts, the long, muscled legs, the bulgeless, sagless bodies are everywhere. Beautiful women, everywhere, telling the rest of us how to stand, how to swing our hair, how slim we must be.

Actually, all this flawless beauty is the product of illusion, generated with body doubles, computers, artful retouching. "Steal this look!" the lifestyles magazines urge women; it's clear from the photo that great new haircut of Sharon Stone's could change a woman's life. But in this era of digital retouching not even Sharon Stone looks like Sharon Stone. (Isabella Rossellini, who used to be the Lancôme girl before she got too old, has said that her photos are so enhanced that when people meet her they tell her, "Your sister is so beautiful.") Still, we try to accomplish the impossible, and often get into trouble. Illusions set the standard for real women, and they spawn special disorders and addictions: in trying to become as fat-free and poreless as the ads, one's fleshly body is pushed to achieve the impossible.

I had a student who admitted to me in her journal that she had a makeup addiction. This young woman was unable to leave the house — not even to walk down to the corner mailbox — without a full face and body cover-up that took her over an hour and a half to apply. In her journal, she described having escalated over a year or so from minimal "touching-up" to a virtual mask of foundation, powder, eyebrow pencil, eye shadow, eyeliner, mascara, lip liner, lipstick — a mask so thorough, so successful in its illusionary reality that her own naked face now looked grotesque to her, mottled, pasty, featureless. She dreaded having sex with her boyfriend, for fear some of the mask might come off and he would see what she looked like underneath. As soon as they were done, she would race to the bathroom to reapply; when he stayed over, she would make sure to sleep lightly, in order to wake up earlier than he. It's funny — and not really funny. My student's disorder may be one generated by a superficial, even insane culture, a disorder befitting the Oprah show rather than a PBS documentary. But a disorder nonetheless. Real. Painful. Deforming of her life.

So, too, for the eating disorders that run rampant among girls and women. In much of my writing on the female body, I've chronicled how these disorders have spread across race, class, and ethnic differences in this culture. Today, serious problems with food, weight, and body image are no longer (if they ever were) the province of pampered, narcissistic, heterosexual white girls. To imagine that they are is to view black, Asian, Latin, lesbian, and working-class women as outside the loop of the dominant culture and untouched by its messages about what is beautiful — a mistake that has left many women feeling abandoned and alone with a disorder they weren't "supposed" to have. Today, eating problems are virtually the norm among high school and college women — and even younger girls. Yes, of course there are far greater tragedies in life than gaining five pounds. But try to reassure a fifteen-year-old girl that her success in life doesn't require a slender body, and she will think you dropped from another planet. *She* knows what's demanded; she's learned it from the movies, the magazines, the soap operas.

There, the "progressive" message conveyed by giving the girls and women depicted great careers or exciting adventures is overpowered, I think, by the more potent example of their perfect bodies. The plots may say: "The world is yours." The bodies caution: "But only if you aren't fat." What counts as "fat" today? Well, Alicia Silverstone was taunted by the press when she appeared at the Academy Awards barely ten pounds heavier than her (extremely) svelte self in *Clueless*. Janeane Garofalo was the "fat one" in *The Truth About Cats and Dogs*. Reviews of *Titanic* described Kate Winslett as plump, overripe, much too hefty for ethereal Leonardo DiCaprio. Any anger you detect here is personal too. I ironed my hair in the sixties, have dieted all my life, continue to be deeply ashamed of those parts of my body — like my peasant legs and zaftig behind — that our culture has coded as ethnic excess. I suspect it's only an accident of generational timing or a slight warp in the fabric of my cultural environment that prevented me from developing an eating disorder. I'm not a makeup junky like my student, but I am becoming somewhat addicted nowadays to alpha-hydroxies, skin drenchers, quenchers, and other "age-defying" potions.

No, I don't think the business of beauty is without its pleasures. It offers a daily ritual of transformation, renewal. Of "putting oneself together" and walking out into the world, more confident than you were, anticipating attraction, flirtation, sexual play. I love shopping for makeup with my friends. (Despite what Rush Limbaugh tells you, feminism — certainly not feminism in the nineties—is not synonymous with unshaved legs.) Women bond over shared makeup, shared beauty tips. It's fun. Too often, though, our bond is over shared pain—over "bad" skin, "bad" hair, "bad" legs. There's always that constant judgment and evaluation—not only by actual, living men but by an ever-present, watchful cultural gaze which always has its eye on our thighs—no matter how much else we accomplish. We judge each other that way too, sometimes much more nastily than men. Some of the bitchiest comments about Marcia Clark's hair and Hillary Clinton's calves have come from women. But if we are sometimes our "own worst enemies," it's usually because we see in each other not so much competition as a reflection of our fears and anxieties about ourselves. In this culture, all women suffer over their bodies. A demon is loose in our consciousness and can't easily be controlled. We see the devil, fat calves, living on Hillary's body. We point our fingers, like the accusers at Salem. Root him out, kill *her*!

And now men are suddenly finding that devil living in their flesh. If someone had told me in 1977 that in 1997 *men* would comprise over a quarter of cosmetic-surgery patients, I would have been astounded. I never dreamed that "equality" would move in the direction of men worrying *more* about their looks rather than women worrying less. I first suspected that something major was going on when the guys in my gender classes stopped yawning and passing snide notes when we discussed body issues, and instead began to protest when the women talked as though they were the only ones "oppressed" by standards of beauty. After my book *Unbearable Weight* appeared, I received several letters from male anorexics, reminding me that the incidence of such disorders among men was on the rise. Today, as many as a million men—and eight million women—have an eating disorder.

I NEVER DREAMED THAT "EQUALITY" WOULD MOVE IN THE DIRECTION OF MEN WORRYING *MORE* ABOUT THEIR LOOKS RATHER THAN WOMEN WORRYING LESS.

Then I began noticing all the new men's "health" magazines on the newsstands, dispensing diet and exercise advice ("A Better Body in Half the Time," "50 Snacks That Won't Make You Fat") in the same cheerleader-ish mode that Betty Friedan had once chastised the women's magazines for: "It's Chinese New Year, so make a resolution to custom-order your next takeout. Ask that they substitute wonton soup for oil. Try the soba noodles instead of plain noodles. They're richer in nutrients and contain much less fat." I guess the world doesn't belong to the meat-eaters anymore, Mr. Ben Quick.

It used to be a truism among those of us familiar with the research on body-image problems that most men (that is, most straight men, on whom the studies were based) were largely immune. Women, research showed, were chronically dissatisfied with themselves. But men tended, if anything, to see themselves as better-looking than they (perhaps) actually were. Peter Richmond, in a 1987 piece in *Glamour*, describes his "wonderful male trick" for seeing what he wants to see when he looks in the mirror:

> I edit out the flaws. Recently, under the influence of too many Heinekens in a strange hotel room, I stood in front of a wrap-around full-length mirror and saw, in a moment of nauseous clarity, how unshapely my stomach and butt have become. The next morning, looking again in the same mirror, ready to begin another business day, I simply didn't see these offending areas.

Notice all the codes for male "action" that Richmond has decorated his self-revelation with. "Too many Heinekens," "another business day"—all reassurances that other things matter more to him than his appearance. But a decade later, it's no longer so easy for men to perform these little tricks. Getting ready for the business day is apt to exacerbate rather than divert male anxieties about the body, as men compete with fitter, younger men and fitter, more self-sufficient women. In a 1994 survey, 6,000 men ages eighteen to fifty-five were asked how they would like to see themselves. Three of men's top six answers were about looks: attractive to women, sexy, good-looking. Male "action" qualities—assertiveness, decisiveness—trailed at numbers eight and nine.

"Back when bad bodies were the norm," claims *Fortune* writer Alan Farnham (again, operating with the presumption of heterosexuality), "money distinguished male from male. Now muscles have devalued money," and the market for products and procedures "catering to male vanity" (as *Fortune* puts it) is $9.5 billion or so a year. "It's a Face-Lifted, Tummy-Tucked Jungle Out There," reports *The New York Times*. To compete, a man

> could buy Rogaine to thicken his hair. He could invest in Body-Slimmers underwear for men, by the designer Nancy Ganz, with built-in support to suck in the waist. Or he could skip the aloe skin cream and go on to a more drastic measure, new to the male market: alpha-hydroxy products that slough off dead skin. Or he could rub on some belly- and thigh-shrinking creams. . . . If rubbing cream seems too strenuous, [he] can just don an undershirt from Mountainville House, to "shape up and pull in loose stomachs and sagging chests," with a diamond-shaped insert at the gut for "extra control." . . . Plastic surgery offers pectoral implants to make the chest appear more muscular, and calf muscle implants to give the leg a bodybuilder shape. There is liposuction to counter thickening middles and accumulating breast and fatty tissue in the chest...and a half-dozen surgical methods for tightening skin.

Some writers blame all this on sexual equality in the workplace. Anthropologist Lionel Tiger offers this explanation: "Once," he says, "men could fairly well control their destiny through providing resources to women, but now that the female is obliged to earn a living, he himself becomes a resource. He becomes his own product: Is he good-looking? Does he smell good? Before, when he had to provide for the female, he could have a potbelly. Now he has to appear attractive in the way the female had to be." Some evidence does support this. A *Psychology Today* survey found that the more financially secure the woman, the more important a man's looks were to her.

I, however, tend to see consumer capitalism rather than women's expectations or proclivities as the true motor driving male concern with appearance. Calvin gave us those muscled men in underwear. Then the cosmetics, diet, exercise, and surgery industries elbowed in, providing the means for everyone to develop that great Soloflex body. After all, why should they restrict themselves to female markets if they can convince men that their looks need constant improvement too? The management and enhancement of the body is a gold mine for consumerism, and one whose treasures are inexhaustible, as women know. Dieting and staving off aging are never-ending processes. Ideals of beauty can be endlessly tinkered with by fashion designers and cosmetic manufacturers, remaining continually elusive, requiring constant new purchases, new kinds of work on the body.

John Berger's opposition of "acting" and "appearing," this body work reveals, is something of a false duality — and always has been. "Feminine" attention to appearance is hardly the absence of activity, as men are learning. It takes time, energy, creativity, dedication. It can *hurt*. Nowadays, the "act/appear" duality is even less meaningful, as the cultivation of the suitably fit appearance has become not just a matter of sexual allure but also a demonstration that one has the "right stuff": will, discipline, the ability to stop whining and "just do it." When I was growing up in the sixties, a muscular male body meant beefy but dumb jock; a middle-class girl could drool over him but probably wouldn't want to marry him. Today, with a booming "gymnasium culture" existing (as in ancient Greece) for professional men and with it a revival of the Greek idea that a good mind and a good body are not mutually exclusive, even Jeff Goldblum has got muscles, and the only type of jock he plays is a computer jock.

All of this, as physicians have begun to note, is landing more and more men straight into the formerly female territory of body-image dysfunction, eating disorders, and exercise compulsions. Last year, I read a survey that reported that 90 percent of male undergraduates believe that they are not muscular enough. That sent warning bells clanging in my mind, and sure enough, there's now a medical category for "muscle dysmorphia" (or "bigorexia," as it's actually sometimes called!), a kind of reverse anorexia in which the sufferer sees his muscles as never massive enough. Researchers are "explaining" bigorexia in the same dumb way they've tended to approach women's disorders — as a combination of bad biochemistry and "triggering events," such as being picked on. They just don't seem to fully appreciate the fact that bigorexia — like anorexia — only blooms in a very particular cultural soil. Not even the ancient Greeks — who revered athletic bodies and scorned weaklings, but also advised moderation in all things — produced "muscle dysmorphics." (Or at least, none of the available medical texts mention anything like it.) Anorexia and bigorexia, like so many contemporary disorders, are diseases of a culture that doesn't know when to stop.

Those beautiful bodies of Greek statues may be the historical inspiration for the muscled men in underwear of the Calvin Klein ads. But the fact is that studying the ancient Greeks reveals a different set of attitudes toward beauty and the body than our contemporary ideals, both homosexual and heterosexual. As is well known by now (although undiscussed when I studied philosophy as an undergraduate), Plato was not above appreciating a beautiful young body. In *Symposium*, he describes the beauty of the body as evidence of the presence of the divine on earth, and the original spur to all "higher" human endeavors (as well as earthly, sexual love). We see someone dazzling, and he or she awakens the soul to its natural hunger to be lifted above the mundane, transitory, mortal world. Some people seek that transcendence through ordinary human intercourse, and achieve the only immortality they will know through the begetting of human offspring and the continuation of the human race. For others, the beautiful body of another becomes the inspiration for a lifelong search for beauty in all its forms, the creation of beautiful art, beautiful words, beautiful ideals, beautiful cities. They will achieve their immortality through communion with something beyond the body — the idea of Beauty itself.

So human beauty is a pretty far-ranging and powerful thing for Plato, capable of evoking worlds beyond itself, even recalling a previous life when we dwelt among timeless, perfect forms. But human beauty, significantly (in fact, all earthly beauty), can only offer a glimpse of heavenly perfection. It's our nature to be imperfect, after all, and anyone who tries to overcome that limitation on earth is guilty of hubris — according to the Greeks. Our own culture, in contrast, is one without "limits" (a frequent theme of advertisements and commercials) and seemingly without any fear of hubris. Not only do we expect perfection in the bodies of others (just take a gander at some personal ads), we are constantly encouraged to achieve it ourselves, with the help of science and technology and the products and services they make available to us. "This body could be yours," the chiseled Greek statue in the Soloflex commercial tells us (and for only twenty minutes three times a week — give me a break!). "Timeless Beauty Is Within Your Reach," reads an ad for cosmetic surgery. Plato is rolling over in his grave.

For Plato (unlike Descartes) there are no "mere" physical bodies; bodies are lit with meaning, with memory. Our culture is more Cartesian; we like to think of our bodies as so much stuff, which can be tinkered with without any consequences for our soul. We bob our "family noses," lift our aging faces, suction extra fat, remove minor "flaws" with seemingly little concern for any "deep" meaning that our bodies might have, as repositories of our histories, our ethnic and racial and family lineage, our personalities. Actually, much of the time our intentions are to deliberately shed those meanings: to get rid of that Jewish nose, to erase the years from our faces. Unlike the Platonic philosopher, we aren't content to experience timelessness in philosophy, art, or even the beautiful bodies of others; we want to stop time on our own bodies too. In the process, we substitute individualized beauty — the distinctive faces of the generation of beautiful actresses of my own age, for example — for generic, very often racialized, reproducible codes of youth.

The fact is that we're not only Cartesian but Puritan in our attitudes toward the body. The Greeks went for muscles, sure, but they would have regarded our exercise compulsions as evidence of a system out of control. They thought it unseemly — and a failure of will — to get too self-obsessed with *any*thing. They were into the judicious "management" of the body (as French philosopher Michel Foucault has put it), not its utter subjugation. We, on the other hand, can become what our culture considers to be sexually alluring only if we're willing to regard our flesh as recalcitrant metal, to be pummeled, burned, and tempered into steel, day in and day out. No pain, no gain. Obsessively pursuing these ideals has deprived both men *and* women of the playful eros of beauty, turned it all into constant, hard work. I love gay and black body cultures for their flirtatiousness, their tongue-in-cheekness, their irony, their "let's dress up and have some fun" attitudes. Consumer culture, unfortunately, can even grind playfulness into a commodity, a required item for this year's wardrobe.

For all its idealization of the beauty of the body, Greek culture also understood that beauty could be "inner." In the *Symposium*, a group of elite Greeks discourse on the nature of love. Everyone except for Socrates and Aristophanes is in love with someone else at the party, and they're madly flirting, advancing their own romantic agendas through their speeches. Among the participants are the most beautiful young men of their crowd. Socrates himself is over fifty at the time, and not a pretty man to look at (to put it generously). Yet as we're told at the beginning (and this seems to have been historically true), nearly everyone has at one time or another been "obsessed" with him, "transported, completely possessed" — by his cleverness, his irony, his ability to weave a spell with words and ideas. Even the most dazzling Athenian of them all — soldier superhero Alcibiades, generally regarded as one of the sexiest, handsomest men in town, who joins the party late (and drunk) with a beautiful wreath of violets and ivy and ribbons in his hair — is totally, madly smitten with Socrates.

Alcibiades' love for Socrates is *not* "Platonic" in the sense in which we have come to understand that term. In fact, Alcibiades is insulted because Socrates has refused to have sex with him. "The moment he starts to speak," he tells the crowd of his feelings for Socrates, "I am beside myself: my heart starts leaping in my chest, the tears come streaming down my face." This is not the way it usually goes. In the more normal Greek scheme of things, it's the beautiful young man — like Alcibiades — who is supposed to start the heart of the older man thumping, and who flirtatiously withholds his favors while the older lover does his best to win him. Alcibiades is in a state about this role reversal, but he understands why it has happened. He compares Socrates to a popular kind of satyr statue, which (like the little lacquered Russian dolls we're more familiar with) could be opened to reveal another figure within. Socrates may be ugly as a satyr on the outside, but "once I had a glimpse of the figures within — they were so godlike, so bright and beautiful, so utterly amazing, that I no longer had a choice — I just had to do whatever he told me."

We pay constant lip service to beauty that is more than skin-deep. The talk shows frequently parade extreme May-December matings for our ogling too. But the fact is that the idea of a glamorous young man being romantically, *sexually* obsessed with someone old and "ugly" — same-sex or other-sex and no matter what other sterling qualities he or she may have — is pretty much beyond us. Historically, men have benefited from a double standard which culturally codes their gray hair, middle-age paunches, facial lines, as signs of wisdom and experience rather than advancing decrepitude. My older gay male friends lament that those days are over for them. And if those new polls about women's attitudes are to be believed, the clock is ticking on that double standard for heterosexual men, too — no matter how hard Hollywood tries to preserve it. With more and more expectation that men be as physically well-tended as women, those celluloid pairings of Woody Allen and women half as old and forty-six times as good-looking are becoming more of a hoot every day.

There is something anti-sensual to me about current aesthetics. There's so much that my younger friends go "uggh" over. Fat — yecch! Wrinkles —yuck! They live in a constant state of squeamishness about the flesh. I find that finely muscled young Calvin Klein model beautiful and sexy, sure. But I also was moved by Clint Eastwood's aging chest in *The Bridges of Madison County*. Deflated, skin loose around the waistband of his pants, not a washboard ridge in sight — for me, they signaled that Eastwood (at least for this role) had put Dirty Harry away for good, become a real, warm, penetrable, vulnerable human being instead of a make-my-day machine. Call me old-fashioned, but I find that very sexy. For a culture obsessed with youth and fitness, in contrast, sagging flesh is almost the ultimate signifier of decay and disorder. We prefer the clean machine — and are given it, in spades. Purified of "flaws," all loose skin tightened, armored with implants, digitally enhanced, the bodies of most movie stars and models are fully dressed even when naked.

In *Saturday Night Fever*, John Travolta had been trim, but (by contemporary standards) a bit "soft." Six years later, Travolta re-created Tony Manero in the sequel, *Staying Alive*. This time, however, the film was directed by Sylvester Stallone, who showed Travolta a statue of a discus thrower and asked, "How would you like to look like that?" "Terrific," Travolta replied, and embarked on a seven-month program of fitness training that literally redesigned his body into a carbon copy of Sly's. In the film, his body was "perfect": gleaming and muscular, without an ounce of fat. He was nice to look at. But if I had to choose between the Tony Manero of *Fever* and the Tony Manero of *Staying Alive*, it'd be no contest. I'd rather spend time (and have sex) with a dancing man with love handles than with a Greek statue who gets in a nasty mood if he misses a workout.

NOTE

[1] Not that women's beauty was dispensable. Concern for her looks symbolized that although she worked as hard as a man, a woman's mind was still on the *real* men who were fighting for her freedom. (An ad for Tangee lipstick describes "a woman's lipstick [as] an instrument of personal morale that helps her to conceal heartbreak or sorrow; gives her self-confidence when it's badly needed. . . . It symbolizes one of the reasons why we are fighting . . . the precious right of women to be feminine and lovely — under any circumstances.") The woman of this period was a creature of both "appearance" *and* "action" — a kind of forerunner to today's superwoman. [Note is Bordo's.]

BIBLIOGRAPHY

Beauvoir, Simone de. (1952). *The Second Sex*. New York: Vintage Books.
Berger, John. (1972). *Ways of Seeing*. Great Britain: Penguin Books.
Blum, Deborah. (1997). *Sex on the Brain: The Biological Differences Between Men and Women*. New York: Viking Penguin.
Boyd, Herbert, and Robert Allen (eds.). (1995). *Brotherman*. New York: Ballantine.
Clark, Danae. (1995). "Commodity Lesbianism." In Kate Meuhuron and Gary Persecute (eds.). *Free Spirits*. Englewood Cliffs, NJ: Prentice Hall, pp. 82–94.
Clarkson, Wensley. (1997). *John Travolta: Back in Character*. Woodstock: Overlook Press.
Ellenzweig, Allen. (1992). *The Homoerotic Photograph*. New York: Columbia University Press.
Farnham, Alan. (1996). "You're So Vain," *Fortune*, September 9, pp. 66–82.
Foucault, Michel. (1985). *The Use of Pleasure*. New York: Vintage Books.
Friday, Nancy. (1996). *The Power of Beauty*. New York: HarperCollins.
Gaines, Steven, and Sharon Churcher. (1994). *Obsession: The Lives and Times of Calvin Klein*. New York: Avon Books.
Gilmore, David. (1990). *Manhood in the Making*. New Haven: Yale University Press.
Gladwell, Malcolm. (1997). "Listening to Khakis," *The New Yorker*, July 28, pp. 54–58.
Hollander, Anne. (1994). *Sex and Suits: The Evolution of Modern Dress*. New York: Kodansha International.
Long, Ron. (1997). "The Fitness of the Gym," *Harvard Gay and Lesbian Review*, Vol. IV, No. 3, Summer, pp. 20–22.
Majors, Richard, and Janet Mancini Billson. (1992). *Cool Pose: The Dilemmas of Black Manhood in America*. New York: Lexington Books.
Piess, Kathy. (1998). *Hope in a Jar: The Making of America's Beauty Culture*. New York: Metropolitan Books.
Pieterse, Jan Nederveen. (1990). *White on Black: Images of Africa and Blacks in Western Popular Culture*. New Haven: Yale University Press.
Plato. (1989). *Symposium*. Trans. Alexander Nehama. Indianapolis: Hackett Publishing.
Richmond, Peter. (1987). "How Do Men Feel About Their Bodies?" *Glamour*, April, pp. 312–13, 369–72.
Rotundo, E. Anthony. (1993). *American Manhood: Transformations in Masculinity from the Revolution to the Modern Era*. New York: Basic Books.
Sartre, Jean-Paul. (1966). *Being and Nothingness*. New York: Washington Square Press.
Shaw, Dan. (1994). "Mirror, Mirror," *New York Times*, May 29, Section 9, pp. 1, 6.
Sheets-Johnstone, Maxine. (1994). *The Roots of Power: Animate Form and Gendered Bodies*. Chicago: Open Court.
Spindler, Amy. (1996). "It's a Face-Lifted, Tummy-Tucked Jungle Out There," *New York Times*, June 9.
Taylor, John. (1995). "The Long Hard Days of Dr. Dick," *Esquire*, September, pp. 120–30.
White, Shane, and Graham White. (1998). *Stylin'*. Ithaca: Cornell University Press.

QUESTIONS FOR A SECOND READING

1. This is a long essay. The writing operates under a set of expectations that does not value efficiency. The writing says, "It is better to take time with this, better to take time rather than hurry, rather than rushing to say what must be said, rather than pushing to be done. Slow down, relax, take your time. This can be fun." While there is attention to a "thesis," the organizing principle of this essay is such that the real work and the real pleasure lie elsewhere. Work and pleasure. As you reread, pay particular attention to how Bordo controls the pace and direction of the essay, where she prolongs the discussion and where and when she shifts direction. Think of this as a way for her (and you) to get work done. And think about it as a way of organizing the pleasure of the text. Be prepared to describe how she does this and whether it works for you (or doesn't). And be prepared to talk about the possibilities of adapting this strategy (a strategy of more rather than less) in your own writing.

2. This is a long essay divided into subsections. The subsections mark stages in the presentation. The subsections allow you to think about form in relation to units larger than the paragraph but smaller than the essay. As you reread, pay attention to these sections. How are they organized internally? How are they arranged? How do they determine the pace or rhythm of your reading, the tonality or phrasing of the text? Which is the slowest, for example? Which is the loudest? And why? And where are they placed? What do they do to the argument?

3. Bordo is a distinctive and stylish writer. She is also one of many writers who are thinking about visual culture and popular culture (about movies, TV, and advertisements) in relation to (what Bordo refers to as) "consumer capitalism." For those who know this work, she makes use of some terms and strategies common to cultural studies. One is to think about "subject position." Bordo says that when she saw the Calvin Klein ad, " I had my first real taste of what it's like to inhabit this visual culture as a man." Another related strategy is to think about how and where one is positioned, as subject or object, in the moment of vision, a moment of looking, when you are defined by the "gaze" of another or when your "gaze" is the source of definition. She says, for example, "For many men, both gay and straight, to be so passively dependent on the gaze of another person for one's sense of self-worth is incompatible with being a real man." She works this out in the section where she talks about Jean-Paul Sartre and Simone de Beauvoir (pp. 192–93). As you reread the chapter, pay particular attention to where and how Bordo invokes and/or inhabits the "subject position" of people different from herself. How are these differences defined? (You might make a list.) Where is she most convincing? least convincing? And, finally, be prepared to speak back to the text from what you take to be your own "subject position." How does it look to you?

4. At one point, Bordo speaks directly to you and invites you into her project: "So the next time you see a Dockers or Haggar ad, think of it not only as an advertisement for khakis but also as an advertisement for a certain notion of what it means to be a man." You don't have to be limited to Dockers, Haggar, or khaki, but as you reread the essay, keep your eye out for advertisements that come your way, advertisements that seem perfect for thinking along with Bordo, for thinking her thoughts but also for thinking about how things have changed or might be seen differently. Clip these or copy them and bring them to class.

ASSIGNMENTS FOR WRITING

1. Bordo looks back to the history of advertising (the "cultural genealogy of the ads I've been discussing"), and she works directly with the ads that prompted and served this chapter in her book. These images are a key part of the writing.

   Bordo also speaks directly to you and invites you into her project: "So the next time you see a Dockers or Haggar ad, think of it not only as an advertisement for khakis but also as an advertisement for a certain notion of what it means to be a man." You don't have to be limited to Dockers, Haggar, or khaki, but as you reread the essay and prepare for this writing assignment, keep your eye out for advertisements that come your way, advertisements that seem perfect for thinking along with Bordo (or advertisements that seem like interesting counter-examples). Clip these or copy them so that you can use them, as she does, as material for writing.

   Write an essay in which you take up Bordo's invitation. You should assume an audience that has not read Bordo (or not read her work recently), so you will need to take time to present the terms and direction of her argument. Your goal, however, is to extend her project to your moment in time, where advertising may very well have moved on to different images or men and strategies of presentation. Bordo is quite specific about her age and experience, her point of view. You should be equally specific. You, too, should establish your point of view. You are placed at a different moment in time, your experience is different, your exposure to images has prepared you differently. You write from a different subject position. Your job, then, is not simply to reproduce Bordo's project but to extend it, to refine it, to put it to the test.

2. The first two second-reading questions (p. 234) point attention to the length of the essay and to its organization. Here, in effect, is what they say:

   > "Beauty (Re)discovers the Male Body" is a long essay. The writing operates under a set of expectations that does not value efficiency. The writing says, "It is better to take time with this, better to take time rather than hurry, rather than rushing to say what must be

> said, rather than pushing to be done. Slow down, relax, take your time. This can be fun." While there is attention to a "thesis," the organizing principle of this essay is such that the real work and the real pleasure lie elsewhere. Work and pleasure. As you reread, pay particular attention to how Bordo controls the pace and direction of the essay, where she prolongs the discussion and where and when she shifts direction. Think of this as a way for her (and you) to get work done. And think about it as a way of organizing the pleasure of the text.
>
> This is a long essay divided into subsections. The subsections mark stages in the presentation. The subsections allow you to think about form in relation to units larger than the paragraph but smaller than the essay. As you reread, pay attention to these sections. How are they organized internally? How are they arranged? How do they determine the pace or rhythm of your reading, the tonality or phrasing of the text? Which is the slowest, for example? Which is the loudest? And why? And where are they placed? What do they do to the argument?

Take time to reread and to think these questions through. It has become common for scholars and teachers to think about the pleasure, even the "erotics" of the text. This is not, to be sure, the usual language of the composition classroom. Write an essay in which you describe the pleasures (and, if you choose, the problems) of Bordo's writing. Describe how it is organized, and how it organizes your time and attention. Describe how it works (or doesn't) for you as a reader, how it works (or doesn't) for her as a writer and thinker. You can, to be sure, make reference to other things you are reading or have read or to the writing you are doing (and have done) in school.

3. Bordo assumes, always, that the representations of men's bodies are generally read (or viewed) in the context of the similar use of women's bodies — in art, in advertising, in visual popular culture (including film and television). For this assignment, choose two sources — one ad directed, you feel, primarily to men and another ad directed primarily to women — or you might look more generally at all of the ads in two magazines, one directed (you feel) primarily to men and another to women. Write an essay in which you use Bordo's essay, and its claims, to think through your examples. You will need to take time to present your examples (including, ideally, the images) and Bordo's understanding of the role of gender in the ways images of the body are designed, presented, and read. How, that is, can you both present *and* extend Bordo's work on gender and advertising?

4. Bordo says that when she saw the Calvin Klein ad, "I had my first real taste of what it's like to inhabit this visual culture as a man." Throughout the essay she makes reference to her "subject position" and to the subject position of other viewers, both real and imagined — viewers younger or older, viewers of another race or ethnicity, men, viewers who are gay rather

than straight. As you prepare to write this essay, reread the chapter (see the "Questions for a Second Reading," p. 234), and pay particular attention to those moments when Bordo speaks to the effects of particular ads, and when she speaks from her or from another subject position. Think carefully about how she is "reading" and responding to these images. Think with equal care about what you see and how you respond; think, that is, about how you might articulate the reactions from your "subject position" or from those that Bordo has not yet been able to imagine. Choose one or two of her examples and write about them as she sees and understands them, but also as you see or understand them. How do these images look to you and at you? How might you speak back to Bordo? Make sure to develop both positions with care and detail. And, at the end, think about how you might best explain the differences.

MAKING CONNECTIONS

1. In "Beauty (Re)discovers the Male Body," Bordo refers to John Berger and his work in *Ways of Seeing* (p. 141), although she refers to a different chapter than the one included here. In general, however, both Berger and Bordo are concerned with how we see and read images; both are concerned to correct the ways images are used and read; both trace the ways images serve the interests of money and power; both texts are written to teach readers how and why they should pay a different kind of attention to the images around them.

   For this assignment, use Bordo's work to reconsider Berger's. Write an essay in which you consider the two chapters as examples of an ongoing project. Berger's essay precedes Bordo's by about a quarter of a century. If you look closely at one or two of their examples, and if you look at the larger concerns of their arguments, are they saying the same things? doing the same work? If so, how? And why is such work still necessary? If not, how do their projects differ? And how might you explain those differences?

2. Like Bordo, Laura Kipnis in "Love's Labors" (p. 391) and Susan Griffin in "Our Secret" (p. 335) are working as feminist social historians. They take familiar social practices (advertising, representations of the past and of the self) and attempt to help readers see them differently, not as simply natural or arbitrary but as practices that have important social and political consequences. Choose one of these texts and read it alongside Bordo's. Write an essay in which you explore and describe the reading and writing strategies employed by the two writers you have chosen. As researchers, how do they gather their materials, weigh them, think them through? What do they notice, and what do they do with what they notice? What makes each project historical? What makes it feminist? How might the two texts speak to each other? Looking at characteristic examples drawn from both writers, what might you conclude about the relative value — to you and to history — of each writer's project?

JUDITH Butler

Judith Butler is the Maxine Elliot Professor in the departments of rhetoric and comparative literature at the University of California at Berkeley. She is also the Hannah Arendt Professor of Philosophy at the European Graduate School in Saas-Fee, Switzerland, where she teaches an intensive summer seminar. She was an undergraduate at Bennington College and then Yale University; she received her PhD in philosophy from Yale in 1984. Her first training as a philosopher, she said, was at the synagogue in her hometown, Cleveland.

Butler is a prolific and controversial writer; her topics are gender, sexuality, and, most recently, war. Her books include *Subjects of Desire: Hegelian Reflections in Twentieth-Century France* (1987); *Gender Trouble: Feminism and the Subversion of Identity* (1990); *Bodies That Matter: On the Discursive Limits of "Sex"* (1993); *The Psychic Life of Power: Theories of Subjection* (1997); *Excitable Speech: A Politics of the Performative* (1997); *Antigone's Claim: Kinship between Life and Death* (2000); *Hegemony, Contingency, Universality* (2000, with Ernesto Laclau and Slavoj Žižek); *Precarious Life: Powers of Violence and Mourning* (2004); *Undoing Gender*, a collection of essays, including the selection that follows (2004); *Giving an Account of Oneself* (2005); and *Frames of War: When Is Life Grievable?* (2009).

Butler's second book, *Gender Trouble*, was extraordinarily successful — that is, it was widely read around the world, translated into several languages, taught in graduate and undergraduate seminars, and referenced in thousands of books and essays. It is, perhaps, one of the most important books of its time; it remains profoundly influential. The argument calls into question the commonplace and controlling assumption that human beings are divided into two clear-cut groups, men and women. Butler challenges this binary, demonstrating that much that is taken for granted about gender is problematic, even illogical. Whatever the individual body, gender identity is more complicated, more diverse, more flexible than assumed by a simple binary, male and female. Gender identity, she argues, is "performative"; it is not the natural result of who we are biologically; it is a product, rather, of how we think, act, imagine, and desire, and these performances are subject to change.

> There is no gender identity behind the expressions of gender; . . . identity is performatively constituted by the very "expressions" that are said to be its results. (*Gender Trouble*, p. 25)

This was the compelling and difficult conclusion: although gender identity is shaped by cultural norms and conventions, and although bodies and biology matter, gender identity is mutable, available to change. It is open to revision, resistance, subversion, and improvisation—sometimes willed, sometimes not. This thought was terrifying for some and liberating for others.

Butler is known for the difficulty of her prose. In fact, the difficulty could be said to be exemplary. In 1998, she was announced as the "winner" of a Bad Writing Contest sponsored by the journal *Philosophy and Literature*, where her prose was singled out for its "anxiety-inducing obscurity." The incident garnered substantial attention in the academic and popular press and became an important point of reference as the nation tried to sort out its relation to the academy, to intellectuals, and to their attempts to bring critical theory to bear on matters of daily life and common concern. In her response to the award, Butler pointed out that the "winners" tended to be people who were writing against common-sense understandings of gender, race, class, and nation. She argued that prose is easy to read when it says what we already know and believe, but that it is harder to read (and to write) a prose that is struggling against the usual ways of thinking and speaking.

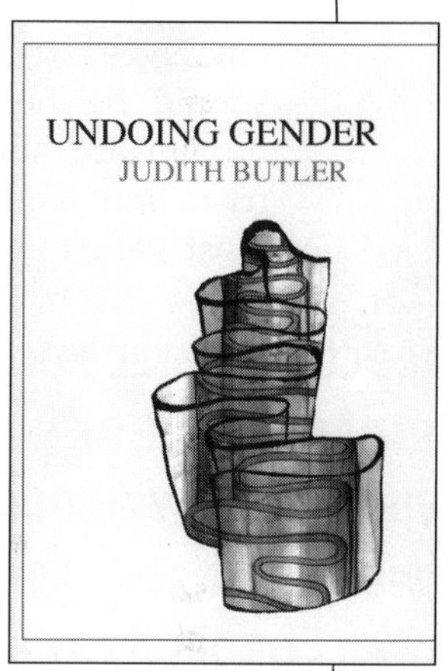

> There is a lot in ordinary language and in received grammar that constrains our thinking. . . . I'm not sure we're going to be able to struggle effectively against those constraints or work within them in a productive way unless we see the ways in which grammar is both producing and constraining our sense of what the world is. (*Excitable Speech: The Politics of the Performative,* pp. 732–33)

Anxiety, perhaps, is the necessary effect of such a project, an alternative to complacency. And so, she concluded in a *New York Times* op-ed article, the controversy was not so much about her prose as about what was appropriate in the classroom and in academic life. "We have an intellectual disagreement about what kind of world we want to live in, and what intellectual resources we must preserve as we make our way toward the politically new."

The other side of the argument is easier to grasp and easier to represent—that such prose is self-indulgent, divisive, posturing, disrespectful of its audience. One thing is certain, however. Butler is widely read and widely cited and is one of the most important, controversial, and influential theorists of our time. Her writing has changed the ways we think, speak, and write about sexuality, gender, and desire. The selection that follows thinks about gender identity in relation to the question of what "constitutes the human," who is granted this recognition and who is not. Butler raises this as a philosophical question, but she is also very interested in the political, in the actual human beings whose lives bear the consequence of being understood as impossible, illegible, and thereby alien, located outside the common understandings of what it means to be a person.

Beside Oneself: On the Limits of Sexual Autonomy

What makes for a livable world is no idle question. It is not merely a question for philosophers. It is posed in various idioms all the time by people in various walks of life. If that makes them all philosophers, then that is a conclusion I am happy to embrace. It becomes a question for ethics, I think, not only when we ask the personal question, what makes my own life bearable, but when we ask, from a position of power, and from the point of view of distributive justice, what makes, or ought to make, the lives of others bearable? Somewhere in the answer we find ourselves not only committed to a certain view of what life is, and what it should be, but also of what constitutes the human, the distinctively human life, and what does not. There is always a risk of anthropocentrism here if one assumes that the distinctively human life is valuable — or most valuable — or is the only way to think the problem of value. But perhaps to counter that tendency it is necessary to ask both the question of life and the question of the human, and not to let them fully collapse into one another.

WE ARE CONSTITUTED POLITICALLY IN PART BY VIRTUE OF THE SOCIAL VULNERABILITY OF OUR BODIES; WE ARE CONSTITUTED AS FIELDS OF DESIRE AND PHYSICAL VULNERABILITY, AT ONCE PUBLICLY ASSERTIVE AND VULNERABLE.

I would like to start, and to end, with the question of the human, of who counts as the human, and the related question of whose lives count as lives, and with a question that has preoccupied many of us for years: what makes for a grievable life? I believe that whatever differences exist within the international gay and lesbian community, and there are many, we all have some notion of what it is to have lost somebody. And if we've lost, then it seems to follow that we have had, that we have desired and loved, and struggled to find the conditions for our desire. We have all lost someone in recent decades from AIDS, but there are other losses that inflict us, other diseases; moreover, we are, as a community, subjected to violence, even if some of us individually have not been. And this means that we are constituted politically in part by virtue of the social vulnerability of our bodies; we are constituted as fields of desire and physical vulnerability, at once publicly assertive and vulnerable.

I am not sure I know when mourning is successful, or when one has fully mourned another human being. I'm certain, though, that it does not mean that one has forgotten the person, or that something else comes along to take his or her place. I don't think it works that way. I think instead that one mourns when one accepts the fact that the loss one undergoes will be one that changes you, changes you possibly forever, and that mourning has to do with agreeing to undergo a transformation the full result of which you cannot know in advance. So there is losing, and there is the transformative effect of loss, and this latter cannot be charted or planned. I don't think, for instance, you can invoke a Protestant ethic when it comes to loss. You can't say, "Oh, I'll go through loss this way, and that will be the result, and I'll apply myself to the task, and I'll endeavor to achieve the resolution of grief that is before me." I think one is hit by waves, and that one starts out the day with an aim, a project, a plan, and one finds oneself foiled. One finds oneself fallen. One is exhausted but does not know why. Something is larger than one's own deliberate plan or project, larger than one's own knowing. Something takes hold, but is this something coming from the self, from the outside, or from some region where the difference between the two is indeterminable? What is it that claims us at such moments, such that we are not the masters of ourselves? To what are we tied? And by what are we seized?

It may seem that one is undergoing something temporary, but it could be that in this experience something about who we are is revealed, something that delineates the ties we have to others, that shows us that those ties constitute a sense of self, compose who we are, and that when we lose them, we lose our composure in some fundamental sense: we do not know who we are or what to do. Many people think that grief is privatizing, that it returns us to a solitary situation, but I think it exposes the constitutive sociality of the self, a basis for thinking a political community of a complex order.

It is not just that I might be said to "have" these relations, or that I might sit back and view them at a distance, enumerating them, explaining what this friendship means, what that lover meant or means to me. On the contrary, grief displays the way in which we are in the thrall of our relations with others that we cannot always recount or explain, that often interrupts the self-conscious account of ourselves we might try to provide in ways that challenge the very notion of ourselves as autonomous and in control. I might try to tell a story about what I am feeling, but it would have to be a story in which the very "I" who seeks to tell the story is stopped in the midst of the telling. The very "I" is called into question by its relation to the one to whom I address myself. This relation to the Other does not precisely ruin my story or reduce me to speechlessness, but it does, invariably, clutter my speech with signs of its undoing.

Let's face it. We're undone by each other. And if we're not, we're missing something. If this seems so clearly the case with grief, it is only because it was already the case with desire. One does not always stay intact. It may be that one wants to, or does, but it may also be that despite one's best efforts, one is undone, in the face of the other, by the touch, by the scent, by the feel, by the prospect of the touch, by the memory of the feel. And so when we speak about *my* sexuality or *my* gender, as we do (and as we must) we mean something complicated by it. Neither of these is precisely a possession, but both are to be understood as *modes of being dispossessed,* ways of being for another or, indeed, by virtue of another. It does not suffice to say that I am promoting a relational view of the self over an autonomous one, or trying to redescribe autonomy in terms of relationality. The term "relationality" sutures the rupture in the relation we seek to describe, a rupture that is constitutive of identity itself. This means that we will have to approach the problem of conceptualizing dispossession with circumspection. One way of doing this is through the notion of ecstasy.

We tend to narrate the history of the broader movement for sexual freedom in such a way that ecstasy figures in the 60s and 70s and persists midway through the 80s. But maybe ecstasy is more historically persistent than that, maybe it is with us all along. To be ec-static means, literally, to be outside oneself, and this can have several meanings: to be transported beyond oneself by a passion, but also to be *beside oneself* with rage or grief. I think that if I can still speak to a "we," and include myself within its terms, I am speaking to those of us who are living in certain ways *beside ourselves*, whether it is in sexual passion, or emotional grief, or political rage. In a sense, the predicament is to understand what kind of community is composed of those who are beside themselves.

We have an interesting political predicament, since most of the time when we hear about "rights," we understand them as pertaining to individuals, or when we argue for protection against discrimination, we argue as a group or a class. And in that language and in that context, we have to present ourselves as bounded beings, distinct, recognizable, delineated, subjects before the law, a community defined by sameness. Indeed, we had better be able to use that language to secure legal protections and entitlements. But perhaps we make a mistake if we take the definitions of who we are, legally, to be adequate descriptions of what we are about. Although this language might well establish our legitimacy within a legal framework ensconced in liberal versions of human ontology, it fails to do justice to passion and grief and rage, all of which tear us from ourselves, bind us to others, transport us, undo us, and implicate us in lives that are not are own, sometimes fatally, irreversibly.

It is not easy to understand how a political community is wrought from such ties. One speaks, and one speaks for another, to another, and yet there is no way to collapse the distinction between the other and myself. When we say "we" we do nothing more than designate this as very problematic. We do not solve it. And perhaps it is, and ought to be, insoluble. We ask that the state, for instance, keep its laws off our bodies, and we call for principles of bodily self-defense and bodily integrity to be accepted as political goods. Yet, it is through the body that gender and sexuality become exposed to others, implicated in social processes, inscribed by cultural norms, and apprehended in their social meanings. In a sense, to be a body is to be given over to others even as a body is, emphatically, "one's own," that over which we must claim rights of autonomy. This is as true for the claims made by lesbians, gays, and bisexuals in favor of sexual freedom as it is for transsexual and transgender claims to self-determination;

as it is for intersex claims to be free of coerced medical, surgical, and psychiatric interventions; as it is for all claims to be free from racist attacks, physical and verbal; and as it is for feminism's claim to reproductive freedom. It is difficult, if not impossible, to make these claims without recourse to autonomy and, specifically, a sense of bodily autonomy. Bodily autonomy, however, is a lively paradox. I am not suggesting, though, that we cease to make these claims. We have to, we must. And I'm not saying that we have to make these claims reluctantly or strategically. They are part of the normative aspiration of any movement that seeks to maximize the protection and the freedoms of sexual and gender minorities, of women, defined with the broadest possible compass, of racial and ethnic minorities, especially as they cut across all the other categories. But is there another normative aspiration that we must also seek to articulate and to defend? Is there a way in which the place of the body in all of these struggles opens up a different conception of politics?

The body implies mortality, vulnerability, agency: the skin and the flesh expose us to the gaze of others but also to touch and to violence. The body can be the agency and instrument of all these as well, or the site where "doing" and "being done to" become equivocal. Although we struggle for rights over our own bodies, the very bodies for which we struggle are not quite ever only our own. The body has its invariably public dimension; constituted as a social phenomenon in the public sphere, my body is and is not mine. Given over from the start to the world of others, bearing their imprint, formed within the crucible of social life, the body is only later, and with some uncertainty, that to which I lay claim as my own. Indeed, if I seek to deny the fact that my body relates me — against my will and from the start — to others I do not choose to have in proximity to myself (the subway or the tube are excellent examples of this dimension of sociality), and if I build a notion of "autonomy" on the basis of the denial of this sphere or a primary and unwilled physical proximity with others, then do I precisely deny the social and political conditions of my embodiment in the name of autonomy? If I am struggling *for* autonomy, do I not need to be struggling for something else as well, a conception of myself as invariably in community, impressed upon by others, impressing them as well, and in ways that are not always clearly delineable, in forms that are not fully predictable?

Is there a way that we might struggle for autonomy in many spheres but also consider the demands that are imposed upon us by living in a world of beings who are, by definition, physically dependent on one another, physically vulnerable to one another? Is this not another way of imagining community in such a way that it becomes incumbent upon us to consider very carefully when and where we engage violence, for violence is, always, an exploitation of that primary tie, that primary way in which we are, as bodies, outside ourselves, for one another?

If we might then return to the problem of grief, to the moments in which one undergoes something outside of one's control and finds that one is beside oneself, not at one with oneself, we can say grief contains within it the possibility of apprehending the fundamental sociality of embodied life, the ways in which we are from the start, and by virtue of being a bodily being, already given over, beyond ourselves, implicated in lives that are not our own. Can this situation, one that is so dramatic for sexual minorities, one that establishes a very specific political perspective for anyone who works in the field of sexual and gender politics, supply a perspective with which to begin to apprehend the contemporary global situation?

Mourning, fear, anxiety, rage. In the United States after September 11, 2001, we have been everywhere surrounded with violence, of having perpetrated it, having suffered it, living in fear of it, planning more of it. Violence is surely a touch of the worst order, a way in which the human vulnerability to other humans is exposed in its most terrifying way, a way in which we are given over, without control, to the will of another, the way in which life itself can be expunged by the willful action of another. To the extent that we commit violence, we are acting upon another, putting others at risk, causing damage to others. In a way, we all live with this particular vulnerability, a vulnerability to the other that is part of bodily life, but this vulnerability becomes highly exacerbated under certain social and political conditions. Although the dominant mode in the United States has been to shore up sovereignty and security to minimize or, indeed, foreclose this vulnerability, it can serve another function and another ideal. The fact that our lives are dependent on others can become the basis of claims for nonmilitaristic political solutions, one which we cannot will away, one which we must attend to, even abide by, as we begin to think about what politics might be implied by staying with the thought of corporeal vulnerability itself.

Is there something to be gained from grieving, from tarrying with grief, remaining exposed to its apparent tolerability and not endeavoring to seek a resolution for grief through violence? Is there something to be gained in the political domain by maintaining grief as part of the framework by which we think our international ties? If we stay with the sense of loss, are we left feeling only passive and powerless, as some fear? Or are we, rather, returned to a sense of human vulnerability, to our collective responsibility for the physical lives of one another? The attempt to foreclose that vulnerability, to banish it, to make ourselves secure at the expense [of] every other human consideration, is surely also to eradicate one of the most important resources from which we must take our bearings and find our way.

To grieve, and to make grief itself into a resource for politics, is not to be resigned to a simple passivity or powerlessness. It is, rather, to allow oneself to extrapolate from this experience of vulnerability to the vulnerability that others suffer through military incursions, occupations, suddenly declared wars, and police brutality. That our very survival can be determined by those we do not know and over whom there is no final control means that life is precarious, and that politics must consider what forms of social and political organization seek best to sustain precarious lives across the globe.

There is a more general conception of the human at work here, one in which we are, from the start, given over to the other, one in which we are, from the start, even prior to individuation itself, and by virtue of our embodiment, given over to an other: this makes us vulnerable to violence, but also to another range of touch, a range that includes the eradication of our being at the one end, and the physical support for our lives, at the other.

We cannot endeavor to "rectify" this situation. And we cannot recover the source of this vulnerability, for it precedes the formation of "I." This condition of being laid bare from the start, dependent on those we do not know, is one with which we cannot precisely argue. We come into the world unknowing and dependent, and, to a certain degree, we remain that way. We can try, from the point of view of autonomy, to argue with this situation, but we are perhaps foolish, if not dangerous, when we do. Of course, we can say that for some this primary scene is extraordinary, loving, and receptive, a warm tissue of relations that support and nurture life in its infancy. For others, this is, however, a scene of abandonment or violence or starvation; they are bodies given over to nothing, or to brutality, or to no sustenance. No matter what the valence of that scene is, however, the fact remains that infancy constitutes a necessary dependency, one that we never fully leave behind. Bodies still must be apprehended as given over. Part of understanding the oppression of lives is precisely to understand that there is no way to argue away this condition of a primary vulnerability, of being given over to the touch of the other, even if, or precisely when, there is no other there, and no support for our lives. To counter oppression requires that one understand that lives are supported and maintained differentially, that there are radically different ways in which human physical vulnerability is distributed across the globe. Certain lives will be highly protected, and the abrogation of their claims to sanctity will be sufficient to mobilize the forces of war. And other lives will not find such fast and furious support and will not even qualify as "grievable."

What are the cultural contours of the notion of the human at work here? And how do the contours that we accept as the cultural frame for the human limit the extent to which we can avow loss as loss? This is surely a question that lesbian, gay, and bi-studies has asked in relation to violence against sexual minorities, and that transgendered people have asked as they have been singled out for harassment and sometimes murder, and that intersexed people have asked, whose formative years have so often been marked by an unwanted violence against their bodies in the name of a normative notion of human morphology. This is no doubt as well the basis of a profound affinity between movements centered on gender and sexuality with efforts to counter the normative human morphologies and capacities that condemn or efface those who are physically challenged. It must, as well, also be part of the affinity with antiracist struggles, given the racial differential that undergirds the culturally viable notions of the human—ones that we see acted out in dramatic and terrifying ways in the global arena at the present time.

So what is the relation between violence and what is "unreal," between violence and unreality that attends to those who become the victims of violence, and where does the notion of the ungrievable life come in? On the level of discourse, certain lives are not considered lives at all, they cannot be humanized; they fit no dominant frame for the human, and their dehumanization occurs first, at this level. This level then gives rise to a physical violence that in some sense delivers the message of dehumanization, which is already at work in the culture.

So it is not just that a discourse exists in which there is no frame and no story and no name for such a life, or that violence might be said to realize or apply this discourse. Violence against those who are already not quite lives, who are living in a state of suspension between life and death, leaves a mark that is no mark. If there is a discourse, it is a silent and melancholic writing in which there have been no lives, and no losses, there has been no common physical condition, no vulnerability that serves as the basis for an apprehension of our commonality, and there has been no sundering of that commonality. None of this takes place on the order of the event. None of this takes place. How many lives have been lost from AIDS in Africa in the last few years? Where are the media representations of this loss, the discursive elaborations of what these losses mean for communities there?

AS BODIES, WE ARE ALWAYS FOR SOMETHING MORE THAN, AND OTHER THAN, OURSELVES.

I began this chapter with a suggestion that perhaps the interrelated movements and modes of inquiry that collect here might need to consider autonomy as one dimension of their normative aspirations, one value to realize when we ask ourselves, in what direction ought we to proceed, and what kinds of values ought we to be realizing? I suggested as well that the way in which the body figures in gender and sexuality studies, and in the struggles for a less oppressive social world for the otherwise gendered and for sexual minorities of all kinds, is precisely to underscore the value of being beside oneself, of being a porous boundary, given over to others, finding oneself in a trajectory of desire in which one is taken out of oneself, and resituated irreversibly in a field of others in which one is not the presumptive center. The particular sociality that belongs to bodily life, to sexual life, and to becoming gendered (which is always, to a certain extent, becoming gendered *for others*) establishes a field of ethical enmeshment with others and a sense of disorientation for the first-person, that is, the perspective of the ego. As bodies, we are always for something more than, and other than, ourselves. To articulate this as an entitlement is not always easy, but perhaps not impossible. It suggests, for instance, that "association" is not a luxury, but one of the very conditions and prerogatives of freedom. Indeed, the kinds of associations we maintain importantly take many forms. It will not do to extol the marriage norm as the new ideal for this movement, as the Human Rights Campaign has erroneously done.[1] No doubt, marriage and same-sex domestic partnerships should certainly be available as options, but to install either as a model for sexual legitimacy is precisely to constrain the sociality of the body in acceptable ways. In light of seriously damaging judicial decisions against second parent adoptions in recent years, it is crucial to expand our notions of kinship beyond the heterosexual frame. It would be a mistake, however, to reduce kinship to family, or to assume that all sustaining community and friendship ties are extrapolations of kin relations.

I make the argument [elsewhere] . . . that kinship ties that bind persons to one another may well be no more or less than the intensification of community ties, may or may not be based on enduring or exclusive sexual relations, may well consist of ex-lovers, nonlovers, friends, and community members. The relations of kinship cross the boundaries between community and family and sometimes redefine the meaning of friendship as well. When these modes of intimate association produce sustaining webs of relationships, they constitute a "breakdown" of traditional kinship that displaces the presumption that biological and sexual relations structure kinship centrally. In addition, the incest taboo that governs kinship ties, producing a necessary exogamy, does not necessarily operate among friends in the same way or, for that matter, in networks of communities. Within these frames, sexuality is no longer exclusively regulated by the rules of kinship at the same time that the durable tie can be situated outside of the conjugal frame. Sexuality becomes open to a number of social articulations that do not always imply binding relations or conjugal ties. That not all of our relations last or are meant to, however, does not mean that we are immune to grief. On the contrary, sexuality outside the field of monogamy well may open us to a different sense of community, intensifying the question of where one finds enduring ties, and so become the condition for an attunement to losses that exceed a discretely private realm.

Nevertheless, those who live outside the conjugal frame or maintain modes of social organization for sexuality that are neither monogamous nor quasi-marital are more and more considered unreal, and their lows and losses less than "true" loves and "true" losses. The derealization of this domain of human intimacy and sociality works by denying reality and truth to the relations at issue.

The question of who and what is considered real and true is apparently a question of knowledge. But it is also, as Michel Foucault makes plain, a question of power. Having or bearing "truth" and "reality" is an enormously powerful prerogative within the social world, one way that power dissimulates as ontology. According to Foucault, one of the first tasks of a radical critique is to discern the relation "between mechanisms of coercion and elements of knowledge."[2] Here we are confronted with the limits of what is knowable, limits that exercise a certain force, but are not grounded in any necessity, limits that can only be read or interrogated by risking a certain security through departing from an established ontology: "[N]othing can exist as an element of knowledge if, on the one hand, it . . . does not conform to a set of rules and constraints characteristic, for example, of a given type of scientific discourse in a given period, and if, on the other hand, it does not possess the effects of coercion or simply the incentives peculiar to what is scientifically validated or simply rational or simply generally accepted, etc."[3] Knowledge and power are not finally separable but work together to establish a set of subtle and explicit criteria for thinking the world: "It is therefore not a matter of describing what knowledge is and what power is and how one would repress the other or how the other would abuse the one, but rather, a nexus of knowledge-power has to be described so that we can grasp what constitutes the acceptability of a system. . . ."[4]

What this means is that one looks *both* for the conditions by which the object field is constituted, and for *the limits* of those conditions. The limits are to be found where the reproducibility of the conditions is not secure, the site where conditions are contingent, transformable. In Foucault's terms, "schematically speaking, we have perpetual mobility, essential fragility or rather the complex interplay between what replicates the same process and what transforms it."[5] To intervene in the name of transformation means precisely to disrupt what has become settled knowledge and knowable reality, and to use, as it were, one's unreality to make an otherwise impossible or illegible claim. I think that when the unreal lays claim to reality, or enters into its domain, something other than a simple assimilation into prevailing norms can and does take place. The norms themselves can become rattled, display their instability, and become open to resignification.

In recent years, the new gender politics has offered numerous challenges from transgendered and transsexual peoples to established feminist and lesbian/gay frameworks, and the intersex movement has rendered more complex the concerns and demands of sexual rights advocates. If some on the Left thought that these concerns were not properly or substantively political, they have been under pressure to rethink the political sphere in terms of its gendered and sexual presuppositions. The suggestion that butch, femme, and transgendered lives are not essential referents for a refashioning of political life, and for a more just and equitable society, fails to acknowledge the violence that the otherwise gendered suffer in the public world and fails as well to recognize that embodiment denotes a contested set of norms governing who will count as a viable subject within the sphere of politics. Indeed, if we consider that human bodies are not experienced without recourse to some ideality, some frame for experience itself, and that this is as true for the experience of one's own body as it is for experiencing another, and if we accept that that ideality and frame are socially articulated, we can see how it is that embodiment is not thinkable without a relation to a norm, or a set of norms. The struggle to rework the norms by which bodies are experienced is thus crucial not only to disability politics, but to the intersex and transgendered movements as they contest forcibly imposed ideals of what bodies ought to be like. The embodied relation to the norm exercises a transformative potential. To posit possibilities beyond the norm or, indeed, a different future for the norm itself, is part of the work of fantasy when we understand fantasy as taking the body as a point of departure for an articulation that is not always constrained by the body as it is. If we accept that altering these norms that decide normative human morphology gives differential "reality" to different kinds of humans as a result, then we are compelled to affirm that transgendered lives have a potential and actual impact on political life at its most fundamental level, that is, who counts as a human, and what norms govern the appearance of "real" humanness.

Moreover, fantasy is part of the articulation of the possible; it moves us beyond what is merely actual and present into a realm of possibility, the not yet actualized or the not actualizable. The struggle to survive is not really separable from the cultural life of fantasy, and the foreclosure of fantasy — through censorship, degradation, or other means — is one strategy for providing for the social death of persons. Fantasy is not the opposite of reality; it is what reality forecloses, and, as a result, it defines the limits of reality, constituting it as its constitutive outside. The critical promise of fantasy, when and where it exists, is to challenge the contingent limits of what will and will not be called reality. Fantasy is what allows us to imagine ourselves and others otherwise; it establishes the possible in excess of the real; it points elsewhere, and when it is embodied, it brings the elsewhere home.

How do drag, butch, femme, transgender, transsexual persons enter into the political field? They make us not only question what is real, and what "must" be, but they also show us how the norms that govern contemporary notions of reality can be questioned and how new modes of reality can become instituted. These practices of instituting new modes of reality take place in part through the scene of embodiment, where the body is not understood as a static and accomplished fact, but as an aging process, a mode of becoming that, in becoming otherwise, exceeds the norm, reworks the norm, and makes us see how realities to which we thought we were confined are not written in stone. Some people have asked me what is the use of increasing possibilities for gender. I tend to answer: Possibility is not a luxury; it is as crucial as bread. I think we should not underestimate what the thought of the possible does for those for whom the very issue of survival is most urgent. If the answer to the question, is life possible, is yes, that is surely something significant. It cannot, however, be taken for granted as the answer. That is a question whose answer is sometimes "no," or one that has no ready answer, or one that bespeaks an ongoing agony. For many who can and do answer the question in the affirmative, that answer is hard won, if won at all, an accomplishment that is fundamentally conditioned by reality being structured or restructured in such a way that the affirmation becomes possible.

One of the central tasks of lesbian and gay international rights is to assert in clear and public terms the reality of homosexuality, not as an inner truth, not as a sexual practice, but as one of the defining features of the social world in its very intelligibility. In other words, it is one thing to assert the reality of lesbian and gay lives as a reality, and to insist that these are lives worthy of protection in their specificity and commonality; but it is quite another to insist that the very public assertion of gayness calls into question what counts as reality and what counts as a human life. Indeed, the task of international lesbian and gay politics is no less than a remaking of reality, a reconstituting of the human, and a brokering of the question, what is and is not livable? So what is the injustice opposed by such work? I would put it this way: to be called unreal and to have that call, as it were, institutionalized as a form of differential treatment, is to become the other against whom (or against which) the human is made. It is the inhuman, the beyond the human, the less than human, the border that secures the human in its ostensible reality. To be called a copy, to be called unreal, is one way in which one can be oppressed, but consider that it is more fundamental than that. To be oppressed means that you already exist as a subject of some kind, you are there as the visible and oppressed other for the master subject, as a possible or potential subject, but to be unreal is something else again. To be oppressed you must first become intelligible. To find that you are fundamentally unintelligible (indeed, that the laws of culture and of language find you to be an impossibility) is to find that you have not yet achieved access to the human, to find yourself speaking only and always *as if you were* human, but with the sense that you are not, to find that your language is hollow, that no recognition is forthcoming because the norms by which recognition takes place are not in your favor.

We might think that the question of how one does one's gender is a merely cultural question, or an indulgence on the part of those who insist on exercising bourgeois freedom in excessive dimensions. To say, however, that gender is performative is not simply to insist on a right to produce a pleasurable and subversive spectacle but to allegorize the spectacular and consequential ways in which reality is both reproduced and contested. This has consequences for how gender presentations are criminalized and pathologized, how subjects who cross gender risk internment and imprisonment, why violence against transgendered subjects is not recognized as violence, and why this violence is sometimes inflicted by the very states that should be offering such subjects protection from violence.

What if new forms of gender are possible? How does this affect the ways that we live and the concrete needs of the human community? And how are we to distinguish between forms of gender possibility that are valuable and those that are not? I would say that it is not a question merely of producing a new future for genders that do not yet exist. The genders I have in mind have been in existence for a long time, but they have not been admitted into the terms that govern reality. So it is a question of developing within law, psychiatry, social, and literary theory a new legitimating lexicon for the gender complexity that we have been living for a long time. Because the norms governing reality have not admitted these forms to be real, we will, of necessity, call them "new."

What place does the thinking of the possible have within political theorizing? Is the problem that we have no norm to distinguish among kinds of possibility, or does that only appear to be a problem if we fail to comprehend "possibility" itself as a norm? Possibility is an aspiration, something we might hope will be equitably distributed, something that might be socially secured, something that cannot be taken for granted, especially if it is apprehended phenomenologically. The point is not to prescribe new gender norms, as if one were under an obligation to supply a measure, gauge, or norm for the adjudication of competing gender presentations. The normative aspiration at work here has to do with the ability to live and breathe and move and would no doubt belong somewhere in what is called a philosophy of freedom. The thought of a possible life is only an indulgence for those who already know themselves to be possible. For those who are still looking to become possible, possibility is a necessity.

It was Spinoza who claimed that every human being seeks to persist in his own being, and he made this principle of self-persistence, the *conatus,* into the basis of his ethics and, indeed, his politics. When Hegel made the claim that desire is always a desire for recognition, he was, in a way, extrapolating upon this Spinozistic point, telling us, effectively, that to persist in one's own being is only possible on the condition that we are engaged in receiving and offering recognition. If we are not recognizable, if there are no norms of recognition by which we are recognizable, then it is not possible to persist in one's own being, and we are not possible beings; we have been foreclosed from possibility. We think of norms of recognition perhaps as residing already in a cultural world into which we are born, but these norms change, and with the changes in these norms come changes in what does and does not count as recognizably human. To twist the Hegelian argument in a Foucaultian direction: norms of recognition function to produce and to deproduce the notion of the human. This is made true in a specific way when we consider how international norms work in the context of lesbian and gay human rights, especially as they insist that certain kinds of violences are impermissible, that certain lives are vulnerable and worthy of protection, that certain deaths are grievable and worthy of public recognition.

To say that the desire to persist in one's own being depends on norms of recognition is to say that the basis of one's autonomy, one's persistence as an "I" through time, depends fundamentally on a social norm that exceeds that "I," that positions that "I" ec-statically, outside of itself in a world of complex and historically changing norms. In effect, our lives, our very persistence, depend upon such norms or, at least, on the possibility that we will be able to negotiate within them, derive our agency from the field of their operation. In our very ability to persist, we are dependent on what is outside of us, on a broader sociality, and this dependency is the basis of our endurance and survivability. When we assert our "right," as we do and we must, we are not carving out a place for our autonomy — if by autonomy we mean a state of individuation, taken as self-persisting prior to and apart from any relations of dependency on the world of others. We do not negotiate with norms or with Others subsequent to our coming into the world. We come into the world on the condition that the social world is already there, laying the groundwork for us. This implies that I cannot persist without norms of recognition that support my persistence: the sense of possibility pertaining to me must first be imagined from somewhere else before I can begin to imagine myself. My reflexivity is not only socially mediated, but socially constituted. I cannot be who I am without drawing upon the sociality of norms that precede and exceed me. In this sense, I am outside myself from the outset, and must be, in order to survive, and in order to enter into the realm of the possible.

To assert sexual rights, then, takes on a specific meaning against this background. It means, for instance, that when we struggle for rights, we are not simply struggling for rights that attach to my person, but we are struggling *to be conceived as persons.* And there is a difference between the former and the latter. If we are struggling for rights that attach, or should attach, to my personhood, then we assume that personhood as already constituted. But if we are struggling not only to be conceived as persons, but to create a social transformation of the very meaning of personhood, then the assertion of rights becomes a way of intervening into the social and political process by which the human is articulated. International human rights is always in the process of subjecting the human to redefinition and renegotiation. It mobilizes the human in the service of rights, but also rewrites the human and rearticulates the human when it comes up against the cultural limits of its working conception of the human, as it does and must.

I CANNOT BE WHO I AM WITHOUT DRAWING UPON THE SOCIALITY OF NORMS THAT PRECEDE AND EXCEED ME.

Lesbian and gay human rights takes sexuality, in some sense, to be its issue. Sexuality is not simply an attribute one has or a disposition or patterned set of inclinations. It is a mode of being disposed toward others, including in the mode of fantasy, and sometimes only in the mode of fantasy. If we are outside of ourselves as sexual beings, given over from the start, crafted in part through primary relations of dependency and attachment, then it would seem that our being beside ourselves, outside ourselves, is there as a function of sexuality itself, where sexuality is not this or that dimension of our existence, not the key or bedrock of our existence, but, rather, as coextensive with existence, as Merleau-Ponty once aptly suggested.[6]

I have tried here to argue that our very sense of personhood is linked to the desire for recognition, and that desire places us outside ourselves, in a realm of social norms that we do not fully choose, but that provides the horizon and the resource for any sense of choice that we have. *This means that the ec-static character of our existence is essential to the possibility of persisting as human.* In this sense, we can see how sexual rights brings together two related domains of ec-stasy, two connected ways of being outside of ourselves. As sexual, we are dependent on a world of others, vulnerable to need, violence, betrayal, compulsion, fantasy; we project desire, and we have it projected onto us. To be part of a sexual minority means, most emphatically, that we are also dependent on the protection of public and private spaces, on legal sanctions that protect us from violence, on safeguards of various institutional kinds against unwanted aggression imposed upon us, and the violent actions they sometimes instigate. In this sense, our very lives, and the persistence of our desire, depend on there being norms of recognition that produce and sustain our viability as human. Thus, when we speak about sexual rights, we are not merely talking about rights that pertain to our individual desires but to the norms on which our very individuality depends. That means that the discourse of rights avows our dependency, the mode of our being in the hands of others, a mode of being with and for others without which we cannot be.

I served for a few years on the board of the International Gay and Lesbian Human Rights Commission, a group that is located in San Francisco. It is part of a broad international coalition of groups and individuals who struggle to establish both equality and justice for sexual minorities, including transgender and intersexed individuals as well as persons with HIV or AIDS.[7] What astonished me time and again was how often the organization was asked to respond to immediate acts of violence against sexual minorities, especially when that violence was not redressed in any way by local police or government in various places in the globe. I had to reflect on what sort of anxiety is prompted by the public appearance of someone who is openly gay, or presumed to be gay, someone whose gender does not conform to norms, someone whose sexuality defies public prohibitions, someone whose body does not conform with certain morphological ideals. What motivates those who are driven to kill someone for being gay, to threaten to kill someone for being intersexed, or would be driven to kill because of the public appearance of someone who is transgendered?

The desire to kill someone, or killing someone, for not conforming to the gender norm by which a person is "supposed" to live suggests that life itself requires a set of sheltering norms, and that to be outside it, to live outside it, is to court death. The person who threatens violence proceeds from the anxious and rigid belief that a sense of world and a sense of self will be radically undermined if such a being, uncategorizable, is permitted to live within the social world. The negation, through violence, of that body is a vain and violent effort to restore order, to renew the social world on the basis of intelligible gender, and to refuse the challenge to rethink that world as something other than natural or necessary. This is not far removed from the threat of death, or the murder itself, of transsexuals in various countries, and of gay men who read as "feminine" or gay women who read as "masculine." These crimes are not always immediately recognized as criminal acts. Sometimes they are denounced by governments and international agencies; sometimes they are not included as legible or real crimes against humanity by those very institutions.

If we oppose this violence, then we oppose it in the name of what? What is the alternative to this violence, and for what transformation of the social world do I call? This violence emerges from a profound desire to keep the order of binary gender natural or necessary, to make of it a structure, either natural or cultural, or both, that no human can oppose, and still remain human. If a person opposes norms of binary gender not just by having a critical point of view about them, but by incorporating norms critically, and that stylized opposition is legible, then it seems that violence emerges precisely as the demand to undo that legibility, to question its possibility, to render it unreal and impossible in the face of its appearance to the contrary. This is, then, no simple difference in points of view. To counter that embodied opposition by violence is to say, effectively, that this body, this challenge to an accepted version of the world is and shall be unthinkable. The effort to enforce the boundaries of what will be regarded as real requires stalling what is contingent, frail, open to fundamental transformation in the gendered order of things.

An ethical query emerges in light of such an analysis: how might we encounter the difference that calls our grids of intelligibility into question without trying to foreclose the challenge that the difference delivers? What might it mean to learn to live in the anxiety of that challenge, to feel the surety of one's epistemological and ontological anchor go, but to be willing, in the name of the human, to allow the human to become something other than what it is traditionally assumed to be? This means that we must learn to live and to embrace the destruction and rearticulation of the human in the name of a more capacious and, finally, less violent world, not knowing in advance what precise form our humanness does and will take. It means we must be open to its permutations, in the name of nonviolence. As Adriana Cavarero points out, paraphrasing Arendt, the question we pose to the Other is simple and unanswerable: "who are you?"[8] The violent response is the one that does not ask, and does not seek to know. It wants to shore up what it knows, to expunge what threatens it with not-knowing, what forces it to reconsider the presuppositions of its world, their contingency, their malleability. The nonviolent response lives with its unknowingness about the Other in the face of the Other, since sustaining the bond that the question opens is finally more valuable than knowing in advance what holds us in common, as if we already have all the resources we need to know what defines the human, what its future life might be.

THAT WE CANNOT PREDICT OR CONTROL WHAT PERMUTATIONS OF THE HUMAN MIGHT ARISE DOES NOT MEAN THAT WE MUST VALUE ALL POSSIBLE PERMUTATIONS OF THE HUMAN.

That we cannot predict or control what permutations of the human might arise does not mean that we must value all possible permutations of the human; it does not mean that we cannot struggle for the realization of certain values, democratic and nonviolent, international and antiracist. The point is only that to struggle for those values is precisely to avow that one's own position is not sufficient to elaborate the spectrum of the human, that one must enter into a collective work in which one's own status as a subject must, for democratic reasons, become disoriented, exposed to what it does not know.

The point is not to apply social norms to lived social instances, to order and define them (as Foucault has criticized), nor is it to find justificatory mechanisms for the grounding of social norms that are extrasocial (even as they operate under the name of the social). There are times when both of these activities do and must take place: we level judgments against criminals for illegal acts, and so subject them to a normalizing procedure; we consider our grounds for action in collective contexts and try to find modes of deliberation and reflection about which we can agree. But neither of these is all we do with norms. Through recourse to norms, the sphere of the humanly intelligible is circumscribed, and this circumscription is consequential for any ethics and any conception of social transformation. We might try to claim that we must *first* know the fundamentals of the human in order to preserve and promote human life as we know it. But what if the very categories of the human have excluded those who should be described and sheltered within its terms? What if those who ought to belong to the human do not operate within the modes of reasoning and justifying validity claims that have been proffered by western forms of rationalism? Have we ever yet known the human? And what might it take to approach that knowing? Should we be wary of knowing it too soon or of any final or definitive knowing? If we take the field of the human for granted, then we fail to think critically and ethically about the consequential ways that the human is being produced, reproduced, and deproduced. This latter inquiry does not exhaust the field of ethics, but I cannot imagine a responsible ethics or theory of social transformation operating without it.

The necessity of keeping our notion of the human open to a future articulation is essential to the project of international human rights discourse and politics. We see this time and again when the very notion of the human is presupposed; the human is defined in advance, in terms that are distinctively western, very often American, and, therefore, partial and parochial. When we start with the human as a foundation, then the human at issue in human rights is already known, already defined. And yet, the human is supposed to be the ground for a set of rights and obligations that are global in reach. How we move from the local to the international (conceived globally in such a way that it does not recirculate the presumption that all humans belong to established nation-states) is a major question for international politics, but it takes a specific form for international lesbian, gay, bi-, trans-, and intersex struggles as well as for feminism. An anti-imperialist or, minimally, nonimperialist conception of international human rights must call into question what is meant by the human and learn from the various ways and means by which it is defined across cultural venues. This means that local conceptions of what is human or, indeed, of what the basic conditions and needs of human life are, must be subjected to reinterpretation, since there are historical and cultural circumstances in which the human is defined differently. Its basic needs and, hence, basic entitlements are made known through various media, through various kinds of practices, spoken and performed.

A reductive relativism would say that we cannot speak of the human or of international human rights, since there are only and always local and provisional understandings of these terms, and that the generalizations themselves do violence to the specificity of the meanings in question. This is not my view. I'm not ready to rest there. Indeed, I think we are compelled to speak of the human, and of the international, and to find out in particular how human rights do and do not work, for example, in favor of women, of what women are, and what they are not. But to speak in this way, and to call for social transformations in the name of women, we must also be part of a critical democratic project. Moreover, the category of women has been used differentially and with exclusionary aims, and not all women have been included within its terms; women have not been fully incorporated into the human. Both categories are still in process, underway, unfulfilled, thus we do not yet know and cannot ever definitively know in what the human finally consists. This means that we must follow a double path in politics: we must use this language to assert an entitlement to conditions of life in ways that affirm the constitutive role of sexuality and gender in political life, and we must also subject our very categories to critical scrutiny. We must find out the limits of their inclusivity and translatability, the presuppositions they include, the ways in which they must be expanded, destroyed, or reworked both to encompass and open up what it is to be human and gendered. When the United Nations conference at Beijing met a few years ago, there was a discourse on "women's human rights" (or when we hear of the International Gay and Lesbian Human Rights Commission), which strikes many people as a paradox. Women's human rights? Lesbian and gay human rights? But think about what this coupling actually does. It performs the human as contingent, a category that has in the past, and continues in the present, to define a variable and restricted population, which may or may not include lesbians and gays, may or may not include women, which has several racial and ethnic differentials at work in its operation. It says that such groups have their own set of human rights, that what human may mean when we think about the humanness of women is perhaps different from what human has meant when it has functioned as presumptively male. It also says that these terms are defined, variably, in relation to one another. And we could certainly make a similar argument about race. Which populations have qualified as the human and which have not? What is the history of this category? Where are we in its history at this time?

I would suggest that in this last process, we can only rearticulate or resignify the basic categories of ontology, of being human, of being gendered, of being recognizably sexual, to the extent that we submit ourselves to a process of cultural translation. The point is not to assimilate foreign or unfamiliar notions of gender or humanness into our own as if it is simply a matter of incorporating alienness into an established lexicon. Cultural translation is also a process of yielding our most fundamental categories, that is, seeing how and why they break up, require resignification when they encounter the limits of an available episteme: what is unknown or not yet known. It is crucial to recognize that the notion of the human will only be built over time in and by the process of cultural translation, where it is not a translation between two languages that stay enclosed, distinct, unified. But rather, *translation will compel each language to change in order to apprehend the other,* and this apprehension, at the limit of what is familiar, parochial, and already known, will be the occasion for both an ethical and social transformation. It will constitute a loss, a disorientation, but one in which the human stands a chance of coming into being anew.

When we ask what makes a life livable, we are asking about certain normative conditions that must be fulfilled for life to become life. And so there are at least two senses of life, the one that refers to the minimum biological form of living, and another that intervenes at the start, which establishes minimum conditions for a livable life with regard to human life.[9] And this does not imply that we can disregard the merely living in favor of the livable life, but that we must ask, as we asked about gender violence, what humans require in order to maintain and reproduce the conditions of their own livability. And what are our politics such that we are, in whatever way is possible, both conceptualizing the possibility of the livable life, and arranging for its institutional support? There will always be disagreement about what this means, and those who claim that a single political direction is necessitated by virtue of this commitment will be mistaken. But this is only because to live is to live a life politically, in relation to power, in relation to others, in the act of assuming responsibility for a collective future. To assume responsibility for a future, however, is not to know its direction fully in advance, since the future, especially the future with and for others, requires a certain openness and unknowingness; it implies becoming part of a process the outcome of which no one subject can surely predict. It also implies that a certain agonism and contestation over the course of direction will and must be in play. Contestation must be in play for politics to become democratic. Democracy does not speak in unison; its tunes are dissonant, and necessarily so. It is not a predictable process; it must be undergone, like a passion must be undergone. It may also be that life itself becomes foreclosed when the right way is decided in advance, when we impose what is right for everyone and without finding a way to enter into community, and to discover there the "right" in the midst of cultural translation. It may be that what is right and what is good consist in staying open to the tensions that beset the most fundamental categories we require, in knowing unknowingness at the core of what we know, and what we need, and in recognizing the sign of life in what we undergo without certainty about what will come.

NOTES

[1] The Human Rights Campaign is the main lobbying organization for lesbian and gay rights in the United States. Situated in Washington, D.C., it has maintained that gay marriage is the number one priority of lesbian and gay politics in the U.S. See www.hrc.org. [All notes are Butler's.]

[2] Michel Foucault, "What is Critique?" in *The Politics of Truth,* 50. This essay is reprinted with an essay by me entitled "Critique as Virtue" in David Ingram, *The Political.*

[3] "What is Critique?" 52.

[4] Ibid., 52–53.

[5] Ibid., 58.

[6] Maurice Merleau-Ponty, *The Phenomenology of Perception.*

[7] See www.iglhrc.org for more information on the mission and accomplishments of this organization.

[8] See Adriana Cavarero, *Relating Narratives,* 20–29 and 87–92.

[9] See Giorgio Agamben, *Homo Sacer: Sovereign Power and Bare Life,* 1–12.

BIBLIOGRAPHY

Agamben, Giorgio. *Homo Sacer: Sovereign Power and Bare Life.* Translated by Daniel Heller-Roazen. Stanford: Stanford University Press, 1998.

Cavarero, Adriana. *Relating Narratives: Storytelling and Selfhood.* Translated by Paul A. Kottman. London: Routledge, 2000.

Foucault, Michel. "What is Critique?" *The Politics of Truth,* edited by Sylvere Lotringer and Lysa Hochroth. New York: Semiotext(e), 1997.

Ingram, David. *The Political.* San Francisco: Wiley-Blackwell, 2002.

Merleau-Ponty, Maurice. "The Body in its Sexual Being." *The Phenomenology of Perception.* Translated by Colin Smith. New York: Routledge, 1967.

QUESTIONS FOR A SECOND READING

1. Butler's "Beside Oneself: On the Limits of Sexual Autonomy" is a philosophical essay, and one of the difficulties it presents to a reader is its emphasis on conceptual language. The sentences most often refer to concepts or ideas rather than to people, places, or events in the concrete, tangible, or observable world. It refers to the *human* or to the *body*, but without telling the stories of particular humans or particular bodies. And this can be frustrating. Without something concrete, without some situation or context in which the conceptual can take shape, these conceptual terms can lose their force or meaning. (If there is a story here, it is the story of a struggle to understand and to articulate a response to the essay's opening question: What makes for a livable world?)

   As you reread Butler, pay attention to the conceptual terms that recur. Words like *ethics*, *power*, *life*, *grief*, *agency*, and *possibility* punctuate this essay, and it is through these key terms that Butler attempts to describe and theorize the world we live in. Pick one of these terms (or one of your own choosing) and pay particular attention to the ways it is used. How is it defined in its initial context? Beyond its dictionary definition, what does this particular term come to mean for Butler? For you as a reader? And how is its meaning elaborated or consolidated or complicated by its uses later in the text?

2. At one point Butler says, "I might try to tell a story about what I am feeling, but it would have to be a story in which the very 'I' who seeks to tell the

story is stopped in the midst of the telling. The very 'I' is called into question by its relation to the one to whom I address myself" (p. 241).

As you reread, pay attention to personal pronouns, such as "I," "we," "one," "you," "our," "my," and "your." In an essay about how we are "constituted," the struggle to claim identity in relation to others is played out in the arena of the sentence. Choose a paragraph where the play of personal pronouns is particularly odd or rich, and be prepared to describe what Butler is doing. And be prepared to think out loud (or to think on the page) about the relationship between what the writer is doing (the deed of writing) and what the paragraph says.

3. Judith Butler writes in the field of Queer Theory. Queer theorists are concerned with queer lives, queer writing, and the study of gender and sexuality. In "Beside Oneself: On the Limits of Sexual Autonomy," Butler raises questions about the visibility, intelligibility, and recognition of gays and lesbians and also about the lives of those who may not conform to any fixed or binary gender norms. She writes:

> To find that you are fundamentally unintelligible (indeed, that the laws of culture and of language find you to be an impossibility) is to find that you have not yet achieved access to the human, to find yourself speaking only and always *as if you were* human, but with the sense that you are not, to find that your language is hollow, that no recognition is forthcoming because the norms by which recognition takes place are not in your favor. (p. 250)

This is a long sentence, and a complicated one. Butler knows this; she knows that it will be difficult for a reader, so she provides what help she can with the parenthetical phrase and the italics. It is useful, as Butler's reader, to practice reading and rereading her sentences, to unfold them slowly, word by word. What does it mean to be "unintelligible"? Why might being unintelligible also mean not having "access to the human" or having a "hollow" language? What examples can you think of that might help someone to better understand Butler's claim about gender and sexuality? And finally, what seems to be at stake in making this claim?

As an exercise in reading and in understanding, write a paraphrase, a translation of this sentence (or a Butler sentence of your own choosing). And in the sentence or sentences of your paraphrase, imitate Butler's rhythm and style.

4. The opening lines of Butler's essay might be understood as an invitation to participate with her in one of the traditions of philosophy. She writes:

> What makes for a livable world is no idle question. It is not merely a question for philosophers. It is posed in various idioms all the time by people in various walks of life. If that makes them all philosophers, then that is a conclusion I am happy to embrace. (p. 240)

Stylistically, Butler makes use of questions as a way of enacting philosophical inquiry. As you reread, pay attention to Butler's questions and, through these, to the method and the rhythm of philosophical inquiry. How would you describe the use, placement, and pacing of her questions? How does one question seem to lead to another? Where do they come from? How do they work together to make an argument?

ASSIGNMENTS FOR WRITING

1. The opening lines of Butler's essay might be understood as an invitation to participate with her in one of the traditions of philosophy. She writes:

   > What makes for a livable world is no idle question. It is not merely a question for philosophers. It is posed in various idioms all the time by people in various walks of life. If that makes them all philosophers, then that is a conclusion I am happy to embrace. It becomes a question for ethics, I think, not only when we ask the personal question, what makes my own life bearable, but when we ask, from a position of power, and from the point of view of distributive justice, what makes, or ought to make, the lives of others bearable? Somewhere in the answer we find ourselves not only committed to a certain view of what life is, and what it should be, but also of what constitutes the human, the distinctively human life, and what does not. (p. 240)

   Write an essay that takes up this invitation—and that takes it up in specific reference to what Butler has offered in "Beside Oneself: On the Limits of Sexual Autonomy." You will need, then, to take some time to represent her essay—both what it says and what it does. The "Questions for a Second Reading" should be helpful in preparing for this. Imagine an audience of smart people, people who may even know something about Butler but who have not read this essay. You have read it, and you want to give them a sense of how and why you find it interesting and important. But you'll also need to take time to address her questions in your own terms: What makes for a livable world? What constitutes the human? Don't slight this part of your essay. Give yourself as many pages as you gave Butler. You should, however, make it clear that you are writing in response to what you have read. You'll want to indicate, both directly and indirectly, how your thoughts are shaped by, indebted to, or in response to hers.

2. Consider the following passage from Butler's "Beside Oneself: On the Limits of Sexual Autonomy":

   > To be ec-static means, literally, to be outside oneself, and this can have several meanings: to be transported beyond oneself by a passion, but also to be *beside oneself* with rage or grief. I think that

> if I can still speak to a "we," and include myself within its terms, I am speaking to those of us who are living in certain ways *beside ourselves*, whether it is in sexual passion, or emotional grief, or political rage. In a sense, the predicament is to understand what kind of community is composed of those who are beside themselves. (p. 242)

To be *beside oneself* is an idiomatic phrase—which suggests that the meaning of the phrase cannot be determined literally but rather has some figurative connotation. In this sense, for someone not familiar with the idiom, the phrase might even be misleading or misunderstood. Butler takes this idiomatic phrase to its theoretical and social conclusions, thinking carefully about what exactly the figurative expression means to say, what it wants us to say, how it has been used, and how it might be made to serve as a fresh tool for thinking. This is a bold project, and one that takes both a critical eye and creative thought.

We might think of all idiomatic expressions as carrying important social, political, and emotional meanings that, while they might not always be visible on the surface or in everyday conversation, propose a way of thinking: *Blood is thicker than water. I was out of my mind. He is out of touch. She has gone out on a limb. It is all water under the bridge.* For this assignment, write an essay that takes up a particular idiomatic phrase as a tool for thinking through an issue that is important to you. Choose carefully—both the issue and the idiom. There should be an urgency in your writing, as there is in Butler's. And, to locate your essay as a reading of Butler, the urgency should be similarly thoughtful and modulated. You are offering your essay as a response to hers, as a similar exercise in thinking.

MAKING CONNECTIONS

1. At a key point in her essay, Butler refers to the work of Michel Foucault:

> The question of who and what is considered real and true is apparently a question of knowledge. But it is also, as Michel Foucault makes plain, a question of power. Having or bearing "truth" and "reality" is an enormously powerful prerogative within the social world, one way that power dissimulates as ontology. According to Foucault, one of the first tasks of a radical critique is to discern the relation "between mechanisms of coercion and elements of knowledge." (p. 247)

And she goes on for some length to work with passages from Foucault, although not from his book *Discipline and Punish*. One of its chapters, "Panopticism," is a selection in *Ways of Reading*. Take some time to reread Butler's essay, paying particular attention to her use of Foucault. Where and why is Foucault helpful to her? In what ways is she providing a new argument or a counterargument? And take time to reread "Panopticism." What passages might be useful in extending or challenging Butler's argument in "Beside Oneself"? Using these two sources, write an essay in which you talk about Butler and Foucault and their engagement with what might be called "radical critique," an effort (in the terms offered above) to "discern the relation 'between mechanisms of coercion and elements of knowledge.'"

Note: The assignment limits you to these two sources, the two selections in the textbook. Butler and Foucault have written much, and their work circulates widely. You are most likely not in a position to speak about everything they have written or about all that has been written about them. We wanted to define a starting point that was manageable. Still, if you wanted to do more research, you might begin by reading the Foucault essay that Butler cites, "What Is Critique?"; you might go to the library to look through books by Butler and Foucault, choosing one or two that seem to offer themselves as next steps; or you could go to essays written by scholars who, like you, are trying to think about the two together.

2. In his essay "States," Edward Said theorizes about the notion of exile in relation to Palestinian identity, offering a study of exile and dislocation through his analysis of photographs taken by Jean Mohr. Consider the following passage:

> We turn ourselves into objects not for sale, but for scrutiny. People ask us, as if looking into an exhibit case, "What is it you Palestinians want?"—as if we can put our demands into a single neat phrase. All of us speak of *awdah*, "return," but do we mean that literally, or do we mean "we must restore ourselves to ourselves"? (p. 560)

When Said talks about being looked at as though in an exhibit case, we might understand him as being concerned with the problem of dehumanization. After all, to be in an exhibit case is to be captured, trapped, or even dead. We might understand Butler as also wrestling with the problem of dehumanization; she writes: "I would like to start, and to end, with the question of the human, of who counts as the human, and the related question of whose lives count as lives, and with a question that has preoccupied many of us for years: what makes for a grievable life?"

Write an essay in which you consider the ways Said and Butler might be said to be speaking with each other. How might the condition of exile be like the condition of being *beside oneself*? What kind of connections—whether you see them as productive or problematic, or both at once—can be made between the ways Said talks about nation, identity, and home, and the ways Butler talks about gender and sexuality? What passages from each seem to have the other in mind? How does each struggle with reference, with pronouns like "we" and "our"?

3. Richard Miller, in "The Dark Night of the Soul," asks a simple and disturbing question. Institutions of higher education teach, and have taught, the "literate arts," reading and writing, always with the assumption that they improve our lives and make us better as human beings. But do they? Miller asks, "Is there any way to justify or explain a life spent working with—and teaching others to work with—texts?"

Miller's essay is divided into sections; most sections consider a particular text: Krakauer's *Into the Wild*, Descartes's *Meditations*, Mary Karr's *The Liar's Club*. Reread Miller in order to get a sense of his argument, style, and method, and then write a section that could be added to "The Dark Night of the Soul" with Butler's "Beside Oneself" as its subject. You could talk about your reading of the text—and what it has to offer. You could talk about its use, as represented in this textbook, in your class, or in the writing of your colleagues. You might also talk about where you might insert your entry into the essay "The Dark Night of the Soul."

ANNE Carson

Anne Carson (b. 1950) grew up in small towns in Ontario, Canada. She was raised in an Irish Catholic family with parents who had active reading lives: her father, a banker, was an avid reader of history books, and her mother read the many books that arrived in the *Reader's Digest* collections. As a teenager, Carson became determined to study ancient Greek and found a teacher to help her during the lunch period. She attended the University of Toronto, where she studied Latin and Greek, and earned a BA in 1974 and a master's degree in classics in 1975. Carson has taught at McGill University in Montreal, Princeton, Emory University, and the University of Michigan. She is a poet, an essayist, a novelist, a translator, a librettist, and a literary critic. She is one of the most versatile, dynamic, and respected writers of our time.

In addition to *Short Talks* (1992), from which the following selection is taken, she has published a number of critically acclaimed and often genre-bending works, including *Eros the Bittersweet* (1986); *Plainwater* (1995); *Autobiography of Red* (1998); *Men in the Off Hours* (2001); *The Beauty of the Husband* (2002), which won the T. S. Eliot Poetry Prize, making Carson the first woman to have been given this honor; and a collection of essays entitled *Decreation: Poetry, Essays, Opera* (2005). Carson has also translated several collections of classic Greek poetry, including *If Not, Winter: Fragments of Sappho* (2002) and *An Oresteia: Agamemnon by Aiskhylos; Elektra by Sophokles; Orestes by Euripides* (2009). Carson has been the recipient of a significant number of prizes and awards—among them a Guggenheim Fellowship, a Lannan Award, a Pushcart Prize, the Griffin Poetry Prize, and a 2000 MacArthur "Genius" Award.

The entries in Carson's *Short Talks* have been called prose poems, miniature lectures, flash fiction, meditations, even essays. And, as with much of Carson's work, *Short Talks* seems to resist classification as any particular *kind* of literature. Carson has said the pieces emerged out of "a bunch of drawings which [she] put titles on, and then the titles got longer and longer until the drawings disappeared." Carson is a particularly erudite writer, drawing from various fields of knowledge and enacting innovative and often playful experiments with language and thought. In a 2006 interview in *The Guardian*, Carson said: "I don't know that we really think any thoughts; we think connections between thoughts. That's where the mind moves, that's what's new, and the thoughts themselves have probably been there in my head or lots of other people's heads for a long time. But the jumps between them are entirely at that moment." This nontraditional way of thinking *about* thinking itself seems one of the qualities that drives Carson's work.

Short Talks

INTRODUCTION

Early one morning words were missing. Before that, words were not. Facts were, faces were. In a good story, Aristotle tells us, everything that happens is pushed by something else. Three old women were bending in the fields. What use is it to question us? they said. Well it shortly became clear that they knew everything there is to know about the snowy fields and the blue-green shoots and the plant called "audacity," which poets mistake for violets. I began to copy out everything that was said. The marks construct an instant of nature gradually, without the boredom of a story. I emphasize this. I will do anything to avoid boredom. It is the task of a lifetime. You can never know enough, never work enough, never use the infinitives and participles oddly enough, never impede the movement harshly enough, never leave the mind quickly enough.

ON *HOMO SAPIENS*

With small cuts Cro-Magnon man recorded the moon's phases on the handles of his tools, thinking about her as he worked. Animals. Horizon. Face in a pan of water. In every story I tell comes a point where I can see no further. I hate that point. It is why they call storytellers blind — a taunt.

ON GERTRUDE STEIN ABOUT 9:30

How curious. I had no idea! Today has ended.

ON TROUT

In haiku there are various sorts of expressions about trout — "autumn trout" and "descending trout" and "rusty trout" are some I have heard. Descending trout and rusty trout are trout that have laid their eggs. Worn out, completely exhausted, they are going down to the sea. Of course there were occasionally trout that spent the winter in deep pools. These were called "remaining trout."

ON PARMENIDES

We pride ourselves on being civilized people. Yet what if the names for things were utterly different? Italy, for example. I have a friend named Andreas, an Italian. He has lived in Argentina as well as England, and also

Costa Rica for some time. Everywhere he lives, he invites people over for supper. It is a lot of work. Artichoke pasta. Peaches. His deep smile never fades. What if the proper name for Italy turns out to be Brzoy—will Andreas continue to travel the world like the wandering moon with her borrowed light? I fear we failed to understand what he was saying or his reasons. What if every time he said *cities,* he meant *delusion,* for example.

ON MAJOR AND MINOR

Major things are wind, evil, a good fighting horse, prepositions, inexhaustible love, the way people choose their king. Minor things include dirt, the names of schools of philosophy, mood and not having a mood, the correct time. There are more major things than minor things overall, yet there are more minor things than I have written here, but it is disheartening to list them. When I think of you reading this, I do not want you to be taken captive, separated by a wire mesh lined with glass from your life itself, like some Elektra.

ON THE RULES OF PERSPECTIVE

A bad trick. Mistake. Dishonesty. These are the views of Braque. Why? Braque rejected perspective. Why? Someone who spends his life drawing profiles will end up believing that man has one eye, Braque felt. Braque wanted to take full possession of objects. He said as much in published interviews. Watching the small shiny planes of the landscape recede out of his grasp filled Braque with loss so he smashed them. *Nature morte,* said Braque.

ON *LE BONHEUR D'ETRE BIEN AIMÉE*

Day after day I think of you as soon as I wake up. Someone has put cries of birds on the air like jewels.

ON RECTIFICATION

Kafka liked to have his watch an hour and a half fast. Felice kept setting it right. Nonetheless for five years they almost married. He made a list of arguments for and against marriage, including inability to bear the assault of his own life (for) and the sight of the nightshirts laid out on his parents' beds at 10:30 (against). Hemorrhage saved him. When advised not to speak by doctors in the sanatorium, he left glass sentences all over the floor. Felice, says one of them, had too much nakedness left in her.

ON WALKING BACKWARDS

My mother forbad us to walk backwards. That is how the dead walk, she would say. Where did she get this idea? Perhaps from a bad translation. The dead, after all, do not walk backwards but they do walk behind us. They have no lungs and cannot call out but would love for us to turn around. They are victims of love, many of them.

ON THE MONA LISA

Every day he poured his question into her, as you pour water from one vessel into another, and it poured back. Don't tell me he was painting his mother, lust, et cetera. There is a moment when the water is not in one vessel nor in the other – what a thirst it was, and he supposed that when the canvas became completely empty he would stop. But women are strong. She knew vessels, she knew water, she knew mortal thirst.

ON WATERPROOFING

Franz Kafka was Jewish. He had a sister, Ottla, Jewish. Ottla married a jurist, Josef David, not Jewish. When the Nuremberg Laws were introduced to Bohemia-Moravia in 1942, quiet Ottla suggested to Josef David that they divorce. He at first refused. She spoke about sleep shapes and property and their two daughters and a rational approach. She did not mention, because she did not yet know the word, Auschwitz, where she would die in October 1943. After putting the apartment in order she packed a rucksack and was given a good shoeshine by Josef David. He applied a coat of grease. Now they are waterproof, he said.

ON SYLVIA PLATH

Did you see her mother on television? She said plain, burned things. She said I thought it an excellent poem but it hurt me. She did not say jungle fear. She did not say jungle hatred wild jungle weeping chop it back chop it. She said self-government she said end of the road. She did not say humming in the middle of the air what you came for chop.

ON READING

Some fathers hate to read but love to take the family on trips. Some children hate trips but love to read. Funny how often these find themselves passengers in the same automobile. I glimpsed the stupendous clear-cut shoulders of the Rockies from between paragraphs of *Madame Bovary.* Cloud shadows roved languidly across her huge rock throat, traced her fir flanks. Since those days, I do not look at hair on female flesh without thinking, Deciduous?

ON SUNDAY DINNER WITH FATHER

Are you going to put that chair back where it belongs or just leave it there looking like a uterus? (Our balcony is a breezy June balcony.) Are you going to let your face distorted by warring desires pour down on us all through the meal or tidy yourself so we can at least enjoy our dessert? (We weight down the corners of everything on the table with little solid-silver laws.) Are you going to nick your throat open on those woodpecker scalps as you do every Sunday night or just sit quietly while Laetitia plays her clarinet for us? (My father, who smokes a brand of cigar called Dimanche Eternel, uses them as ashtrays.)

ON HEDONISM

Beauty makes me hopeless. I don't care why anymore I just want to get away. When I look at the city of Paris I long to wrap my legs around it. When I watch you dancing there is a heartless immensity like a sailor in a dead-calm sea. Desires as round as peaches bloom in me all night, I no longer gather what falls.

ON SHELTER

You can write on a wall with a fish heart, it's because of the phosphorus. They eat it. There are shacks like that down along the river. I am writing this to be as wrong as possible to you. Replace the door when you leave, it says. Now you tell me how wrong that is, how long it glows. Tell me.

QUESTIONS FOR A SECOND READING

1. As you reread "Short Talks," you may not be familiar with all the names or texts that serve as quick points of reference: from Aristotle to Gertrude Stein to Sylvia Plath to *Madame Bovary*. Choose one reference that seems interesting or compelling to you and, in groups or on your own, go to the library (as well as the Internet) to gather materials and to take notes. (We ask you to use the library so that you can learn your way around it, but also so that you can put your hands on books. It makes a difference.) Here are some questions to ask: Who is this person? What is this text? How does it (or he or she) serve as a point of reference in "Short Talks"? What is Carson doing here?

   In preparation for class discussion, write a gloss, an explanatory paragraph outlining your responses to these questions that can be of use to other students in your class.

2. "Short Talks" provides references to writers and artists. It is also often voiced as a personal narrative, a familiar example of someone telling you something about their thoughts and experiences. As you reread, pull out the threads of this personal narrative. Who is speaking? About what? To what ends? With what urgency? How would you characterize the speaker in this text?

3. The form of Carson's "Short Talks" presents challenges, but it also presents opportunities. As you reread, think about this text as a type of experimental essay. How does it draw on the conventions of the essay? How does it defy or revise those conventions? How would you describe its formal features in

relation to what you understand to be conventional essay form? How does "Short Talks" satisfy or challenge a reader's expectations?

Be prepared to discuss these questions in class—and come with other questions of your own. Also prepare a Carson-like text—four paragraphs, each with a subheading, that seem like "Short Talks" in style and intent.

ASSIGNMENTS FOR WRITING

1. In the "Introduction" in "Short Talks," Carson says:

> You can never know enough, never work enough, never use the infinitives and participles oddly enough, never impede the movement harshly enough, never leave the mind quickly enough. (p. 266)

This passage may or may not be a way of announcing the essay's subject or topic. As you reread "Short Talks," read it with the goal of taking a position on what this essay is "about." What is it "about"? And what might be the connections between its subject and its style or method, these short units of prose, each with a subheading?

Write an essay in which you present your understanding of "Short Talks," what it does and what it has to say. You can take as your audience your colleagues in class, or you could be addressing readers like you who will be coming to "Short Talks" for the first time. Be sure to work closely from examples, examples drawn both from the text and from your experience as a reader of this text.

2. The form of Carson's "Short Talks" presents challenges, but it also presents opportunities. This assignment takes the third of the "Questions for a Second Reading" and converts it into a more ambitious writing assignment. Let's begin with what we said before:

> As you reread, think about this text as a type of experimental essay. How does it draw on the conventions of the essay? How does it defy or revise those conventions? How would you describe its formal features in relation to what you understand to be conventional essay form? How does "Short Talks" satisfy or challenge a reader's expectations?

Prepare an essay that is Carson-like. It should be, at minimum, as long as hers. It should be similar in style and intent. Her work is your model and inspiration, and yet this project is also yours. A reader should be able to see where and how your work is in conversation with hers; a reader should also be able to see what you bring to the table. Be sure that your essay has an "Introduction," something to orient a reader to what follows. (Introductions often are either written last or seriously revised once the project is complete.)

MAKING CONNECTIONS

1. Reread Brian Doyle's "Joyas Voladoras" and Antonio Porchia's excerpt from *Voices*. These pieces, like Carson's "Short Talks," blur the boundaries of genre. They are and aren't essays. As a mental exercise, let's think of them as experimental essays, essays that push the boundaries of essay form. They raise questions about what prose can do, about what it might be good for.

   Reread "Short Talks" alongside one (or both) of these selections, noting as you read the distinctive features of each writer's style. It will be up to you to identify and name them. It will be useful, as well, to note commonalities, the stylistic overlaps between texts.

   Write an essay in which you consider the genre of the essay—its form and style, its limits and possibilities—through your examination of these examples. You'll need to work closely with examples, both from the text and from your experience as a reader of these texts.

2. Consider the following sentence from Alberto Ríos's "Translating Translation: Finding the Beginning": "Linguists, by using electrodes on the vocal chords, have been able to demonstrate that English has tenser vowels than, for example, Spanish." Or this sentence from Anne Carson's "Short Talks": "Kafka liked to have his watch an hour and a half fast." Or this statement from Susan Griffin's "Our Secret": "The life plan of the body is encoded in the DNA molecule, a substance that has the ability to hold information and to replicate itself." Or this sentence from Walker Percy's "The Loss of the Creature": "Garcia López de Cárdenas discovered the Grand Canyon and was amazed at the sight." Or this statement from Brian Doyle's "Joyas Voladoras": "The biggest heart in the world is inside the blue whale."

   All of the statements above might be considered "facts" or called "factual information." Each writer is making a declarative statement that makes a claim about what is so. Using the quotations above, or perhaps using other quotations from other selections in *Ways of Reading*, write an essay in which you consider each writer's use of declarative statements or "facts." What, in your understanding, is a fact? How do the writers you have chosen to examine challenge or support your notion of facts? What are their facts for? What, in other words, are some of the ways these writers use facts—for what purposes or to what ends?

BRIAN Doyle

Brian Doyle (b. 1956) lives in Portland, Oregon, where he is the editor of the University of Portland's *Portland Magazine*. Doyle's essays have appeared in such nationally renowned journals as *Harper's Magazine*, *Atlantic Monthly*, *The American Scholar*, and *Orion*. He won an *American Scholar* best essay award in 2000.

Doyle has published more than ten books, including *Two Voices* (1996), written with his father and winner of both the Catholic Press Association Book Award and a Christopher Award; *Credo: Essays on Grace, Altar Boys, Bees, Kneeling, Saints, the Mass, Priests, Strong Women, Epiphanies, a Wake, and the Haunting Thin Energetic Dusty Figure* (1999); *Saints Passionate and Peculiar* (2002); *Leaping: Revelations and Epiphanies* (2003); *Spirited Men: Story, Soul and Substance* (2004), a collection of essays about musicians and writers from William Blake to Van Morrison; and *Epiphanies and Elegies: Very Short Stories* (2007). His book *The Wet Engine: Exploring the Mad Wild Miracle of the Heart* (2005) is a long essay and meditation inspired by the experience of having a son, Liam, who was born with three rather than four chambers in his heart. In honor of his work, Doyle was the recipient of the 2008 American Academy of Arts and Letters Award in Literature.

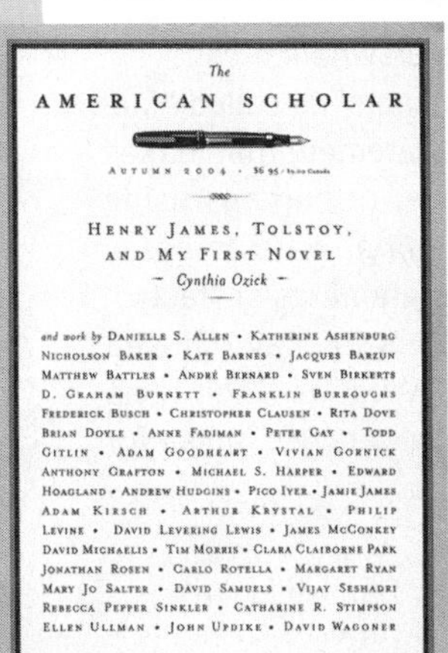

Doyle has said that he sees writing as a form of meditation and contemplation, and his essays display deep examination and keen observation. He has said of himself as a writer: "I am a small man who writes small essays about small matters." The essay that follows, "Joyas Voladoras," opens with something small, a hummingbird's heart. But, as is the case for most of Doyle's work, the essay turns the reader's attention to things much larger. "Joyas Voladoras" was originally published in *The American Scholar* (Autumn 2004); it was selected for *Best American Essays, 2005*.

Joyas Voladoras

Consider the hummingbird for a long moment. A hummingbird's heart beats ten times a second. A hummingbird's heart is the size of a pencil eraser. A hummingbird's heart is a lot of the hummingbird. *Joyas Voladoras,* flying jewels, the first white explorers in the Americas called them, and the white men had never seen such creatures, for hummingbirds came into the world only in the Americas, nowhere else in the universe, more than three hundred species of them whirring and zooming and nectaring in hummer time zones nine times removed from ours, their hearts hammering faster than we could clearly hear if we pressed our elephantine ears to their infinitesimal chests.

Each one visits a thousand flowers a day. They can dive at sixty miles an hour. They can fly backwards. They can fly more than five hundred miles without pausing to rest. But when they rest they come close to death: on frigid nights, or when they are starving, they retreat into torpor, their metabolic rate slowing to a fifteenth of their normal sleep rate, their hearts sludging nearly to a halt, barely beating, and if they are not soon warmed, if they do not soon find that which is sweet, their hearts grow cold, and they cease to be. Consider for a moment those hummingbirds who did not open their eyes again today, this very day, in the Americas: bearded helmet-crests and booted racket-tails, violet-tailed sylphs and violet-capped wood-nymphs, crimson topazes and purple-crowned fairies, red-tailed comets and amethyst woodstars, rainbow-bearded thornbills and glittering-bellied emeralds, velvet-purple coronets and golden-bellied star-frontlets, fiery-tailed awlbills and Andean hillstars, spatuletails and pufflegs, each the most amazing thing you have never seen, each thunderous wild heart the size of an infant's fingernail, each mad heart silent, a brilliant music stilled.

Hummingbirds, like all flying birds but more so, have incredible enormous immense ferocious metabolisms. To drive those metabolisms they have race-car hearts that eat oxygen at an eye-popping rate. Their hearts are built of thinner, leaner fibers than ours. Their arteries are stiffer and more taut. They have more mitochondria in their heart muscles – anything to gulp more oxygen. Their hearts are stripped to the skin for the war against gravity and inertia, the mad search for food, the insane idea of flight. The price of their ambition is a life closer to death; they suffer heart attacks and aneurysms and ruptures more than any other living creature. It's expensive to fly. You burn out. You fry the machine. You melt the engine.

Every creature on earth has approximately two billion heartbeats to spend in a lifetime. You can spend them slowly, like a tortoise, and live to be two hundred years old, or you can spend them fast, like a hummingbird, and live to be two years old.

The biggest heart in the world is inside the blue whale. It weighs more than seven tons. It's as big as a room. It *is* a room, with four chambers. A child could walk around in it, head high, bending only to step through the valves. The valves are as big as the swinging doors in a saloon. This house of a heart drives a creature a hundred feet long. When this creature is born it is twenty feet long and weighs four tons. It is waaaaay bigger than your car. It drinks a hundred gallons of milk from its mama every day and gains two hundred pounds a day and when it is seven or eight years old it endures an unimaginable puberty and then it essentially disappears from human ken, for next to nothing is known of the mating habits, travel patterns, diet, social life, language, social structure, diseases, spirituality, wars, stories, despairs, and arts of the blue whale. There are perhaps ten thousand blue whales in the world, living in every ocean on earth, and of the largest mammal who ever lived we know nearly nothing. But we know this: the animals with the largest hearts in the world generally travel in pairs, and their penetrating moaning cries, their piercing yearning tongue, can be heard underwater for miles and miles.

SO MUCH HELD IN A HEART IN A LIFETIME. SO MUCH HELD IN A HEART IN A DAY, AN HOUR, A MOMENT.

Mammals and birds have hearts with four chambers. Reptiles and turtles have hearts with three chambers. Fish have hearts with two chambers. Insects and mollusks have hearts with one chamber. Worms have hearts with one chamber, although they may have as many as eleven single-chambered hearts. Unicellular bacteria have no hearts at all; but even they have fluid eternally in motion, washing from one side of the cell to the other, swirling and whirling. No living being is without interior liquid motion. We all churn inside.

So much held in a heart in a lifetime. So much held in a heart in a day, an hour, a moment. We are utterly open with no one, in the end — not mother and father, not wife or husband, not lover, not child, not friend. We open windows to each but we live alone in the house of the heart. Perhaps we must. Perhaps we could not bear to be so naked, for fear of a constantly harrowed heart. When young we think there will come one person who will savor and sustain us always; when we are older we know this is the dream of a child, that all hearts finally are bruised and scarred, scored and torn, repaired by time and will, patched by force of character, yet fragile and rickety forevermore, no matter how ferocious the defense and how many bricks you bring to the wall. You can brick up your heart as stout and tight and hard and cold and impregnable as you possibly can and down it comes in an instant, felled by a woman's second glance, a child's apple breath, the shatter of glass in the road, the words *I have something to tell you,* a cat with a broken spine dragging itself into the forest to die, the brush of your mother's papery ancient hand in the thicket of your hair, the memory of your father's voice early in the morning echoing from the kitchen where he is making pancakes for his children.

QUESTIONS FOR A SECOND READING

1. One of the fascinating aspects of Doyle's short essay is the way he is able to move from talking about hummingbirds, blue whales, and hearts to sentences that are about something else — or at least seem to be pointing to something else, pointing *away* from hummingbirds, blue whales, and hearts and pointing *toward*—well, what?

   Reread Doyle's essay with particular attention to moments you see this pointing *away* from the subject. Perhaps you might underline any sentences that seem to want us to think about more than the literal subject at hand. Once you've identified these moments in the essay, consider the following questions: How can you tell that Doyle is moving your attention away from the literal content of the essay? What signals seem to indicate that movement? And finally, can you see anything that Doyle does to prepare you for these moments — what gestures, grammatical constructions, phrases seem to let us know that his piece is going to be about something more than hummingbirds?

2. On the surface, some moments in Doyle's essay may seem as though he is merely supplying his reader with facts about hummingbirds, blue whales, and hearts. But given the rest of the essay, for Doyle, offering his reader facts seems to be about something more than providing information. As you reread Doyle's essay, think carefully about what the "facts" in his essay are doing. Are they providing information? What kind? What else can these "facts" be said to be doing in the essay? If Doyle is not meaning to write a report on the size of hearts, then why does he give all of this information about hearts? What are these sentences for?

3. From its opening sentence, Doyle's essay "Joyas Voladoras" is addressed directly to you: "Consider the hummingbird for a long moment." And, at the end, Doyle writes as though he can speak for you, using "we" freely and with a confident eloquence: "When young we think there will come one person who will savor and sustain us always; when we are older we know

this is the dream of a child." Does this work? Do you, in fact, inhabit these sentences in the ways the writer seems to assume you will?

As you reread, pay attention to the ways you are addressed in this essay, the ways you are invited (or pulled) into the text. How does Doyle do this? Why does he do this? Could the essay have been written otherwise? (Could you rewrite a paragraph to show a different style of address?) Does it work for you?

4. As you reread, pay attention to sentences and paragraphs and the spaces in between. Choose a characteristic sentence, a characteristic paragraph, and a characteristic moment of transition. Be prepared to describe what each is doing and how each works—how it works for the reader, how it works for the writer. And, as an exercise, write a Doyle-like sentence of your own, one with the shape and rhythm of the sentence you have chosen.

ASSIGNMENTS FOR WRITING

1. The form of Doyle's "Joyas Voladoras" could be said to present challenges, but it could also be said to present pleasure and opportunity. As you reread, think about this text as a type of experimental essay. How does it draw on the conventions of the essay? How does it defy or revise those conventions? How would you describe its formal features in relation to what you understand to be conventional essay form? How does "Joyas Voladoras" engage a reader? How does it satisfy or challenge a reader's expectations?

   Prepare an essay that is Doyle-like. It should be, at minimum, as long as his. It should be similar in style and intent. His work is your model and inspiration, and yet this project is also yours. A reader should be able to see where and how your work is in conversation with his; a reader should also be able to see what you bring to the table. And, when you are done, write a brief "Introduction" or "Afterword," something to orient your reader to what follows or something to provide your reader with a context at the end.

2. We suspect that at some point in your educational history, someone has asked you to "find the main idea" of an essay. Often when students are asked to do this kind of work, there is one central argument or one significant point. Your job is to find it and bring it home. "Joyas Voladoras" is an essay without such a structure, without a conventional "thesis statement," without a conventional introduction and conclusion.

   It can be read, of course, as though it presented a conventional challenge. As you reread the essay, and in preparation for writing an essay of your own, ask yourself, "What is this essay about?" How do these six paragraphs come to a single conclusion? What is this conclusion? (And why is Doyle so hesitant to write it out?) Write this essay, making good use of examples from the text. You will be demonstrating your ability, as a reader, to find meaning in what you read. Let this serve as "Part One."

In "Part Two," write briefly, and perhaps in a different, more reflective style, about what you have done and about what is lost in "Joyas Voladoras" (or in the experience of its reader) when such a reading is imposed upon the essay.

(Note: What is a "more reflective style"? Doyle provides an example. A reflective style can also simply rely on sentences that are tentative, questioning, exploratory, sentences that look at things from various angles—"not only this but, perhaps, also that.")

MAKING CONNECTIONS

1. Consider the following sentence from Alberto Ríos's "Translating Translation: Finding the Beginning": "Linguists, by using electrodes on the vocal chords, have been able to demonstrate that English has tenser vowels than, for example, Spanish." Or this sentence from Anne Carson's "Short Talks": "Kafka liked to have his watch an hour and a half fast." Or this statement from Susan Griffin's "Our Secret": "The life plan of the body is encoded in the DNA molecule, a substance that has the ability to hold information and to replicate itself." Or this sentence from Walker Percy's "The Loss of the Creature": "Garcia López de Cárdenas discovered the Grand Canyon and was amazed at the sight." Or this statement from Brian Doyle's "Joyas Voladoras": "The biggest heart in the world is inside the blue whale."

   All of the above statements might be considered "facts" or called "factual information." Each writer is making a declarative statement that makes a claim about what is so. Using the quotations above, or perhaps using other quotations from other selections in *Ways of Reading*, write an essay in which you consider each writer's use of declarative statements or "facts." What, in your understanding, is a fact? How do the writers you have chosen to examine challenge or support your notion of facts? What are their facts for? What, in other words, are some of the ways these writers use facts—for what purposes or to what ends?

2. Reread Anne Carson's "Short Talks" and Antonio Porchia's excerpt from *Voices*. These pieces, like Doyle's "Joyas Voladoras," blur the boundaries of genre. They are and aren't essays. As a mental exercise, let's think of them as experimental essays, essays that push the boundaries of essay form. They raise questions about what prose can do, about what it might be good for.

   Reread "Joyas Voladoras" alongside one (or both) of these selections, noting as you read the distinctive features of each writer's style. It will be up to you to identify and name them. It will be useful, as well, to note commonalities, the stylistic overlaps between texts.

Write an essay in which you consider the genre of the essay—its form and style, its limits and possibilities—through your examination of these examples. You'll need to work closely with examples, both from the text and from your experience as a reader of these texts.

MICHEL

Foucault

Michel Foucault (1926–1984) stands at the beginning of the twenty-first century as one of the world's leading intellectuals. He was trained as a philosopher, but much of his work, like that presented in *Discipline and Punish: The Birth of the Prison* (1975), traces the presence of certain ideas across European history. So he could also be thought of as a historian, but a historian whose goal is to revise the usual understanding of history—not as a progressive sequence but as a series of repetitions governed by powerful ideas, terms, and figures. Foucault was also a public intellectual, involved in such prominent issues as prison reform. He wrote frequently for French newspapers and reviews. His death from AIDS was front-page news in *Le Monde*, the French equivalent of the *New York Times*. He taught at several French universities and in 1970 was appointed to a professorship at the Collège de France, the highest position in the French system. He traveled widely, visiting and lecturing at universities throughout the world.

Foucault's work is central to much current work in the humanities and the social sciences. In fact, it is hard to imagine any area of the academy that has not been influenced by his writing. There is a certain irony in all this, since Foucault argued persuasively that we need to give up thinking about knowledge as individually produced; we have to stop thinking the way we do about the "author" or the "genius," about individuality or creativity; we have to stop thinking as though there were truths that stand beyond the interests of a given moment. It is both dangerous and wrong, he argued, to assume that knowledge is disinterested. Edward Said had this to say of Foucault:

> His great critical contribution was to dissolve the anthropological models of identity and subjecthood underlying research in the humanistic and social sciences. Instead of seeing everything in culture and society as ultimately emanating from either a sort of unchanging Cartesian ego or a heroic solitary artist, Foucault proposed the much juster notion that all work, like social life itself, is collective. The principal task therefore is to circumvent or break down the ideological biases that prevent us from saying that what enables a doctor to practice medicine or a historian to write history is not mainly a set of

> individual gifts, but an ability to follow rules that are taken for granted as an unconscious a priori by all professionals. More than anyone before him, Foucault specified rules for those rules, and even more impressively, he showed how over long periods of time the rules became epistemological enforcers of what (as well as of how) people thought, lived, and spoke.

These rules, these unconscious enforcers, are visible in "discourse" — ways of thinking and speaking and acting that we take for granted as naturally or inevitably there but that are constructed over time and preserved by those who act without question, without stepping outside the discourse and thinking critically. But, says Foucault, there is no place "outside" the discourse, no free, clear space. There is always only another discursive position. A person in thinking, living, and speaking expresses not merely himself or herself but the thoughts and roles and phrases governed by the available ways of thinking and speaking. The key questions to ask, then, according to Foucault, are not Who said this? or Is it original? or Is it true? or Is it authentic? but Who talks this way? or What unspoken rules govern this way of speaking? or Where is this discourse used? Who gets to use it? when? and to what end?

The following selection is the third chapter of *Discipline and Punish: The Birth of the Prison* (translated from the French by Alan Sheridan). In this book, Foucault is concerned with the relationships between knowledge and power, arguing that knowledge is not pure and abstract but is implicated in networks of power relations. Or, as he puts it elsewhere, people govern themselves "through the production of truth." This includes the "truths" that determine how we imagine and manage the boundaries between the "normal" and the transgressive, the lawful and the delinquent. In a characteristic move, Foucault reverses our intuitive sense of how things are. He argues, for example, that it is not the case that prisons serve the courts and a system of justice but that the courts are the products, the servants of "the prison," the prison as an idea, as the central figure in a way of thinking about transgression, order, and the body, a way of thinking that is persistent and general, present, for example, through all efforts to produce the normal or "disciplined individual": "in the central position that [the prison] occupies, it is not alone, but linked to a whole series of 'carceral' mechanisms which seem distinct enough — since they are intended to alleviate pain, to cure, to comfort — but which all tend, like the prison, to exercise a power of normalization." Knowledge stands in an antagonistic role in *Discipline and Punish*; it is part of a problem, not a route to a solution.

You will find "Panopticism" difficult reading. All readers find Foucault's prose tough going. It helps to realize that it is necessarily difficult. Foucault, remember, is trying to work outside of, or in spite of, the usual ways of thinking and writing. He is trying not to reproduce the standard discourse but to point to what it cannot or will not say. He is trying to make gestures beyond what is ordinarily, normally said. So his prose struggles with its own situation. Again, as Edward Said says, "What [Foucault] was interested in . . . was 'the more' that can be discovered lurking in signs and discourses but that is irreducible to language and speech; 'it is this "more,"' he said, 'that we must reveal and describe.' Such a concern appears to be both devious and obscure, yet it accounts for a lot that is especially unsettling in Foucault's writing. There is no such thing as being at home in his writing, neither for reader nor for writer." While readers find Foucault difficult, he is widely read and widely cited. His books include *The Birth of the Clinic: An Archaeology of Medical Perception* (1963), *The Order of Things: An Archaeology of the Human Sciences* (1966), *The Archaeology of Knowledge* (1969), *Madness and Civilization* (1971), and the three-volume *History of Sexuality* (1976, 1979, 1984).

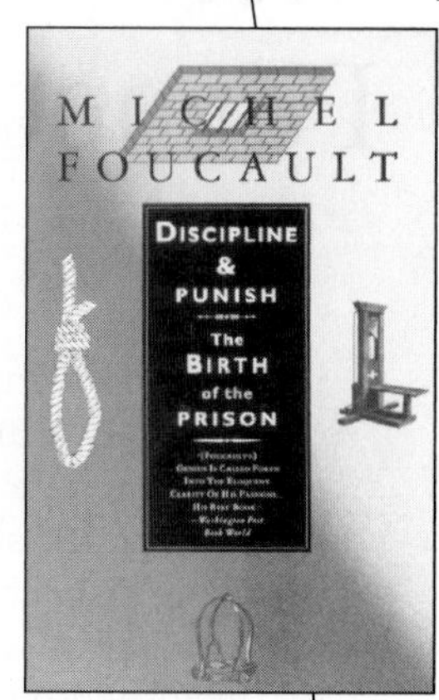

Panopticism

The following, according to an order published at the end of the seventeenth century, were the measures to be taken when the plague appeared in a town.[1]

First, a strict spatial partitioning: the closing of the town and its outlying districts, a prohibition to leave the town on pain of death, the killing of all stray animals; the division of the town into distinct quarters, each governed by an intendant. Each street is placed under the authority of a syndic, who keeps it under surveillance; if he leaves the street, he will be condemned to death. On the appointed day, everyone is ordered to stay indoors: it is forbidden to leave on pain of death. The syndic himself comes to lock the door of each house from the outside; he takes the key with him and hands it over to the intendant of the quarter; the intendant keeps it until the end of the quarantine. Each family will have made its own provisions; but, for bread and wine, small wooden canals are set up between the street and the interior of the houses, thus allowing each person to receive his ration without communicating with the suppliers and other residents; meat, fish, and herbs will be hoisted up into the houses with pulleys and baskets. If it is absolutely necessary to leave the house, it will be done in turn, avoiding any meeting. Only the intendants, syndics, and guards will move about the streets and also, between the infected houses, from one corpse to another, the "crows," who can be left to die: these are "people of little substance who carry the sick, bury the dead, clean, and do many vile and abject offices." It is a segmented, immobile, frozen space. Each individual is fixed in his place. And, if he moves, he does so at the risk of his life, contagion, or punishment.

EVERYONE LOCKED UP IN HIS CAGE, EVERYONE AT HIS WINDOW, ANSWERING TO HIS NAME AND SHOWING HIMSELF WHEN ASKED — IT IS THE GREAT REVIEW OF THE LIVING AND THE DEAD.

Inspection functions ceaselessly. The gaze is alert everywhere: "A considerable body of militia, commanded by good officers and men of substance," guards at the gates, at the town hall, and in every quarter to ensure the prompt obedience of the people and the most absolute authority of the magistrates, "as also to observe all disorder, theft and extortion." At each of the town gates there will be an observation post; at the end of each street sentinels. Every day, the intendant visits the quarter in his charge, inquires whether the syndics have carried out their tasks, whether the inhabitants have anything to complain of; they "observe their actions." Every day, too, the syndic goes into the street for which he is responsible;

stops before each house: gets all the inhabitants to appear at the windows (those who live overlooking the courtyard will be allocated a window looking onto the street at which no one but they may show themselves); he calls each of them by name; informs himself as to the state of each and every one of them — "in which respect the inhabitants will be compelled to speak the truth under pain of death"; if someone does not appear at the window, the syndic must ask why: "In this way he will find out easily enough whether dead or sick are being concealed." Everyone locked up in his cage, everyone at his window, answering to his name and showing himself when asked — it is the great review of the living and the dead.

This surveillance is based on a system of permanent registration: reports from the syndics to the intendants, from the intendants to the magistrates or mayor. At the beginning of the "lock up," the role of each of the inhabitants present in the town is laid down, one by one; this document bears "the name, age, sex of everyone, notwithstanding his condition": a copy is sent to the intendant of the quarter, another to the office of the town hall, another to enable the syndic to make his daily roll call. Everything that may be observed during the course of the visits — deaths, illnesses, complaints, irregularities — is noted down and transmitted to the intendants and magistrates. The magistrates have complete control over medical treatment; they have appointed a physician in charge; no other practitioner may treat, no apothecary prepare medicine, no confessor visit a sick person without having received from him a written note "to prevent anyone from concealing and dealing with those sick of the contagion, unknown to the magistrates." The registration of the pathological must be constantly centralized. The relation of each individual to his disease and to his death passes through the representatives of power, the registration they make of it, the decisions they take on it.

Five or six days after the beginning of the quarantine, the process of purifying the houses one by one is begun. All the inhabitants are made to leave; in each room "the furniture and goods" are raised from the ground or suspended from the air; perfume is poured around the room; after carefully sealing the windows, doors, and even the keyholes with wax, the perfume is set alight. Finally, the entire house is closed while the perfume is consumed; those who have carried out the work are searched, as they were on entry, "in the presence of the residents of the house, to see that they did not have something on their persons as they left that they did not have on entering." Four hours later, the residents are allowed to reenter their homes.

This enclosed, segmented space, observed at every point, in which the individuals are inserted in a fixed place, in which the slightest movements are supervised, in which all events are recorded, in which an uninterrupted work of writing links the center and periphery, in which power is exercised without division, according to a continuous hierarchical figure, in which each individual is constantly located, examined, and distributed among the living beings, the sick, and the dead — all this constitutes a compact model of the disciplinary mechanism. The plague is met by order;

its function is to sort out every possible confusion: that of the disease, which is transmitted when bodies are mixed together; that of the evil, which is increased when fear and death overcome prohibitions. It lays down for each individual his place, his body, his disease, and his death, his well-being, by means of an omnipresent and omniscient power that subdivides itself in a regular, uninterrupted way even to the ultimate determination of the individual, of what characterizes him, of what belongs to him, of what happens to him. Against the plague, which is a mixture, discipline brings into play its power, which is one of analysis. A whole literary fiction of the festival grew up around the plague: suspended laws, lifted prohibitions, the frenzy of passing time, bodies mingling together without respect, individuals unmasked, abandoning their statutory identity and the figure under which they had been recognized, allowing a quite different truth to appear. But there was also a political dream of the plague, which was exactly its reverse: not the collective festival, but strict divisions; not laws transgressed, but the penetration of regulation into even the smallest details of everyday life through the mediation of the complete hierarchy that assured the capillary functioning of power; not masks that were put on and taken off, but the assignment to each individual of his "true" name, his "true" place, his "true" body, his "true" disease. The plague as a form, at once real and imaginary, of disorder had as its medical and political correlative discipline. Behind the disciplinary mechanisms can be read the haunting memory of "contagions," of the plague, of rebellions, crimes, vagabondage, desertions, people who appear and disappear, live and die in disorder.

If it is true that the leper gave rise to rituals of exclusion, which to a certain extent provided the model for and general form of the great Confinement, then the plague gave rise to disciplinary projects. Rather than the massive, binary division between one set of people and another, it called for multiple separations, individualizing distributions, an organization in depth of surveillance and control, an intensification and a ramification of power. The leper was caught up in a practice of rejection, of exile-enclosure; he was left to his doom in a mass among which it was useless to differentiate; those sick of the plague were caught up in a meticulous tactical partitioning in which individual differentiations were the constricting effects of a power that multiplied, articulated, and subdivided itself; the great confinement on the one hand; the correct training on the other. The leper and his separation; the plague and its segmentations. The first is marked; the second analyzed and distributed. The exile of the leper and the arrest of the plague do not bring with them the same political dream. The first is that of a pure community, the second that of a disciplined society. Two ways of exercising power over men, of controlling their relations, of separating out their dangerous mixtures. The plague-stricken town, traversed throughout with hierarchy, surveillance, observation, writing; the town immobilized by the functioning of an extensive power that bears in a distinct way over all individual bodies — this is the utopia of the perfectly governed city. The plague (envisaged as a possibility at least) is the trial in the course of which one may define ideally the exercise of disciplinary power. In order to make rights and laws function according to pure theory, the jurists place themselves in imagination in the state of nature; in order to see perfect disciplines functioning, rulers dreamed of the state of plague. Underlying disciplinary projects the image of the plague stands for all forms of confusion and disorder; just as the image of the leper, cut off from all human contact, underlies projects of exclusion.

They are different projects, then, but not incompatible ones. We see them coming slowly together, and it is the peculiarity of the nineteenth century that it applied to the space of exclusion of which the leper was the symbolic inhabitant (beggars, vagabonds, madmen, and the disorderly formed the real population) the technique of power proper to disciplinary partitioning. Treat "lepers" as "plague victims," project the subtle segmentations of discipline onto the confused space of internment, combine it with the methods of analytical distribution proper to power, individualize the excluded, but use procedures of individualization to mark exclusion — this is what was operated regularly by disciplinary power from the beginning of the nineteenth century in the psychiatric asylum, the penitentiary, the reformatory, the approved school, and to some extent, the hospital. Generally speaking, all the authorities exercising individual control function according to a double mode; that of binary division and branding (mad/sane; dangerous/harmless; normal/abnormal); and that of coercive assignment, of differential distribution (who he is; where he must be; how he is to be characterized; how he is to be recognized; how a constant surveillance is to be exercised over him in an individual way, etc.). On the one hand, the lepers are treated as plague victims; the tactics of individualizing disciplines are imposed on the excluded; and, on the other hand, the universality of disciplinary controls makes it possible to brand the "leper" and to bring into play against him the dualistic mechanisms of exclusion. The constant division between the normal and the abnormal, to which every individual is subjected, brings us back to our own time, by applying the binary branding and exile of the leper to quite different objects; the existence of a whole set of techniques and institutions for measuring, supervising, and correcting the abnormal brings into play the disciplinary mechanisms to which the fear of the plague gave rise. All the mechanisms of power which, even today, are disposed around the abnormal individual, to brand him and to alter him, are composed of those two forms from which they distantly derive.

Bentham's *Panopticon* is the architectural figure of this composition. We know the principle on which it was based: at the periphery, an annular building; at the center, a tower; this tower is pierced with wide windows that open onto the inner side of the ring; the peripheric building is divided into cells, each of which extends the whole width of the building; they have two windows, one on the inside, corresponding to the windows of the tower; the other, on the outside, allows the light to cross the cell from one end to the other. All that is needed, then, is to place a supervisor in a

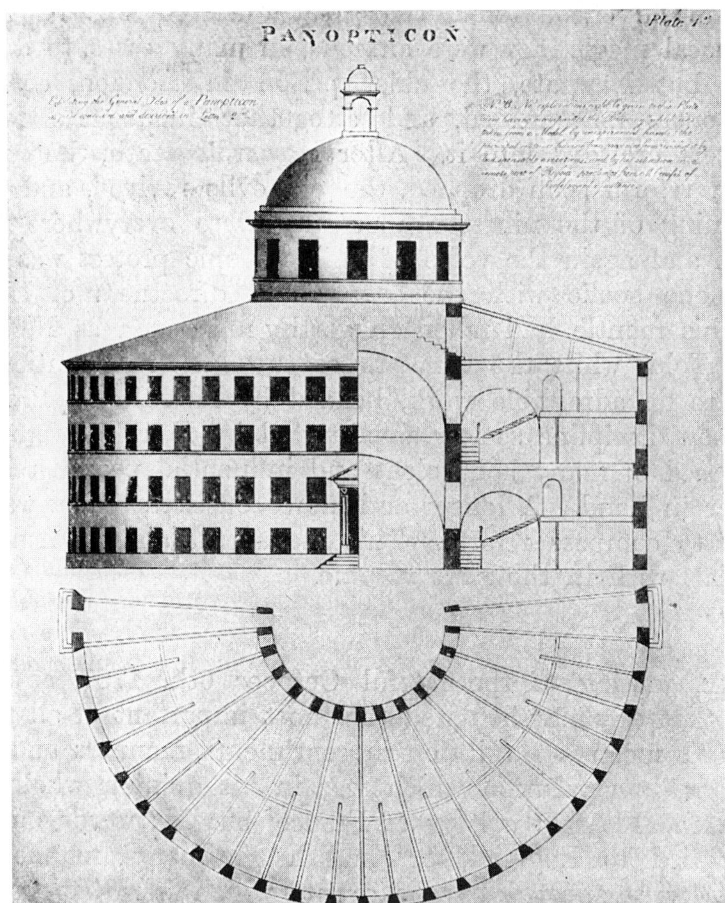

Plan of the Panopticon by J. Bentham (*The Works of Jeremy Bentham*, ed. Bowring, vol. IV, 1843, 172–73).

central tower and to shut up in each cell a madman, a patient, a condemned man, a worker, or a schoolboy. By the effect of backlighting, one can observe from the tower, standing out precisely against the light, the small captive shadows in the cells of the periphery. They are like so many cages, so many small theaters, in which each actor is alone, perfectly individualized and constantly visible. The panoptic mechanism arranges spatial unities that make it possible to see constantly and to recognize immediately. In short, it reverses the principle of the dungeon; or rather of its three functions — to enclose, to deprive of light, and to hide — it preserves only the first and eliminates the other two. Full lighting and the eye of a supervisor capture better than darkness, which is ultimately protected. Visibility is a trap.

To begin with, this made it possible — as a negative effect — to avoid those compact, swarming, howling masses that were to be found in places of confinement, those painted by Goya or described by Howard. Each individual, in his place, is securely confined to a cell from which he is seen from the front by the supervisor; but the side walls prevent him from coming into contact with his companions. He is seen, but he does not see; he is the object of information, never a subject in communication. The arrangement of his room, opposite the central tower, imposes on him an axial visibility; but the divisions of the ring, those separated cells, imply a lateral invisibility. And this invisibility is a guarantee of order. If the inmates are convicts, there is no danger of a plot, an attempt at collective escape, the planning of new crimes for the future, bad reciprocal influences; if they are patients, there is no danger of contagion; if they are madmen, there is no risk of their committing violence upon one another;

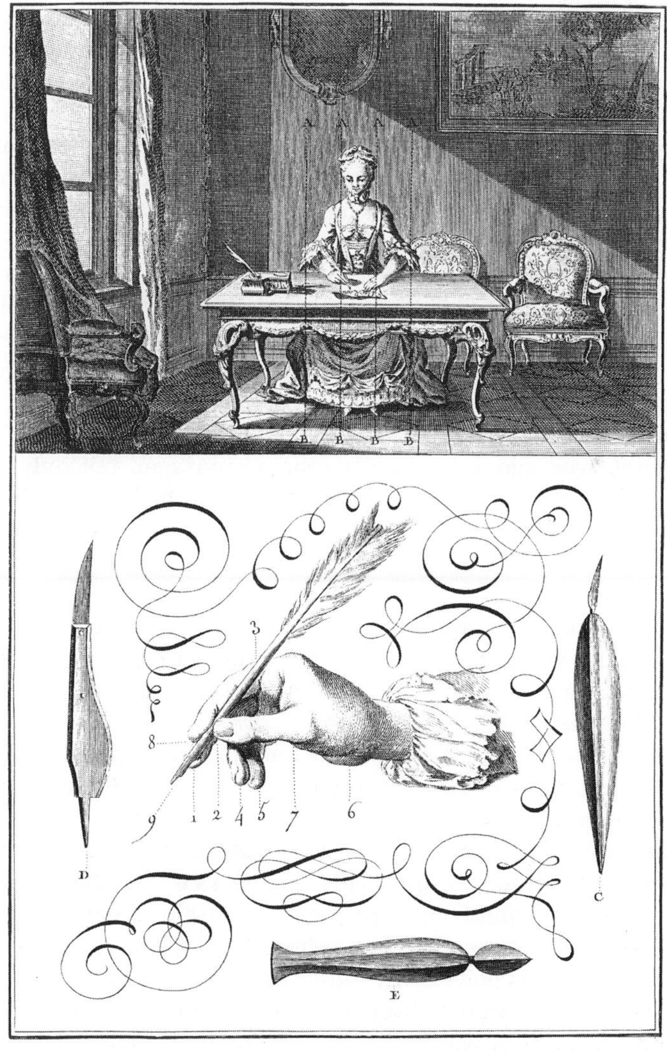

Handwriting model. *Collections historiques de l'I.N.R.D.P.*

if they are schoolchildren, there is no copying, no noise, no chatter, no waste of time; if they are workers, there are no disorders, no theft, no coalitions, none of those distractions that slow down the rate of work, make it less perfect, or cause accidents. The crowd, a compact mass, a locus of multiple exchanges, individualities merging together, a collective effect, is abolished and replaced by a collection of separated individualities. From the point of view of the guardian, it is replaced by a multiplicity that can be numbered and supervised; from the point of view of the inmates, by a sequestered and observed solitude (Bentham 60–64).

Hence the major effect of the Panopticon: to induce in the inmate a state of conscious and permanent visibility that assures the automatic functioning of power. So to arrange things that the surveillance is permanent in its effects even if it is discontinuous in its action; that the perfection of power should tend to render its actual exercise unnecessary; that this architectural apparatus should be a machine for creating and sustaining a power relation independent of the person who exercises it; in short, that the inmates should be caught up in a power situation of which they are themselves the bearers. To achieve this, it is at once too much and too little that the prisoner should be constantly observed by an inspector: too little, for what matters is that he knows himself to be observed; too much, because he has no need in fact of being so. In view of this, Bentham laid down the principle that power should be visible and unverifiable. Visible: the inmate will constantly have before his eyes the tall outline of the central tower from which he is spied upon. Unverifiable: the inmate must never know whether he is being looked at at any one moment; but he must be sure that he may always be so. In order to make the presence or absence of the inspector unverifiable, so that the prisoners, in their cells, cannot even see a shadow, Bentham envisaged not only venetian blinds on the windows of the central observation hall, but, on the inside, partitions that intersected the hall at right angles and, in order to pass from one quarter to the other, not doors but zigzag openings; for the slightest noise, a gleam of light, a brightness in a half-opened door would betray the presence of the guardian.[2] The Panopticon is a machine for dissociating the see/being seen dyad: in the peripheric ring, one is totally seen, without ever seeing; in the central tower, one sees everything without ever being seen.[3]

It is an important mechanism, for it automatizes and disindividualizes power. Power has its principle not so much in a person as in a certain concerted distribution of bodies, surfaces, lights, gazes; in an arrangement whose internal mechanisms produce the relation in which individuals are caught up. The ceremonies, the rituals, the marks by which the sovereign's surplus power was manifested are useless. There is a machinery that assures dissymmetry, disequilibrium, difference. Consequently, it does not matter who exercises power. Any individual, taken almost at random, can operate the machine: in the absence of the director, his family, his friends, his visitors, even his servants (Bentham 45). Similarly, it does not matter what motive animates him: the curiosity of the indiscreet, the malice of a

Interior of the penitentiary at Stateville, United States, twentieth century.

child, the thirst for knowledge of a philosopher who wishes to visit this museum of human nature, or the perversity of those who take pleasure in spying and punishing. The more numerous those anonymous and temporary observers are, the greater the risk for the inmate of being surprised and the greater his anxious awareness of being observed. The Panopticon is a marvelous machine which, whatever use one may wish to put it to, produces homogeneous effects of power.

A real subjection is born mechanically from a fictitious relation. So it is not necessary to use force to constrain the convict to good behavior, the madman to calm, the worker to work, the schoolboy to application, the patient to the observation of the regulations. Bentham was surprised that panoptic institutions could be so light: there were no more bars, no more

Lecture on the evils of alcoholism in the auditorium of Fresnes prison.

chains, no more heavy locks; all that was needed was that the separations should be clear and the openings well arranged. The heaviness of the old "houses of security," with their fortresslike architecture, could be replaced by the simple, economic geometry of a "house of certainty." The efficiency of power, its constraining force have, in a sense, passed over to the other side — to the side of its surface of application. He who is subjected to a field of visibility, and who knows it, assumes responsibility for the constraints of power; he makes them play spontaneously upon himself; he inscribes in himself the power relation in which he simultaneously plays both roles; he becomes the principle of his own subjection. By this very fact, the external power may throw off its physical weight; it tends to the noncorporal; and, the

HE WHO IS SUBJECTED TO A FIELD OF VISIBILITY, AND WHO KNOWS IT, ASSUMES RESPONSIBILITY FOR THE CONSTRAINTS OF POWER.

more it approaches this limit, the more constant, profound, and permanent are its effects: it is a perpetual victory that avoids any physical confrontation and which is always decided in advance.

Bentham does not say whether he was inspired, in his project, by Le Vaux's menagerie at Versailles: the first menagerie in which the different elements are not, as they traditionally were, distributed in a park (Loisel 104–7). At the center was an octagonal pavilion which, on the first floor, consisted of only a single room, the king's *salon*; on every side large windows looked out onto seven cages (the eighth side was reserved for the entrance), containing different species of animals. By Bentham's time, this menagerie had disappeared. But one finds in the program of the Panopticon a similar concern with individualizing observation, with characterization and classification, with the analytical arrangement of space. The Panopticon is a royal menagerie; the animal is replaced by man, individual distribution by specific grouping, and the king by the machinery of a furtive power. With this exception, the Panopticon also does the work of a naturalist. It makes it possible to draw up differences: among patients, to observe the symptoms of each individual, without the proximity of beds, the circulation of miasmas, the effects of contagion confusing the clinical tables; among schoolchildren, it makes it possible to observe performances (without there being any imitation or copying), to map aptitudes, to assess characters, to draw up rigorous classifications, and in relation to normal development, to distinguish "laziness and stubbornness" from "incurable imbecility"; among workers, it makes it possible to note the aptitudes of each worker, compare the time he takes to perform a task, and if they are paid by the day, to calculate their wages (Bentham 60–64).

So much for the question of observation. But the Panopticon was also a laboratory; it could be used as a machine to carry out experiments, to alter behavior, to train or correct individuals. To experiment with medicines and monitor their effects. To try out different punishments on prisoners, according to their crimes and character, and to seek the most effective ones. To teach different techniques simultaneously to the workers, to decide which is the best. To try out pedagogical experiments — and in particular to take up once again the well-debated problem of secluded education, by using orphans. One would see what would happen when, in their sixteenth or eighteenth year, they were presented with other boys or girls; one could verify whether, as Helvetius thought, anyone could learn anything; one would follow "the genealogy of every observable idea"; one could bring up different children according to different systems of thought, making certain children believe that two and two do not make four or that the moon is a cheese, then put them together when they are twenty or twenty-five years old; one would then have discussions that would be worth a great deal more than the sermons or lectures on which so much money is spent; one would have at least an opportunity of making discoveries in the domain of metaphysics. The Panopticon is a privileged place for experiments on men, and for analyzing with complete certainty the transformations that may be obtained from them. The Panopticon may even provide an apparatus for supervising its own mechanisms. In this central tower, the director may spy on all the employees that he has under his orders: nurses, doctors, foremen, teachers, warders; he will be able to judge them continuously, alter their behavior, impose upon them the methods he thinks best; and it will even be possible to observe the director himself. An inspector arriving unexpectedly at the center of the Panopticon will be able to judge at a glance, without anything being concealed from him, how the entire establishment is functioning. And, in any case, enclosed as he is in the middle of this architectural mechanism, is not the director's own fate entirely bound up with it? The incompetent physician who has allowed contagion to spread, the incompetent prison governor or workshop manager will be the first victims of an epidemic or a revolt. "'By every tie I could devise,' said the master of the Panopticon, 'my own fate had been bound up by me with theirs'" (Bentham 177). The Panopticon functions as a kind of laboratory of power. Thanks to its mechanisms of observation, it gains in efficiency and in the ability to penetrate into men's behavior; knowledge follows the advances of power, discovering new objects of knowledge over all the surfaces on which power is exercised.

The plague-stricken town, the panoptic establishment — the differences are important. They mark, at a distance of a century and a half, the transformations of the disciplinary program. In the first case, there is an exceptional situation: against an extraordinary evil, power is mobilized; it makes itself everywhere present and visible; it invents new mechanisms; it separates, it immobilizes, it partitions; it constructs for a time what is both a counter-city and the perfect society; it imposes an ideal functioning, but one that is reduced, in the final analysis, like the evil that it combats, to a simple dualism of life and death: that which moves brings death, and one kills that which moves. The Panopticon, on the other hand, must be understood as a generalizable model of functioning; a way of defining power relations in terms of the everyday life of men. No doubt Bentham presents it as a particular institution, closed in upon itself. Utopias, perfectly closed in upon themselves, are common enough. As opposed to the ruined prisons, littered with mechanisms of torture, to be seen in Piranese's engravings, the Panopticon presents a cruel, ingenious cage. The fact that it should have given rise, even in our own time, to so many variations, projected or realized, is evidence of the imaginary intensity that it has possessed for almost two hundred years. But the Panopticon must not be understood as a dream building: it is the diagram of a mechanism of power reduced to its ideal form; its functioning, abstracted from any obstacle, resistance, or friction, must be represented as a pure architectural and optical system: it is in fact a figure of political technology that may and must be detached from any specific use.

It is polyvalent in its applications; it serves to reform prisoners, but also to treat patients, to instruct schoolchildren, to confine the insane, to supervise workers, to put beggars and idlers to work. It is a type of location of bodies in space, of distribution of individuals in relation to one another, of hierarchical organization, of disposition of centers and channels of power, of definition of the instruments and modes of intervention of power, which can be implemented in hospitals, workshops, schools, prisons. Whenever one is dealing with a multiplicity of individuals on whom a task or a particular form of behavior must be imposed, the panoptic schema may be used. It is — necessary modifications apart — applicable "to all establishments whatsoever, in which, within a space not too large to be covered or commanded by buildings, a number of persons are meant to be kept under inspection" (Bentham 40; although Bentham takes the penitentiary house as his prime example, it is because it has many different functions to fulfill — safe custody, confinement, solitude, forced labor, and instruction).

In each of its applications, it makes it possible to perfect the exercise of power. It does this in several ways: because it can reduce the number of those who exercise it, while increasing the number of those on whom it is exercised. Because it is possible to intervene at any moment and because the constant pressure acts even before the offenses, mistakes, or crimes have been committed. Because, in these conditions, its strength is that it never intervenes, it is exercised spontaneously and without noise, it constitutes a mechanism whose effects follow from one another. Because, without any physical instrument other than architecture and geometry, it acts directly on individuals; it gives "power of mind over mind." The panoptic schema makes any apparatus of power more intense: it assures its economy (in material, in personnel, in time); it assures its efficacity by its preventative character, its continuous functioning, and its automatic mechanisms. It is a way of obtaining from power "in hitherto unexampled quantity," "a great and new instrument of government . . . ; its great excellence consists in the great strength it is capable of giving to *any* institution it may be thought proper to apply it to" (Bentham 66).

It's a case of "it's easy once you've thought of it" in the political sphere. It can in fact be integrated into any function (education, medical treatment, production, punishment); it can increase the effect of this function, by being linked closely with it; it can constitute a mixed mechanism in which relations of power (and of knowledge) may be precisely adjusted, in the smallest detail, to the processes that are to be supervised; it can establish a direct proportion between "surplus power" and "surplus production." In short, it arranges things in such a way that the exercise of power is not added on from the outside, like a rigid, heavy constraint, to the functions it invests, but is so subtly present in them as to increase their efficiency by itself increasing its own points of contact. The panoptic mechanism is not simply a hinge, a point of exchange between a mechanism of power and a function; it is a way of making power relations function in a function, and of making a function function through these power relations. Bentham's preface to *Panopticon* opens with a list of the benefits to be obtained from his "inspection-house": *"Morals reformed — health preserved — industry invigorated — instruction diffused — public burthens lightened* — Economy seated, as it were, upon a rock — the gordian knot of the Poor-Laws not cut, but untied — all by a simple idea in architecture!" (Bentham 39).

Furthermore, the arrangement of this machine is such that its enclosed nature does not preclude a permanent presence from the outside: we have seen that anyone may come and exercise in the central tower the functions of surveillance, and that, this being the case, he can gain a clear idea of the way in which the surveillance is practiced. In fact, any panoptic institution, even if it is as rigorously closed as a penitentiary, may without difficulty be subjected to such irregular and constant inspections: and not only by the appointed inspectors, but also by the public; any member of society will have the right to come and see with his own eyes how the schools, hospitals, factories, prisons function. There is no risk, therefore, that the increase of power created by the panoptic machine may degenerate into tyranny; the disciplinary mechanism will be democratically controlled, since it will be constantly accessible "to the great tribunal committee of the world."[4] This Panopticon, subtly arranged so that an observer may observe, at a glance, so many different individuals, also enables everyone to come and observe any of the observers. The seeing machine was once a sort of dark room into which individuals spied; it has become a transparent building in which the exercise of power may be supervised by society as a whole.

The panoptic schema, without disappearing as such or losing any of its properties, was destined to spread throughout the social body; its vocation was to become a generalized function. The plague-stricken town provided an exceptional disciplinary model: perfect, but absolutely violent; to the disease that brought death, power opposed its perpetual threat of death; life inside it was reduced to its simplest expression; it was, against the power of death, the meticulous exercise of the right of the sword. The Panopticon, on the other hand, has a role of amplification; although it arranges power, although it is intended to make it more economic and more effective, it does so not for power itself, nor for the immediate salvation of a threatened society: its aim is to strengthen the social forces — to increase production, to develop the economy, spread education, raise the level of public morality; to increase and multiply.

How is power to be strengthened in such a way that, far from impeding progress, far from weighing upon it with its rules and regulations, it actually facilitates such progress? What intensificator of power will be able at the same time to be a multiplicator of production? How will power, by increasing its forces, be able to increase those of society instead of confiscating them or impeding them? The Panopticon's solution to this problem is that the productive increase of power can be assured only if, on the one hand, it can be exercised continuously in the very foundations of society, in the subtlest possible way, and if, on the other hand, it functions outside these sudden, violent, discontinuous forms that are bound up with the exercise of sovereignty. The body of the king, with its strange material and physical presence, with the force that he himself deploys or transmits to some few others, is at the opposite extreme of this new physics of power represented by panopticism; the domain of panopticism is, on the contrary, that whole lower region, that region of irregular bodies, with their details, their multiple movements, their heterogeneous forces, their spatial relations; what are required are mechanisms that analyze distributions, gaps, series, combinations, and which use instruments that render visible, record, differentiate, and compare: a physics of a relational and multiple power, which has its maximum intensity not in the person of the king, but in the bodies that can be individualized by these relations. At the theoretical level, Bentham defines another way of analyzing the social body and the power relations that traverse it; in terms of practice, he defines a procedure of subordination of bodies and forces that must increase the utility of power while practicing the economy of the prince. Panopticism is the general principle of a new "political anatomy" whose object and end are not the relations of sovereignty but the relations of discipline.

The celebrated, transparent, circular cage, with its high tower, powerful and knowing, may have been for Bentham a project of a perfect disciplinary institution; but he also set out to show how one may "unlock" the disciplines and get them to function in a diffused, multiple, polyvalent way throughout the whole social body. These disciplines, which the classical age had elaborated in specific, relatively enclosed places — barracks, schools, workshops — and whose total implementation had been imagined only at the limited and temporary scale of a plague-stricken town, Bentham dreamed of transforming into a network of mechanisms that would be everywhere and always alert, running through society without interruption in space or in time. The panoptic arrangement provides the formula for this generalization. It programs, at the level of an elementary and easily transferable mechanism, the basic functioning of a society penetrated through and through with disciplinary mechanisms.

There are two images, then, of discipline. At one extreme, the discipline-blockade, the enclosed institution, established on the edges of society, turned inwards towards negative functions: arresting evil, breaking communications, suspending time. At the other extreme, with panopticism, is the discipline-mechanism: a functional mechanism that must improve the exercise of power by making it lighter, more rapid, more effective, a design of subtle coercion for a society to come. The movement from one project to the other, from a schema of exceptional discipline to one of a generalized surveillance, rests on a historical transformation: the gradual extension of the mechanisms of discipline throughout the seventeenth and eighteenth centuries, their spread throughout the whole social body, the formation of what might be called in general the disciplinary society.

A whole disciplinary generalization — the Benthamite physics of power represents an acknowledgment of this — had operated throughout the classical age. The spread of disciplinary institutions, whose network was beginning to cover an ever larger surface and occupying above all a less and less marginal position, testifies to this: what was an islet, a privileged place, a circumstantial measure, or a singular model, became a general formula; the regulations characteristic of the Protestant and pious armies of William of Orange or of Gustavus Adolphus were transformed into regulations for all the armies of Europe; the model colleges of the Jesuits, or the schools of Batencour or Demia, following the example set by Sturm, provided the outlines for the general forms of educational discipline; the ordering of the naval and military hospitals provided the model for the entire reorganization of hospitals in the eighteenth century.

But this extension of the disciplinary institutions was no doubt only the most visible aspect of various, more profound processes.

1. *The functional inversion of the disciplines*. At first, they were expected to neutralize dangers, to fix useless or disturbed populations, to avoid the inconveniences of over-large assemblies; now they were being asked to play a positive role, for they were becoming able to do so, to increase the possible utility of individuals. Military discipline is no longer a mere means of preventing looting, desertion, or failure to obey orders among the troops; it has become a basic technique to enable the army to exist, not as an assembled crowd, but as a unity that derives from this very unity an increase in its forces; discipline increases the skill of each individual, coordinates these skills, accelerates movements, increases fire power, broadens the fronts of attack without reducing their vigor, increases the capacity for resistance, etc. The discipline of the workshop, while remaining a way of enforcing respect for the regulations and authorities, of preventing thefts or losses, tends to increase aptitudes, speeds, output, and therefore profits; it still exerts a moral influence over behavior, but more and more it treats actions in terms of their results, introduces bodies into a machinery, forces into an economy. When, in the seventeenth century, the provincial schools or the Christian elementary schools were founded, the justifications given for them were above all negative: those poor who were unable to bring up their children left them "in ignorance of their obligations: given the difficulties they have in earning a living, and themselves having been badly brought up, they are unable to communicate a sound upbringing that they themselves never had"; this involves three major inconveniences: ignorance of God, idleness (with its consequent drunkenness, impurity, larceny, brigandage), and the formation of those gangs of beggars, always ready to stir up public disorder and "virtually to exhaust the funds of the Hôtel-Dieu" (Demia 60–61). Now, at the beginning of the Revolution, the end laid down for primary education was to be, among other things, to "fortify," to "develop the body," to prepare the child "for a future in some mechanical work," to give him "an observant eye, a sure hand and prompt habits" (Talleyrand's Report to the Constituent Assembly, 10 September 1791, quoted by Léon 106). The disciplines function increasingly as techniques for making useful individuals. Hence their emergence from a marginal position on the confines of society, and detachment from the forms of exclusion or expiation, confinement, or retreat. Hence the slow loosening of their kinship with religious regularities and enclosures. Hence also their rooting in the most important, most central, and most productive sectors of society. They become attached to some of the great essential functions: factory production, the transmission of knowledge, the diffusion of aptitudes and skills, the war-machine. Hence, too, the double tendency one sees developing

throughout the eighteenth century to increase the number of disciplinary institutions and to discipline the existing apparatuses.

2. *The swarming of disciplinary mechanisms*. While, on the one hand, the disciplinary establishments increase, their mechanisms have a certain tendency to become "deinstitutionalized," to emerge from the closed fortresses in which they once functioned and to circulate in a "free" state; the massive, compact disciplines are broken down into flexible methods of control, which may be transferred and adapted. Sometimes the closed apparatuses add to their internal and specific function a role of external surveillance, developing around themselves a whole margin of lateral controls. Thus the Christian School must not simply train docile children; it must also make it possible to supervise the parents, to gain information as to their way of life, their resources, their piety, their morals. The school tends to constitute minute social observatories that penetrate even to the adults and exercise regular supervision over them: the bad behavior of the child, or his absence, is a legitimate pretext, according to Demia, for one to go and question the neighbors, especially if there is any reason to believe that the family will not tell the truth; one can then go and question the parents themselves, to find out whether they know their catechism and the prayers, whether they are determined to root out the vices of their children, how many beds there are in the house and what the sleeping arrangements are; the visit may end with the giving of alms, the present of a religious picture, or the provision of additional beds (Demia 39–40). Similarly, the hospital is increasingly conceived of as a base for the medical observation of the population outside; after the burning down of the Hôtel-Dieu in 1772, there were several demands that the large buildings, so heavy and so disordered, should be replaced by a series of smaller hospitals; their function would be to take in the sick of the quarter, but also to gather information, to be alert to any endemic or epidemic phenomena, to open dispensaries, to give advice to the inhabitants, and to keep the authorities informed of the sanitary state of the region.[5]

ONE ALSO SEES THE SPREAD OF DISCIPLINARY PROCEDURES, NOT IN THE FORM OF ENCLOSED INSTITUTIONS, BUT AS CENTERS OF OBSERVATION DISSEMINATED THROUGHOUT SOCIETY.

One also sees the spread of disciplinary procedures, not in the form of enclosed institutions, but as centers of observation disseminated throughout society. Religious groups and charity organizations had long played this role of "disciplining" the population. From the Counter-Reformation to the philanthropy of the July monarchy, initiatives of this type continued to increase; their aims were religious (conversion and moralization), economic (aid and encouragement to work), or political (the struggle against discontent or agitation). One has only to cite by way of example the regulations for the charity associations in the Paris parishes. The territory to be covered was divided into quarters and cantons and the members of the associations divided themselves up along the same lines.

These members had to visit their respective areas regularly. "They will strive to eradicate places of ill-repute, tobacco shops, life-classes, gaming houses, public scandals, blasphemy, impiety, and any other disorders that may come to their knowledge." They will also have to make individual visits to the poor; and the information to be obtained is laid down in regulations: the stability of the lodging, knowledge of prayers, attendance at the sacraments, knowledge of a trade, morality (and "whether they have not fallen into poverty through their own fault"); lastly, "one must learn by skillful questioning in what way they behave at home. Whether there is peace between them and their neighbors, whether they are careful to bring up their children in the fear of God . . . , whether they do not have their older children of different sexes sleeping together and with them, whether they do not allow licentiousness and cajolery in their families, especially in their older daughters. If one has any doubts as to whether they are married, one must ask to see their marriage certificate."[6]

3. *The state-control of the mechanisms of the discipline*. In England, it was private religious groups that carried out, for a long time, the functions of social discipline (cf. Radzinovitz 203–14); in France, although a part of this role remained in the hands of parish guilds or charity associations, another — and no doubt the most important part — was very soon taken over by the police apparatus.

The organization of a centralized police had long been regarded, even by contemporaries, as the most direct expression of royal absolutism; the sovereign had wished to have "his own magistrate to whom he might directly entrust his orders, his commissions, intentions, and who was entrusted with the execution of orders and orders under the King's private seal" (a note by Duval, first secretary at the police magistrature, quoted in Funck-Brentano, I). In effect, in taking over a number of preexisting functions — the search for criminals, urban surveillance, economic and political supervision — the police magistratures and the magistrature-general that presided over them in Paris transposed them into a single, strict, administrative machine: "All the radiations of force and information that spread from the circumference culminate in the magistrate-general. . . . It is he who operates all the wheels that together produce order and harmony. The effects of his administration cannot be better compared than to the movement of the celestial bodies" (Des Essarts 344, 528).

But, although the police as an institution were certainly organized in the form of a state apparatus, and although this was certainly linked directly to the center of political sovereignty, the type of power that it exercises, the mechanisms it operates, and the elements to which it applies them are specific. It is an apparatus that must be coextensive with the entire social body and not only by the extreme limits that it embraces, but by the minuteness of the details it is concerned with. Police power must bear "over everything": it is not, however, the totality of the state nor of the kingdom as visible and invisible body of the monarch; it is the dust of events, actions, behavior, opinions — "everything that happens";[7] the police are concerned with "those things of every moment," those "unimportant things," of which

Catherine II spoke in her Great Instruction (Supplement to the *Instruction for the Drawing Up of a New Code*, 1769, article 535). With the police, one is in the indefinite world of a supervision that seeks ideally to reach the most elementary particle, the most passing phenomenon of the social body: "The ministry of the magistrates and police officers is of the greatest importance; the objects that it embraces are in a sense definite, one may perceive them only by a sufficiently detailed examination" (Delamare, unnumbered preface): the infinitely small of political power.

And, in order to be exercised, this power had to be given the instrument of permanent, exhaustive, omnipresent surveillance, capable of making all visible, as long as it could itself remain invisible. It had to be like a faceless gaze that transformed the whole social body into a field of perception: thousands of eyes posted everywhere, mobile attentions ever on the alert, a long, hierarchized network which, according to Le Maire, comprised for Paris the forty-eight *commissaires*, the twenty *inspecteurs*, then the "observers," who were paid regularly, the *"basses mouches,"* or secret agents, who were paid by the day, then the informers, paid according to the job done, and finally the prostitutes. And this unceasing observation had to be accumulated in a series of reports and registers; throughout the eighteenth century, an immense police text increasingly covered society by means of a complex documentary organization (on the police registers in the eighteenth century, cf. Chassaigne). And, unlike the methods of judicial or administrative writing, what was registered in this way were forms of behavior, attitudes, possibilities, suspicions — a permanent account of individuals' behavior.

Now, it should be noted that, although this police supervision was entirely "in the hands of the king," it did not function in a single direction. It was in fact a double-entry system: it had to correspond, by manipulating the machinery of justice, to the immediate wishes of the king, but it was also capable of responding to solicitations from below; the celebrated *lettres de cachet*, or orders under the king's private seal, which were long the symbol of arbitrary royal rule and which brought detention into disrepute on political grounds, were in fact demanded by families, masters, local notables, neighbors, parish priests; and their function was to punish by confinement a whole infrapenality, that of disorder, agitation, disobedience, bad conduct; those things that Ledoux wanted to exclude from his architecturally perfect city and which he called "offenses of nonsurveillance." In short, the eighteenth-century police added a disciplinary function to its role as the auxiliary of justice in the pursuit of criminals and as an instrument for the political supervision of plots, opposition movements, or revolts. It was a complex function since it linked the absolute power of the monarch to the lowest levels of power disseminated in society; since, between these different, enclosed institutions of discipline (workshops, armies, schools), it extended an intermediary network, acting where they could not intervene, disciplining the nondisciplinary spaces; but it filled in the gaps, linked them together, guaranteed with its armed force an interstitial discipline and a metadiscipline. "By means of a wise police, the sovereign accustoms the people to order and obedience" (Vattel 162).

The organization of the police apparatus in the eighteenth century sanctioned a generalization of the disciplines that became coextensive with the state itself. Although it was linked in the most explicit way with everything in the royal power that exceeded the exercise of regular justice, it is understandable why the police offered such slight resistance to the rearrangement of the judicial power; and why it has not ceased to impose its prerogatives upon it, with ever-increasing weight, right up to the present day; this is no doubt because it is the secular arm of the judiciary; but it is also because, to a far greater degree than the judicial institution, it is identified, by reason of its extent and mechanisms, with a society of the disciplinary type. Yet it would be wrong to believe that the disciplinary functions were confiscated and absorbed once and for all by a state apparatus.

"Discipline" may be identified neither with an institution nor with an apparatus; it is a type of power, a modality for its exercise, comprising a whole set of instruments, techniques, procedures, levels of application, targets; it is a "physics" or an "anatomy" of power, a technology. And it may be taken over either by "specialized" institutions (the penitentiaries or "houses of correction" of the nineteenth century), or by institutions that use it as an essential instrument for a particular end (schools, hospitals), or by preexisting authorities that find in it a means of reinforcing or reorganizing their internal mechanisms of power (one day we should show how intrafamilial relations, essentially in the parents-children cell, have become "disciplined," absorbing since the classical age external schemata, first educational and military, then medical, psychiatric, psychological, which have made the family the privileged locus of emergence for the disciplinary question of the normal and the abnormal), or by apparatuses that have made discipline their principle of internal functioning (the disciplinarization of the administrative apparatus from the Napoleonic period), or finally by state apparatuses whose major, if not exclusive, function is to assure that discipline reigns over society as a whole (the police).

On the whole, therefore, one can speak of the formation of a disciplinary society in this movement that stretches from the enclosed disciplines, a sort of social "quarantine," to an indefinitely generalizable mechanism of "panopticism." Not because the disciplinary modality of power has replaced all the others; but because it has infiltrated the others, sometimes undermining them, but serving as an intermediary between them, linking them together, extending them, and above all making it possible to bring the effects of power to the most minute and distant elements. It assures an infinitesimal distribution of the power relations.

A few years after Bentham, Julius gave this society its birth certificate (Julius 384–86). Speaking of the panoptic principle, he said that there was much more there than architectural ingenuity: it was an event in the "history of the human mind." In appearance, it is merely the solution of a technical problem; but, through it, a whole type of society emerges. Antiquity had been a civilization of spectacle. "To render accessible to a multitude of men the inspection of a small number of objects": this was the problem to which the architecture of temples, theaters, and circuses responded. With spectacle, there was a predominance of public life, the intensity of festivals, sensual proximity. In these rituals in which blood flowed, society found new vigor and formed for a moment a single great body. The modern age poses the opposite problem: "To procure for a small number, or even for a single individual, the instantaneous view of a great multitude." In a society in which the principal elements are no longer the community and public life, but, on the one hand, private individuals and, on the other, the state, relations can be regulated only in a form that is the exact reverse of the spectacle: "It was to the modern age, to the ever-growing influence of the state, to its ever more profound intervention in all the details and all the relations of social life, that was reserved the task of increasing and perfecting its guarantees, by using and directing towards that great aim the building and distribution of buildings intended to observe a great multitude of men at the same time."

Julius saw as a fulfilled historical process that which Bentham had described as a technical program. Our society is one not of spectacle, but of surveillance; under the surface of images, one invests bodies in depth; behind the great abstraction of exchange, there continues the meticulous, concrete training of useful forces; the circuits of communication are the supports of an accumulation and a centralization of knowledge; the play of signs defines the anchorages of power; it is not that the beautiful totality of the individual is amputated, repressed, altered by our social order, it is rather that the individual is carefully fabricated in it, according to a whole technique of forces and bodies. We are much less Greeks than we believe. We are neither in the amphitheater, nor on the stage, but in the panoptic machine, invested by its effects of power, which we bring to ourselves since we are part of its mechanism. The importance, in historical mythology, of the Napoleonic character probably derives from the fact that it is at the point of junction of the monarchical, ritual exercise of sovereignty and the hierarchical, permanent exercise of indefinite discipline. He is the individual who looms over everything with a single gaze which no detail, however minute, can escape: "You may consider that no part of the Empire is without surveillance, no crime, no offense, no contravention that remains unpunished, and that the eye of the genius who can enlighten all embraces the whole of this vast machine, without, however, the slightest detail escaping his attention" (Treilhard 14). At the moment of its full blossoming, the disciplinary society still assumes with the Emperor the old aspect of the power of spectacle. As a monarch who is at one and the same time a usurper of the ancient throne and the organizer of the new state, he combined into a single symbolic, ultimate figure the whole of the long process by which the pomp of sovereignty, the necessarily spectacular manifestations of power, were extinguished one by one in the daily exercise of surveillance, in a panopticism in which the vigilance of intersecting gazes was soon to render useless both the eagle and the sun.

The formation of the disciplinary society is connected with a number of broad historical processes — economic, juridico-political, and lastly, scientific — of which it forms part.

1. Generally speaking, it might be said that the disciplines are techniques for assuring the ordering of human multiplicities. It is true that there is nothing exceptional or even characteristic in this: every system of power is presented with the same problem. But the peculiarity of the disciplines is that they try to define in relation to the multiplicities a tactics of power that fulfills three criteria: firstly, to obtain the exercise of power at the lowest possible cost (economically, by the low expenditure it involves; politically, by its discretion, its low exteriorization, its relative invisibility, the little resistance it arouses); secondly, to bring the effects of this social power to their maximum intensity and to extend them as far as possible, without either failure or interval; thirdly, to link this "economic" growth of power with the output of the apparatuses (educational, military, industrial, or medical) within which it is exercised; in short, to increase both the docility and the utility of all the elements of the system. This triple objective of the disciplines corresponds to a well-known historical conjuncture. One aspect of this conjuncture was the large demographic thrust of the eighteenth century; an increase in the floating population (one of the primary objects of discipline is to fix; it is an antinomadic technique); a change of quantitative scale in the groups to be supervised or manipulated (from the beginning of the seventeenth century to the eve of the French Revolution, the school population had been increasing rapidly, as had no doubt the hospital population; by the end of the eighteenth century, the peacetime army exceeded 200,000 men). The other aspect of the conjuncture was the growth in the apparatus of production, which was becoming more and more extended and complex; it was also becoming more costly and its profitability had to be increased. The development of the disciplinary methods corresponded to these two processes, or rather, no doubt, to the new need to adjust their correlation. Neither the residual forms of feudal power nor the structures of the administrative monarchy, nor the local mechanisms of supervision, nor the unstable, tangled mass they all formed together could carry out this role: they were hindered from doing so by the irregular and inadequate extension of their network, by their often conflicting functioning, but above all by the "costly" nature of the power that was exercised in them. It was costly in several senses: because directly it cost a great deal to the Treasury; because the system of corrupt offices and farmed-out taxes weighed indirectly, but very heavily, on the population; because the resistance it encountered forced it into a cycle of perpetual reinforcement; because it proceeded essentially by levying (levying on money or products by royal, seigniorial, ecclesiastical taxation; levying on men or time by *corvées* of press-ganging, by locking up or banishing vagabonds). The development of the disciplines marks the appearance of elementary techniques belonging to a quite different economy: mechanisms of power which, instead of proceeding by deduction, are integrated into the productive efficiency of the apparatuses from

within, into the growth of this efficiency and into the use of what it produces. For the old principle of "levying-violence," which governed the economy of power, the disciplines substitute the principle of "mildness-production-profit." These are the techniques that make it possible to adjust the multiplicity of men and the multiplication of the apparatuses of production (and this means not only "production" in the strict sense, but also the production of knowledge and skills in the school, the production of health in the hospitals, the production of destructive force in the army).

In this task of adjustment, discipline had to solve a number of problems for which the old economy of power was not sufficiently equipped. It could reduce the inefficiency of mass phenomena: reduce what, in a multiplicity, makes it much less manageable than a unity; reduce what is opposed to the use of each of its elements and of their sum; reduce everything that may counter the advantages of number. That is why discipline fixes; it arrests or regulates movements; it clears up confusion; it dissipates compact groupings of individuals wandering about the country in unpredictable ways; it establishes calculated distributions. It must also master all the forces that are formed from the very constitution of an organized multiplicity; it must neutralize the effects of counterpower that spring from them and which form a resistance to the power that wishes to dominate it: agitations, revolts, spontaneous organizations, coalitions — anything that may establish horizontal conjunctions. Hence the fact that the disciplines use procedures of partitioning and verticality, that they introduce, between the different elements at the same level, as solid separations as possible, that they define compact hierarchical networks, in short, that they oppose to the intrinsic, adverse force of multiplicity the technique of the continuous, individualizing pyramid. They must also increase the particular utility of each element of the multiplicity, but by means that are the most rapid and the least costly, that is to say, by using the multiplicity itself as an instrument of this growth. Hence, in order to extract from bodies the maximum time and force, the use of those overall methods known as timetables, collective training, exercises, total and detailed surveillance. Furthermore, the disciplines must increase the effect of utility proper to the multiplicities, so that each is made more useful than the simple sum of its elements: it is in order to increase the utilizable effects of the multiple that the disciplines define tactics of distribution, reciprocal adjustment of bodies, gestures, and rhythms, differentiation of capacities, reciprocal coordination in relation to apparatuses or tasks. Lastly, the disciplines have to bring into play the power relations, not above but inside the very texture of the multiplicity, as discreetly as possible, as well articulated on the other functions of these multiplicities and also in the least expensive way possible: to this correspond anonymous instruments of power, coextensive with the multiplicity that they regiment, such as hierarchical surveillance, continuous registration, perpetual assessment, and classification. In short, to substitute for a power that is manifested through the brilliance of those who exercise it, a power that insidiously objectifies those on whom it is applied; to form a body of knowledge about these individuals, rather than to deploy the ostentatious signs of sovereignty. In a word, the disciplines are the ensemble of minute technical inventions that made it possible to increase the useful size of multiplicities by decreasing the inconveniences of the power which, in order to make them useful, must control them. A multiplicity, whether in a workshop or a nation, an army or a school, reaches the threshold of a discipline when the relation of the one to the other becomes favorable.

If the economic take-off of the West began with the techniques that made possible the accumulation of capital, it might perhaps be said that the methods for administering the accumulation of men made possible a political take-off in relation to the traditional, ritual, costly, violent forms of power, which soon fell into disuse and were superseded by a subtle, calculated technology of subjection. In fact, the two processes — the accumulation of men and the accumulation of capital — cannot be separated; it would not have been possible to solve the problem of the accumulation of men without the growth of an apparatus of production capable of both sustaining them and using them; conversely, the techniques that made the cumulative multiplicity of men useful accelerated the accumulation of capital. At a less general level, the technological mutations of the apparatus of production, the division of labor and the elaboration of the disciplinary techniques sustained an ensemble of very close relations (cf. Marx, *Capital,* vol. I, chapter XIII and the very interesting analysis in Guerry and Deleule). Each makes the other possible and necessary; each provides a model for the other. The disciplinary pyramid constituted the small cell of power within which the separation, coordination, and supervision of tasks was imposed and made efficient; and analytical partitioning of time, gestures, and bodily forces constituted an operational schema that could easily be transferred from the groups to be subjected to the mechanisms of production; the massive projection of military methods onto industrial organization was an example of this modeling of the division of labor following the model laid down by the schemata of power. But, on the other hand, the technical analysis of the process of production, its "mechanical" breaking-down, were projected onto the labor force whose task it was to implement it: the constitution of those disciplinary machines in which the individual forces that they bring together are composed into a whole and therefore increased is the effect of this projection. Let us say that discipline is the unitary technique by which the body is reduced as a "political" force at the least cost and maximized as a useful force. The growth of a capitalist economy gave rise to the specific modality of disciplinary power, whose general formulas, techniques of submitting forces and bodies, in short, "political anatomy," could be operated in the most diverse political regimes, apparatuses, or institutions.

2. The panoptic modality of power — at the elementary, technical, merely physical level at which it is situated — is not under the immediate dependence or a direct extension of the great juridico-political structures of a society; it is nonetheless not absolutely independent. Historically, the process by which the bourgeoisie became in the course of the eighteenth

century the politically dominant class was masked by the establishment of an explicit, coded, and formally egalitarian juridical framework, made possible by the organization of a parliamentary, representative regime. But the development and generalization of disciplinary mechanisms constituted the other, dark side of these processes. The general juridical form that guaranteed a system of rights that were egalitarian in principle was supported by these tiny, everyday, physical mechanisms, by all those systems of micropower that are essentially nonegalitarian and asymmetrical that we call the disciplines. And although, in a formal way, the representative regime makes it possible, directly or indirectly, with or without relays, for the will of all to form the fundamental authority of sovereignty, the disciplines provide, at the base, a guarantee of the submission of forces and bodies. The real, corporal disciplines constituted the foundation of the formal, juridical liberties. The contract may have been regarded as the ideal foundation of law and political power; panopticism constituted the technique, universally widespread, of coercion. It continued to work in depth on the juridical structures of society, in order to make the effective mechanisms of power function in opposition to the formal framework that it had acquired. The "Enlightenment," which discovered the liberties, also invented the disciplines.

In appearance, the disciplines constitute nothing more than an infralaw. They seem to extend the general forms defined by law to the infinitesimal level of individual lives; or they appear as methods of training that enable individuals to become integrated into these general demands. They seem to constitute the same type of law on a different scale, thereby making it more meticulous and more indulgent. The disciplines should be regarded as a sort of counter-law. They have the precise role of introducing insuperable asymmetries and excluding reciprocities. First, because discipline creates between individuals a "private" link, which is a relation of constraints entirely different from contractual obligation; the acceptance of a discipline may be underwritten by contract; the way in which it is imposed, the mechanisms it brings into play, the nonreversible subordination of one group of people by another, the "surplus" power that is always fixed on the same side, the inequality of position of the different "partners" in relation to the common regulation, all these distinguish the disciplinary link from the contractual link, and make it possible to distort the contractual link systematically from the moment it has as its content a mechanism of discipline. We know, for example, how many real procedures undermine the legal fiction of the work contract: workshop discipline is not the least important. Moreover, whereas the juridical systems define juridical subjects according to universal norms, the disciplines characterize, classify, specialize; they distribute along a scale, around a norm, hierarchize individuals in relation to one another and, if necessary, disqualify and invalidate. In any case, in the

THE DEVELOPMENT AND GENERALIZATION OF DISCIPLINARY MECHANISMS CONSTITUTED THE OTHER, DARK SIDE OF THESE PROCESSES.

space and during the time in which they exercise their control and bring into play the asymmetries of their power, they effect a suspension of the law that is never total, but is never annulled either. Regular and institutional as it may be, the discipline, in its mechanism, is a "counterlaw." And, although the universal juridicism of modern society seems to fix limits on the exercise of power, its universally widespread panopticism enables it to operate, on the underside of the law, a machinery that is both immense and minute, which supports, reinforces, multiplies the asymmetry of power and undermines the limits that are traced around the law. The minute disciplines, the panopticisms of every day may well be below the level of emergence of the great apparatuses and the great political struggles. But, in the genealogy of modern society, they have been, with the class domination that traverses it, the political counterpart of the juridical norms according to which power was redistributed. Hence, no doubt, the importance that has been given for so long to the small techniques of discipline, to those apparently insignificant tricks that it has invented, and even to those "sciences" that give it a respectable face; hence the fear of abandoning them if one cannot find any substitute; hence the affirmation that they are at the very foundation of society, and an element in its equilibrium, whereas they are a series of mechanisms for unbalancing power relations definitively and everywhere; hence the persistence in regarding them as the humble, but concrete form of every morality, whereas they are a set of physico-political techniques.

To return to the problem of legal punishments, the prison with all the corrective technology at its disposal is to be resituated at the point where the codified power to punish turns into a disciplinary power to observe; at the point where the universal punishments of the law are applied selectively to certain individuals and always the same ones; at the point where the redefinition of the juridical subject by the penalty becomes a useful training of the criminal; at the point where the law is inverted and passes outside itself, and where the counterlaw becomes the effective and institutionalized content of the juridical forms. What generalizes the power to punish, then, is not the universal consciousness of the law in each juridical subject; it is the regular extension, the infinitely minute web of panoptic techniques.

3. Taken one by one, most of these techniques have a long history behind them. But what was new, in the eighteenth century, was that, by being combined and generalized, they attained a level at which the formation of knowledge and the increase of power regularly reinforce one another in a circular process. At this point, the disciplines crossed the "technological" threshold. First the hospital, then the school, then, later, the workshop were not simply "reordered" by the disciplines; they became, thanks to them, apparatuses such that any mechanism of objectification could be used in them as an instrument of subjection, and any growth of power could give rise in them to possible branches of knowledge; it was this link, proper to the technological systems, that made possible within the disciplinary element the formation of clinical

medicine, psychiatry, child psychology, educational psychology, the rationalization of labor. It is a double process, then: an epistemological "thaw" through a refinement of power relations; a multiplication of the effects of power through the formation and accumulation of new forms of knowledge.

The extension of the disciplinary methods is inscribed in a broad historical process: the development at about the same time of many other technologies – agronomical, industrial, economic. But it must be recognized that, compared with the mining industries, the emerging chemical industries or methods of national accountancy, compared with the blast furnaces or the steam engine, panopticism has received little attention. It is regarded as not much more than a bizarre little utopia, a perverse dream – rather as though Bentham had been the Fourier of a police society, and the Phalanstery had taken on the form of the Panopticon. And yet this represented the abstract formula of a very real technology, that of individuals. There were many reasons why it received little praise; the most obvious is that the discourses to which it gave rise rarely acquired, except in the academic classifications, the status of sciences; but the real reason is no doubt that the power that it operates and which it augments is a direct, physical power that men exercise upon one another. An inglorious culmination had an origin that could be only grudgingly acknowledged. But it would be unjust to compare the disciplinary techniques with such inventions as the steam engine or Amici's microscope. They are much less; and yet, in a way, they are much more. If a historical equivalent or at least a point of comparison had to be found for them, it would be rather in the "inquisitorial" technique.

The eighteenth century invented the techniques of discipline and the examination, rather as the Middle Ages invented the judicial investigation. But it did so by quite different means. The investigation procedure, an old fiscal and administrative technique, had developed above all with the reorganization of the Church and the increase of the princely states in the twelfth and thirteenth centuries. At this time it permeated to a very large degree the jurisprudence first of the ecclesiastical courts, then of the lay courts. The investigation as an authoritarian search for a truth observed or attested was thus opposed to the old procedures of the oath, the ordeal, the judicial duel, the judgment of God, or even of the transaction between private individuals. The investigation was the sovereign power arrogating to itself the right to establish the truth by a number of regulated techniques. Now, although the investigation has since then been an integral part of Western justice (even up to our own day), one must not forget either its political origin, its link with the birth of the states and of monarchical sovereignty, or its later extension and its role in the formation of knowledge. In fact, the investigation has been the no doubt crude, but fundamental, element in the constitution of the empirical sciences; it has been the juridico-political matrix of this experimental knowledge, which, as we know, was very rapidly released at the end of the Middle Ages. It is perhaps true to say that, in Greece, mathematics were born from techniques of measurement; the sciences of nature, in any case, were born, to some extent, at the end of the Middle Ages, from the practices of investigation. The great empirical knowledge that covered the things of the world and transcribed them into the ordering of an indefinite discourse that observes, describes, and establishes the "facts" (at a time when the Western world was beginning the economic and political conquest of this same world) had its operating model no doubt in the Inquisition — that immense invention that our recent mildness has placed in the dark recesses of our memory. But what this politico-juridical, administrative, and criminal, religious and lay, investigation was to the sciences of nature, disciplinary analysis has been to the sciences of man. These sciences, which have so delighted our "humanity" for over a century, have their technical matrix in the petty, malicious minutiae of the disciplines and their investigations. These investigations are perhaps to psychology, psychiatry, pedagogy, criminology, and so many other strange sciences, what the terrible power of investigation was to the calm knowledge of the animals, the plants, or the earth. Another power, another knowledge. On the threshold of the classical age, Bacon, lawyer and statesman, tried to develop a methodology of investigation for the empirical sciences. What Great Observer will produce the methodology of examination for the human sciences? Unless, of course, such a thing is not possible. For, although it is true that, in becoming a technique for the empirical sciences, the investigation has detached itself from the inquisitorial procedure, in which it was historically rooted, the examination has remained extremely close to the disciplinary power that shaped it. It has always been and still is an intrinsic element of the disciplines. Of course it seems to have undergone a speculative purification by integrating itself with such sciences as psychology and psychiatry. And, in effect, its appearance in the form of tests, interviews, interrogations, and consultations is apparently in order to rectify the mechanisms of discipline: educational psychology is supposed to correct the rigors of the school, just as the medical or psychiatric interview is supposed to rectify the effects of the discipline of work. But we must not be misled; these techniques merely refer individuals from one disciplinary authority to another, and they reproduce, in a concentrated or formalized form, the schema of power-knowledge proper to each discipline (on this subject, cf. Tort). The great investigation that gave rise to the sciences of nature has become detached from its politico-juridical model; the examination, on the other hand, is still caught up in disciplinary technology.

In the Middle Ages, the procedure of investigation gradually superseded the old accusatory justice, by a process initiated from above; the disciplinary technique, on the other hand, insidiously and as if from below, has invaded a penal justice that is still, in principle, inquisitorial. All the great movements of extension that characterize modern penality — the problematization of the criminal behind his crime, the concern with a punishment that is a correction, a therapy, a normalization, the division of the act of judgment between various authorities that are supposed to measure, assess, diagnose, cure, transform individuals — all this betrays the penetration of the disciplinary examination into the judicial inquisition.

What is now imposed on penal justice as its point of application, its "useful" object, will no longer be the body of the guilty man set up against the body of the king; nor will it be the juridical subject of an ideal contract; it will be the disciplinary individual. The extreme point of penal justice under the Ancien Régime was the infinite segmentation of the body of the regicide: a manifestation of the strongest power over the body of the greatest criminal, whose total destruction made the crime explode into its truth. The ideal point of penality today would be an indefinite discipline: an interrogation without end, an investigation that would be extended without limit to a meticulous and ever more analytical observation, a judgment that would at the same time be the constitution of a file that was never closed, the calculated leniency of a penalty that would be interlaced with the ruthless curiosity of an examination, a procedure that would be at the same time the permanent measure of a gap in relation to an inaccessible norm and the asymptotic movement that strives to meet in infinity. The public execution was the logical culmination of a procedure governed by the Inquisition. The practice of placing individuals under "observation" is a natural extension of a justice imbued with disciplinary methods and examination procedures. Is it surprising that the cellular prison, with its regular chronologies, forced labor, its authorities of surveillance and registration, its experts in normality, who continue and multiply the functions of the judge, should have become the modern instrument of penalty? Is it surprising that prisons resemble factories, schools, barracks, hospitals, which all resemble prisons?

NOTES

[1] Archives militaires de Vincennes, A 1,516 91 sc. Pièce. This regulation is broadly similar to a whole series of others that date from the same period and earlier. [All notes are Foucault's.]

[2] In the *Postscript to the Panopticon*, 1791, Bentham adds dark inspection galleries painted in black around the inspector's lodge, each making it possible to observe two stories of cells.

[3] In his first version of the *Panopticon*, Bentham had also imagined an acoustic surveillance, operated by means of pipes leading from the cells to the central tower. In the *Postscript* he abandoned the idea, perhaps because he could not introduce into it the principle of dissymmetry and prevent the prisoners from hearing the inspector as well as the inspector hearing them. Julius tried to develop a system of dissymmetrical listening (Julius 18).

[4] Imagining this continuous flow of visitors entering the central tower by an underground passage and then observing the circular landscape of the Panopticon, was Bentham aware of the Panoramas that Barker was constructing at exactly the same period (the first seems to have dated from 1787) and in which the visitors, occupying the central place, saw unfolding around them a landscape, a city, or a battle? The visitors occupied exactly the place of the sovereign gaze.

[5] In the second half of the eighteenth century, it was often suggested that the army should be used for the surveillance and general partitioning of the population. The army, as yet to undergo discipline in the seventeenth century, was regarded as a force capable of instilling it. Cf., for example, Servan, *Le Soldat citoyen*, 1780.

[6] Arsenal, MS. 2565. Under this number, one also finds regulations for charity associations of the seventeenth and eighteenth centuries.

[7] Le Maire in a memorandum written at the request of Sartine, in answer to sixteen questions posed by Joseph II on the Parisian police. This memorandum was published by Gazier in 1879.

BIBLIOGRAPHY

Archives militaires de Vincennes, A 1,516 91 sc.
Bentham, J., *Works*, ed. Bowring, IV, 1843.
Chassaigne, M., *La Lieutenance générale de police*, 1906.
Delamare, N., *Traité de police*, 1705.
Demia, C., *Règlement pour les écoles de la ville de Lyon*, 1716.
Des Essarts, T. N., *Dictionnaire universel de police*, 1787.
Funck-Brentano, F., *Catalogue des manuscrits de la bibliothèque de l'Arsenal*, IX.
Guerry, F., and Deleule, D., *Le Corps productif*, 1973.
Julius, N. H., *Leçons sur les prisons*, I, 1831 (Fr. trans.).
Léon, A., *La Révolution française et l'éducation technique*, 1968.
Loisel, G., *Histoire des ménageries*, II, 1912.
Marx, Karl, *Capital*, vol. I, ed. 1970.
Radzinovitz, L., *The English Criminal Law*, II, 1956.
Servan, J., *Le Soldat citoyen*, 1780.
Tort, Michel, *Q.I.*, 1974.
Treilhard, J. B., *Motifs du code d'instruction criminelle*, 1808.
Vattel, E. de, *Le Droit des gens*, 1768.

QUESTIONS FOR A SECOND READING

1. Foucault's text begins with an account of a system enacted in the seventeenth century to control the spread of plague. After describing this system of surveillance, he compares it to the "rituals of exclusion" used to control lepers. He says, "The exile of the leper and the arrest of the plague do not bring with them the same political dream." At many points he sets up similar pairings, all in an attempt to understand the relations of power and knowledge in modern public life.

   As you reread, mark the various points at which Foucault works out the differences between a prior and the current "political dream" of order. What techniques or instruments belong to each? What moments in history are defined by each? How and where are they visible in public life?

2. Toward the end of the chapter Foucault says, "The extension of the disciplinary methods is inscribed in a broad historical process." Foucault writes a difficult kind of history (at one point he calls it a genealogy), since it does not make use of the usual form of historical narrative—with characters, plots, scenes, and action. As you reread, take notes that will allow you to trace time, place, and sequence (and, if you can, agents and agency) in Foucault's account of the formation of the disciplinary society based on technologies of surveillance. Why do you think he avoids a narrative mode of presentation?

3. As you reread Foucault's text, bring forward the stages in his presentation (or the development of his argument). Mark those moments that you consider key or central to the working out of his argument concerning the panopticon. What sentences of his would you use to represent key moments in the text? The text at times turns to numbered sections. How, for example,

do they function? Describe the beginning, middle, and end of the essay. Describe the skeleton or understructure of the chapter. What are its various stages or steps? How do they relate to one another?

ASSIGNMENTS FOR WRITING

1. About three-quarters of the way into this chapter, Foucault says,

> Our society is one not of spectacle, but of surveillance; under the surface of images, one invests bodies in depth; behind the great abstraction of exchange, there continues the meticulous, concrete training of useful forces; the circuits of communication are the supports of an accumulation and a centralization of knowledge; the play of signs defines the anchorages of power; it is not that the beautiful totality of the individual is amputated, repressed, altered by our social order, it is rather that the individual is carefully fabricated in it, according to a whole technique of forces and bodies. (p. 301)

This prose is eloquent and insists on its importance to our moment and our society; it is also very hard to read or to paraphrase. Who is doing what to whom? How do we think about the individual's being carefully fabricated in the social order?

Take this chapter as a problem to solve. What is it about? What are its key arguments? its examples and conclusions? Write an essay that summarizes "Panopticism." Imagine that you are writing for readers who have read the chapter (although they won't have the pages in front of them). You will need to take time to present and discuss examples from the text. Your job is to help your readers figure out what it says. You get the chance to take the lead and be the teacher. You should feel free to acknowledge that you don't understand certain sections even as you write about them.

So, how do you write about something you don't completely understand? Here's a suggestion. When you have completed your summary, read it over and treat it as a draft. Ask questions like these: What have I left out? What was I tempted to ignore or finesse? Go back to those sections of the chapter that you ignored and bring them into your essay. Revise by adding discussions of some of the very sections you don't understand. You can write about what you think Foucault *might* be saying—you can, that is, be cautious and tentative; you can admit that the text is what it is, hard to read. You don't have to master this text. You do, however, need to see what you can make of it.

2. About a third of the way through his text, Foucault asserts, "The Panopticon is a marvelous machine which, whatever use one may wish to put it to, produces homogeneous effects of power." Write an essay in which you explain the machinery of the panopticon as a mechanism of power. Paraphrase Foucault and,

where it seems appropriate, use his words. Present Foucault's account as you understand it. As part of your essay, and in order to explain what he is getting at, include two examples—one of his, perhaps, and then one of your own.

3. Perhaps the most surprising thing about Foucault's argument in "Panopticism" is the way it equates prisons with schools, hospitals, and workplaces, sites we are accustomed to imagining as very different from a prison. Foucault argues against our commonly accepted understanding of such things.

   At the end of the chapter Foucault asks two questions. These are rhetorical questions, strategically placed at the end. Presumably we are prepared to feel their force and to think of possible answers.

   > Is it surprising that the cellular prison, with its regular chronologies, forced labor, its authorities of surveillance and registration, its experts in normality, who continue and multiply the functions of the judge, should have become the modern instrument of penalty? Is it surprising that prisons resemble factories, schools, barracks, hospitals, which all resemble prisons? (p. 309)

   For this assignment, take the invitation of Foucault's conclusion. No, you want to respond, it is not surprising that "experts in normality, who continue and multiply the functions of the judge, should have become the modern instrument of penalty." No, it is not surprising that "prisons resemble factories, schools, barracks, hospitals, which all resemble prisons." Why isn't it surprising? Or, why isn't it surprising if you are thinking along with Foucault?

   Write an essay in which you explore one of these possible resemblances. You may, if you choose, cite Foucault. You can certainly pick up some of his key terms or examples and put them into play. You should imagine, however, that it is your turn. With your work on Foucault behind you, you are writing to a general audience about "experts in normality" and the key sites of surveillance and control.

MAKING CONNECTIONS

1. Both John Berger in "Ways of Seeing" (p. 141) and Michel Foucault in "Panopticism" discuss what Foucault calls "power relations." Berger claims that "the entire art of the past has now become a political issue," and he makes a case for the evolution of a "new language of images" which could "confer a new kind of power" if people were to understand history in art. Foucault argues that the Panopticon signals an "inspired" change in power relations. "It is," he says,

   > an important mechanism, for it automatizes and disindividualizes power. Power has its principle not so much in a person as in a certain concerted distribution of bodies, surfaces, lights, gazes; in an arrangement whose internal mechanisms produce the relation in which individuals are caught up. (p. 288)

Both Berger and Foucault create arguments about power, its methods and goals. As you read through their essays, mark passages you might use to explain how each author thinks about power—where it comes from, who has it, how it works, where you look for it, how you know when you see it, what it does, where it goes. You should reread the essays as a pair, as part of a single project in which you are looking to explain theories of power.

Write an essay in which you present and explain "Ways of Seeing" and "Panopticism" as examples of Berger's and Foucault's theories of power. Both Berger and Foucault are arguing against usual understandings of power and knowledge and history. In this sense, their projects are similar. You should be sure, however, to look for differences as well as similarities.

2. At the end of "Panopticism," Foucault asks two questions. These are rhetorical questions, strategically placed at the end. Presumably we are prepared to feel their force and to think of possible answers.

> Is it surprising that the cellular prison, with its regular chronologies, forced labor, its authorities of surveillance and registration, its experts in normality, who continue and multiply the functions of the judge, should have become the modern instrument of penalty? Is it surprising that prisons resemble factories, schools, barracks, hospitals, which all resemble prisons? (p. 309)

Is Foucault making the same argument as Paulo Freire, in "The 'Banking' Concept of Education" (p. 318)? Reread the Freire essay with Foucault's general argument in mind and thinking through the particular image (and institution) of the panopticon. How might you summarize these two arguments and their take on schooling? Freire, who speaks of a revolution in education, imagines a future in which students might be "free." Free in what sense? Does he have an answer to Foucault's concerns? Or does Foucault have an argument that might trump Freire's optimism?

You should assume an audience interested in education. It will not be the case, however, that they have read these two essays. You will need, then, to be careful in providing summary, paraphrase, and quotation. You will need to provide the background to an argument that you (and your readers) can identify as *yours*.

3. At a key point in her essay "Beside Oneself: On the Limits of Sexual Autonomy" (p. 240), Judith Butler refers to the work of Michel Foucault:

> The question of who and what is considered real and true is apparently a question of knowledge. But it is also, as Michel Foucault makes plain, a question of power. Having or bearing "truth" and "reality" is an enormously powerful prerogative within the social world, one way that power dissimulates as ontology. According to Foucault, one of the first tasks of a radical critique is to discern the relation "between mechanisms of coercion and elements of knowledge." (p. 247)

And she goes on for some length to work with passages from Foucault, although not from his book *Discipline and Punish*.

Take some time to reread Butler's essay, paying particular attention to her use of Foucault. Where and why is Foucault helpful to her? In what ways is she providing a new argument or a counterargument? And take time to reread "Panopticism." What passages might be useful in extending or challenging Butler's argument in "Beside Oneself"? Using these two sources, write an essay in which you talk about Butler and Foucault and their engagement with what might be called "radical critique," an effort (in the terms offered above) to "discern the relation 'between mechanisms of coercion and elements of knowledge.'"

Note: The assignment limits you to these two sources, the two selections in the textbook. Butler and Foucault have written much, and their work circulates widely. You are most likely not in a position to speak about everything they have written or about all that has been written about them. We wanted to define a starting point that was manageable. Still, if you want to do more research, you might begin by reading the Foucault essay that Butler cites, "What Is Critique?"; you might go to the library to look through books by Butler and Foucault, choosing one or two that seem to offer themselves as next steps; or you could go to essays written by scholars who, as you are, are trying to think about the two together.

4. Both Laura Kipnis in "Love's Labors" (p. 391) and Michel Foucault in "Panopticism" write about power relations. Foucault's essay is more theoretical in its approach, whereas Kipnis treads a bit more lightly, poking fun at our strange attempts to meet the oppressive cultural norms of domesticity. Nevertheless, there are strong connections between Foucault's analysis of the "mechanisms of coercion" that assert control over individuals in a disciplined society and Kipnis's critique of the ways in which conformity is compelled without the use of physical force. Write an essay in which you put Foucault's and Kipnis's essays into dialogue with each other.

   You might begin by working with the unique voices adopted by the two writers — both relate to readers in rather unconventional ways. If it helps, try rewriting some representative passages from Foucault's essay as you imagine Kipnis would write them or vice versa. In addition to noticing distinctions in tone and voice, pay attention to pronoun use. Who or what tends to be the subject of each writer's sentences, and what might this reveal about their interests, about the kind of story each wants to tell? Also consider the kinds of evidence on which each writer relies. How do Kipnis and Foucault attempt to make visible the disciplinary forces that people usually do not notice or regard as oppressive?

   At some point, you will want to consider how these writers' stylistic differences reflect diverse interests and ways of thinking about power and the individual. How does each writer represent the forces that control and discipline us? Who is doing what to whom and for what reasons? What is the place of the individual in relation to these larger normalizing forces, and what are the possibilities for resisting or altering these power relations? Finally, what might be the consequences, for you as an individual, of thinking about these two essays in relation to each other?

Note: You should imagine that your readers, while they might be familiar with both texts, do not have them in front of them. Therefore, you will need to do the work of presentation and summary.

PAULO Freire

Paulo Freire (pronounce it "Fr-air-ah" unless you can make a Portuguese "r") was one of the most influential radical educators of our world. A native of Recife, Brazil, he spent most of his early career working in poverty-stricken areas of his homeland, developing methods for teaching illiterate adults to read and write and (as he would say) to think critically and, thereby, to take power over their own lives. Because he has created a classroom where teachers and students have equal power and equal dignity, his work has stood as a model for educators around the world. It led also to sixteen years of exile after the military coup in Brazil in 1964. During that time he taught in Europe and in the United States and worked for the Allende government in Chile, training the teachers whose job it would be to bring modern agricultural methods to the peasants.

Freire (1921–1997) worked with the adult education programs of UNESCO, the Chilean Institute of Agrarian Reform, and the World Council of Churches. He was professor of educational philosophy at the Catholic University of São Paulo. He is the author of *Education for Critical Consciousness, The Politics of Education, Pedagogy of the Oppressed, Revised Edition* (from which the following essay is drawn), and *Learning to Question: A Pedagogy of Liberation* (with Antonio Faundez). *Pedagogy of Indignation*, the first English translations of Freire's late-life reflections on personal development, was published in 2004.

For Freire, education is not an objective process, if by objective we mean "neutral" or "without bias or prejudice." Because teachers could be said to have something that their students lack, it is impossible to have a "neutral" classroom; and when teachers present a subject to their students, they also present a point of view on that subject. The choice, according to Freire, is fairly simple: teachers either work "for the liberation of the people—their humanization—or for their domestication, their domination." The practice of teaching, however, is anything but simple. According to Freire, a teacher's most crucial skill is his or her ability to assist students' struggle to gain control over the conditions of their lives, and this means helping them not only to know but "to know that they know."

Freire edited, along with Henry A. Giroux, a series of books on education and teaching. In *Literacy: Reading the Word and the World*, a book for the series, Freire describes the interrelationship between reading the written word and understanding the world that surrounds us.

> My parents introduced me to reading the word at a certain moment in this rich experience of understanding my immediate world. Deciphering the word flowed naturally from reading my particular world; it was not something superimposed on it. I learned to read and write on the grounds of the backyard of my house, in the shade of the mango trees, with words from my world rather than from the wider world of my parents. The earth was my blackboard, the sticks my chalk.

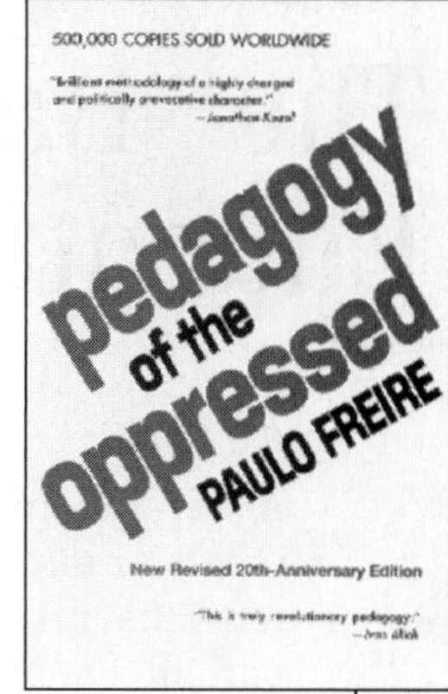

For Freire, reading the written word involves understanding a text in its very particular social and historical context. Thus reading always involves "critical perception, interpretation, and *rewriting* of what is read."

The "Banking" Concept of Education

A careful analysis of the teacher-student relationship at any level, inside or outside the school, reveals its fundamentally *narrative* character. This relationship involves a narrating Subject (the teacher) and patient, listening objects (the students). The contents, whether values or empirical dimensions of reality, tend in the process of being narrated to become lifeless and petrified. Education is suffering from narration sickness.

The teacher talks about reality as if it were motionless, static, compartmentalized, and predictable. Or else he expounds on a topic completely alien to the existential experience of the students. His task is to "fill" the students with the contents of his narration — contents which are detached from reality, disconnected from the totality that engendered them and could give them significance. Words are emptied of their concreteness and become a hollow, alienated, and alienating verbosity.

The outstanding characteristic of this narrative education, then, is the sonority of words, not their transforming power. "Four times four is sixteen; the capital of Pará is Belém." The student records, memorizes, and repeats these phrases without perceiving what four times four really means, or realizing the true significance of "capital" in the affirmation "the capital of Pará is Belém," that is, what Belém means for Pará and what Pará means for Brazil.

EDUCATION THUS BECOMES AN ACT OF DEPOSITING, IN WHICH THE STUDENTS ARE THE DEPOSITORIES AND THE TEACHER IS THE DEPOSITOR.

Narration (with the teacher as narrator) leads the students to memorize mechanically the narrated content. Worse yet, it turns them into "containers," into "receptacles" to be "filled" by the teacher. The more completely she fills the receptacles, the better a teacher she is. The more meekly the receptacles permit themselves to be filled, the better students they are.

Education thus becomes an act of depositing, in which the students are the depositories and the teacher is the depositor. Instead of communicating, the teacher issues communiqués and makes deposits which the students patiently receive, memorize, and repeat. This is the "banking" concept of education, in which the scope of action allowed to the students extends only as far as receiving, filing, and storing the deposits. They do, it is true, have the opportunity to become collectors or cataloguers of the things they store. But in the last analysis, it is the people themselves who are filed away through the lack of creativity, transformation, and knowledge in this (at best) misguided system. For apart from inquiry, apart from the praxis, individuals cannot be truly human. Knowledge emerges only through invention and re-invention, through the restless, impatient, continuing, hopeful inquiry human beings pursue in the world, with the world, and with each other.

In the banking concept of education, knowledge is a gift bestowed by those who consider themselves knowledgeable upon those whom they consider to know nothing. Projecting an absolute ignorance onto others, a characteristic of the ideology of oppression, negates education and knowledge as processes of inquiry. The teacher presents himself to his students as their necessary opposite; by considering their ignorance absolute, he justifies his own existence. The students, alienated like the slave in the Hegelian dialectic, accept their ignorance as justifying the teacher's existence — but, unlike the slave, they never discover that they educate the teacher.

The *raison d'être* of libertarian education, on the other hand, lies in its drive towards reconciliation. Education must begin with the solution of the teacher-student contradiction, by reconciling the poles of the contradiction so that both are simultaneously teachers *and* students.

This solution is not (nor can it be) found in the banking concept. On the contrary, banking education maintains and even stimulates the contradiction through the following attitudes and practices, which mirror oppressive society as a whole:

a. the teacher teaches and the students are taught;
b. the teacher knows everything and the students know nothing;
c. the teacher thinks and the students are thought about;
d. the teacher talks and the students listen — meekly;
e. the teacher disciplines and the students are disciplined;
f. the teacher chooses and enforces his choice, and the students comply;
g. the teacher acts and the students have the illusion of acting through the action of the teacher;
h. the teacher chooses the program content, and the students (who were not consulted) adapt to it;
i. the teacher confuses the authority of knowledge with his or her own professional authority, which she and he sets in opposition to the freedom of the students;
j. the teacher is the Subject of the learning process, while the pupils are mere objects.

It is not surprising that the banking concept of education regards men as adaptable, manageable beings. The more students work at storing the deposits entrusted to them, the less they develop the critical consciousness which would result from their intervention in the world as transformers of that world. The more completely they accept the passive role imposed on them, the more they tend simply to adapt to the world as it is and to the fragmented view of reality deposited in them.

The capability of banking education to minimize or annul the students' creative power and to stimulate their credulity serves the interests of the oppressors, who care neither to have the world revealed nor to see it transformed. The oppressors use their "humanitarianism" to preserve a profitable situation. Thus they react almost instinctively against any experiment in education which stimulates the critical faculties and is not content with a partial view of reality but always seeks out the ties which link one point to another and one problem to another.

Indeed, the interests of the oppressors lie in "changing the consciousness of the oppressed, not the situation which oppresses them";[1] for the more the oppressed can be led to adapt to that situation, the more easily they can be dominated. To achieve this end, the oppressors use the banking concept of education in conjunction with a paternalistic social action apparatus, within which the oppressed receive the euphemistic title of "welfare recipients." They are treated as individual cases, as marginal persons who deviate from the general configuration of a "good, organized, and just" society. The oppressed are regarded as the pathology of the healthy society, which must therefore adjust these "incompetent and lazy" folk to its own patterns by changing their mentality. These marginals need to be "integrated," "incorporated" into the healthy society that they have "forsaken."

The truth is, however, that the oppressed are not "marginals," are not people living "outside" society. They have always been "inside" — inside the structure which made them "beings for others." The solution is not to "integrate" them into the structure of oppression, but to transform that structure so that they can become "beings for themselves." Such transformation, of course, would undermine the oppressors' purposes; hence their utilization of the banking concept of education to avoid the threat of student *conscientização*.[2]

The banking approach to adult education, for example, will never propose to students that they critically consider reality. It will deal instead with such vital questions as whether Roger gave green grass to the goat, and insist upon the importance of learning that, on the contrary, Roger gave green grass to the rabbit. The "humanism" of the banking approach masks the effort to turn women and men into automatons — the very negation of their ontological vocation to be more fully human.

Those who use the banking approach, knowingly or unknowingly (for there are innumerable well-intentioned bank-clerk teachers who do not realize that they are serving only to dehumanize), fail to perceive that the deposits themselves contain contradictions about reality. But, sooner or later, these contradictions may lead formerly passive students to turn against their domestication and the attempt to domesticate reality. They may discover through existential experience that their present way of life is irreconcilable with their vocation to become fully human. They may perceive through their relations with reality that reality is really a *process*, undergoing constant transformation. If men and women are searchers and their ontological vocation is humanization, sooner or later they may perceive the contradiction in which banking education seeks to maintain them, and then engage themselves in the struggle for their liberation.

But the humanist, revolutionary educator cannot wait for this possibility to materialize. From the outset, her efforts must coincide with those of the students to engage in critical thinking and the quest for mutual humanization. His efforts must be imbued with a profound trust in people and their creative power. To achieve this, they must be partners of the students in their relations with them.

The banking concept does not admit to such partnership — and necessarily so. To resolve the teacher-student contradiction, to exchange the role of depositor, prescriber, domesticator, for the role of student among students would be to undermine the power of oppression and serve the cause of liberation.

Implicit in the banking concept is the assumption of a dichotomy between human beings and the world: a person is merely *in* the world, not *with* the world or with others; the individual is spectator, not re-creator. In this view, the person is not a conscious being (*corpo consciente*); he or she is rather the possessor of *a* consciousness: an empty "mind" passively open to the reception of deposits of reality from the world outside. For example, my desk, my books, my coffee cup, all the objects before me — as bits of the world which surrounds me — would be "inside" me, exactly as I am inside my study right now. This view makes no distinction between being accessible to consciousness and entering consciousness. The distinction, however, is essential: the objects which surround me are simply accessible to my consciousness, not located within it. I am aware of them, but they are not inside me.

It follows logically from the banking notion of consciousness that the educator's role is to regulate the way the world "enters into" the students. The teacher's task is to organize a process which already occurs spontaneously, to "fill" the students by making deposits of information which he or she considers to constitute true knowledge.[3] And since people "receive" the world as passive entities, education should make them more passive still, and adapt them to the world. The educated individual is the adapted person, because she or he is better "fit" for the world. Translated into practice, this concept is well suited to the purposes of the oppressors, whose tranquility rests on how well people fit the world the oppressors have created, and how little they question it.

The more completely the majority adapt to the purposes which the dominant minority prescribe for them (thereby depriving them of the right to their own purposes), the more easily the minority can continue to prescribe. The theory and practice of banking education serve this end quite efficiently. Verbalistic lessons, reading requirements,[4] the methods for evaluating "knowledge," the distance between the teacher and the taught, the criteria for promotion: everything in this ready-to-wear approach serves to obviate thinking.

The bank-clerk educator does not realize that there is no true security in his hypertrophied role, that one must seek to live *with* others in solidarity. One cannot impose oneself, nor even merely co-exist with one's students. Solidarity requires true communication, and the concept by which such an educator is guided fears and proscribes communication.

Yet only through communication can human life hold meaning. The teacher's thinking is authenticated only by the authenticity of the students' thinking. The teacher cannot think for her students, nor can she impose her thoughts on them. Authentic thinking, thinking that is concerned about *reality*, does not take place in ivory tower isolation, but only in communication. If it is true that thought has meaning only when generated by action upon the world, the subordination of students to teachers becomes impossible.

Because banking education begins with a false understanding of men and women as objects, it cannot promote the development of what Fromm calls "biophily," but instead produces its opposite: "necrophily."

> While life is characterized by growth in a structured, functional manner, the necrophilous person loves all that does not grow, all that is mechanical. The necrophilous person is driven by the desire to transform the organic into the inorganic, to approach life mechanically, as if all living persons were things. . . . Memory, rather than experience; having, rather than being, is what counts. The necrophilous person can relate to an object — a flower or a person — only if he possesses it; hence a threat to his possession is a threat to himself; if he loses possession he loses contact with the world. . . . He loves control, and in the act of controlling he kills life.[5]

Oppression — overwhelming control — is necrophilic; it is nourished by love of death, not life. The banking concept of education, which serves the interests of oppression, is also necrophilic. Based on a mechanistic, static, naturalistic, spatialized view of consciousness, it transforms students into receiving objects. It attempts to control thinking and action, leads women and men to adjust to the world, and inhibits their creative power.

When their efforts to act responsibly are frustrated, when they find themselves unable to use their faculties, people suffer. "This suffering due to impotence is rooted in the very fact that the human equilibrium has been disturbed."[6] But the inability to act which causes people's anguish also causes them to reject their impotence, by attempting

> to restore [their] capacity to act. But can [they], and how? One way is to submit to and identify with a person or group having power. By this symbolic participation in another person's life, [men have] the illusion of acting, when in reality [they] only submit to and become part of those who act.[7]

Populist manifestations perhaps best exemplify this type of behavior by the oppressed, who, by identifying with charismatic leaders, come to feel that they themselves are active and effective. The rebellion they express as they emerge in the historical process is motivated by that desire to act effectively. The dominant elites consider the remedy to be more domination and repression, carried out in the name of freedom, order, and social peace (that is, the peace of the elites). Thus they can condemn — logically, from their point of view — "the violence of a strike by workers and [can] call upon the state in the same breath to use violence in putting down the strike."[8]

Education as the exercise of domination stimulates the credulity of students, with the ideological intent (often not perceived by educators) of indoctrinating them to adapt to the world of oppression. This accusation is not made in the naïve hope that the dominant elites will thereby simply abandon the practice. Its objective is to call the attention of true humanists to the fact that they cannot use banking educational methods in the pursuit of liberation, for they would only negate that very pursuit. Nor may a revolutionary society inherit these methods from an oppressor society. The revolutionary society which practices banking education is either misguided or mistrusting of people. In either event, it is threatened by the specter of reaction.

Unfortunately, those who espouse the cause of liberation are themselves surrounded and influenced by the climate which generates the banking concept, and often do not perceive its true significance or its dehumanizing power. Paradoxically, then, they utilize this same instrument of alienation in what they consider an effort to liberate. Indeed, some "revolutionaries" brand as "innocents," "dreamers," or even "reactionaries" those who would challenge this educational practice. But one does not liberate people by alienating them. Authentic liberation — the process of humanization — is not another deposit to be made in men. Liberation is a praxis: the action and reflection of men and women upon their world in order to transform it. Those truly committed to the cause of liberation can accept neither the mechanistic concept of consciousness as an empty vessel to be filled, nor the use of banking methods of domination (propaganda, slogans — deposits) in the name of liberation.

Those truly committed to liberation must reject the banking concept in its entirety, adopting instead a concept of women and men as conscious beings, and consciousness as consciousness intent upon the world. They must abandon the educational goal of deposit-making and replace it with the posing of the problems of human beings in their relations with the world. "Problem-posing" education, responding to the essence of consciousness — *intentionality* — rejects communiqués and embodies communications. It epitomizes the special characteristic of consciousness: being *conscious of,* not only as intent on objects but as turned in upon itself in a Jasperian "split" — consciousness as consciousness *of* consciousness.

Liberating education consists in acts of cognition, not transferrals of information. It is a learning situation in which the cognizable object (far from being the end of the cognitive act) intermediates the cognitive actors — teacher on the one hand and students on the other. Accordingly, the practice of problem-posing education entails at the outset that the teacher-student contradiction be resolved. Dialogical relations — indispensable to the capacity of cognitive actors to cooperate in perceiving the same cognizable object — are otherwise impossible.

Indeed, problem-posing education, which breaks with the vertical patterns characteristic of banking education, can fulfill its function as the practice of freedom only if it can overcome the above contradiction. Through dialogue, the teacher-of-the-students and the students-of-the-teacher cease to exist and a new term emerges: teacher-student with students-teachers. The teacher is no longer merely the-one-who-teaches, but one who is himself taught in dialogue with the students, who in turn while being taught also teach. They become jointly responsible for a process in which all grow. In this process, arguments based on "authority" are no longer valid; in order to function, authority must be *on the side of* freedom, not *against* it. Here, no one teaches another, nor is anyone self-taught. People teach each other, mediated by the world, by the cognizable objects which in banking education are "owned" by the teacher.

The banking concept (with its tendency to dichotomize everything) distinguishes two stages in the action of the educator. During the first, he cognizes a cognizable object while he prepares his lessons in his study or his laboratory; during the second, he expounds to his students about that object. The students are not called upon to know, but to memorize the contents narrated by the teacher. Nor do the students practice any act of cognition, since the object towards which that act should be directed is the property of the teacher rather than a medium evoking the critical reflection of both teacher and students. Hence in the name of the "preservation of culture and knowledge" we have a system which achieves neither true knowledge nor true culture.

The problem-posing method does not dichotomize the activity of the teacher-student: she is not "cognitive" at one point and "narrative" at another. She is always "cognitive," whether preparing a project or engaging in dialogue with the students. He does not regard cognizable objects as his private property, but as the object of reflection by himself and the students. In this way, the problem-posing educator constantly re-forms his reflections in the reflection of the students. The students — no longer docile listeners — are now critical co-investigators in dialogue with the teacher. The teacher presents the material to the students for their consideration, and re-considers her earlier considerations as the students express their own. The role of the problem-posing educator is to create, together with the students, the conditions under which knowledge at the level of the *doxa* is superseded by true knowledge, at the level of the *logos*.

Whereas banking education anesthetizes and inhibits creative power, problem-posing education involves a constant unveiling of reality. The former attempts to maintain the *submersion* of consciousness; the latter strives for the *emergence* of consciousness and *critical intervention* in reality.

Students, as they are increasingly posed with problems relating to themselves in the world and with the world, will feel increasingly challenged and obliged to respond to that challenge. Because they apprehend the challenge as interrelated to other problems within a total context, not as a theoretical question, the resulting comprehension tends to be increasingly critical and thus constantly less alienated. Their response to the challenge evokes new challenges, followed by new understandings; and gradually the students come to regard themselves as committed.

Education as the practice of freedom — as opposed to education as the practice of domination — denies that man is abstract, isolated, independent, and unattached to the world; it also denies that the world exists as a reality apart from people. Authentic reflection considers neither abstract man nor the world without people, but people in their relations with the world. In these relations consciousness and world are simultaneous: consciousness neither precedes the world nor follows it.

> La conscience et le monde sont donnés d'un même coup: extérieur par essence à la conscience, le monde est, par essence relatif à elle.[9]

In one of our culture circles in Chile, the group was discussing (based on a codification) the anthropological concept of culture. In the midst of the discussion, a peasant who by banking standards was completely ignorant said: "Now I see that without man there is no world." When the educator responded: "Let's say, for the sake of argument, that all the men on earth were to die, but that the earth itself remained, together with trees, birds, animals, rivers, seas, the stars . . . wouldn't all this be a world?" "Oh no," the peasant replied emphatically. "There would be no one to say: 'This is a world.'"

AUTHENTIC REFLECTION CONSIDERS NEITHER ABSTRACT MAN NOR THE WORLD WITHOUT PEOPLE, BUT PEOPLE IN THEIR RELATIONS WITH THE WORLD.

The peasant wished to express the idea that there would be lacking the consciousness of the world which necessarily implies the world of consciousness. *I* cannot exist without a *not-I*. In turn, the *not-I* depends on that existence. The world which brings consciousness into existence becomes the world *of* that consciousness. Hence, the previously cited affirmation of Sartre: *"La conscience et le monde sont donnés d'un même coup."*

As women and men, simultaneously reflecting on themselves and on the world, increase the scope of their perception, they begin to direct their observations towards previously inconspicuous phenomena:

> In perception properly so-called, as an explicit awareness [*Gewahren*], I am turned towards the object, to the paper, for instance. I apprehend it as being this here and now. The apprehension is a singling out, every object having a background in experience. Around and about the paper lie books, pencils, inkwell, and so forth, and these in a certain sense are also "perceived," perceptually there, in the "field of intuition"; but while I was turned towards the paper there was no turning in their direction, nor any apprehending of them, not even in a secondary sense. They appeared and yet were not singled out, were not posited on their own account.

> Every perception of a thing has such a zone of background intuitions or background awareness, if "intuiting" already includes the state of being turned towards, and this also is a "conscious experience," or more briefly a "consciousness of" all indeed that in point of fact lies in the co-perceived objective background.[10]

That which had existed objectively but had not been perceived in its deeper implications (if indeed it was perceived at all) begins to "stand out," assuming the character of a problem and therefore of challenge. Thus, men and women begin to single out elements from their "background awarenesses" and to reflect upon them. These elements are now objects of their consideration, and, as such, objects of their action and cognition.

In problem-posing education, people develop their power to perceive critically *the way they exist* in the world *with which* and *in which* they find themselves; they come to see the world not as a static reality, but as a reality in process, in transformation. Although the dialectical relations of women and men with the world exist independently of how these relations are perceived (or whether or not they are perceived at all), it is also true that the form of action they adopt is to a large extent a function of how they perceive themselves in the world. Hence, the teacher-student and the students-teachers reflect simultaneously on themselves and the world without dichotomizing this reflection from action, and thus establish an authentic form of thought and action.

Once again, the two educational concepts and practices under analysis come into conflict. Banking education (for obvious reasons) attempts, by mythicizing reality, to conceal certain facts which explain the way human beings exist in the world; problem-posing education sets itself the task of demythologizing. Banking education resists dialogue; problem-posing education regards dialogue as indispensable to the act of cognition which unveils reality. Banking education treats students as objects of assistance; problem-posing education makes them critical thinkers. Banking education inhibits creativity and domesticates (although it cannot completely destroy) the *intentionality* of consciousness by isolating consciousness from the world, thereby denying people their ontological and historical vocation of becoming more fully human. Problem-posing education bases itself on creativity and stimulates true reflection and action upon reality; thereby responding to the vocation of persons as beings who are authentic only when engaged in inquiry and creative transformation. In sum: banking theory and practice, as immobilizing and fixating forces, fail to acknowledge men and women as historical beings; problem-posing theory and practice take the people's historicity as their starting point.

Problem-posing education affirms men and women as beings in the process of *becoming* — as unfinished, uncompleted beings in and with a likewise unfinished reality. Indeed, in contrast to other animals who are unfinished, but not historical, people know themselves to be unfinished;

they are aware of their incompletion. In this incompletion and this awareness lie the very roots of education as an exclusively human manifestation. The unfinished character of human beings and the transformational character of reality necessitate that education be an ongoing activity.

Education is thus constantly remade in the praxis. In order to *be*, it must *become*. Its "duration" (in the Bergsonian meaning of the word) is found in the interplay of the opposites *permanence* and *change*. The banking method emphasizes permanence and becomes reactionary; problem-posing education — which accepts neither a "well-behaved" present nor a predetermined future — roots itself in the dynamic present and becomes revolutionary.

Problem-posing education is revolutionary futurity. Hence, it is prophetic (and, as such, hopeful). Hence, it corresponds to the historical nature of humankind. Hence, it affirms women and men as beings who transcend themselves, who move forward and look ahead, for whom immobility represents a fatal threat, for whom looking at the past must only be a means of understanding more clearly what and who they are so that they can more wisely build the future. Hence, it identifies with the movement which engages people as beings aware of their incompletion — an historical movement which has its point of departure, its Subjects and its objective.

The point of departure of the movement lies in the people themselves. But since people do not exist apart from the world, apart from reality, the movement must begin with the human-world relationship. Accordingly, the point of departure must always be with men and women in the "here and now," which constitutes the situation within which they are submerged, from which they emerge, and in which they intervene. Only by starting from this situation — which determines their perception of it — can they begin to move. To do this authentically they must perceive their state not as fated and unalterable, but merely as limiting — and therefore challenging.

Whereas the banking method directly or indirectly reinforces men's fatalistic perception of their situation, the problem-posing method presents this very situation to them as a problem. As the situation becomes the object of their cognition, the naïve or magical perception which produced their fatalism gives way to perception which is able to perceive itself even as it perceives reality, and can thus be critically objective about that reality.

A deepened consciousness of their situation leads people to apprehend that situation as an historical reality susceptible of transformation. Resignation gives way to the drive for transformation and inquiry, over which men feel themselves to be in control. If people, as historical beings necessarily engaged with other people in a movement of inquiry, did not control that movement, it would be (and is) a violation of their humanity. Any situation in which some individuals prevent others from engaging in the process of inquiry is one of violence. The means used are not important; to alienate human beings from their own decision making is to change them into objects.

This movement of inquiry must be directed towards humanization — the people's historical vocation. The pursuit of full humanity, however, cannot be carried out in isolation or individualism, but only in fellowship and solidarity; therefore it cannot unfold in the antagonistic relations between oppressors and oppressed. No one can be authentically human while he prevents others from being so. Attempting *to be more* human, individualistically, leads to *having more*, egotistically, a form of dehumanization. Not that it is not fundamental *to have* in order *to be* human. Precisely because it *is* necessary, some men's *having* must not be allowed to constitute an obstacle to others' *having*, must not consolidate the power of the former to crush the latter.

Problem-posing education, as a humanist and liberating praxis, posits as fundamental that the people subjected to domination must fight for their emancipation. To that end, it enables teachers and students to become Subjects of the educational process by overcoming authoritarianism and an alienating intellectualism; it also enables people to overcome their false perception of reality. The world — no longer something to be described with deceptive words — becomes the object of that transforming action by men and women which results in their humanization.

Problem-posing education does not and cannot serve the interests of the oppressor. No oppressive order could permit the oppressed to begin to question: Why? While only a revolutionary society can carry out this education in systematic terms, the revolutionary leaders need not take full power before they can employ the method. In the revolutionary process, the leaders cannot utilize the banking method as an interim measure, justified on grounds of expediency, with the intention of *later* behaving in a genuinely revolutionary fashion. They must be revolutionary — that is to say, dialogical — from the outset.

NOTES

[1] Simone de Beauvoir, *La pensée de droite, aujourd'hui* (Paris); ST, *El pensamiento político de la derecha* (Buenos Aires, 1963), p. 34. [All notes are Freire's, unless indicated by Eds.]

[2] According to Freire's translator, "The term *conscientização* refers to learning to perceive social, political, and economic contradictions, and to take action against the oppressive elements of reality" [Eds.].

[3] This concept corresponds to what Sartre calls the "digestive" or "nutritive" concept of education, in which knowledge is "fed" by the teacher to the students to "fill them out." See Jean-Paul Sartre, "Une idée fundamentale de la phénomenologie de Husserl: L'intentionalité," *Situations* I (Paris, 1947).

[4] For example, some professors specify in their reading lists that a book should be read from pages 10 to 15 — and do this to "help" their students!

[5] Erich Fromm, *The Heart of Man* (New York, 1966), p. 41.

[6] Ibid., p. 31.

[7] Ibid.

[8] Reinhold Niebuhr, *Moral Man and Immoral Society* (New York, 1960), p. 130.

[9] Sartre, op. cit., p. 32. [The passage is obscure but could be read as "Consciousness and the world are given at one and the same time: the exterior world as it enters consciousness is relative to our ways of seeing and understanding that world." — Eds.]

[10] Edmund Husserl, *Ideas — General Introduction to Pure Phenomenology* (London, 1969), pp. 105–6.

QUESTIONS FOR A SECOND READING

1. While Freire speaks powerfully about the politics of the classroom, he provides few examples of actual classroom situations. As you go back through the essay, try to ground (or to test) what he says with examples of your own. What would take place in a "problem-posing" class in English, history, psychology, or math? What is an "authentic form of thought and action"? How might you describe what Freire refers to as "reflection"? What, really, might teachers be expected to learn from their students? What example can you give of a time when you were "conscious of consciousness" and it made a difference to you with your schoolwork?

    You might also look for moments when Freire does provide examples of his own. On page 321, for example, Freire makes the distinction between a student's role as "spectator" and as "re-creator" by referring to his own relationship to the objects on his desk. How might you explain this distinction? Or, how might you use the example of his books and coffee cup to explain the distinction he makes between "being accessible to consciousness" and "entering consciousness"?

2. Freire uses two terms drawn from Marxist literature: *praxis* and *alienation*. From the way these words are used in the essay, how would you define them? And how might they be applied to the study of education?

3. A writer can be thought of as a teacher and a reader as a student. If you think of Freire as your teacher in this essay, does he enact his own principles? Does he speak to you as though he were making deposits in a bank? Or is there a way in which the essay allows for dialogue? Look for sections in the essay you could use to talk about the role Freire casts you in as a reader.

ASSIGNMENTS FOR WRITING

1. Surely all of us, anyone who has made it through twelve years of formal education, can think of a class, or an occasion outside of class, to serve as a quick example of what Freire calls the "banking" concept of education, where students were turned into "containers" to be "filled" by their teachers. If Freire is to be useful to you, however, he must do more than enable you to call up quick examples. He should allow you to say more than that a teacher once treated you like a container or that a teacher once gave you your freedom.

    Write an essay that focuses on a rich and illustrative incident from your own educational experience and read it (that is, interpret it) as Freire would. You will need to provide careful detail: things that were said and done, perhaps the exact wording of an assignment, a textbook, or a teacher's comments. And you will need to turn to the language of Freire's argument, to take key phrases and passages and see how they might be used to investigate your case.

To do this, you will need to read your account as not simply the story of you and your teacher, since Freire is writing not about individual personalities (an innocent student and a mean teacher, a rude teacher, or a thoughtless teacher) but about the roles we are cast in, whether we choose to be or not, by our culture and its institutions. The key question, then, is not who you were or who your teacher was but what roles you played and how those roles can lead you to better understand the larger narrative or drama of Education (an organized attempt to "regulate the way the world 'enters into' the students").

Freire would not want you to work passively or mechanically, however, as though you were following orders. He would want you to make your own mark on the work he has begun. Use your example, in other words, as a way of testing and examining what Freire says, *particularly those passages that you find difficult or obscure.*

2. Problem-posing education, according to Freire, "sets itself the task of demythologizing"; it "stimulates true reflection and action"; it allows students to be "engaged in inquiry and creative transformation." These are grand and powerful phrases, and it is interesting to consider what they might mean if applied to the work of a course in reading and writing.

   If the object for study were Freire's essay "The 'Banking' Concept of Education," what would Freire (or a teacher determined to adapt his practices) ask students to *do* with the essay? What writing assignment might he set for his students? Prepare that assignment, or a set of questions or guidelines or instructions (or whatever) that Freire might prepare for his class.

   Once you've prepared the writing assignment, write the essay that you think would best fulfill it. And once you've completed the essay, go on, finally, to write the teacher's comments on it—to write what you think Freire, or a teacher following his example, might write on a piece of student work.

MAKING CONNECTIONS

1. Freire says,

> Students, as they are increasingly posed with problems relating to themselves in the world and with the world, will feel increasingly challenged and obliged to respond to that challenge. Because they apprehend the challenge as interrelated to other problems within a total context, not as a theoretical question, the resulting comprehension tends to be increasingly critical and thus constantly less alienated. (pp. 324–25)

Students learn to respond, Freire says, through dialogue with their teachers. Freire could be said to serve as your first teacher here. He has raised the issue for you and given you some language you can use to frame questions and to imagine the possibilities of response.

Using one of the essays in this book as a starting point, pose a problem that challenges you and makes you feel obliged to respond, a problem that, in Freire's terms, relates to you "in the world and with the world." This is a chance for you, in other words, to pose a Freirian question and then to write a Freirian essay, all as an exercise in the practice of freedom.

When you are done, you might reread what you have written to see how it resembles or differs from what you are used to writing. What are the indications that you are working with greater freedom? If you find evidence of alienation or "domination," to what would you attribute it, and what, then, might you do to overcome it?

2. Freire writes about the distribution of power and authority in the classroom and argues that education too often alienates individuals from their own historical situation. Richard Rodriguez, in "The Achievement of Desire" (p. 515), writes about his education as a process of difficult but necessary alienation from his home, his childhood, and his family. And he writes about power—about the power that he gained and lost as he became increasingly successful as a student.

   But Freire and Rodriguez write about education as a central event in the shaping of an adult life. It is interesting to imagine what they might have to say to each other. Write a dialogue between the two in which they discuss what Rodriguez has written in "The Achievement of Desire." What would they say to each other? What questions would they ask? How would they respond to each other in the give-and-take of conversation?

   Note: This should be a dialogue, not a debate. Your speakers are trying to learn something about each other and about education. They are not trying to win points or convince a jury.

3. While they do not explicitly use the term or define the genre as Laura Kipnis does in "Love's Labors" (p. 391), Paulo Freire's "The 'Banking' Concept of Education" and the two selections from Gloria Anzaldúa's *Borderlands/La frontera* (p. 72) can be classified as polemics, works that attempt to "shake things up," to provoke readers and poke holes in "cultural pieties." Polemics, Kipnis explains, often bend or break conventional rules or expectations for argumentation. "Be advised," she warns us: "polemics aren't measured; they don't tell 'both sides of the story.' They overstate the case. They toss out provocations and occasionally mockery, usually because they're arguing against something so unquestionable and deeply entrenched it's the only way to make even a dent in the usual story."

Write an essay in which you present "The 'Banking' Concept of Education" as an example of polemical writing. You may want to begin by thinking about what has drawn the writer to the polemical form. What is "the usual story" that the polemicist wants to dislodge? What kinds of opposition from readers might the writer anticipate, and how does he or she address or attempt to counter resistance? As a reader, how did you respond to this attack on "received wisdom"?

Kipnis also tells us that "polemics aren't necessarily unconflicted (nor are the polemicists); rhetoric and sentiment aren't always identical twins." If you find evidence that the polemicist might be "conflicted," how does he or she deal with such conflicts and / or contradictions? Does your analysis of Freire's text offer some new insights into polemical writing—its social function, its merits, its risks—that Kipnis has not elucidated?

SUSAN Griffin

Susan Griffin (b. 1943) is a well-known and respected feminist writer, poet, essayist, lecturer, teacher, playwright, and filmmaker. She has published more than twenty books, including an Emmy Award–winning play, *Voices*, with a preface by Adrienne Rich (1975); three books of poetry, *Like the Iris of an Eye* (1976), *Unremembered Country* (1987), and *Bending Home: Selected and New Poems* (1998); and four books of nonfiction that have become key feminist texts, *Women and Nature: The Roaring inside Her* (1978), *Rape: The Power of Consciousness* (1979), *Pornography and Silence: Culture's Revenge against Nature* (1981), and *A Chorus of Stones: The Private Life of War* (1992). Her most recent books are *The Eros of Everyday Life* (1996), a collection of essays on women in Western culture; *What Her Body Thought: A Journey into the Shadows* (1999), on her battle with illness; *The Book of the Courtesans: A Catalog of Their Virtues* (2002), which includes biographies of courtesans throughout history; and *Wrestling with the Angel of Democracy: On Being an American Citizen* (2008), an examination of democratic ideals.

"Our Secret" is a chapter from Susan Griffin's moving and powerful book *A Chorus of Stones*, winner of the Bay Area Book Reviewers Association Award and a finalist for the Pulitzer Prize in nonfiction. The book explores the connections between present and past, public life and private life, an individual life and the lives of others. Griffin writes, for example, "I do not see my life as separate from history. In my mind my family secrets mingle with the secrets of statesmen and bombers." In one section of the book she writes of her mother's alcoholism and her father's response to it. In another she writes of her paternal grandmother, who was banished from the family for reasons never spoken. Next to these she thinks about Heinrich Himmler, head of the Nazi secret police, or Hugh Trenchard of the British Royal Air Force, who introduced the saturation bombing of cities and civilians to modern warfare, or Wernher von Braun and the development of rockets and rocketry. "As I held these [figures and scenes] in my mind," she writes, "a certain energy was generated between them. There were two subjects but one theme: denying and bearing witness."

A Chorus of Stones combines the skills of a careful researcher working with the documentary records of war, the imaginative powers of a novelist entering the lives and experiences of those long dead, and a poet's attention to language. It is a remarkable piece of writing, producing in its form and style the very experience of surprise and connectedness that Griffin presents as the product of her research. "It's not a historian's history," she once told an interviewer. "What's in it is true, but I think of it as a book that verges on myth and legend, because those are the ways we find the deepest meanings and significance of events."

Griffin's history is not a historian's history; her sociology is not a sociologist's; her psychology is not written in conventional forms or registers. She is actively engaged in the key research projects of our time, providing new knowledge and new ways of thinking and seeing, but she works outside the usual forms and boundaries of the academic disciplines. There are other ways of thinking about this, she seems to say. There are other ways to do this work. Her book on rape, for example, ends with a collage of women's voices, excerpts from public documents, and bits and pieces from the academy.

"Our Secret" has its own peculiar structure and features—the sections in italics, for example. As a piece of writing, it proceeds with a design that is not concerned to move quickly or efficiently from introduction to conclusion. It is, rather, a kind of collage or collection of stories, sketches, anecdotes, fragments. While the sections in the essay are presented as fragments, the essay is not, however, deeply confusing or disorienting. The pleasure of the text, in fact, is moving from here to there, feeling a thread of connection at one point, being surprised by a new direction at another. The writing is careful, thoughtful, controlled, even if this is not the kind of essay that announces its thesis and then collects examples for support. It takes a different attitude toward examples—and toward the kind of thinking one might bring to bear in gathering them and thinking them through. As Griffin says, "the telling and hearing of a story is not a simple act." It is not simple and, as her writing teaches us, it is not straightforward. As you read this essay, think of it as a lesson in reading, writing, and thinking. Think of it as a lesson in working differently. And you might ask why it is that this kind of writing is seldom taught in school.

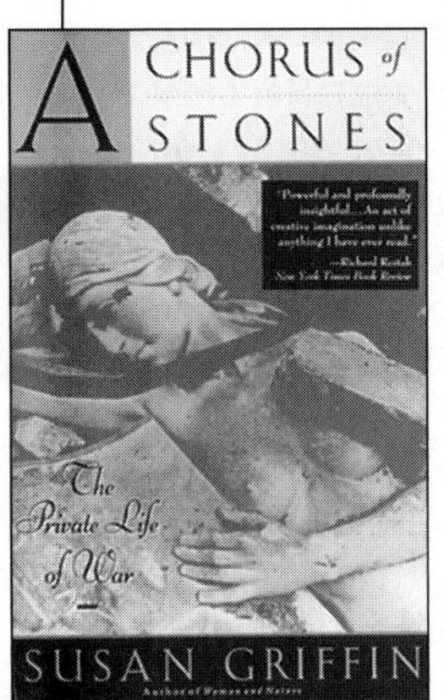

Our Secret

The nucleus of the cell derives its name from the Latin nux, *meaning nut. Like the stone in a cherry, it is found in the center of the cell, and like this stone, keeps its precious kernel in a shell.*

She is across the room from me. I am in a chair facing her. We sit together in the late darkness of a summer night. As she speaks the space between us grows larger. She has entered her past. She is speaking of her childhood. Her father. The war. Did I know her father fought in the Battle of the Bulge? What was it for him, this great and terrible battle? She cannot say. He never spoke of it at home. They knew so little, her mother, her brothers, herself. Outside, the sea has disappeared. One finds the water now only by the city lights that cease to shine at its edges. California. She moved here with her family when her father became the commander of a military base. There were nuclear missiles standing just blocks from where she lived. But her father never spoke about them. Only after many years away from home did she learn what these weapons were.

The first guided missile is developed in Germany, during World War II. It is known as the Vergeltungswaffe, *or the Vengeance weapon. Later, it will be called the V-1 rocket.*

She is speaking of another life, another way of living. I give her the name Laura here. She speaks of the time after the war, when the cold war was just beginning. The way we are talking now, Laura tells me, was not possible in her family. I nod in recognition. Certain questions were never answered. She learned what not to ask. She begins to tell me a story. Once when she was six years old she went out with her father on a long trip. It was not even a year since the war ended. They were living in Germany.

They drove for miles and miles. Finally they turned into a small road at the edge of a village and drove through a wide gate in a high wall. The survivors were all gone. But there were other signs of this event beyond and yet still within her comprehension. Shoes in great piles. Bones. Women's hair, clothes, stains, a terrible odor. She began to cry a child's frightened tears and then to scream. She had no words for what she saw. Her father admonished her to be still. Only years later, and in a classroom, did she find out the name of this place and what had happened here.

The shell surrounding the nucleus is not hard and rigid; it is a porous membrane. These pores allow only some substances to pass through them, mediating the movement of materials in and out of the nucleus.

Often I have looked back into my past with a new insight only to find that some old, hardly recollected feeling fits into a larger pattern of meaning. Time can be measured in many ways. We see time as moving forward and hope that by our efforts this motion is toward improvement. When the atomic bomb exploded, many who survived the blast say time stopped with the flash of light and was held suspended until the ash began to descend. Now, in my mind, I can feel myself moving backward in time. I am as if on a train. And the train pushes into history. This history seems to exist somewhere, waiting, a foreign country behind a border and, perhaps, also inside me. From the windows of my train, I can see what those outside do not see. They do not see each other, or the whole landscape through which the track is laid. This is a straight track, but still there are bends to fit the shape of the earth. There are even circles. And returns.

The missile is guided by a programmed mechanism. There is no electronic device that can be jammed. Once it is fired it cannot stop.

It is 1945 and a film is released in Germany. This film has been made for other nations to see. On the screen a train pulls into a station. The train is full of children. A man in a uniform greets the children warmly as they step off the train. Then the camera cuts to boys and girls who are swimming. The boys and girls race to see who can reach the other side of the pool first. Then a woman goes to a post office. A man goes to a bank. Men and women sit drinking coffee at a cafe. The film is called *The Führer Presents the Jews with a City*. It has been made at Terezin concentration camp.

Through the pores of the nuclear membrane a steady stream of ribonucleic acid, RNA, the basic material from which the cell is made, flows out.

It is wartime and a woman is writing a letter. *Everyone is on the brink of starvation*, she says. In the right-hand corner of the page she has written *Nordhausen, Germany 1944*. She is writing to Hans. *Do you remember*, she asks, the day this war was declared? The beauty of the place. The beauty of the sea. *And I bathed in it that day, for the last time.*

In the same year, someone else is also writing a letter. In the right-hand corner he has put his name followed by a title. *Heinrich Himmler. Reichsführer, SS. Make no mention of the special treatment of the Jews*, he says, use only the words Transportation of the Jews toward the Russian East.

A few months later this man will deliver a speech to a secret meeting of leaders in the district of Posen. *Now you know all about it, and you will keep quiet*, he will tell them. Now we share a secret and *we should take our secret to our graves.*

The missile flies from three to four thousand feet above the earth and this makes it difficult to attack from the ground.

The woman who writes of starvation is a painter in her seventy-seventh year. She has lost one grandchild to this war. And a son to the war before. Both boys were named Peter. Among the drawings she makes which have already become famous: a terrified mother grasps a child, *Death Seizes Children*; an old man curls over the bent body of an old woman, *Parents*; a thin face emerges white from charcoal, *Beggars*.

A small but critical part of the RNA flowing out of the pores holds most of the knowledge issued by the nucleus. These threads of RNA act as messengers.

Encountering such images, one is grateful to be spared. But is one ever really free of the fate of others? I was born in 1943, in the midst of this war. And I sense now that my life is still bound up with the lives of those who lived and died in this time. Even with Heinrich Himmler. All the details of his existence, his birth, childhood, adult years, death, still resonate here on earth.

The V-1 rocket is a winged plane powered by a duct motor with a pulsating flow of fuel.

I SENSE NOW THAT MY LIFE IS STILL BOUND UP WITH THE LIVES OF THOSE WHO LIVED AND DIED IN THIS TIME. EVEN WITH HEINRICH HIMMLER.

It is April 1943, Heinrich Himmler, Reichsführer SS, has gained control of the production of rockets for the Third Reich. The SS Totenkampf stand guard with machine guns trained at the entrance to a long tunnel, two miles deep, fourteen yards wide and ten yards high, sequestered in the Harz Mountains near Nordhausen. Once an old mining shaft, this tunnel serves now as a secret factory for the manufacture of V-1 and V-2 missiles. The guards aim their machine guns at the factory workers who are inmates of concentration camp Dora.

Most of the RNA flowing out of the cell is destined for the construction of a substance needed to compensate for the continual wearing away of the cell.

It is 1925. Heinrich Himmler, who is now twenty-five years old, has been hired as a secretary by the chief of the Nazi Party in Landshut. He sits behind a small desk in a room overcrowded with party records, correspondence, and newspaper files. On the wall facing him he can see a portrait of Adolf Hitler. He hopes one day to meet the Führer. In anticipation of that day, while he believes no one watches, he practices speaking to this portrait.

It is 1922. Heinrich visits friends who have a three-year-old child. Before going to bed this child is allowed to run about naked. And this disturbs Heinrich. He writes in his diary, *One should teach a child a sense of shame.*

It is the summer of 1910. Heinrich begins his first diary. He is ten years old. He has just completed elementary school. His father tells him his childhood is over now. In the fall he will enter Wilhelms Gymnasium. There the grades he earns will determine his prospects for the future. From now on he must learn to take himself seriously.

• • • • • • •

Eight out of ten of the guided missiles will land within eight miles of their targets.

His father Gebhard is a schoolmaster. He knows the requirements. He provides the boy with pen and ink. Gebhard was once a tutor for Prince Heinrich of Wittelsbach. He has named his son Heinrich after this prince. He is grateful that the prince consented to be Heinrich's godparent. Heinrich is to write in his diary every day. Gebhard writes the first entry in his son's diary, to show the boy how it is to be done.

July 13, Departed at 11:50 and arrive safely on the bus in L. We have a very pretty house. In the afternoon we drink coffee at the coffee house.

I open the cover of the journal I began to keep just as I started my work on this book. I want to see what is on the first page. *It is here I begin a new life,* I wrote. Suffering many losses at once, I was alone and lonely. Yet suddenly I felt a new responsibility for myself. *The very act of keeping a journal,* I sensed, would help me into this life that would now be my own.

Inside the nucleus is the nucleolus where the synthesis of RNA takes place. Each nucleolus is filled with a small jungle of fern-like structures all of whose fronds and stalks move and rotate in perfect synchrony.

It is 1910. The twenty-second of July. Gebhard adds the words *first swim* to his son's brief entry, *thirteenth wedding anniversary of my dear parents.* 1911. Over several entries Heinrich lists each of thirty-seven times he takes a swim, in chronological order. *11:37 A.M. Departed for Lindau.* He does not write of his feelings. *August 8, Walk in the park.* Or dreams. *August 10, Bad weather.*

In the last few years I have been searching, though for what precisely I cannot say. Something still hidden which lies in the direction of Heinrich Himmler's life. I have been to Berlin and Munich on this search, and I have walked over the gravel at Dachau. Now as I sit here I read once again the fragments from Heinrich's boyhood diary that exist in English. I have begun to think of these words as ciphers. Repeat them to myself, hoping to find a door into the mind of this man, even as his character first forms so that I might learn how it is he becomes himself.

The task is not easy. The earliest entries in this diary betray so little. Like the words of a schoolboy commanded to write what the teacher requires of him, they are wooden and stiff. The stamp of his father's character is so heavy on this language that I catch not even a breath of a self here. It is easy to see how this would be true. One simply has to imagine Gebhard standing behind Heinrich and tapping his foot.

His father must have loomed large to him. Did Gebhard lay his hand on Heinrich's shoulder? The weight of that hand would not be comforting. It would be a warning. A reminder. Heinrich must straighten up now and be still. Yet perhaps he turns his head. Maybe there is a sound outside. A bird. Or his brother Gebhard's voice. But from the dark form behind him he hears a name pronounced. This is his name, *Heinrich*. The sound rolls sharply off his father's tongue. He turns his head back. He does not know what to write. He wants to turn to this form and beseech him, but this man who is his father is more silent than stone. And now when Heinrich can feel impatience all around him, he wants to ask, *What should I write?* The edge of his father's voice has gotten sharper. *Why can't you remember?* Just write what happened yesterday. And make sure you get the date right. *Don't you remember?* We took a walk in the park together and we ran into the duchess. Be certain you spell her name correctly. And look here, you must get the title right. That is extremely important. Cross it out. Do it again. *The title.*

The boy is relieved. His mind has not been working. His thoughts were like paralyzed limbs, immobile. Now he is in motion again. He writes the sentences as they are dictated to him. *The park.* He crosses out the name. He writes it again. Spelling it right. *The duchess.* And his father makes one more correction. The boy has not put down the correct time for their walk in the park.

And who is the man standing behind? In a photograph I have before me of the aging Professor and Frau Himmler, as they pose before a wall carefully composed with paintings and family portraits, Frau Himmler adorned with a demure lace collar, both she and the professor smiling kindly from behind steel-rimmed glasses, the professor somewhat rounded with age, in a dark three-piece suit and polka-dot tie, looks so ordinary.

The missile carries a warhead weighing 1,870 pounds. It has three different fuses to insure detonation.

Ordinary. What an astonishing array of images hide behind this word. The ordinary is of course never ordinary. I think of it now as a kind of mask, not an animated mask that expresses the essence of an inner truth, but a mask that falls like dead weight over the human face, making flesh a stationary object. One has difficulty penetrating the heavy mask that Gebhard and his family wore, difficulty piercing through to the creatures behind.

It must not have been an easy task to create this mask. One detects the dimensions of the struggle in the advice of German child-rearing experts from this and the last century. *Crush the will*, they write. *Establish dominance. Permit no disobedience. Suppress everything in the child.*

I have seen illustrations from the books of one of these experts, perhaps the most famous of these pedagogues, Dr. Daniel Gottlieb Moritz Schreber. At first glance these pictures recall images of torture. But they are instead pictures of children whose posture or behavior is being corrected. A brace up the spine, a belt tied to a waist and the hair at the back of the neck so the child will be discouraged from slumping, a metal plate at the edge of a desk keeping the child from curling over her work, a child tied to a bed to prevent poor sleeping posture or masturbation. And there are other methods recommended in the text. An enema to be given before bedtime. The child immersed in ice-cold water up to the hips, before sleep.

The nightmare images of the German child-rearing practices that one discovers in this book call to mind the catastrophic events of recent German history. I first encountered this pedagogy in the writing of Alice Miller. At one time a psychoanalyst, she was haunted by the question, *What could make a person conceive the plan of gassing millions of human beings to death?* In her work, she traces the origins of this violence to childhood.

Of course there cannot be one answer to such a monumental riddle, nor does any event in history have a single cause. Rather a field exists, like a field of gravity that is created by the movements of many bodies. Each life is influenced and it in turn becomes an influence. Whatever is a cause is also an effect. Childhood experience is just one element in the determining field.

As a man who made history, Heinrich Himmler shaped many childhoods, including, in the most subtle of ways, my own. And an earlier history, a history of governments, of wars, of social customs, an idea of gender, the history of a religion leading to the idea of original sin, shaped Heinrich Himmler's childhood as certainly as any philosophy of child raising. One can take for instance any formative condition of his private life, the fact that he was a frail child, for example, favored by his mother, who could not meet masculine standards, and show that this circumstance derived its real meaning from a larger social system that gave inordinate significance to masculinity.

Yet to enter history through childhood experience shifts one's perspective not away from history but instead to an earlier time just before history has finally shaped us. Is there a child who existed before the conventional history that we tell of ourselves, one who, though invisible to us, still shapes events, even through this absence? How does our sense of history change when we consider childhood, and perhaps more important, why is it that until now we have chosen to ignore this point of origination, the birthplace and womb of ourselves, in our consideration of public events?

In the silence that reverberates around this question, an image is born in my mind. I can see a child's body, small, curled into itself, knees bent toward the chest, head bending softly into pillows and blankets, in a posture thought unhealthy by Dr. Schreber, hand raised to the face, delicate mouth making a circle around the thumb. There is comfort as well as sadness in this image. It is a kind of a self-portrait, drawn both from memory and from a feeling that is still inside me. As I dwell for a moment with this image I can imagine Heinrich in this posture, silent, curled, fetal, giving comfort to himself.

But now, alongside this earlier image, another is born. It is as if these two images were twins, always traveling in the world of thought together. One does not come to mind without the other. In this second portrait, which is also made of feeling and memory, a child's hands are tied into mittens. And by a string extending from one of the mittens, her hand is tied to the bars of her crib. She is not supposed to be putting her finger in her mouth. And she is crying out in rage while she yanks her hand violently trying to free herself of her bonds.

To most of existence there is an inner and an outer world. Skin, bark, surface of the ocean open to reveal other realities. What is inside shapes and sustains what appears. So it is too with human consciousness. And yet the mind rarely has a simple connection to the inner life. At a certain age we begin to define ourselves, to choose an image of who we are. I am this and not that, we say, attempting thus to erase whatever is within us that does not fit our idea of who we should be. In time we forget our earliest selves and replace that memory with the image we have constructed at the bidding of others.

One can see this process occur in the language of Heinrich's diaries. If in the earliest entries, except for the wooden style of a boy who obeys authority, Heinrich's character is hardly apparent, over time this stilted style becomes his own. As one reads on, one no longer thinks of a boy who is forced to the task, but of a prudish and rigid young man.

In Heinrich's boyhood diaries no one has been able to find any record of rage or of events that inspire such rage. Yet one cannot assume from this evidence that such did not exist. His father would have permitted neither anger nor even the memory of it to enter these pages. That there must be no visible trace of resentment toward the parent was the pedagogy of the age. Dr. Schreber believed that children should learn to be grateful. The pain and humiliation children endure are meant to benefit them. The parent is only trying to save the child's soul.

Now, for different reasons, I too find myself on the track of a child's soul. The dimensions of Heinrich Himmler's life have put me on this track. I am trying to grasp the inner state of his being. For a time the soul ceased to exist in the modern mind. One thought of a human being as a kind of machine, or as a cog in the greater mechanism of society, operating within another machine, the earth, which itself operates within the greater mechanical design of the universe.

When I was in Berlin, I spoke to a rabbi who had, it seemed to me, lost his faith. When I asked him if he still believed in God, he simply shook his head and widened his eyes as if to say, *How is this possible?* He had been telling me about his congregation: older people, many of Polish origin, survivors of the holocaust who were not able to leave Germany after the war because they were too ill to travel. He was poised in this painful place by choice. He had come to lead this congregation only temporarily but, once feeling the condition of his people, decided to stay. Still, despite his answer, and as much as the holocaust made a terrible argument for the death of the spirit, talking in that small study with this man, I could feel from him the light of something surviving.

The religious tradition that shaped Heinrich's childhood argues that the soul is not part of flesh but is instead a prisoner of the body. But suppose the soul is meant to live in and through the body and to know itself in the heart of earthly existence?

Then the soul is an integral part of the child's whole being, and its growth is thus part of the child's growth. It is, for example, like a seed planted underground in the soil, naturally moving toward the light. And it comes into its fullest manifestation thus only when seen, especially when self meeting self returns a gaze.

What then occurs if the soul in its small beginnings is forced to take on a secret life? A boy learns, for instance, to hide his thoughts from his father simply by failing to record them in his journals. He harbors his secrets in fear and guilt, confessing them to no one until in time the voice of his father chastising him becomes his own. A small war is waged in his mind. Daily implosions take place under his skin, by which in increments something in him seems to disappear. Gradually his father's voice subsumes the vitality of all his desires and even his rage, so that now what he wants most passionately is his own obedience, and his rage is aimed at his own failures. As over time his secrets fade from memory, he ceases to tell them, even to himself, so that finally a day arrives when he believes the image he has made of himself in his diaries is true.

The child, Dr. Schreber advised, *should be permeated by the impossibility of locking something in his heart.* The doctor who gave this advice had a son who was hospitalized for disabling schizophrenia. Another of his children committed suicide. But this was not taken as a warning against his approach. His methods of educating children were so much a part of the canon of everyday life in Germany that they were introduced into the state school system.

That this philosophy was taught in school gives me an interior view of the catastrophe to follow. It adds a certain dimension to my image of these events to know that a nation of citizens learned that no part of themselves could be safe from the scrutiny of authority, nothing locked in the heart, and at the same time to discover that the head of the secret police of this nation was the son of a schoolmaster. It was this man, after all, Heinrich Himmler, Reichsführer SS, who was later to say, speaking of the mass arrests of Jews, *Protective custody is an act of care.*

The polite manner of young Heinrich's diaries reminds me of life in my grandmother's home. Not the grandmother I lost and later found, but the one who, for many years, raised me. She was my mother's mother. The family would assemble in the living room together, sitting with a certain reserve, afraid to soil the surfaces. What was it that by accident might have been made visible?

All our family photographs were posed. We stood together in groups of three or four and squinted into the sun. My grandmother directed us to smile. I have carried one of these photographs with me for years without acknowledging to myself that in it my mother has the look she always had when she drank too much. In another photograph, taken near the time of my parents' divorce, I can see that my father is almost crying, though I could not see this earlier. I must have felt obliged to see only what my grandmother wanted us to see. Tranquil, domestic scenes.

In the matrix of the mitochondria all the processes of transformation join together in a central vortex.

We were not comfortable with ourselves as a family. There was a great shared suffering and yet we never wept together, except for my mother, who would alternately weep and then rage when she was drunk. Together, under my grandmother's tutelage, we kept up appearances. Her effort was ceaseless.

When at the age of six I went to live with her, my grandmother worked to reshape me. I learned what she thought was correct grammar. The manners she had studied in books of etiquette were passed on to me, not by casual example but through anxious memorization and drill. Napkin to be lifted by the corner and swept onto the lap. Hand to be clasped firmly but not too firmly.

We were not to the manner born. On one side my great-grandfather was a farmer, and on the other a butcher newly emigrated from Ireland, who still spoke with a brogue. Both great-grandfathers drank too much, the one in public houses, the other more quietly at home. The great-grandfather who farmed was my grandmother's father. He was not wealthy but he aspired to gentility. My grandmother inherited both his aspiration and his failure.

We considered ourselves finer than the neighbors to our left with their chaotic household. But when certain visitors came, we were as if driven by an inward, secret panic that who we really were might be discovered. Inadvertently, by some careless gesture, we might reveal to these visitors who were our betters that we did not belong with them, that we were not real. Though of course we never spoke of this, to anyone, not even ourselves.

Gebhard Himmler's family was newly risen from poverty. Just as in my family, the Himmlers' gentility was a thinly laid surface, maintained no doubt only with great effort. Gebhard's father had come from a family of peasants and small artisans. Such a living etched from the soil, and by one's hands, is tenuous and hard. As is frequently the case with young men born to poverty, Johann became a soldier. And, like many young soldiers, he got himself into trouble more than once for brawling and general mischief. On one occasion he was reproved for what was called *immoral behavior with a low woman.* But nothing of this history survived in his son's version of him. By the time Gebhard was born, Johann was fifty-six years old and had reformed his ways. Having joined the royal police force of Bavaria, over the years he rose to the rank of sergeant. He was a respectable man, with a respectable position.

Perhaps Gebhard never learned of his father's less than respectable past. He was only three years old when Johann died. If he had the slightest notion, he did not breathe a word to his own children. Johann became the icon of the Himmler family, the heroic soldier who single-handedly brought his family from the obscurity of poverty into the warm light of the favored. Yet obscure histories have a way of casting a shadow over the present. Those who are born to propriety have a sense of entitlement, and this affords them some ease as they execute the correct mannerisms of their class. More recent members of the elect are less certain of themselves; around the edges of newly minted refinement one discerns a certain fearfulness, expressed perhaps as uncertainty, or as its opposite, rigidity.

One can sense that rigidity in Gebhard's face as a younger man. In a photograph of the Himmler family, Gebhard, who towers in the background, seems severe. He has the face of one who looks for mistakes. He is vigilant. Heinrich's mother looks very small next to him, almost as if she is cowering. She has that look I have seen many times on my father's face, which one can only describe as ameliorating. Heinrich is very small. He stands closest to the camera, shimmering in a white dress. His face is pretty, even delicate.

HE HAS THE FACE OF ONE WHO LOOKS FOR MISTAKES. HE IS VIGILANT.

I am looking now at the etching called *Poverty*, made in 1897. Near the center, calling my attention, a woman holds her head in her hands. She stares through her hands into the face of a sleeping infant. Though the infant and the sheet and pillow around are filled with light, one recognizes that the child is dying. In a darker corner, two worried figures huddle, a father and another child. Room, mother, father, child exist in lines, a multitude of lines, and each line is filled with a rare intelligence.

Just as the physicist's scrutiny changes the object of perception, so does art transmute experience. One cannot look upon what Käthe Kollwitz has drawn without feeling. The lines around the child are bleak with unreason. Never have I seen so clearly that what we call poverty is simply a raw exposure to the terror and fragility of life. But there is more in this image. There is meaning in the frame. One can feel the artist's eyes. Her gaze is in one place soft, in another intense. Like the light around the infant, her attention interrupts the shadow that falls across the room.

The artist's choice of subject and the way she saw it were both radical departures, not only from certain acceptable assumptions in the world of art, but also from established social ideas because the poor were thought of as less than human. The death of a child to a poor parent was supposed to be a less painful event. In her depiction, the artist told a different story.

Heinrich is entering a new school now, and so his father makes a list of all his future classmates. Beside the name of each child he writes the child's father's name, what this father does for a living, and his social position. Heinrich must be careful, Gebhard tells him, to choose whom he befriends. In his diaries the boy seldom mentions his friends by name. Instead he writes that he played, for instance, with the landlord's child.

There is so much for Heinrich to learn. Gebhard must teach him the right way to bow. The proper forms of greeting. The history of his family; the history of his nation. Its heroes. His grandfather's illustrious military past. There is an order in the world and Heinrich has a place in this order which he must be trained to fill. His life is strictly scheduled. At this hour a walk in the woods so that he can appreciate nature. After that a game of chess to develop his mind. And after that piano, so that he will be cultured.

If a part of himself has vanished, that part of the self that feels and wants, and from which hence a coherent life might be shaped, Heinrich is not at sea yet. He has no time to drift or feel lost. Each moment has been spoken for, every move prescribed. He has only to carry out his father's plans for him.

But everything in his life is not as it should be. He is not popular among his classmates. Should it surprise us to learn that he has a penchant for listening to the secrets of his companions, and that afterward he repeats these secrets to his father, the schoolmaster? There is perhaps a secret he would like to learn and one he would like to tell, but this has long since been forgotten. Whatever he learns now he must tell his father. He must not keep anything from him. He must keep his father's good will at all costs. For, without his father, he does not exist.

And there is another reason Heinrich is not accepted by his classmates. He is frail. As an infant, stricken by influenza, he came close to perishing and his body still retains the mark of that illness. He is not strong. He is not good at the games the other boys play. At school he tries over and over to raise himself on the crossbars, unsuccessfully. He covets the popularity of his stronger, more masculine brother, Gebhard. But he cannot keep up with his brother. One day, when they go out for a simple bicycle ride together, Heinrich falls into the mud and returns with his clothes torn.

It is 1914. A war begins. There are parades. Young men marching in uniform. Tearful ceremonies at the railway station. Songs. Decorations. Heinrich is enthusiastic. The war has given him a sense of purpose in life. Like other boys, he plays at soldiering. He follows the war closely, writing in his diary of the progress of armies, *This time with 40 Army Corps and Russia and France against Germany.* The entries he makes do not seem so listless now; they have a new vigor. As the war continues, a new ambition gradually takes the shape of determination. Is this the way he will finally prove himself? Heinrich wants to be a soldier. And above all he wants a uniform.

It is 1915. In her journal Käthe Kollwitz records a disturbing sight. The night before at the opera she found herself sitting next to a young soldier. He was blinded. He sat *without stirring, his hands on his knees, his head erect.* She could not stop looking at him, and the memory of him, she writes now, *cuts her to the quick.*

It is 1916. As Heinrich comes of age he implores his father to help him find a regiment. He has many heated opinions about the war. But his thoughts are like the thoughts and feelings of many adolescents; what he expresses has no steady line of reason. His opinions are filled with contradictions, and he lacks that awareness of self which can turn ambivalence into an inner dialogue. Yet, beneath this amorphous bravado, there is a pattern. As if he were trying on different attitudes, Heinrich swings from harshness to compassion. In one place he writes, *The Russian prisoners multiply like vermin.* (Should I write here that this is a word he will one day use for Jews?) But later he is sympathetic to the same prisoners because they are so far away from home. Writing once of *the silly old women and petty bourgeois . . . who so dislike war,* in another entry, he remembers the young men he has seen depart on trains and he asks, *How many are alive today?*

Is the direction of any life inevitable? Or are there crossroads, points at which the direction might be changed? I am looking again at the Himmler family. Heinrich's infant face resembles the face of his mother. His face is soft. And his mother? In the photograph she is a fading presence. She occupied the same position as did most women in German families, secondary and obedient to the undisputed power of her husband. She has a slight smile which for some reason reminds me of the smile of a child I saw in a photograph from an album made by the SS. This child's image was captured as she stood on the platform at Auschwitz. In the photograph she emanates a certain frailty. Her smile is a very feminine smile. Asking, or perhaps pleading, *Don't hurt me.*

Is it possible that Heinrich, looking into that child's face, might have seen himself there? What is it in a life that makes one able to see oneself in others? Such affinities do not stop with obvious resemblance. There is a sense in which we all enter the lives of others.

It is 1917, and a boy who will be named Heinz is born to Catholic parents living in Vienna. Heinz's father bears a certain resemblance to Heinrich's father. He is a civil servant and, also like Gebhard, he is pedantic and correct in all he does. Heinrich will never meet this boy. And yet their paths will cross.

Early in the same year as Heinz's birth, Heinrich's father has finally succeeded in getting him into a regiment. As the war continues for one more year, Heinrich comes close to achieving his dream. He will be a soldier. He is sent to officer's training. Yet he is not entirely happy. *The food is bad,* he writes to his mother, *and there is not enough of it. It is cold. There are bedbugs. The room is barren.* Can she send him food? A blanket? Why doesn't she write him more often? Has she forgotten him? They are calling up troops. Suppose he should be called to the front and die?

But something turns in him. Does he sit on the edge of a neat, narrow military bunk bed as he writes in his diary that he does not want to be like a boy who whines to his mother? Now, he writes a different letter: *I am once more a soldier body and soul.* He loves his uniform; the oath he has learned to write; the first inspection he passes. He signs his letters now, *Miles Heinrich.* Soldier Heinrich.

I am looking at another photograph. It is of two boys. They are both in military uniform. Gebhard, Heinrich's older brother, is thicker and taller. Next to him Heinrich is still diminutive. But his face has become harder, and his smile, though faint like his mother's smile, has gained a new quality, harsh and stiff like the little collar he wears.

Most men can remember a time in their lives when they were not so different from girls, and they also remember when that time ended. In ancient Greece a young boy lived with his mother, practicing a feminine life in her household, until the day he was taken from her into the camp of men. From this day forward the life that had been soft and graceful became rigorous and hard, as the older boy was prepared for the life of a soldier.

My grandfather on my mother's side was a contemporary of Heinrich Himmler. He was the youngest boy in the family and an especially pretty child. Like Heinrich and all small boys in this period, he was dressed in a lace gown. His hair was long and curled about his face. Like Heinrich, he was his mother's favorite. She wanted to keep him in his finery. He was so beautiful in it, and he was her last child. My great-grandmother Sarah had a dreamy, artistic nature, and in his early years my grandfather took after her. But all of this made him seem girlish. And his father and older brothers teased him mercilessly. Life improved for him only when he graduated to long pants. With them he lost his dreamy nature too.

The soul is often imagined to be feminine. All those qualities thought of as soulful, a dreaminess or artistic sensibility, are supposed to come more naturally to women. Ephemeral, half seen, half present, nearly ghostly, with only the vaguest relation to the practical world of physical law, the soul appears to us as lost. The hero, with his more masculine virtues, must go in search of her. But there is another, older story of the soul. In this story she is firmly planted on the earth. She is incarnate and visible everywhere. Neither is she faint of heart, nor fading in her resolve. It is she, in fact, who goes bravely in search of desire.

1918. Suddenly the war is over. Germany has lost. Heinrich has failed to win his commission. He has not fought in a single battle. Prince Heinrich, his namesake, has died. The prince will be decorated for heroism, after his death. Heinrich returns home, not an officer or even a soldier any longer. He returns to school, completing his studies at the gymnasium and then the university. But he is adrift. Purposeless. And like the world he belongs to, dissatisfied. Neither man nor boy, he does not know what he wants.

Until now he could rely on a strict regimen provided by his father. Nothing was left uncertain or undefined for long in his father's house. The thoroughness of Gebhard's hold over his family comes alive for me through this procedure: every package, letter, or money order to pass through the door was by Gebhard's command to be duly recorded. And I begin to grasp a sense of Gebhard's priorities when I read that Heinrich, on one of his leaves home during the war, assisted his mother in this task. The shadow of his father's habits will stretch out over history. They will fall over an office in Berlin through which the SS, and the entire network of concentration camps, are administered. Every single piece of paper issued with regard to this office will pass over Heinrich's desk, and to each page he will add his own initials. Schedules for trains. Orders for building supplies. Adjustments in salaries. No detail will escape his surmise or fail to be recorded.

But at this moment in his life Heinrich is facing a void. I remember a similar void, when a long and intimate relationship ended. What I felt then was fear. And at times panic. In a journal I kept after this separation, I wrote, *Direct knowledge of the illusory nature of panic. The feeling that I had let everything go out of control.* I could turn in only one direction: inward. Each day I abated my fears for a time by observing myself. But what exists in that direction for Heinrich? He has not been allowed to inhabit that terrain. His inner life has been sealed off both from his father and himself.

I am not certain what I am working for, he writes, and then, not able to let this uncertainty remain, he adds, *I work because it is my duty.* He spends long hours in his room, seldom leaving the house at all. He is at sea. Still somewhat the adolescent, unformed, not knowing what face he should put on when going out into the world, in his journal he confesses that he still lacks that *naturally superior kind of manner that he would dearly like to possess.*

Is it any wonder then that he is so eager to rejoin the army? The army gave purpose and order to his life. He wants his uniform again. In his uniform he knows who he is. But his frailty haunts him. Over and over he shows up at recruiting stations throughout Bavaria only to be turned away each time, with the single word, *Untauglich*. Unfit. At night the echo of this word keeps him awake.

When he tries to recover his pride, he suffers another failure of a similar kind. A student of agriculture at the university, now he dreams of becoming a farmer. He believes he can take strength and vitality from the soil. After all his own applications are rejected, his father finds him a position in the countryside. He rides toward his new life on his motorcycle and is pelted by torrents of rain. Though he is cold and hungry, he is also exuberant. He has defeated his own weakness. But after only a few weeks his body fails him again. He returns home ill with typhus and must face the void once more.

What Germany needs now is a man of iron. How easy it is to hear the irony of these words Heinrich records in his journal. But at this moment in history, he is hearing another kind of echo. There are so many others who agree with him. The treaty of Versailles is taken as a humiliation. An unforgivable weakness, it is argued, has been allowed to invade the nation.

1920. 1922. 1923. Heinrich is twenty, twenty-two, twenty-three. He is growing up with the century. And he starts to adopt certain opinions popular at this time. As I imagine myself in his frame of mind, facing a void, cast into unknown waters, these opinions appear like rescue ships on the horizon, a promise of *terra firma*, the known.

It is for instance fashionable to argue that the emergence of female equality has drained the nation of its strength. At social gatherings Heinrich likes to discuss the differences between men and women. That twilight area between the certainties of gender, homosexuality, horrifies him. A man should be a man and a woman a woman. Sexually explicit illustrations in a book by Oscar Wilde horrify him. Uncomfortable with the opposite sex, so much so that one of his female friends believes he hates women, he has strong feelings about how men and women ought to relate. *A real man,* he sets down in his diary, *should love a woman as a child who must be admonished perhaps even punished, when she is foolish, though she must also be protected and looked after because she is so weak.*

As I try to enter Heinrich's experience, the feeling I sense behind these words is of immense comfort. I know who I am. My role in life, what I am to feel, what I am to be, has been made clear. I am a man. I am the strong protector. And what's more, I am needed. There is one who is weak. One who is weaker than I am. And I am the one who must protect her.

And yet behind the apparent calm of my present mood, there is an uneasiness. Who is this one that I protect? Does she tell me the truth about herself? I am beginning to suspect that she hides herself from me. There is something secretive in her nature. She is an unknown, even dangerous, territory.

The year is 1924. And Heinrich is still fascinated with secrets. He discovers that his brother's fiancée has committed one or maybe even two indiscretions. At his urging, Gebhard breaks off the engagement. But Heinrich is still not satisfied. He writes a friend who lives near his brother's former fiancée, *Do you know of any other shameful stories?* After this, he hires a private detective to look into her past.

Is it any coincidence that in the same year he writes in his diary that he has met a *great man, genuine and pure?* This man, he notes, may be the new leader Germany is seeking. He finds he shares a certain drift of thought with this man. He is discovering who he is now, partly by affinity and partly by negation. In his picture of himself, a profile begins to emerge cast in light and shadow. He knows now who he is and who he is not. He is not Jewish.

And increasingly he becomes obsessed with who he is not. In this pursuit, his curiosity is fed by best-selling books, posters, films, journals; he is part of a larger social movement, and this no doubt gives him comfort, and one cannot, in studying the landscape of his mind as set against the landscape of the social body, discover where he ends and the milieu of this time begins. He is perhaps like a particle in a wave, a wave which has only the most elusive relationship with the physical world, existing as an afterimage in the mind.

I can imagine him sitting at a small desk in his bedroom, still in his father's home. Is it the same desk where he was required to record some desultory sentences in his diary every day? He is bent over a book. It is evening. The light is on, shining on the pages of the book. Which book among the books he has listed in his journal does he read now? Is it *Das Liebesnest* (*The Lovenest*), telling the story of a liaison between a Jewish man and a gentile woman? *Rasse*? Explaining the concept of racial superiority? Or is it *Juden Schuldbuch* (*The Book of Jewish Guilt*). Or *Die Sünde wider das Blut* (*The Sin Against the Blood*).

One can follow somewhat his train of thought here and there where he makes comments on what he reads in his journal. When he reads *Tscheka*, for instance, a history of the secret police in Russia, he says he is disappointed. *Everyone knows*, he writes, that the Jews control the secret police in Russia. But nowhere in the pages of this book does he find a mention of this "fact."

His mind has begun to take a definite shape, even a predictable pattern. Everywhere he casts his eyes he will discover a certain word. Wherever his thoughts wander he brings them back to this word. *Jew. Jude. Jew.* With this word he is on firm ground again. In the sound of the word, a box is closed, a box with all the necessary documents, with all the papers in order.

My grandfather was an anti-Semite. He had a long list of enemies that he liked to recite. Blacks were among them. And Catholics. And the English. He was Protestant and Irish. Because of his drinking he retired early (though we never discussed the cause). In my childhood I often found him sitting alone in the living room that was darkened by closed venetian blinds which kept all our colors from fading. Lonely myself, I would try to speak with him. His repertoire was small. When I was younger he would tell me stories of his childhood, and I loved those stories. He talked about the dog named Blackie that was his then. A ceramic statue of a small black dog resembling him stood near the fireplace. He loved this dog in a way that was almost painful to hear. But he could never enter that intricate world of expressed emotion in which the shadings of one's life as it is felt and experienced become articulated. This way of speaking was left to the women of our family. As I grew older and he could no longer tell me the story of his dog, he would talk to me about politics. It was then that, with a passion he revealed nowhere else, he would recite to me his long list filled with everyone he hated.

I did not like to listen to my grandfather speak this way. His face would get red, and his voice took on a grating tone that seemed to abrade not only the ears but some other slower, calmer velocity within the body of the room. His eyes, no longer looking at me, blazed with a kind of blindness. There was no reaching him at these moments. He was beyond any kind of touch or remembering. Even so, reciting the long list of those he hated, he came temporarily alive. Then, once out of this frame of mind, he lapsed into a kind of fog which we called, in the family, his retirement.

There was another part of my grandfather's mind that also disturbed me. But this passion was veiled. I stood at the borders of it occasionally catching glimpses. He had a stack of magazines by the chair he always occupied. They were devoted to the subject of crime, and the crimes were always grisly, involving photographs of women or girls uncovered in ditches, hacked to pieces or otherwise mutilated. I was never supposed to look in these magazines, but I did. What I saw there could not be reconciled with the other experience I had of my grandfather, fond of me, gentle, almost anachronistically protective.

THERE WAS NO REACHING HIM AT THESE MOMENTS. HE WAS BEYOND ANY KIND OF TOUCH OR REMEMBERING.

Heinrich Himmler was also fascinated with crime. Along with books about Jews, he read avidly on the subjects of police work, espionage, torture. Despite his high ideals regarding chastity, he was drawn to torrid, even pornographic fiction, including *Ein Sadist im Priesterrock* (*A Sadist in Priestly Attire*) which he read quickly, noting in his journal that it was a book *about the corruption of women and girls . . . in Paris.*

Entering the odd and often inconsistent maze of his opinions, I feel a certain queasiness. I cannot find a balance point. I search in vain for some center, that place which is in us all, and is perhaps even beyond nationality, or even gender, the felt core of existence, which seems to be at the same time the most real. In Heinrich's morass of thought there are no connecting threads, no integrated whole. I find only the opinions themselves, standing in an odd relation to gravity, as if hastily formed, a rickety, perilous structure.

I am looking at a photograph. It was taken in 1925. Or perhaps 1926. A group of men pose before a doorway in Landshut. Over this doorway is a wreathed swastika. Nearly all the men are in uniform. Some wear shiny black boots. Heinrich is among them. He is the slightest, very thin. Heinrich Himmler. He is near the front. At the far left there is the blurred figure of a man who has been caught in motion as he rushes to join the other men. Of course I know his feeling. The desire to partake, and even to be part of memory.

Photographs are strange creations. They are depictions of a moment that is always passing; after the shutter closes, the subject moves out of the frame and begins to change outwardly or inwardly. One ages. One shifts to a different state of consciousness. Subtle changes can take place in an instant, perhaps one does not even feel them — but they are perceptible to the camera.

The idea we have of reality as a fixed quantity is an illusion. Everything moves. And the process of knowing oneself is in constant motion too, because the self is always changing. Nowhere is this so evident as in the process of art which takes one at once into the self and into *terra incognita*, the land of the unknown. *I am groping in the dark*, the artist Käthe Kollwitz writes in her journal. Here, I imagine she is not so much uttering a cry of despair as making a simple statement. A sense of emptiness always precedes creation.

Now, as I imagine Himmler, dressed in his neat uniform, seated behind his desk at party headquarters, I can feel the void he feared begin to recede. In every way his life has taken on definition. He has a purpose and a schedule. Even the place left by the cessation of his father's lessons has now been filled. He is surrounded by men whose ideas he begins to adopt. From Alfred Rosenberg he learns about the history of Aryan blood, a line Rosenberg traces back to thousands of years before Christ. From Walther Darré he learns that the countryside is a source of Nordic strength. (And that Jews gravitate toward cities.)

Yet I do not find the calmness of a man who has found himself in the descriptions I have encountered of Heinrich Himmler. Rather, he is filled with an anxious ambivalence. If there was once someone in him who felt strongly one way or the other, this one has long ago vanished. In a room filled with other leaders, he seems to fade into the woodwork, his manner obsequious, his effect inconsequential. He cannot make a decision alone. He is known to seek the advice of other men for even the smallest decisions. In the years to come it will be whispered that he is being led by his own assistant, Reinhard Heydrich. He has made only one decision on his own with a consistent resolve. Following Hitler with unwavering loyalty, he is known as *der treue Heinrich*, true Heinrich. He describes himself as an instrument of the Führer's will.

But still he has something of his own. Something hidden. And this will make him powerful. He is a gatherer of secrets. As he supervises the sale of advertising space for the Nazi newspaper, *Völkischer Beobachter*, he instructs the members of his staff to gather information, not only on the party enemies, the socialists and the communists, but on Nazi Party members themselves. In his small office he sits surrounded by voluminous files that are filled with secrets. From this he will build his secret police. By 1925, with an order from Adolf Hitler, the Schutzstaffel, or SS, has become an official institution.

His life is moving now. Yet in this motion one has the feeling not of a flow, as in the flow of water in a cell, nor as the flow of rivers toward an ocean, but of an engine, a locomotive moving at high speed, or even a missile, traveling above the ground. History has an uncanny way of creating its own metaphors. In 1930, months after Himmler is elected to the Reichstag, Wernher von Braun begins his experiments with liquid fuel missiles that will one day soon lead to the development of the V-2 rocket.

The successful journey of a missile depends upon the study of ballistics. Gravitational fields vary at different heights. The relationship of a projectile to the earth's surface will determine its trajectory. The missile may give the illusion of liberation from the earth, or even abandon. Young men dreaming of space often invest the missile with these qualities. Yet, paradoxically, one is more free of the consideration of gravity while traveling the surface of the earth on foot. There is no necessity for mathematical calculation for each step, nor does one need to apply Newton's laws to take a walk. But the missile has in a sense been forced away from its own presence; the wisdom that is part of its own weight has been transgressed. It finds itself thus careening in a space devoid of memory, always on the verge of falling, but not falling and hence like one who is constantly afraid of illusion, gripped by an anxiety that cannot be resolved even by a fate that threatens catastrophe.

The catastrophes which came to pass after Heinrich Himmler's astonishing ascent to power did not occur in his own life, but came to rest in the lives of others, distant from him, and out of the context of his daily world. It is 1931. Heinz, the boy born in Vienna to Catholic parents, has just turned sixteen, and he is beginning to learn something about himself. All around him his school friends are falling in love with girls. But when he searches inside himself, he finds no such feelings. He is pulled in a different direction. He finds that he is still drawn to another boy. He does not yet know, or even guess, that these feelings will one day place him in the territory of a target.

It is 1933. Heinrich Himmler, Reichsführer SS, has become President of the Bavarian police. In this capacity he begins a campaign against *subversive elements*. Opposition journalists, Jewish business owners, Social Democrats, Communists — names culled from a list compiled on index cards by Himmler's deputy, Reinhard Heydrich — are rounded up and arrested. When the prisons become too crowded, Himmler builds temporary camps. Then, on March 22, the Reichsführer opens the first official and permanent concentration camp at Dachau.

It is 1934. Himmler's power and prestige in the Reich are growing. Yet someone stands in his way. Within the hierarchy of the state police forces, Ernst Röhm, Commandant of the SA, stands over him. But Himmler has made an alliance with Hermann Göring, who as President Minister of Prussia controls the Prussian police, known as the Gestapo. Through a telephone-tapping technique Göring has uncovered evidence of a seditious plot planned by Röhm against the Führer, and he brings this evidence to Himmler. The Führer, having his own reasons to proceed against

Röhm, a notorious homosexual and a socialist, empowers the SS and the Gestapo to form an execution committee. This committee will assassinate Röhm, along with the other leaders of the SA. And in the same year, Göring transfers control of the Gestapo to the SS.

But something else less easy to conquer stands in the way of his dreams for himself. It is his own body. I can see him now as he struggles. He is on a playing field in Berlin. And he has broken out in a sweat. He has been trying once again to earn the Reich's sports badge, an honor whose requirements he himself established but cannot seem to fulfill. For three years he has exercised and practiced. On one day he will lift the required weights or run the required laps, but at every trial he fails to throw the discus far enough. His attempt is always a few centimeters short.

And once he is Reichsführer, he will set certain other standards for superiority that, no matter how heroic his efforts, he will never be able to meet. A sign of the *Übermensch*, he says, is blondness, but he himself is dark. He says he is careful to weed out any applicant for the SS who shows traces of a mongolian ancestry, but he himself has the narrow eyes he takes as a sign of such a descent. *I have refused to accept any man whose size was below six feet because I know only men of a certain size have the necessary quality of blood*, he declares, standing just five foot seven behind the podium.

It is the same year, and Heinz, who is certain now that he is a homosexual, has decided to end the silence which he feels to be a burden to him. From the earliest years of his childhood he has trusted his mother with all of his secrets. Now he will tell her another secret, the secret of whom he loves. *My dear child*, she tells him, *it is your life and you must live it.*

It is 1936. Though he does not know it, Himmler is moving into the sphere of Heinz's life now. He has organized a special section of the Gestapo to deal with homosexuality and abortion. On October 11, he declares in a public speech, *Germany's forebears knew what to do with homosexuals. They drowned them in bogs.* This was not punishment, he argues, but *the extermination of unnatural existence.*

As I read these words from Himmler's speech, they call to mind an image from a more recent past, an event I nearly witnessed. On my return from Berlin and after my search for my grandmother, I spent a few days in Maine, close to the city of Bangor. This is a quiet town, not much used to violence. But just days before I arrived a young man had been murdered there. He was a homosexual. He wore an earring in one ear. While he walked home one evening with another man, three boys stopped him on the street. They threw him to the ground and began to kick him. He had trouble catching his breath. He was asthmatic. They picked him up and carried him to a railing of a nearby bridge. He told them he could not swim. Yet still, they threw him over the railing of the bridge into the stream, and he drowned. I saw a picture of him printed in the newspaper. That kind of beauty only very graceful children possess shined through his adult features. It was said that he had come to New England to live with his lover. But the love had failed, and before he died he was piecing his life back together.

When Himmler heard that one of his heroes, Frederick the Great, was a homosexual, he refused to believe his ears. I remember the year when my sister announced to my family that she was a lesbian. I can still recall the chill of fear that went up my spine at the sound of the word "queer." We came of age in the fifties; this was a decade of conformity, awash with mood both public and private, bearing on the life of the body and the body politic. Day after day my grandfather would sit in front of the television set watching as Joseph McCarthy interrogated witnesses about their loyalty to the flag. At the same time, a strict definition of what a woman or a man is had returned to capture the shared imagination. In school I was taught sewing and cooking, and I learned to carry my books in front of my chest to strengthen the muscles which held up my breasts.

I was not happy to hear that my sister was a homosexual. Moved from one member of my family to another, I did not feel secure in the love of others. As the child of divorce I was already different. *Where are your mother and father? Why don't you live with them?* I dreaded these questions. Now my sister, whom I adored and in many ways had patterned myself after, had become an outcast, moved even further out of the circle than I.

It is March 1938. Germany has invaded Austria. Himmler has put on a field-gray uniform for the occasion. Two hand grenades dangle from his Sam Browne belt. Accompanied by a special command unit of twenty-eight men armed with tommy guns and light machine guns, he proceeds to Vienna. Here he will set up Gestapo headquarters in the Hotel Metropole before he returns to Berlin.

It is a Friday, in March of 1939. Heinz, who is twenty-two years old now, and a university student, has received a summons. He is to appear for questioning at the Hotel Metropole. Telling his mother it can't be anything serious, he leaves. He enters a room and stands before a desk. The man behind the desk does not raise his head to nod. He continues to write. When he puts his pen down and looks up at the young man, he tells him, *You are a queer, homosexual, admit it.* Heinz tries to deny this. But the man behind the desk pulls out a photograph. He sees two faces here he knows. His own face and the face of his lover. He begins to weep.

I have come to believe that every life bears in some way on every other. The motion of cause and effect is like the motion of a wave in water, continuous, within and not without the matrix of being, so that all consequences, whether we know them or not, are intimately embedded in our experience. But the missile, as it hurls toward its target, has lost its context. It has been driven farther than the eye can see. How can one speak of direction any longer? Nothing in the space the missile passes through can seem familiar. In the process of flight, alienated by terror, this motion has become estranged from life, has fallen out of the natural rhythm of events.

I am imagining Himmler as he sits behind his desk in January of 1940. The procedures of introduction into the concentration camps have all been outlined or authorized by Himmler himself. He supervises every detail of these operations. Following his father's penchant for order, he makes many very explicit rules, and requires that reports be filed continually. Train schedules, orders for food supplies, descriptions of punishments all pass over his desk. He sits behind a massive door of carved wood, in his office, paneled in light, unvarnished oak, behind a desk that is normally empty, and clean, except for the bust of Hitler he displays at one end, and a little drummer boy at the other, between which he reads, considers and initials countless pieces of paper.

One should teach a child a sense of shame. These words of Himmler's journals come back to me as I imagine Heinz now standing naked in the snow. The weather is below zero. After a while he is taken to a cold shower, and then issued an ill-fitting uniform. Now he is ordered to stand with the other prisoners once more out in the cold while the commandant reads the rules. All the prisoners in these barracks are homosexuals. There are pink triangles sewn to their uniforms. They must sleep with the light on, they are told, and with their hands outside their blankets. This is a rule made especially for homosexual men. Any man caught with his hands under his blankets will be taken outside into the icy night where several bowls of water will be poured over him, and where he will he made to stand for an hour.

Except for the fact that this punishment usually led to death from cold and exposure, this practice reminds me of Dr. Schreber's procedure for curing children of masturbation. Just a few nights ago I woke up with this thought: *Was Dr. Schreber afraid of children?* Or the child he once was? Fear is often just beneath the tyrant's fury, a fear that must grow with the trajectory of his flight from himself. At Dachau I went inside a barrack. It was a standard design, similar in many camps. The plan of the camps too was standard, and resembled, so I was told by a German friend, the camp sites designed for the Hitler Youth. This seemed to me significant, not as a clue in an analysis, but more like a gesture that colors and changes a speaker's words.

It is the summer of 1940. After working for nearly a decade on liquid fuel rockets, Wernher von Braun begins to design a missile that can be used in the war. He is part of a team trying to meet certain military specifications.

The missile must be carried through railway tunnels. It must cover a range of 275 kilometers and carry a warhead weighing one metric ton. The engineers have determined that the motor of this rocket, a prototype of the V-2, will need to be fueled by a pump, and now a pump has been made. Von Braun is free to turn his attention to the turbine drive.

When I think of this missile, or of men sleeping in a barrack, hands exposed, lying on top of worn blankets, an image of Himmler's hands comes to me. Those who remember him say that as he conducted a conversation, discussing a plan, for example, or giving a new order, his hands would lie on top of his desk, limp and inert. He did not like to witness the consequences of his commands. His plans were launched toward distant targets and blind to the consequences of flesh.

After a few months, in one of countless orders which mystify him, coming from a nameless source, and with no explanation, but which he must obey, Heinz is transferred from Sachsenhausen to Flossenbürg. The regime at this camp is the same, but here the commandant, unlike Himmler, does not choose to distance himself from the suffering of others. He is instead drawn to it. He will have a man flogged for the slightest infraction of the rules, and then stand to watch as this punishment is inflicted. The man who is flogged is made to call out the number of lashes as he is lashed, creating in him, no doubt, the feeling that he is causing his own pain. As the man's skin bursts open and he cries out in pain, the commandant's eyes grow excited. His face turns red. His hand slips into his trousers, and he begins to handle himself.

Was the commandant in this moment in any way an extension of the Reichsführer, living out a hidden aspect of this man, one who takes pleasure in the pain of others? This explanation must shed some light, except perhaps as it is intended through the category of an inexplicable perversity to put the crimes Himmler committed at a distance from any understanding of ourselves. The Reichsführer's sexuality is so commonplace. He was remarkable only for the extent of his prudery as a young man. Later, like so many men, he has a wife, who dominates him, and a mistress, younger, more docile, adoring, whom he in turn adores. It has been suggested that he takes pleasure in seeing the naked bodies of boys and young men. If he has a sexual fetish it is certainly this, the worship of physical perfection in the male body. And this worship has its sadistic aspects: his efforts to control reproduction, to force SS men to procreate with many women, the kidnapping from occupied countries of children deemed worthy. Under the veneer of his worship, an earlier rage must haunt him. The subject of cruel insults from other boys with hardier bodies, and the torturous methods his father used to raise him, does he not feel rage toward his persecutors, a rage that, in the course of time, enters history? Yet this is an essential part of the picture: he is dulled to rage. So many of his feelings are inaccessible to him. Like the concentration camps he commands, in many ways he remains absent to himself. And in this he is not so different from the civilization that produced him.

Writing this, I have tried to find my own rage. The memory is immediate. I am a child, almost nine years old. I sit on the cold pavement of a winter day in Los Angeles. My grandmother has angered me. There is a terrible injustice. A punishment that has enraged me. As I sit picking blades of grass and arranging them into piles, I am torturing her in my mind. I have tied her up and I am shouting at her. Threatening her. Striking her. I batter her, batter her as if with each blow, each landing of my hand against her flesh, I can force my way into her, I can be inside her, I can grab hold of someone inside her, someone who feels, who feels as I do, who feels the hurt I feel, the wound I feel, who feels pain as I feel pain. I am forcing her to feel what I feel. I am forcing her to know me. And as I strike her, blow after blow, a shudder of weeping is released in me, and I become utterly myself, the weeping in me becoming rage, the rage turning to tears, all the time my heart beating, all the time uttering a soundless, bitter, passionate cry, a cry of vengeance and of love.

Is this what is in the torturer's heart? With each blow of his whip does he want to make the tortured one feel as he himself has felt? The desire to know and be known is strong in all of us. Many years after the day I imagined myself as my grandmother's torturer I came to understand that, just as I had wanted my grandmother to feel what I had felt, she wanted me to feel as she had felt. Not what she felt as a woman, but what she had felt long ago as a child. Her childhood was lost to her, the feelings no longer remembered. One way or another, through punishment, severity, or even ridicule, she could goad me into fury and then tears. I expressed for her all she had held inside for so long.

IS THIS WHAT IS IN THE TORTURER'S HEART? WITH EACH BLOW OF HIS WHIP DOES HE WANT TO MAKE THE TORTURED ONE FEEL AS HE HIMSELF HAS FELT?

One day, the commandant at Flossenbürg encounters a victim who will not cry and Heinz is a witness to this meeting. As usual this prisoner must count out the number of blows assigned to him. The beating commences. And the prisoner counts out the numbers. But otherwise he is silent. Except for the numbers, not a cry, not a sound, passes his lips. And this puts the commandant in a rage. He orders the guard to strike harder with the lash; he increases the number of lashes; he orders the prisoner to begin counting from zero again. Finally, the beating shall continue *until the swine starts screaming*, he shouts. And now, when the prisoner's blood is flowing to the ground, he starts to howl. And with this, the commandant's face grows red, and his hands slip into his trousers again.

A connection between violence and sexuality threads its way through many histories. As we sit in the living room together, looking out over the water, Laura's stories move in and out of the world of her family, and of our shared world, its habits, its wars. She is telling me another story about her father, the general. They were living on the missile base. She had been out late baby-sitting. When she returned home the house was dark. She had no key. It was raining hard. She rang. There was no answer. Then she began to pound on the door. Suddenly the door opened. The hallway was dark. She was yanked into this darkness by her father. He was standing naked. Without speaking to her he began to slap her hard across the face, again and again, and did not stop until her mother, appearing in the stairs in a bathrobe, stood between them. *I knew*, she told me, *they had been making love*.

What was the source of his rage? Did it come from childhood, or battle, or both, the battle awakening the panic of an earlier abuse? The training a soldier receives is to wreak his anger on others. Anyone near receives it. I have heard stories of a man waking at night screaming in terror, reaching for a gun hidden under the pillow, and pointing it or even firing at his own family. In a play about Heracles by Euripides, the great warrior, who has just returned from the underworld, thinking that he has vanquished death, is claimed by madness. He believes himself to be in the home of his enemy. But he is in his own home and, finding his own children, mistakes them for the children of his enemy, clubs one to death and then kills the other two with arrows.

But it is not only warriors who wreak vengeance on their own children. Suffering is passed on from parent to child unto many generations. Did I know as a child that my grandmother's unclaimed fury had made its way into my mother's psyche too? With all her will my mother tried not to repeat against her own children the crimes that had battered her. Where my grandmother was tyrannical, my mother was tolerant and gave free rein. Where my grandmother goaded with critical remarks, my mother was encouraging, and even elaborately praising. But, like my grandfather, my mother drank too much. It was a way of life for her. Sooner or later the long nights would come. Every time I returned home, either to live with her or to visit, I prayed she would not drink again, while I braced myself for what I knew to be inevitable. The evening would begin with a few beers at home, followed by an endless tour of several bars. Either I went along and waited in cars, or I waited at home. In the early morning she would return, her eyes wandering like moths in their sockets. We would sit in two chairs opposite each other, as if these were prearranged places, marked out for us on the stage by a powerful but invisible director. She would start by joking with me. She was marvelously witty when she was drunk. All her natural intelligence was released then and allowed to bloom. But this performance was brief. Her humor turned by dark degrees to meanness. What must have daily constricted her, a kind of sea monster, feeding beneath the waters of her consciousness, and strong, would rise up to stop her glee and mine. Then she would strike. If I was not in my chair to receive her words, she would come and get me. What she said was viperous to me, sank like venom into my veins, and burned a path inside me. Even today I can remember very few of the words she used. She said that my laugh was too loud, or ugly. That I was incapable of loving. I am thankful now that, because she was not in her right mind, I knew at least in a part of myself that these accusations were unfounded. Yet they produced a doubt in me, a lingering shadow, the sense that perhaps I deserved whatever suffering befell me, and that shadow lingers.

Even if a feeling has been made secret, even if it has vanished from memory, can it have disappeared altogether? A weapon is lifted with the force of a forgotten memory. The memory has no words, only the insistence of a pain that has turned into fury. A body, tender in its childhood or its nakedness, lies under this weapon. And this body takes up the rage, the pain, the disowned memory with each blow.

1893. *Self-portrait at Table.* An etching and aquatint, the first in a long series of self-portraits that span the artist's life. A single lamp illuminates her face, the upper part of the body and the table where she sits. Everything else is in darkness. At first glance one thinks of loneliness. But after a moment it is solitude one sees. And a single moment in that solitude, as if one note of music, resonant and deep, played uninterrupted, echoing from every surface, coming to full consciousness in this woman, who in this instant looks out to those who will return her gaze with a face that has taken in and is expressing the music in the air about her. Solemnly and with a quiet patience, her hands pause over the etching she makes, a form she is bringing into being, the one she recognizes as herself.

Who are we? The answer is not easy. There are so many strands to the story, and one must trace every strand. I begin to suspect each thread goes out infinitely and touches everything, everyone. I read these words from an ancient gnostic text, words that have been lost to us for a long time: *For I am the first and the last.* Though in another account we have heard the beginning of this speech spoken by Jesus, here these words come to us in the voice of the goddess. *I am the honored one and scorned one*, the older text goes on. *I am the whore and the holy one. I am the wife and the virgin. I am the barren one, and many are her sons.* These words take on a new meaning for me, as I remember them now. *I am the silence that is incomprehensible*, the text reads, and ends, *I am the utterance of my name.*

Were you to trace any life, and study even the minute consequences, the effect, for instance, of a three-minute walk over a patch of grass, of words said casually to a stranger who happens to sit nearby in a public place, the range of that life would extend way beyond the territory we imagine it to inhabit. This is of course less difficult to understand when imagining the boundaries of a life such as Heinrich Himmler had.

After my visit to Dachau, I went to Paris where, in the fourteenth arrondissement, in the Métro station, I met Hélène. She stopped to help me read my map. We found we were going in the same direction, and thus it was on our way there that we began to speak. Something told me she had survived a concentration camp. And she had. She too fell into the circle of Himmler's life and its consequences. Himmler never went to Paris. At the time of the first mass arrests there he was taking a group of high Nazi officials on a tour of Auschwitz. During the tour, by his orders, the prisoners were made to stand at attention for six hours under the hot sun, but that is another story. Under his command, the Gestapo in Paris began to prepare for the mass arrests of Jews.

Paris had fallen to the German armies in July 1940. By September of that year a notice went up in all the neighborhoods. *Avis aux Israélites*, it read. *Notice to Israelites. By the demand of the occupying authorities, Israelites must present themselves, by October 2, without delay, equipped with identification papers, to the office of the Censor, to complete an identity card.* The notice was signed by the mayor and threatened the most severe punishment for the failure to comply. Through this process vital information was recorded about each Jewish family. Names, ages, addresses, occupations, places of work. An index card was made up for each person. And each card was then duplicated and sent to the offices of the Gestapo on Avenue Foch. There, the cards were duplicated several more times so that the names could be filed by several categories, alphabetically by surname, by address, by arrondissement, occupation, and nationality. At this point in history, work that would be done by computer now was painstakingly completed by countless men and women. Their labor continued feverishly almost until the hour of the first mass arrests, the *rafles*, two years later.

One can trace every death to an order signed by Himmler, yet these arrests could never have taken place on such a massive scale without this vast system of information. What did they think, those who were enlisted for this work? They were civilians. French. There were of course Nazi collaborators, among them, those who shared the same philosophy, or who simply obeyed and profited from whoever might be in power. But among the men and women who did this work, my suspicion is, there were many who tried to keep from themselves the knowledge of what they did. Of course, the final purpose of their labors was never revealed to those who prepared the machinery of arrest. If a man allowed his imagination to stray in the direction of this purpose, he could no doubt comfort himself with the argument that he was only handling pieces of paper. He could tell himself that matters were simply being set in order. The men and women who manufacture the trigger mechanisms for nuclear bombs do not tell themselves they are making weapons. They say simply that they are metal forgers.

There are many ways we have of standing outside ourselves in ignorance. Those who have learned as children to become strangers to themselves do not find this a difficult task. Habit has made it natural not to feel. To ignore the consequences of what one does in the world becomes ordinary. And this tendency is encouraged by a social structure that makes fragments of real events. One is never allowed to see the effects of what one does. But this ignorance is not entirely passive. For some, blindness becomes a kind of refuge, a way of life that is chosen, even with stubborn volition, and does not yield easily even to visible evidence.

The arrests were accompanied by an elaborate procedure, needed on some level, no doubt, for practical reasons, but also serving another purpose. They garbed this violence in the cloak of legality. A mind separated from the depths of itself cannot easily tell right from wrong. To this mind, the outward signs of law and order signify righteousness. That Himmler had such a mind was not unique in his generation, nor, I suspect, in ours.

In a museum in Paris I found a mimeographed sheet giving instructions to the Parisian police on how to arrest Jews. They must always carry red pencils, the sheet admonished, because all records regarding the arrests of Jews must be written in red. And the instructions went on to specify that, regarding the arrests of Jews, all records must be made in triplicate. Finally, the sheet of instructions included a way to categorize those Jews arrested. I could not make any sense of the categories. I only knew them to be crucial. That they might determine life and death for a woman, or man, or child. And that in the mind that invented these categories they had to have had some hidden significance, standing, like the crudely shaped characters of a medieval play, for shades of feeling, hidden states of being, secret knowledge.

For the most part, the men who designed the first missiles were not interested in weapons so much as flight. In his account of the early work at Peenemünde laboratories, Wernher von Braun explains that the scientists there had discovered a way to fund their research by making rockets appeal to the military. Colonel Dornberger told the other scientists that they could not hope to continue if all they created were experimental rockets. All Wernher von Braun wanted was to design vehicles that would travel to the moon. In the early fifties, in a book he wrote with two other scientists, he speaks of the reasons for such a flight. Yes, he says, curiosity and adventure play a part. But the primary reason is *to increase man's knowledge of the universe.*

To tell a story, or to hear a story told, is not a simple transmission of information. Something else in the telling is given too, so that, once hearing, what one has heard becomes a part of oneself. Hélène and I went to the museum in Paris together. There, among photographs of the first mass arrests and the concentration camp at Drancy, she told me this story. Reading the notice signed by the mayor, she presented herself immediately at the office of the censor. She waited with others, patiently. But when her turn in line came, the censor looked at her carefully. She was blond and had blue eyes. *Are you really Jewish?* he asked her.

The question of who was and who was not Jewish was pivotal to the Nazi mind and much legal controversy hung in the balance of this debate. For a few years, anyone with three Jewish grandparents was considered Jewish. An ancestor who belonged to the faith, but was not of Jewish blood would be Jewish. One who did not belong to the faith, but was of Jewish blood, was also Jewish. At the heart of this controversy, I hear the whisper of ambivalence, and perhaps the smallest beginning of compassion. For, to this mind, the one who is not Jewish becomes recognizable as like oneself.

Yes, I am Jewish, she said. *But your mother*, he asked again. *Can you be certain? Yes*, she said. *Ask her, go home and ask her*, he said, putting his stamp away. *But my mother is dead*, she protested. Then, he said, keeping his stamp in the drawer, *Your father. Your father must not be Jewish. Go home and ask him. I know he is Jewish*, Hélène answered. *There is no doubt that he is Jewish. He has always been Jewish, and I am Jewish too*. Then the man was silent, he shook his head. And, looking past her, said, *Perhaps your father was not really your father. Have you thought of that? Perhaps he was not your father?* She was young. *Of course he's my father. How can you say that? Certainly he is my father*, she insisted. *He is Jewish and so am I.* And she demanded that her papers be stamped.

What was in this man's mind as he questioned her? Did he say to himself, Perhaps here is someone I can save? Did he have what Pierre Sauvage has called *a moment of goodness*? What we know as goodness is not a static quality but arrives through a series of choices, some imperceptible, which are continually presented to us.

It is 1941. And Heinrich Himmler pays a visit to the Russian front. He has been put in charge of organizing the *Einsatzgruppen*, moving groups of men who carry out the killing of civilians and partisans. He watches as a deep pit is dug by the captured men and women. Then, suddenly, a young man catches his eye. He is struck by some quality the man possesses. He takes a liking to him. He has the commandant of the *Einsatzgruppen* bring the young man to him. *Who was your father?* he asks. *Your mother? Your grandparents? Do you have at least one grandparent who was not Jewish?* He is trying to save the young man. But he answers no to all the questions. So Himmler, strictly following the letter of the law, watches as the young man is put to death.

The captured men, women, and children are ordered to remove their clothing then. Naked, they stand before the pit they have dug. Some scream. Some attempt escape. The young men in uniform place their rifles against their shoulders and fire into the naked bodies. They do not fall silently. There are cries. There are open wounds. There are faces blown apart. Stomachs opened up. The dying groan. Weep. Flutter. Open their mouths.

There is no photograph of the particular moment when Heinrich Himmler stares into the face of death. What does he look like? Is he pale? He is stricken, the accounts tell us, and more than he thought he would be. He has imagined something quieter, more efficient, like the even rows of numbers, the alphabetical lists of names he likes to put in his files. Something he might be able to understand and contain. But one cannot contain death so easily.

• • • ● • • •

Death with Girl in Her Lap. One of many studies the artist did of death. A girl is drawn, her body dead or almost dead, in that suspended state where the breath is almost gone. There is no movement. No will. The lines the artist has drawn are simple. She has not rendered the natural form of head, arm, buttock, thigh exactly. But all these lines hold the feeling of a body in them. And as my eyes rest on this image, I can feel my own fear of death, and also, the largeness of grief, how grief will not let you remain insulated from your own feelings, or from life itself. It is as if I knew this girl. And death, too, appears to know her, cradling the fragile body with tenderness; she seems to understand the sorrow of dying. Perhaps this figure has taken into herself all the deaths she has witnessed. And in this way, she has become merciful.

Because Himmler finds it so difficult to witness these deaths, the commandant makes an appeal to him. If it is hard for you, he says, think what it must be for these young men who must carry out these executions, day after day. Shaken by what he has seen and heard, Himmler returns to Berlin resolved to ease the pain of these men. He will consult an engineer and set him to work immediately on new designs. Before the year has ended, he presents the *Einsatzgruppen* with a mobile killing truck. Now the young men will not have to witness death day after day. A hose from the exhaust pipe funnels fumes into a chamber built on the bed of a covered truck, which has a red cross painted on its side so its passengers will not be alarmed as they enter it.

To a certain kind of mind, what is hidden away ceases to exist.

Himmler does not like to watch the suffering of his prisoners. In this sense he does not witness the consequences of his own commands. But the mind is like a landscape in which nothing really ever disappears. What seems to have vanished has only transmuted to another form. Not wishing to witness what he has set in motion, still, in a silent part of himself, he must imagine what takes place. So, just as the child is made to live out the unclaimed imagination of the parent, others under Himmler's power were made to bear witness for him. Homosexuals were forced to witness and sometimes take part in the punishment of other homosexuals, Poles of other Poles, Jews of Jews. And as far as possible, the hands of the men of the SS were protected from the touch of death. Other prisoners were required to bury the bodies, or burn them in the ovens.

Hélène was turned in by a Jewish man who was trying, no doubt, to save his own life, and she was put under arrest by another Jewish man, an inmate of the same camp to which she was taken. She was grateful that she herself had not been forced to do harm. But something haunted her. A death that came to stand in place of her own death. As we walked through the streets of Paris she told me this story.

By the time of her arrest she was married and had a young son. Her husband was taken from their apartment during one of the mass arrests that began in July of 1942. Hélène was out at the time with her son. For some time she wandered the streets of Paris. She would sleep at night at the homes of various friends and acquaintances, leaving in the early morning so that she would not arouse suspicion among the neighbors. This was the hardest time, she told me, because there was so little food, even less than she was to have at Drancy. She had no ration card or any way of earning money. Her whole existence was illegal. She had to be as if invisible. She collected scraps from the street. It was on the street that she told me this story, as we walked from the fourth arrondissement to the fifth, crossing the bridge near Notre Dame, making our way toward the Boulevard St. Michel.

Her husband was a citizen of a neutral country and for this reason legally destined for another camp. From this camp he would not be deported. Instead he was taken to the French concentration camp at Drancy. After his arrest, hoping to help him, Hélène managed to take his papers to the Swiss Consulate. But the papers remained there. After her own arrest she was taken with her son to Drancy, where she was reunited with her husband. He told her that her efforts were useless. But still again and again she found ways to smuggle out letters to friends asking them to take her husband's papers from the Swiss Consulate to the camp at Drancy. One of these letters was to save their lives.

After a few months, preparations began to send Hélène and her family to Auschwitz. Along with many other women, she was taken to have her hair cut short, though those consigned to that task decided she should keep her long, blond hair. Still, she was herded along with the others to the train station and packed into the cars. Then, just two hours before the train was scheduled to leave, Hélène, her son, and her husband were pulled from the train. Her husband's papers had been brought by the Swiss consul to the camp. The Commandant, by assuming Hélène shared the same nationality with her husband, had made a fortuitous mistake.

IN HÉLÈNE'S PLACE THE GUARDS BROUGHT A YOUNG MAN. SHE WOULD NEVER FORGET HIS FACE, SHE TOLD ME, OR HIS NAME. LATER SHE TRIED TO FIND OUT WHETHER HE HAD LIVED OR DIED BUT COULD LEARN NOTHING.

But the train had to have a specific number of passengers before it could leave. In Hélène's place the guards brought a young man. She would never forget his face, she told me, or his name. Later she tried to find out whether he had lived or died but could learn nothing.

Himmler did not partake in the actual preparations for what he called "the final solution." Nor did he attend the Wannsee Conference where the decision to annihilate millions of human beings was made. He sent his assistant Heydrich. Yet Heydrich, who was there, did not count himself entirely present. He could say that each decision he made was at the bequest of Heinrich Himmler. In this way an odd system of insulation was created. These crimes, these murders of millions, were all carried out in absentia, as if by no one in particular.

This ghostlike quality, the strange absence of a knowing conscience, as if the living creature had abandoned the shell, was spread throughout the entire chain of command. So a French bureaucrat writing a letter in 1942 speaks in detail of the mass arrests that he himself supervised as if he had no other part in these murders except as a kind of spiritless cog in a vast machine whose force compelled him from without. *The German authorities have set aside especially for that purpose enough trains to transport 30,000 Jews,* he writes. *It is therefore necessary that the arrests made should correspond to the capacity of the trains.*

It is August 23, 1943. The first inmates of concentration camp Dora have arrived. Is there some reason why an unusually high percentage of prisoners ordered to work in this camp are homosexuals? They are set to work immediately, working with few tools, often with bare hands, to convert long tunnels carved into the Harz Mountains into a factory for the manufacture of missiles. They work for eighteen hours each day. Six of these hours are set aside for formal procedures, roll calls, official rituals of the camp. For six hours they must try to sleep in the tunnels, on the damp earth, in the same area where the machines, pickaxes, explosions, and drills are making a continually deafening noise, twenty-four hours of every day. They are fed very little. They see the daylight only once a week, at the Sunday roll call. The tunnels themselves are illuminated with faint light bulbs. The production of missiles has been moved here because the factories at Peenemünde were bombed. Because the secret work at Peenemünde had been revealed to the Allies by an informer, after the bombing the Reichsführer SS proposed that the factories should be installed in a concentration camp. Here, he argued, security could be more easily enforced; only the guards had any freedom, and they were subject to the harsh discipline of the SS. The labor itself could be hidden under the soil of the Harz Mountains.

Memory can be like a long, half-lit tunnel, a tunnel where one is likely to encounter phantoms of a self, long concealed, no longer nourished with the force of consciousness, existing in a tortured state between life and death. In his account of his years at Peenemünde, Wernher von Braun never mentions concentration camp Dora. Yet he was seen there more than once by inmates who remembered him. As the designing engineer, he had to supervise many details of production. Conditions at camp Dora could not have escaped his attention. Dora did not have its own crematorium. And so many men and women died in the course of a day that the bodies waiting to be picked up by trucks and taken to the ovens of Buchenwald were piled high next to the entrance to the tunnels.

Perhaps von Braun told himself that what went on in those tunnels had nothing to do with him. He had not wished for these events, had not wanted them. The orders came from someone who had power over him. In the course of this writing I remembered a childhood incident that made me disown myself in the same way. My best friend, who was my neighbor, had a mean streak and because of this had a kind of power over the rest of us who played with her. For a year I left my grandmother's house to live with my mother again. On my return I had been replaced by another little girl, and the two of them excluded me. But finally my chance arrived. My friend had a quarrel with her new friend and enlisted me in an act of revenge. Together we cornered her at the back of a yard, pushing her into the garbage cans, yelling nasty words at her, throwing things at her.

My friend led the attack, inventing the strategies and the words which were hurled. With part of myself I knew what it was to be the object of this kind of assault. But I also knew this was the way to regain my place with my friend. Later I disowned my acts, as if I had not committed them. Because I was under the sway of my friend's power, I told myself that what I did was really her doing. And in this way became unreal to myself. It was as if my voice threatening her, my own anger, and my voice calling names, had never existed.

I was told this story by a woman who survived the holocaust. The war had not yet begun. Nor the exiles. Nor the mass arrests. But history was on the point of these events, tipping over, ready to fall into the relentless path of consequences. She was then just a child, playing games in the street. And one day she found herself part of a circle of other children. They had surrounded a little boy and were calling him names because he was Jewish. He was her friend. But she thought if she left this circle, or came to his defense, she herself would lose her standing among the others. Then, suddenly, in an angry voice her mother called her in from the street. As soon as the door shut behind her, her mother began to shout, words incomprehensible to her, and slapped her across the face. *Your father*, her mother finally said, after crying, and in a quieter voice, *was Jewish.* Her father had been dead for three years. Soon after this day her mother too would die. As the danger grew worse her gentile relatives would not harbor her any longer, and she joined the fate of those who tried to live in the margins, as if invisible, as if mere shadows, terrified of a direct glance, of recognition, existing at the unsteady boundary of consciousness.

In disowning the effects we have on others, we disown ourselves. My father watched the suffering of my childhood and did nothing. He was aware of my mother's alcoholism and the state of her mind when she drank. He knew my grandmother to be tyrannical. We could speak together of these things almost dispassionately, as if both of us were disinterested witnesses to a fascinating social drama. But after a day's visit with him, spent at the park, or riding horses, or at the movies, he would send me back into that world of suffering we had discussed so dispassionately.

His disinterest in my condition was not heartless. It reflected the distance he kept from his own experience. One could sense his suffering but he never expressed it directly. He was absent to a part of himself. He was closer to tears than many men, but he never shed those tears. If I cried he would fall into a frightened silence. And because of this, though I spent a great deal of time with him, he was always in a certain sense an absent father. Unknowingly I responded in kind, for years, feeling a vaguely defined anger that would neither let me love nor hate him.

My father learned his disinterest under the guise of masculinity. Boys don't cry. There are whole disciplines, institutions, rubrics in our culture which serve as categories of denial.

Science is such a category. The torture and death that Heinrich Himmler found disturbing to witness became acceptable to him when it fell under this rubric. He liked to watch the scientific experiments in the concentration camps. And then there is the rubric of military order. I am looking at a photograph. It was taken in 1941 in the Ukraine. The men of an *einsatzgruppen* are assembled in a group pose. In front of them their rifles rest in ceremonial order, composed into tripods. They stand straight and tall. They are clean-shaven and their uniforms are immaculate, in *apple-pie order*, as we would say in America.

It is not surprising that cleanliness in a profession that sheds blood would become a compulsion. Blood would evidence guilt and fear to a mind trying to escape the consequence of its decisions. It is late in the night when Laura tells me one more story. Her father is about to be sent to Europe, where he will fight in the Battle of the Bulge and become a general. For weeks her mother has prepared a party. The guests begin to arrive in formal dress and sparkling uniforms. The white-gloved junior officers stand to open the doors. Her mother, regal in satin and jewels, starts to descend the staircase. Laura sits on the top stair watching, dressed in her pajamas. Then suddenly a pool of blood appears at her mother's feet, her mother falls to the floor, and almost as quickly, without a word uttered, a junior officer sweeps up the stairs, removes her mother into a waiting car, while another one cleans up the blood. No one tells Laura that her mother has had a miscarriage, and the party continues as if no event had taken place, no small or large death, as if no death were about to take place, nor any blood be spilled.

But the nature of the material world frustrates our efforts to remain free of the suffering of others. The mobile killing van that Himmler summoned into being had some defects. Gas from the exhaust pipes leaked into the cabin where the drivers sat and made them ill. When they went to remove the bodies from the van they were covered with blood and excrement, and their faces bore expressions of anguish. Himmler's engineers fixed the leak, increased the flow of gas so the deaths would be quicker, and built in a drain to collect the bodily fluids that are part of death.

There are times when no engineers can contain death. Over this same landscape through which the mobile killing vans traveled, an invisible cloud would one day spread, and from it would descend a toxic substance that would work its way into the soil and the water, the plants and the bodies of animals, and into human cells, not only in this landscape of the Ukraine, but in the fjords of Norway, the fields of Italy and France, and even here, in the far reaches of California, bringing a death that recalled, more than forty years later, those earlier hidden deaths.

You can see pictures of them. Whole families, whole communities. The fabric on their backs almost worn through. Bodies as if ebbing away before your eyes. Poised on an edge. The cold visible around the thin joints of arms and knees. A bed made in a doorway. Moving then, over time, deeper and deeper into the shadows. Off the streets. Into back rooms, and then to the attics or the cellars. Windows blackened. Given less and less to eat. Moving into smaller and smaller spaces. Sequestered away like forbidden thoughts, or secrets.

Could he have seen in these images of those he had forced into hiding and suffering, into agony and death, an image of the outer reaches of his own consciousness? It is only now that I can begin to see he has become part of them. Those whose fate he sealed. Heinrich Himmler. A part of Jewish history. Remembered by those who fell into the net of his unclaimed life. Claimed as a facet of the wound, part of the tissue of the scar. A mark on the body of our minds, both those of us who know this history and those who do not.

For there is a sense in which we are all witnesses. Hunger, desperation, pain, loneliness, these are all visible in the streets about us. The way of life we live, a life we have never really chosen, forces us to walk past what we see. And out at the edge, beyond what we see or hear, we can feel a greater suffering, cries from a present or past starvation, a present or past torture, cries of those we have never met, coming to us in our dreams, and even if these cries do not survive in our waking knowledge, still, they live on in the part of ourselves we have ceased to know.

I think now of the missile again and how it came into being. Scientific inventions do not spring whole like Athena from the head of Zeus from the analytic implications of scientific discoveries. Technological advance takes shape slowly in the womb of society and is influenced and fed by our shared imagination. What we create thus mirrors the recesses of our own minds, and perhaps also hidden capacities. Television mimics the ability to see in the mind's eye. And the rocket? Perhaps the night flight of the soul, that ability celebrated in witches to send our thoughts as if through the air to those distant from us, to send images of ourselves, and even our secret feelings, out into an atmosphere beyond ourselves, to see worlds far flung from and strange to us becomes manifest in a sinister fashion in the missile.

Self-portrait in charcoal. Since the earliest rendering she made of her own image, much time has passed. The viewer here has moved closer. Now the artist's head fills the frame. She is much older in years and her features have taken on that androgyny which she thought necessary to the work of an artist. Her hair is white on the paper where the charcoal has not touched it. She is in profile and facing a definite direction. Her eyes look in that direction. But they do not focus on anyone or anything. The portrait is soft, the charcoal rubbed almost gently over the surface, here light, here dark. Her posture is one not so much of resolution as resignation. The portrait was drawn just after the First World War, the war in which her son Peter died. I have seen these eyes in the faces of those who grieve, eyes that are looking but not focused, seeing perhaps what is no longer visible.

After the war, German scientists who developed the V-1 and V-2 rocket immigrate to the United States where they continue to work on rocketry. Using the Vengeance weapon as a prototype, they develop the first ICBM missiles.

On the twenty-third of May 1945, as the war in Europe comes to an end, Heinrich Himmler is taken prisoner by the Allied command. He has removed the military insignia from his clothing, and he wears a patch over one eye. Disguised in this manner, and carrying the identity papers of a man he had condemned to death, he attempts to cross over the border at Bremervörde. No one at the checkpoint suspects him of being the Reichsführer SS. But once under the scrutiny of the guards, all his courage fails him. Like a trembling schoolboy, he blurts out the truth. Now he will be taken to a center for interrogation, stripped of his clothing and searched. He will refuse to wear the uniform of the enemy, so he will be given a blanket to wrap over his underclothing. Taken to a second center for interrogation, he will be forced to remove this blanket and his underclothes. The interrogators, wishing to make certain he has no poison hidden anywhere, no means by which to end his life and hence avoid giving testimony, will surround his naked body. They will ask him to open his mouth. But just as one of them sees a black capsule wedged between his teeth, he will jerk his head away and swallow. All attempts to save his life will fail. He will not survive to tell his own story. His secrets will die with him.

There were many who lived through those years who did not wish to speak of what they saw or did. None of the German rocket engineers bore witness to what they saw at concentration camp Dora. Common rank and file members of the Nazi Party, those without whose efforts or silent support the machinery could not have gone on, fell almost as a mass into silence. In Berlin and Munich I spoke to many men and women, in my generation or younger, who were the children of soldiers, or party members, or SS men, or generals, or simply believers. Their parents would not speak to them of what had happened. The atmosphere in both cities was as if a pall had been placed over memory. And thus the shared mind of this nation has no roots, no continuous link with what keeps life in a pattern of meaning.

Lately I have come to believe that an as yet undiscovered human need and even a property of matter is the desire for revelation. The truth within us has a way of coming out despite all conscious efforts to conceal it. I have heard stories from those in the generation after the war, all speaking of the same struggle to ferret truth from the silence of their parents so that they themselves could begin to live. One born the year the war ended was never told a word about concentration camps, at home or in school. She began to wake in the early morning hours with nightmares which mirrored down to fine and accurate detail the conditions of the camps. Another woman searching casually through some trunks in the attic of her home found a series of pamphlets, virulently and cruelly anti-Semitic, which had been written by her grandfather, a high Nazi official. Still another pieced together the truth of her father's life, a member of the Gestapo, a man she remembered as playful by contrast to her stern mother. He died in the war. Only over time could she put certain pieces together. How he had had a man working under him beaten. And then, how he had beaten her.

Many of those who survived the holocaust could not bear the memories of what happened to them and, trying to bury the past, they too fell into silence. Others continue to speak as they are able. The manner of speech varies. At an artist's retreat in the Santa Cruz Mountains I met a woman who survived Bergen Belsen and Auschwitz. She inscribes the number eight in many of her paintings. And the number two. This is the story she is telling with those numbers. It was raining the night she arrived with her mother, six brothers and sisters at Auschwitz. It fell very hard, she told me. We were walking in the early evening up a hill brown in the California fall. The path was strewn with yellow leaves illuminated by the sun in its descent. They had endured the long trip from Hungary to Poland, without food or water. They were very tired. Now the sky seemed very black but the platform, lit up with stadium lights, was blinding after the darkness of the train. She would never, she told me, forget the shouting. It is as if she still cannot get the sound out of her ears. The Gestapo gave one shrill order after another, in a language she did not yet understand. They were herded in confusion, blows coming down on them randomly from the guards, past a tall man in a cape. This was Dr. Mengele. He made a single gesture toward all her family and continued it toward her but in a different direction. For days, weeks, months after she had learned what their fate had been she kept walking in the direction of their parting and beyond toward the vanishing point of her vision of them.

There were seven from her family who died there that night. The eighth to die was her father. He was sent to a different camp and died on the day of liberation. Only two lived, she and one brother. The story of one life cannot be told separately from the story of other lives. Who are we? The question is not simple. What we call the self is part of a larger matrix of relationship and society. Had we been born to a different family, in a different time, to a different world, we would not be the same. All the lives that surround us are in us.

• • • • • • •

On the first day that I met Lenke she asked a question that stays with me still. Why do some inflict on others the suffering they have endured? What is it in a life that makes one choose to do this, or not? It is a question I cannot answer. Not even after several years pondering this question in the light of Heinrich Himmler's soul. Two years after my conversation with Lenke, as if there had been a very long pause in our dialogue, I was given a glimpse in the direction of an answer. Leo told me his story; it sounded back over time, offering not so much solution as response.

The nucleus of every cell in the human body contains the genetic plan for the whole organism.

We sat together in a large and noisy restaurant, light pouring through the windows, the present clamoring for our attention, even as we moved into the past. Leo was nine years old when the war entered his life. He remembers standing in a crowd, he told me, watching as a partisan was flogged and executed by the Germans. *What do you think I felt?* he asked me, the irony detectable in his voice. What he told me fell into his narration as part of a larger picture. The capture, the roughness, the laceration of flesh, the sight of death, all this excited him.

Violence was not new to him. Through bits and pieces surrounding the central line of his story I came to some idea of what his childhood must have been. His father was a cold man, given to rages over small errors. Leo was beaten often. Such attacks had already forced his older half brother out of the house. It was to this brother that Leo bonded and gave his love.

EVERYTHING HE HEARD FROM HIS BROTHER HE TOOK INTO HIMSELF. SUCH LOVE AS LEO HAD FOR HIS BROTHER CAN BE A FORCEFUL TEACHER.

Leo remembered a party before the war. The room was lively with talk until his older brother arrived. Then a silence fell over everyone. The older men were afraid of this young man, even his father. And to Leo, his brother, with his air of power and command, was a hero. He could scarcely understand the roots of this power, moored in a political system of terror so effective, few even spoke of it. Leo's brother was a young member of Stalin's secret police. Cast into the streets while still a boy, he learned the arts of survival. Eventually he was arrested for assaulting and robbing a man. It was under this circumstance that he offered himself to the NKVD, the forerunner of the KGB, as an interrogator. He learned to torture men and women suspected of treason or of harboring secrets.

He wore high black leather boots and a black leather jacket, which impressed Leo. Leo followed him about, and they would take long walks together, his brother telling him the stories he could tell no one else. How he had tortured a woman. How he had made blood flow from the nipples of her breasts.

Everything he heard from his brother he took into himself. Such love as Leo had for his brother can be a forceful teacher. He did not see his brother often, nor was his intimacy with him great enough to create familiarity. What he had was a continual taste awakening hunger. Never did he know the daily presence of the beloved, or all his imperfections, the real person dwelling behind the mask of the ideal, the shiny and impervious leather. To fill the nearly perpetual absence of his brother he clung to this ideal. An appearance of strength. A certain arrogance in the face of violence, promising an even greater violence. Love always seeks a resting place.

I knew a similar attachment to my sister. Separated when I was six and she was thirteen, the experience of love I knew with her was longing, and over time this bonded me to longing itself. And to the books she brought me to read, the poems she read to me, worlds she pointed me toward.

And the German occupation of the Ukraine? The accident at Chernobyl had taken place just weeks before we met. But long before this event, the same land suffered other wounds. As the Soviet army retreated, they burned crops and killed livestock. Even before the German invasion, the land was charred and black for miles around. Then when the German army came, the executions began. And the deportations. Many were taken away to forced labor camps. Leo was among them.

His father was an agronomist with some knowledge of how to increase crop yields. The whole family was transported to Germany, but at the scientist's camp Leo was transported in another direction. His father watched him go, Leo told me, with no protest, not even the protestation of tears.

What was it like for him in the labor camp to which he was sent? His telling of the past existed in a framework of meaning he had built slowly over the years, and with great pain, forced to this understanding by events that he himself had brought into being, later in his life.

It is a question of passion, he told me. While he was in the camps, he began to worship the uniformed members of the SS and the SA, just as he had loved his brother. Their strength, their ideals, their willingness to do violence, to live for something beyond themselves, the black leather they wore, the way they were clean and polished and tall. He saw those who, like himself, were imprisoned as small and demeaned, caught in the ugliness of survival, lacking any heroism, cowardly, petty. Even now, as he looked back himself with another eye, his disdain for those who suffered persisted in a phantom form, in the timbre of his voice.

The punishment of the guards did not embitter him. In his mind he believed he himself was always justly punished. Once, against the rules, he stole food, honey, while he was working. He did not accept his own hunger as an argument for kindness. He admired the strength with which he was hit. Even the intimacy of the blows gave him a certain pride in himself. Loving the arms that hit him, he could think of this power as his own.

But there were two assaults which he could not forgive. They humiliated him. Now as I write I can see that to him his attackers must have been unworthy of his admiration. He was on a work detail in the neighboring village when a boy his own age slapped him. And later an old woman spat in his face.

This was all he told me of his time of imprisonment. After the liberation, he went into Germany to search for his family. Did he believe that perhaps, even now, something outside of the circle drawn by what he had suffered existed for him? Was there a seed of hope, a wish that made him, thin, weak, on shaking legs, travel the hundreds of miles, sleeping in trains and train stations, to search? He was exhausted, I can imagine, past that edge of weariness in which whatever is real ceases entirely to matter and existence itself is just a gesture, not aimed any longer at outcome, but just a simple expression of what remains and so can seem even brighter. He was making a kind of pilgrimage.

It is in this way, coldness beyond cold, frailty beyond endurance, that sorrow becomes a power. A light begins to shine past the fire of ovens, yet from them, as if stars, or turning leaves, falling and trapped in their fall, nevertheless kept their brilliance, and this brilliance a beacon, like a code, flashes out the precise language of human suffering. Then we know that what we suffer is not going to pass by without meaning.

Self-portrait, 1923. The artist's face is drawn of lines left white on the page which seem as if they were carved out of night. We are very close to her. It is only her face we see. Eye to eye, she looks directly at us. But her eyes are unfocused and weary with that kind of tiredness that has accumulated over so much time we think of it as aging. Her mouth, wide and frank, does not resist gravity any longer. This mouth smiles with an extraordinary subtlety. We can almost laugh with this mouth, drawn with lines which, like all the lines on the page, resemble scars, or tears in a fabric.

A story is told as much by silence as by speech. Like the white spaces in an etching, such silences render form. But unlike an etching in which the whole is grasped at once, the silence of a story must be understood over time. Leo described to me what his life was like after he found his parents, but he did not describe the moment, or even the day or week, when he found them. Only now as I write these words does the absence of joy in this reunion begin to speak to me. And in the space of this absence I can feel the kind of cold that can extinguish the most intense of fires.

Leo was soon streetwise. His family was near starvation. He worked the black market. Older men buying his goods would ask him for women, and he began to procure for them. He kept his family alive. His father, he told me, never acknowledged his effort. When they moved to America a few years later and Leo reminded him that his work had fed him, his father exclaimed, in a voice of shock and disparagement, *And what you did!*

In 1957, the Soviet Union develops the SS-6, a surface-to-surface missile. It is launched with thirty-two engines. Failing as a weapon, this device is used to launch the first satellite into space. In 1961, the Soviet Union develops the

SS-7. These missiles carry nuclear warheads. They are launched from hardened silos to protect them from attack.

In America he was sent to high school. But he did not know how to be an ordinary boy among boys. He became a street fighter. Together with a group of boys among whom he was the toughest, he would look for something to happen. More than once they devised a trap for homosexual men. They would place the prettiest boy among them on a park bench and wait behind the trees and bushes. Usually a man would pull up in his car and go to sit on the bench next to the boy. When this man made any gesture of seduction, or suggested the boy leave with him, the boys would suddenly appear and, surrounding him, beat him and take his money.

I am thinking of these boys as one after another they forced the weight of their bodies into another man's body and tried to hurt him, to bloody him, to defeat him. I know it is possible to be a stranger to one's feelings. For the years after I was separated from my mother, I forgot that I missed her. My feeling was driven so deep, it was imperceptible, so much a part of me, I would not have called it grief. It is said that when boys or young men attack a man they find effeminate or believe to be homosexual they are trying to put at a distance all traces of homosexuality in themselves. But what does this mean? What is the central passion in this issue of manhood, proven or disproven? In my imagination I witness again the scene that Leo described to me. It is a passionate scene, edged by a love the boys feel for each other, and by something more, by a kind of grief, raging because it is buried so deep inside. Do they rage against this man's body because of what has been withheld from them, held back, like the food of intimacy, imprisoned and guarded in the bodies of older men, in the bodies of fathers? Is it this rage that fires the mettle of what we call manhood?

Yet, are we not all affected by this that is withheld in men? Are we not all forged in the same inferno? It was never said directly, but I know my great-grandfather beat my grandfather, and lectured him, drunkenly, humiliating and shaming him. I am told that as adults they quarreled violently over politics. No one in my family can remember the substance of the disagreement, only the red faces, the angry voices. Now, as I look back to imagine my grandfather passionately reciting the list of those he hated, our black neighbors, the Jews, the Communists, I follow the path of his staring eyes and begin to make out a figure. It is my great-grandfather Colvin, receiving even after his death too indifferently the ardent and raging pleas of his son. And hearing that voice again, I hear an echo from my grandfather's daughter, my mother, whose voice when she had been drinking too much had the same quality, as of the anguish of feeling held back for so long it has become monstrous, the furies inside her unleashed against me.

Leo's telling had a slightly bitter edge, a style which felt like the remnant of an older harshness. He kept looking at me as if to protect himself from any sign of shock in my face. Now he was not certain he would tell me the rest of his story. But he did.

Just after he graduated from high school, the Korean War began. He was drafted, and sent directly to Korea. Was he in combat? Leo shook his head. He was assigned to an intelligence unit. He spoke Russian. And he was directed to interrogate Russian prisoners who were captured behind enemy lines. He told me this story. He was given two men to question. With the first man he made every kind of threat. But he carried nothing out. The man was resolutely silent. And Leo learned nothing from him. He left the room with all his secrets. *You can never,* Leo told me later, *let any man get the better of you.* With the second man he was determined not to fail. He would get him to tell whatever he knew. He made the same threats again, and again met silence. Then, suddenly, using his thumb and finger, he put out the man's eye. And as the man was screaming and bleeding, he told him he would die one way or the other. He was going to be shot. But he had the choice now of seeing his executioners or not, of dying in agony or not. And then the man told him his secrets.

Self-portrait, 1927. She has drawn herself in charcoal again, and in profile. And she still looks out but now her eyes are focused. She is looking at something visible, distant, but perhaps coming slowly closer. Her mouth still turns down, and this must be a characteristic expression because her face is lined in that direction. The form of her face is drawn with soft strokes, blended into the page, as one life blends into another life, or a body into earth. There is something in the quality of her attention, fine lines sketched over her eyebrow. A deeper black circle under her eye. With a resolute, unhappy awareness, she recognizes what is before her.

The life plan of the body is encoded in the DNA molecule, a substance that has the ability to hold information and to replicate itself.

Self-portrait, 1934. As I look now I see in her face that whatever it was she saw before has now arrived. She looks directly at us again and we are even closer to her than before. One finger at the edge of the frame pulls against her eyebrow, against lines drawn there earlier, as if to relieve pain. All the lines lead downward, like rain. Her eyes are open but black, at once impenetrable and infinite. There is a weariness here again, the kind from which one never recovers. And grief? It is that grief I have spoken of earlier, no longer apart from the flesh and bone of her face.

After many years of silence, my mother and I were able to speak of what happened between us and in our family. It was healing for us, to hear and speak the truth, and made for a closeness we had not felt before. Both of us knew we were going to speak before we did.

Before a secret is told one can often feel the weight of it in the atmosphere. Leo gazed at me for a long moment. There was more he wanted to tell me and that I wanted to hear. The rest of his story was elsewhere, in the air, in our hands, the traffic on the street, felt. He shook his head again before he began. The war was over, but he had started in a certain direction and now he could not stop. He befriended a young man from the army. This man looked up to him the way he had to his brother. He wanted to teach the younger man what he knew. He had already committed several robberies, and he wanted an accomplice. They went out together, looking for an easy target for the young man to practice on. They found someone who was easy. He was old, and black. Leo showed his friend how to hold his gun, up close to the temple, pointing down. The boy did this. But the old man, terrified, simply ran. As Leo directed him, the younger man held the gun out in front of him to shoot and he pulled the trigger. But the cartridge of the bullet stuck in the chamber. So the man, still alive, kept running. Then, as Leo urged him on, his friend ran after the old man and, jumping on his back, began to hit him on the head with the butt of his pistol. The moment overtook him. Fear, and exhilaration at mastering fear, a deeper rage, all made a fuel for his fury. He hit and hit again and again. He drew blood. Then the man ceased to cry out, ceased to struggle. He lay still. And the younger man kept on hitting, so that the moment of the older man's death was lost in a frenzy of blows. Then finally there was silence. The young man, knowing he had caused a death, stood up shaking and walked away. He was stunned, as if he himself had been beaten. And Leo, who had been calling and shouting to encourage his friend, who had been laughing, he said, so hard he had to hold himself, was silent too. He went to stand by the body of the old man. Blood poured profusely from the wounds on his head. He stared into the face of this dead man. And now in his telling of the story he was crying. He paused. What was it there in that face for him, broken, afraid, shattered, flesh and bone past repair, past any effort, any strength? *I could see,* he told me, *that this man was just like me.*

In 1963 America develops a new missile, the Titan II. It has a larger range, a larger carrying capacity, a new guidance system, and an improved vehicle for reentry. These missiles are still being deployed.

1938. *Self-portrait.* The artist is once again in profile. But now she faces another direction. The bones of her cheeks, mouth, nose, eyes are still all in shadow. Her eyebrows arch in tired anticipation. She has drawn herself with the simplest of strokes. Charcoal blending softly downward, all the strokes moving downward. This is old age. Not a single line drawn for vanity, or for the sake of pretense, protects us from her age. She is facing toward death.

We knew, both Leo and I, that now he was telling me what was most crucial to him. In the telling, some subtle change passed through him. Something unknown was taking shape here, both of us witnesses, both of us part of the event. This that he lived through was what I was seeking to understand. What he saw in the face of the dead man did not leave him. For a long time he was afraid of his own dreams. Every night, the same images returned to him, but images in motion, belonging to a longer narration. He dreamed that he entered a park and began to dig up a grave there. Each night he would plunge his hands in the earth and find the body buried there. But each night the body he found was more and more eroded. This erosion filled him with horror. He could not sleep alone. Every night he would find a different woman to sleep with him. Every night he would drink himself into insensibility. But the images of dreams began to come to him even in his waking hours. And so he began to drink ceaselessly. Finally he could not go on as before. Two months after the death he had witnessed he confessed his part in it.

For many reasons his sentence was light. Both he and his friend were young. They had been soldiers. He knew that, had the man he helped to kill not been black, his sentence would have been longer; or he may himself have been put to death. He said nothing of his years of imprisonment. Except that these years served to quiet the dreams that had haunted him. His wit, his air of toughness, all he had seen make him good at the work he does now with boys who have come into conflict with society, a work which must in some way be intended as restitution.

Yet, as he spoke, I began to see that he believed some part of his soul would never be retrieved. *There is a circle of humanity,* he told me, *and I can feel its warmth. But I am forever outside.*

I made no attempt to soften these words. What he said was true. A silence between us held what had been spoken. Then gradually we began to make small movements. Hands reaching for a key, a cigarette. By a quiet agreement, his story was over, and we were in the present again.

The telling and the hearing of a story is not a simple act. The one who tells must reach down into deeper layers of the self, reviving old feelings, reviewing the past. Whatever is retrieved is reworked into a new form, one that narrates events and gives the listener a path through these events that leads to some fragment of wisdom. The one who hears takes the story in, even to a place not visible or conscious to the mind, yet there. In this inner place a story from another life suffers a subtle change. As it enters the memory of the listener it is augmented by reflection, by other memories, and even the body hearing and responding in the moment of the telling. By such transmissions, consciousness is woven.

Over a year has passed now since I heard Leo's story. In my mind's eye, I see the events of his life as if they were carved out in woodblock prints, like the ones Käthe Kollwitz did. Of all her work, these most resemble Expressionist art. Was it intended that the form be so heavy, as if drawn centuries back into a mute untold history? Her work, and the work of the Expressionist movement, was called degenerate by the Nazis. These images, images of tumultuous inner feelings, or of suffering caused and hidden by social circumstance, were removed from the walls of museums and galleries.

When I was in Munich, a German friend told me that her generation has been deprived of German culture. What existed before the Third

Reich was used in Nazi propaganda, and so has become as if dyed with the stain of that history. The artists and writers of the early twentieth century were silenced; they went into exile or perished. The link with the past was broken. Yet, even unremembered, the past never disappears. It exists still and continues under a mantle of silence, invisibly shaping lives.

The DNA molecule is made of long, fine, paired strands. These strands are helically coiled.

What is buried in the past of one generation falls to the next to claim. The children of Nazis and survivors alike have inherited a struggle between silence and speech.

The night I met Hélène at a Métro station in Paris I was returning from dinner with a friend. Ten years older than I, Jewish, French, in 1942, the year before my own birth, Natalie's life was put in danger. She was given false papers and shepherded with other children out of Paris through an underground movement. She lived out the duration of war in the countryside in the home of an ambassador who had diplomatic immunity. A woman who has remained one of her closest friends to this day was with her in this hiding place. The night we had dinner Natalie told me a story about her. This friend, she said, grew up determined to shed her past. She made Natalie promise never to reveal who she was or what had happened to her. She changed her name, denied that she was Jewish, and raised her children as gentiles. Then, opening her hands in a characteristic gesture, Natalie smiled at me. The story was to take a gently ironic turn. The past was to return. This summer, she told me, she had held one end of a bridal canopy, what in a Jewish wedding is called a chuppa, at the wedding of her friend's daughter. This girl was marrying the son of an Orthodox rabbi. And her son too, knowing nothing of his mother's past, had gravitated toward Judaism.

WHAT IS BURIED IN THE PAST OF ONE GENERATION FALLS TO THE NEXT TO CLAIM.

In 1975 the SS-19 missile is deployed in the Soviet Union. It carries several warheads, each with a different target. A computer within it controls and detects deviations from its programmed course.

One can find traces of every life in each life. There is a story from my own family history that urges its way onto the page here. Sometime in the eighteenth century three brothers migrated from Scotland to the United States. They came from Aberdeen and bore the name Marks, a name common in that city to Jewish families who had immigrated from Germany to escape the pogroms. Jacob Marks, who descended from these brothers, was my great-great-grandfather. The family story was that he was descended from Huguenots. In our family, only my sister and I speak of the possibility that he could have been Jewish. Jacob married Rosa and they gave birth to a daughter whom they named Sarah. She married Thomas Colvin, and their last son was Ernest Marks Colvin, my grandfather, the same grandfather who would recite to me his furious list of those he hated, including Jews.

Who would my grandfather, I wonder now, have been if he had known his own history. Could he then have seen the shape of his life as part of a larger configuration? Wasn't he without this knowledge like the missile, or the neutron torn away from gravity, the matrix that sustains and makes sense of experience?

In any given cell only a small fraction of the genes are active. Messages to awaken these genes are transmitted by the surrounding cytoplasm, messages from other cells, or from outside substances.

I cannot say for certain what our family history was. I know only that I did gravitate myself toward what seemed missing or lost in me. In my first years of high school I lived alone with my father. He was often gone, at work or staying with his girlfriend. I adopted the family of a school friend, spending hours with them, baby-sitting their younger children, helping with household tasks, sharing meals, spending an evening speaking of art or politics. Then one evening, as I returned home, I saw a strange man standing near my door. He had come to tell me my father was dead, struck by an automobile while he was crossing the street in the light of dusk. I turned for solace and finally shelter to my adopted family. In the short time we lived together, out of my love for them, I took on their gestures, the manner and rhythm of their thought, ways of cooking, cadences, a sprinkling of Yiddish vocabulary. I became in some ways Jewish.

In the late seventies the United States develops a circuitry for the Minuteman rocket which allows for a target to be changed in the midst of flight.

Is there any one of us who can count ourselves outside the circle circumscribed by our common past? Whether or not I was trying to reweave threads severed from my family history, a shared heritage of despair and hope, of destruction and sustenance, was within me. What I received from my adopted family helped me to continue my life. My suffering had been placed, even wordlessly, in a larger stream of suffering, and as if wrapped and held by a culture that had grown up to meet suffering, to retell the tales and place them in a larger context by which all life continues.

L'chayim. Life. Held to even at the worst times. The dream of a better world. The schoolbook, tattered, pages flying loose, gripped in the hands of a young student, his coat open at the shoulder and along the front where the fabric was worn. The ghetto of Slonim. 1938. The Passover cup, fashioned secretly by inmates at Terezin, the Passover plate, the menorah, made at the risk of death from purloined materials. Pictures drawn by those who were there. Despair, the attrition of pain, daily cold, hunger somehow entering the mark of pencil or brush. Butterflies painted by children who all later perished. Stitches made across Lenke's drawings, reminding us of the stitches she sustained in one operation after another, after her liberation, when she was stricken with tuberculosis of the spine. The prisoner forced to pick up discarded clothing of those sent to the gas chambers, who said that among this clothing, as he gathered it, he saw *Stars of David like a drift of yellow flowers.*

As the fertilized egg cell starts to divide, all the daughter cells have identical DNA, but the cells soon cease to look alike, and in a few weeks, a number of different kinds of cells can be recognized in the embryo.

I am thinking again of a child's body. Curled and small. Innocent. The skin soft like velvet to the touch. Eyes open and staring without reserve or calculation, quite simply, into the eyes of whoever appears in this field of vision. Without secrets. Arms open, ready to receive or give, just in the transpiration of flesh, sharing the sound of the heartbeat, the breath, the warmth of body on body.

In 1977 the Soviet Union puts the SS-NX-17 and SS N-18 into service. These are ballistic missiles to be launched from submarines. In 1978 the United States perfects the underwater launch system of the Tomahawk missile.

I could not, in the end, for some blessed reason, turn away from myself. Not at least in this place. The place of desire. I think now of the small lines etching themselves near the eyes of a woman's face I loved. And how, seeing these lines, I wanted to stroke her face. To lean myself, my body, my skin into her. A part of me unravels as I think of this, and I am taken toward longing, and beyond, into another region, past the walls of this house, or all I can see, stretching farther than the horizon where right now sea and sky blend. It is as if my cells are moving in a larger wave, a wave that takes in every history, every story.

At the end of nine months a multitude of different cells make up the newborn infant's body, including nerve cells, muscle cells, skin cells, retinal cells, liver cells, brain cells, cells of the heart that beats, cells of the mouth that opens, cells of the throat that cries . . .

When I think of that young man now, who died in the river near the island of my father's birth, died because he loved another man, I like to imagine his body bathed in the pleasure of that love. To believe that the hands that touched this young man's thighs, his buttocks, his penis, the mouth that felt its way over his body, the man who lay himself between his legs, or over, around his body did this lovingly, and that then the young man felt inside his flesh what radiated from his childlike beauty. Part angel. Bathed in a passionate sweetness. Tasting life at its youngest, most original center, the place of reason, where one is whole again as at birth.

In the last decade the Soviet Union improves its antiballistic missiles to make them maneuverable and capable of hovering in midair. The United States continues to develop and test the MX missile, with advanced inertial guidance, capable of delivering ten prearmed electronically guided warheads, each with maneuverability, possessing the power and accuracy to penetrate hardened silos. And the Soviet Union begins to design a series of smaller one-warhead mobile missiles, the SS-25, to be driven around by truck, and the SS-X-24, to be drawn on railroad tracks. And the United States develops a new warhead for the Trident missile carrying fourteen smaller warheads that can be released in a barrage along a track or a road.

A train is making its way through Germany. All along its route those who are in the cars can look out and see those who are outside the cars. And those who are outside can see those who are inside. Sometimes words are exchanged. Sometimes there is a plea for water. And sometimes, at the risk of life, water is given. Sometimes names are called out, or curses are spoken, under the breath. And sometimes there is only silence.

Who are those on the inside and where are they going? There are rumors. It is best not to ask. There are potatoes to buy with the last of the rations. There is a pot boiling on the stove. And, at any rate, the train has gone; the people have vanished. You did not know them. You will not see them again. Except perhaps in your dreams. But what do those images mean? Images of strangers. Agony that is not yours. A face that does not belong to you. And so in the daylight you try to erase what you have encountered and to forget those tracks that are laid even as if someplace in your body, even as part of yourself.

QUESTIONS FOR A SECOND READING

1. One of the challenges a reader faces with Griffin's text is knowing what to make of it. It's a long piece, but the reading is not difficult. The sections are short and straightforward. While the essay is made up of fragments, the arrangement is not deeply confusing or disorienting. Still, the piece has no single controlling idea; it does not move from thesis to conclusion. One way of reading the essay is to see what one can make of it, what it might add up to. In this sense, the work of reading is to find one idea, passage, image, or metaphor—something in the text—and use this to organize the essay.

   As you prepare to work back through the text, think about the point of reference you could use to organize your reading. Is the essay "about" Himmler? secrets? fascism? art? Germany? the United States? families and child-rearing? gay and lesbian sexuality? Can one of the brief sections be taken as a key to the text? What about the italicized sections—how are they to be used?

   You should not assume that one of these is the right way to read. Assume, rather, that one way of working with the text is to organize it around a single point of reference, something you could say that Griffin "put there" for you to notice and to use.

Or you might want to do this in your name rather than Griffin's. That is, you might, as you reread, chart the connections *you* make, connections that you feel belong to you (to your past, your interests, your way of reading), and think about where and how you are drawn into the text (and with what you take to be Griffin's interests and desires). You might want to be prepared to talk about why you sum things up the way you do.

2. Although this is not the kind of prose you would expect to find in a textbook for a history course, and although the project is not what we usually think of as a "research" project, Griffin is a careful researcher. The project is serious and deliberate; it is "about" history, both family history and world history. Griffin knows what she is doing. So what *is* Griffin's project? As you reread, look to those sections where Griffin seems to be speaking to her readers about her work—about how she reads and how she writes, about how she gathers her materials and how she studies them. What is she doing? What is at stake in adopting such methods? How and why might you teach someone to do this work?

ASSIGNMENTS FOR WRITING

1. Griffin's text gathers together related fragments and works on them, but does so without yoking examples to a single, predetermined argument or thesis. In this sense, it is a kind of anti-essay. One of the difficulties readers of this text face is in its retelling. If someone says to you, "Well, what was it about?" the answer is not easy or obvious. The text is so far-reaching, so carefully composed of interrelated stories and reflections, and so suggestive in its implications and in the connections it enables that it is difficult to summarize without violence, without seriously reducing the text.

   But, imagine that somebody asks, "Well, what was it about?" Write an essay in which you present your reading of "Our Secret." You want to give your reader a sense of what the text is like (or what it is like to read the text), and you want to make clear that the account you are giving is your reading, your way of working it through. You might, in fact, want to suggest what you leave out or put to the side. (The first second-reading question might help you prepare for this.)

2. Griffin argues that we—all of us, especially all of us who read her essay—are part of a complex web of connections. At one point she says,

   > Who are we? The question is not simple. What we call the self is part of a larger matrix of relationship and society. Had we been born to a different family, in a different time, to a different world, we would not be the same. All the lives that surround us are in us. (p. 371)

At another point she asks, "Is there any one of us who can count ourselves outside the circle circumscribed by our common past?" She speaks of a "field,"

> like a field of gravity that is created by the movements of many bodies. Each life is influenced and it in turn becomes an influence. Whatever is a cause is also an effect. Childhood experience is just one element in the determining field. (p. 340)

One way of thinking about this concept of the self (and of interrelatedness), at least under Griffin's guidance, is to work on the connections that she implies and asserts. As you reread the selection, look for powerful and surprising juxtapositions, fragments that stand together in interesting and suggestive ways. Think about the arguments represented by the blank space between those sections. (And look for Griffin's written statements about "relatedness.") Look for connections that seem important to the text (and to you) and representative of Griffin's thinking (and yours). Then, write an essay in which you use these examples to think through your understanding of Griffin's claims for this "larger matrix," the "determining field," or our "common past."

3. It is useful to think of Griffin's prose as experimental. She is trying to do something that she can't do in the "usual" essay form. She wants to make a different kind of argument or engage her reader in a different manner. And so she mixes personal and academic writing. She assembles fragments and puts seemingly unrelated material into surprising and suggestive relationships. She breaks the "plane" of the page with italicized intersections. She organizes her material, but not in the usual mode of thesis-example-conclusion. The arrangement is not nearly so linear. At one point, when she seems to be prepared to argue that German child-rearing practices produced the Holocaust, she quickly says:

> Of course there cannot be one answer to such a monumental riddle, nor does any event in history have a single cause. Rather a field exists, like a field of gravity that is created by the movements of many bodies. Each life is influenced and it in turn becomes an influence. Whatever is a cause is also an effect. Childhood experience is just one element in the determining field. (p. 340)

Her prose serves to create a "field," one where many bodies are set in relationship.

It is useful, then, to think about Griffin's prose as the enactment of a method, as a way of doing a certain kind of intellectual work. One way to study this, to feel its effects, is to imitate it, to take it as a model. For this assignment, write a Griffin-like essay, one similar in its methods of organization and argument. You will need to think about the stories you might tell, about the stories and texts you might gather (stories and texts not your own). As you write, you will want to think carefully about arrangement and about commentary (about where, that is, you will speak to your reader *as* the writer of the piece). You should not feel bound to Griffin's subject matter, but you should feel that you are working in her spirit.

MAKING CONNECTIONS

1. Is it surprising that prisons resemble factories, schools, barracks, hospitals, which all resemble prisons? (p. 309)

— MICHEL FOUCAULT
Panopticism

The child, Dr. Schreber advised, *should be permeated by the impossibility of locking something in his heart. . . .*

That this philosophy was taught in school gives me an interior view of the catastrophe to follow. It adds a certain dimension to my image of these events to know that a nation of citizens learned that no part of themselves could be safe from the scrutiny of authority, nothing locked in the heart, and at the same time to discover that the head of the secret police of this nation was the son of a schoolmaster. It was this man, after all, Heinrich Himmler, Reichsführer SS, who was later to say, speaking of the mass arrests of Jews, *Protective custody is an act of care.* (p. 342)

— SUSAN GRIFFIN
Our Secret

Both Griffin and Foucault write about the "fabrication" of human life and desire within the operations of history and of specific social institutions—the family, the school, the military, the factory, the hospital. Both are concerned with the relationship between forces that are hidden, secret, and those that are obvious, exposed. Both write with an urgent concern for the history of the present, for the ways our current condition is tied to history, politics, and culture.

And yet these are very different pieces to read. They are written differently—that is, they differently invite a reader's participation and understanding. They take different examples from history. They offer different accounts of the technologies of order and control. It can even be said that they do their work differently and that they work toward different ends.

Write an essay in which you use one of the essays to explain and to investigate the other—where you use Griffin as a way of thinking about Foucault or Foucault as a way of thinking about Griffin. "To explain," "to investigate"—perhaps you would prefer to think of this encounter as a dialogue or a conversation, a way of bringing the two texts together. You should imagine that your readers are familiar with both texts, but have not yet thought of the two together. You should imagine that your readers do not have the texts in front of them, that you will need to do the work of presentation and summary.

2. Both Gloria Anzaldúa in the two chapters reprinted here from her book *Borderlands/La frontera* (p. 72) and Susan Griffin in "Our Secret" write mixed texts, or what might be called "montages." Neither of their pieces proceeds as simply a story or an essay, although both have elements of

fiction and nonfiction in them (and, in Anzaldúa's case, poetry). They both can be said to be making arguments and to be telling stories. Anzaldúa, in her chapters, is directly concerned with matters of identity and the ways identity is represented through sexuality, religion, and culture. Griffin is concerned with the "self" as "part of a larger matrix of relationship and society."

Write an essay in which you present and explain Anzaldúa's and Griffin's key arguments about the relation of identity, history, culture, and society. What terms and examples do they provide? What arguments or concerns? What different positions do they take? And what about their writing styles? How might their concerns be reflected in the ways they write?

3. John Edgar Wideman, in "Our Time" (p. 657), uses personal history to think about and to represent forces beyond the individual that shape human life and possibility—family, national history, and race. Susan Griffin is engaged in a similar project; she explains her motives this way: "One can find traces of every life in each life."

   Perhaps. It is a bold step to think that this is true and to believe that one can, or should, write the family into the national or international narrative. Write an essay in which you read "Our Secret" alongside Wideman's "Our Time." Your goal is not only to discuss how these writers do what they do, and to what conclusions and to what ends, but also to discuss your sense of what is at stake in each project. How does a skilled writer handle such a project? What are the technical issues? What would lead a writer to write like this? Would you do the same? Where and how? For whose benefit?

4. One way to imagine Susan Griffin's project in "Our Secret" is to think of her study of Heinrich Himmler as a journey through texts. She spends a significant amount of time attending to Himmler's journals and writings, looking at the way he stood in photographs, closely reading the words he chose as a child and later as a Nazi soldier. Griffin says she herself has been "searching" through these documents. She writes:

   > Now as I sit here I read once again the fragments from Heinrich's boyhood diary that exist in English. I have begun to think of these words as ciphers. Repeat them to myself, hoping to find a door into the mind of this man, even as his character first forms so that I might learn how it is he becomes himself. (p. 338)

   Considering the journals and memoirs he consults, one might think of Richard E. Miller, in "The Dark Night of the Soul" (p. 420), as having a similar project to Griffin's, one of sifting through texts in order to uncover their relationships to the human beings who read and wrote these texts. Miller writes:

   > Asking why a Steve Cousins or an Eric Harris or a Dylan Klebold is violent is itself a meaningless act, not because the motivation is too deeply buried or obscurely articulated to ever be known, but

> because we no longer live in a world where human action can be explained. We have plenty of information; it just doesn't amount to anything. This is the logic of the history of increasing humiliation working itself out over time. (p. 426)

Write an essay in which you discuss Griffin's project of looking at Himmler in relation to Miller's examination of Eric Harris and Dylan Klebold. How do Miller's words above help to illuminate, expand, or complicate Susan Griffin's thoughts in "Our Secret"? What does Griffin mean when she says she thinks of Himmler's words as ciphers? In what ways do Griffin and Miller seem to be engaging in a similar inquiry or investigation? What does each text offer as its theory of writing and reading?

LAURA Kipnis

Laura Kipnis is a professor in the department of radio/television/film at Northwestern University. She is a leading cultural theorist and critic, whose writings on sex, love, pornography, and the body have captured a wide, international audience. She has received grants and fellowships from the Guggenheim Foundation, the Rockefeller Foundation, the National Endowment for the Arts, and Yaddo.

She began her career as a painter and then a video artist, with a BFA from the San Francisco Art Institute and an MFA from the Nova Scotia College of Art and Design. Her video productions include *Your Money or Your Life* (1982), *Ecstasy Unlimited: The Interpenetration of Sex and Capital* (1985), *A Man's Woman* (1988), and *Marx: The Video* (1990). In the early 1990s, she turned to prose; her first book, *Ecstasy Unlimited: On Sex, Capital, Gender and Aesthetics* (1993), was a reworking of the arguments of her 1985 video. She has published essays and reviews available to a variety of audiences, in academic journals such as *Critical Inquiry* and *Social Text* and in general-audience magazines like *Harper's*, *The Nation*, and the *New York Times Magazine*. Her other books include *Bound and Gagged: Pornography and the Politics of Fantasy in America* (1996), *Against Love: A Polemic* (2003), and *The Female Thing: Dirt, Sex, Envy, Vulnerability* (2006). Her current project is *How to Become a Scandal*, a book that examines our preoccupation with the sexual behavior of public figures.

Of all her books, *Against Love*, from which the following selections are taken, is the most striking and unusual in method, voice, and style. Jeffrey Williams asked her about this in a 2003 interview for *Minnesota Review*. She said,

> Yes, there's a performance aspect to the writing — the voice isn't precisely "me," it's some far more vivacious and playful version of me. It's a polemic, so there are certain questions I don't have to address, or complications I don't have to go into. I can be completely irresponsible. I love it.

And, she added,

> I would say that something's happened to my relation to writing recently, which is moving more into a condition of unconsciousness

about it, or lately being more interested in creativity than theory. I trace it back to my art school origins. I started as a painter, actually, and there's something about the writing I've been doing lately which has gotten really intricate and worked over, that reminds me of my origins as a painter. I've started to write in a painterly way, dabbing at it, endless revising. But there's another aspect, something about the performance of voice that also has a degree of unconsciousness about it, a form of play, I'd like to think.

Also, I think I was trying to recapture something of the experience of being in love, and writing from the psychical or libidinal position of, for example, somebody writing love letters, trying to capture the complicated act that writing is in that kind of moment. You know, where you're trying to entice and seduce somebody and win their love or keep their love, or when you know somebody's way in love with you and you're feeling incredibly charming and sexy. I was trying to reproduce that experience in the writing.

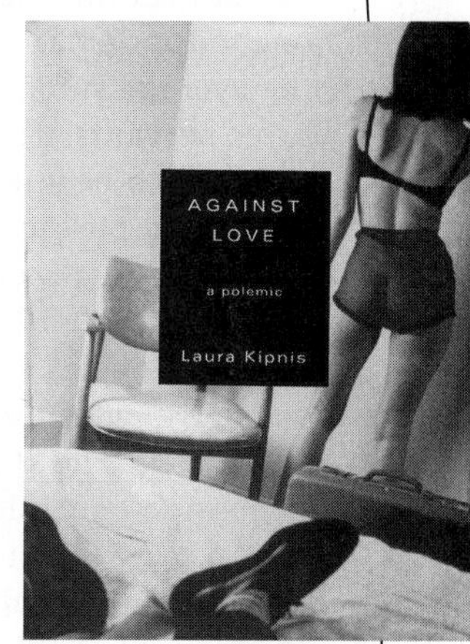

Seduction and enticement. How often are you offered this in a textbook!

Against Love is not an advice column or a self-help book. Kipnis announces it as a "polemic," a sharply worded, controversial argument, one that is more interested in being effective than in being fair. This genre, however, allows her to ask big questions about the limits imposed on our thoughts and actions.

Reader Advisory

Please fasten your seatbelts: we are about to encounter contradictions. The subject is love, and things may get bumpy.

To begin with, who would dream of being against love? No one. Love is, as everyone knows, a mysterious and all-controlling force, with vast power over our thoughts and life decisions. Love is boss, and a demanding one too: it demands our loyalty. We, in turn, freely comply — or as freely as the average subject in thrall to an all-powerful master, as freely as indentured servants. It's a new form of mass conscription: meaning it's out of the question to be summoned by love, issued your marching orders, and then decline to pledge body and being to the cause. There's no way of being against love precisely because we moderns are constituted as beings yearning to be filled, craving connection, needing to adore and be adored, because love is vital plasma and everything else in the world just tap water. We prostrate ourselves at love's portals, anxious for entry, like social strivers waiting at the ropeline outside some exclusive club hoping to gain admission to its plushy chambers, thereby confirming our essential worth and making us interesting to ourselves.

But is there also something a bit worrisome about all this uniformity of opinion? Is this the one subject about which no disagreement will be entertained, about which one truth alone is permissible? (Even cynics and anti-romantics: obviously true believers to the hilt.) Consider that the most powerful organized religions produce the occasional heretic; every ideology has its apostates; even sacred cows find their butchers. Except for love.

Hence the necessity for a polemic against it. Polemics exist to poke holes in cultural pieties and turn received wisdom on its head, even about sacrosanct subjects like love. A polemic is designed to be the prose equivalent of a small explosive device placed under your E-Z-Boy lounger. It won't injure you (well not severely); it's just supposed to shake things up and rattle a few convictions. Be advised: polemics aren't measured; they don't tell "both sides of the story." They overstate the case. They toss out provocations and occasionally mockery, usually because they're arguing against something so unquestionable and deeply entrenched it's the only way to make even a dent in the usual story. Modern love may be a company town — it may even come with company housing (also known as "domesticity") — but are we such social marionettes that we automatically buy all usual stories, no questions asked?

Please note that "against" is also a word with more than one meaning. Polemics aren't necessarily unconflicted (nor are the polemicists); rhetoric and sentiment aren't always identical twins. Thus, please read on in a conflicted and contradictory spirit. Such is the nature of our subject.

Love's Labors

Will all the adulterers in the room please stand up? This means all you cheating wives, philandering husbands, and straying domestic partners, past, present, and future. Those who find themselves fantasizing a lot, please rise also. So may those who have ever played supporting roles in the adultery melodrama: "other man," "other woman," suspicious spouse or marital detective (*"I called your office at three and they said you'd left!"*), or least fun of all, the miserable cuckold or cuckoldess. Which, of course, you may be, without (at least, consciously) knowing that you are. Feel free to take a second to mull this over, or to make a quick call: *"Hi hon, just checking in!"*

It will soon become clear to infidelity cognoscenti that we're not talking about your one-night stands here: not about those transient out-of-town encounters, those half-remembered drunken fumblings, those remaining enclaves of suburban swinging — or any of the other casual opportunities for bodies to collide in relatively impersonal ways in postmodern America. We live in sexually interesting times, meaning a culture which manages to be simultaneously hypersexualized and to retain its Puritan underpinnings, in precisely equal proportions. Estimates of the percentage of those coupled who have strayed at least once vary from 20 to 70 percent, meaning that you can basically select any statistic you like to support whatever position you prefer to take on the prevalence of such acts. Whatever the precise number — and really, must we join the social scientists and pen-protector brigades and fetishize numbers? — apparently, taking an occasional walk on the wild side while still wholeheartedly pledged to a monogamous relationship isn't an earthshaking contradiction. Many of us manage to summon merciful self-explanations as required ("Shouldn't drink on an empty stomach") or have learned over the years to deploy the strategic exception ("Out-of-town doesn't count," "Oral sex doesn't count") with hairsplitting acumen. Perhaps a few foresightful types have even made prior arrangements with the partner to cover such eventualities — the "one time rule," the "must-confess-all rule" (though such arrangements are said to be more frequent these days among our nonheterosexual denominations). Once again, statistics on such matters are spotty.[1]

But we're not talking about "arrangements" with either self or spouse, or when it's "just sex," or no big thing. We will be talking about what feels like a big thing: the love affair. Affairs of the heart. Exchanges of intimacy, reawakened passion, confessions, idealization, and declarations — along with favorite books, childhood stories, relationship complaints, and deepest selves, often requiring agonized consultation with close friends or professional listeners at outrageous hourly rates because one or both parties are married or committed to someone else, thus all this merging and ardor takes place in nervous hard-won secrecy and is turning your world upside down. In other words, we will be talking about *contradictions,* large, festering contradictions at the epicenter of love in our time. Infidelity will serve as our entry point to this teeming world of ambivalence and anxiety, and as our lens on the contemporary ethos of love — as much an imaginary space as an actual event. (Commitment's dark other, after all — its dialectical pal.) Meaning whether or not you signed up for the gala cruise, we're all in this boat one way or another — if only by virtue of vowing not to be.

So just as a thought experiment — though it will never happen to *you* and certainly never has — please imagine finding yourself in the contradictory position of having elected to live a life from which you now plot intricate and meticulous escapes: a subdivision getaway artist, a Houdini of the homefront. You didn't plan it, yet . . . somehow here you are, buffeted by conflicting emotions, and the domesticity you once so earnestly pledged to uphold now a tailor-made straitjacket whose secret combination is the ingenious (and hopefully undetectable) excuses you concoct to explain your mounting absences (or mounting phone bills for you long-distance strayers; thank God for those prepaid phone cards, an adulterer's telephonic godsend). When defenses are down, or some minor domestic irritant unaccountably becomes an epic dispute — which happens even in the best of times, not only when you're preoccupied by thoughts of where you'd rather be and with whom — or when the yearning becomes physically painful, or you're spending an inordinate amount of time sobbing in the bathroom, this turn of events may raise fundamental questions about what sort of emotional world you want to inhabit, or what fulfillments you're entitled to, or — for a daring few — even the nerve-rattling possibility of actually *changing your life.* (Alternatively, forgo hard questions and just up the Prozac dosage, which will probably take care of that resurgent libido problem too.)

INFIDELITY WILL SERVE AS OUR ENTRY POINT TO THIS TEEMING WORLD OF AMBIVALENCE AND ANXIETY, AND AS OUR LENS ON THE CONTEMPORARY ETHOS OF LOVE — AS MUCH AN IMAGINARY SPACE AS AN ACTUAL EVENT.

A note on terminology: while adultery traditionally requires the prior condition of a state-issued marriage license for at least one of the parties, for the purposes of the ensuing discussion any coupled relationship based on the assumption of sexual fidelity will count as "married." And with gay populations now demanding official entry to state-sanctioned nuptials too, no longer is this the heterosexual plight alone: welcome aboard all commitment-seeking queer, bi, and transgendered compatriots. But gay or straight, licensed or not, anywhere the commitment to monogamy reigns, adultery provides its structural transgression — sexual exclusivity being the cornerstone of modern coupledom, or such is the premise — and for the record, you can also commit it with any sex or gender your psyche can manage to organize its desires around; this may not always be the same one that shapes your public commitments.

An additional terminological point. As our focus will be on "social norms" and "mainstream conventions" of love rather than exceptions and anomalies (and on the interesting penchant for inventing conventions that simultaneously induce the desire for flight), for the purposes of discussion terms like "love" and "coupledom," or "coupled" and "married," will often be used interchangably. Though coupledom is not always the sole outcome of romantic love, nor does love necessarily persist throughout coupledom's duration; though not all couples have joined into legal marriage contracts with the state; though a few iconoclasts do manage to love to the beat of a different drummer, let's agree at the outset that the sequence "love-couple-marriage" does structure prevailing social expectations, regardless of variations in individual practices. Feel free to make whatever semantic adjustments are required should some idiosyncrasy (or prolonged adolescent rebellion or bad luck streak or terminal ambivalence) on your part necessitate a different terminology. "Domestic partners," "significant others," even you "commitment-phobes": keep reading. There are a million stories in love's majestic empire, and yours is in here too.

And while we're clarifying terms, a note on gender. These days either partner can play either gender role, masculine or feminine, regardless of sex or sexual orientation. Thus, gender will not be a significant aspect of our discussion. Whoever waits at home, whoever "has their suspicions," is the wife. Whoever "wants more freedom" is the guy. And if the married-male/single-female configuration is still the most prevalent adultery form, all indications are that female straying is on the rise: clearly all that was required were more opportunities for women to get out of the house. (And more academic degrees: sociologists report that the higher a woman's education level, the more likely she is to have affairs; when the female partner has more education than the male, she's the one more likely to stray.) While feminism typically gets the credit (or blame) for propelling women out of the domicile and into the job market, let's give credit where credit is due: thanks must go too to economic downturns and stagnating real wages — although if it now takes two incomes to support a household, maybe this was not exactly what the term "women's liberation" was designed to mean.[2]

And, finally, a note on genre. This *is* a polemic. If there is scant attention paid to the delights of coupled fidelity and the rewards of long-term intimacies or the marvelousness of love itself, please remember that the polemicist's job is not to retell the usual story, and that one is well rehearsed enough that it should not need rehearsing once more here. Should its absence cause anxiety, if frequent bouts of sputtering are occluding your reading experience, just append where necessary.

Adulterers: you may now be seated. Will all those in Good Relationships please stand? Thank you, feel free to leave if this is not your story — you for whom long-term coupledom is a source of optimism and renewal, not emotional anesthesia. Though before anyone rushes for the exits, a point of clarification: a "good relationship" would probably include having — and wanting to have — sex with your spouse or spouse-equivalent on something more than a quarterly basis. (Maybe with some variation in choreography?) It would mean inhabiting an emotional realm in which monogamy isn't giving something up (your "freedom," in the vernacular) because such cost-benefit calculations just don't compute. It would mean a domestic sphere in which faithfulness wasn't preemptively secured through routine interrogations (*"Who was that on the phone, dear?"*), surveillance (*"Do you think I didn't notice how much time you spent talking to X at the reception?"*), or impromptu search and seizure. A "happy" state of monogamy would be defined as a state you don't have to *work* at maintaining. After all, doesn't the demand for fidelity beyond the duration of desire *feel* like work — or work as currently configured for so many of us handmaidens to the global economy: alienated, routinized, deadening, and not something you would choose to do if you actually had a choice in the matter?

Yes, we all know that Good Marriages Take Work: we've been well tutored in the catechism of labor-intensive intimacy. Work, work, work: given all the heavy lifting required, what's the difference between work and "after work" again? Work/home, office/bedroom: are you ever *not* on the clock? Good relationships may take work, but unfortunately, when it comes to love, trying is always trying too hard: work doesn't work. Erotically speaking, play is what works. Or as psychoanalyst Adam Phillips puts it: "In our erotic life . . . it is no more possible to work at a relationship than it is to will an erection or arrange to have a dream. In fact when you are working at it you know it has gone wrong, that something is already missing."

Yet here we are, toiling away. Somehow — how exactly did this happen? — the work ethic has managed to brownnose its way into all spheres of human existence. No more play — *or* playing around — even when off the clock. Of course, the work ethic long ago penetrated the leisure sphere; leisure, once a respite from labor, now takes quite a lot of work itself. (Think about it the next time you find yourself repetitively lifting heavy pieces of metal after work: in other words, "working out.") Being wedded to the work ethic is not exactly a new story; this strain runs deep in middle-class culture: think about it the next time you're lying awake contemplating any of those 4 A.M. raison d'être questions about your self-worth or social value. (*"What have I really accomplished?"*)[3] But when did the rhetoric of the factory become the default language of love — and does this mean that collective bargaining should now replace marriage counseling when negotiating for improved domestic conditions?

When monogamy becomes labor, when desire is organized contractually, with accounts kept and fidelity extracted like labor from employees, with marriage a domestic factory policed by means of rigid shop-floor discipline designed to keep the wives and husbands and domestic partners of the world choke-chained to the status quo machinery — is this really what we mean by a "good relationship"?

Back in the old days, social brooders like Freud liked to imagine that there was a certain basic lack of fit between our deepest instincts and society's requirements of us, which might have left us all a little neurosis-prone, but at least guaranteed some occasional resistance to the more stifling demands of socialization. But in the old days, work itself occasionally provided motives for resistance: the struggle over wages and conditions of course, and even the length of the workday itself. Labor and capital may have eventually struck a temporary truce at the eight-hour day, but look around: it's an advance crumbling as we speak. Givebacks are the name of the game, and not just on the job either: with the demands of labor-intensive intimacy and "working on your relationship," now it's double-shifting for everyone.[4] Or should we just call it vertical integration: the same compulsory overtime and capricious directives, the dress codes and attitude assessments, those dreaded annual performance reviews — and don't forget "achieving orgasm."

But recall that back in the old days the promise of technological progress was actually supposed to be *less* work rather than more. Now that's an antiquated concept, gone the way of dodo birds and trade unionism. How can you not admire a system so effective at swallowing all alternatives to itself that it can make something as abject as "working for love" sound admirable? Punching in, punching out; trying to wrest love from the bosses when not busily toiling in the mine shafts of domesticity — or is it the other way around? It should come as no surprise, as work sociologist Arlie Russell Hochschild reports, that one of the main reasons for the creeping expansion of the official workday is that a large segment of the labor force put in those many extra hours because they're avoiding going home. (Apparently domestic life has become such a chore that staying at the office is more relaxing.)

HOW CAN YOU NOT ADMIRE A SYSTEM SO EFFECTIVE AT SWALLOWING ALL ALTERNATIVES TO ITSELF THAT IT CAN MAKE SOMETHING AS ABJECT AS "WORKING FOR LOVE" SOUND ADMIRABLE?

So when does domestic overwork qualify as a labor violation and where do you file the forms? For guidance on such questions, shall we go straight to the horse's mouth? This, of course, would be Marx, industrial society's *poète maudit,* so little read yet so vastly reviled, who started so much trouble so long ago by asking a very innocent question: "What is a working day?" For this is the simple query at the heart of *Capital* (which took three volumes to answer). As we see, Marx's question remains our own to this day: just how long should we have to work before we get to quit and goof around, and still get a living wage? Or more to our point, if private life in post-industrialism means that relationships now take work too, if love is the latest form of alienated labor, would rereading *Capital* as a marriage manual be the most appropriate response?

What people seem to forget about Marx (too busy blaming him for all those annoying revolutions) is how evocatively he writes about *feelings.* Like the feeling of overwork. The motif of workers being bled dry keeps cropping up in his funny, mordant prose, punctuated by flurries of over-the-top Gothic metaphors about menacing deadness. The workday is a veritable graveyard, menaced by gruesome creatures and ghouls from the world of the ambulatory dead; overwork produces "stunted monsters," the machinery is a big congealed mass of dead labor, bosses are "blood-sucking vampires," so ravenous to extract more work from the employees to feed their endless werewolf-like hunger for profit, that if no one fought about the length of the workday it would just go on and on, leaving us crippled monstrosities in the process, with more and more alienated labor demanded from our tapped-out bodies until we dropped dead just from exhaustion.

Funny, the metaphors of the homefront seem to have acquired a rather funereal ring these days too: *dead* marriages, *mechanical* sex, *cold* husbands, and *frigid* wives, all going through the motions and keeping up appearances. Your desire may have withered long ago, you may yearn — in inchoate, stumbling ways — for "something else," but you're indentured nevertheless. *Nothing must change.* Why? Because you've poured so much of yourself into the machinery already — your lifeblood, your history — which paradoxically imbues it with magical powers. Thus will social institutions (factories in *Capital,* but love is a social institution too) come to subsume and dominate their creators, who don't see it happening, or what they've lost, or that the thing they themselves invented and bestowed with life has taken them over like a hostile alien force, like it had a life of its own. Or so Marx diagnosed the situation at the advent of industrialism.

A doleful question lingers, and with no answer yet in sight: *Why work so hard?* Because there's no other choice? But maybe there is. After all, technological progress could reduce necessary labor to a minimum had this ever been made a social goal — if the goal of progress were freeing us from necessity instead of making a select few marvelously rich while the luckless rest toil away. Obviously the more work anyone has to do, the less gratification it yields — no doubt true even when "working on your relationship" — whereas, being freed from work would (to say the least!) alter the entire structure of human existence, not to mention jettison all those mildewed work-ethic relationship credos too — into the dustbin of history they go. "Free time and you free people," as the old labor slogan used to go. Of course, free people might pose social dangers. Who knows what mischief they'd get up? What other demands would come next?

As Marx should have said, if he didn't: "Why work when you can play? Or play around?" (Of course, playing around sometimes gets to be serious business too; about which, more to come.) Historical footnote: Marx was quite the adulterer himself.

Whining about working conditions won't make you too popular with management though, so keep your complaints to yourself. Obviously the well-publicized desperation of single life — early death for men; statistical improbability of ever finding mates for women — is forever wielded against reform-minded discontented couple-members, much as the grimness of the USSR once was against anyone misguided enough to argue for systematic social reforms in a political argument (or rash enough to point out that the "choices" presented by the liberal democracies are something less than an actual choice). *"Hey, if you don't like it here, just see how you like it over there."* Obviously, couple economies too are governed — like our economic system itself — by scarcity, threat, and internalized prohibitions, held in place by those incessant assurances that there are "no viable alternatives." (What an effective way of preventing anyone from thinking one up.) Let's note in passing that the citizenship-as-marriage analogy has been a recurring theme in liberal-democratic political theory for the last couple of hundred years or so, from Rousseau on: these may feel like entirely personal questions, but perhaps they're also not without a political dimension? (More on this to come.)

How we love and how we work can hardly be separate questions: we're social creatures after all — despite all those enlightening studies of sexual behavior in bonobos and red-winged blackbirds claiming to offer important insights into the nuances of human coupling. Harkening back to some remote evolutionary past for social explanations does seem to be a smoke screen for other agendas, usually to tout the "naturalness" of capitalist greed or the "naturalness" of traditional gender roles. Man as killer ape; woman as nurturing turtledove, or name your own bestial ancestor as circumstance requires. (When sociobiologists start shitting in their backyards with dinner guests in the vicinity, maybe their arguments about innateness over culture will start seeming more persuasive.) No, we're social creatures to a fault, and apparently such malleable ones that our very desires manage to keep lockstep with whatever particular social expectations of love prevail at the moment. What else would explain a polity so happily reconciled to social dictates that sex and labor could come to function like one inseparable unit of social machinery? Where's the protest? Where's the outrage? So effectively weeded out — and in the course of just a few short generations too — that social criticism is now as extraneous as a vestigial organ. Note that the rebellion of desire against social constrictions was once a favorite cultural theme, pulsing through so many of our literary classics — consider *Romeo and Juliet* or *Anna Karenina*. Now apparently we've got that small problem solved and can all love the way that's best for society: busy worker bees and docile nesters all.

Despite the guise of nature and inevitability that attaches itself to these current arrangements, the injunction to work at love is rather a recent cultural dictate, and though the vast majority of the world's inhabitants may organize themselves into permanent and semi-permanent arrangements of two, even the most cursory cross-cultural glance reveals that the particulars of these arrangements vary greatly. In our own day and part of the globe, they take the form of what historians of private life have labeled the "companionate couple," voluntary associations based (at least in principle) on intimacy, mutuality, and equality; falling in love as the prerequisite to a lifelong commitment that unfolds in conditions of shared domesticity, the expectation of mutual sexual fulfillment. And by the way, you will have sex with this person and this person alone for the rest of eternity (at least in principle).

The odd thing is that such overwhelming cultural uniformity is also so endlessly touted as the triumph of freedom and individuality over the shackling social conventions of the past (and as if the distinctly regulatory aspect of these arrangements didn't cancel out all such emancipatory claims in advance). Equally rickety is the alternate view that these arrangements somehow derive from natural law — love as an eternal and unchanging essence which finds its supreme realization in our contemporary approach to experiencing it. The history of love is written differently by every historian who tackles the subject; without becoming mired in their internecine debates, we can still say with certainty that nothing in the historical or the anthropological record indicates that our amorous predecessors were "working on their relationships." Nor until relatively recently was marriage the expected venue for Eros or romantic love, nor was the presumptive object of romantic love your own husband or wife (more likely someone else's), nor did anyone expect it to endure a lifetime: when practiced, it tended to be practiced episodically and largely outside the domicile.

But our focus here is not historical, so let's stick to modern love and its claims. Freedom over shackling social conventions — really? If love has power over us, what a sweepingly effective form of power this proves to be, with every modern psyche equally subject to its caprices, all of us allied in fearsome agreement that a mind somehow unsusceptible to love's new conditions is one requiring professional ministrations. Has any despot's rule ever so successfully infiltrated every crevice of a population's being, into its movements and gestures, penetrated its very soul? In fact it creates the modern notion of a soul — one which experiences itself as empty without love. Saying "no" to love isn't just heresy, it's tragedy: for our sort the failure to achieve what is most essentially human. And not just tragic, but abnormal. (Of course the concept of normalcy itself is one of the more powerful social management tools devised to date.) The diagnosis? It can only be that dread modern ailment, "fear of intimacy." Extensive treatment will be required, and possibly social quarantine to protect the others from contamination.

If without love we're losers and our lives bereft, how susceptible we'll also be to any social program promoted in its name. And not only the work ethic: take a moment to consider domestic coupledom itself. What a feat of social engineering to shoehorn an entire citizenry (minus the occasional straggler) into such uniform household arrangements, all because everyone knows that true love demands it and that any reluctance to participate signals an insufficiency of love. What a startling degree of conformity is so meekly accepted — and so desired! — by a species, *homo Americanus,* for whom other threats to individuality do so often become fighting matters, a people whose jokes (and humor is nothing if not an act of cultural self-definition) so frequently mock others for their behavioral uniformity — communism for its apparatchiks, lemmings for their skills as brainless followers — yet somehow fails to notice its own regimentation in matters at least as defining as toeing a party line, and frequently no more mindful than diving off high cliffs en masse.

Of course love may have its way with us, but it's also a historical truism that no form of power is so absolute that it completely quashes every pocket of resistance. We may prostrate ourselves to love — and thus to domestic coupledom, modern love's mandatory barracks — but it's not as though protest movements don't exist. (If you're willing to look in the right places.) Regard those furtive breakaway factions periodically staging dangerous escape missions, scaling barbed-wire fences and tunneling for miles with sharpened spoons just to emancipate themselves — even temporarily.

Yes, *adulterers*: playing around, breaking vows, causing havoc. Or . . . maybe not just playing around? After all, if adultery is a de facto referendum on the sustainability of monogamy — and it would be difficult to argue that it's not — this also makes it the nearest thing to a popular uprising against the regimes of contemporary coupledom. But let's consider this from a wider angle than the personal dimension alone. After all, social theorists and political philosophers have often occupied themselves with similar questions: the possibilities of liberty in an administered society, the social meaning of obligation, the genealogy of morality — even the status of the phrase "I do" as a performative utterance, a mainstay question of the branch of philosophy known as speech act theory. Might we entertain the possibility that posing philosophical questions isn't restricted to university campuses and learned tomes, that maybe it's something everyone does in the course of everyday life — if not always in an entirely knowing fashion? If adultery is more of a critical practice than a critical theory, well, acting out *is* what happens when knowledge or consciousness about something is foreclosed. Actually, that's what acting out is for. Why such knowledge is foreclosed is a question yet to be considered — though how much do any of us know about our desires and motivations, or the contexts that produce them? We can be pretty clueless. We say things like "Something just happened to me," as if it were an explanation.

MIGHT WE ENTERTAIN THE POSSIBILITY THAT POSING PHILOSOPHICAL QUESTIONS ISN'T RESTRICTED TO UNIVERSITY CAMPUSES AND LEARNED TOMES, THAT MAYBE IT'S SOMETHING EVERYONE DOES IN THE COURSE OF EVERYDAY LIFE?

Social historians assessing the shape of societies past often do look to examples of bad behavior and acting out, to heretics, rebels, criminals — or question who receives those designations — because ruptures in the social fabric also map a society's structuring contradictions, exposing the prevailing systems of power and hierarchy and the weak links in social institutions. If adultery is a special brand of heresy in the church of modern love, clearly it's a repository for other social contradictions and ruptures as well.[5] This isn't to say that adultery is a new story — it's hardly that. It does mean that it's a story that gets reshaped by every era as required. Ours, for instance, made it into the basis for an extended period of national political scandal — this after decades, if not centuries, of relative inattention to the matter. And after previously handing politicians carte blanche to stray with impunity, suddenly yanking back the privilege. Why?

One consequence (if not a cause) was the opportunity it created for exiled questions about the governing codes of intimate life — including how well or badly individuals negotiate them — to enter the national political discussion. Clearly there's pervasive dissatisfaction with the state of marriage: the implosion rate is high and climbing. Equally clearly, the reasons for that dissatisfaction is a discussion that can't publicly take place. Understandably: consider the network of social institutions teetering precariously on companionate love's rickety foundations — which means, frankly, that large chunks of contemporary social existence are built on the silt of unconsciousness, including large sectors of the economy itself. Given the declining success story of long-term marriages, as reported in the latest census, we're faced with a social institution in transition, and no one knows where it's going to land. The reasonable response would be to factor these transitions into relevant policy and social welfare decisions; this is apparently impossible. Instead, we're treated to a parade of elected representatives moralizing in public and acting out their own marital dissatisfactions in private, as if the entire subject had been exiled to the outer boroughs of unconsciousness — there to be performed à deux for the citizenry by naked politicians pantomiming the issues like players in some new avant garde form of national political dinner theater. But given the levels of confusion (and disavowal) surrounding these questions, is it so surprising that they just keep popping up unbidden into public view like a chronic rash or an unsightly nervous condition? Or surprising that they'd be channeled into scandal, the social ritual of choice for exposing open secrets (and for ritually shaming anyone they can be pinned to, thus exempting the rest of us and temporarily healing the rupture)? Scandal is the perfect package for circulating such dilemmas. More on this to come.

To recap. Among the difficult (and important) questions our adulterer-philosophers and roving politicians have put before us is this: Just how much renunciation of desire does society demand of us versus the degree of gratification it provides? The adulterer's position — following a venerable tradition of radical social theory — would be: "*Too much.*" Or this: Is it the persistence of the work ethic that ties us to the companionate couple and its workaday regimes, or is it the ethos of companionate coupledom that ties us to soul-deadening work regimes? On this one the jury is still out.

Adultery is not, of course, minus its own contradictions. Foremost among them: What are these domestic refuseniks and matrimonial escape artists escaping *to*, with such determination and cunning? Well, it appears that they're escaping to . . . *love*. As should be clear, ours is a story with a significant degree of unconsciousness, and not a little internal incoherence.

(Or as Laura puts it to Alec in *Brief Encounter,* the classic infidelity story: "I love you with all my heart and soul. I want to die.")

Thus, please read on in a tolerant spirit.

If adultery is the sit-down strike of the love-takes-work ethic, regard the assortment of company goons standing by to crush any dissent before it even happens. (Recall too the fate of labor actions past, as when the National Guard was ordered to fire on striking workers to convince them how great their jobs were, in case there were any doubts.) Needless to say, any social program based on something as bleak as working for love will also require an efficient enforcement wing to ply its dismal message. These days we call it "therapy." Yes, we weary ambivalent huddled masses of discontent will frequently be found scraping for happier consciousness in the discreetly soundproofed precincts of therapy, a newly arisen service industry owing its pricey existence to the cheery idea that ambivalence is a curable condition, that "growth" means adjustment to prevailing conditions, and that rebellion is neurotic — though thankfully, curable.

But no rest for the weary when you're in therapy! Resenting the boss? Feeling overworked or bored or dissatisfied? Getting complaints about your attitude? Whether it's "on the relationship" or "on the job," get yourself right to the therapist's office, pronto. The good news is that there are only two possible diagnoses for all such modern ailments (as all we therapy-savants know): it's going to be either "intimacy issues" or "authority issues." The bad news is that you'll soon discover that the disease doubles as the prescription at this clinic: you're just going to have to "work harder on yourself." If a nation gets the leaders it deserves, can the same be said for its therapies?

Of course according to Freud — arguably a better theorist than therapist himself (he could get a little pushy with the patients) — desire *is* regressive, and antisocial, and *there's no cure,* which is what makes it the wild card in our little human drama. (And also so much fun.) It screws up all well-ordered plans and lives, and to be alive is to be fundamentally split, fundamentally ambivalent, and unreconciled to the trade-offs of what Freud called, just a bit mockingly, "civilized sexual morality."[6] But Freud was long ago consigned to conformist therapy's historical ash can, collectively pilloried for his crimes against decency and empiricism (Philip Wylie: "Unfortunately, Americans, who are the most prissy people on earth, have been unable to benefit from Freud's wisdom because they can *prove* that they do not, by and large, sleep with their mothers"). So don't sign up for therapy if you're looking for radical social insights — or social insights at all actually: what's for sale here is "self-knowledge." (Only a cynic could suspect it of being remedial socialization in party clothes.) As you will soon discover under the tutelage of your kindly therapist, all those excess desires have their roots in some childhood deprivation or trauma, which has led to lack of self-esteem or some other impeded development which has made you unable to achieve proper intimacy and thus prone to searching for it in all the wrong places, namely anywhere outside the home. (You can be fairly certain it's not going to be those social norms that need a tune up; sorry, hon — it's you.) Conflicts in the realm of desire act out something "unresolved" in the self, a deeply buried trove of childhood memories or injuries that you will spend years excavating, in regular office visits and at no small cost. But don't resist! The more you resist the longer it takes, and the more you'll pay — in forty-five-minute increments, and at fees far exceeding the median daily wage. But happily, you will soon be feeling far better about yourself, and at peace with your desires and conflicts; if not, the same results can be attained in easy-to-swallow capsule form. With an estimated thirty million Americans — or around 10 percent of the adult population — having ingested antidepressants to date (GPs apparently hand them out like lollipops), better living through chemistry is now the favored social solution. Just say goodbye to your sex life.[7]

Another of the company goons: Culture. Consider the blaringly omnipresent propaganda beaming into our psyches on an hourly basis: the millions of images of lovestruck couples looming over us from movie screens, televisions, billboards, magazines, incessantly strong-arming us onboard the love train. Every available two-dimensional surface touts love. So deeply internalized is our obedience to this capricious despot that artists create passionate odes to its cruelty; audiences seem never to tire of the most repetitive and deeply unoriginal mass spectacles devoted to rehearsing the litany of its torments, forking over hard-earned dollars to gaze enraptured at the most blatantly propagandistic celebrations of its power, fixating all hopes on the narrowest glimmer of its fleeting satisfactions. But if pledging oneself to love is the human spirit triumphal, or human nature, or consummately "normal," why does it require such vast PR expenditures? Why so much importuning of the population?

Could there be something about contemporary coupled life itself that requires all this hectoring, from the faux morality of the work ethic to the incantations of therapists and counselors to the inducements of the entertainment industries, just to keep a truculent citizenry immobilized within it? Absent the sell tactics, would the chickens soon fly the coop, at least once those initial surges of longing and desire wear off? (Or more accurately, flap off in even greater numbers than the current 50 percent or so that do?) As we know, "mature love," that magical elixir, is supposed to kick in when desire flags, but could that be the problem right there? Mature love: it's kind of like denture adhesive. Yes, it's supposed to hold things in place; yes, it's awkward for everyone when it doesn't; but unfortunately there are some things that glue just won't glue, no matter how much you apply.

Clearly the couple form as currently practiced is an ambivalent one — indeed, a form in decline say those census-takers — and is there any great mystery why? On the one hand, the yearning for intimacy, on the other, the desire for autonomy; on the one hand, the comfort and security of routine, on the other, its soul-deadening predictability; on the one side, the pleasure of being deeply known (and deeply knowing another person), on the other, the straitjacketed roles that such familiarity predicates — the shtick of couple interactions; the repetition of the arguments; the boredom and the rigidities which aren't about to be transcended in this or any other lifetime, and which harden into those all-too-familiar couple routines: the

Stop Trying To Change Me routine and the Stop Blaming Me For Your Unhappiness routine. (Novelist Vince Passaro: "It is difficult to imagine a modern middle-class marriage not syncopated by rage.") Not to mention the *regression,* because, after all, you've chosen your parent (or their opposite), or worse, you've become your parent, tormenting (or withdrawing from) the mate as the same-or-opposite-sex parent once did, replaying scenes you were once subjected to yourself as a helpless child — or some other variety of family repetition that will keep those therapists guessing for years. Given everything, a success rate of 50 percent seems about right (assuming that success means longevity).

Or here's another way to tell the story of modern love. Let's imagine that to achieve consensus and continuity, any society is required to produce the kinds of character structures and personality types it needs to achieve its objective — to perpetuate itself — molding a populace's desires to suit particular social purposes. Those purposes would not be particularly transparent to the characters in question, to those who live out the consequent emotional forms as their truest and most deeply felt selves. (That would be us.)

Take the modern consumer. (Just a random example.) Clearly, routing desire into consumption would be necessary to sustain a consumer society — a citizenry who fucked in lieu of shopping would soon bring the entire economy grinding to a standstill. Or better still, take the modern depressive. What a boon to both the pharmaceutical and the social-harmony industries such a social type would be. These are merely hypotheticals, of course, since it's not as if we live in a society of consumers and depressives, or as if the best therapy for the latter weren't widely held to be strategically indulging in the activities of the former — "retail therapy" in urban parlance.

But perhaps there would be social benefits to cultivating a degree of emotional stagnation in the populace? Certain advantages to social personality types who gulped down disappointment like big daily doses of Valium, who were so threatened by the possibility of change that the anarchy of desire was forever tamed and a commitment to perfect social harmony effortlessly achieved? Advantages to a citizenry of busy utilitarians, toiling away, working harder, with all larger social questions (is this *really* as good as it gets?) pushed aside or shamed, since it's not like you have anything to say about it anyway.

Some of our gloomier thinkers have argued that there is indeed a functional fit between such social purposes and modes of inner life, a line of thinking associated with the generation of social theorists known as the Frankfurt School, who witnessed the rise of fascism in Germany first-hand and started connecting the dots between authoritarian personality types, the family forms that produced them, and the political outcomes. In fact, according to renegade psychoanalyst Wilhelm Reich, a Frankfurt School fellow traveler, the only social purpose of compulsory marriage for life is to produce the submissive personality types that mass society requires. He also took the view — along with Freud — that suppressing sexual curiosity leads to general intellectual atrophy, including the loss of any power to rebel. (Not a point destined to attract large numbers of adherents, since, if true, the consequent intellectual atrophy would presumably prevent recognition of the condition.) A variation on the argument has it that social forms—economic forms too—arise on the basis of the personality types already in place. Capitalism itself clearly requires certain character structures to sustain it, and would never have gotten off the ground, according to early sociologist Max Weber, if it weren't for the prep work of religious asceticism. Capitalism only succeeded, says Weber, because it happened along at the heyday of Calvinism, already busy churning out personalities so steeped in sacrifice that the capitalist work ethic wasn't a difficult sell.[8] Personality types will continue to be tweaked as necessary: once consumer capitalism arrived it required an overlay of hedonism on top of the productivity, at least to the extent that hedonism can be channeled into consumption. Witness the results: a society of happy shopaholics for whom shopping is not just a favored form of recreation, it's an identity.

Though when it comes to repression, perhaps we also come equipped with a secret talent for it? So intimated Freud, its most savvy chronicler. A certain degree of basic repression is necessary for any civilization to survive: if we were all just humping each other freely whenever the impulse arose, what energy would be left for erecting a culture? But with civilization achieved and now on firm enough footing, do we push it further than necessary, churning out *surplus repression,* in the phrase of another Frankfurt fellow traveler, Herbert Marcuse? Could we be a little nervous about the possibility of our own freedom? Consider how little resistance those repressive forces meet as they ooze their way into the neighborhoods of daily life. Resistance? More like mademoiselles greeting the occupying fascist troops with flirtatious glances and coy inviting smiles. *"What cute jackboots, monsieur."* Basking in their warm welcome from a docile populace, those repressive tendencies, now completely emboldened, reemerge unfettered in the guise of social character types, marching in goose step to the particular requirements of the day: the "professional," the "disciplinarian," the "boss," the "efficiency expert." Observe such types—your friends and neighbors—toiling away at work and home, each accompanied by an internal commanding officer (the collaborationist within) issuing a steady string of silent directives. "Willpower!" "Grow up!" "Be realistic!" "Get busy!" "Don't play around!" And thus we become psyches for whom repression has its own seductions. How *virtuous* it feels, trading play for industry, freedom for authority, and any lingering errant desires for "mature" realizations like Good Relationships Take Work.

Us, rebel? More like trained poodles prancing on hind legs, yipping for approval and doggie treats. So exiled have even basic questions of freedom become from the political vocabulary that they sound musty and ridiculous, and vulnerable to the ultimate badge of shame—"That's so '60s!"—the entire decade having been mocked so effectively that social protest seems outlandish and "so last-century," just another style excess like love beads and Nehru jackets. No, rebellion won't pose a problem for this social order. But just in case, any vestiges of freedom (or any tattered remnants still viable after childhood's brute socialization) will need to be checked at the door before entering the pleasure palace of domestic coupledom. Should you desire entry, that is. And who among us does not—because who can be against love?

But just for fun, try this quick thought experiment. Imagine the most efficient kind of social control possible. It wouldn't be a soldier on every corner—too expensive, too crass. Wouldn't the most elegant means of producing acquiescence be to somehow transplant those social controls so seamlessly into the guise of individual needs that the difference between them dissolved? And here we have the distinguishing political feature of the liberal democracies: their efficiency at turning out character types who identify so completely with society's agenda for them that they volunteer their very beings to the cause. But . . . *how* would such a feat be accomplished? *What* mysterious force or mind-altering substance could compel an entire population into such total social integration without them even noticing it happening, or uttering the tiniest peep of protest?

What if it could be accomplished through *love*? If love, that fathomless, many-splendored thing, that most mutable yet least escapable of all human experiences, that which leads the soul forward toward wisdom and beauty, were also the special potion through which renunciation could, paradoxically, be achieved? The paradox being that falling in love is the nearest most of us come to glimpsing utopia in our lifetimes (with sex and drugs as fallbacks), and harnessing our most utopian inclinations to the project of social control would be quite a singular achievement in the annals of modern population management. Like soma in *Brave New World,* it's the perfect drug. "Euphoric, narcotic, pleasantly hallucinant," as one character describes it. "All the advantages of Christianity and alcohol; none of their defects," quips another.

Powerful, mind-altering utopian substances do tend to be subject to social regulation in industrialized societies (as with sex and drugs): we like to worry about whether people will make wise use of these things. What if they impede productivity! So we make them scarce and shroud them in prohibitions, thus reinforcing their danger, along with the justification for social controls.

Clearly love is subject to just as much regulation as any powerful pleasure-inducing substance. Whether or not we fancy that we love as we please, free as the birds and butterflies, an endless quantity of social instruction exists to tell us what it is, and what to do with it, and how, and when. And tell us, and tell us: the quantity of advice on the subject of how to love properly is almost as infinite as the sanctioned forms it takes are limited. Love's proper denouement, matrimony, is also, of course, the social form regulated by the state, which refashions itself as benevolent pharmacist, doling out the addictive substance in licensed doses. (It could always be worse: the other junkies are forced to huddle outside neighborhood clinics in the cold for their little paper cups; love at least gets treated with a little pomp and ceremony.) Of course, no one is physically held down and forced to swallow vows, and not all those who love acquire the proper licenses to do so, but what a remarkable compliance rate is nevertheless achieved. Why bother to make marriage compulsory when informal compulsions work so well that even gays—once such paragons of unregulated sexuality, once so contemptuous of whitebread hetero lifestyles—are now demanding state regulation too? What about re-envisioning the form;

rethinking the premises? What about just insisting that social resources and privileges not be allocated on the basis of marital status? No, let's *demand regulation*! (Not that it's particularly easy to re-envision anything when these intersections of love and acquiescence are the very backbone of the modern self, when every iota of self-worth and identity hinge on them, along with insurance benefits.)

So, here you are, gay or straight, guy or gal, with matrimony (or some functional equivalent) achieved, domestication complete, steadfastly pledged and declawed. A housetrained kitten. But wait: what's that nagging little voice at the edge of your well-being, the one that refuses to shut up, even when jabbed with the usual doses of shame. The one that says: *"Isn't there supposed to be something more?"* Well maybe there is, but don't go getting any "ideas," because an elaborate domestic security apparatus is on standby, ready to stomp the life out of them before they can breed — stomp them dead like the filthy homewrecking cockroaches they are.

Sure, we all understand jealousy. Aren't all precarious regimes inherently insecure, casting watchful eyes on their citizenry's fidelity, ready to spring into action should anything threaten the exclusivity of those bonds? Every regime also knows that good intelligence props up its rule, so it's best to figure you're always being watched — you never know exactly from where, but a file is being compiled. Like seasoned FBI agents, longtime partners learn to play both sides of the good cop / bad cop routine. *"Just tell me, I promise I'll understand. . . . You did WHAT?!"* Once suspicions are aroused, the crisis alarm starts shrilling, at which point any tactics are justified to ensure your loyalty. Since anything can arouse suspicion, "preventative domestic policing" will always be an option: loyalty tests, trick questions, psychological torture, and carefully placed body blows that leave no visible marks. (Private detectives are also an option, or if you like, a Manhattan company called Check-a-Mate will send out attractive sexual decoys to see if your mate will go for the bait, then issue a full report.)[9]

Sure, easy to feel sympathetic to wronged partners: humiliated, undesired, getting fat, deserving better. The question of why someone cheats on you or leaves you can never be adequately explained. ("Intimacy issues," no doubt.) Realizing that people are talking, that friends knew and you didn't, that someone else has been poaching in your pasture and stealing what is by law yours *is* a special circle of hell. And even if you don't much want to have sex with the mate anymore, it's a little galling that someone else does. (Though this knowledge sometimes sparks a belated resurgence of desire: the suspicion-ridden marriage bed can be a pretty steamy place.)

But here's a question for you spouse-detectives as you're combing through credit card receipts, or cracking e-mail passwords, or perfecting the art of noiselessly lifting up phone extensions, counting condoms or checking the diaphragm case: What are you hoping to find? If you're looking, you basically know the answer, right? And if you don't find anything this time, are you willing to declare the matter settled? Hardly! Suspicion is addictive, sometimes even gratifying. After all, rectitude is on your side, and you want those promises kept, damn it. You want those vows *obeyed.* You want security, and of course you want love — since don't we all? But you'll settle for obedience, and when all else fails, ultimatums might work. But it's not as though you don't know when you're being lied to (though what constitutes "knowing" and "not knowing" in this regard could fill another book) and having transformed yourself into a one-person citizen-surveillance unit, how can you not hate the mate for forcing you to act with such a lack of dignity?

Here we come to the weak link in the security-state model of long-term coupledom: *desire.* It's ineradicable. It's roving and inchoate, we're inherently desiring creatures, and sometimes desire just won't take no for an answer, particularly when some beguiling and potentially available love-object hoves into your sight lines, making you feel what you'd forgotten how to feel, which is *alive,* even though you're supposed to be channeling all such affective capacities into the "appropriate" venues, and everything (Social Stability! The National Fabric! Being a Good Person!) hinges on making sure that you do. But renunciation chafes, particularly when the quantities demanded begin to exceed the amount of gratification achieved, for instance when basic monogamy evolves, as it inevitably does under such conditions, into *surplus monogamy*: enforced compliance rather than a free expression of desire. (Or "repressive satisfaction" in Marcuse's still handy, still stinging phrase.) The problem is that maybe we're really *not* such acquiescent worker bees in our desires, and maybe there actually *isn't* consent about being reduced to the means to an end, especially when the end is an overused platitude about the social fabric, whatever that is. Meaning what? — that we'll all just churn out the proper emotions to uphold calcified social structures like cows produce milk, like machines spit out O-rings?

But start thinking like that, and who knows what can happen? And that's the problem with dissatisfaction — it gives people "ideas." Maybe even critical ideas. First a glimmering, then an urge, then a transient desire, soon a nascent thought: *"Maybe there's something else."* Recall that the whole bothersome business with labor unions and workers demanding things like shorter workdays started out the same way: a few troublemakers got fed up with being treated like machines, word spread, and pretty soon there was a whole movement. "Wanting more" is a step on the way to a political idea, or so say political theorists, and ideas can have a way of turning themselves into demands. In fact, "wanting more" is the simple basis of all utopian thinking, according to philosopher Ernst Bloch. "Philosophies of utopia begin at home," Bloch liked to say — found in the smallest sensations of pleasure and fun, or even in daydreams, exactly because they reject inhibitions and daily drudgery. Utopianism always manages to find an outlet too, operating in disguise when necessary, turning up in all sorts of far-flung places. Or right under our noses, because utopianism is an aspect of anything that opens up the possibilities for different ways of thinking about the world. For madcap utopian Bloch, the most tragic form of loss wasn't the loss of security, it was the loss of the capacity to imagine that things could be different.

And for us? If philosophies of utopia begin at home, if utopianism is buried deep in those small, lived epiphanies of pleasure, in sensations of desire, and fun, and play, in love, in transgression, in the rejection of drudgery and work, well . . . no one *works* at adultery, do they? If this makes it a personal lab experiment in reconfiguring the love-to-work ratio, or a makeshift overhaul of the gratification-to-renunciation social equation, then it's also a test run for the most verboten fly-in-the-ointment question of all: *"Could things be different?"* No, it may not be particularly thought-out, or even articulable, but what else is behind these furtive little fantasies and small acts of resistance — playing around, acting out, chasing inchoate desires and longings — but just trying to catch fleeting glimpses of what "something else" could feel like? (Not that anyone here is endorsing adultery! After all, it hardly needs endorsements, it's doing quite well on its own. New recruits are signing up by the minute.)

Sure, adulterers behave badly. Deception rules this land, self-deception included. Not knowing what you're doing risks bad faith, and living exclusively in the present, and leaving sodden emotional disasters strewn behind. But note the charges typically leveled against the adulterer: "immaturity" (failure to demonstrate the requisite degree of civilized repression); "selfishness" (failure to work for the collective good — a somewhat selectively imposed requirement in corporate America); "boorishness" (failure to achieve proper class behavior). Or the extra fillip of moral trumping: "People will get hurt!" (Though perhaps amputated desires hurt too.) True, typically in outbursts of mass dissatisfaction — strikes, rebellions, sedition, coups — people sometimes get hurt: beware of sharp rocks and flying debris. But if adultery summons all the shaming languages of bad citizenship, it also indicates the extent to which domestic coupledom is the boot camp for compliant citizenship, a training ground for gluey resignation and immobility. The partner plays drill sergeant and anything short of a full salute to existing conditions is an invitation to the stockades — or sometimes a dishonorable discharge.

Still, conflicted desires and divided loyalties don't present a pretty picture when seen up close: the broken promises, the free-range seductiveness, the emotional unreliability, all perched a little precariously on that chronic dissatisfaction, crashing up against the rocky shoals of desperation. Ambivalence, universal though it may be, isn't much fun for anyone. (Least of all when you're on the receiving end. Deceived partners everywhere: our sympathies.) Ambivalence may fade into resignation, and given a high enough tolerance for swallowing things, this is supposed to count as a happy ending. But ambivalence can also be another way of saying that we social citizens have a constitutive lack of skill at changing things. Understandably — who gets any training at this? Even when not entirely resigned to the social institutions we're handed, who has a clue how to remake them, and why commit to them if there could be something better? Unfortunately, "something better" is also an idea so derided it's virtually prohibited entry to consciousness, and consequently available primarily in dreamlike states: romantic love and private utopian experiments like adultery (or secondhand, in popular fantasy genres like romance and myth).

But after all, we don't make history under conditions of our own choosing, and private life is pretty much all we have to work with when it comes to social experiments in our part of the world these days, where consumer durables and new technologies come equipped with planned obsolescence, and social institutions are as petrified as Mesozoic rock formations.

Still, before signing up for the thrill ride of adultery, a word to the wise. Let's all be aware that passionate love involves alarmingly high degrees of misrecognition in even the best of cases (that poignant Freudian paradigm), which means that we players in the adultery drama will be especially beset, madly flinging ourselves down uncharted paths in states of severe aporia, the impediments to self-knowledge joined at the hip to the lures of disavowal. All of us risk drowning in those swirling tidal waves of emotion and lust, cramped up and overwhelmed, having thought ourselves shrewd and agile enough to surf the crest despite the posted danger signs. You may say you're not going to get in too deep, you may say you just want to have fun, but before you know it you're flattened by a crashing wave from nowhere and left gasping for air with a mouthful of sand. (Translation: you're in love, or you're in lust, and not with your mate, and your life feels out of control, and maybe you've been waiting your whole life to feel this way about someone, which means you're in big trouble.)

So watch out, baby — a few missteps, a couple of late-night declarations, and everything could be up for grabs. What started as a fling has somehow turned serious; the supplement has started to supersede the thing that needed supplementing. Perhaps unplanned exposures have forced things into the open, or those "contradictions" of yours have started announcing themselves in some unpleasant somatic form that eventually can't be ignored. Insomnia. Migraines. Cold sores. Digestive ailments. Heart palpitations. Sexual difficulties. (Sometimes bodies just won't play along, even when instructed otherwise.) Choices will need to be made. Choices that you, with your terminal ambivalence and industrial-strength guilt, are not capable of making. Antacids aren't working. Work is suffering. The shrink just says, "What do you think?" But about what? Love is also a way of forgetting what the question is. Using love to escape love, groping for love outside the home to assuage the letdowns of love at home — it's kind of like smoking and wearing a nicotine patch at the same time: two delivery systems for an addictive chemical substance that feels vitally necessary to your well-being at the moment, even if likely to wreak unknown havoc in the deepest fibers of your being at some unspecified future date.

The best polemic against love would be to mimic in prose the erratic and overheated behavior of its hapless practitioners: the rushes and excesses, the inconsistent behavior and inchoate longings, the moment-by-moment vacillations between self-doubt (*"What am I doing?"*) and utter certainty (*"You're the one"*), all in quest of something transformative and unknown. It would replicate in form the impediments and trade-offs and fumbling around, all the things felt but not understood, and the tension of being caught in-between — between mates and lovers or between rival ways of telling such conflicted tales, each beckoning with its own sultry and alluring vocabulary: social theory and love affairs, Marx and Freud, utopia and pragmatics, parody and sentimentality. "Just pick one and settle down already," you can hear people saying. But what if you just keep finding yourself looking "elsewhere" as much as you tell yourself not to, because this is really no way to act? Yes, just like all you adultery clowns out there tripping over your big floppy shoes and chasing improbable fulfillment, knowing it has the whiff of a doomed undertaking and making up the rules as you go along, we polemicists too are propelled to (intellectual) promiscuity, rashness and blind risks and becoming the neighborhood pariah (or joke) just for thinking there could be reasons to experiment with reimagining things.

But to those feeling a little stultified and contemplating a spin down Reinvention Road: do weigh your options carefully. Don't forget that all outbreaks of love outside sanctioned venues still invite derisive epitaphs like "cheating" or "mid-life crisis," while those that play by the rules will be community-sanctified with champagne and gifts in the expensive over-rehearsed costume rituals of the wedding-industrial complex (its participants stiffly garbed in the manner of landed gentry from some non-existent epoch: clearly, playing out unnatural roles is structured into these initiation rites as a test of the participants' stamina for role-playing as a social enterprise and as a measure of their resolve and ability to keep doing so in perpetuity).

Consider this not just a polemic, but also an elegy: an elegy for all the adultery clowns crying on the inside, with our private experiments and ragtag utopias. The elegiac mode traditionally allows a degree of immoderation, so please read on in an excessive and mournful spirit — or at least with some patience for the bad bargains and compensatory forms the discontented classes engineer for themselves in daily life. So many have met such dismal, joyless fates, dutifully renouncing all excess desires, and along with them any hopes that the world could deliver more than it currently does — or could if anyone had the temerity to fight about it, and face down the company goons, then face down the ritual shaming, and last but not least the massive self-inflicted guilt shortly to follow.

But beware their seductive and dangerous lures too, those beguiling adulterers, dangerous as pirate ships lying in wait to cadge any unguarded troves of emotion and pleasure, promises brandished like a swashbuckler's sword, slicing through qualms like they were air. Was ever there a more seductive seducer, or a more captivating captor, than an emotionally starving human with potential ardor in sight? (*"Trust me, things will work out."*) But to all you temporary utopians and domestic escape artists who couldn't sustain your own wishes for more courageous selves or different futures or love on better terms, who could only filch a few brief moments of self-reinvention and fun before being drop-kicked, guilt-ridden and self-loathing, back to the domestic gulags, the compartmentalization, the slow death of "maturity" (because risking stagnation is obviously preferable to risking change in the prevailing emotional economy): we mourn your deaths. We leave big immoderate bouquets at your gravesides.

NOTES

[1] Sexual self-reporting is notoriously unreliable. Consider the statistical problems plaguing the 1994 survey on sexual behavior by the University of Chicago National Opinion Research Center. Though touted as the most authoritative and thorough sex survey ever conducted, there was a small problem with the data: 64 percent of male sexual contacts reported couldn't be accounted for — or rather, they could if, in a pool of 3,500 responses, ten different women had each had 2,000 partners they didn't report. Sociologist Martina Morris, writing in the journal *Nature,* proposed a solution: eliminate the answers of male respondents who reported more than twenty partners in their lifetime or more than five in the previous year, which would make the numbers come out right. Leaving aside the question of whether men over-report more than women under-report sexual activity, or whether accumulating more than twenty partners in a lifetime defies probability, we might ask, does tweaking the data on the basis of such assumptions make statistics any more reliable than guesses? As it happens, the Chicago survey reported quite low adultery rates (men 21 percent, women 11 percent), figures which are still widely quoted in current news stories on adultery. By comparison, the Kinsey reports pegged male adultery at 50 percent (in 1948) and female adultery (in 1953) at 26 percent. [All notes are Kipnis's.]

[2] It remains to be seen whether feminism's greatest accomplishment was the liberation of women or whether it was redistributing feminine submission more equally between the genders: this question will hover in the background of our discussion. Note that gender equity isn't necessarily synonymous with greater freedom; it can simply mean equality in submission. The wave of civil and constitutional reforms that took place throughout the liberal democracies during much of the twentieth century did grant women equal status as legal subjects and did reform marital property laws; the questions being posed here will take up less evident forms of subjection, which intersect variously with gender reforms.

[3] Note that sociologists have devised a somewhat ironical term for nonworking populations — the unemployed, the welfare classes, the elderly, or criminals — presumably meant to reflect how they're seen by society. The term is "social garbage."

[4] But which sphere models the other? Recent United Nations statistics show employed Americans working an average of 49½ hours a week, and that's just at paid labor. This is an average of 3½ weeks a year more than Japanese workers (the previous world leaders), 6½ weeks more than British workers, and 12½ weeks more than German workers. Said the economist who compiled the report, "It has a lot to do with the American psyche, with American culture."

[5] Of course, heretics also invariably fascinate — entire Inquisitions are devoted to probing their views. (See Carlo Ginzburg's *The Cheese and the Worms,* an ingenious case study of one medieval heretic and the fascination he exerted over his inquisitors.)

[6] And was Freud an adulterer? It seems unlikely, though one of his would-be debunkers, a rather singular historian of psychoanalysis named Peter Swales, has made it his life's work (these debunkers are a zealous bunch) to prove that Freud and his sister-in-law Minna Bernays were an item.

[7] Harvard psychiatrist Joseph Glenmullen, author of *Prozac Backlash,* estimates that up to 60 percent of those who take Prozac or other SSRIs (the most widely prescribed category of antidepressants) experience drug-induced sexual dysfunction as a side effect.

[8] Weber, who coined the term "work ethic": yet another major adulterer. And one so transformed by his belated awakening to erotic experience, according to biographers, that it propelled the direction of his later (some say best) work on the conflicts between eroticism or other varieties of mystical religiosity and the processes of rationality. (Yes, adultery's eternal dilemma.)

[9] Or consider the possibilities opened up by new technologies. A Web site called Adulteryandcheating.com counsels tactics like satellite tracking and cyber-spying to nab cheating partners; spy equipment stores are also promoting new keystroke-capture programs as a surveillance system for suspicious spouses, which, once installed on a home computer, will record your partner's e-mail exchanges and Web site visits for your later review.

SELECTED BIBLIOGRAPHY

A Note on Sources

The uses made of innocent books and authors has been frequently speculative and occasionally contrarian: this should probably be regarded as a list of incitations rather than citations in the usual sense. Principal inciters: Chapter 1: Herbert Marcuse, *One-Dimensional Man* (Boston: Beacon Press, 1964); Chapter 2: Michel Foucault, *Discipline and Punish: The Birth of the Prison,* trans. Alan Sheridan (New York: Vintage Books, 1977); Chapter 3: Michel de Certeau, *The Practice of Everyday Life,* trans. Steven Rendall (Berkeley and Los Angeles: University of California Press, 1984), and Peter Bürger, *Theory of the Avant Garde,* trans. Michael Shaw (Minneapolis: University of Minnesota Press, 1984); Chapter 4: Fredric Jameson, *The Political Unconscious: Narrative as a Socially Symbolic Act* (Ithaca, N.Y.: Cornell University Press, 1981).

Inciters—or intellectual dads? But you know how it is with dads: half the time you love them, half the time you want to kill them and eat them. (Or so speculates uber-dad Freud.)

Additional Sources

Bloch, Ernst. *The Utopian Function of Art and Literature.* Cambridge, Mass.: MIT Press, 1988.

Freud, Sigmund. *Civilization and Its Discontents.* New York: J. Cape and H. Smith, 1930.

——. "'Civilized' Sexual Morality and Modern Nervous Illness." In *The Standard Edition of the Complete Psychological Works of Sigmund Freud.* Vol. 9. London: Hogarth Press, 1953–74.

Ginzburg, Carlo. *The Cheese and the Worms: The Cosmos of a Sixteenth Century Miller.* Trans. John Tedeschi and Anne Tedeschi. New York: Penguin, 1982.

Hochschild, Arlie Russell. *The Time Bind: When Work Becomes Home and Home Becomes Work.* New York: Metropolitan Books, 1997.

Marcuse, Herbert. *Eros and Civilization: A Philosophical Inquiry into Freud.* Boston: Beacon Press, 1955.

Marx, Karl. *Capital, A Critique of Political Economy: Volume One.* Trans. Ben Fowkes. New York: Penguin, 1976.

Weber, Max. *The Protestant Work Ethic and the Spirit of Capitalism.* Trans. Talcott Parsons. New York. Scribner, 1976.

QUESTIONS FOR A SECOND READING

1. Although she gives her book the provocative title *Against Love: A Polemic*, thereby aligning herself with a long tradition of polemical writing, it is not necessarily love itself to which Laura Kipnis is objecting—or at least not love alone. "Polemics exist," she explains, "to poke holes in cultural pieties and turn received wisdom on its head, even about sacrosanct subjects like love." What "cultural pieties" and "received wisdom" does Kipnis seem to be attacking here and for what reasons? As you reread, mark sentences or phrases from "Love's Labors" that you would draw upon in order to explain the various targets for Kipnis's critique.

2. By beginning her book with a "Reader Advisory," Kipnis suggests (a bit tongue in cheek perhaps) that there is something unconventional, perhaps even unsettling, about what we are about to read. "A polemic is designed," she warns us, "to be the prose equivalent of a small explosive device placed under your E-Z-Boy lounger. It won't injure you (well not severely); it's just supposed to shake things up and rattle a few convictions" (p. 390). As you reread "Love's Labors," keep a list of what you might call the "weapons" in Kipnis's arsenal. Paying careful attention not only to *what* she writes but also to *how* she writes, what surprises do you find in Kipnis's prose? What strategies does she rely on as a writer attempting to "shake things up" and "rattle" her readers' convictions? Of the "weapons" you identify, which do you think are mainstays of polemical writing, and which seem particular to Kipnis? To what extent might these tactics be translatable to nonpolemical forms of writing?

3. For some readers, particularly those who are young or have never been married, Kipnis's detailed anecdotes about infidelity and the shackles of long-term committed coupledom may seem remote. And yet she claims from the beginning that "this could be anyone's story." As you read through the

essay a second time, look for passages that suggest connections to your own life. To what extent do the anecdotes, behaviors, or ideas Kipnis writes about dovetail your own experiences or those of people you know?

4. At one level, "Love's Labors" seems almost painfully direct and "to the point"; its style is hard-hitting, aggressive. And yet, at the sentence level, dashes, ellipses, and parentheses—marks facilitating digression and interruption—play an important role in Kipnis's repertoire. As you reread, mark characteristic sentences in which Kipnis uses these forms of punctuation. Choosing two or three particularly compelling examples as models, craft a few sentences of your own in which you imitate Kipnis as closely as you can. Looking over Kipnis's sentences and your own, why do you think she has composed these sentences this way? What effects do they achieve? Be prepared to talk about what they *do* as well as what they say.

5. Another striking feature of Kipnis's prose is her use of metaphors. She often uses metaphors, either in single sentences or in more extended ways, to provide concrete correlatives for abstract ideas ("matrimonial escape artists," "adultery is the sit-down strike of the love-takes-work ethic"). Sometimes she calls attention to the implications of the figurative language that we unthinkingly use in our everyday speech—the language of work that "has managed to brownnose its way" into our thinking about intimate relationships, for example. As you work your way through the chapter, pay special attention to the various uses Kipnis makes of metaphor and choose two examples for discussion. How do these metaphors work? How are they helpful? Where (or when) do they break down?

6. *Against Love* is filled with technical terms or phrases that seem more appropriate to textbooks than to lovers. Here are a few: dialectic, structural transgression, social management tools, gender role, redistributed feminine submission, the Frankfurt School. As you reread, make a list of what you take to be the key terms and references representing this register in Kipnis's prose. What are the effects and consequences of these shifts in tone and reference? ("Rhetoric and sentiment," she says in the reader's advisory, "aren't always identical twins.") Who talks like this? Where, when, and to whom?

   And, to prepare material for class discussion, choose three terms, the ones you take to be the most interesting, and prepare glosses or translations: "By 'structural transgression,' I think Kipnis means..."

ASSIGNMENTS FOR WRITING

1. In the "Reader Advisory" that opens *Against Love*, Kipnis posits that polemics are not necessarily required to adhere to conventional rules or expectations for argumentation. "Be advised," she warns us:

> polemics aren't measured; they don't tell "both sides of the story." They overstate the case. They toss out provocations and occasionally mockery, usually because they're arguing against something so unquestionable and deeply entrenched it's the only way to make even a dent in the usual story. (p. 390)

She further suggests that "polemics aren't necessarily unconflicted (nor are the polemicists); rhetoric and sentiment aren't always identical twins."

While she does not provide a "measured" account that carefully records "both sides of the story" and hides all evidence of ambivalence, the text is nonetheless an argument, one which attempts to persuade readers of the merits of its thesis. Write an essay in which you describe and reflect on the way in which Kipnis presents her argument. As you reread "Love's Labors," pay close attention to how Kipnis positions you as a reader and herself as a writer. By what means does Kipnis seek to persuade, garner authority, or support her claims? On what evidence does she rely? What are her signature moves? In what ways does the polemic (or the polemicist) appear to be "conflicted," and how does she deal with those conflicts?

A good way to focus your analysis is to home in on a few key passages, reading small sections closely and carefully in order to illuminate something about the text as a whole. As you work with these passages, think about the choices Kipnis has made as a writer and what particular effects those choices produce. After you have analyzed Kipnis's strategies, you might find that you have some new insights about the merits as well as the risks of polemical writing.

2. If you have ever tried to argue with someone about something in which they believe quite strongly, you have no doubt noticed that there is more at stake than logic alone. Allegiances to ideas, particularly those that are firmly entrenched, are tied up with a person's identity, self-image, pride. Breaking through the barriers that people construct to protect unquestioned assumptions or cherished delusions is no easy task. Polemics, according to Kipnis, can be an effective means of doing so.

   This assignment invites you to try your hand at writing a polemic in the spirit of *Against Love*. You do not need to title your essay "Against X," but you should strive, like Kipnis, to "poke holes in cultural pieties and turn received wisdom on its head." The success of your essay will depend heavily on your selected topic, so be sure to give this considerable thought. Avoid selecting a topic that we've all heard debated repeatedly (death penalty, welfare, etc.). Instead, consider challenging an idea or a belief people tend to unthinkingly take as a given, something that goes deeper than consciously chosen political positions. You might begin by asking, "Why do so many people assume that...?" Talk to your friends; if they say, "I've never thought of it like that before" or "No one could be against X," then you're on the right track.

As you compose your essay, you will certainly find it helpful to enlist some of the methods employed by Kipnis. What strategies does she use in order to "shake things up and rattle a few convictions," and how might you achieve similar effects? What research might you need to do in order to prepare to write? Bear in mind Kipnis's claim that polemics (and polemicists) are not necessarily "unconflicted." If you find that your "sentiment" does not necessarily conform to your "rhetoric," consider how you will deal with those conflicts in your writing.

3. Kipnis says:

> Might we entertain the possibility that posing philosophical questions isn't restricted to university campuses and learned tomes, that maybe it's something everyone does in the course of everyday life — if not always in an entirely knowing fashion? If adultery is more of a critical practice than a critical theory, well, acting out *is* what happens when knowledge or consciousness about something is foreclosed. Actually, that's what acting out is for. Why such knowledge is foreclosed is a question yet to be considered — though how much do any of us know about our desires and motivations, or the contexts that produce them? We can be pretty clueless. We say things like "Something just happened to me," as if it were an explanation. (p. 399)

Kipnis points to a "critical practice" rather than a critical theory. What other forms of critical practice might you observe, or have you observed, in "everyday life"? Working as a social historian — using Kipnis's study of adultery as a model — conduct your own analysis of a divergent "critical practice" that you think reveals something about our society's "structuring contradictions." What might your analysis teach us about our "prevailing systems of power" and/or "the weak links in social institutions"? How is your work informed by your reading of Kipnis? Where might it diverge?

4. "There are a million stories in love's majestic empire," Kipnis writes, "and yours is in here too." One way of testing this assertion is to take an episode from your life or the life around you — an episode that seems relevant to Kipnis's argument — and examine it through the lens provided by *Against Love*. Yours does not have to be a story of love (in fact, love stories are the hardest to write), but it should be about a real or imagined or never-to-be-thought-of transgression. Take time to tell the story fully and well — with attention to scene, character, and dialogue. (As an alternative to writing about your own experience, you could select a text or an event that has had a strong effect on you — a film, perhaps, a song, or an incident from the news.)

Your essay should, however, also be a reading of Kipnis and in conversation with *Against Love*. If Kipnis were to write about this experience, for example, what would she notice? What details would interest her, and how would she interpret them? What terms would she bring to her analysis, and what conclusions might she draw? But this is your essay, too: Where or how might you take the discussion one step further? How might your essay be against *Against Love*?

MAKING CONNECTIONS

1. While they do not explicitly use the term or define the genre as Kipnis does, Paulo Freire's "The 'Banking' Concept of Education" (p. 318) and the two selections in this anthology reprinted from Gloria Anzaldúa's *Borderlands/La frontera* (p. 72) can be classified as polemics, works that attempt to "shake things up," to provoke readers and poke holes in "cultural pieties." Polemics, Kipnis explains, often bend or break conventional rules or expectations for argumentation. "Be advised," she warns us: "polemics aren't measured; they don't tell 'both sides of the story.' They overstate the case. They toss out provocations and occasionally mockery, usually because they're arguing against something so unquestionable and deeply entrenched it's the only way to make even a dent in the usual story" (p. 390).

   Write an essay in which you present either "The 'Banking' Concept of Education" or the sections from *Borderlands/La frontera* as an example of polemical writing. You may want to begin by thinking about what has drawn the writer to the polemical form. What is "the usual story" that the polemicist wants to dislodge? What kinds of opposition from readers might the writer anticipate, and how does he or she address or attempt to counter resistance? As a reader, how did you respond to this attack on "received wisdom"?

   Kipnis also tells us that "polemics aren't necessarily unconflicted (nor are the polemicists); rhetoric and sentiment aren't always identical twins." If you find evidence that the polemicist might be "conflicted," how does the writer deal with such conflicts and/or contradictions? Does your analysis of Freire's or Anzaldúa's text offer some new insights into polemical writing—its social function, its merits, its risks—that Kipnis has not elucidated?

2. Both Laura Kipnis in "Love's Labors" and Michel Foucault in "Panopticism" (p. 282) write about power relations. Foucault's essay is theoretical, whereas Kipnis treads more lightly, poking fun at our strange attempts to meet the oppressive cultural norms of domesticity. Nevertheless, there are strong connections between Foucault's analysis of the "mechanisms of power" that assert control over individuals in a disciplined society and Kipnis's critique of the ways in which conformity is compelled without the use of physical force. Write an essay in which you put Foucault's and Kipnis's essays into dialogue with each other.

   You might begin by working with the distinctive voices adopted by the two writers—both relate to readers in rather unconventional ways. If it helps, try rewriting some representative passages from Foucault's essay as you imagine Kipnis would write them or vice versa. In addition to noticing distinctions in tone and voice, pay attention to pronoun use. Who or what tends to be the subject of each writer's sentences, and what might this reveal about their interests, about the kind of story each wants to tell? Also consider the kinds of evidence on which each writer relies. How do they attempt to make visible the disciplinary forces that people usually do not notice or regard as oppressive?

At some point, you will want to consider how these writers' stylistic differences reflect diverse interests and ways of thinking about power and the individual. How does each writer represent the forces that control and discipline us? Who is doing what to whom and for what reasons? What is the place of the individual in relation to these larger normalizing forces, and what are the possibilities for resisting or altering these power relations? Finally, what might be the consequences, for you as an individual, of thinking about these two essays in relation to each other?

Note: You should imagine that your readers, while they might be familiar with both texts, do not have them in front of them. Therefore, you will need to do the work of presentation and summary.

3. Like Kipnis, Susan Bordo in "Beauty (Re)discovers the Male Body" (p. 189) and Susan Griffin in "Our Secret" (p. 335) are working as feminist social historians. They take familiar social practices (advertising, representations of the past and of the self) and attempt to help readers see them differently, not as simply natural or arbitrary but as practices that have important social and political consequences. Choose one of these texts and read it alongside Kipnis's. Write an essay in which you explore and describe the reading and writing strategies employed by the two writers you have chosen. As researchers, how do they gather their materials, weigh them, think them through? What do they notice, and what do they do with what they notice? What makes each project historical? What makes it feminist? How might the two texts speak to each other? Looking at characteristic examples drawn from both writers, what might you conclude about the relative value—to you and to history—of each writer's project?

4. Both "Against Love" and "Authority and American Usage" by David Foster Wallace (p. 622) are serious essays written in an unconventional style—or in a style not usually found in academic writing. A character emerges in these essays, figures representing differing versions of a well-schooled, learned, and articulate adult. These are intellectuals, people who read widely, who think closely and freshly and methodically about big questions, people with ideas and with style, people who define themselves in relation to sources—to books and to other writers. And yet, the figures they strike are unusual in academic settings. Both Wallace and Kipnis know this; the desire to be different motivates how they write and what they do in these essays.

   Write an essay in which you discuss the figure of the intellectual as represented in these two essays. You'll need to work closely with a few key and representative moments in each text. You'll need to make clear distinctions between Kipnis and Wallace (the Kipnis and Wallace who appear on the page). And write an essay in which you assess this figure in relation to your own education—better yet, in relation to the figure you intend to cut as a well-schooled adult, as an intellectual, as a person with ideas and knowledge and something to say.

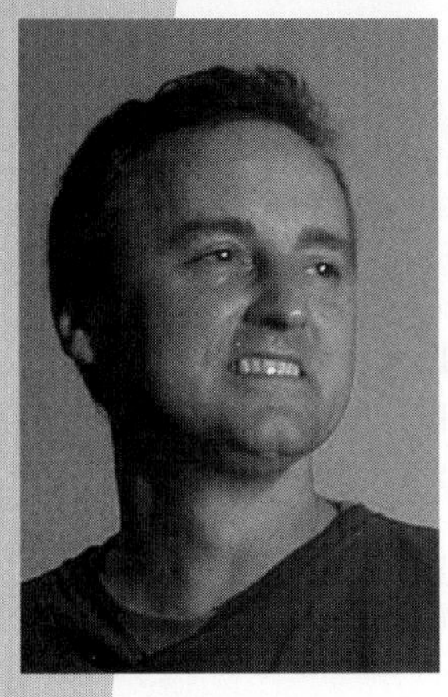

RICHARD E. Miller

Richard E. Miller is professor of English and the executive director of the Plangere Writing Center at Rutgers University. He received his BA from St. John's University, his MA from the University of Massachusetts at Boston, and his PhD from the University of Pittsburgh. He is the author of *As If Learning Mattered: Reforming Higher Education* (1998), *Writing at the End of the World* (2005), and, with Kurt Spellmeyer, a textbook, *The New Humanities Reader* (third edition, 2008).

Throughout his career, Miller has looked at schooling in the United States and, in particular, at the required curriculum in English — a literature course and a composition course — and he has asked big questions. For example, in *Writing at the End of the World*, he says:

> In a secular society, education is the most powerful resource citizens have to ensure a brighter future for themselves. But what is one to do when the future includes a radioactive wasteland in the northern Ukraine? The smoldering ruins of the World Trade Center? Looted museums in a bombed-out Baghdad? No meaningful discussion of the humanities can proceed without confronting such examples of human depravity and indifference. Who, surveying the ruins at Chernobyl, would be persuaded either by Matthew Arnold's argument that we are ennobled by studying the best that has been thought and said in our time or by those who maintain that the work in the humanities provides the foundation for a critical engagement with the world? (pp. ix–x)

Here is what Miller says about his own teaching. Since he is referring, in part, to his teaching in first-year writing courses, a course occupying the same curricular slot as the one you are taking, this is worth quoting at length.

> When I am back in the classroom, I work at getting the students to use their writing not just as a tool for making arguments, but also as a lens for exploring complexity and a vehicle for arriving at nuanced understandings of a lived reality that is inescapably characterized by ambiguities, shades of meaning, contradictions, and gaps. That's a long way to try to take undergraduates in one course in one semester, but

> this is what I believe the function of a secular public education should be: to provide training in the arts of solving the problems of this world, training that recognizes that people, who never leave behind their embodied histories and their cherished beliefs, can't be revised the way papers can. (pp. 196–97)

His goal, he says, for himself and for his students, is

> learning how to speak in ways that others can hear, in finding a way to move and be in more than one world at once. This isn't the only answer and it isn't always the answer, but learning how to look for such answers and finding out how to implement the evanescent solutions the search itself suggests is the primary function of the humanities as I conceive them. The practice of the humanities, so defined, is not about admiration or greatness or appreciation or depth of knowledge or scholarly achievement; it's about the movement between worlds, arms out, balancing; it's about making the connections that count. (p. 198)

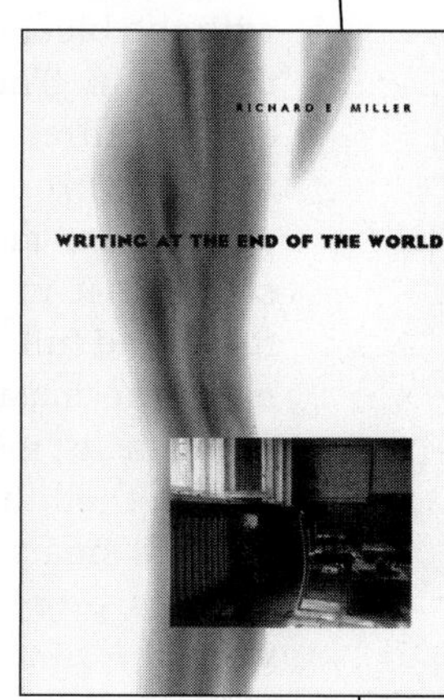

Miller is a brilliant essayist and an innovative thinker. He has turned his attention increasingly to multimedia composition, composition in digital environments, both in his own writing and as a necessary next step for the teaching of English. For an example of this work, at nmc.org you can access a presentation he gave to the Modern Language Association: "This Is How We Dream, Parts 1 and 2."

The Dark Night of the Soul

Though they may already have faded from memory, driven off by more recent and yet more spectacular horrors, for a few short weeks in 1999, the events at Columbine High School mesmerized the nation. There was the live footage of students fleeing in terror across the green, the boy with the bleeding head being dropped from the window, the SWAT teams moving in. There was the discovery of what lay beyond the eye of the camera: fifteen dead, a cache of weapons, a large homemade bomb made with two propane tanks and a gasoline canister, the eventual disclosure of an even more sinister fantasy that involved hijacking a plane and crashing it in New York City.[1] There was the ongoing effort to present fuller and fuller portraits of Eric Harris and Dylan Klebold, the two young men who masterminded the slaughter: they were outsiders, video-game enthusiasts, members of the Trench Coat Mafia, neo-Nazis, two boys who couldn't tell their alcohol-fueled dreams from reality, a leader and a follower, a smart kid and a loser, specimens of a middle-class value system in crisis, proof of the need for stricter gun-control laws. And finally, there were the funerals, the white caskets covered in writing from those left behind, the doves released into the air, and all those inspirational speeches about healing and hope.

Any major social cataclysm produces in its wake two responses; First, there is the search for causes: Why did this happen? Who is to blame? And second, there is an appeal to some greater authority to assist in preventing such upheavals in the future. Following Columbine, fingers were pointed at everyone and everything: inattentive parents, indifferent guidance counselors, insensitive jocks, the entertainment industry, powerful gun lobbyists, the media, the Internet, the military-industrial complex, a president who couldn't keep his pants on.[2] And then, as one would expect, there were calls both for increased external controls — new laws, regulations, supervisory agencies — and for increased internal controls — educational interventions, moral training, prayer. Surely, more laws, more education, and more religious instruction would bring these violent students back into line.

Despite heightened sensitivity and increased security, however, the schoolyard massacre has proven to be a remarkably durable and recurring social cataclysm. In February 1997, a sixteen-year-old in Bethel, Alaska, entered his high school and murdered the principal and another student. In October 1997, another sixteen-year-old, this one living in Pearl, Mississippi, killed his mother, then went to school and killed two more students. In December 1997, a fourteen-year-old took aim at a prayer circle in West Paducah, Kentucky, killing three. In March 1998, two boys, eleven and thirteen, pulled a fire alarm and gunned down students exiting Westside Middle School in Jonesboro, Arkansas, leaving five dead. And the list goes on with additional shootings over the past five years at high schools in Fayetteville, Tennessee; Springfield, Oregon; Richmond, Virginia; Conyers, Georgia; Deming, New Mexico; and Cold Spring, Minnesota. In March 2001, a skinny kid, whom classmates called "Anorexic Andy," walked into his high school in Santee, California, to reenact his version of Columbine. He killed two and wounded thirteen before being subdued. And in April 2002, Robert Steinhaeuser returned to Johann Gutenberg High School in Erfurt, Germany, to avenge his expulsion for forging a doctor's note: he killed two students and thirteen teachers before turning his gun on himself.

It's reassuring to think that either the work of the legal system or the educational system can reduce or eliminate altogether the threat of the unpredictable and the unforeseen. This is why we have childproof medicine bottles, penalties for not buckling up, informational literature on family planning for students in junior high school: these are all examples of reasonable responses to known problems. But the schoolyard massacre seems a problem of a different order. What legal or educational response could be equal to the challenge of controlling the behavior of so many students from such varied backgrounds? Just how much surveillance would be required to bring the marginalized fraction of the student population back into the fold? How invasive would a curricular intervention have to be to succeed in instilling a set of preferable values in those who currently feel so deeply alienated while at school? While the answers to these questions are unknown, what we do know is this: the day after Columbine High School reopened, after all the public and private soul-searching in the community about the killings, after all the media coverage and analysis, after an enormous pep rally replete with bouncing cheerleaders, enthusiastic athletes, and all the mandatory school spirit one could ever hope for, swastikas were found scratched in a stall in one of the high school's newly painted bathrooms.

WHAT LEGAL OR EDUCATIONAL RESPONSE COULD BE EQUAL TO THE CHALLENGE OF CONTROLLING THE BEHAVIOR OF SO MANY STUDENTS FROM SUCH VARIED BACKGROUNDS?

Eric Harris certainly didn't accept the idea that anyone was to blame for his actions or that anything could have been done to stop him or Dylan Klebold in going forward with their plan. Anticipating speculation of just this kind, Harris wrote in his diary:

> i want to leave a lasting impression on the world, and god damnit do not blame anyone else besides me and V for this. dont blame my family, they had no clue and there is nothing they could have done, they brought me up just fucking fine, dont blame toy stores or any other stores for selling us ammo, bomb materials or anything like that because its not their fault.

> i dont want no fucking laws on buying fucking PVC pipes. we are kind of a select case here so dont think this will happen again. dont blame the school. dont fucking put cops all over the place just because we went on a killing spree doesnt mean everyone else will and hardly ever do people bring bombs or guns to school anyway. the admin. is doing a fine job as it is. i dont know who will be left after we kill but dammit don't change any policies just because of us. it would be stupid and if there is any way in this fucked up universe we can come back as ghosts we will haunt the life out of anyone who blames anyone besides me and V.[3]

If one accepts Harris's assertions, then the events at Columbine are largely without motive or meaning: the killing spree was a misguided grab for immortality by two young men at loose ends. If one rejects Harris's assertions, though, and persists in the pursuit for causes, one is left with the inescapable fact that the hierarchical, exclusionary environment of mandatory schooling fosters feelings of rage and helplessness that cannot be contained. The law drives everyone into the schoolhouse; the educational system then sifts and sorts its way through the masses, raising expectations and crushing dreams as it goes. Eventually, something has to give.[4]

What is to be done? What is to be done? Only those utterly indifferent to the suffering of others can forestall asking this question for long. And, after any tragedy that involves the death of young people, it doesn't take long for someone to make the case that the problem lies with advanced technology and all the fantasy factories that it has spawned, which together have blurred the line between fact and fiction. After the Columbine shootings, Pat Schroeder, the former congresswoman from Colorado who now runs the Association of American Publishers, was among those who argued that we've reached the point where suburban kids are becoming mass murderers because we've created domestic spaces that isolate individuals in a technological sea of entertainment—the TV, the VCR, the computer, the entertainment center, the Internet, a different toy for everyone. "*This* is the beautiful family of America living the American dream," Schroeder observed wryly. "But we need some ways to relate to each other as human beings. We need to work on getting connected." Convinced that the virtual connections available in cyberspace tend to be divisive, Schroeder has committed herself to protecting the practice of reading books. Schroeder believes that book clubs and coffee bars provide a kind of embodied community unavailable on the Internet. These places where people go to discuss the printed word are, she says, "among the few civil institutions left. [They are] places to go see other people" (qtd. in Gross).

I share Schroeder's desire for a future where physical communion with others is still an option. You might say, in fact, that Schroeder and I come from the same secular faith tradition, that we share the same belief in reading's potentially redemptive power. And yet, there are dark days when I doubt the activities of reading and writing have much of a future. Indeed, after Columbine, it seems almost ludicrous to suggest that the social, psychological, and biochemical problems that contributed to this massacre might have been peacefully resolved if only Harris and Klebold had spent more time talking about what they were reading. Does reading really possess such curative powers? Does writing? Does group discussion?

Reading, writing, talking, meditating, speculating, arguing: these are the only resources available to those of us who teach the humanities and they are, obviously, resources that can be bent to serve any purpose. Harris and Klebold, in fact, wrote and produced for all different sorts of media; they read a range of material that supported their beliefs and that taught them how to put together their incendiary devices; they hung out with like-minded individuals and discussed their ideas. They relied on writing to post their scathing observations about their peers on Harris's Web site; they composed poems in their creative writing class that their teacher described as "dark and sad"; they created a video for a class project in which they acted out their fantasy of moving through the school gunning down their tormentors (Pooley 30–32). Harris even had the affectation of an English teacher, declaring on his Web site that one of the many habits he found unforgivable in his peers was the tendency to pronounce the "t" in "often": "Learn to speak correctly, you morons," he commands (Barron). They read, they wrote, they talked. And at the end of the process, they tried to kill everyone they could.

For some, it will hardly come as a surprise to learn that reading and writing have no magically transformative powers. But for those of us who have been raised into the teaching and publishing professions, it can be quite a shock to confront the possibility that reading and writing and talking exercise almost *none* of the powers we regularly attribute to them in our favorite stories. The dark night of the soul for literacy workers comes with the realization that training students to read, write, and talk in more critical and self-reflective ways cannot protect them from the violent changes our culture is undergoing. Helen Keller learning to see the world through a language traced into the palm of her hand; Malcolm X in prison memorizing the dictionary word by word; Paulo Freire moving among the illiterate masses in Brazil: we tell ourselves and our students over and over again about the power of reading and writing while the gap between rich and poor grows greater, the Twin Towers come crashing down, and somewhere some other group of angry young men is at work silently stockpiling provisions for the next apocalypse.

If you're in the business of teaching others how to read and write with care, there's no escaping the sense that your labor is increasingly irrelevant. Indeed, one way to understand the dark, despairing character of so much of the critical and literary theory that has come to dominate the humanities over the past two decades is to see this writing as the defensive response of those who have recognized but cannot yet admit that the rise of technology and the emergence of the globalized economy have diminished the academy's cultural significance. And so, to fight off the sense that words exercise less and less power in world affairs, one can declare that discourse plays a fundamental role in the constitution of reality. Rather than concede that reading as an activity has come to consume less and less time in the average person's life, one can insist that the canon wars are the ground upon which the nation's political future is being determined; rather than accept the fact that technological advances have taken control of publishing out of the hands of the few and transformed everyone with access to the Internet into a potential author and critic, one can decry the movement of our culture's critical center from the university to the sound stage of the Oprah Winfrey Show. What is unthinkable in such pronouncements about the centrality of academic work is the possibility that the vast majority of the reading and writing that teachers and their students do about literature and culture more generally might not be all that important. It could all just be a rather labored way of passing the time.

I have these doubts, you see, doubts silently shared by many who spend their days teaching others the literate arts. Aside from gathering and organizing information, aside from generating critiques and analyses that forever fall on deaf ears, what might the literate arts be said to be good for? How — and in what limited ways — might reading and writing be made to matter in the new world that is evolving before our eyes? Is there any way to justify or explain a life spent working with — and teaching others to work with — texts? These are the questions that animate the meditations that follow. Those who have never felt the inner urgency of such questions need read no further.

THE PRINCE OF DARKNESS

> In a million millennia, the sun will be bigger. It will feel nearer. In a million millennia, if you are still reading me, you can check these words against personal experience, because the polar ice caps have melted and Norway enjoys the climate of North Africa.
>
> Later still, the oceans will be boiling. The human story, or at any rate, the terrestrial story, will be coming to an end. I don't honestly expect you to be reading me then.
>
> — MARTIN AMIS
> *The Information*

In *The Information,* Martin Amis's bleak and scorching send-up of the literary professions, the following beliefs are gleefully debunked: that reading makes you a better person; that writers of merit are driven to write by virtue of their deep insights into the human spirit; that a world filled with artistic creations is superior to one filled with the castoffs of consumer culture; that writing provides access to immortality. To stage his skewering of these cultural commonplaces, Amis pits two writers against each other: Richard Tull, the author of artistic, experimental (that is to say, unreadable) novels; and Gwyn Barry, who is vapid and soulless, but whose eventless, multicultural, utopian novel, *Amelior,* has become an international phenomenon. To the degree that *The Information* has a plot, it revolves around Tull's repeated efforts to punish Barry for having met with popular literary success. To Tull's way of thinking, Barry's greatest literary achievement is a work of no consequence: as he describes it, *Amelior* "was about a group of fair-minded young people who, in an unnamed country, strove to establish a rural community. And they succeeded. And then it ended. Not worth writing in the first place, the finished book was, in Richard's view, a ridiculous failure" (28). And yet, in the world Amis has created for his readers, pretentious, sentimental slop of this kind has adulation heaped upon it, while work like the kind Richard Tull produces — work that strains mightily to achieve a high seriousness, work that is replete with veiled literary references, work that endlessly announces its indebtedness to the earlier classics — actually physically harms the few who can bear to read it, causing migraines, seeing disorders, and even forced hospitalizations.

Tull, who is unable to find a publisher and whose previous novels are out of print, can only view his friend's success as a cruel joke the universe is playing on him, one he's determined to counteract. But, as Tull eventually discovers, there's no fighting the ways of the universe. In the grand scheme of things, he is insignificant, and what lies in store for him is what lies in store for us all — a story of increasing humiliation. In fact, *The History of Increasing Humiliation* is one of the many books for which Tull has received an advance but has yet to write, one which is to contain his theory about "the decline in the status and virtue of literary protagonists" (92). As Tull sees it, there's a direct connection between the decline in the status of heroes in the novel and the growth in our understanding of the dimensions of the universe: with each advance in astronomical studies, "we get smaller" (93). We can see the effects of this in our literary creations, Tull argues: "First gods, then demigods, then kings, then great warriors, great lovers, then burghers and merchants and vicars and doctors and lawyers. Then social realism: you. Then irony: me. Then maniacs and murderers, tramps, mobs, rabble, flotsam, vermin" (92). And indeed, Amis uses Tull as a vehicle to prove this theory, assaulting the pieties of those who would privilege the acts of reading and writing by showing artists to be indistinguishable from criminals. By this, Amis does not mean that all criminals are like Hannibal Lecter, all-knowing virtuosos who transgress and transcend social bonds at will. Rather, as Amis puts it, "the criminal *is* like an artist (though not for the reasons usually given, which merely depend on immaturity and the condition of self-employment): the criminal resembles the artist in his pretension, his incompetence, and his self-pity" (76). One could hardly say that the status of the criminal has been elevated through such a comparison.

When Tull's initial efforts to harm his rival fail, he turns to Steve Cousins, a financially secure, semi-retired criminal, who now entertains himself by pursuing "recreational" adventures in his profession: his specialty, as he defines it, is "fuck[ing] people up" for sport (116). And, for reasons that are never quite clear, "Scozzy," as his mates call him, is determined to hurt a writer, preferably Gwyn Barry. Scozzy may be motivated by his own hatred of *Amelior,* which he refers to as a "total crock" and "complete crap" (114); he may be driven by the autodidact's sense of inferiority (113); he may be acting out the aggressions of an abandoned child (Amis repeatedly links Scozzy to the wild boy of Aveyron). But to seek motivation for Scozzy's actions is, within Amis's cosmology, to misunderstand the criminal's place in the universe and our own as well. Asking why a Steve Cousins or an Eric Harris or a Dylan Klebold is violent is itself a meaningless act, not because the motivation is too deeply buried or obscurely articulated to ever be known, but because we no longer live in a world where human action can be explained. We have plenty of information; it just doesn't amount to anything. This is the logic of the history of increasing humiliation working itself out over time.

At one point in the novel, Tull's wife, Gina, is reading the newspaper in horror, trying to make sense of the actions of a child-murderer. "Words," says Gina, " — words fail me. *Why?* Won't someone tell me?" (123). Amis then interrupts this scene to introduce his own commentary on how we are to make sense of these senseless acts, the ones which rob us of speech, the ones which drive us to ask why. "A contemporary investigator will tell you that he hardly ever thinks about motive. It's no help. He's sorry, but it's no help. Fuck the why, he'll say. Look at the how, which will give you the who. But fuck the why" (124). There is no ultimate explanation for these acts of brutality, which is something the little boy, who apologized to the man who was about to murder him, could not understand: "the little boy was searching for motivation in the contemporary playground. Don't look. You won't find it, because it's gone. I'm sorry. I'm sorry" (124).[5]

As it goes with the world, so it goes with the novel: to seek out what motivates Tull to try to destroy Gwyn Barry, to try to understand why Scozzy would want to hurt Barry, to see some reason in Gina's betrayal of Tull — these are all fruitless acts in Amis's cosmos, where only the naive believe that violence is the result of some ultimately discernable act of volition. Tull understands that he lives in a world defined by random acts of violence and he is afraid, not for his own safety, but for his son's: "violence would come, if it came, from the individual, from left field, denuded of motive. The urban pastoral was all left field. There was no right field. And violence wouldn't come for Richard. It would come for Marco" (99). And, indeed, this very scenario is acted out in the conclusion to *The Information,* with Scozzy, bent on revenge for having been publicly insulted by Tull, heading to Tull's neighborhood determined to kidnap Marco. Unaware of the danger his son is in, drunkenly planning one final plot to bring Barry down, Tull stumbles into his apartment only to discover Barry in the act of sodomizing his wife. Meanwhile, outside in the park, Barry's bodyguards happen to intercept Scozzy before he is able to harm Marco. Broken and defeated, Tull belatedly realizes that he owes his son's life to the man he viewed as being in every way his inferior. As the novel ends, with Barry proudly sauntering off victorious, Tull climbs the stairs back to his apartment "working on a way of forgiving Gina. A form of words. Because if he forgave her, she could never leave him now. Who was he? Who had he been throughout? Who would he always be?" (373). Tull, "a failed book reviewer who comes on like Dr. Johnson" (286), has been shown to be a fool who can't even read the intentions and the capabilities of those closest to him. Barry, the avowed fraud and hypocrite, gets everything — fame, fortune, even "the Profundity Requital," which guarantees him lifetime support so he can devote himself to thinking about the social good.

Although Amis explicitly outlaws such a question, one can't help but wonder why a writer would produce such a scathing portrait of the literary world and its denizens. If this is Amis's assessment both of his peers and of the reading public, then why go on writing? Is he, like Gwyn Barry, just along for the ride, cynically "doing what every man would do if he thought he could get away with it" (286)?[6] *The Information* might best be read as a meditation on the fact that sooner or later all writers encounter something that robs them of their sleep, something that deprives them of feeling that what they do matters. As the novel opens, Richard Tull is crying in his sleep, crying because the night had brought "all its unwelcome information" (4). And when he wakes, he considers calling Gwyn Barry, for whom "there would be no information, or the information, such as it was, would all be good" (5). Tull and Barry are both entering their forties and the information that awaits them on this threshold communicates different messages: Gina has given Tull an additional year to complete his latest and perhaps final novel, *Untitled,* after which time — the novel's failure being a foregone conclusion — Tull will have to commit himself to more gainful employment. Barry, on the other hand, has written two bestsellers; his marriage has been featured on the BBC; he's got an international promotional tour lined up; he's been nominated for the Profundity Requital. Tull is having "a crisis of the middle years," a crisis Amis himself has been through. Citing what are presumably notes from his own writing journal, Amis observes, "intimations of monstrousness are common, are perhaps universal, in early middle age" (44). One form this takes is a preoccupation with the question, "how can I ever play the omniscient, the all-knowing, when I don't know *anything?"* (43).

So the information that comes with age, the information that comes at night, brings news of futility, ignorance, insignificance, humiliation: "When we die, our bodies will eventually go back where they came from: to a dying star, our own, five billion years from now, some time around the year 5,000,001,995" (45). With the aging of the body and the foreclosing of future possibilities, all the inbound information serves to turn one's attention to mortality: "the information is telling me to stop saying *hi* and to start saying *bye"* (89). Throughout the novel, Amis concedes that he is not in control of what is happening, that events are unfolding and characters are developing without reference to any greater design on his part. "I don't come at these people," Amis explains in the middle of the novel, "They come at me. They come at me like information formed in the night. I don't make them. They're already there" (190–91). Whether Amis is genuinely haunted by these characters or is only mocking the terror that lesser writers experience when they lose control of their material is a matter of importance only to those who wish to argue over Amis's own literary achievements. For the purposes of this discussion, though, the salient point is to note the ways in which Amis's novel brings together the aging body, the activity of writing, and the inbound information to explore — and I would say produce — feelings of hopelessness. We live in the Information Age and all the information is telling us that whatever we have done, whatever we are doing, and whatever we plan to do will never have any lasting significance.

FOLLOWING THE WORD

> You know, Eric, you can read about this stuff, but you can't understand it until you live it.
>
> — CHRIS McCANDLESS in Jon Krakauer's *Into the Wild*

Chris McCandless's misadventures in the Alaskan wilderness are now well known, thanks to Jon Krakauer's best-selling account of the young man's disappearance and death in *Into the Wild.* These are the facts: after graduating from Emory in 1990, McCandless donated the remains of his college trust fund to Oxfam, burned what money remained, along with his identification papers, and disappeared. Two years later, in the fall of 1992, his emaciated body was found, along with his favorite books and his journal, in a school bus deep in the Alaskan wilds. Something about McCandless's quest and his ultimate fate captured the imagination of readers across the country. For some, the story is a tragedy, one that concerns a deadly conflict between youthful idealism and a brutal, unforgiving reality. For those reading this version of McCandless's life, the loss of a young man who wanted to commune with the natural world and the disappearance of a world untouched by the mercenary desires of human society are developments to be mourned. For others, though, McCandless's story is just another example of the foolishness of those who believe more in the power of books than in the power of the natural world. For these readers, McCandless is a stock figure, a suburban rube, a dreamer who neither understood nor respected the very forces he sought to embrace. For these readers, McCandless got what he deserved.

McCANDLESS STANDS AS EVIDENCE THAT THERE CONTINUE TO BE REAL READERS WHO INVEST THE ACTIVITIES OF READING AND WRITING WITH GREAT SIGNIFICANCE.

I am interested in McCandless not because of the debate his death has sparked, but because he provides us with an opportunity to consider a reader who differs from Amis's characters in one critical regard: regardless of whether or not Amis himself actually believes that knowledge of the size of the cosmos robs the activities of reading and writing of any lasting meaning, McCandless stands as evidence that there continue to be real readers who invest the activities of reading and writing with great significance. In this respect, McCandless is just the kind of reader that Amis's character Richard Tull (and almost every English teacher) is looking for: a reader who savors the words that others have produced, who seeks guidance from the printed page, who dreams of inhabiting the landscapes that his or her most-admired authors describe in such loving detail. While one could argue that some similar utopian longing is there to be found boiling beneath Amis's bleak account of these information-saturated times, it is much more immediately clear that McCandless actually believed that it was possible to escape the bonds of the corporatized world and reach a space of greater calm. He knew this because his books told him so.

What makes *Into the Wild* remarkable is Krakauer's ability to get some purchase on McCandless's actual reading practice, which, in turn, enables him to get inside McCandless's head and speculate with considerable authority about what ultimately led the young man to abandon the comforts of home and purposefully seek out mortal danger. Krakauer is able to do this, in part, because he has access to the books that McCandless read, with all their underlinings and marginalia, as well as to his journals and the postcards and letters McCandless sent to friends during his journey. Working with these materials and his interviews with McCandless's family and friends, Krakauer develops a sense of McCandless's inner life and eventually comes to some understanding of why the young man was so susceptible to being seduced by the writings of London, Thoreau, Muir, and Tolstoy. Who McCandless is and what becomes of him are, it turns out, intimately connected to the young man's approach to reading — both what he chose to read and how he chose to read it.

After graduating from college, McCandless hopped in his car and headed west, embarking on a journey that, since Kerouac, has become a cliché for the dispossessed male. McCandless told no one where he was going or what his plans were. When his car broke down, he abandoned it and began hitchhiking. He renamed himself "Alexander Supertramp." He kept a journal and took photographs to record his adventure. He traveled to California, canoed down into Mexico, made his way toward Alaska. Along the way, he met people who looked out for him and he, more often than not, would return their kindness by encouraging them to read the books that had so moved him. To one, McCandless wrote: "Wayne, you really should read *War and Peace.* I meant it when I said you had one of the highest characters of any man I'd met. That is a very powerful and highly symbolic book. It has things in it that I think you will understand. Things that escape most people" (Krakauer 33). He took a job working at a flea market selling used paperbacks and lost himself in the pleasure of organizing merchandise and assisting in the very kind of commercial transactions he elsewhere despised. His boss reported: "Alex was big on the classics: Dickens, H. G. Wells, Mark Twain, Jack London. London was his favorite. He'd try to convince every snowbird who walked by that they should read *Call of the Wild*" (43–44). In the abandoned bus where McCandless's body was eventually found, there were books by Tolstoy and

Thoreau with highlighted passages celebrating chastity and moral purity (65–66). On some plywood he had written what Krakauer calls McCandless's "declaration of independence":

> AND NOW AFTER TWO RAMBLING YEARS COMES THE FINAL AND GREATEST ADVENTURE. THE CLIMACTIC BATTLE TO KILL THE FALSE BEING WITHIN AND VICTORIOUSLY CONCLUDE THE SPIRITUAL PILGRIMAGE. . . . NO LONGER TO BE POISONED BY CIVILIZATION HE FLEES, AND WALKS ALONE UPON THE LAND TO BECOME *LOST IN THE WILD.* (163; capitals and italics in original)

Like most readers, McCandless surrounded himself with books that reinforced his own beliefs — in this case, texts that confirmed his sense that he was living honorably by attempting to follow his beliefs *to the letter.* Alternately the evangelist and the pilgrim, McCandless moved through the world trying to convert others to his point of view and turning away from anyone who sought to make more intimate contact with him personally. As Alex, he was a hobo, a vagabond, the self-defined "super" tramp, someone who had neither the need nor the desire for human relationships: his books and his solo adventures satisfied his yearnings for connection. Or, as Krakauer puts it in his summary judgment of McCandless's motivations: "Unlike Muir and Thoreau, McCandless went into the wilderness not primarily to ponder nature or the world at large but, rather, to explore the inner country of his own soul" (183).

As much as Krakauer admires McCandless for having embarked upon such a spiritual journey, he is careful to point out that McCandless was ultimately undone by the great trust he placed in the written word. The harshest judgment Krakauer offers in his account emerges in his discussion of McCandless's way of reading Jack London's stories about life in Alaska: "He was so enthralled by these tales . . . that he seemed to forget they were works of fiction, constructions of the imagination that had more to do with London's romantic sensibilities than with the actualities of life in the subarctic wilderness. McCandless conveniently overlooked the fact that London himself had spent just a single winter in the North and that he'd died by his own hand on his California estate at the age of forty, a fatuous drunk, obese and pathetic, maintaining a sedentary existence that bore scant resemblance to the ideals he espoused in print" (44). What most interests me about Krakauer's critique of London is its vehemence: Krakauer's rage here is for an author whose life and words don't align. Because McCandless wanted to believe in the world London invented, because McCandless wanted to be enchanted, he failed to ask the question that Krakauer believes must be of concern to all readers: namely, what is the relationship between what the author says and the way the author lives? London used his writing as a place to store his fantasies about struggling to survive, about lonely battles against the elements, about the animal within, fantasies that have trapped and — Krakauer's language suggests — even killed some of those naive enough to believe them.

While Krakauer faults McCandless for being fooled by London's prose, he goes to great lengths to defend McCandless against charges of recklessness or incompetence. It is true, Krakauer concedes, that McCandless could have taken any number of actions to avoid dying in the woods. The young man could have taken a map with him; he could have done a better job exploring the banks of the suddenly uncrossable river that prevented him from returning by the route he came in on; he could even have started a forest fire to alert the authorities to his plight. But for those who see McCandless's death by starvation as irrefutable proof of his failure as an outdoorsman, Krakauer has another explanation: McCandless died in the woods not because he couldn't find enough food to survive, but because he ate seeds that no one knew to be poisonous. Relying on *Tanaina Plantlore* to guide his gatherings in the wild, McCandless trusted its author completely. As he grew weaker and as game grew scarcer, McCandless began to eat the roots of a species of wild potato that the book identified as nontoxic. The book said nothing about the seeds of the wild potato and it is Krakauer's hypothesis that, as he grew more desperate, McCandless took the book's silence on the seeds as permission to ingest them. If Krakauer is right, one could say that McCandless was killed off by a reading practice that placed too much faith in books, a practice that forgets that the world in all its infinite complexity and particularity will always exceed the explanatory grasp of any single text and, indeed, of all texts taken in their totality.

Whenever I've taught this book — and I've used it with first-year students, undergraduate literature majors, and advanced graduate students — the issue of trust inevitably arises as a problem. Why accept Krakauer's account when he is so obviously invested in defending McCandless from his critics? The fact that Krakauer is so openly identified with the subject of his research is a sign, I would say, that he is producing a kind of writing that can and should still matter. Because Krakauer has inhabited the same clichés that captured McCandless, because he understands their pull from the inside, he is able to offer an account of the young man's motivations that is simultaneously sympathetic *and* critical. By working on the materials of McCandless's life, Krakauer learns how to do what McCandless was unable or unwilling to do: he comes to understand and respect the thoughts of those who were appalled by his behavior. He is doing the work of making peace with his past. Thus, although Krakauer claims he is just trying to make sense of "why some people seem to despise [McCandless] so intensely for having died" in the Alaskan wilds, the truth is that Krakauer is equally interested in using McCandless as a vehicle for making sense of his own turbulent, and occasionally self-destructive, youth. As it turns out, McCandless and Krakauer had much in common. They read and were moved by many of the same authors; they fell in love, like many lonely, alienated, introspective young men before them, with a stark, unforgiving beauty that they could only find in books and in the natural world; and, finally, when the time was right, they both ran away from a world that did not live up to their expectations.

From a certain vantage point, McCandless's Alaskan odyssey and Krakauer's harrowing attempt to climb the Devils Thumb are clichés of modernity: they are the stories of young men, fed up with society, determined to get away from it all. (One version of this cliché involves heading off into the wild; a more recent version, as we've seen, involves entering the schoolyard armed to the teeth.) Now that he has safely made the passage into middle age, Krakauer can see that there's nothing particularly original about embarking on such a journey and he is reluctant to require that such adventures be treated either with reverence or with scorn. On his own journey, Krakauer discovered just how fleeting the profound and transformative experience of scaling a mountain peak can be. Less than a month after realizing his dream, he found himself back in Colorado, pounding nails into frames for townhouses. Over the years that followed, Krakauer came to a different realization: "I was a raw youth who mistook passion for insight and acted according to an obscure, gap-ridden logic. I thought climbing the Devils Thumb would fix all that was wrong with my life. In the end, of course, it changed almost nothing" (155).

Since Krakauer and McCandless moved through the same experiential world for a time, Krakauer seems to know, intuitively, where to look to find a final explanation for McCandless's aberrant behavior. Why would a young man with so much going for him throw it all away? Unlike Amis, Krakauer cannot accept a world without motive, so he continues to probe until he discovers what he believes to be the series of events that alienated McCandless from his family and friends. The ultimate cause of McCandless's disaffection, it would appear, was that his father had conducted an extended affair when McCandless was a small child. Years later, unbeknownst to his parents, McCandless found out about his father's double life and confided in his sister that this discovery made his "entire childhood seem like a fiction" (121–23). To some, it will seem that in uncovering this information, Krakauer has simply succeeded in moving McCandless from one familiar narrative to another, finding at the heart of his desire to escape nothing more than another primordial example of the Oedipal struggle. However accurate such an assessment might be, I would argue that the true significance of Krakauer's discovery lies elsewhere. Having learned this dark family secret, Krakauer is able to provide us with a glimpse of how McCandless responded when confronted with a reality quite unlike the one contained in the books he had chosen to surround himself with. With his childhood transformed into a fiction, McCandless understood himself to have received a warrant to embark on a new life. He believed he was alone. He believed he owed no one anything. He believed he was free.

ON MEDITATIVE WRITING AND ITS CONSEQUENCES

Several years have now passed since I first realized how numerous were the false opinions that in my youth I had taken to be true, and thus how doubtful were all those that I had subsequently built upon them. And thus

> I realized that once in my life I had to raze everything to the ground and begin again from the original foundations, if I wanted to establish anything firm and lasting in the sciences.
>
> — RENÉ DESCARTES, *Meditations on First Philosophy*

All these unhappy men, the betrayed and the betrayers, the real and the fictional. Is there any hope for them? Or for the wasted worlds they've left in their wake? Thinking about these lives, so deeply entangled with violence, neglect, and lies; watching the news, which is forever reporting that another angry man has entered some building or schoolyard, guns blazing; feeling the weight of these stories, and knowing their inevitable movement towards death, destruction, and humiliation: such thoughts only serve to plunge one deeper into the darkness. Amis's fiction clearly offers no escape from such ruminations. And Krakauer's real-life account confirms the fact that relying on reading as a mode of escape has its own unique set of dangers. Against the backdrop of Columbine (or Kosovo or Rwanda or September 11 or Afghanistan or Iraq — the news never fails to offer up another example), there is little these authors can do. The senseless loss of life always trumps the efforts of the meaning makers. Why bother with reading and writing when the world is so obviously going to hell?

WHY BOTHER WITH READING AND WRITING WHEN THE WORLD IS SO OBVIOUSLY GOING TO HELL?

One could say that the course of Western philosophy was forever altered by an encounter with a differently phrased version of this question. When Descartes reached that point in his life when he felt that nothing he had been told in the past could be trusted, he, too, sealed himself off from the rest of society and contemplated the dark possibility that he might be doomed to live out the rest of his days in a dream world. This, at any rate, is the opening conceit of his *Meditations on First Philosophy.* To rid himself of all the false opinions that he had been fed in his youth, Descartes tells us that he waited until he had both the maturity and the free time necessary to devote to the harrowing task of self-purification. In his mid-forties, he sits by the fire, in his dressing gown, all alone. He is transported by the idea that he can attack his past and demolish it. He, too, wants to be free. And so Descartes settles down to the task of dismantling and reassembling his cosmology, a process that takes him six days to complete.[7]

On the first day of his meditations, everything collapses under the force of Descartes' determined skepticism. There is nothing Descartes has ever thought or felt that cannot also be doubted. Since everything that comes to him through his senses is misleading, he finds it impossible to distinguish dream states from states of consciousness. He even imagines the possibility that there might well be "an evil genius, supremely powerful and clever" who whiles away his time deceiving him at every turn (62). While the first act of the God of Genesis is to separate light from darkness, Descartes' accomplishment, on his first day, is to plunge his readers into the pitch of night. In the inverted world he has created with his skepticism, one dreams in the light and fears waking to toil "among the inextricable shadows of the difficulties" that have been produced by the workings of his mind (63).

On the second day, Descartes sets out to inhabit the world of doubt he has created: "I suppose that everything I see is false. I believe that none of what my deceitful memory represents ever existed" (63). Shorn of his past, of his body with all its misleading signals and vague impressions, Descartes discovers his true essence: he is first and foremost a "thing that thinks" (*une chose qui pense*) (65). And as a "thing that thinks," he determines that the senses are not to be trusted: in the midst of this meditation, Descartes looks out the window and believes he sees men walking by on the street. "[Y]et," Descartes asks,"but what do I see aside from hats and coats, which could conceal automata?" (68). To get to the essence of any thing, be it a man or a piece of wax, we must strip "it of its clothing" and "look at [it] in its nakedness" (68): we must remove all outward appearances and get to that which does not change.

On the third day, having shut his eyes, stopped up his ears, withdrawn all his senses, and abandoned his past, Descartes surveys the world of his creation and determines that he is alone. The only way out of this bleak environment that is haunted by malicious demons and the illusory reports of the senses is to posit the existence of a firm foundation, which, for reasons we'll discuss shortly, Descartes designates "God." Descartes' "proof" or "discovery" of God's existence is well known: God is the perfection that Descartes can conceive of but does not actually possess in his thoughts. Since Descartes' thoughts cannot be the cause of this state of perfection (because "what is more perfect [that is, what contains in itself more reality] cannot come into being from what is less perfect"), this perfection must exist outside of him (73). From this, "it necessarily follows that I am not alone in the world, but that something else, which is the cause of this idea, also exists" (74).

Alone with his God in the fourth meditation, Descartes turns his thoughts to an issue that has been at the center of our current discussion: how to distinguish between truth and falsity. For Descartes, the crucial task before him is to explain how God, who is perfect, could have created a thinking thing so defective that it struggles to distinguish fact from fiction, truth from lies. Setting to the side the question of *why* his creator elected to design him in this way, Descartes posits that his own errors result from the fact that he has been endowed by his creator with a will that has a much wider scope than his intellect. On the fifth and sixth days of his meditations, in a repetition that bespeaks a certain anxiety, Descartes once again proves the existence of God and then, after some deft negotiations, is returned to his body and the sensuous world. Before resting, Descartes looks back on where his thinking has taken him and concludes that "the hyperbolic doubts of the last few days ought to be rejected as ludicrous" (103). By doubting everything, he has found the firm ground that is necessary for going on: there is a God; everything that happens is not a lie; the mind can provide us with direct access to the truth. Descartes, it would appear, is home free.

Why should the thoughts this lonely man had more than 350 years ago warrant our attention now? Descartes contributed to the larger effort to liberate reason from the prison of religious dogma and he did this, in part, by driving a wedge between the mind, which traffics in clear and distinct ideas, and the body, which transmits and receives the innately imperfect data of the senses. Fearful of how his thoughts might be received at the time, Descartes had his meditations published first in Latin in Paris and only later allowed them to be translated into French and reprinted in Holland where he was staying. He also placed at the front of his meditations an open letter "to the Most Wise and Distinguished Men, the Dean and Doctors of the Faculty of Sacred Theology of Paris," explaining his reasons for seeking to make public the transcripts, as it were, of his own encounter with the darkness. For those readers prone to skipping such front matter and jumping straight to the body of the text, it will probably come as something of a surprise to learn that Descartes' meditations, which seem like such an earnest attempt to find some solid bedrock upon which to build a life free of falsehoods, are actually a ruse. As Descartes makes clear in his letter to the faculty, he never really had any doubts at all about God or the eternal life of the soul: he's simply trying to put together an argument that will persuade the "unbelievers" (*infidèles*) of what he and his fellow believers "believe by faith" (47). So, the darkness, the radical doubt, the mind floating free of the body are all just props to add to the drama of the fiction he's created — ways of getting those outside the circle of believers to share in his illusion.

That's one way to read Descartes' opening remarks to the Faculty of Sacred Theology. There is, however, yet another possibility. (There always is.) Maybe the letter to the deans and doctors is the sham, just Descartes whispering sweet nothings to those in power in hopes of securing a protected space where he can carry out his scientific research without threat of being harassed. And, given that Descartes is so good at creating the illusion of compliance, what can the illustrious deans and faculty do? He's poured it on so thick — he's just doing what any fellow believer would do, contributing to the cause, etc. — that they just have to get out of the way. If the God that emerges from Descartes' meditations is one more likely to be found residing in the theorems of analytical geometry than in the sanctuaries of the Vatican, what's the harm? That's how advertising works: it's just food for the infidels. It poses no threat to the believers, for what true believer would doubt the existence of God or that the soul separates from the body at death?

There's no resolving the question of whether or not Descartes was being completely sincere when he wrote to the deans and doctors of the Faculty of Sacred Theology in Paris seeking their protection. All we can know is that he had good reason to fear their powers and the institution they represented. For our purposes, what matters most is pausing to take note of the intellectual regime that has risen in the wake of Descartes' effort to break free of dogmatic belief by locating the self at the nexus of reason and the will. To resolve his crisis in certainty and construct a working space that is not contaminated by the lies of the past, Descartes established an internal hierarchy that gives primacy to the mind and its universal truths — truths that, like the properties of a triangle, are clear, distinct, and without a history. The body and its voyage through time are without interest: nothing is to be gained by exploring what happens to the body as it moves through the social institutions that govern life. These are just accidents of time and place. The mind is where the action is.

Whether Descartes himself learned anything as a result of writing down these meditations isn't clear. We know only that Descartes' meditations were designed to provide their author with a method for protecting himself from being deceived by the world and its denizens. Encased in this regulatory mechanism, Descartes is, I believe, more alone at the end of his meditations than when he started. For now that he has rid himself of his fictions and screwed himself into the real, he has no need to consider these fundamental matters any further: "I will say in addition that these arguments are such that I believe there is no way open to the human mind whereby better ones could ever be found" (48). True to this claim, Descartes spends much of the rest of his life defending the veracity of his proofs and the cogency of his line of reasoning. He wanders off into the dreamy world of argumentation.

JOINING THE LIARS' CLUB: WRITING AND THE GENERATION OF HOPE

I never knew despair could lie.

— MARY KARR, *The Liars' Club*

It's safe to say that the spirit of our time differs markedly from the spirit of Descartes' time. While he wrote to banish the particular and to revel in the universal, now that we inhabit the age of the memoir, we find ourselves surrounded by those who write to distinguish themselves from the crowd by capturing the deep particularity and pathos of their own past experiences. Frank McCourt describes the grueling poverty of the Irish immigrant; former Princeton professor Michael Ryan records having sex with his dog; Kathryn Harrison, sex with her father; David Denby, sex with himself (while reading the Great Books no less); James McBride, what it's like to grow up black while having a white mother; Susanna Kaysen, what it's like to be institutionalized. The list goes on and on, because every shoe salesman and waitress, every schoolteacher and cop, every politician and pundit has a story to tell and wants to share it now via the Internet, on some television talk show, or on the printed page. The chosen media doesn't seem to matter. The stories will out.

While there has been much fretting in the critical community about this "turn to the personal" and all that it may be said to signify, the memoirs just keep coming, flooding over the outstretched arms of all those who would like to contain the spread of this genre. That the memoirs, in general, return to scenes of violence and violation is worth pondering, for here one finds evidence of one way in which writing continues to matter at the current moment: the memoir allows one to plunge into the darkness of the past; it provides the means both for evoking and for making sense of that past; and it can be made to generate a sense of possibility, a sense that a better, brighter future is out there to be secured. When judged by these criteria, Mary Karr's *The Liars' Club* stands out as one of the most remarkable representatives of the genre.

The Liars' Club opens with fragments of a recovered memory, "a single instant surrounded by dark": Karr, at seven years old, being inspected by her family doctor; the Sheriff and his deputies moving through her house; the backyard on fire; her mother being taken away; the concerted effort to find a place for the children to stay (3). One of the central projects of *The Liars' Club* is to make sense of these fragments, to relocate them in a more coherent, more comprehensive account of Karr's past. What happened that night? Why did no one ever speak of it again? To answer these questions, Karr has to wade through the faulty, inexact evidence that her family — which is its own liars' club — makes available to her and then find a way to tell not only her story, but also the stories of Pete Karr, her father, Charlie Marie Moore Karr, her mother, and Lecia, her sister.

By the middle of Karr's memoir, she has succeeded in finding out what led to the appearance of the police and the firemen in her house. She eventually remembers being with her sister, hiding in the dark, their mother in the bedroom doorway holding a knife and then, moments later, her mother in the hallway calling the police, saying, "Get over here. I just killed them both. Both of them. I've stabbed them both to death" (157). But to get to this moment, Karr must first detail: life among the working poor in Leechfield, Texas; the odd union of her father, an oil worker, and her mother, a highly educated woman with artistic aspirations; her parents' spiral into alcoholism, the violent fights, the long separations; the slow, agonizingly painful death of the grandmother; her own rape by a neighborhood boy. She is participating in a form of revelation, a ritual of purging and purification. She is telling the family secrets, pulling the ghosts out of the closets, waking the dead, and she does so with no overt sign of shame.

At one point, in retaliation for a beating she received in a fight with the boys who lived next door, Karr credits herself with going on "a rampage that prefigured what Charles Whitman — the guy who shot and killed thirteen people from the tower at the University of Texas — would do a few years later" (161). She got a BB gun, climbed a tree, and waited for her victims to walk out into a nearby field. And when the enemy clan appeared, Karr opened fire, hitting one of the children in the neck before the family fled out of range. When one of the boys hid behind his father, Karr reports that her response was as follows: *"You pussy,* I thought, as if Rickey's not wanting to get shot were a defining mark against his manhood" (162). For this activity, Karr received a whipping. She notes, as well, that her "morning as sniper won [her] a grudging respect. Kids stopped mouthing off about Mother" (162). Violence silenced her tormenters and it kept the enemies at bay. Within the psychic economy of the world Karr inhabited at the time, this doubtless seemed the only rational response available to her.

Eventually, Karr recovers the psychically charged world surrounding her memory of that dark night. Trapped in a life she never wanted serving as a "hausfrau" to an oilman in a "crackerbox house," surrounded by people she despised, Charlie Marie Karr tried to set her world on fire. She burned down her studio. She made a bonfire of her paintings, the children's toys, their books, their furniture, their clothes, their shoes.

As Mary and her sister mutely look on, they are transformed by the experience: they are ready to be led into the fire themselves. "We are in the grip of some big machine grinding us along. The force of it simplifies everything. A weird calm has settled over me from the inside out. What is about to happen to us has stood in line to happen. All the roads out of that instant have been closed, one by one" (152).

They are doomed.

No neighbor intervenes to stop what is happening. No one calls the police. The children don't run away to save themselves. The father doesn't appear to rescue them. The mother is not restrained by some maternal instinct. On the familial level, this is the apocalypse: this is a time without hope. And yet, for reasons that are never explained and perhaps never can be, Charlie Marie doesn't actually go through with murdering her children. She only thinks she has. The disaster passes. The mother is institutionalized. Mary takes her BB gun into the tree. And eventually Charlie Marie comes back home.

From a certain vantage point, this would appear to be the logical place for Karr to end her meditation. She's cast light into her memory of that dark night in the bedroom and now knows what happened. Why keep *The Liars' Club* going for another two hundred pages? What else is there to know? The story continues, I would argue, for two interrelated reasons. First, Karr only knows the *how* and the *what* regarding that night; she does not know *why* her mother went over the edge. Second, Karr's writing has not yet delivered her from those memories because she knows only the facts, not the truth of what happened. At the age of seven, thinking magically, she understood only that her mother had tried to kill her for failing to clean up her room. By the middle of the book, she recognizes the inadequacy of such an explanation. Without the *why* she has nothing, just information coming in the dead of night.

Pursuing the question of motivation takes Karr into still darker waters. After her mother's psychotic episode, her parents move to Colorado and eventually divorce. Her mother remarries and sinks deeper into a drunken stupor. Karr walks in on her mother having sex with another man; Karr is raped again; Charlie Marie tries to kill her new husband, buys a bar, stays up late reading French philosophy and "talking in a misty-eyed way about suicide" (230). Eventually, Charlie Marie puts the girls on a plane back to their father, but it's the wrong plane and they end up flying to Mexico. The calamities continue without ever exposing the cause of all this senseless, self-destructive behavior. Why is it that no one seeks help? What is it that fuels Charlie Marie's all-encompassing sense of despair? Why is it that Pete Karr seeks refuge with the other members of "the Liars' Club," a group of men who drink together and tell tall tales that keep their pasts shrouded in darkness?

When Karr finally finds the key that unlocks the mystery of her family's past, it is long after she has grown up and moved away. Her parents have reunited. She has watched her father's steady decline after a stroke, sat by his side during his final days, listened to him ramble on about his life in the war, a time he never before mentioned. She discovers that he was wounded twice, one time stuck with "a bayonet through his forearm, leaving a scar [she'd] seen a thousand times and never once asked about" (307), the other time left for dead under the rubble of a bridge he'd helped to explode. This last news sends Karr up to the family attic in search of military papers that might be used to get her father additional medical assistance. While moving amongst the family's remains, she discovers four jewelry boxes, each containing a wedding ring. She has, quite unexpectedly, found her mother's hidden past and she then finds the strength to use this material evidence to compel her mother to speak. As Karr confronts her ever-reticent mother, she observes: "Few born liars ever intentionally embark in truth's direction, even those who believe that such a journey might axiomatically set them free" (311).

Karr uncovers the systemic violence that defined her mother's past — the sudden, inexplicable disappearance of her first husband and her first two children, the years she spent trying to find her first family, the reunion where she was convinced to leave the children with their father and return to her studio apartment in Texas — and as she does so the fragmented pieces of her own life begin to fall into place. In the end, the mystery is not so mysterious: "Those were my mother's demons, then, two small children, whom she longed for and felt ashamed for having lost." The explanation for Charlie Marie's years of silence about her past is both simple and profound. She tells her daughter that she kept these events a secret because she was afraid that, if Mary knew, she "wouldn't like [her] anymore" (318).

It would be easy to ridicule such an explanation. After all, Charlie Marie has done much in her life that her daughter did know about that would have justified rejection. She neglected her children, placed them in harm's way, tried to kill herself, tried to kill them. Karr herself finds her mother's reasoning to be "pathetic" (318). However one judges Charlie Marie's excuse, though, the fact that she cannot produce a satisfying or reasonable account for her silence is compelling evidence of just how much power stories *can* exercise over the lives of individuals. By clinging to her silence, by keeping her story trapped inside, she invested her untold story with such a monstrous power that she came to believe that speaking it aloud would make her essentially unlikable. Left alone with this story, Charlie Marie transformed a series of events where she was outmatched, unprepared, and cruelly victimized into irrefutable proof of her own unworthiness as a mother. Without some other connection to the world, without some other voice to counter her interpretations, Charlie Marie was left to suffer her own perpetually punishing judgments. Within this psychic economy, the only possible way for Charlie Marie to remain likable was to keep her story a secret. To remain likable, she had to lie.

The revelation of Charlie Marie's story did not produce the anticipated effect, though.

As Karr puts it: "what Mother told absolved us both, in a way. All the black crimes we believed ourselves guilty of were myths, stories we'd cobbled together out of fear. We expected no good news interspersed with the bad. Only the dark aspect of any story sank in. I never knew despair could lie." As the book ends, Karr escapes the darkness that has defined her past and contemplates "the cool tunnel of white light the spirit might fly into at death." Acknowledging that this description of what it's like to die may simply be an account of "death's neurological fireworks, the brain's last light show," Karr insists that this is a lie she can live with. She is content to at least entertain the possibility of a future communion with her loved ones, a time when "all your beloveds hover before you, their lit arms held out in welcome" (320).

In Karr's hands, the memoir thus becomes a vehicle for arriving at an understanding that produces forgiveness. Writing, as she uses it, is a hermeneutic practice that involves witnessing the mundane horrors of the past in order to make peace with that past. And, as the preceding account makes clear, it also becomes, however briefly, a means for gaining access to the light of the universal. While the other writers and events I've discussed here have turned our attention to death and decay, Karr offers an encounter with the prospect of one's mortality that leads neither to despair nor cynicism nor violence nor suicide nor escape. Even if it's a lie, the lie Karr tells herself at the end of *The Liars' Club* is a lie that keeps her inside the realm of social relations, helping her make what she can of what life has put before her.

AN EXPERIMENT IN INSTITUTIONAL AUTOBIOGRAPHY

It might seem that, by organizing these readings in this way, I've been building up to a spirited defense of the social and therapeutic value of writing one's memoirs. After all, this kind of writing worked for Karr, why shouldn't it work for us all? But the genre of the memoir is no more likely to compel a writer to make peace with the past or to find some sense of connection with others than is poetry, fiction, the meditative essay, the policy statement, the well-honed critique, the bulleted memo, the forced confession, the suicide note. When Martin Amis composed his memoirs, for instance, the genre didn't force him to shift his world view: he ends *Experience* with atrocity, Auschwitz, ruminations on the murder of one of his cousins, and "the usual articles of faith for a man of fifty . . . : that the parents are going, the children are staying, and I am somewhere in between" (371). When Eric Harris began his diary with the statement, "I hate the fucking world," he wasn't laying the groundwork for a transformative inner voyage; he was girding himself for battle.

If we accept Amis's bleak view of the future of publishing – and I think we should – then the challenge, for all whose lives are inextricably bound to the literate arts, is to make a compelling case for why writing might be said to matter in the twenty-first century. Amis taking the long view, Alex Supertramp running into the wild, Descartes alone with his thoughts: it is clear that these men knew that writing could be used to articulate and extend one's sense of despair and one's sense of superiority. What isn't clear, though, is whether these men knew what Karr knows – namely, how to use writing as a practice for constructing a sense of hope and optimism atop the ruins of previous worlds. Is it possible to produce writing that generates a greater sense of connection to the world and its inhabitants? Of self-understanding? Writing that moves out from the mundane, personal tragedies that mark any individual life into the history, the culture, and the lives of the institutions that surround us all?

In working my way up to this set of questions, I have unexpectedly found myself relying on words and phrases that immediately produce religious connotations: the dark night of the soul, the generation of hope, the power of forgiveness. While I did not set out to consider religious matters, the language I've fallen into using has inevitably led me to a set of concerns that tends to be avoided by those who share my secular sensibilities. Under normal circumstances, I might find other, less volatile terms. But these aren't normal circumstances. There will never again be a book that can credibly be labeled "great," not because outstanding books are no longer being produced, but because the world is now awash with writing that no one reads, with last year's blockbusters ending up in the dump next to this year's most insightful critiques. If one is in search of fame or truth and one has placed all one's hopes on the activity of writing, this fact can be a devastating blow. But, however painful it may be to admit, it is clear that those of us who remain committed to books are part of a residual culture whose days are numbered. The fetishization of the written word is coming to an end and in its place one finds a fascination with moving what is known from here to there in the shortest amount of time and with the elusive pleasures of religious conviction. One finds as well a haunting sense of disconnection, as one tightly wound individual after another hatches a plot to make others pay for these ambient feelings of placelessness. The world as we have known it is passing away and the world that is emerging is one that appears to be fraught with danger.

IS IT POSSIBLE TO PRODUCE WRITING THAT GENERATES A GREATER SENSE OF CONNECTION TO THE WORLD AND ITS INHABITANTS? OF SELF-UNDERSTANDING?

What to do? These concerns about the diminishing power of reading and writing serve as the launching point for a sustained investigation into the value of humanistic inquiry at the present moment. In fashioning the oxymoronic phrase "institutional autobiography" to describe the collection of meditations that follows,[8] I mean to highlight a brand of intellectual inquiry that is centrally concerned with what might best be termed "the felt experience of the impersonal." The course of any given individual life cuts through or around a set of institutions charged with responsibility for nurturing both a sense of self and a sense of connection between self and society — the family, the school, and, for some, the church or the house of worship. It goes without saying that the relative influence each of these institutions has on any given individual depends on a number of variables, including race, class, and gender. By linking the institutional with the autobiographic, my goal is not to draw attention away from our individual differences, but rather to show that we all internalize institutional influences in ways that are both idiosyncratic and historically situated, open-ended and overdetermined, liberating and confining. We all go to school, bringing both our minds and our embodied histories: what happens there is both utterly predictable and utterly mysterious, the circumscribed movement of a statistical norm and the free flight of aberrant data.

Historically, schooling in the United States has served as the battleground where the nation works out its evolving understanding of social justice — through, for example, busing, affirmative action, the student loan program, the multicultural curriculum. What has changed recently, though, is the power of weaponry that students bring to the schoolyard and the magnitude of the notoriety that accrues to those who show up ready for a fight. The police investigating the actions of Harris and Klebold concluded that the two young men were driven, above all, by a desire for fame: "[A]ll the rest of the justifications are just smoke. They certainly wanted the media to write stories about them every day. And they wanted cult followings. They [were] going to become superstars by getting rid of bad people" (Cullen, "Kill Mankind"). We might say that Harris and Klebold wanted what all writers are said to want, what Richard Tull and Alexander Supertramp dreamed of and what Gwyn Barry, Amis, Krakauer, Descartes, and Karr have all, to varying degrees, achieved. The costs of such fame are quite high and the benefits fleeting at best.

Can secular institutions of higher education be taught to use writing to foster a kind of critical optimism that is able to transform idle feelings of hope into viable plans for sustainable action? Can the first year writing course become a place where we engage productively with the dark realities of our time: violence, suicide, war, and terrorism, as well as fraudulence, complicity, and trauma? Can teachers of first year writing be moved beyond praising students for generating arguments without consequence, thought with no interest in action? If there is to be lasting hope for the future of higher education, that hope can only be generated by confronting our desolate world and its threatening, urgent realities. The only way out is through.

NOTES

[1] The boys' larger plans were laid out in Harris's diary, in which he fantasized about going to an island after the massacre or, "if there isn't such a place," he wrote, "then we will hijack a hell of a lot of bombs and crash a plane into NYC with us inside [f]iring away as we go down." Eric Harris, personal diary. For a discussion of inaccuracies in the initial characterization of the boys' interests and beliefs, see Cullen, "Inside." [All notes are Miller's, unless indicated by Eds.]

[2] Michael Moore's *Bowling for Columbine* rebuts these familiar explanations for the massacre in Littleton and makes the compelling argument that it is a culture of fear, particularly fear of the racialized other, that is the source of America's violent ways.

[3] Harris, personal diary. "V" is short for "Vodka," Harris's code name for Dylan Klebold. For more on the contents of Harris's diary, see Cullen, "Kill Mankind," and Prendergast.

[4] Harris, who was in the final semester of his senior year, had been rejected from a number of colleges in the weeks prior to carrying out the attack on Columbine. And, just before the attack, he had been rejected by the Marine Corps, apparently because he was taking the antidepressant Luvox. Although both Harris and Klebold were considered by their peers to be "brilliant, particularly in math and computers," it was Klebold who seemed to have had everything going for him: unlike Harris, he had had a date for the senior prom and he had just returned from a trip with his parents to visit the University of Arizona, where he had been admitted for the following fall (Pooley 28). Whatever their shared experiences moving through the school system and the juvenile penal system had been, it was clear to both that their paths would begin to diverge radically after graduation.

[5] Kate Battan, lead investigator of the Columbine shootings, is quoted as having said, as she completed her report: "Everybody wants a quick answer. They want an easy answer so that they can sleep at night and know this is not going to happen tomorrow at their school. And there is no such thing in this case. There's not an easy answer. I've been working on this nonstop daily [for six months] since April 20th and I can't tell you why it happened" (qtd. in Cullen, "Inside").

[6] Amis does, in fact, share much in common with his successful character: he thrives on publicity; he made a name for himself early on as a modern Lothario, and his insistence during contract negotiations for *The Information* on receiving the largest advance ever given in Britain for a literary novel earned him the enmity of much of the literary community (Lyall C13).

[7] Descartes was trained by the Jesuits, the religious order founded by Ignatius Loyola who became a committed Christian after a transformative experience reading *The Life of Christ.* Part of the training Descartes received involved going on a series of retreats where initiates meditated on passages from Scripture in the hope that this practice would help them to achieve a deeper understanding of the text and a more loving response to the world. That Descartes returned to the meditational form later in life is evidence of its lasting pedagogical value.

[8] Miller refers to the chapters in *Writing at the End of the World* that follow this one, essays of a similar method. These chapters, some of which draw on his own experience, are not included in this selection. [Eds.]

BIBLIOGRAPHY

Amis, Martin. *Experience: A Memoir.* New York: Hyperion, 2000.

——. *The Information.* New York: Harmony, 1995.

Barron, James. "Warnings from a Student Turned Killer." *New York Times,* May 1, 1999: A12.

Bowling for Columbine. Dir. Michael Moore. United Artists, 2002.

Cullen, Dave. "Inside the Columbine High Investigation." *Salon.com,* Sept. 23, 1999. Feb. 22, 2003 <http://www.salon.com/news/feature/1999/09/23/columbine>.

——."Kill Mankind. No One Should Survive." *Salon.com,* Sept. 23,1999. Feb. 19, 2003 <http://www.salon.com/news/feature/1999/09/23/journal>.

Denby, David. *Great Books: My Adventures with Homer, Rousseau, Woolf, and Other Indestructible Writers of the Western World.* New York: Simon, 1996.

Descartes, René. *Discourse on Method and Meditations on First Philosophy.* Trans. Donald A. Cress. 4th ed. Indianapolis: Hackett, 1998.

Gross, Jane. "Out of the House, but Still Focused on Family." *New York Times,* Apr. 29, 1999: B2.

Harris, Eric. Personal diary (excerpts). *Westword.com,* Dec. 12, 2002 <http://www.westword.com/special_reports/columbine/files/index_html>.

Harrison, Kathryn. *The Kiss.* New York: Bard, 1996.

Karr, Mary. *The Liars' Club.* New York: Viking, 1995.

Kaysen, Susanna. *Girl, Interrupted.* New York: Vintage, 1994.

Krakauer, Jon. *Into the Wild.* New York: Villard, 1996.

Lyall, Sarah. "Martin Amis's Big Deal Leaves Literati Fuming." *New York Times,* Jan. 31,1995: C13.

McBride, James. *The Color of Water: A Black Man's Tribute to His White Mother.* New York: Riverhead, 1996.

McCourt, Frank. *Angela's Ashes: A Memoir*. New York: Scribner, 1996.
Pooley, Eric. "Portrait of a Deadly Bond." *Time*, May 10,1999: 26–32.
Prendergast, Alan. "I'm Full of Hate and I Love It." *Denver Westword*, Dec. 6, 2001. Feb. 25, 2003 <http://www.westword.com/issues/2001-12-06/news.html/l/index.html>.
Ryan, Michael. *Secret Life: An Autobiography*. New York: Vintage, 1996.

QUESTIONS FOR A SECOND READING

1. "The Dark Night of the Soul" is the first chapter in Richard Miller's book *Writing at the End of the World*. The chapter, which we are inviting you to read as an essay, is organized by subheadings. You might think of these as a way of *punctuating* the essay, and you might think of this technique as a tool for your own toolkit.

   As you reread the essay, pay attention to each unit marked off by a subheading, and pay attention to the progression or arrangement of these units. How might they mark stages or strategies for the writer? for the reader? (Are they big paragraphs, for example, or mini-essays, or stanzas, or something else?) How might you describe the principle of selection and organization? Can you imagine bringing this strategy into your own writing?

2. In the final chapter of *Writing at the End of the World*, Miller says the following about his own writing:

   > While the assessments, evaluations, proposals, reports, commentaries, and critiques I produce help to keep the bureaucracy of higher education going, there is another kind of writing I turn to in order to sustain the ongoing search for meaning in a world no one controls. This writing asks the reader to make imaginative connections between disparate elements; it tracks one path among many possible ones across the glistening water. (p. 196)

   We can assume that this is the kind of writing present in "The Dark Night of the Soul." And he says this about English and the humanities:

   > The practice of the humanities . . . is not about admiration or greatness or appreciation or depth of knowledge or scholarly achievement; it's about the movement between worlds, arms out, balancing; it's about making the connections that count. (p. 198)

   This latter is a pretty bold statement, since English departments have traditionally defined their job as teaching students to read deeply, to conduct scholarly research, and to appreciate great works of literature. What Miller has to offer, rather, is "movement between worlds, arms out, balancing" or "making the connections that count."

   As you reread "The Dark Night of the Soul," be prepared to talk about connections—about the connections Miller makes, about the ways he makes them, and about the ways you as a reader are (or are not) invited into this process. Is Miller's description of his project, as represented above, accurate or sufficient? If what is represented in Miller's writing can suggest a goal for a curriculum or an imperative for English instruction in high schools and in colleges, what changes would need to be made? What would a course look like? What would its students do? Would you want to take such a course?

3. For the sake of argument, let's say that Jon Krakauer and Mary Karr are the key figures in this essay—Krakauer as a reader, Karr as a writer. As you reread, pay particular attention to these two sections. What are the appropriate goals and methods for reading, if Krakauer is to serve as a model? What are the appropriate goals and methods for writing, if Karr is to serve as a model? And do you agree with the initial assumption, that Krakauer and Karr are the key figures in this essay?

   For further research: Two chapters in *Writing at the End of the World* are, at least in part, autobiographical. In them Miller writes about his own family, and the story he tells is a difficult one. You could read these chapters to add a third key figure to this mix—Miller himself. Does Miller read Karr as an exemplary figure? With this example in mind, how do you read Miller? How might you place his writing in relation to hers?

4. Miller introduces two phrases in the final paragraphs of "The Dark Night of the Soul": "the felt experience of the impersonal" and "critical optimism." He introduces these to set up key terms a reader can use in reading the chapters that follow in his book. You don't have these chapters to refer to. Still, the chapter that you read should serve as suitable preparation for a reader to make sense of these terms. As you reread "The Dark Night of the Soul," keep these key terms in mind. And be prepared to write one-paragraph definitions of each. What do they mean for Miller? What do they mean in relation to the work he does in "The Dark Night of the Soul"? Each paragraph should include a reference (with a block quotation) to one of Miller's examples.

5. Richard E. Miller has recently turned his attention to multimedia composition, composition in digital environments, both in his own writing and as a necessary next step for the teaching of English. You can access an example of this work at nmc.org: "This Is How We Dream, Parts 1 and 2." Watch this video presentation, and as you reread, take the notes you will need to be prepared to talk about new media in relation to the concerns expressed in "The Dark Night of the Soul."

ASSIGNMENTS FOR WRITING

1. Miller's essay opens with a list of fatal shootings in school—troublingly, an incomplete list. As the essay builds to questions—questions for educators and for students—the specters of violence and alienation remain, changing how we think about the reading and writing school endeavors to teach us. "I have these doubts, you see," Miller writes of academic work, "doubts

silently shared by many who spend their days teaching others the literate arts. Aside from gathering and organizing information, aside from generating critiques and analyses that forever fall on deaf ears, what might the literate arts be said to be good for?" (p. 424).

Write an essay that takes up this question—"what might the literate arts be good for?"—and that takes it up from your range of reference and from your point of view—or, more properly, from the point of view of you and people like you, the group you feel prepared to speak for. As an exercise in understanding, your essay should be modeled on one (or more) of the sections in "The Dark Night of the Soul." You can choose the text—and the text can be anything that might serve as an example of the literate arts, things in print but also including songs, films, and TV shows. But your presentation and discussion of the text should be in conversation with Miller—with his concerns, his key terms, his examples, and his conclusions.

2. In the final chapter of *Writing at the End of the World*, Miller says the following about English and the humanities:

> The practice of the humanities . . . is not about admiration or greatness or appreciation or depth of knowledge or scholarly achievement; it's about the movement between worlds, arms out, balancing; it's about making the connections that count. (p. 198)

This latter is a pretty bold statement, since English departments have traditionally defined their job as teaching students to read deeply, to conduct scholarly research, and to appreciate great works of literature. What Miller has to offer, rather, is "movement between worlds, arms out, balancing" or "making the connections that count."

"The Dark Night of the Soul" could be said to be about the teaching of English. Reread it, taking notes and marking sections you might use to think about Miller's concerns and his contributions and about schooling and the teaching of the "literate arts." This is a subject about which you already have some considerable experience. Write an essay in response to "The Dark Night of the Soul," one in which you engage Miller's argument from the point of view of the student. If what is represented in Miller's writing can suggest a goal for a curriculum or an imperative for English instruction in high schools and in colleges, what changes would need to be made? What would a course look like? What would its students do? Would you want to take such a course?

3. In the final chapter of *Writing at the End of the World*, Miller says the following about his own writing:

> While the assessments, evaluations, proposals, reports, commentaries, and critiques I produce help to keep the bureaucracy of higher education going, there is another kind of writing I turn to in order to sustain the ongoing search for meaning in a world no one controls. This writing asks the reader to make imaginative connections between disparate elements; it tracks one path among many possible ones across the glistening water. (p. 196)

We can assume that this is the kind of writing present in "The Dark Night of the Soul."

Reread "The Dark Night of the Soul" with particular attention to Miller's method, which is, in simplest terms, putting one thing next to another. Pay attention to the connections Miller makes, to the ways he makes them, and to the ways as a reader you are (or are not) invited into this process. And write a Miller-like essay. To give the project some shape and limit, let's say that it should bring together at least three "disparate elements," three examples you can use to think about whatever it is you want to think about. You don't need to be constrained to Miller's subject—writing, reading, and schooling—although this subject might be exactly the right one for you. Your writing should, however, be like Miller's in its sense of urgency. Write about something that matters to you—in other words, that you care about, that touches you personally and deeply.

4. Consider the following passage from Miller's "The Dark Night of the Soul":

> What makes *Into the Wild* remarkable is Krakauer's ability to get some purchase on McCandless's actual reading practice, which, in turn, enables him to get inside McCandless's head and speculate with considerable authority about what ultimately led the young man to abandon the comforts of home and purposefully seek out mortal danger. Krakauer is able to do this, in part, because he has access to the books that McCandless read, with all their underlinings and marginalia, as well as to his journals and the postcards and letters McCandless sent to friends during his journey. Working with these materials and his interviews with McCandless's family and friends, Krakauer develops a sense of McCandless's inner life and eventually comes to some understanding of why the young man was so susceptible to being seduced by the writings of London, Thoreau, Muir, and Tolstoy. Who McCandless is and what becomes of him are, it turns out, intimately connected to the young man's approach to reading—both what he chose to read and how he chose to read it. (p. 429)

When Miller is writing about Krakauer's *Into the Wild*, he seems to suggest that what we read, and how we read, can say something about who we are and about what we might become. This is a very bold claim.

Think of a book that made a difference to you, that captured you, maybe one you have read more than once, maybe one that you've made marks in or that still sits on your bookshelf. Or, if not a book, think of your favorite song or album or movie or TV show, something that engaged you at least potentially as McCandless was engaged by London, Thoreau, Muir, and Tolstoy. What was it that you found there? What kind of reader were you? And what makes this a story in the past tense? How and why did you move on? (Or if it is not a story in the past tense, where are you now, and are you, like McCandless, in any danger?)

MAKING CONNECTIONS

1. After years spent unwilling to admit its attractions, I gestured nostalgically toward the past. I yearned for that time when I had not been so alone. I became impatient with books. I wanted experience more immediate. I feared the library's silence. I silently scorned the gray, timid faces around me. I grew to hate the growing pages of my dissertation on genre and Renaissance literature. (In my mind I heard relatives laughing as they tried to make sense of its title.) I wanted something — I couldn't say exactly what. (p. 531)

— RICHARD RODRIGUEZ
The Achievement of Desire

For some, it will hardly come as a surprise to learn that reading and writing have no magically transformative powers. But for those of us who have been raised into the teaching and publishing professions, it can be quite a shock to confront the possibility that reading and writing and talking exercise almost *none* of the powers we regularly attribute to them in our favorite stories. The dark night of the soul for literacy workers comes with the realization that training students to read, write, and talk in more critical and self-reflective ways cannot protect them from the violent changes our culture is undergoing. (p. 423)

— RICHARD E. MILLER
The Dark Night of the Soul

Both Richard E. Miller and Richard Rodriguez are concerned with the limits (and the failures) of education, with particular attention to the humanities and to the supposed benefits to be found in reading and writing. "I have these doubts, you see," Miller writes of academic work, "doubts silently shared by many who spend their days teaching others the literate arts. Aside from gathering and organizing information, aside from generating critiques and analyses that forever fall on deaf ears, what might the literate arts be said to be good for?" (p. 424).

Write an essay that takes up this question — "what might the literate arts be said to be good for?" — and that takes it up with these two essays, Miller's "The Dark Night of the Soul" and Rodriguez's "The Achievement of Desire" (p. 515), as your initial points of reference. What does each say? How might they be said to speak to each other? And, finally, where are you in this? Where are you, and people like you, the group for whom you feel prepared to speak? You, too, have been and will continue to be expected to take courses in reading and writing, to read, write, and talk in "critical and self-reflective ways." Where are you in this conversation?

2. After years spent unwilling to admit its attractions, I gestured nostalgically toward the past. I yearned for that time when I had not been so alone. I became impatient with books. I wanted experiences more immediate. I feared the library's silence. I silently scorned

> the gray, timid faces around me. I grew to hate the growing pages of my dissertation on genre and Renaissance literature. (In my mind I heard relatives laughing as they tried to make sense of its title.) I wanted something — I couldn't say exactly what. (p. 531)
>
> — RICHARD RODRIGUEZ
> *The Achievement of Desire*

> I could not, in the end, for some blessed reason, turn away from myself. Not at least in this place. The place of desire. I think now of the small lines etching themselves near the eyes of a woman's face I loved. And how, seeing these lines, I wanted to stroke her face. To lean myself, my body, my skin into her. A part of me unravels as I think of this, and I am taken toward longing, and beyond, into another region, past the walls of this house, or all I can see, stretching farther than the horizon where right now sea and sky blend. It is as if my cells are moving in a larger wave, a wave that takes in every history, every story. (p. 381)
>
> — SUSAN GRIFFIN
> *Our Secret*

We typically think of desire as something that leads us toward something, not as an achievement in and of itself, but as a process. Both Rodriguez and Griffin embody desire in different ways in their essays. If Richard Miller were to read these writers for their desires, what do you think he would notice?

Write an essay in which you think through the relationship between writing and desire. With Miller in mind, consider how Rodriguez's or Griffin's essay enacts a set of desires. What seems to propel their writing? What interests or concerns move them from one subject to another? At the same time, what desires do they come to as the essay unfolds? What do they seem to move closer to, and what do they seem to leave behind? Use this opportunity to reflect on your own writing and the changing desires that propel you or slow you down, the set of desires that may or may not be found in Miller's ideals, Rodriguez's reflections, or Griffin's imaginings.

3. One way to imagine Susan Griffin's project in "Our Secret" (p. 335) is to think of her study of Heinrich Himmler as a journey through texts. She spends a significant amount of time attending to Himmler's journals and writings, looking at the way he stood in photographs, closely reading the words he chose as a child and later as a Nazi soldier. Griffin says that she has been "searching" through these documents. She writes:

> Now as I sit here I read once again the fragments from Heinrich's boyhood diary that exist in English. I have begun to think of these words as ciphers. Repeat them to myself, hoping to find a door into the mind of this man, even as his character first forms so that I might learn how it is he becomes himself. (p. 338)

Considering the journals and memoirs he consults, one might think of Richard Miller as having a similar project to Griffin's, one of sifting through texts in order to uncover their relationships to the human beings who read and wrote these texts. Miller writes:

> Asking why a Steve Cousins or an Eric Harris or a Dylan Klebold is violent is itself a meaningless act, not because the motivation is too deeply buried or obscurely articulated to ever be known, but because we no longer live in a world where human action can be explained. We have plenty of information; it just doesn't amount to anything. This is the logic of the history of increasing humiliation working itself out over time. (p. 426)

Write an essay in which you discuss Griffin's project of looking at Himmler in relation to Miller's examination of Eric Harris and Dylan Klebold. How do Miller's words above help to illuminate, expand, or complicate Susan Griffin's thoughts in "Our Secret"? What does Griffin mean when she says she thinks of Himmler's words as ciphers? In what ways do Griffin and Miller seem to be engaging in a similar inquiry or investigation? What does each text offer as its theory of writing and reading?

4. In his essay "Our Time" (p. 657) John Edgar Wideman worries over the problems of representation, of telling his brother's story. He speaks directly to the fundamental problem writers face when they try to represent the lives of others: "I'd slip unaware out of his story and into one of my own. I'd be following him, an obedient shadow, then a cloud would blot the sun and I'd be gone, unchained, a dark form still skulking behind him but no longer in tow" (p. 672). Wideman goes on to say:

> The hardest habit to break . . . would be listening to myself listen to him. That habit would destroy any chance of seeing my brother on his terms; and seeing him in his terms, learning his terms, seemed the whole point of learning his story. . . . I had to teach myself to listen. Start fresh, clear the pipes, resist too facile an identification, tame the urge to take off with Robby's story and make it my own. (p. 672)

Richard E. Miller, in "The Dark Night of the Soul," is also concerned with the problems of representation. He provides readings of the lives of others — from Eric Harris to Chris McCandless to Martin Amis to René Descartes and Mary Karr — who are also engaged with the problems of representation and understanding. Write an essay about writing and representation, about the real world and the world of texts, with Wideman and Miller as your primary points of reference. How do they understand representation as a problem for writers and readers? How is that understanding represented (or enacted) in their own work? Which might have something to learn from the example of the other?

5. Both Richard Miller, in "The Dark Night of the Soul," and Judith Butler, in "Beside Oneself: On the Limits of Sexual Autonomy" (p. 240), are concerned with the fundamental question of what, in Butler's terms, "makes for a livable world." How would Miller read, appropriate, and understand Butler's essay?

   "The Dark Night of the Soul" is divided into sections; most sections consider a particular text: Krakauer's *Into the Wild*, Descartes's *Meditations*, Karr's *The Liars' Club*. Reread Miller in order to get a sense of his argument, style, and method, and then write a section that could be added to "The Dark Night of the Soul" with Butler's "Beside Oneself" as its subject.

ENGAGING WITH STUDENT WRITING

You will find below a couple of responses to Richard Miller written by students using the "Assignments for Writing" in *Ways of Reading*. The essays included here are previously unpublished, but we invite you to read them in much the same way as you would read the other essays collected in this book. They are meant to serve not as models or examples, but as opportunities to work on an essay as a reader and as a writer. Response to question 2 in "Assignments for Writing":

Books Aren't Enough

By Austin Crull

Perched on a shelf above my bed are a few dozen novels with worn covers and faded letters written down their spines. These books fit right in with their surroundings. A messy bed, clothes strewn about the room, and a desk with just about any item you could think of spread randomly across it. Yet there is a distinct difference here. The books are worn, but they stand neatly in line. Their spines are cracked, yet they emanate a feeling of composition rather than chaos. In their pages are stories about wizards, elves, and tons of other imaginative creatures that can only be found on the pages of fantasy novels. What can a book say about a person? And how can we discover this answer if that which we are searching for is about ourselves? It seems that self-analysis is the only means of reaching these answers. In a way, we must step outside ourselves in order to truly find what makes us who we are. In this instance, books are the evidence collected for self-inspection, and just as Jon Krakauer studied Chris McCandless in his book *Into the Wild*, we too can gain a wealth of knowledge about ourselves through the books we read.

Stepping over and around the mess on the floor, I step directly in front of the bookshelf of a nineteen-year-old college student. One book stands out from the rest. It is larger than the rest, but that's not what makes it so apparent to me. While the entire collection looks well used, this book in particular looks as though it has been picked up far more than the rest. *The Lord of the Rings* by J. R. R. Tolkien is inscribed down the side in faded golden letters. The story is well known—one of unlikely friendships, good versus evil, and overcoming seemingly insurmountable obstacles. So what does this tell us? That this person has friends? That this person hates evil and maybe has overcome a few obstacles in his life? Were this the case, then it seems we've discovered the identity of just about every kid in the world. It is not these truths that we are searching for. They speak neither to the complexities of a person nor to the depths of human emotion. What about this one book tells something that nothing else in the room could possibly reveal? The fact that it has been read numerous times says something in and of itself. This book is important. Something is locked within the text of these pages that enthralls the reader so much that he comes back and reads it time and time again.

One of these components is the sheer depth of this novel. Its author, Tolkien, spent a lifetime writing the pages of this book, leaving no question unanswered and no detail overlooked. Perhaps this says something about its reader. A book like this may reveal the curiosity of our subject. He is someone who searches for every answer and needs to know every detail. Another component may be the magnitude of the story. In the book the fate of the world rests on the shoulders of some of the smallest and seemingly most insignificant characters. To an outsider this can suggest the insecurities of the reader. Perhaps the reader connects with the insignificance of the characters. There is hope in the story and reassurance that no one is truly insignificant. Our reader no doubt finds comfort in these ideas. In addition to these ideas, one notion is quite evident that our reader may identify with. Adventure. Looking around this room, you can see textbooks everywhere. It is a college kid's dorm after all. This book no doubt offers an escape from the exams, a relief from the readings about molecules and economics. This book provides excitement, and it disconnects readers from mediocre reality.

So what does this all really say about our subject? He has insecurities. Sometimes he wishes to break free from the bonds of reality. These conclusions seem to be similar to the few that were drawn earlier. They are shared by nearly everyone. These conclusions don't seem to create an identity as much as they create the picture of humanity. It is at this point where I notice the problem with our question. There is no sense of individuality when we look upon the books in this room. Thousands of people have read all these books. They provide a blank page when we try to interpret a person through them. It is the mind we are trying to unlock which creates the interpretation for us. Without seeing how someone reacts to the pages of *The Lord of the Rings*, we have no chance of discovering who they are. Our thoughts and actions are what reveal our identities—not those of an author. It is at these moments, when we think we understand someone, that we fall short.

In Richard Miller's *Writing at the End of the World*, he mentions that the author of *Into the Wild*, Jon Krakauer, researches who his subject (Chris McCandless) is through his readings. No doubt this is true; however, Krakauer also researches McCandless through interviews with family and friends, his writings, and his actions. That is how Krakauer develops an identity for his subject. The human mind is so complex that it takes more than one medium for us to develop an identity for another person. And even with all the resources at Krakauer's fingertips, who's to say that his suggestions are accurate? It seems an insurmountable challenge to create an identity for someone else no matter what the resources at your disposal.

Austin Crull's essay, "Books Aren't Enough," seems to both enact *and* challenge Miller's arguments about how reading might shape a human mind. Crull speculates about himself through the books he finds in his room, but he also reflects on the room itself and on the condition of the books he finds there. It seems he wants us to consider not only the books but also the context in which they are found. Ultimately, he tells us: "Without seeing how someone reacts to the pages of *The Lord of the Rings*, we have no chance of discovering who they are. Our thoughts and actions are what reveal our identities—not those of an author." What does Crull seem to be arguing in this statement? How does he want to intervene in Miller's questions about literacy and the way reading might reflect one's "inner life"? Why do you suppose Crull wants to focus on "how someone reacts"? Is this issue of reaction one Miller misses or neglects? How might you position Crull and Miller as contributing to the same conversation? How do they converge, collaborate, or challenge each other?

Response to question 2 in "Assignments for Writing":

Dreams: The Core of One's Identity?

By Brady Bartlett

Sigmund Freud believed that dreams are the symbolic language of the subconscious mind. So what does that tell us? Are dreams impulses or desires that are too harmful or disturbing to our conscious mind? Are they suppressed feelings that we have shoved deep inside of ourselves? A person's superego keeps the subconscious mind from acting out—one's superego is shut off during the dream state—so are dreams the profound hidden passions that drive and influence somebody?

My roommate keeps a journal of the dreams he has. He wakes up in the morning and writes them down to make sure he doesn't miss any details. What would somebody be able to learn about Obi if they stumbled on his journal of dreams? Is it fair to make assumptions about Obi's motives or thoughts based on complex symbolic dreams? His dreams could be nothing but exaggerations of thoughts and interactions that occurred throughout the day. Is it fair for me to make these assumptions about Obi based on his subconscious mind?

I am on a bridge. It is a brown bridge, and I am running. The city is behind me. Some force starts to push me. I start to fall off the bridge to the left. I am falling in air. Right before I hit the ground, I wake up.

Does Obi live in the city? Maybe he is afraid of the city and does not want to be stuck there his whole life. He feels threatened about his surroundings—he no longer wants to be there—he runs. Obi is on the bridge, on his way out of the city, and then he falls off of the bridge. Obi does not believe in himself. Instead of seeing himself get out of the city, he falls off before he gets away from the danger. He thinks that he will not be able to make it away from the city. He worries that he does not have what it takes to get out.

I'm in the woods with my older brother. We are climbing this big rock in the woods. All of a sudden a few giant robot monkeys start coming toward my brother and me. They have guns! My brother tells me to hide. He starts shooting them, but is shot in the leg. I run up next to him. I grab the gun and start shooting. They are getting closer. I wake up.

Obi's brother takes the normal older brother role in life. His older brother protects him even if it is a life-and-death situation. There is definite trust that his older brother will watch out for him, even against giant robot monkeys. The point right after his older brother gets shot in the leg and Obi runs to his aid shows that the trust and love are mutual. His brother is willing to risk his life to save him, and Obi has his brother's back also. The fact that he grabbed the gun and started shooting back probably means he is pretty brave or at least in the face of danger he stands up. He is not a coward. He is a person who cares greatly about his family.

I'm on a trip to California. I am going to see the Dodgers vs. Indians baseball game. At the game I get the urge to play floor hockey. Next thing I know I am playing floor hockey at USC. While playing, I look up and see my buddy from home (who goes there), and after I finish the game, I go give him a hug. I wake up.

This friend of his is probably pretty close to him. Maybe they have talked about visiting each other, and that is what brought this dream about. He misses his friend and wants to see him. Seeing him reminds him of home, which he also misses, but not enough to go home. He is happy being independent but still wanted to get that sense of home. He is also probably someone who likes sports, seeing as in his dream he both watched one and played one.

I am older; in my thirties if I had to guess. I am dressed in a suit, and my date is wearing a gorgeous blue dress. We are at a fancy restaurant. Suddenly we're in a hot tub at a mansion. Nobody is around but us. It is quiet. The sun is setting, and the view out to the ocean is breathtaking. As I lean in for a kiss, the alarm goes off . . . of course.

From this I get that Obi is ambitious. I think that a normal life is not in his plans for the future. He has bigger plans. This may not be his ideal dream house or girl, but he is hoping that he lives nicely when he is older. He could be high maintenance and used to this type of living, or he does not live like this and aspires to be successful. If he aspires to be like this, his standards are high. Instead of being content with a nice family in the countryside, he goes for the gold. Fancy suit, beautiful girl, expensive restaurant, mansion, ocean view. He thinks this is what will make him happy in life.

Certainly one cannot figure out a great deal about people through their dreams. Think of a dream that you have had more than once. One that sticks with you. What does it say about you? Why do you think you had it? The problem with dreams is that they are not fully understood. Even I cannot tell you what my dreams mean. My guess would be a more educated guess because I know more about myself, but a guess nonetheless. This extends beyond dreams. You cannot judge someone or try to figure them out through dreams, their writing, what they read, or what music they listen to. To understand somebody, you have to communicate with them and try to get to know them.

When you read someone's things to try to get a sense of who they are, too much is left for assumption and interpretation. Too many factors are not taken into consideration by the reader, like their mood. If I write something while I am in an angry mood, what is said will come off a lot differently than if I were in a very happy state of mind. Reading someone else's dreams is very appealing because it is always interesting to see what goes on in somebody's mind when they no longer have control. During dreams your morals are put to the side, and that barrier is no longer there. Your mind is free to do what it likes. Feelings that are so deep that you do not even acknowledge their existence may arise during dreams. The dream could be a fantasy that is not possible to achieve in real life.

Do dreams really mean anything to someone? Perhaps they are just some connections to something still on the conscious mind. Maybe somebody just told Obi a story or he watched a movie, and in his dream state it was taken to a completely different level. In the dream state there are no boundaries. You can fly, be invisible, never die, be wealthy, or even not look the same. You are at the mercy of your subconscious mind. If someone tries to interpret these images made from your subconscious mind, it is simply unfair. You are not even sure what these symbolic messages mean, so how would somebody else know? Next time you have a dream, write it down and think of what might be said about you if a total stranger tried to interpret it.

Brady Bartlett experiments with form in this essay. He moves back and forth between his thinking about Obi's dream journal and quotations from the journal. We might understand Bartlett's essay as experimenting with shifts in perspective, just as Susan Griffin's essay "Our Secret" does. However, rather than writing an essay that engages with a text that Obi reads, Bartlett chooses to engage with a text that Obi *writes*, a text that is intended to record the images and narratives of his subconscious mind. Austin Crull, in his essay "Books Aren't Enough," seems to suggest that reactions might be more telling than merely what one reads. Does Bartlett's essay spend time thinking about reactions as well? What does Bartlett seem to suggest about how literacy practices (reading and writing) shape and reflect lives? Bartlett interprets Obi through his dreams; however, at the close of his essay, he seems to be questioning whether this is a legitimate or fair strategy for interpretation. What appears to be his concern? Does Miller have similar concerns as he offers his interpretations of Eric Harris's journal? Consider Bartlett, Crull, and Miller as three writers who are all trying to tackle the difficult project of representing their own and others' readings. How would you describe each of their approaches? What are they saying *to* one another?

WALKER Percy

Walker Percy, in his midforties, after a life of relative obscurity and after a career as, he said, a "failed physician," wrote his first novel, *The Moviegoer*. It won the National Book Award for fiction in 1962, and Percy emerged as one of this country's leading novelists. Little in his background would have predicted such a career.

After graduating from Columbia University's medical school in 1941, Percy (1916–1990) went to work at Bellevue Hospital in New York City. He soon contracted tuberculosis from performing autopsies on derelicts and was sent to a sanitorium to recover, where, as he said, "I was in bed so much, alone so much, that I had nothing to do but read and think. I began to question everything I had once believed." He returned to medicine briefly but suffered a relapse and during his long recovery began "to make reading a full-time occupation." He left medicine, but not until 1954, almost a decade later, did he publish his first essay, "Symbol as Need."

The essays that followed, including "The Loss of the Creature," all dealt with the relationships between language and understanding or belief, and they were all published in obscure academic journals. In the later essays, Percy seemed to turn away from academic forms of argument and to depend more and more on stories or anecdotes from daily life—to write, in fact, as a storyteller and to be wary of abstraction or explanation. Robert Coles has said that Percy's failure to find a form that would reach a larger audience may have led him to try his hand at a novel. You will notice in the essay that follows that Percy delights in piling example upon example; he never seems to settle down to a topic sentence, or any sentence for that matter, that sums everything up and makes the examples superfluous.

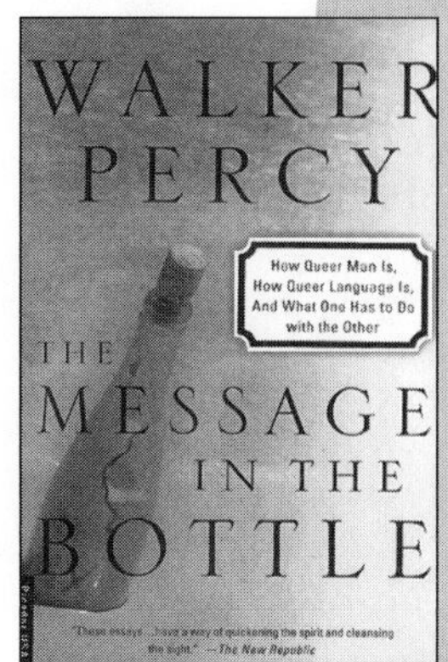

In addition to *The Moviegoer*, Percy has written five other novels, including *Lancelot* (1977), *Love in the Ruins* (1971), and *The Thanatos Syndrome* (1987). He has published two books of essays, *The Message in the Bottle: How Queer Man Is, How*

Queer Language Is, and What One Has to Do with the Other (1975, from which "The Loss of the Creature" is taken), and *Lost in the Cosmos: The Last Self-Help Book* (1983). Walker Percy died at his home in Covington, Louisiana, on May 10, 1990, leaving a considerable amount of unpublished work, some of which has been gathered into a posthumous collection, *Signposts in a Strange Land* (1991). *The Correspondence of Shelby Foote and Walker Percy* was published in 1996.

The Loss of the Creature

I

Every explorer names his island Formosa, beautiful. To him it is beautiful because, being first, he has access to it and can see it for what it is. But to no one else is it ever as beautiful — except the rare man who manages to recover it, who knows that it has to be recovered.

Garcia López de Cárdenas discovered the Grand Canyon and was amazed at the sight. It can be imagined: One crosses miles of desert, breaks through the mesquite, and there it is at one's feet. Later the government set the place aside as a national park, hoping to pass along to millions the experience of Cárdenas. Does not one see the same sight from the Bright Angel Lodge that Cárdenas saw?

The assumption is that the Grand Canyon is a remarkably interesting and beautiful place and that if it had a certain value *P* for Cárdenas, the same value *P* may be transmitted to any number of sightseers — just as Banting's discovery of insulin can be transmitted to any number of diabetics. A counterinfluence is at work, however, and it would be nearer the truth to say that if the place is seen by a million sightseers, a single sightseer does not receive value *P* but a millionth part of value *P*.

THE THING IS NO LONGER THE THING AS IT CONFRONTED THE SPANIARD; IT IS RATHER THAT WHICH HAS ALREADY BEEN FORMULATED — BY PICTURE POSTCARD, GEOGRAPHY BOOK, TOURIST FOLDERS, AND THE WORDS *GRAND CANYON.*

It is assumed that since the Grand Canyon has the fixed interest value *P*, tours can be organized for any number of people. A man in Boston decides to spend his vacation at the Grand Canyon. He visits his travel bureau, looks at the folder, signs up for a two-week tour. He and his family take the tour, see the Grand Canyon, and return to Boston. May we say that this man has seen the Grand Canyon? Possibly he has. But it is more likely that what he has done is the one sure way not to see the canyon.

Why is it almost impossible to gaze directly at the Grand Canyon under these circumstances and see it for what it is — as one picks up a strange object from one's back yard and gazes directly at it? It is almost impossible because the Grand Canyon, the thing as it is, has been appropriated by the symbolic complex which has already been formed in the sightseer's mind. Seeing the canyon under approved circumstances is seeing the symbolic complex head on. The thing is no longer the thing as it confronted the Spaniard; it is rather that which has already been formulated — by picture postcard, geography book, tourist folders, and the words *Grand Canyon*. As a result of this preformulation, the source of the sightseer's pleasure undergoes a shift. Where the wonder and delight of the Spaniard arose from his penetration of the thing itself, from a progressive discovery of depths, patterns, colors, shadows, etc., now the sightseer measures his satisfaction *by the degree to which the canyon conforms to the preformed complex.* If it does so, if it looks just like the postcard, he is pleased; he might even say, "Why it is every bit as beautiful as a picture postcard!" He feels he has not been cheated. But if it does not conform, if the colors are somber, he will not be able to see it directly; he will only be conscious of the disparity between what it is and what it is supposed to be. He will say later that he was unlucky in not being there at the right time. The highest point, the term of the sightseer's satisfaction, is not the sovereign discovery of the thing before him; it is rather the measuring up of the thing to the criterion of the preformed symbolic complex.

Seeing the canyon is made even more difficult by what the sightseer does when the moment arrives, when sovereign knower confronts the thing to be known. Instead of looking at it, he photographs it. There is no confrontation at all. At the end of forty years of preformulation and with the Grand Canyon yawning at his feet, what does he do? He waives his right of seeing and knowing and records symbols for the next forty years. For him there is no present; there is only the past of what has been formulated and seen and the future of what has been formulated and not seen. The present is surrendered to the past and the future.

The sightseer may be aware that something is wrong. He may simply be bored; or he may be conscious of the difficulty: that the great thing yawning at his feet somehow eludes him. The harder he looks at it, the less he can see. It eludes everybody. The tourist cannot see it; the bellboy at the Bright Angel Lodge cannot see it: for him it is only one side of the space he lives in, like one wall of a room; to the ranger it is a tissue of everyday signs relevant to his own prospects — the blue haze down there means that he will probably get rained on during the donkey ride.

How can the sightseer recover the Grand Canyon? He can recover it in any number of ways, all sharing in common the stratagem of avoiding the approved confrontation of the tour and the Park Service.

It may be recovered by leaving the beaten track. The tourist leaves the tour, camps in the back country. He arises before dawn and approaches the South Rim through a wild terrain where there are no trails and no railed-in lookout points. In other words, he sees the canyon by avoiding all the facilities for seeing the canyon. If the benevolent Park Service hears about this fellow and thinks he has a good idea and places the following notice in the Bright Angel Lodge: *Consult ranger for information on getting off the beaten track* — the end result will only be the closing of another access to the canyon.

It may be recovered by a dialectical movement which brings one back to the beaten track but at a level above it. For example, after a lifetime of avoiding the beaten track and guided tours, a man may deliberately seek out the most beaten track of all, the most commonplace tour imaginable:

he may visit the canyon by a Greyhound tour in the company of a party from Terre Haute — just as a man who has lived in New York all his life may visit the Statue of Liberty. (Such dialectical savorings of the familiar as the familiar are, of course, a favorite stratagem of *The New Yorker* magazine.) The thing is recovered from familiarity by means of an exercise in familiarity. Our complex friend stands behind his fellow tourists at the Bright Angel Lodge and sees the canyon through them and their predicament, their picture taking and busy disregard. In a sense, he exploits his fellow tourists; he stands on their shoulders to see the canyon.

Such a man is far more advanced in the dialectic than the sightseer who is trying to get off the beaten track — getting up at dawn and approaching the canyon through the mesquite. This stratagem is, in fact, for our complex man the weariest, most beaten track of all.

It may be recovered as a consequence of a breakdown of the symbolic machinery by which the experts present the experience to the consumer. A family visits the canyon in the usual way. But shortly after their arrival, the park is closed by an outbreak of typhus in the south. They have the canyon to themselves. What do they mean when they tell the home folks of their good luck: "We had the whole place to ourselves"? How does one see the thing better when the others are absent? Is looking like sucking: the more lookers, the less there is to see? They could hardly answer, but by saying this they testify to a state of affairs which is considerably more complex than the simple statement of the schoolbook about the Spaniard and the millions who followed him. It is a state in which there is a complex distribution of sovereignty, of zoning.

It may be recovered in a time of national disaster. The Bright Angel Lodge is converted into a rest home, a function that has nothing to do with the canyon a few yards away. A wounded man is brought in. He regains consciousness; there outside his window is the canyon.

The most extreme case of access by privilege conferred by disaster is the Huxleyan novel of the adventures of the surviving remnant after the great wars of the twentieth century. An expedition from Australia lands in Southern California and heads east. They stumble across the Bright Angel Lodge, now fallen into ruins. The trails are grown over, the guard rails fallen away, the dime telescope at Battleship Point rusted. But there is the canyon, exposed at last. Exposed by what? By the decay of those facilities which were designed to help the sightseer.

This dialectic of sightseeing cannot be taken into account by planners, for the object of the dialectic is nothing other than the subversion of the efforts of the planners.

The dialectic is not known to objective theorists, psychologists, and the like. Yet it is quite well known in the fantasy-consciousness of the popular arts. The devices by which the museum exhibit, the Grand Canyon, the ordinary thing, is recovered have long since been stumbled upon. A movie shows a man visiting the Grand Canyon. But the movie maker knows something the planner does not know. He knows that one cannot take the sight frontally. The canyon must be approached by the stratagems we have mentioned: the Inside Track, the Familiar Revisited, the Accidental Encounter. Who is the stranger at the Bright Angel Lodge? Is he the ordinary tourist from Terre Haute that he makes himself out to be? He is not. He has another objective in mind, to revenge his wronged brother, counterespionage, etc. By virtue of the fact that he has other fish to fry, he may take a stroll along the rim after supper and then we can see the canyon through him. The movie accomplishes its purpose by concealing it. Overtly the characters (the American family marooned by typhus) and we the onlookers experience pity for the sufferers, and the family experience anxiety for themselves; covertly and in truth they are the happiest of people and we are happy through them, for we have the canyon to ourselves. The movie cashes in on the recovery of sovereignty through disaster. Not only is the canyon now accessible to the remnant: the members of the remnant are now accessible to each other, a whole new ensemble of relations becomes possible — friendship, love, hatred, clandestine sexual adventures. In a movie when a man sits next to a woman on a bus, it is necessary either that the bus break down or that the woman lose her memory. (The question occurs to one: Do you imagine there are sightseers who see sights just as they are supposed to? a family who live in Terre Haute, who decide to take the canyon tour, who go there, see it, enjoy it immensely, and go home content? a family who are entirely innocent of all the barriers, zones, losses of sovereignty I have been talking about? Wouldn't most people be sorry if Battleship Point fell into the canyon, carrying all one's fellow passengers to their death, leaving one alone on the South Rim? I cannot answer this. Perhaps there are such people. Certainly a great many American families would swear they had no such problems, that they came, saw, and went away happy. Yet it is just these families who would be happiest if they had gotten the Inside Track and been among the surviving remnant.)

It is now apparent that as between the many measures which may be taken to overcome the opacity, the boredom, of the direct confrontation of the thing or creature in its citadel of symbolic investiture, some are less authentic than others. That is to say, some stratagems obviously serve other purposes than that of providing access to being — for example, various unconscious motivations which it is not necessary to go into here.

Let us take an example in which the recovery of being is ambiguous, where it may under the same circumstances contain both authentic and unauthentic components. An American couple, we will say, drives down into Mexico. They see the usual sights and have a fair time of it. Yet they are never without the sense of missing something. Although Taxco and Cuernavaca are interesting and picturesque as advertised, they fall short of "it." What do the couple have in mind by "it"? What do they really hope for? What sort of experience could they have in Mexico so that upon their return, they would feel that "it" had happened? We have a clue: Their hope has something to do with their own role as tourists in a foreign country and the way in which they conceive this role. It has something to do with other American tourists. Certainly they feel that they are very far from "it" when, after traveling five thousand miles, they arrive at the plaza in Guanajuato only to find themselves surrounded by a dozen other couples from the Midwest.

Already we may distinguish authentic and unauthentic elements. First, we see the problem the couple faces and we understand their efforts to surmount it. The problem is to find an "unspoiled" place. "Unspoiled" does not mean only that a place is left physically intact; it means also that it is not encrusted by renown and by the familiar (as in Taxco), that it has not been discovered by others. We understand that the couple really want to get at the place and enjoy it. Yet at the same time we wonder if there is not something wrong in their dislike of their compatriots. Does access to the place require the exclusion of others?

Let us see what happens.

The couple decide to drive from Guanajuato to Mexico City. On the way they get lost. After hours on a rocky mountain road, they find themselves in a tiny valley not even marked on the map. There they discover an Indian village. Some sort of religious festival is going on. It is apparently a corn dance in supplication of the rain god.

The couple know at once that this is "it." They are entranced. They spend several days in the village, observing the Indians and being themselves observed with friendly curiosity.

Now may we not say that the sightseers have at last come face to face with an authentic sight, a sight which is charming, quaint, picturesque, unspoiled, and that they see the sight and come away rewarded? Possibly this may occur. Yet it is more likely that what happens is a far cry indeed from an immediate encounter with being, that the experience, while masquerading as such, is in truth a rather desperate impersonation. I use the word *desperate* advisedly to signify an actual loss of hope.

The clue to the spuriousness of their enjoyment of the village and the festival is a certain restiveness in the sightseers themselves. It is given expression by their repeated exclamations that "this is too good to be true," and by their anxiety that it may not prove to be so perfect, and finally by their downright relief at leaving the valley and having the experience in the bag, so to speak — that is, safely embalmed in memory and movie film.

What is the source of their anxiety during the visit? Does it not mean that the couple are looking at the place with a certain standard of performance in mind? Are they like Fabre, who gazed at the world about him with wonder, letting it be what it is; or are they not like the overanxious mother who sees her child as one performing, now doing badly, now doing well? The village is their child and their love for it is an anxious love because they are afraid that at any moment it might fail them.

We have another clue in their subsequent remark to an ethnologist friend. "How we wished you had been there with us! What a perfect goldmine of folkways! Every minute we would say to each other, if only you were here! You must return with us." This surely testifies to a generosity of spirit, a willingness to share their experience with others, not at all like their feelings toward their fellow Iowans on the plaza at Guanajuato!

I am afraid this is not the case at all. It is true that they longed for their ethnologist friend, but it was for an entirely different reason. They wanted him, not to share their experience, but to certify their experience as genuine.

"This is it" and "Now we are really living" do not necessarily refer to the sovereign encounter of the person with the sight that enlivens the mind and gladdens the heart. It means that now at last we are having the acceptable experience. The present experience is always measured by a prototype, the "it" of their dreams. "Now I am really living" means that now I am filling the role of sightseer and the sight is living up to the prototype of sights. This quaint and picturesque village is measured by a Platonic ideal of the Quaint and the Picturesque.

Hence their anxiety during the encounter. For at any minute something could go wrong. A fellow Iowan might emerge from a 'dobe hut; the chief might show them his Sears catalog. (If the failures are "wrong" enough, as these are, they might still be turned to account as rueful conversation pieces. "There we were expecting the chief to bring us a churinga and he shows up with a Sears catalog!") They have snatched victory from disaster, but their experience always runs the danger of failure.

They need the ethnologist to certify their experience as genuine. This is borne out by their behavior when the three of them return for the next corn dance. During the dance, the couple do not watch the goings-on; instead they watch the ethnologist! Their highest hope is that their friend should find the dance interesting. And if he should show signs of true absorption, an interest in the goings-on so powerful that he becomes oblivious of his friends — then their cup is full. "Didn't we tell you?" they say at last. What they want from him is not ethnological explanations; all they want is his approval.

What has taken place is a radical loss of sovereignty over that which is as much theirs as it is the ethnologist's. The fault does not lie with the ethnologist. He has no wish to stake a claim to the village; in fact, he desires the opposite: he will bore his friends to death by telling them about the village and the meaning of the folkways. A degree of sovereignty has been surrendered by the couple. It is the nature of the loss, moreover, that they are not aware of the loss, beyond a certain uneasiness. (Even if they read this and admitted it, it would be very difficult for them to bridge the gap in their confrontation of the world. Their consciousness of the corn dance cannot escape their consciousness of their consciousness, so that with the onset of the first direct enjoyment, their higher consciousness pounces and certifies: "Now you are doing it! Now you are really living!" and, in certifying the experience, sets it at nought.)

Their basic placement in the world is such that they recognize a priority of title of the expert over his particular department of being. The whole horizon of being is staked out by "them," the experts. The highest satisfaction of the sightseer (not merely the tourist but any layman seer of sights) is that his sight should be certified as genuine. The worst of this impoverishment is that there is no sense of impoverishment. The surrender of title is so complete that it never even occurs to one to reassert title. A poor man may envy the rich man, but the sightseer does not envy the expert. When a caste system becomes absolute, envy disappears. Yet the caste of layman-expert is not the fault of the expert. It is due altogether to the eager surrender of sovereignty by the layman so that he may take up the role not of the person but of the consumer.

I do not refer only to the special relation of layman to theorist. I refer to the general situation in which sovereignty is surrendered to a class of privileged knowers, whether these be theorists or artists. A reader may surrender sovereignty over that which has been written about, just as a consumer may surrender sovereignty over a thing which has been theorized about. The consumer is content to receive an experience just as it has been presented to him by theorists and planners. The reader may also be content to judge life by whether it has or has not been formulated by those who know and write about life. A young man goes to France. He too has a fair time of it, sees the sights, enjoys the food. On his last day, in fact as he sits in a restaurant in Le Havre waiting for his boat, something happens. A group of French students in the restaurant get into an impassioned argument over a recent play. A riot takes place. Madame la concierge joins in, swinging her mop at the rioters. Our young American is transported. This is "it." And he had almost left France without seeing "it"!

WHEN A CASTE SYSTEM BECOMES ABSOLUTE, ENVY DISAPPEARS. YET THE CASTE OF LAYMAN-EXPERT IS NOT THE FAULT OF THE EXPERT. IT IS DUE ALTOGETHER TO THE EAGER SURRENDER OF SOVEREIGNTY BY THE LAYMAN.

But the young man's delight is ambiguous. On the one hand, it is a pleasure for him to encounter the same Gallic temperament he had heard about from Puccini and Rolland. But on the other hand, the source of his pleasure testifies to a certain alienation. For the young man is actually barred from a direct encounter with anything French excepting only that which has been set forth, authenticated by Puccini and Rolland — those who know. If he had encountered the restaurant scene without reading Hemingway, without knowing that the performance was so typically, charmingly French, he would not have been delighted. He would only have been anxious at seeing things get so out of hand. The source of his delight is the sanction of those who know.

This loss of sovereignty is not a marginal process, as might appear from my example of estranged sightseers. It is a generalized surrender of the horizon to those experts within whose competence a particular segment of the horizon is thought to lie. Kwakiutls are surrendered to Franz Boas; decaying Southern mansions are surrendered to Faulkner and Tennessee Williams. So that, although it is by no means the intention of the expert to expropriate sovereignty — in fact he would not even know what sovereignty meant in this context — the danger of theory and consumption is a seduction and deprivation of the consumer.

In the New Mexico desert, natives occasionally come across strange-looking artifacts which have fallen from the skies and which are stenciled: *Return to U.S. Experimental Project, Alamogordo. Reward.* The finder returns the object and is rewarded. He knows nothing of the nature of the object he has found and does not care to know. The sole role of the native, the highest role he can play, is that of finder and returner of the mysterious equipment.

The same is true of the laymen's relation to *natural* objects in a modern technical society. No matter what the object or event is, whether it is a star, a swallow, a Kwakiutl, a "psychological phenomenon," the layman who confronts it does not confront it as a sovereign person, as Crusoe confronts a seashell he finds on the beach. The highest role he can conceive himself as playing is to be able to recognize the title of the object, to return it to the appropriate expert and have it certified as a genuine find. He does not even permit himself to see the thing — as Gerard Hopkins could see a rock or a cloud or a field. If anyone asks him why he doesn't look, he may reply that he didn't take that subject in college (or he hasn't read Faulkner).

This loss of sovereignty extends even to oneself. There is the neurotic who asks nothing more of his doctor than that his symptoms should prove interesting. When all else fails, the poor fellow has nothing to offer but his own neurosis. But even this is sufficient if only the doctor will show interest when he says, "Last night I had a curious sort of dream; perhaps it will be significant to one who knows about such things. It seems I was standing in a sort of alley — " (I have nothing else to offer you but my own unhappiness. Please say that it, at least, measures up, that it is a *proper* sort of unhappiness.)

II

A young Falkland Islander walking along a beach and spying a dead dogfish and going to work on it with his jackknife has, in a fashion wholly unprovided in modern educational theory, a great advantage over the Scarsdale high-school pupil who finds the dogfish on his laboratory desk. Similarly the citizen of Huxley's *Brave New World* who stumbles across a volume of Shakespeare in some vine-grown ruins and squats on a potsherd to read it is in a fairer way of getting at a sonnet than the Harvard sophomore taking English Poetry II.

The educator whose business it is to teach students biology or poetry is unaware of a whole ensemble of relations which exist between the student and the dogfish and between the student and the Shakespeare sonnet. To put it bluntly: A student who has the desire to get at a dogfish or a Shakespeare sonnet may have the greatest difficulty in salvaging the creature itself from the educational package in which it is presented. The great difficulty is that he is not aware that there is a difficulty; surely, he thinks, in such a fine classroom, with such a fine textbook, the sonnet must come across! What's wrong with me?

The sonnet and the dogfish are obscured by two different processes. The sonnet is obscured by the symbolic package which is formulated not by the sonnet itself but by the *media* through which the sonnet is transmitted, the media which the educators believe for some reason to be transparent. The new textbook, the type, the smell of the page, the classroom, the aluminum windows and the winter sky, the personality of Miss Hawkins — these media which are supposed to transmit the sonnet may only succeed in transmitting themselves. It is only the hardiest and cleverest of students who can salvage the sonnet from this many-tissued package. It is only the rarest student who knows that the sonnet must be salvaged from the package. (The educator is well aware that something is wrong, that there is a fatal gap between the student's learning and the student's life: the student reads the poem, appears to understand it, and gives all the answers. But what does he recall if he should happen to read a Shakespeare sonnet twenty years later? Does he recall the poem or does he recall the smell of the page and the smell of Miss Hawkins?)

One might object, pointing out that Huxley's citizen reading his sonnet in the ruins and the Falkland Islander looking at his dogfish on the beach also receive them in a certain package. Yes, but the difference lies in the fundamental placement of the student in the world, a placement which makes it possible to extract the thing from the package. The pupil at Scarsdale High sees himself placed as a consumer receiving an experience-package; but the Falkland Islander exploring his dogfish is a person exercising the sovereign right of a person in his lordship and mastery of creation. He too could use an instructor and a book and a technique, but he would use them as his subordinates, just as he uses his jackknife. The biology student does not use his scalpel as an instrument, he uses it as a magic wand! Since it is a "scientific instrument," it should do "scientific things."

IT IS ONLY THE HARDIEST AND CLEVEREST OF STUDENTS WHO CAN SALVAGE THE SONNET FROM THIS MANY-TISSUED PACKAGE.

The dogfish is concealed in the same symbolic package as the sonnet. But the dogfish suffers an additional loss. As a consequence of this double deprivation, the Sarah Lawrence student who scores A in zoology is apt to know very little about a dogfish. She is twice removed from the dogfish, once by the symbolic complex by which the dogfish is concealed, once again by the spoliation of the dogfish by theory which renders it invisible. Through no fault of zoology instructors, it is nevertheless a fact that the zoology laboratory at Sarah Lawrence College is one of the few places in the world where it is all but impossible to see a dogfish.

The dogfish, the tree, the seashell, the American Negro, the dream, are rendered invisible by a shift of reality from concrete thing to theory which Whitehead has called the fallacy of misplaced concreteness. It is the mistaking of an idea, a principle, an abstraction, for the real. As a consequence of the shift, the "specimen" is seen as less real than the theory of the specimen. As Kierkegaard said, once a person is seen as a specimen of a race or a species, at that very moment he ceases to be an individual. Then there are no more individuals but only specimens.

To illustrate: A student enters a laboratory which, in the pragmatic view, offers the student the optimum conditions under which an educational experience may be had. In the existential view, however — that view of the student in which he is regarded not as a receptacle of experience but as a knowing being whose peculiar property it is to see himself as being in a certain situation — the modern laboratory could not have been more effectively designed to conceal the dogfish forever.

The student comes to his desk. On it, neatly arranged by his instructor, he finds his laboratory manual, a dissecting board, instruments, and a mimeographed list:

Exercise 22: Materials
1 dissecting board
1 scalpel
1 forceps
1 probe
1 bottle india ink and syringe
1 specimen of *Squalus acanthias*

The clue of the situation in which the student finds himself is to be found in the last item: 1 specimen of *Squalus acanthias*.

The phrase *specimen of* expresses in the most succinct way imaginable the radical character of the loss of being which has occurred under his very nose. To refer to the dogfish, the unique concrete existent before him, as a "specimen of *Squalus acanthias*" reveals by its grammar the spoliation of the dogfish by the theoretical method. This phrase, *specimen of*, example of, instance of, indicates the ontological status of the individual creature in the eyes of the theorist. The dogfish itself is seen as a rather shabby expression of an ideal reality, the species *Squalus acanthias*. The result is the radical devaluation of the individual dogfish. (The *reductio ad absurdum* of Whitehead's shift is Toynbee's employment of it in his historical method. If a gram of NaCl is referred to by the chemist as a "sample of" NaCl, one may think of it as such and not much is missed by the oversight of the act of being of this particular pinch of salt, but when the Jews and the Jewish religion are understood as — in Toynbee's favorite phrase — a "classical example of" such and such a kind of *Voelkerwanderung*, we begin to suspect that something is being left out.)

If we look into the ways in which the student can recover the dogfish (or the sonnet), we will see that they have in common the stratagem of avoiding the educator's direct presentation of the object as a lesson to be learned and restoring access to sonnet and dogfish as beings to be known, reasserting the sovereignty of knower over known.

In truth, the biography of scientists and poets is usually the story of the discovery of the indirect approach, the circumvention of the educator's presentation — the young man who was sent to the *Technikum* and on his way fell into the habit of loitering in book stores and reading poetry;

or the young man dutifully attending law school who on the way became curious about the comings and goings of ants. One remembers the scene in *The Heart Is a Lonely Hunter* where the girl hides in the bushes to hear the Capehart in the big house play Beethoven. Perhaps she was the lucky one after all. Think of the unhappy souls inside, who see the record, worry about scratches, and most of all worry about whether they are *getting it*, whether they are bona fide music lovers. What is the best way to hear Beethoven: sitting in a proper silence around the Capehart or eavesdropping from an azalea bush?

However it may come about, we notice two traits of the second situation: (1) an openness of the thing before one — instead of being an exercise to be learned according to an approved mode, it is a garden of delights which beckons to one; (2) a sovereignty of the knower — instead of being a consumer of a prepared experience, I am a sovereign wayfarer, a wanderer in the neighborhood of being who stumbles into the garden.

One can think of two sorts of circumstances through which the thing may be restored to the person. (There is always, of course, the direct recovery: A student may simply be strong enough, brave enough, clever enough to take the dogfish and the sonnet by storm, to wrest control of it from the educators and the educational package.) First by ordeal: The Bomb falls; when the young man recovers consciousness in the shambles of the biology laboratory, there not ten inches from his nose lies the dogfish. Now all at once he can see it directly and without let, just as the exile or the prisoner or the sick man sees the sparrow at his window in all its inexhaustibility; just as the commuter who has had a heart attack sees his own hand for the first time. In these cases, the simulacrum of everydayness and of consumption has been destroyed by disaster; in the case of the bomb, literally destroyed. Secondly, by apprenticeship to a great man: one day a great biologist walks into the laboratory; he stops in front of our student's desk; he leans over, picks up the dogfish, and, ignoring instruments and procedure, probes with a broken fingernail into the little carcass. "Now here is a curious business," he says, ignoring also the proper jargon of the specialty. "Look here how this little duct reverses its direction and drops into the pelvis. Now if you would look into a coelacanth, you would see that it — "And all at once the student can see. The technician and the sophomore who loves his textbooks are always offended by the genuine research man because the latter is usually a little vague and always humble before the thing; he doesn't have much use for the equipment or the jargon. Whereas the technician is never vague and never humble before the thing; he holds the thing disposed of by the principle, the formula, the textbook outline; and he thinks a great deal of equipment and jargon.

But since neither of these methods of recovering the dogfish is pedagogically feasible — perhaps the great man even less so than the Bomb — I wish to propose the following educational technique which should prove equally effective for Harvard and Shreveport High School. I propose that English poetry and biology should be taught as usual, but that at irregular intervals, poetry students should find dogfishes on their desks and biology students should find Shakespeare sonnets on their dissection boards. I am serious in declaring that a Sarah Lawrence English major who began poking about in a dogfish with a bobby pin would learn more in thirty minutes than a biology major in a whole semester; and that the latter upon reading on her dissecting board

> That time of year Thou may'st in me behold
> When yellow leaves, or none, or few, do hang
> Upon those boughs which shake against the cold —
> Bare ruin'd choirs where late the sweet birds sang

might catch fire at the beauty of it.

The situation of the tourist at the Grand Canyon and the biology student are special cases of a predicament in which everyone finds himself in a modern technical society — a society, that is, in which there is a division between expert and layman, planner and consumer, in which experts and planners take special measures to teach and edify the consumer. The measures taken are measures appropriate to the consumer: the expert and the planner *know* and *plan*, but the consumer *needs* and *experiences*.

There is a double deprivation. First, the thing is lost through its packaging. The very means by which the thing is presented for consumption, the very techniques by which the thing is made available as an item of need-satisfaction, these very means operate to remove the thing from the sovereignty of the knower. A loss of title occurs. The measures which the museum curator takes to present the thing to the public are self-liquidating. The upshot of the curator's efforts are not that everyone can see the exhibit but that no one can see it. The curator protests: Why are they so indifferent? Why do they even deface the exhibit? Don't they know it is theirs? But it is not theirs. It is his, the curator's. By the most exclusive sort of zoning, the museum exhibit, the park oak tree, is part of an ensemble, a package, which is almost impenetrable to them. The archaeologist who puts his find in a museum so that everyone can see it accomplishes the reverse of his expectations. The result of his action is that no one can see it now but the archaeologist. He would have done better to keep it in his pocket and show it now and then to strangers.

The tourist who carves his initials in a public place, which is theoretically "his" in the first place, has good reasons for doing so, reasons which the exhibitor and planner know nothing about. He does so because in his role of consumer of an experience (a "recreational experience" to satisfy a "recreational need") he knows that he is disinherited. He is deprived of his title over being. He knows very well that he is in a very special sort of zone in which his only rights are the rights of a consumer. He moves like a ghost through schoolroom, city streets, trains, parks, movies. He carves his initials as a last desperate measure to escape his ghostly role of consumer. He is saying in effect: I am not a ghost after all; I am a sovereign person. And he establishes title the only way remaining to him, by staking his claim over one square inch of wood or stone.

Does this mean that we should get rid of museums? No, but it means that the sightseer should be prepared to enter into a struggle to recover a sight from a museum.

The second loss is the spoliation of the thing, the tree, the rock, the swallow, by the layman's misunderstanding of scientific theory. He believes that the thing is *disposed of* by theory, that it stands in the Platonic relation of being a *specimen* of such and such an underlying principle. In the transmission of scientific theory from theorist to layman, the expectation of the theorist is reversed. Instead of the marvels of the universe being made available to the public, the universe is disposed of by theory. The loss of sovereignty takes this form: as a result of the science of botany, trees are not made available to every man. On the contrary. The tree loses its proper density and mystery as a concrete existent and, as merely another *specimen* of a species, becomes itself nugatory.

Does this mean that there is no use taking biology at Harvard and Shreveport High? No, but it means that the student should know what a fight he has on his hands to rescue the specimen from the educational package. The educator is only partly to blame. For there is nothing the educator can do to provide for this need of the student. Everything the educator does only succeeds in becoming, for the student, part of the educational package. The highest role of the educator is the maieutic role of Socrates: to help the student come to himself not as a consumer of experience but as a sovereign individual.

The thing is twice lost to the consumer. First, sovereignty is lost: it is theirs, not his. Second, it is radically devalued by theory. This is a loss which has been brought about by science but through no fault of the scientist and through no fault of scientific theory. The loss has come about as a consequence of the seduction of the layman by science. The layman will be seduced as long as he regards beings as consumer items to be experienced rather than prizes to be won, and as long as he waives his sovereign rights as a person and accepts his role of consumer as the highest estate to which the layman can aspire.

As Mounier said, the person is not something one can study and provide for; he is something one struggles for. But unless he also struggles for himself, unless he knows that there is a struggle, he is going to be just what the planners think he is.

QUESTIONS FOR A SECOND READING

1. Percy's essay proceeds by adding example to example, one after another. If all the examples were meant to illustrate the same thing, the same general point or idea, then one would most likely have been enough. The rest would have been redundant. It makes sense, then, to assume that

each example gives a different view of what Percy is saying, that each modifies the others, or qualifies them, or adds a piece that was otherwise lacking. It's as though Percy needed one more to get it right or to figure out what was missing along the way. As you read back through the essay, pay particular attention to the *differences* between the examples (between the various tourists going to the Grand Canyon, or between the tourists at the Grand Canyon and the tourists in Mexico). Also note the logic or system that leads from one to the next. What progress of thought is represented by the movement from one example to another, or from tourists to students?

2. The essay is filled with talk about "loss" — the loss of sovereignty, the loss of the creature — but it is resolutely ambiguous about what it is that we have lost. As you work your way back through, note the passages that describe what we are missing and why we should care. Are we to believe, for example, that Cárdenas actually had it (whatever "it" is) — that he had no preconceived notions when he saw the Grand Canyon? Mightn't he have said, "I claim this for my queen" or "There I see the glory of God" or "This wilderness is not fit for man"? To whom, or in the name of what, is this loss that Percy chronicles such a matter of concern? If this is not just Percy's peculiar prejudice, if we are asked to share his concerns, whose interests or what interests are represented here?

3. The essay is made up of stories or anecdotes, all of them fanciful. Percy did not, in other words, turn to first-person accounts of visitors to the Grand Canyon or to statements by actual students or teachers. Why not, do you suppose? What does this choice say about his "method" — about what it can and can't do? As you reread the essay, look for sections you could use to talk about the power and limits of Percy's method.

ASSIGNMENTS FOR WRITING

1. Percy tells several stories — some of them quite good stories — but it is often hard to know just what he is getting at, just what point he is trying to make. If he's making an argument, it's not the sort of argument that is easy to summarize. And if the stories (or anecdotes) are meant to serve as examples, they are not the sort of examples that lead directly to a single, general conclusion or that serve to clarify a point or support an obvious thesis. In fact, at the very moment when you expect Percy to come forward and pull things together, he offers yet another story, as though another example, rather than any general statement, would get you closer to what he is saying.

   There are, at the same time, terms and phrases to suggest that this is an essay with a point to make. Percy talks, for example, about "the loss of sovereignty," "symbolic packages," "consumers of experience," and "dialectic," and it seems that these terms and phrases are meant to name or comment on key scenes, situations, or characters in the examples.

For this assignment, tell a story of your own, one that is suggested by the stories Percy tells — perhaps a story about a time you went looking for something or at something, or about a time when you did or did not find a dogfish in your Shakespeare class. You should imagine that you are carrying out a project that Walker Percy has begun, a project that has you looking back at your own experience through the lens of "The Loss of the Creature," noticing what Percy would notice and following the paths that he would find interesting. Try to bring the terms that Percy uses — like "sovereign," "consumer," "expert," and "dialectic" — to bear on the story you have to tell. Feel free to imitate Percy's style and method in your essay.

2. Percy charts several routes to the Grand Canyon: you can take the packaged tour, you can get off the beaten track, you can wait for a disaster, you can follow the "dialectical movement which brings one back to the beaten track but at a level above it." This last path (or stratagem), he says, is for the complex traveler.

> Our complex friend stands behind his fellow tourists at the Bright Angel Lodge and sees the canyon through them and their predicament, their picture taking and busy disregard. In a sense, he exploits his fellow tourists; he stands on their shoulders to see the canyon. (p. 461)

The complex traveler sees the Grand Canyon through the example of the common tourists with "their predicament, their picture taking and busy disregard." He "stands on their shoulders" to see the canyon. This distinction between complex and common approaches is an important one in the essay. It is interesting to imagine how the distinction could be put to work to define ways of reading.

Suppose that you read "The Loss of the Creature" as a common reader. What would you see? What would you identify as key sections of the text? What would you miss? What would you say about what you see?

If you think of yourself, now, as a complex reader, modeled after any of Percy's more complex tourists or students, what would you see? What would you identify as key sections of the text? What would you miss? What would you say about what you see?

For this assignment, write an essay with three sections. You may number them, if you choose. The first section should represent the work of a common reader with "The Loss of the Creature," and the second should represent the work of a complex reader. The third section should look back and comment on the previous two. In particular, you might address these questions: Why might a person prefer one reading over the other? What is to be gained or lost with both?

MAKING CONNECTIONS

1. There is much that is similar to Percy's concerns in David Abram's "Animism and the Alphabet" (p. 28). In fact, it is easy to imagine Abram using the same title—"The Loss of the Creature." They ask similar questions; they write with a similar urgency; they are even similar in method.

   Let's take the similarities as a starting point. As you reread the essays, then, think primarily about the differences. Both are concerned with loss. What, for each, has been lost? What are the reasons? What are the consequences? What options are available for restoration? Write an essay that begins with Abram's point of view, a concern over "modern civilization's evident disregard for the needs of the natural world," and that thinks, then, about Percy's understanding of loss, its origins and consequences.

2. > But the difference lies in the fundamental placement of the student in the world. . . . (Walker Percy, p. 467)

   > What I am about to say to you has taken me more than twenty years to admit: *A primary reason for my success in the classroom was that I couldn't forget that schooling was changing me and separating me from the life I enjoyed before becoming a student.* (Richard Rodriguez, p. 516)

   Both Percy and Richard Rodriguez, in "The Achievement of Desire" (p. 515), write about students and how they are "placed" in the world by teachers and by the way schools characteristically represent knowledge, the novice, and the expert. And both tell stories to make their points, stories of characteristic students in characteristic situations. Write an essay in which you tell a story of your own, one meant to serve as a corrective or a supplement to the stories Percy and Rodriguez tell. You will want both to tell your story and to use it as a way of returning to and commenting on Percy and Rodriguez and the arguments they make. Your authority can rest on the fact that you are a student and as a consequence have ways of understanding that position that they do not.

ANTONIO
Porchia

Antonio Porchia (1885–1968) was born in Conflenti, Italy, where he lived until 1902 when his recently widowed mother, following on the path of many Calabrian families of the time, relocated her family to Argentina. Porchia, the eldest of seven children, made wages as a basket weaver and potter; he later founded a small printing press and was involved in attempts to organize labor. The first of his short assembled aphorisms, "Voces," ("Voices") were published in a small left-wing newspaper, *La Fragua* (*The Forge*). In 1936, Porchia left the printing press to care for nieces and nephews whose mother had died. Porchia was said to be of "unlimited kindness, he was never heard speaking ill of any-body and he hosted many friends in his house, some of whom were painters, others were writers."

The first substantial collection of these short writings, also titled *Voices,* appeared in a private edition in 1943, prepared and paid for by Porchia. The collection attracted little attention until 1949, when the French intellectual and critic Roger Callois translated Porchia's work into French. With the publication in France, Porchia gained (and retains) a wide international following, including substantial recognition in Argentina, where Porchia would read from *Voices* on the radio, as the municipal station shut down at midnight. Among his admirers are Jorge Luis Borges, André Breton, and Henry Miller.

Voices is Porchia's only published work, and it was translated into English by W. S. Merwin in 1969. Merwin selected some 250 poems out of the 600 that appeared in the various editions of *Voices* published since 1943. Merwin writes that Porchia had "no doctrinal allegiances, nor any attempt at dogmatic system." He goes on to say that "Porchia's utterances are obviously, in this sense, a spiritual, quite as much as literary, testament."

For as much as we know, Porchia was untaught in any formal sense; he had not been guided or educated by any specific writers or influences. This seems to be one of the characteristics of his writing that readers and major literary figures of the time found compelling about his work. He seemed to stand for the possibility that an individual could become wise and literary by constantly turning over thoughts and small phrases. Porchia denied ever having even heard of those writers who are taken by critics and scholars to have been his influences, writers like Franz Kafka, the influential novelist and short story writer, or Lao-Tzu, the Taoist philosopher and author of many Buddhist koans.

It has been said that upon being considered for a writing award in France, Porchia sent word declining the French Book Club's invitation to visit, characteristically saying, as if he were writing another aphorism for his collection, "Distances mean nothing. Everything is here." And that too is the challenge of reading Porchia. As he says in one of his aphorisms, he knows what he has given us, but not what we have received. In a time like ours, when writers are expected to be prolific and productive in their output, it's difficult to imagine a writer spending his or her life thinking over the same 600 sentences. And yet these brief statements have been important to readers across time and across continents. They raise interesting questions for a reader. What do you do with them? How do you read them? How do you read them together, in sequence? How do we make sense of the voices we hear in Porchia's work?

Voices

Before I travelled my road I was my road.

I found the whole of my first world in my meager bread.

My father, when he went, made my childhood a gift of a half a century.

The little things are what is eternal, and the rest, all the rest, is brevity, extreme brevity.

Without this ridiculous vanity that takes the form of self-display, and is part of everything and everyone, we would see nothing, and nothing would exist.

Truth has very few friends and those few are suicides.

• • • • • • •

He who holds me by a thread is not strong; the thread is strong.

• • • • • • •

A door opens to me. I go in and am faced with a hundred closed doors.

My poverty is not complete: it lacks me.

If you do not raise your eyes you will think that you are the highest point.

• • ● ● ● • •

One lives in the hope of becoming a memory.

I have scarcely touched clay and I am made of it.

• • ● ● ● • •

Man talks about everything, and he talks about everything as though the understanding of everything were all inside him.

Nothing that is complete breathes.

• • ● ● ● • •

You will find the distance that separates you from them, by joining them.

• • ● ● ● • •

The far away, the very far, the farthest, I have found only in my own blood.

The mystery brings peace to my eyes, not blindness.

When your suffering is a little greater than my suffering I feel that I am a little cruel.

He who tells the truth says almost nothing.

• • • • • • •

Mud, when it leaves the mud, stops being mud.

• • • • • • •

When I come upon some idea that is not of this world, I feel as though this world had grown wider.

• • • • • • •

Only the wound speaks its own word.

• • • • • • •

Yes, I will try to be. Because I believe that not being is arrogant.

QUESTIONS FOR A SECOND READING

1. One way we might understand Porchia's sentences would be to read them as literary aphorisms. Literary aphorisms are intended to make powerful statements in very concise sentences. Porchia's aphorisms, then, might be read as an attempt at this kind of resonance and power, much in the same way as haiku poetry can leave us with a single image that resonates far beyond the length of the poem. As you reread this selection, choose one of Porchia's aphorisms that you think is particularly powerful. What gives the statement its power? What image, word, or feeling are you left with after reading it? What are the features of its sentences? What do you notice about their syntax, grammatical structure, vocabulary?

2. Despite the seriousness of many of Porchia's statements, these aphorisms can also be read as playful—and as inviting playfulness in return. As you reread "Voices," think about ways that you might play with the text. For example, try typing the aphorisms into your computer as one long paragraph. What happens when you present them in this form? Change the order, or add transitions, again with the goal of creating a paragraph from these sentences. What is this paragraph about? What threads of argument or meaning, if any, can tie these sentences together? Or were they always a kind of whole?

ASSIGNMENTS FOR WRITING

1. It is easy to read and remember, to clip and save, one of Porchia's aphorisms. Reading a collection of them, thinking about them as an example of a writer's project, this is another matter altogether. To think about these odd sentences, it helps to read them over and over again; it helps to write some Porchia-like sentences of your own.

   Do this. Read them over and over; write some sentences of your own. Do this until these sentences begin to take shape for you as a whole, as a project, not just as one-liners. And write an essay, one that works closely from examples, explaining how we might understand Porchia's project as a writer. Porchia devoted his life to writing these. Why might a writer return to these sentences again and again? They have been valued by readers across generations and continents. Why, do you suppose?

2. There are several steps to this writing assignment. First, choose one of Porchia's aphorisms, one that seems to you to be rich with meaning or possibility. Then, over a period of days, write ten responses to it. You could

write about what it seems to mean, or why you find it compelling, or where it sends your thinking, or how you have learned to read it. Try for variety in your ten responses—in style, tone, and topic. It might help to write out the aphorism and to put it in sight: on a notebook cover, taped to your mirror, typed into your computer's screensaver, or anywhere else you know you will see it.

When you have completed ten responses, gather them together as a numbered set, revise them as appropriate, and provide an introduction or an afterword — a piece of writing where you speak to your reader about what you have done and why the aphorism might be understood as an interesting or compelling genre.

MAKING CONNECTIONS

1. Antonio Porchia and Anne Carson both work in short forms: Porchia writes aphorisms, usually a single sentence long; Carson writes "short talks," brief titled paragraphs. There are two steps in this writing assignment.

   In the first, prepare your own set of Carson-like "short talks" (a minimum of 5 sections) and your own set of Porchia-like aphorisms (a minimum of 10). Your work should be similar in style and intent. Their work is your model and inspiration, and yet this project is also yours. A reader should be able to see where and how your work is in conversation with theirs; a reader should also be able to see what you bring to the table.

   When you are done, gather your work together, revise, format, and organize as appropriate, and provide an introduction or an afterword — a piece of writing where you speak to your reader about what you have done and why the short form might be understood as an interesting or compelling genre.

2. This is the final sentence of Brian Doyle's "Joyas Voladoras":

   > You can brick up your heart as stout and tight and hard and cold and impregnable as you possibly can and down it comes in an instant, felled by a woman's second glance, a child's apple breath, the shatter of glass in the road, the words *I have something to tell you,* a cat with a broken spine dragging itself into the forest to die, the brush of your mother's papers ancient hand in the thicket of your hair, the memory of your father's voice early in the morning echoing from the kitchen where he is making pancakes for his children. (p. 275)

   It is safe to say that Doyle is going for maximum effect in this sentence. It is a sentence that is meant to register, to resonate, to be memorable, and, in this case, to bring an essay to a satisfying close.

Gather five such sentences from "Joyas Voladoras" (or, if you choose, five sentences from other selections in *Ways of Reading*). Place them alongside your five favorite aphorisms from "Voices." Porchia's sentences, too, are carefully crafted for maximum effect. (You can be a critic as well as a promoter of such sentences.) Write an essay in which you present these 10 sentences, looking more for differences than for similarities in your examples, and all as part of a general discussion of the sentence as a device, a flexible form a writer can use for meaning and effect.

MARY LOUISE Pratt

Mary Louise Pratt (b. 1948) grew up in Listowel, Ontario, a small Canadian farm town. She got her BA at the University of Toronto and her PhD from Stanford University, where for nearly thirty years she was a professor in the departments of comparative literature and Spanish and Portuguese. At Stanford, she was one of the cofounders of the new freshman culture program, a controversial series of required courses that replaced the old Western civilization core courses. The course she is particularly associated with is called "Europe and the Americas"; it brings together European representations of the Americas with indigenous American texts. As you might guess from the essay that follows, the program at Stanford expanded the range of countries, languages, cultures, and texts that are seen as a necessary introduction to the world; it also, however, revised the very idea of culture that many of us take for granted—particularly the idea that culture, at its best, expresses common values in a common language. Among other awards and honors, Pratt is the recipient of a Guggenheim Fellowship and a Fellowship at the Center for Advanced Study in the Behavioral Sciences, Stanford University. She is Silver Professor in the Department of Spanish and Portuguese at New York University. She served as president of the Modern Language Association for 2003.

Pratt is the author of *Toward a Speech Act Theory of Literary Discourse* (1977) and coauthor of *Women, Culture, and Politics in Latin America* (1990), the textbook *Linguistics for Students of Literature* (1980), *Amor Brujo: The Images and Culture of Love in the Andes* (1990), and *Imperial Eyes: Studies in Travel Writing and Transculturation* (1992). The essay that follows was revised to serve as the introduction to *Imperial Eyes*, which examines European travel writing in the eighteenth and nineteenth centuries, when Europe was "discovering" Africa and the Americas. It argues that travel writing produced "the rest of the world" for European readers. It didn't "report" on Africa or South America; it produced an "Africa" or an "America" for European consumption. Travel writing produced places that could be thought of as barren, empty, undeveloped, inconceivable, needful of European influence and control, ready to serve European industrial, intellectual, and commercial interests. The reports of travelers or, later, scientists and anthropologists are part of a more general process by which the emerging industrial nations took possession of new territory.

The European understanding of Peru, for example, came through European accounts, not from attempts to understand or elicit responses from Andeans, Peruvian natives. Such a response was delivered when an Andean, Guaman Poma, wrote to King Philip III of Spain, but his letter was unreadable. Pratt is interested in just those moments of contact between peoples and cultures. She is interested in how King Philip read (or failed to read) a letter from Peru, but also in how someone like Guaman Poma prepared himself to write to the king of Spain. To fix these moments, she makes use of a phrase she coined, the "contact zone," which, she says,

> I use to refer to the space of colonial encounters, the space in which peoples geographically and historically separated come into contact with each other and establish ongoing relations, usually involving conditions of coercion, radical inequality, and intractable conflict. . . . By using the term "contact," I aim to foreground the interactive, improvisational dimensions of colonial encounters so easily ignored or suppressed by diffusionist accounts of conquest and domination. A "contact" perspective emphasizes how subjects are constituted in and by their relations to each other. It treats the relations among colonizers and colonized, or travelers and "travelees," not in terms of separateness or apartheid, but in terms of copresence, interaction, interlocking understandings and practices.

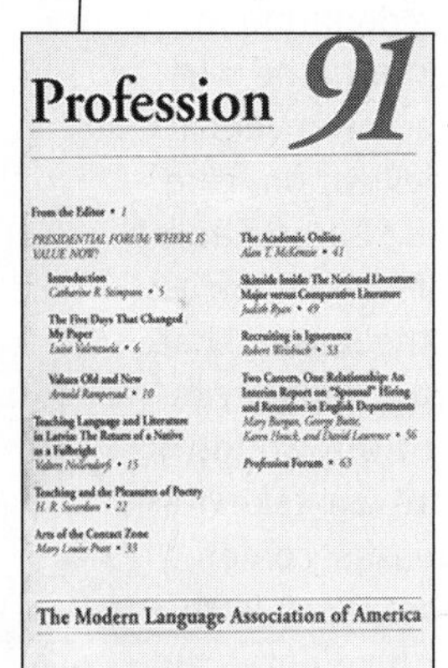

"Arts of the Contact Zone" was first written as a lecture. It was delivered as a keynote address at the second Modern Language Association Literacy Conference, held in Pittsburgh, Pennsylvania, in 1990.

Arts of the Contact Zone

Whenever the subject of literacy comes up, what often pops first into my mind is a conversation I overheard eight years ago between my son Sam and his best friend, Willie, aged six and seven, respectively: "Why don't you trade me Many Trails for Carl Yats . . . Yesits . . . Ya-strum-scrum." "That's not how you say it, dummy, it's Carl Yes . . . Yes . . . oh, I don't know." Sam and Willie had just discovered baseball cards. Many Trails was their decoding, with the help of first-grade English phonics, of the name Manny Trillo. The name they were quite rightly stumped on was Carl Yastrzemski. That was the first time I remembered seeing them put their incipient literacy to their own use, and I was of course thrilled.

Sam and Willie learned a lot about phonics that year by trying to decipher surnames on baseball cards, and a lot about cities, states, heights, weights, places of birth, stages of life. In the years that followed, I watched Sam apply his arithmetic skills to working out batting averages and subtracting retirement years from rookie years; I watched him develop senses of patterning and order by arranging and rearranging his cards for hours on end, and aesthetic judgment by comparing different photos, different series, layouts, and color schemes. American geography and history took shape in his mind through baseball cards. Much of his social life revolved around trading them, and he learned about exchange, fairness, trust, the importance of processes as opposed to results, what it means to get cheated, taken advantage of, even robbed. Baseball cards were the medium of his economic life too. Nowhere better to learn the power and arbitrariness of money, the absolute divorce between use value and exchange value, notions of long- and short-term investment, the possibility of personal values that are independent of market values.

Baseball cards meant baseball card shows, where there was much to be learned about adult worlds as well. And baseball cards opened the door to baseball books, shelves and shelves of encyclopedias, magazines, histories, biographies, novels, books of jokes, anecdotes, cartoons, even poems. Sam learned the history of American racism and the struggle against it through baseball; he saw the Depression and two world wars from behind home plate. He learned the meaning of commodified labor, what it means for one's body and talents to be owned and dispensed by another. He knows something about Japan, Taiwan, Cuba, and Central America and how men and boys do things there. Through the history and experience of baseball stadiums he thought about architecture, light, wind, topography, meteorology, the dynamics of public space. He learned the meaning of expertise, of knowing about something well enough that you can start a conversation with a stranger and feel sure of holding your own. Even with an adult — especially with an adult. Throughout his preadolescent years, baseball history was Sam's luminous point of contact with grown-ups, his lifeline to caring. And, of course, all this time he was also playing baseball, struggling his way through the stages of the local Little League system, lucky enough to be a pretty good player, loving the game and coming to know deeply his strengths and weaknesses.

Literacy began for Sam with the newly pronounceable names on the picture cards and brought him what has been easily the broadest, most varied, most enduring, and most integrated experience of his thirteen-year life. Like many parents, I was delighted to see schooling give Sam the tools with which to find and open all these doors. At the same time I found it unforgivable that schooling itself gave him nothing remotely as meaningful to do, let alone anything that would actually take him beyond the referential, masculinist ethos of baseball and its lore.

However, I was not invited here to speak as a parent, nor as an expert on literacy. I was asked to speak as an MLA [Modern Language Association] member working in the elite academy. In that capacity my contribution is undoubtedly supposed to be abstract, irrelevant, and anchored outside the real world. I wouldn't dream of disappointing anyone. I propose immediately to head back several centuries to a text that has a few points in common with baseball cards and raises thoughts about what Tony Sarmiento, in his comments to the conference, called new visions of literacy. In 1908 a Peruvianist named Richard Pietschmann was exploring in the Danish Royal Archive in Copenhagen and came across a manuscript. It was dated in the city of Cuzco in Peru, in the year 1613, some forty years after the final fall of the Inca empire to the Spanish and signed with an unmistakably Andean indigenous name: Felipe Guaman Poma de Ayala. Written in a mixture of Quechua and ungrammatical, expressive Spanish, the manuscript was a letter addressed by an unknown but apparently literate Andean to King Philip III of Spain. What stunned Pietschmann was that the letter was twelve hundred pages long. There were almost eight hundred pages of written text and four hundred of captioned line drawings. It was titled *The First New Chronicle and Good Government.* No one knew (or knows) how the manuscript got to the library in Copenhagen or how long it had been there. No one, it appeared, had ever bothered to read it or figured out how. Quechua was not thought of as a written language in 1908, nor Andean culture as a literate culture.

THE LETTER GOT THERE, ONLY 350 YEARS TOO LATE, A MIRACLE AND A TERRIBLE TRAGEDY.

Pietschmann prepared a paper on his find, which he presented in London in 1912, a year after the rediscovery of Machu Picchu by Hiram Bingham. Reception, by an international congress of Americanists, was apparently confused. It took twenty-five years for a facsimile edition of the work to appear in Paris. It was not till the late 1970s, as positivist reading habits gave way to interpretive studies and colonial elitisms to post-colonial pluralisms, that Western scholars found ways of reading Guaman Poma's *New Chronicle and Good Government* as the extraordinary intercultural tour de force that it was. The letter got there, only 350 years too late, a miracle and a terrible tragedy.

I propose to say a few more words about this erstwhile unreadable text, in order to lay out some thoughts about writing and literacy in what I like to call the *contact zones*. I use this term to refer to social spaces where cultures meet, clash, and grapple with each other, often in contexts of highly asymmetrical relations of power, such as colonialism, slavery, or their aftermaths as they are lived out in many parts of the world today. Eventually I will use the term to reconsider the models of community that many of us rely on in teaching and theorizing and that are under challenge today. But first a little more about Guaman Poma's giant letter to Philip III.

Insofar as anything is known about him at all, Guaman Poma exemplified the sociocultural complexities produced by conquest and empire. He was an indigenous Andean who claimed noble Inca descent and who had adopted (at least in some sense) Christianity. He may have worked in the Spanish colonial administration as an interpreter, scribe, or assistant to a Spanish tax collector — as a mediator, in short. He says he learned to write from his half brother, a mestizo whose Spanish father had given him access to religious education.

Guaman Poma's letter to the king is written in two languages (Spanish and Quechua) and two parts. The first is called the *Nueva corónica,* "New Chronicle." The title is important. The chronicle of course was the main writing apparatus through which the Spanish presented their American conquests to themselves. It constituted one of the main official discourses. In writing a "new chronicle," Guaman Poma took over the official Spanish genre for his own ends. Those ends were, roughly, to construct a new picture of the world, a picture of a Christian world with Andean rather than European peoples at the center of it — Cuzco, not Jerusalem. In the *New Chronicle* Guaman Poma begins by rewriting the Christian history of the world from Adam and Eve (Fig. 1), incorporating the Amerindians into it as offspring of one of the sons of Noah. He identifies five ages of Christian history that he links in parallel with the five ages of canonical Andean history — separate but equal trajectories that diverge with Noah and reintersect not with Columbus but with Saint Bartholomew, claimed to have preceded Columbus in the Americas. In a couple of hundred pages, Guaman Poma constructs a veritable encyclopedia of Inca and pre-Inca history, customs, laws, social forms, public offices, and dynastic leaders. The depictions resemble European manners and customs description, but also reproduce the meticulous detail with which knowledge in Inca society was stored on *quipus* and in the oral memories of elders.

Guaman Poma's *New Chronicle* is an instance of what I have proposed to call an *autoethnographic* text, by which I mean a text in which people undertake to describe themselves in ways that engage with representations others have made of them. Thus if ethnographic texts are those in which European metropolitan subjects represent to themselves their others (usually their conquered others), autoethnographic texts are representations that the so-defined others construct *in response to* or in dialogue with those

Figure 1. Adam and Eve.

texts. Autoethnographic texts are not, then, what are usually thought of as autochthonous forms of expression or self-representation (as the Andean *quipus* were). Rather they involve a selective collaboration with and appropriation of idioms of the metropolis or the conqueror. These are merged or infiltrated to varying degrees with indigenous idioms to create self-representations intended to intervene in metropolitan modes of understanding. Autoethnographic works are often addressed to both metropolitan audiences and the speaker's own community. Their reception is thus highly indeterminate. Such texts often constitute a marginalized group's point of entry into the dominant circuits of print culture. It is interesting to think, for example, of American slave autobiography in its autoethnographic dimensions, which in some respects distinguish it from Euramerican autobiographical tradition. The concept might help explain why some of the earliest published writing by Chicanas took the form of folkloric manners and customs sketches written in English and published in English-language newspapers or folklore magazines (see Treviño). Autoethnographic representation often involves concrete collaborations between people, as between literate ex-slaves and abolitionist intellectuals, or between Guaman Poma and the Inca elders who were his informants. Often, as in Guaman Poma, it involves more than one language. In recent decades autoethnography, critique, and resistance have reconnected with writing in a contemporary creation of the contact zone, the *testimonio*.

Guaman Poma's *New Chronicle* ends with a revisionist account of the Spanish conquest, which, he argues, should have been a peaceful encounter of equals with the potential for benefiting both, but for the mindless greed of the Spanish. He parodies Spanish history. Following contact with the Incas, he writes, "In all Castille, there was a great commotion. All day and at night in their dreams the Spaniards were saying, 'Yndias, yndias, oro, plata, oro, plata del Piru'" ("Indies, Indies, gold, silver, gold, silver from Peru") (Fig. 2). The Spanish, he writes, brought nothing of value to share with the Andeans, nothing "but armor and guns con la codicia de oro, plata, oro y plata, yndias, a las Yndias, Piru" ("with the lust for gold, silver, gold and silver, Indies, the Indies, Peru") (p. 372). I quote these words as an example of a conquered subject using the conqueror's language to construct a parodic, oppositional representation of the conqueror's own speech. Guaman Poma mirrors back to the Spanish (in their language,

Figure 2. Conquista. Meeting of Spaniard and Inca. The Inca says in Quechua, "You eat this gold?" Spaniard replies in Spanish, "We eat this gold."

which is alien to him) an image of themselves that they often suppress and will therefore surely recognize. Such are the dynamics of language, writing, and representation in contact zones.

The second half of the epistle continues the critique. It is titled *Buen gobierno y justicia,* "Good Government and Justice," and combines a description of colonial society in the Andean region with a passionate denunciation of Spanish exploitation and abuse. (These, at the time he was writing, were decimating the population of the Andes at a genocidal rate. In fact, the potential loss of the labor force became a main cause for reform of the system.) Guaman Poma's most implacable hostility is invoked by the clergy, followed by the dreaded *corregidores,* or colonial overseers (Fig. 3). He also praises good works, Christian habits, and just men where he finds them, and offers at length his views as to what constitutes "good government and justice." The Indies, he argues, should be administered through a collaboration of Inca and Spanish elites. The epistle ends with an imaginary question-and-answer session in which, in a reversal of hierarchy, the king is depicted asking Guaman Poma questions about how to reform the empire—a dialogue imagined across the many lines that

Figure 3. Corregidor de minas. Catalog of Spanish abuses of indigenous labor force.

divide the Andean scribe from the imperial monarch, and in which the subordinated subject single-handedly gives himself authority in the colonizer's language and verbal repertoire. In a way, it worked — this extraordinary text did get written — but in a way it did not, for the letter never reached its addressee.

To grasp the import of Guaman Poma's project, one needs to keep in mind that the Incas had no system of writing. Their huge empire is said to be the only known instance of a full-blown bureaucratic state society built and administered without writing. Guaman Poma constructs his text by appropriating and adapting pieces of the representational repertoire of the invaders. He does not simply imitate or reproduce it; he selects and adapts it along Andean lines to express (bilingually, mind you) Andean interests and aspirations. Ethnographers have used the term *transculturation* to describe processes whereby members of subordinated or marginal groups select and invent from materials transmitted by a dominant or metropolitan culture. The term, originally coined by Cuban sociologist Fernando Ortiz in the 1940s, aimed to replace overly reductive concepts of acculturation and assimilation used to characterize culture under conquest. While subordinate peoples do not usually control what emanates from the dominant culture, they do determine to varying extents what gets absorbed into their own and what it gets used for. Transculturation, like autoethnography, is a phenomenon of the contact zone.

TRANSCULTURATION, LIKE AUTOETHNOGRAPHY, IS A PHENOMENON OF THE CONTACT ZONE.

As scholars have realized only relatively recently, the transcultural character of Guaman Poma's text is intricately apparent in its visual as well as its written component. The genre of the four hundred line drawings is European — there seems to have been no tradition of representational drawing among the Incas — but in their execution they deploy specifically Andean systems of spatial symbolism that express Andean values and aspirations.[1]

In Figure 1, for instance, Adam is depicted on the left-hand side below the sun, while Eve is on the right-hand side below the moon, and slightly lower than Adam. The two are divided by the diagonal of Adam's digging stick. In Andean spatial symbolism, the diagonal descending from the sun marks the basic line of power and authority dividing upper from lower, male from female, dominant from subordinate. In Figure 2, the Inca appears in the same position as Adam, with the Spaniard opposite, and the two at the same height. In Figure 3, depicting Spanish abuses of power, the symbolic pattern is reversed. The Spaniard is in a high position indicating dominance, but on the "wrong" (right-hand) side. The diagonals of his lance and that of the servant doing the flogging mark out a line of illegitimate, though real, power. The Andean figures continue to occupy the left-hand side of the picture, but clearly as victims. Guaman Poma wrote that the Spanish conquest had produced *"un mundo al revés,"* "a world in reverse."

In sum, Guaman Poma's text is truly a product of the contact zone. If one thinks of cultures, or literatures, as discrete, coherently structured, monolingual edifices, Guaman Poma's text, and indeed any autoethnographic work, appears anomalous or chaotic — as it apparently did to the European scholars Pietschmann spoke to in 1912. If one does not think of cultures this way, then Guaman Poma's text is simply heterogeneous, as the Andean region was itself and remains today. Such a text is heterogeneous on the reception end as well as the production end: it will read very differently to people in different positions in the contact zone. Because it deploys European and Andean systems of meaning making, the letter necessarily means differently to bilingual Spanish-Quechua speakers and to monolingual speakers in either language; the drawings mean differently to monocultural readers, Spanish or Andean, and to bicultural readers responding to the Andean symbolic structures embodied in European genres.

In the Andes in the early 1600s there existed a literate public with considerable intercultural competence and degrees of bilingualism. Unfortunately, such a community did not exist in the Spanish court with which Guaman Poma was trying to make contact. It is interesting to note that in the same year Guaman Poma sent off his letter, a text by another Peruvian was adopted in official circles in Spain as the canonical Christian mediation between the Spanish conquest and Inca history. It was another huge encyclopedic work, titled the *Royal Commentaries of the Incas,* written, tellingly, by a mestizo, Inca Garcilaso de la Vega. Like the mestizo half brother who taught Guaman Poma to read and write, Inca Garcilaso was the son of an Inca princess and a Spanish official, and had lived in Spain since he was seventeen. Though he too spoke Quechua, his book is written in eloquent, standard Spanish, without illustrations. While Guaman Poma's life's work sat somewhere unread, the *Royal Commentaries* was edited and reedited in Spain and the New World, a mediation that coded the Andean past and present in ways thought unthreatening to colonial hierarchy.[2] The textual hierarchy persists; the *Royal Commentaries* today remains a staple item on PhD reading lists in Spanish, while the *New Chronicle and Good Government,* despite the ready availability of several fine editions, is not. However, though Guaman Poma's text did not reach its destination, the transcultural currents of expression it exemplifies continued to evolve in the Andes, as they still do, less in writing than in storytelling, ritual, song, dance-drama, painting and sculpture, dress, textile art, forms of governance, religious belief, and many other vernacular art forms. All express the effects of long-term contact and intractable, unequal conflict.

Autoethnography, transculturation, critique, collaboration, bilingualism, mediation, parody, denunciation, imaginary dialogue, vernacular expression — these are some of the literate arts of the contact zone. Miscomprehension, incomprehension, dead letters, unread masterpieces, absolute heterogeneity of meaning — these are some of the perils of writing in the contact zone. They all live among us today in the transnationalized metropolis of the United States and are becoming more widely visible, more pressing, and, like Guaman Poma's text, more decipherable to those who once would have ignored them in defense of a stable, centered sense of knowledge and reality.

CONTACT AND COMMUNITY

The idea of the contact zone is intended in part to contrast with ideas of community that underlie much of the thinking about language, communication, and culture that gets done in the academy. A couple of years ago, thinking about the linguistic theories I knew, I tried to make sense of a utopian quality that often seemed to characterize social analyses of language by the academy. Languages were seen as living in "speech communities," and these tended to be theorized as discrete, self-defined, coherent entities, held together by a homogeneous competence or grammar shared identically and equally among all the members. This abstract idea of the speech community seemed to reflect, among other things, the utopian way modern nations conceive of themselves as what Benedict Anderson calls "imagined communities."[3] In a book of that title, Anderson observes that with the possible exception of what he calls "primordial villages," human communities exist as *imagined* entities in which people "will never know most of their fellow-members, meet them or even hear of them, yet in the mind of each lives the image of their communion." "Communities are distinguished," he goes on to say, "not by their falsity/genuineness, but by *the style in which they are imagined*" (15; emphasis mine). Anderson proposes three features that characterize the style in which the modern nation is imagined. First, it is imagined as *limited*, by "finite, if elastic, boundaries"; second, it is imagined as *sovereign*; and, third, it is imagined as *fraternal*, "a deep, horizontal comradeship" for which millions of people are prepared "not so much to kill as willingly to die" (15). As the image suggests, the nation-community is embodied metonymically in the finite, sovereign, fraternal figure of the citizen-soldier.

Anderson argues that European bourgeoisies were distinguished by their ability to "achieve solidarity on an essentially imagined basis" (74) on a scale far greater than that of elites of other times and places. Writing and literacy play a central role in this argument. Anderson maintains, as have others, that the main instrument that made bourgeois nation-building projects possible was print capitalism. The commercial circulation of books in the various European vernaculars, he argues, was what first created the invisible networks that would eventually constitute the literate elites and those they ruled as nations. (Estimates are that 180 million books were put into circulation in Europe between the years 1500 and 1600 alone.)

Now obviously this style of imagining of modern nations, as Anderson describes it, is strongly utopian, embodying values like equality, fraternity, liberty, which the societies often profess but systematically fail to realize. The prototype of the modern nation as imagined community was, it seemed to me, mirrored in ways people thought about language and the speech community. Many commentators have pointed out how modern views of language as code and competence assume a unified and homogeneous social world in which language exists as a shared patrimony — as a device, precisely, for imagining community. An image of a universally shared literacy is also part of the picture. The prototypical manifestation of language is generally taken to be the speech of individual adult native speakers face-to-face (as in Saussure's famous diagram) in monolingual, even monodialectal situations — in short, the most homogeneous case linguistically and socially. The same goes for written communication. Now one could certainly imagine a theory that assumed different things — that argued, for instance, that the most revealing speech situation for understanding language was one involving a gathering of people each of whom spoke two languages and understood a third and held only one language in common with any of the others. It depends on what workings of language you want to see or want to see first, on what you choose to define as normative.

In keeping with autonomous, fraternal models of community, analyses of language use commonly assume that principles of cooperation and shared understanding are normally in effect. Descriptions of interactions between people in conversation, classrooms, medical and bureaucratic settings, readily take it for granted that the situation is governed by a single set of rules or norms shared by all participants. The analysis focuses then on how those rules produce or fail to produce an orderly, coherent exchange. Models involving games and moves are often used to describe interactions. Despite whatever conflicts or systematic social differences might be in play, it is assumed that all participants are engaged in the same game and that the game is the same for all players. Often it is. But of course it often is not, as, for example, when speakers are from different classes or cultures, or one party is exercising authority and another is submitting to it or questioning it. Last year one of my children moved to a new elementary school that had more open classrooms and more flexible curricula than the conventional school he started out in. A few days into the term, we asked him what it was like at the new school. "Well," he said, "they're a lot nicer, and they have a lot less rules. But know *why* they're nicer?" "Why?" I asked. "So you'll obey all the rules they don't have," he replied. This is a very coherent analysis with considerable elegance and explanatory power, but probably not the one his teacher would have given.

When linguistic (or literate) interaction is described in terms of orderliness, games, moves, or scripts, usually only legitimate moves are actually named as part of the system, where legitimacy is defined from the point of view of the party in authority — regardless of what other parties might see themselves as doing. Teacher-pupil language, for example, tends to be described almost entirely from the point of view of the teacher and teaching, not from the point of view of pupils and pupiling (the word doesn't even exist, though the thing certainly does). If a classroom is analyzed as a social world unified and homogenized with respect to the teacher, whatever students do other than what the teacher specifies is invisible or anomalous to the analysis. This can be true in practice as well. On several occasions my fourth grader, the one busy obeying all the rules they didn't have, was given writing assignments that took the form of answering a series of questions to build up a paragraph. These questions often asked him to identify with the interests of those in power over him — parents, teachers, doctors, public authorities. He invariably sought ways to resist or subvert these assignments. One assignment, for instance, called for imagining "a helpful invention." The students were asked to write single-sentence responses to the following questions:

> What kind of invention would help you?
> How would it help you?
> Why would you need it?
> What would it look like?
> Would other people be able to use it also?
> What would be an invention to help your teacher?
> What would be an invention to help your parents?

Manuel's reply read as follows:

> A grate adventchin
>
> Some inventchins are GRATE!!!!!!!!!!! My inventchin would be a shot that would put every thing you learn at school in your brain. It would help me by letting me graduate right now!! I would need it because it would let me play with my friends, go on vacachin and, do fun a lot more. It would look like a regular shot. Ather peaple would use to. This inventchin would help my teacher parents get away from a lot of work. I think a shot like this would be GRATE!

Despite the spelling, the assignment received the usual star to indicate the task had been fulfilled in an acceptable way. No recognition was available, however, of the humor, the attempt to be critical or contestatory, to parody the structures of authority. On that score, Manuel's luck was only slightly better than Guaman Poma's. What is the place of unsolicited oppositional discourse, parody, resistance, critique in the imagined classroom community? Are teachers supposed to feel that their teaching has been most successful when they have eliminated such things and unified the social world, probably in their own image? Who wins when we do that? Who loses?

Such questions may be hypothetical, because in the United States in the 1990s, many teachers find themselves less and less able to do that even if they want to. The composition of the national collectivity is changing and so are the styles, as Anderson put it, in which it is being imagined. In the 1980s in many nation-states, imagined national syntheses that had retained hegemonic force began to dissolve. Internal social groups with histories and lifeways different from the official ones began insisting on those histories and lifeways *as part of their citizenship*, as the very mode of their membership in the national collectivity. In their dialogues with dominant institutions, many groups began asserting a rhetoric of belonging that made demands beyond those of representation and basic rights granted from above. In universities we started to hear, "I don't just want you to let me be here, I want to belong here; this institution should belong to me as much as it does to anyone else." Institutions have responded with, among other things, rhetorics of diversity and multiculturalism whose import at this moment is up for grabs across the ideological spectrum.

These shifts are being lived out by everyone working in education today, and everyone is challenged by them in one way or another. Those of us committed to educational democracy are particularly challenged as that notion finds itself besieged on the public agenda. Many of those who govern us display, openly, their interest in a quiescent, ignorant, manipulable electorate. Even as an ideal, the concept of an enlightened citizenry seems to have disappeared from the national imagination. A couple of years ago the university where I work went through an intense and wrenching debate over a narrowly defined Western-culture requirement that had been instituted there in 1980. It kept boiling down to a debate over the ideas of national patrimony, cultural citizenship, and imagined community. In the end, the requirement was transformed into a much more broadly defined course called Cultures, Ideas, Values.[4] In the context of the change, a new course was designed that centered on the Americas and the multiple cultural histories (including European ones) that have intersected here. As you can imagine, the course attracted a very diverse student body. The classroom functioned not like a homogeneous community or a horizontal alliance but like a contact zone. Every single text we read stood in specific historical relationships to the students in the class, but the range and variety of historical relationships in play were enormous. Everybody had a stake in nearly everything we read, but the range and kind of stakes varied widely.

THE VERY NATURE OF THE COURSE PUT IDEAS AND IDENTITIES ON THE LINE.

It was the most exciting teaching we had ever done, and also the hardest. We were struck, for example, at how anomalous the formal lecture became in a contact zone (who can forget Atahuallpa throwing down the Bible because it would not speak to him?). The lecturer's traditional (imagined) task — unifying the world in the class's eyes by means of a monologue that rings equally coherent, revealing, and true for all, forging an ad hoc community, homogeneous with respect to one's own words — this task became not only impossible but anomalous and unimaginable. Instead, one had to work in the knowledge that whatever one said was going to be systematically received in radically heterogeneous ways that we were neither able nor entitled to prescribe.

The very nature of the course put ideas and identities on the line. All the students in the class had the experience, for example, of hearing their culture discussed and objectified in ways that horrified them; all the students saw their roots traced back to legacies of both glory and shame; all the students experienced face-to-face the ignorance and incomprehension, and occasionally the hostility, of others. In the absence of community values and the hope of synthesis, it was easy to forget the positives; the fact, for instance, that kinds of marginalization once taken for granted were gone. Virtually every student was having the experience of seeing the world described with him or her in it. Along with rage, incomprehension, and pain, there were exhilarating moments of wonder and revelation, mutual understanding, and new wisdom — the joys of the contact zone. The sufferings and revelations were, at different moments to be sure, experienced by every student. No one was excluded, and no one was safe.

The fact that no one was safe made all of us involved in the course appreciate the importance of what we came to call "safe houses." We used the term to refer to social and intellectual spaces where groups can constitute themselves as horizontal, homogeneous, sovereign communities with high degrees of trust, shared understandings, temporary protection from legacies of oppression. This is why, as we realized, multicultural curricula should not seek to replace ethnic or women's studies, for example. Where there are legacies of subordination, groups need places for healing and mutual recognition, safe houses in which to construct shared understandings, knowledges, claims on the world that they can then bring into the contact zone.

Meanwhile, our job in the Americas course remains to figure out how to make that crossroads the best site for learning that it can be. We are looking for the pedagogical arts of the contact zone. These will include, we are sure, exercises in storytelling and in identifying with the ideas, interests, histories, and attitudes of others; experiments in transculturation and collaborative work and in the arts of critique, parody, and comparison (including unseemly comparisons between elite and vernacular cultural forms); the redemption of the oral; ways for people to engage with suppressed aspects of history (including their own histories), ways to move *into and out of* rhetorics of authenticity; ground rules for communication across lines of difference and hierarchy that go beyond politeness but maintain mutual respect; a systematic approach to the all-important concept of *cultural mediation*. These arts were in play in every room at the extraordinary Pittsburgh conference on literacy. I learned a lot about them there, and I am thankful.

NOTES

[1] For an introduction in English to these and other aspects of Guaman Poma's work, see Rolena Adorno. Adorno and Mercedes Lopez-Baralt pioneered the study of Andean symbolic systems in Guaman Poma.

[2] It is far from clear that the *Royal Commentaries* was as benign as the Spanish seemed to assume. The book certainly played a role in maintaining the identity and aspirations of indigenous elites in the Andes. In the mid-eighteenth century, a new edition of the *Royal Commentaries* was suppressed by Spanish authorities because its preface included a prophecy by Sir Walter Raleigh that the English would invade Peru and restore the Inca monarchy.

[3] The discussion of community here is summarized from my essay "Linguistic Utopias."
[4] For information about this program and the contents of courses taught in it, write Program in Cultures, Ideas, Values (CIV), Stanford Univ., Stanford, CA 94305.

BIBLIOGRAPHY

Adorno, Rolena. *Guaman Poma de Ayala: Writing and Resistance in Colonial Peru*. Austin: U of Texas P, 1986.
Anderson, Benedict. *Imagined Communities: Reflections on the Origins and Spread of Nationalism*. London: Verso, 1984.
Garcilaso de la Vega, El Inca. *Royal Commentaries of the Incas*. 1613. Austin: U of Texas P, 1966.
Guaman Poma de Ayala, Felipe. *El primer nueva corónica y buen gobierno*. Manuscript. Ed. John Murra and Rolena Adorno. Mexico: Siglo XXI, 1980.
Pratt, Mary Louise. "Linguistic Utopias." *The Linguistics of Writing*. Ed. Nigel Fabb et al. Manchester: Manchester UP, 1987. 48–66.
Treviño, Gloria. "Cultural Ambivalence in Early Chicano Prose Fiction." Diss. Stanford U, 1985.

QUESTIONS FOR A SECOND READING

1. Perhaps the most interesting question "Arts of the Contact Zone" raises for its readers is how to put together the pieces: the examples from Pratt's children, the discussion of Guaman Poma and the *New Chronicle and Good Government*, the brief history of European literacy, and the discussion of curriculum reform at Stanford. The terms that run through the sections are, among others, these: "contact," "community," "autoethnography," "transculturation." As you reread, mark those passages you might use to trace the general argument that cuts across these examples.

2. This essay was originally delivered as a lecture. Before you read Pratt's essay again, create a set of notes on what you remember as important, relevant, or worthwhile. Imagine yourself as part of her audience. Then reread the essay. Where would you want to interrupt her? What questions could you ask her that might make "Arts of the Contact Zone" more accessible to you?

3. This is an essay about reading and writing and teaching and learning, about the "literate arts" and the "pedagogical arts" of the contact zone. Surely the composition class, the first-year college English class, can be imagined as a contact zone. And it seems in the spirit of Pratt's essay to identify (as a student) with Guaman Poma. As you reread, think about how and where this essay might be said to speak directly to you about your education as a reader and writer in a contact zone.

4. There are some difficult terms in this essay: "autochthonous," "autoethnography," "transculturation." The last two are defined in the text; the first you will have to look up. (We did.) In some ways, the slipperiest of the key words in the essay is "culture." At one point Pratt says,

   > If one thinks of cultures, or literatures, as discrete, coherently structured, monolingual edifices, Guaman Poma's text, and indeed

> any autoethnographic work, appears anomalous or chaotic — as it apparently did to the European scholars Pietschmann spoke to in 1912. If one does not think of cultures this way, then Guaman Poma's text is simply heterogeneous, as the Andean region was itself and remains today. Such a text is heterogeneous on the reception end as well as the production end: it will read very differently to people in different positions in the contact zone. (p. 492)

If one thinks of cultures as "coherently structured, monolingual edifices," the text appears one way; if one thinks otherwise, the text is "simply heterogeneous." What might it mean to make this shift in the way one thinks of culture? Can you do it—that is, can you read the *New Chronicle* from both points of view, make the two points of view work in your own imagining? Can you, for example, think of a group that you participate in as a "community"? Then can you think of it as a "contact zone"? Which one seems "natural" to you? What does Pratt assume to be the dominant point of view now, for *her* readers?

As you reread, not only do you want to get a sense of how to explain these two attitudes toward culture, but you also need to practice shifting your point of view from one to the other. Think, from inside the position of each, of the things you would be expected to say about Poma's text, Manuel's invention, and your classroom.

ASSIGNMENTS FOR WRITING

Here, briefly, are two descriptions of the writing one might find or expect in the "contact zone." They serve as an introduction to the three writing assignments.

> Autoethnography, transculturation, critique, collaboration, bilingualism, mediation, parody, denunciation, imaginary dialogue, vernacular expression — these are some of the literate arts of the contact zone. Miscomprehension, incomprehension, dead letters, unread masterpieces, absolute heterogeneity of meaning — these are some of the perils of writing in the contact zone. They all live among us today in the transnationalized metropolis of the United States and are becoming more widely visible, more pressing, and, like Guaman Poma's text, more decipherable to those who once would have ignored them in defense of a stable, centered sense of knowledge and reality. (pp. 492–93)

> We are looking for the pedagogical arts of the contact zone. These will include, we are sure, exercises in storytelling and in identifying with the ideas, interests, histories, and attitudes of others; experiments in transculturation and collaborative work and in the arts of critique, parody, and comparison (including unseemly comparisons between elite and vernacular cultural forms); the redemption of the oral; ways for people to engage with suppressed aspects of history (including their own histories), ways to move *into and out of* rhetorics of authen-

ticity; ground rules for communication across lines of difference and hierarchy that go beyond politeness but maintain mutual respect; a systematic approach to the all-important concept of *cultural mediation*. (p. 497)

1. One way of working with Pratt's essay, of extending its project, would be to conduct your own local inventory of writing from the contact zone. You might do this on your own or in teams with others from your class. You will want to gather several similar documents, your "archive," before you make your final selection. Think about how to make that choice. What makes one document stand out as representative? Here are two ways you might organize your search:

   a. You could look for historical documents. A local historical society might have documents written by Native Americans ("Indians") to the white settlers. There may be documents written by slaves to masters or to northern whites explaining their experience with slavery. There may be documents by women (like suffragists) trying to negotiate for public positions and rights. There may be documents from any of a number of racial or ethnic groups — Hispanic, Jewish, Irish, Italian, Polish, Swedish — trying to explain their positions to the mainstream culture. There may, perhaps at union halls, be documents written by workers to owners. Your own sense of the heritage of your area should direct your search.

   b. Or you could look for contemporary documents in the print that is around you, things that you might otherwise overlook. Pratt refers to one of the characteristic genres of the Hispanic community, the *"testimonio."* You could look at the writing of any marginalized group, particularly writing intended, at least in part, to represent the experience of outsiders to the dominant culture (or to be in dialogue with that culture or to respond to that culture). These documents, if we follow Pratt's example, would encompass the work of young children or students, including college students.

   Once you have completed your inventory, choose a document you would like to work with and present it carefully and in detail (perhaps in even greater detail than Pratt's presentation of the *New Chronicle*). You might imagine that you are presenting this to someone who would not have seen it and would not know how to read it, at least not as an example of the literate arts of the contact zone.

2. Another way of extending the project of Pratt's essay would be to write your own autoethnography. It should not be too hard to locate a setting or context in which you are the "other" — the one who speaks from outside rather than inside the dominant discourse. Pratt says that the position of the outsider is marked not only by differences of language and ways of thinking and speaking but also by differences in power, authority, status. In a sense,

she argues, the only way those in power can understand you is in *their* terms. These are terms you will need to use to tell your story, but your goal is to describe your position in ways that "engage with representations others have made of [you]" without giving in or giving up or disappearing in their already formed sense of who you are.

This is an interesting challenge. One of the things that will make the writing difficult is that the autoethnographic or transcultural text calls upon skills not usually valued in American classrooms: bilingualism, parody, denunciation, imaginary dialogue, vernacular expression, storytelling, unseemly comparisons of high and low cultural forms—these are some of the terms Pratt offers. These do not fit easily with the traditional genres of the writing class (essay, term paper, summary, report) or its traditional values (unity, consistency, sincerity, clarity, correctness, decorum).

You will probably need to take this essay (or whatever it should be called) through several drafts. It might be best to begin as Pratt's student, using her description as a preliminary guide. Once you get a sense of your own project, you may find that you have terms or examples to add to her list of the literate arts of the contact zone.

3. Citing Benedict Anderson and what he calls "imagined communities," Pratt argues that our idea of community is "strongly utopian, embodying values like equality, fraternity, liberty, which the societies often profess but systematically fail to realize." Against this utopian vision of community, Pratt argues that we need to develop ways of understanding (even noticing) social and intellectual spaces that are not homogeneous, unified; we need to develop ways of understanding and valuing difference.

   Think of a community of which you are a member, a community that is important to you. And think about the utopian terms you are given to name and describe this community. Think, then, about this group in Pratt's terms—as a "contact zone." How would you name and describe this social space? Write an essay in which you present these alternate points of view on a single social group. You will need to present this discussion fully, so that someone who is not part of your group can follow what you say, and you should take time to think about the consequences (for you, for your group) of this shift in point of view, in terms.

MAKING CONNECTIONS

1. Here, from "Arts of the Contact Zone," is Mary Louise Pratt on the "autoethnographic" text:

   > Guaman Poma's *New Chronicle* is an instance of what I have proposed to call an *autoethnographic* text, by which I mean a text in which people undertake to describe themselves in ways that engage with representations others have made of them. Thus if ethnographic texts are those in which European metropolitan subjects

> represent to themselves their others (usually their conquered others), autoethnographic texts are representations that the so-defined others construct *in response to* or in dialogue with those texts. . . . They involve a selective collaboration with and appropriation of idioms of the metropolis or the conqueror. These are merged or infiltrated to varying degrees with indigenous idioms to create self-representations intended to intervene in metropolitan modes of understanding. . . . Such texts often constitute a marginalized group's point of entry into the dominant circuits of print culture. It is interesting to think, for example, of American slave autobiography in its autoethnographic dimensions, which in some respects distinguish it from Euramerican autobiographical tradition. (pp. 487–88)

John Edgar Wideman's "Our Time" (p. 657) and the excerpts from Gloria Anzaldúa's *Borderlands / La frontera* (p. 72) could serve as twentieth-century examples of autoethnographic texts. Choose one of these selections and reread it with "Arts of the Contact Zone" in mind. Write an essay that presents the selection as an example of autoethnographic and/or transcultural texts. You should imagine that you are working to put Pratt's ideas to the test (*do* they do what she says such texts must do?), but also add what you have to say concerning this text as a literate effort to be present in the context of difference.

2. In the selection titled "States" (p. 541), Edward Said says,

> All cultures spin out a dialectic of self and other, the subject "I" who is native, authentic, at home, and the object "it" or "you," who is foreign, perhaps threatening, different, out there. From this dialectic comes the series of heroes and monsters, founding fathers and barbarians, prized masterpieces and despised opponents that express a culture from its deepest sense of national self-identity to its refined patriotism, and finally to its coarse jingoism, xenophobia, and exclusivist bias. (p. 565)

This is as true of the Palestinians as it is of the Israelis — although, he adds, "For Palestinian culture, the odd thing is that its own identity is more frequently than not perceived as 'other.' "

Citing Benedict Anderson and what he refers to as "imagined communities," Mary Louise Pratt in "Arts of the Contact Zone" argues that our idea of community is "strongly utopian, embodying values like equality, fraternity, liberty, which the societies often profess but systematically fail to realize." Against this utopian vision of community, Pratt argues that we need to develop ways of understanding (noticing or creating) social and intellectual spaces that are not homogeneous or unified — contact zones. She argues that we need to develop ways of understanding and valuing difference.

There are similar goals and objects to these projects. Reread Pratt's essay with Said's "States" in mind. As she defines what she refers to as the "literate arts of the contact zone," can you find points of reference in Said's text? Said's thinking always attended to the importance and the conditions of writing, including his own. There are ways that "States" could be imagined as both "autoethnographic" and "transcultural." How might Said's work allow you to understand the "literate arts of the contact zone" in practice? How might his work allow you to understand the problems and possibilities of such writing beyond what Pratt has imagined, presented, and predicted?

3. In "Arts of the Contact Zone," Mary Louise Pratt defines contact zones as "social spaces where cultures meet, clash, and grapple with each other, often in contexts of highly asymmetrical relations of power." While we don't ordinarily think of the natural world as a culture, David Abram, in "Animism and the Alphabet" (p. 28), writes about the environment as if it were a culture of sorts — speaking to us, writing to us, attempting to communicate if only we are willing and able to listen. Abram might argue as well that the environment speaks in a context of "highly asymmetrical relations of power," where people — like the Spaniards in Pratt's central example — hold the dominant position, often exhibiting little interest in the "languages" spoken by mountains, rivers, animals, and clouds.

   Write an essay in which you consider how Pratt's concept of the contact zone might be useful in helping us consider our relationship with the natural world. Is the environment trying to speak to us as Guaman Poma tried to speak to his Spanish conquerors? In what ways is this analogy useful or productive, and in what ways does it fall short? Where would we find the "autoethnographic texts" produced by the natural world, and how can we learn to read them? Can you locate environmental versions of what Pratt calls "critique, collaboration, bilingualism, mediation, parody, denunciation, imaginary dialogue, [and] vernacular expression"? What are the possibilities for — and the problems with — "translating" messages from the natural world into languages we understand?

ALBERTO ÁLVARO Ríos

Alberto Álvaro Ríos (b. 1952) holds the Katharine C. Turner Endowed Chair in English at Arizona State University. He is the recipient of many distinguished awards for his writing, among them fellowships from the National Endowment for the Arts and the Guggenheim Foundation. He has been awarded six Pushcart Prizes and the Arizona Governor's Arts Award. While Ríos began his career primarily as a poet, this short essay brings to light his work as a teacher and an essayist. His poetry and prose often examine geographic, cultural, and spiritual aspects of borders, location, and language. As his essay "Translating Translation: Finding the Beginning" puts it, Ríos understands language and translation in complex and layered ways. In an interview, he said:

> I've come to the realization that my first language was really what I've called the "language of listening." What came out of my mouth was not nearly so important as what entered my ear. For me Spanish was all around me, but my mother was there, too — with a British accent. I had a zoo of sounds. If I had to say it succinctly, I would say that I write in Spanish — it just looks like English.

Rather than simplify ideas about what it means to translate, to move between one language and another, Ríos seems to want to open up the idea and the act of translation by presenting translation as a metaphor for the ways language, what it says, and how it says it are always being figured and refigured by those speaking and listening and writing and reading.

Ríos was born in Nogales, Arizona, to a Mexican father and an English mother; he has spent a large part of his life in Arizona. He spoke both English and Spanish until junior high, when he was stopped from speaking Spanish at his American public school. He began writing poetry at this time. He earned two bachelor's degrees (in English and psychology) and a master of fine arts in poetry from the University of Arizona.

Working in and across many genres of writing, Ríos has published ten books of poetry, including *Elk Heads on the Wall* (1979); *Whispering to Fool the Wind* (1982), winner of the Walt Whitman Award; *The Lime Orchard Woman* (1988); *The Smallest Muscle in the Human Body* (2002), nominated for a National Book Award; *The Theatre of Night* (2006); and *The Dangerous Shirt* (2009). He has also published three collections of short stories: *Pig Cookies* (1995), *The Iguana Killer* (1998), and *Curtain of Trees* (1999). *Capirotada: A Nogales Memoir* (1999) describes his experiences growing up in a small southwestern border town. In the essay that follows, first published in *Prairie Schooner*, Ríos tackles the problems of cultural, linguistic, and perhaps even emotional translation, conveying the challenges that he and his students face.

Translating Translation: Finding the Beginning

Linguists, by using electrodes on the vocal cords, have been able to demonstrate that English has tenser vowels than, for example, Spanish. The body itself speaks a language differently, so that moving from one language to another is more than translating words. It's getting the body ready as well. It's getting the heart ready along with the mind.

I've been intrigued by this information. It addresses the physicality of language in a way that perhaps surprises us. In this sense, we forget that words aren't simply what they mean — they are also physical acts.

I often talk about the duality of language using the metaphor of binoculars, how by using two lenses one might see something better, closer, with more detail. The apparatus, the binoculars, are of course physically clumsy — as is the learning of two languages, and all the signage and so on that this entails — they're clumsy, but once put to the eyes a new world in that moment opens up to us. And it's not a new world at all — it's the same world, but simply better seen, and therefore better understood.

When I was three or four, my parents bought a new house in what would later become a small suburb of Nogales, Arizona, on the border of Mexico, some four miles outside town. My father was born in Mexico, on the border of Guatemala, and my mother was born in England. I had languages.

As we kept driving out to watch the house being built, my mother got to make a number of choices regarding details, among which was the color of various rooms.

My mother, when asked what color she wanted the kitchen, said to the workers who were all Mexican, and who spoke very little English, *límon*. She said it both because she wanted the kitchen to be yellow and because she wanted to start learning Spanish. The workers nodded yes. But when we came back the next day, the kitchen was painted bright green, like a small jungle. Mexican *limones,* my mother found out, are small and green, that color exactly, no mistake.

So that's the color that wall stayed for the next eight years. She said it was a reminder to us all that there was a great deal to learn in the world. You might laugh at first, but after eight years you start to think about it.

And she was right. It was a perfect, small example of that other way to see things, and for eight years the kitchen for us was, perhaps in a very large way, an even better place than school.

Let me tell another story. Several years ago, a man, who only spoke Spanish, was arrested for illegally crossing the border from Mexico into the United States at Douglas, Arizona. He was put in a cell, but it was late in the day, the shift was changing, and the jailer forgot to tell the next shift that someone was back there. It's apparently a small jail, and nobody thought to look since no one heard anything. The man was left there from a Thursday to a Saturday, when a janitor found him.

But why didn't you say something, he was asked. Yet this very question underscores exactly the lack of understanding between the man and his jailers. The man, who was not a criminal, simply did what he was supposed to do. He had manners.

But manners don't always mean good manners.

We try to do what people want, but they have to know what they're asking for. That search for understanding is often itself a search for, and an act of, translation as well.

Several years ago I was doing an Artists in the Schools residency at the high school in Eloy, Arizona. Two memorable events occurred. The first was among a group of gifted students: a fire alarm rang, but nobody got up. We were having such a good time, nobody seemed willing to stop. One student said, "It's probably fake anyway. Couldn't we just send someone out to check?"

That was nice, but something else occurred on the same day, a Thursday. I was also working with a group of — what to call them, what were they called? Non-gifted students? In this class, there was an attentive group of four or five students in front, but in back and to the sides students were in various states of engagement, the most active of which was a poker game.

The students were Mexican and Chicano, mostly, migrant worker children, and those not being entirely attentive comprised mostly *cholos*. *Cholos* are what Pachucos used to be. The young men, in particular, have a uniform: chino pants, black belt, thick, black shoes, two T-shirts — a regular one over a thin-strapped one — and a hair net.

The hair net by itself is interesting, and to an outsider perhaps effeminate. But there were many reasons for a hair net. These boys' older brothers often worked, for example, in fast-food restaurants, and had to wear nets. And a net, it was a show of attitude — you took your net off when the important things happened. School was not that.

In working with these students, I was also faced with a substitute teacher, who had no ideas on how to control the class and who was very glad that I was the one standing up in front.

The week went its own way, with me talking and reading, the students in front responding, and the others playing cards and throwing pencils. But I know this classroom, and that was the thing. I also understood what happened next.

On this Thursday of the week, one of the boys in back got up, starting walking his walk to the front, ostensibly to sharpen a pencil, but he kind of hung around me at the desk. I was done for the day, and everyone was working, or supposed to be working, on a writing assignment.

"Hey, *ese,*" he said to me, with a small pointing of the right hand.

"Hey," I said.

He nodded his head. "You really like this poetry shit," he asked.

"Yes." I said.

And then he followed with the very best thing I could have hoped for. "So, how many fights you had?"

In that moment I knew exactly what he was asking me. He was trying to understand, to make some bridge, to make some sense for himself. It was a moment I won't forget. Whatever I answered doesn't finally matter. He had already found some kind of answer in his question.

He was looking for an equation, for something to understand. And he said it in the best way he could.

AND THEN HE FOLLOWED WITH THE VERY BEST THING I COULD HAVE HOPED FOR. "SO, HOW MANY FIGHTS YOU HAD?"

Language is more than what we say—it's also how we say it, and whether or not we even understand what we are saying. Language is manners, then, well-said or not; language is the attempt to understand as much as the understanding itself. It is the how as much as the what, form as much as content, intent as much as words.

These are the lateral muscles and physical directions of language that translation often fails to use. I had to be able to hear what this young man was asking me, whether or not I was prepared. It was another vocabulary altogether, yet filled with familiar words.

But maybe that's all right. Maybe that's exactly what keeps a computer or a book from doing the job. Maybe that's what keeps us human, and engaged, and necessary.

How many fights have I had? he asked.

Just one, I said, like you.

QUESTIONS FOR A SECOND READING

1. One way to begin thinking about Alberto Álvaro Ríos's essay is to focus our attention on the title of the piece. What might it mean to "translate translation"? What passages in the essay seem to speak directly to the meaning of his title? His subtitle is "Finding the Beginning." To what "beginning" do you think Ríos refers?

2. Ríos writes that language is "more than what we say—it's also how we say it" and that language is "the how as much as the what, form as much as content, intent as much as words." We might consider, then, *how* Ríos says what he says. If you were to describe *how* Ríos's essay is written, *how* he says what he says, what would you say? How would you describe the form of Ríos's essay? How does he approach its organization or design? As you reread, think about the relationship between the *how* and the *what* of the essay.

3. Ríos tells several stories in his essay—each of them occurring at a different time and place and each of them distinct from the others. Two of the stories he tells have to do with his own history—one from his childhood and the other from his experience as a teacher of writing. He also tells a story in which he is not one of the characters, a story about the arrest of a man he does not appear to know personally. Why does he choose these three stories to tell? As you reread, think about the ways these stories speak to one another. Where are you invited to make connections? How might you make the case for this as a unified essay, as a piece of writing with a single goal in mind?

ASSIGNMENTS FOR WRITING

1.

> I often talk about the duality of language using the metaphor of binoculars, how by using two lenses one might see something better, closer, with more detail. The apparatus, the binoculars, are of course physically clumsy — as is the learning of two languages, and all the signage and so on that this entails — they're clumsy, but once put to the eyes a new world in that moment opens up to us. And it's not a new world at all — it's the same world, but simply better seen, and therefore better understood. (p. 506)

Write an essay in which you take up the metaphor of the binoculars. How does it serve or illuminate the central concerns of the essay? What does it have to do with translation, for example? What are the metaphor's limits; where does it break down or no longer continue to serve? And, finally, how useful is it to you, both as a reader and as a person who has experienced the "duality of languages"? (You may not have learned a second language, like Spanish, but you have certainly moved between worlds that have their own particular and distinctive ways of speaking.)

2. "Translating Translation" is divided into five sections, each separated by white space on the page. In the middle are two stories: one from his childhood and one from his experience as a teacher. As you reread, think about the form of the essay. How do these sections work together? How do they organize the work of a reader? What advantage do they allow the writer?

   For this assignment, write an essay using the form and method of "Translating Translation"—four sections, two stories in the middle. You might borrow some of the phrases that begin Ríos's paragraphs: "I've been intrigued by" or "I often talk about" or "Let me tell another story."

MAKING CONNECTIONS

1. Consider the final section of "Translating Translation: Finding the Beginning":

> He was looking for an equation, for something to understand. And he said it in the best way he could.
>
> Language is more than what we say — it's also how we say it, and whether or not we even understand what we are saying. Language is manners, then, well-said or not; language is the attempt to understand as much as the understanding itself. It is the how as much as the what, form as much as content, intent as much as words.
>
> These are the lateral muscles and physical directions of language that translation often fails to use. I had to be able to hear what this young man was asking me, whether or not I was prepared. It was another vocabulary altogether, yet filled with familiar words.
>
> But maybe that's all right. Maybe that's exactly what keeps a computer or a book from doing the job. Maybe that's what keeps us human, and engaged, and necessary.
>
> How many fights have I had? he asked.
>
> Just one, I said, like you. (p. 508)

This essay doesn't end in textbook fashion. It does not, exactly, come to conclusions, as we might expect it to. There are many ways to write and conclude an essay, and many of those ways do not necessarily involve coming to any actual conclusions. For this assignment, read several concluding paragraphs of essays in *Ways of Reading*. These may be essays you've read before, or perhaps essays you've never read. As you read, pay specific attention to the kinds of concluding paragraphs you are reading. How do these essays end? What kinds of moves do these writers make?

Write an essay in which you examine the art of the conclusion. What are the distinctive features in the closing paragraphs you've chosen from the selections in *Ways of Reading*? What are the key differences? What strategies are represented in your examples? What do they demand of a reader? Of a writer? Where and how might you imagine bringing these techniques into your own work?

2. Gloria Anzaldúa, in "Entering into the Serpent" (p. 72), coins the phrase *la facultad*:

> *La facultad* is the capacity to see in surface phenomena the meaning of deeper realities, to see the deep structure below the surface. It is an instant "sensing," a quick perception arrived at without conscious reasoning. It is an acute awareness mediated by the part of the psyche that does not speak, that communicates in images and symbols. . . . (p. 82)

Both Anzaldúa and Ríos could be said to be trying to convey this capacity of *la facultad* in their writing—both through what they and through what their subjects see and say. Write an essay in which you articulate your understanding of *la facultad*. It may help to return to Anzaldúa's essay and to reread this passage in the context of her essay. Once you have offered a meaningful discussion of *la facultad*, use this concept as a lens through which to examine Ríos's "Translating Translation: Finding the Beginning." Are there moments when Ríos seems to be concerned with "the part of the psyche that does not speak," despite the fact that his piece is about language? How do you see Ríos communicating in "images and symbols"? What do you think the "structure [or structures] below the surface" are for Ríos? What kinds of structures are these?

3. Consider the following sentence from Alberto Álvaro Ríos's "Translating Translation: Finding the Beginning": "Linguists, by using electrodes on the vocal chords, have been able to demonstrate that English has tenser vowels than, for example, Spanish." Or this sentence from Anne Carson's "Short Talks" (p. 266): "Kafka liked to have his watch an hour and a half fast." Or this statement from Susan Griffin's "Our Secret" (p. 335): "The life plan of the body is encoded in the DNA molecule, a substance that has the ability to hold information and to replicate itself." Or this statement from Walker Percy's "The Loss of the Creature" (p. 459): "Garcia López de Cárdenas discovered the Grand Canyon and was amazed at the sight." Or this sentence from Brian Doyle's "Joyas Voladoras" (p. 273): "The biggest heart in the world is inside the blue whale."

All of the above are statements of fact. Each writer is offering a declarative sentence that makes a claim about what is (or was) so. Using the passage above, or perhaps using passages from other selections in *Ways of Reading*, write an essay in which you consider each writer's use of such statements of fact. As you review your examples, what are the different or distinctive ways the writers use facts? To what purposes are they used? To what ends? How do these sentences serve the larger project, the essay? Does it matter whether these statements are true? Should the essay be held to the same standards of reporting and objectivity as, say, newspaper journalism?

RICHARD

Rodriguez

Richard Rodriguez, the son of Mexican immigrants, was born in San Francisco in 1944. He grew up in Sacramento, where he attended Catholic schools before going on to Stanford University, Columbia University, the Warburg Institute in London, and the University of California at Berkeley, eventually pursuing a PhD in English Renaissance literature. His essays have been published in *Saturday Review, The American Scholar, Change*, and elsewhere. He now lives in San Francisco and works as a lecturer, an educational consultant, and a freelance writer. He has published several books: *Hunger of Memory: The Education of Richard Rodriguez* (1981), *Days of Obligation: An Argument with My Mexican Father* (1992), and *Brown: The Last Discovery of America* (2002).

In *Hunger of Memory*, a book of autobiographical essays that the *Christian Science Monitor* called "beautifully written, wrung from a sore heart," Rodriguez tells the story of his education, paying particular attention to both the meaning of his success as a student and, as he says, "its consequent price—the loss." Rodriguez's loss is represented most powerfully by his increased alienation from his parents and the decrease of intimate exchanges in family life. His parents' primary language was Spanish; his, once he became eager for success in school, was English. But the barrier was not only a language barrier. Rodriguez discovered that the interests he developed at school and through his reading were interests he did not share with those at home—in fact, his desire to speak of them tended to threaten and humiliate his mother and father.

This separation, Rodriguez argues, is a necessary part of every person's development, even though not everyone experiences it so dramatically. We must leave home and familiar ways of speaking and understanding in order to participate in public life. On these grounds, Rodriguez has been a strong voice against bilingual education, arguing that classes conducted in Spanish will only reinforce Spanish-speaking students' separateness from mainstream American life. Rodriguez's book caused a great deal of controversy upon publication, particularly in the Hispanic community. As one critic argued, "It is indeed painful that Mr. Rodriguez has come to identify himself so completely with the majority culture that he must propagandize for a system of education which can only produce other deprived and impoverished souls like himself." In his second book, *Days of Obligation: An*

Argument with My Mexican Father, Rodriguez continues to explore his relationship with his family and with his Mexican heritage; here, however, he also writes of his life as a gay male and the forms of alienation entailed by his sexuality, including his sense of distance from gay lifestyles and culture, both popular and academic.

The selection that follows, Chapter 2 of *Hunger of Memory*, deals with Rodriguez's experiences in school. "If," he says, "because of my schooling I had grown culturally separated from my parents, my education finally had given me ways of speaking and caring about that fact." This essay is a record of how he came to understand the changes in his life. A reviewer writing in the *Atlantic Monthly* concluded that *Hunger of Memory* will survive in our literature "not because of some forgotten public issues that once bisected Richard Rodriguez's life, but because his history of that life has something to say about what it means to be American . . . and what it means to be human."

The Achievement of Desire

I stand in the ghetto classroom — "the guest speaker" — attempting to lecture on the mystery of the sounds of our words to rows of diffident students. "Don't you hear it? Listen! The music of our words. *'Sumer is icumen in. . . .'* And songs on the car radio. We need Aretha Franklin's voice to fill plain words with music — her life." In the face of their empty stares, I try to create an enthusiasm. But the girls in the back row turn to watch some boy passing outside. There are flutters of smiles, waves. And someone's mouth elongates heavy, silent words through the barrier of glass. Silent words — the lips straining to shape each voiceless syllable: *"Meet meee late errr."* By the door, the instructor smiles at me, apparently hoping that I will be able to spark some enthusiasm in the class. But only one student seems to be listening. A girl, maybe fourteen. In this gray room her eyes shine with ambition. She keeps nodding and nodding at all that I say; she even takes notes. And each time I ask a question, she jerks up and down in her desk like a marionette, while her hand waves over the bowed heads of her classmates. It is myself (as a boy) I see as she faces me now (a man in my thirties).

The boy who first entered a classroom barely able to speak English, twenty years later concluded his studies in the stately quiet of the reading room in the British Museum. Thus with one sentence I can summarize my academic career. It will be harder to summarize what sort of life connects the boy to the man.

THE BOY WHO FIRST ENTERED A CLASSROOM BARELY ABLE TO SPEAK ENGLISH, TWENTY YEARS LATER CONCLUDED HIS STUDIES IN THE STATELY QUIET OF THE READING ROOM IN THE BRITISH MUSEUM.

With every award, each graduation from one level of education to the next, people I'd meet would congratulate me. Their refrain [was] always the same: "Your parents must be very proud." Sometimes then they'd ask me how I managed it — my "success." (How?) After a while, I had several quick answers to give in reply. I'd admit, for one thing, that I went to an excellent grammar school. (My earliest teachers, the nuns, made my success their ambition.) And my brother and both my sisters were very good students. (They often brought home the shiny school trophies I came to want.) And my mother and father always encouraged me. (At every graduation they were behind the stunning flash of the camera when I turned to look at the crowd.)

As important as these factors were, however, they account inadequately for my academic advance. Nor do they suggest what an odd success I managed. For although I was a very good student, I was also a very bad student. I was a "scholarship boy," a certain kind of scholarship boy. Always successful, I was always unconfident. Exhilarated by my progress. Sad. I became the prized student — anxious and eager to learn. Too eager, too anxious — an imitative and unoriginal pupil. My brother and two sisters enjoyed the advantages I did, and they grew to be as successful as I, but none of them ever seemed so anxious about their schooling. A second-grade student, I was the one who came home and corrected the "simple" grammatical mistakes of our parents. ("Two negatives make a positive.") Proudly I announced — to my family's startled silence — that a teacher had said I was losing all trace of a Spanish accent. I was oddly annoyed when I was unable to get parental help with a homework assignment. The night my father tried to help me with an arithmetic exercise, he kept reading the instructions, each time more deliberately, until I pried the textbook out of his hands, saying, "I'll try to figure it out some more by myself."

When I reached the third grade, I outgrew such behavior. I became more tactful, careful to keep separate the two very different worlds of my day. But then, with ever-increasing intensity, I devoted myself to my studies. I became bookish, puzzling to all my family. Ambition set me apart. When my brother saw me struggling home with stacks of library books, he would laugh, shouting: "Hey, Four Eyes!" My father opened a closet one day and was startled to find me inside, reading a novel. My mother would find me reading when I was supposed to be asleep or helping around the house or playing outside. In a voice angry or worried or just curious, she'd ask: "What do you see in your books?" It became the family's joke. When I was called and wouldn't reply, someone would say I must be hiding under my bed with a book.

(How did I manage my success?)

What I am about to say to you has taken me more than twenty years to admit: *A primary reason for my success in the classroom was that I couldn't forget that schooling was changing me and separating me from the life I enjoyed before becoming a student.* That simple realization! For years I never spoke to anyone about it. Never mentioned a thing to my family or my teachers or classmates. From a very early age, I understood enough, just enough about my classroom experiences to keep what I knew repressed, hidden beneath layers of embarrassment. Not until my last months as a graduate student, nearly thirty years old, was it possible for me to think much about the reasons for my academic success. Only then. At the end of my schooling, I needed to determine how far I had moved from my past. The adult finally confronted, and now must publicly say, what the child shuddered from knowing and could never admit to himself or to those many faces that smiled at his every success. ("Your parents must be very proud. . . .")

I

At the end, in the British Museum (too distracted to finish my dissertation) for weeks I read, speed-read, books by modern educational theorists, only to find infrequent and slight mention of students like me. (Much more is written about the more typical case, the lower-class student who barely is helped by his schooling.) Then one day, leafing through Richard Hoggart's *The Uses of Literacy*, I found, in his description of the scholarship boy, myself. For the first time I realized that there were other students like me, and so I was able to frame the meaning of my academic success, its consequent price — the loss.

Hoggart's description is distinguished, at least initially, by deep understanding. What he grasps very well is that the scholarship boy must move between environments, his home and the classroom, which are at cultural extremes, opposed. With his family, the boy has the intense pleasure of intimacy, the family's consolation in feeling public alienation. Lavish emotions texture home life. *Then*, at school, the instruction bids him to trust lonely reason primarily. Immediate needs set the pace of his parents' lives. From his mother and father the boy learns to trust spontaneity and nonrational ways of knowing. *Then*, at school, there is mental calm. Teachers emphasize the value of a reflectiveness that opens a space between thinking and immediate action.

Years of schooling must pass before the boy will be able to sketch the cultural differences in his day as abstractly as this. But he senses those differences early. Perhaps as early as the night he brings home an assignment from school and finds the house too noisy for study.

> He has to be more and more alone, if he is going to "get on." He will have, probably unconsciously, to oppose the ethos of the hearth, the intense gregariousness of the working-class family group. Since everything centres upon the living-room, there is unlikely to be a room of his own; the bedrooms are cold and inhospitable, and to warm them or the front room, if there is one, would not only be expensive, but would require an imaginative leap — out of the tradition — which most families are not capable of making. There is a corner of the living-room table. On the other side Mother is ironing, the wireless is on, someone is singing a snatch of song or Father says intermittently whatever comes into his head. The boy has to cut himself off mentally, so as to do his homework, as well as he can.[1]

The next day, the lesson is as apparent at school. There are even rows of desks. Discussion is ordered. The boy must rehearse his thoughts and raise his hand before speaking out in a loud voice to an audience of classmates. And there is time enough, and silence, to think about ideas (big ideas) never considered at home by his parents.

Not for the working-class child alone is adjustment to the classroom difficult. Good schooling requires that any student alter early childhood habits. But the working-class child is usually least prepared for the change. And, unlike many middle-class children, he goes home and sees in his parents a way of life not only different but starkly opposed to that of the classroom. (He enters the house and hears his parents talking in ways his teachers discourage.)

Without extraordinary determination and the great assistance of others — at home and at school — there is little chance for success. Typically most working-class children are barely changed by the classroom. The exception succeeds. The relative few become scholarship students. Of these, Richard Hoggart estimates, most manage a fairly graceful transition. Somehow they learn to live in the two very different worlds of their day. There are some others, however, those Hoggart pejoratively terms "scholarship boys," for whom success comes with special anxiety. Scholarship boy: good student, troubled son. The child is "moderately endowed," intellectually mediocre, Hoggart supposes — though it may be more pertinent to note the special qualities of temperament in the child. High-strung child. Brooding. Sensitive. Haunted by the knowledge that one *chooses* to become a student. (Education is not an inevitable or natural step in growing up.) Here is a child who cannot forget that his academic success distances him from a life he loved, even from his own memory of himself.

Initially, he wavers, balances allegiance. ("The boy is himself [until he reaches, say, the upper forms] very much of *both* the worlds of home and school. He is enormously obedient to the dictates of the world of school, but emotionally still strongly wants to continue as part of the family circle.") Gradually, necessarily, the balance is lost. The boy needs to spend more and more time studying, each night enclosing himself in the silence permitted and required by intense concentration. He takes his first step toward academic success, away from his family.

From the very first days, through the years following, it will be with his parents — the figures of lost authority, the persons toward whom he feels deepest love — that the change will be most powerfully measured. A separation will unravel between them. Advancing in his studies, the boy notices that his mother and father have not changed as much as he. Rather, when he sees them, they often remind him of the person he once was and the life he earlier shared with them. He realizes what some Romantics also know when they praise the working class for the capacity for human closeness, qualities of passion and spontaneity, that the rest of us experience in like measure only in the earliest part of our youth. For the Romantic, this doesn't make working-class life childish. Working-class life challenges precisely because it is an *adult* way of life.

The scholarship boy reaches a different conclusion. He cannot afford to admire his parents. (How could he and still pursue such a contrary life?) He permits himself embarrassment at their lack of education. And to evade nostalgia for the life he has lost, he concentrates on the benefits education will bestow upon him. He becomes especially ambitious. Without the support of old certainties and consolations, almost mechanically, he assumes the procedures and doctrines of the classroom. The kind of allegiance the young student might have given his mother and father only days earlier, he transfers to the teacher, the new figure of authority. "[The scholarship boy] tends to make a father-figure of his form-master," Hoggart observes.

But Hoggart's calm prose only makes me recall the urgency with which I came to idolize my grammar school teachers. I began by imitating their accents, using their diction, trusting their every direction. The very first facts they dispensed, I grasped with awe. Any book they told me to read, I read — then waited for them to tell me which books I enjoyed. Their every casual opinion I came to adopt and to trumpet when I returned home. I stayed after school "to help" — to get my teacher's undivided attention. It was the nun's encouragement that mattered most to me. (She understood exactly what — my parents never seemed to appraise so well — all my achievements entailed.) Memory gently caressed each word of praise bestowed in the classroom so that compliments teachers paid me years ago come quickly to mind even today.

The enthusiasm I felt in second-grade classes I flaunted before both my parents. The docile, obedient student came home a shrill and precocious son who insisted on correcting and teaching his parents with the remark: "My teacher told us. . . ."

I intended to hurt my mother and father. I was still angry at them for having encouraged me toward classroom English. But gradually this anger was exhausted, replaced by guilt as school grew more and more attractive to me. I grew increasingly successful, a talkative student. My hand was raised in the classroom; I yearned to answer any question. At home, life was less noisy than it had been. (I spoke to classmates and teachers more often each day than to family members.) Quiet at home, I sat with my papers for hours each night. I never forgot that schooling had irretrievably changed my family's life. That knowledge, however, did not weaken ambition. Instead, it strengthened resolve. Those times I remembered the loss of my past with regret, I quickly reminded myself of all the things my teachers could give me. (They could make me an educated man.) I tightened my grip on pencil and books. I evaded nostalgia. Tried hard to forget. But one does not forget by trying to forget. One only remembers. I remembered too well that education had changed my family's life. I would not have become a scholarship boy had I not so often remembered.

Once she was sure that her children knew English, my mother would tell us, "You should keep up your Spanish." Voices playfully groaned in response. *"¡Pochos!"* my mother would tease. I listened silently.

After a while, I grew more calm at home. I developed tact. A fourth-grade student, I was no longer the show-off in front of my parents. I became a conventionally dutiful son, politely affectionate, cheerful enough, even — for reasons beyond choosing — my father's favorite. And much about my family life was easy then, comfortable, happy in the rhythm of our living together: hearing my father getting ready for work; eating the breakfast my mother had made me; looking up from a novel to hear my brother or one of my sisters playing with friends in the backyard; in winter, coming upon the house all lighted up after dark.

But withheld from my mother and father was any mention of what most mattered to me: the extraordinary experience of first-learning. Late afternoon: in the midst of preparing dinner, my mother would come up behind me while I was trying to read. Her head just over mine, her breath warmly scented with food. "What are you reading?" Or, "Tell me all about your new courses." I would barely respond, "Just the usual things, nothing special." (A half smile, then silence. Her head moving back in the silence. Silence! Instead of the flood of intimate sounds that had once flowed smoothly between us, there was this silence.) After dinner, I would rush to a bedroom with papers and books. As often as possible, I resisted parental pleas to "save lights" by coming to the kitchen to work. I kept so much, so often, to myself. Sad. Enthusiastic. Troubled by the excitement of coming upon new ideas. Eager. Fascinated by the promising texture of a brand-new book. I hoarded the pleasures of learning. Alone for hours. Enthralled. Nervous. I rarely looked away from my books — or back on my memories. Nights when relatives visited and the front rooms were warmed by Spanish sounds, I slipped quietly out of the house.

It mattered that education was changing me. It never ceased to matter. My brother and sisters would giggle at our mother's mispronounced words. They'd correct her gently. My mother laughed girlishly one night, trying not to pronounce *sheep* as *ship*. From a distance I listened sullenly. From that distance, pretending not to notice on another occasion, I saw my father looking at the title pages of my library books. That was the scene on my mind when I walked home with a fourth-grade companion and heard him say that his parents read to him every night. (A strange-sounding book — *Winnie the Pooh*.) Immediately, I wanted to know, "What is it like?" My companion, however, thought I wanted to know about the plot of the book. Another day, my mother surprised me by asking for a "nice" book to read. "Something not too hard you think I might like." Carefully I chose one, Willa Cather's *My Ántonia*. But when, several weeks later, I happened to see it next to her bed unread except for the first few pages, I was furious and suddenly wanted to cry. I grabbed up the book and took it back to my room and placed it in its place, alphabetically on my shelf.

"Your parents must be very proud of you." People began to say that to me about the time I was in sixth grade. To answer affirmatively, I'd smile. Shyly I'd smile, never betraying my sense of the irony: I was not proud of my mother and father. I was embarrassed by their lack of education. It was not that I ever thought they were stupid, though stupidly I took for granted their enormous native intelligence. Simply, what mattered to me was that they were not like my teachers.

But, "Why didn't you tell us about the award?" my mother demanded, her frown weakened by pride. At the grammar school ceremony several weeks after, her eyes were brighter than the trophy I'd won. Pushing back the hair from my forehead, she whispered that I had "shown" the *gringos*. A few minutes later, I heard my father speak to my teacher and felt ashamed of his labored, accented words. Then guilty for the shame. I felt such contrary feelings. (There is no simple road-map through the heart of the scholarship boy.) My teacher was so soft-spoken and her words were edged sharp and clean. I admired her until it seemed to me that she spoke too carefully. Sensing that she was condescending to them, I became nervous. Resentful. Protective. I tried to move my parents away. "You both must be very proud of Richard," the nun said. They responded quickly. (They were proud.) "We are proud of all our children." Then this afterthought: "They sure didn't get their brains from us." They all laughed. I smiled.

Tightening the irony into a knot was the knowledge that my parents were always behind me. They made success possible. They evened the path. They sent their children to parochial schools because the nuns "teach better." They paid a tuition they couldn't afford. They spoke English to us.

For their children my parents wanted chances they never had—an easier way. It saddened my mother to learn that some relatives forced their children to start working right after high school. To *her* children she would say, "Get all the education you can." In schooling she recognized the key to job advancement. And with the remark she remembered her past.

As a girl new to America my mother had been awarded a high school diploma by teachers too careless or busy to notice that she hardly spoke English. On her own, she determined to learn how to type. That skill got her jobs typing envelopes in letter shops, and it encouraged in her an optimism about the possibility of advancement. (Each morning when her sisters put on uniforms, she chose a bright-colored dress.) The years of young womanhood passed, and her typing speed increased. She also became an excellent speller of words she mispronounced. "And I've never been to college," she'd say, smiling, when her children asked her to spell words they were too lazy to look up in a dictionary.

Typing, however, was dead-end work. Finally frustrating. When her youngest child started high school, my mother got a full-time office job once again. (Her paycheck combined with my father's to make us—in fact—what we had already become in our imagination of ourselves—middle class.) She worked then for the (California) state government in numbered civil service positions secured by examinations. The old ambition of her youth was rekindled. During the lunch hour, she consulted bulletin boards for announcements of openings. One day she saw mention of something called an "anti-poverty agency." A typing job. A glamorous job, part of the governor's staff. "A knowledge of Spanish required." Without hesitation she applied and became nervous only when the job was suddenly hers.

"Everyone comes to work all dressed up," she reported at night. And didn't need to say more than that her co-workers wouldn't let her answer the phones. She was only a typist, after all, albeit a very fast typist. And an excellent speller. One morning there was a letter to be sent to a Washington cabinet officer. On the dictating tape, a voice referred to urban guerrillas. My mother typed (the wrong word, correctly): "gorillas." The mistake horrified the anti-poverty bureaucrats who shortly after arranged to have her returned to her previous position. She would go no further. So she willed her ambition to their children. "Get all the education you can; with an education you can do anything." (With a good education *she* could have done anything.)

When I was in high school, I admitted to my mother that I planned to become a teacher someday. That seemed to please her. But I never tried to explain that it was not the occupation of teaching I yearned for as much as it was something more elusive: I wanted to *be* like my teachers, to possess their knowledge, to assume their authority, their confidence, even to assume a teacher's persona.

In contrast to my mother, my father never verbally encouraged his children's academic success. Nor did he often praise us. My mother had to remind him to "say something" to one of his children who scored some academic success. But whereas my mother saw in education the opportunity for job advancement, my father recognized that education provided an even more startling possibility: it could enable a person to escape from a life of mere labor.

In Mexico, orphaned when he was eight, my father left school to work as an "apprentice" for an uncle. Twelve years later, he left Mexico in frustration and arrived in America. He had great expectations then of becoming an engineer. ("Work for my hands and my head.") He knew a Catholic priest who promised to get him money enough to study full time for a high school diploma. But the promises came to nothing. Instead there was a dark succession of warehouse, cannery, and factory jobs. After work he went to night school along with my mother. A year, two passed. Nothing much changed, except that fatigue worked its way into the bone; then everything changed. He didn't talk anymore of becoming an engineer. He stayed outside on the steps of the school while my mother went inside to learn typing and shorthand.

IT WAS MY FATHER WHO LAUGHED WHEN I CLAIMED TO BE TIRED BY READING AND WRITING.

By the time I was born, my father worked at "clean" jobs. For a time he was a janitor at a fancy department store. ("Easy work; the machines do it all.") Later he became a dental technician. ("Simple.") But by then he was pessimistic about the ultimate meaning of work and the possibility of ever escaping its claims. In some of my earliest memories of him, my father already seems aged by fatigue. (He has never really grown old like my mother.) From boyhood to manhood, I have remembered him in a single image: seated, asleep on the sofa, his head thrown back in a hideous corpselike grin, the evening newspaper spread out before him. "But look at all you've accomplished," his best friend said to him once. My father said nothing. Only smiled.

It was my father who laughed when I claimed to be tired by reading and writing. It was he who teased me for having soft hands. (He seemed to sense that some great achievement of leisure was implied by my papers and books.) It was my father who became angry while watching on television some woman at the Miss America contest tell the announcer that she was going to college. ("Majoring in fine arts.") "College!" he snarled. He despised the trivialization of higher education, the inflated grades and cheapened diplomas, the half education that so often passed as mass education in my generation.

It was my father again who wondered why I didn't display my awards on the wall of my bedroom. He said he liked to go to doctors' offices and see their certificates and degrees on the wall. ("Nice.") My citations from school got left in closets at home. The gleaming figure astride one of my trophies was broken, wingless, after hitting the ground. My medals were placed in a jar of loose change. And when I lost my high school diploma, my father found it as it was about to be thrown out with the trash. Without telling me, he put it away with his own things for safe-keeping.

These memories slammed together at the instant of hearing that refrain familiar to all scholarship students: "Your parents must be proud. . . ." Yes, my parents were proud. I knew it. But my parents regarded my progress with more than mere pride. They endured my early precocious behavior — but with what private anger and humiliation? As their children got older and would come home to challenge ideas both of them held, they argued before submitting to the force of logic or superior factual evidence with the disclaimer, "It's what we were taught in our time to believe." These discussions ended abruptly, though my mother remembered them on other occasions when she complained that our "big ideas" were going to our heads. More acute was her complaint that the family wasn't close anymore, like some others she knew. Why weren't we close, "more in the Mexican style"? Everyone is so private, she added. And she mimicked the yes and no answers she got in reply to her questions. Why didn't we talk more? (My father never asked.) I never said.

I was the first in my family who asked to leave home when it came time to go to college. I had been admitted to Stanford, one hundred miles away. My departure would only make physically apparent the separation that had occurred long before. But it was going too far. In the months preceding my leaving, I heard the question my mother never asked except indirectly. In the hot kitchen, tired at the end of her workday, she demanded to know, "Why aren't the colleges here in Sacramento good enough for you? They are for your brother and sister." In the middle of a car ride, not turning to face me, she wondered, "Why do you need to go so far away?" Late at night, ironing, she said with disgust, "Why do you have to put us through this big expense? You know your scholarship will never cover it all." But when September came there was a rush to get everything ready. In a bedroom that last night I packed the big brown valise, and my mother sat nearby sewing initials onto the clothes I would take. And she said no more about my leaving.

Months later, two weeks of Christmas vacation: the first hours home were the hardest. ("What's new?") My parents and I sat in the kitchen for a conversation. (But, lacking the same words to develop our sentences and to shape our interests, what was there to say? What could I tell them of the term paper I had just finished on the "universality of Shakespeare's appeal"?) I mentioned only small, obvious things: my dormitory life; weekend trips I had taken; random events. They responded with news of their own. (One was almost grateful for a family crisis about which there was much to discuss.) We tried to make our conversation seem like more than an interview.

II

From an early age I knew that my mother and father could read and write both Spanish and English. I had observed my father making his way through what, I now suppose, must have been income tax forms. On other occasions I waited apprehensively while my mother read onion-paper letters airmailed from Mexico with news of a relative's illness or death. For both my parents, however, reading was something done out of necessity and as quickly as possible. Never did I see either of them read an entire book. Nor did I see them read for pleasure. Their reading consisted of work manuals, prayer books, newspaper, recipes.

Richard Hoggart imagines how, at home,

> [the scholarship boy] sees strewn around, and reads regularly himself, magazines which are never mentioned at school, which seem not to belong to the world to which the school introduces him; at school he hears about and reads books never mentioned at home. When he brings those books into the house they do not take their place with other books which the family are reading, for often there are none or almost none; his books look, rather, like strange tools.

In our house each school year would begin with my mother's careful instruction: "Don't write in your books so we can sell them at the end of the year." The remark was echoed in public by my teachers, but only in part: "Boys and girls, don't write in your books. You must learn to treat them with great care and respect."

OPEN THE DOORS OF YOUR MIND WITH BOOKS, read the red and white poster over the nun's desk in early September. It soon was apparent to me that reading was the classroom's central activity. Each course had its own book. And the information gathered from a book was unquestioned. READ TO LEARN, the sign on the wall advised in December. I privately wondered: What was the connection between reading and learning? Did one learn something only by reading it? Was an idea only an idea if it could be written down? In June, CONSIDER BOOKS YOUR BEST FRIENDS. Friends? Reading was, at best, only a chore. I needed to look up whole paragraphs of words in a dictionary. Lines of type were dizzying, the eye having to move slowly across the page, then down, and across. . . . The sentences of the first books I read were coolly impersonal. Toned hard. What most bothered me, however, was the isolation reading required. To console myself for the loneliness I'd feel when I read, I tried reading in a very soft voice. Until: "Who is doing all that talking to his neighbor?" Shortly after, remedial reading classes were arranged for me with a very old nun.

At the end of each school day, for nearly six months, I would meet with her in the tiny room that served as the school's library but was actually only a storeroom for used textbooks and a vast collection of *National Geographics*. Everything about our sessions pleased me: the smallness of the room; the noise of the janitor's broom hitting the edge of the long hallway outside the door; the green of the sun, lighting the wall; and the old woman's face blurred white with a beard. Most of the time we took turns. I began with my elementary text. Sentences of astonishing simplicity seemed to me lifeless and drab: "The boys ran from the rain. . . . She wanted to sing. . . . The kite rose in the blue." Then the old nun would read from her favorite books, usually biographies of early American presidents. Playfully she ran through complex sentences, calling the words alive with her voice, making it seem that the author somehow was speaking directly to me. I smiled just to listen to her. I sat there and sensed for the very first time some possibility of fellowship between a reader and a writer, a communication, never *intimate* like that I heard spoken words at home convey, but one nonetheless *personal*.

One day the nun concluded a session by asking me why I was so reluctant to read by myself. I tried to explain; said something about the way written words made me feel all alone – almost, I wanted to add but didn't, as when I spoke to myself in a room just emptied of furniture. She studied my face as I spoke; she seemed to be watching more than listening. In an uneventful voice she replied that I had nothing to fear. Didn't I realize that reading would open up whole new worlds? A book could open doors for me. It could introduce me to people and show me places I never imagined existed. She gestured toward the bookshelves. (Bare-breasted African women danced, and the shiny hubcaps of automobiles on the back covers of the *Geographic* gleamed in my mind.) I listened with respect. But her words were not very influential. I was thinking then of another consequence of literacy, one I was too shy to admit but nonetheless trusted. Books were going to make me "educated." *That* confidence enabled me, several months later, to overcome my fear of the silence.

In fourth grade I embarked upon a grandiose reading program. "Give me the names of important books," I would say to startled teachers. They soon found out that I had in mind "adult books." I ignored their suggestion of anything I suspected was written for children. (Not until I was in college, as a result, did I read *Huckleberry Finn* or *Alice's Adventures in Wonderland*.) Instead, I read *The Scarlet Letter* and Franklin's *Autobiography*. And whatever I read I read for extra credit. Each time I finished a book, I reported the achievement to a teacher and basked in the praise my effort earned. Despite my best efforts, however, there seemed to be more and more books I needed to read. At the library I would literally tremble as I came upon whole shelves of books I hadn't read. So I read and I read and I read: *Great Expectations*; all the short stories of Kipling; *The Babe Ruth Story*; the entire first volume of the *Encyclopedia Britannica* (A–ANSTEY); the *Iliad*; *Moby Dick*; *Gone with the Wind*; *The Good Earth*; *Ramona*; *Forever Amber*; *The Lives of the Saints*; *Crime and Punishment*; *The Pearl*. . . . Librarians who initially frowned when I checked out the maximum ten books at a time started saving books they thought I might like. Teachers would say to the rest of the class, "I only wish the rest of you took reading as seriously as Richard obviously does."

But at home I would hear my mother wondering, "What do you see in your books?" (Was reading a hobby like her knitting? Was so much reading even healthy for a boy? Was it the sign of "brains"? Or was it just a convenient excuse for not helping about the house on Saturday mornings?) Always, "What do you see. . .?"

What *did* I see in my books? I had the idea that they were crucial for my academic success, though I couldn't have said exactly how or why. In the sixth grade I simply concluded that what gave a book its value was some major idea or theme it contained. If that core essence could be mined and memorized, I would become learned like my teachers. I decided to record in a notebook the themes of the books that I read. After reading *Robinson Crusoe*, I wrote that its theme was "the value of learning to live by oneself." When I completed *Wuthering Heights*, I noted the danger of "letting emotions get out of control." Rereading these brief moralistic appraisals usually left me disheartened. I couldn't believe that they were really the source of reading's value. But for many more years, they constituted the only means I had of describing to myself the educational value of books.

In spite of my earnestness, I found reading a pleasurable activity. I came to enjoy the lonely good company of books. Early on weekday mornings, I'd read in my bed. I'd feel a mysterious comfort then, reading in the dawn quiet — the blue-gray silence interrupted by the occasional churning of the refrigerator motor a few rooms away or the more distant sounds of a city bus beginning its run. On weekends I'd go to the public library to read, surrounded by old men and women. Or, if the weather was fine, I would take my books to the park and read in the shade of a tree. A warm summer evening was my favorite reading time. Neighbors would leave for vacation and I would water their lawns. I would sit through the twilight on the front porches or in backyards, reading to the cool, whirling sounds of the sprinklers.

I also had favorite writers. But often those writers I enjoyed most I was least able to value. When I read William Saroyan's *The Human Comedy*, I was immediately pleased by the narrator's warmth and the charm of his story. But as quickly I became suspicious. A book so enjoyable to read couldn't be very "important." Another summer I determined to read all the novels of Dickens. Reading his fat novels, I loved the feeling I got — after the first hundred pages — of being at home in a fictional world where I knew the names of the characters and cared about what was going to happen to them. And it bothered me that I was forced away at the conclusion, when the fiction closed tight, like a fortune-teller's fist — the futures of all the major characters neatly resolved. I never knew how to take such feelings seriously, however. Nor did I suspect that these experiences could be part of a novel's meaning. Still, there were pleasures to sustain me after I'd finish my books. Carrying a volume back to the library, I would be pleased by its weight. I'd run my fingers along the edge of the pages and marvel at the breadth of my achievement. Around my room, growing stacks of paperback books reenforced my assurance.

I entered high school having read hundreds of books. My habit of reading made me a confident speaker and writer of English. Reading also enabled me to sense something of the shape, the major concerns, of Western thought. (I was able to say something about Dante and Descartes and Engels and James Baldwin in my high school term papers.) In these various ways, books brought me academic success as I hoped that they would. But I was not a good reader. Merely bookish, I lacked a point of view when I read. Rather, I read in order to acquire a point of view. I vacuumed books for epigrams, scraps of information, ideas, themes — anything to fill the hollow within me and make me feel educated. When one of my teachers suggested to his drowsy tenth-grade English class that a person could not have a "complicated idea" until he had read at least two thousand books, I heard the remark without detecting either its irony or its very complicated truth. I merely determined to compile a list of all the books I had ever read. Harsh with myself, I included only once a title I might have read several times. (How, after all, could one read a book more than once?) And I included only those books over a hundred pages in length. (Could anything shorter be a book?)

There was yet another high school list I compiled. One day I came across a newspaper article about the retirement of an English professor at a nearby state college. The article was accompanied by a list of the "hundred most important books of Western Civilization." "More than anything else in my life," the professor told the reporter with finality, "these books have made me all that I am." That was the kind of remark I couldn't ignore. I clipped out the list and kept it for the several months it took me to read all of the titles. Most books, of course, I barely understood. While reading Plato's *Republic*, for instance, I needed to keep looking at the book jacket comments to remind myself what the text was about. Nevertheless, with the special patience and superstition of a scholarship boy, I looked at every word of the text. And by the time I reached the last word, relieved, I convinced myself that I had read *The Republic*. In a ceremony of great pride, I solemnly crossed Plato off my list.

THE SCHOLARSHIP BOY PLEASES MOST WHEN HE IS YOUNG — THE WORKING-CLASS CHILD STRUGGLING FOR ACADEMIC SUCCESS.

III

The scholarship boy pleases most when he is young — the working-class child struggling for academic success. To his teachers, he offers great satisfaction; his success is their proudest achievement. Many other persons offer to help him. A businessman learns the boy's story and promises to underwrite part of the cost of his college education. A woman leaves him her entire library of several hundred books when she moves. His progress is featured in a newspaper article. Many people seem happy for him. They marvel. "How did you manage so fast?" From all sides, there is lavish praise and encouragement.

In his grammar school classroom, however, the boy already makes students around him uneasy. They scorn his desire to succeed. They scorn him for constantly wanting the teacher's attention and praise. "Kiss Ass," they call him when his hand swings up in response to every question he hears. Later, when he makes it to college, no one will mock him aloud. But he detects annoyance on the faces of some students and even some teachers who watch him. It puzzles him often. In college, then in graduate school, he behaves much as he always has. If anything is different about him it is that he dares to anticipate the successful conclusion of his studies. At last he feels that he belongs in the classroom, and this is exactly the source of the dissatisfaction he causes. To many persons around him, he appears too much the academic. There may be some things about him that recall his beginnings — his shabby clothes; his persistent poverty; or his dark skin (in those cases when it symbolizes his parents' disadvantaged condition) — but they only make clear how far he has moved from his past. He has used education to remake himself.

It bothers his fellow academics to face this. They will not say why exactly. (They sneer.) But their expectations become obvious when they are disappointed. They expect — they want — a student less changed by his schooling. If the scholarship boy, from a past so distant from the classroom, could remain in some basic way unchanged, he would be able to prove that it is possible for anyone to become educated without basically changing from the person one was.

Here is no fabulous hero, no idealized scholar-worker. The scholarship boy does not straddle, cannot reconcile, the two great opposing cultures of his life. His success is unromantic and plain. He sits in the classroom and offers those sitting beside him no calming reassurance about their own lives. He sits in the seminar room — a man with brown skin, the son of working-class Mexican immigrant parents. (Addressing the professor at the head of the table, his voice catches with nervousness.) There is no trace of his parents in his speech. Instead he approximates the accents of teachers and classmates. Coming from *him* those sounds seem suddenly odd. Odd too is the effect produced when *he* uses academic jargon — bubbles at the tip of his tongue: "*Topos* . . . negative capability . . . vegetation imagery in Shakespearean comedy." He lifts an opinion from Coleridge, takes something else from Frye or Empson or Leavis. He even repeats exactly his professor's earlier comment. All his ideas are clearly borrowed. He seems to have no thought of his own. He chatters while his listeners smile — their look one of disdain.

When he is older and thus when so little of the person he was survives, the scholarship boy makes only too apparent his profound lack of *self*-confidence. This is the conventional assessment that even Richard Hoggart repeats:

> [The scholarship boy] tends to over-stress the importance of examinations, of the piling-up of knowledge and of received opinions. He discovers

> a technique of apparent learning, of the acquiring of facts rather than of the handling and use of facts. He learns how to receive a purely literate education, one using only a small part of the personality and challenging only a limited area of his being. He begins to see life as a ladder, as permanent examination with some praise and some further exhortation at each stage. He becomes an expert imbiber and doler-out; his competence will vary, but will rarely be accompanied by genuine enthusiasms. He rarely feels the reality of knowledge, of other men's thoughts and imaginings, on his own pulses. . . . He has something of the blinkered pony about him. . . .

But this is criticism more accurate than fair. The scholarship boy is a very bad student. He is the great mimic; a collector of thoughts, not a thinker; the very last person in class who ever feels obliged to have an opinion of his own. In large part, however, the reason he is such a bad student is because he realizes more often and more acutely than most other students — than Hoggart himself — that education requires radical self-reformation. As a very young boy, regarding his parents, as he struggles with an early homework assignment, he knows this too well. That is why he lacks self-assurance. He does not forget that the classroom is responsible for remaking him. He relies on his teacher, depends on all that he hears in the classroom and reads in his books. He becomes in every obvious way the worst student, a dummy mouthing the opinions of others. But he would not be so bad — nor would he become so successful, a *scholarship* boy — if he did not accurately perceive that the best synonym for primary "education" is "imitation."

Those who would take seriously the boy's success — and his failure — would be forced to realize how great is the change any academic undergoes, how far one must move from one's past. It is easiest to ignore such considerations. So little is said about the scholarship boy in pages and pages of educational literature. Nothing is said of the silence that comes to separate the boy from his parents. Instead, one hears proposals for increasing the self-esteem of students and encouraging early intellectual independence. Paragraphs glitter with a constellation of terms like *creativity* and *originality*. (Ignored altogether is the function of imitation in a student's life.) Radical educationalists meanwhile complain that ghetto schools "oppress" students by trying to mold them, stifling native characteristics. The truer critique would be just the reverse: not that schools change ghetto students too much, but that while they might promote the occasional scholarship student, they change most students barely at all.

From the story of the scholarship boy there is no specific pedagogy to glean. There is, however, a much larger lesson. His story makes clear that education is a long, unglamorous, even demeaning process — *a nurturing never natural to the person one was before one entered a classroom*. At once different from most other students, the scholarship boy is also the archetypal "good student." He exaggerates the difficulty of being a student, but his exaggeration reveals a general predicament. Others are changed by their schooling as much as he. They too must re-form themselves. They must develop the skill of memory long before they become truly critical thinkers. And when they read Plato for the first several times, it will be with awe more than deep comprehension.

The impact of schooling on the scholarship boy is only more apparent to the boy himself and to others. Finally, although he may be laughable — a blinkered pony — the boy will not let his critics forget their own change. He ends up too much like them. When he speaks, they hear themselves echoed. In his pedantry, they trace their own. His ambitions are theirs. If his failure were singular, they might readily pity him. But he is more troubling than that. They would not scorn him if this were not so.

IV

Like me, Hoggart's imagined scholarship boy spends most of his years in the classroom afraid to long for his past. Only at the very end of his schooling does the boy-man become nostalgic. In this sudden change of heart, Richard Hoggart notes:

> He longs for the membership he lost, "he pines for some Nameless Eden where he never was." The nostalgia is the stronger and the more ambiguous because he is really "in quest of his own absconded self yet scared to find it." He both wants to go back and yet thinks he has gone beyond his class, feels himself weighted with knowledge of his own and their situation, which hereafter forbids him the simpler pleasures of his father and mother. . . .

According to Hoggart, the scholarship boy grows nostalgic because he remains the uncertain scholar, bright enough to have moved from his past, yet unable to feel easy, a part of a community of academics.

This analysis, however, only partially suggests what happened to me in my last year as a graduate student. When I traveled to London to write a dissertation on English Renaissance literature, I was finally confident of membership in a "community of scholars." But the pleasure that confidence gave me faded rapidly. After only two or three months in the reading room of the British Museum, it became clear that I had joined a lonely community. Around me each day were dour faces eclipsed by large piles of books. There were the regulars, like the old couple who arrived every morning, each holding a loop of the shopping bag which contained all their notes. And there was the historian who chattered madly to herself. ("Oh dear! Oh! Now, what's this? What? Oh, my!") There were also the faces of young men and women worn by long study. And everywhere eyes turned away the moment our glance accidentally met. Some persons I sat beside day after day, yet we passed silently at the end of the day, strangers. Still, we were united by a common respect for the written word and for scholarship. We did form a union, though one in which we remained distant from one another.

More profound and unsettling was the bond I recognized with those writers whose books I consulted. Whenever I opened a text that hadn't been used for years, I realized that my special interests and skills united me to a mere handful of academics. We formed an exclusive — eccentric! — society, separated from others who would never care or be able to share our concerns. (The pages I turned were stiff like layers of dead skin.) I began to wonder: Who, beside my dissertation director and a few faculty members, would ever read what I wrote? And: Was my dissertation much more than an act of social withdrawal? These questions went unanswered in the silence of the Museum reading room. They remained to trouble me after I'd leave the library each afternoon and feel myself shy — unsteady, speaking simple sentences at the grocer's or the butcher's on my way back to my bed-sitter.

Meanwhile my file cards accumulated. A professional, I knew exactly how to search a book for pertinent information. I could quickly assess and summarize the usability of the many books I consulted. But whenever I started to write, I knew too much (and not enough) to be able to write anything but sentences that were overly cautious, timid, strained brittle under the heavy weight of footnotes and qualifications. I seemed unable to dare a passionate statement. I felt drawn by professionalism to the edge of sterility, capable of no more than pedantic, lifeless, unassailable prose.

Then nostalgia began.

After years spent unwilling to admit its attractions, I gestured nostalgically toward the past. I yearned for that time when I had not been so alone. I became impatient with books. I wanted experience more immediate. I feared the library's silence. I silently scorned the gray, timid faces around me. I grew to hate the growing pages of my dissertation on genre and Renaissance literature. (In my mind I heard relatives laughing as they tried to make sense of its title.) I wanted something — I couldn't say exactly what. I told myself that I wanted a more passionate life. And a life less thoughtful. And above all, I wanted to be less alone. One day I heard some Spanish academics whispering back and forth to each other, and their sounds seemed ghostly voices recalling my life. Yearning became preoccupation then. Boyhood memories beckoned, flooded my mind. (Laughing intimate voices. Bounding up the front steps of the porch. A sudden embrace inside the door.)

For weeks after, I turned to books by educational experts. I needed to learn how far I had moved from my past — to determine how fast I would be able to recover something of it once again. But I found little. Only a chapter in a book by Richard Hoggart. . . . I left the reading room and the circle of faces.

I came home. After the year in England, I spent three summer months living with my mother and father, relieved by how easy it was to be home. It no longer seemed very important to me that we had little to say. I felt easy sitting and eating and walking with them. I watched them, nevertheless, looking for evidence of those elastic, sturdy strands that bind generations in a web of inheritance. I thought as I watched my mother one night: of course a friend had been right when she told me that I gestured and laughed just like my mother. Another time I saw for myself: my father's eyes were much like my own, constantly watchful.

But after the early relief, this return, came suspicion, nagging until I realized that I had not neatly sidestepped the impact of schooling. My desire to do so was precisely the measure of how much I remained an academic. *Negatively* (for that is how this idea first occurred to me): my need to think so much and so abstractly about my parents and our relationship was in itself an indication of my long education. My father and mother did not pass their time thinking about the cultural meanings of their experience. It was I who described their daily lives with airy ideas. And yet, *positively*: the ability to consider experience so abstractly allowed me to shape into desire what would otherwise have remained indefinite, meaningless longing in the British Museum. If, because of my schooling, I had grown culturally separated from my parents, my education finally had given me ways of speaking and caring about that fact.

My best teachers in college and graduate school, years before, had tried to prepare me for this conclusion, I think, when they discussed texts of aristocratic pastoral literature. Faithfully, I wrote down all that they said. I memorized it: "The praise of the unlettered by the highly educated is one of the primary themes of 'elitist' literature." But, "the importance of the praise given the unsolitary, richly passionate and spontaneous life is that it simultaneously reflects the value of a reflective life." I heard it all. But there was no way for any of it to mean very much to me. I was a scholarship boy at the time, busily laddering my way up the rungs of education. To pass an examination, I copied down exactly what my teachers told me. It would require many more years of schooling (an inevitable miseducation) in which I came to trust the silence of reading and the habit of abstracting from immediate experience — moving away from a life of closeness and immediacy I remembered with my parents, growing older — before I turned unafraid to desire the past, and thereby achieved what had eluded me for so long — the end of education.

NOTE

[1] All quotations in this essay are from Richard Hoggart, *The Uses of Literacy* (London: Chatto and Windus, 1957), chapter 10. [Author's note]

QUESTIONS FOR A SECOND READING

1. In *Hunger of Memory*, the book from which "The Achievement of Desire" is drawn, Rodriguez says several times that the story he tells, although it is very much his story, is also a story of our common experience — growing up, leaving home, becoming educated, entering the world. When you reread this essay, look particularly for sections or passages you might bring forward as evidence that this is, in fact, an essay which can give you a way of looking at your own life, and not just his. And look for sections that defy

universal application. To what degree *is* his story the story of our common experience? Why might he (or his readers) want to insist that his story is everyone's story?

2. At the end of the essay, Rodriguez says:

> It would require many more years of schooling (an inevitable mis-education) in which I came to trust the silence of reading and the habit of abstracting from immediate experience — moving away from a life of closeness and immediacy I remembered with my parents, growing older — before I turned unafraid to desire the past, and thereby achieved what had eluded me for so long — the end of education. (p. 532)

What do you think, as you reread this essay, is the "end of education"? And what does that end (that goal? stopping point?) have to do with "miseducation," "the silence of reading," "the habit of abstracting from immediate experience," and "desir[ing] the past"?

ASSIGNMENTS FOR WRITING

1. You could look at the relationship between Richard Rodriguez and Richard Hoggart as a case study of the relation of a reader to a writer or a student to a teacher. Look closely at Rodriguez's references to Hoggart's book, *The Uses of Literacy*, and at the way Rodriguez made use of that book to name and describe his own experience as a student. (An extended selection of *The Uses of Literacy* can be found on pages 752–59.) What did he find in the book? How did he use it? How does he use it in his own writing?

   Write an essay in which you discuss Rodriguez's use of Hoggart's *The Uses of Literacy*. How, for example, would you compare Rodriguez's version of the "scholarship boy" with Hoggart's? (At one point, Rodriguez says that Hoggart's account is "more accurate than fair." What might he have meant by that?) And what kind of reader is the Rodriguez who is writing "The Achievement of Desire" — is he still a "scholarship boy," or is that description no longer appropriate?

   Note: You might begin your research with what may seem to be a purely technical matter, examining how Rodriguez handles quotations and works Hoggart's words into paragraphs of his own. On the basis of Rodriguez's use of quoted passages, how would you describe the relationship between Hoggart's words and Rodriguez's? Who has the greater authority? Who is the expert, and under what conditions? What "rules" might Rodriguez be said to follow or to break? Do you see any change in the course of the essay in how Rodriguez uses block quotations? in how he comments on them?

2. Rodriguez insists that his story is also everyone's story. Take an episode from your life, one that seems in some way similar to one of the episodes in "The Achievement of Desire," and cast it into a shorter version of Rodriguez's essay. Your job here is to look at your experience in Rodriguez's terms, which means thinking the way he does, noticing what he would notice, interpreting details in a similar fashion, using his key terms, seeing through his point of view; it could also mean imitating his style of writing, working with quotations from other writers, doing whatever it is you see him doing characteristically while he writes. Imitation, Rodriguez argues, is not necessarily a bad thing; it can, in fact, be one of the powerful ways in which a person learns.

   Note: This assignment can also be used to read against "The Achievement of Desire." Rodriguez insists on the universality of his experience leaving home and community and joining the larger public life. You could highlight the differences between your experience and his. You should begin by imitating Rodriguez's method; you do not have to arrive at his conclusions, however.

3. > What I am about to say to you has taken me more than twenty years to admit: *A primary reason for my success in the classroom was that I couldn't forget that schooling was changing me and separating me from the life I enjoyed before becoming a student.* (p. 516)
   >
   > If, because of my schooling, I had grown culturally separated from my parents, my education finally had given me ways of speaking and caring about that fact. (p. 532)

   As you reread Rodriguez's essay, what would you say are his "ways of speaking and caring"? One way to think about this question is to trace how the lessons he learned about reading, education, language, family, culture, and class shifted as he moved from elementary school through college and graduate school to his career as a teacher and a writer. What scholarly abilities did he learn that provided him with "ways of speaking and caring" valued in the academic community? Where and how do you see him using them in his essay?

   Write an essay in which you discuss how Rodriguez reads (reviews, summarizes, interprets) his family, his teachers, his schooling, himself, and his books. What differences can you say such reading makes to those ways of speaking and caring that you locate in the text?

MAKING CONNECTIONS

1. Paulo Freire, in "The 'Banking' Concept of Education" (p. 318), discusses the political implications of the relations between teachers and students. Some forms of schooling, he says, can give students control over their lives, but most schooling teaches students only to submit to domination by

others. If you look closely at the history of Rodriguez's schooling from the perspective of Freire's essay, what do you see? Write an essay describing how Freire might analyze Rodriguez's education. How would he see the process as it unfolds throughout Rodriguez's experience, as a student, from his early schooling (including the study he did on his own at home), through his college and graduate studies, to the position he takes, finally, as the writer of "The Achievement of Desire"?

2. Here, from "Arts of the Contact Zone" (p. 485), is Mary Louise Pratt on the "autoethnographic" text:

> Guaman Poma's *New Chronicle* is an instance of what I have proposed to call an *autoethnographic* text, by which I mean a text in which people undertake to describe themselves in ways that engage with representations others have made of them. Thus if ethnographic texts are those in which European metropolitan subjects represent to themselves their others (usually their conquered others), autoethnographic texts are representations that the so-defined others construct *in response to* or in dialogue with those texts. . . . They involve a selective collaboration with and appropriation of idioms of the metropolis or the conqueror. These are merged or infiltrated to varying degrees with indigenous idioms to create self-representations intended to intervene in metropolitan modes of understanding. . . . Such texts often constitute a marginalized group's point of entry into the dominant circuits of print culture. (pp. 487–88)

Richard Rodriguez's "The Achievement of Desire" could be considered "autoethnography." He is clearly working to explain himself, to account for who he is and who he has become. But to whom? Who is identified as his audience? Can you talk here about "indigenous idioms" or the "idioms of the metropolis"?

Reread "The Achievement of Desire" with Pratt's essay in mind. And write an essay in which you discuss "The Achievement of Desire" as an example of an autoethnographic and/or a transcultural text. You should imagine that you are working to put Pratt's ideas to the test (does it present itself as a convenient example?), but also add what you have to say about the ways this autobiography defines its audience, speaker, and purpose.

3. Richard Rodriguez in "The Achievement of Desire," Susan Griffin in "Our Secret" (p. 335), and John Edgar Wideman in "Our Time" (p. 657) use a life story to think about and to represent forces beyond the individual that shape life and possibility—family, war, race, and ethnicity. Susan Griffin explains her motive this way: "One can find traces of every life in each life." Perhaps. It is a bold step to think that this is true and to believe that one can, or should, use autobiography as a way to understand the national or international narrative. Write an essay in which you read "The Achievement of Desire" alongside one of the other two essays. Your goal is not only to discuss how these writers do what they do, and to what conclusions and to what ends, but also to discuss your sense of what is at stake in such a

project. How are their accounts of family different? How do they connect the structure of the family to larger structural concerns? What are the key differences, and how might you explain them?

4. After years spent unwilling to admit its attractions, I gestured nostalgically toward the past. I yearned for that time when I had not been so alone. I became impatient with books. I wanted experience more immediate. I feared the library's silence. I silently scorned the gray, timid faces around me. I grew to hate the growing pages of my dissertation on genre and Renaissance literature. (In my mind I heard relatives laughing as they tried to make sense of its title.) I wanted something — couldn't say exactly what. (p. 531)

— RICHARD RODRIGUEZ
The Achievement of Desire

For some, it will hardly come as a surprise to learn that reading and writing have no magically transformative powers. But for those of us who have been raised into the teaching and publishing professions, it can be quite a shock to confront the possibility that reading and writing and talking exercise almost *none* of the powers we regularly attribute to them in our favorite stories. The dark night of the soul for literacy workers comes with the realization that training students to read, write, and talk in more critical and self-reflective ways cannot protect them from the violent changes our culture is undergoing. (p. 423)

— RICHARD E. MILLER
The Dark Night of the Soul

Both Richard E. Miller and Richard Rodriguez are concerned with the limits (and the failures) of education, with particular attention to the humanities and to the supposed benefits to be found in reading and writing. "I have these doubts, you see," Miller writes of academic work, "doubts silently shared by many who spend their days teaching others the literate arts. Aside from gathering and organizing information, aside from generating critiques and analyses that forever fall on deaf ears, what might the literate arts be said to be good for?" (p. 424).

Write an essay that takes up this question — "what might the literate arts be said to be good for?" — and that takes it up with these two essays, Miller's "The Dark Night of the Soul" (p. 420) and Rodriguez's "The Achievement of Desire," as your initial points of reference. What does each say? How might they be said to speak to each other? And, finally, where are you in this? Where are you, and people like you, the group for whom you feel prepared to speak? You, too, have been and will continue to be expected to take courses in reading and writing, to read, write, and talk in "critical and self-reflective ways." Where are you in this conversation?

EDWARD Said

Edward Said (1935–2003) was one of the world's most distinguished literary critics and scholars, distinguished (among other things) for his insistence on the connectedness of art and politics, literature and history. As he argues in his influential essay "The World, the Text, the Critic,"

> Texts have ways of existing, both theoretical and practical, that even in their most rarefied form are always enmeshed in circumstance, time, place, and society — in short, they are in the world, and hence worldly. The same is doubtless true of the critic, as reader and as writer.

Said (pronounced "sigh-eed") was a "worldly" reader and writer, and the selection that follows is a case in point. It is part of his long-term engagement with the history and politics of the Middle East, particularly of the people we refer to as Palestinians. His critical efforts, perhaps best represented by his most influential book, *Orientalism* (1978), examine the ways the West has represented and understood the East ("They cannot represent themselves; they must be represented"), demonstrating how Western journalists, writers, artists, and scholars have created and preserved a view of Eastern cultures as mysterious, dangerous, unchanging, and inferior.

Said was born in Jerusalem, in what was at that time Palestine, to parents who were members of the Christian Palestinian community. In 1947, as the United Nations was establishing Israel as a Jewish state, his family fled to Cairo. In the introduction to *After the Last Sky: Palestinian Lives* (1986), the book from which the following selection was taken, he says,

> I was twelve, with the limited awareness and memory of a relatively sheltered boy. By the mid-spring of 1948 my extended family in its entirety had departed, evicted from Palestine along with almost a million other Palestinians. This was the *nakba*, or catastrophe, which heralded the destruction of our society and our dispossession as a people.

Said was educated in English-speaking schools in Cairo and Massachusetts; he completed his undergraduate training at Princeton and received his PhD from Harvard in 1964. He was a member of the English department at Columbia University in New York from 1963 until his death from leukemia. In the 1970s, he began writing to a broad public on the situation of the Palestinians; from 1977 to 1991, he served on the Palestinian National Council, an exile government. In 1991, he split from the Palestine Liberation Organization (PLO) over its Gulf War policy (Yasir Arafat's support of Saddam Hussein) and, as he says, for "what I considered to be its new defeatism."

The peculiar and distinctive project represented by *After the Last Sky* began in the 1980s, in the midst of this political engagement. "In 1983," Said writes in the introduction,

> while I was serving as a consultant to the United Nations for its International Conference on the Question of Palestine (ICQP), I suggested that photographs of Palestinians be hung in the entrance hall to the main conference site in Geneva. I had of course known and admired Mohr's work with John Berger, and I recommended that he be commissioned to photograph some of the principal locales of Palestinian life. Given the initial enthusiasm for the idea, Mohr left on a special UN-sponsored trip to the Near East. The photographs he brought back were indeed wonderful; the official response, however, was puzzling and, to someone with a taste for irony, exquisite. You can hang them up, we were told, but no writing can be displayed with them.

In response to a UN mandate, Said had also commissioned twenty studies for the participants at the conference. Of the twenty, only three were accepted as "official documents." The others were rejected "because one after another Arab state objected to this or that principle, this or that insinuation, this or that putative injury to its sovereignty." And yet, Said argues, the complex experience, history, and identity of the people known as Palestinians remained virtually unknown, particularly in the West (and in the United States). To most, Said says, "Palestinians are visible principally as fighters, terrorists, and lawless pariahs." When Jean Mohr, the photographer, told a friend that he was preparing an exhibition on the Palestinians, the friend responded, "Don't you think the subject's a bit dated? Look, I've taken photographs of Palestinians too, especially in the refugee camps . . . it's really sad! But these days, who's interested in people who eat off the ground with their hands? And then there's all that terrorism. . . . I'd have thought you'd be better off using your energy and capabilities on something more worthwhile."

For both Said and Mohr, these rejections provided the motive for *After the Last Sky*. Said's account, from the book's introduction, is worth quoting at length for how well it represents the problems of writing:

> Let us use photographs and a text, we said to each other, to say something that hasn't been said about Palestinians. Yet the problem of writing about and representing — in all senses of the word — Palestinians in some fresh way is part of a much larger problem. For it is not as if no one speaks about or portrays the Palestinians. The difficulty is that everyone, including the Palestinians themselves, speaks a very great deal. A huge body of literature has grown up, most of it polemical, accusatory, denunciatory. At this point, no one writing about Palestine — and

> indeed, no one going to Palestine — starts from scratch: We have all been there before, whether by reading about it, experiencing its millennial presence and power, or actually living there for periods of time. It is a terribly crowded place, almost too crowded for what it is asked to be by way of history or interpretation of history.

The resulting book is quite a remarkable document. The photos are not the photos of a glossy coffee-table book, and yet they are compelling and memorable. The prose at times leads to the photos; at times it follows as meditation or explanation, an effort to get things right — "things like exile, dispossession, habits of expression, internal and external landscapes, stubbornness, poignancy, and heroism." It is a writing with pictures, not a writing to which photos were later added. Said had, in fact, been unable to return to Israel/Palestine for several years. As part of this project, he had hoped to be able to take a trip to the West Bank and Gaza in order to see beyond Mohr's photographs, but such a trip proved to be unsafe and impossible — both Arab and Israeli officials had reason to treat him with suspicion. The book was written in exile; the photos, memories, books, and newspapers, these were the only vehicles of return.

After the Last Sky is, Said wrote in 1999, "an unreconciled book, in which the contradictions and antinomies of our lives and experiences remain as they are, assembled neither (I hope) into neat wholes nor into sentimental ruminations about the past. Fragments, memories, disjointed scenes, intimate particulars." The Palestinians, Said wrote in the introduction, fall between classifications. "We are at once too recently formed and too variously experienced to be a population of articulate exiles with a completely systematic vision and too voluble and trouble making to be simply a pathetic mass of refugees." And he adds, "The whole point of this book is to engage this difficulty, to deny the habitually simple, even harmful representations of Palestinians, and to replace them with something more capable of capturing the complex reality of their experience."

Furthermore, he says, "just as Jean Mohr and I, a Swiss and a Palestinian, collaborated in the process, we would like you — Palestinians, Europeans, Americans, Africans, Latin Americans, Asians — to do so also." This is both an invitation and a challenge. While there is much to learn about the Palestinians, the people and their history, the opening moment in the collaborative project is to learn to look and to read in the service of a complex and nuanced act of understanding.

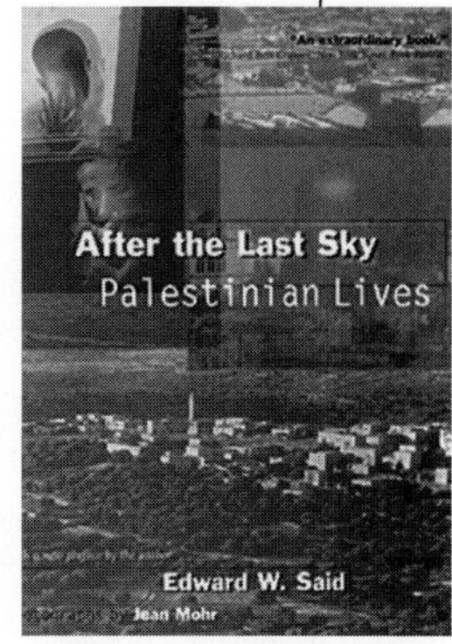

Said is the author of many books and collections, including *Joseph Conrad and the Fiction of Autobiography* (1966), *Beginnings: Intention and Method* (1975), *Orientalism* (1978), *The Question of Palestine* (1979), *Covering Islam: How the Media and the Experts Determine How We See the Rest of the World* (1981), *Blaming the Victims* (1988), *Musical Elaborations* (1991), *Culture and Imperialism* (1993), *The Politics of Dispossession: The Struggle for Palestinian Self-Determination, 1989–1994* (1994), *Representations of the Intellectual* (1994), *Peace and Its*

Discontents: Essays on Palestine in the Middle East Peace Process (1995), *Out of Place: A Memoir* (2000), *Reflections on Exile* (2000), *The Edward Said Reader* (2000), *The End of the Peace Process: Oslo and After* (2001), *Power, Politics, and Culture* (2001), *Mona Hatoum: The Entire World as a Foreign Land* (2001), *On Late Style: Music and Literature Against the Grain* (2006), and *Music at the Limits* (2007).

Jean Mohr has worked as a photographer for UNESCO, the World Health Organization, and the International Red Cross. He has collaborated on four books with John Berger: *Ways of Seeing* (1972; see excerpt on p. 141), *A Seventh Man* (1975), *Another Way of Telling* (1982), and *A Fortunate Man* (1967).

States

Caught in a meager, anonymous space outside a drab Arab city, outside a refugee camp, outside the crushing time of one disaster after another, a wedding party stands, surprised, sad, slightly uncomfortable. Palestinians — the telltale mixture of styles and attitudes is so evidently theirs — near Tripoli in northern Lebanon. A few months after this picture was taken their camp was ravaged by intra-Palestinian fighting. Cutting across the wedding party's path here is the ever-present Mercedes, emblazoned with its extra mark of authenticity, the proud *D* for *Deutschland*. A rare luxury in the West, the Mercedes — usually secondhand and smuggled in — is the commonest of cars in the Levant. It has become what horse, mule, and camel were, and then much more. Universal taxi, it is a symbol of modern technology domesticated, of the intrusion of the West into traditional life, of illicit trade. More important, the Mercedes is the all-purpose conveyance, something one uses for everything — funerals, weddings, births, proud display, leaving home, coming home, fixing, stealing, reselling, running away in, hiding in. But because Palestinians have

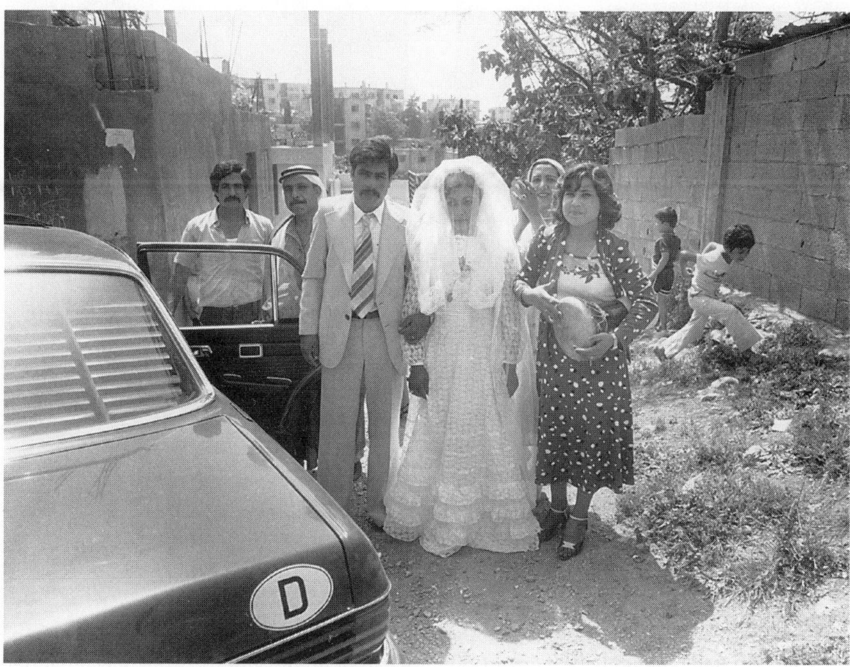

Tripoli, Badawi camp, May 1983.

no state of their own to shield them, the Mercedes, its provenance and destination obscure, seems like an intruder, a delegate of the forces that both dislocate and hem them in. "The earth is closing on us, pushing us through the last passage," writes the poet Mahmoud Darwish.

The paradox of mobility and insecurity. Wherever we Palestinians are, we are not in our Palestine, which no longer exists. You travel, from one end of the Arab world to the other, in Europe, Africa, the Americas, Australia, and there you find Palestinians like yourself who, like yourself, are subject to special laws, a special status, the markings of a force and violence not yours. Exiles at home as well as abroad, Palestinians also still inhabit the territory of former Palestine (Israel, the West Bank, Gaza), in sadly reduced circumstances. They are either "the Arabs of Judea and Samaria," or, in Israel, "non-Jews." Some are referred to as "present absentees." In Arab countries, except for Jordan, they are given special cards identifying them as "Palestinian refugees," and even where they are respectable engineers, teachers, business people, or technicians, they know that in the eyes of their host country they will always be aliens. Inevitably, photographs of Palestinians today include this fact and make it visible.

Memory adds to the unrelieved intensity of Palestinian exile. Palestine is central to the cultures of Islam, Christianity, and Judaism; Orient and Occident have turned it into a legend. There is no forgetting it, no way of overlooking it. The world news is often full of what has happened in Palestine-Israel, the latest Middle East crisis, the most recent Palestinian

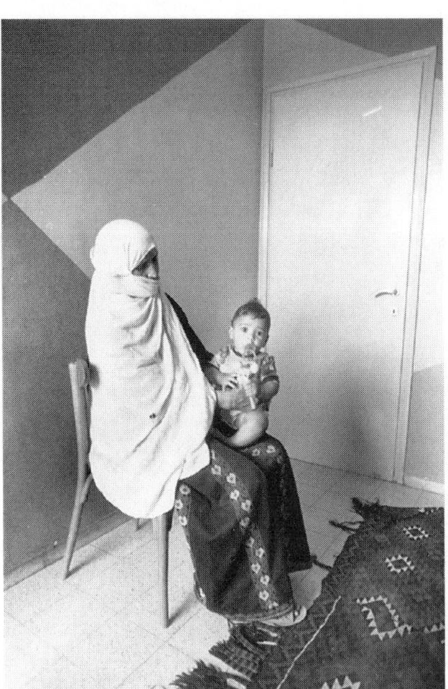

Tel Sheva, 1979. A village of settled nomads near Bersheeba. Some years ago, these people still lived in a tent, under the desert sky. The carpet on the ground is the only reminder of that earlier period.

exploits. The sights, wares, and monuments of Palestine are the objects of commerce, war, pilgrimage, cults, the subjects of literature, art, song, fantasy. East and West, their high and their commercial cultures, have descended on Palestine. Bride and groom wear the ill-fitting nuptial costumes of Europe, yet behind and around them are the clothes and objects of their native land, natural to their friends and attendants. The happiness of the occasion is at odds with their lot as refugees with nowhere to go. The children playing nearby contrast starkly with the unappealing surroundings; the new husband's large workman's hands clash with his wife's delicate, obscuring white. When we cross from Palestine into other territories, even if we find ourselves decently in new places, the old ones loom behind us as tangible and unreal as reproduced memory or absent causes for our present state.

Sometimes the poignancy of resettlement stands out like bold script imposed on faint pencil traces. The fit between body and new setting is not good. The angles are wrong. Lines supposed to decorate a wall instead form an imperfectly assembled box in which we have been put. We perch on chairs uncertain whether to address or evade our interlocutor. This child is held out, and yet also held in. Men and women re-express the unattractiveness around them: The angle made across her face by the woman's robe duplicates the ghastly wall pattern, the man's crossed feet repeat and contradict the outward thrust of the chair leg [p. 542]. He seems unsettled, poised for departure. Now what? Now where? All at once it is our transience and impermanence that our visibility expresses, for we can be seen as figures forced to push on to another house, village, or region. Just as we once were taken from one "habitat" to a new one, we can be moved again.

Exile is a series of portraits without names, without contexts. Images that are largely unexplained, nameless, mute. I look at them without precise anecdotal knowledge, but their realistic exactness nevertheless makes a deeper impression than mere information. I cannot reach the actual people who were photographed, except through a European photographer who saw them for me. And I imagine that he, in turn, spoke to them through an interpreter. The one thing I know for sure, however, is that they treated him politely but as someone who came from, or perhaps acted at the direction of, those who put them where they so miserably are. There was the embarrassment of people uncertain why they were being looked at and recorded. Powerless to stop it.

When A. Z.'s father was dying, he called his children, one of whom is married to my sister, into his room for a last family gathering. A frail, very old man from Haifa, he had spent his last thirty-four years in Beirut in a state of agitated disbelief at the loss of his house and property. Now he murmured to his children the final faltering words of a penniless, helpless patriarch. "Hold on to the keys and the deed," he told them, pointing to a battered suitcase near his bed, a repository of the family estate salvaged from Palestine when Haifa's Arabs were expelled. These intimate mementos of a past irrevocably lost circulate among us, like the genealogies and fables of a wandering singer of tales. Photographs, dresses, objects severed from their original locale, the

Amman, 1984. A visit to the former mayor of Jerusalem and his wife, in exile in Jordan.

rituals of speech and custom: Much reproduced, enlarged, thematized, embroidered, and passed around, they are strands in the web of affiliations we Palestinians use to tie ourselves to our identity and to each other.

Sometimes these objects, heavy with memory — albums, rosary beads, shawls, little boxes — seem to me like encumbrances. We carry them about, hang them up on every new set of walls we shelter in, reflect lovingly on them. Then we do not notice the bitterness, but it continues and grows nonetheless. Nor do we acknowledge the frozen immobility of our attitudes. In the end the past owns us. My father spent his life trying to escape these

Ramallah, 1979. An everyday street scene, banal and reassuring. And yet, the tension is constant. A passing military jeep, a flying stone — the incident, the drama, can occur at any moment.

objects, "Jerusalem" chief among them — the actual place as much as its reproduced and manufactured self. Born in Jerusalem, as were his parents, grandparents, and all his family back in time to a distant vanishing point, he was a child of the Old City who traded with tourists in bits of the true cross and crowns of thorn. Yet he hated the place; for him, he often said, it meant death. Little of it remained with him except a fragmentary story or two, an odd coin or medal, one photograph of his father on horseback, and two small rugs. I never even saw a picture of my grandmother's face. But as he grew older, he reverted to old Jerusalemite expressions that I did not understand, never having heard them during the years of my youth.

Identity — who we are, where we come from, what we are — is difficult to maintain in exile. Most other people take their identity for granted. Not the Palestinian, who is required to show proofs of identity more or less constantly. It is not only that we are regarded as terrorists, but that our existence as native Arab inhabitants of Palestine, with primordial rights there (and not elsewhere), is either denied or challenged. And there is more. Such as it is, our existence is linked negatively to encomiums about Israel's democracy, achievements, excitement; in much Western rhetoric we have slipped into the place occupied by Nazis and anti-Semites; collectively, we can aspire to little except political anonymity and resettlement; we are known for no actual achievement, no characteristic worthy of esteem, except the effrontery of disrupting Middle East peace. Some Israeli settlers on the West Bank say: "The Palestinians can stay here, with no rights, as resident aliens." Other Israelis are less kind. We have no known Einsteins, no Chagall, no Freud or Rubinstein to protect us with a legacy of glorious achievements. We have had no Holocaust to protect us with the world's compassion. We are "other," and opposite, a flaw in the geometry of resettlement and exodus. Silence and discretion veil the hurt, slow the body searches, soothe the sting of loss.

A zone of recollected pleasure surrounds the few unchanged spots of Palestinian life in Palestine. The foodsellers and peddlers — itinerant vendors of cakes or corn — are still there for the casual eye to see, and they still provoke the appetite. They seem to travel not only from place to place,

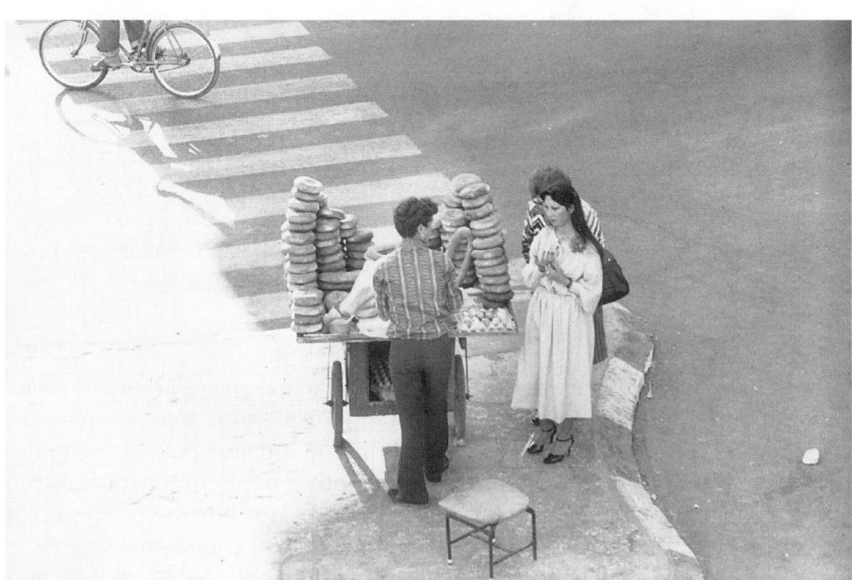

but from an earlier time to the present, carrying with them the same clientele — the young girls and boys, the homeward-bound cyclist, the loitering student or clerk — now as then. We buy their wares with the same surreptitiously found change (who can remember the unit? was it a piaster? fils? shilling?) spent on the same meager object, neither especially good nor especially well prepared. The luxurious pleasure of tasting the vendor's *sim-sim*, the round sesame cakes dipped in that tangy mixture of thyme and sumac, or his *durra*, boiled corn sprayed with salt, surpasses the mere act of eating and opens before us the altogether agreeable taste of food not connected with meals, with nourishment, with routine. But what a distance now actually separates me from the concreteness of that life. How easily traveled the photographs make it seem, and how possible to suspend the barriers keeping me from the scenes they portray.

For the land is further away than it has ever been. Born in Jerusalem in late 1935, I left mandatory Palestine permanently at the end of 1947. In the spring of 1948, my last cousin evacuated our family's house in West Jerusalem; Martin Buber subsequently lived there till his death, I have been told. I grew up in Egypt, then came to the United States as a student. In 1966 I visited Ramallah, part of the Jordanian West Bank, for a family wedding. My father, who was to die five years later, accompanied my sister and me. Since our visit, all the members of my family have resettled — in Jordan, in Lebanon, in the United States, and in Europe. As far as I know, I have no relatives who still live in what was once Palestine. Wars, revolutions, civil struggles have changed the countries I have lived in — Lebanon, Jordan, Egypt — beyond recognition. Until thirty-five years ago I could travel from Cairo to Beirut overland, through territories held or in other ways controlled by rival colonial powers. Now, although my mother lives in Beirut, I have not visited her since the Israeli invasion of 1982: Palestinians are no longer welcome there. The fact is that today I can neither return to the places of my youth, nor voyage freely in the countries and places that mean the most to me, nor feel safe from arrest or violence even in the countries I used to frequent but whose governments and policies have changed radically in recent times. There is little that is more unpleasant for me these days than the customs and police check upon entering an Arab country.

WHAT A DISTANCE NOW ACTUALLY SEPARATES ME FROM THE CONCRETENESS OF THAT LIFE. HOW EASILY TRAVELED THE PHOTOGRAPHS MAKE IT SEEM.

Consider the tremendous upheavals since 1948 each of which effectively destroyed the ecology of our previous existence. When I was born, we in Palestine felt ourselves to be part of a small community, presided over by the majority community and one or another of the outside powers holding sway over the territory. My family and I, for example, were members of a tiny Protestant group within a much larger Greek Orthodox Christian minority, within the larger Sunni Islam majority; the important outside power was Britain, with its great rival France a close second. But then after World War II Britain and France lost their hold, and for the first time we directly confronted the colonial legacy — inept rulers, divided populations, conflicting promises made to resident Arabs and mostly European Jews with incompatible claims. In 1948 Israel was established; Palestine was destroyed, and the great Palestinian dispossession began. In 1956 Egypt was invaded by Britain, France, and Israel, causing what was left of the large Levantine communities there (Italian, Greek, Jewish, Armenian, Syrian) to leave. The rise of Abdel Nasser fired all Arabs — especially Palestinians — with the hope of a revived Arab nationalism, but after the union of Syria with Egypt failed in 1961, the Arab cold war, as it has been called, began in earnest; Saudi Arabia versus Egypt, Jordan versus Syria, Syria versus Iraq. . . . A new population of refugees, migrant workers, and traveling political parties crisscrossed the Arab world. We Palestinians immersed ourselves in the politics of Baathism in Syria and Iraq, of Nasserism in Egypt, of the Arab Nationalist Movement in Lebanon.

The 1967 war was followed shortly after by the Arab oil boom. For the first time, Palestinian nationalism arose as an independent force in the Middle East. Never did our future seem more hopeful. In time, however, our appearance on the political scene stimulated, if it did not actually cause, a great many less healthy phenomena: fundamentalist Islam, Maronite nationalism, Jewish zealotry. The new consumer culture, the computerized economy, further exacerbated the startling disparities in the Arab world between rich and poor, old and new, privileged and disinherited. Then, starting in 1975, the Lebanese civil war pitted the various Lebanese sects, the Palestinians, and a number of Arab and foreign powers against each other. Beirut was destroyed as the intellectual and political nerve center of Arab life; for us, it was the end of our only important, relatively independent center of Palestinian nationalism, with the Palestinian Liberation Organization at its heart. Anwar Sadat recognized Israel, and Camp David further dismantled the region's alliances and disrupted its balance. After the Iranian revolution in 1979 came the Iran-Iraq war. Israel's 1982 invasion of Lebanon put more Palestinians on the move, as the massacres in the Palestinian refugee camps of Sabra and Shatila reduced the community still further. By the end of 1983, Palestinians were fighting each other, and Syria and Libya were directly involved, supporting Palestinian dissidents against PLO loyalists. With the irony typical of our political fate, however, in mid-1985 we were united together in Sabra and Shatila to fight off a hostile Shi'ite militia patronized by Syria.

The stability of geography and the continuity of land — these have completely disappeared from my life and the life of all Palestinians. If we are not stopped at borders, or herded into new camps, or denied reentry and residence, or barred from travel from one place to another, more of our land is taken, our lives are interfered with arbitrarily, our voices are prevented from reaching each other, our identity is confined to frightened little islands in an inhospitable environment of superior military force sanitized by the clinical jargon of pure administration. On the West Bank and in Gaza we confront several Zionist "master plans"—which, according to Meron Benvenisti, ex-deputy mayor of Jerusalem, are "explicitly sectarian." He continues:

> The criteria established to determine priorities of settlement regions are "*interconnection* [*havirah*] between existing Jewish areas for the creation of [Jewish] settlement continuity" and "*separation* [*hayitz*] to restrict uncontrolled Arab settlement and the prevention of Arab settlement blocs"; "*scarcity* [*hesech*] refers to areas devoid of Jewish settlement." In these criteria "pure planning and political planning elements are included."
>
> *(The West Bank Data Project: A Survey of Israeli Policies)*

Continuity for *them*, the dominant population; discontinuity for *us*, the dispossessed and dispersed.

The circle is completed, though, when we Palestinians acknowledge that much the same thesis is adhered to by Arab and other states where sizable Palestinian communities exist. There too we are in dispersed camps, regions, quarters, zones; but unlike their Israeli counterparts, these places are not the scientific product of "pure planning" or "political planning." The Baqa'a camp in Amman, the Palestinian quarter of Hawaly in Kuwait, are simply there.

All forms of Palestinian activity, all attempts at unity, are suspect. On the West Bank and Gaza, "development" (the systematic strengthening of Palestinian economic and social life) is forbidden, whereas "improvement" is tolerated so long as there isn't too much of it; so long as it doesn't

Tyre, South Lebanon, 1983. Bourj el-Shemali camp. The car bears witness to a drama, circumstances unknown. The flowers: the month of May, it is spring. The children: wearing smart clothes, almost certainly donated by a charity. They are refugees — the children of refugees.

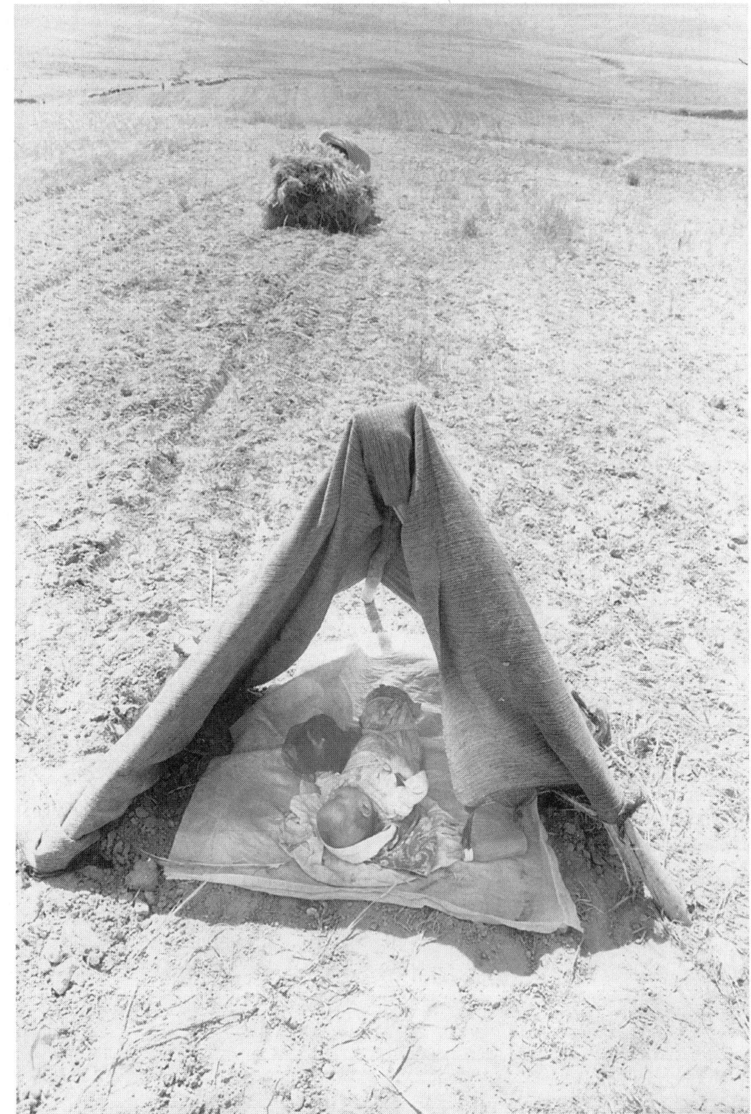

Bedouin encampment near Bersheeba, 1979.

become development. The colors of the Palestinian flag are outlawed by Israeli military law; Fathi Gabin of Gaza, an artist, was given a six-month prison sentence for using black, green, red, and white in one of his works. An exhibit of Palestinian culture at al-Najah University in Nablus earned the school a four-month closing. Since our history is forbidden, narratives are rare; the story of origins, of home, of nation is underground. When it appears it is broken, often wayward and meandering in the extreme, always coded, usually in outrageous forms — mock-epics, satires, sardonic parables, absurd rituals — that make little sense to an outsider. Thus Palestinian life is scattered, discontinuous, marked by the artificial and imposed arrangements of interrupted or confined space, by the dislocations and unsynchronized rhythms of disturbed time. Across our children's lives, in the open fields in which they play, lie the ruins of war, of a borrowed or imported industrial technology, of cast-off or abandoned forms. How odd the conjuncture, and yet for Palestinians, how fitting. For where no straight line leads from home to birthplace to school to maturity, all events are accidents, all progress is a digression, all residence is exile. We linger in nondescript places, neither here nor there; we peer through windows without glass, ride conveyances without movement or power. Resourcefulness and receptivity are the attitudes that serve best.

The difference between the new generation of Palestinians and that of 1948 is striking. Our parents bore on their faces the marks of disaster uncomprehended. Suddenly their past had been interrupted, their society obliterated, their existence radically impoverished. Refugees, all of them. Our children know no such past. Cars are equally for riding or, ruined, for playing in. Everything around them seems expendable, impermanent, unstable, especially where — as in Lebanon — Palestinian communities have been disastrously depleted or destroyed, where much of their life is undocumented, where they themselves are uncounted.

No Palestinian census exists. There is no line that can be drawn from one Palestinian to another that does not seem to interfere with the political designs of one or another state. While all of us live among "normal" people, people with complete lives, they seem to us hopelessly out of reach, with their countries, their familial continuity, their societies intact. How does a Palestinian father tell his son and daughter that Lebanon (Egypt, Syria, Jordan, New York) is where we are, but not where we are *from*? How does a mother confirm her intimate recollections of childhood in Palestine to her children, now that the facts, the places, even the names, are no longer allowed to exist?

So we borrow and we patch things together. Palestinians retain the inflections of Jaffa, of Hebron, of Jerusalem and other cities left behind, even as their dialect becomes that of Beirut, Detroit, or Paris. I have found out much more about Palestine and met many more Palestinians than I ever did, or perhaps could have, in pre-1948 Palestine. For a long time I thought that this was so because I was a child then, somewhat sheltered, a member of a minority. But my experience is confirmed by my oldest and closest Palestinian friend, Ibrahim Abu-Lughod. Although he was more in and of pre-1948 Palestine — because older, more conscious and active — than I ever was, he too says that he is much more in contact with Palestinians today than when he was in Palestine. He writes,

> Thanks to modern technological progress, Palestinian families, and Palestinian society as a whole, have been able to forge very numerous human, social, and political links. By getting on a plane I can see the majority of my friends. It's because of this that our family has remained unified. I see all the members of my family at least once or twice a year. Being in Jaffa, I could never have seen relatives who lived in Gaza, for example.

Gaza, 1979. Refugee camp. A boy of unknown age.

But Ibrahim does not celebrate this sociability: "I constantly experience the sense that something is missing for me. To compensate for this lack, I multiply and intensify human contacts."

Over the missing "something" are superimposed new realities. Plane travel and phone conversations nourish and connect the fortunate; the symbols of a universal pop culture enshroud the vulnerable.

There can be no orderly sequence of time. You see it in our children who seem to have skipped a phase of growth or, more alarming, achieved an out-of-season maturity in one part of their body or mind while the rest remains childlike. None of us can forget the whispers and occasional proclamations that our children are "the population factor" — to be feared, and hence to be deported — or constitute special targets for death. I heard it said in Lebanon that Palestinian children in particular should be killed because each of them is a potential terrorist. Kill them before they kill you.

Tel Sheva, 1979. A group portrait, taken at the request of the children.

How rich our mutability, how easily we change (and are changed) from one thing to another, how unstable our place — and all because of the missing foundation of our existence, the lost ground of our origin, the broken link with our land and our past. There are no Palestinians. Who are the Palestinians? "The inhabitants of Judea and Samaria." Non-Jews. Terrorists. Troublemakers. DPs.* Refugees. Names on a card. Numbers on a list. Praised in speeches — *el pueblo palestino, il popolo palestino, le peuple*

* ***DPs*** Displaced persons or displaced people. [Eds.]

palestinien — but treated as interruptions, intermittent presences. Gone from Jordan in 1970, now from Lebanon.

None of these departures and arrivals is clean, definitive. Some of us leave, others stay behind. Remnants, new arrivals, old residents. Two great images encapsulate our unresolved existence. One is the identity card (passport, travel document, laissez-passer), which is never Palestinian but always something else; it is the subject of our national poem, Mahmoud Darwish's "Bitaqit Hawia": "Record! I am an Arab/Without a name — without title/patient in a country/with people enraged." And the second is Emil Habiby's invention the Pessoptimist (*al-mutasha'il*), the protagonist of a disorderly and ingenious work of Kafkaesque fiction, which has become a kind of national epic. The Pessoptimist is being half here, half not here, part historical creature, part mythological invention, hopeful and hopeless, everyone's favorite obsession and scapegoat. Is Habiby's character fiction, or does his extravagant fantasy only begin to approximate the real? Is he a made-up figure or the true essence of our existence? Is Habiby's jamming-together of words — *mutafa'il* and *mutasha'im* into *mutasha'il*, which repeats the Palestinian habit of combining opposites like *la* ("no") and *na'am* ("yes") into *la'am* — a way of obliterating distinctions that do not apply to us, yet must be integrated into our lives?

Emil Habiby is a craggy, uncompromisingly complex, and fearsomely ironic man from Haifa, son of a Christian family, Communist party stalwart, long-time Knesset member, journalist, editor. His novel about the Pessoptimist (whose first name, incidentally, is Said) is chaotic because it mixes time,

Bersheeba, 1979. Near a Bedouin encampment, a little kitchen garden — and its scarecrow of bits and pieces.

characters, and places; fiction, allegory, history, and flat statement, without any thread to guide the reader through its complexities. It is the best work of Palestinian writing yet produced, precisely because the most seemingly disorganized and ironic. In it we encounter characters whose names are of particular significance to Palestinians: The name of Yuaad, the work's female lead, means "it shall be repeated," a reference to the string of defeats that mark our history, and the fatalistic formulae that color our discourse. One of the other characters is Isam al-Bathanjani — Isam the Eggplant, a lawyer who is not very helpful to Said but who keeps turning up just the same. So it is with eggplants in Palestine. My family — my father in particular — has always been attached to eggplants from Battir, and during the many years since any of us had Battiri eggplants the seal of approval on good eggplants was that "they're almost as good as the Battiris."

Today when I recall the tiresome paeans to Battiris, or when in London and Paris I see the same Jaffa oranges or Gaza vegetables grown in the *bayarat* ("orchards") and fields of my youth, but now marketed by Israeli export companies, the contrast between the inarticulate rich *thereness* of what we once knew and the systematic export of the produce into the hungry mouths of Europe strikes me with its unkind political message. The land and the peasants are bound together through work whose products seem always to have meant something to other people, to have been destined for consumption elsewhere. This observation holds force not just because the Carmel boxes and the carefully wrapped eggplants are emblems of the power that rules the sprawling fertility and enduring human labor of Palestine, but also because the discontinuity between me, out here, and the actuality there is so much more compelling now than my receding memories and experiences of Palestine.

EXILE AGAIN. THE FACTS OF MY BIRTH ARE SO DISTANT AND STRANGE AS TO BE ABOUT SOMEONE I'VE HEARD OF RATHER THAN SOMEONE I KNOW.

Another, far more unusual, item concerning this vegetable appears in an article by Avigdor Feldman, "The New Order of the Military Government: State of Israel Against the Eggplant," which appeared in the journal *Koteret Rashit*, August 24, 1983. Laws 1015 and 1039, Feldman reports, stipulate that any Arab on the West Bank and Gaza who owns land must get written permission from the military governor before planting either a new vegetable — for example, an eggplant — or fruit tree. Failure to get permission risks one the destruction of the tree or vegetable plus one year's imprisonment.

Exile again. The facts of my birth are so distant and strange as to be about someone I've heard of rather than someone I know. Nazareth — my mother's town. Jerusalem — my father's. The pictures I see display the same produce, presented in the same carelessly plentiful way, in the same rough wooden cases. The same people walk by, looking at the same posters and trinkets, concealing the same secrets, searching for the same profits, pleasures, and goals. The same as what? There is little that I can

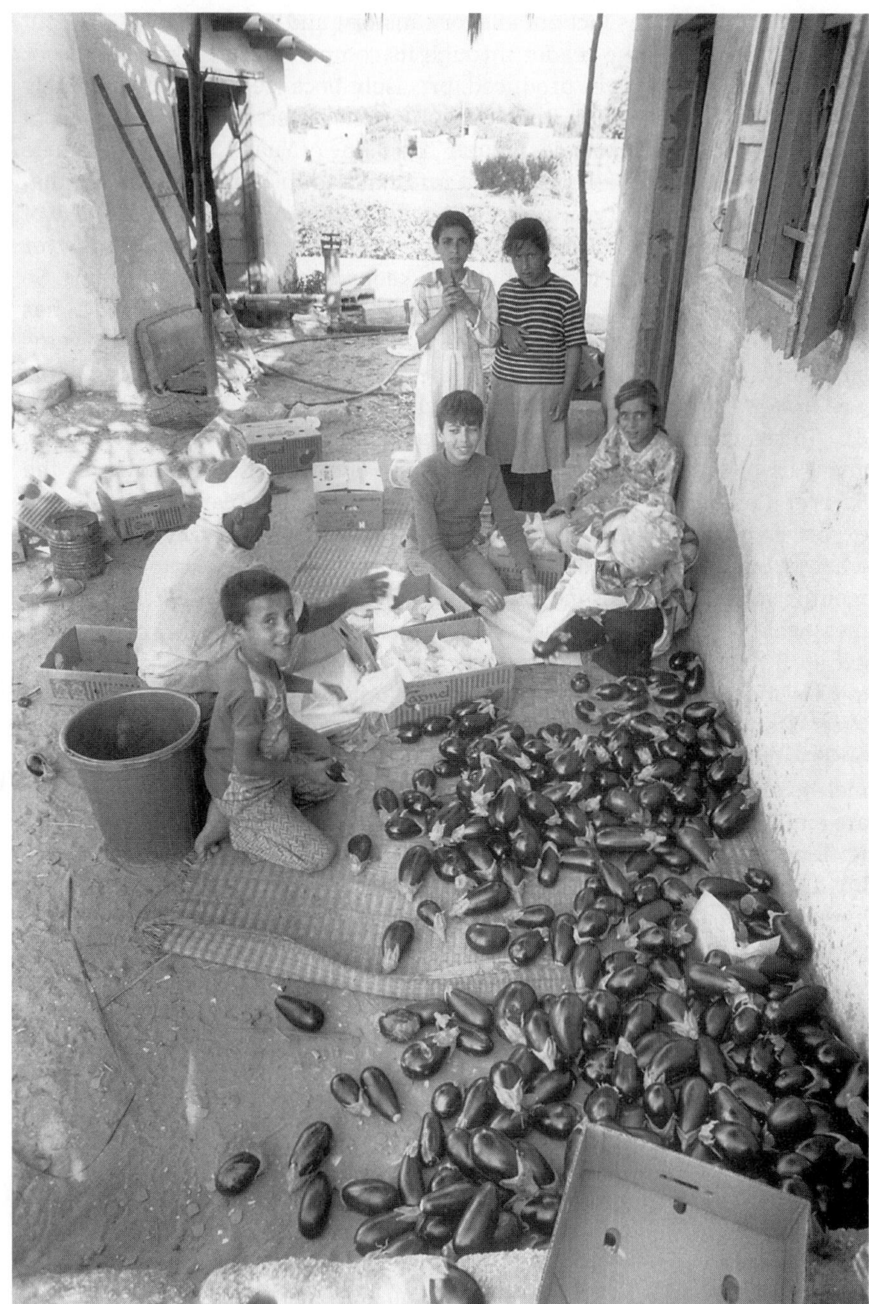

Gaza, 1979. Farm using refugee labor.

truly remember about Jerusalem and Nazareth, little that is specific, little that has the irreducible durability of tactile, visual, or auditory memories that concede nothing to time, little — and this is the "same" I referred to — that is not confused with pictures I have seen or scenes I have glimpsed elsewhere in the Arab world.

Palestine is exile, dispossession, the inaccurate memories of one place slipping into vague memories of another, a confused recovery of general wares, passive presences scattered around in the Arab environment. The story of Palestine cannot be told smoothly. Instead, the past, like the present, offers only occurrences and coincidences. Random. The man enters a quiet alley where he will pass cucumbers on his right, tomatoes on his left; a priest walks down the stairs, the boy dashes off, satchel under arm, other boys loiter, shopkeepers look out for business; carrying an airline bag, a man advances past a display of trinkets, a young man disappears around the corner, two boys idle aimlessly. Tomatoes, watermelons, arcades, cucumbers, posters, people, eggplants — not simply there, but represented by photographs as being there — saturated with meaning and memory, and still very far away. Look more closely and think through these possibilities: The poster is about Egypt. The trinkets are made in Korea or Hong Kong. The scenes are surveyed, enclosed, and surrounded by Israelis. European and Japanese tourists have more access to Jerusalem and Nazareth than I do. Slowly, our lives — like Palestine itself — dissolve into something else. We can't hold to the center for long.

Exile. At a recent conference in America featuring a "dialogue" between Israeli and Palestinian intellectuals with reconciliation high on the agenda,

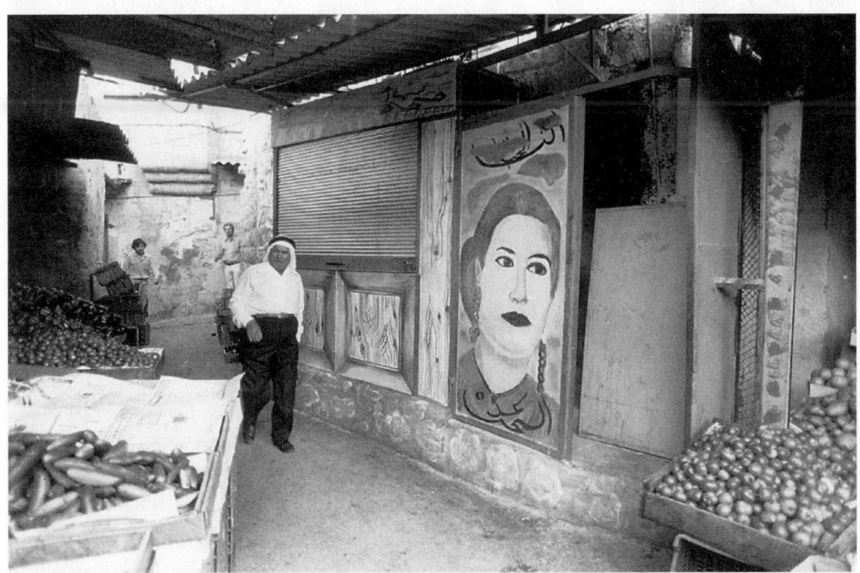

Nazareth, 1979. Portrait of Om Kalsoum.

Jerusalem, 1979. A snapshot.

Jerusalem, 1979. A snapshot.

a man rises from the audience to pose a question. "I am a Palestinian, a peasant. Look at my hands. I was kicked out in 1948 and went to Lebanon. Then I was driven out, and went to Africa. Then to Europe. Then to here. Today [he pulls out an envelope] I received a paper telling me to leave this country. Would one of you scholars tell me please: Where am I supposed to go now?" No one had anything to tell him. He was an embarrassment, and I have no idea what in fact he did, what became of him. My shame.

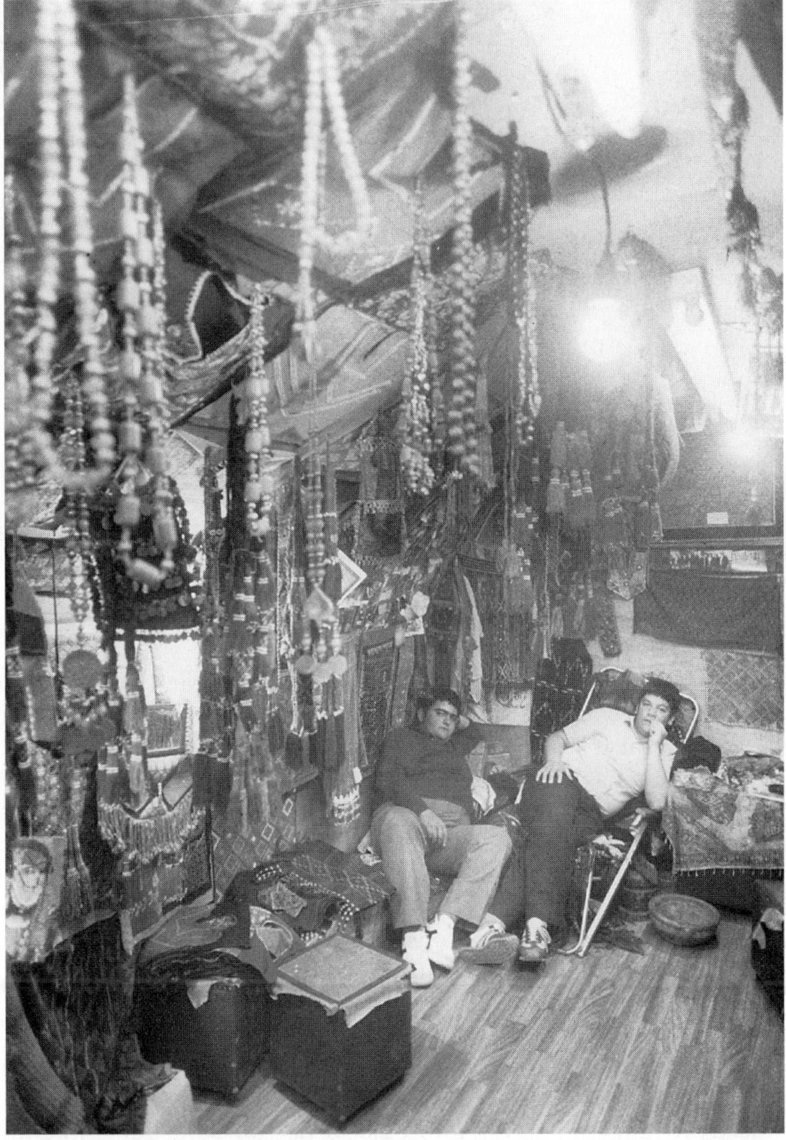

Old City of Jerusalem, 1984. A tourist shop. Customers are rare. Will they be American, Swiss, or Israeli?

The Palestinian's claims on Israel are generally unacknowledged, much less seen as directly connected to the founding of the state. On the Arabs there is an ambivalent Palestinian claim, recognized in Arab countries by countless words, gestures, threats, and promises. Palestine, after all, is the centerpiece of Arab nationalism. No Arab leader since World War II has failed to make Palestine a symbol of his country's nationalist foreign policy. Yet, despite the avowals, we have no way of knowing really how they — all the "theys" — feel about us. Our history has cost every one of our friends a great deal. It has gone on too long.

Jerusalem, 1979.

Let Ghassan Kanafani's novella *Men in the Sun* stand for the fear we have that unless we press "them" they will allow us to disappear, and the equal worry that if we press them they will either decry our hectoring presence, and quash it in their states, or turn us into easy symbols of their nationalism. Three refugees concealed in the belly of a tanker truck are being transported illegally across the border into Kuwait. As the driver converses with the guards, the men (Palestinians) die of suffocation—in the sun, forgotten. It is not the driver's forgetfulness that nags at him. It is their silence. "Why didn't you knock on the sides of the tank? Why didn't you bang the sides of the tank? Why? Why? Why?" Our fear to press.

The Palestinians as commodity. Producing ourselves much as the *masabih*, lamps, tapestries, baskets, embroideries, mother-of-pearl trinkets are produced. We turn ourselves into objects not for sale, but for scrutiny. People ask us, as if looking into an exhibit case, "What is it you Palestinians want?"—as if we can put our demands into a single neat phrase. All of us speak of *awdah*, "return," but do we mean that literally, or do we mean "we must restore ourselves to ourselves"? The latter is the real point, I think, although I know many Palestinians who want their houses and their way of life back, exactly. But is there any place that fits us, together with our accumulated memories and experiences?

Do we exist? What proof do we have?

The further we get from the Palestine of our past, the more precarious our status, the more disrupted our being, the more intermittent our presence. When did we become "a people"? When did we stop being one? Or are we in the process of becoming one? What do those big questions have to do with our intimate relationships with each other and with others? We frequently end our letters with the mottoes "Palestinian love" or "Palestinian kisses." Are there really such things as Palestinian intimacy and embraces, or are they simply intimacy and embraces, experiences common to everyone, neither politically significant nor particular to a nation or a people?

The politics of such a question gets very close to our central dilemma: We all know that we are Arabs, and yet the concept, not to say the lived actuality, of Arabism — once the creed and the discourse of a proud Arab nation, free of imperialism, united, respected, powerful — is fast disappearing, cut up into the cautious defensiveness of relatively provincial Arab states, each with its own traditions — partly invented, partly real — each with its own nationality and restricted identity. In addition, Palestine has been replaced by an Israel whose aggressive sense of itself as the state of the Jewish people fuels the exclusivity of a national identity won and maintained to a great extent at our expense. We are not Jews, we have no place there except as resident aliens, we are outsiders. In the Arab states we are in a different position. There we are Arabs, but it is the process of nationalization that excludes us: Egypt is for and by Egyptians, Iraq is for and by Iraqis, in ways that cannot include Palestinians whose intense national revival is a separate phenomenon. Thus we are the same as other Arabs, and yet different. We cannot exist except as Arabs, even though "the Arabs" exist otherwise as Lebanese, Jordanians, Moroccans, Kuwaitis, and so forth.

Add to this the problems we have of sustaining ourselves as a collective unit and you then get a sense of how *abstract*, how very solitary and unique, we tend to feel.

Strip off the occasional assertiveness and stridency of the Palestinian stance and you may catch sight of a much more fugitive, but ultimately quite beautifully representative and subtle, sense of identity. It speaks in languages not yet fully formed, in settings not completely constituted, like the shy glance of a child holding her father's knee while she curiously and tentatively examines the stranger who photographs her. Her look conjures up the unappreciated fact of birth, that sudden, unprepared-for depositing of a small bundle of self on the fields of the Levant after which comes the trajectory of dispossession, military and political violence, and that constant, mysterious entanglement with monotheistic religion at its most profound — the Christian Incarnation and Resurrection, the Ascension to heaven of the Prophet Mohammed, the Covenant of Yahweh with his people — that is knotted definitively in Jerusalem, center of the world, *locus classicus* of Palestine, Israel, and Paradise.

A secular world of fatigue and miraculously renewed energies, the world of American cigarettes and an unending stream of small papers pulled out of miscellaneous notebooks or "blocnotes," written on with disposable pens, messages of things wanted, of people missing, of requests to the bureaucracy. The Palestinian predicament: finding an "official" place for yourself in a system that makes no allowances for

Village of Ramah, Galilee, 1979. A secular high school with students from thirty-six neighboring villages.

you, which means endlessly improvising solutions for the problem of finding a missing loved one, of planning a trip, of entering a school, on whatever bit of paper is at hand. Constructed and deconstructed, ephemera are what we negotiate with, since we authorize no part of the world and only influence increasingly small bits of it. In any case, we keep going.

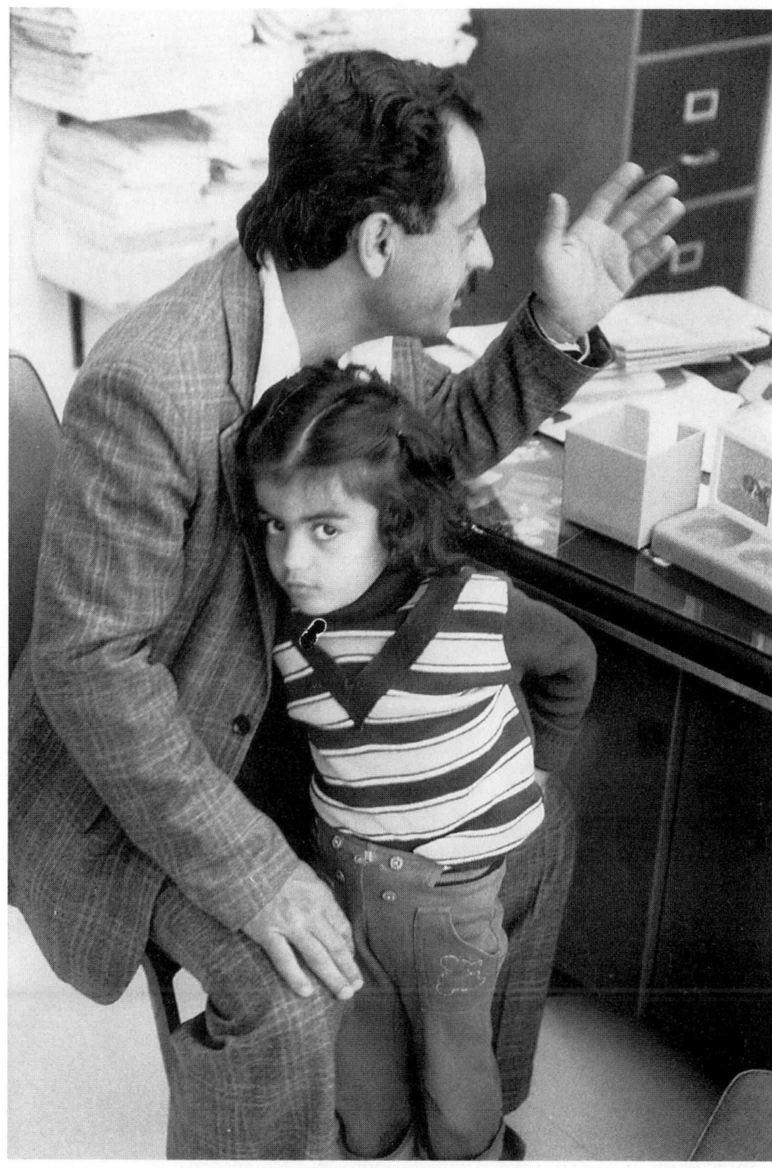

Amman, 1984. Pediatric clinic.

The striking thing about Palestinian prose and prose fiction is its formal instability: Our literature in a certain very narrow sense *is* the elusive, resistant reality it tries so often to represent. Most literary critics in Israel and the West focus on what is said in Palestinian writing, who is described, what the plot and contents deliver, their sociological and political meaning. But it is *form* that should be looked at. Particularly in fiction, the struggle to achieve form expresses the writer's efforts to construct a coherent scene,

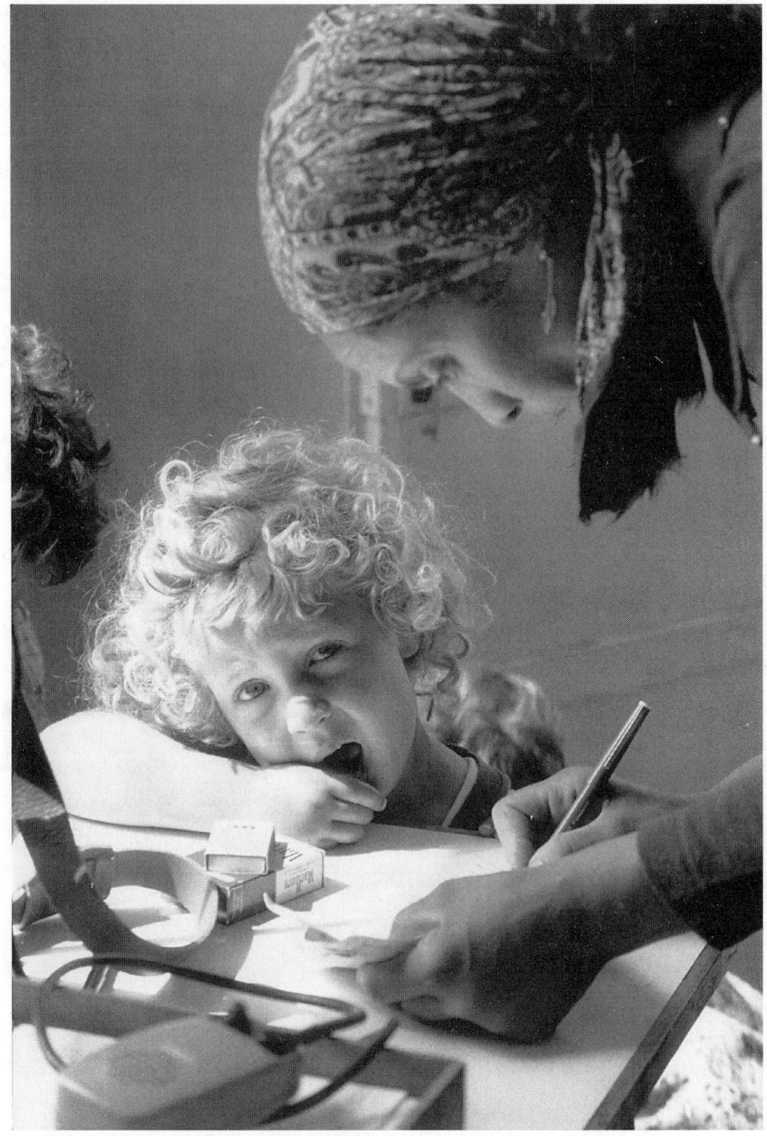

Sidon, South Lebanon, 1983. A refugee writes out a message destined for her husband, a prisoner in the camp at Ansar.

a narrative that might overcome the almost metaphysical impossibility of representing the present. A typical Palestinian work will always be concerned with this peculiar problem, which is at once a problem of plot and an enactment of the writer's enterprise. In Kanafani's *Men in the Sun* much of the action takes place on the dusty streets of an Iraqi town where three Palestinian men must petition, plead, and bargain with "specialists" to smuggle them across the border into Kuwait. Impelled by exile and dislocation, the Palestinians need to carve a path for themselves in existence, which for them is by no means a given or stable reality. Like the history of the lands they left, their lives seem interrupted just before they could come to maturity and satisfaction; thus each man leaves behind family and responsibilities, to whose exigencies he must answer — unsuccessfully — here in the present. Kanafani's very sentences express instability and fluctuation — the present tense is subject to echoes from the past, verbs of sight give way to verbs of sound or smell, and one sense interweaves with another — in an effort to defend against the harsh present and to protect some particularly cherished fragment of the past. Thus, the precarious actuality of these men in the sun reproduces the precarious status of the writer, each echoing the other.

Our characteristic mode, then, is not a narrative, in which scenes take place *seriatim*, but rather broken narratives, fragmentary compositions, and self-consciously staged testimonials, in which the narrative voice keeps stumbling over itself, its obligations, and its limitations.

Each Palestinian structure presents itself as a potential ruin. The theme of the formerly proud family house (village, city, camp) now wrecked, left behind, or owned by someone else, turns up everywhere in our literature and cultural heritage. Each new house is a substitute, supplanted in turn by yet another substitute. The names of these places extend all the way from the private (my friend Mohammed Tarbush expatiates nobly on the beauties of Beit Natif, a village near Bethlehem that was wiped out of existence by Israeli bulldozers in 1948; his widowed mother now lives in Jarash, Jordan, he in Paris) to the official, or institutionalized, sites of ruin — Deir Yassin, Tell el-Zaatar, Birim and Ikrit, Ein el-Hilwé, Sabra, Shatila, and more. Even "Palestine" itself is such a place and, curiously, already appears as a subject of elegy in journalism, essays, and literature of the early twentieth century. In the works of Halim Nassar, Ezzat Darwaza, Khallil Beidas, and Aref el-Aref, Palestine's destruction is predicted.

IMPELLED BY EXILE AND DISLOCATION, THE PALESTINIANS NEED TO CARVE A PATH FOR THEMSELVES IN EXISTENCE, WHICH FOR THEM IS BY NO MEANS A GIVEN OR STABLE REALITY.

All cultures spin out a dialectic of self and other, the subject "I" who is native, authentic, at home, and the object "it" or "you," who is foreign, perhaps threatening, different, out there. From this dialectic comes the series of heroes and monsters, founding fathers and barbarians, prized masterpieces and despised opponents that express a culture from its deepest sense of national self-identity to its refined patriotism, and finally to its coarse jingoism, xenophobia, and exclusivist bias. For Palestinian culture, the odd thing is that its own identity is more frequently than not perceived as "other." "Palestine" is so charged with significance for others that Palestinians cannot perceive it as intimately theirs without a simultaneous sense of its urgent importance for others as well. "Ours" but not

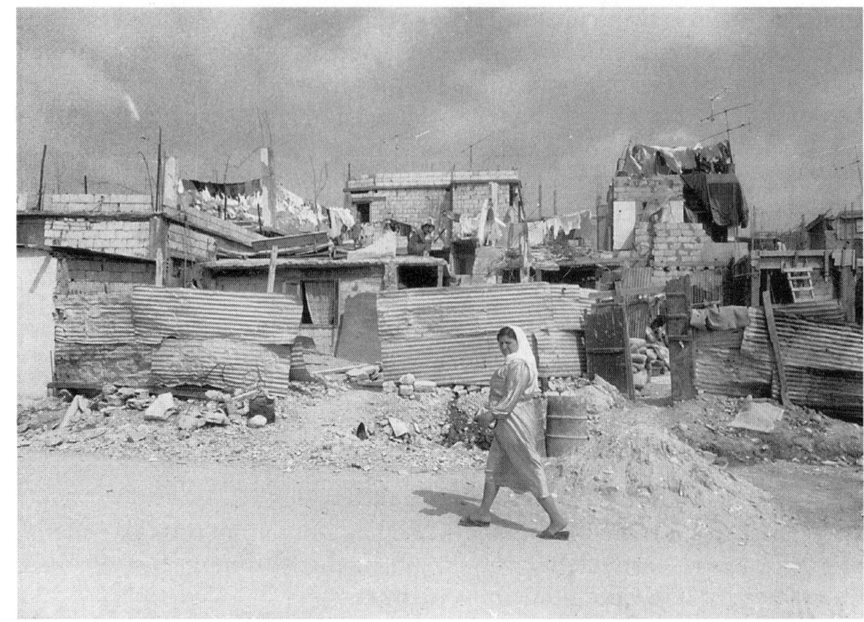

Sidon, South Lebanon, 1983. Camp at Ein el-Hilwé. Time passes: destruction, reconstruction, redestruction.

yet fully "ours." Before 1948, Palestine had a central agonistic meaning both for Arab nationalism and for the Zionist movement. After 1948, the parts of Palestine still inhabited by Arabs took on the additional label of the "non-Jewish" part of the Jewish state. Even a picture of an Arab town — like Nazareth where my mother was born and grew up — may express this alienating perspective. Because it is taken from outside Nazareth (in fact, from Upper Nazareth, a totally Jewish addition to the town, built on the surrounding hills), the photograph renders Palestine as "other." I never knew Nazareth, so this is my only image of it, an image of the "other," from the "outside," Upper Nazareth.

Thus the insider becomes the outsider. Not only have the interpositions between us and Palestine grown more formidable over time, but, to make matters worse, most of us pass our lives separated from each other. Yet we live in comradely communication despite the barriers. Today the Palestinian genius expresses itself in crossings-over, in clearing hurdles, activities that do not lessen the alienation, discontinuity, and dispossession, but that dramatize and clarify them instead. We have remained; in the words of Tawfik Zayyad's famous poem, "The Twenty Impossibles," it would be easier "to catch fried fish in the Milky Way,/to plow the sea,/to teach the alligator speech" than to make us leave. To the Israelis, whose incomparable military and political power dominates us, we are at the periphery, the image that will not go away. Every assertion of our nonexistence, every attempt to spirit us away, every new effort to prove that we were never really there, simply raises the question of why so much denial

Arab Nazareth, 1979. Viewed from Upper Nazareth.

of, and such energy expended on, what was not there? Could it be that even as alien outsiders we dog their military might with our obdurate moral claim, our insistence (like that of Bartleby the Scrivener) that "we would prefer not to," not to leave, not to abandon Palestine forever?

The proof of whatever small success we have had is not that we have regained a homeland, or acquired a new one; rather, it is that some Israelis have admitted the possibility of sharing a common space with us, in Palestine. The proposed modes of such a sharing are adventurous and utopian in the present context of hostility between Arabs and Jews, but on an intellectual level they are actual, and to some of us — on both sides — they make sense. Most Palestinians have their own special instance of the Israeli who reached out across the barricade most humanly. For some it is the intrepid Israeli lawyer defending Palestinian political prisoners, or trying to prevent land expropriations and collective punishment; for others it is — the testimony of Salah Ta'amari, leader of the Palestinian prisoners rounded up during the Israeli invasion and put in the Ansar prison camp, comes to mind — an Israeli in a position of authority (prison guard or army officer) who prevented some atrocity or showed some clear sign of humanity and fellow feeling. For my part, removed from the terrible pressures of the scene, I think of all the Israeli (or non-Israeli) Jews whose articulate witness to the injustice of their people against mine has marked out a communal territory. The result has usually been a friendship whose depth is directly proportional to the admiration I feel for their tenacity of conscience and belief in the face of the most slanderous attacks. Surely few have equaled the courage and

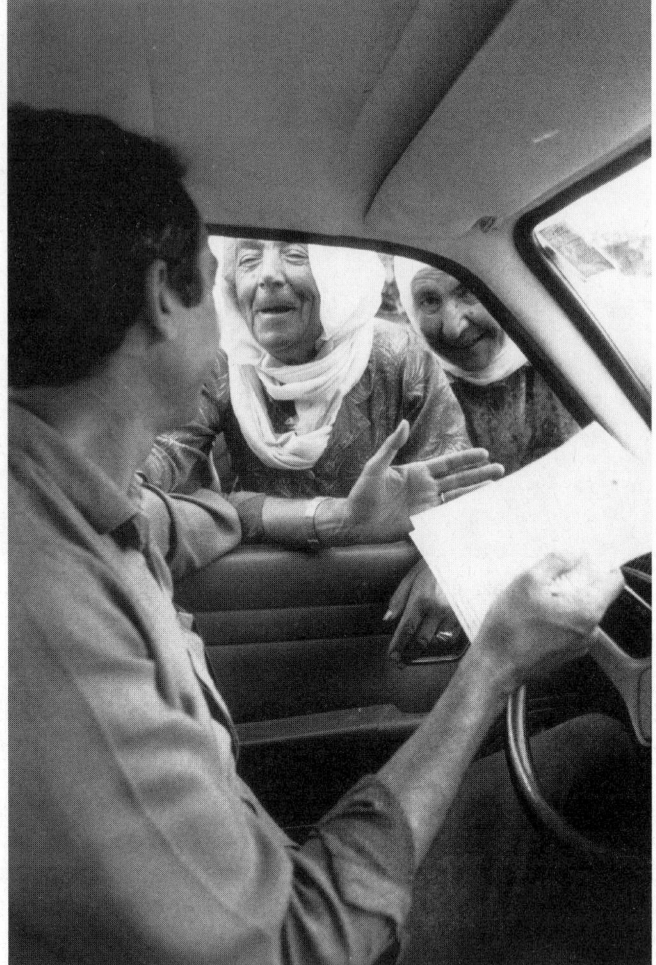

Tyre, South Lebanon, 1983. Rashidyé camp: A local official collects messages from the relations of refugees for the International Red Cross.

principle of Israel Shahak, of Leah Tsemal and Felicia Langer, of Noam Chomsky, of Izzy Stone, of Elmer Berger, of Matti Peled, of so many others who stood up bravely during the events in Lebanon.

There are few opportunities for us Palestinians, or us Palestinians *and* Israelis, to learn anything about the world we live in that is *not* touched by, indeed soaked in, the hostilities of our struggle. And if it isn't the Palestinian-Zionist struggle, there are the pressures of religion, of every conceivable ideology, of family, peers, and compatriots, each of them bearing down upon us, pushing, kneading, prodding every one of us from childhood to maturity.

In such an environment, learning itself is a chancy, hybrid activity, laced with the unresolvable antitheses of our age. The child is full of the

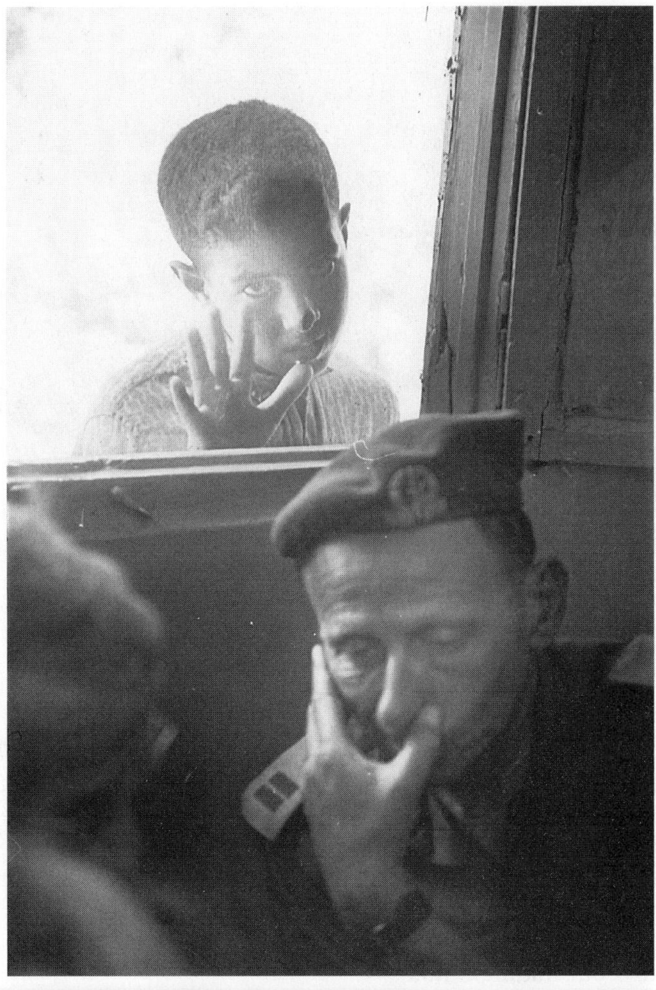

Kalandia (near Ramallah), 1967. A few days after the end of the June War: in the foreground, an Israeli officer, lost in thought. Behind the window, a young villager.

curious hope and undirected energy that attract the curatorial powers of both church and state. Fortunately, here the spirit of the creative urge in all human activity asserts itself — neither church nor state can ultimately exhaust, or control, the possibilities latent in the classroom, playground, or family. An orderly row of chairs and tables, a disciplined recitation circle in a Catholic school with a nun in charge, are also places for the absorption of more knowledge and experience than authorities impart — places where the child explores here and there, his/her mind and body wandering in space and time despite the constraints in each. In a school where the teacher is a devout Muslim, the child's propensity for disturbing or opposing the schemes of knowledge and discipline causes him/her to leave the table, disrupt the pattern, seek unthought-of possibilities. The tension

Jerusalem, 1979. A dialogue between left-wing Israeli and Arab intellectuals.

between teachers and students remains, but better the tension than the peace of passivity, or the unresisting assent to authority.

The pressures of the here and now require an answer to the Palestinian crisis here and now. Whereas our interlocutors, our "others" — the Arab states, the United States, the USSR, Israel, our friends and enemies — have the luxury of a state in which institutions do their work undisturbed by the question of existence-or-not, we lead our lives under a sword of Damocles, whose dry rhetorical form is the query "When are you Palestinians going to accept a solution?" — the implication being that if we don't, we'll disappear. This, then, is our midnight hour.

It is difficult to know how much the often stated, tediously reiterated worries about us, which include endless lectures on the need for a clear Palestinian statement of the desire for peace (as if we controlled the decisive factors!), are malicious provocation and how much genuine, if sympathetic, ignorance. I don't think any of us reacts as impatiently to such things as we did, say, five years ago. True, our collective situation is more precarious now than it was, but I detect a general turning inward among Palestinians, as if many of us feel the need to consolidate and collect the shards of Palestinian life still present and available to us. This is not quietism at all, nor is it resignation. Rather, it springs from the natural impulse to stand back when the headlong rush of events gets to be too much, perhaps, for us to savor life as life, to reflect at some distance from politics on where we came from and where we are, to regrasp, revise, recomprehend the tumultuous experiences at whose center, quite without our consent, we have been made to stand.

Jean Mohr's photograph [p. 574] of a small but clearly formed human group surrounded by a dense and layered reality expresses very well what

Nazareth, 1979. A municipal kindergarten, looked after by nuns.

we experience during that detachment from an ideologically saturated world. This image of four people seen at a distance near Ramallah, in the middle of and yet separated from thick foliage, stairs, several tiers of terraces and houses, a lone electricity pole off to the right, is for me a private, crystallized, almost Proustian evocation of Palestine. Memory: During the summer of 1942 – I was six – we rented a house in Ramallah. My father, I recall, was ill with high blood pressure and recovering from a nervous breakdown. I remember him as withdrawn and constantly smoking. My mother took me to a variety show at the local Friends school. During the second half I left the hall to go to the toilet, but for reasons I could not (and still do not) grasp, the boy-scout usher would not let me back in. I recall with ever-renewed poignancy the sudden sense of distance I experienced from what was familiar and pleasant – my mother, friends, the show; all at once the rift introduced into the cozy life I led taught me the meaning of

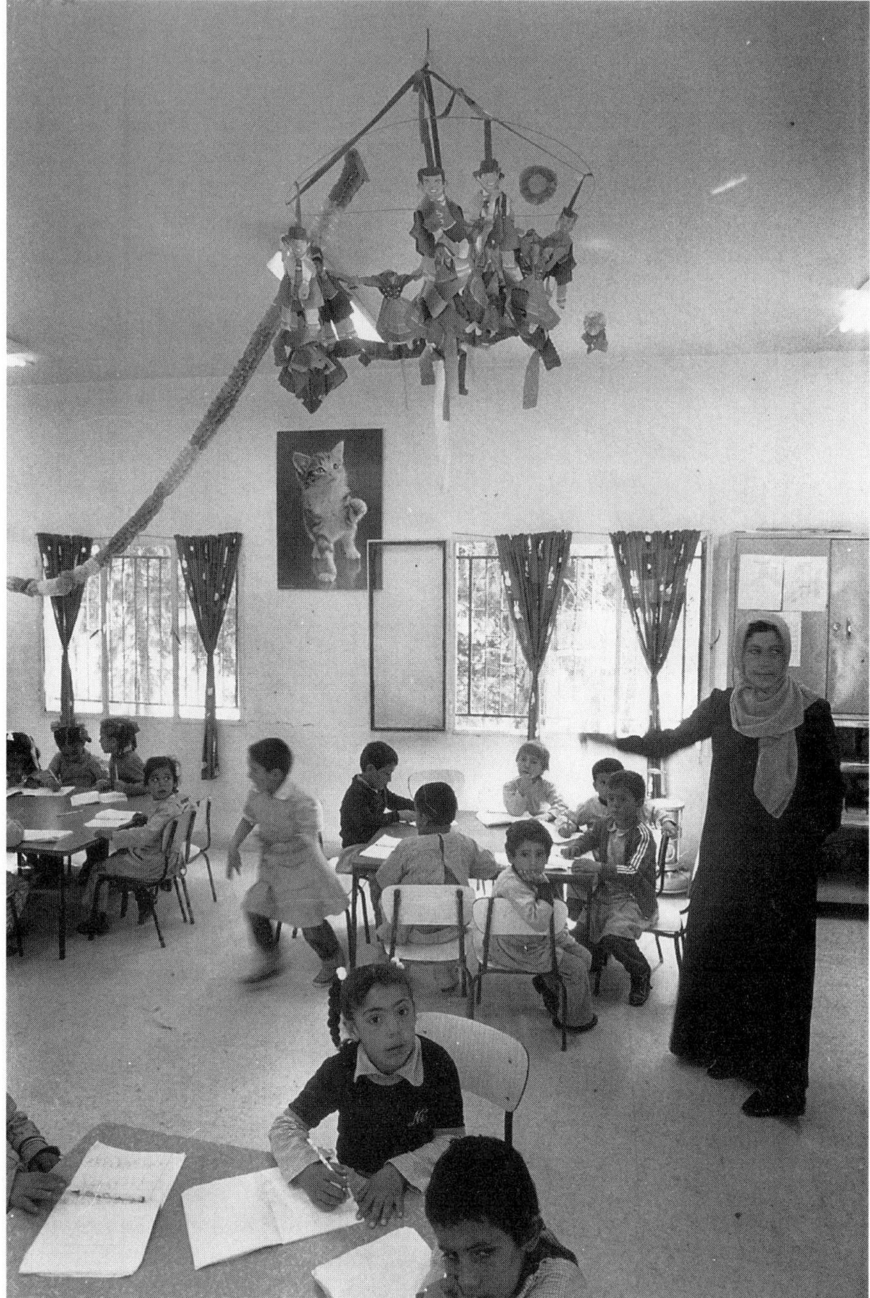

Amman, 1984. Camp at Baqa'a, one of the oldest in Jordan. The YWCA looks after some of the kindergartens.

Jerusalem, 1984.

separation, of solitude, and of anguished boredom. There was nothing to do but wait, although my mother did appear a little later to find out what had happened to me. We left immediately, but not before I furtively took a quick look back through the door window at the lighted stage. The telescoped vision of small figures assembled in a detached space has remained with me for over forty years, and it reappears in the adjusted and transformed center of Jean's 1983 picture. I never ventured anywhere near that part of Ramallah again. I would no more know it than I would the precise place of this photo; and yet I am sure it would be familiar, the way this one immediately seemed.

My private past is inscribed on the surface of this peaceful but somehow brooding pastoral scene in the contemporary West Bank. I am not the only one surveying the scene. There is the child on the left who looks on. There are also the Swiss photographer, compassionate, curious, silent, and of course the ever-present Israeli security services, who hold the West Bank and its population in the vise of occupation. As for those terraces and multiple levels: Do they serve the activities of daily life or are they the haunted stairs of a prison which, like Piranesi's, lead nowhere, confining their human captives? The dense mass of leaves, right and left, lend their bulk to the frame, but they too impinge on the slender life they surround, like memory or a history too complex to be sorted out, bigger than its subject, richer than any consciousness one might have of it.

The power grid recalls the Mercedes in Tripoli. Unassimilated, its modernity and power have been felt with considerable strength in our lives here and there throughout the Third World. Another childhood memory: Driving through the Sinai from Egypt into Palestine, we would see the row

Near Senjel, a village between Ramallah and Nablus, 1979.

I NEVER VENTURED ANYWHERE NEAR THAT PART OF RAMALLAH AGAIN. I WOULD NO MORE KNOW IT THAN I WOULD THE PRECISE PLACE OF THIS PHOTO; AND YET I AM SURE IT WOULD BE FAMILIAR.

of telephone and electricity pylons partnering the empty macadamized road that cut through an even emptier desert. Who are they, I would ask myself. What do they think when we are not here? When we stopped to stretch our legs, I would go up to a pole and look at its dull brown surface for some sign of life, identity, or awareness. Once I marked one with my initials EWS, hoping to find it again on the trip back. All of them looked exactly the same as we hurtled by. We never stopped. I never drove there again, nor can I now. Futile efforts to register my presence on the scene.

Intimate memory and contemporary social reality seem connected by the little passage between the child, absorbed in his private, silent sphere, and the three older people, who are the public world of adults, work, and community. It is a vacant, somewhat tenuously maintained space, however; sandy, pebbly, and weedy. All the force in the photograph moves dramatically from trees left to trees right, from the visible enclave of domesticity (stairs, houses, terrace) to the unseen larger world of power and authority beyond. I wonder whether the four people are in fact connected, or whether as a group they simply happen to be in the way of unseen forces totally indifferent to the dwelling and living space these people inhabit. This is also, then, a photograph of latent, of impending desolation, and once again I am depressed by the transience of Palestinian life, its vulnerability and all too easy dislocation. But another movement, another feeling, asserts itself in response, set in motion by the two strikingly marked openings in the buildings, openings that suggest rich, cool interiors which outsiders cannot penetrate. Let us enter.

QUESTIONS FOR A SECOND READING

1. The first three paragraphs provide a "reading" of the opening photograph, "Tripoli, Badawi camp, May 1983." Or, to put it another way, the writing evolves from and is in response to that photograph. As you reread these paragraphs, pay close attention to what Said is doing, to what he notices, to what prompts or requires commentary. How would you describe and explain the writing that follows? What is he doing with the photo? What is he doing as a writer? What is he doing for a reader? (How does he position a reader?)

   It might be useful to begin by thinking about what Said is *not* doing. It is not, for example, the presentation one might expect in a slide show on travel in Lebanon. Nor is it the kind of presentation one might expect while seeing the slides of family or friends, or slides in an art history or art appreciation class.

   Once you have worked through the opening three paragraphs, reread the essay paying attention to Said's work with all the photographs. Is there a pattern? Do any of the commentaries stand out for their force, variety, innovation?

2. Here is another passage from the introduction to *After the Last Sky*:

   > Its style and method — the interplay of text and photos, the mixture of genres, modes, styles — do not tell a consecutive story, nor do they constitute a political essay. Since the main features of our present existence are dispossession, dispersion, and yet also a kind of power incommensurate with our stateless exile, I believe that essentially unconventional, hybrid, and fragmentary forms of expression should be used to represent us. What I have quite consciously designed, then, is an alternative mode of expression to the one usually encountered in the media, in works of social science, in popular fiction. (p. 6)

   And later:

   > The multifaceted vision is essential to any representation of us. Stateless, dispossessed, de-centered, we are frequently unable either to speak the "truth" of our experience or to make it heard. We do not usually control the images that represent us; we have

> been confined to spaces designed to reduce or stunt us; and we have often been distorted by pressures and powers that have been too much for us. An additional problem is that our language, Arabic, is unfamiliar in the West and belongs to a tradition and civilization usually both misunderstood and maligned. Everything we write about ourselves, therefore, is an interpretive translation—of our language, our experience, our senses of self and others. (p. 6)

And from "States":

> The striking thing about Palestinian prose and prose fiction is its formal instability: Our literature in a certain very narrow sense *is* the elusive, resistant reality it tries so often to represent. Most literary critics in Israel and the West focus on what is said in Palestinian writing, who is described, what the plot and contents deliver, their sociological and political meaning. But it is *form* that should be looked at. Particularly in fiction, the struggle to achieve form expresses the writer's efforts to construct a coherent scene, a narrative that might overcome the almost metaphysical impossibility of representing the present. (pp. 563–64)

As you reread, think about form—organization, arrangement, and genre. What *is* the order of the writing in this essay? (We will call it an essay for lack of a better term.) How might you diagram or explain its organization? By what principle(s) is it ordered and arranged? The essay shifts genres —memoir, history, argument. It is, as Said says, "hybrid." What surprises are there? or disappointments? How might you describe the writer's strategy as he works on his audience, on readers? And, finally, do you find Said's explanation sufficient or useful—does the experience of exile produce its own inevitable style of report and representation?

3. The essay is filled with references to people (including writers), places, and events that are, most likely, foreign to you. Choose one that seems interesting or important, worth devoting time to research. Of course the Internet will be a resource, but you should also use the library, if only to become aware of the different opportunities and materials it provides. Compile a report of the additional information; be prepared to discuss how the research has served or changed your position as a reader of "States."

4. The final chapter of *After the Last Sky* ends with this:

> I would like to think, though, that such a book not only tells the reader about us, but in some way also reads the reader. I would like to think that we are not just the people seen or looked at in these photographs: We are also looking at our observers. (p. 166)

Read back through Said's essay by looking at the photos with this reversal in mind—looking in order to see yourself as the one who is being looked at, as the one observed. How are you positioned by the photographer,

Jean Mohr? How are you positioned by the person in the scene, always acknowledging your presence? What are you being told?

Once you have read through the photographs, reread the essay with a similar question in mind. This time, however, look for evidence of how Said positions you, defines you, invents you as a presence in the scene.

ASSIGNMENTS FOR WRITING

1. Compose a similar project, a Said-like reading of a set of photos. These can be photos prepared for the occasion (by you or a colleague); they could also be photos already available. Whatever their source, they should represent people and places, a history and/or geography that you know well, that you know to be complex and contradictory, and that you know will not be easily or readily understood by others, both the group for whom you will be writing (most usefully the members of your class) and readers more generally. You must begin with a sense that the photos cannot speak for themselves; you must speak for them.

   In preparation, you should reread closely to come to a careful understanding of Said's project. (The first and second "Questions for a Second Reading" should be useful for this.) To prepare a document that is Said-like (one that shows your understanding of what Said is doing), you will need an expert's sense of how to write from and to photographs, and you will need to consider questions of form — of order, arrangement, and genre.

2. While "States" does not present itself as polemical writing — an argument in defense of Palestinian rights, an argument designed to locate blame or propose national or international policy — it is, still, writing with a purpose. It has an argument, it has a particular project in mind, and it wants something to happen.

   Write an essay that represents the argument or the project of "States" for someone who has not read it. You will need, in other words, to establish a context and to summarize. You should also work from passages (and images) to give your reader a sense of the text, its key terms and language. And write about "States" as though it has something to do with you.

   Your essay is not just summary, in other words, but summary in service of statement, response, or extension. As you are invited to think about the Palestinians, or about exile more generally, or about the texts and images that are commonly available, what do you think? What do you have to add?

3. The final chapter of *After the Last Sky* ends with this:

   > I would like to think, though, that such a book not only tells the reader about us, but in some way also reads the reader. I would like to think that we are not just the people seen or looked at in these photographs: We are also looking at our observers. (p. 166)

The fourth question in "Questions for a Second Reading" sets a strategy for rereading with this passage in mind — looking in order to see yourself as the one who is being looked at, as the one observed. Write an essay in which you think this through by referring specifically to images and to text. How are you positioned? by whom and to what end?

4. Said insists upon our recognizing the contemporary social, political, and historic context for intimate scenes he (and Jean Mohr) present of people going about their everyday lives. The Palestinian people are still much in the news — photographs of scenes from their lives are featured regularly in newspapers, in magazines, and on the Internet. Collect a series of these images from a particular and defined recent period of time — a week or a month, say, when the Palestinians have been in the news. Using these images, and putting them in conversation with some of the passages and images in "States," write an essay in the manner of Said's essay, with text and image in productive relationship. The goal of your essay should be to examine how Said's work, in "States," can speak to us (or might speak to us) today.

MAKING CONNECTIONS

1. Edward Said talks about the formal problems in the writing of "States" (and for more on this, see the second of the "Questions for a Second Reading"):

> The striking thing about Palestinian prose and prose fiction is its formal instability: Our literature in a certain very narrow sense *is* the elusive, resistant reality it tries so often to represent. Most literary critics in Israel and the West focus on what is said in Palestinian writing, who is described, what the plot and contents deliver, their sociological and political meaning. But it is *form* that should be looked at. Particularly in fiction, the struggle to achieve form expresses the writer's efforts to construct a coherent scene, a narrative that might overcome the almost metaphysical impossibility of representing the present. (pp. 563–64)

And here is a similar discussion from the introduction to *After the Last Sky*:

> The multifaceted vision is essential to any representation of us. Stateless, dispossessed, de-centered, we are frequently unable either to speak the "truth" of our experience or to make it heard. We do not usually control the images that represent us; we have been confined to spaces designed to reduce or stunt us; and we have often been distorted by pressures and powers that have been too much for us. An additional problem is that our language, Arabic, is unfamiliar in the West and belongs to a tradition and civilization usually both misunderstood and maligned. Everything we write about ourselves, therefore, is an interpretive translation — of our language, our experience, our senses of self and others. (p. 6)

Edward Said's sense of his project as a writing project, a writing project requiring formal experimentation, is similar to Gloria Anzaldúa's in *Borderlands/La frontera*. In the two chapters represented in *Ways of Reading*, "Entering into the Serpent" (p. 72) and "How to Tame a Wild Tongue" (p. 85), Anzaldúa is also writing (and resisting) "interpretive translation." In place of the photographs in "States," she offers poems, stories, and myths, as well as passages in Spanish.

Write an essay in which you consider these selections as writing projects. The formal experimentation in each is said by the writers to be fundamental, necessary, a product of the distance between a particular world of experience and the available modes of representation. In what ways are the essays similar? In what ways are they different? Where and how is a reader (where and how are you) positioned in each? What is the experience of reading them? What does one need to learn to be their ideal reader?

2. There are several writers in *Ways of Reading* whose writing could be called unconventional, even experimental. A short list includes Gloria Anzaldúa, Anne Carson, Susan Griffin, and John Edgar Wideman. (We can imagine arguments for several other selections as well.)

   Choose a selection from one of these writers to read alongside Edward Said's "States." As you read the two, pay particular attention to what the writing does, to how it works. This is not quite the same as paying attention to what it says. What does this way of writing allow each writer to do that another style, perhaps "topic sentence, examples, and conclusion," would not? What does it offer a reader—or what does it allow a reader to do? Write an essay in which you compare the styles of these two selections. Is there one that you find compelling or attractive? If each provides a textbook example, what are you invited to think about as you consider the possibilities and limits of your own style? of "standard" or "school" style? In what ways might this work be seen as a way of working on the problems of writing? And what might this work have to do with you, a student in a writing class?

3. Said says,

   > All cultures spin out a dialectic of self and other, the subject "I" who is native, authentic, at home, and the object "it" or "you," who is foreign, perhaps threatening, different, out there. From this dialectic comes the series of heroes and monsters, founding fathers and barbarians, prized masterpieces and despised opponents that express a culture from its deepest sense of national self-identity to its refined patriotism, and finally to its coarse jingoism, xenophobia, and exclusivist bias. (p. 565)

   This is as true of the Palestinians as it is of the Israelis—although, he adds, "For Palestinian culture, the odd thing is that its own identity is more frequently than not perceived as 'other.'"

Citing Benedict Anderson and what he refers to as "imagined communities," Mary Louise Pratt in "Arts of the Contact Zone" (p. 485) argues that our idea of community is "strongly utopian, embodying values like equality, fraternity, liberty, which the societies often profess but systematically fail to realize." Against this utopian vision of community, Pratt argues that we need to develop ways of understanding (noticing or creating) social and intellectual spaces that are not homogeneous or unified—contact zones. She argues that we need to develop ways of understanding and valuing difference.

There are similar goals and objects to these projects. Reread Pratt's essay with Said's "States" in mind. Recalling what she refers to as the "literate arts of the contact zone," can you find points of reference in Said's text? Said's thinking always attended to the importance and the conditions of writing, including his own. There are ways that "States" could be imagined as both "autoethnographic" and "transcultural." How might his work allow you to understand the "literate arts of the contact zone" in practice? How might his work allow you to understand the problems and possibilities of such writing beyond what Pratt has imagined, presented, and predicted?

4. Jean Mohr's collaboration with John Berger was important to Said, particularly in the 1975 book *A Seventh Man*, a photographic essay on migrant workers in Europe. Find a copy of *A Seventh Man* (in a library or a bookstore or online) and write an essay on what you think it was in Mohr's work, and in his collaboration with Berger, that was most compelling to Said.

5. In Edward Said's essay "States," he theorizes about the notion of exile in relation to Palestinian identity, offering a study of exile and dislocation through his analysis of photographs taken by Jean Mohr. Consider the following passage:

> We turn ourselves into objects not for sale, but for scrutiny. People ask us, as if looking into an exhibit case, "What is it you Palestinians want?"—as if we can put our demands into a single neat phrase. All of us speak of *awdah*, "return," but do we mean that literally, or do we mean "we must restore ourselves to ourselves"? (p. 560)

When Said talks about being looked at as though in an exhibit case, we might understand him as being concerned with the problem of dehumanization. After all, to be in an exhibit case is to be captured, trapped, or even dead. In her essay "Beside Oneself: On the Limits of Sexual Autonomy" (p. 240), Judith Butler might be understood to be considering a similar problem. She writes, "I would like to start, and to end, with the question of the human, of who counts as the human, and the related question of whose lives count as lives, and with a question that has preoccupied many of us for years: what makes for a grievable life?"

Write an essay in which you consider the ways Said and Butler might be said to be speaking with each other. How might the condition of exile be like the condition of being *beside oneself*? What kind of connections – whether you see them as productive or problematic, or both at once – can be made between the ways Said talks about nation, identity, and home, and the ways Butler talks about gender and sexuality? What passages from each seem to have the other in mind? How does each struggle with reference, with pronouns like "we" and "our"?

TOMMIE Shelby

Tommie Shelby is Professor of African American Studies and Professor of Philosophy at Harvard University. He received his BA from Florida A&M University in 1990 and his PhD from the University of Pittsburgh in 1998. Before joining the faculty at Harvard, Shelby was a member of The Ohio State University department of philosophy. Although still early in his career, Shelby has published two well-received books: *Hip Hop and Philosophy: Rhyme 2 Reason* (with Derrick Darby, 2005); and *We Who Are Dark: The Philosophical Foundations of Black Solidarity* (2005), chosen by *New York Magazine* as a "best academic book" (2009). Shelby is also editor of the journal *Transition*.

In the preface to *We Who Are Dark*, Shelby tells the story of his undergraduate education and his growing interest in questions of black solidarity. It is worth quoting at length:

> I first began to think systematically and critically about the meaning of black solidarity as an undergraduate at Florida A&M University (FAMU), a historically black university in Tallahassee. Although I had previously attended de facto racially segregated public schools (in Jacksonville, Florida, and in Los Angeles), FAMU was the first school I attended that regarded the education of black youth for leadership as part of its official mission. Looking back on that time, I can see that several events and chance encounters had a big impact on my intellectual development and outlook on black politics.
>
> Like many in the student body, I initially majored in business administration. It was at one of the biweekly forums organized by the School of Business and Industry, during which one or another high-ranking executive from the corporate world would speak, that I first heard "Lift Every Voice and Sing." Or at least, that day in the fall of 1986 was the first time I remember hearing the song, despite the fact that I grew up in James Weldon Johnson's hometown. Listening to the words then, sung by my fellow students and faculty, stirred my pride in blackness and my sense of unity with other African Americans, past and present. I suspect that every person in the hall felt a similar connectedness — both to one another and to our ancestors who

> had fought so hard to make equal citizenship a reality for those of us singing the "Black National Anthem." But how many of us had thought deeply about what solidarity requires of us? I certainly hadn't. As business students at a black college, were we to carry out the project of black capitalism in the spirit of Booker T. Washington or embrace the teachings of Marcus Garvey? Were we to continue the protest tradition of W. E. B. Du Bois and the NAACP, or should we take the more revolutionary approach of the African Blood Brotherhood or the Black Panthers? Were we to build and maintain black institutions like the one we were attending? What, if any, of the legacy of the civil rights movement or Black Power should we carry forward? What part, if any, ought we leave behind? I didn't have any answers to these questions and, frankly, didn't spend much time looking for them. Yet I was convinced that African Americans should possess a strong black identity and should maintain their bonds of solidarity. I figured that the precise content of that identity and unity could be worked out later. (pp. x–xi)

These questions, and the courses he took in the humanities and social sciences, led Shelby to "perhaps the most impractical of all majors for a first generation college student—philosophy" (p. xi). And, in his junior year, he had the chance to hear and to meet a guest speaker on his campus, Kwame Anthony Appiah, who had come to FAMU to encourage promising black students to consider academic careers. His encounter with Appiah, and later study of Appiah's ideas, forced him "to rethink [his] uncritical belief in black solidarity" (p. xi).

The selection that follows is chapter 6 from *We Who Are Dark*. Given our standard practice in *Ways of Reading*, we will refer to it as an essay, as a single unit of work, one that can be read on its own. Occasionally, however, Shelby refers to previous chapters. In the chapters that precede chapter 6, Shelby develops and then relies on a distinction between "classical black nationalism" and "pragmatic nationalism" as he thinks about the history (and the future) of arguments for and against black solidarity. For Shelby, classical black nationalism assumes that

> black solidarity and self-realization must be rooted in a shared African or Pan-African ethnoracial identity, which black Americans must reclaim and develop. This group consciousness, which some have termed "Afrocentric" or "Afrikan," is held to be a necessary and proper foundation for a transnational and self-determining black community. (p. 10)

Pragmatic nationalism refers to the view that "black solidarity is merely a contingent strategy for creating greater freedom and social equality for blacks, a pragmatic yet principled approach to achieving racial justice" (p. 10). And, he concludes, "On a variety of grounds, I urge the rejection of classical black nationalism. Yet I defend a version of pragmatic nationalism as an alternative" (p. 10).

Social Identity and Group Solidarity

> We are one with you under the ban of prejudice and proscription — one with you under the slander of inferiority — one with you in social and political disfranchisement. What you suffer, we suffer; what you endure, we endure. We are indissolubly united, and must fall or flourish together.
>
> — FREDERICK DOUGLASS, "To Our Oppressed Countrymen" (1847)

In an effort to liberate blacks from the burdens of racial injustice, blacks frequently call upon, even pressure, one another to become a more unified collective agent for social change. There are, of course, critics who think such solidarity irrational, impractical, and even morally objectionable.[1] Yet many people, both black and nonblack, continue to believe that black solidarity is essential to achieve the full freedom and social equality that American ideals promise. . . . Even among those who agree that black solidarity is important for bringing about racial justice, there is substantial disagreement over the precise meaning of this group commitment. Such disagreement can be quite fundamental, as can be seen by comparing classical and pragmatic nationalism.

Recall that, according to classical nationalism, black solidarity and voluntary separation under conditions of equality and self-determination is a worthwhile end in itself. On this account, blacks should unite and work together because they are a people with their own distinctive ethnoracial identity; and as a cohesive national group, blacks have interests that are best pursued by their seeking group autonomy within some relatively independent institutional framework. However, according to pragmatic nationalism, blacks should unite and work together because they suffer a common oppression; and given the current political climate they can make progress in overcoming or ameliorating their shared condition only if they embrace black solidarity. Here, black unity is merely a contingent strategy for creating greater freedom and equality for blacks.

Though similar in underlying motivation, the two strains within the nationalist tradition are importantly different. The pragmatic account, the least radical of the two, simply acknowledges the negative historical impact and current existence of antiblack racism in America and calls on those who suffer because of these injustices to act collectively to end them or at least to reduce their impact on their lives. The goal of this political program, then, is to free blacks from racism and its burdensome legacy, and it regards black solidarity as a necessary means to that end. The classical nationalist, on the other hand, maintains that blacks are a people whose members need to work together to bring about their collective self-realization as a people. Generally more pessimistic about the prospects for ending, or even sharply reducing, antiblack racism, this program seeks relief for black people through collective autonomy and self-organization and it calls for black solidarity to bring this about.

In previous chapters, I have highlighted the weaknesses in the classical program, problems that I believe are insurmountable. I have also tried to show that interpretations of pragmatic nationalism as community nationalism, political corporatism, or cultural nationalism are also untenable. My concern in this chapter will be to further clarify the practical implications of a viable pragmatic nationalism and to more sharply distinguish it from its classical rival. I shall do so by scrutinizing a doctrine that is often thought to be a component of any conception of black solidarity.

COLLECTIVE IDENTITY THEORY

Collective identity theory holds that a shared black identity is essential for an effective black solidarity whose aim is liberation from racial oppression, and thus blacks who are committed to emancipatory group solidarity must steadfastly embrace their distinctive black identity. It is clear why the advocate of classical nationalism would accept this view, since it is the distinctive social identity of blacks that, on this account, constitutes them as a "people," which in turn grounds the claim of group self-determination. Without such an identity, the goal of black collective self-realization loses its rationale and much of its appeal. For the pragmatic nationalist, too, collective identity theory seems to have much going for it. In particular, it would appear to help with overcoming two serious obstacles to black collective action against racial injustice.

COLLECTIVE IDENTITY THEORY HOLDS THAT A SHARED BLACK IDENTITY IS ESSENTIAL FOR AN EFFECTIVE BLACK SOLIDARITY WHOSE AIM IS LIBERATION FROM RACIAL OPPRESSION.

First, there is the familiar free-rider problem. Although many blacks, even some who are well off, are willing to make the relevant sacrifices to bring about racial justice, many are also complacent, narrowly self-interested, or simply weary of carrying on the struggle. Their inaction weakens the collective effort. It also breeds resentment and mistrust, as some are seen as benefiting from the sacrifices of others without contributing to what should be a group endeavor. Collective identity theory suggests a (perhaps only partial) solution: namely, by cultivating a common conception of who they are as a people, blacks can strengthen the bonds of identification, loyalty, special concern, and trust that would enable them to overcome these barriers to collective action. Such an identity could also give blacks a foundation for mutual identification across class lines, something that is sorely needed in this time of increasing intraracial economic stratification.

Second, there is the general problem that the mere acceptance of abstract principles of justice is often insufficient to motivate people to contribute the time and resources necessary for effecting meaningful social change. This difficulty affects the collective will of blacks as well, despite the fact that they, perhaps more than any other racialized group in America, desperately want to see an end to unfair racial disadvantage. We have noted several broad principles — antiracism, racial equality, equal educational opportunity, and antipoverty — that all blacks can be expected to support. But getting blacks (or any other group) to act upon these principles is another matter. Again, a collective identity would seem to help: viewing one another as black brothers and sisters with a shared social identity in blackness may, like the familiar motivating force of kinship relations, make blacks more inclined to help each other in a movement to eradicate racial injustice and its negative consequences.

Many influential theorists in the history of black political thought have defended or implicitly relied upon collective identity theory. The tendency to link the demand for collective self-definition with emancipatory black solidarity can be found in the writings and speeches of quite diverse black thinkers.[2] For purposes of illustrating this tendency, I will, once again, focus on Du Bois and his well-known essay "The Conservation of Races" (1897). In that early essay, Du Bois explicitly advocates a particularly strong form of emancipatory black solidarity: "It is our [American Negroes'] *duty* to conserve our physical powers, our intellectual endowments, our spiritual ideals; as a race we must strive by race organization, by race solidarity, by race unity *to the realization of that broader humanity which freely recognizes differences in men, but sternly deprecates inequality in their opportunities of development.*"[3] . . . Du Bois believed that black solidarity is necessary for overcoming racial oppression and insuring that blacks make their unique cultural contribution to humanity. He also insisted that blacks should "conserve" their racial identity rather than allow themselves to be absorbed completely into Anglo-American culture, for the goals of emancipatory black solidarity cannot be achieved without the preservation of a distinctive black identity: "We believe it the *duty* of the Americans of Negro descent, *as a body,* to maintain their race identity *until* this mission of the Negro people is accomplished, and the ideal of human brotherhood has become a practical possibility."[4] Although Du Bois often suggested that he would like to see black identity, in particular its cultural dimensions, preserved even beyond that time when social equality becomes a reality, here he emphasizes the "duty" of blacks to maintain their identity "until" such equality is realized.

Even in his early reconstruction of the concept of "race," Du Bois emphasized the link between racial identity and race solidarity: "[A race] is a vast family of human beings, generally of common blood and language, always of common history, traditions and impulses, *who are both voluntarily and involuntarily striving together for the accomplishment of certain more or less vividly conceived ideals of life.*"[5]

There has recently been a lively philosophical debate over the exact meaning of Du Bois's conception of race as defined in his "Conservation" essay.[6] Much of this debate has focused on the metaphysics of race — on what would make a group of people a "race," what it would mean for races to be "real," and, given what we now know about human variety, whether any races actually exist. In light of his avowed philosophical proclivities, it is safe to assume that Du Bois was concerned with such abstract ontological questions. Yet his interest in the reality of races was also based on his desire to lay a firm foundation for black solidarity, to forge or construct a collective black identity that would enable "the Negro" to become a more unified force for social change. Du Bois was convinced that a collective black identity — based primarily on a shared history and culture, and only secondarily, if at all, on a common biological inheritance — is a necessary component of an emancipatory black solidarity. Much of black political thought has followed him in this. Indeed, among advocates of black solidarity, collective identity theory is often regarded as a truism.

I will argue, however, that blacks should reject this conception of pragmatic nationalism, because cultivating a collective black identity is unnecessary for forging effective bonds among blacks, would create (or exacerbate an already) undue constraint on individual freedom, and is likely, in any case, to be self-defeating. I will urge the disentanglement of the call for an emancipatory black political solidarity from the call for a collective black identity. A black solidarity based on the common experience of antiblack racism and the joint commitment to bringing it to an end can and should play an important role in the fight against racial injustice. But a form of black unity that emphasizes the need to positively affirm a "racial," ethnic, cultural, or national identity is a legacy of black political thought that must now be abandoned for the sake of the struggle against racial domination and black disadvantage.

Before proceeding further, two caveats are in order. First, my concern in this chapter, as throughout the book, is with that form of group solidarity that has as its primary goal the liberation of black people from the burdens of injustice. Thus, when I speak of black solidarity I refer to this type of political or emancipatory solidarity. But of course not everything that could rightly be called a form of black solidarity is, strictly speaking, directly bound up with politics. There are other collective goals or values that might be thought to serve as a basis for building black unity. For instance, there is a form of black solidarity that has as its end the nurturing of communal relations among blacks, a solidarity that is not treated as a means to some other external objective but as valuable in itself. Some may seek solidarity with other blacks simply because they see intrinsic value in the social interaction and the feelings of community that it brings. Nothing I say here should be taken to preclude or disparage this type of *social* solidarity. The form of emancipatory political solidarity that I would defend is perfectly compatible with it. Indeed, sometimes black social solidarity can foster black political solidarity and vice versa. Second, . . . some blacks might want to work together to cultivate and preserve black culture. They may also see this collective project as important quite apart from its relationship to the struggle against injustice. Provided such a project is not treated as a necessary component of black political solidarity, it is not threatened by the rejection of the collective identity theory. It may, however, suffer from other conceptual and normative difficulties. . . .

MODES OF BLACKNESS

Before submitting it to critical scrutiny, it will be useful to specify the collective identity theory in a bit more detail. This will require discussing a long-standing philosophical conundrum — the meaning of "blackness." According to collective identity theory, black people must embrace and preserve their distinctive black identity if a politically progressive solidarity is to flourish among them. Thus it is necessary to know what group of people the label *black* is supposed to be picking out here and what the nature of this "black identity" is that they must embrace and preserve. I want to approach these two questions by building upon a distinction . . . between "thin" and "thick" conceptions of black identity. Relying on this distinction, we will see, among other things, that the collective identity theorist urges the cultivation of thick blackness.

. . . On a thin conception of black identity, blackness is a vague and socially imposed category of "racial" difference that serves to distinguish groups on the basis of their members having certain visible, inherited physical characteristics and a particular biological ancestry. There are widely shared, nationally variable, intersubjective criteria for the classification of individuals into racial groupings. The prevailing (though not uncontested) thin conception of black identity in the United States, a conception that has its social heritage in chattel slavery and Jim Crow domination, holds that *blacks* include both (1) those persons who have certain easily identifiable, inherited physical traits (such as dark skin, tightly curled or "kinky" hair, a broad flat nose, and thick lips) and who are descendants of peoples from sub-Saharan Africa; and (2) those persons who, while not meeting or only ambiguously satisfying the somatic criteria, are descendants of Africans who are widely presumed to have had these physical characteristics. Thus, on a thin view, blacks are persons who (more or less) fit a particular phenotypic profile and certain genealogical criteria and/or who are generally believed to have biological ancestors who fit the relevant profile.

For those who meet these criteria, there is little room for choice about one's "racial" identity. One cannot simply refuse to be thinly black — as the African American folk saying goes, "the only thing I *have* to do is stay black and die." If, say, one were to assimilate completely to so-called white culture, one's thin blackness would nevertheless remain intact, for cultural conversion provides no escape. No amount of wealth, income, social status, or education can erase one's thin blackness, which of course is not to deny that these advantages might mitigate some of its negative consequences. One might alter her physical appearance so as not to "look black," or if she doesn't look black, she might then conceal her genealogy — as those who "pass" do — but in either case, she would still *be* black, in the thin sense, even if never found out.[7] It is an individual's thin blackness that makes her vulnerable to antiblack racism despite her law-abiding conduct and good character, her commitment to civic and personal responsibility, the extent of her assimilation to mainstream bourgeois or mass culture, her middle-class income and professional status, her educational success and intellectual achievement, or her nonblack physical appearance.[8] Thus the category of thin blackness, as an official "racial" classification, is all that would be needed for the administration of civil rights laws and the enforcement of antidiscrimination statutes.

A *thick* conception of black identity, which usually includes a thin component, always requires something more, or something other, than a common physical appearance and African ancestry.[9] Here the social category "black" has a narrower social meaning, with specific and sometimes quite austere criteria for who qualifies as black. Unlike thin blackness, thick blackness can be adopted, altered, or lost through individual action. Drawing on the history of black social thought, five familiar modes of thick blackness can be distinguished.

First, there is the *racialist* mode.[10] On this conception, black identity is based on the supposed presence of a special genotype in the biological makeup of all (fully) black people that does not exist among nonblacks. On this view, an underlying cluster of genes, transmitted through biological reproduction, accounts not only for the relatively superficial phenotypic traits that satisfy the criteria for thin blackness but also explains more socially significant traits, such as temperament, aesthetic sensibility, and certain innate talents. It is the possession of this genotype that defines membership in the black race. There is of course a racialist conception that holds that the black essence significantly determines the native intelligence, reproductive traits and tendencies, and moral character of those who possess it. However, blacks generally regard this strong form of biological determinism as false and insulting, and so I shall proceed on the assumption that the collective identity theorist, as an advocate for black freedom and equality, does not endorse it either.

Second, there is the *ethnic* conception of blackness, which treats black identity as a matter of shared ancestry and common cultural heritage. On such an account, there is no assumption that two people of the same ethnicity must necessarily share the same racial genotype. To be sure, as a result of their shared biological ancestry the members of an ethnic group may share certain physical traits — for instance, dark skin or the capacity to grow an Afro — and they may even value their possession of these traits as part of their ethnic identity. But these ethnic traits need not be viewed as indicating an underlying biological essence that explains black behavioral or psychological dispositions. Indeed, the ethnic conception of blackness is consistent with the complete rejection of racialism.

There are two dominant conceptions of black ethnicity among black Americans. One emphasizes the fact that black Americans are descendants of certain sub-Saharan African peoples, and it maintains that they share a culture that is traceable to the culture of those ancestors. The other stresses both the experiences of blacks with oppression in the New World and the rich culture they have created in the context of that oppression since being forcibly removed from Africa. On either version, though, one does not have a black ethnic identity, in the thick sense, unless one has the relevant lineage and embraces, to some significant degree, the corresponding cultural traits.

Third, there is blackness as *nationality*. "Nationality" has at least two meanings. It is often used to mean citizenship in a territorially sovereign state. A person would therefore have a black national identity if he or she were a citizen of a (predominantly) black nation-state (such as Ghana, Haiti, or Nigeria). But "nationality" also has a meaning that is quite similar to that of ethnicity. An ethnic identity can be considered a national one when the people in question think of themselves and their culture as derived from a particular geographical location, where the relevant territory is considered an ancestral "homeland" and a source of group pride. In the case of black Americans, this geographical region is, again, typically (some part of) sub-Saharan Africa. However, I will treat black nationality, in both its senses, as a variant of the ethnic conception, for the differences between ethnicity and nationality, as here defined, will not affect the argument to follow.

Fourth, there is the *cultural* conception of blackness. It rests on the claim that there is an identifiable ensemble of beliefs, values, conventions, traditions, and practices (that is, a culture or subculture) that is distinctively black. . . . Though this culture is thought to be the creative product of those who satisfy the criteria for thin blackness, the continued reproduction of the culture does not depend solely on the activities of these blacks, because nonblacks may participate in sustaining and developing it as well. On this model, thick black identity is tied neither to race nor to biological descent. Anyone could, in principle, embrace and cultivate a black cultural identity, in much the same way that anyone could, again in principle, become a practicing Christian.

Finally, there is the historically influential *kinship* mode of blackness. This view conceptualizes black identity on the model of the family — recall Du Bois's conception of race as a "vast family" or consider the common use of "brother" and "sister" to affectionately refer to fellow blacks.[11] Of course blacks are not a family, not even an extended one, in any ordinary sense. And earlier I criticized the invocation of this idiom insofar as it is meant to underwrite contemporary black political solidarity. . . . So what is it about familial relations that could plausibly constitute a basis or suggest an analogous foundation for a thick black identity? There seem to be three possibilities. First, one could understand blackness in terms of biological relatedness or genealogy — "blood ties." But then the kinship conception can be adequately expressed in terms of the racialist view, the ethnic view without the cultural requirement, or the thin conception of black identity.[12] Second, one could treat black identity as a matter not merely of biology but of the reproduction of a common way of life. But here the idea could be fully captured by the ethnic conception of blackness (perhaps with some additional racialist assumptions). Or third, like familial relations formed through marriage or adoption (whether formal or informal), blackness could be thought to rest on voluntary affiliation, custom, or (legal) convention. This form of blackness, however, would be simply a version of the cultural conception, a matter of *joining* the relevant group. The familiar kinship view is not, therefore, a conception of blackness distinct from the ones already considered, just a convenient (though often misleading) trope used to signify one or more of them. Now of course members of a family often share important experiences that contribute to their feelings of connectedness, trust, and loyalty. And in a similar way, black people have a common history of racial oppression and share a common vulnerability to racial discrimination. However, as I will argue below, these commonalities can form the basis for group solidarity without relying at all on a thick collective black identity.

There are several things to notice about thin and thick black identities and their interrelations. First, a person who satisfies the thin social criteria for being classified as black may nevertheless choose, with varying degrees of psychological difficulty and against various forms of social pressure, not to define his or her self-conception in terms of "blackness" at all. That is, such a person may choose not to subjectively identify with the label *black* or to conform to its associated behavioral norms.[13] Some nationalists contend that those so-called blacks who refuse to self-identify as black are denying something important about themselves, usually out of racially motivated self-hate. But a different, more respectable, reason for rejecting a black identity, one that does not necessarily involve self-deception or bad faith, is that one may believe that the designation *black,* with its typical connotations, is not an apt characterization of either who one is or who one would like to be. Or one might think that a black identity, while perhaps perfectly appropriate for some, is too limiting in one's own case. Yet another reason might be that one believes it to be an inherently invidious and repressive social distinction that should thus be repudiated on moral or political grounds. It should be clear, however, that the choice not to self-identify as black, whatever its rationale, does *not* dissolve the often constraining social realities that are created by the fact that *others* may insist on ascribing such an identity to one and consequently may treat one accordingly, whether for good or ill.

Second, black identity is not only multidimensional — involving the thin/thick distinction and often including various types of thickness — but the content of each mode is intensely contested. This circumstance makes possible the familiar but controversial discourse of black authenticity. It sometimes happens, for example, that an individual who satisfies the thin criteria for blackness possesses only a subset of the three modes of thick blackness under consideration — for instance, the thinly black person may (seem to) embody the racialist dimension without exemplifying the cultural dimension. There is intense disagreement among African Americans about whether anyone who identifies as black along one dimension should also, perhaps as a test of group loyalty or trustworthiness, identify as black along all the others — to be, in a sense, "fully" black. It is also possible for an individual to exemplify each of these modes but to different extents; for example, a person might have dark skin and love hip hop but have little fondness for or knowledge of African cultures and no interest at all in the blues. Recognition of this fact has also sometimes given rise to talk of "degrees" of blackness. Moreover, because the boundaries of each mode are both vague and fiercely disputed, there is often deep disagreement among African Americans about exactly when the label *black* applies in a given case, a circumstance that sometimes produces seemingly irresolvable questions about whether certain persons are "really" black.

Now given the thin/thick distinction, we can understand what it would mean to say of someone who is clearly black according to the thin criteria but who fails to satisfy the relevant criteria for thick blackness (whatever they turn out to be) that he or she isn't "really" black — a claim that is sometimes thought to be essentialist and paradoxical, if not completely incoherent.[14] Here is how we might make sense of that familiar charge without relying on racialism and within the context of thinking about the relevance of a collective identity for black solidarity. Though a person cannot choose whether to be black in the thin sense, she can, as we've said, decide what significance she will attach to her thin blackness. This includes deciding whether to commit herself to pragmatic black nationalism. But if she does so commit, either explicitly or implicitly, then she could rightly be criticized for failing to live up to obligations she has voluntarily accepted as a member of that solidarity group. For instance, she might be criticized for not being sufficiently faithful to the goal of racial equality.

OF COURSE WE ALL, WHETHER BLACK OR NOT, HAVE AN OBLIGATION TO RESIST RACIAL INJUSTICE.

Of course we all, whether black or not, have an obligation to resist racial injustice. The obligations of blacks in this regard are certainly no greater than those of nonblacks.[15] But blacks would arguably have an obligation to pursue their antiracism *through* black solidarity if in its absence racial justice could not be achieved. Such an obligation would follow from the principle that if one wills the end, one also wills the necessary means, provided of course these means are morally permissible. If such a position is sound, then blacks who fail to commit to black solidarity are open to criticism. And thus if collective identity theory is correct, any thinly black person who does not affirm thick blackness as part of his identity, whether he has made a commitment to black solidarity or not, would be vulnerable to criticism. In this book, I leave open the question of whether a commitment to black political solidarity is strictly obligatory, for answering it would require resolving the difficult empirical question of whether such solidarity is absolutely necessary to achieve racial justice. Instead I focus on what should and should not be required of those who *choose* to fight antiblack racism through black political solidarity, noting, as I have emphasized throughout, that such group efforts are a legitimate and constructive means to effect social change. This leaves open the possibility that it is permissible for blacks to work for racial justice through some other means, whether group-based or not.

Thus, if we think of authenticity, not as a matter of acting in conformity to or fully realizing one's inherent essence, but as being faithful to the practical principles that one has freely adopted, then black "inauthenticity" could be understood as not living up to one's solidaristic commitments (whatever these turn out to entail). If the goals of black solidarity cannot be achieved without a thick shared identity, as collective identity theory maintains, then a person who has signed on to this emancipatory project, but fails to identify as thickly black, may rightly be criticized for being "inauthentic" — fraudulent or fake. By using the thin/thick distinction, then, we can more clearly discuss the discourse of black authenticity and what role, if any, it has to play in black solidarity.

Finally, it is clear that among those who satisfy the criteria for thin blackness, many spontaneously embrace a thick black identity without treating this as a conscious strategy and without being concerned for how this would impact black politics. Even for those who do deliberately choose to cultivate a thick black identity, they do so for the most varied reasons, many doubtless having to do with resisting racial injustice but some having more to do with cultivating self-esteem, wanting a rich and relatively stable conception of who they are, or desiring a strong sense of community. It is moreover probably rare that blacks consciously embrace a thick black identity solely for political purposes. In fact, in order for such an identity to have a positive effect on black solidarity, it may be necessary for some to embrace it for reasons apart from its political value. The collective identity theorist could concede all this but nevertheless insist that were a sufficient number of blacks, for whatever reason, to reject or distance themselves from thick blackness, this would seriously hamper, if not undermine, emancipatory black solidarity, especially given the collective action problems that blacks currently face. Indeed, the familiar policing of social identities that takes place among black Americans — which often frustrates those who seek greater freedom in the construction of their social identities — arguably functions to strengthen the bonds of solidarity necessary for effective resistance against racial oppression. It is for this reason that the advocate of collective identity theory urges blacks to accept a thick black identity, even if some will do so for reasons having little to do with antiracist politics.

Given the above distinctions and caveats, the collective identity theory can now be given a more precise formulation: There are persons who meet the criteria for thin blackness who also have available to them a black identity that is "deeper," that is, *thicker,* than their thin blackness, and these persons must positively affirm and preserve their thick blackness if collectively they are to overcome their racial oppression through group solidarity. Thus, for the remainder of this chapter, when I speak of the alleged need for a common black identity, I will be using the term *black* in the thick sense, and when I speak of "black people" or simply "blacks," I will mean "black" in the thin sense, unless otherwise indicated.

IS A COLLECTIVE IDENTITY NECESSARY?

On a racialist conception of blackness, with its commitment to a more-than-skin-deep racial essence, embracing and preserving black identity would entail, at a minimum, fostering intraracial reproduction between blacks and, perhaps more importantly, discouraging interracial reproduction between blacks and nonblacks. This practice of racial endogamy is supposed to help keep the black essence intact and protect blacks from the dangers of racial hybridity. However, this view has a number of well-known problems. For one thing, it is now generally acknowledged that no "pure" biological races exist. Indeed, many biologists and anthropologists question the very idea of "racial" difference.[16] But even if there are (or once were) pure racial groups, those Americans who are black by the prevailing thin criteria certainly would not qualify as such a group (or even a proper subset thereof), because most (by some estimates as many as 80 percent) have some European or Native American ancestry.[17] Limiting black solidarity to only "pure(er)" blacks would exclude many victims of antiblack racism, contrary to the point of the enterprise. It would also run the risk of creating a "reverse" color prejudice — a preference for darker skin rather than the more familiar but no less problematic preference for lighter skin — among those who identify or are identified as black. Harold Cruse has rightly emphasized this danger: "In the United States, the American Negro group is too large and mixed with too many racial strains for the ideology of black-skin supremacy to function within the group. It can lead to the reasoning that 'I'm blacker than you, and so is my mama, so I'm purer than you and your mama. Therefore, I am also more nationalistic than you, and more politically trustworthy than you and your mama, in the interests of Black Power.' But inside America this is a pure fiction."[18]

A racialist justification for the principle of black endogamy would be no more plausible if the more inclusive "one-drop rule" were adopted.[19] Such a conception of black identity would hardly justify prohibiting "race mixing" in the name of black solidarity. If anything, it suggests that blacks should make it their policy to produce "mixed" progeny, because this would only increase their numbers and thereby perhaps their collective strength.[20]

Given the obvious problems with its racialist version, most advocates of the collective identity theory have adopted the more plausible position that blacks should embrace and preserve their distinctive *ethnic* or *cultural* identity. Recall that the main difference between these two conceptions of blackness is that the ethnic version requires black ancestry while the cultural version does not. But because collective identity theory calls on blacks alone to embrace thick blackness, those who do so will have the appropriate ancestry by default; that is, the thinly black who have a black cultural identity will thereby be ethnically black. Thus for present purposes, the ethnic and cultural versions of collective identity theory come to the same thing, and I will therefore treat them as one "ethnocultural" conception of blackness.

Yet perhaps this is too quick. The ethnic version of collective identity theory may urge blacks to *affirm* their black ancestry in some special way. Provided it is devoid of any racialist assumptions, there seem to be three important ways this affirmation could be carried out. First, one could honor the memory of one's black ancestors by embracing and passing on their cultural legacy. This view, however, is just a variant of the cultural version of collective identity theory. Second, it might be thought that because one's black bodily appearance is the result of one's black racial pedigree, one should honor one's black ancestors by being proud of that appearance and perhaps accentuating it. This might seem all the more important once one considers the fact that racists have often maintained that blacks are physically unattractive, even repulsive. Being proud of "looking black" can be expressed by, for example, wearing one's hair "natural" and prominently featuring one's other prototypical "black features" — big lips, noses, and hips. Yet doing so would be a matter of observing certain norms of conduct or fashion imperatives, and thus this account of the alleged independent significance of black ancestry is also a variant of the cultural version of collective identity theory, one that attaches positive meaning to outward bodily appearance. Third, one might affirm one's black ancestry by honoring the sacrifices that previous generations of blacks have made for the benefit of future generations. Setting aside the option of paying such homage through cultural identification and preservation . . . , I would argue that the best way to honor the heroic efforts of previous generations of blacks is to continue their struggle for racial justice and black liberation. This view, however, is consistent with a pragmatic nationalist conception of solidarity whether or not a thick identity is thought to be a necessary component, as either the thin or thick variant would urge blacks to work for racial equality and black freedom.

Now the ethnocultural version of collective identity theory requires blacks to identify with black culture, insisting that blacks view it as (at least partly) constitutive of who they are. Note, though, that if this ethnocultural identity is to have a positive impact on black solidarity — providing a basis for mutual identification, engendering a sense of special concern, reinforcing their commitment to common values or goals, and creating stronger bonds of loyalty and trust — then it cannot be a passive or merely internal acknowledgement of the value of black culture. Rather, blacks must actively perform or display their cultural identity for other blacks (and perhaps nonblacks) to see. They must demonstrate their knowledge and appreciation of black culture by, for example, participating in it, preserving or developing it, and exposing others to it, especially their children. However this is accomplished, there must be some means by which blacks publicly signify their allegiance to ethnocultural blackness.

There is a strong and weak version of the ethnocultural view. On the strong version, a collective black ethnocultural identity is a *necessary* component of black solidarity; that is, failing to cultivate such a collective identity would undermine the effort to build black unity. On the weak version, a collective identity is not claimed to be necessary for black solidarity, since blacks might get by without one, but it is thought that such an identity would strengthen the bonds of unity by giving blacks more in common than just their history of oppression and vulnerability to racism. However, I maintain that neither version is sound. Focusing on the strong version first, I will argue that there is little reason to suppose that blacks must share a collective identity in order for them to exhibit, as a group, each of the five characteristics of robust solidarity [identification with the group, a special concern for the group, shared values and goals, loyalty, and mutual trust].

At the outset, it might be thought that if blacks are to *identify* with each other, they must share an ethnocultural identity (or at least they must *believe* themselves to share such an identity). Yet there are clearly other, and more politically reliable, bases for identification. Blacks could, for example, identify with each other because they believe themselves to suffer the same form of racial subordination, to have experienced the degradation and insult of antiblack racism, or to share a common interest in ending racial inequality and racialized poverty. The mutual recognition of such commonality could produce, and arguably already has produced, empathetic understanding of a deeply felt kind between blacks. Thus, quite apart from their supposed common "racial" characteristics, ethnicity, or culture, each could come to see and feel that a significant part of himself or herself is to be found in the others, so that it becomes meaningful to speak about and act on the basis of what "we" experience, "we" believe, and "we" desire.

In fact, members of oppressed groups often experience a common fate because of a social identity that they only *appear* to share, as it is not unusual for the dominant group to construct an identity for those it oppresses (and for itself) in order to justify the ill treatment and deplorable condition of the subordinate group.[21] Such imputed or ascribed social identities are sometimes entirely fictional, maliciously fabricated by oppressor groups. Consider, for example, the old myth that blacks are the descendants of Ham and thus are forever cursed to toil for the benefit of whites. But even when the ascribed identity is based in something real, members of the subordinate group may still find it more pragmatic to build solidarity on the basis of their common oppression and their desire to overcome it, for some of them might not value or identify with the ascription.

The special concern that is typical of solidarity groups often has little to do with a shared culture. Sometimes this concern is rooted in mutual identification itself, which, as I have said, does not require a common ethnoracial identity and often extends across lines of cultural difference. Consider the mutual concern that binds together some women in their fight to end patriarchy and gender discrimination. Such women come from a variety of ethnocultural backgrounds and yet are able, imperfectly to be sure, to identify with one another's burdens, fears, and pain.[22] But special concern does not even require such identification — that sense of "we-ness." Mere empathy is often sufficient. Such empathy is rooted in the feeling that "had things gone a little differently, I could be in your unfortunate position" or perhaps "I have been in your position, and thus I can understand what you are going through and may be well situated to lead you out of it." This kind of imaginative self-projection into the shoes of another can move individuals to the kind of special concern that is characteristic of solidarity, a form of caring that is not limited to those with whom one shares an ethnocultural identity.

Black solidarity does require a shared set of values or goals. But this normative commitment need not involve embracing black culture as the basis of a collective identity. One does not have to possess a black cultural identity — indeed one does not have to be black at all — to appreciate the value of racial equality, to condemn racism, or to abhor poverty. Of course, values are components of culture, and black cultural forms are among those that sometimes express or embody principles of social equality, which can be a legitimate source of black pride. Nevertheless, the basis of blacks' commitment to equality should be that this is what justice demands, not simply that such values are embedded in black cultural traditions. Now, to the extent that black culture expresses or embodies principles of justice, this might provide those who embrace a black ethnocultural identity with a *further* reason to cling to these principles. But if, as is not unreasonable to suppose, there were components of black culture that did not extol the virtues of racial justice but instead emphasized black supremacy or, worse, black inferiority, then blacks would of course need to reject these components of their culture and embrace social equality instead, whatever its ethnocultural roots.

Loyalty, too, can exist between blacks with a wide range of ethnocultural identities. Consider, for example, the loyalty that sometimes exists between the diverse members of labor organizations. Despite differences in age, race, gender, sexual orientation, religion, region, ethnicity, occupation, and many other things, some workers have been intensely loyal to one another, especially when confronted with threatening or dire circumstances. Moreover, they often maintain this loyalty with little more in common than their shared vulnerability as workers and their will to improve their lot. There is no reason why blacks cannot do the same, for they, too, are vulnerable to a threatening social force — antiblack racism. And just as workers can unite in the name of economic justice without sharing a conception of the value of labor or a desire to preserve their "identity" as workers, blacks can unite in the name of racial justice without sharing a conception of the value of black culture or a desire to conserve ethnocultural blackness.

It is also clear that blacks can foster mutual trust among themselves without sharing a common ethnocultural identity. A common culture would undoubtedly create a type of familiarity and ease of intercourse that could contribute to the building of mutual trust. And, in general, it is easier to trust those with whom one shares a social identity. However, trust can be facilitated in other ways as well. One can, for instance, demonstrate one's trustworthiness by openly making efforts to advance the cause of black liberation. Working together with other blacks to accomplish limited, short-term goals — for example, collectively boycotting a known racist establishment or putting concerted pressure on political leaders to heed black concerns — can also foster trust. This makes the participants only minimally vulnerable to one another, while at the same time creating seeds of trust that can grow through future collective efforts. In any case, . . . using one's talents and resources to promote an antiracist agenda is surely a better sign of one's trustworthiness in the struggle against racial oppression than expressing one's solidarity with other blacks through exhibiting pride in one's black ethnocultural identity.

Against this view, Laurence Thomas has argued that there can be no "genuine cooperation" among blacks until they develop what he calls a "group narrative" — defined as "a set of stories which defines values and entirely positive goals, which specifies a set of fixed points of historical significance, and which defines a set of ennobling rituals to be regularly performed" — for, according to him, such a narrative provides the basis for mutual trust.[23] Moreover, Thomas claims that a people cannot genuinely cooperate with each other simply on account of their desire to defeat a common enemy, because the existence of such an enemy cannot form the basis of mutual trust.

I disagree. First, if the civil rights movement did not constitute genuine cooperation among blacks, then I'm not sure what would. Thomas may not count the movement as genuine cooperation, because it did not operate on the basis of what he regards as "group autonomy"; that is, blacks were not generally regarded as the foremost interpreters of their history and cultural traditions. But unless the goal is black collective self-realization *as a people* or *cultural* self-determination, then the narrative-free black solidarity that held together the civil rights movement should be sufficient for the post–civil rights era as well. Second, Thomas's account of group narrative would seem to suggest that blacks need something comparable to an ethnic religion if they are to form bonds of mutual trust. But I see no reason to believe that, because, as I argued above, there are less restrictive and more reliable routes to that end.

WOULD A SHARED IDENTITY HELP?

So far I have argued that a collective ethnocultural identity is not a necessary condition for the creation and maintenance of robust black solidarity. But, as I mentioned earlier, some collective identity theorists endorse a slightly weaker position. Instead of claiming that a collective black identity is necessary, they claim that, while perhaps not necessary for black solidarity, such an identity would create stronger bonds of unity. Prima facie, this seems quite plausible. Yet this weaker version is also unsound, as it is much more likely, at least presently, that the requirement of a common identity would weaken, if not undermine, black solidarity. There are a number of reasons for thinking this to be the case, some of which have already been reviewed.

For one thing, the push for a collective black identity would probably worsen existing intragroup antagonisms . . . and might even produce new ones. The types of internal conflict and competition among blacks that I have in mind would be likely to show up in several domains; here I mention four salient ones.

First, the imperative to conform to black culture would require individual blacks to possess the capacity to identify, if only implicitly and roughly, which elements are components of their culture and which are not. The problem is that there is no consensus on just what characteristics these are or on how they are to be distinguished from elements of white culture. In fact, what is culturally black is one of the most contested issues within the greater black population. Thus the question inevitably arises: Who has the authority and expertise to specify the content and define the parameters of black culture?

There is no black plural subject that can define itself culturally, only individual blacks who, perhaps working together or, more likely, struggling against one another, choose to cultivate this or that cultural identity — to take up various beliefs, values, practices, and modes of expression that they regard as "black." Even among those who most earnestly seek to maintain black cultural integrity (perhaps especially among them), there is often intense disagreement on just what elements constitute authentic black culture and which elements represent a bastardization or abandonment of the truly black. In light of this inevitable cultural friction, it is hard to imagine how an inclusive and democratic form of cultural autonomy could emerge. Should black Americans see themselves as essentially tied to Africa, and if so, what African culture(s) should be given privileged status? Can this shared identity include elements from European, Anglo-American, or Western culture and still be authentically black, or must it remain, in some sense, "pure"? How much, if any, of the cultural legacy of slavery — for example, southern Negro folk culture — should blacks embrace? Given historical migration patterns, should blacks from northeastern, West Coast, or midwestern urban centers or those with a southern sensibility be seen as more paradigmatically black? Should black identity be tied to a particular religious tradition, and if so, should this be Christianity, Islam, or some indigenous traditional African religion? Are there distinctively black norms of etiquette or black social values? Is there a black ethics, epistemology, or aesthetic? Are there uniquely black styles of dress, hairstyles, or modes of speech? While some of these are no doubt interesting questions, there is no reason to believe, and in fact every reason to doubt, that blacks can achieve anything like

THERE IS NO BLACK PLURAL SUBJECT THAT CAN DEFINE ITSELF CULTURALLY, ONLY INDIVIDUAL BLACKS.

consensus on such matters. And the endless and often acrimonious disagreements over what constitutes the real meaning of blackness can easily become so all-consuming that blacks lose sight of the *sources* of their anxiety about who they are — such as antiblack racism, social exclusion, persistent racial inequality, and severe urban poverty — which should be the primary focus of their collective political energies.

Second, class differences among blacks will complicate any attempt to sustain a common black ethnocultural identity.[24] First of all, it is not clear that the black professional elite, the black middle class, the black working class, and the black urban poor share more cultural traits with each other as a group than they do with nonblacks of their respective economic station and educational level. Moreover, for decades now there has been an ongoing contest between blacks of different socioeconomic status over who has the standing to define black identity; that is, over who is best positioned to have the authentic black experience and to represent "the race" in the public eye. It is also clear that the growing physical separation of the black middle class from the black urban poor — the former sometimes living in the suburbs and the latter mainly in central cities — is likely to exacerbate this conflict. Given the increasing intragroup stratification of blacks and the well-known correlation between class position and cultural identification, we can expect this internal struggle over the meaning of blackness to continue and perhaps intensify. Yet if blacks were to drop the requirement of a common ethnocultural identity, which as I have argued is not necessary for the success of pragmatic nationalism anyway, this might reduce the negative effects that class differences have on black solidarity. I say *reduce,* not eliminate, for class differences among blacks pose a real and serious threat to pragmatic nationalism. My main point here, though, is that insisting on a common black ethnocultural identity can only worsen this already challenging problem.

Third, the requirement of a common black identity would surely aggravate the antagonism between black men and black women over the meaning of blackness as it relates to gender and the family. Historically, the content of black identity, including gender roles and norms governing family structure, has largely been prescribed by black men — that is, when it wasn't being defined by other ideological and structural forces within the larger society — most often leading to greater sacrifice and less freedom for black women. Moreover, the attempt to maintain a "positive" and cohesive group identity will likely have the effect, as it often has, of subordinating or ignoring the legitimate concerns of black women. Because black women are situated at the intersection of racial and sexist oppression, they have experiences and interests that are peculiar to their complex social condition.

But many black men fail to see, acknowledge, or take seriously these gendered experiences and interests. When black women voice, let alone attempt to aggressively deal with, their political concerns — such as sexual assault, domestic violence, inequality within the domestic sphere, degrading representations of women in the media, sexual and reproductive freedom, gender discrimination and harassment on the job, access to positions of leadership and authority — this is often wrongly seen as a divisive attempt to embarrass black men or as an imprudent move that threatens to worsen the public image of blacks. Rather than listening to black women and thinking of their concerns as integral to the freedom struggle, many black men have tried to silence them and have remained complicit in the perpetuation of patriarchy, often in the name of "unity." Given the prevalence of sexist attitudes and behavior among black men (and even some women), and the continuing unequal power relations between the sexes, male-centered conceptions of blackness are likely to predominate, though not, of course, without resistance. Witness, for example, the mixed reaction among black Americans, and especially black women, to the nomination of Clarence Thomas to the Supreme Court or to the call for a Million Man March on Washington. Though black feminist perspectives are growing in influence, even among some black men, until greater strides are made against (black) male hegemony, a shared and progressive view of what it means to be black is unlikely to develop.[25]

And fourth, there is a generational divide that can only be made worse by insisting that all blacks share an ethnocultural identity. Many of those who came of age during the civil rights era have a different understanding of what it means to be culturally black than those who grew up after Jim Crow was abolished. This is most evident in the intense intergenerational disagreement over the value and positive or negative influence of hip-hop culture.[26] Some of this disagreement is political. Some blacks contest the political content of rap lyrics and the images seen in music videos and hip-hop-inspired advertisements. Many feel that hip-hop representations degrade women, glorify violence, belittle the value of education, make light of drug abuse, reproduce pathological behavior, and reinforce negative stereotypes about blacks. Those who identify with the culture believe that it affirms women's sexual freedom, accurately depicts the grim realities of ghetto life, critiques a failing school system, highlights the hypocrisy of the war on drugs, provides a soul-preserving source of comfort in impoverished conditions, and furnishes black youth with an identity that is not beholden to the politics of respectability. Such debate is healthy and, in any case, unavoidable if black political solidarity is to be sustained in the post–civil rights era. Some of the generational conflict surrounding hip-hop culture is simply aesthetic: blacks have sharply divergent views about whether the culture contains beauty and genuine artistry. Debate over such questions can also be healthy — and fun. Yet consensus on the aesthetic worth of hip hop is not on the horizon.

However, all blacks have a vested interest in racial equality, regardless of their cultural identification, class position, gender, or age (though the urgency with which one pursues racial justice will likely depend on, among other things, whether one also suffers under class subordination, male domination, both, or neither). And given their common classification as thinly black, blacks can identify with each other across these differences, for they share the susceptibility to antiblack racism that this classification makes possible. As Du Bois often emphasized, recognition of this common interest and mutual identification can lend much-needed motivational strength to a morally based, joint commitment to ending racism, especially when it is accompanied by the special concern, loyalty, and trust that are characteristic of solidarity. Moreover, as Orlando Patterson has argued, though both blacks and whites have an interest in overcoming racism and racial antagonism, blacks must play a larger part in bringing this about, not only because they stand to gain more from it, but because whites have much less to lose from the status quo.[27]

It is doubtful that blacks will ever come to consensus on the meaning of "blackness." Though the quest for collective self-definition may not be an entirely futile one, blacks cannot afford to rest their hopes for racial justice on its success. And they certainly should not postpone the collective effort to bring about such justice until they secure this elusive common identity. Blacks can and should agree, in the present, to collectively resist racial injustice, not only because it is the morally responsible thing to do but also because it negatively affects them all, albeit to varying degrees and in different ways. Mobilizing and coordinating this effort will be difficult enough without adding the unnecessary and divisive requirement that blacks embrace and preserve a distinctive ethnocultural identity.

One final reason to doubt that a common identity would contribute to black solidarity and thus to the elimination of racial injustice is that if blacks were to push for a thicker collective identity, this would strain their already delicate bonds of unity. For although most blacks believe in the struggle for racial equality and the value of black communal relations, they also value the freedom to choose their cultural affiliations and to decide on their own conception of human flourishing.[28] If there is group pressure to conform to some prototype of blackness, which collective identity theory would seem to require, this would likely create "core" and "fringe" subgroups, thus alienating those on the fringe and providing them with an incentive to defect from the collective effort. Those who only marginally fit the black prototype may feel that accepting a conventional black identity is unduly burdensome and consequently may only half-heartedly participate, if at all, in the black fight against racism, especially if by acting alone they can manage, perhaps through their superior class position, to escape some of the more severe forms of racial injustice. Thus, a prescribed black identity could have the unintended consequence of inviting blacks who do not identify with the prevailing conception of blackness to protest against black intolerance, to form alternative alliances, to become egoistic, or to be simply complacent.

At this point, a critic might ask: But what about the assimilated black who has rejected his black identity in favor of a white persona and cultural lifestyle; can other blacks in the collective struggle really trust him when he shows no loyalty to black culture? The answer depends on how he conducts himself in other contexts, especially those that bear directly on the struggle for racial justice. Granted, sometimes when a black person chooses not to identify with black culture, this is accompanied by a lack of identification with the struggle against racial injustice. And cultural identification has long been a test of group loyalty and critical consciousness among blacks, as many realize that some among them will inevitably attempt to escape the stigma of blackness by taking on cultural attributes associated with "respectable" whites. Though this sometimes happens, especially among elites, it would be unjustified to presume that every time a black person adopts a "white" cultural identity, he or she is effectively lost to the struggle.

Sometimes nonblack modes of self-presentation are taken up so that the person can gain entry into institutions and social environments dominated by whites. Sometimes such a person was not socialized into black culture to begin with, and so is not presenting a persona at all. Sometimes she may simply find an alternative cultural identity more intrinsically appealing. And sometimes she may be operating with an unconventional though no less valid interpretation of blackness. As I argued earlier, we cannot simply infer a lack of loyalty and trustworthiness from the fact that a person does not define herself in terms of black culture. Many so-called assimilated blacks have played important roles in the struggle against racism, and it would be unreasonable and insulting to doubt their commitment to black solidarity simply because they did not embrace what some define as an appropriate black ethnocultural identity. As Bernard Boxill wisely reminds us (though his black trope is now somewhat dated), "it is false and vicious to infer that every assimilated black, or every black-skinned writer or poet who does not display 'soul,' is imitative and servile."[29] In short, the cultural test of group loyalty often produces false negatives.

The fact is, a person can show loyalty to the cause of black liberation and thus her trustworthiness as an ally in black resistance to racism through ways other than cultural identification. She can, for example, work to help ensure that the next generation of blacks has a lighter burden of racial oppression than the present one. Such work and protest against racism and its legacy should be sufficient to eliminate any suspicion that might arise due to the person's lack of black cultural identification. If the person were truly self-hating and servile, then she would be unlikely to openly struggle and sacrifice to advance the interests of the very group whose abject status is the source of her self-contempt. Blacks should be careful not to reject potential allies on the ground that these persons do not share their ethnocultural identity. It is much more important, indeed critical, that race-conscious blacks seek solidarity with others who share their antiracist values, along with their commitment to eliminating racial oppression and the social problems it causes.

VIRTUES OF PLURALISM AND INCLUSIVENESS

One response to these considerations is to insist that there already exists an inclusive and widely shared black identity and thus that blacks need only preserve it. Yet this claim is simply implausible. Blacks, taken in the thin sense, are an ethnically and culturally diverse group. This diversity includes differences in physical appearance, language, customs, religion, political outlook, moral values, aesthetic tastes, cuisine, fashion, traditions, national origin, and more.[30] The cultural and ethnic diversity of blacks should be especially obvious once we consider the various cultural traits embraced by recent black immigrants from Africa, Latin America, Europe, and the Caribbean. These other communities of African descent are themselves subject to antiblack prejudice in the United States and beyond. One could of course mean to include under "black identity" *all* of the cultural traits that are embraced and reproduced by blacks. This, however, would have the effect of rendering collective identity theory vacuous, because blacks cannot help taking on cultural traits of one sort or another, and therefore the imperative to "conserve blackness" would have no prescriptive force—it would not require blacks to do anything but literally "be themselves." If we view everything that black people do as "black," then blackness becomes a matter of ontology, sinking us right back into the quicksand of essentialism from which we should be actively trying to escape.

Alternatively, one might argue that it is possible to construct a pluralistic and nuanced conception of black identity, rather than a monolithic and unduly restrictive one. Again, this may be true. Yet no matter where one sets the boundaries of thick blackness, if it is meaningful enough to have normative, and not merely descriptive, force, some blacks will be left out or forced into submission. The collective identity theorist might not be troubled by this result, because he may insist that not all blacks are needed in the struggle against antiblack racism and some, if not most, will be indifferent to the fight for racial justice anyway. However, . . . we cannot determine on the basis of cultural identification alone who will or won't be willing to make such a solidaristic commitment. Thus it is more reasonable to be as inclusive as is consistent with the basic goals of such unity, as there is power in numbers. Indeed, it may turn out that the least "black" among us are among those most dedicated to the cause of racial justice, despite the widespread assumption to the contrary.[31] In any case, insisting on a specific conception of black identity, regardless of how pluralistic it is taken to be, is still vulnerable to the criticisms raised earlier against an essentialist discourse of black authenticity: blacks will find themselves in an unnecessary, contentious, distracting, and interminable debate over what counts as "black" and who will decide.

ONE MIGHT ARGUE THAT IT IS POSSIBLE TO CONSTRUCT A PLURALISTIC AND NUANCED CONCEPTION OF BLACK IDENTITY, RATHER THAN A MONOLITHIC AND UNDULY RESTRICTIVE ONE.

But let us suppose that cultivating a collective black identity were a realistic possibility for the near future. It might nevertheless be too dangerous to try to bring this about, for it is possible to go too far in creating group cohesiveness. The attempt to forge a collective black identity could unwittingly produce a groupthink mentality. The symptoms of groupthink include such things as collective efforts to rationalize the group's subordinate condition; social pressure on fellow members who reject in-group or out-group stereotypes; self-censorship of deviations from some presumed group consensus; and allegiance to ideologues who screen the group from information that might threaten its self-image. Striving to create a shared black identity could lead to this uncritical and often unconscious drive for unanimity and positive self-conception. This would have disastrous consequences for the cause of black liberation, by engendering defective collective decision-making, such as assuming that traditional solutions to black oppression must be correct; failing to reconsider initially discarded strategies or programs of action; dismissing criticisms of conventional narratives and goals; and ignoring social-scientific analyses that diverge from black common sense. Blacks must avoid these pitfalls, but unfortunately they have not always done so.[32]

One such pitfall deserves further comment. Many conceptions of black identity include, if only implicitly, an account of the nature of black oppression. In the black nationalist tradition, these narratives generally emphasize the pervasiveness of white supremacy. The legacy of slavery and current racism are treated as the primary obstacles to black flourishing, and shared narratives about racial oppression are reproduced as a part of black cultural heritage. To the extent that this cultural inheritance is embraced as an essential core of black identity itself, it could prove to be a self-imposed obstacle to black emancipation. Thus, for example, when a person accepts a particular analysis of the black condition *as a black person* — as a feature of who he *is* and not just what he believes — this can lead him to be stubbornly resistant to changing his view of the nature and causes of the black condition in the face of overwhelming evidence. To change his mind about such fundamental social matters would be to him (though he may not consciously recognize it as such) not just a shift in opinion based on evidence but a tragic loss of self-identity, which few are willing to consider, let alone seriously countenance. Now when a whole community accepts a particular analysis of their collective condition as a necessary component of who they are *as a people,* this can make it extremely difficult for them to reevaluate their shared standing or to recognize differences in standing between the various subgroups within the community. The point here is that an uncritical attachment to a particular conception of blackness where this includes a common narrative about the social status and material conditions of the group can undermine the group's ability to arrive at an objective assessment of their shared problems and possible solutions. Given the need to distinguish between the impact on blacks' life prospects of current racism, historical racism, and nonracial social dynamics, it is essential that blacks not embrace a collective ethnocultural identity that collapses these distinctions or misconstrues their current significance.

What must be recognized here is that "blackness," as a modality or child of "race," is an ideological construct that African-descended peoples have inherited as a legacy of the transatlantic slave trade. Like many such constructs, including "nation" and "ethnicity," it is extremely malleable and capacious, and so blacks have naturally fought — sometimes with their oppressors, sometimes with each other—to remold it to suit their own purposes. Consequently, blackness can be, and has been, given multiple meanings, which vary with the interpreters, their motives for using the notion, and the social circumstances. Thus, despite the obvious practical significance of the label *black,* agreement on its positive meaning must be limited to the claim that there are a number of loosely associated and variously interpreted *black identities.* The one link that often does exist between these multiple identities, however, is that many of them have been formed in an antiblack social environment, and each, in its own way, will likely bear the marks of race-based ill treatment. Yet the aim of black political solidarity should not be to discover the essential group-affirming core of all modalities of blackness, but to release all of these identities from racial stigma.

Paul Gilroy has advocated a conception of black identity based on a set of loosely related narratives that, according to him, have been produced in response to the experience of transatlantic black oppression. The multiple and globally dispersed practices that reproduce these stories can be viewed as constituting a sort of "tradition," which all blacks may identify with and participate in. Such an account, if adequate, could allow us to speak intelligibly and somewhat concretely of "black identities." However, such a conception of black identity would be of little help to the collective identity theorist, for at least two reasons. First, as Gilroy emphasizes, the Black Atlantic tradition is not rooted in a particular culture or ethnic heritage but is transnational, syncretic, unstable, and always mutating. Part of this lack of "purity" has to do with the inclusion of many European, Anglo-American, and Latin American cultural forms and modes of expression. Thus, although blacks can identify with and lay claim to the Black Atlantic tradition, so can many whites. Second, the Black Atlantic tradition, as Gilroy conceives of it, is nonessentialist. Therefore, there is nothing built into the content or structure of the tradition that determines who can or should identify with it or how any individual should relate to it. A black person who does not identify with it is not thereby inauthentic, and one may appreciate its depth, value, and beauty without necessarily defining one's identity in terms of it. Given the abstract and inclusive nature of the Black Atlantic tradition, there is room for many black identities and no basis for insisting on any one of them as the "real" social identity of blacks.

Although I find the idea of a Black Atlantic cultural tradition appealing, for the reasons given above I would stop short of including it as a necessary component of contemporary black American political engagement. I would urge blacks living in the United States, and by extension those in other parts of the world, to identify with each other on the basis of their experience of racial oppression and commitment to collectively resist it. From the standpoint of black political solidarity, each should be allowed to interpret "blackness" however he or she sees fit, provided the interpretation does not advocate anything immoral and is consistent with the collective struggle for racial justice.[33] In saying this, I am not suggesting, as some have, that individual blacks should give up their various black identities in favor of an American, a cosmopolitan, or simply a "human" identity. Though there should be more mindfulness of the dangers and limitations of "blackness," I see no reason to object to blacks identifying with what they regard as their ethnocultural heritage. What I resist is the tendency to think that blacks must *share* a distinctive black identity if they are to be a unified force against racial injustice.

IS THIN BLACKNESS TOO THIN?

The advocate of collective identity theory might object as follows: Surely a black solidarity that focuses on resisting racial oppression must at least require that blacks identify with their *thin* blackness, for without such a common identity they will lack a stable foundation for mutual identification. Yet this objection fails. Consider the following variant of the well-worn but still instructive witch analogy.[34] Historically, for example, in medieval Europe and in Salem, Massachusetts, in the late seventeenth century, the trial and subsequent punishment of "witches" was ostensibly based on the claim that the accused had communed with the forces of the underworld. Though this accusation was certainly unfounded, these so-called witches nevertheless suffered a common fate. Now let us suppose for a moment that some of the accused really did practice witchcraft — that they engaged in sorcery, sought to conspire with the Devil, surreptitiously corrupted good Christians, and so on. Suppose further that, at various points, some of their number, for whatever reason, ceased practicing witchcraft and no longer self-identified as "witches." And finally, suppose that at least some of these practitioners of witchcraft believed that there were some among them who were *frauds,* not "real" witches, according to some commonly accepted criteria for being a witch or according to some more controversial and strict criteria. Despite all this, it seems clear that all of these erstwhile, quasi, pseudo-, and would-be witches could have shared bonds of solidarity with each other, not based on their common affirmation of a "witch identity" (for *ex hypothesi* the existence of a *shared* identity was in doubt), but based on their common persecution. For purposes of collective resistance to unjust persecution, they simply could have put aside the question of who was and who was not an authentic witch and focused their attention and energy on overcoming their common plight.

Black solidarity could have, and should have, an analogous foundation. Just as a common belief in the value of "black magic" is not a necessary foundation for "witch" resistance to their unjust persecution, a shared belief in the value of a common "black identity" is not needed to ground "black" solidarity against racial domination. The basis of blacks' group identification is not their attachment to their thin black identity but rather their shared experience with antiblack racism and their mutual commitment to ending it. Blacks need only recognize that part of the reason they often suffer mistreatment is that others see them as thickly black (their thin blackness being merely a "sign" of a deeper difference), and this racialized perception leads their oppressors to devalue them.[35] Identification between members of the racially oppressed group can therefore be based on their common recognition of this sad and disturbing fact. It would not undermine black solidarity if the physical and genealogical characteristics that constitute their thin blackness, apart from the unjust treatment that they engender, were to have no intrinsic significance for the members of the united oppressed group. Once a racially just social order is achieved, thin blackness may in fact lose all social and political significance.

Some might suggest that even this stripped-down common-oppression theory commits itself to a version of the collective identity view, for despite its pretensions to have transcended identity politics, it nevertheless endorses the cultivation of a thick collective black identity: it urges blacks to see themselves as racially oppressed. This shared identity is based not on race, ethnicity, nationality, or culture, but on the common experience of antiblack racism. Thus, those blacks who are united by ties of solidarity will still have a collective identity, and one that is not reducible to their political principles. This identity might aptly be described as "victims of antiblack racial oppression."

One response to this objection is to simply concede it; that is, we could accept that the one "thick" collective black identity that continues to be a realistic possibility is constituted by victim status in an antiblack social world. This approach to the meaning of blackness is not self-defeating or divisive like the other conceptions considered, because the vast majority of blacks rightly accept that antiblack racism continues to exist (though of course they have no wish to preserve the conditions under which an oppression-based identity would be advantageous or desirable).[36] Such an identity would not gratuitously add to individual unfreedom, for it is nonracialist and perfectly consistent with tolerance for ethnocultural diversity. Moreover, blacks should not have to go to great lengths to cultivate this identity, for regrettably there is more than enough antiblack sentiment and discrimination still around to sustain it — though, admittedly, it may be necessary to convince some people of the depth of the problem.[37] But this view of "blackness" would not give the collective identity theorist all that he or she wants, for the search for a collective black identity has generally been a struggle to discover or construct a *positive* social identity, one that could be a basis for pride, dignity, and collective self-affirmation. A common identity based on nothing more than the shared experience of racism cannot provide such an identity, for this would, perversely, treat victimhood as something to be proud of — which is not, of course, to say that it is something blacks ought to be ashamed of. . . .

Some might argue that a collective identity constituted by a shared oppressed condition can be seen to be positive and group-affirming if viewed from a black theological perspective, say, Christian or Muslim.[38] On this view, God embraces blacks *because* they are oppressed; and he is concerned to help them liberate themselves from their evil oppressors.

However, the positive dimension of this kind of blackness is surely derived, not from the oppression itself, but from the virtue associated with the steadfast pursuit of truth and justice *despite* being oppressed and/or from the promise that, through faith and collective struggle, blacks will ultimately be delivered from that oppression. If God did not love what is good and hate what is evil, or if he could help liberate blacks from undeserved domination but did not, then they could hardly take just pride in being "chosen" by him. Yet even if black theology could find in black oppression something to be proud of, a theological account of this sort will not resonate with all blacks, because not all are religious. At best, then, "victims of antiblack racial oppression" could be a positive identity for some. Thus, blacks clearly need a nonsectarian basis for their political solidarity.

IS PRAGMATIC BLACK SOLIDARITY (STILL) TOO BLACK?

Some will surely wonder why *black* solidarity is needed at all, especially because racism is not unique to the experience of blacks and, as has been emphasized throughout this book, solidarity between antiracist blacks and nonblacks is both possible and necessary. Should we not just reject black solidarity and embrace interracial, antiracist solidarity instead? Anthony Appiah, for example, raises this kind of objection against Du Bois's conception of racial solidarity.[39]

Although blacks should surely work with antiracist nonblacks against racism and other forms of social injustice, there is no principled reason why blacks must give up their solidaristic commitment to each other to do so. The two forms of solidarity are not mutually exclusive. There is room for nested and overlapping forms of antiracist solidarity, just as there is space for more or less exclusive and inclusive collective struggles at other sites of oppression, such as class, gender, culture, and sexuality. Broader forms of antiracist solidarity and coalition building should be cultivated, but there are several reasons why it is prudent for blacks to hold on to their narrower commitment to each other as well, at least for the time being.

First, antiblack racial injustice — like anti-Semitism, anti-Asian racism, the oppression of American Indians, the denial of equal citizenship to Latino groups, and the more recent profiling and harassment of Arab Americans — has features that make it unique as a form of racial subjection in the United States. The enslavement and brutalization of Africans in the New World, the subsequent exclusion of blacks from the mainstream of American civic, economic, and social life, and the peculiar content of antiblack racist ideology, with its images of blacks as lazy, stupid, incompetent, hypersexual, and disposed to gratuitous acts of violence, have combined to give antiblack race prejudice a distinctive character among American forms of racism. There are also severe social problems — joblessness, alarmingly high rates of incarceration, concentrated poverty, failing schools, a violent drug trade — that plague some black communities and that are partly the result of past and present racial discrimination against black people in particular. Although a joint commitment to fighting racial injustice in all its forms can help create interracial solidarity, it is often the shared experience of *specific* forms of racial injustice that creates the strongest motivation to act and the most enduring bonds among victims of racism.[40] This additional motivational impetus is needed to overcome the moral complacency and conservative resistance that inhibit political reform in the racial arena, a political momentum that cannot be achieved by mere abstract calls for greater social justice.[41]

Second, the black experience with racism in America makes it difficult for many blacks to fully trust nonblacks when it comes to fighting against racism, for they have too often been victimized by the racism of nonblacks, even by some who are racially oppressed themselves. What is more, other ethnoracial minority groups have solidaristic commitments of their own, which have sometimes been used to exploit the economic and political disadvantages of African Americans as a group. And whites in power sometimes favor these other groups over blacks, creating resentment and competition between minority groups. In light of this, it should be clear that many black Americans justifiably feel the need to protect themselves against the dangers that may result from competing group loyalties and group interests. A unilateral laying down of solidaristic arms, as it were, would needlessly increase black vulnerability to marginalization. Thus, on pragmatic grounds, blacks should maintain their political solidarity with each other while simultaneously cultivating greater bonds of unity with progressive members of other racial groups.

Finally, the common experience of antiblack racism has for centuries provided a firm and well-recognized basis for mutual identification and special concern among blacks. This shared experience partially accounts for the bonds that exist today, for blacks understand one another's burdens and empathize with each other on this basis. In light of this common understanding and identification, the legacy of collective struggle to remove this burden is a cherished inheritance for many black Americans. As we seek to establish stronger interracial forms of solidarity in our fight against social injustice, we should not underestimate or devalue the social bond among blacks. Historically, it has been a great source of strength and hope, and a highly effective means for mobilizing the population to work for social justice. I believe that it can, and should, continue to do so. In holding out this hope, however, I am not suggesting that black collective action, founded on pragmatic black solidarity, would be sufficient to eliminate racism. Indeed, it might be that nothing blacks do, even with the help of members from other ethnoracial groups, will end antiblack racism.[42] Perhaps the most that can be realistically hoped for, at least in the foreseeable future, is that black solidarity affords blacks a limited form of collective self-defense against some of the more burdensome kinds of racial injustice. But this, I should think, would be sufficient to make the effort worthwhile.

NOTES

[1] See, for example, Kwame Anthony Appiah, "Racisms," in *Anatomy of Racism,* ed. David Theo Goldberg (Minneapolis: University of Minnesota Press, 1990); Randall Kennedy, "My Race Problem — And Ours," *Atlantic Monthly* (May 1997): 55–66; and Paul Gilroy, *Against Race: Imagining Political Culture beyond the Color Line* (Cambridge, Mass.: Harvard University Press, 2000). [All notes are Shelby's.]

[2] See Martin R. Delany, "The Political Destiny of the Colored Race," in *The Ideological Origins of Black Nationalism,* ed. Sterling Stuckey (Boston: Beacon Press, 1972); Edward W. Blyden, "The Call of Providence to the Descendants of Africa in America," in *Negro Social and Political Thought,* ed. Howard Brotz (New York: Basic Books, 1966), pp. 112–26; Alexander Crummell, "The Relations and Duties of Free Colored Men in America to Africa," in Brotz, *Negro Social and Political Thought,* pp. 171–80; W. E. B. Du Bois, "The Conservation of Races," in Brotz, *Negro Social and Political Thought,* pp. 483–92; Marcus Garvey, *The Philosophy and Opinions of Marcus Garvey: Or, Africa for the Africans,* ed. Amy Jacques Garvey (Dover, Mass.: Majority Press, 1986); Alain Locke, "The New Negro," in *The New Negro,* ed. Alain Locke (New York: Atheneum, 1969), pp. 3–16; Malcolm X, "Black Man's History," in *The End of White World Supremacy: Four Speeches by Malcolm X,* ed. Imam Benjamin Karim (New York: Arcade, 1971), pp. 23–66; Amiri Baraka, "The Legacy of Malcolm X, and the Coming of the Black Nation," in *The LeRoi Jones/Amiri Baraka Reader,* ed. William J. Harris (New York: Thunder's Mouth Press, 1991), pp. 161–69; Harold Cruse, *The Crisis of the Negro Intellectual* (New York: Quill, 1984); Kwame Ture (Stokely Carmichael) and Charles V. Hamilton, *Black Power: The Politics of Liberation in America* (New York: Vintage, 1992); Cornel West, *Prophesy Deliverance! An Afro-American Revolutionary Christianity* (Philadelphia: Westminster Press, 1982); Maulana Karenga, "Society, Culture, and the Problem of Self-Consciousness: A Kawaida Analysis," in *Philosophy Born of Struggle: Anthology of Afro-American Philosophy from 1917,* ed. Leonard Harris (Dubuque, Iowa: Kendall/Hunt, 1983), pp. 212–28; Molefi Kete Asante, *The Afrocentric Idea* (Philadelphia: Temple University Press, 1998); and Lucius T. Outlaw Jr., *On Race and Philosophy* (New York: Routledge, 1996), chap. 6. Though not all of these thinkers explicitly defend the collective identity theory, each at least implicitly relies upon it. Moreover, it is arguable that some of them, such as Delany and Du Bois, came to deemphasize the importance of a collective black identity to black solidarity, which is why I say that the view can be found in their "writings and speeches."

[3] Du Bois, "Conservation of Races," p. 489; emphasis added.

[4] Ibid., p. 491; emphasis added.

[5] Ibid., p. 485; emphasis added.

[6] See, for example, Kwame Anthony Appiah, *In My Father's House: Africa in the Philosophy of Culture* (New York: Oxford University Press, 1992), pp. 28–46; Frank M. Kirkland, "Modernity and Intellectual Life in Black," *Philosophical Forum* 24 (1992–1993): 136–65; Lucius Outlaw, "On W. E. B. Du Bois's 'The Conservation of Races,'" in *Overcoming Racism and Sexism,* ed. Linda A. Bell and David Blumenfeld (Lanham, Md.: Rowman and Littlefield, 1995), pp. 79–102; Robert Gooding-Williams, "Outlaw, Appiah, and Du Bois's 'The Conservation of Races,'" in *W. E. B. Du Bois on Race and Culture,* ed. Bernard W. Bell, Emily R. Grosholz, and James B. Stewert (New York: Routledge, 1996), pp. 39–56; Bernard R. Boxill, "Du Bois on Cultural Pluralism," in Bell et al., *Du Bois on Race and Culture,* pp. 61–65; Tommy L. Lott, *The Invention of Race: Black Culture and the Politics of Representation* (Malden, Mass.: Blackwell, 1999), pp. 47–66; Paul C. Taylor, "Appiah's Uncompleted Argument: W. E. B. Du Bois and the Reality of Race," *Social Theory and Practice* 26 (2000): 103–28; Patrick Goodin, "Du Bois and Appiah: The Politics of Race and Racial Identity," in *The Quest for Community and Identity: Critical Essays in Africana Social Philosophy,* ed. Robert E. Birt (Lanham, Md.: Rowman and Littlefield, 2002), pp. 73–83.

[7] For an illuminating set of personal and philosophical reflections on racial passing in America, see Adrian Piper, "Passing for White, Passing for Black," *Transition* 58 (1992): 4–32.

[8] For a similar conception of blackness, which the above account attempts to build upon, see Bernard R. Boxill, *Blacks and Social Justice,* rev. ed. (Lanham, Md.: Rowman and Littlefield, 1992), p. 178.

[9] Those thick conceptions that require something *other,* rather than just something *more,* than the thin criteria for blackness will entail, if only implicitly, a critique and rejection of the thin criteria.

[10] Appiah, "Racisms," pp. 4–5.

[11] For attempts to make a strong analogy between families and races, see Anna Stubblefield, "Races as Families," *Journal of Social Philosophy* 32 (Spring 2001): 99–112; and Yalonda Howze and David Weberman, "On Racial Kinship," *Social Theory and Practice* 27 (2001): 419–36.

[12] For an interpretive reconstruction of the discourse of black kinship that fits the model of thin blackness, see Lionel K. McPherson and Tommie Shelby, "Blackness and Blood: Interpreting African American Identity," *Philosophy and Public Affairs* 32 (2004): 171–92.

[13] For illuminating discussions of the relationship between third-person racial ascription and first-person racial self-identification, see Anna Stubblefield, "Racial Identity and Non-Essentialism about Race," *Social Theory and Practice* 21 (1995): 341–68; K. Anthony Appiah,

"Race, Culture, Identity: Misunderstood Connections," in K. Anthony Appiah and Amy Gutmann, *Color Conscious: The Political Morality of Race* (Princeton: Princeton University Press, 1996), pp. 76–80; and Robert Gooding-Williams, "Race, Multiculturalism and Democracy," *Constellations* 5 (1998): 18–41.

[14] For someone who doubts "the value of the distinction between being authentically black and being inauthentically black," see Gooding-Williams, "Race, Multiculturalism and Democracy," p. 25. Also see Anthony Appiah, "'But Would That Still Be Me?' Notes on Gender, 'Race,' and Ethnicity, as Sources of 'Identity,'" *Journal of Philosophy* 87 (1990): 493–99. For useful discussions of the different claims of black authenticity, see K. Anthony Appiah, "Identity, Authenticity, and Survival: Multicultural Societies and Social Reproduction," in *Multiculturalism: Examining the Politics of Recognition,* ed. Amy Gutmann (Princeton: Princeton University Press, 1994), pp. 149–63; Lani Guinier, *The Tyranny of the Majority: Fundamental Fairness in Representative Democracy* (New York: Free Press, 1994), pp. 54–58; and Naomi Zack, *Thinking about Race* (Belmont, Calif.: Wadsworth, 1998), pp. 70–72.

[15] For an interesting recent discussion of the obligations of subordinate groups in the fight against injustice, see Amy Gutmann, *Identity and Democracy* (Princeton: Princeton University Press, 2003), pp. 138–44.

[16] See the statement on "race" by the American Anthropological Association: www.aaanet.org/stmts/racepp.htm (accessed 1/10/05); and the American Association of Physical Anthropologists, "Statement on Biological Aspects of Race," *American Journal of Physical Anthropology* 101 (1996): 569–70.

[17] Naomi Zack, *Race and Mixed Race* (Philadelphia: Temple University Press, 1993), p. 75.

[18] Cruse, *Crisis of the Negro Intellectual,* p. 556.

[19] Gunnar Myrdal, *An American Dilemma: The Negro Problem and Modern Democracy* (New York: Harper and Row, 1944), pp. 113–17; and F. James Davis, *Who Is Black? One Nation's Definition* (University Park: Pennsylvania State University Press, 1991).

[20] For instructive discussions of the black "no race-mixing" policy, see Charles W. Mills, "Do Black Men Have a Moral Duty to Marry Black Women?" *Journal of Social Philosophy,* 25th Anniversary Special Issue (1994): 131–53; and Anita L. Allen, *Why Privacy Isn't Everything: Feminist Reflections on Personal Accountability* (Lanham, Md.: Rowman and Littlefield, 2003), pp. 97–107.

[21] Robert Miles, *Racism* (London: Routledge, 1989), pp. 11–40.

[22] See bell hooks, *Feminist Theory: From Margin to Center,* 2nd ed. (Cambridge, Mass.: South End Press, 1984); and Elizabeth V. Spelman, *Inessential Woman: Problems of Exclusion in Feminist Thought* (Boston: Beacon Press, 1988).

[23] See Laurence Mordekhai Thomas, "Group Autonomy and Narrative Identity," in *Color, Class, Identity: The New Politics of Race,* ed. John Arthur and Amy Shapiro (Boulder: Westview Press, 1996), pp. 182–83.

[24] For important discussions of this issue, see E. Franklin Frazier, *Black Bourgeoisie* (New York: Free Press, 1957); William Julius Wilson, *The Declining Significance of Race* (Chicago: University of Chicago Press, 1978); Manning Marable, *How Capitalism Underdeveloped Black America* (Boston: South End Press, 1983), chap. 5; Michael C. Dawson, *Behind the Mule: Race and Class in African-American Politics* (Princeton: Princeton University Press, 1994); Kevin K. Gaines, *Uplifting the Race: Black Leadership, Politics, and Culture in the Twentieth Century* (Chapel Hill: University of North Carolina Press, 1996); and Adolph Reed Jr., *Stirrings in the Jug: Black Politics in the Post-Segregation Era* (Minneapolis: University of Minnesota Press, 1999).

[25] For important discussions of the relationship between black identity, gender, and politics, see Michele Wallace, *Black Macho and the Myth of the Superwoman* (New York: Dial, 1978); Angela Y. Davis, *Women, Race, and Class* (New York: Random House, 1981); bell hooks, *Ain't I a Woman: Black Women and Feminism* (Boston: South End Press, 1981); Gloria T. Hull, Patricia Bell-Scott, and Barbara Smith, eds., *All the Women Are White, All the Men Are Black, but Some of Us Are Brave: Black Women's Studies* (Old Westbury, N.Y.: Feminist Press, 1982); Paula Giddings, *When and Where I Enter: The Impact of Black Women on Race and Sex in America* (New York: Morrow, 1984); Patricia Hill Collins, *Black Feminist Thought: Knowledge, Consciousness, and the Politics of Empowerment* (New York: Routledge, 1990); Cornel West, *Race Matters* (New York: Vintage, 1994), chap. 2; Evelyn Brooks Higginbotham, *Righteous Discontent: The Women's Movement in the Black Baptist Church, 1880–1920* (Cambridge, Mass.: Harvard University Press, 1993); Hazel V. Carby, *Race Men* (Cambridge, Mass.: Harvard University Press, 1998); Joy James and T. Denean Sharpley-Whiting, eds., *The Black Feminist Reader* (Malden, Mass.: Blackwell, 2000); and E. Frances White, *Dark Continent of Our Bodies; Black Feminism and the Politics of Respectability* (Philadelphia: Temple University Press, 2001).

[26] See, for example, Derrick Darby and Tommie Shelby, eds., *Hip Hop and Philosophy: Rhyme 2 Reason* (Chicago: Open Court, 2005); Imani Perry, *Prophets of the Hood: Politics and Poetics in Hip Hop* (Durham: Duke University Press, 2004); Cornel West, *Democracy Matters: Winning the Fight against Imperialism* (New York: Penguin, 2004), chap. 6; Todd Boyd, *The New H.N.I.C.: The Death of Civil Rights and the Reign of Hip Hop* (New York: New York University Press, 2003); Bakari Kitwana, *The Hip Hop Generation: Young Blacks and the Crisis in African American Culture* (New York: Basic Books, 2002); S. Craig Watkins, "'Black Is Back, and It's Bound to Sell!': Nationalist Desire and the

Production of Black Popular Culture," in *Is It Nation Time? Contemporary Essays on Black Power and Black Nationalism,* ed. Eddie S. Glaude Jr. (Chicago: University of Chicago Press, 2002), pp. 189–214; Joan Morgan, *When Chickenheads Come Home to Roost: A Hip-Hop Feminist Breaks It Down* (New York: Touchstone, 2000); William Eric Perkins, ed., *Droppin' Science: Critical Essays on Rap Music and Hip Hop Culture* (Philadelphia: Temple University Press, 1996); and Tricia Rose, *Black Noise: Rap Music and Black Culture in Contemporary America* (Hanover, N.H.: University Press of New England, 1994).

[27] Orlando Patterson, *The Ordeal of Integration: Progress and Resentment in America's "Racial" Crisis* (Washington, D.C.: Civitas, 1997), p. 202.

[28] For helpful discussions of the threat to individual freedom posed by racial identities, see Stubblefield, "Racial Identity and Non-Essentialism about Race"; and Appiah, "Race, Culture, Identity," pp. 97–99.

[29] Boxill, *Blacks and Social Justice,* p. 181.

[30] Michael Omi and Howard Winant, *Racial Formation in the United States: From the 1960's to the 1990's* (New York: Routledge, 1994), pp. 22–23; and Appiah, "Race, Culture, Identity," pp. 85–90.

[31] See Jennifer L. Hochschild, *Facing Up to the American Dream: Race, Class, and the Soul of the Nation* (Princeton: Princeton University Press, 1995).

[32] The symptoms of groupthink are summarized in Michael A. Hogg, *The Social Psychology of Group Cohesiveness: From Attraction to Social Identity* (New York: New York University Press, 1992), pp. 135–37. Hogg bases his summary on I. L. Janis, *Groupthink: Psychological Studies of Policy Decisions and Fiascoes,* 2nd ed. (Boston: Houghton Mifflin, 1982).

[33] See Paul Gilroy, *The Black Atlantic: Modernity and Double Consciousness* (Cambridge, Mass.: Harvard University Press, 1993); also see bell hooks, "Postmodern Blackness," in *Yearning: Race, Gender, and Cultural Politics* (Boston: South End Press, 1990); and Linda Martín Alcoff, "Philosophy and Racial Identity," *Philosophy Today* 41 (1997): 67–76.

[34] Philosophers often invoke the "witch" as an example of a nonexistent entity, but I think Appiah was the first to use the witch analogy in the context of the metaphysics of race. See, for example, his article on "race" in *Africana: The Encyclopedia of African and African-American Experience,* ed. Kwame Anthony Appiah and Henry Louis Gates Jr. (New York: Basic Books, 1999).

[35] For illuminating philosophical reflections on the subtle workings of the "racial gaze," see Jean-Paul Sartre, *Anti-Semite and Jew* (New York: Schocken, 1948); West, *Prophesy Deliverance,* pp. 50–65; Adrian M. S. Piper, "Higher-Order Discrimination," in *Identity, Character, and Morality: Essays in Moral Psychology,* ed. Owen Flanagan and Amelie Rorty (Cambridge, Mass.; MIT Press, 1990); Robert Gooding-Williams, "'Look, a Negro!'" in *Reading Rodney King, Reading Urban Uprising,* ed. Robert Gooding-Williams (New York: Routledge, 1993), pp. 157–77; and Linda Martín Alcoff, "Towards a Phenomenology of Racial Embodiment," *Radical Philosophy* 95 (1999): 15–26.

[36] For empirical evidence in support of the claim that blacks overwhelmingly view racism and racial inequality as serious social problems, see Howard Schuman, Charlotte Steeh, Lawrence Bobo, and Maria Krysan, *Racial Attitudes in America: Trends and Interpretations,* rev. ed. (Cambridge, Mass.: Harvard University Press, 1997); Hochschild, *Facing Up;* and Donald R. Kinder and Lynn M. Sanders, *Divided By Color: Racial Politics and Democratic Ideals* (Chicago: University of Chicago Press, 1996).

[37] According to Orlando Patterson, "All things considered, it is reasonable to estimate that about a quarter of the Euro-American population harbors at least mildly racist feelings toward Afro-Americans and that one in five is a hard-core racist. . . . However one may wish to quibble over the meaning of attitude surveys and other data, this is real progress, an enormous change from the fifties and sixties, when the great majority of Euro-Americans were openly racists, measured by whatever means. Nonetheless, when roughly a quarter of all Euro-Americans are racists, it still remains the case that for every two Afro-American persons there are three Euro-American racists. In spite of all the progress among Euro-Americans, this is still an outrageous situation for any Afro-American" (Patterson, *The Ordeal of Integration,* p. 61). Also see Schuman et al., *Racial Attitudes;* David O. Sears, Colette van Laar, Mary Carrillo, and Rick Kosterman, "Is It Really Racism? The Origins of White Americans' Opposition to Race-Targeted Policies," *Public Opinion Quarterly* 61 (1997): 16–53; Lawrence Bobo, James R. Klugel, and Ryan A. Smith, "Laissez-Faire Racism: The Crystallization of a Kinder, Gentler, Antiblack Ideology," in *Racial Attitudes in the 1990s,* ed. Steven A. Tuch and Jack K. Martin (Westport, Conn.: Praeger, 1997), pp. 15–41; David O. Sears, Jim Sidanius, and Lawrence Bobo, eds., *Racialized Politics: The Debate about Racism in America* (Chicago: University of Chicago Press, 2000); and Michael K. Brown, Martin Carnoy, Elliot Currie, Troy Duster, David B. Oppenheimer, Marjorie M. Shultz, and David Wellman, *Whitewashing Race: The Myth of a Color-Blind Society* (Berkeley: University of California Press, 2003).

[38] See, for example, Alexander Crummell, "The Progress of Civilization along the West Coast of Africa," in *Classical Black Nationalism: From the American Revolution to Marcus Garvey,* ed. Wilson J. Moses (New York: New York University Press, 1996); James H. Cone, *A Black Theology of Liberation* (Maryknoll, N.Y.: Orbis, 1990); and Elijah Muhammad, *Message to the Blackman in America* (Atlanta: Messenger Elijah Muhammad Propagation Society, 1997).

[39] See Appiah, *In My Father's House,* p. 42. Although Appiah's criticism of Du Bois's Pan-Africanism is quite telling, it has little force against the version of black solidarity defended here, for that version, in contrast to Du Bois's, does not rely on the doctrine of racialism, it does not presuppose a common black culture, and it is rooted in the specificity of black oppression in America.

[40] For a helpful analysis of the subjective experience of *particular* forms of racism and of the phenomenology of black subordination, see Lewis Gordon, *Existentia Africana: Understanding Africana Thought* (New York: Routledge, 2000), chap. 4.

[41] For more on this point, see Lani Guinier and Gerald Torres, *The Miner's Canary: Enlisting Race, Resisting Power, Transforming Democracy* (Cambridge, Mass.: Harvard University Press, 2002).

[42] See Derrick Bell, *Faces at the Bottom of the Well: The Permanence of Racism* (New York: Basic Books, 1992).

QUESTIONS FOR A SECOND READING

1. One difficulty with this text is that Shelby is often speaking from within positions that are not his own. He is, in a sense, ventriloquizing arguments made by others, writing within the "discourse," for example, of black authenticity or of "collective identity theory." As you reread, pay particular attention to the sources of the language (or languages) in this text. Where, for example, can you find Tommie Shelby? How would you define and characterize the author *as he is present* in this text? And with whom is he arguing? How would you define and characterize his presumed and/or ideal audience? And if, as we are assuming, it is hard to figure out who is speaking and to whom, how might you account for this? Let's not assume that this is Shelby's "failure" as a writer. Let's assume that this is a strategy or an achievement or a necessary accommodation.

2. It is common to talk about punctuation in relation to the sentence. Writers use marks of punctuation (commas, dashes, colons, semicolons, parentheses) to organize a sentence and to help readers locate themselves in relation to what they are reading. Shelby provides a useful example. You can notice immediately, for example, how he uses white space and subheadings to organize the essay into sections. He often leads with a quick summary of what he intends to conclude. He also frequently enumerates points in the subsections: first, second, third, and so on.

   As you reread, take note of these (and perhaps other) strategies he uses to organize his work, to locate himself as you imagine him writing, and to locate you, as you read, in relation to the larger project. When you are done, go back over your notes to identify distinct strategies, to see if your examples cluster into types. Give them a name and prepare a list you can use to talk about Shelby's characteristic style as an essayist. What works best for you? What works not so well? How might you imagine his work at the computer, writing and revising to prepare this chapter? What does Shelby offer you that you might want to add to your toolkit?

3. Shelby's endnotes often offer a kind of mini-course on whatever issue he has under discussion. Endnote 1, for instance, gives a reading list of critics who think black solidarity to be "irrational, impractical, and even morally

objectionable." Endnote 2 provides references to a long list of black writers who have linked "the demand for collective self-definition with emancipatory black solidarity." Using the library (so that you can put your hands on books and scholarly journals) and, perhaps, working with a group, skim through the items in one of the more extended footnotes. Who are these writers, what do they say, how do they approach the subject, and why would they be interesting or important or useful or memorable for Shelby?

4. This chapter, or essay, is an extended consideration of the implications and limits of "collective identity theory." As an exercise in understanding, prepare a paraphrase, one long paragraph, to explain this theory and one instance of Shelby's response to it. As you do this (and again as an exercise in understanding), include a passage in block quotation—that is, an extended passage that you will introduce, include (following the appropriate conventions), and then discuss. Choose a passage to represent Shelby's position. Choose carefully and thoughtfully; your writing will be the most engaged if you choose a passage that you find particularly useful or interesting or perplexing or challenging.

ASSIGNMENTS FOR WRITING

1. > *Collective identity theory* holds that a shared black identity is essential for an effective black solidarity whose aim is liberation from racial oppression, and thus blacks who are committed to emancipatory group solidarity must steadfastly embrace their distinctive black identity. (p. 585)

Shelby invokes *collective identity theory* to discuss the history and future of black citizens of the United States. This theory, however, has broad application: it does not apply only to discussions of black nationalism or racial solidarity. It could apply as well to people who identify collectively on the basis of age (your generation) or gender or sexuality or ethnicity or social class or region or religion, or (to keep the list going) it could refer to any number of subcultures with which you might be familiar. (We should be quick to add: You are certainly invited to consider black nationalism or racial solidarity. Our goal above was to extend the invitation more broadly.)

Write an essay that captures the term *collective identity theory*, that adopts the phrase and uses it to consider an instance of social identity and group solidarity that has particular meaning for you. You'll need to take time to define this term *collective identity theory* and to credit Shelby and his use of the term. But the bigger task will be to bring Shelby's work and his example to bear on issues and examples of your own choosing. Because you are engaged in a Shelby-like project (or because he is your starting point), as you work on your essay, see what use you might make of Shelby's distinctions between "thick" and "thin," "classic" and "pragmatic."

2. In the introduction to *We Who Are Dark*, Shelby says:

> Still, my book is not a manifesto. Nor do I specify a political agenda that activists can readily put into action. I aim to articulate and defend the basic moral and political principles that should undergird contemporary African American political unity. My focus on philosophical foundations is not a search for fundamental premises that are self-evident or beyond criticism and revision (as if there could be such), but a self-conscious, critical engagement with basic conceptual and normative questions, the answers to which are too often merely assumed rather than closely examined and argued for. (p. 20)

Read back through the selection to think about the argument *as* argument—to think about what it does, how it works, as well as what it says. The tone and method are very different from what you find now in talk radio or in the staged debates represented in television news. And the style and method are different from what you find in the popular media, from op-ed pages to editorials.

Write an essay that considers and evaluates the argumentative style. For the sake of your reader, you will need to present the substance of the argument, its direction and conclusion. But we'd like you also to think about Shelby's essay as exemplary, as representing a particular mode of thought and persuasion. What are its advantages and disadvantages? What does it assume about reader, audience, and occasion? Who is speaking, and to whom? And in what setting? How might this mode of argumentation serve you (and your generation)?

Question 4 in "Questions for a Second Reading" is a useful exercise in preparation for this writing assignment. It might also be useful to read aloud the opening and closing paragraphs of Shelby's text—to get a sense of voice, pacing, and address.

3. Write an essay that engages Shelby's argument. As you reread the selection, imagine that it is addressed specifically to you. Whether you are, in the terms of his essay, black or white, it speaks to the ways *you* (and people like you) rely on and identify with a group, a collective.

Write an essay that engages Shelby's argument in "Social Identity and Group Solidarity." And write your essay in a form and style that are responsive to his. In this sense, your essay will also be an exercise in imitation or homage. Because this assignment makes demands similar to those in question 2 above, let us repeat some of the advice we provided there.

In the introduction to *We Who Are Dark*, Shelby says:

> Still, my book is not a manifesto. Nor do I specify a political agenda that activists can readily put into action. I aim to articulate and defend the basic moral and political principles that should undergird contemporary African American political unity. My focus on philosophical foundations is not a search for fundamental premises that are self-evident or beyond criticism and revision (as if

> there could be such), but a self-conscious, critical engagement with basic conceptual and normative questions, the answers to which are too often merely assumed rather than closely examined and argued for. (p. 20)

As you reread, think about the argument *as* argument—think about what it does, how it works, about method as well as content. The tone and method are very different from what you hear now in talk radio or in the staged debates represented in television news. And the style and method are different from what you find in the popular media, from op-ed pages to editorials. When you have completed your essay, you should be able to refer to the ways you consider it to be Shelby-like.

4. One difficulty with Tommie Shelby's essay "Social Identity and Group Solidarity" is that Shelby is often speaking from within positions that are not his own. He is, in a sense, ventriloquizing arguments made by others, writing within the "discourse," for example, of black authenticity or of "collective identity theory," taking positions that are not his own. In a sense, the problems in the essay enact the conceptual and political problems Shelby is addressing—what are the possible relationships between an individual and the group?

   As you reread, pay particular attention to the sources of the language (or languages) in this text. Where, for example, can you find Tommie Shelby? How would you define and characterize the author *as he is present* in this text? And with whom is he arguing? How would you define and characterize his presumed and/or ideal audience? And if, as we are assuming, it is hard to figure out who is speaking and to whom, how might you account for this? Let's not assume that this is Shelby's "failure" as a writer. Let's assume that this is a strategy or an achievement or a necessary accommodation.

   Choose three or four sections of the text that, for you, provide interesting and representative examples, and write an essay that considers the difficulty of writing and reading "Social Identity and Group Solidarity."

MAKING CONNECTIONS

1.

> *Collective identity theory* holds that a shared black identity is essential for an effective black solidarity whose aim is liberation from racial oppression, and thus blacks who are committed to emancipatory group solidarity must steadfastly embrace their distinctive black identity. (p. 585)

Shelby invokes *collective identity theory* to discuss the history and future of black citizens of the United States. This theory, however, has broad application: it does not apply only to discussions of black nationalism or racial solidarity. It could apply as well to people who identify collectively on the basis of age (your generation) or gender or sexuality or ethnicity or social class or region or religion, or (to keep the list going) it could refer to any number of subcultures with which you might be familiar.

This edition of *Ways of Reading* collects several writers who are thinking about collective identity and individual freedoms: Judith Butler, in "Beside Oneself: On the Limits of Sexual Autonomy" (p. 240); Gloria Anzaldúa, in the two chapters from *Borderlands/La frontera* (p. 72); and John Edgar Wideman, in "Our Time" (p. 657).

Choose one of these to read along with "Social Identity and Group Solidarity." And write an essay that explores the term *collective identity theory*, that adopts the phrase and uses it to consider the arguments developed by Butler, Anzaldúa, or Wideman — arguments developed in the text but also enacted in its style and method. You'll need to take time to define the term *collective identity theory* and to credit Shelby. But the bigger task will be to bring Shelby's work and his example to bear on this other text and the example it presents. (You are certainly invited to bring in examples of your own choosing as well.) Because you are engaged in a Shelby-like project (or because he is your starting point), as you work on your essay, see what use you might make of Shelby's distinctions between "thick" and "thin," "classic" and "pragmatic."

2.

> First, I want to explain why American social distinctions cannot be understood in terms of the concept of race: the only race in the United States, I shall argue, is *the* human race. (p. 102)
>
> — KWAME ANTHONY APPIAH
> *Race, Culture, Identity: Misunderstood Connections*

> I would urge blacks living in the United States, and by extension those in other parts of the world, to identify with each other on the basis of their experience of racial oppression and commitment to collectively resist it. From the standpoint of black political solidarity, each should be allowed to interpret "blackness" however he or she sees fit, provided the interpretation does not advocate anything immoral and is consistent with the collective struggle for racial justice. In saying this, I am not suggesting, as some have, that individual blacks should give up their various black identities in favor of an American, a cosmopolitan, or simply a "human" identity. (pp. 606–07)
>
> — TOMMIE SHELBY
> *Social Identity and Group Solidarity*

Kwame Anthony Appiah is a generation ahead of Tommie Shelby, who is a young scholar (*We Who Are Dark* is his first book); Shelby credits Appiah's influence on his thinking and his work — even his decision to turn to philosophy and to pursue an academic career. Appiah is present in Shelby's endnotes. It is useful and appropriate, then, to consider "Social Identity and Group Solidarity" as a response to Appiah, who is represented in *Ways of Reading* through his essay "Race, Culture, Identity," a chapter from *Color Conscious: The Political Morality of Race*.

As you reread them (first Appiah, then Shelby), think about questions of priority and influence and take notes where, for example, Appiah could be said to be addressing the next generation, and where Shelby, whether he acknowledges it or not, is addressing Appiah (and his generation). How would you characterize the exchange: a dialogue? a debate? a clash of wills? a failure to communicate? a classic example of . . . what? And where do you stand in relation to the two—how do their essays address you and your concerns?

Write an essay to represent the exchange. You will need to find time to represent the general argument in each essay, as well as the moments when they most seem to be writing to each other. And you'll need to take time (and space) to represent your own position.

3. In the introduction to *We Who Are Dark*, Shelby says:

> Still, my book is not a manifesto. Nor do I specify a political agenda that activists can readily put into action. I aim to articulate and defend the basic moral and political principles that should undergird contemporary African American political unity. My focus on philosophical foundations is not a search for fundamental premises that are self-evident or beyond criticism and revision (as if there could be such), but a self-conscious, critical engagement with basic conceptual and normative questions, the answers to which are too often merely assumed rather than closely examined and argued for. (p. 20)

Laura Kipnis's "Love's Labors" (p. 391) *is* a manifesto. It is a "critical engagement," but in a very different register and with very different methods. As you reread these two essays, think about the arguments *as* arguments—think about what they do, how they work, about method as well as content. Both write as though something important were at stake—something they feel personally. So what *are* the key differences—the differences that matter to you as a writer, thinker, and citizen? Academia, we think it is safe to say, prefers Shelby's style and method over Kipnis's. Why, do you suppose? And what is your position on this?

4. Both Tommie Shelby's "Social Identity and Group Solidarity" and Kwame Anthony Appiah's "Race, Culture, Identity" (p. 101) call attention to the difficulties of representing and understanding the experience of those whom we call African Americans—the difficulty of telling the story, of getting it right, of recovering experience from the representations of others.

Read one, or both, of these essays alongside John Edgar Wideman's "Our Time" (p. 657) and write an essay in which you represent these texts as examples of writers working on a problem that has a particular urgency for black Americans. How might you name this problem? How might you illustrate it? What examples are available? What do you find compelling in each of these approaches to the problem? And what might this problem have to do with you—as a writer, a thinker, a citizen?

DAVID FOSTER Wallace

David Foster Wallace (1962–2008) wrote big books and big essays, books and essays with long sentences and long footnotes, and yet, for most readers, his prose was like riding a roller coaster—scary, fun, compelling, exuberant, impossible to resist. In Wallace's *New York Times* obituary, Bruce Weber described Wallace as a "versatile writer of seemingly bottomless energy, . . . a maximalist, exhibiting in his work a huge, even manic curiosity—about the physical world, about the much larger universe of human feelings and about the complexity of living in America at the end of the 20th century." Wallace's sentences, he said, show the "playfulness of a master punctuater and the inventiveness of a genius grammarian."

Wallace grew up in Illinois, in an academic family (his father was a philosopher; his mother was an English teacher—and a teacher of composition); he graduated from Amherst College in 1985 with a double honors degree in English and philosophy. His philosophy thesis won the Gail Kennedy Memorial Prize; his English thesis became his first novel, *The Broom of the System* (1987). He took graduate courses in philosophy at Harvard; he received a master of fine arts degree in fiction from the University of Arizona in 1987. He taught creative writing at Illinois State University. In 2002, he became the Roy E. Disney Professor of Creative Writing at Pomona College, of the Claremont Colleges in California. He won a Whiting Writers' Award (1987), a Lannan Literary Award (1996), a Salon Book Award (1996), the Aga Kahn Prize for Fiction (1997), and a John D. and Catherine T. MacArthur Foundation Fellowship (1997), commonly known as the "Genius Award."

Wallace wrote novels, short stories, and essays. His second novel, *Infinite Jest* (1996), placed him as one of the most important, innovative, and influential writers of his generation. At more than 1,000 pages, it was, as the *New York Times* said, "a whopper." Sven Birketts, in a review for the *Atlantic Monthly,* called it "resourceful, hilarious, intelligent, and unique." Wallace published three collections of short stories—*Girl with Curious Hair* (1989), *Brief Interviews with Hideous Men* (1999), and *Oblivion: Stories* (2004). He was also a prolific and much-admired essayist. In fact, although his fiction sparked controversy among the critics, his nonfiction was almost universally praised. In a lovely *Rolling Stone* essay (October 30, 2008) celebrating Wallace's life and work, David Lipsky said:

> When people tell you they're fans of David Foster Wallace, what they're often telling you is that they've read the cruise-ship piece [an essay written for *Harper's Magazine*]; Wallace would make it the title essay in his first collection of journalism, *A Supposedly Fun Thing I'll Never Do Again*. In a way, the difference between the fiction and the nonfiction reads as the difference between Wallace's social self and his private self. The essays were endlessly charming, they were the best friend you'd ever have, spotting everything, whispering jokes, sweeping you past what was irritating or boring or awful in humane style. Wallace's fiction, especially after *Infinite Jest*, would turn chilly, dark, abstract. You could imagine the author of the fiction sinking into a depression. The nonfiction writer was an impervious sun.

Wallace's nonfiction books include *Signifying Rappers: Rap and Race in the Urban Present* (1990, with Mark Costello); *A Supposedly Fun Thing I'll Never Do Again* (1990); *Everything and More: A Compact History of Infinity* (2003); *Consider the Lobster: And Other Essays* (2005); *McCain's Promise: Aboard the Straight Talk Express with John McCain and a Whole Bunch of Actual Reporters, Thinking about Hope* (2008); and, posthumously, *This Is Water: Some Thoughts, Delivered on a Significant Occasion, about Living a Compassionate Life* (2009), the transcription of a commencement speech Wallace delivered at Kenyon College in 2005.

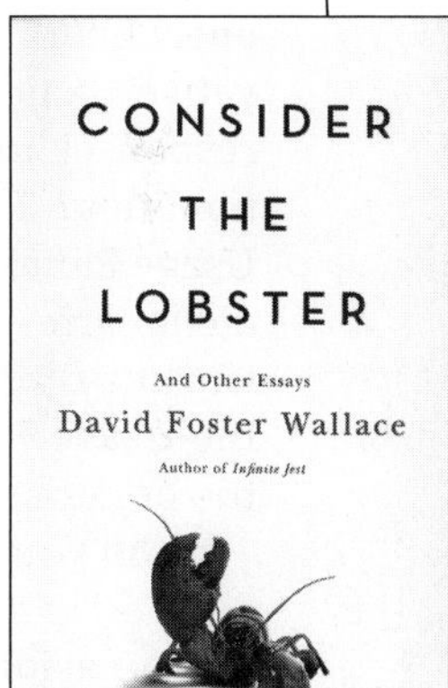

The essay that follows, "Authority and American Usage," was originally published in *Harper's Magazine* (April 2001) under the title "Tense Present: Democracy, English, and the Wars over Usage." It was republished with the current title in *Consider the Lobster.*

Authority and American Usage*

Dilige et quod vis fac.
—Augustine

Did you know that probing the seamy underbelly of US lexicography reveals ideological strife and controversy and intrigue and nastiness and fervor on a near-Lewinskian scale?

For instance, did you know that some modern dictionaries are notoriously liberal and others notoriously conservative, and that certain conservative dictionaries were actually conceived and designed as corrective responses to the "corruption" and "permissiveness" of certain liberal dictionaries? That the oligarchic device of having a special "Distinguished Usage Panel . . . of outstanding professional speakers and writers" is some dictionaries' attempt at a compromise between the forces of egalitarianism and traditionalism in English, but that most linguistic liberals dismiss the Usage Panel device as mere sham-populism, as in e.g. "Calling upon the opinions of the elite, it claims to be a democratic guide"?

Did you know that US lexicography even *had* a seamy underbelly?

The occasion for this article is Oxford University Press's recent release of Mr. Bryan A. Garner's *A Dictionary of Modern American Usage*, a book that Oxford is marketing aggressively and that it is my assigned function to review. It turns out to be a complicated assignment. In today's US, a typical book review is driven by market logic and implicitly casts the reader in the role of consumer. Rhetorically, its whole project is informed by a question that's too crass ever to mention up front: "Should you buy this book?" And because Bryan A. Garner's usage dictionary belongs to a particular subgenre of a reference genre that is itself highly specialized and particular, and because at least a dozen major usage guides have been published in the last couple years and some of them have been quite good indeed,[1] the central unmentionable question here appends the prepositional comparative ". . . rather than *that* book?" to the main clause and so entails a discussion of whether and how *ADMAU* is different from other recent specialty-products of its kind.

* (or, "Politics and the English Language" Is Redundant)

[1] (the best and most substantial of these being *The American Heritage Book of English Usage*, Jean Eggenschwiler's *Writing: Grammar, Usage, and Style*, and Oxford/Clarendon's' own *The New Fowler's Modern English Usage*)

The fact of the matter is that Garner's dictionary is extremely good, certainly the most comprehensive usage guide since E. W. Gilman's *Webster's Dictionary of English Usage,* now a decade out of date.[2] But the really salient and ingenious features of *A Dictionary of Modern American Usage* involve issues of rhetoric and ideology and style, and it is impossible to describe why these issues are important and why Garner's management of them borders on genius without talking about the historical context[3] in which *ADMAU* appears, and this context turns out to be a veritable hurricane of controversies involving everything from technical linguistics and public education to political ideology,[4] and these controversies take a certain amount of time to unpack before their relation to what makes Garner's dictionary so eminently worth your hard-earned reference-book dollar can even be established; and in fact there's no way even to begin the whole harrowing polymeric discussion without first taking a moment to establish and define the highly colloquial term *SNOOT.*

From one perspective, a certain irony attends the publication of any good new book on American usage. It is that the people who are going to be interested in such a book are also the people who are least going to need it — i.e., that offering counsel on the finer points of US English is preaching to the choir. The relevant choir here comprises that small percentage of American citizens who actually care about the current status of double modals and ergative verbs. The same sorts of people who watched *The Story of English* on PBS (twice) and read Safire's column with their half-caff every Sunday. The sorts of people who feel that special blend of wincing despair and sneering superiority when they see EXPRESS LANE — 10 ITEMS OR LESS or hear *dialogue* used as a verb or realize that the founders of the Super 8 Motel chain must surely have been ignorant of the meaning of *suppurate.* There are lots of epithets for people like

---

[2] *The New Fowler's* is also extremely comprehensive and fine, but its emphasis is on British usage.

[3] Sorry about this phrase; I hate this phrase, too. This happens to be one of those very rare times when "historical context" is the phrase to use and there is no equivalent phrase that isn't even worse (I actually tried "lexico-temporal backdrop" in one of the middle drafts, which I think you'll agree is not preferable).

INTERPOLATION

The above ¶ is motivated by the fact that this reviewer nearly always sneers and/or winces when he sees a phrase like "historical context" deployed in a piece of writing and thus hopes to head off any potential sneers/winces from the reader here, especially in an article about felicitous usage. One of the little personal lessons I've learned in working on this essay is that being chronically inclined to sneer/wince at other people's usage tends to make me chronically anxious about other people's sneering/wincing at my usage. It is, of course, possible that this bivalence is news to nobody but me; it may be just a straightforward instance of Matt 7:1's thing about "Judge not lest ye be judged." In any case, the anxiety seems worth acknowledging up front.

[4] One of the claim-clusters I'm going to spend a lot of both our time arguing for is that issues of English usage are fundamentally and inescapably political, and that putatively disinterested linguistic authorities like dictionaries are always the products of certain ideologies, and that as authorities they are accountable to the same basic standards of sanity and honesty and fairness as our political authorities.

this — Grammar Nazis, Usage Nerds, Syntax Snobs, the Grammar Battalion, the Language Police. The term I was raised with is *SNOOT*.[5] The word might be slightly self-mocking, but those other terms are outright dysphemisms. A SNOOT can be loosely defined as somebody who knows what *dysphemism* means and doesn't mind letting you know it.

I submit that we SNOOTs are just about the last remaining kind of truly elitist nerd. There are, granted, plenty of nerd-species in today's America, and some of these are elitist within their own nerdy purview (e.g., the skinny, carbuncular, semi-autistic Computer Nerd moves instantly up on the totem pole of status when your screen freezes and now you need his help, and the bland condescension with which he performs the two occult keystrokes that unfreeze your screen is both elitist and situationally valid). But the SNOOT's purview is interhuman life itself. You don't, after all (despite withering cultural pressure), have to use a computer, but you can't escape language: language is everything and everywhere; it's what lets us have anything to do with one another; it's what separates us from animals; Genesis 11:7–10 and so on. And we SNOOTs know when and how to hyphenate phrasal adjectives and to keep participles from dangling, and we know that we know, and we know how very few other Americans know this stuff or even care, and we judge them accordingly.

I SUBMIT THAT WE SNOOTS ARE JUST ABOUT THE LAST REMAINING KIND OF TRULY ELITIST NERD.

In ways that certain of us are uncomfortable with, SNOOTs' attitudes about contemporary usage resemble religious/political conservatives' attitudes about contemporary culture.[6] We combine a missionary zeal and a near-neural faith in our beliefs' importance with a curmudgeonly hell-in-a-handbasket despair at the way English is routinely defiled by

---

[5] SNOOT (*n*) (*highly colloq*) is this reviewer's nuclear family's nickname à clef for a really extreme usage fanatic, the sort of person whose idea of Sunday fun is to hunt for mistakes in the very prose of Safire's column. This reviewer's family is roughly 70 percent SNOOT, which term itself derives from an acronym, with the big historical family joke being that whether S.N.O.O.T. stood for "Sprachgefühl Necessitates Our Ongoing Tendance" or "Syntax Nudniks Of Our Time" depended on whether or not you were one.

[6] This is true in my own case, at any rate — plus also the "uncomfortable" part. I teach college English part-time. Mostly Lit, not Composition. But I am so pathologically obsessed with usage that every semester the same thing happens: once I've had to read my students' first set of papers, we immediately abandon the regular Lit syllabus and have a three-week Emergency Remedial Usage and Grammar Unit, during which my demeanor is basically that of somebody teaching HIV prevention to intravenous-drug users. When it emerges (as it does, every term) that 95 percent of these intelligent upscale college students have never been taught, e.g., what a clause is or why a misplaced *only* can make a sentence confusing or why you don't just automatically stick in a comma after a long noun phrase, I all but pound my head on the blackboard; I get angry and self-righteous; I tell them they should sue their hometown school boards, and mean it. The kids end up scared, both of me and for me. Every August I vow silently to *chill about usage* this year, and then by Labor Day there's foam on my chin. I can't seem to help it. The truth is that I'm not even an especially good or dedicated teacher; I don't have this kind of fervor in class about anything else, and I know it's not a very productive fervor, nor a healthy one — it's got elements of fanaticism and rage to it, plus a snobbishness that I know I'd be mortified to display about anything else.

supposedly literate adults.[7] Plus a dash of the elitism of, say, Billy Zane in *Titanic* — a fellow SNOOT I know likes to say that listening to most people's public English feels like watching somebody use a Stradivarius to pound nails. We[8] are the Few, the Proud, the More or Less Constantly Appalled at Everyone Else.

THESIS STATEMENT FOR WHOLE ARTICLE

Issues of tradition vs. egalitarianism in US English are at root political issues and can be effectively addressed only in what this article hereby terms a "Democratic Spirit." A Democratic Spirit is one that combines rigor and humility, i.e., passionate conviction plus a sedulous respect for the convictions of others. As any American knows, this is a difficult spirit to cultivate and maintain, particularly when it comes to issues you feel strongly about. Equally tough is a DS's criterion of 100 percent intellectual integrity — you have to be willing to look honestly at yourself and at your motives for believing what you believe, and to do it more or less continually.

This kind of stuff is advanced US citizenship. A true Democratic Spirit is up there with religious faith and emotional maturity and all those other top-of-the-Maslow-Pyramid-type qualities that people spend their whole lives working on. A Democratic Spirit's constituent rigor and humility and self-honesty are, in fact, so hard to maintain on certain issues that it's almost irresistibly tempting to fall in with some established dogmatic camp and to follow that camp's line on the issue and to let your position harden within the camp and become inflexible and to believe that the other camps[9] are either evil or insane and to spend all your time and energy trying to shout over them.

I submit, then, that it is indisputably easier to be Dogmatic than Democratic, especially about issues that are both vexed and highly

---

[7] N.B. that this article's own title page features blocks of the typical sorts of contemporary boners and clunkers and oxymorons and solecistic howlers and bursts of voguish linguistic methane that tend to make a SNOOT's cheek twitch and forehead darken. (N.B. further that it took only about a week of semi-attentive listening and note-taking to assemble these blocks — the Evil is all around us.)

[8] Please note that the strategically repeated I-P pronoun is meant to iterate and emphasize that this reviewer is very much one too, a SNOOT, plus to connote the nuclear family mentioned *supra*. SNOOTitude runs in families. In *ADMAU*'s preface, Bryan Garner mentions both his father and grandfather and actually uses the word *genetic*, and it's probably true: 90 percent of the SNOOTs I know have at least one parent who is, by profession or temperament or both, a SNOOT. In my own case, my mom is a Comp teacher and has written remedial usage books and is a SNOOT of the most rabid and intractable sort. At least part of the reason I am a SNOOT is that for years my mom brainwashed us in all sorts of subtle ways. Here's an example. Family suppers often involved a game: if one of us children made a usage error, Mom would pretend to have a coughing fit that would go on and on until the relevant child had identified the relevant error and corrected it. It was all very self-ironic and lighthearted; but still, looking back, it seems a bit excessive to pretend that your small child is actually *denying you oxygen* by speaking incorrectly. The really chilling thing, though, is that I now sometimes find myself playing this same "game" with my own students, complete with pretend pertussion.

[9] (It seems to be a natural law that camps form only in opposition to other camps and that there are always at least two w/r/t any difficult issue.)

charged. I submit further that the issues surrounding "correctness" in contemporary American usage are both vexed and highly charged, and that the fundamental questions they involve are ones whose answers have to be literally *worked out* instead of merely found.

A distinctive feature of *ADMAU* is that its author is willing to acknowledge that a usage dictionary is not a bible or even a textbook but rather just the record of one bright person's attempts to work out answers to certain very difficult questions. This willingness appears to me to be informed by a Democratic Spirit. The big question is whether such a spirit compromises Bryan Garner's ability to present himself as a genuine "authority" on issues of usage. Assessing Garner's book, then, requires us to trace out the very weird and complicated relationship between Authority and Democracy in what we as a culture have decided is English. That relationship is, as many educated Americans would say, still in process at this time.

A Dictionary of Modern American Usage has no Editorial Staff or Distinguished Panel. It's been conceived, researched, and written *ab ovo usque ad mala* by Mr. Bryan A. Garner. This Garner is an interesting guy. He's both a lawyer and a usage expert (which seems a bit like being both a narcotics wholesaler and a DEA agent). His 1987 *A Dictionary of Modern Legal Usage* is already a minor classic; and now, instead of practicing law anymore, he goes around conducting writing seminars for JDs and doing prose-consulting for various judicial bodies. Garner's also the founder of something called the H. W. Fowler Society,[10] a worldwide group of usage Trekkies who like to send one another linguistic boners clipped from different periodicals. You get the idea. This Garner is one serious and very hard-core SNOOT.

The lucid, engaging, and extremely sneaky preface to *ADMAU* serves to confirm Garner's SNOOTitude in fact while undercutting it in tone. For one thing, whereas the traditional usage pundit cultivates a remote and imperial persona — the kind who uses *one* or *we* to refer to himself — Garner gives us an almost Waltonishly endearing sketch of his own background:

> I realized early — at the age of 15[11] — that my primary intellectual interest was the use of the English language. . . . It became an all-consuming passion. . . . I read everything I could find on the subject. Then, on a wintry evening while visiting New Mexico at the age of 16, I discovered Eric Partridge's *Usage and Abusage*. I was enthralled. Never had I held a more exciting book. . . . Suffice it to say that by the time I was 18, I had committed to memory most of Fowler, Partridge, and their successors.

---

[10] If Samuel Johnson is the Shakespeare of English usage, think of Henry Watson Fowler as the Eliot or Joyce. His 1926 *A Dictionary of Modern English Usage* is the granddaddy of modern usage guides, and its dust-dry wit and blushless imperiousness have been models for every subsequent classic in the field, from Eric Partridge's *Usage and Abusage* to Theodore Bernstein's *The Careful Writer* to Wilson Follett's *Modern American Usage* to Gilman's '89 *Webster's*.

[11] (Garner prescribes spelling out only numbers under ten. I was taught that this rule applies just to Business Writing and that in all other modes you spell out one through nineteen and start using cardinals at 20. *De gustibus non est disputandum*.)

Although this reviewer regrets the bio-sketch's failure to mention the rather significant social costs of being an adolescent whose overriding passion is English usage,[12] the critical hat is off to yet another personable preface-section, one that Garner entitles "First Principles": "Before going any further, I should explain my approach. That's an unusual thing for the author of a usage dictionary to do — unprecedented, as far as I know. But a guide to good writing is only as good as the principles on which it's based. And users should be naturally interested in those principles. So, in the interests of full disclosure . . ."[13]

The "unprecedented" and "full disclosure" here are actually good-natured digs at Garner's Fowlerite predecessors, and a slight nod to one camp in the wars that have raged in both lexicography and education ever since the notoriously liberal *Webster's Third New International Dictionary* came out in 1961 and included terms like *heighth* and *irregardless* without any monitory labels on them. You can think of *Webster's Third* as sort of the Fort Sumter of the contemporary Usage Wars. These wars are both the context and the target of a very subtle rhetorical strategy in *A Dictionary of Modern American Usage,* and without talking about them it's impossible to explain why Garner's book is both so good and so sneaky.

We regular citizens tend to go to The Dictionary for authoritative guidance.[14] Rarely, however, do we ask ourselves who exactly decides what gets in The Dictionary or what words or spellings or pronunciations get deemed substandard or incorrect. Whence the authority of dictionary-makers to decide what's OK and what isn't? Nobody elected them, after all. And simply appealing to precedent or tradition won't work, because what's considered correct changes over time. In the 1600s, for instance, the second-singular took a singular conjugation — "You is." Earlier still, the standard 2-S pronoun wasn't *you* but *thou*. Huge numbers of now-acceptable words like *clever, fun, banter,* and *prestigious* entered English as what usage authorities considered errors or egregious slang. And not just usage conventions but English itself changes over time; if it didn't, we'd all still be talking like Chaucer. Who's to say which changes are natural and good and which are corruptions? And when Bryan Garner or E. Ward Gilman do in fact presume to say, why should we believe them?

---

[12] From personal experience, I can assure you that any kid like this is going to be at best marginalized and at worst savagely and repeatedly Wedgied — see *sub.*

[13] What follow in the preface are "the ten critical points that, after years of working on usage problems, I've settled on." These points are too involved to treat separately, but a couple of them are slippery in the extreme — e.g., "10. **Actual Usage.** In the end, the actual usage of educated speakers and writers is the overarching criterion for correctness," of which both "educated" and "actual" would really require several pages of abstract clarification and qualification to shore up against Usage Wars–related attacks, but which Garner rather ingeniously elects to define and defend via their application in his dictionary itself. Garner's ability not only to stay out of certain arguments but to render them irrelevant ends up being very important — see much *sub.*

[14] There's no better indication of The Dictionary's authority than that we use it to settle wagers. My own father is still to this day living down the outcome of a high-stakes bet on the correct spelling of *meringue,* a bet made on 14 September 1978.

These sorts of questions are not new, but they do now have a certain urgency. America is in the midst of a protracted Crisis of Authority in matters of language. In brief, the same sorts of political upheavals that produced everything from Kent State to Independent Counsels have produced an influential contra-SNOOT school for whom normative standards of English grammar and usage are functions of nothing but custom and the ovine docility of a populace that lets self-appointed language experts boss them around. See for example MIT's Steven Pinker in a famous *New Republic* article — "Once introduced, a prescriptive rule is very hard to eradicate, no matter how ridiculous. Inside the writing establishment, the rules survive by the same dynamic that perpetuates ritual genital mutilations" — or, at a somewhat lower emotional pitch, Bill Bryson in *Mother Tongue: English and How It Got That Way*:

> Who sets down all those rules that we know about from childhood — the idea that we must never end a sentence with a preposition or begin one with a conjunction, that we must use *each other* for two things and *one another* for more than two . . . ? The answer, surprisingly often, is that no one does, that when you look into the background of these "rules" there is often little basis for them.

In *ADMAU*'s preface, Garner himself addresses the Authority question with a Trumanesque simplicity and candor that simultaneously disguise the author's cunning and exemplify it:

> As you might already suspect, I don't shy away from making judgments. I can't imagine that most readers would want me to. Linguists don't like it, of course, because judgment involves subjectivity.[15] It isn't scientific. But rhetoric and usage, in the view of most professional writers,[16]

---

[15] This is a clever half-truth. Linguists compose only one part of the anti-judgment camp, and their objections to usage judgments involve way more than just "subjectivity."

[16] Notice, please, the subtle appeal here to the same "writing establishment" that Steven Pinker scorns. This isn't accidental; it's rhetorical.* What's crafty is that this is one of several places where Garner uses professional writers and editors as support for his claims, but in the preface he also treats these language pros as the primary *audience* for *ADMAU,* as in e.g. "The problem for professional writers and editors is that they can't wait idly to see what direction the language takes. Writers and editors, in fact, influence that direction: they must make decisions. . . . That has traditionally been the job of the usage dictionary: to help writers and editors solve editorial predicaments."

This is the same basic rhetorical move that President R. W. Reagan perfected in his televised Going-Over-Congress's-Head-to-the-People addresses, one that smart politicians ever since have imitated. It consists in citing the very audience you're addressing as the source of support for your proposals: "I'm pleased to announce tonight that we are taking the first steps toward implementing the policies that you elected me to implement," etc. The tactic is crafty because it (1) flatters the audience, (2) disguises the fact that the rhetor's purpose here is actually to persuade and rally support, not to inform or celebrate, and (3) preempts charges from the loyal opposition that the actual policy proposed is in any way contrary to the interests of the audience. I'm not suggesting that Bryan Garner has any particular political agenda. I'm simply pointing out that *ADMAU*'s preface is fundamentally rhetorical in the same way that Reagan's little Chats With America were.

* (In case it's not totally obvious, be advised that this article is using the word *rhetoric* in its strict traditional sense, something like "the persuasive use of language to influence the thoughts and actions of an audience.")

> aren't scientific endeavors. You[17] don't want dispassionate descriptions; you want sound guidance. And that requires judgment.

Whole monographs could be written just on the masterful rhetoric of this passage. Besides the FN 16 stuff, note for example the ingenious equivocation of *judgment,* which in "I don't shy away from making judgments" means actual rulings (and thus invites questions about Authority), but in "And that requires judgment" refers instead to perspicacity, discernment, reason. As the body of *ADMAU* makes clear, part of Garner's overall strategy is to collapse these two different senses of *judgment,* or rather to use the second sense as a justification for the first. The big things to recognize here are (1) that Garner wouldn't be doing any of this if he weren't *keenly* aware of the Authority Crisis in modern usage, and (2) that his response to this crisis is — in the best Democratic Spirit — rhetorical.

So . . .

COROLLARY TO THESIS STATEMENT FOR WHOLE ARTICLE

The most salient and timely feature of Bryan A. Garner's dictionary is that its project is both lexicographical and rhetorical. Its main strategy involves what is known in classical rhetoric as the Ethical Appeal. Here the adjective, derived from the Greek *ēthos,* doesn't mean quite what we usually mean by *ethical.* But there are affinities. What the Ethical Appeal amounts to is a complex and sophisticated "Trust me." It's the boldest, most ambitious, and also most democratic of rhetorical Appeals because it requires the rhetor to convince us not just of his intellectual acuity or technical competence but of his basic decency and fairness and sensitivity to the audience's own hopes and fears.[18]

These latter are not qualities one associates with the traditional SNOOT usage-authority, a figure who for many Americans exemplifies snobbishness and anality, and one whose modern image is not helped by stuff like *The American Heritage Dictionary*'s Distinguished Usage Panelist Morris Bishop's "The arrant solecisms of the ignoramus are here often omitted entirely, 'irregardless' of how he may feel about this neglect" or critic John Simon's "The English language is being treated nowadays exactly as slave traders once handled their merchandise." Compare those lines' authorial personas with Garner's in, e.g., "English usage is so challenging that even experienced writers need guidance now and then."

The thrust here is going to be that *A Dictionary of Modern American Usage* earns Garner pretty much all the trust his Ethical Appeal asks us for. What's interesting is that this trust derives not so much from the

---

[17] See?

[18] In this last respect, recall for example W. J. Clinton's "I feel your pain," which was a blatant if not especially deft Ethical Appeal.

book's lexicographical quality as from the authorial persona and spirit it cultivates. *ADMAU* is a feel-good usage dictionary in the very best sense of *feel-good.* The book's spirit marries rigor and humility in such a way as to let Garner be extremely prescriptive without any appearance of evangelism or elitist put-down. This is an extraordinary accomplishment. Understanding why it's basically a *rhetorical* accomplishment, and why this is both historically significant and (in this reviewer's opinion) politically redemptive, requires a more detailed look at the Usage Wars.

You'd definitely know that lexicography had an underbelly if you read the different little introductory essays in modern dictionaries — pieces like *Webster's DEU*'s "A Brief History of English Usage" or *Webster's Third*'s "Linguistic Advances and Lexicography" or *AHD-2*'s "Good Usage, Bad Usage, and Usage" or *AHD-3*'s "Usage in the Dictionary: The Place of Criticism." But almost nobody ever bothers with these little intros, and it's not just their six-point type or the fact that dictionaries tend to be hard on the lap. It's that these intros aren't actually written for you or me or the average citizen who goes to The Dictionary just to see how to spell (for instance) *meringue*. They're written for other lexicographers and critics; and in fact they're not really introductory at all, but polemical. They're salvos in the Usage Wars that have been under way ever since editor Philip Gove first sought to apply the value-neutral principles of structural linguistics to lexicography in *Webster's Third.* Gove's now-famous response to conservatives who howled[19] when *W3* endorsed *OK* and described *ain't* as "used colloquially by educated speakers in many regions of the United States" was this: "A dictionary should have no truck with artificial notions of correctness or superiority. It should be descriptive and not prescriptive." Gove's terms stuck and turned epithetic, and linguistic conservatives are now formally known as Prescriptivists and linguistic liberals as Descriptivists.

The former are better known, though not because of dictionaries' prologues or scholarly Fowlerites. When you read the columns of William Safire or Morton Freeman or books like Edwin Newman's *Strictly Speaking* or John Simon's *Paradigms Lost,* you're actually reading Popular Prescriptivism, a genre sideline of certain journalists (mostly older males, the majority of whom actually do wear bow ties[20]) whose bemused irony often masks a Colonel Blimp's rage at the way the beloved English of their

---

[19] Really, *howled:* Blistering reviews and outraged editorials from across the country — from the *Times* and *The New Yorker* and the *National Review* and good old *Life,* or see e.g. this from the January '62 *Atlantic Monthly*: "We have seen a novel dictionary formula improvised, in great part, out of snap judgments and the sort of theoretical improvement that in practice impairs; and we have seen the gates propped wide open in enthusiastic hospitality to miscellaneous confusions and corruptions. In fine, the anxiously awaited* work that was to have crowned cisatlantic linguistic scholarship with a particular glory turns out to be a scandal and a disaster."

* (*Sic* — should obviously be "eagerly awaited." *Nemo mortalium omnibus horis sapit.*)

[20] It's true: Newman, Simon, Freeman, James J. Kilpatrick . . . can George F. Will's best-seller on usage be long in coming?

youth is being trashed in the decadent present. Some Pop Prescriptivism is funny and smart, though much of it just sounds like old men grumbling about the vulgarity of modern mores.[21] And some PP is offensively small-minded and knuckle-dragging, such as *Paradigms Lost*'s simplistic dismissal of Standard Black English: "As for 'I be,' 'you be,' 'he be,' etc., which should give us all the heebie-jeebies, these may indeed be comprehensible, but they go against all accepted classical and modern grammars and are the product not of a language with its roots in history but of ignorance of how a language works." But what's really interesting is that the plutocratic tone and styptic wit of Newman and Safire and the best of the Pop Prescriptivists are modeled after the mandarin-Brit personas of Eric Partridge and H. W. Fowler, the same twin towers of scholarly Prescriptivism whom Garner talks about revering as a kid.[22]

Descriptivists, on the other hand, don't have weekly columns in the *Times*. These guys tend to be hard-core academics, mostly linguists or Comp theorists. Loosely organized under the banner of structural (or "descriptive") linguistics, they are doctrinaire positivists who have their intellectual roots in Comte and Saussure and L. Bloomfield[23] and their ideological roots firmly in the US Sixties. The brief explicit mention Garner's preface gives this crew—

> Somewhere along the line, though, usage dictionaries got hijacked by the descriptive linguists,[24] who observe language scientifically. For the pure descriptivist, it's impermissible to say that one form of language is any better than another: as long as a native speaker says it, it's OK—and anyone who takes a contrary stand is a dunderhead. . . . Essentially, descriptivists and prescriptivists are approaching different problems. Descriptivists want to record language as it's actually used, and they perform a useful

---

[21] Even Edwin Newman, the most thoughtful and least hemorrhoidal of the pop SNOOTs, sometimes lets his Colonel B. poke out, as in e.g. "I have no wish to dress as many younger people do nowadays. . . . I have no wish to impair my hearing by listening to their music, and a communication gap between an electronic rock group and me is something I devotedly cherish and would hate to see disappear."

[22] Note for instance the mordant pith (and royal *we*) of this random snippet from Partridge's *Usage and Abusage:*

> **anxious of.** 'I am not hopeless of our future. But I am profoundly anxious of it,' Beverley Nichols, *News of England,* 1938: which made us profoundly anxious *for* (or *about*)—not *of*—Mr. Nichols's literary future.

Or observe the near-Himalayan condescension of Fowler, here on some people's habit of using words like *viable* or *verbal* to mean things the words don't really mean:

> **slipshod extension** . . . is especially likely to occur when some accident gives currency among the uneducated to words of learned origin, & the more if they are isolated or have few relatives in the vernacular. . . . The original meaning of *feasible* is simply doable (L. *facere* do); but to the unlearned it is a mere token, of which he has to infer the value from the contexts in which he hears it used, because such relatives as it has in English—*feat, feature, faction,* &c.—either fail to show the obvious family likeness to which he is accustomed among families of indigenous words, or are (like *malfeasance*) outside his range.

[23] FYI, Leonard Bloomfield's 1933 *Language* pretty much founded descriptive linguistics by claiming that the proper object of study was not language but something called "language behavior."

[24] Utter bushwa: As *ADMAU's* body makes clear, Garner knows precisely where along the line the Descriptivists started influencing usage guides.

> function — although their audience is generally limited to those willing to pore through vast tomes of dry-as-dust research.[25]

— is disingenuous in the extreme, especially the "approaching different problems" part, because it vastly underplays the Descriptivists' influence on US culture. For one thing, Descriptivism so quickly and thoroughly took over English education in this country that just about everybody who started junior high after c. 1970 has been taught to write Descriptively — via "freewriting," "brainstorming," "journaling" — a view of writing as self-exploratory and expressive rather than as communicative, an abandonment of systematic grammar, usage, semantics, rhetoric, etymology. For another thing, the very language in which today's socialist, feminist, minority, gay, and environmental movements frame their sides of political debates is informed by the Descriptivist belief that traditional English is conceived and perpetuated by Privileged WASP Males[26] and is thus inherently capitalist, sexist, racist, xenophobic, homophobic, elitist: unfair. Think Ebonics. Think Proposition 227. Think of the involved contortions people undergo to avoid using *he* as a generic pronoun, or of the tense, deliberate way white males now adjust their vocabularies around non-w.m.'s. Think of the modern ubiquity of spin or of today's endless rows over just the *names* of things — "Affirmative Action" vs. "Reverse Discrimination," "Pro-Life" vs. "Pro-Choice," "Undocumented Worker" vs. "Illegal Alien," "Perjury" vs. "Peccadillo," and so on.

DESCRIPTIVISM SO QUICKLY AND THOROUGHLY TOOK OVER ENGLISH EDUCATION IN THIS COUNTRY THAT JUST ABOUT EVERYBODY WHO STARTED JUNIOR HIGH AFTER C. 1970 HAS BEEN TAUGHT TO WRITE DESCRIPTIVELY.

The Descriptivist revolution takes a little time to unpack, but it's worth it. The structural linguists' rejection of conventional usage rules in English depends on two main kinds of argument. The first is academic and methodological. In this age of technology, some Descriptivists contend, it's the scientific method — clinically objective, value-neutral, based on direct observation and demonstrable hypothesis — that should determine both the content of dictionaries and the standards of "correct" English. Because language is constantly evolving, such standards will always be fluid. Philip

---

[25] His SNOOTier sentiments about linguists' prose emerge in Garner's preface via his recollection of studying under certain eminent Descriptivists in college: "The most bothersome thing was that they didn't write well: their offerings were dreary gruel. If you doubt this, go pick up any journal of linguistics. Ask yourself whether the articles are well-written. If you haven't looked at one in a while, you'll be shocked."

INTERPOLATION

Garner's aside about linguists' writing has wider applications, though *ADMAU* mostly keeps them implicit. The truth is that most US academic prose is appalling — pompous, abstruse, claustral, inflated, euphuistic, pleonastic, solecistic, sesquipidelian, Heliogabaline, occluded, obscure, jargon-ridden, empty: resplendently dead. . . .

[26] (which is in fact true)

Gove's now-classic introduction to *Webster's Third* outlines this type of Descriptivism's five basic edicts: "1 — Language changes constantly; 2 — Change is normal; 3 — Spoken language *is* the language; 4 — Correctness rests upon usage; 5 — All usage is relative."

These principles look prima facie OK — simple, commonsensical, and couched in the bland s.-v.-o. prose of dispassionate science — but in fact they're vague and muddled and it takes about three seconds to think of reasonable replies to each one of them, viz.:

1 — All right, but how much and how fast?

2 — Same thing. Is Hericlitean flux as normal or desirable as gradual change? Do some changes serve the language's overall pizzazz better than others? And how many people have to deviate from how many conventions before we say the language has actually changed? Fifty percent? Ten percent? Where do you draw the line? Who draws the line?

3 — This is an old claim, at least as old as Plato's *Phaedrus*. And it's specious. If Derrida and the infamous Deconstructionists have done nothing else, they've successfully debunked the idea that speech is language's primary instantiation.[27] Plus consider the weird arrogance of Gove's (3) with respect to correctness. Only the most mullah-like Prescriptivists care all that much about spoken English; most Prescriptive usage guides concern Standard *Written* English.[28]

4 — Fine, but whose usage? Gove's (4) begs the whole question. What he wants to suggest here, I think, is a reversal of the traditional entailment-relation between abstract rules and concrete usage: instead of usage's ideally corresponding to a rigid set of regulations, the regulations ought to correspond to the way real people are actually using the language. Again, fine, but which people? Urban Latinos? Boston Brahmins? Rural Midwesterners? Appalachian Neogaelics?

5 — *Huh?* If this means what it seems to mean, then it ends up biting Gove's whole argument in the ass. Principle (5) appears to imply that the correct answer to the above "which people?" is: All of them. And it's easy to show why this will not stand up as a lexicographical principle. The most obvious problem with it is that not everything can go in The Dictionary. Why not? Well, because you can't actually observe and record every last bit of every last native speaker's "language behavior," and even if you

---

27 (Q.v. the "Pharmakon" stuff in Derrida's *La dissémination* — but you'd probably be better off just trusting me.)

28 Standard Written English (SWE) is sometimes called Standard English (SE) or Educated English, but the basic inditement-emphasis is the same. See for example *The Little, Brown Handbook*'s definition of Standard English as "the English normally expected and used by educated readers and writers."

SEMI-INTERPOLATION

Plus let's note that Garner's preface explicitly characterizes his dictionary's intended audience as "writers and editors." And even the recent ads for *ADMAU* in organs like the *New York Review of Books* are built around the slogan "If you like to WRITE . . . **Refer to us**."*

* (Your SNOOT reviewer cannot help observing, w/r/t this ad, that the opening ***r*** in its **Refer** shouldn't be capitalized after a dependent clause + ellipsis. (*Quandoque bonus dormitat Homerus*.)

could, the resultant dictionary would weigh four million pounds and need to be updated hourly.[29] The fact is that any real lexicographer is going to have to make choices about what gets in and what doesn't. And these choices are based on . . . what? And so we're right back where we started.

It is true that, as a SNOOT, I am naturally predisposed to look for flaws in Gove et al.'s methodological argument. But these flaws still seem awfully easy to find. Probably the biggest one is that the Descriptivists' "scientific lexicography" — under which, keep in mind, the ideal English dictionary is basically number-crunching: you somehow observe every linguistic act by every native/naturalized speaker of English and put the sum of all these acts between two covers and call it The Dictionary — involves an incredibly crude and outdated understanding of what *scientific* means. It requires a naive belief in scientific Objectivity, for one thing. Even in the physical sciences, everything from quantum mechanics to Information Theory has shown that an act of observation is itself part of the phenomenon observed and is analytically inseparable from it.

If you remember your old college English classes, there's an analogy here that points up the trouble scholars get into when they confuse observation with interpretation. It's the New Critics.[30] Recall their belief that literary criticism was best conceived as a "scientific" endeavor: the critic was a neutral, careful, unbiased, highly trained observer whose job was to find and objectively describe meanings that were right there, literally inside pieces of literature. Whether you know what happened to New Criticism's reputation depends on whether you took college English after c. 1975; suffice it to say that its star has dimmed. The New Critics had the same basic problem as Gove's Methodological Descriptivists: they believed that there was such a thing as unbiased observation. And that linguistic meanings could exist "Objectively," separate from any interpretive act.

The point of the analogy is that claims to Objectivity in language study are now the stuff of jokes and shudders. The positivist assumptions that underlie Methodological Descriptivism have been thoroughly confuted and displaced — in Lit by the rise of post-structuralism, Reader-Response Criticism, and Jaussian Reception Theory, in linguistics by the rise of Pragmatics — and it's now pretty much universally accepted that (a) meaning is inseparable from some act of interpretation and (b) an act of interpretation is always somewhat biased, i.e., informed by the interpreter's particular ideology. And the consequence of (a) + (b) is that there's no way around it — decisions about what to put in The Dictionary and what to exclude are going to be based on a lexicographer's ideology. And every lexicographer's got one. To presume that dictionary-making

---

[29] Granted, some sort of 100 percent compendious real-time Megadictionary might conceivably be possible online, though it would take a small army of lexical webmasters and a much larger army of *in situ* actual-use reporters and surveillance techs; plus it'd be GNP-level expensive (. . . plus what would be the point?).

[30] *New Criticism* refers to T. S. Eliot and I. A. Richards and F. R. Leavis and Cleanth Brooks and Wimsatt & Beardsley and the whole autotelic Close Reading school that dominated literary criticism from the Thirties to well into the Seventies.

can somehow avoid or transcend ideology is simply to subscribe to a particular ideology, one that might aptly be called Unbelievably Naive Positivism.

There's an even more important way Descriptivists are wrong in thinking that the scientific method developed for use in chemistry and physics is equally appropriate to the study of language. This one doesn't depend on stuff about quantum uncertainty or any kind of postmodern relativism. Even if, as a thought experiment, we assume a kind of 19th-century scientific realism — in which, even though some scientists' interpretations of natural phenomena might be biased,[31] the natural phenomena themselves can be supposed to exist wholly independent of either observation or interpretation — it's still true that no such realist supposition can be made about "language behavior," because such behavior is both *human* and fundamentally *normative*.

To understand why this is important, you have only to accept the proposition that language is by its very nature public — i.e., that there is no such thing as a private language[32] — and then to observe the way Descriptivists seem either ignorant of this fact or oblivious to its consequences, as in for example one Dr. Charles Fries's introduction to an epigone of *Webster's Third* called *The American College Dictionary*:

> A dictionary can be an "authority" only in the sense in which a book of chemistry or physics or of botany can be an "authority" — by the accuracy and the completeness of its record of the observed facts of the field examined, in accord with the latest principles and techniques of the particular science.

This is so stupid it practically drools. An "authoritative" physics text presents the results of *physicists'* observations and *physicists'* theories about those observations. If a physics textbook operated on Descriptivist principles, the fact that some Americans believe electricity flows better downhill (based on the observed fact that power lines tend to run high above the homes they serve) would require the Electricity Flows Better Downhill Hypothesis to be included as a "valid" theory in the textbook — just as, for Dr. Fries, if some Americans use *infer* for *imply* or *aspect* for *perspective,* these usages become *ipso facto* "valid" parts of the language. The truth is that structural linguists like Gove and Fries are not scientists at all; they're pollsters who misconstrue the importance of the "facts" they are recording. It isn't scientific phenomena they're observing and tabulating, but rather a set of human behaviors, and a lot of human behaviors are — to be blunt — moronic. Try, for instance, to imagine an "authoritative" ethics textbook whose principles were based on what most people actually *do*.

[31] ("EVIDENCE OF CANCER LINK REFUTED BY TOBACCO INSTITUTE RESEARCHERS")

[32] This proposition is in fact true, . . . and although the demonstration is persuasive it is also . . . lengthy and involved and rather, umm, dense, so that once again you'd maybe be better off simply granting the truth of the proposition and forging on with the main text.

Grammar and usage conventions are, as it happens, a lot more like ethical principles than like scientific theories. The reason the Descriptivists can't see this is the same reason they choose to regard the English language as the sum of all English utterances: they confuse mere regularities with *norms.*

Norms aren't quite the same as rules, but they're close. A norm can be defined here simply as something that people have agreed on as the optimal way to do things for certain purposes. Let's keep in mind that language didn't come into being because our hairy ancestors were sitting around the veldt with nothing better to do. Language was invented to serve certain very specific purposes—"That mushroom is poisonous"; "Knock these two rocks together and you can start a fire"; "This shelter is mine!" and so on. Clearly, as linguistic communities evolve over time, they discover that some ways of using language are better than others—not better *a priori,* but better with respect to the community's purposes. If we assume that one such purpose might be communicating which kinds of food are safe to eat, then we can see how, for example, a misplaced modifier could violate an important norm: "People who eat that kind of mushroom often get sick" confuses the message's recipient about whether he'll get sick only if he eats the mushroom frequently or whether he stands a good chance of getting sick the very first time he eats it. In other words, the fungiphagic community has a vested practical interest in excluding this kind of misplaced modifier from acceptable usage; and, given the purposes the community uses language for, the fact that a certain percentage of tribesmen screw up and use misplaced modifiers to talk about food safety does not *eo ipso* make m.m.'s a good idea.

Maybe now the analogy between usage and ethics is clearer. Just because people sometimes lie, cheat on their taxes, or scream at their kids, this doesn't mean that they think those things are "good."[33] The whole point of establishing norms is to help us evaluate our actions (including utterances) according to what we as a community have decided our real interests and purposes are. Granted, this analysis is oversimplified; in practice it's incredibly hard to arrive at norms and to keep them at least minimally fair or sometimes even to agree on what they are (see e.g. today's Culture Wars). But the Descriptivists' assumption that all usage norms are arbitrary and dispensable leads to—well, have a mushroom.

The different connotations of *arbitrary* here are tricky, though—and this sort of segues into the second main kind of Descriptivist argument. There is a sense in which specific linguistic conventions really *are* arbitrary. For instance, there's no particular metaphysical reason why our word for a four-legged mammal that gives milk and goes moo is *cow* and

---

[33] In fact, the Methodological Descriptivists' reasoning is known in social philosophy as the "Well, Everybody Does It" fallacy—i.e., if a lot of people cheat on their taxes, that means it's somehow morally OK to cheat on your taxes. Ethics-wise, it takes only two or three deductive steps to get from there to the sort of State of Nature where everybody's hitting each other over the head and stealing their groceries.

not, say, *prtlmpf.* The uptown term for this is "the arbitrariness of the linguistic sign,"[34] and it's used, along with certain principles of cognitive science and generative grammar, in a more philosophically sophisticated version of Descriptivism that holds the conventions of SWE to be more like the niceties of fashion than like actual norms. This "Philosophical Descriptivism" doesn't care much about dictionaries or method; its target is the standard SNOOT claim that prescriptive rules have their ultimate justification in the community's need to make its language meaningful and clear.

Steven Pinker's 1994 *The Language Instinct* is a good and fairly literate example of this second kind of Descriptivist argument, which, like the Gove-et-al. version, tends to deploy a jr.-high-filmstrip SCIENCE: POINTING THE WAY TO A BRIGHTER TOMORROW–type tone:

> [T]he words "rule" and "grammar" have very different meanings to a scientist and a layperson. The rules people learn (or, more likely, fail to learn) in school are called "prescriptive" rules, prescribing how one *ought* to talk. Scientists studying language propose "descriptive" rules, describing how people *do* talk. Prescriptive and descriptive grammar are simply different things.[35]

The point of this version of Descriptivism is to show that the descriptive rules are more fundamental and way more important than the prescriptive rules. The argument goes like this. An English sentence's being *meaningful* is not the same as its being *grammatical.* That is, such clearly ill-formed constructions as "Did you seen the car keys of me?" or "The show was looked by many people" are nevertheless comprehensible; the sentences do, more or less, communicate the information they're trying to get across. Add to this the fact that nobody who isn't damaged in some profound Oliver Sacksish way actually ever makes these sorts of very deep syntactic errors[36] and you get the basic proposition of N. Chomsky's generative linguistics, which is that there exists a Universal Grammar beneath and common to all languages, plus that there is probably an actual

---

[34] This phrase is attributable to Ferdinand de Saussure, the Swiss philologist who more or less invented modern technical linguistics, separating the study of language as an abstract formal system from the historical and comparative emphases of 19th-century philology. Suffice it to say that the Descriptivists like Saussure a *lot*. Suffice it also to say that they tend to misread him and take him out of context and distort his theories in all kinds of embarrassing ways — e.g., Saussure's "arbitrariness of the linguistic sign" means something other and far more complicated than just "There's no ultimate necessity to English speakers' saying *cow*." (Similarly, the structural linguists' distinction between "language behavior" and "language" is based on a simplistic misreading of Saussure's distinction between *"parole"* and *"langue."*)

[35] (If that last line of Pinker's pourparler reminds you of Garner's "Essentially, descriptivists and prescriptivists are approaching different problems," be advised that the similarity is neither coincidence nor plagiarism. One of the many cunning things about *ADMAU*'s preface is that Garner likes to take bits of Descriptivist rhetoric and use them for very different ends.)

[36] Pinker puts it this way: "No one, not even a valley girl, has to be told not to say *Apples the eat boy* or *The child seems sleeping* or *Who did you meet John and?* or the vast, vast majority of the millions of trillions of mathematically possible combinations of words."

part of the human brain that's imprinted with this Universal Grammar the same way birds' brains are imprinted with Fly South and dogs' with Sniff Genitals. There's all kinds of compelling evidence and support for these ideas, not least of which are the advances that linguists and cognitive scientists and AI researchers have been able to make with them, and the theories have a lot of credibility, and they are adduced by the Philosophical Descriptivists to show that since the really *important* rules of language are at birth already hardwired into people's neocortex, SWE prescriptions against dangling participles or mixed metaphors are basically the linguistic equivalent of whalebone corsets and short forks for salad. As Steven Pinker puts it, "When a scientist considers all the high-tech mental machinery needed to order words into everyday sentences, prescriptive rules are, at best, inconsequential decorations."

SWE PRESCRIPTIONS AGAINST DANGLING PARTICIPLES OR MIXED METAPHORS ARE BASICALLY THE LINGUISTIC EQUIVALENT OF WHALEBONE CORSETS AND SHORT FORKS FOR SALAD.

This argument is not the barrel of drugged trout that Methodological Descriptivism was, but it's still vulnerable to objections. The first one is easy. Even if it's true that we're all wired with a Universal Grammar, it doesn't follow that *all* prescriptive rules are superfluous. Some of these rules really do seem to serve clarity and precision. The injunction against two-way adverbs ("People who eat this often get sick") is an obvious example, as are rules about other kinds of misplaced modifiers ("There are many reasons why lawyers lie, some better than others") and about relative pronouns' proximity to the nouns they modify ("She's the mother of an infant daughter who works twelve hours a day").

Granted, the Philosophical Descriptivist can question just how absolutely necessary these rules are: it's quite likely that a recipient of clauses like the above could figure out what they mean from the sentences on either side or from the overall context or whatever.[37] A listener can usually figure out what I really mean when I misuse *infer* for *imply* or say *indicate* for *say,* too. But many of these solecisms — or even just clunky redundancies like "The door was rectangular in shape" — require at least a couple extra nanoseconds of cognitive effort, a kind of rapid sift-and-discard process, before the recipient gets it. Extra work. It's debatable just how much extra work, but it seems indisputable that we put *some* extra interpretive burden on the recipient when we fail to honor certain conventions. W/r/t confusing clauses like the above, it simply seems more "considerate" to follow the rules of correct English . . . just as it's more "considerate" to de-slob your home before entertaining guests or to brush your teeth before picking up a date. Not just more considerate but more

[37] (FYI, there happens to be a whole subdiscipline of linguistics called Pragmatics that essentially studies the way statements' meanings are created by various contexts.)

respectful somehow—both of your listener/reader and of what you're trying to get across. As we sometimes also say about elements of fashion and etiquette, the way you use English "makes a statement" or "sends a message"—even though these statements/messages often have nothing to do with the actual information you're trying to communicate.

We've now sort of bled into a more serious rejoinder to Philosophical Descriptivism: from the fact that linguistic communication is not strictly dependent on usage and grammar it does *not* necessarily follow that the traditional rules of usage and grammar are nothing but "inconsequential decorations." Another way to state this objection is that something's being "decorative" does not necessarily make it "inconsequential." Rhetoric-wise, Pinker's flip dismissal is very bad tactics, for it invites precisely the question it's begging: inconsequential *to whom*?

A key point here is that the resemblance between usage rules and certain conventions of etiquette or fashion is closer than the Philosophical Descriptivists know and far more important than they understand. Take, for example, the Descriptivist claim that so-called correct English usages like *brought* rather than *brung* and *felt* rather than *feeled* are arbitrary and restrictive and unfair and are supported only by custom and are (like irregular verbs in general) archaic and incommodious and an all-around pain in the ass. Let us concede for the moment that these claims are 100 percent reasonable. Then let's talk about pants. Trousers, slacks. I suggest to you that having the so-called correct subthoracic clothing for US males be pants instead of skirts is arbitrary (lots of other cultures let men wear skirts), restrictive and unfair (US females get to wear either skirts or pants), based solely on archaic custom (I think it's got to do with certain traditions about gender and leg-position, the same reasons women were supposed to ride sidesaddle and girls' bikes don't have a crossbar), and in certain ways not only incommodious but illogical (skirts are more comfortable than pants;[38] pants ride up; pants are hot; pants can squish the 'nads and reduce fertility; over time pants chafe and erode irregular sections of men's leg-hair and give older men hideous half-denuded legs; etc. etc.). Let us grant—as a thought experiment if nothing else—that these are all sensible and compelling objections to pants as an androsartorial norm. Let us, in fact, in our minds and hearts say yes—*shout* yes—to the skirt, the kilt, the toga, the sarong, the jupe. Let us dream of or even in our spare time work toward an America where nobody lays any arbitrary sumptuary prescriptions on anyone else and we can all go around as comfortable and aerated and unchafed and motile as we want.

And yet the fact remains that in the broad cultural mainstream of millennial America, men do not wear skirts. If you, the reader, are a US male, and even if you share my personal objections to pants and dream as I do of a cool and genitally unsquishy American Tomorrow, the odds are still 99.9 percent that in 100 percent of public situations you wear

---

[38] (presumably)

pants/slacks/shorts/trunks. More to the point, if you are a US male and also have a US male child, and if that child might happen to come to you one evening and announce his desire/intention to wear a skirt rather than pants to school the next day, I am 100 percent confident that you are going to discourage him from doing so. *Strongly* discourage him. You could be a Molotov-tossing anti-pants radical or a kilt manufacturer or Dr. Steven Pinker himself—you're going to stand over your kid and be prescriptive about an arbitrary, archaic, uncomfortable, and inconsequentially decorative piece of clothing. Why? Well, because in modern America any little boy who comes to school in a skirt (even, say, a modest all-season midi) is going to get stared at and shunned and beaten up and called a total geekoid by a whole lot of people whose approval and acceptance are important to him.[39] In our present culture, in other words, a boy who wears a skirt is "making a statement" that is going to have all kinds of gruesome social and emotional consequences for him.

You can probably see where this is headed. I'm going to describe the intended point of the pants analogy in terms that I'm sure are simplistic—doubtless there are whole books in Pragmatics or psycholinguistics or something devoted to unpacking this point. The weird thing is that I've seen neither Descriptivists nor SNOOTs deploy it in the Wars.[40,41]

When I say or write something, there are actually a whole lot of different things I am communicating. The propositional content (i.e., the verbal information I'm trying to convey) is only one part of it. Another part is stuff about me, the communicator. Everyone knows this. It's a function of the fact that there are so many different well-formed ways to say the same basic thing, from e.g. "I was attacked by a bear!" to "Goddamn bear tried to kill me!" to "That ursine juggernaut did essay to sup upon my person!" and so on. Add the Saussurian/Chomskian consideration that many grammatically ill-formed sentences can also get the propositional content across—"Bear attack Tonto, Tonto heap scared!"—and the number of subliminal options we're scanning/sorting/interpreting as we communicate with one another goes transfinite very quickly. And different levels of diction and formality are only the simplest kinds of distinction; things get way more complicated in the sorts of interpersonal

---

[39] In the case of little Steve Pinker Jr., these people are the boy's peers and teachers and crossing guards. In the case of adult cross-dressers and drag queens who have jobs in the straight world and wear pants to those jobs, it's bosses and coworkers and customers and people on the subway. For the die-hard slob who nevertheless wears a coat and tie to work, it's mostly his boss, who doesn't want his employees' clothes to send clients "the wrong message." But it's all basically the same thing.

[40] Even Garner scarcely mentions it, and just once in his dictionary's miniessay on CLASS DISTINCTIONS: "[M]any linguistic pratfalls can be seen as class indicators—even in a so-called classless society such as the United States." And when Bryan A. Garner uses a clunky passive like "can be seen" as to distance himself from an issue, you know something's in the air.

[41] In fact, pretty much the only time one ever hears the issue made wholly explicit is in radio ads for tapes that promise to improve people's vocabularies. These ads tend to be extremely ominous and intimidating and always start out with "DID YOU KNOW PEOPLE JUDGE YOU BY THE WORDS YOU USE?"

communication where social relations and feelings and moods come into play. Here's a familiar kind of example. Suppose that you and I are acquaintances and we're in my apartment having a conversation and that at some point I want to terminate the conversation and not have you be in my apartment anymore. Very delicate social moment. Think of all the different ways I can try to handle it: "Wow, look at the time"; "Could we finish this up later?"; "Could you please leave now?"; "Go"; "Get out"; "Get the hell out of here"; "Didn't you say you had to be someplace?"; "Time for you to hit the dusty trail, my friend"; "Off you go then, love"; or that sly old telephone-conversation-ender: "Well, I'm going to let you go now"; etc. etc.[n] And then think of all the different factors and implications of each option.[42]

The point here is obvious. It concerns a phenomenon that SNOOTs blindly reinforce and that Descriptivists badly underestimate and that scary vocab-tape ads try to exploit. People really do judge one another according to their use of language. Constantly. Of course, people are constantly judging one another on the basis of all kinds of things — height, weight, scent, physiognomy, accent, occupation, make of vehicle[43] — and, again, doubtless it's all terribly complicated and occupies whole battalions of sociolinguists. But it's clear that at least one component of all this interpersonal semantic judging involves *acceptance,* meaning not some touchy-feely emotional affirmation but actual acceptance or rejection of someone's bid to be regarded as a peer, a member of somebody else's collective or community or Group. Another way to come at this is to acknowledge something that in the Usage Wars gets mentioned only in very abstract terms: "correct" English usage is, as a practical matter, a function of whom you're talking to and of how you want that person to respond — not just to your utterance but also to *you.* In other words, a large part of the project of any communication is rhetorical and depends on what some rhet-scholars call "Audience" or "Discourse Community."[44] It is the present existence in the United States of an enormous number

---

[42] To be honest, the example here has a special personal resonance for this reviewer because in real life I always seem to have a hard time winding up a conversation or asking somebody to leave, and sometimes the moment becomes so delicate and fraught with social complexity that I'll get overwhelmed trying to sort out all the different possible ways of saying it and all the different implications of each option and will just sort of blank out and do it totally straight — "I want to terminate the conversation and not have you be in my apartment anymore" — which evidently makes me look either as if I'm very rude and abrupt or as if I'm semi-autistic and have no sense of how to wind up a conversation gracefully. Somehow, in other words, my reducing the statement to its bare propositional content "sends a message" that is itself scanned, sifted, interpreted, and judged by my auditor, who then sometimes never comes back. I've actually lost friends this way.

[43] (. . . not to mention color, gender, ethnicity — you can see how fraught and charged all this is going to get)

[44] *Discourse Community* is a rare example of academic jargon that's actually a valuable addition to SWE because it captures something at once very complex and very specific that no other English term quite can.*

* (The above, while true, is an obvious attempt to preempt readerly sneers/winces at the term's continued deployment in this article.)

of different Discourse Communities, plus the fact that both people's use of English and their interpretations of others' use are influenced by rhetorical assumptions, that are central to understanding why the Usage Wars are so politically charged and to appreciating why Bryan Garner's *ADMAU* is so totally sneaky and brilliant and modern.

Fact: There are all sorts of cultural/geographical dialects of American English — Black English, Latino English, Rural Southern, Urban Southern, Standard Upper-Midwest, Maine Yankee, East-Texas Bayou, Boston Blue-Collar, on and on. Everybody knows this. What not everyone knows — especially not certain Prescriptivists — is that many of these non-SWE-type dialects have their own highly developed and internally consistent grammars, and that some of these dialects' usage norms actually make more linguistic/aesthetic sense than do their Standard counterparts.* Plus, of course, there are also innumerable sub- and subsubdialects[45] based on all sorts of things that have nothing to do with locale or ethnicity — Medical-School English, Twelve-Year-Old-Males-Whose-Worldview-Is-Deeply-Informed-by-*South-Park* English — that are nearly incomprehensible to anyone who isn't inside their very tight and specific Discourse Community (which of course is part of their function[46]).

***INTERPOLATION**

POTENTIALLY DESCRIPTIVIST-LOOKING EXAMPLE OF SOME GRAMMATICAL ADVANTAGES OF A NON-STANDARD DIALECT THAT THIS REVIEWER ACTUALLY KNOWS ABOUT FIRSTHAND

I happen to have two native English dialects — the SWE of my hyper-educated parents and the hard-earned Rural Midwestern of most of my peers. When I'm talking to RMs, I tend to use constructions like "Where's it at?" for "Where is it?" and sometimes "He don't" instead of "He doesn't." Part of this is a naked desire to fit in and not get rejected as an egghead or fag (see *sub*). But another part is that I, SNOOT or no, believe that these RMisms are in certain ways superior to their Standard equivalents.

---

[45] Just how tiny and restricted a subdialect can get and still be called a subdialect isn't clear; there might be very firm linguistic definitions of what's a dialect and what's a subdialect and what's a subsub-, etc. Because I don't know any better and am betting you don't either, I'm going to use *subdialect* in a loose inclusive way that covers idiolects as distinctive as Peorians-Who-Follow-Pro-Wrestling-Closely or Geneticists-Who-Specialize-in-Hardy-Weinberg-Equilibrium. *Dialect* should probably be reserved for major players like Standard Black English et al.

[46] (Plus it's true that whether something gets called a "subdialect" or "jargon" seems to depend on how much it annoys people outside its Discourse Community. Garner himself has miniessays on AIRPLANESE, COMPUTERESE, LEGALESE, and BUREAUCRATESE, and he more or less calls all of them jargon. There is no *ADMAU* miniessay on DIALECTS, but there is one on JARGON, in which such is Garner's self-restraint that you can almost hear his tendons straining, as in "[Jargon] arises from the urge to save time and space — and occasionally to conceal meaning from the uninitiated.")

For a dogmatic Prescriptivist, "Where's it at?" is double-damned as a sentence that not only ends with a preposition but whose final preposition forms a redundancy with *where* that's similar to the redundancy in "the reason is because" (which latter usage I'll admit makes me dig my nails into my palms). Rejoinder: First off, the avoid-terminal-prepositions rule is the invention of one Fr. R. Lowth, an 18th-century British preacher and indurate pedant who did things like spend scores of pages arguing for *hath* over the trendy and degenerate *has*. The a.-t.-p. rule is antiquated and stupid and only the most ayotolloid SNOOT takes it seriously. Garner himself calls the rule "stuffy" and lists all kinds of useful constructions like "a person I have great respect for" and "the man I was listening to" that we'd have to discard or distort if we really enforced it.

Plus, the apparent redundancy of "Where's it at?"[47] is offset by its metrical logic: what the *at* really does is license the contraction of *is* after the interrogative adverb. You can't say "Where's it?" So the choice is between "Where is it?" and "Where's it at?", and the latter, a strong anapest, is prettier and trips off the tongue better than "Where is it?", whose meter is either a clunky monosyllabic-foot + trochee or it's nothing at all.

Using "He don't" makes me a little more uncomfortable; I admit that its logic isn't quite as compelling. Nevertheless, a clear trend in the evolution of English from Middle to Modern has been the gradual regularizing of irregular present-tense verbs,[48] a trend justified by the fact that irregulars are hard to learn and to keep straight and have nothing but history going for them. By this reasoning, Standard Black English is way out on the cutting edge of English with its abandonment of the 3-S present in *to do* and *to go* and *to say* and its marvelously streamlined six identical present-tense inflections of *to be*. (Granted, the conjugation "he be" always sounds odd to me, but then SBE is not one of my dialects.)

This is probably the place for your SNOOT reviewer openly to concede that a certain number of traditional prescriptive rules really are stupid and that people who insist on them (like the legendary assistant to Margaret Thatcher who refused to read any memo with a split infinitive in it, or the jr.-high teacher I had who automatically graded you down if you started a sentence with *Hopefully*) are that very most contemptible and dangerous kind of SNOOT, the SNOOT Who Is Wrong. The injunction against split infinitives, for instance, is a consequence of the weird fact that English grammar is modeled on Latin even though Latin is a synthetic language and English is an analytic

---

[47] (a redundancy that's a bit arbitrary, since "Where's it *from*?" isn't redundant [mainly because *whence* has receded into semi-archaism])

[48] E.g., for a long time English had a special 2-S present conjugation — "thou lovest," "thou sayest" — that now survives only in certain past tenses (and in the present of *to be*, where it consists simply in giving the 2-S a plural inflection).

language.[49] Latin infinitives consist of one word and are impossible to as it were split, and the earliest English Prescriptivists — so enthralled with Latin that their English usage guides were actually *written* in Latin[50] — decided that English infinitives shouldn't be split either. Garner himself takes out after the s.i. rule in his miniessays on both SPLIT INFINITIVES and SUPERSTITIONS.[51] And *Hopefully* at the beginning of a sentence, as a certain cheeky eighth-grader once (to his everlasting social cost) pointed out in class, actually functions not as a misplaced modal auxiliary or as a manner adverb like *quickly* or *angrily* but as a sentence adverb (i.e., as a special kind of "veiled reflexive that indicates the speaker's attitude about the state of affairs described by the rest of the sentence — examples of perfectly OK sentence adverbs are *clearly, basically, luckily*), and only SNOOTs educated in the high-pedantic years 1940–1960 blindly proscribe it or grade it down.

WHETHER WE'RE CONSCIOUS OF IT OR NOT, MOST OF US ARE FLUENT IN MORE THAN ONE MAJOR ENGLISH DIALECT.

The cases of split infinitives and *Hopefully* are in fact often trotted out by dogmatic Descriptivists as evidence that all SWE usage rules are arbitrary and dumb (which is a bit like pointing to Pat Buchanan as evidence that all Republicans are maniacs). FYI, Garner rejects *Hopefully*'s knee-jerk proscription, too, albeit grudgingly, saying "the battle is lost" and including the adverb in his miniessay on SKUNKED TERMS, which is his phrase for a usage that is "hotly disputed . . . any use of it is likely to distract some readers." (Garner also points out something I'd never quite realized, which is that *hopefully*, if misplaced/mispunctuated in the body of a sentence, can create some of the same two-way ambiguities as other adverbs, as in e.g. "I will borrow your book and hopefully read it soon."

Whether we're conscious of it or not, most of us are fluent in more than one major English dialect and in several subdialects and are probably at least passable in countless others. Which dialect you choose to use depends, of course, on whom you're addressing. More to the point, I submit that the

---

[49] A synthetic language uses grammatical inflections to dictate syntax, whereas an analytic languages uses word order. Latin, German, and Russian are synthetic; English and Chinese are analytic.

[50] (Q.v. for example Sir Thomas Smith's cortex-withering *De Recta et Emendata Linguae Anglicae Scriptione Dialogus* of 1568.)

[51] N.B., though, that he's sane about it. Some split infinitives really are clunky and hard to parse, especially when there are a lot of words between *to* and the verb ("We will attempt to swiftly and to the best of our ability respond to these charges"), which Garner calls "wide splits" and sensibly discourages. His overall verdict on split infinitives — which is that some are "perfectly proper" and some iffy and some just totally bad news, and that no one wide tidy dogmatic ukase can handle all s.i. cases, and thus that "knowing when to split an infinitive requires a good ear and a keen eye" — is a fine example of the way Garner distinguishes sound and helpful Descriptivist objections from wacko or dogmatic objections and then incorporates the sound objections into a smarter and more flexible Prescriptivism.

dialect you use depends mostly on what sort of Group your listener is part of and on whether you wish to present yourself as a fellow member of that Group. An obvious example is that traditional upper-class English has certain dialectal differences from lower-class English and that schools used to have courses in elocution whose whole *raison* was to teach people how to speak in an upper-class way. But usage-as-inclusion is about much more than class. Try another sort of thought experiment: A bunch of US teenagers in clothes that look several sizes too large for them are sitting together in the local mall's food court, and imagine that a 53-year-old man with jowls, a comb-over, and clothes that fit perfectly comes over to them and says he was scoping them and thinks they're totally rad and/or phat and asks is it cool if he just kicks it and chills with them here at their table. The kids' reaction is going to be either scorn or embarrassment for the guy — most likely a mix of both. Q: Why? Or imagine that two hard-core young urban black guys are standing there talking and I, who am resoundingly and in all ways white, come up and greet them with "Yo" and address one or both as "Brother" and ask "s'up, s'goin' on," pronouncing *on* with that NYCish o͞o-ŏ diphthong that Young Urban Black English deploys for a standard o. Either these guys are going to think that I am mocking them and be offended or they are going to think I am simply out of my mind. No other reaction is remotely foreseeable. Q: Why?

Why: A dialect of English is learned and used either because it's your native vernacular or because it's the dialect of a Group by which you wish (with some degree of plausibility) to be accepted. And although it is a major and vitally important one, SWE is only one dialect. And it is never, or at least hardly ever,[52] anybody's only dialect. This is because there are — as you and I both know and yet no one in the Usage Wars ever seems to mention — situations in which faultlessly correct SWE is *not* the appropriate dialect.

Childhood is full of such situations. This is one reason why SNOOTlets tend to have such a hard social time of it in school. A SNOOTlet is a little kid who's wildly, precociously fluent in SWE (he is often, recall, the offspring of SNOOTs). Just about every class has a SNOOTlet, so I know you've seen them — these are the sorts of six-to-twelve-year-olds who use *whom* correctly and whose response to striking out in T-ball is to shout "How incalculably dreadful!" The elementary-school SNOOTlet is one of the earliest identifiable species of academic geekoid and is duly despised by his peers and praised by his teachers. These teachers usually don't see the incredible amounts of punishment the SNOOTlet is receiving from his classmates, or if they do see it they blame the classmates and shake their heads sadly at the vicious and arbitrary cruelty of which children are capable.

---

[52] (It is, admittedly, difficult to imagine William F. Buckley using or perhaps even being aware of anything besides SWE.)

Teachers who do this are dumb. The truth is that his peers' punishment of the SNOOTlet is not arbitrary at all. There are important things at stake. Little kids in school are learning about Group-inclusion and -exclusion and about the respective rewards and penalties of same and about the use of dialect and syntax and slang as signals of affinity and inclusion. They're learning about Discourse Communities. Little kids learn this stuff not in Language Arts or Social Studies but on the playground and the bus and at lunch. When his peers are ostracizing the SNOOTlet or giving him monstrous quadruple Wedgies or holding him down and taking turns spitting on him, there's serious learning going on. Everybody here is learning except the little SNOOT[53] — in fact, what the SNOOTlet is being punished for is precisely his *failure* to learn. And his Language Arts teacher — whose own Elementary Education training prizes "linguistic facility" as one of the "social skills" that ensure children's "developmentally appropriate peer rapport,"[54] but who does not or cannot consider the possibility that linguistic facility might involve more than lapidary SWE — is unable to see that her beloved SNOOTlet is actually *deficient* in Language Arts. He has only one dialect. He cannot alter his vocabulary, usage, or grammar, cannot use slang or vulgarity; and it's these abilities that are really required for "peer rapport," which is just a fancy academic term for being accepted by the second-most-important Group in the little kid's

---

53 AMATEUR DEVELOPMENTAL-SOCIOLINGUISTIC INTERPOLATION #1

The SNOOTlet is, as it happens, an indispensable part of the other children's playground education. School and peers are kids' first socialization outside the family. In learning about Groups and Group tectonics, the kids are naturally learning that a Group's identity depends as much on exclusion as inclusion. They are, in other words, starting to learn about Us and Them, and about how an Us always needs a Them because being not-Them is essential to being Us. Because they're little children and it's school, the obvious Them is the teachers and all the values and appurtenances of the teacher-world.* This teacher-Them helps the kids see how to start to be an Us, but the SNOOTlet completes the puzzle by providing a kind of missing link: he is the traitor, the Us who is in fact not Us but *Them.* The SNOOTlet, who at first appears to be one of Us because like Us he's three feet tall and runny-nosed and eats paste, nevertheless speaks an erudite SWE that signals membership not in Us but in Them, which since Us is defined as not-Them is equivalent to a rejection of Us that is also a *betrayal* of Us precisely because the SNOOTlet is a kid, i.e., one of Us.

Point: The SNOOTlet is teaching his peers that the criteria for membership in Us are not just age, height, paste-ingestion, etc., that in fact Us is primarily a state of mind and a set of sensibilities. An ideology. The SNOOTlet is also teaching the kids that Us has to be *extremely vigilant* about persons who may at first appear to be Us but are in truth *not* Us and may need to be identified and excluded *at a moment's notice*. The SNOOTlet is not the only type of child who can serve as traitor: the Teacher's Pet, the Tattletale, the Brown-Noser, and the Mama's Boy can also do nicely . . . just as the Damaged and Deformed and Fat and Generally Troubled children all help the nascent mainstream Us-Groups refine the criteria for in- and exclusion.

In these crude and fluid formations of ideological Groupthink lies American kids' real socialization. We all learn early that community and Discourse Community are the same thing, and a fearsome thing indeed. It helps to know where We come from.

* (Plus, because the teacher-Them are tall humorless punishers/rewarders, they come to stand for all adults and — in a shadowy, inchoate way — for the Parents, whose gradual shift from composing Us to defining Them is probably the biggest ideological adjustment of childhood.)

54 (Elementary Ed professors really do talk this way.)

life.[55] If he is sufficiently in thrall to his teachers and those teachers are sufficiently clueless, it may take years and unbelievable amounts of punishment before the SNOOTlet learns that you need more than one dialect to get along in school.

This reviewer acknowledges that there seems to be some, umm, personal stuff getting dredged up and worked out here;[56] but the stuff is germane. The point is that the little A+ SNOOTlet is actually in the same dialectal position as the class's "slow" kid who can't learn to stop using *ain't* or *bringed.* Exactly the same position. One is punished in class, the other on the playground, but both are deficient in the same linguistic skill — viz., the ability to move between various dialects and levels of "correctness," the ability to communicate one way with peers and another way with teachers and another with family and another with T-ball coaches and so on. Most of these dialectal adjustments are made below the level of conscious awareness, and our ability to make them seems part psychological and part something else — perhaps something hardwired into the same motherboard as Universal Grammar — and in truth this ability is a much better indicator of a kid's raw "verbal IQ" than test scores or grades, since US English classes do far more to retard dialectal talent than to cultivate it.

---

55 AMATEUR DEVELOPMENTAL-SOCIOLINGUISTIC INTERPOLATION #2

And by the time the SNOOTlet hits adolescence it'll have supplanted the family to become the *most* important Group. And it will be a Group that depends for its definition on a rejection of traditional Authority.* And because it is the recognized dialect of mainstream adult society, there is no better symbol of traditional Authority than SWE. It is not an accident that adolescence is the time when slang and code and subdialects of subdialects explode all over the place and parents begin to complain that they can hardly even understand their kids' language. Nor are lyrics like "I can't get no/Satisfaction" an accident or any kind of sad commentary on the British educational system. Jagger et al. aren't stupid; they're rhetoricians, and they know their audience.

* (That is, the teacher-/parent-Them becomes the Establishment, Society — Them becomes THEM.)

56 (The skirt-in-school scenario was not personal stuff, though, FYI.)

A NOTE TO READERS FROM BARTHOLOMAE AND PETROSKY: For reasons we struggle to understand, David Foster Wallace's publisher would give us permission to reprint only about two-thirds of the essay "Authority and American Usage." As we made the cuts, we made sure that the essay retained a shape and a conclusion. Still, we thought you might be interested in a quick, summary account of what comes *after* the section you just read.

1. *The Teaching of Writing.* Wallace argues that teachers need to develop "overt, honest, and compelling arguments for why SWE is a dialect worth learning." And these arguments are hard to make because they are elitist. He says, "The real truth, of course, is that SWE is the dialect of the American elite." Wallace concludes this discussion by turning specifically to the problems this argument presents to those whose ways of speaking and writing place them outside the

circle of the elite, including "students of color." In his own teaching, Wallace says the following to his students (and he says it in his "official teacher-voice"):

> I don't know whether anybody's told you this or not, but when you're in a college English class you're basically studying a foreign dialect. This dialect is Standard Written English. . . . In my class, you have to learn and write in SWE. If you want to study your own primary dialect and its rules and history and how it's different from SWE, fine — there are some great books by scholars of Black English, and I'll help you find some and talk about them with you if you want. But that will be outside class. In class — in my English class — you will have to master and write in Standard Written English, which we might just as well call "Standard White English" because it was developed by white people and is used by white people, especially educated, powerful white people. . . . (p. 108)

He adds: "I should note here that a couple of the students I've said this stuff to were offended — one lodged an Official Complaint — and that I have had more than one colleague profess to find my spiel 'racially insensitive.' Perhaps you do too." And he concludes: "This reviewer's own humble opinion is that some of the cultural and political realities of American life are themselves racially insensitive and elitist and offensive and unfair, and that pussyfooting around these realities with euphemistic doublespeak is not only hypocritical but toxic to the project of ever really changing them."

2. *Why Bryan A. Garner Is a Genius*. Wallace concludes that Garner is a genius. And his genius is present in the quality of his writing. Although Garner is making judgments throughout *A Dictionary of Modern American Usage*, the persona that emerges is "disinterested," "reasonable," "objective," and compelling. It is neither elitist nor fussy (like a SNOOT). Garner appears not as "a cop or a judge" but more as an interested and passionate professional, like a doctor or a lawyer. Wallace says, "[Garner's] argumentative strategy is totally brilliant and totally sneaky, and part of both qualities is that it usually doesn't seem like there's an argument going on at all."

   Bryan Garner understood something that made his dictionary of American usage different from those that came before it: "the lexicographer's challenge now is to be not just accurate and comprehensive but *credible*. . . . [I]n the absence of capital-A Authority in language, the reader must now be moved or persuaded to grant a dictionary its authority, freely and for what appear to be good reasons." The autobiographical moments in Garner's introduction are part of the ethical appeal of his writing — a reader is asked to identify with this person, to trust him, and to admire him. And Wallace concludes:

   > Probably the most ingenious and attractive thing about his dictionary's Ethical Appeal . . . is Garner's scrupulousness about considering the reader's own hopes and fears and reasons for caring enough about usage to bother with something like *ADMAU* at all. These reasons, as Garner makes clear, tend to derive from a reader's concern about his/her *own* linguistic authority and rhetorical persona and

> ability to convince an audience that he/she cares. Again and again, Garner frames his prescriptions in rhetorical terms: "To the writer or speakers for whom credibility is important, it's a good idea to avoid distracting *any* readers or listeners"; "Whatever you do, if you use *data* in a context in which its number becomes known, you'll bother some of your readers." *A Dictionary of Modern Usage*'s real thesis, in other words, is that the purposes of the expert authority and the purposes of the lay reader are identical, and identically rhetorical — which is about as Democratic these days as you're going to get. (p. 124)

QUESTIONS FOR A SECOND READING

1. It is common to talk about punctuation in relation to the sentence. Writers use marks of punctuation (commas, dashes, colons, semicolons, parentheses) to organize a sentence and to help readers locate themselves in relation to what they are reading. Writers also, however, punctuate essays or chapters — longer units of text. Wallace provides an excellent — and distinctive — example of this practice. You can notice immediately, for example, how he uses white space and subheadings to organize the essay into sections. There are also italics, "interpolations," enumerations, footnotes, footnotes to footnotes, all deployed to shape a reader's encounter with the text. Some are designed to be helpful; some, you might say, are deliberately designed to get in a reader's way.

   As you reread, take note of the places where Wallace could be said to be "punctuating" this essay. (You can do this in the margins.) When you are done, go back over your notes to see if there are distinct strategies, to see if your examples cluster into types. What, as a writer, is Wallace doing in each case? Why? What are the consequences for a reader? What attracts you as a writer?

2. Wallace's essay is purportedly a book review of Bryan A. Garner's *A Dictionary of Modern American Usage*. It is a long review. It provides an account of Garner's book while also placing it in relation to current issues, writers, and texts concerning the making of dictionaries and the correct and incorrect uses of words. It participates in a genre common in academic circles, a "review of the literature," and yet it has a different feel or sound than most academic writing. It has "style," you might say. You might say that there is a surprising, interesting, and distinctive character speaking in this text.

   As you reread, think about the speaker as a character, as an invention of David Foster Wallace, the writer (who could, at least hypothetically, have written about dictionaries in a different voice and in a different form). And mark moments when this character seems most distinctively present or alive. This character (whom we might also call Wallace) is a figure who reads in the field, who thinks about these issues, and who speaks with authority. He has a distinctive personality, way of thinking, view of the world. (Students are often invited, for example, to think of the "Thoreau" in *Walden* in just these terms, to think of him as a great American character.) When you are done, be prepared to talk about this as a strategy. Why would Wallace, the writer, present himself (or enter the conversation) in just these ways? What was at stake for him?

3. At several places in his essay, Wallace applauds Bryan Garner for being "rhetorical" and "totally sneaky." These seem unusual terms with which to signal praise. Indeed, "rhetoric" is often associated with being sneaky, as in the politician who sneakily avoids a question or converts an opponent's strength into a weakness. As you reread, look again at Wallace's uses of the term *rhetoric*. What does it come to mean? What work does it do for him? With what terms is it paired or opposed?

   When you are done, and as an exercise in understanding, prepare a paraphrase, one long paragraph, to explain what "rhetoric" comes to mean for Wallace. As you do this (and again as an exercise in understanding), include a passage in block quotation—that is, an extended passage that you will introduce, include (following the appropriate conventions), and then discuss.

4. The structure of Wallace's text is complex, with its footnotes, interpolations, digressions, numbered lists, and assorted oddities. Though he mentions a "thesis" at several points, he doesn't announce a thesis in the opening paragraph and then dutifully follow it with examples and the way to a conclusion. As you reread, pay attention to the argument (or arguments) that are developed in this essay. What are the key terms? Where does Wallace begin, and where does he move thereafter? What are his major contentions? How does he support them? Where does he end?

   When you are done, and as an exercise in understanding, prepare a paraphrase, one long paragraph, to explain what you take to be the key argument in this essay. As you do this (and again as an exercise in understanding), include a passage in block quotation—that is, an extended passage that you will introduce, include (following the appropriate conventions), and then discuss.

5. The Latin phrase by Augustine—*Dilige et quod vis fac*—that Wallace uses as his epigraph means "Love, and do what thou wilt." Wallace doesn't offer any explanation of this epigraph in his text. As you reread, reflect on how it might relate to his arguments about language use.

6. According to Bruce Weber, writing for the *New York Times,* Wallace's sentences showed the "playfulness of a master punctuator and the inventiveness of a genius grammarian." As you reread, choose a sentence that might fit this description. Type it out; and then create a sentence of your own in direct imitation—the same length, punctuation, grammar, and rhythm, but with new words and a different topic. When you are done, be prepared to talk about what a sentence like this *does*—not what it says but what it *does*—the sentence as a gesture, an action, a deed in words.

7. If you are interested in reading this essay in its entirety, you'll likely find it at your college or university library in a collection titled *Consider the Lobster: And Other Essays* (2005), by David Foster Wallace. It is also interesting to read this essay, and to think about its style, in relationship to other essays in that collection. Those we would recommend as starters would be the title essay, "Consider the Lobster," on the Maine Lobster Festival, and "Some Remarks on Kafka's Funniness from Which Probably Not Enough Has Been Removed," about the difficulty of teaching the novelist and short story writer Franz Kafka in college literature courses.

ASSIGNMENTS FOR WRITING

1. At certain moments in his essay, Wallace describes his approach as a teacher of college students. He tells us in footnote 6, for instance, that while he teaches literature courses, he usually abandons the syllabus after he reads his students' first papers in order to hold "a three-week Emergency Remedial Usage and Grammar Unit, during which my demeanor is basically that of somebody teaching HIV prevention to intravenous-drug users." And later he provides a representation of a lengthy speech he gives to individual college students who struggle with Standard Written English. He says,

> I'm not trying to suggest here that an effective SWE pedagogy would require teachers to wear sunglasses and call students Dude. What I am suggesting is that the rhetorical situation of a US English class — a class composed wholly of young people whose Group identity is rooted in defiance of Adult Establishment values, plus also composed partly of minorities whose primary dialects are different from SWE — requires a teacher to come up with overt, honest, and compelling arguments for why SWE is a dialect worth learning. (p. 107)

But Wallace also teaches writing by example — that is, by what he says in this essay about effective writing and by the way he chooses to write. In this sense, "Authority and American Usage" offers a writing lesson.

Write an essay in which you take up the invitation to engage Wallace's argument about U.S. English, about SWE, about rhetoric, and about the function and importance of a writing class. You will need to work directly in reference to what Wallace says in the text. In other words, you'll need to work with sentences and examples. But you also bring experience to the table. From your point of view, and from the point of view of students like you, what is at stake? How and where might you enter this conversation? Where are you in the settings Wallace invokes? in his arguments?

2. A character emerges in this essay, a figure representing one version of a well-schooled, learned, and articulate adult, an intellectual, someone who reads widely, who thinks closely and freshly and methodically about big questions, someone with ideas and with style, someone who is defined in relation to sources—to books and to other writers. (The second of the "Questions for a Second Reading" is designed to help you locate this character as a figure in a text, as a writer's invention.)

   Write an essay in which you discuss the figure of the intellectual represented in the essay "Authority and American Usage." You'll need to work closely with a few key and representative moments in the text. And write an essay in which you assess this figure in relation to your own education—better yet, in relation to the figure you intend to cut as a well-schooled adult, as an intellectual, as a person with ideas and knowledge and something to say.

3. Wallace's essay is purportedly a book review of Bryan A. Garner's *A Dictionary of Modern American Usage*. It is a long review. It provides an account of Garner's book while also placing it in relation to current issues, writers, and texts concerning the making of dictionaries and the correct and incorrect uses of words. It participates in a genre common in academic circles, a "review of the literature," and yet it has a different feel or sound than most academic writing. It has "style," you might say. And it has a method. (The first and fourth of the "Questions for a Second Reading" are designed to help you locate key features of this method.)

   Write something *like* this essay, something Wallace-like, in relation to a book (or an essay) you have read. The subject or topic does not have to be related to dictionaries or to usage. This could well be something you have read for this class or for another class, something you may have already written about, but differently, not in a Wallace-like way. Your range of reference may not be as great as Wallace's, but you should bring one or two other writers into play, others who have thought and written about the topic. The most important thing, however, is to make this an exercise in adopting and experimenting with Wallace's method and style.

MAKING CONNECTIONS

1. Like David Foster Wallace, David Abram in "Animism and the Alphabet" (p. 28) is concerned with the value of—and the cultural problems that come with—advanced literacy. Both writers look carefully at the functions of writing, and both consider the ethical dimension of language. Yet their works are also quite different. As you reread their essays, take note of their attitudes toward writing and its uses. How do their arguments about the value and purpose of writing differ from each other? What does each writer notice that the other overlooks?

Write an essay in which you compare Wallace and Abram as writers on writing. Look closely not only at what they say but also at what they do—the kinds of moves they make as writers and the effects of their choices. How does the fact that they are making use of writing even as they discuss it affect their work on the page? In what ways do they implicitly model (or fail to model) the kinds of writing they explicitly claim to respect and appreciate? Finally, how do Wallace's and Abram's values as writers differ from your own? This is an opportunity for you, too, to exhibit awareness that your writing can display the virtues for which you argue in your essay.

2. In his essay "The Dark Night of the Soul" (p. 420), Richard E. Miller notes that, at times, Eric Harris, one of two teens who killed thirteen people at Columbine High School in 1999,

> had the affectation of an English teacher, declaring on his Web site that one of the many habits he found unforgivable in his peers was the tendency to pronounce the "t" in "often": "Learn to speak correctly, you morons," he commands. . . . (p. 423)

Reading this passage, we might recall the discussion of "SNOOTs" and other "Prescriptivists" in "Authority and American Usage" by David Foster Wallace, who confesses he finds it difficult to tolerate usage that departs from Standard Written English. Both Foster and Miller are concerned with the future of print-based literacy—with the ways in which the reading and writing of books will (or won't) matter to our culture in the years to come. Wallace worries that schools will quit teaching standard conventions for communication in writing, while Miller worries that "training students to read and write in more critical and self-reflective ways cannot protect them from the violent changes our culture is undergoing."

Write an essay in which you discuss your own sense of the future of American literacy and its relationship to cultural change, paying particular attention to the language habits of your generation. Based on what you've observed among your peers, do you find Foster's and Miller's anxieties well founded? overwrought? reflective of something they don't examine? How do you respond to their concern that books and teachers are losing their authority? Focus your essay on a moment or a series of moments in your experience or observation that speaks to Foster's and Miller's fears about the fate of reading and writing in the twenty-first century.

3. Both Kwame Anthony Appiah's "Race, Culture, Identity: Misunderstood Connections" (p. 101) and David Foster Wallace's "Authority and American Usage" have a distinctive style, voice, and method. A character emerges in each essay, a figure representing one version of a well-schooled, learned, and articulate adult, an intellectual, someone who reads widely, who thinks closely and freshly and methodically about big questions, someone with ideas and with style, someone who is defined in relation to sources—to books and to other writers—and someone who takes pains to address his

readers. This is an intellectual, then, with a desire to reach others, to engage them, and to bring them into his point of view.

Write an essay in which you discuss the figure of the intellectual represented in these two essays. You'll need to work closely with a few key and representative moments in the texts. And write an essay in which you assess this figure in relation to your own education — better yet, in relation to the figure you intend to cut as a well-schooled adult, as an intellectual, as a person with ideas and knowledge and something to say.

JOHN EDGAR Wideman

John Edgar Wideman was born in 1941 in Washington, D.C., but spent most of his youth in Homewood, a neighborhood in Pittsburgh. He earned a BA from the University of Pennsylvania and taught at the University of Wyoming and the University of Massachusetts at Amherst. He is currently Asa Messer Professor and Professor of Africana Studies and English at Brown University. In addition to the nonfiction work *Brothers and Keepers* (1984), from which this selection is drawn, Wideman has published a number of critically acclaimed works of fiction, including *The Lynchers* (1986); *Reuben* (1989); *Fever: Twelve Stories* (1989); *Philadelphia Fire: A Novel* (1991); and a series of novels set in Homewood: *Damballah* (1981), *Hiding Place* (1982), and *Sent for You Yesterday* (which won the 1984 PEN/Faulkner Award). The latter novels have been reissued as a set, titled *The Homewood Trilogy*. His most recent books include *The Cattle Killing* (1996), *Two Cities* (1998), *Hoop Roots* (2001), *The Island, Martinique* (2003), *God's Gym* (2005), and *Fanon* (2008). In 1994, Wideman published another work of nonfiction, *Fatheralong: A Meditation on Fathers and Sons, Race and Society*.

In the preface to *The Homewood Trilogy*, Wideman writes,

> The value of black life in America is judged, as life generally in this country is judged, by external, material signs of success. Urban ghettoes are dangerous, broken-down, economically marginal pockets of real estate infected with drugs, poverty, violence, crime, and since black life is seen as rooted in the ghetto, black people are identified with the ugliness, danger, and deterioration surrounding them. This logic is simpleminded and devastating, its hold on the American imagination as old as slavery; in fact, it recycles the classic justification for slavery, blaming the cause and consequences of oppression on the oppressed. Instead of launching a preemptive strike at the flawed assumptions that perpetuate racist thinking, blacks and whites are doomed to battle endlessly with the symptoms of racism.
>
> In these three books again bound as one I have set myself to the task of making concrete those invisible planes of existence that bear witness to the fact that black life, for all its material impoverishment,

continues to thrive, to generate alternative styles, redemptive strategies, people who hope and cope. But more than attempting to prove a "humanity," which should be self-evident anyway to those not blinded by racism, my goal is to celebrate and affirm. *Where did I come from? Who am I? Where am I going?*

Brothers and Keepers is a family story; it is about Wideman and his brother Robby. John went to Oxford as a Rhodes scholar, and Robby went to prison for his role in a robbery and a murder. In the section that follows, "Our Time," Wideman tries to understand his brother, their relationship, where they came from, where they are going. In this account, you will hear the voices of Robby, John, and people from the neighborhood, but also the voice of the writer, speaking about the difficulty of writing and the dangers of explaining away Robby's life.

Brothers and Keepers is not the first time Wideman has written to or about his brother. The first of the Homewood series, *Damballah*, is dedicated to Robby. The dedication reads:

> Stories are letters. Letters sent to anybody or everybody. But the best kind are meant to be read by a specific somebody. When you read that kind you know you are eavesdropping. You know a real person somewhere will read the same words you are reading and the story is that person's business and you are a ghost listening in.
>
> Remember. I think it was Geral I first heard call a watermelon a letter from home. After all these years I understand a little better what she meant. She was saying the melon is a letter addressed to us. A story for us from down home. Down Home being everywhere we've never been, the rural South, the old days, slavery, Africa. That juicy, striped message with red meat and seeds, which always looked like roaches to me, was blackness as cross and celebration, a history we could taste and chew. And it was meant for us. Addressed to us. We were meant to slit it open and take care of business.
>
> Consider all these stories as letters from home. I never liked watermelon as a kid. I think I remember you did. You weren't afraid of becoming instant nigger, of sitting barefoot and goggle-eyed and Day-Glo black and drippy-lipped on massa's fence if you took one bite of the forbidden fruit. I was too scared to enjoy watermelon. Too self-conscious. I let people rob me of a simple pleasure. Watermelon's still tainted for me. But I know better now. I can play with the idea even if I can't get down and have a natural ball eating a real one.
>
> Anyway . . . these stories are letters. Long overdue letters from me to you. I wish they could tear down the walls. I wish they could snatch you away from where you are.

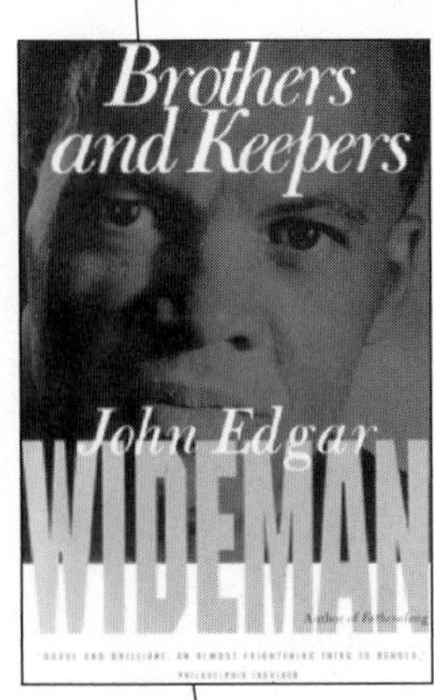

Our Time

You remember what we were saying about young black men in the street-world life. And trying to understand why the "square world" becomes completely unattractive to them. It has to do with the fact that their world is the GHETTO and in that world all the glamour, all the praise and attention is given to the slick guy, the gangster especially, the ones that get over in the "life." And it's because we can't help but feel some satisfaction seeing a brother, a black man, get over on these people, on their system without playing by their rules. No matter how much we have incorporated these rules as our own, we know that they were forced on us by people who did not have our best interests at heart. So this hip guy, this gangster or player or whatever label you give these brothers that we like to shun because of the poison that they spread, we, black people, still look at them with some sense of pride and admiration, our children openly, us adults somewhere deep inside. We know they represent rebellion — what little is left in us. Well, having lived in the "life," it becomes very hard — almost impossible — to find any contentment in joining the status quo. Too hard to go back to being nobody in a world that hates you. Even if I had struck it rich in the life, I would have managed to throw it down the fast lane. Or have lost it on a revolutionary whim. Hopefully the latter.

I have always burned up in my fervent passions of desire and want. My senses at times tingle and itch with my romantic, idealistic outlook on life, which has always made me keep my distance from reality, reality that was a constant insult to my world, to my dream of happiness and peace, to my people-for-people kind of world, my easy-cars-for-a-nickel-or-a-dime sorta world. And these driving passions, this sensitivity to the love and good in people, also turned on me because I used it to play on people and their feelings. These aspirations of love and desire turned on me when I wasn't able to live up to this sweet-self morality, so I began to self-destruct, burning up in my sensitivity, losing direction, because nowhere could I find this world of truth and love and harmony.

In the real world, the world left for me, it was unacceptable to be "good," it was square to be smart in school, it was jive to show respect to people outside the street world, it was cool to be cold to your woman and the people that loved you. The things we liked we called "bad." "Man, that was a bad girl." The world of the angry black kid growing up in the sixties was a world in which to be in was to be out — out of touch with the square world and all of its rules on what's right and wrong. The thing was to make your own rules, do your own thing, but make sure it's contrary to what society says or is.

I SHALL ALWAYS PRAY

I

Garth looked bad. Real bad. Ichabod Crane anyway, but now he was a skeleton. Lying there in the bed with his bones poking through his skin, it made you want to cry. Garth's barely able to talk, his smooth, medium-brown skin yellow as pee. Ichabod legs and long hands and long feet, Garth could make you laugh just walking down the street. On the set you'd see him coming a far way off. Three-quarters leg so you knew it had to be Garth the way he was split up higher in the crotch than anybody else. Wilt the Stilt with a lean bird body perched on top his high waist. Size-fifteen shoes. Hands could palm a basketball easy as holding a pool cue. Fingers long enough to wrap round a basketball, but Garth couldn't play a lick. Never could get all that lankiness together on the court. You'd look at him sometimes as he was trucking down Homewood Avenue and think that nigger ain't walking, he's trying to remember how to walk. Awkward as a pigeon on roller skates. Knobby joints out of whack, arms and legs flailing, going their separate ways, his body jerking to keep them from going too far. Moving down the street like that wouldn't work, didn't make sense if you stood back and watched, if you pretended you hadn't seen Garth get where he was going a million times before. Nothing funny now, though. White hospital sheets pulled to his chest. Garth's head always looked small as a tennis ball way up there on his shoulders. Now it's a yellow, shrunken skull.

Ever since Robby had entered the ward, he'd wanted to reach over and hide his friend's arm under the covers. For two weeks Gar had been wasting away in the bed. Bad enough knowing Gar was dying. Didn't need that pitiful stick arm reminding him how close to nothing his main man had fallen. So fast. It could happen so fast. If Robby tried to raise that arm it would come off in his hand. As gentle as he could would not be gentle enough. The arm would disintegrate, like a long ash off the end of a cigarette.

Time to leave. No sense in sitting any longer. Garth not talking, no way of telling whether he was listening either. And Robby has nothing more to say. Choked up the way he gets inside hospitals. Hospital smell and quiet, the bare halls and bare floors, the echoes, something about all that he can't name, wouldn't try to name, rises in him and chills him. Like his teeth are chattering the whole time he's inside a hospital. Like his entire body is trembling uncontrollably, only nobody can see it or hear it but him. Shaking because he can't breathe the stuffy air. Hot and cold at the same time. He's been aching to leave since he entered the ward. Aching to get up and bust through the big glass front doors. Aching to pounce on that spidery arm flung back behind Gar's head. The arm too wasted to belong to his friend. He wants to grab it and hurl it away.

Robby pulls on tight white gloves the undertaker had dealt out to him and the rest of the pallbearers. His brown skin shows through the thin material, turns the white dingy. He's remembering that last time in Garth's ward. The hospital stink. Hot, chilly air. A bare arm protruding from the sleeve of the hospital gown, more dried-up toothpick than arm, a withered twig, with Garth's fingers like a bunch of skinny brown bananas drooping from the knobby tip.

Robby had studied the metal guts of the hospital bed, the black scuff marks swirling around the chair's legs. When he'd finally risen to go, his chair scraping against the vinyl floor broke a long silence. The noise must have roused Garth's attention. He'd spoken again.

You're good, man. Don't ever forget, Rob. You're the best.

Garth's first words since the little banter back and forth when Robby had entered the ward and dragged a chair to the side of Gar's bed. A whisper scarcely audible now that Robby was standing. Garth had tried to grin. The best he could manage was a pained adjustment of the bones of his face, no more than a shadow scudding across the yellow skull, but Robby had seen the famous smile. He hesitated, stopped rushing toward the door long enough to smile back. Because that was Gar. That was the way Gar was. He always had a smile and a good word for his cut buddies. Garth's grin was money in the bank. You could count on it like you could count on a good word from him. Something in his face would tell you you were alright, better than alright, that he believed in you, that you were, as he'd just whispered, "the best." You could depend on Garth to say something to make you feel good, even though you knew he was lying. With that grin greasing the lie you had to believe it, even though you knew better. Garth was the gang's dreamer. When he talked, you could see his dreams. That's why Robby had believed it, seen the grin, the bright shadow lighting Garth's face an instant. Out of nothing, out of pain, fear, the certainty of death gripping them both, Garth's voice had manufactured the grin.

Now they had to bury Garth. A few days after the visit to the hospital the phone rang and it was Garth's mother with the news of her son's death. Not really news. Robby had known it was just a matter of time. Of waiting for the moment when somebody else's voice would pronounce the words he'd said to himself a hundred times. *He's gone. Gar's dead.* Long gone before the telephone rang. Gar was gone when they stuck him up in the hospital bed. By the time they'd figured out what ailed him and admitted him to the hospital, it was too late. The disease had turned him to a skeleton. Nothing left of Garth to treat. They hid his messy death under white sheets, perfumed it with disinfectant, pumped him full of drugs so he wouldn't disturb his neighbors.

The others had squeezed into their pallbearers' gloves. Cheap white cotton gloves so you could use them once and throw them away like the rubber ones doctors wear when they stick their fingers up your ass. Michael, Cecil, and Sowell were pallbearers, too. With Robby and two men from Garth's family they would carry the coffin from Gaines Funeral Parlor to the hearse. Garth had been the dreamer for the gang. Robby counted four black fingers in the white glove. Garth was the thumb. The hand would be clumsy, wouldn't work right without him. Garth was different. But everybody else was different, too. Mike, the ice man, supercool. Cecil indifferent, ready to do most anything or nothing and couldn't care less which it was. Sowell wasn't really part of the gang; he didn't hang with them, didn't like to take the risks that were part of the "life." Sowell kept a good job. The "life" for him was just a way to make quick money. He didn't shoot up; he thought of himself as a businessman, an investor not a partner in their schemes. They knew Sowell mostly through Garth. Perhaps things would change now. The four survivors closer after they shared the burden of Gar's coffin, after they hoisted it and slid it on steel rollers into the back of Gaines's Cadillac hearse.

Robby was grateful for the gloves. He'd never been able to touch anything dead. He'd taken a beating once from his father rather than touch the bloody mousetrap his mother had nudged to the back door with her toe and ordered him to empty. The brass handle of the coffin felt damp through the glove. He gripped tighter to stop the flow of blood or sweat, whatever it was leaking from him or seeping from the metal. Garth had melted down to nothing by the end so it couldn't be him nearly yanking off Robby's shoulder when the box shifted and its weight shot forward. Felt like a coffin full of bricks. Robby stared across at Mike but Mike was a soldier, eyes front, riveted to the yawning rear door of the hearse. Mike's eyes wouldn't admit it, but they'd almost lost the coffin. They were rookie pallbearers and maneuvering down the carpeted front steps of Gaines Funeral Parlor they'd almost let Garth fly out their hands. They needed somebody who knew what he was doing. An old, steady head to show them the way. They needed Garth. But Garth was long gone. Ashes inside the steel box.

They began drinking later that afternoon in Garth's people's house. Women and food in one room, men hitting the whiskey hard in another. It was a typical project apartment. The kind everybody had stayed in or visited one time or another. Small, shabby, featureless. Not a place to live. No matter what you did to it, how clean you kept it or what kind of furniture you loaded it with, the walls and ceilings were not meant to be home for anybody. A place you passed through. Not yours, because the people who'd been there before you left their indelible marks everywhere and you couldn't help adding your bruises and knots for the next tenants. You could rent a kitchen and bedroom and a bathroom and a living room, the project flats were laid out so you had a room for each of the things people did in houses. Problem was, every corner was cut. Living cramped is one thing and people can get cozy in the closest quarters. It's another thing to live in a place designed to be just a little less than adequate. No slack, no space to personalize, to stamp the flat with what's peculiar to your style. Like a man sitting on a toilet seat that's too small and the toilet too close to the bathtub so his knees shove against the enamel edge. He can move his bowels that way and plenty of people in the world have a lot less but he'll never enjoy sitting there, never feel the deep down comfort of belonging where he must squat.

Anyway, the whiskey started flowing in that little project apartment. Robby listened, for Garth's sake, as long as he could to old people reminiscing about funerals they'd attended, about all the friends and relatives they'd escorted to the edge of Jordan, old folks sipping good whiskey and moaning and groaning till it seemed a sin to be left behind on this side of the river after so many saints had crossed over. He listened to people express their grief, tell sad, familiar stories. As he got high he listened less closely to the words. Faces and gestures revealed more than enough. When he split with Mike and Cecil and their ladies, Sowell tagged along. By then the tacky, low-ceilinged rooms of the flat were packed. Loud talk, laughter, storytellers competing for audiences. Robby half expected the door he pushed shut behind himself to pop open again, waited for bottled-up noise to explode into the funky hallway.

Nobody thinking about cemeteries now. Nobody else needs to be buried today, so it was time to get it on. Some people had been getting close to rowdy. Some people had been getting mad. Mad at one of the guests in the apartment, mad at doctors and hospitals and whites in general who had the whole world in their hands but didn't have the slightest idea what to do with it. A short, dark man, bubble-eyed, immaculately dressed in a three-piece, wool, herringbone suit, had railed about the callousness, the ignorance of white witch doctors who, by misdiagnosing Garth's illness, had sealed his doom. His harangue had drawn a crowd. He wasn't just talking, he was testifying, and a hush had fallen over half the room as he dissected the dirty tricks of white folks. If somebody ran to the hospital and snatched a white-coated doctor and threw him into the circle surrounding the little fish-eyed man, the mourners would tear the pale-faced devil apart. Robby wished he could feed them one. Remembered Garth weak and helpless in the bed and the doctors and nurses flitting around in the halls, jiving the other patients, ignoring Gar like he wasn't there. Garth was dead because he had believed them. Dead because he had nowhere else to turn when the pain in his gut and the headaches grew worse and worse. Not that he trusted the doctors or believed they gave a flying fuck about him. He'd just run out of choices and had to put himself in their hands. They told him jaundice was his problem, and while his liver rotted away and pain cooked him dizzy Garth assured anyone who asked that it was just a matter of giving the medicine time to work. To kill the pain he blew weed as long as he had strength to hold a joint between his lips. Take a whole bunch of smoke to cool me out these days. Puffing like a chimney till he lost it and fell back and Robby scrambling to grab the joint before Garth torched hisself.

When you thought about it, Garth's dying made no sense. And the more you thought the more you dug that nothing else did neither. The world's a stone bitch. Nothing true if that's not true. The man had you coming and going. He owned everything worth owning and all you'd ever get was what he didn't want anymore, what he'd chewed and spit out and left in the gutter for niggers to fight over. Garth had pointed to the street and said, If we ever make it, it got to come from there, from the curb. We got to melt that rock till we get us some money. He grinned then, Ain't no big thing. We'll make it, brother man. We got what it takes. It's our time.

Something had crawled in Garth's belly. The man said it wasn't nothing. Sold him some aspirins and said he'd be alright in no time. The man killed Garth. Couldn't kill him no deader with a .357 magnum slug, but ain't no crime been committed. Just one those things. You know, everybody makes mistakes. And a dead nigger ain't really such a big mistake when you think about it. Matter of fact you mize well forget the whole thing. Nigger wasn't going nowhere, nohow. I mean he wasn't no brain surgeon or astronaut, no movie star or big-time athlete. Probably a dope fiend or gangster. Wind up killing some innocent person or wasting another nigger. Shucks. That doctor ought to get a medal.

Hey, man. Robby caught Mike's eye. Then Cecil and Sowell turned to him. They knew he was speaking to everybody. Late now. Ten, eleven, because it had been dark outside for hours. Quiet now. Too quiet in his pad. And too much smoke and drink since the funeral. From a bare bulb in the kitchen ceiling light seeped down the hallway and hovered dimly in the doorway of the room where they sat. Robby wondered if the others felt as bad as he did. If the cemetery clothes itched their skin. If they could smell grave dust on their shoes. He hoped they'd finish this last jug of wine and let the day be over. He needed sleep, downtime to get the terrible weight of Garth's death off his mind. He'd been grateful for the darkness. For the company of his cut buddies after the funeral. For the Sun Ra tape until it ended and plunged them into a deeper silence than any he'd ever known. Garth was gone. In a few days people would stop talking about him. He was in the ground. Stone-cold dead. Robby had held a chunk of crumbly ground in his white-gloved fingers and mashed it and dropped the dust into the hole. Now the ground had closed over Garth and what did it mean? Here one day and gone the next and that was that. They'd bury somebody else out of Gaines tomorrow. People would dress up and cry and get drunk and tell lies and next day it'd be somebody else's turn to die. Which one of the shadows in this black room would go first? What did it matter? Who cared? Who would remember their names; they were ghosts already. Dead as Garth already. Only difference was, Garth didn't have it to worry about no more. Garth didn't have to pretend he was going anywhere cause he was there. He'd made it to the place they all were headed fast as their legs could carry them. Every step was a step closer to the stone-cold ground, the pitch-black hole where they'd dropped Garth's body.

Hey, youall. We got to drink to Garth one last time.

They clinked glasses in the darkness. Robby searched for something to say. The right words wouldn't come. He knew there was something proper and precise that needed to be said. Because the exact words eluded him, because only the right words would do, he swallowed his gulp of heavy, sweet wine in silence.

He knew he'd let Garth down. If it had been one of the others dead, Michael or Cecil or Sowell or him, Garth wouldn't let it slide by like this, wouldn't let it end like so many other nights had ended, the fellows nodding off one by one, stupefied by smoke and drink, each one beginning to shop around in his mind, trying to figure whether or not he should turn in or if there was a lady somewhere who'd welcome him in her bed. No. Garth would have figured a way to make it special. They wouldn't be hiding in the bushes. They'd be knights in shining armor around a big table. They'd raise their giant, silver cups to honor the fallen comrade. Like in the olden days. Clean, brave dudes with gold rings and gold chains. They'd draw their blades. Razor-edged swords that gleam in the light with jewels sparkling in the handles. They'd make a roof over the table when they stood and raised their swords and the points touched in the sky. A silver dagger on a satin pillow in the middle of the table. Everybody roll up their sleeves and prick a vein and go round, each one touching everybody else so the blood runs together and we're brothers forever, brothers as long as blood flows in anybody's arm. We'd ride off and do unbelievable shit. The dead one always with us cause we'd do it all for him. Swear we'd never let him down.

It's our time now. We can't let Garth down. Let's drink this last one for him and promise him we'll do what he said we could. We'll be the best. We'll make it to the top for him. We'll do it for Garth.

Glasses rattled together again. Robby empties his and thinks about smashing it against a wall. He'd seen it done that way in movies but it was late at night and these crazy niggers might not know when to stop throwing things. A battlefield of broken glass for him to creep through when he gets out of bed in the morning. He doesn't toss the empty glass. Can't see a solid place anyway where it would strike clean and shatter to a million points of light.

My brother had said something about a guy named Garth during one of my visits to the prison. Just a name mentioned in passing. *Garth* or *Gar*. I'd asked Robby to spell it for me. Garth had been a friend of Robby's, about Robby's age, who died one summer of a mysterious disease. Later when Robby chose to begin the story of the robbery and killing by saying, "It all started with Gar dying," I remembered that first casual mention and remembered a conversation with my mother. My mom and I were in the kitchen of the house on Tokay Street. My recollection of details was vague at first but something about the conversation had made a lasting impression because, six years later, hearing Robby say the name *Garth* brought back my mother's words.

My mother worried about Robby all the time. Whenever I visited home, sooner or later I'd find myself alone with Mom and she'd pour out her fears about Robby's *wildness,* the deep trouble he was bound for, the web of entanglements and intrigues and bad company he was weaving around himself with a maddening disregard for the inevitable consequences.

I don't know. I just don't know how to reach him. He won't listen. He's doing wrong and he knows it but nothing I say makes any difference. He's not like the rest of youall. You'd misbehave but I could talk to you or smack you if I had to and you'd straighten up. With Robby it's like talking to a wall.

I'd listen and get angry at my brother because I registered not so much the danger he was bringing on himself, but the effect of his escapades on the woman who'd brought us both into the world. After all, Robby was no baby. If he wanted to mess up, nobody could stop him. Also Robby was my brother, meaning that his wildness was just a stage, a chaotic phase of his life that would only last till he got his head together and decided to start doing right. Doing as the rest of us did. He was my brother. He couldn't fall too far. His brushes with the law (I'd had some, too), the time he'd spent in jail, were serious but temporary setbacks. I viewed his troubles, when I thought about them at all, as a form of protracted juvenile delinquency, and fully expected Robby would learn his lesson sooner or later and return to the fold, the prodigal son, chastened, perhaps a better person for the experience. In the meantime the most serious consequence of his wildness was Mom's devastating unhappiness. She couldn't sustain the detachment, the laissez-faire optimism I had talked myself into. Because I was two thousand miles away, in Wyoming, I didn't have to deal with the day-to-day evidence of Robby's trouble. The syringe Mom found under his bed. The twenty-dollar bill missing from her purse. The times he'd cruise in higher than a kite, his pupils reduced to pinpricks, with his crew and they'd raid the refrigerator and make a loud, sloppy feast, all of them feeling so good they couldn't imagine anybody not up there on cloud nine with them enjoying the time of their lives. Cruising in, then disappearing just as abruptly, leaving their dishes and pans and mess behind. Robby covering Mom with kisses and smiles and drowning her in babytalk hootchey-coo as he staggers through the front door. Her alone in the ravaged, silent kitchen, listening as doors slam and a car squeals off on the cobblestones of Tokay, wondering where they're headed next, wishing, praying Robby will return and eat and eat and eat till he falls asleep at the table so she can carry him upstairs and tuck him in and kiss his forehead and shut the door gently on his sleep.

I WASN'T AROUND FOR ALL THAT. DIDN'T WANT TO KNOW HOW BAD THINGS WERE FOR HIM.

I wasn't around for all that. Didn't want to know how bad things were for him. Worrying about my mother was tough enough. I could identify with her grief, I could blame my brother. An awful situation, but simple too. My role, my responsibilities and loyalties were clear. The *wildness* was to blame, and it was a passing thing, so I just had to help my mother survive the worst of it, then everything would be alright. I'd steel myself for the moments alone with her when she'd tell me the worst. In the kitchen, usually, over a cup of coffee with the radio playing. When my mother was alone in the house on Tokay, either the TV or a radio or both were always on. Atop the kitchen table a small clock radio turned to WAMO, one of Pittsburgh's soul stations, would background with scratchy gospel music whatever we said in the morning in the kitchen. On a morning like that in 1975, while I drank a cup of coffee and part of me, still half-asleep, hidden, swayed to the soft beat of gospel, my mother had explained how upset Robby was over the death of his friend, Garth.

It was a terrible thing. I've known Garth's mother for years. He was a good boy. No saint for sure, but deep down a good boy. Like your brother. Not a mean bone in his body. Out there in the street doing wrong, but that's where most of them are. What else can they do, John? Sometimes I can't blame them. No jobs, no money in their pockets. How they supposed to feel like men? Garth did better than most. Whatever else he was into, he kept that little job over at Westinghouse and helped out his mother. A big, playful kid. Always smiling. I think that's why him and Robby were so tight. Neither one had good sense. Giggled and acted like fools. Garth no wider than my finger. Straight up and down. A stringbean if I ever saw one. When Robby lived here in the house with me, Garth was always around. I know how bad Robby feels. He hasn't said a word but I know. When Robby's quiet, you know something's wrong. Soon as his eyes pop open in the morning he's looking for the party. First thing in the morning he's chipper and chattering. Looking for the party. That's your brother. He had a match in Garth.

Shame the way they did that boy. He'd been down to the clinic two or three times but they sent him home. Said he had an infection and it would take care of itself. Something like that anyway. You know how they are down there. Have to be spitting blood to get attention. Then all they give you is a Band-Aid. He went back two times, but they kept telling him the same dumb thing. Anybody who knew Garth could see something awful was wrong. Circles under his eyes. Sallow look to his skin. Losing weight. And the poor thing didn't have any weight to lose. Last time I saw him I was shocked. Just about shocked out my shoes. Wasn't Garth standing in front of me. Not the boy I knew.

Well, to make a long story short, they finally took him in the hospital but it was too late. They let him walk the streets till he was dead. It was wrong. Worse than wrong how they did him, but that's how those dogs do us every day God sends here. Garth's gone, so nothing nobody can say will do any good. I feel so sorry for his mother. She lived for that boy. I called her and tried to talk but what can you say? I prayed for her and prayed for Garth and prayed for Robby. A thing like that tears people up. It's worse if you keep it inside. And that's your brother's way. He'll let it eat him up and then go out and do something crazy.

Until she told me Garth's story I guess I hadn't realized how much my mother had begun to change. She had always seemed to me to exemplify the tolerance, the patience, the long view epitomized in her father. John French's favorite saying was, Give 'em the benefit of the doubt. She could get as ruffled, as evil as the rest of us, cry and scream or tear around the house fit to be tied. She had her grudges and quarrels. Mom could let it all hang out, yet most of the time she radiated a deep calm. She reacted strongly to things but at the same time held judgment in abeyance. Events, personalities always deserved a second, slower appraisal, an evaluation outside the sphere of everyday hassles and vexations. You gave people the benefit of the doubt. You attempted to remove your ego, acknowledge the limitations of your individual view of things. You consulted as far as you were equipped by temperament and intelligence a broader, more abiding set of relationships and connections.

You tried on the other person's point of view. You sought the other, better person in yourself who might talk you into relinquishing for a moment your selfish interest in whatever was at issue. You stopped and considered the long view, possibilities other than the one that momentarily was leading you by the nose. You gave yourself and other people the benefit of the doubt.

My mother had that capacity. I'd admired, envied, and benefited infinitely from its presence. As she related the story of Garth's death and my brother's anger and remorse, her tone was uncompromisingly bitter. No slack, no margin of doubt was being granted to the forces that destroyed Garth and still pursued her son. She had exhausted her reserves of understanding and compassion. The long view supplied the same ugly picture as the short. She had an enemy now. It was that revealed truth that had given the conversation its edge, its impact. *They* had killed Garth, and his dying had killed part of her son; so the battle lines were drawn. Irreconcilably. Absolutely. The backside of John French's motto had come into play. Giving someone the benefit of the doubt was also giving him enough rope to hang himself. If a person takes advantage of the benefit of the doubt and keeps on taking and taking, one day the rope plays out. The piper must be paid. If you've been the one giving, it becomes incumbent on you to grip your end tight and take away. You turn the other cheek, but slowly, cautiously, and keep your fist balled up at your side. If your antagonist decides to smack rather than kiss you or leave you alone, you make sure you get in the first blow. And make sure it's hard enough to knock him down.

Before she told Garth's story, my mother had already changed, but it took years for me to realize how profoundly she hated what had been done to Garth and then Robby. The gentleness of my grandfather, like his fair skin and good French hair, had been passed down to my mother. Gentleness styled the way she thought, spoke, and moved in the world. Her easy disposition and sociability masked the intensity of her feelings. Her attitude to authority of any kind, doctors, clerks, police, bill collectors, newscasters, whites in general partook of her constitutional gentleness. She wasn't docile or cowed. The power other people possessed or believed they possessed didn't frighten her; she accommodated herself, offered something they could accept as deference but that was in fact the same resigned, alert attention she paid to roaches or weather or poverty, any of the givens outside herself that she couldn't do much about. She never engaged in public tests of will, never pushed herself or her point of view on people she didn't know. Social awkwardness embarrassed her. Like most Americans she didn't like paying taxes, was suspicious of politicians, resented the disparity between big and little people in our society and the double standard that allowed big shots to get away with murder. She paid particular attention to news stories that reinforced her basic political assumption that power corrupts. On the other hand she knew the world was a vale of tears and one's strength, granted by God to deal with life's inevitable calamities, should not be squandered on small stuff.

In spite of all her temperamental and philosophic resistance to extremes, my mother would be radicalized. What the demonstrations, protest marches, and slogans of the sixties had not effected would be accomplished by Garth's death and my brother's troubles. She would become an aggressive, acid critic of the status quo in all its forms: from the President ("If it wasn't for that rat I'd have a storm door to go with the storm windows but he cut the program") on down to bank tellers ("I go there every Friday and I'm one of the few black faces she sees all day and she knows me as well as she knows that wart on her cheek but she'll still make me show my license before she'll cash my check"). A son she loved would be pursued, captured, tried, and imprisoned by the forces of law and order. Throughout the ordeal her love for him wouldn't change, couldn't change. His crime tested her love and also tested the nature, the intent of the forces arrayed against her son. She had to make a choice. On one side were the stark facts of his crime: robbery, murder, flight; her son an outlaw, a fugitive; then a prisoner. On the other side the guardians of society, the laws, courts, police, judges, and keepers who were responsible for punishing her son's transgression.

She didn't invent the two sides and initially didn't believe there couldn't be a middle ground. She extended the benefit of the doubt. Tried to situate herself somewhere in between, acknowledging the evil of her son's crime while simultaneously holding on to the fact that he existed as a human being before, after, and during the crime he'd committed. He'd done wrong but he was still Robby and she'd always be his mother. Strangely, on the dark side, the side of the crime and its terrible consequences, she would find room to exercise her love. As negative as the elements were, a life taken, the grief of the survivors, suffering, waste, guilt, remorse, the scale was human; she could apply her sense of right and wrong. Her life to that point had equipped her with values, with tools for sorting out and coping with disaster. So she would choose to make her fight there, on treacherous yet familiar ground — familiar since her son was there — and she could place herself, a woman, a mother, a grieving, bereaved human being, there beside him.

Nothing like that was possible on the other side. The legitimacy of the other side was grounded not in her experience of life, but in a set of rules seemingly framed to sidestep, ignore, or replace her sense of reality. Accepting the version of reality encoded in *their* rules would be like stepping into a cage and locking herself in. Definitions of her son, herself, of need and frailty and mercy, of blackness and redemption and justice had all been neatly formulated. No need here for her questions, her uncertainty, her fear, her love. Everything was clean and clear. No room for her sense that things like good and evil, right and wrong bleed into each other and create a dreadful margin of ambiguity no one could name but could only enter, enter at the risk of everything because everything is at stake and no one on earth knows what it means to enter or what will happen if and when the testing of the margin is over.

She could love her son, accept his guilt, accept the necessity of punishment, suffer with him, grow with him past the stage of blaming everyone but himself for his troubles, grieve with him when true penitence began to exact its toll. Though she might wish penance and absolution could be achieved in private, without the intervention of a prison sentence, she understood dues must be paid. He was her son but he was also a man who had committed a robbery in the course of which another woman's son had been killed. What would appall her and what finally turned her against the forces of law and order was the incapacity of the legal system to grant her son's humanity. "Fair" was the word she used — a John French word. She expected them to treat Robby fair. Fairness was what made her willing to give him up to punishment even though her love screamed no and her hands clung to his shoulders. Fairness was what she expected from the other side in their dealings with her and her son.

She could see their side, but they steadfastly refused to see hers. And when she realized fairness was not forthcoming, she began to hate. In the lack of reciprocity, in the failure to grant that Robby was first a man, then a man who had done wrong, the institutions and individuals who took over control of his life denied not only his humanity but the very existence of the world that had nurtured him and nurtured her — the world of touching, laughing, suffering black people that established Robby's claim to something more than a number.

Mom expects the worst now. She's peeped their hole card. She understands they have a master plan that leaves little to accident, that most of the ugliest things happening to black people are not accidental but the predictable results of the working of the plan. What she learned about authority, about law and order didn't make sense at first. It went against her instincts, what she wanted to believe, against the generosity she'd observed in her father's interactions with other Homewood people. He was fair. He'd pick up the egg rolls he loved from the back kitchen door of Mr. Wong's restaurant and not blame Wong, his old talking buddy and card-playing crony, for not serving black people in his restaurant. Wong had a family and depended on white folks to feed them, so Wong didn't have any choice and neither did John French if he wanted those incredible egg rolls. He treated everyone, high and low, the same. He said what he meant and meant what he said. John French expected no more from other people than he expected from himself. And he'd been known to mess up many a time, but that was him, that was John French, no better, no worse than any man who pulls on his britches one leg at a time. He needed a little slack, needed the benefit of that blind eye people who love, or people who want to get along with other people, must learn to cast. John French was grateful for the slack, so was quick to extend it to others. Till they crossed him.

My mother had been raised in Homewood. The old Homewood. Her relations with people in that close-knit, homogeneous community were based on trust, mutual respect, common spiritual and material concerns. Face-to-face contact, shared language and values, a large fund of communal experience rendered individual lives extremely visible in Homewood. Both a person's self-identity ("You know who you are") and accountability ("Other people know who you are") were firmly established.

If one of the Homewood people said, "That's the French girl" or, "There goes John French's daughter," a portrait with subtle shading and complex resonance was painted by the words. If the listener addressed was also a Homewood resident, the speaker's voice located the young woman passing innocently down Tioga Street in a world invisible to outsiders. A French girl was somebody who lived in Cassina Way, somebody you didn't fool with or talk nasty to. Didn't speak to at all except in certain places or on certain occasions. French girls were church girls, Homewood African Methodist Episcopal Zion Sunday-school-picnic and social-event young ladies. You wouldn't find them hanging around anywhere without escorts or chaperones. French girls had that fair, light, bright, almost white redbone complexion and fine blown hair and nice big legs but all that was to be appreciated from a distance because they were nice girls and because they had this crazy daddy who wore a big brown country hat and gambled and drank wine and once ran a man out of town, ran him away without ever laying a hand on him or making a bad-mouthed threat, just cut his eyes a certain way when he said the man's name and the word went out and the man who had cheated a drunk John French with loaded dice was gone. Just like that. And there was the time Elias Brown was cleaning his shotgun in his backyard. Brown had his double-barreled shotgun across his knees and a jug of Dago Red on the ground beside him and it was a Saturday and hot and Brown was sweating through his BVD undershirt and paying more attention to the wine than he was to the gun. Next thing you know, *Boom!* Off it goes and buckshot sprayed down Cassina Way, and it's Saturday and summer like I said, so chillens playing everywhere but God watches over fools and babies so nobody hit bad. Nobody hit at all except the little French girl, Geraldine, playing out there in the alley and she got nicked in her knee. Barely drew blood. A sliver of that buckshot musta ricocheted off the cobblestones and cut her knee. Thank Jesus she the only one hit and she ain't hit bad. Poor Elias Brown don't quite know what done happened till some the mens run over in his yard and snatch the gun and shake the wine out his head. What you doing, fool? Don't you know no better all those children running round here? Coulda killed one these babies. Elias stone drunk and don't hear nothing, see nothing till one the men say French girl. Nicked the little French girl, Geraldine. Then Elias woke up real quick. His knees, his dusty butt, everything he got starts to trembling and his eyes get big as dinner plates. Then he's gone like a turkey through the corn. Nobody seen Elias for a week. He's in Ohio at his sister's next time anybody hear anything about Elias. He's cross there in Ohio and still shaking till he git word John French ain't after him. It took three men gon over there telling the same story to get Elias back to Homewood. John French ain't mad. He *was* mad but he ain't mad now. Little girl just nicked is all and French ain't studying you, Brown.

You heard things like that in Homewood names. Rules of etiquette, thumbnail character sketches, a history of the community. A dire warning to get back could be coded into the saying of a person's name, and a further inflection of the speaker's voice could tell you to ignore the facts, forget what he's just reminded you to remember and go on. Try your luck.

Because Homewood was self-contained and possessed such a strong personality, because its people depended less on outsiders than they did on each other for so many of their most basic satisfactions, they didn't notice the net settling over their community until it was already firmly in place. Even though the strands of the net — racial discrimination, economic exploitation, white hate and fear — had existed time out of mind, what people didn't notice or chose not to notice was that the net was being drawn tighter, that ruthless people outside the community had the power to choke the life out of Homewood, and as soon as it served their interests would do just that. During the final stages, as the net closed like a fist around Homewood, my mother couldn't pretend it wasn't there. But instead of setting her free, the truth trapped her in a cage as tangible as the iron bars of Robby's cell.

Some signs were subtle, gradual. The A & P started to die. Nobody mopped filth from the floors. Nobody bothered to restock empty shelves. Fewer and fewer white faces among the shoppers. A plate-glass display window gets broken and stays broken. When they finally close the store, they paste the going-out-of-business notice over the jagged, taped crack. Other signs as blatant, as sudden as fire engines and patrol cars breaking your sleep, screaming through the dark Homewood streets. First Garth's death, then Robby's troubles brought it all home. My mother realized her personal unhappiness and grief were inseparable from what was happening *out there*. Out there had never been further away than the thousand insults and humiliations she had disciplined herself to ignore. What she had deemed petty, not worth bothering about, were strings of the net just as necessary, as effective as the most dramatic intrusions into her life. She decided to stop letting things go by. No more benefit of the doubt. Doubt had been cruelly excised. She decided to train herself to be as wary, as unforgiving as she'd once been ready to live and let live. My mother wouldn't become paranoid, not even overtly prickly or bristling. That would have been too contrary to her style, to what her blood and upbringing had instilled. The change was inside. What she thought of people. How she judged situations. Things she'd say or do startled me, set me back on my heels because I didn't recognize my mother in them. I couldn't account for the stare of pure unadulterated hatred she directed at the prison guard when he turned away from her to answer the phone before handing her the rest-room key she'd requested, the vehemence with which she had cussed Richard Nixon for paying no taxes when she, scraping by on an income of less than four thousand dollars a year, owed the IRS three hundred dollars.

Garth's death and Robby's troubles were at the center of her new vision. Like a prism, they caught the light, transformed it so she could trace the seemingly random inconveniences and impositions coloring her life to their source in a master plan.

I first heard Garth's story in the summer of 1975, the summer my wife carried our daughter Jamila in her belly, the summer before the robbery and killing. The story contained all the clues I'm trying to decipher now. Sitting in the kitchen vaguely distracted by gospel music from the little clock radio atop the table, listening as my mother expressed her sorrow, her indignation at the way Garth was treated, her fears for my brother, I was hearing a new voice. Something about the voice struck me then, but I missed what was novel and crucial. I'd lost my Homewood ear. Missed all the things unsaid that invested her words with special urgency. People in Homewood often ask: You said that to say what? The impacted quality of an utterance either buries a point too obscurely or insists on a point so strongly that the listener wants the meat of the message repeated, wants it restated clearly so it stands alone on its own two feet. If I'd been alert enough to ask that question, to dig down to the root and core of Garth's story after my mother told it, I might have understood sooner how desperate and dangerous Homewood had become. Six years later my brother was in prison, and when he began the story of his troubles with Garth's death, a circle completed itself; Robby was talking to me, but I was still on the outside, looking in.

I WAS HEARING A NEW VOICE. SOMETHING ABOUT THE VOICE STRUCK ME THEN, BUT I MISSED WHAT WAS NOVEL AND CRUCIAL. I'D LOST MY HOMEWOOD EAR.

That day six years later, I talked with Robby three hours, the maximum allotted for weekday visits with a prisoner. It was the first time in life we'd ever talked that long. Probably two and a half hours longer than the longest, unbroken, private conversation we'd ever had. And it had taken guards, locks, and bars to bring us together. The ironies of the situation, the irony of that fact, escaped neither of us.

I listened mostly, interrupting my brother's story a few times to clarify dates or names. Much of what he related was familiar. The people, the places. Even the voice, the words he chose were mine in a way. We're so alike, I kept thinking, anticipating what he would say next, how he would say it, filling in naturally, easily with my words what he left unsaid. Trouble was our minds weren't interchangeable. No more than our bodies. The guards wouldn't have allowed me to stay in my brother's place. He was the criminal. I was the visitor from outside. Different as night and day. As Robby talked I let myself forget that difference. Paid too much attention to myself listening and lost some of what he was saying. What I missed would have helped define the difference. But I missed it. It was easy to half listen. For both of us to pretend to be closer than we were. We needed the closeness. We were brothers. In the prison visiting lounge I acted toward my brother the way I'd been acting toward him all my life, heard what I wanted to hear, rejected the rest.

When Robby talked, the similarity of his Homewood and mine was a trap. I could believe I knew exactly what he was describing. I could relax into his story, walk down Dunfermline or Tioga, see my crippled grandmother sitting on the porch of the house on Finance, all the color her pale face had lost blooming in the rosebush beneath her in the yard, see Robby in the downstairs hall of the house on Marchand, rapping with his girl on the phone, which sat on a three-legged stand just inside the front door. I'd slip unaware out of his story into one of my own. I'd be following him, an obedient shadow, then a cloud would blot the sun and I'd be gone, unchained, a dark form still skulking behind him but no longer in tow.

The hardest habit to break, since it was the habit of a lifetime, would be listening to myself listen to him. That habit would destroy any chance of seeing my brother on his terms; and seeing him in his terms, learning his terms, seemed the whole point of learning his story. However numerous and comforting the similarities, we were different. The world had seized on the difference, allowed me room to thrive, while he'd been forced into a cage. Why did it work out that way? What was the nature of the difference? Why did it haunt me? Temporarily at least, to answer these questions, I had to root my fiction-writing self out of our exchanges. I had to teach myself to listen. Start fresh, clear the pipes, resist too facile an identification, tame the urge to take off with Robby's story and make it my own.

I understood all that, but could I break the habit? And even if I did learn to listen, wouldn't there be a point at which I'd have to take over the telling? Wasn't there something fundamental in my writing, in my capacity to function, that depended on flight, on escape? Wasn't another person's skin a hiding place, a place to work out anxiety, to face threats too intimidating to handle in any other fashion? Wasn't writing about people a way of exploiting them?

A stranger's gait, or eyes, or a piece of clothing can rivet my attention. Then it's like falling down to the center of the earth. Not exactly fear or panic but an uneasy, uncontrollable momentum, a sense of being swallowed, engulfed in blackness that has no dimensions, no fixed points. That boundless, incarcerating black hole is another person. The detail grabbing me functions as a door and it swings open and I'm drawn, sucked, pulled in head over heels till suddenly I'm righted again, on track again and the peculiarity, the ordinariness of the detail that usurped my attention becomes a window, a way of seeing out of another person's eyes, just as for a second it had been my way in. I'm scooting along on short, stubby legs and the legs are not anybody else's and certainly not mine, but I feel for a second what it's like to motor through the world atop these peculiar duck thighs and foreshortened calves and I know how wobbly the earth feels under those run-over-at-the-heel, split-seamed penny loafers. Then just as suddenly I'm back. I'm me again, slightly embarrassed, guilty because I've been trespassing and don't know how long I've been gone or if anybody noticed me violating somebody else's turf.

Do I write to escape, to make a fiction of my life? If I can't be trusted with the story of my own life, how could I ask my brother to trust me with his?

The business of making a book together was new for both of us. Difficult. Awkward. Another book could be constructed about a writer who goes to a prison to interview his brother but comes away with his own story. The conversations with his brother would provide a stage for dramatizing the writer's tortured relationship to other people, himself, his craft. The writer's motives, the issue of exploitation, the inevitable conflict between his role as detached observer and his responsibility as a brother would be at the center of such a book. When I stopped hearing Robby and listened to myself listening, that kind of book shouldered its way into my consciousness. I didn't like the feeling. That book compromised the intimacy I wanted to achieve with my brother. It was as obtrusive as the Wearever pen in my hand, the little yellow sheets of Yard Count paper begged from the pad of the guard in charge of overseeing the visiting lounge. The borrowed pen and paper (I was not permitted into the lounge with my own) were necessary props. I couldn't rely on memory to get my brother's story down and the keepers had refused my request to use a tape recorder, so there I was. Jimmy Olson, cub reporter, poised on the edge of my seat, pen and paper at ready, asking to be treated as a brother.

We were both rookies. Neither of us had learned very much about sharing our feelings with other family members. At home it had been assumed that each family member possessed deep, powerful feelings and that very little or nothing at all needed to be said about these feelings because we all were stuck with them and talk wouldn't change them. Your particular feelings were a private matter and family was a protective fence around everybody's privacy. Inside the perimeter of the fence each family member resided in his or her own quarters. What transpired in each dwelling was mainly the business of its inhabitant as long as nothing generated within an individual unit threatened the peace or safety of the whole. None of us knew how traditional West African families were organized or what values the circular shape of their villages embodied, but the living arrangements we had worked out among ourselves resembled the ancient African patterns. You were granted emotional privacy, independence, and space to commune with your feelings. You were encouraged to deal with as much as you could on your own, yet you never felt alone. The high wall of the family, the collective, communal reality of other souls, other huts like yours eliminated some of the dread, the isolation experienced when you turned inside and tried to make sense out of the chaos of your individual feelings. No matter how grown you thought you were or how far you believed you'd strayed, you knew you could cry *Mama* in the depths of the night and somebody would tend to you. Arms would wrap round you, a soft soothing voice lend its support. If not a flesh-and-blood mother then a mother in the form of song or story or a surrogate, Aunt Geral, Aunt Martha, drawn from the network of family numbers.

Privacy was a bridge between you and the rest of the family. But you had to learn to control the traffic. You had to keep it uncluttered, resist the temptation to cry wolf. Privacy in our family was a birthright, a union card granted with family membership. The card said you're one of us but also certified your separateness, your obligation to keep much of what defined your separateness to yourself.

An almost aesthetic consideration's involved. Okay, let's live together. Let's each build a hut and for security we'll arrange the individual dwellings in a circle and then build an outer ring to enclose the whole village. Now your hut is your own business, but let's in general agree on certain outward forms. Since we all benefit from the larger pattern, let's compromise, conform to some degree on the materials, the shape of each unit. Because symmetry and harmony please the eye. Let's adopt a style, one that won't crimp anybody's individuality, one that will buttress and enhance each member's image of what a living place should be.

So Robby and I faced each other in the prison visiting lounge as familiar strangers, linked by blood and time. But how do you begin talking about blood, about time? He's been inside his privacy and I've been inside mine, and neither of us in thirty-odd years had felt the need to exchange more than social calls. We shared the common history, values, and style developed within the tall stockade of family, and that was enough to make us care about each other, enough to insure a profound depth of mutual regard, but the feelings were undifferentiated. They'd seldom been tested specifically, concretely. His privacy and mine had been exclusive, sanctioned by family traditions. Don't get too close. Don't ask too many questions or give too many answers. Don't pry. Don't let what's inside slop out on the people around you.

The stories I'd sent to Robby were an attempt to reveal what I thought about certain matters crucial to us both. Our shared roots and destinies. I wanted him to know what I'd been thinking and how that thinking was drawing me closer to him. I was banging on the door of his privacy. I believed I'd shed some of my own.

We were ready to talk. It was easy to begin. Impossible. We were neophytes, rookies. I was a double rookie. A beginner at this kind of intimacy, a beginner at trying to record it. My double awkwardness kept getting in the way. I'd hidden the borrowed pen by dropping my hand below the level of the table where we sat. Now when in hell would be the right moment to raise it? To use it? I had to depend on my brother's instincts, his generosity. I had to listen, listen.

Luckily there was catching up to do. He asked me about my kids, about his son, Omar, about the new nieces and nephews he'd never seen. That helped. Reminded us we were brothers. We got on with it. Conditions in the prisons. Robby's state of mind. The atmosphere behind the prison walls had been particularly tense for over a year. A group of new, younger guards had instituted a get-tough policy. More strip searches, cell shakedowns, strict enforcement of penny-ante rules and regulations. Grown men treated like children by other grown men. Inmates yanked out of line and punished because a button is undone or hair uncombed. What politicians demanded in the free world was being acted out inside the prison. A crusade, a war on crime waged by a gang of gung-ho guards against men who were already certified casualties, prisoners of war. The walking wounded being beaten and shot up again because they're easy targets. Robby's closest friends, including Cecil and Mike, are in the hole. Others who were considered potential troublemakers had been transferred to harsher prisons. Robby was warned by a guard. We ain't caught you in the shit yet, but we will. We know what you're thinking and we'll catch you in it. Or put you in it. Got your buddies and we'll get you.

The previous summer, 1980, a prisoner, Leon Patterson, had been asphyxiated in his cell. He was an asthma sufferer, a convicted murderer who depended on medication to survive the most severe attacks of his illness. On a hot August afternoon when the pollution index had reached its highest count of the summer, Patterson was locked in his cell in a cell block without windows and little air. At four o'clock, two hours after he'd been confined to the range, he began to call for help. Other prisoners raised the traditional distress signal, rattling tin cups against the bars of their cells. Patterson's cries for help became screams, and his fellow inmates beat on the bars and shouted with him. Over an hour passed before any guards arrived. They carted away Patterson's limp body. He never revived and was pronounced dead at 10:45 that evening. His death epitomized the polarization in the prison. Patterson was seen as one more victim of the guards' inhumanity. A series of incidents followed in the ensuing year, hunger strikes, melees between guards and prisoners, culminating in a near massacre when the dog days of August hung once more over the prison.

One of the favorite tactics of the militant guards was grabbing a man from the line as the prisoners moved single-file through an archway dividing the recreation yard from the main cell blocks. No reason was given or needed. It was a simple show of force, a reminder of the guards' absolute power, their right to treat the inmates any way they chose, and do it with impunity. A sit-down strike in the prison auditorium followed one of the more violent attacks on an inmate. The prisoner who had resisted an arbitrary seizure and strip search was smacked in the face. He punched back and the guards jumped him, knocked him to the ground with their fists and sticks. The incident took place in plain view of over a hundred prisoners and it was the last straw. The victim had been provoked, assaulted, and surely would be punished for attempting to protect himself, for doing what any man would and should do in similar circumstances. The prisoner would suffer again. In addition to the physical beating they'd administered, the guards would attack the man's record. He'd be written up. A kangaroo court would take away his *good time*, thereby lengthening the period he'd have to wait before becoming eligible for probation or parole. Finally, on the basis of the guards' testimony he'd probably get a sixty-day sojourn in the hole. The prisoners realized it was time to take a stand. What had happened to one could happen to any of them. They rushed into the auditorium and locked themselves in. The prisoners held out till armed state troopers and prison guards in riot gear surrounded the building. Given the mood of that past year and the unmistakable threat in the new warden's voice as he repeated through a loudspeaker his refusal to meet with the prisoners and discuss their grievances, everybody inside the building knew that the authorities meant business, that the forces of law and order would love nothing better than an excuse to turn the auditorium into a shooting gallery. The strike was broken. The men filed out. A point was driven home again. Prisoners have no rights the keepers are bound to respect.

That was how the summer had gone. Summer was bad enough in the penitentiary in the best of times. Warm weather stirred the prisoners' blood. The siren call of the streets intensified. Circus time. The street blooming again after the long, cold winter. People outdoors. On their stoops. On the corners. In bright summer clothes or hardly any clothes at all. The free-world sounds and sights more real as the weather heats up. Confinement a torture. Each cell a hotbox. The keepers take advantage of every excuse to keep you out of the yard, to deprive you of the simple pleasure of a breeze, the blue sky. Why? So that the pleasant weather can be used as a tool, a boon to be withheld. So punishment has a sharper edge. By a perverse turn of the screw something good becomes something bad. Summer a bitch at best, but this past summer as the young turks among the guards ran roughshod over the prisoners, the prison had come close to blowing, to exploding like a piece of rotten fruit in the sun. And if the lid blew, my brother knew he'd be one of the first to die. During any large-scale uprising, in the first violent, chaotic seconds no board of inquiry would ever be able to reconstruct, scores would be settled. A bullet in the back of the brain would get rid of troublemakers, remove potential leaders, uncontrollable prisoners the guards hated and feared. You were supremely eligible for a bullet if the guards couldn't press your button. If they hadn't learned how to manipulate you, if you couldn't be bought or sold, if you weren't into drug and sex games, if you weren't cowed or depraved, then you were a threat.

Robby understood that he was sentenced to die. That all sentences were death sentences. If he didn't buckle under, the guards would do everything in their power to kill him. If he succumbed to the pressure to surrender dignity, self-respect, control over his own mind and body, then he'd become a beast, and what was good in him would die. The death sentence was unambiguous. The question for him became: How long could he survive in spite of the death sentence? Nothing he did would guarantee his safety. A disturbance in a cell block halfway across the prison could provide an excuse for shooting him and dumping him with the other victims. Anytime he was ordered to go with guards out of sight of other prisoners, his escorts could claim he attacked them, or attempted to escape. Since the flimsiest pretext would make murdering him acceptable, he had no means of protecting himself. Yet to maintain sanity, to minimize their opportunities to destroy him, he had to be constantly vigilant. He had to discipline himself to avoid confrontations, he had to weigh in terms of life and death every decision he made; he had to listen and obey his keepers' orders, but he also had to determine in certain threatening situations whether it was better to say no and keep himself out of a trap or take his chances that this particular summons was not the one inviting him to his doom. Of course to say no perpetuated his reputation as one who couldn't be controlled, a bad guy, a guy you never turn your back on, one of the prisoners out to get the guards. That rap made you more dangerous in the keepers' eyes and therefore increased the likelihood they'd be frightened into striking first. Saying no put you in no less jeopardy than going along with the program. Because the program was contrived to kill you. Directly or indirectly, you knew where you were headed. What you didn't know was the schedule. Tomorrow. Next week. A month. A minute. When would one of them get itchy, get beyond waiting a second longer? Would there be a plan, a contrived incident, a conspiracy they'd talk about and set up as they drank coffee in the guards' room or would it be the hair-trigger impulse of one of them who held a grudge, harbored an antipathy so elemental, so irrational that it could express itself only in a burst of pure, unrestrained violence?

If you're Robby and have the will to survive, these are the possibilities you must constantly entertain. Vigilance is the price of survival. Beneath the vigilance, however, is a gnawing awareness boiling in the pit of your stomach. You can be as vigilant as you're able, you can keep fighting the good fight to survive, and still your fate is out of your hands. If they decide to come for you in the morning, that's it. Your ass is grass and those minutes, and hours, days and years you painfully stitched together to put off the final reckoning won't matter at all. So the choice, difficult beyond words, to say yes or say no is made in light of the knowledge that in the end neither your yes nor your no matters. Your life is not in your hands.

The events, the atmosphere of the summer had brought home to Robby the futility of resistance. Power was absurdly apportioned all on one side. To pretend you could control your own destiny was a joke. You learned to laugh at your puniness, as you laughed at the stink of your farts lighting up your cell. Like you laughed at the seriousness of the masturbation ritual that romanticized, cloaked in darkness and secrecy, the simple, hungry shaking of your penis in your fist. You had no choice, but you always had to decide to go on or stop. It had been a stuttering, stop, start, maybe, fuck it, bitch of a summer, and now, for better or worse, we were starting up something else. Robby backtracks his story from Garth to another beginning, the house on Copeland Street in Shadyside where we lived when he was born.

I know that had something to do with it. Living in Shadyside with only white people around. You remember how it was. Except for us and them couple other families it was a all-white neighborhood. I got a thing about black. See, black was like the forbidden fruit. Even when we went to Freed's in Homewood, Geraldine and them never let me go no farther than the end of the block. All them times I stayed over there I didn't go past Mr. Conrad's house by the vacant lot or the other corner where Billy Shields and them stayed. Started to wondering what was so different about a black neighborhood. I was just a little kid and I was curious.

I really wanted to know why they didn't want me finding out what was over there. Be playing with the kids next door to Freed, you know, Sonny and Gumpy and them, but all the time I'm wondering what's round the corner, what's up the street. Didn't care if it was *bad* or good or dangerous or what, I had to find out. If it's something bad I figured they would have told me, tried to scare me off. But nobody said nothing except, No. Don't you go no farther than the corner. Then back home in Shadyside nothing but white people so I couldn't ask nobody what was special about black. Black was a mystery and in my mind I decided I'd find out what it was all about. Didn't care if it killed me, I was going to find out.

One time, it was later, I was close to starting high school, I overheard Mommy and Geraldine and Sissy talking in Freed's kitchen. They was talking about us moving from Shadyside back to Homewood. The biggest thing they was worried about was me. How would it be for me being in Homewood and going to Westinghouse? I could tell they was scared. Specially Mom. You know how she is. She didn't want to move. Homewood scared her. Not so much the place but how I'd act if I got out there in the middle of it. She already knew I was wild, hard to handle. There'd be too much mess for me to get into in Homewood. She could see trouble coming.

And she was right. Me and trouble hooked up. See, it was a question of being somebody. Being my own person. Like youns had sports and good grades sewed up. Wasn't nothing I could do in school or sports that youns hadn't done already. People said, Here comes another Wideman. He's gon be a good student like his brothers and sister. That's the way it was spozed to be. I was another Wideman, the last one, the baby, and everybody knew how I was spozed to act. But something inside me said no. Didn't want to be like the rest of youns. Me, I had to be a rebel. Had to get out from under youns' good grades and do. Way back then I decided I wanted to be a star. I wanted to make it big. My way. I wanted the glamour. I wanted to sit high up.

Figured out school and sports wasn't the way. I got to thinking my brothers and sister was squares. Loved youall but wasn't no room left for me. Had to figure out a new territory. I had to be a rebel.

Along about junior high I discovered Garfield. I started hanging out up on Garfield Hill. You know, partying and stuff in Garfield cause that's where the niggers was. Garfield was black, and I finally found what I'd been looking for. That place they was trying to hide from me. It was heaven. You know. Hanging out with the fellows. Drinking wine and trying anything else we could get our hands on. And the ladies. Always a party on the weekends. Had me plenty sweet little soft-leg Garfield ladies. Niggers run my butt off that hill more than a couple times behind messing with somebody's piece but I'd be back next weekend. Cause I'd found heaven. Looking back now, wasn't much to Garfield. Just a rinky-dink ghetto up on a hill, but it was the street. I'd found my place.

Having a little bit of a taste behind me I couldn't wait to get to Homewood. In a way I got mad with Mommy and the rest of them. Seemed to me like they was trying to hold me back from a good time. Seemed like they just didn't want me to have no fun. That's when I decided I'd go on about my own business. Do it my way. Cause I wasn't getting no slack at home. They still expected me to be like my sister and brothers. They didn't know I thought youns was squares. Yeah. I knew I was hipper and groovier than youns ever thought of being. Streetwise, into something. Had my own territory and I was bad. I was a rebel. Wasn't following in nobody's footsteps but my own. And I was a hip cookie, you better believe it. Wasn't a hipper thing out there than your brother, Rob. I couldn't wait for them to turn me loose in Homewood.

Me being the youngest and all, the baby in the family, people always said, ain't he cute. That Robby gon be a ladykiller. Been hearing that mess since day one so ain't no surprise I started to believing it. Youns had me pegged as a lady's man so that's what I was. The girls be talking the same trash everybody else did. Ain't he cute. Be petting me and spoiling me like I'm still the baby of the family and I sure ain't gon tell them stop. Thought I was cute as the girls be telling me. Thought sure enough, I'm gon be a star. I loved to get up and show my behind. Must have been good at it too cause the teacher used to call me up in front of the class to perform. The kids'd get real quiet. That's probably why the teacher got me up. Keep the class quiet while she nods off. Cause they'd listen to me. Sure nuff pay attention.

Performing always come natural to me. Wasn't nervous or nothing. Just get up and do my thing. They liked for me to do impressions. I could mimic anybody. You remember how I'd do that silly stuff around the house. Anybody I'd see on TV or hear on a record I could mimic to a T. Bob Hope, Nixon, Smokey Robinson, Ed Sullivan. White or black. I could talk just like them or sing a song just like they did. The class yell out a famous name and I'd do the one they wanted to hear. If things had gone another way I've always believed I could have made it big in show business. If you could keep them little frisky kids in Liberty School quiet you could handle any audience. Always could sing and do impressions. You remember Mom asking me to do them for you when you came home from college.

I still be performing. Read poetry in the hole. The other fellows get real quiet and listen. Sing down in there too. Nothing else to do, so we entertain each other. They always asking me to sing or read. "Hey, Wideman. C'mon man and do something." Then it gets quiet while they waiting for me to start. Quiet and it's already dark. You in your own cell and can't see nobody else. Barely enough light to read by. The other fellows can hear you but it's just you and them walls so it feels like being alone much as it feels like you're singing or reading to somebody else.

Yeah. I read my own poems sometimes. Other times I just start in on whatever book I happen to be reading. One the books you sent me, maybe. Fellows like my poems. They say I write about the things they be thinking. Say it's like listening to their own self thinking. That's cause we all down there together. What else you gonna do but think of the people on the outside. Your woman. Your kids or folks, if you got any. Just the same old sad shit we all be thinking all the time. That's what I write and the fellows like to hear it.

Funny how things go around like that. Go round and round and keep coming back to the same place. Teacher used to get me up to pacify the class and I'm doing the same thing in prison. You said your teachers called on you to tell stories, didn't they? Yeah. It's funny how much we're alike. In spite of everything I always believed that. Inside. The feeling side. I always believed we was the most alike out of all the kids. I see stuff in your books. The kinds of things I be thinking or feeling.

Your teachers got you up, too. To tell stories. That's funny, ain't it.

I listen to my brother Robby. He unravels my voice. I sit with him in the darkness of the Behavioral Adjustment Unit. My imagination creates something like a giant seashell, enfolding, enclosing us. Its inner surface is velvet-soft and black. A curving mirror doubling the darkness. Poems are Jean Toomer's petals of dusk, petals of dawn. I want to stop. Savor the sweet, solitary pleasure, the time stolen from time in the hole. But the image I'm creating is a trick of the glass. The mirror that would swallow Robby and then chime to me: You're the fairest of them all. The voice I hear issues from a crack in the glass. I'm two or three steps ahead of my brother, making fiction out of his words. Somebody needs to snatch me by the neck and say, Stop. Stop and listen, listen to him.

The Behavioral Adjustment Unit is, as one guard put it, "a maximum-security prison within a maximum-security prison." The "Restricted Housing Unit" or "hole" or "Home Block" is a squat, two-story cement building containing thirty-five six-by-eight-foot cells. The governor of Pennsylvania closed the area in 1972 because of "inhumane conditions," but within a year the hole was reopened. For at least twenty-three hours a day the prisoners are confined to their cells. An hour of outdoor exercise is permitted only on days the guards choose to supervise it. Two meals are served three hours apart, then nothing except coffee and bread for the next twenty-one. The regulation that limits the time an inmate can serve in the BAU for a single offense is routinely sidestepped by the keepers. "Administrative custody" is a provision allowing officials to cage men in the BAU indefinitely. Hunger strikes are one means the prisoners have employed to protest the harsh conditions of the penal unit. Hearings prompted by the strikes have produced no major changes in the way the hole operates. Law, due process, the rights of the prisoners are irrelevant to the functioning of this prison within a prison. Robby was sentenced to six months in the BAU because a guard suspected he was involved in an attempted escape. The fact that a hearing, held six months later, established Robby's innocence, was small consolation since he'd already served his time in the hole.

I LISTEN TO MY BROTHER ROBBY. HE UNRAVELS MY VOICE.

Robby tells me about the other side of being the youngest: Okay, you're everybody's pet and that's boss, but on the other hand you sometimes feel you're the least important. Always last. Always bringing up the rear. You learn to do stuff on your own because the older kids are always busy, off doing their things, and you're too young, left behind because you don't fit, or just because they forget you're back here, at the end, bringing up the rear. But when orders are given out, you sure get your share. "John's coming home this weekend. Clean up your room." Robby remembers being forced to get a haircut on the occasion of one of my visits. Honor thy brother. Get your hair cut, your room rid up, and put on clean clothes. He'll be here with his family and I don't want the house looking like a pigpen.

I have to laugh at the image of myself as somebody to get a haircut for. Robby must have been fit to be tied.

Yeah, I was hot. I mean, you was doing well and all that, but shit, you were my brother. And it was my head. What's my head got to do with you? But you know how Mommy is. Ain't no talking to her when her mind gets set. Anything I tried to say was "talking *back*," so I just went ahead to the man and got my ears lowered.

I was trying to be a rebel but back then the most important thing still was what the grown-ups thought about me. How they felt meant everything. Everything. Me and Tish and Dave were the ones at home then. You was gone and Gene was gone so it was the three of us fighting for attention. And we fought. Every crumb, everytime something got cut up or parceled out or it was Christmas or Easter, we so busy checking out what the other one got wasn't hardly no time to enjoy our own. Like a dogfight or cat fight all the time. And being the youngest I'm steady losing ground most the time. Seemed like to me, Tish and Dave the ones everybody talked about. Seemed like my time would never come. That ain't the way it really was, I know. I had my share cause I was the baby and ain't he cute and lots of times I know I got away with outrageous stuff or got my way cause I could play that baby mess to the hilt. Still it seemed like Dave and Tish was the ones really mattered. Mommy and Daddy and Sis and Geral and Big Otie and Ernie always slipping some change in their pockets or taking them to the store or letting them stay over all night in Homewood. I was a jealous little rascal. Sometimes I thought everybody thought I was just a spoiled brat. I'd say damn all youall. I'd think, Go on and love those square turkeys, but one day I'll be the one coming back with a suitcase full of money and a Cadillac. Go on and love them good grades. Robby gon do it his own way.

See, in my mind I was Superfly. I'd drive up slow to the curb. My hog be half a block long and these fine foxes in the back. Everybody looking when I ease out the door clean and mean. Got a check in my pocket to give to Mom. Buy her a new house with everything in it new. Pay her back for the hard times. I could see that happening as real as I can see your face right now. Wasn't no way it wasn't gon happen. Rob was gon make it big. I'd be at the door, smiling with the check in my hand and Mommy'd be so happy she'd be crying.

Well, it's a different story ain't it. Turned out different from how I used to think it would. The worst thing I did, the thing I feel most guilty behind is stealing Mom's life. It's like I stole her youth. Can't nothing change that.

I can't give back what's gone. Robbing white people didn't cause me to lose no sleep back then. Couldn't feel but so bad about that. How you gon feel sorry when society's so corrupt, when everybody got their hand out or got their hand in somebody else's pocket and ain't no rules nobody listens to if they can get away with breaking them? How you gon apply the rules? It was dog eat dog out there, so how was I spozed to feel sorry if I was doing what everybody else doing. I just got caught is all. I'm sorry about that, and damned sorry that guy Stavros got killed, but as far as what I did, as far as robbing white people, ain't no way I was gon torture myself over that one.

I tried to write Mom a letter. Not too long ago. Should say I did write the letter and put it in a envelope and sent it cause that's what I did, but I be crying so much trying to write it I don't know what wound up in that letter. I wanted Mom to know I knew what I'd done. In a way I wanted to say I was sorry for spoiling her life. After all she did for me I turned around and made her life miserable. That's the wrongest thing I've done and I wanted to say I was sorry but I kept seeing her face while I was writing the letter. I'd see her face and it would get older while I was looking. She'd get this old woman's face all lined and wrinkled and tired about the eyes. Wasn't nothing I could do but watch. Cause I'd done it and knew I done it and all the letters in the world ain't gon change her face. I sit and think about stuff like that all the time. It's better now. I think about other things too. You know like trying to figure what's really right and wrong, but there be days the guilt don't never go away.

I'm the one made her tired, John. And that's my greatest sorrow. All the love that's in me she created. Then I went and let her down.

When you in prison you got plenty of time to think, that's for damned sure. Too much time. I've gone over and over my life. Every moment. Every little thing again and again. I lay down on my bed and watch it happening over and over. Like a movie. I get it all broke down in pieces then I break up the pieces then I take the pieces of the pieces and run them through my hands so I remember every word a person said to me or what I said to them and weigh the words till I think I know what each and every one meant. Then I try to put it back together. Try to understand where I been. Why I did what I did. You got time for that in here. Time's all you got in here.

Going over and over things sometimes you can make sense. You know. Like the chinky-chinky Chinaman sittin' on the fence. You put it together and you think, yes. That's why I did thus and so. Yeah. That's why I lost that job or lost that woman or broke that one's heart. You stop thinking in terms of something being good or being evil, you just try to say this happened because that happened because something else came first. You can spend days trying to figure out just one little thing you did. People out there in the world walk around in a daze cause they ain't got time to think. When I was out there, I wasn't no different. Had this Superfly thing and that was the whole bit. Nobody could tell me nothing.

Seems like I should start the story back in Shadyside. In the house on Copeland Street. Nothing but white kids around. Them little white kids had everything, too. That's what I thought, anyway. Nice houses, nice clothes. They could buy pop and comic books and candy when they wanted to. We wasn't that bad off, but compared to what them little white kids had I always felt like I didn't have nothing. It made me kinda quiet and shy around them. Me knowing all the time I wanted what they had. Wanted it bad. There was them white kids with everything and there was the black world Mommy and them was holding back from me. No place to turn, in a way. I guess you could say I was stuck in the middle. Couldn't have what the white kids in Shadyside had, and I wasn't allowed to look around the corner for something else. So I'd start the story with Shadyside, the house on Copeland.

Another place to start could be December 29, 1950 — the date of Robby's birth. For some reason — maybe my mother and father were feuding, maybe we just happened to be visiting my grandmother's house when my mother's time came — the trip to the hospital to have Robby began from Finance Street, from the house beside the railroad tracks in Homewood. What I remember is the bustle, people rushing around, yelling up and down the stairwell, doors slammed, drawers being opened and shut. A cold winter day so lots of coats and scarves and galoshes. My mother's face was very pale above the dark cloth coat that made her look even bigger than she was, carrying Robby the ninth month. On the way out the front door she stopped and stared back over her shoulder like she'd forgotten something. People just about shoving her out the house. Lots of bustle and noise getting her through the crowded hallway into the vestibule. Somebody opened the front door and December rattled the glass panes. Wind gusting and whistling, everybody calling out last-minute instructions, arrangements, goodbyes, blessings, prayers. My mother's white face calm, hovering a moment above it all as she turned back toward the hall, the stairs where I was planted, halfway to the top. She didn't find me, wasn't looking for me. A thought had crossed her mind and carried her far away. She didn't know why so many hands were rushing her out the door. She didn't hear the swirl of words, the icy blast of wind. Wrapped in a navy-blue coat, either Aunt Aida's or an old one of my grandmother's, which didn't have all its black buttons but stretched double over her big belly, my mother was wondering whether or not she'd turned off the water in the bathroom sink and deciding whether or not she should return up the stairs to check. Something like that crossing her mind, freeing her an instant before she got down to the business of pushing my brother into the world.

Both my grandfathers died on December 28. My grandmother died just after dawn on December 29. My sister lost a baby early in January. The end of the year has become associated with mournings, funerals; New Year's Day arrives burdened by a sense of loss, bereavement. Robby's birthday became tainted. To be born close to Christmas is bad enough in and of itself. Your birthday celebration gets upstaged by the orgy of gift giving on Christmas Day. No matter how many presents you receive on

December 29, they seem a trickle after the Christmas flood. Plus there's too much excitement in too brief a period. Parents and relatives are exhausted, broke, still hung over from the Christmas rush, so there just isn't very much left to work with if your birthday comes four short days after Jesus'. Almost like not having a birthday. Or even worse, like sharing it with your brothers and sister instead of having the private oasis of your very own special day. So Robby cried a lot on his birthdays. And it certainly wasn't a happy time for my mother. Her father, John French, died the year after Robby was born, one day before Robby's birthday. Fifteen years and a day later Mom would lose her mother. The death of the baby my sister was carrying was a final, cruel blow, scaring my mother, jinxing the end of the year eternally. She dreaded the holiday season, expected it to bring dire tidings. She had attempted at one point to consecrate the sad days, employ them as a period of reflection, quietly, privately memorialize the passing of the two people who'd loved her most in the world. But the death of my father's father, then the miscarriage within this jinxed span of days burst the fragile truce my mother had effected with the year's end. She withdraws into herself, anticipates the worst as soon as Christmas decorations begin appearing. In 1975, the year of the robbery and murder, Robby was on the run when his birthday fell. My mother was sure he wouldn't survive the deadly close of the year.

Robby's birthday is smack dab in the middle of the hard time. Planted like a flag to let you know the bad time's arrived. His adult life, the manhood of my mother's last child, begins as she is orphaned, as she starts to become nobody's child.

I named Robby. Before the women hustled my mother out the door into a taxi, I jumped down the stairs, tugged on her coattail, and reminded her she'd promised it'd be Robby. No doubt in my mind she'd bring me home a baby brother. Don't ask me why I was certain. I just was. I hadn't even considered names for a girl. Robby it would be. Robert Douglas. Where the Douglas came from is another story, but the Robert came from me because I liked the sound. Robert was formal, dignified, important. Robert. And that was nearly as nice as the chance I'd have to call my little brother Rob and Robby.

He weighed seven pounds, fourteen ounces. He was born in Allegheny Hospital at 6:30 in the evening, December 29, 1950. His fingers and toes were intact and quite long. He was a plump baby. My grandfather, high on Dago Red, tramped into the maternity ward just minutes after Robby was delivered. John French was delighted with the new baby. Called him Red. A big fat little red nigger.

December always been a bad month for me. One the worst days of my life was in December. It's still one the worst days in my life even after all this other mess. Jail. Running. The whole bit. Been waiting to tell you this a long time. Ain't no reason to hold it back no longer. We into this telling-the-truth thing so mize well tell it all. I'm still shamed, but there it is. You know that TV of youall's got stolen from Mommy's. Well, I did it. Was me and Henry took youall's TV that time and set the house up to look like a robbery. We did it. Took my own brother's TV. Couldn't hardly look you in the face for a long time after we done it. Was pretty sure youall never knowed it was me, but I felt real bad round youns anyway. No way I was gon confess though. Too shamed. A junkie stealing from his own family. See. Used to bullshit myself. Say I ain't like them other guys. They stone junkies, they hooked. Do anything for a hit. But me, I'm Robby. I'm cool. I be believing that shit, too. Fooling myself. You got to bullshit yourself when you falling. Got to do it to live wit yourself. See but where it's at is you be doing any goddam thing for dope. You hooked and that's all's to it. You a stone junkie just like the rest.

Always wondered if you knew I took it.

Mom was suspicious. She knew more than we did then. About the dope. The seriousness of it. Money disappearing from her purse when nobody in the house but the two of you. Finding a syringe on the third floor. Stuff like that she hadn't talked about to us yet. So your stealing the TV was a possibility that came up. But to me it was just one of many. One of the things that could have happened along with a whole lot of other possibilities we sat around talking about. An unlikely possibility as far as I was concerned. Nobody wanted to believe it was you. Mom tried to tell us how it *could* be but in my mind you weren't the one. Haven't thought about it much since then. Except as one of those things that make me worry about Mom living in the house alone. One of those things making Homewood dangerous, tearing it down.

I'm glad I'm finally getting to tell you. I never could get it out. Didn't want you to think I'd steal from my own brother. Specially since all youall done to help me out. You and Judy and the kids. Stealing youall's TV. Don't make no sense, does it? But if we gon get the story down mize well get it all down.

It was a while ago. Do you remember the year?

Nineteen seventy-one was Greens. When we robbed Greens and got in big trouble so it had to be the year before that, 1970. That's when it had to be. Youns was home for Christmas. Mommy and them was having a big party. A reunion kinda cause all the family was together. Everybody home for the first time in a long time. Tish in from Detroit. David back from Philly. Youns in town. My birthday, too. Party spozed to celebrate my birthday too, since it came right along in there after Christmas. Maybe that's why I was feeling so bad. Knowing I had a birthday coming and knowing at the same time how fucked up I was.

Sat in a chair all day. I was hooked for the first time. Good and hooked. Didn't know how low you could feel till that day. Cold and snowing outside. And I got the stone miseries inside. Couldn't move. Weak and sick. Henry too. He was wit me in the house feeling bad as I was. We was two desperate dudes. Didn't have no money and that Jones down on us.

Mommy kept asking, What's wrong with you two? She was on my case all day. What ails you, Robby? Got to be about three o'clock. She come in the room again: You better get up and get some decent clothes on. We're leaving for Geral's soon. See cause it was the day of the big Christmas party. Geral had baked a cake for me. Everybody was together and they'd be singing Happy Birthday Robby and do. The whole bit an I'm spozed to be guest of honor and can't even move out the chair. Here I go again disappointing everybody. Everybody be at Geral's looking for me and Geral had a cake and everything. Where's Robby? He's home dying cause he can't get no dope.

Feeling real sorry for myself but I'm hating me too. Wrapped up in a blanket like some damned Indin. Shivering and wondering how the hell Ima go out in this cold and hustle up some money. Wind be howling. Snow pitching a bitch. There we is. Stuck in the house. Two pitiful junkies. Scheming how we gon get over. Some sorry-assed dudes. But it's comical in a way too, when you look back. To get well we need to get money. And no way we gon get money less we go outside and get sicker than we already is. Mom peeking in the room, getting on my case. Get up out that chair, boy. What are you waiting for? We're leaving in two minutes.

So I says, Go on. I ain't ready. Youns go on. I'll catch up with youns at Geral's.

Mommy standing in the doorway. She can't say too much, cause youns is home and you ain't hip to what's happening. C'mon now. We can't wait any longer for you. Please get up. Geral baked a cake for you. Everybody's looking forward to seeing you.

Seem like she stands there a hour begging me to come. She ain't mad no more. She's begging. Just about ready to cry. Youall in the other room. You can hear what she's saying but you can't see her eyes and they tearing me up. Her eyes begging me to get out the chair and it's tearing me up to see her hurting so bad, but ain't nothing I can do. Jones sitting on my chest and ain't no getup in me.

Youns go head, Mommy. I'll be over in a little while. Be there to blow them candles out and cut the cake.

She knew better. Knew if I didn't come right then, chances was I wasn't coming at all. She knew but wasn't nothing she could do. Guess I knew I was lying too. Nothing in my mind cept copping that dope. Yeah, Mom. Be there to light them candles. I'm grinning but she ain't smiling back. She knows I'm in trouble, deep trouble. I can see her today standing in the doorway begging me to come with youns.

But it ain't meant to be. Me and Henry thought we come up with a idea. Henry's old man had some pistols. We was gon steal em and hock em. Take the money and score. Then we be better. Wouldn't be no big thing to hustle some money, get the guns outa hock. Sneak the pistols back in Henry's house, everything be alright. Wouldn't even exactly be stealing from his old man. Like we just borrowing the pistols till we score and take care business. Henry's old man wouldn't even know his pistols missing. Slick. Sick as we was, thinking we slick.

A hundred times. Mom musta poked her head in the room a hundred times.

What's wrong with you?

Like a drum beating in my head. What's wrong with you? But the other thing is stronger. The dope talking to me louder. It says get you some. It says you ain't never gon get better less you cop.

We waited long as we could but it didn't turn no better outside. Still snowing. Wind shaking the whole house. How we gon walk to Henry's and steal them pistols? Henry live way up on the hill. And the way up Tokay then you still got a long way to go over into the projects. Can't make it. No way we gon climb Tokay. So then what? Everybody's left for Geral's. Then I remembers the TV youns brought. A little portable Sony black-and-white, right? You and Judy sleeping in Mom's room and she has her TV already in there, so the Sony ain't unpacked. Saw it sitting with youall's suitcases over by the dresser. On top the dresser in a box. Remembered it and soon's I did I knew we had to have it. Sick as I was that TV had to go. Wouldn't really be stealing. Borrow it instead of borrowing the pistols. Pawn it. Get straight. Steal some money and buy it back. Just borrowing youall's TV.

Won't take me and Henry no time to rob something and buy back the TV. We stone thieves. Just had to get well first so we could operate. So we took youns TV and set the house up to look like a robbery.

I'm remembering the day. Wondering why it had slipped completely from my mind. I feel like a stranger. Yet as Robby talks, my memory confirms details of his recollection. I admit, yes. I was there. That's the way it was. But *where* was I? Who was I? How did I miss so much?

His confessions make me uncomfortable. Instead of concentrating on what he's revealing, I'm pushed into considering all the things I could be confessing, should be confessing but haven't and probably won't ever. I feel hypocritical. Why should I allow my brother to repose a confidence in me when it's beyond my power to reciprocate? Shouldn't I confess that first? My embarrassment, my uneasiness, the clinical, analytic coldness settling over me when I catch on to what's about to happen.

I have a lot to hide. Places inside myself where truth hurts, where incriminating secrets are hidden, places I avoid, or deny most of the time. Pulling one piece of that debris to the surface, airing it in the light of day doesn't accomplish much, doesn't clarify the rest of what's buried down there. What I feel when I delve deeply into myself is chaos. Chaos and contradiction. So how up front can I get? I'm moved by Robby's secrets. The heart I have is breaking. But what that heart is and where it is I can't say. I can't depend on it, so he shouldn't. Part of me goes out to him. Heartbreak is the sound of ice cracking. Deep. Layers and layers muffling the sound.

I listen but I can't trust myself. I have no desire to tell everything about myself so I resist his attempt to be up front with me. The chaos at my core must be in his. His confession pushes me to think of all the stuff I should lay on him. And that scares the shit out of me. I don't like to feel dirty, but that's how I feel when people try to come clean with me.

Very complicated and very simple too. The fact is I don't believe in clean. What I know best is myself and, knowing what I know about myself, clean seems impossible. A dream. One of those better selves occasionally in the driver's seat but nothing more. Nothing to be depended upon. A self no more or less in control than the countless other selves who each, for a time, seem to be running things.

Chaos is what he's addressing. What his candor, his frankness, his confession echo against. Chaos and time and circumstances and the old news, the bad news that we still walk in circles, each of us trapped in his own little world. Behind bars. Locked in our cells.

But my heart can break, does break listening to my brother's pain. I just remember differently. Different parts of the incident he's describing come back. Strange thing is my recollections return through the door he opened. My memories needed his. Maybe the fact that we recall different things is crucial. Maybe they are foreground and background, propping each other up. He holds on to this or that scrap of the past and I listen to what he's saved and it's not mine, not what I saw or heard or felt. The pressure's on me then. If his version of the past is real, then what's mine? Where does it fit? As he stitches his memories together they bridge a vast emptiness. The time lost enveloping us all. Everything. And hearing him talk, listening to him try to make something of the nothing, challenges me. My sense of the emptiness playing around his words, any words, is intensified. Words are nothing and everything. If I don't speak I have no past. Except the nothing, the emptiness. My brother's memories are not mine, so I have to break into the silence with my own version of the past. My words. My whistling in the dark. His story freeing me, because it forces me to tell my own.

I'm sorry you took so long to forgive yourself. I forgave you a long time ago, in advance for a sin I didn't even know you'd committed. You lied to me. You stole from me. I'm in prison now listening because we committed those sins against each other countless times. I want your forgiveness. Talking about debts you owe me makes me awkward, uneasy. We remember different things. They set us apart. They bring us together searching for what is lost, for the meaning of difference, of distance.

For instance, the Sony TV. It was a present from Mort, Judy's dad. When we told him about the break-in and robbery at Mom's house, he bought us another Sony. Later we discovered the stolen TV was covered by our homeowner's policy even though we'd lost it in Pittsburgh. A claim was filed and eventually we collected around a hundred bucks. Not enough to buy a new Sony but a good portion of the purchase price. Seemed a lark when the check arrived. Pennies from heaven. One hundred dollars free and clear since we already had the new TV Mort had surprised us with. About a year later one of us, Judy or I, was telling the story of the robbery and how well we came out of it. Not until that very moment when I caught a glimpse of Mort's face out of the corner of my eye did I realize what we'd done. Judy remembers urging me to send Mort that insurance check and she probably did, but I have no recollection of an argument. In my mind there had never been an issue. Why shouldn't we keep the money? But when I saw the look of surprise and hurt flash across Mort's face, I knew the insurance check should have gone directly to him. He's a generous man and probably would have refused to accept it, but we'd taken advantage of his generosity by not offering the check as soon as we received it. Clearly the money belonged to him. Unasked, he'd replaced the lost TV. I had treated him like an institution, one of those faceless corporate entities like the gas company or IRS. By then, by the time I saw the surprise in Mort's face and understood how selfishly, thoughtlessly, even corruptly I'd behaved, it was too late. Offering Mort a hundred dollars at that point would have been insulting. Anything I could think of saying sounded hopelessly lame, inept. I'd fucked up. I'd injured someone who'd been nothing but kind and generous to me. Not intentionally, consciously, but that only made the whole business worse in a way because I'd failed him instinctively. The failure was a measure of who I was. What I'd unthinkingly done revealed something about my relationship to Mort I'm sure he'd rather not have discovered. No way I could take my action back, make it up. It reflected a truth about who I was.

That memory pops right up. Compromising, ugly. Ironically, it's also about stealing from a relative. Not to buy dope, but to feed a habit just as self-destructive. The habit of taking good fortune for granted, the habit of blind self-absorption that allows us to believe the world owes us everything and we are not responsible for giving anything in return. Spoiled children. The good coming our way taken as our due. No strings attached.

Lots of other recollections were triggered as Robby spoke of that winter and the lost TV. The shock of walking into a burgled house. How it makes you feel unclean. How quickly you lose the sense of privacy and security a house, any place you call home, is supposed to provide. It's a form of rape. Forced entry, violation, brutal hands defiling what's personal, and precious. The aftershock of seeing your possessions strewn about, broken. Fear gnawing at you because what you thought was safe isn't safe at all. The worst has happened and can happen again. Your sanctuary has been destroyed. Any time you walk in your door you may be greeted by the same scene. Or worse. You may stumble upon the thieves themselves. The symbolic rape of your dwelling place enacted on your actual body. Real screams. Real blood. A knife at your throat. A stranger's weight bearing down.

Mom put it in different words but she was as shaken as I was when we walked into her house after Geral's party. Given what I know now, she must have been even more profoundly disturbed than I imagined. A double bind. Bad enough to be ripped off by anonymous thieves. How much worse if the thief is your son? For Mom the robbery was proof Robby was gone. Somebody else walking round in his skin. Mom was wounded in ways I hadn't begun to guess at. At the root of her pain were your troubles, the troubles stealing you away from her, from all of us. The troubles thick in the air as that snow you are remembering, the troubles falling on your head and mine, troubles I refused to see. . . .

Snowing and the hawk kicking my ass but I got to have it. TV's in a box under my arm and me and Henry walking down Bennett to Homewood Avenue. Need thirty dollars. Thirty dollars buy us two spoons. Looking for One-Arm Ralph, the fence. Looking for him or that big white Cadillac he drives.

Wind blowing snow all up in my face. Thought I's bout to die out there. Nobody on the avenue. Even the junkies and dealers inside today. Wouldn't put no dog out in weather like that. So cold my teeth is chattering, talking to me. No feeling in my hands but I got to hold on to that TV. Henry took it for a little while so's I could put both my hands in my pockets. Henry lookin bad as I'm feeling. Thought I was gon puke. But it's too goddamn cold to puke.

Nobody in sight. Shit and double shit's what I'm thinking. They got to be somewhere. Twenty-four hours a day, seven days a week somebody doing business. Finally we seen One-Arm Ralph come out the Hi Hat.

This TV, man, Lemme hold thirty dollars on it.

Ralph ain't goin for it. Twenty-five the best he say he can do. Twenty-five don't do us no good. It's fifteen each for a spoon. One spoon ain't enough. We begging the dude now. We got to have it, man. Got to get well. We good for the money. Need thirty dollars for two hits. You get your money back.

Too cold to be standing around arguing. The dude go in his pocket and give us the thirty. He been knowing us. He know we good for it. I'm telling him don't sell the TV right away. Hold it till tomorrow we have his money. He say, You don't come back tonight you blow it. Ralph a hard motherfucker and don't want him changing his mind again about the thirty so I say, We'll have the money tonight. Hold the TV till tonight, you get your money.

Now all we got to do is find Goose. Goose always be hanging on the set. Ain't nobody else dealing, Goose be out there for his people. Goose an alright dude, but even Goose ain't out in the street on no day like this. I know the cat stays over the barbershop on Homewood Avenue. Across from Murphy's five-and-ten. I goes round to the side entrance, the alleyway tween Homewood and Kelly. That's how you get to his place. Goose lets me in and I cop. For some reason I turn up the alley and go toward Kelly instead of back to Homewood the way I came in. Don't know why I did it. Being slick. Being scared. Henry's waiting on the avenue for me so I go round the long way just in case somebody pinned him. I can check out the scene before I come back up the avenue. That's probably what I'm thinking. But soon's I turn the corner of Kelly, Bam. Up pops the devil.

Up against the wall, Squirrel.

It's Simon and Garfunkel, two jive undercover cops. We call them that, you dig. Lemme tell you what kind of undercover cops these niggers was. Both of em wearing Big Apple hats and jackets like people be wearing then but they both got on police shoes. Police brogans you could spot a mile away. But they think they slick. They disguised, see. Apple hats and hippy-dip jackets. Everybody knew them chumps was cops. Ride around in a big Continental. Going for bad. Everybody hated them cause everybody knew they in the dope business. They bust a junkie, take his shit and sell it. One them had a cousin. Biggest dealer on the Hill. You know where he getting half his dope. Be selling again what Simon and Garfunkel stole from junkies. Some rotten dudes. Liked to beat on people too. Wasn't bad enough they robbing people. They whipped heads too.

Soon's I turn the corner they got me. Bams me up against the wall. They so lame they think they got Squirrel. Think I'm Squirrel and they gon make a big bust. We got you, Squirrel. They happy, see, cause Squirrel dealing heavy then. Thought they caught them a whole shopping bag of dope.

Wearing my double-breasted pea coat. Used to be sharp but it's raggedy now. Ain't worth shit in cold weather like that. Pockets got holes and the dope dropped down in the lining so they don't find nothing the first time they search me. Can tell they mad. Thought they into something big and don't find shit. Looking at each other like, What the fuck's going on here? We big-time undercover supercops. This ain't spozed to be happening to us. They roughing me up too. Pulling my clothes off and shit. Hands all down in my pockets again. It's freezing and I'm shivering but these fools don't give a fuck. Rip my goddamn pea coat off me. Shaking it. Tearing it up. Find the two packs of dope inside the lining this time. Ain't what they wanted but they pissed off now. Take what they can get now.

What's this, Squirrel? Got your ass now.

Slinging me down the alley. I'm stone sick now. Begging these cats for mercy. Youall got me. You got your bust. Lemme snort some the dope, man. Little bit out each bag. You still got your bust. I'm dying. Little taste fore you lock me up.

Rotten motherfuckers ain't going for it. They see I'm sick as a dog. They know what's happening. Cold as it is, the sweat pouring out me. It's sweat but it's like ice. Like knives cutting me. They ain't give back my coat. Snowing on me and I'm shaking and sweating and sick. They can see all this. They know what's happening but ain't no mercy in these dudes. Henry's cross the street watching them bust me. Tears in his eyes. Ain't nothing he can do. The street's empty. Henry's bout froze too. Watching them sling my ass in their Continental. Never forget how Henry looked that day. All alone on the avenue. Tears froze in his eyes. Seeing him like that was a sad thing. Last thing I saw was him standing there across Homewood Avenue before they slammed me up in the car. Like I was in two places. That's me standing there in the snow. That's me so sick and cold I'm crying in the empty street and ain't a damn thing I can do about it.

By the time they get me down to the Police Station, down to No. 5 in East Liberty, I ain't no more good, sure nuff. Puking. Begging them punks not to bust me. Just bout out my mind. Must have been a pitiful sight. Then's when Henry went to Geral's house and scratched on the window and called David out on the porch. That's when youall found out I was in trouble and had to come down and get me. Right in the middle of the party and everything. Henry's sick too and he been walking round Homewood in the cold didn't know what to do. But he's my man. He got to Geral's so youall could come down and help me. Shamed to go in so he scratched on the window to get Dave on the porch.

Party's over and youns go to Mommy's and on top everything else find the house broke in and the TV gone. All the stuff's going through my mind. I'm on the bottom now. Low as you can go. Had me in a cell and I was lying cross the cot staring at the ceiling. Bars all round. Up cross the ceiling too. Like in a cage in the zoo. Miserable as I could be. All the shit staring me in the face. You're a dope fiend. You stole your brother's TV. You're hurting Mommy again. Hurting everybody. You're sick. You're nothing. Looking up at the bars on the ceiling and wondering if I could tie my belt there. Stick my neck in it. I wanted to be dead.

Tied my belt to the ceiling. Then this guard checking on me he starts to hollering.

What you doing? Hey, Joe. This guy's trying to commit suicide.

They take my clothes. Leave me nothing but my shorts. I'm lying there shivering in my underwear and that's the end. In a cage naked like some goddamn animal. Shaking like a leaf. Thinking maybe I can beat my head against the bars or maybe jump down off the bed head first on the concrete and bust my brains open. Dead already. Nothing already. Low as I can go.

Must have passed out or gone to sleep or something, cause it gets blurry round in here. Don't remember much but they gave back my clothes and took me Downtown and there was a arraignment next morning.

Mommy told me later, one the cops advised her not to pay my bond. Said the best thing for him be to stay in jail awhile. Let him see how it is inside. Scare im. But I be steady beggin. Please, please get me out here. Youns got soft-hearted. Got the money together and paid the bond.

What would have happened if you left me to rot in there till my hearing? Damned if I know. I probably woulda went crazy, for one thing. I do know that. Know I was sick and scared and cried like a baby for Mommy and them to get me out. Don't think it really do no good letting them keep me in there. I mean the jail's a terrible place. You can get everything in jail you get in the street. No different. Cept in jail it's more dangerous cause you got a whole bunch of crazies locked up in one little space. Worse than the street. Less you got buddies in there they tear you up. Got to learn to survive quick. Cause jail be the stone jungle. Call prison the House of Knowledge cause you learns how to be a sure nuff criminal. Come in lame you leave knowing all kinds of evil shit. You learn quick or they eats you up. That's where it's at. So you leave a person in there, chances are they gets worse. Or gets wasted.

But Mom has that soft heart anyway and she ain't leaving her baby boy in no miserable jail. Right or wrong, she ain't leaving me in no place like that. Daddy been talking to Simon and Garfunkel. Daddy's hip, see. He been out there in the street all his life and he knows what's to it. Knows those guys and knows how rotten they is. Ain't no big thing they catch one pitiful little junkie holding two spoons. They wants dealers. They wants to look good Downtown. They wants to bust dealers and cop beaucoup dope so's they can steal it and get rich. Daddy makes a deal with them rats. Says if they drop the charges he'll make me set up Goose. Finger Goose and then stay off Homewood Avenue. Daddy says I'll do that so they let me go.

No way Ima squeal on Goose but I said okay, it's a deal. Soon's I was loose I warned Goose. Pretend like I'm trying to set him up so the cops get off my ass but Goose see me coming know the cops is watching. Helped him, really. Like a lookout. Them dumb motherfuckers got tired playing me. Simon got greedy. Somebody set him up. He got busted for drugs. Still see Garfunkel riding round in his Continental but they took him off the avenue. Too dangerous. Everybody hated them guys.

My lowest day. Didn't know till then I was strung out. That's the first time I was hooked. Started shooting up with Squirrel and Bugs Johnson when Squirrel be coming over to Mom's sometimes. Get up in the morning, go up to the third floor, and shoot up. They was like my teachers. Bugs goes way back. He started with Uncle Carl. Been shooting ever since. Dude's old now. Call him King of the Junkies, he been round so long. Bugs seen it all. You know junkies don't hardly be getting old. Have their day then they gone. Don't see em no more. They in jail or dead. Junkie just don't have no long life. Fast life but your average dopehead ain't round long. Bugs different. He was a pal of Uncle Carl's back in the fifties. Shot up together way back then. Now here he is wit Squirrel and me, still doing this thing. Everybody knows Bugs. He the King.

Let me shoot up wit em but they wouldn't let me go out in the street and hustle wit em. Said I was too young. Too green.

Learning from the King, see. That's how I started the heavy stuff. Me and Squirrel and Bugs first thing in the morning when I got out of bed. Mom was gone to work. They getting themselves ready to hit the street. Make that money. Just like a job. Wasn't no time before I was out there, too. On my own learning to get money for dope. Me and my little mob. We was ready. Didn't take us no time fore we was gangsters. Gon be the next Bugs Johnson. Gon make it to the top.

Don't take long. One day you the King. Next day dope got you and it's the King. You ain't nothing. You lying there naked bout to die and it don't take but a minute. You fall and you gone in a minute. That's the life. That's how it is. And I was out there. I know. Now they got me jammed up in the slammer. That's the way it is. But nobody could tell me nothing then. Hard head. You know. Got to find out for myself. Nobody could tell me nothing. Just out of high school and my life's over and I didn't even know it. Too dumb. Too hardheaded. I was gon do it my way. Youns was square. Youns didn't know nothing. Me, I was gon make mine from the curb. Hammer that rock till I was a supergangster. Be the one dealing the shit. Be the one running the junkies. That's all I knew. Street smarts. Stop being a chump. Forget that nickel-dime hoodlum bag. Be a star. Rise to the top.

You know where that got me. You heard that story. Here I sit today behind that story. Nobody to blame but my ownself. I know that now. But things was fucked up in the streets. You could fall in them streets, Brother. Low. Them streets could snatch you bald-headed and turn you around and wring you inside out. Streets was a bitch. Wake up some mornings and you think you in hell. Think you died and went straight to hell. I know cause I been there. Be days I wished I was dead. Be days worser than that.

QUESTIONS FOR A SECOND READING

1. Wideman frequently interrupts this narrative to talk about the problems he is having as a writer. He says, for example, "The hardest habit to break, since it was the habit of a lifetime, would be listening to myself listen to him. That habit would destroy any chance of seeing my brother on his terms; and seeing him in his terms, learning his terms, seemed the whole point of learning his story" (p. 672). What might Wideman mean by this — listening to himself listen? As you reread "Our Time," note the sections in which Wideman speaks to you directly as a writer. What is he saying? Where and how are you surprised by what he says?

   Wideman calls attention to the problems he faces. How does he try to solve them? Are you sympathetic? Do the solutions work, so far as you are concerned?

2. Wideman says that his mother had a remarkable capacity for "[trying] on the other person's point of view." Wideman tries on another point of view himself, speaking to us in the voice of his brother Robby. As you reread this selection, note the passages spoken in Robby's voice and try to infer Robby's point of view from them. If you look at the differences between John and Robby as evidenced by the ways they use language to understand and represent the world, what do you notice?

3. Wideman talks about three ways he could start Robby's story: with Garth's death, with the house in Shadyside, and with the day of Robby's birth. What difference would it make in each case if he chose one and not the others? What's the point of presenting all three?

ASSIGNMENTS FOR WRITING

1. At several points in the essay, Wideman discusses his position as a writer, telling Robby's story, and he describes the problems he faces in writing this piece (or in "reading" the text of his brother's life). You could read this selection, in other words, as an essay about reading and writing.

   Why do you think Wideman talks about these problems here? Why not keep quiet and hope that no one notices? Choose three or four passages in which Wideman refers directly or indirectly to his work as a writer, and write an essay defining the problems Wideman faces and explaining why you think he raises them as he does. Finally, what might this have to do with your work as a writer — or as a student in this writing class?

2. Wideman tells Robby's story in this excerpt, but he also tells the story of his neighborhood, Homewood; of his mother; and of his grandfather John French. Write an essay retelling one of these stories and explaining what it might have to do with Robby and John's.

3. "Our Time" is a family history, but it is also a meditation on the problems of writing family histories — or, more generally, the problems of writing about the "real" world. There are sections in "Our Time" where Wideman speaks directly about the problems he faces as a writer. And the unusual features in the prose stand as examples of how he tried to solve these problems — at certain points Wideman writes as an essayist, at others like a storyteller; at certain points he switches voices; the piece breaks up into sections, it doesn't move from introduction to conclusion. Think of these as part of Wideman's method, as his way of working on the problems of writing as practical problems, where he is trying to figure out how to do justice to his brother and his story.

   As you prepare to write this assignment, read back through the selection to think about it as a way of doing one's work, as a project, as a way of writing. What are the selection's key features? What is its shape or design? How does Wideman, the writer, do what he does? And you might ask: What would it take to learn to write like this? How is this writing related to the writing taught in school? Where and how might it serve you as a student?

   Once you have developed a sense of Wideman's method, write a Wideman-like piece of your own, one that has the rhythm and the moves, the shape and the design of "Our Time." As far as subject matter is concerned, let Wideman's text stand as an invitation (inviting you to write about family and neighborhood), but don't feel compelled to follow his lead. You can write about anything you want. The key is to follow the essay as an example of a *way* of writing — moving slowly, turning this way and that, combining stories and reflection, working outside of a rigid structure of thesis and proof.

MAKING CONNECTIONS

1. Various selections in this textbook can be said to be "experimental" in their use of nonfiction prose. These are essays that don't do what essays are supposed to do. They break the rules. They surprise. The writers work differently than most writers. They imagine a different project (or they imagine their project differently).

   Although any number of the selections in *Ways of Reading* might be read alongside "Our Time," here are some that have seemed interesting to our students: Gloria Anzaldúa, the essays from *Borderlands/La frontera* (pp. 72, 85); Susan Griffin, "Our Secret" (p. 335); and Richard E. Miller, "The Dark Night of the Soul" (p. 420).

Choose one selection to compare with Wideman's and write an essay in which you both explain and explore the projects represented by the two pieces of writing. How do they address a reader's expectations? How do they manipulate the genre? How do they reimagine the features we take for granted in the genre of the essay—sentences and paragraphs; introductions and conclusions; argument, narrative, and exposition? And what is to be gained (or what is at stake) in writing this way? (Would you, for example, argue that these forms of writing should be taught in college?) You should assume that you are writing for someone who is a sophisticated reader but who is not familiar with these particular essays. You will need, that is, to be careful in choosing and presenting examples.

2. Both Kwame Anthony Appiah, in "Race, Culture, Identity: Misunderstood Connections" (p. 101), and Wideman speak directly to the reader. They seem to feel that there are problems of understanding in the stories they have to tell and in their relations to their subjects and audiences. Look back over both stories and mark the passages in which the authors address you as a reader. Ask yourself why the authors might do this. What do they reveal about their work as writers at such moments? How would you describe the relationship each writer has with his subject matter? As a reader of each of these stories, how would you describe the relationship between the authors and yourself as the "audience"?

   After you have completed this preliminary research, write an essay in which you discuss these two acts of writing *as* acts of writing—that is, as stories in which the writers are self-conscious about their work as writers and make their audience aware of their self-consciousness. What differences or connections exist between you, the authors, and their subject matter? How do these differences or connections influence you as a reader?

3. Both Tommie Shelby's "Social Identity and Group Solidarity" (p. 584) and Kwame Anthony Appiah's "Race, Culture, Identity: Misunderstood Connections" (p. 101) call attention to the difficulties of representing and understanding the experience of those whom we call African Americans—the difficulty of telling the story, of getting it right, of recovering experience from the representations of others.

   Read one, or both, of these essays alongside "Our Time" and write an essay in which you represent these texts as examples of writers working on a problem that has a particular urgency for black Americans. How might you name this problem? How might you illustrate it? What examples are available? What do you find compelling in each of these approaches to the problem? And what might this problem have to do with you—as a writer, a thinker, a citizen?

4. In his essay "Our Time," John Edgar Wideman worries over the problems of representation, of telling his brother's story. He speaks directly to the fundamental problem writers face when they try to represent the lives of others: "I'd slip unaware out of his story and into one of my own. I'd be following him, an obedient shadow, then a cloud would blot the sun and I'd be gone, unchained, a dark form still skulking behind him but no longer in tow" (p. 672). Wideman goes on to say:

   > The hardest habit to break . . . would be listening to myself listen to him. That habit would destroy any chance of seeing my brother on his terms; and seeing him in his terms, learning his terms, seemed the whole point of learning his story. . . . I had to teach myself to listen. Start fresh, clear the pipes, resist too facile an identification, tame the urge to take off with Robby's story and make it my own. (p. 672)

   Richard E. Miller, in "The Dark Night of the Soul" (p. 420), is also concerned with the problems of representation. He provides readings of the lives of others — from Eric Harris to Chris McCandless to Martin Amis to René Descartes and Mary Karr — who are also engaged with the problems of representation and understanding. Write an essay about writing and representation, about the real world and the world of texts, with Wideman and Miller as your primary points of reference. How do they understand representation as a problem for writers and readers? How is that understanding represented (or enacted) in their own work? Which writer might have something to learn from the example of the other?

Assignment SEQUENCES

Working with Assignment Sequences

Ten assignment sequences follow. (Another nine sequences are included in *Resources for Teaching Ways of Reading.*) These assignment sequences are different from the single writing assignments at the end of each essay. The single writing assignments are designed to give you a way back into the works you have read. They define the way you, the reader, can work on an essay by writing about it—testing its assumptions, probing its examples, applying its way of thinking to a new setting or to new material. A single assignment might ask you to read what Paulo Freire has to say about education and then, as a writer, to use Freire's terms and methods to analyze a moment from your own schooling. The single assignments are designed to demonstrate how a student might work on an essay, particularly an essay that is long or complex, and they are designed to show how pieces that might seem daunting are open, manageable, and managed best by writing.

The assignment sequences have a similar function, but with one important difference. Instead of writing one paper, or working on one or two selections from the book, you will be writing several essays and reading several selections. Your work will be sequential as well as cumulative. The work you do on Freire, for example, will give you a way of beginning with Mary Louise Pratt or Judith Butler. It will give you an angle of vision. You won't be a newcomer to such discussions. Your previous reading will make the new essay rich with association. Passages or examples will jump out, as if magnetized, and demand your attention. And by reading these essays in context, you will see each writer as a single voice in a larger discussion. Neither Freire, nor Pratt, nor Butler, after all, has had the last word on the subject of education. It is not as though, by working on one of the essays, you have wrapped the subject up, ready to be put on the shelf.

The sequences are designed, then, so that you will be working not only on essays but on a subject, like education (or history, or culture, or the autobiography), a subject that can be examined, probed, and understood through the various frames provided by your reading. Each essay becomes a way of seeing a problem or a subject; it becomes a tool for thinking, an example of how a mind might work, a way of using language to make a subject rich and alive. In the assignment sequences, your reading is not random. Each sequence provides a set of readings that can be pulled together into a single project.

The sequences allow you to participate in an extended academic project, one with several texts and several weeks' worth of writing. You are not just adding one essay to another (Freire + Pratt = ?) but trying out an approach to a subject by revising it, looking at new examples, hearing what someone else has to say, and beginning again to take a position of your own. Projects like these take time. It is not at all uncommon for professional writers to devote weeks or even months to a single essay, and the essay they write marks not the end of their thinking on the subject, but only one stage. Similarly, when readers are working on a project, the pieces they read accumulate on their desks and in their minds and become part of an extended conversation with several speakers, each voice offering a point of view on a subject, a new set of examples, or a new way of talking that resonates with echoes from earlier reading.

A student may read many books, take several courses, write many papers; ideally each experience becomes part of something larger, an education. The work of understanding, in other words, requires time and repeated effort. The power that comes from understanding cannot be acquired quickly—by reading one essay or working for a few hours. A student, finally, is a person who choreographs such experiences, not someone who passes one test only to move on to another. And the assignment sequences are designed to reproduce, although in a condensed period of time, the rhythm and texture of academic life. They invite you to try on its characteristic ways of seeing, thinking, and writing. The work you do in one week will not be lost when it has bearing on the work you do in the next. If an essay by Susan Griffin has value for you, it is not because you proved to a teacher that you read it, but because you have put it to work and made it a part of your vocabulary as a student.

WORKING WITH A SEQUENCE

Here is what you can expect as you work with a sequence. You begin by working with a single story or essay. You will need to read each piece twice, the second time with the "Questions for a Second Reading" and the assignment sequence in mind. Before rereading the selection, in other words, you should read through the assignments to get a sense of where you will be headed. And you should read the questions at the end of each selection. (You can use those questions to help frame questions of your own.) The purpose of all these questions, in a sense, is to prepare the text to speak—to bring it to life and insist that it respond to your attention, answer your questions. If you think of the authors as people you can talk to, if you think of their pages as occasions for dialogue (as places where you get to ask questions and insist on responses) — if you prepare your return to those pages in these ways, you are opening up the essays or stories (not closing them down or finishing them off) and creating a scene where you get to step forward as a performer.

While each sequence moves from selection to selection in *Ways of Reading*, the most significant movement in the sequence is defined by the essays you write. Your essays provide the other major texts for the course. In fact, when we teach these sequences, we seldom have any discussion of the assigned readings before our students have had a chance to write. When we talk as a group about John Berger's "Ways of Seeing," for example, we begin by reproducing one or two student essays, handing them out to the class, and using them as the basis for discussion. We want to start, in other words, by looking at ways of reading Berger's essay — not at his essay alone.

The essays you write for each assignment in a sequence might be thought of as works-in-progress. Your instructor will tell you the degree to which each essay should be finished — that is, the degree to which it should be revised and copyedited and worked into a finished performance. In our classes, most writing assignments go through at least one revision. After we have had a chance to see a draft (or after a draft has been seen by others in the class), and after we have had some discussion of sample student essays, we ask students to read the assigned essay or story one more time and to rework their essays to bring their work one step further — not necessarily to finish the essays (as though there would be nothing else to say) but to finish up this stage in their work and to feel their achievement in a way a writer simply cannot the first time through. Each assignment, then, really functions as two assignments in the schedule for the course. As a consequence, we don't "cover" as many essays in a semester as students might in another class. But coverage is not our goal. In a sense, we are teaching our students how to read slowly and closely, to return to a text rather than set it aside, to take the time to reread and rewrite and to reflect on what these activities entail. Some of these sequences, then, contain more readings or more writing assignments than you can address in a quarter or semester. Different courses work at different paces. It is important, however, to preserve time for rereading and rewriting. The sequences were written with the assumption that they would be revised to meet the needs of teachers, students, and programs. As you look at your syllabus, you may find, then, that reading or writing assignments have been changed, added, or dropped. There are alternative selections and assignments at the end of most of these sequences so that the sequences can be customized. Your instructor may wish to replace some of the selections and assignments in the sequence with alternatives.

You will be writing papers that can be thought of as single essays. But you will also be working on a project, something bigger than its individual parts. From the perspective of the project, each piece you write is part of a larger body of work that evolves over the term. You might think of each sequence as a revision exercise, where the revision looks forward to what comes next as well as backward to what you have done. This form of revision asks you to do more than complete a single paper; it invites you to resee a subject or reimagine what you might say about it from a new point of view. You should feel free, then, to draw on your earlier essays when you work on one of the later assignments. There is every reason for you to reuse ideas, phrases, sentences, even paragraphs as your work builds from one week to the next. The advantage of works-in-progress is that you are not starting over completely every time you sit down to write. You've been over this territory before. You've developed some expertise in your subject. There is a body of work behind you.

Most of the sequences bring together several essays from the text and ask you to imagine them as an extended conversation, one with several speakers. The assignments are designed to give you a voice in the conversation as well, to allow you to speak in turn and to take your place in the company of other writers. This is the final purpose of the assignment sequence: after several weeks' work on the essays and on the subject that draws them together, you will begin to establish your own point of view. You will develop a position from which you can speak with authority, drawing strength from the work you have done as well as from your familiarity with the people who surround you.

This book brings together some of the most powerful voices of our culture. They speak in a manner that asks for response. The assignments at the end of each selection and, with a wider range of reference, the assignment sequences here at the end of the book demonstrate that there is no reason for a student, in such company, to remain silent.

SEQUENCE ONE

The Aims of Education

Paulo Freire
Mary Louise Pratt
Richard Rodriguez
Richard E. Miller

ALTERNATIVE:

Susan Griffin

You have been in school for many years, long enough for your experiences in the classroom to seem natural, inevitable. The purpose of this sequence is to invite you to step outside a world you may have begun to take for granted, to look at the ways you have been taught and at the unspoken assumptions behind your education. The seven assignments that follow bring together four essays that discuss how people (and particularly students) become trapped inside habits of thought. These habits of thought become invisible (or seem natural) because of the ways our schools work or because of the ways we have traditionally learned to use language when we speak, read, or write.

ASSIGNMENT 1

Applying Freire to Your Own Experience as a Student

PAULO FREIRE

> The teacher talks about reality as if it were motionless, static, compartmentalized, and predictable. Or else he expounds on a topic completely alien to the existential experience of the students. His task is to "fill" the students with the contents of his

> narration — contents which are detached from reality, disconnected from the totality that engendered them and could give them significance. Words are emptied of their concreteness and become a hollow, alienated, and alienating verbosity. (p. 318)
>
> — PAULO FREIRE
> *The "Banking" Concept of Education*

Surely, anyone who has made it through twelve years of formal education can think of a class, or an occasion outside of class, to serve as a quick example of what Freire calls the "banking" concept of education, where students are turned into "containers" to be "filled" by their teachers. If Freire is to be useful to you, however, he must do more than call up quick examples. He should allow you to say more than that a teacher once treated you like a container (or that a teacher once gave you your freedom).

Write an essay that focuses on a rich and illustrative incident from your own educational experience and read it (that is, interpret it) as Freire would. You will need to provide careful detail: things that were said and done, perhaps the exact wording of an assignment, a textbook, or a teacher's comments. And you will need to turn to the language of Freire's argument, to take key phrases and passages from his argument and see how they might be used to investigate your case.

To do this, you will need to read your account as not simply the story of you and your teacher, since Freire is not writing about individual personalities (an innocent student and a mean teacher, a rude teacher, or a thoughtless teacher) but about the roles we are cast in, whether we choose to be or not, by our culture and its institutions. The key question, then, is not who you were or who your teacher was but what roles you played and how those roles can lead you to better understand the larger narrative or drama of Education (an organized attempt to "regulate the way the world 'enters into' the students").

Note: Freire would not want you to work passively or mechanically, as though you were merely following orders. He would want you to make your own mark on the work he has begun. Use your example, in other words, as a way of testing and examining what Freire says, particularly those passages that you find difficult or obscure.

ASSIGNMENT 2

The Contact Zone

MARY LOUISE PRATT

> The idea of the contact zone is intended in part to contrast with ideas of community that underlie much of the thinking about language, communication, and culture that gets done in the academy. (p. 493)
>
> — MARY LOUISE PRATT
> *Arts of the Contact Zone*

Citing Benedict Anderson and what he calls "imagined communities," Pratt argues that our idea of community is "strongly utopian, embodying values like equality, fraternity, liberty, which the societies often profess but systematically fail to realize." Against this utopian vision of community, Pratt argues that we need to develop ways of understanding (even noticing) social and intellectual spaces that are not homogeneous, unified; we need to develop ways of understanding and valuing difference. And, for Pratt, the argument extends to schooling. "What is the place," she asks,

> of unsolicited oppositional discourse, parody, resistance, critique in the imagined classroom community? Are teachers supposed to feel that their teaching has been most successful when they have eliminated such things and unified the social world, probably in their own image? Who wins when we do that? Who loses? (p. 495)

Such questions, she says, "may be hypothetical, because in the United States in the 1990s, many teachers find themselves less and less able to do that even if they want to."

"In the United States in the 1990s." "The imagined classroom community." From your experience, what scenes might be used to represent schooling in the 1990s and beyond? How are they usually imagined (idealized, represented, interpreted, valued)? What are the implications of Pratt's argument?

Write an essay in which you use Pratt's terms to examine a representative scene from your own experience with schools and schooling. What examples, stories, or images best represent your experience? How might they be interpreted as examples of community? as examples of "contact zones"? As you prepare your essay, you will want to set the scene as carefully as you can, so that someone who was not there can see it fully. Think about how someone who has not read Pratt might interpret the scene. And think through the various ways *you* might interpret your example. And you should also think about your position in an argument about school as a contact zone. What do you (or people like you) stand to gain or lose when you adopt Pratt's point of view?

ASSIGNMENT 3

The Pedagogical Arts of the Contact Zone

MARY LOUISE PRATT

> Meanwhile, our job in the Americas course remains to figure out how to make that crossroads the best site for learning that it can be. We are looking for the pedagogical arts of the contact zone. These will include, we are sure, exercises in storytelling and in identifying with the ideas, interests, histories, and attitudes of others; experiments in

> transculturation and collaborative work and in the arts of critique, parody, and comparison (including unseemly comparisons between elite and vernacular cultural forms); the redemption of the oral; ways for people to engage with suppressed aspects of history (including their own histories), ways to move *into and out of* rhetorics of authenticity; ground rules for communication across lines of difference and hierarchy that go beyond politeness but maintain mutual respect; a systematic approach to the all-important concept of *cultural mediation*. (p. 497)
>
> — MARY LOUISE PRATT
> *Arts of the Contact Zone*

Pratt writes generally about culture and history, but also about reading and writing and teaching and learning, about the "literate" and "pedagogical" arts of this place she calls the contact zone. Think about the class you are in — its position in the curriculum, in the institution. Think about its official goals (and its unofficial goals). Think about the positions represented by the students, the teacher. Think about how to think about the class, in Pratt's terms, as a contact zone.

And think about the unusual exercises represented by her list: "storytelling," "experiments in transculturation," "critique," "parody," "unseemly comparisons," moving into and out of "rhetorics of authenticity" — these are some of them. Take one of these suggested exercises, explain what you take it to mean, and then go on to discuss how it might be put into practice in a writing class. What would students do? to what end? How would their work be evaluated? What place would the exercise have in the larger sequence of assignments over the term, quarter, or semester? In your terms, and from your point of view, what might you learn from such an exercise?

Or you could think of the question this way: What comments would a teacher make on one of the papers you have written so far in order that its revision might stand as one of these exercises? How would the revision be different from what you are used to doing?

Write an essay in which you present and discuss an exercise designed to serve the writing class as a contact zone.

ASSIGNMENT 4

Ways of Reading, Ways of Speaking, Ways of Caring

RICHARD RODRIGUEZ

> What I am about to say to you has taken me more than twenty years to admit: *A primary reason for my success in the classroom was that I couldn't forget that schooling was changing me and*

> *separating me from the life I enjoyed before becoming a student.* (p. 516)
>
> If, because of my schooling, I had grown culturally separated from my parents, my education finally had given me ways of speaking and caring about that fact. (p. 532)
>
> — RICHARD RODRIGUEZ
> *The Achievement of Desire*

As you reread Rodriguez's essay, what would you say are his "ways of speaking and caring"? One way to think about this question is to trace how the lessons he learned about reading, education, language, family, culture, and class shifted as he moved from elementary school through college and graduate school to his career as a teacher and a writer. What scholarly abilities did he learn that provided him with "ways of speaking and caring" valued in the academic community? Where and how do you see him using them in his essay?

Write an essay in which you discuss how Rodriguez reads (reviews, summarizes, interprets) his family, his teachers, his schooling, himself, and his books. What differences can you say such reading makes to those ways of speaking and caring that you locate in the text?

ASSIGNMENT 5
A Story of Schooling
RICHARD RODRIGUEZ

Rodriguez insists that his story is also everyone's story. Take an episode from your life, one that seems in some way similar to one of the episodes in "The Achievement of Desire," and cast it into a shorter version of Rodriguez's essay. Your job here is to look at your experience in Rodriguez's terms, which means thinking the way he does, noticing what he would notice, interpreting details in a similar fashion, using his key terms, seeing through his point of view; it could also mean imitating his style of writing, working with quotations from other writers, doing whatever it is you see him doing characteristically while he writes. Imitation, Rodriguez argues, is not necessarily a bad thing; it can, in fact, be one of the powerful ways in which a person learns.

Note: This assignment can also be used to read against "The Achievement of Desire." Rodriguez insists on the universality of his experience leaving home and community and joining the larger public life. You could highlight the differences between your experience and his. You should begin by imitating Rodriguez's method; you do not have to arrive at his conclusions, however.

ASSIGNMENT 6

The Literate Arts

RICHARD E. MILLER

Miller's essay opens with a list of fatal shootings in school—troublingly, an incomplete list. As the essay builds to questions—questions for educators and for students—the specters of violence and alienation remain, changing how we think about the reading and writing school endeavors to teach us. "I have these doubts, you see," Miller writes of academic work, "doubts silently shared by many who spend their days teaching others the literate arts. Aside from gathering and organizing information, aside from generating critiques and analyses that forever fall on deaf ears, what might the literate arts be said to be good for?" (p. 424).

Write an essay that takes up this question — "what might the literate arts be said to be good for?" — and that takes it up from your range of reference and from your point of view—or, more properly, from the point of view of you and people like you, the group you feel prepared to speak for. As an exercise in understanding, your essay should be modeled on one (or more) of the sections in "The Dark Night of the Soul." You can choose the text—and the text can be anything that might serve as an example of the literate arts, things in print but also including songs, films, and TV shows. But your presentation and discussion of the text should be in conversation with Miller—with his concerns, his key terms, his examples, and his conclusions.

ASSIGNMENT 7

Making Connections

PAULO FREIRE, MARY LOUISE PRATT,

RICHARD RODRIGUEZ, RICHARD E. MILLER

> After years spent unwilling to admit its attractions, I gestured nostalgically toward the past. I yearned for that time when I had not been so alone. I became impatient with books. I wanted experience more immediate. I feared the library's silence. I silently scorned the gray, timid faces around me. I grew to hate the growing pages of my dissertation on genre and Renaissance literature. (In my mind I heard relatives laughing as they tried to make sense of its title.) I wanted something — I couldn't say exactly what. (p. 531)
>
> —RICHARD RODRIGUEZ
>
> *The Achievement of Desire*

> For some, it will hardly come as a surprise to learn that reading and writing have no magically transformative powers. But for those of us who have been raised into the teaching and publishing professions, it can be quite a shock to confront the possibility that reading and writing and talking exercise almost *none* of the powers we regularly attribute to them in our favorite stories. The dark night of the soul for literacy workers comes with the realization that training students to read, write, and talk in more critical and self-reflective ways cannot protect them from the violent changes our culture is undergoing. (p. 423)
>
> — RICHARD MILLER
> *The Dark Night of the Soul*

"I have these doubts, you see," Miller writes of academic work, "doubts silently shared by many who spend their days teaching others the literate arts. Aside from gathering and organizing information, aside from generating critiques and analyses that forever fall on deaf ears, what might the literate arts be said to be good for?" (p. 424).

These questions are repeated, in different contexts and with different inflections, by all of the writers you have been reading: Freire, Pratt, Rodriguez, and Miller. All are concerned with the limits (and the failures) of education, with particular attention to the humanities and to the supposed benefits to be found in reading and writing.

Write an essay that takes up this question — "what might the literate arts be said to be good for?" — and that takes it up with these writers and these essays as your initial point of reference. What do they say? How might they be said to speak to one another? And, finally, where are you in this? Where are you, and people like you, the group for whom you feel prepared to speak? You, too, have been and will continue to be expected to take courses in reading and writing, to read, write, and talk in critical and self-reflective ways. Where are you in this conversation?

ALTERNATIVE ASSIGNMENT

Writing Against the Grain

SUSAN GRIFFIN

As you reread "Our Secret," think of Griffin's prose as experimental, as deliberate and crafted. She is trying to do something that she can't do in the "usual" essay form. She wants to make a different kind of argument and engage her reader in a different manner. And so she mixes personal and academic writing. She assembles fragments and juxtaposes seemingly unrelated material in surprising and suggestive relationships. She breaks the "plane" of the page with italicized inter-sections. She organizes her material, that is, but not in the usual mode of thesis-example-conclusion. The arrangement is not nearly so linear. At one point, when she seems to be prepared to argue that German child-rearing practices produced the Holocaust, she quickly says:

> Of course there cannot be one answer to such a monumental riddle, nor does any event in history have a single cause. Rather a field exists, like a field of gravity that is created by the movements of many bodies. Each life is influenced and it in turn becomes an influence. Whatever is a cause is also an effect. Childhood experience is just one element in the determining field. (p. 340)

Her prose serves to create a "field," one where many bodies are set in relationship.

It is useful, then, to think about Griffin's prose as the enactment of a method, as a way of doing a certain kind of intellectual work. One way to study this, to feel its effects, is to imitate it, to take it as a model. For this assignment, write a Griffin-like essay, one similar in its methods or organization and argument. You will need to think about the stories you might tell, about the stories and texts you might gather (stories and texts not your own). As you write, you will want to think carefully about arrangement and about commentary (about where, that is, you will speak to your reader *as* the writer of the piece). You should not feel bound to Griffin's subject matter, but you should feel that you are working in her spirit.

ALTERNATIVE ASSIGNMENT

The Task of Attention

SUSAN GRIFFIN

> I am looking now at the etching called *Poverty*, made in 1897. Near the center, calling my attention, a woman holds her head in her hands. (p. 344)
>
> — SUSAN GRIFFIN
> *Our Secret*

This is one of the many moments when Griffin speaks to us as though in the midst of her work. The point of this assignment is to think about that work — what it is, how she does it, and what it might have to do with schools and schooling. She is, after all, doing much of the traditional work of scholars — going to the archive, studying old materials, traveling and interviewing subjects, learning and writing history.

And yet this is not the kind of prose you would expect to find in a textbook for a history course. Even if the project is not what we usually think of as a research project, Griffin is a careful researcher. Griffin knows what she is doing. Go back to look again (this time with a writer's eye) at both the features of Griffin's prose and the way she characterizes her work as a scholar, gathering and studying her materials.

Write an essay in which you present an account of *how* Griffin does her work. You should use her words and examples from the text, but you should also feel that it is your job to explain what you present and to comment on it from the point of view of a student. As you reread, look to those sections where Griffin seems to be speaking to her readers about her work—about how she reads and how she writes, about how she gathers her materials and how she studies them. What is she doing? What is at stake in adopting such methods? How might they be taught? Where in the curriculum might (should?) such lessons be featured?

SEQUENCE TWO

The Arts of the Contact Zone

Mary Louise Pratt
Gloria Anzaldúa
John Edgar Wideman
Edward Said

ALTERNATIVES:

David Abram
Tommie Shelby
Alberto Álvaro Ríos

This sequence allows you to work closely with the argument of Mary Louise Pratt's "Arts of the Contact Zone," not so much through summary (repeating the argument) as through extension (working under its influence, applying its terms and protocols). In particular, you are asked to try your hand at those ways of reading and writing Pratt defines as part of the "literate arts of the contact zone," ways of reading and writing that have not historically been taught or valued in American schools.

Pratt is one of the country's most influential cultural critics. In "Arts of the Contact Zone," she makes the argument that our usual ways of reading and writing assume identification—that is, we learn to read and write the texts that express our own position and point of view. As a result, texts that reproduce different ways of thinking, texts that allude to different cultural systems, seem flawed, wrong, or inscrutable. As a counterposition, Pratt asks us to imagine scenes of reading, writing, teaching, and learning as "contact zones," places of contact between people who can't or don't or won't necessarily identify with one another.

In the first assignment, you are asked to search for or produce a document to exemplify the arts of the contact zone, working in library archives, searching the streets, surfing the Internet, or writing an "autoethnography." This is a big job, and probably new to most students; it is a project you will want to come back to and revise. The remaining assignments outline a project in which you examine other selections from *Ways of Reading* that exemplify or present moments of cultural contact.

ASSIGNMENT 1

The Literate Arts of the Contact Zone

MARY LOUISE PRATT

Here, briefly, are two descriptions of the writing one might find or expect in the contact zone:

> Autoethnography, transculturation, critique, collaboration, bilingualism, mediation, parody, denunciation, imaginary dialogue, vernacular expression—these are some of the literate arts of the contact zone. Miscomprehension, incomprehension, dead letters, unread masterpieces, absolute heterogeneity of meaning—these are some of the perils of writing in the contact zone. They all live among us today in the transnationalized metropolis of the United States and are becoming more widely visible, more pressing, and, like Guaman Poma's text, more decipherable to those who once would have ignored them in defense of a stable, centered sense of knowledge and reality. (pp. 492–93)

> We are looking for the pedagogical arts of the contact zone. These will include, we are sure, exercises in storytelling and in identifying with the ideas, interests, histories, and attitudes of others; experiments in transculturation and collaborative work and in the arts of critique, parody, and comparison (including unseemly comparisons between elite and vernacular cultural forms); the redemption of the oral; ways for people to engage with suppressed aspects of history (including their own histories), ways to move *into and out of* rhetorics of authenticity; ground rules for communication across lines of difference and hierarchy that go beyond politeness but maintain mutual respect; a systematic approach to the all-important concept of *cultural mediation*. (p. 497)

Here are two ways of working on Pratt's idea of the contact zone. Choose one.

1. One way of working with Pratt's essay, of extending its project, would be to conduct your own local inventory of writing from the contact zone. You might do this on your own or in teams, with others from your class. You will want to gather several similar documents, your "archive," before you make a final

selection. Think about how to make that choice. What makes one document stand out as representative? Here are two ways you might organize your search:

a. You could look for historical documents. A local historical society might have documents written by Native Americans ("Indians") to the white settlers. There may be documents written by slaves to masters or to northern whites explaining their experience. There may be documents written by women (suffragists, for example) trying to negotiate for public positions or rights. There may be documents from any of a number of racial or ethnic groups—Hispanic, Jewish, Irish, Italian, Polish, Swedish—trying to explain their positions to the mainstream culture. There may, perhaps at union halls, be documents written by workers to owners. Your own sense of the heritage of your area should direct your search.
b. Or you could look at contemporary documents in the print that is around you, texts that you might otherwise overlook. Pratt refers to one of the characteristic genres of the Hispanic community, the "*testimonio*." You could look for songs, testimonies, manifestos, statements by groups on campus, stories, autobiographies, interviews, letters to the editor, Web pages. You could look at the writing of any marginalized group, particularly writing intended, at least in part, to represent the experience of outsiders to the dominant culture (or to be in dialogue with that culture or to respond to that culture). These documents, if we follow Pratt's example, would encompass the work of young children or students, including college students.

Once you have completed your inventory, choose a document you would like to work with and write an essay that presents it carefully and in detail (perhaps in even greater detail than Pratt's presentation of the *New Chronicle*). You will, in other words, need to set the scene, summarize, explain, and work block quotations into your essay. You might imagine that you are presenting this to someone who would not have seen it and would not know how to read it, at least not as an example of the literate arts of the contact zone.

2. Another way of extending the project of Pratt's essay would be to write your autoethnography. It should not be too hard to locate a setting or context in which you are the "other"—the one who speaks from outside rather than inside the dominant discourse. Pratt says that the position of the outsider is marked not only by differences of language and ways of thinking and speaking but also by differences in power, authority, status. In a sense, she argues, the only way those in power can understand you is in *their* terms. These are terms you will need to use to tell your story, but your goal is to describe your position in ways that "engage with representations others have made of [you]" without giving in or giving up or disappearing in their already formed sense of who you are.

   This is an interesting challenge. One of the things that will make the writing difficult is that the autoethnographic or transcultural text calls upon skills not usually valued in American classrooms: bilingualism, parody, denunciation, imaginary dialogue, vernacular expression, storytelling, unseemly comparisons of high and low cultural forms—these are some of the terms Pratt offers. These do not fit easily with the traditional genres of the writing class (essay, term paper, summary, report) or its traditional values (unity, consistency, sincerity, clarity, correctness, decorum).

You will probably need to take this essay (or whatever it should be called) through several drafts. (In fact, you might revise this essay after you have completed assignments 2 and 3.) It might be best to begin as Pratt's student, using her description as a preliminary guide. Once you get a sense of your own project, you may find that you have terms or examples to add to her list of the literate arts of the contact zone.

ASSIGNMENT 2
Borderlands
MARY LOUISE PRATT, GLORIA ANZALDÚA

In "Arts of the Contact Zone," Pratt talks about the "autoethnographic" text, "a text in which people undertake to describe themselves in ways that engage with representations others have made of them," and about "transculturation," the "processes whereby members of subordinated or marginal groups select and invent from the materials transmitted by a dominant or metropolitan culture."

Write an essay in which you present a reading of *Borderlands/La frontera* as an example of an autoethnographic and/or transcultural text. You should imagine that you are writing to someone who is not familiar with either Pratt's argument or Anzaldúa's thinking. Part of your work, then, is to present Anzaldúa's text to readers who don't have it in front of them. You have the example of Pratt's reading of Guaman Poma's *New Chronicle and Good Government*. And you have her discussion of the literate arts of the contact zone. Think about how Anzaldúa's text might be similarly read and about how her text does and doesn't fit Pratt's description. Your goal should be to add an example to Pratt's discussion and to qualify it, to alter or reframe what she has said now that you have had a chance to look at an additional example.

ASSIGNMENT 3
Counterparts
JOHN EDGAR WIDEMAN

Here, from "Arts of the Contact Zone," is Mary Louise Pratt on the autoethnographic text:

> Guaman Poma's *New Chronicle* is an instance of what I have proposed to call an *autoethnographic* text, by which I mean a text in which people undertake to describe themselves in ways that engage with representations others have made of them. Thus if

> ethnographic texts are those in which European metropolitan subjects represent to themselves their others (usually their conquered others), autoethnographic texts are representations that the so-defined others construct *in response to* or in dialogue with those texts. . . . [T]hey involve a selective collaboration with and appropriation of idioms of the metropolis or the conqueror. These are merged or infiltrated to varying degrees with indigenous idioms to create self-representations intended to intervene in metropolitan modes of understanding. . . . Such texts often constitute a marginalized group's point of entry into the dominant circuits of print culture. It is interesting to think, for example, of American slave autobiography in its autoethnographic dimensions, which in some respects distinguish it from Euramerican autobiographical tradition. (pp. 487–88)

John Edgar Wideman's "Our Time" (p. 657) could serve as a twentieth-century counterpart to the *New Chronicle*. Reread it with "Arts of the Contact Zone" in mind. Write an essay that presents "Our Time" as an example of autoethnographic and/or transcultural text. You should imagine that you are working to put Pratt's ideas to the test (*does* it do what she says such texts must do?), but also add what you have to say concerning this text as a literate effort to be present in the context of difference.

ASSIGNMENT 4

A Dialectic of Self and Other

MARY LOUISE PRATT, EDWARD SAID

In "States," an account of Palestinian life written by a Palestinian in exile, Edward Said says,

> All cultures spin out a dialectic of self and other, the subject "I" who is native, authentic, at home, and the object "it" or "you," who is foreign, perhaps threatening, different, out there. From this dialectic comes the series of heroes and monsters, founding fathers and barbarians, prized masterpieces and despised opponents that express a culture from its deepest sense of national self-identity to its refined patriotism, and finally to its coarse jingoism, xenophobia, and exclusivist bias. (p. 565)

This is as true of the Palestinians as it is of the Israelis — although, he adds, "For Palestinian culture, the odd thing is that its own identity is more frequently than not perceived as 'other.'"

Pratt argues that our idea of community is "strongly utopian, embodying values like equality, fraternity, liberty, which the societies often profess but systematically fail to realize." Against this utopian vision of community, Pratt argues that we need to develop ways of understanding (noticing or creating) social and intellectual spaces that are not homogeneous or unified—contact zones. She argues that we need to develop ways of understanding and valuing difference.

There are similar goals and objects to these projects. Reread Pratt's essay with Said's "States" in mind. As she defines what she refers to as the "literate arts of the contact zone," can you find points of reference in Said's text? Said's thinking always attended to the importance and the conditions of writing, including his own. There are ways that "States" could be imagined as both autoethnographic and transcultural. How might his work allow you to understand the literate arts of the contact zone in practice? How might his work allow you to understand the problems and possibilities of such writing beyond what Pratt has imagined, presented, and predicted?

ASSIGNMENT 5
On Culture
MARY LOUISE PRATT, GLORIA ANZALDÚA, JOHN EDGAR WIDEMAN, EDWARD SAID

In some ways, the slipperiest of the key words in Pratt's essay "Arts of the Contact Zone" is "culture." At one point Pratt says,

> If one thinks of cultures, or literatures, as discrete, coherently structured, monolingual edifices, Guaman Poma's text, and indeed any autoethnographic work, appears anomalous or chaotic—as it apparently did to the European scholars Pietschmann spoke to in 1912. If one does not think of cultures this way, then Guaman Poma's text is simply heterogeneous, as the Andean region was itself and remains today. Such a text is heterogeneous on the reception end as well as the production end: it will read very differently to people in different positions in the contact zone. (p. 492)

If one thinks of cultures as "coherently structured, monolingual edifices," the text appears one way; if one thinks otherwise, the text is "simply heterogeneous." What might it mean to make this shift in the way one thinks of culture? Can you do it—that is, can you read the *New Chronicle* (or its excerpts) from both points of view? Better yet—what about your own culture and its key texts? Can you, for example, think of a group that you participate in as a "community"? Where and how does it represent itself to others? Where and how does it do this in writing? What are its "literate arts"?

The assignments in this sequence are an exercise in reading texts as heterogeneous, as contact zones. As a way of reflecting on your work in this sequence, write an essay in which you explain the work you have been doing to someone not in the course, someone who is interested in reading, writing, and learning, but who has not read Pratt, Anzaldúa, Wideman, or Said.

ALTERNATIVE ASSIGNMENT

Writing Language Back into the Land

DAVID ABRAM

In "Arts of the Contact Zone," Mary Louise Pratt defines contact zones as "social spaces where cultures meet, clash, and grapple with each other, often in contexts of highly asymmetrical relations of power." While we don't ordinarily think of the natural world as a culture, David Abram, in "Animism and the Alphabet," writes about the environment as if it were a culture of sorts—speaking to us, writing to us, attempting to communicate if only we are willing and able to listen. Abram might argue as well that the environment speaks in a context of "highly asymmetrical relations of power," in which people—like the Spaniards in Pratt's central example—hold the dominant position, often exhibiting little interest in the "languages" spoken by mountains, rivers, animals, or clouds.

Write an essay in which you consider how Pratt's concept of the contact zone might be useful in helping us consider our relationship with the natural world. Is the environment trying to speak to us as Guaman Poma tried to speak to his Spanish conquerors? In what ways is this analogy useful or productive, and in what ways does it fall short? Where would we find the "autoethnographic texts" produced by the natural world, and how can we learn to read them? Can you locate environmental versions of what Pratt calls "critique, collaboration, bilingualism, mediation, parody, denunciation, imaginary dialogue, [and] vernacular expression"? What are the possibilities for—and the problems with—"translating" messages from the natural world into languages we understand?

ALTERNATIVE ASSIGNMENT

We Who Are Dark

TOMMIE SHELBY

In the introduction to *We Who Are Dark*, Tommie Shelby says:

> Still, my book is not a manifesto. Nor do I specify a political agenda that activists can readily put into action. I aim to articulate and defend the basic moral and political principles that should undergird contemporary African American political unity. My focus on philosophical foundations is not a search for fundamental premises that are self-evident or beyond criticism and revision (as if there could be such), but a self-conscious, critical engagement with basic conceptual and normative questions, the answers to which are too often merely assumed rather than closely examined and argued for. (p. 20)

Read back through the selection to think about the ways the argument addresses its various audiences—to think about what it does, how it works, as well as what it says. The tone and method are very different from what you find now in talk radio or in the staged debates represented in television news. And the style and method are different from what you find in the popular media, from op-ed pages to editorials.

Then write an essay that considers and evaluates the argumentative style. For the sake of your reader, you will need to present the substance of the argument, its direction and conclusion. But we'd like you also to think about Shelby's essay as exemplary, as representing a particular mode of thought and persuasion. What are its advantages and disadvantages? What does it assume about reader, audience, and occasion? Who is speaking, and to whom? And in what setting? Can Mary Louise Pratt's essay on the "contact zone" be of use to you here?

ALTERNATIVE ASSIGNMENT

Binocular Vision

ALBERTO ÁLVARO RÍOS

> I often talk about the duality of language using the metaphor of binoculars, how by using two lenses one might see something better, closer, with more detail. The apparatus, the binoculars, are of course physically clumsy — as is the learning of two languages, and all the signage and so on that this entails — they're clumsy, but once put to the eyes a new world in that moment opens up to us. And it's not a new world and all — it's the same world, but simply better seen, and therefore better understood. (p. 506)
>
> — ALBERTO ÁLVARO RÍOS
>
> *Translating Translation: Finding the Beginning*

One way to understand Ríos's essay is as a collection of stories placed side by side to illuminate the complex ways that meanings are made through language. Rios uses three main narratives in this piece: the story of his mother's kitchen, the story of the man who is arrested for illegal border crossing, and finally the story of his teaching for Artists in the Schools. These three narratives drive the essay; they are responsible for leading us to think not only about what each narrative wants to say but also about what these three narratives say to one another. You may also notice that Ríos does not end his essay with any final thoughts or reflections, but with a single line of dialogue: "Just one, I said, like you."

Write an essay in which you think about this text, and the way it addresses its audiences, through Pratt's metaphor of the contact zone. In what ways might this text serve as an illustration of the "arts" of the contact zone? (Where is "translation" in her account?) In what ways might it challenge and/or extend her argument?

SEQUENCE THREE

Autobiographical Explorations

Richard Rodriguez
Edward Said
Susan Griffin
Richard E. Miller

ALTERNATIVES:

John Edgar Wideman
Gloria Anzaldúa

Autobiographical writing has been a regular feature of writing courses since the nineteenth century. There are a variety of reasons for the prevalence of autobiography, not the least of which is the pleasure students take in thinking about and writing about their lives and their world. There is also a long tradition of published autobiographical writing, particularly in the United States. The title of this sequence puts a particular spin on that tradition, since it points to a more specialized use of autobiography, phrased here as "exploration." What is suggested by the title is a use of writing (and the example of one's experience, including intellectual experience) to investigate, question, explore, inquire. Often the genre is not used for these purposes at all. Autobiographical writing is often used for purposes of display or self-promotion, or to further (rather than question) an argument (about success, about how to live a good or proper or fulfilling life).

There are two threads to this sequence. The first is to invite you to experiment with the genre of "autobiographical exploration." The second is to foreground the relationship between your work and the work of others, to think about how and why and where you are prepared to write autobiographically (prepared not only by the lessons you've learned in school but also by the culture and the way it invites you to tell — and live — the story of your life). And, if you are working inside a conventional field, a predictable way of writing, the sequence asks where and how you might make your mark or assert your position — your identity as a person (a character in a life story) and as a writer (someone working with the conventions of life-writing).

The alternative assignments that follow provide similar assignments but with different readings. They can be substituted for or added to the assignments in this sequence.

ASSIGNMENT 1

Desire, Reading, and the Past

RICHARD RODRIGUEZ

In "The Achievement of Desire," Richard Rodriguez tells stories of home but also stories of reading, of moments when things he read allowed him a way of reconsidering or revising ("framing," he calls it) the stories he would tell himself about himself. It is a very particular account of neighborhood, family, ethnicity, and schooling.

At the same time, Rodriguez insists that his story is also everyone's story — that his experience is universal. Take an episode from your life, one that seems in some ways similar to one of the episodes in "The Achievement of Desire," and cast it into a shorter version of Rodriguez's essay. Try to make use of your reading in ways similar to his. Think about what you have read lately in school, perhaps in this anthology.

In general, however, your job in this assignment is to look at your experience in Rodriguez's terms, which means thinking the way he does, noticing what he would notice, interpreting details in a similar fashion, using his key terms, seeing through his point of view; it could mean imitating his style of writing, doing whatever it is you see him doing characteristically when he writes. Imitation, Rodriguez argues, is not necessarily a bad thing; it can, he argues, be one of the powerful ways a person learns. Let this assignment serve as an exercise.

ASSIGNMENT 2

A Photographic Essay

EDWARD SAID

Edward Said, in the introduction to *After the Last Sky*, says of his method in "States":

> Its style and method — the interplay of text and photos, the mixture of genres, modes, styles — do not tell a consecutive story, nor do they constitute a political essay. Since the main features of our

> present existence are dispossession, dispersion, and yet also a kind of power incommensurate with our stateless exile, I believe that essentially unconventional, hybrid, and fragmentary forms of expression should be used to represent us. What I have quite consciously designed, then, is an alternative mode of expression to the one usually encountered in the media, in works of social science, in popular fiction. (p. 6)

And later:

> The multifaceted vision is essential to any representation of us. Stateless, dispossessed, de-centered, we are frequently unable either to speak the "truth" of our experience or to make it heard. We do not usually control the images that represent us; we have been confined to spaces designed to reduce or stunt us; and we have often been distorted by pressures and powers that have been too much for us. An additional problem is that our language, Arabic, is unfamiliar in the West and belongs to a tradition and civilization usually both misunderstood and maligned. Everything we write about ourselves, therefore, is an interpretive translation — of our language, our experience, our senses of self and others. (p. 6)

Reread "States," paying particular attention to the relationship of text and photograph, and paying attention to form. What *is* the order of the writing in this essay? (We will call it an essay for lack of a better term.) How might you diagram or explain its organization? By what principle(s) is it ordered and arranged? The essay shifts genres — memoir, history, argument. It is, as Said comments, "hybrid." What surprises are there? or disappointments? How might you describe the writer's strategy as he works on his audience, on readers? And, finally, do you find Said's explanation sufficient or useful — does the experience of exile produce its own inevitable style of report and representation?

For this assignment, compose a similar project, a Said-like reading of a set of photos. These can be photos prepared for the occasion (by you or a colleague); they could also be photos already available. Whatever their source, they should represent people and places, a history and/or geography that you know well, that you know to be complex and contradictory, and that you know will not be easily or readily understood by others, both the group for whom you will be writing (most usefully the members of your class) and readers more generally. You must begin with a sense that the photos cannot speak for themselves; you must speak for them.

In preparation, you should reread closely to come to a careful understanding of Said's project. (The first and second "Questions for a Second Reading," on p. 575, should be useful for this.)

ASSIGNMENT 3
The Matrix
SUSAN GRIFFIN

At several points in her essay "Our Secret," Susan Griffin argues that we—all of us—are part of a complex web of connections. We live in history, and history is determining. At one point she says:

> Who are we? The question is not simple. What we call the self is part of a larger matrix of relationship and society. Had we been born to a different family, in a different time, to a different world, we would not be the same. All the lives that surround us are in us. (p. 371)

At another point she asks, "Is there any one of us who can count ourselves outside the circle circumscribed by our common past?" She speaks of a "field"

> like a field of gravity that is created by the movements of many bodies. Each life is influenced and it in turn becomes an influence. Whatever is a cause is also an effect. Childhood experience is just one element in the determining field. (p. 340)

One way of thinking about this concept of the self (and of interrelatedness), at least under Griffin's guidance, is to work on the connections that she implies and asserts. As you reread the selection, look for powerful and surprising juxtapositions, fragments that stand together in interesting and suggestive ways. Think about the arguments represented by the blank spaces on the page or the jumps from section to section. (And look for Griffin's written statements about relatedness.) Look for connections that seem important to the text (and to you) and to be representative of Griffin's thinking (and useful to yours).

Write an essay in which you use these examples to think through the ways Griffin answers the question she raises: Who are we?

ASSIGNMENT 4
The Experience of Thought
RICHARD E. MILLER

In the final chapter of *Writing at the End of the World*, Richard E. Miller says the following about his own writing:

> While the assessments, evaluations, proposals, reports, commentaries, and critiques I produce help to keep the bureaucracy of higher education going, there is another kind of writing I turn to

> in order to sustain the ongoing search for meaning in a world no one controls. This writing asks the reader to make imaginative connections between disparate elements; it tracks one path among many possible ones across the glistening water. (p. 196)

We can assume that this is the kind of writing present in "The Dark Night of the Soul."

Reread "The Dark Night of the Soul" with particular attention to Miller's method, which is, in simplest terms, putting one thing next to another. Pay attention to the connections Miller makes, to the ways he makes them, and to the ways as a reader you are (or are not) invited into this process. And write a Miller-like essay. To give the project some shape and limit, let's say that it should bring together at least three "disparate elements," three examples you can use to think about whatever it is you want to think about. You don't need to be constrained to Miller's subject—writing, reading, and schooling—although this subject might be exactly the right one for you. Your writing should, however, be like Miller's in its sense of urgency. In other words, write about something that matters to you, that you care about, that touches you personally and deeply.

ASSIGNMENT 5

The "I" of the Personal Essay

RICHARD RODRIGUEZ, EDWARD SAID, RICHARD E. MILLER

The assignments in this sequence have been designed to prompt autobiographical writing. They have been invitations for you to tell your story and to think about the ways stories represent a person and a life. They have also, of course, been exercises in imitation, in writing like Rodriguez, Said, and Miller, in casting your story in their terms. These exercises highlight the ways in which your story is never just your own but also written through our culture's sense of what it means to be a person, to live, grow, change, learn, experience. No writer simply gets to invent childhood. Childhood, like adulthood, is a category already determined by hundreds of thousands of representations of life—in books, in songs, on TV, in paintings, in the stories we tell ourselves about ourselves. As you have written these four personal narratives, you have, of course, been telling the truth, just as you have also, of course, been creating a character, setting scenes, providing certain representations that provide a version of (but that don't begin to sum up) your life.

Read back over the essays you have written (and perhaps revised). As you read, look for examples of where you feel you were doing your best work, where you are proud of the writing and interested in what it allows you to see or to think (where the "investigations" seem most worthwhile).

And think about what is *not* contained in these essays. What experiences are missing? what point of view? what ways of speaking or thinking or writing? If you were to go back to assemble these pieces into a longer essay, what would you keep, and what would you add or change? What are the problems facing a writer, like you, trying to write a life, to take experience and represent it in sentences?

With these questions in mind, reread the essays you have written and write a preface, a short piece introducing a reader to what you have written (to your work—and perhaps work you may do on these essays in the future).

ALTERNATIVE ASSIGNMENT

Old Habits

JOHN EDGAR WIDEMAN

Wideman frequently interrupts the narrative in "Our Time" to talk about the problems he is having as a writer. He says, for example, "The hardest habit to break, since it was the habit of a lifetime, would be listening to myself listen to him. That habit would destroy any chance of seeing my brother on his terms; and seeing him in his terms, learning his terms, seemed the whole point of learning his story" (p. 672).

Wideman gives you the sense of a writer who is aware from the inside, while writing, of the problems inherent in the personal narrative. This genre always shades and deflects; it is always partial and biased; in its very attempts to be complete, to understand totally, it reduces its subject in ways that are unacceptable. And so you can see Wideman's efforts to overcome these problems—he writes in Robby's voice; he starts his story three different times, first with Garth, later with the neighborhood, hoping that a variety of perspectives will overcome the limits inherent in each; he stops and speaks to us not as the storyteller but as the writer, thinking about what he is doing and not doing.

Let Wideman's essay provide a kind of writing lesson. It highlights problems; it suggests alternatives. Using Wideman, then, as your writing teacher, write a family history of your own. Yours will most likely be shorter than Wideman's, but let its writing be the occasion for you also to work on a personal narrative as a writing problem, an interesting problem that forces a writer to think about the limits of representation and point of view (about who gets to speak and in whose terms, about who sums things up and what is left out in this accounting).

ALTERNATIVE ASSIGNMENT

La Conciencia de la Mestiza/Toward a New Consciousness

GLORIA ANZALDÚA

We've included two chapters from Gloria Anzaldúa's *Borderlands/La frontera*. The style of these chapters is unconventional, experimental.

As you reread Anzaldúa, think about her chapters as forming an argument. How does the argument develop? To whom is it directed? What are its key terms and examples? What are the conclusions? To what degree is the style of these chapters part of the argument (or a subtext or a counterpoint)? Write an essay in which you summarize Anzaldúa's argument in these two chapters. Place it in the context of at least one of the texts you have already read in this sequence.

SEQUENCE FOUR

Experts and Expertise

Kwame Anthony Appiah
Judith Butler
Edward Said
Walker Percy

ALTERNATIVES:

Richard E. Miller
David Abram
Anne Carson

The first three assignments in this sequence give you the chance to think about familiar settings or experiences through the work of writers who have had a significant effect on contemporary thought: Kwame Anthony Appiah, Judith Butler, and Edward Said.

In each case, you will be given the opportunity to work alongside these thinkers as an apprentice, carrying out work they have begun. The final assignment in the sequence will ask you to look back on what you have done, to take stock, and, with Walker Percy's account of the oppressive nature of expertise in mind, to draw some conclusions about the potential and consequences of this kind of intellectual apprenticeship. There are three alternative assignments following the sequence. Any of these could be used in place of the assignments in the sequence.

ASSIGNMENT 1

Ideational/Representational

KWAME ANTHONY APPIAH

Central to Appiah's method in his essay "Race, Culture, Identity: Misunderstood Connections" is his use of two concepts taken from his reading in the philosophy of language: the "ideational" view of meaning and the "referential" view of meaning. (The fourth of the "Questions for a Second Reading," on p. 134, can provide a preliminary exercise for this writing assignment.) Write an essay in which you use this method to examine a key word (or phrase) in your discursive world — a word or phrase with consequences (like "race"). You'll need to take some time to present your key term and the complications or controversies it entails. And then, following Appiah, you can work from "ideational" to "referential" as you examine the ways it is (and has been) used and understood.

Appiah says (and shows) that the referential theory requires an examination of the history of the term and its use. Although you may not have the range of reference evident in Appiah's essay, it is important that you do this work, that you look for examples across time. The range may not be as great (from the eighteenth century on), but it is important that you locate your key term in instances of its use in print as well as in common speech. You can turn to historical dictionaries, like the *Oxford English Dictionary*. You can turn to newspapers, magazines, books, films, and popular culture. This is a research project, in other words.

ASSIGNMENT 2
A Question for Philosophers
JUDITH BUTLER

The opening lines of Judith Butler's essay "Beside Oneself: On the Limits of Sexual Autonomy" might be understood as an invitation to participate with her in one of the traditions of philosophy. She writes:

> What makes for a livable world is no idle question. It is not merely a question for philosophers. It is posed in various idioms all the time by people in various walks of life. If that makes them all philosophers, then that is a conclusion I am happy to embrace. It becomes a question for ethics, I think, not only when we ask the personal question, what makes my own life bearable, but when we ask, from a position of power, and from the point of view of distributive justice, what makes, or ought to make, the lives of others bearable? Somewhere in the answer we find ourselves not only committed to a certain view of what life is, and what it should be, but also of what constitutes the human, the distinctively human life, and what does not. (p. 240)

Write an essay that takes up this invitation — and that takes it up in specific reference to what Butler has offered in "Beside Oneself: On the Limits of Sexual Autonomy." You will need, then, to take some time to represent her essay — both what it says and what it does. The "Questions for a Second Reading" (p. 258) should be helpful in preparing for this. Imagine an audience of smart people, people who may even know something about Butler, but who have not read this essay. You have read it, and you want to give them a sense of how and why you find it interesting and important.

But you'll also need to take time to address her questions in your own terms: What makes for a livable world? What constitutes the human? Don't slight this part of your essay. Give yourself as many pages as you gave Butler. You should, however, make it clear that you are writing in response to what you have read. You'll want to indicate, both directly and indirectly, how your thoughts are shaped by, indebted to, or in response to hers.

ASSIGNMENT 3

On Representation

EDWARD SAID

In his essay "States," Edward Said insists on our recognizing the contemporary social, political, and historical context for intimate scenes he (and Jean Mohr) present of people going about their everyday lives. The Palestinian people are still much in the news—photographs of scenes from their lives are featured regularly in newspapers, in magazines, and on the Internet. Collect a series of these images from a particular and defined recent period of time—a week or a month, say, when the Palestinians have been in the news. Using these images, and putting them in conversation with some of the passages and images in "States," write an essay in the manner of Said's essay, with text and image in productive relationship. The goal of your essay should be to examine how Said's work in "States" can speak to us (or might speak to us) today.

ASSIGNMENT 4

On Experts and Expertise

KWAME ANTHONY APPIAH, JUDITH BUTLER,

EDWARD SAID, WALKER PERCY

> The whole horizon of being is staked out by "them," the experts. The highest satisfaction of the sightseer (not merely the tourist but any layman seer of sights) is that his sight should be certified as genuine. The worst of this impoverishment is that there is no sense of impoverishment. (p. 464)
>
> I refer to the general situation in which sovereignty is surrendered to a class of privileged knowers, whether these be theorists or artists. A reader may surrender sovereignty over that which has been written about, just as a consumer may surrender sovereignty over a thing which has been theorized about. The consumer is content to

> receive an experience just as it has been presented to him by theorists and planners. The reader may also be content to judge life by whether it has or has not been formulated by those who know and write about life. (p. 465)
>
> — WALKER PERCY
> *The Loss of the Creature*

In the last three assignments you were asked to try on other writers' ways of seeing the world. You looked at what you had read or done, and at scenes from your own life, casting your experience in the terms of others.

Percy, in "The Loss of the Creature," offers what might be taken as a critique of such activity. "A reader," he says, "may surrender sovereignty over that which has been written about, just as a consumer may surrender sovereignty over a thing which has been theorized about." Appiah, Butler, and Said have all been presented to you as, in a sense, "privileged knowers." You have been asked to model your own work on their examples.

It seems safe to say that, at least so far as Percy is concerned, surrendering sovereignty is not a good thing to do. If Percy were to read over your work in these assignments, how do you think he would describe what you have done? If he were to take your work as an example in his essay, where might he place it? And how would his reading of your work fit with your sense of what you have done? Would Percy's assessment be accurate, or is there something he would be missing, something he would fail to see?

Write an essay in which you describe and comment on your work in this sequence, looking at it both from Percy's point of view and from your own, but viewing that work as an example of an educational practice, a way of reading (and writing) that may or may not have benefits for the reader.

Note: You will need to review carefully those earlier papers and mark sections that you feel might serve as interesting examples in your discussion. You want to base your conclusions on the best evidence you can. When you begin writing, it might be useful to refer to the writer of those earlier papers as a "he" or a "she" who played certain roles and performed his or her work in certain characteristic ways. You can save the first person, the "I," for the person who is writing this assignment and looking back on those texts.

ALTERNATIVE ASSIGNMENT

A Story of Reading

RICHARD E. MILLER

Consider the following passage from Richard E. Miller's "The Dark Night of the Soul":

> What makes *Into the Wild* remarkable is Krakauer's ability to get some purchase on McCandless's actual reading practice, which, in turn, enables him to get inside McCandless's head and speculate

> with considerable authority about what ultimately led the young man to abandon the comforts of home and purposefully seek out mortal danger. Krakauer is able to do this, in part, because he has access to the books that McCandless read, with all their underlinings and marginalia, as well as to his journals and the postcards and letters McCandless sent to friends along his journey. Working with these materials and his interviews with McCandless's family and friends, Krakauer develops a sense of McCandless's inner life and eventually comes to some understanding of why the young man was so susceptible to being seduced by the writings of London, Thoreau, Muir, and Tolstoy. Who McCandless is and what becomes of him are, it turns out, intimately connected to the young man's approach to reading — both what he chose to read and how he chose to read it. (p. 429)

When Miller is writing about Krakauer's *Into the Wild*, he seems to suggest that what we read, and how we read, can say something about who we are and about what we might become. This is a very bold claim.

Think of a book that made a difference to you, that captured you, maybe one you have read more than once, maybe one that you've made marks in or that still sits on your bookshelf. Or, if not a book, think of your favorite song or album or movie or TV show, something that engaged you at least potentially as McCandless was engaged by London, Thoreau, Muir, and Tolstoy. What was it that you found there? What kind of reader were you? And what makes this a story in the past tense? How and why did you move on? (Or, if it is not a story in the past tense, where are you now, and are you, like McCandless, in any danger?)

ALTERNATIVE ASSIGNMENT

The Loss of the Creature

DAVID ABRAM

There is much that is similar to Walker Percy's concerns in David Abram's "Animism and the Alphabet." In fact, it is easy to imagine Abram using the same title — "The Loss of the Creature." They ask similar questions; they write with a similar urgency; they are even similar in method.

Let's take the similarities as a starting point. As you reread the essays, then, think primarily about the differences. Both are concerned with loss. What, for each, has been lost? What are the reasons? What are the consequences? What options are available for restoration? Write an essay that begins with Abram's point of view, a concern over "modern civilization's evident disregard for the needs of the natural world," and that thinks, then, about Percy's understanding of loss, its origins and consequences.

ALTERNATIVE ASSIGNMENT

Short Talks

ANNE CARSON

The form of Carson's "Short Talks" presents challenges, but it also presents opportunities. As you reread, think about this text as a type of experimental essay. How does it draw upon the conventions of the essay? How does it defy or revise those conventions? How would you describe its formal features in relation to what you understand to be conventional essay form? How does "Short Talks" satisfy or challenge a reader's expectations?

Prepare an essay that is Carson-like. It should be, at minimum, as long as hers. It should be similar in style and intent. Her work is your model and inspiration, and yet this project is also yours. A reader should be able to see where and how your work is in conversation with hers; a reader should also be able to see what you bring to the table. Be sure that your essay has an "Introduction," something to orient a reader to what follows. ("Introductions" are often either written last or seriously revised once the project is complete.)

SEQUENCE FIVE

On Difficulty

Michel Foucault
Judith Butler
Kwame Anthony Appiah
David Foster Wallace

ALTERNATIVES:

Tommie Shelby
Antonio Porchia
John Edgar Wideman

The assignments in this sequence invite you to consider the nature of difficult texts and how the problems they pose might be said to belong simultaneously to language, to readers, and to writers. The sequence presents four difficult essays (and three alternatives, should you wish to alter the sequence). The assumption the sequence makes is that they are difficult for all readers, not just for students, and that the difficulty is necessary, strategic, not a mistake or evidence of a writer's failure.

ASSIGNMENT 1

Foucault's Fabrication

MICHEL FOUCAULT

About three-quarters of the way into "Panopticism," Foucault says,

> Our society is one not of spectacle, but of surveillance; under the surface of images, one invests bodies in depth; behind the great abstraction of exchange, there continues the meticulous, concrete training of useful

> forces; the circuits of communication are the supports of an accumulation and a centralization of knowledge; the play of signs defines the anchorages of power; it is not that the beautiful totality of the individual is amputated, repressed, altered by our social order, it is rather that the individual is carefully fabricated in it, according to a whole technique of forces and bodies. (p. 301)

This prose is eloquent and insists on its importance to our moment and our society; it is also very hard to read or to paraphrase. Who is doing what to whom? How do we think about the individual being carefully fabricated in the social order?

Take this selection as a problem to solve. What is it about? What are its key arguments, its examples and conclusions? Write an essay that summarizes "Panopticism." Imagine that you are writing for readers who have read the chapter (although they won't have the pages in front of them) and who are at sea as to its argument. You will need to take time to present and discuss examples from the text. Your job is to help your readers figure out what it says. You get the chance to take the lead and be the teacher. In addition, you should feel free to acknowledge that you don't understand certain sections even as you write about them.

So how do you write about something you don't completely understand? Here's a suggestion. When you have completed your summary, read it over and treat it as a draft. Ask questions like these: What have I left out? What was I tempted to ignore or finesse? Go back to those sections of the chapter that you ignored and bring them into your essay. Revise by adding discussions of some of the very sections you don't understand. You can write about what you think Foucault might be saying—you can, that is, be cautious and tentative; you can admit that the text is what it is, hard to read. You don't have to master this text. You do, however, need to see what you can make of it.

ASSIGNMENT 2

Concept and Example

JUDITH BUTLER

Judith Butler's "Beside Oneself: On the Limits of Sexual Autonomy" is a philosophical essay, and one of the difficulties it presents to a reader is its emphasis on conceptual language. The sentences most often refer to concepts or ideas rather than to people, places, or events in the concrete, tangible, observable world. It refers to the *human* or to the *body*, but without telling the stories of particular humans or particular bodies. In fact, as a reader, you can feel her pull back at the very moments when she begins to speak in the first person, to personalize the essay. Without something concrete, without some situation or context in which the conceptual can take shape, these conceptual terms can lose their force or meaning. (If there is a story in this essay, it is not the story of the loss of a particular friend or love; it is the "story" of a struggle to understand and to articulate a response to the essay's opening question: what makes for a livable world?)

Reread this essay, noting particular moments (sentences, passages, and paragraphs) that make things hard for you, that are difficult for you as a reader. Choose four that seem to you to be the most representative. How are they hard? How would you characterize the difficulties they present? Where and how do you see Butler trying to help her readers? Where and how does she leave you on your own?

As an exercise, prepare a brief paraphrase or translation of each of these four representative moments: "What I think Butler is saying is . . ." And, finally, write an essay in which you discuss the essay, its argument, its methods, and the difficulties it presents to a reader.

ASSIGNMENT 3

A Reader-Friendly Text

KWAME ANTHONY APPIAH

Compared to Butler's "Beside Oneself," Kwame Anthony Appiah's essay "Race, Culture, Identity: Misunderstood Connections" is a reader-friendly text—that is, it goes out of its way to address, engage, anticipate, and entertain its readers. For example, it begins: "Imagine yourself on Angel Island in the 1920s. You are helping an inquisitive immigrant from Canton to fill in an immigration form." This engagement is a *technical* feat; it is a strategy; it is the result of something Appiah does as a writer. It is not just a quality of his character.

Still, Appiah's essay could also be said to be difficult—to be a challenge to read. It contains quick references to the names of writers and scholars whom you may not recognize. In the first few pages, he mentions Jorge Garcia, David Wong, Houston Baker, Samuel Delaney, I. A. Richards, Frank Ramsey, and W. V. O. Quine, to list just a few. It works with complicated ideas and relies on technical terms, some of them coined by Appiah himself: "racialism," "semantic deference," "biological concept," for example. And it poses an argument that not only runs against common assumptions but also raises difficult political questions about race and identity.

As you reread, take note of the places in the text where the writer addresses you or, if not through direct address, where the writer seems to have you in mind. And take note of those places where you find yourself to be most challenged, where the text becomes difficult to read.

When you are done, go back over your notes to see if there are distinct strategies, to see if your examples cluster into types. And write an essay in which you discuss "Race, Culture, Identity," its argument, its methods, and the difficulties it presents to a reader. If it is helpful, you might draw on passages from Foucault or Butler for additional examples.

ASSIGNMENT 4

The Figure of the Writer as an Intellectual

DAVID FOSTER WALLACE

A character emerges in David Foster Wallace's essay "Authority and American Usage," a figure representing one version of a well-schooled, learned, and articulate adult, an intellectual, someone who reads widely, who thinks closely and freshly and methodically about big questions, someone with ideas and with style, someone who is defined in relation to sources—to books and to other writers, someone whose writing requires footnotes and long digressions.

As you reread, think about the speaker as a character, as an invention of David Foster Wallace, the writer (who could, at least hypothetically, have written about dictionaries in a different voice and in a different form). And mark moments when this character seems most distinctively present or alive. This character (whom we might also call Wallace) is a figure who reads in the field, who thinks about these issues, and who speaks with authority. He has a distinctive personality, way of thinking, view of the world. (Students are often invited, for example, to think of the "Thoreau" in *Walden* in just these terms, to think of him as a great American character.) Why would Wallace, the writer, present himself (or enter the conversation) in just these ways? What was at stake for him?

Having done this preparatory work, write an essay in which you discuss the figure of the intellectual represented in the essay "Authority and American Usage." You'll need to work closely with a few key and representative moments in the text. And write an essay in which you assess this figure in relation to your own education—better yet, in relation to the figure you intend to cut as a well-schooled adult, as an intellectual, as a person with ideas and knowledge and something to say.

ASSIGNMENT 5

A Theory of Difficulty

MICHEL FOUCAULT, JUDITH BUTLER, KWAME ANTHONY APPIAH, DAVID FOSTER WALLACE

Now that you have worked with these four texts, you are in a good position to review what you have written about each of them in order to say something more general about difficulty—difficulty in writing, difficulty in reading.

Write an essay in which you present a theory of difficulty, a kind of guide, something that might be useful to students who are regularly asked to confront difficult assignments. You will want to work from your previous essays—pulling out sections, revising, reworking examples for this new essay. Don't let your earlier work go unacknowledged. But, at the same time, feel free to move out from these readings to other materials, examples, or situations.

ALTERNATIVE ASSIGNMENT

Speaker and Audience

TOMMIE SHELBY

One difficulty with Tommie Shelby's essay "Social Identity and Group Solidarity" is that Shelby is often speaking from within positions that are not his own. He is, in a sense, ventriloquizing arguments made by others, writing within the "discourse," for example, of black authenticity or of "collective identity theory," taking positions that are not his own. In a sense, the problems in the essay enact the conceptual and political problems Shelby is addressing—what are the possible relationships between an individual and the group?

As you reread, pay particular attention to the sources of the language (or languages) in this text. Where, for example, can you find Tommie Shelby? How would you define and characterize the author *as he is present* in this text? And with whom is he arguing? How would you define and characterize his presumed and/or ideal audience? And if, as we are assuming, it is hard to figure out who is speaking and to whom, how might you account for this? Let's not assume that this is Shelby's "failure" as a writer. Let's assume that this is a strategy or an achievement or a necessary accommodation.

Choose three or four sections of the text that, for you, provide interesting and representative examples, and write an essay that considers the difficulty of writing and reading "Social Identity and Group Solidarity."

ALTERNATIVE ASSIGNMENT

Reading and Reading Again

ANTONIO PORCHIA

It is easy to read and remember, to clip and save, one of Porchia's aphorisms. Reading a collection of them, thinking about them as an example of a writer's project, this is another matter altogether. To think about these odd sentences, it helps to read them over and over again; it helps to write some Porchia-like sentences of your own.

Do this. Read them over and over; write some sentences of your own. Do this until these sentences begin to take shape for you as a whole, as a project, not just as one-liners. And write an essay, one that works closely from examples, explaining how we might understand Porchia's project as a writer. Porchia devoted his life to writing these. Why might a writer return to these sentences again and again? They have been valued by readers across generations and continents. Why, do you suppose?

ALTERNATIVE ASSIGNMENT

A Story of Reading

JOHN EDGAR WIDEMAN

At several points in "Our Time," Wideman interrupts the narrative to discuss his position as a writer telling Robby's story. He describes the problems he faces in writing this piece (or in reading the text of his brother's life). You could read this selection, in other words, as an essay about reading and writing. It is Wideman's account of his work.

As a narrative, "Our Time" is made up of sections, fragments, different voices. It is left to the reader, in a sense, to put the pieces together and complete the story. There is work for a reader to do, in other words, and one way to account for that work is to call it "practice" or "training." Wideman wants to force a reader's attention by offering a text that makes unusual demands, a text that teaches a reader to read differently. If you think of your experience with the text, of how you negotiated its terrain, what is the story of reading you might tell? In what way do your difficulties parallel Wideman's—at least those he tells us about when he stops to talk about the problems he faces as a writer?

Write an essay in which you tell the story of what it was like to read "Our Time" and compare your experience working with this text with Wideman's account of his own.

A story of reading—this is not a usual school exercise. Usually you are asked what texts mean, not what it was like to read them. As you prepare for this assignment, think back as closely as you can to your experience the first time through. And you will want to reread, looking for how and where Wideman seems to be deliberately working on his reader, defying expectation and directing response. You want to tell a story that is rich in detail, precise in accounting for moments in the text. You want to bring forward the features that can make your story a good story to read—suspense, action, context, drama. Since this is your story, you are one of the characters. You will want to refer to yourself as you were at the moment of reading while also reserving a space for you to speak from your present position, as a person thinking about what it was like to read the text, and as a person thinking about Wideman and about reading. You are telling a story, but you will need to break the narrative (as Wideman breaks his) to account in more general terms for the demands Wideman makes on readers. What habits does he assume a reader will bring to this text? How and why does he want to break them?

SEQUENCE SIX

Reading Culture

John Berger
Susan Bordo
Laura Kipnis
Michel Foucault

ALTERNATIVES:

Richard E. Miller
David Foster Wallace
David Abram

In this sequence, you will be reading and writing about culture. Not Culture, something you get if you go to the museum or a concert on Sunday, but culture—the images, words, and sounds that pervade our lives and organize and represent our common experience. This sequence invites your reflection on the ways culture "works" in and through the lives of individual consumers.

The difficulty of this sequence lies in the way it asks you to imagine that you are not a sovereign individual, making your own choices and charting the course of your life. This is conceptually difficult, but it can also be distasteful, since we learn at an early age to put great stock in imagining our own freedom. Most of the readings that follow ask you to imagine that you are the product of your culture; that your ideas, feelings, and actions, your ways of thinking and being, are constructed for you by a large, organized, pervasive force (sometimes called history, sometimes called culture, sometimes called ideology). You don't feel this to be the case, but that is part of the power of culture, or so the argument goes. These forces hide themselves. They lead you to believe that their constructions are naturally, inevitably there, that things are the way they are because that is just "the way things are." The assignments in this sequence ask you to read against your common sense. You will be expected to try on the role of the critic—to see how and where it might be useful to recognize complex motives in ordinary expressions.

The authors in this sequence all write as though, through great effort, they could step outside culture to see and criticize its workings. The assignments in this sequence will ask you both to reflect on this type of criticism and to participate in it.

ASSIGNMENT 1

Looking at Pictures

JOHN BERGER

> Original paintings are silent and still in a sense that information never is. Even a reproduction hung on a wall is not comparable in this respect for in the original the silence and stillness permeate the actual material, the paint, in which one follows the traces of the painter's immediate gestures. This has the effect of closing the distance in time between the painting of the picture and one's own act of looking at it. . . . What we make of that painted moment when it is before our eyes depends upon what we expect of art, and that in turn depends today upon how we have already experienced the meaning of paintings through reproductions. (p. 158)
>
> — JOHN BERGER
> *Ways of Seeing*

While Berger describes original paintings as silent in this passage, it is clear that these paintings begin to speak if one approaches them properly, if one learns to ask "the right questions of the past." Berger demonstrates one route of approach, for example, in his reading of the Hals paintings, where he asks questions about the people and objects and their relationship to the painter and the viewer. What the paintings might be made to say, however, depends on the viewer's expectations, his or her sense of the questions that seem appropriate or possible. Berger argues that because of the way art is currently displayed, discussed, and reproduced, the viewer expects only to be mystified.

For this assignment, imagine that you are working against the silence and mystification Berger describes. Go to a museum — or, if that is not possible, to a large-format book of reproductions in the library (or, if that is not possible, to the Internet) — and select a painting that seems silent and still, yet invites conversation. Your job is to figure out what sorts of questions to ask, to interrogate the painting, to get it to speak, to engage with the past in some form of dialogue. Write an essay in which you record this process and what you have learned from it. Somewhere in your essay, perhaps at the end, turn back to Berger's chapter to talk about how this process has or hasn't confirmed what you take to be Berger's expectations.

Note: If possible, include with your essay a reproduction of the painting you select. (Check the postcards at the museum gift shop.) In any event, you want to make sure that you describe the painting in sufficient detail for your readers to follow what you say.

ASSIGNMENT 2

Berger and After

JOHN BERGER, SUSAN BORDO

In "Beauty (Re)discovers the Male Body," Bordo refers to John Berger and his work in *Ways of Seeing*, although she refers to a different chapter than the one included here. In general, however, both Berger and Bordo are concerned with how we see and read images; both are concerned to correct the ways images are used and read; both trace the ways images serve the interests of money and power; both are written to teach readers how and why they should pay a different kind of attention to the images around them.

For this assignment, use Bordo's work to reconsider Berger's. Write an essay in which you consider the two chapters as examples of an ongoing project. Berger's essay precedes Bordo's by about a quarter of a century. If you look closely at one or two of their examples, and if you look at the larger concerns of their arguments, are they saying the same things? doing the same work? If so, how? And why is such work still necessary? If not, how do their projects differ? And how might you explain those differences?

ASSIGNMENT 3

Reading the Body

SUSAN BORDO

In "Beauty (Re)discovers the Male Body," Bordo looks back to the history of advertising (the "cultural genealogy of the ads I've been discussing") and works directly with the ads that prompted and served this chapter in her book. These images are a key part of the writing.

Bordo also speaks directly to you and invites you into her project: "So the next time you see a Dockers or a Haggar ad, think of it not only as an advertisement for khakis but also as an advertisement for a certain notion of what it means to be a man." You don't have to be limited to Dockers, Haggar, or khaki, but as you reread the essay and prepare for this writing assignment, keep your eye out for advertisements that come your way, advertisements that seem perfect for thinking along with Bordo (or advertisements that seem like interesting counterexamples). Clip these or copy them so that you can use them, as she does, as material for writing.

Write an essay in which you take up Bordo's invitation. You should assume an audience that has not read Bordo (or not read her work recently), so you will need to take time to present the terms and direction of her argument. Your goal, however, is to extend her project to your moment in time, when advertising may very well have moved on to different images of men and strategies of presentation. Bordo is quite specific about her age and experience, her point of view. You should be equally specific. You, too, should establish your point of view. You are placed at a different moment in time; your experience is different; your exposure to images has prepared you differently. You write from a different subject position. Your job, then, is not simply to reproduce Bordo's project but to extend it, to refine it, to put it to the test.

ASSIGNMENT 4
A Critical Practice
LAURA KIPNIS

Laura Kipnis's essay, "Love's Labors" considers the social text rather than particular images. She writes about love, desire, marriage, and adultery. At one point in her essay, she says:

> Might we entertain the possibility that posing philosophical questions isn't restricted to university campuses and learned tomes, that maybe it's something everyone does in the course of everyday life — if not always in an entirely knowing fashion? If adultery is more of a critical practice than a critical theory, well, acting out *is* what happens when knowledge or consciousness about something is foreclosed. Why such knowledge is foreclosed is a question yet to be considered — though how much do any of us know about our desires and motivations, or the contexts that produce them? We can be pretty clueless. We say things like "Something just happened to me," as if that were an explanation. (p. 399)

Kipnis refers to adultery as a "critical practice" rather than a critical theory. What other forms of critical practice might you observe, or have you observed, in "everyday life"? Working as a social historian — using Kipnis's study of adultery as a model — conduct your own analysis of a divergent "critical practice" that you think reveals something about our society's "structuring contradictions." What might your analysis teach us about our "prevailing systems of power" and/or "the weak links in social institutions"? How is your work informed by your reading of Kipnis? Where might it diverge?

ASSIGNMENT 5
On Agency
JOHN BERGER, SUSAN BORDO, LAURA KIPNIS, MICHEL FOUCAULT

> [The Panopticon] is an important mechanism, for it automatizes and disindividualizes power. Power has its principle not so much in a person as in a certain concerted distribution of

> bodies, surfaces, lights, gazes; in an arrangement whose internal mechanisms produce the relation in which individuals are caught up. The ceremonies, the rituals, the marks by which the sovereign's surplus power was manifested are useless. There is a machinery that assures dissymmetry, disequilibrium, difference. Consequently, it does not matter who exercises power. Any individual, taken almost at random, can operate the machine: in the absence of the director, his family, his friends, his visitors, even his servants. Similarly, it does not matter what motive animates him: the curiosity of the indiscreet, the malice of a child, the thirst for knowledge of a philosopher who wishes to visit this museum of human nature, or the perversity of those who take pleasure in spying and punishing. The more numerous those anonymous and temporary observers are, the greater the risk for the inmate of being surprised and the greater his anxious awareness of being observed. The Panopticon is a marvelous machine which, whatever use one may wish to put it to, produces homogeneous effects of power. (pp. 288–89)
>
> —MICHEL FOUCAULT
> *Panopticism*

Foucault's work has changed our ways of thinking about "who is doing what to whom." Write an essay in which you explain Foucault's understanding of the Panopticon as a mechanism of power. You will need to paraphrase Foucault's argument, translate his terms, and, where appropriate, cite and deploy his terms. Present Foucault's account as you understand it, and be willing to talk about what you don't understand — or don't quite understand.

As part of your essay, and in order to examine his argument and his terms, use Foucault as a way of thinking about the work of Berger, Bordo, and Kipnis. How might Foucault treat the material they select for their examples? (As you write, it would be strategically useful to limit yourself to one example from each.) How does each of the three writers account for *agency* in their descriptions of the workings of power? What do you make of the differences in their accounts of power and knowledge? What do they imply about how one might live in or understand the world? What might they have to do with the ways you, or people like you, live in and understand the world?

ASSIGNMENT 6

Reading Culture

JOHN BERGER, SUSAN BORDO, LAURA KIPNIS, MICHEL FOUCAULT

Write an essay in which you revise and bring together the essays you have written for this sequence. You can treat them as individual statements, revising each, ordering them, writing an introduction, a conclusion, and necessary transitions.

Or you can revise more radically and combine what you have into some other form.

Your goal should be to bring the writers into conversation with each other, to use one selection to weigh, evaluate, and understand another. And your goal should be to find a way, yourself, to enter the conversation—to find a space, a voice, a set of examples and concerns. Where and how do these issues touch you and people like you (some group for whom you feel authorized to speak)? Where do you feel a similar urgency? Where and how would you qualify or challenge the position of these other writers? Where and how would you join them?

ALTERNATIVE ASSIGNMENT

What Is It Good For?

RICHARD E. MILLER

Richard E. Miller's essay "The Dark Night of the Soul" opens with a list of fatal shootings in school—troublingly, an incomplete list. As the essay builds to questions—questions for educators and for students—the specters of violence and alienation remain, changing how we think about the reading and writing that school endeavors to teach us. "I have these doubts, you see," Miller writes of academic work, "doubts silently shared by many who spend their days teaching others the literate arts. Aside from gathering and organizing information, aside from generating critiques and analyses that forever fall on deaf ears, what might the literate arts be said to be good for?" (p. 424).

Write an essay that takes up this question—"what might the literate arts be said to be good for?"—and that takes it up from your range of reference and from your point of view—or, more properly, from the point of view of you and people like you, the group you feel prepared to speak for. As an exercise in understanding, your essay should be modeled on one (or more) of the sections in "The Dark Night of the Soul." You can choose the text—and the text can be anything that might serve as an example of the literate arts, things in print but also including songs, films, and TV shows. But your presentation and discussion of the text should be in conversation with Miller—with his concerns, his key terms, his examples, and his conclusions.

ALTERNATIVE ASSIGNMENT

Standard English in a Democratic Culture

DAVID FOSTER WALLACE

At certain moments in his essay "Authority and American Usage," David Foster Wallace describes his approach as a teacher of college students. He tells us in footnote 6, for instance, that while he teaches literature courses, he usually abandons the syllabus after he reads his students' first papers in order to hold "a three-week Emergency Remedial Usage and Grammar Unit, during which my demeanor is basically that of somebody teaching HIV prevention to intravenous-drug users." And later he provides a representation of a lengthy speech he gives to individual college students who struggle with Standard Written English. He says,

> I'm not trying to suggest here that an effective SWE pedagogy would require teachers to wear sunglasses and call students Dude. What I am suggesting is that the rhetorical situation of a US English class — a class composed wholly of young people whose Group identity is rooted in defiance of Adult Establishment values, plus also composed partly of minorities whose primary dialects are different from SWE — requires a teacher to come up with overt, honest, and compelling arguments for why SWE is a dialect worth learning. (p. 107)

But Wallace also teaches writing by example — that is, by what he says in this essay about effective writing and by the way he chooses to write. In this sense, "Authority and American Usage" offers a writing lesson.

Write an essay in which you take up the invitation to engage Wallace's argument about U.S. English, about SWE, about rhetoric, and about the function and importance of a writing class. You will need to work directly in reference to what Wallace says in the text. In other words, you'll need to work with sentences and examples. But you also bring experience to the table. From your point of view, and from the point of view of students like you, what is at stake? How and where might you enter this conversation? Where are you in the settings Wallace invokes? in his arguments?

ALTERNATIVE ASSIGNMENT

Digital Environments

DAVID ABRAM

Though David Abram spends most of his essay "Animism and the Alphabet" looking at a significant cultural shift that took place many centuries ago, he briefly observes that we are currently undergoing a change of similar magnitude as we move from print-based literacy to electronic literacy. But Abram claims that our immersion in this change makes it impossible for us to analyze it properly:

> [T]oday we are simply unable to discern with any clarity the manner in which our own perceptions and thoughts are being shifted by our sensory involvement with electronic technologies, since any thinking that discerns such a shift is itself subject to the very effect that it strives to thematize. Nevertheless, we may be sure that the shapes of our consciousness *are* shifting in tandem with the technologies that engage our senses . . . . (p. 44)

In other words, we can't yet understand the impact of electronic (and digital) environments on reading and writing because we can't see outside of what is currently shaping our vision. We can only know that we are in the midst of a powerful transformation.

There is a challenge here — and an invitation. How might new media, which combine image, sound, and text, complicate Abram's argument about the effects of writing and our divorce from the natural world? There is a generation of students emerging for whom digital environments have been everyday experiences. You can speak for them. Write an essay that extends or challenges Abram's arguments by looking at developments in new media. Your essay should be similar to Abram's in language, spirit, and tone. While generalizing, he also speaks from his own experience. You should too. Your essay should be a response to his, which means that you will need to provide summary and paraphrase; you should also, however, make a point of picking up his key terms or phrases to see how they work in the context of your experience and your argument. And it is probably best, at least at the outset, to take a measured and skeptical stance toward new media.

SEQUENCE SEVEN

The Uses of Reading (I)

Richard Rodriguez and Richard Hoggart
Susan Bordo and John Berger
David Bartholomae and Anthony Petrosky

ALTERNATIVE:

Richard Rodriguez and Richard Hoggart

This sequence focuses attention on authors as readers, on the use of sources, and on the art of reading as a writer. It combines technical lessons with lessons on the practice and rhetoric of citation. The assignments ask you to think again about how writers use the writing that precedes them in order to move forward, to get work done, to define a position for writing and thinking. The final assignment returns attention to attitudes toward reading and writing in contemporary American education, with *Ways of Reading* offered as an example.

ASSIGNMENT 1

The Scholarship Boy (I)

RICHARD RODRIGUEZ, RICHARD HOGGART

You could look at the relationship between Richard Rodriguez and Richard Hoggart as a case study of the relation of a reader to a writer or of a student to a teacher. Look closely at Rodriguez's references to Hoggart's book *The Uses of Literacy* and at the way Rodriguez made use of that book to name and describe his own experience as a student. (An extended selection of *The Uses of Literacy* can be found in the alternative assignment.) What did he find in the book? How did he use it? How does he use it in his own writing?

Write an essay in which you discuss Rodriguez's use of Hoggart's *The Uses of Literacy*. How, for example, would you compare Rodriguez's version of the "scholarship boy" with Hoggart's? (At one point, Rodriguez says that Hoggart's account is "more accurate than fair." What might he have meant by that?) And what kind of reader is the Rodriguez who is writing "The Achievement of Desire"—is he still a "scholarship boy," or is that description no longer appropriate?

Note: You might begin your research with what may seem to be a purely technical matter, examining how Rodriguez handles quotations and works Hoggart's words into paragraphs of his own. On the basis of Rodriguez's use of quoted passages, how would you describe the relationship between Hoggart's words and Rodriguez's? Who has the greater authority? Who is the expert, and under what conditions? What rules might Rodriguez be said to follow or to break? Do you see any change in the course of the essay in how Rodriguez uses block quotations? in how he comments on them?

ASSIGNMENT 2

Sources

SUSAN BORDO, JOHN BERGER

In "Beauty (Re)discovers the Male Body," Bordo refers to John Berger and his work in *Ways of Seeing*, although she refers to a different chapter than the one included here. In general, however, both Berger and Bordo are concerned with how we see and read images; both are concerned to correct the ways images are used and read; both trace the ways images serve the interests of money and power; both are written to teach readers how and why they should pay a different kind of attention to the images around them.

For this assignment, use Bordo's work to reconsider Berger's. As you reread each essay, mark passages that you might be able to put into interesting conversation with each other. And, when you have completed this work, write an essay in which you consider the two chapters as examples of an ongoing project. Berger's essay precedes Bordo's by about a quarter of a century. If you look closely at one or two of their examples, and if you look at the larger concerns of their arguments, are they saying the same things? doing the same work? If so, how? And why is such work still necessary? If not, how do their projects differ? And how might you explain those differences?

ASSIGNMENT 3

Ways of Reading

DAVID BARTHOLOMAE AND ANTHONY PETROSKY

Reread the introduction to *Ways of Reading*. Given the work that you have done in this sequence, you are prepared to read it not as a simple statement of "how things are" but as a position taken in a tradition of concern over the role of reading in the education of Americans. Write an essay in which you consider the introduction in relation to Rodriguez, Hoggart, Bordo, and Berger, and the ways they articulate the proper uses of reading.

And what about you — do you see your own interests and concerns, the values you hold (or those held by people you admire), the abilities you might need or hope to gain — do you see these represented in what you have read?

ALTERNATIVE ASSIGNMENT

The Scholarship Boy (II)

RICHARD RODRIGUEZ, RICHARD HOGGART

At the end of this assignment, you will find an extended section from Richard Hoggart's *The Uses of Literacy*. This is the book Rodriguez found in the British Museum, the book he used, he says, to "frame the meaning of my academic success." The section here is the one that surrounds the passages Rodriguez cites in "The Achievement of Desire." Read the Hoggart excerpt and think about these questions: How might you compare Rodriguez's version of the "scholarship boy" with Hoggart's? How might you explain the importance of Hoggart's book to Rodriguez? What kind of reader is the Rodriguez who is writing "The Achievement of Desire" — is he still a "scholarship boy," or is that description no longer appropriate?

You could look at the relationship between Rodriguez and Hoggart as a case study in the possible relations between a writer and a prior text or between a student and a teacher. Read the two together, taking notes to assist such a comparative reading. As you read Rodriguez's discussion of Hoggart's book, pay attention to both the terms and passages Rodriguez selects and those he ignores, and pay attention to what Rodriguez *does* with what he selects. Look closely at how Rodriguez reads and presents Hoggart's text.

As you read Hoggart's account of the scholarship boy, try to read from outside Rodriguez's point of view. How else might these passages be read? In what ways might Hoggart be said to be saying what Rodriguez says he is saying? In what ways might he be said to be saying something else, something Rodriguez misses or ignores? In what ways might Hoggart be said to be making a different argument, telling a different story? What position or point of view or set of beliefs would authorize this other reading, the reading from outside Rodriguez's point of view? And, if you can establish this "alternative" reading, what does that tell you about the position or point of view or set of beliefs that authorize Rodriguez's use of the text?

As you prepare to write about Rodriguez's use of Hoggart, think about how you will describe his performance. What, for example, might you attribute to strategy, to Rodriguez's intent? What might you attribute to blindness (a failure to see or notice something in the text)? What might you attribute to the unconscious (a fear of the text, a form of repression, a desire to transform the text into something else)? These are conventional ways of telling the story of reading. What use are they to your project? Can you imagine others?

Write an essay in which you discuss Rodriguez as an example of a reader and writer working with a prior text. Your goal should be to understand Rodriguez and "The Achievement of Desire" better but also to think about the implications of his "case" for readers and writers in the undergraduate curriculum. You should feel free to use sentences and paragraphs, arguments, or ideas you developed in the first assignment in this sequence.

A SCHOLARSHIP BOY

> For my part I am very sorry for him. It is an uneasy lot at best, to be what we call highly taught and yet not to enjoy: to be present at this great spectacle of life and never to be liberated from a small hungry shivering self.
>
> —GEORGE ELIOT

This is a difficult chapter to write, though one that should be written. As in other chapters, I shall be isolating a group of related trends: but the consequent dangers of over-emphasis are here especially acute. The three immediately preceding chapters have discussed attitudes which could from one point of view appear to represent a kind of poise. But the people most affected by the attitudes now to be examined — the "anxious and the uprooted" — are to be recognized primarily by their lack of poise, by their uncertainty. About the self-indulgences which seem to satisfy many in their class they tend to be unhappily superior: they are much affected by the cynicism which affects almost everyone, but this is likely to increase their lack of purpose rather than tempt them to "cash in" or to react into further indulgence.

In part they have a sense of loss which affects some in all groups. With them the sense of loss is increased precisely because they are emotionally uprooted from their class, often under the stimulus of a stronger critical intelligence or imagination, qualities which can lead them into an unusual self-consciousness before their own situation (and make it easy for a sympathizer to dramatize their "*Angst*"). Involved with this may be a physical uprooting from their class through the medium of the scholarship system. A great many seem to me to be affected in this way, though only a very small proportion badly; at one boundary the group includes psychotics; at the other, people leading apparently normal lives but never without an underlying sense of some unease.

It will be convenient to speak first of the nature of the uprooting which some scholarship boys experience. I have in mind those who, for a number of years, perhaps for a very long time, have a sense of no longer really belonging to any group. We all know that many do find a poise in their new situations. There are "declassed" experts and specialists who go into their own spheres after the long scholarship climb has led them to a PhD. There are brilliant individuals who become fine administrators and officials, and find themselves thoroughly at home. There are some, not necessarily so gifted, who reach a kind of poise which is yet not a passivity nor even a failure in awareness, who are at ease in their new group without any ostentatious adoption of the protective coloring of that group, and who have an easy relationship with their working-class relatives, based not on a form of patronage but on a just respect. Almost every working-class boy who goes through the process of further education by scholarships finds himself chafing against his environment during adolescence. He is at the friction-point of two cultures; the test of his real education lies in his ability, by about the age of twenty-five, to smile at his father with his whole face and to respect his flighty young sister and his slower brother. I shall be concerned with those for whom the uprooting is particularly troublesome, not because I underestimate the gains which this kind of selection gives, nor because I wish to stress the more depressing features in contemporary life, but because the difficulties of some people illuminate much in the wider discussion of cultural change. Like transplanted stock, they react to a widespread drought earlier than those who have been left in their original soil.

I am sometimes inclined to think that the problem of self-adjustment is, in general, especially difficult for those working-class boys who are only moderately endowed, who have talent sufficient to separate them from the majority of their working-class contemporaries, but not to go much farther. I am not implying a correlation between intelligence and lack of unease; intellectual people have their own troubles: but this kind of anxiety often seems most to afflict those in the working-classes who have been pulled one stage away from their original culture and yet have not the intellectual equipment which would then cause them to move on to join the "declassed" professionals and experts. In one sense, it is true, no one is ever "declassed"; and it is interesting to see how this occasionally obtrudes (particularly today, when ex-working-class boys move in all the managing areas of society) — in the touch of insecurity, which often appears as an undue concern to establish "presence" in an otherwise quite professional professor, in the intermittent rough homeliness of an important executive and committee-man, in the tendency to vertigo which betrays a lurking sense of uncertainty in a successful journalist.

But I am chiefly concerned with those who are self-conscious and yet not self-aware in any full sense, who are as a result uncertain, dissatisfied, and gnawed by self-doubt. Sometimes they lack will, though they have intelligence, and "it takes will to cross this waste." More often perhaps, though they have as much will as the majority, they have not sufficient to resolve the complex tensions which their uprooting, the peculiar problems of their particular domestic settings, and the uncertainties common to the time create.

As childhood gives way to adolescence and that to manhood, this kind of boy tends to be progressively cut off from the ordinary life of his group. He is marked out early: and here I am thinking not so much of his teachers in the "elementary" school as of fellow-members of his family. "'E's got brains," or "'E's bright," he hears constantly; and in part the tone is one of pride and admiration. He is in a way cut off by his parents as much as by his talent which urges him to break away from his group. Yet on their side this is not altogether from admiration: "'E's got brains," yes, and he is expected to follow the trail that opens. But there can also be a limiting quality in the tone with which the phrase is used; character counts more. Still, he has brains — a mark of pride and almost a brand; he is heading for a different world, a different sort of job.

He has to be more and more alone, if he is going to "get on." He will have, probably unconsciously, to oppose the ethos of the hearth, the intense gregariousness of the working-class family group. Since everything centers upon the living-room, there is unlikely to be a room of his own; the bedrooms are cold and inhospitable, and to warm them or the front room, if there is one, would not only be expensive, but would require an imaginative leap — out of the tradition — which most families are not capable of making. There is a corner of the living-room table. On the other side Mother is ironing, the wireless is on, someone is singing a snatch of song, or Father says intermittently whatever comes into his head. The boy has to cut himself off mentally, so as to do his homework, as well as he can. In summer, matters can be easier; bedrooms are warm enough to work in: but only a few boys, in my experience, take advantage of this. For the boy is himself (until he reaches, say, the upper forms) very much of *both* the worlds of home and school. He is enormously obedient to the dictates of the world of school, but emotionally still strongly wants to continue as part of the family circle.

So the first big step is taken in the progress towards membership of a different sort of group or to isolation, when such a boy has to resist the central domestic quality of working-class life. This is true, perhaps particularly true, if he belongs to a happy home, because the happy homes are often the more gregarious. Quite early the stress on solitariness, the encouragement towards strong self-concern, is felt; and this can make it more difficult for him to belong to another group later.

At his "elementary" school, from as early as the age of eight, he is likely to be in some degree set apart, though this may not happen if his school is in an area which each year provides a couple of dozen boys from "the scholarship form" for the grammar-schools. But probably he is in an area predominantly working-class and his school takes up only a few scholarships a year. The situation is altering as the number of scholarships increases, but in any case human adjustments do not come as abruptly as administrative changes.

He is similarly likely to be separated from the boys' groups outside the home, is no longer a full member of the gang which clusters round the lampposts in the evenings; there is homework to be done. But these are the male groups among which others in his generation grew up, and his detachment from them is emotionally linked with one more aspect of his home situation — that he now tends to be closer to the women of the house than to the men. This is true, even if his father is not the kind who dismisses books and reading as "a woman's game." The boy spends a large part of his time at the physical center of the home, where the woman's spirit rules, quietly getting on with his work whilst his mother gets on with her jobs — the father not yet back from work or out for a drink with his mates. The man and the boy's brothers are outside, in the world of men; the boy sits in the women's world. Perhaps this partly explains why many authors from the working-classes, when they write about their childhood, give the women in it so tender and central a place. There is bound to be occasional friction, of course — when they wonder whether the boy is "getting above himself," or when he feels a strong reluctance to break off and do one of the odd jobs a boy is expected to do. But predominantly the atmosphere is likely to be intimate, gentle, and attractive. With one ear he hears the women discussing their worries and ailments and hopes, and he tells them at intervals about his school and the work and what the master said. He usually receives boundless uncomprehending sympathy: he knows they do not understand, but still he tells them; he would like to link the two environments.

This description simplifies and overstresses the break; in each individual case there will be many qualifications. But in presenting the isolation in its most emphatic form the description epitomizes what is very frequently found. For such a boy is between two worlds, the worlds of school and home; and they meet at few points. Once at the grammar-school, he quickly learns to make use of a pair of different accents, perhaps even two different apparent characters and differing standards of value. Think of his reading-material, for example: at home he sees strewn around and reads regularly himself, magazines which are never mentioned at school, which seem not to belong to the world to which the school introduces him; at school he hears about and reads books never mentioned at home. When he brings those books into the house they do not take their place with other books which the family are reading, for often there are none or almost none; his books look, rather, like strange tools.

He will perhaps, especially today, escape the worst immediate difficulties of his new environment, the stigma of cheaper clothes, of not being able to afford to go on school-holiday trips, of parents who turn up for the grammar-school play looking shamefully working-class. But as a grammar-school boy, he is likely to be anxious to do well, to be accepted or even to catch the eye as he caught the eye, because of his brains, at the "elementary" school. For brains are the currency by which he has bought his way, and increasingly brains seem to be the currency that tells. He tends to make his schoolmasters over-important, since they are the cashiers in the new world of brain-currency. In his home-world his father is still his father; in the other world of school his father can have little place: he tends to make a father-figure of his form-master.

Consequently, even though his family may push him very little, he will probably push himself harder than he should. He begins to see life, for as far as he can envisage it, as a series of hurdle-jumps, the hurdles of scholarships which are won by learning how to amass and manipulate the new currency. He tends to over-stress the importance of examinations, of the piling-up of knowledge and of received opinions. He discovers a technique of apparent learning, or acquiring of facts rather than of the handling and use of facts. He learns how to receive a purely literate education, one using only a small part of the personality and challenging only a limited area of his being. He begins to see life as a ladder, as a permanent examination with some praise and some further exhortation at each stage. He becomes an expert imbiber and doler-out; his competence will vary, but will rarely be accompanied by genuine enthusiasms. He rarely feels the reality of knowledge, of other men's thoughts and imaginings, of his own pulses; he rarely discovers an author for himself and on his own. In this half of his life he can respond only if there is a direct connection with the system of training. He has something of the blinkered pony about him; sometimes he is trained by those who have been through the same regimen, who are hardly unblinkered themselves, and who praise him in the degree to which he takes comfortably to their blinkers. Though there is a powerful, unidealistic, unwarmed realism about his attitude at bottom, that is his chief form of initiative; of other forms — the freely ranging mind, the bold flying of mental kites, the courage to reject some "lines" even though they are officially as important as all the rest — of these he probably has little, and his training does not often encourage them. This is not a new problem; Herbert Spencer spoke of it fifty years ago: but it still exists: "The established systems of education, whatever their matter may be, are fundamentally vicious in their manner. They encourage *submissive receptivity* instead of *independent activity*."

There is too little stress on action, on personal will and decision; too much goes on in the head, with the rather-better-than-normal intellectual machine which has brought him to his grammar-school. And because so often the "good" boy, the boy who does well, is the one who with his conscientious passivity meets the main demand of his new environment, he gradually loses spontaneity so as to acquire examination-passing reliability. He can snap his fingers at no one and nothing; he seems set to make an adequate, reliable, and unjoyous kind of clerk. He has been too long "afraid of all that has to be obeyed." Hazlitt, writing at the beginning of the nineteenth century, made a wider and more impassioned judgment on trends in his society; but it has some relevance here and now:

> Men do not become what by nature they are meant to be, but what society makes them. The generous feelings, and high propensities of the soul are, as it were, shrunk up, seared, violently wrenched, and amputated, to fit us for our intercourse with the world, something in the manner that beggars maim and mutilate their children, to make them fit for their future situation in life.

Such a scholarship boy has lost some of the resilience and some of the vitality of his cousins who are still knocking about the streets. In an earlier generation, as one of the wicker-witted persons born into the working-classes, he would in all probability have had those wits developed in the jungle of the slums, where wit had to ally itself to energy and initiative. He plays little on the streets; he does not run round delivering newspapers: his sexual growth is perhaps delayed. He loses something of the gamin's resilience and carelessness, of his readiness to take a chance, of his perkiness and boldness, and he does not acquire the unconscious confidence of many a public-school-trained child of the middle-classes. He has been trained like a circus-horse, for scholarship winning.

As a result, when he comes to the end of the series of set-pieces, when he is at last put out to raise his eyes to a world of tangible and unaccommodating things, of elusive and disconcerting human beings, he finds himself with little inner momentum. The driving-belt hangs loosely, disconnected from the only machine it has so far served, the examination-passing machine. He finds difficulty in choosing a direction in the world where there is no longer a master to please, a toffee-apple at the end of each stage, a certificate, a place in the upper half of the assessable world. He is unhappy in a society which presents largely a picture of disorder, which is huge and sprawling, not limited, ordered, and centrally heated; in which the toffee-apples are not accurately given to those who work hardest nor even to the most intelligent: but in which disturbing imponderables like "character," "pure luck," "ability to mix," and "boldness" have a way of tipping the scales.

His condition is made worse because the whole trend of his previous training has made him care too much for marked and ticketed success. This world, too, cares much for recognizable success, but does not distribute it along the lines on which he has been trained to win it. He would be happier if he cared less, if he could blow the gaff for himself on the world's success values. But they too closely resemble the values of school; to reject them he would have first to escape the inner prison in which the school's tabulated rules for success have immured him.

He does not wish to accept the world's criterion — get on at any price (though he has an acute sense of the importance of money). But he has been equipped for hurdle-jumping; so he merely dreams of getting on, but somehow not in the world's way. He has neither the comforts of simply accepting the big world's values, nor the recompense of feeling firmly critical towards them.

He has moved away from his "lower" origins, and may move farther. If so, he is likely to be nagged underneath by a sense of how far he has come, by the fear and shame of a possible falling-back. And this increases his inability to leave himself alone. Sometimes the kind of job he gets only increases this slightly dizzy sense of still being on the ladder; unhappy on it, but also proud and, in the nature of his condition, usually incapable of jumping-off, of pulling-out of that particular race:

> Pale, shabby, tightly strung, he had advanced from post to post in his insurance office with the bearing of a man about to be discharged. . . . Brains had only meant that he must work harder in the elementary school than those born free of them. At night he could still hear the malicious chorus

> telling him that he was a favorite of the master. . . . Brains, like a fierce heat, had turned the world to a desert round him, and across the sands in the occasional mirage he saw the stupid crowds, playing, laughing, and without thought enjoying the tenderness, the compassion, the companionship of love.

That is over-dramatized, not applicable to all or even to most — but in some way affecting many. It affects also that larger group, to which I now turn, of those who in some ways ask questions of themselves about their society, who are because of this, even though they may never have been to grammar-schools, "between two worlds, one dead, the other powerless to be born." They are the "private faces in public places" among the working-classes; they are Koestler's "thoughtful corporals"; they are among those, though not the whole of those, who take up many kinds of self-improvement. They may be performing any kind of work, from manual labor to teaching; but my own experience suggests that they are to be found frequently among minor clerks and similarly black-coated workers, and among elementary school-teachers, especially in the big cities. Often their earnestness for improvement shows itself as an urge to act like some people in the middle-classes; but this is not a political betrayal: it is much nearer to a mistaken idealism.

This kind of person, and we have seen that this is his first great loss, belongs now to no class, usually not even to what is called, loosely enough, the "classless intelligentsia." He cannot face squarely his own working-class, for that, since the intuitive links have gone, would require a greater command in facing himself than he is capable of. Sometimes he is ashamed of his origins; he has learned to "turn up his nose," to be a bit superior about much in working-class manners. He is often not at ease about his own physical appearance which speaks too clearly of his birth; he feels uncertain or angry inside when he realizes that that, and a hundred habits of speech and manners, can "give him away" daily. He tends to visit his own sense of inadequacy upon the group which fathered him; and he provides himself with a mantle of defensive attitudes. Thus he may exhibit an unconvincing pride in his own gaucheness at practical things — "brain-workers" are never "good with their hands." Underneath he knows that his compensatory claim to possess finer weapons, to be able to handle "book-knowledge," is insecurely based. He tries to read all the good books, but they do not give him that power of speech and command over experience which he seeks. He is as gauche there as with the craftsman's tools.

He cannot go back; with one part of himself he does not want to go back to a homeliness which was often narrow: with another part he longs for the membership he has lost, "he pines for some Nameless Eden where he never was." The nostalgia is the stronger and the more ambiguous because he is really "in quest of his own absconded self yet scared to find it." He both wants to go back and yet thinks he has gone beyond his class, feels himself weighted with knowledge of his own and their situation, which hereafter forbids him the simpler pleasures of his father and mother. And this is only one of his temptations to self-dramatization.

If he tries to be "pally" with working-class people, to show that he is one of them, they "smell it a mile off." They are less at ease with him than with some in other classes. With them they can establish and are prepared to honor, seriously or as a kind of rather ironical game, a formal relationship; they "know where they are with them." But they can immediately detect the uncertainty in his attitudes, that he belongs neither to them nor to one of the groups with which they are used to performing a hierarchical play of relations; the odd man out is still the odd man out.

He has left his class, at least in spirit, by being in certain ways unusual; and he is still unusual in another class, too tense and overwound. Sometimes the working-classes and the middle-classes can laugh together. He rarely laughs; he smiles constrainedly with the corner of his mouth. He is usually ill at ease with the middle-classes because with one side of himself he does not want them to accept him; he mistrusts or even a little despises them. He is divided here as in so many other ways. With one part of himself he admires much he finds in them: a play of intelligence, a breadth of outlook, a kind of style. He would like to be a citizen of that well-polished, prosperous, cool, book-lined, and magazine-discussing world of the successful intelligent middle-class which he glimpses through doorways or feels awkward among on short visits, aware of his grubby finger-nails. With another part of himself he develops an asperity towards that world: he turns up his nose at its self-satisfactions, its earnest social concern, its intelligent coffee-parties, its suave sons at Oxford, and its Mrs. Miniverish or Mrs. Ramseyish cultural pretensions. He is rather over-ready to notice anything which can be regarded as pretentious or fanciful, anything which allows him to say that these people do not know what life is really like. He wavers between scorn and longing.

— RICHARD HOGGART
The Uses of Literacy (1957)

SEQUENCE EIGHT

The Uses of Reading (II)

Judith Butler
Michel Foucault
Tommie Shelby
Kwame Anthony Appiah
David Bartholomae and Anthony Petrosky

ALTERNATIVE:

Richard E. Miller

This sequence provides an alternative set of readings and assignments to the previous sequence. It again focuses attention on authors as readers, on the uses of sources, and on the art of reading as a writer.

ASSIGNMENT 1

Sources

JUDITH BUTLER, MICHEL FOUCAULT

At a key point in her essay "Beside Oneself: On the Limits of Sexual Autonomy," Judith Butler refers to the work of Michel Foucault:

> The question of who and what is considered real and true is apparently a question of knowledge. But it is also, as Michel Foucault makes plain, a question of power. Having or bearing "truth" and "reality" is an enormously powerful prerogative within the social

> world, one way that power dissimulates as ontology. According to Foucault, one of the first tasks of a radical critique is to discern the relation "between mechanisms of coercion and elements of knowledge." (p. 247)

And she goes on for some length to work with passages from Foucault, although not from his book *Discipline and Punish.*

Take some time to reread Butler's essay, paying particular attention to her use of Foucault. Where and why is Foucault helpful to her? In what ways is she providing a new argument or a counterargument? And take time to reread "Panopticism." What passages might be useful in extending or challenging Butler's argument in "Beside Oneself"? Using these two sources, write an essay in which you talk about Butler and Foucault and their engagement with what might be called "radical critique," an effort (in the terms offered above) to "discern the relation 'between mechanisms of coercion and elements of knowledge.'"

Note: The assignment limits you to these two sources, the two selections in the textbook. Butler and Foucault have written much, and their work circulates widely. You are most likely not in a position to speak about everything they have written or about all that has been written about them. We wanted to define a starting point that was manageable. Still, if you want to do more research, you might begin by reading the Foucault essay that Butler cites, "What Is Critique?"; you might go to the library to look through books by Butler and Foucault, choosing one or two that seem to offer themselves as next steps; or you could go to essays written by scholars who, as you are, are trying to think about the two together.

ASSIGNMENT 2

A Student and His Teacher

KWAME ANTHONY APPIAH, TOMMIE SHELBY

> First, I want to explain why American social distinctions cannot be understood in terms of the concept of race: the only race in the United States, I shall argue, is *the* human race. (p. 102)
>
> — KWAME ANTHONY APPIAH
> *Race, Culture, Identity: Misunderstood Connections*

> I would urge blacks living in the United States, and by extension those in other parts of the world, to identify with each other on the basis of their experience of racial oppression and commitment to

> collectively resist it. From the standpoint of black political solidarity, each should be allowed to interpret "blackness" however he or she sees fit, provided the interpretation does not advocate anything immoral and is consistent with the collective struggle for racial justice. In saying this, I am not suggesting, as some have, that individual blacks should give up their various black identities in favor of an American, a cosmopolitan, or simply a "human" identity. (pp. 606–07)
>
> — TOMMIE SHELBY
> *Social Identity and Group Solidarity*

Kwame Anthony Appiah is a generation ahead of Tommie Shelby, who is a young scholar (*We Who Are Dark* is his first book); Shelby credits Appiah's influence on his thinking and his work—even his decision to turn to philosophy and to pursue an academic career. Appiah is present in Shelby's footnotes. It is useful and appropriate, then, to consider "Social Identity and Group Solidarity" as a response to Appiah, who is represented in *Ways of Reading* through his essay "Race, Culture, Identity: Misunderstood Connections," a chapter from the book *Color Conscious: The Political Morality of Race.*

As you reread them (first Appiah, then Shelby), think about questions of priority and influence and take notes where, for example, Appiah could be said to be addressing the next generation and where Shelby, whether he acknowledges it or not, is addressing Appiah (and his generation). How would you characterize the exchange: a dialogue? a debate? a clash of wills? a failure to communicate? a classic example of . . . what? And where do you stand in relation to the two—how do their essays address you and your concerns?

ASSIGNMENT 3

Ways of Reading

DAVID BARTHOLOMAE AND ANTHONY PETROSKY

Reread the introduction to *Ways of Reading*. Given the work that you have done in this sequence, you are prepared to read it not as a simple statement of "how things are" but as a position taken in a tradition of concern over the role of reading in the education of Americans. Write an essay in which you consider the introduction in relation to Butler, Foucault, Shelby, and Appiah, and the ways they articulate the proper uses of reading.

And think about your own interests and concerns, the values you hold (or those held by people you admire), the abilities you might need or hope to gain. Do you see these represented in what you have read?

ALTERNATIVE ASSIGNMENT

A Story of Reading

RICHARD E. MILLER

Consider the following passage from Richard E. Miller's "The Dark Night of the Soul":

> What makes *Into the Wild* remarkable is Krakauer's ability to get some purchase on McCandless's actual reading practice, which, in turn, enables him to get inside McCandless's head and speculate with considerable authority about what ultimately led the young man to abandon the comforts of home and purposefully seek out mortal danger. Krakauer is able to do this, in part, because he has access to the books that McCandless read, with all their underlinings and marginalia, as well as to his journals and the postcards and letters McCandless sent to friends along his journey. Working with these materials and his interviews with McCandless's family and friends, Krakauer develops a sense of McCandless's inner life and eventually comes to some understanding of why the young man was so susceptible to being seduced by the writings of London, Thoreau, Muir, and Tolstoy. Who McCandless is and what becomes of him are, it turns out, intimately connected to the young man's approach to reading — both what he chose to read and how he chose to read it. (p. 429)

When Miller is writing about Krakauer's *Into the Wild*, he seems to suggest that what we read, and how we read, can say something about who we are and about what we might become. This is a very bold claim.

Think of a book that made a difference to you, that captured you, maybe one you have read more than once, maybe one that you've made marks in or that still sits on your bookshelf. Or, if not a book, think of your favorite song or album or movie or TV show, something that engaged you at least potentially as McCandless was engaged by London, Thoreau, Muir, and Tolstoy. What was it that you found there? What kind of reader were you? And what makes this a story in the past tense? How and why did you move on? (Or, if it is not a story in the past tense, where are you now, and are you, like McCandless, in any danger?)

SEQUENCE NINE

The Art of Argument

Anne Carson
Antonio Porchia
Alberto Álvaro Ríos
Brian Doyle

Writing courses have traditionally included a unit on argumentation. The assignments in this sequence ask you to consider arguments in unusual settings. The assignments ask you not only to identify and explore writers' arguments but also to explore how they are enacted. You don't need technical terms for these assignments (like *induction* and *deduction*); you will be asked to develop your own terms, your own ways of describing the arguments you find.

ASSIGNMENT 1

Short Talks

ANNE CARSON

Carson, we might assume, writes these short talks with a purpose, perhaps to say something, to persuade her readers, or to take a stand on an issue or a subject. In this sense, we might think of Carson's "Short Talks" as an argument, or as a series of arguments. Below are two options for writing about "Short Talks." Choose one.

a. Select one of the short talks and write an essay in which you explain what you see as its argument. Is Carson writing to persuade you about something? What does she assume it is that keeps you from thinking as she does? Who would disagree? Why argue, in other words? What features of Carson's writing in this short talk indicate to you that an argument is being made—what words or grammatical constructions suggest this? How might this particular short talk raise questions about what it means to *make an argument* in the first place?

b. Think about Carson's "Short Talks" as a coherent whole, as an essay. Imagine that the short talks are making one argument or (perhaps) a series of connected arguments, an argument by steps or stages. What is the argument as you understand it? To whom is it addressed? Who would disagree? What strategies does she use to bring a reader to her side?

As you think back on what you have written, what is the lesson to be learned here? How might Carson's writing be said to be powerful or compelling? In what ways does it fall short?

ASSIGNMENT 2

Theories of Persuasion

ANNE CARSON, ANTONIO PORCHIA

Read Antonio Porchia's excerpt from *Voices* and reread Anne Carson's "Short Talks." Both of these pieces make arguments in interesting and unexpected ways. Reread each of these selections together (you may even want to do this reading more than once), noting as you read any moments when they seem to reveal a *theory* of argument. How do they address their readers? In what ways might their writing be said to be "winning"?

Write an essay in which you consider the issue of persuasion through your examination of these two pieces of writing. What theories of persuasion are revealed in each? Be sure to work closely with examples, including block quotations. How do they differ? And what do the differences say to you as a writer? What can you learn from their example? What can't you learn?

ASSIGNMENT 3

How Do You Say It?

ALBERTO ÁLVARO RÍOS

Read Alberto Álvaro Ríos's "Translating Translation: Finding the Beginning" and reread Antonio Porchia's aphorisms. Ríos writes: "Language is more than what we say—it's also how we say it" (p. 508). Use Ríos's claim about language to write an essay in which you study Ríos's own sense of what it means to be persuasive. What does he say? How does he say it? And, from your perspective, what makes his writing persuasive or compelling or convincing? Where does it fall short?

ASSIGNMENT 4

What Are Facts For?

ALBERTO ÁLVARO RÍOS, ANNE CARSON, BRIAN DOYLE

Consider the following sentence from Alberto Álvaro Ríos's "Translating Translation: Finding the Beginning": "Linguists, by using electrodes on the vocal chords, have been able to demonstrate that English has tenser vowels than, for example, Spanish." Or this sentence from Anne Carson's "Short Talks": "Kafka liked to have his watch an hour and a half fast." Or this statement from Brian Doyle's "Joyas Voladoras": "The biggest heart in the world is inside the blue whale."

All of the above statements might be considered "facts" or called "factual information." Each writer is making a declarative statement that makes a claim about what is so. Using the quotations above, or perhaps using other quotations from these selections, write an essay in which you consider each writer's use of declarative statements or "facts" as part of his or her argument. What, in your understanding, is a fact? What is the relationship between *facts* and *arguments*? How do these writers challenge or support your notion of facts? What are their facts for? What, in other words, are some of the ways these writers use facts—for what purposes or to what ends? And how are their "facts" connected to, or perhaps even disconnected from, their arguments?

ASSIGNMENT 5

Retrospective

ANNE CARSON, BRIAN DOYLE, ANTONIO PORCHIA, ALBERTO ÁLVARO RÍOS

We said at the outset that we would be asking you to look for arguments in unusual places. None of these writers presents an argument in debate form. All, however, aim to be persuasive or compelling; all could be said to engage a reader and to ask that reader to identify with their way of thinking. As you think back over the work you have done in this sequence, what lessons are there for a writer of your age and generation? Of the group whose work you have read—Carson, Doyle, Porchia, and Ríos—to whom would you turn first? How does their work speak back and forth, one to the other? What does it have to say to you?

SEQUENCE TEN

Working with Metaphor

Alberto Álvaro Ríos
Antonio Porchia
Brian Doyle
Anne Carson
Eula Biss

ALTERNATIVE:

Susan Griffin

A metaphor is a comparison, where two seemingly disparate thoughts, images, or objects are linked together. The (often) surprising combination presents a new level of thought or understanding, one fixed in an image: "He is drowning in money." Metaphors are indispensable to thought and language. Everyone who writes and talks uses them. Each of the writers in this sequence uses metaphor in interesting and distinctive ways. The assignments ask you to think about metaphors and how they work for writers and readers.

ASSIGNMENT 1

Binoculars

ALBERTO ÁLVARO RÍOS

I often talk about the duality of language using the metaphor of binoculars, how by using two lenses one might see something better, closer, with more detail. The apparatus, the binoculars, are of

> course physically clumsy — as is the learning of two languages, and all the signage and so on that this entails — they're clumsy, but once put to the eyes a new world in that moment opens up to us. And it's not a new world at all — it's the same world, but simply better seen, and therefore better understood. (p. 506)

Write an essay in which you take up the metaphor of the binoculars. How does it serve or illuminate the central concerns of the essay? What does it have to do with translation, for example? What are the metaphor's limits; where does it break down or no longer continue to serve? And, finally, how useful is it to you, both as a reader and as a person who has experienced the "duality of languages"? (You may not have learned a second language, like Spanish, but you have certainly moved between worlds that have their own particular and distinctive ways of speaking.)

ASSIGNMENT 2

Thread, Mud, Door, Clay, Wound

ALBERTO ÁLVARO RÍOS, ANTONIO PORCHIA

Reread the following five aphorisms in Antonio Porchia's "Voices":

> He who holds me by a thread is not strong; the thread is strong.
> Mud, when it leaves the mud, stops being mud.
> A door opens to me. I go in and am faced with a hundred closed doors.
> I have scarcely touched the clay and I am made of it.
> Only the wound speaks its own word. (pp. 477, 478)

The thread, the mud, the door, the clay, or the wound—you are asked to think about each of these as both a word in normal use (where mud is mud) but also to think of it as outside of normal use, where it is now referring to something else. Choose two of these aphorisms and write an essay that attempts to bring together the following:

A description, one written as closely as possible, of what you take each aphorism to mean. This will require an explication of the metaphor, a parsing out of what it seems to say.

An account, one written as technically as possible, of how each metaphor works—or how it worked for you. What was hard? What was fun? What was surprising?

A theory of metaphor as a way of thinking, seeing and writing. (In this account, Ríos might also serve as a point of reference.)

ASSIGNMENT 3

On Your Own

BRIAN DOYLE, ANNE CARSON

One way to better understand metaphor, what it is and how it works, is to practice writing your own. Choose one of the following two essay options:

a. One of the distinctive features in Brian Doyle's short essay, "Joyas Voladoras," is the way it moves from hummingbirds, blue whales and hearts to something else—or at least seems to be pointing to something else, pointing *away* from hummingbirds, blue whales and hearts and pointing *toward*—well, what? The movement is metaphorical; one thing stands for another.

   Prepare an essay that is Doyle-like. It should be, at minimum, as long as his. It should be similar in style and intent. It should be organized into six sections, each separated by additional white space. Each should have some Doyle-like sentences. It should make similar metaphorical demands on its readers.

   His work is your model and inspiration, and yet this project is also yours. A reader should be able to see where and how your work is in conversation with his; a reader should also be able to see what you bring to the table. And, when you are done, write a brief "Introduction" or "Afterword," something to orient your reader to what follows or something to provide your reader with a context at the end.

b. One way to read Anne Carson's "Short Talks" is to think of each section as offering a metaphor. One might say, for example, that "On Trout" is not really about trout but about something else.

   Prepare an essay that is Carson-like. It should be, at minimum, as long as hers. It should be similar in style and intent. It should have an equal series of paragraphs (or sections), each headed by subtitles; it should make similar metaphorical demands on its readers.

   Her work is your model and inspiration, and yet this project is also yours. A reader should be able to see where and how your work is in conversation with hers; a reader should also be able to see what you bring to the table. Be sure that your essay has an "Introduction," something to orient a reader to what follows. ("Introductions" are often either written last or seriously revised once the project is complete.)

ASSIGNMENT 4

The Pain Scale

EULA BISS

Read Eula Biss's essay "The Pain Scale." As you read, mark passages where you find yourself thinking that Biss is being figurative, or that what she is saying has both a literal meaning *and* a figurative meaning. As you mark passages, remember that metaphor is not a closed system; there is no "right" or "correct" implied meaning that you are searching for. These are meanings you will make and build as you read, thinking about both the context of the essay and your own experiences. Once you have read the essay and marked passages that seem more than literal to you, choose a few of the most powerful moments you have identified in Biss's essay.

Write an essay in which you imagine yourself as a guide who will steer some other reader through the implied, metaphorical implications of Biss's essay. Imagine yourself as a teacher. What would you ask your students to notice? How would you advise them to make meaning out of the passages you've chosen? What might you hope the students that you are guiding will understand about reading and writing through your guidance? How might you explain metaphor?

ALTERNATIVE ASSIGNMENT

Parts and Wholes

SUSAN GRIFFIN AND ONE OTHER

It is useful to think of Griffin's essay as experimental. She tries to do something that she cannot do in a more "traditional" essay form. She wants to make a different kind of argument or engage her reader in a different manner. She assembles fragments and puts seemingly unrelated material into surprising and suggestive relationships. One way to think about Griffin's essay is to think about each of her brief italicized sections as developing metaphors for her entire project—the cell, the missile, the etchings, and so on. Choose one passage from Griffin's series of italicized passages, a passage that will help you unearth an aspect of Griffin's essay.

Then turn to one of the other writers in this sequence (Ríos, Porchia, Doyle, Carson, or Biss). Find a passage in this author's writing that you think helps to unlock his or her essay (or fragments) in a similar way to Griffin. Remember that the content of the essay need not be linked to Griffin (though it might be), but you should look for writerly moves, ways that the metaphor operates in the context of a larger project. Rather than think of this as a kind of "compare and contrast" essay, think of your essay as an exploration of how metaphors work to bring together the larger project of an essay. How do these parts equal their wholes? How do they enrich the larger project of each writer?

Text Credits

David Abram. From *The Spell of the Sensuous* by David Abram, copyright © 1996 by David Abram. Used by permission of Pantheon Books, a division of Random House, Inc.

Gloria Anzaldúa. "Entering into the Serpent" and "How to Tame a Wild Tongue." From *Borderlands/La Frontera: The New Mestiza.* Copyright © 1987, 1999, 2007 by Gloria Anzaldúa. Reprinted by permission of Aunt Lute Books.

Kwame Anthony Appiah. "Race, Culture, Identity: Misunderstood Connections." K. Appiah Anthony, *Color Conscious.* © 1996 Princeton University Press. 1998 paperback edition. Reprinted by permissions of Princeton University Press.

John Berger. "Chapter 1" from *Ways of Seeing*. Copyright © 1972 by John Berger. Used by permission of Viking Penguin, a division of Penguin Group (USA) Inc.

John Berger. From *And Our Faces, My Heart, Brief as Photos* by John Berger, copyright © 1984 by John Berger. Used by permission of Pantheon Books, a division of Random House, Inc.

Eula Biss. "The Pain Scale." Reprinted with the permission of the author. Copyright © Eula Biss.

Susan Bordo. "Beauty (Re)Discovers the Male Body" from *The Male Body* by Susan Bordo. Copyright © 1999 by Susan Bordo. Reprinted by permission of Farrar, Straus and Giroux, LLC.

Judith Butler. Copyright © 2004 from *Undoing Gender* by Judith Butler. Reproduced by permission of Taylor and Francis Group, LLC, a division of Informa, plc.

Anne Carson. From *Plainwater: Essays and Poetry* by Anne Carson, copyright © 1995 by Anne Carson. Used by permission of Alfred A. Knopf, a division of Random House, Inc.

Brian Doyle. "Joyas Voladoras." From *The American Scholar,* Volume 73, No. 4, Autumn 2004. Used by permission of The American Scholar.

Michel Foucault. "Panopticism." From *Discipline and Punish* by Michel Foucault. English translation copyright © 1977 by Alan Sheridan (New York: Pantheon). Originally published in French as *Surveiller et Punir*. Copyright © 1975 by Editions Gallimard. Reprinted by permission of Georges Borchardt, Inc., for Editions Gallimard.

Paulo Freire. Excerpt from *Pedagogy of the Oppressed,* by Paulo Freire, © 1970, 1993. Reprinted by permission of the Continuum International Publishing Group.

Susan Griffin. From *Chorus of Stones* by Susan Griffin, copyright © 1992 by Susan Griffin. Used by permission of Doubleday, a division of Random House, Inc.

Richard Hoggart. From *The Uses of Literacy* by Richard Hoggart, published by Chatto & Windus. Reprinted by permission of The Random House Group Ltd.

Laura Kipnis. From *Against Love: A Polemic* by Laura Kipnis, copyright © 2003 by Laura Kipnis. Used by permission of Pantheon Books, a division of Random House, Inc.

Richard E. Miller. "The Dark Night of the Soul" from *Writing at the End of the World,* by Richard E. Miller, © 2005. Reprinted by permission of the University of Pittsburgh Press.

Walker Percy. "The Loss of the Creature" from *The Message in the Bottle* by Walker Percy. Copyright © 1975 by Walker Percy. Reprinted by permission of Farrar, Straus and Giroux, LLC.

Antonio Porchia. From *Voices* by Antonio Porchia, translated by W. S. Merwin, translation copyright © 1969 by W. S. Merwin. Used by permission of Alfred A. Knopf, a division of Random House, Inc.

Mary Louise Pratt. "Arts of the Contact Zone" from *Profession 91*. Copyright © 1991. Reprinted by permission of the Modern Language Association of America.

Alberto Álvaro Ríos. "Translating Translation: Finding the Beginning." Reprinted from *Prairie Schooner*, volume 68, number 4 (winter 1994) by permission of the University of Nebraska Press. Copyright 1994 by the University of Nebraska Press.

Richard Rodriguez. *Hunger of Memory: The Education of Richard Rodriguez* by Richard Rodriguez. Reprinted by permission of David R. Godine Publishers, Inc. Copyright © 1982 by Richard Rodriguez.

Edward Said. "States" from *After the Last Sky*. Copyright © 1999 by Columbia University Press.

Tommie Shelby. "Social Identity and Group Solidarity," reprinted by permission of the publisher from *We Who Are Dark: The Philosophical Foundations of Black Solidarity* by Tommie Shelby, pp. 201–242, Cambridge, Mass.: Harvard University Press, Copyright © 2005 by the President and Fellows of Harvard College.

David Foster Wallace. From *Consider the Lobster* by David Foster Wallace. Copyright © 2006 by David Foster Wallace. By permission of Little, Brown and Company.

John Edgar Wideman. "Our Time" from *Brothers and Keepers* by John Edgar Wideman. Copyright © 1984 by John Edgar Wideman, reprinted with permission of The Wylie Agency, LLC.

Art Credits

David Abram photograph courtesy of David Abram. Jacket cover copyright © 1997 by Vintage Books. From *The Spell of the Sensuous* by David Abram. Used by permission of Vintage Books, a division of Random House, Inc.

Gloria Anzaldúa photograph © Jean Weisinger. Cover design from *Borderlands/La Frontera: The New Mestiza*, copyright © 1987, 1999, 2007 by Gloria Anzaldúa. Reproduced by permission of Aunt Lute Books.

Kwame Anthony Appiah photograph courtesy of Office of Communications/ Princeton University. Cover design from K. Anthony Appiah, *Color Conscious* © 1996 Princeton University Press, 1998 paperback edition. Reprinted by permission of Princeton University Press.

John Berger photograph © Henri Cartier-Bresson/Magnum Photos. Cover design from *Ways of Seeing* by John Berger, copyright © 1972 by John Berger. Used by permission of Viking Penguin, a division of Penguin Group (USA) Inc. Jacket cover copyright © 1994 by Pantheon Books, a division of Random House, Inc. Jacket cover from *And Our Faces, My Heart, Brief as Photos* by John Berger. Used by permission of Pantheon Books, a division of Random House, Inc. Rene Magritte, "The Key of Dreams" © 2010 C. Herscovici, London / Artists Rights Society (ARS), New York. Frans Hals, "Regents of the Old Men's Alms House" and "Regentesses of the Old Men's Alms House" reprinted by permission of Frans Halsmuseum. Pablo Picasso, "Still Life with a Wicker Chair" © 2010 Estate of Pablo Picasso / Artists Rights Society (ARS), New York. Leonardo da Vinci, "The Virgin of the Rocks" © National Gallery, London / Art Resource, NY. Leonardo da Vinci, "The Madonna of the Rocks, c. 1483" Louvre Museum, Paris. Photo Credit: Scala / Art Resource, NY. Leonardo da Vinci, "The Virgin of the Rocks." Reproduced by courtesy of the Trustees, The National Gallery, London. Sandro Botticelli, "Venus and Mars." Reproduced by courtesy of the Trustees, The National Gallery, London / Art Resource, NY. Details of Pieter Brueghel the Elder, "Jesus Carrying the Cross, or the Way to Calvary, 1564." Photo Credit: Erich Lessing / Art Resource, NY. Vincent van Gogh, "Wheatfield with Crows." Van Gogh Museum Foundation, Amsterdam, The Netherlands. Art Resource, NY. Jan Vermeer, "The Kitchenmaid" Rijkmuseum, Amsterdam, The Netherlands. Art Resource, NY. Rembrandt, "Woman in Bed." National Gallery of Scotland. Michaelangelo Merisi daCaravaggio, "The Calling of St. Matthew." Photo Credit: Scala / Art Resource, NY.

Eula Biss photograph courtesy of Eula Biss. Cover of *Seneca Review* courtesy of *Seneca Review*.

Susan Bordo photograph courtesy of the University of Kentucky. Jacket design by Susan Mitchell from *The Male Body* by Susan Bordo. Copyright © 1999 by Susan Mitchell. Jacket art © The Special Photographer Co./Photonica. Reprinted by permission of Farrar, Straus and Giroux LLC.

Judith Butler photograph © Markus Kirchgessner/Redux Pictures. Cover Copyright 2010 from *Undoing Gender* by Judith Butler. Reproduced by permission of Taylor and Francis Group, LLC, a division of Informa, plc.

Anne Carson photograph © Peter Smith. Cover of *Short Talks* by Anne Carson reprinted by permission of Brick Books.

Brian Doyle photograph © Jerry Hart, courtesy of the author. Cover reprinted from *The American Scholar*, Volume 73, No. 4, Autumn 2004. Copyright © 2004 by The Phi Beta Kappa Society.

Michel Foucault photograph © Jerry Bauer. Jacket cover copyright © 1979 by Vintage Books, a division of Random House, Inc. from *Discipline and Punish* by Michel Foucault, translated by Alan Sheridan. Used by permission of Pantheon Books, a division of Random House, Inc. Panopticon photograph © Mansell/Time & Life Pictures/Getty Images. Handwriting model © The Granger Collection, New York. Stateville penitentiary photograph © Bettmann/CORBIS. Evils of alcoholism © Mary Evans Picture Library/Alamy.

Paulo Freire photograph courtesy Juca Martins/OLHAR IMAGEM. Cover design from *Pedagogy of the Oppressed* by Paulo Freire © 1970, 2000. Reprinted with the permission of the publisher, The Continuum International Publishing Group.

Susan Griffin photograph courtesy of the California Institute of Integral Studies. Jacket cover copyright © 1992 by Doubleday, a division of Random House, Inc. from *Chorus of Stones* by Susan Griffin. Used by permission of Doubleday, a division of Random House, Inc.

Laura Kipnis photograph courtesy of Laura Kipnis. Jacket cover copyright © 2003 by Pantheon Books. From *Against Love: A Polemic* by Laura Kipnis. Used by permission of Pantheon Books, a division of Random House, Inc.

Richard E. Miller photograph courtesy of Richard E. Miller. Cover from *Writing at the End of the World*, by Richard E. Miller, © 2005. Reprinted by permission of the University of Pittsburgh Press.

Walker Percy photograph © Rhoda K. Faust, New Orleans, LA. Jacket design by Janet Halverson from *The Message in the Bottle* by Walker Percy. Jacket design copyright © 1975 by Janet Halverson. Reprinted by permission of Farrar, Straus and Giroux, LLC.

Antonio Porchia photograph by Chandler-Zuretti. Cover of Antonio Porchia *Voices* © 2003. Reprinted by permission of Copper Canyon Press, www.coppercanyonpress.org.

Mary Louise Pratt photograph © Linda A. Cicero / Stanford News Service. Cover design for *Profession 91* reprinted by permission of the Modern Language Association of America. Adam and Eve, Conquista: Meeting of Spaniards and Inca, Corregidor de Minas from Guaman Poma de Ayala manuscript. Original in the archives of the State Library of Denmark.

Alberto Álvaro Ríos photograph courtesy of the Trustees, Arizona State University. *The Best of Prairie Schooner: Personal Essays* edited by Hilda Raz and Kate Flaherty is available wherever books are sold or from the University of Nebraska Press 800.848.6224 and on the web at nebraskapress.unl.edu.

Richard Rodriguez photograph © 2001 Christine Alicino. Jacket for *Hunger of Memory* by Richard Rodriguez, reproduced by permission of David R. Godine, Publisher. Copyright © 1982 by David R. Godine, Publisher.

Edward Said photograph © Jerry Bauer. Cover image from *After the Last Sky* designed by Benjamin Shin Farber with photographs by Jean Mohr, reprinted by permission of Columbia University Press. All photographs accompanying Edward Said's *After the Last Sky* © Jean Mohr, Geneva.

Tommie Shelby photograph © Marcus Halevi. Book cover from *We Who Are Dark* by Tommie Shelby appears courtesy of Harvard University Press, Copyright © 2005 by the President and Fellows of Harvard College. Cover photo © Stuart McClymont/Getty Images.

David Foster Wallace photograph © Gary Hannabarger/CORBIS. Cover reprint from *Consider the Lobster* by David Foster Wallace, used by permission of Little Brown and Company, a division of the Hachette Book Group.

John Edgar Wideman photograph courtesy of the University of Massachusetts, Amherst. Jacket cover copyright © 1995 by Vintage Books, a division of Random House, Inc. from *Brothers and Sisters* by John Edgar Wideman Used by permission of Vintage Books, a division of Random House, Inc.